April 22–25, 2012
Boston, MA, USA

I0027526

**Association for
Computing Machinery**

Advancing Computing as a Science & Profession

ICPE'12

Proceedings of the 3rd Joint WOSP/SIPEW International Conference on
Performance Engineering

Sponsored by:
SPEC, ACM SIGMETRICS, and ACM SIGSOFT

Supported by:
Hewlett Packard & SAP

**Association for
Computing Machinery**

Advancing Computing as a Science & Profession

The Association for Computing Machinery
2 Penn Plaza, Suite 701
New York, New York 10121-0701

Notice to Past Authors of ACM-Published Articles
ACM intends to create a complete electronic archive of all articles and/or other material previously published by ACM. If you have written a work that has been previously published by ACM in any journal or conference proceedings prior to 1978, or any SIG Newsletter at any time, and you do NOT want this work to appear in the ACM Digital Library, please inform permissions@acm.org, stating the title of the work, the author(s), and where and when published.

ISBN: 978-1-4503-1202-8 (Digital)

ISBN: 978-1-4503-1725-2 (Print)

Additional copies may be ordered prepaid from:

ACM Order Department
PO Box 30777
New York, NY 10087-0777, USA

Phone: 1-800-342-6626 (USA and Canada)
+1-212-626-0500 (Global)
Fax: +1-212-944-1318
E-mail: acmhelp@acm.org
Hours of Operation: 8:30 am – 4:30 pm ET

Printed in the USA

General Co-Chairs' Welcome

It is our pleasure to welcome you to Boston for the third joint International Conference on Performance Engineering (ICPE 2012). ICPE brings together the Standard Performance Evaluation Corporation (SPEC) International Performance Evaluation Workshop (SIPEW) and ACM's Workshop on Software and Performance (WOSP) communities. Performance engineering is of great importance to society and industry. We are pleased to bring you an interesting program to advance the state of the art that includes research contributions from both academia and industry. The technical program includes 25 high quality papers and 9 poster presentations. We also have a day of compelling tutorials and 2 keynote speakers as part of the technical program. Prof. William H. Sanders will talk about "Assuring the Trustworthiness of the Smarter Electric Grid," including a discussion of research opportunities in performance engineering. Amnon Naamad, Senior Director of Innovation at EMC, will present "New Challenges in Performance Engineering,"

The conference would not have been possible without the community that supports ICPE. This starts with researchers submitting high quality papers and of course includes those who have worked hard to organize the conference itself. Diwakar Krishnamurthy and Lizy John, the Program Chairs, have prepared an excellent technical program. Stephen Dawson has prepared a tutorial program that will be of interest to both those new to performance engineering and those of us who have been around for a while. Ningfang Mi prepared our demos and posters session. Pankaj Garg worked tirelessly to keep everyone on track as Publications chair. Greg Franks and Rob Bell did an excellent job publicizing the event. Kai Sachs was very helpful as finance chair. Xiaoyun Zhu did a splendid job ensuring a smooth registration process for this joint event. Very special thanks go to Michael Faber who served as Web Chair. Samuel Kounev and Vittorio Cortellessa, General co-Chairs for ICPE 2011, provided guidance throughout the year to help us prepare for this event.

Dianne Rice of SPEC was very helpful throughout the process of preparing for ICPE 2012. We are indebted to her for her support. We also appreciate the help of the student volunteers from the Northeastern University Computer Architecture Research Lab. We also very much appreciate the support and guidance of April Mosqus and Ann Lane of ACM and to Lisa Tolles at Sheridan Printing Company for her help with the proceedings. We thank the corporate sponsors Hewlett Packard, SAP, EMC and SPEC who helped us to keep registration costs low and allow us to offer travel grants to students.

The WOSP community was founded and has been led by Connie Smith since its first workshop in Santa Fe New Mexico in 1998. We have all been inspired by her work. This year Connie passed the leadership baton for the WOSP steering committee on to Andre Bondi. We are all very grateful to Connie for the guidance, leadership, and friendship she has offered to the community over these years. We are thankful to André for taking on this role.

Finally, we thank you for participating in ICPE and wish you an exciting conference and stay in Boston.

General Co-Chairs

David Kaeli, *Northeastern University, Boston, MA, USA*

Jerry Rolia, *Hewlett Packard Labs, Palo Alto, CA, USA*

Program Chairs' Welcome

It is our great pleasure to welcome you to the Third ACM/SPEC International Conference on Performance Engineering (ICPE 2012). The primary goal of the conference is to integrate theory and practice in the field of performance engineering by providing a forum for sharing ideas and experiences between industry and academia. This year's conference brings together researchers and industry practitioners to share and present their experiences, discuss challenges, and report on both state-of-the-art research and work-in-progress on performance engineering of software and systems, including performance measurement, modeling, benchmark design, and run-time performance management. ICPE gives researchers and practitioners a unique opportunity to share their perspectives with others interested in the various aspects of computer systems performance engineering.

The calls for papers attracted 66 paper submissions across three different tracks namely, research, industry, and work-in-progress/vision. Papers were submitted from Asia, Australia, Europe, North America and South America. Each paper went through a rigorous peer review process involving at least 3 and in most cases 4 program committee members. The program committee accepted 19 full research papers, 2 short research papers, 2 industrial papers, and 10 work-in-progress/vision papers. These papers cover a variety of topics, including performance modeling, performance and software development processes, benchmarking, energy efficiency, and performance evaluation of cloud and adaptive systems. The program is further enriched with 3 tutorials, 2 presentations from SPEC Distinguished Dissertation Award Winners, and 9 poster/demo exhibitions.

In addition to the paper presentations, the conference offers two keynote speakers of international prestige:

- William H. Sanders, Professor, University of Illinois at Urbana-Champaign (USA), presenting "Assuring the Trustworthiness of the Smarter Electric Grid"

- Amnon Naamad, Senior Director of Innovation, EMC (USA), presenting "New Challenges in Performance Engineering"

Altogether there are 33 peer-reviewed papers that have been selected from high quality submissions for presentation at this year's conference in Boston. We are confident that you will find the program stimulating and that it will provide you with many new ideas and insights.

Welcome to Boston, and many thanks for your participation!

Lizy John	**Diwakar Krishnamurthy**
ICPE 2012 Program co-chair	*ICPE 2012 Program co-chair*

Table of Contents

Tutorial 1

Tutorial 2

Keynote Address 1
Session Chair: Jerry Rolia *(Hewlett Packard Laboratories)*

Session: 1: Performance Prediction Techniques for Software and Systems

Session 2: Performance Modeling and Evaluation of Adaptive

Session 3: Performance and Software Development Processes

Session 4: Performance and Energy Efficiency

Keynote Address 2

Session Chair: David Kaeli *(Northeastern University)*

Session 5: Benchmarking

Session 6: Performance Modeling of Software and Systems

Session 7: Poster Preview Presentations

Session 8: Work-in-Progress/Vision Track

Session 9: Performance Measurement and Experimental Analysis

2012 ICPE Conference Organization

General Chairs: David Kaeli *(Northeastern University, USA)*
Jerry Rolia *(Hewlett Packard Labs, USA)*

Program Chairs: Lizy John *(University of Texas at Austin, USA)*
Diwakar Krishnamurthy *(University of Calgary, Canada)*

Industrial Chair: John Henning *(Oracle, USA)*

Tutorial Chair: Stephen Dawson *(SAP Research, UK)*

Poster Chair: Ningfang Mi *(Northeastern University, USA)*

Publication Chair: Pankaj Garg *(ZeeSource, USA)*

Publicity Chairs: Rob Bell *(IBM, USA)*
Greg Franks *(Carleton University, Canada)*

Finance Chair: Kai Sachs *(SAP, Germany)*

Registration Chair: Xiaoyun Zhu *(VMware, USA)*

Award Chairs: Rema Hariharan *(AMD, USA)*
Virgilio Almeida *(UFMG, Brazil)*

Web Chair: Michael Faber *(KIT, Germany)*

Steering Committee Chairs: André Bondi *(Siemens, USA)*
Samuel Kounev *(KIT, Germany)*

Program Committee: Martin Arlitt *(HP Labs, USA)*
Jose Nelson Amaral *(University of Alberta, Canada)*
Alberto Avritzer *(Siemens Corporate Research, USA)*
Simonetta Balsamo *(Università Ca' Foscari di Venezia, Italy)*
Giuliano Casale *(Imperial College, UK)*
Lawrence Chung *(University of Texas at Dallas, USA)*
Jeanine Cook *(New Mexico State University, USA)*
Vittorio Cortellessa *(Universita' dell'Aquila, Italy)*
Susanna Donatelli *(University of Torino, Italy)*
Lieven Eeckhout *(Ghent University, Belgium)*
Manoj Franklin *(University of Maryland, USA)*
Rema Hariharan *(AMD, USA)*

Program Committee
(continued): John Henning *(Oracle, USA)*

Ravi Iyer *(Intel Research, USA)*

Mathew Jacob *(IISC, India)*

Carlos Juiz *(Universitat de les Illes Balears, Spain)*

Dimitris Kaseridis *(ARM, USA)*

Samuel Kounev *(KIT, Germany)*

Klaus Lange *(HP, USA)*

David Lilja *(University of Minnesota, USA)*

Jenny Liu *(PNNL, USA)*

Catalina Llado *(Universitat de les Illes Balears, Spain)*

Anirban Mahanti *(NICTA, Australia)*

Pat Martin *(Queen's University, Canada)*

Raffaela Mirandola *(Politecnico di Milano, Italy)*

Dorina Petriu *(Carleton University, Canada)*

Ralf Reussner *(KIT, Germany)*

Alma Riska *(EMC, USA)*

Kai Sachs *(SAP, Germany)*

Seetharami Seelam *(IBM Research, USA)*

Anand Sivasubramanian *(Penn State University, USA)*

Mark Squillante *(IBM Research, USA)*

Malgorzata Steinder *(IBM Research, USA)*

Bronis Supinski *(LLNL, USA)*

Pat Teller *(University of Texas at El Paso, USA)*

Mirco Tribastone *(LMU, Germany)*

Petr Tuma *(Charles University, Czech Republic)*

Akshat Verma *(IBM Research, India)*

Tom Wenisch *(University of Michigan, USA)*

Zhibin Yu *(Huazhong University, China)*

ICPE 2012 Sponsors & Supporters

Sponsors:

Supporters:

Best Practices for Writing and Managing Performance Requirements: A Tutorial

André B. Bondi

Siemens Corporation, Corporate
Research and Technologies
755 College Road East
Princeton, NJ 08540 USA

+1 609 734 3578

andre.bondi@siemens.com

ABSTRACT

Performance requirements are one of the main drivers of architectural decisions. Because many performance problems have their roots in architectural decisions, and since poor performance is a principal cause of software project risk, it is essential that performance requirements be developed early in the software lifecycle, and that they be clearly formulated. In this tutorial, we shall look at criteria for high-quality performance requirements, including algebraic consistency, measurability, testability, and linkage to business and engineering needs. While focus of this tutorial is on practice, we shall show how the drafting of performance requirements can be aided by performance modeling. We shall show methods for presenting and managing performance requirements that will improve their chances of being accepted by architects, developers, testers, contract negotiators, and purchasers; and of their being successfully implemented and tested.

Categories and Subject Descriptors

C.4 **[Computer Systems Organization]**: Performance of systems; D.2.1 **[Software Engineering]**: Requirements specification.

General Terms

Measurement, documentation, performance.

Keywords

System performance, performance requirements.

1. INTRODUCTION

Poor computer system performance has been called the single most frequent cause of the failure of software projects [13, 1]. Among the causes of poor performance are poor architectural choices and inadequately specified performance requirements. In our experience and that of several performance engineers and developers with whom we have spoken, performance requirements may be vaguely written, or might not even have been written at all by the time the project is close to completion.

The absence of performance requirements increases the risk that performance will receive inadequate attention during the

architectural, development, and functional testing phases of a software project. Performance requirements are drivers of computer and software architecture.

Since performance problems often have their roots in poor architectural decisions, the early establishment of performance requirements for a new system is crucial to the project's success.

The lack of well specified performance requirements places the burden on the performance tester to identify the ranges of workloads to which the system should be subjected before delivery. In such cases, performance testers must make conjectures about the anticipated system load and use case mix, and then devise load tests accordingly. If the tests are well structured, they can tell us whether the system has desirable performance properties under designated loads, but the tested loads may not be close to those envisioned for the system.

We have found that poorly written performance requirements incur an insidious cost. They cause confusion among the developers charged with meeting them, as well as among the performance testers who must verify that they are met. The confusion must be resolved in meetings to try to understand what was meant. In the author's experience, clarification of the performance requirements often means rewriting them in keeping with the spirit in which they were meant, and then communicating the revisions to the various stakeholders for approval.

Whether or not they are well formulated, performance requirements are a key ingredient of customer expectations of what the system will do. Therefore, they may constitute part of an agreement about what the supplier is supposed to deliver. It follows that poorly drafted requirements increase the prospect of incurring customer ill will, which can have undesirable consequences, including loss of business and even litigation.

In this tutorial, we identify best practices for specifying performance requirements, and examine the risks and pitfalls of building a software system in cases in which the requirements are either absent or written in a form that makes them inherently untestable or unachievable. We argue that performance requirements should possess the same good qualities as functional requirements, such as traceability, measurability, and unambiguousness [6], and be linked to business, engineering, or regulatory needs. By ensuring measurability, we reduce the possibility of adopting performance requirements that are unachievable or that impose constraints that have no impact on performance at all. The linkage may help to overcome the problem that slogans masquerading as performance requirements are sometimes neither achievable nor testable. Demanding this linkage also ensures the traceability of a performance requirement by answering why the requirement was specified in the first place.

Confusion can also arise when a performance requirement has been written for no apparent reason, or when it is in conflict with other performance requirements. The guidelines we propose are intended to reduce the risk of these difficulties.

2. RELATION TO PREVIOUS WORK

Smith and Williams state that performance requirements are a precondition for good system performance [13]. Nixon describes a framework for managing them during the course of a project, and how they should be arranged to facilitate the identification of performance goals [10]. Ho *et al* [5] advocate the incremental formulation of performance requirements and conduct of performance tests in an Agile development process. They identify three levels of performance requirements. Level 1 performance requirements are related to system performance in single user mode. Level 2 performance requirements specify the performance requirements when the system is supporting a specific transaction rate. Level 3 requirements are similar to Level 2 requirements, but relate to the peak rate.

The emphasis in the present tutorial is on the practice of performance requirements engineering. We begin with a discussion of the performance metrics that are used in performance requirements, because a clear definition of performance metrics is necessary to ensure that performance requirements are unambiguous. As we describe below, the desirable attributes of performance requirements are closely related to those of functional requirements, for example as described in [6].

3. PERFORMANCE METRICS

It is essential to describe the performance of a system in terms that are commonly understood and unambiguously defined and related to the problem domain. Performance is described in terms of quantities known as *metrics*. A metric is defined as a standard of measurement [14]. Metrics should be defined in terms that aid the understanding of the system from both engineering and business perspectives. A comprehensive discussion of performance metrics is contained in [7]. The values of performance metrics should be obtainable by direct measurement or by arithmetic manipulation of direct measurement or the values of other metrics. Performance metrics such as average response times are based on sample statistics. Performance metrics such as average utilizations are based on time-averaged statistics.

A performance metric should inform us about the behavior of the system in the context of its domain of application and/or in the context of its resource usage. What is informative depends on the point of view of a particular stakeholder as well as on the domain itself. For example, an accountant may be interested in the monthly transaction volume of a system. By contrast, an individual user of the system may only be interested in its response time during a period of peak usage. This means that the system must be engineered to handle a set number of transactions per second in the peak hour. The latter quantity is of interest to the performance engineer. It is only of interest to the accountant to the extent that it is directly related to the total monthly volume. If the two metrics are to be used interchangeably, there must be a well known understanding and agreement about the relationship between them. Such an example exists in telephony. In the latter part of the 20th Century, it was understood that about 10% of the calls on a weekday occur during the busy hour. In the USA, this is true of both local call traffic and long distance traffic observed concurrently in multiple time zones. It is also understood that the number of relevant business days in a month is about 22. Thus, thus the monthly traffic volume would be approximately 22 times the busy hour volume, divided by 10%. For example, if 50,000 calls occur in a network in the busy hour, the number of calls per month could be approximately estimated as 22 x 50,000/10% = 22 x 500,000 = 11,000,000 calls. This relationship must be stated in the performance requirements if any requirement relies on it.

Lilja has identified the following useful properties of performance metrics [7]. Among these are linearity (meaning that the performance of a system improves by the same ratio as the metric describing it), reliability (meaning that System A outperforms System B when the metric indicates that it does), repeatability (meaning that if the same experiment is run more than once under identical load conditions with identical configurations, the resulting metric will always have the same value), ease of measurement, consistency (meaning that the metric has the same meaning across all systems), and independence (meaning that it does not reflect the bias of any stakeholder).

More than one metric may be needed to describe the performance of a system. For on-line transaction processing systems, such as a brokerage system or an online airline reservation system, the metrics of interest will be the response times and transaction rates for each type of transaction, usually measured in the hour when the traffic is heaviest. The transaction loss rate, i.e., the fraction of submitted transactions that were not completed for whatever reason, is another measure of performance. It should be very low. We see immediately that one performance metric on its own is not sufficient to tell us about the performance of a system or about the quality of service it provides. The tendency to fixate on a single number or to focus too much on a single metric, termed *mononumerosis* by Odlyzsko [11], can result in a poor design or purchasing decision, because the chosen metric may not reflect critical system characteristics that are described by other metrics. One cannot rely on a single number to tell us the whole story about the performance of a system. For example, a low system response time may be accompanied by a high transaction loss rate, because the loss rate reduces the waiting times of the transactions that have not been lost, or because lost transactions may have been more likely to suffer long delays.

4. GUIDELINES FOR SPECIFYING PERFORMANCE REQUIREMENTS

The criteria for performance requirements are a superset of those in [6] for functional requirements. In particular, like functional requirements, performance requirements must be unambiguous, traceable, verifiable, complete, and correct. Additional criteria relate to the quantitative nature of performance requirements. To be useful, they must be written in measurable terms, expressed in correct statistical terms, and written in terms of one or more metrics that are informative about the problem domain. They must also be written in terms of metrics suitable for the time scale within which the system must respond to stimuli. In addition, the requirements must be mathematically consistent. Finally, all performance requirements must be linked to business, regulatory, and engineering needs. We now elaborate on each of these criteria in turn.

4.1 Unambiguousness

First and foremost, a performance requirement must be unambiguous. Ambiguity arises primarily from a poor choice of wording, but it can also arise from a poor choice of metrics.

- **Example 1.** "The response times shall be less than 5 seconds 95% of the time."

This requirement is ambiguous. It opens the question of whether this must be true during 95% of the busy hour, 95% of the busiest 5 minutes of the busy hour (both of which may be hard to satisfy), or during 95% of the year (which might be easy to satisfy if quiet periods are included in the average). In any case, the response time is a sampled discrete observation, not a quantity averaged over time. Consider an alternative formulation:

- "The average response time shall be 2 seconds or less in each 5-minute period beginning on the hour. Ninety-five percent of all response times shall be less than 5 seconds."

This requirement is very specific as to the periods in which averages will be collected, as well as to the probability of a sampled response time exceeding a specific value.

- **Example 2.** "The system shall support all submitted transactions."

Requiring that a system shall support all submitted transactions is ambiguous, because

1. there is no statement of the rate at which transactions occur,
2. there no statement of what the transactions do,
3. there is no explicit definition of the term "support".

Instead, one might state that the submitted rate of type A transactions is 5 per second, or (equivalently) 60 per minute. If this requirement is coupled with an unambiguous response time requirement such as that given in Example 1, and a further requirement that no errors occur while the transactions are being handled, we may be able to say that the transaction rate is being *supported* if the response time and transaction loss rate requirements are also met. We may also be able to say that a desired transaction rate is *sustainable* all resources in the system are at utilization levels below a stated average utilization that is less than saturation (e.g., 70%) to allow room for spikes in activity when this rate occurs.

4.2 Measurability

A well specified performance requirement must be expressed in terms of quantities that are measurable. If the source of the measurement is not known or is not trustworthy, the requirement will be unenforceable. Therefore, it must be possible to obtain the values of the metric(s) in which the requirement is expressed. To ensure this, the source of the data involved in the requirement should be specified alongside the requirement itself. The source of the data could be a measurement tool embedded in the operating system, a load generator, or a counter generated by the application or one of its supporting platforms, such as an application server or database management system. A performance requirement should not be adopted if it cannot be verified and enforced by measurement.

- **Example 3.** The average, minimum, and maximum response times during an observation interval may be obtained from a commercial load generator, together with a count of the number of attempted, successful, and failed transactions of each type, but only if the load generator is set up to collect them.
- **Example 4.** The sample variance of the response times can only be obtained if the load generator also collects the sum of the squared response times during each observation interval,

or if all response times have been logged, provided always that at least two response times have been collected.

4.3 Verifiability

According to [6], a requirement is verifiable "…if, and only if, there exists some finite cost-effective process with which a person or machine can check that the software product meets the requirement. In general any ambiguous requirement is not verifiable." For performance requirements, this means that the performance requirement is testable, consistent, unambiguous, measurable, and consistent with all other performance and functional requirements pertaining to the system of interest. Where a performance requirement is inherently untestable, such as freedom from deadlock, a procedure should be specified for determining that the design fails to meet at least one of the three necessary conditions for deadlock. These are circular waiting for a resource, mutual exclusion from a resource, and nonpreemption of a resource [3]. On the other hand, if deadlock happens to occur during performance testing, we know that the requirement for freedom from it cannot be met.

4.4 Completeness

A performance requirement is complete if its parameters are fully specified, if it is unambiguous, and if its context is fully specified. A requirement that specifies that a system shall be able to process 50,000 transactions per month is incomplete because the type of transaction has not been specified, the parameters of the transaction have not been specified, and the context has not been specified. In particular, to be able to test the requirement, we have to know how many transactions are requested in the peak hour, and then have some context for inferring that the peak hourly transaction rate is functionally related to the number of transactions per month. We also have to define a performance requirement for the acceptable time to complete the transaction.

4.5 Correctness

In addition to being correct within the context of the application to which it refers, a performance requirement is correct only if it is specified in measurable terms, is unambiguous, and is mathematically consistent with other requirements. In addition, it must be specified with respect to the time scale for which engineering steps must be taken.

4.6 Mathematical Consistency

There are multiple aspects to the mathematical consistency of performance requirements.

- Performance requirements must be mathematically consistent with one another. To verify consistency, one must ensure that no inference can be drawn from any requirement that would conflict with any other requirement. Inferences could be drawn through the use of models. They could also be drawn by deriving an implied requirement from a stated one. If the implied requirement is inconsistent with other requirements, so is the source requirement.
- Each performance requirement must be consistent with stated performance assumptions, e.g., about the traffic conditions and engineering constraints. For example, a message round trip time should be less than the timeout interval, while the produce of the processing time and the system throughput must be less than 100% so that the CPU is not saturated.
- The performance requirements must not specify combinations of loads and anticipated service times that make it unachievable. This will happen if the product of the offered traffic rate and the anticipated average service time

of any device is greater than the number of devices acting in parallel (usually one).

4.7 Testability

We desire that all performance requirements be testable. Testability is closely related to measurability. If a metric mentioned in a performance requirement cannot be measured, the requirement cannot be tested, either.

Not all performance requirements are directly linked to the ability to attain specific values for metrics, though. Moreover, such requirements may be very difficult to test. For example, as discussed above, freedom from deadlock must be verified from the system structure. Since the potential for deadlock can be masked under light loads, and since testing for freedom from deadlock involves the enumeration of all execution paths, freedom from deadlock is not verifiable by performance testing alone.

4.8 Traceability

Like functional requirements, performance requirements must be traceable. Traceability answers questions like the following:

1. Why has this performance requirement been specified?
2. To what business need does the performance requirement respond?
3. To what engineering needs does the performance requirement respond?
4. Does the performance requirement help us conform to a government or industrial regulation?
5. Is the requirement consistent with industrial norms? Is it derived from industrial norms?
6. Who proposed the requirement?
7. If this requirement is based on a mathematical derivation or model, the parameters should be listed and a reference to the model provided.
8. If this requirement is based on the outputs of a load model, a reference and pointer to the load model should be provided, together with the corresponding version number and date of issue.

4.9 Linkage to Business and Engineering Needs

All performance requirements must be linked to business and engineering needs. Linking to a business need reduces the risk of engineering the system to meet a requirement that is unnecessarily stringent, while linking to an engineering need helps us to understand why the requirement was specified in the first place. An example of a business need is the desire to provide a competitive differentiator from a slower product. An example of an engineering need is that a TCP packet must be acknowledged within a certain time interval to prevent timeouts. Another example of an engineering need is the standards requirement that an alarm be delivered to a console and/or sounded within a maximum amount of time from that at which the corresponding problem was detected [9].

5. QUALITATIVE ATTRIBUTES RELATED TO PERFORMANCE

Performance requirements may contain a statement of the form "The system shall be scalable." All too often, there is no mention of the dimension with respect to which the system should be scaled, or the extent to which the system might be scaled in the future. Absent these criteria for scalability, testers will not know how to verify that the system is indeed scalable, and product managers and sales engineers will not be able to manage customer expectations about the ability of the system to be expanded. Characteristics for scalability, such as load scalability, space-time scalability, space scalability, and structural scalability are described in [2]. Examples of the corresponding dimensions include transaction rates, the ability to exploit parallelism, storage available to users and the operating environment, and constraints imposed by the size of the address space.

Stability is a quality attribute that is also related to scalability. If the system runs smoothly when N objects are present but crashes when N+1 objects are present, the scalability of the system is limited by the number of objects the system can support. Clearly, the number of objects the system can support is a dimension of scalability that is limited in this case.

Stability or a tendency to instability are also indicated by characteristics of the performance metrics. For example, during a prolonged period when the average offered transaction rate is constant, one expects (a) that the completion rate to be equal to the transaction rate, (b) that average resource utilizations will be approximately constant, (c) that average response times will be approximately constant, and (d) that memory occupancy will be approximately constant. Performance requirements for these characteristics should be specified. Failure to meet them in performance tests or production should be cause for an investigation. Upward trends in any or all these measures is an indication of saturation or an oncoming crash. In particular, if memory occupancy is increasing, there may be a memory leak that could lead to a system crash.

6. DERIVED AND IMPLICIT PERFORMANCE REQUIREMENTS

While performance requirements about transaction rates, throughputs, and response times are often explicitly stated, consequent requirements on subsystems, including object pool size and memory usage are not. If they are not explicitly stated, they must be derived from the quantities that are given to ensure system stability and to ensure that sufficient numbers of concurrent activities can be supported. In the author's experience, an astute developer and/or tester may ask the performance engineer to specify the maximum size of the object pool so that testing can be done accordingly.

As an example, suppose that a transaction will be dropped if an object pool is exhausted. The required transaction response time may be thought of as an average value for the holding time, while the transaction rate multiplied by the number of times an object will be acquired and released by the transaction. If we require that the probability of object pool exhaustion is 10^{-6} or less, we can approximately size the object pool to achieve this requirement using the Erlang loss formula [4]. The calculated object pool size is the derived requirement needed to achieve the desired probability of pool exhaustion. While the loss probability requirement is inherently hard to test because losses should not occur, the ability to store the desired number of objects is easily tested in principle, provided that the test harness is capable of doing so.

In this context, it is worth noting that freedom from deadlock is always an implicit requirement. It can be derived from any requirement that specifies or implies a non-zero throughput, because a system in deadlock has zero throughput. Freedom from deadlock is a prerequisite for system stability.

7. PATTERNS AND ANTI-PATTERNS IN PERFORMANCE REQUIREMENTS

While performance requirements for specialized embedded systems may take unusual, domain-specific forms, those for transaction-oriented systems tend to fall into patterns for average response time, throughput, and number of supported users. We have already seen some examples of these in the foregoing. Smith and Williams have used the term *performance anti-pattern* to describe an aspect of system structure or algorithmic behaviour that leads to poor performance [13]. We shall use the term *performance requirements anti-pattern* to denote a form of performance requirement that is ambiguous at best and misleading at worst. Anti-patterns are to be avoided, even if they express sentiments that are laudable. We illustrate patterns and anti-patterns with examples encountered by the author.

7.1 Response Time Pattern and Anti-Pattern

The following is an ill-formulated performance requirement.

1. *Ideally, the response time shall be at most one second.*
2. *The response time shall be at most 2 seconds.*

This requirement is problematic. The term "ideally" expresses a sentiment, but does not describe something that is attainable. The two parts of the requirement are mutually inconsistent. The occurrence of a single response time in excess of two seconds would mean that the requirement had not been met. Nothing is stated about when or how often the response time requirement must be met. If a sentiment like that in the first part of the requirement must be documented, it is best to place it in a section on supporting commentary rather than in the body of the requirement itself.

We propose a formulation that expresses the same sentiment while being measurable and testable.

1. *The average response time during the busy hour shall be 1 second.*
2. *99% of all response times shall be less than 2 seconds during the busy hour.*
3. *Both requirements shall be met simultaneously.*

The wording in parts 1 and 2 of this requirement reflects the fact that the average response time is a sample statistic rather than a time-averaged statistic. Notice also that the second part of the requirement does not say that the response time shall be less than 2 seconds 99% of the time, since that would suggest averaging over time rather than over the observed values of the response time.

7.2 "…all the time/…of the time" Anti-Pattern

Were a requirement to say that the response time should be less than 2 seconds 99% of the time, we would have to clarify the requirement by asking whether the requirement for the average response time would be met for 0.99x3600=3564 seconds in every hour, or during some fraction of the year, or some other time interval. The problem may be illustrated by a quote from former President George W. Bush: "I talk to General Petraeus all the time. I say 'all the time' -- weekly; that's all the time – …"[8]. The quantification is ambiguous because the time scale and frequency of interaction are unspecified, and because one cannot tell from colloquial use whether the "…all the time" or "…of the time" refers to a sample statistic such as average response time, a time-averaged statistic such as utilization or queue length, or to a frequency, such as the number of events per second or even the number of communications between a president and a general per month.

7.3 Resource Utilization Anti-Pattern

A requirement that states that the CPU utilization shall be 60% is erroneous because the resource utilization depends on the hardware and on the volume of activity. The desired response time and throughput requirements might well be met at higher utilizations. Furthermore, the requirement would fail to be met under light loads, which is absurd. When confronted with a requirement like this, the performance engineer could ask whether the stakeholder who originated the requirement is concerned about overload, and then offer to reformulate the requirement as an upper bound on processor utilization. Doing so helps to ensure that the system will be able to gracefully deal with transients that could cause the utilization to briefly exceed the stated level under normal conditions. It is entirely appropriate to state a resource utilization requirement of the form "The average utilization of resource X shall be less than Y% in the peak hour." For single server resources, Y might be set to 70%. For a pair of parallel servers in which one acts as a backup for the other, it is appropriate to state that the utilizations of individual processors must not exceed 40%, so that the maximum load on one of them after a failover would be no more than 80%. Anything higher than that could result in system saturation.

8. PERFORMANCE REQUIREMENTS GATHERING

As with functional requirements, the gathering of performance requirements entails interviewing stakeholders from many different teams within the customer and supplier organizations. In the author's experience, the set of stakeholders can include product managers and sales engineers, because they identify the market segments for a system, including customers for large-scale and small-scale systems. Any pertinent regulations that could affect performance requirements must also be identified, such as fire codes in the case of alarm systems. The set of stakeholders also includes architects, designers, developers, and testers. It is important to interview the architects and developers, because they may propose the use of technologies that are incapable of meeting the envisaged system demand.

Stakeholders may be reluctant to commit to a particular set of estimates of demand for system usage because Customer A may argue that his organisation's load is not like Customer B's. For example, the work mix of a small rural clinic may be very different from that of a large hospital using similar sorts of computer-controlled diagnostic equipment for different purposes. Even the workloads of hospitals with similar numbers of beds may differ, because one hospital might specialize in orthopaedics while the other only does cancer care. Their fire alarm systems may be quite different, too, because of the nature of what is stored. Despite these disparities, performance requirements specification and testing should not be avoided. Instead, the project team should resort to the use of a set of *reference scenarios* reflecting standardized mixes of activities. The reference scenarios might be agreed to by product managers and/or sales engineers, and then mapped to the corresponding activities in the computer system, with corresponding workloads. The frequency and delay requirements of these activities form the body of the performance requirements. Under no circumstances should performance requirements be reduced to a single number, because doing so will mask potential complexities and obscure any possibilities for tradeoffs.

9. PERFORMANCE REQUIREMENTS PITFALL: TRANSITION FROM A LEGACY SYSTEM TO A NEW SYSTEM

When transitioning from a legacy system to a new one, it is easy to overlook subtle changes in functionality that might affect the way performance requirements should be formulated. The author encountered this pitfall when transitioning from a 1940s vintage 35mm rangefinder camera to a modern point and shoot digital camera. With the old camera, pressing the shutter button causes the subject to be captured pretty much in the state seen by the user. In this case, the object was a walking cow with a bell hanging from its collar. The digital camera took so much time to capture the image that the resulting photo included the cow's udder, but not the bell. The difficulty was that the shutter reaction time with the digital camera included autofocus and exposure setting. With the vintage camera, these would have been done manually in advance of the shutter being released. The problem occurred because the photographer simply assumed that the digital camera would have the same shutter reaction time as the vintage camera. It does not, and the unexpected image was the result. One might ask whether the comparison of the shutter reaction times is fair, given that the digital camera does so much more when the button is pressed. The answer is that a comparison should reflect expectations of the functionality that will be implemented, and that the user should plan the shot accordingly.

10. STRUCTURE OF A PERFORMANCE REQUIREMENTS DOCUMENT

The structure of a performance requirements document we recommend is quite similar to that recommended in [6] for functional requirements. A section on traffic assumptions specific to the domain should be included to reduce the risk of ambiguity or misunderstanding. This is especially important in a labour force with turnover. Reference work items and reference workloads are needed to establish the context for domain-specific metrics. A reference work item may be a particular kind of transaction or set of transactions and activities. A reference workload specifies the mix and volumes of the transactions and activities. A reference scenario might be a set of workloads, or a set of actions to be carried out upon the occurrence of a specific type of event. For instance, a reference scenario for a fire alarm system might be the occurrence of a fire that triggers summoning the fire brigade, the sounding of alarms, and the automated closure of a defined set of ventilators and doors. The performance metrics used in the requirements, especially those that are specific to the domain, should be defined and mapped to related system actions. The instrumentation used to gather the metrics should also be specified to the extent known, so that one can establish that a mechanism for verifying and enforcing the requirements exists. Figure 1 shows a possible outline for a performance requirements document.

1. Scope and Purpose
2. Intended Audience
3. References (including functional requirements spec)
4. Statement of Assumptions:
   a. Traffic assumptions Specific to the Domain
   b. Definition of reference work items and reference workloads and scenarios
   c. Criteria for load sustainability
   d. Definitions of metrics used in the requirements
   e. Instrumentation to gather the metrics for verification
5. Performance Requirements

Figure 1. Outline of a performance requirements document.

Table 1. Suggested fields of a performance requirements record.

1.	Requirement Number
2.	Title
3.	Statement of requirement
4.	Supporting commentary
5.	List of precedents, sources, standards
6.	Derivation of quantities
7.	List of dependent requirements
8.	List of assumptions and precedent performance requirements
9.	Sources of measurement data.
10.	Name of a subject matter expert on this requirement
11.	Indicator if the requirement is independently modifiable, or if not, why not.
12.	Indicator that the requirement is traceable.
13.	Indicator that the requirement is unambiguous, or if not, why not.
14.	Indicator that the requirement is correct, or, if not, why not.
15.	Indicator that the requirement is complete, and if not, why not.
16.	Indicator that the requirement has passed or failed review, and why.

11. STRUCTURE OF A PERFORMANCE REQUIREMENT

The fields of a performance requirement record suggested below reflect many of the concerns we have described above. Some, like the list of precedents, sources, and standards, are intended to provide traceability. Separating supporting commentary from the statement of the requirement reduces the risk of ambiguity while providing an opportunity to document some of the reasoning behind the requirement and the requirement's purpose. Listing dependent and precedent performance requirements help one to see how requirements are intertwined. A possible list of records is shown in Table 1.

12. THE COMMERCIAL SENSITIVITY OF PERFORMANCE REQUIREMENTS

Disclaimer: This section does not contain legal advice. You should seek the advice of legal counsel when drafting any agreements or documents incorporated into agreements by reference. Legal obligations and practice may differ from one jurisdiction to another. The author is not a lawyer.

12.1 Confidentiality

A great deal can be inferred about the competitiveness of a product or the commercial position of the intended customer by examining performance requirements. For example, the ability of a network management system to handle traps at a given peak rate, combined with knowledge of the number of nodes to be managed and the peak polling rate can tell us about the intended market segment of the product while nourishing speculation about the product's feature set, or even about the nature of the site the system is intended to support. This can affect price negotiations between supplier and buyer, and perhaps the supplier's share price. Therefore, performance requirements and any contractual negotiations related to them should be treated as confidential and perhaps even covered by non-disclosure agreements (NDAs). The release of performance requirements and performance data outside a circle of individuals with a need to know should be handled with great care. Engineering, marketing, legal, and intellectual property departments should all be involved in setting up a formal process to release performance data to the public or to third parties under non-disclosure agreements.

12.2 System Performance and the Relationship Between Buyer and Supplier

Situations may arise in which the supplier has greater expertise in system performance than the buyer, or vice versa. In the author's experience, both are possible whether the buyer is a startup and the supplier is established, both are startups, both are established, or the supplier is a startup and the buyer is established. In any of these cases, transparency and adherence to commonly accepted guidelines for writing requirements, such as those prescribed by IEEE Std 830-1998 for software requirements documents [6] will go a long way to preventing misunderstandings and disputes regarding performance requirements and the interpretation of performance test results.

13. MANAGING PERFORMANCE REQUIREMENTS

Performance requirements play a role in every stage of the software lifecycle, whether the lifecycle is managed using a waterfall process, an Agile process, or something else. To facilitate access by the stakeholders, performance requirements should be centrally stored, perhaps in the same system that is used to store functional requirements. To ensure that performance considerations do not fall into a crack, it is essential that an individual be nominated as their owner, and that this individual be visibly mandated and empowered to communicate with all project stakeholders about performance issues.

In addition to addressing performance concerns, the performance requirements owner will be responsible for managing change control, requirements traceability, as well as ensuring that every change or addition is linked to business and engineering needs. The owner will also play a pivotal role in mediating between different groups of stakeholders when performance requirements are negotiated and written, including architects, designers, and perhaps even lawyers. Involvement with the latter is necessary to ensure that contracted levels of performance are described in measurable terms. If performance requirements are changed, the performance requirements owner must ensure that the changes are understood by architects, developers, and sales engineers, so that the necessary changes to architecture, implementation, and appropriate commitments to customers can be made.

14. CONCLUSION

The foregoing discussion has covered a wide range of topics related to performance requirements. Careful wording of performance requirements is necessary to ensure verifiability and testability. Ambiguity and confusion occur when a performance requirement contains inconsistencies, or when it is inconsistent with other requirements or with standards documents. Ambiguous and otherwise ill-specified requirements lead to time wasted trying to sort out what they mean. The absence of performance requirements can lead to disagreements among stakeholders about performance expectations. We have proposed guidelines for writing and managing performance requirements that are consistent with those for functional requirements. The performance requirements must be formulated in terms of metrics whose values can be measured in testing and in production. The metrics must be relevant to the application domain. We have also shown how reference scenarios and reference workloads can be used to steer stakeholders towards a clear baseline when the possible set of performance requirements is very large. Our experience suggests that adherence to the practices here can be used to avoid many performance pitfalls, while aiding in the smooth application of performance engineering principles in the software lifecycle.

15. ACKNOWLEDGMENTS

The author has benefited from useful discussions with Alberto Avritzer, Brian Berenbach, Dan Paulish, and Bob Schwanke of Siemens Corporate Research, as well as from the experience of teaching performance requirements practices in internal training courses.

16. REFERENCES

[1] Bass, Len, Robert L. Nord, William Wood, David Zubrow: Risk Themes Discovered through Architecture Evaluations. WICSA 2007, Mumbai, January 2007.

[2] Bondi, A. B.: Characteristics of Scalability and Their Impact on Performance. Proc. WOSP2000 (Workshop on Software Performance), 195-203, Ottawa, Canada, September 2000.

[3] Coffman, E., and P. J. Denning. Operating Systems Theory. Prentice Hall, 1973.

[4] Cooper, R. B., Introduction to Queueing Theory, Second Edition, North Holland, 1981.

[5] Ho, C.-W.; Johnson, M.J.; Williams, L., and Maximilen, E.M.: On agile performance requirements specification and testing. Proc. Agile Conference, Minneapolis, 2006,

[6] IEEE Std 830-1998 IEEE Recommended Practice for Software Requirements Specifications –Description

[7] Lilja, D. J. *Measuring Computer Performance: a Practitioner's Guide. Cambridge University Press,* 2000.

[8] http://www.prnewswire.com/cgi-bin/stories.pl?ACCT=104&STORY=/www/story/06-28-2007/0004617850&EDATE=

[9] NFPA 72, National Fire Alarm Code ®, 2007 Edition, NFPA, Quincy, MA 02169-7471.

[10] Nixon, B.A.: Managing performance requirements for information systems. Proc. First WOSP 1998, 131-144, 1998.

[11] Odlyszko, A.M., CMG Magazine, 2000.

[12] R. F. Rey (ed)., Engineering and Operations in the Bell System, AT&T Bell Laboratories, 1983.

[13] Smith, Connie U., and Lloyd G. Williams. Performance Solutions: a Practical Guide to Creating Responsive, Scalable Software. Addison-Wesley, 2000.

[14] Webster's Ninth New Collegiate Dictionary, Merriam Webster, 1988.

Introduction to Queueing Petri Nets:
Modeling Formalism, Tool Support and Case Studies

Samuel Kounev
Karlsruhe Institute of
Technology
Am Fasanengarten 5
Karlsruhe, Germany
kounev@kit.edu

Simon Spinner
FZI Research Center for
Information Technology
Haid-und-Neu-Str. 10-14
Karlsruhe, Germany
spinner@fzi.de

Philipp Meier
Karlsruhe Institute of
Technology
Am Fasanengarten 5
Karlsruhe, Germany
mail@philippmeier.com

ABSTRACT

Queueing Petri nets are a powerful formalism that can be exploited for modeling distributed systems and evaluating their performance and scalability. By combining the modeling power and expressiveness of queueing networks and stochastic Petri nets, queueing Petri nets provide a number of advantages. This tutorial presents an introduction to queueing Petri nets first introducing the modeling formalism itself and then summarizing the results of several modeling case studies which demonstrate how queueing Petri nets can be used for performance modeling and analysis. As part of the tutorial, we present QPME (Queueing Petri net Modeling Environment), an open-source tool for stochastic modeling and analysis of systems using queueing Petri nets. Finally, we briefly present a model-to-model transformation automatically generating a queueing Petri net model from a higher-level software architecture model annotated with performance relevant information.

Categories and Subject Descriptors

C.4 [**Performance Of Systems**]: Modeling Techniques; I.6.5 [**Simulation and Modeling**]: Model Development—*meta-modeling, modeling methodologies*; D.4.8 [**Operating Systems**]: Performance—*Modeling and prediction*

General Terms

Performance, design

Keywords

Performance, stochastic models, system simulation, modeling tools

1. INTRODUCTION

Introduced in 1993 by Falko Bause [1], queueing Petri nets (QPNs) have a number of advantages over conventional modeling formalisms such as queueing networks and stochastic Petri nets. By combining the modeling power and expressiveness of queueing networks and stochastic Petri nets, QPNs enable the integration of hardware and software aspects of system behavior into the same model. In addition to hardware contention and scheduling strategies, QPNs make it easy to model simultaneous resource possession, synchronization, asynchronous processing and software contention. These aspects have significant impact on the performance of modern enterprise software systems.

Another advantage of QPNs is that they can be used to combine qualitative and quantitative system analysis. A number of efficient techniques from Petri net theory can be exploited to verify some important qualitative properties of QPNs. The latter not only help to gain insight into the behavior of the system, but are also essential preconditions for a successful quantitative analysis [4]. Last but not least, QPN models have an intuitive graphical representation that facilitates model development. In [9], we showed how QPNs can be used for modeling distributed e-business applications. Building on this work, we have developed a methodology for performance modeling of distributed component-based systems using QPNs [7]. The methodology has been applied to model a number of systems ranging from simple systems to systems of realistic size and complexity. It can be used as a powerful tool for performance and scalability analysis. Some examples of modeling studies based on QPNs can be found in [7,8,11,12,15,18,19]. These studies consider different types of systems including distributed component-based systems, service-oriented applications, event-based systems and Grid computing environments.

In this tutorial, we present an introduction to queueing Petri nets (QPNs) first introducing the formalism itself. Then we present QPME (Queueing Petri net Modeling Environment) [17], an open-source tool for stochastic modeling and analysis of systems using QPNs. The tool is developed and maintained by the Descartes Research Group [6] at Karlsruhe Institute of Technology (KIT). The first version of the tool was released in January 2007 and since then it has been distributed to more than 130 organizations worldwide (universities, companies and research institutes). Since May 2011, QPME is distributed under the Eclipse Public License.

Afterwards, we summarize the results of several modeling case studies to demonstrate how QPNs can be used for performance modeling and analysis. Finally, as part of the tutorial, we briefly discuss our latest work on developing an automated model-to-model transformation from component-based software architecture models (with performance annotations) to QPN models analyzed using QPME. The transformation allows to specify models of software systems at a higher level of abstraction eliminating the need to build QPN models manually [14].

2. QUEUEING PETRI NETS

The main idea behind the QPN formalism was to add queueing and timing aspects to the places of Colored Generalized Stochastic Petri Nets (CGSPNs) [1]. This is done by allowing queues (service stations) to be integrated into places of CGSPNs. A place of a CGSPN that has an integrated queue is called a *queueing place* and consists of two components, the *queue* and a *depository* for tokens which have completed their service at the queue. This is depicted in Figure 1.

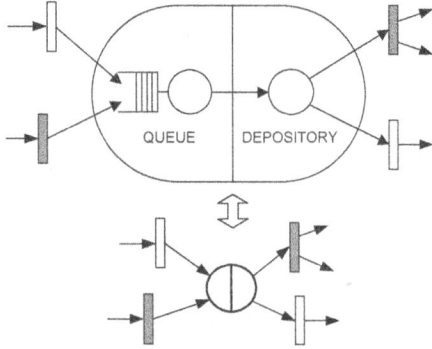

Figure 1: A queueing place and its shorthand notation.

The behavior of the net is as follows: tokens, when fired into a queueing place by any of its input transitions, are inserted into the queue according to the queue's scheduling strategy. Tokens in the queue are not available for output transitions of the place. After completion of its service, a token is immediately moved to the depository, where it becomes available for output transitions of the place. This type of queueing place is called *timed* queueing place. In addition to timed queueing places, QPNs also introduce *immediate* queueing places, which allow pure scheduling aspects to be described. Tokens in immediate queueing places can be viewed as being served immediately. Scheduling in such places has priority over scheduling/service in timed queueing places and firing of timed transitions. The rest of the net behaves like a normal CGSPN. A formal definition of a QPN follows [1]:

DEFINITION 1.
A QPN is an 8-tuple $QPN = (P, T, C, I^-, I^+, M_0, Q, W)$ where:

1. $P = \{p_1, p_2, ..., p_n\}$ *is a finite and non-empty set of places,*

2. $T = \{t_1, t_2, ..., t_m\}$ *is a finite and non-empty set of transitions, $P \cap T = \emptyset$,*

3. C *is a* color function *that assigns a finite and non-empty set of colors to each place and a finite and non-empty set of modes to each transition.*

4. I^- *and I^+ are the* backward *and* forward *incidence functions defined on $P \times T$, such that $I^-(p,t), I^+(p,t) \in [C(t) \to C(p)_{MS}]$, $\forall (p,t) \in P \times T$[1]*

5. M_0 *is a function defined on P describing the initial marking such that $M_0(p) \in C(p)_{MS}$.*

6. $Q = (\tilde{Q}_1, \tilde{Q}_2, (q_1, ..., q_{|P|}))$ *where*

   - $\tilde{Q}_1 \subseteq P$ *is the set of timed queueing places,*
   - $\tilde{Q}_2 \subseteq P$ *is the set of immediate queueing places, $\tilde{Q}_1 \cap \tilde{Q}_2 = \emptyset$ and*
   - q_i *denotes the description of a queue[2] taking all colors of $C(p_i)$ into consideration, if p_i is a queueing place* or *equals the keyword 'null', if p_i is an ordinary place.*

7. $W = (\tilde{W}_1, \tilde{W}_2, (w_1, ..., w_{|T|}))$ *where*

   - $\tilde{W}_1 \subseteq T$ *is the set of timed transitions,*
   - $\tilde{W}_2 \subseteq T$ *is the set of immediate transitions, $\tilde{W}_1 \cap \tilde{W}_2 = \emptyset$, $\tilde{W}_1 \cup \tilde{W}_2 = T$ and*
   - $w_i \in [C(t_i) \longmapsto \mathbb{R}^+]$ *such that $\forall c \in C(t_i)$: $w_i(c) \in \mathbb{R}^+$ is interpreted as a rate of a negative exponential distribution specifying the firing delay due to color c, if $t_i \in \tilde{W}_1$* or *a firing weight specifying the relative firing frequency due to color c, if $t_i \in \tilde{W}_2$.*

For a more detailed introduction to the QPN modeling formalism, the reader is referred to [1, 4, 7].

2.1 Hierarchical Queueing Petri Nets

A major hurdle to the practical application of QPNs is the so-called largeness problem or *state-space explosion problem*: as one increases the number of queues and tokens in a QPN, the size of the model's state space grows exponentially and quickly exceeds the capacity of today's computers. This imposes a limit on the size and complexity of the models that are analytically tractable. An attempt to alleviate this problem was the introduction of *Hierarchically-Combined QPNs (HQPNs)* [2]. The main idea is to allow hierarchical model specification and then exploit the hierarchical structure for efficient numerical analysis. This type of analysis is termed *structured analysis* and it allows models to be solved that are about an order of magnitude larger than those analyzable with conventional techniques. HQPNs are a natural generalization of the original QPN formalism. In HQPNs, a queueing place may contain a whole QPN instead of a single queue. Such a place is called a *subnet place* and is depicted in Figure 2. A subnet place might contain an ordinary QPN or again a HQPN allowing multiple levels of nesting. For simplicity, we restrict ourselves to two-level hierarchies. We use the term *High-Level QPN (HLQPN)* to refer to the upper level of the HQPN and the term *Low-Level QPN (LLQPN)*

---

[1]The subscript MS denotes multisets. $C(p)_{MS}$ denotes the set of all finite multisets of $C(p)$.

[2]In the most general definition of QPNs, queues are defined in a very generic way allowing the specification of arbitrarily complex scheduling strategies taking into account the state of both the queue and the depository of the queueing place [1]. In QPME, we use conventional queues as defined in queueing network theory.

to refer to a subnet of the HLQPN. Every subnet of a HQPN has a dedicated input and output place, which are ordinary places of a CPN. Tokens being inserted into a subnet place after a transition firing are added to the input place of the corresponding HQPN subnet. The semantics of the output place of a subnet place is similar to the semantics of the depository of a queueing place: tokens in the output place are available for output transitions of the subnet place. Tokens contained in all other places of the HQPN subnet are not available for output transitions of the subnet place. Every HQPN subnet also contains a *actual-population* place used to keep track of the total number of tokens fired into the subnet place.

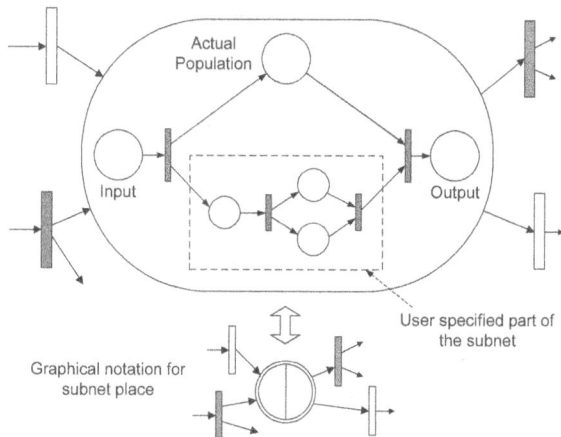

Figure 2: A subnet place and its shorthand notation.

2.2 Departure Disciplines

Departure disciplines are an extension of the QPN modeling formalism introduced in [7] to address a common limitation of QPN models (and of Petri nets in general), i.e., tokens inside ordinary places and depositories are not distinguished in terms of their order of arrival. Departure disciplines are defined for ordinary places or depositories and determine the order in which arriving tokens become available for output transitions. We define two departure disciplines, Normal (used by default) and First-In-First-Out (FIFO). The former implies that tokens become available for output transitions immediately upon arrival just like in conventional QPN models. The latter implies that tokens become available for output transitions in the order of their arrival, i.e., a token can leave the place/depository only after all tokens that have arrived before it have left, hence the term FIFO. For an example of how this feature can be exploited and the benefits it provides we refer the reader to [7]. An alternative approach to introduce token ordering in an ordinary place is to replace the place with an immediate queueing place containing a FCFS queue. The generalized queue definition from [1] can be exploited to define the scheduling strategy of the queue in such a way that tokens are served immediately according to FCFS, but only if the depository is empty [4]. If there is a token in the depository, all tokens are blocked in their current position until the depository becomes free. However, the generalized queue definition from [1], while theoretically powerful, is impractical to implement, so, in practice, it is rarely used and queues in QPNs are usually

treated as conventional queues from queueing network theory.

2.3 Example QPN Model

We now present an example QPN model of a simple Java EE system. The model was taken from [9] and is shown in Figure 3.

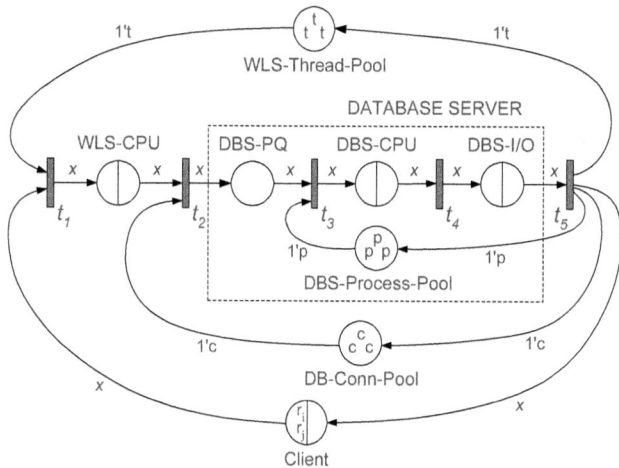

Figure 3: QPN Model of a Java EE System [9].

The system modeled is an e-business application running in a Java EE environment consisting of a WebLogic Server (Java EE application server) hosting the application components and a backend database server used for persisting business data. In the following, we describe the places of the model:

Client Queueing place with IS scheduling strategy representing clients sending requests to the system. Time spent at the queue of this place corresponds to the client think time, i.e., the service time of the queue is equal to the average client think time.

WLS-CPU Queueing place with PS scheduling strategy representing the CPU of the *WebLogic Server (WLS)*.

DBS-CPU Queueing place with PS scheduling strategy representing the CPU of the *database server (DBS)*.

DBS-I/O Queueing place with FCFS scheduling strategy representing the disk subsystem of the DBS.

WLS-Thread-Pool Ordinary place representing the thread pool of the WLS. Each token in this place represents a WLS thread.

DB-Conn-Pool Ordinary place representing the database connection pool of the WLS. Tokens in this place represent database connections to the DBS.

DBS-Process-Pool Ordinary place representing the process pool of the DBS. Tokens in this place represent database processes.

DBS-PQ Ordinary place used to hold incoming requests at the DBS while they wait for a server process to be allocated to them.

The following types of tokens (token colors) are used in the model:

Token 'r_i' represents a request sent by a client for execution of a transaction of class i. For each request class a separate token color is used (e.g., 'r_1', 'r_2', 'r_3',...). Tokens of these colors can be contained only in places `Client`, `WLS-CPU`, `DBS-PQ`, `DBS-CPU` and `DBS-I/O`.

Token 't' represents a WLS thread. Tokens of this color can be contained only in place `WLS-Thread-Pool`.

Token 'p' represents a DBS process. Tokens of this color can be contained only in place `DBS-Process-Pool`.

Token 'c' represents a database connection to the DBS. Tokens of this color can be contained only in place `DB-Conn-Pool`.

We now take a look at the life-cycle of a client request in our system model. Every request (modeled by a token of color 'r_i' for some i) is initially at the queue of place `Client` where it waits for a user-specified think time. After the think time elapses, the request moves to the `Client` depository where it waits for a WLS thread to be allocated to it before its processing can begin. Once a thread is allocated (modeled by taking a token of color 't' from place `WLS-Thread-Pool`), the request moves to the queue of place `WLS-CPU`, where it receives service from the CPU of the WLS. It then moves to the depository of the place and waits for a database connection to be allocated to it. The database connection (modeled by token 'c') is used to connect to the database and make any updates required by the respective transaction. A request sent to the database server arrives at place `DBS-PQ` (DBS Process Queue) where it waits for a server process (modeled by token 'p') to be allocated to it. Once this is done, the request receives service first at the CPU and then at the disk subsystem of the database server. This completes the processing of the request, which is then sent back to place `Client` releasing the held DBS process, database connection and WLS thread.

3. QUEUEING PETRI NET MODELING ENVIRONMENT (QPME)

QPME (Queueing Petri net Modeling Environment) [17] is an open-source tool for stochastic modeling and analysis of systems using QPNs, distributed under the Eclipse Public License. The tool is developed and maintained by the Descartes Research Group [6] at Karlsruhe Institute of Technology (KIT). QPME consists of two main components: a QPN Editor (QPE) and a Simulator for QPNs (SimQPN). In the following, we briefly describe these components.

3.1 Queueing Petri net Editor (QPE)

QPE is a graphical editor for QPNs. The user can create QPN models with a simple drag-and-drop approach. Figure 4 shows the QPE main window which is comprised of four views. The *Main Editor View* displays the graphical representation of the currently edited QPN. The palette contains the set of QPN elements that can be inserted in a QPN model by drag-and-drop, such as places, transitions, and connections. Furthermore, it provides editors for the central definition of colors and queues used in a QPN model. In the *Properties View* the user can edit the properties of the element currently selected in the QPN model. For instance, scheduling strategies and service time distributions of queueing places can be specified in this view. The *Outline View* shows a list of all elements in the QPN model. The *Console View* displays the output when simulating a QPN model.

In a QPN, a transition defines a set of firing modes. An incidence function specifies the behavior of the transition for each of its firing modes in terms of tokens destroyed and/or created in the places of the QPN. Figure 5 shows the *Incidence Function Editor*, which is used to edit the incidence function of a transition. Once opened this editor displays the transition input places on the left, the transition firing modes in the middle and the transition output places on the right. Each place (input or output) is displayed as a rectangle containing a separate circle for each token color allowed in the place. The user can create connections from token colors of input places to modes or from modes to token colors of output places. If a connection is created between a token color of a place and a mode, this means that when the transition fires in this mode, tokens of the respective color are removed from the place. Similarly, if a connection is created between a mode and a token color of an output place, this means that when the transition fires in this mode, tokens of the respective color are deposited in the place.

In addition to the basic features described above, QPE has several characterizing features that improve the model expressiveness of QPNs and simplify the creation of complex QPN models. Special mention must be made of the following features:

- *Central color management.* The user can define token colors globally for the whole QPN instead of on a per place basis. This feature was motivated by the fact that in QPNs typically the same token color (type) is used in multiple places. Instead of having to define the color multiple times, the user can define it one time and then reference it in all places where it is used. This saves time, makes the model definition more compact, and last but not least, it makes the modeling process less error-prone since references to the same token color are specified explicitly.

- *Shared queues.* The user can specify that multiple queueing places share the same underlying physical queue[3]. In QPE, queues are defined centrally (similar to token colors) and once defined they can be referenced from inside multiple queueing places. This allows to use queueing places to represent software entities, e.g., software components, which can then be mapped to different hardware resources modeled as queues [18]. Shared queues are not supported in standard QPN models [18].

- *Hierarchical QPNs.* Subnet places can contain complete child QPN models. Hierarchical QPNs enable to model layered systems and improve the understandability of huge QPNs. QPE fully supports hierarchical QPNs.

---

[3]While the same effect can be achieved by using multiple subnet places mapped to a nested QPN containing a single queueing place, this would require expanding tokens that enter the nested QPN with a *tag* to keep track of their origin as explained in [3].

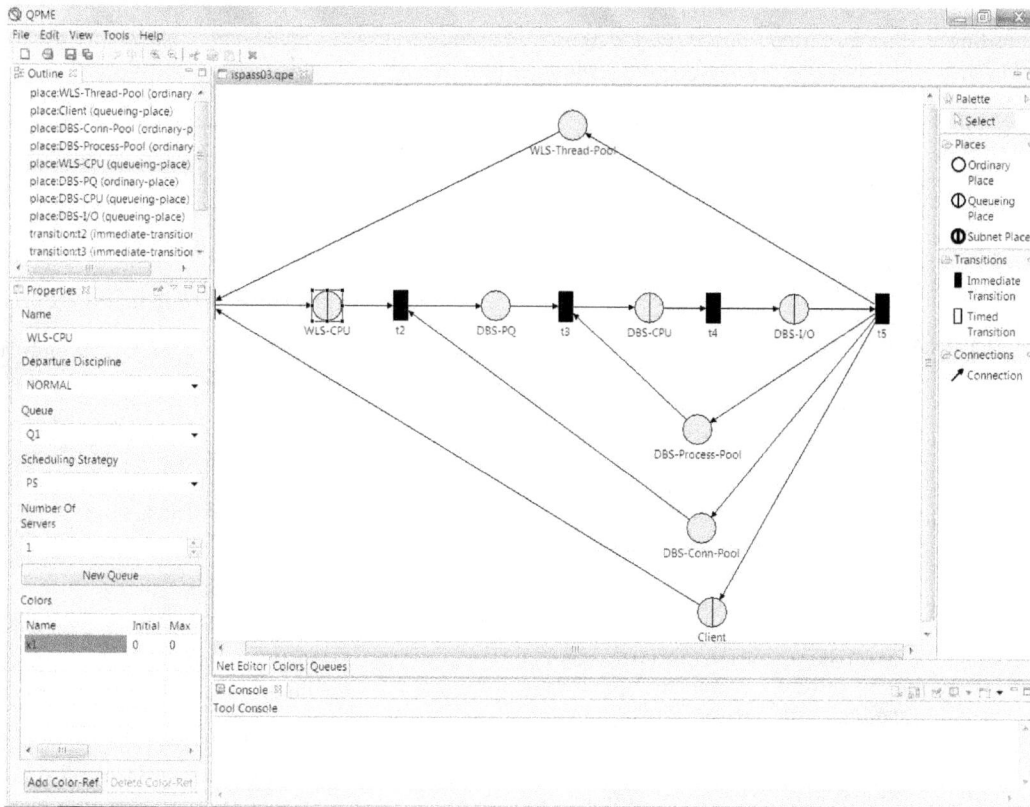

Figure 4: QPE main window.

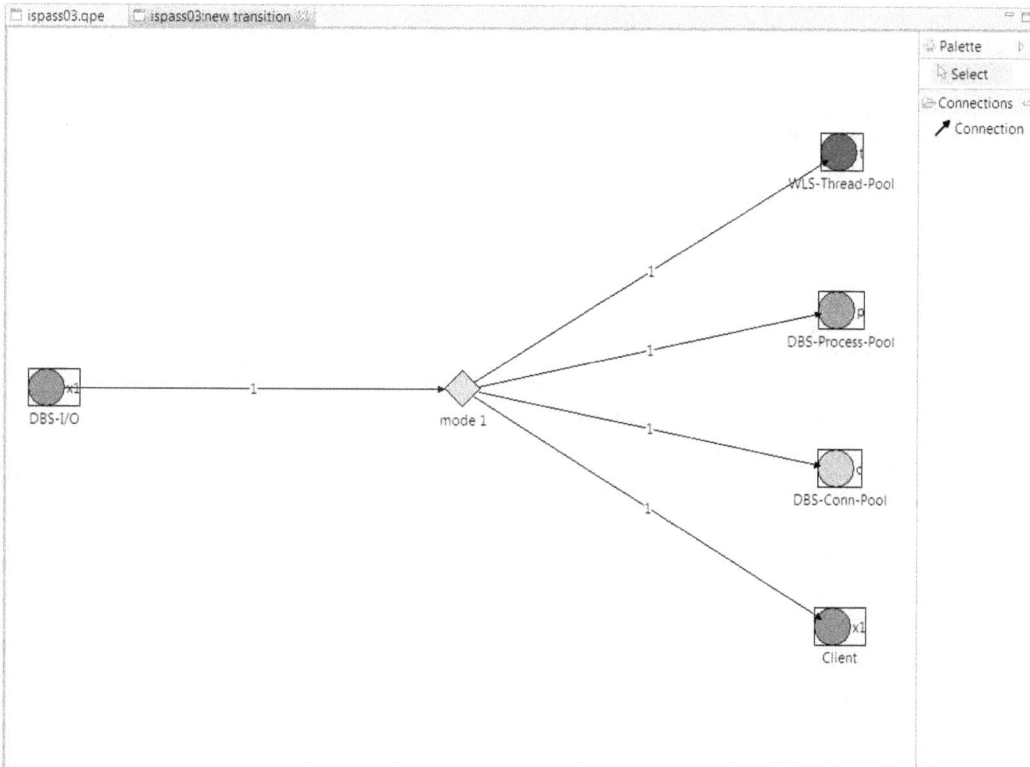

Figure 5: QPE incidence function editor.

- *Departure Disciplines.* Departure disciplines are defined for ordinary places or depositories and determine the order in which arriving tokens become available for output transitions. QPE supports two disciplines: Normal (used by default) and First-In-First-Out (FIFO). The latter implies that tokens become available for output transitions in the order of their arrival whereas the former does not consider the order of arrival of tokens. For an example of how this extension of the QPN formalism can be exploited and the benefits it provides we refer the reader to [7].

3.2 Simulation of QPN Model (SimQPN)

SimQPN is a discrete-event simulation engine specialized for QPNs. It simulates QPN models directly and has been designed to exploit the knowledge of the structure and behavior of QPNs to improve the efficiency of the simulation. Therefore, SimQPN provides much better performance than a general purpose simulator would provide, both in terms of the speed of simulation and the quality of output data provided.

3.2.1 Model Support

SimQPN implements most, but not all of the QPN elements that can be modeled in QPE. It currently supports three different scheduling strategies for queues: First-Come-First-Served (FCFS), Processor-Sharing (PS), and Infinite Server (IS). A wide range of service time distributions are supported including Beta, BreitWigner, ChiSquare, Gamma, Hyperbolic, Exponential, ExponentialPower, Logarithmic, Normal, StudentT, Uniform and VonMises as well as deterministic and empirical distributions. All of the characterizing features of QPE described in Sect. 3.1 are fully supported by the SimQPN simulator. A current limitation of SimQPN is the missing support for timed transitions[4] and immediate queueing places. The spectrum of scheduling strategies and service time distributions supported by SimQPN will be extended. Support for timed transitions and immediate queueing places is also planned for future releases.

3.2.2 Output Data

SimQPN offers the ability to configure what data exactly to collect during the simulation and what statistics to provide at the end of the run. This can be specified on a per *location* basis where location is defined to have one of the following five types: i) ordinary place, ii) queue of a queueing place (considered from the perspective of the place), iii) depository of a queueing place, iv) queue (considered from the perspective of all places it is part of), and v) probe.

A probe enables the user to specify a region of interest for which data should be collected during simulation. The region of a probe includes one or more places and is defined by one start and one end place. The goal is to evaluate the time tokens spend in the region when moving between its begin and end place. The probe starts its measurements for each token entering its region at the start place and updates the statistics when the token leaves at the end place. Probes are realized by attaching timestamps to individual tokens. With probes it is possible to determine statistics for the residence time of tokens in a region of interest.

For each location the user can choose between six modes of data collection . The higher the mode, the more information is collected and the more statistics are provided. Since collecting data costs CPU time, the more data is collected, the slower the simulation would progress. Therefore, with data collection modes the user can speed up the simulation by avoiding the collection of data that is not required. The six data collection modes are defined as follows:

- *Mode 0.* No data is collected.

- *Mode 1.* Only token throughput data is collected.

- *Mode 2.* Additionally, data to compute token population, token occupancy, and queue utilization is collected

- *Mode 3.* Token residence time data is collected (maximum, minimum, mean, standard deviation, steady state mean, and confidence interval of steady state mean).

- *Mode 4.* This mode adds a histogram of observed token residence times.

- *Mode 5.* Additionally token residence times are dumped to a file for further analysis with external tools.

3.2.3 Steady State Analysis

SimQPN supports two methods for the estimation of steady state mean residence times of tokens inside the various locations of the QPN. These are the well-known *Method of Independent Replications* (in its variant referred to as replication/deletion approach) and the classical *Method of Nonoverlapping Batch Means (NOMB)*. We refer the reader to [13, 16] for an introduction to these methods. Both of them can be used to provide point and interval estimates of the steady state mean token residence time.

We have validated the analysis algorithms implemented in SimQPN by subjecting them to a rigorous experimental analysis and evaluating the quality of point and interval estimates [10]. Our analysis showed that data reported by SimQPN is very accurate and stable. Even for residence time, the metric with highest variation, the standard deviation of point estimates did not exceed 2.5% of the mean value. In all cases, the estimated coverage of confidence intervals was less than 2% below the nominal value (higher than 88% for 90% confidence intervals and higher than 93% for 95% confidence intervals).

Furthermore, SimQPN includes an implementation of the *Method of Welch* for determining the length of the initial transient (warm-up period). We have followed the rules in [13] for choosing the number of replications, their length and the window size.

3.2.4 Processing and Visualization of Results

After a successful simulation run, SimQPN saves the results from the simulation in an XML file with a `.simqpn` extension. QPE provides an advanced query engine for the processing and visualization of simulation results. The query engine allows to define queries on the simulation results in order to filter, aggregate and visualize performance data for multiple places, queues and colors of the QPN. The results from the queries can be displayed in textual or graphical form. QPE provides the following two query editors:

---

[4]In most cases a timed transition can be approximated by a serial network consisting of an immediate transition, a queueing place and a second immediate transition.

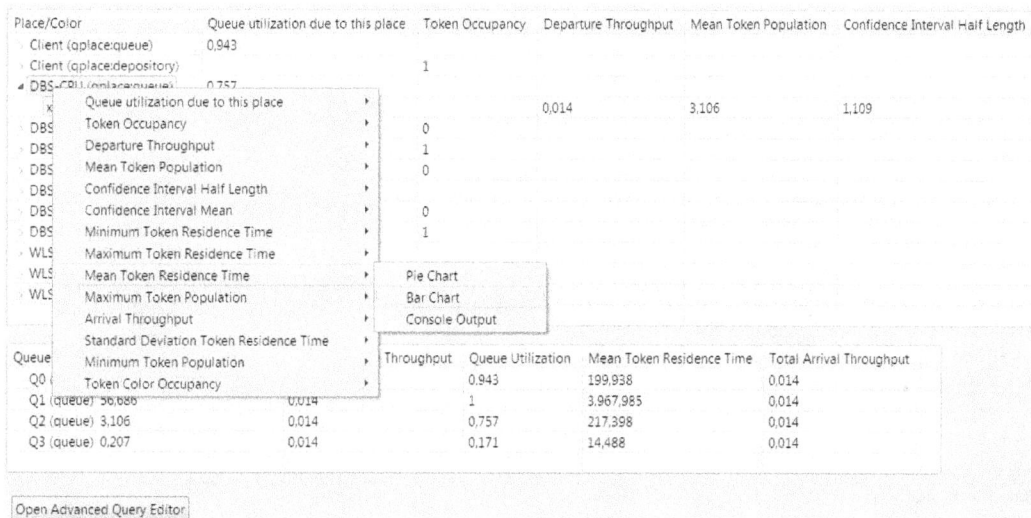

Figure 6: Metrics context menu of the simple query editor.

- *Simple Query Editor.* The user can quickly filter and visualize metrics of a *single* location or token color with a few clicks. Currently, three visualization options are available: "Pie Chart", "Bar Chart" and "Console Output".

- *Advanced Query Editor.* The user can create complex queries including the aggregation of metrics over multiple locations and token colors with a powerful user interface. The following two aggregation operators are currently supported: "Average" and "Sum".

Figure 6 shows an area of the user interface of the simple query editor. The statistics for all QPN places are presented in the table in the background. When opening the context menu of one of the places, a context menu with a set of possible metrics of interest is made available.

4. MODELING CASE STUDIES

In this section, we summarize the results of several case studies in different application domains showing how QPN models can be exploited for performance analysis of different types of computer systems.

4.1 Distributed Component-Based Systems

In [7], we presented a novel case study of a realistic distributed component-based system, showing how QPN models can be exploited as a powerful performance prediction tool in the software engineering process. A detailed system model was built in a step-by-step fashion, validated, and then used to evaluate the system performance and scalability. The system studied in [7] is a deployment of the SPECjAppServer2004 benchmark for J2EE application servers. It models a complete end-to-end application that is designed to be representative of today's real-life distributed component-based systems. Along with the case study, a practical performance modeling methodology was presented in [7] which helps to construct models that accurately reflect the system performance and scalability characteristics. We showed that

by taking advantage of the modeling power and expressiveness of QPNs our approach makes it possible to model the system at a higher degree of accuracy, providing a number of important benefits.

The QPN model of the SPECjAppServer2004 benchmark was validated by comparing the model predictions against measurements from the real system for a number of different transaction mixes. The QPN model we developed according to the presented methodology was able to predict the performance of the system accurately. We then used the validated QPN model to analyze the system with different deployment configurations and workload scenarios in order to analyze its scalability. We were able to correctly identify the load balancer as the bottleneck resource with our model. Furthermore, we showed that the accuracy of the QPN model can be improved further when introducing departure disciplines for places in QPNs. In summary, it was possible to analyze QPN models of realistic size and complexity using SimQPN, taking advantage of the modeling power and expressiveness of the QPN paradigm. Even for the largest and most complex scenarios, the modeling error for transaction response time did not exceed 20.6% and was much lower for transaction throughput and resource utilization.

4.2 Distributed Event-Based Systems

In [12,19], we presented a comprehensive methodology for workload characterization and performance modeling of Distributed Event-Based Systems (DEBS). The methodology helps to identify and eliminate bottlenecks and ensure that systems are designed and sized to meet their QoS requirements. The methodology is based on operational analysis and QPNs. We first used analytical analysis techniques to find the utilization of system components and derive an approximation for the mean event delivery latency. We then showed how more detailed performance models based on QPNs can be built to provide more accurate performance prediction. Modeling DEBS is particularly challenging because of the complete decoupling of communicating parties, on the one hand, and the dynamic changes in the system structure and behavior, on the other hand. When a request is sent in a traditional request/reply-based distributed system, it is sent directly to a given destination which makes it easy to identify the system components and resources involved in its processing. In contrast to this, when an event is published in a DEBS, it is not addressed to a particular destination, but rather routed along all paths that lead to subscribers with matching subscriptions. In this case study, the DEBS was modeled with QPNs because it simplifies the modeling of forks of asynchronous tasks. In [12, 19], we also proposed the extension of the QPN formalism to support queues shared by several queueing places as it eases the modeling of a DEBS. This extension has been meanwhile integrated into QPME.

The SPECjms2007 benchmark was used in this case study to evaluate the performance of the proposed methodology. The SPECjms2007 benchmark is based on an application scenario modeling the supply chain of a supermarket company where RFID technology is used to track the flow of goods. Given the size and complexity of the modeled system, the resulting performance model was much larger and more complex than existing queueing models of message-oriented event-based systems. Overall, the presented model contained a total of 59 queueing places, 76 token colors and 68 transitions with a total of 285 firing modes. The model was analyzed using SimQPN which took less than 5 minutes in all cases. We considered several different scenarios that represent different types of messaging workloads stressing different aspects of the MOM infrastructure including both workloads focused on point-to-point messaging as well as workloads focused on publish/subscribe. In summary, the model proved to be very accurate in predicting the system performance, especially considering the size and complexity of the system that was modeled [19].

4.3 Enterprise Data Fabrics

Enterprise data fabrics are gaining increasing attention in many industry domains including financial services, telecommunications, transportation and health care. Providing a distributed, operational data platform sitting between application infrastructures and back-end data sources, enterprise data fabrics are designed for high performance and scalability. In [8], we presented a case study of a representative enterprise data fabric, the Gem-Fire EDF, presenting a simulation-based tool that we have developed for automated performance prediction and capacity planning. We implemented a tool that automates resource demand estimation, model generation, model analysis and results processing based on QPN models. Given a system configuration and a workload scenario, the tool generates a report showing the predicted system throughput, server utilization and operation response times. The tool uses SimQPN for solving the generated QPN models.

Both, the modeling approach and the model extraction technique were evaluated to demonstrate their effectiveness and practical applicability. We considered several workload and configuration scenarios and compared performance predictions obtained with SimQPN against measurements on the real system. Overall, our experiments showed that predictions of network and server utilization were quite accurate independent of the load level, while predictions of response times were reasonably accurate in the cases where the average server utilization was lower than 75% [8]. We also considered the analysis overhead and showed that the analysis overhead is acceptable for capacity planning purposes and the proposed approach can be applied for scenarios of reasonable size [8].

4.4 Enterprise Grid Environments

In [15], we presented a methodology for designing autonomic Quality of Service (QoS) aware resource managers that have the capability to predict the performance of the Grid components they manage and allocate resources in such a way that service level agreements are honored. Support for advanced features such as autonomic workload characterization on-the-fly, dynamic deployment of Grid servers on demand, as well as dynamic system reconfiguration after a server failure is provided. We implemented a resource manager framework that uses QPNs as online performance models for autonomic QoS control. The QPN models are solved using SimQPN to obtain QoS predictions. The approach was validated in two different experimental setups, the first one with only two Grid servers, the second one with up to nine servers running in a virtualized environment. As a basis for the experiments, we used three sample services each with different behavior and service demands. The results of the predictions from SimQPN were compared to measurements from a real system and to predictions obtained with OMNeT++ models. The results showed that both QPN and OMNeT++ models provided very consistent and accurate predictions of performance metrics. There was hardly any difference between confidence intervals provided by SimQPN and OMNeT++. At the same time, while OMNeT++ results were limited to request response times, SimQPN results were more comprehensive and included estimates of request throughputs, server utilization, queue lengths, etc. In all cases, the modeling error was below 15%. For details about the experiment setup and procedure see [15].

Five different scenarios each focusing on selected aspects of the framework were studied. We compared the behavior of the system in two different configurations - "with QoS Control" vs. "without QoS Control". In the first configuration, the resource manager applied admission control using our resource allocation framework to ensure that SLAs are honored. In the second configuration, the resource manager simply load-balanced the incoming requests over the two servers without considering QoS requirements. In all scenarios with QoS Control enabled, the measured response times were stable and nearly 100% of the client SLAs were fulfilled. The results confirmed the effectiveness of our resource manager architecture in ensuring that QoS requirements are continuously met.

5. MODEL-TO-MODEL TRANSFORMATIONS

In [14], we showed how an automated model-to-model transformation can be used to evaluate the performance of component-based systems modeled at the software architectural level by means of automatically generated QPN models. The source language, in this case, the Palladio Component Model (PCM) [5], is automatically transformed into a suitable QPN representation, which is then solved using the tools introduced earlier. In this section, we briefly discuss PCM and then illustrate the transformation by presenting as an example the mapping of open and closed workloads.

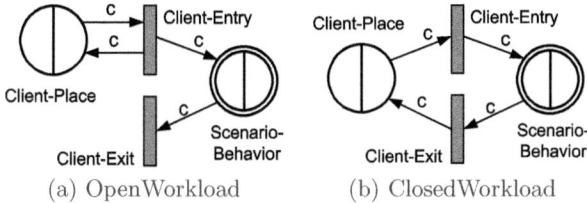

(a) OpenWorkload   (b) ClosedWorkload

Figure 7: Workload QPN.

Finally, we summarize the results from an in-depth evaluation of the transformation.

5.1 Palladio Component Model (PCM)

The Palladio Component Model (PCM) [5] is a meta-model allowing the specification of performance-relevant information of a component-based architecture. It focuses on the software performance engineering (SPE) and component-based software engineering (CBSE) domains. Four factors essentially determine the performance of a software component: its implementation, the performance of external services it requires, the performance of the execution environment it is deployed on, and the usage profile. Each of these aspects is described using parametric dependencies. The PCM provides a domain-specific language for describing component-based software architectures and the performance characteristics of the employed components.

5.2 PCM2QPN Transformation

To illustrate how elements of PCM are mapped to QPN elements, the mapping of closed and open workloads is presented in the following.

The workload in PCM is represented as a number of usage scenarios, running in parallel. Each scenario has a workload specification and contains a specification of the scenario behavior. Two kinds of workloads are supported. An open workload is characterized by an inter-arrival time distribution, which describes the time that elapses between consecutive requests. Figure 7(a) shows how the *OpenWorkload* usage model entity is represented in the generated QPN to achieve the open workload semantics. The *Client-Place* queueing place generates tokens of a color *c* which is different for each *UsageScenario*. It references a client queue with Infinite Server (IS) scheduling strategy. An empirical distribution is used for the *Client-Place* resource demand representing *inter-arrival time* distribution of the *OpenWorkload*. The initial number of tokens is set to 1. For each input token the *Client-Entry* transition creates a new token in the subnet representing the *ScenarioBehavior*. Another token is created in the *Client-Place* queue. The *Client-Exit* transition destroys tokens of color *c* from the *ScenarioBehavior* subnet.

A closed workload is characterized both by an integral population, as well as by a think time distribution. There is a fixed number of requests, each of which has to wait according to the think time after its processing is complete. Figure 7(b) shows the mapping for a *ClosedWorkload*. The difference is that the *Client-Entry* transition does not generate any tokens in the *Client-Place*. Instead, this is done by the *Client-Exit* transition. At the *Client-Place* we use an empirical distribution for the resource demand equal to the

think time distribution of the *ClosedWorkload*. The initial number of tokens is set to the *population* of the closed workload. A new token will now be available after it has passed through the whole *ScenarioBehavior* and after the residence time in the queue, which equals the *think time*.

Other elements of the PCM meta-model are mapped in a similar manner. Also, as part of the transformation, the individual QPN parts of the mapped PCM elements are connected using ordinary places according to the connections within the PCM model. The different possible token colors for each QPN part are similarly derived from the different usages of a component definition within the PCM system model.

5.3 Evaluation

The approach of using an automated transformation for the analysis of PCM models was evaluated in the context of five representative case studies. The details are omitted here for brevity and can be found in [14]. Compared to existing tools to analyze PCM models, our approach leads to performance predictions of mean value metrics with high accuracy at a significantly reduced analysis overhead in many cases by an order of magnitude. Important limitations of the approach are the inability to model the synchronization of multiple requests at a barrier, as well as the inability to represent stochastic dependencies between PCM expression language variables.

6. CONCLUSIONS

In this tutorial, we presented an introduction to the QPN modeling formalism and showed how it can be used for performance modeling of distributed systems. QPNs have a number of benefits compared to traditional queueing networks and stochastic Petri nets. Exploiting the modeling power and expressiveness of QPNs, QPN models can be used to accurately capture both hardware and software aspects of system behavior. We summarized the results from several modeling case studies in different application domains (including distributed component-based systems, distributed event-based systems, enterprise data fabrics, and enterprise grid environments) showing how QPNs can be used for performance modeling in these domains. Furthermore, we briefly introduced QPME, a tool for stochastic modeling and analysis using QPNs. Finally, we showed how software architecture models (with performance annotations capturing performance relevant aspects) can be automatically transformed to QPNs eliminating the need to build QPN models manually.

Acknowledgements

This work was partially funded by the German Research Foundation (DFG) under grant No. KO 3445/6-1.

7. REFERENCES

[1] F. Bause. Queueing Petri Nets - A formalism for the combined qualitative and quantitative analysis of systems. In *Proc. of 5th Intl. Workshop on Petri Nets and Perf. Models, Toulouse, France, Oct. 19-22*, 1993.

[2] F. Bause, P. Buchholz, and P. Kemper. *Hierarchically combined queueing Petri nets*, volume 199 of *Lecture Notes in Control and Information Sciences*, pages 176–182. Springer Berlin / Heidelberg, 1994.

[3] F. Bause, P. Buchholz, and P. Kemper. Integrating Software and Hardware Performance Models Using Hierarchical Queueing Petri Nets. In *Proc. of the 9. ITG / GI - Fachtagung Messung, Modellierung und Bewertung von Rechen- und Kommunikationssystemen, Freiberg, Germany*, 1997.

[4] F. Bause and F. Kritzinger. *Stochastic Petri Nets - An Introduction to the Theory*. Vieweg Verlag, 2002.

[5] S. Becker, H. Koziolek, and R. Reussner. The palladio component model for model-driven performance prediction. *Journal of Systems and Software*, 82(1):3–22, 2009.

[6] Descartes Research Group. http://www.descartes-research.net, November 2011.

[7] S. Kounev. Performance Modeling and Evaluation of Distributed Component-Based Systems using Queueing Petri Nets. *IEEE Transactions on Software Engineering*, 32(7):486–502, July 2006.

[8] S. Kounev, K. Bender, F. Brosig, N. Huber, and R. Okamoto. Automated Simulation-Based Capacity Planning for Enterprise Data Fabrics. In *Proceedings of the 4th International ICST Conference on Simulation Tools and Techniques (SIMUTools 2011), Barcelona, Spain*, 2011.

[9] S. Kounev and A. Buchmann. Performance Modelling of Distributed E-Business Applications using Queuing Petri Nets. In *Proceedings of the 2003 IEEE International Symposium on Performance Analysis of Systems and Software (ISPASS 2003), Austin, USA, March 20-22*, 2003.

[10] S. Kounev and A. Buchmann. SimQPN - a tool and methodology for analyzing queueing Petri net models by means of simulation. *Performance Evaluation*, 63(4-5):364–394, May 2006.

[11] S. Kounev, R. Nou, and J. Torres. Autonomic QoS-Aware Resource Management in Grid Computing using Online Performance Models. In *Proceedings of the 2nd International Conference on Performance Evaluation Methodologies and Tools (VALUETOOLS 2007), Oct. 23-25, Nantes, France*, 2007.

[12] S. Kounev, K. Sachs, J. Bacon, and A. Buchmann. A Methodology for Performance Modeling of Distributed Event-Based Systems. In *Proceedings of the 11th IEEE International Symposium on Object/Component/Service-oriented Real-time Distributed Computing (ISORC 2008), Orlando, USA*, May 2008.

[13] A. Law and D. W. Kelton. *Simulation Modeling and Analysis*. Mc Graw Hill Companies, Inc., third edition, 2000.

[14] P. Meier, S. Kounev, and H. Koziolek. Automated Transformation of Palladio Component Models to Queueing Petri Nets. In *Proceedings of the 19th IEEE/ACM International Symposium on Modeling, Analysis and Simulation of Computer and Telecommunication Systems (MASCOTS 2011)*, Singapore, July 25-27 2011.

[15] R. Nou, S. Kounev, F. Julia, and J. Torres. Autonomic QoS control in enterprise Grid environments using online simulation. *Journal of Systems and Software*, 82(3):486–502, Mar. 2009.

[16] K. Pawlikowski. Steady-State Simulation of Queueing Processes: A Survey of Problems and Solutions. *ACM Computing Surveys*, 22(2):123–170, 1990.

[17] QPME Homepage. http://qpme.sourceforge.net, November 2011.

[18] K. Sachs. *Performance Modeling and Benchmarking of Event-based Systems*. PhD thesis, TU Darmstadt, 2010.

[19] K. Sachs, S. Kounev, and A. Buchmann. Performance Modeling and Analysis of Message-oriented Event-driven Systems. *Journal of Software and Systems Modeling (SoSyM)*, January 2012. To appear.

Keynote Talk

Assuring the Trustworthiness of the Smarter Electric Grid

William H. Sanders
University of Illinois
Urbana-Champaign, Illinois, USA
whs@illinois.edu

Abstract

The vision for a modernized "Smart Grid" involves the use of an advanced computing, communication and control cyber infrastructure for enhancing current grid operations by enabling timely interactions among a range of entities. The coupling between the power grid and its cyber infrastructure is inherent, and the extent to which the Smart Grid vision can be achieved depends upon the trustworthiness of its cyber infrastructure.

This talk describes challenges in assuring the trustworthiness (performance, dependability, and security) of the emerging smart grid, using example of research underway at the DOE- and HHS-funded Trustworthy Cyber Infrastructure for the Power Grid (TCIPG) Center. The goal of TCIPG is to provide trustworthiness in the nation's electric grid cyber infrastructure such that it continues to deliver electricity and maintain critical operations even in the presence of cyber attacks. Achieving this goal will involve the extension, integration, design, and development of IT technologies imbibed with key properties of real-time availability and security. This research area provides many opportunities for performance analysts and engineers to apply and extend their research.

Categories & Subject Descriptors: D.2.1 Requirements/Specifications, D.2.9 Management, I.6 Simulation and Modeling, J.7 Computers in Other Systems

General Terms: Management, Measurement, Performance, Design, Reliability, Security

Keywords: Smart Grid

Bio

William H. Sanders is a Donald Biggar Willett Professor of Engineering and the Director of the Coordinated Science Laboratory (www.csl.illinois.edu) at the University of Illinois at Urbana-Champaign, and was the founding Director Of the Information Trust Institute (www.iti.illinois.edu). He is a professor in the Department of Electrical and Computer Engineering and Affiliate Professor in the Department of Computer Science. He is a Fellow of the IEEE and the ACM, a past Chair of the IEEE Technical Committee on Fault-Tolerant Computing, and past Vice-Chair of the IFIP Working Group 10.4 on Dependable Computing.

On The Accuracy of Cache Sharing Models

Vlastimil Babka
babka@d3s.mff.cuni.cz

Peter Libič
libic@d3s.mff.cuni.cz

Tomáš Martinec
martinec@d3s.mff.cuni.cz

Petr Tůma
tuma@d3s.mff.cuni.cz

Department of Distributed and Dependable Systems
Faculty of Mathematics and Physics, Charles University
Malostranské náměstí 25, Prague 1, 118 00, Czech Republic

ABSTRACT

Memory caches significantly improve the performance of workloads that have temporal and spatial locality by providing faster access to data. Current processor designs have multiple cores sharing a cache. To accurately model a workload performance and to improve system throughput by intelligently scheduling workloads on cores, we need to understand how sharing caches between workloads affects their data accesses.

Past research has developed analytical models that estimate the cache behavior for combined workloads given the stack distance profiles describing these workloads. We extend this research by presenting an analytical model with contributions to accuracy and composability – our model makes fewer simplifying assumptions than earlier models, and its output is in the same format as its input, which is an important property for hierarchical composition during software performance modeling.

To compare the accuracy of our analytical model with earlier models, we attempted to reproduce the reported accuracy of those models. This proved to be difficult. We provide additional insight into the major factors that influence analytical model accuracy.

Categories and Subject Descriptors

C.4 [**Performance of Systems**]: *Modeling techniques, Measurement techniques*; B.3.2 [**Memory Structures**]: Design Styles—*Cache memories*; B.8.2 [**Performance and Reliability**]: Performance Analysis and Design Aids

General Terms

Performance, Measurement, Experimentation

Keywords

processor caches, performance modeling, cache models

1. MOTIVATION

The motivation for this paper originates with our work on software performance modeling. In software performance models, the performance of a software system is typically derived from the performance of the constituting components and the component interactions [7]. The interactions may be explicit, such as method invocation or message passing, or implicit, such as competing for a shared resource. Often, memory caches are one such resource.

Memory caches significantly improve the performance of workloads that have temporal and spatial locality by providing faster access to data. An accurate software performance model may therefore need to capture the performance impact of multiple workloads competing for memory caches [2].

Analytical models that estimate the cache behavior for a combination of workloads have been developed. These models target applications such as processor design or workload scheduling [8, 9, 13, 10]. For application in software performance modeling, additional requirements exist:

- Software performance models typically deal with time. The cache model therefore needs to calculate the timing penalties, rather than only the cache miss counts or the cache miss ratios.

- Software performance models often contain hierarchically composed components. The cache model should therefore permit the corresponding evaluation of hierarchically composed workloads.

Our first contribution is a cache model that reflects these requirements. The model belongs to the family of analytical cache models that use stack distance profiles[1] to describe the workload behavior. As a step towards hierarchical composition, our model calculates the resulting stack distance profile of a combination of workloads in addition to the timing penalties.

An important property of a cache model is its accuracy. The evaluation of accuracy is hindered by two factors: the difficulty in obtaining precise model inputs and the difficulty in creating controlled experimental conditions. Existing research differs in how these difficulties are addressed –

---

[1] A stack distance profile tells the probability of accessing a given number of different cache lines in between consecutive accesses to the same cache line.

striving for more precise inputs and more controlled conditions often implies significant overhead and limited realism, but imprecise inputs and uncontrolled conditions can also be detrimental.

Our second contribution is an evaluation of the modeling accuracy in realistic settings. In particular, we improve the existing methods for collecting the model inputs on real hardware, impose no additional control over the execution phases of the competing workloads, and compare the modeling results with measurements on real hardware.

Because the accuracy of a model depends on multiple factors, interpreting particular accuracy results is difficult. This prevents direct comparison of the accuracy results reported in previous research. It also complicates estimating how much of the reported accuracy is preserved in different settings.

As our third contribution, we use experiments to isolate the individual accuracy factors and provide insights into how the experimental settings impact accuracy. We also develop a method for collecting the stack distance profiles that mediates the influence of the workload profile stability and the replacement policy approximation on accuracy.[2]

The paper is structured as follows. We start by introducing our cache model in Section 2. We explain what tools we use to collect the model inputs in Section 3. In Section 4, we present the evaluation results, first in an overall view and then focusing on the major accuracy factors. In Section 5, we outline the relationship of our model to existing research, both in design and in evaluation. We summarize our contribution in Section 6.

2. CACHE SHARING MODEL

The cache sharing model for a cache with associativity A takes as an input for each workload x the stack distance profile sdp_x, the mean number of cache accesses per instruction API_x, the number of instructions per processor clock cycle when running in isolation IPC_x, and the cache miss penalty in processor clock cycles mp_x. The output consists of modified stack distance profiles, sdp'_x, and modified IPC values, IPC'_x, when each workload is running in parallel with other workloads. The profiles and IPC values can also be combined to get a single profile and IPC value representing the combined workload, for use when the models are composed in hierarchies.

For sake of brevity, we describe the model for two parallel workloads, denoted 1 and 2. The extension for multiple parallel workloads is straightforward.

In principle, the modified stack distance profile of workload 1, when running in parallel with workload 2, is derived in three steps done for each stack distance d, $1 \leq d \leq A$:

1. Calculate the average time (in processor clock cycles) between two consecutive accesses to the same cache line, where the second access has a stack distance d. We call this *reuse time* of stack distance d and denote as r_d.

2. Estimate the number of distinct cache lines accessed by the other workload during the time r_d.

---

[2]See Section 4.5 for workload profile stability and Section 4.6 for replacement policy approximation.

3. Increase the stack distance of accesses for the original stack distance d by the number estimated in step 2.

We now describe the individual steps in detail.

Step 1. To obtain r_d, we observe that during the reuse time, the workload has to access $d-1$ distinct cache lines to build up the distance of the reused cache line in the LRU stack, and then access the reused line. With the assumption of independent accesses, this equals the mean time to achieve cache set occupation from 0 to d distinct cache lines, and can be derived from the stack distance profile as follows.

We model the process of cache set occupation of a workload as a Markov chain, with $d+1$ states representing the number of occupied cache lines between 0 and d. The transition matrix $\mathbf{P}_d$ is defined:[3]

- $p_{0,1} = 1$

- $p_{i,i} = hit(i), 1 \leq i < d$

- $p_{i,i+1} = 1 - hit(i), 1 \leq i < d$

- $p_{d,d} = 1$

- $p_{i,j} = 0$ otherwise, $0 \leq i \leq d$, $0 \leq j \leq d$

In the above, $hit(i)$ is the probability of a cache hit with i lines occupied, and can be derived directly from the stack distance profile:

$$hit(i) = \frac{\sum_{j=1}^{i} sdp_1(j)}{\sum_{j=1}^{A+1} sdp_1(j)} \qquad (1)$$

With the state d being absorbing, we can calculate the expected number of steps t_d from the initial state 0 to the absorption in state d [11]:

$$t_d = \sum_{j=0}^{d-1} \left[(\mathbf{I} - \mathbf{T})^{-1} \right]_{0,j} \qquad (2)$$

where $\mathbf{I}$ is a d-by-d identity matrix, $\mathbf{T} = [p_{i,j}]$, $i, j \in \{0, \ldots, d-1\}$.

The mean number of accesses between reuses of cache lines with stack distance d is equal to t_d and the reuse time (in processor cycles) can be derived:

$$r_d = \frac{t_d}{API_1 \cdot IPC_1} \qquad (3)$$

Step 2. To determine the interference from the second workload, we first calculate the average number of accesses by the second workload during the reuse time of the first workload:

$$a_d = r_d \cdot API_2 \cdot IPC_2 \qquad (4)$$

To calculate how many *distinct* lines exist in a_d consecutive accesses by the second workload, we use the transition matrix of the second workload with the number of occupied cache lines ranging from 0 to the cache associativity A, denoted as $\mathbf{Q}_A$. We derive the probability vectors

---

[3]The indices start from zero to match the states directly.

$\mathbf{D}(n) = \{D_0(n), \dots, D_A(n)\}$, where $D_m(n)$ is the probability of the second workload accessing m distinct cache lines after n accesses, where $0 \leq m \leq A$, as follows [11]:

$$\mathbf{D}(n) = \mathbf{u}\mathbf{Q}_A^n, \tag{5}$$

where $\mathbf{u} = \{u_0, \dots, u_A\}, u_0 = 1$ and $u_m = 0, m > 0$.

The vector $\mathbf{D}(a_d)$ thus gives the probability distribution of the number of distinct cache lines accessed by the second workload. For non-integer values of a_d, the vector is defined as an element-wise linear interpolation between the vectors $\mathbf{D}(\lfloor a_d \rfloor)$ and $\mathbf{D}(\lceil a_d \rceil)$.

Step 3. A partial distance profile pdp'_{1d}, describing the modified stack distances under sharing for accesses with original stack distance d, is calculated by taking the value $sdp_1(d)$ from the original profile and distributing it between distances d to $d + A$ proportionally to the values in $\mathbf{D}(a_d)$. Since accesses with resulting distance larger than $A + 1$ are always misses, we treat them as having the distance of $A+1$:

$$pdp'_{1d}(d + i) = sdp_1(d) \cdot D_i(a_d), 0 \leq i < A + 1 - d$$

$$pdp'_{1d}(A + 1) = sdp_1(d) \cdot \sum_{i=A+1-d}^{A} D_i(a_d) \tag{6}$$

After repeating the three steps for each $d, 1 \leq d \leq A$, the resulting distance profile sdp'_1 can be constructed by adding up the partial distance profiles pdp'_{1d} created in each repetition:

$$sdp'_1(i) = \sum_{d=1}^{A} pdp'_{1d}(i), 1 \leq i \leq A + 1 \tag{7}$$

Cache misses in the original profile, $sdp_1(A+1)$, are simply added to $sdp'_1(A+1)$.

To determine IPC'_1, we consider how the ratio of misses per cache access increases due to the decrease of cache hit probability $hit(A)$ to $hit'(A)$, which is calculated from sdp'_1 using Eq. 1:

$$\Delta MPA_1 = hit(A) - hit'(A) \tag{8}$$

These extra cache misses can be translated to extra CPI using the workload cache miss penalty mp_1:

$$\Delta CPI_1 = \Delta MPA_1 \cdot API_1 \cdot mp_1 \tag{9}$$

The resulting IPC'_1 of the first workload thus follows:

$$IPC'_1 = ((1/IPC_1) + \Delta CPI_1)^{-1} \tag{10}$$

To determine sdp'_2 and IPC'_2, we repeat the whole process with the roles of the first and the second workload exchanged.

In equations 3 and 4, we have used the IPC values from isolated execution, although the workloads are in fact mutually influencing their IPC by executing in parallel over the shared cache. We solve this issue iteratively – in each iteration, new sdp'_x and IPC'_x values are calculated using IPC'_x values from the previous iteration, starting with the isolated IPC_x inputs. Note that the stack distance profiles of the individual workloads are not modified during the iterations – in all steps, the isolated sdp_x profiles are used as inputs. We use a simple ϵ stability criterion on the IPC'_x values to determine solution convergence.

Finally, for composition purposes, the composed stack distance profile is calculated by element-wise averaging the sdp'_x profiles weighted by the memory access frequencies derived from IPC'_x and API_x.

3. EVALUATION TOOL SUPPORT

We evaluate the accuracy of the cache model by carrying out multiple experiments where various workload combinations are executed in parallel on cores that share a cache. The performance of the workload is both modeled and measured and the values are compared. Here, we describe the experimental workloads and the two techniques we use for collecting the stack distance profiles. Because any profiling technique can influence the collected profile, we use two different techniques to understand this influence on the accuracy of the model.

3.1 Experimental Workloads

Our workload combinations are pairs of workloads adopted from the SPEC CPU 2006 benchmark suite [1], supplemented with FFT and LZW calculations. The workloads execute in our experimental framework [3], which separates the initialization and the calculation parts of each workload and runs the calculation parts repeatedly to achieve steady cache sharing conditions. Even though the workloads can have multiple phases with different behavior, we avoid explicit synchronization that would make only particular phases compete against each other.

Depending on various technical properties of the code, getting a benchmark to work in our experimental framework may require a significant effort. To reduce this effort, we only use a subset of the SPEC CPU 2006 benchmark suite, but ensure that the included workloads have sufficient variation in their stack distance profiles. The subset consists of the 401.bzip2, 429.mcf, 444.namd, 458.sjeng, 462.libquantum, 470.lbm, and 473.astar benchmarks, with modifications adjusting the range of the accepted inputs as follows:

- 401.bzip2 was extended with a parameter for configuring the amount of data compressed, in addition to the file containing the data. Eight configurations are used, with the with amount of data set to either 1 MB or 2 MB and the input file set to one of *dryer.jpg*, *input.program*, *text.html* from 401.bzip2 inputs, and *100_100_130_cf_a.of* from 470.lbm inputs.

- 429.mcf uses a randomized subset of the *inp.in* input.

- 444.namd uses the *namd.input* input.

- 458.sjeng uses a subset of the *test.txt* input.

- 462.libquantum was modified to accept the input as arguments rather than reading it from a file. We use two input combinations, $(143, 25)$ and $(39, 25)$.

- 470.lbm was extended with a parameter for configuring the number of iterations performed per invocation. We use the *100_100_130_cf_a.of* input and one iteration per invocation.

- 473.astar uses the *lake.bin* with *lake.cfg* input.

Together with the FFT and LZW calculations, we have 139 workload combinations.

3.2 Stack Distance Collection: Valgrind Extension

The first technique we use for stack distance profile collection extends the cache profiler Cachegrind, which is a part of the Valgrind instrumentation and dynamic analysis tool [12]. When executing an application, Cachegrind observes the memory accesses and dynamically simulates a two-level cache hierarchy that is configured to match the host platform. The number of cache accesses and cache misses can be either reported for the whole program, or reported in more detail for program function and source line.

To simulate the cache hierarchy, Cachegrind maintains a LRU stack of cache line addresses for each cache set. Our extension added counters for all stack distances to produce the stack distance profiles.

To minimize the framework overhead, we use Valgrind Client Control trapdoor mechanism, which can instruct the simulator to start and stop counting, save the results, and reset the counters. We use this mechanism to let the simulator populate the LRU stacks during the warmup cycles, and only count the access distances during the measurement cycles. After measurement, the counters for each set are added together to form a single average profile – modeling with a separate profile for each set is also possible, but not investigated here.

Valgrind ignores hardware prefetching, because it only intercepts memory accesses at software level.

3.3 Stack Distance Collection: Stressmark Workload

The second technique we use for stack distance profile collection uses the Stressmark workload, described in [13]. Stressmark is designed to heavily use a configurable subset of the cache. This reduces the effective cache size for any other workload that runs with Stressmark. Observing the hardware performance event counters for multiple effective cache sizes allows us to derive the stack distance profiles and the miss penalties for the other workload.

During execution, Stressmark strives to occupy a particular number of ways in all cache sets by accessing the cache in a random sequence, going through all sets once for each way to be occupied. This access pattern results in a flat stack distance profile. By observing the shared cache access and miss counters, we calculate the average number of truly occupied ways across all sets as the accessed number of ways times the observed hit rate. By repeating the Stressmark execution for different number of occupied ways, we can observe the miss rate of the profiled workload under different effective cache sizes, which allows us to compute the stack distance profile.

Because the Stressmark workload competes with the profiled workload in all sets, it may not be able to achieve a high number of truly occupied ways against more intensive workloads. This means observations corresponding to small stack distances may be missing. For those distances, we distribute the remaining accesses equally. For observed distances that are not integers, we use linear interpolation.

We make two modifications to Stressmark to improve accuracy. To estimate the cache miss penalty, we use only misses due to sharing, rather than all missess. Specifically, we measure how much the processor clock cycle counter and the shared cache miss counter increase under sharing. The penalty is calculated as the cycle count increase over the miss count increase, with the least-square-error linear regression applied to calculate a single penalty value for each workload. We also use the page coloring-based memory allocator from [5] to ensure that in our Stressmark implementation, all cache sets are accessed and no conflict misses occur.

The Stressmark-based tool interacts with hardware prefetching. In particular, the hardware performance event counters used to determine Stressmark cache occupancy do not distinguish between cache misses due to prefetch hits and prefetch misses. Therefore, either both kinds of cache misses are counted or none are. Stressmark can also suppress prefetches that would otherwise happen [4, 2].

3.4 Stack Distance Collection: Discussion

Despite the instrumentation overhead, collecting profiles with Valgrind is actually faster than using Stressmark, which has to repeat the measurement for each stack distance from zero to the cache associativity. However, Valgrind is not a cycle-accurate simulator. Therefore, we collect the instruction throughput and miss penalty values using Stressmark even when we obtain the stack distance profiles with Valgrind.

4. EVALUATION RESULTS

To evaluate the modeling accuracy, we independently model and measure cache sharing on selected workload combinations, and compare the model predictions to the measurements. Our measurements are obtained on a Dell PowerEdge 1955 system with two Quad-Core Intel Xeon processors (Type E5345, Family 6, Model 15, Stepping 11, Clock 2.33 GHz), 8 GB DDR2-667 memory, Intel 5000P memory controller, Fedora Linux 8, gcc-4.1.2-33.x86 64, glibc-2.7-2.x86 64. The workloads run on cores that have a private 32 KB 8-way set associative instruction L1 cache, a private 32 KB 8-way set associative L1 data cache, and share a 4 MB 16-way set associative L2 unified cache.

In our experiments, we disable hardware prefetching, because neither of our stack distance profile collection techniques is hardware prefetch aware. If needed, the performance impact of hardware prefetching can be evaluated separately from the performance impact of cache sharing [4, 2].

In the following, MR stands for miss rate, IPC stands for instruction throughput, *isol* stands for values measured when running an isolated workload, *real* stands for values measured when running a workload combination, and *pred* stands for values predicted by the model.

4.1 Overview: IPC

As an overview, we plot the relative slowdown prediction, $(IPC_{isol} - IPC_{pred})/IPC_{isol}$, against the relative slowdown measurement, $(IPC_{isol} - IPC_{real})/IPC_{isol}$, for all workload combinations. A workload combination is displayed as two points, one for each workload. A dotted line indicates when the predicted slowdown equals the measured slowdown. Figure 1 plots the predictions based on the Valgrind profiles, Figure 2 plots the predictions based on the Stressmark profiles.

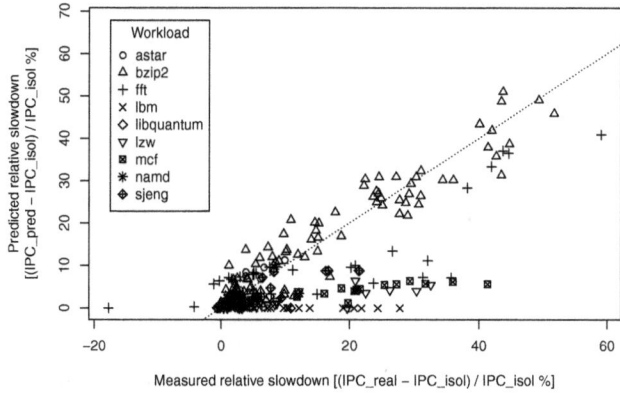

Figure 1: IPC slowdown prediction against IPC slowdown measurement, Valgrind profiles.

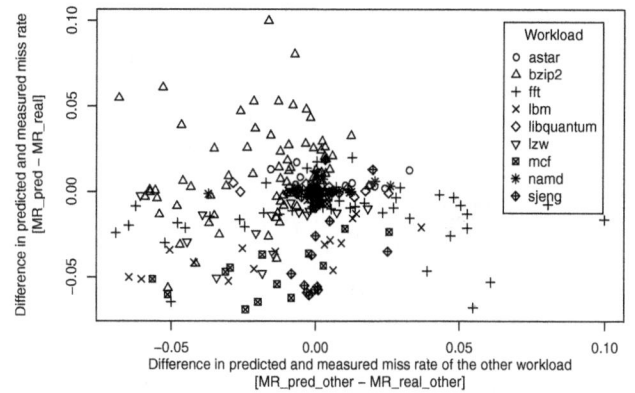

Figure 2: IPC slowdown prediction against IPC slowdown measurement, Stressmark profiles.

The workloads most sensitive to parallel execution are some variants of fft and bzip2. With the Valgrind profiles, their slowdown is predicted with relatively acceptable error, however, for most of the other sensitive workloads, the slowdown prediction is too optimistic. Overall, the Valgrind profiles have a median prediction error of 3.5 %, inter-quartile range 1 % - 8.5 %, where the prediction error is calculated as $|IPC_{pred} - IPC_{real}|/IPC_{real}$. When considering only the upper quartile of workload combinations by sensitivity to paralel execution, we have 70 workloads whose slowdown exceds 19 %. For this group, the median prediction error is 14 %, inter-quartile range 7 % - 27 %.

With the Stressmark profiles and the workloads most sensitive to parallel execution, the slowdown prediction is somewhat pessimistic. Overall, the Stresmark profiles have a median prediction error of 9.6 %, inter-quartile range 4.7 % - 30 %. For the same group of sensitive workloads as above, the median prediction error is 10 %, inter-quartile range 6 % - 27 %. Importantly, the prediction is very pessimistic even for the least sensitive workloads.

The figures indicate that there are also workloads that appear to speed up in parallel execution. Although not intuitive, this is indeed possible, especially where a mostly writing workload executes in combination with a mostly reading workload. In this situation, the reading workload may take over part of the penalty for evicting dirty cache lines from the writing workload [2].

Compared to existing research, which rarely reports errors larger than units of percent, the results on Figures 1 and 2 might appear to be inaccurate. In the related work section, we explain why this is a misleading impression. To justify our claim, we have used the same inputs to perform validation with our implementation of the model in [13], and – although we can never safely exclude potential implementation issues – we have obtained similar modeling accuracy. The details are not included in the text due to lack of space, however, we publish both the sources and the data for interested readers.

4.2 Overview: Miss Rate

We continue with plotting the miss rate prediction error, $MR_{pred} - MR_{real}$, against the miss rate increase of the workload in concurrent execution, $MR_{real} - MR_{isol}$. The

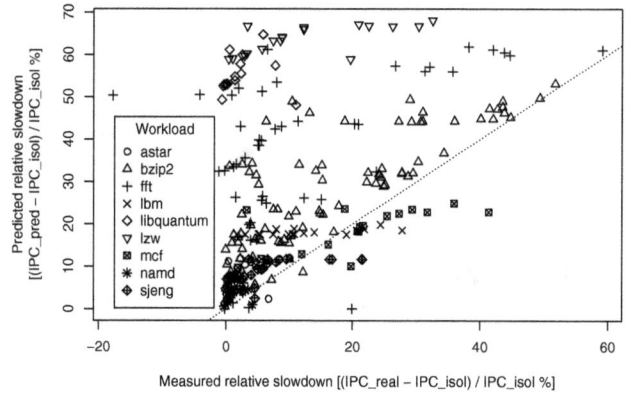

Figure 3: MR prediction error depending on the MR prediction error of the other workload in combination, Valgrind profiles.

predictions based on the Valgrind profiles are in Figure 4, the predictions based on the Stressmark profiles are in Figure 5.

With the Valgrind profiles, the model appears to predict the miss rate with a resolution of about 0.05. The roughly linear cluster of points to the lower left suggests that increases in the miss rate below this resolution are not predicted by the model. We attribute these effects to the detailed behavior of the cache replacement policy.

With the Stressmark profiles, the model appears more pessimistic for less sensitive workloads. This effect is exemplified with lzw, whose Stressmark profile indicates almost 40% of accesses with stack distance just below the cache associativity (see Figure 8). Since these accesses would be very likely to change from hits to misses under concurrent execution, an inaccuracy in this part of the profile would explain the observed effect.

To assess whether both workloads in a workload combination suffer from the same miss rate prediction error, or whether the model favors one workload against the other, we plot the miss rate prediction error of one workload in a combination against the miss rate prediction error of the

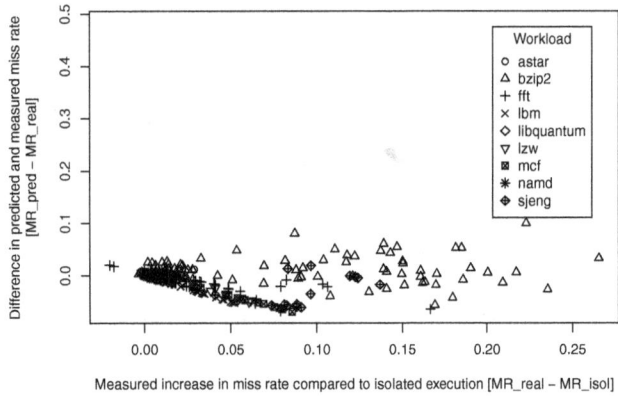

Figure 4: MR prediction error depending on MR increase, Valgrind profiles.

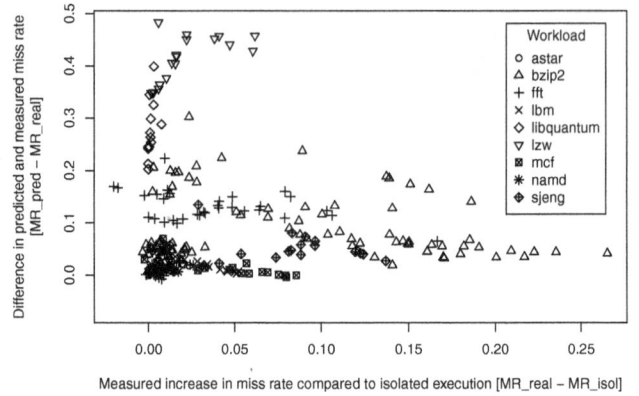

Figure 5: MR prediction error depending on MR increase, Stressmark profiles.

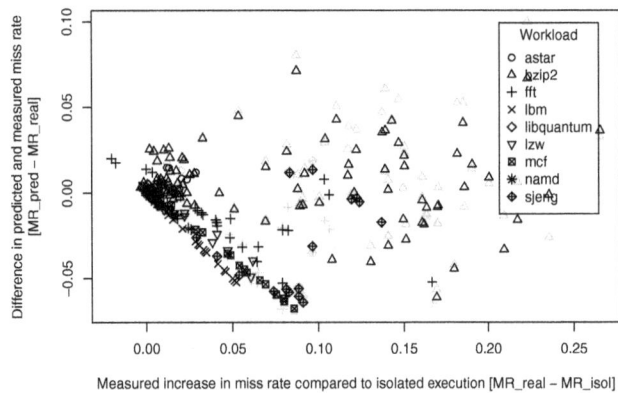

Figure 6: MR prediction error depending on MR increase, Valgrind profiles (grey points). Black points denote prediction with injected IPC_{real}.

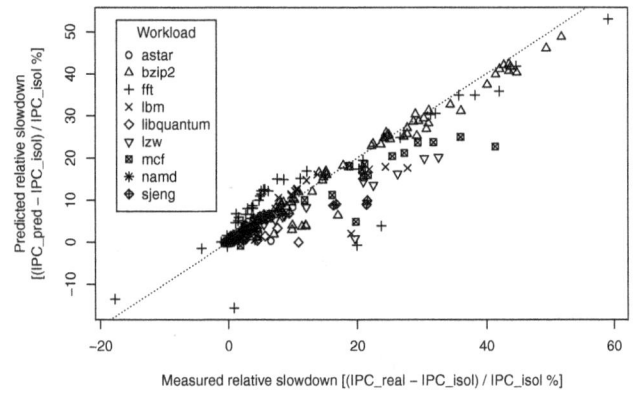

Figure 7: IPC slowdown prediction against IPC slowdown measurement, injected MR_{real}.

other workload. The results for Valgrind profiles on Figure 3 suggest that the error tends to impact both workloads equally, even though there are exceptions. Although not shown separately, the impact on the slowdown prediction is similar.

4.3 Miss Penalty Approximation

The cache model includes interaction between misses and penalties. Next, we investigate measurements that help isolate the effects of poor miss penalty approximation on the miss rate prediction. We do that by injecting IPC_{real} into the calculation where IPC_{pred} would otherwise be calculated.

There are two ways the injection can be performed. Either the iteration in the model is preserved and the measured instruction throughput is used as a seed, or the iteration is removed entirely. For the former option, there is no observable change in results, which confirms the iteration is not hindered by encountering local extremes. For the latter option, the results with Valgrind profiles are on Figure 6, with black points adjusted and grey points original. The difference is in fact relatively small.

4.4 Miss Rate Prediction

Analogously to the previous experiment, we investigate measurements that help isolate the effects of poor miss rate prediction. We do that by injecting MR_{real} into the calculation where MR_{pred} would otherwise be calculated, again removing the iteration entirely. The results on Figure 7 clearly indicate that an improved miss rate prediction would improve the modeling accuracy.

4.5 Workload Profile Stability

The previous experiments indicate the modeling accuracy is related more to the miss rate prediction than to the miss penalty approximation. The Valgrind profiles and the Stressmark profiles yield potentially different prediction results, and profile inaccuracies could explain some observed prediction errors. We therefore investigate the profiles themselves and the role of the assumption that the profiles are stable over time and similar across cache sets.

Our use of two workload profile collecting tools makes it possible to compare the profiles, Valgrind with Stressmark. While each tool has its drawbacks, and neither profile is therefore guaranteed to be correct, significant differences should reveal potential profile accuracy issues. The comparison of the profiles is on Figure 8.

The comparison of the profiles indeed reveals significant differences between Valgrind and Stressmark. The tools inherently differ in their sensitivity to the assumptions of stability over time and similarity across sets – where Valgrind continuously tracks accesses to all sets, Stressmark must compete one set at a time. To investigate this difference, we have developed a synthetic workload that is able to mimic another workload given its stack distance histogram and mean number of cache accesses per instruction, while enforcing both stability over time and similarity across sets. For brevity, we refer to this synthetic workload as Emulator.

The goal of Emulator is to perform independent memory accesses in each cache set that satisfy a given stack distance profile. The difficult part is avoiding access to data controlling Emulator, since that would distort the memory access pattern. Even a pseudocode description of Emulator is rather involved, we therefore only present the basic ideas and invite interested readers to peruse the sources.

In its most basic form, Emulator would need to keep track of the LRU stack for each set, and, for each access, randomly pick a distance from the profile, find the corresponding address in the LRU stack, perform the access and update the LRU stack. To avoid accessing the LRU stack, Emulator prepares the sequence of addresses to access beforehand. To further reduce overhead, the sequence of addresses to access is stored as a chain of pointers at the very addresses to be accessed [5]. Except for locating the first item of the chain, it can thus be traversed without overhead.

Finally, Emulator does not treat each cache set independently. Instead, the sets are assigned and ordered randomly in 16 groups of equal size. Each group has its own chain of pointers that defines the sequence of addresses to access, touching each set of the group once in random order. When executing, Emulator maintains 16 pointers, one for each group, to traverse all sets.

This design reduces the size of data controlling Emulator that has to be read during each iteration to 16 pointers, which on our platform translates into an overhead of accessing 2 extra cache lines per 4096 useful accesses. While this comes at the cost of introducing regularity of accesses among the sets, the independence of accesses within each set is preserved. The relative sizes of the access pattern and the caches also ensure that all accesses spill from the private L1 cache to the shared L2 cache, as is required.

We submit the Valgrind profiles of the original workloads to Emulator to create synthetic workloads with the same stack distance profile that are stable over time and homogeneous across sets. We then collect the Stressmark profiles of the synthetic workloads and use these profiles to model the original workloads. The results are indeed more accurate – across all workloads, the median prediction error is 5.7 %, inter-quartile range 2.4 % - 13 %, across the group of sensitive workloads, the median prediction error is 8 %, inter-quartile range 4.5 % - 15 %. The details are on Figure 9.

Interestingly, the process is not just a more complicated way of updating the Stressmark profiles to match the Valgrind ones – in fact, the Stressmark profiles of the synthetic workloads are not entirely similar to the Valgrind profiles of the original workloads. This is shown on Figure 11. We ex-

plain the reason for this difference and the related modeling accuracy next.

4.6 Cache Replacement Policy

So far, we have put aside the issue of the cache replacement policy. Although the details of the policy are not available in vendor documentation, the hardware most likely implements pseudo LRU in both the private L1 cache and the shared L2 cache. This actually impacts the workload profile collecting tools:

- When Valgrind collects a profile, it has to calculate when accesses spill from L1 to L2. Any deviation from strict LRU in L1 therefore impacts the profile, while deviations in L2 do not. In precise terms, when Valgrind collects a profile, it means that *the measured workload would have this profile in L2 on a platform where L1 uses strict LRU.*

- When Stressmark collects a profile, it has to calculate which position in the stack distance histogram corresponds to L2 misses observed at particular L2 occupancy. Any deviation from strict LRU in L2 therefore impacts the profile, while deviations in L1 do not. In precise terms, when Stressmark collects a profile, it means that *a workload with this profile executing on a platform where L2 uses strict LRU would cause the same number of L2 misses as the measured workload does on a platform where both L1 and L2 use pseudo LRU.*

Our cache model calculates the miss rates under the assumption of strict LRU. The validation compares these with miss rates measured on a platform with pseudo LRU. The mismatch between strict LRU and pseudo LRU exhibits itself differently with the two workload profile collecting tools:

- The Valgrind profile describes how the profiled workload would access L2 if L1 used strict LRU. Then, the model calculates what the miss rate would be if multiple profiled workloads shared an L2 with strict LRU. When using the Valgrind profiles, the model therefore calculates a miss rate on a hypothetical platform with strict LRU.

- The Stressmark profile describes how a hypothetical workload would have to access L2 on a platform with strict LRU to achieve the same miss rates against Stressmark as the profiled workload does on the platform with pseudo LRU. Then, the model calculates what the miss rate would be if multiple hypothetical workloads shared an L2 with strict LRU. When using the Stressmark profiles, the model therefore calculates a miss rate for the hypothetical workloads, which should achieve a similar miss rate on a platform with strict LRU as the profiled workloads do on the platform with pseudo LRU.

This explains the results from Section 4.5, where using the Stressmark profiles of the Emulator workloads, which in turn simulate the Valgrind profiles of the original workloads, yields better accuracy than using either the Stressmark profiles or the Valgrind profiles of the original workloads directly. When collecting the profiles of the original workloads, Valgrind copes better than Stressmark with workloads

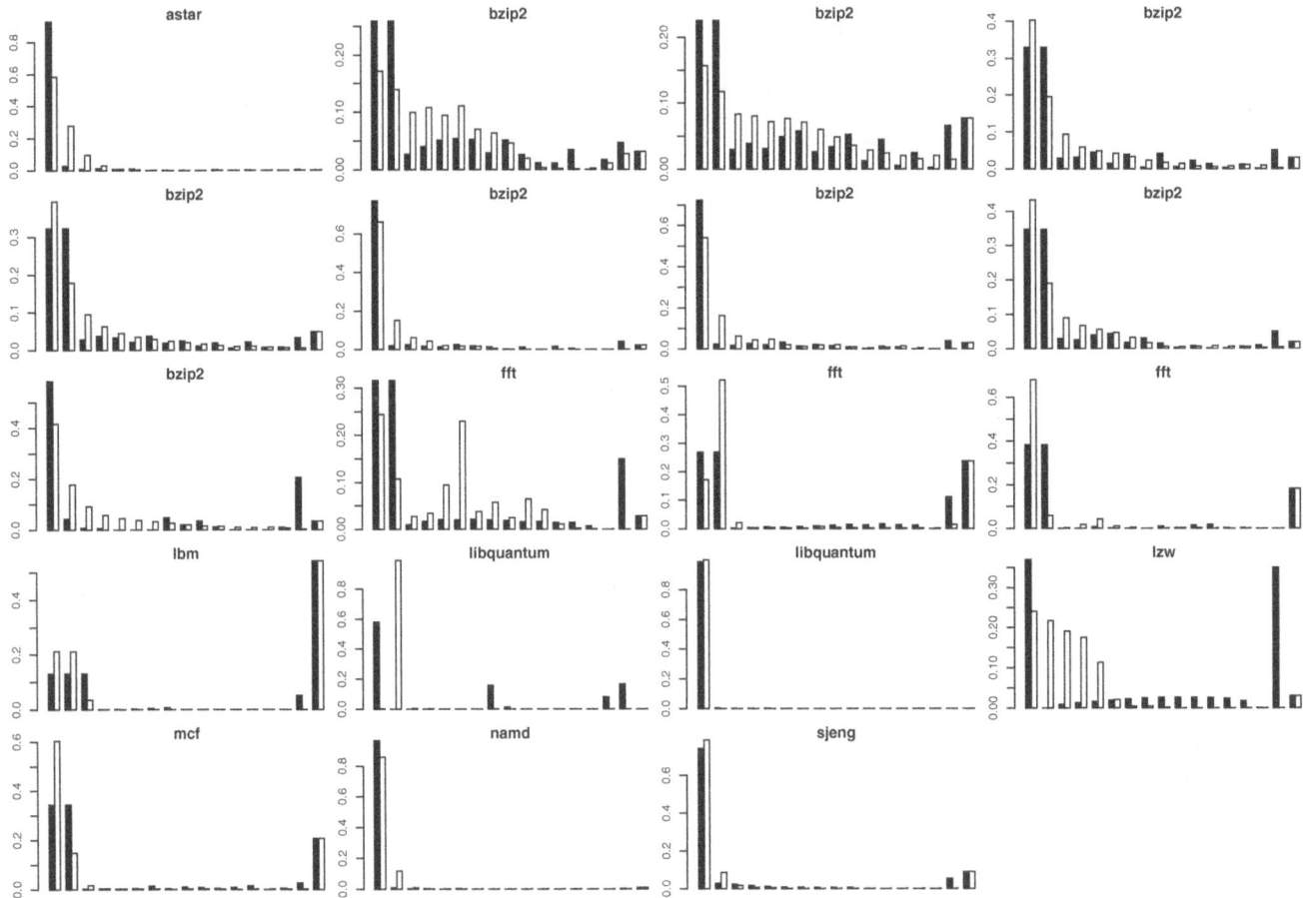

Figure 8: Stressmark profiles (black) and Valgrind profiles (white) of the original workloads. Distances grow from left to right. Multiple profiles of the same name denote the same benchmark with different choices of inputs.

whose profiles change over time and differ across sets. Simulating the original workloads with Emulator ensures stability over time and homogeneity across sets, important for the subsequent use of Stressmark. Finally, Stressmark calculates what profiles would cause the observed cache misses in a cache with strict LRU. These profiles fit the cache model, which estimates the cache misses under the assumption of strict LRU, better than the Valgrind profiles.

Finally, we illustrate the modeling accuracy in a situation where both the workload profile stability issues and the cache replacement policy issues are minimized. Modifying the previous experiment, we submit the Valgrind profiles of the original workloads to Emulator to create synthetic workloads, we then collect the Stressmark profiles of the synthetic workloads, and we use these profiles to model the synthetic workloads. The results, plotting the relative slowdown prediction, $(IPC_{isol} - IPC_{pred})/IPC_{isol}$, against the relative slowdown measurement, $(IPC_{isol} - IPC_{real})/IPC_{isol}$, are on Figure 10. Across all workloads, the median prediction error is 3.2%, inter-quartile range 0.9% - 6.1%, across the group of sensitive workloads, the median prediction error is 3.8%, inter-quartile range 1.6% - 5.9%. Since the results are for the synthetic workloads, they are no longer useful

for modeling the original workloads, but they illustrate the accuracy achievable for workloads with stable profiles.

To conclude, our evaluation has shown the modeling accuracy achievable when the various simplifying assumptions about the workloads and the platform are satisfied only to a degree common in realistic settings. Furthermore, we have shown how enforcing the validity of the individual assumptions contributes to the modeling accuracy. The results indicate that the modeling accuracy is sufficient for application in software performance modeling, especially for workloads sensitive to cache sharing.

5. RELATED WORK

Of the models that estimate the cache miss ratio based on the workload description, we focus on models that rely on access distance profiles for workload description and are capable of handling combinations of workloads. More complex modeling approaches, such as full system simulation, belong to different application domain due to potentially large overhead. Less complex modeling approaches, such as overhead interpolation, were investigated in [6]. For each related model, we consider the internal structure and the evaluation approach separately.

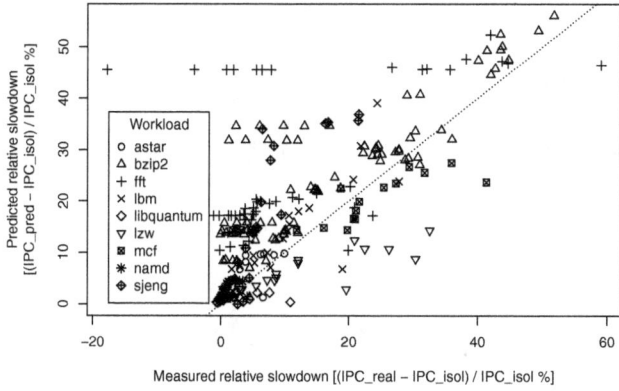

Figure 9: IPC slowdown prediction against IPC slowdown measurement of the *original workloads* with profiles collected by Stressmark on *synthetic workloads*.

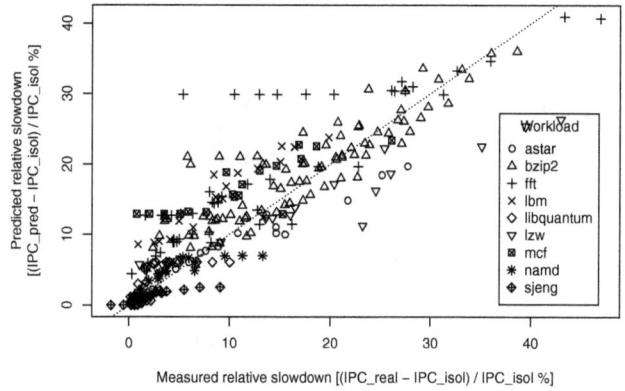

Figure 10: IPC slowdown prediction against IPC slowdown measurement of the *synthetic workloads* with profiles collected by Stressmark (also on synthetic workloads).

In our review, we sometimes have to adjust the discrepancies in terminology. Notably, when talking about the distance between consecutive accesses to the same cache line, we use the term *reuse distance profile* when the distance is expressed in memory accesses, and the term *stack distance profile* when the distance is expressed in unique cache lines.

5.1 Related Model Structure

The statistical model by Chandra et al. [8] is the oldest of the related models listed here. The computational approach follows the general outline of first estimating the time between two consecutive accesses to the same cache line by one workload, then calculating the distribution of accesses to unique cache lines in that time interval by the other workload, and finally determining what percentage of former hits will be turned to misses by those additional accesses.

The most notable difference between their model and ours is in the required inputs. Their model requires not only the stack distance profile, but also a distribution of the intermediate access counts for each distance in the stack distance profile, together denoted as circular sequence profile. In some points of the calculation, parts of the circular sequence profile are averaged over, the contribution of this additional information to accuracy is therefore not clear. The required inputs are also different from the provided outputs, preventing hierarchical model composition.

As another notable difference, their model does not consider the mutual influence between the competing workloads. This is related to the fact that their model only deals with the cache misses and not the timing penalties, and is thus unable to determine how much the additional cache misses due to sharing change the relative speed of the workloads.

Both our model and the model in [8] assume limited associativity. This assumption is important for their model since it uses a recursive formula to calculate the number of accesses to unique cache lines in a given time interval. Because the complexity of the formula grows exponentially with the interval length, the calculation over the entire cache, rather than over a single cache set, is not feasible in their model.

The throughput model by Chen et al. [9] includes a probabilistic cache contention model that extends the model in [8] in two major ways:

- The model compensates for situations where, due to a relatively large number of sets, the competing workloads are not likely to access the same sets in short time intervals. To do that, the model replaces the recursive formula that calculates the number of accesses to unique cache lines in a given time interval with a calculation based on additional input information.

- The model estimates how much the additional cache misses due to sharing change the relative speed of the workloads. Unlike our model, which iterates until convergence, the model in [9] only uses two repetitions.

In addition to the inputs required by the model in [8], the model in [9] also requires the average number of accessed sets and the stack distance profile for accesses in a given time interval, both for multiple groups of time intervals. Again, the required inputs are different from the provided outputs, preventing hierarchical model composition.

Both our model and the model in [9] assume limited associativity. Using the additional input information, their model better describes the situations where the workloads are not likely to compete for the same sets, however, their model still expects that the stack distance profiles are the same for all sets. Given that the choice of the cache sets is typically not controlled by the workload, this expectation appears reasonable.

The model by Xu et al. [13] employs a computational approach based on the properties of a steady state, where the competing workloads occupy their fixed shares of the cache. First, the relationship between the length of a time interval and the number of unique cache lines accessed in the interval is expressed using a recursive formula similar to that in [8]. Next, it is observed that all the competing workloads take the same time to entirely occupy their cache shares, and that the sum of the cache shares is the cache size. This gives a set of equations that can be solved to yield the sizes of the cache shares.

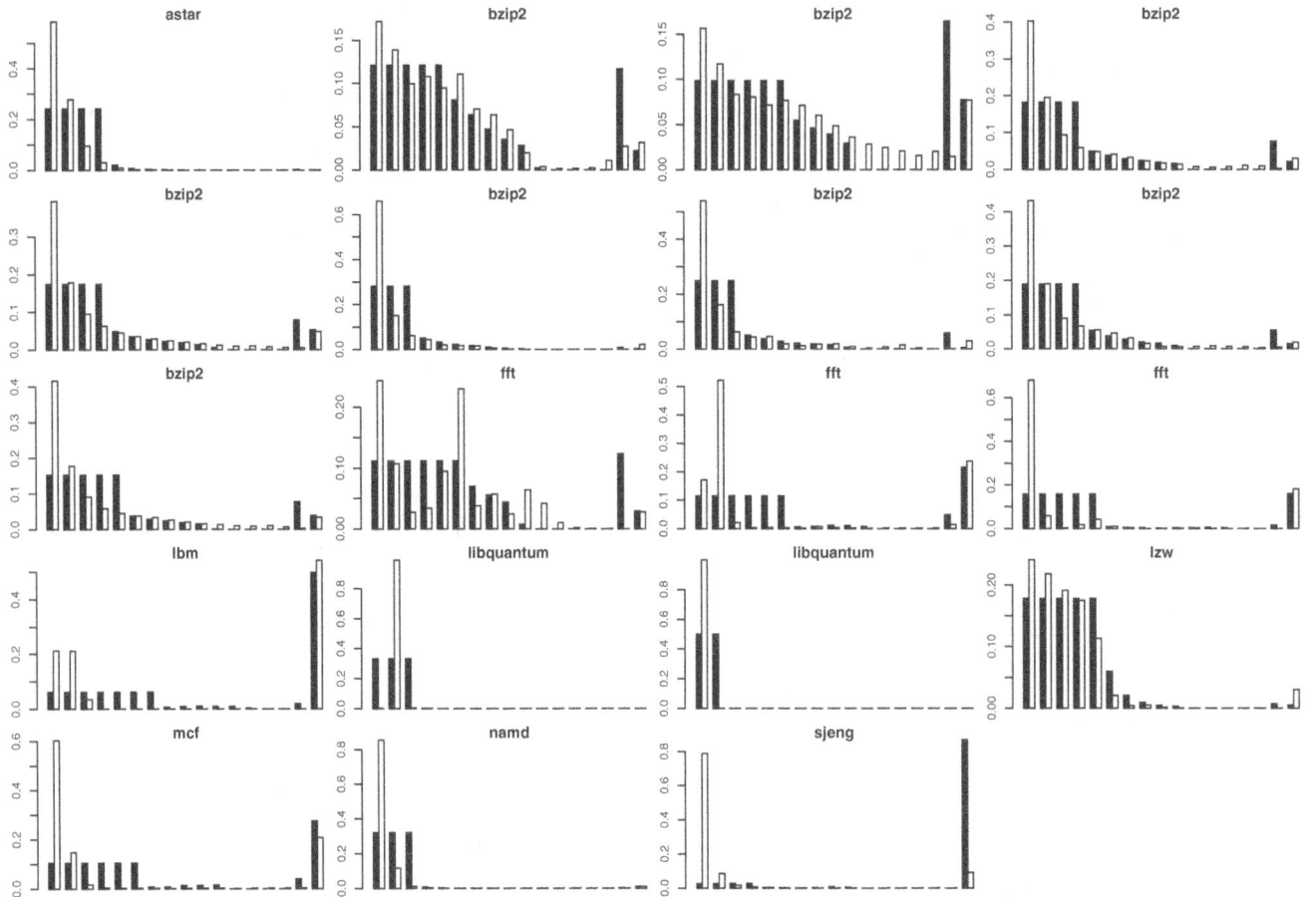

Figure 11: Stressmark profiles of the synthetic workloads (black) and Valgrind profiles of the original workloads (white). Distances grow from left to right.

Both our model and the model in [13] assume limited associativity, expecting that the stack distance profiles are the same for all sets. Their model also requires the same inputs as our model. Again, the required inputs are different from the provided outputs, preventing hierarchical model composition.

The model by Eklov et al. [10] relies on a statistical approach that estimates a stack distance profile from a reuse distance profile. First, scaled versions of the reuse distance profiles of the competing workloads are expressed as functions of the instruction throughputs. The scaled profiles are then merged into a single reuse distance profile. Next, a merged stack distance profile is estimated from the merged reuse distance profile. The merged stack distance profile is then split into the stack distance profiles of the competing workloads. Finally, the instruction throughputs of the competing workloads are expressed as functions of the stack distance profiles. This gives a set of equations that can be solved to yield the instruction throughputs.

Unlike our model, the model in [10] assumes full associativity. The impact of this difference on accuracy depends on the workloads, and is generally difficult to quantify.

The model in [10] requires similar inputs as our model, namely the reuse distance profiles where we require the stack distance profiles. Although technically different, the inputs are of similar nature and scale. Internally, their model performs profile conversions, merges and splits that involve approximations and possibly rounding,[4] which may impact accuracy. Although direct comparison is not possible due to technical differences, we believe that similar impact on our model is smaller, since it uses no rounding and fewer assumptions.

Finally, the required inputs are different from the provided outputs, but since the merged reuse distance profile is considered as an interim information in the model, it is possible that relatively minor modification would remove this obstacle to hierarchical model composition.

To summarize, we show how our model and the reviewed models differ in features such as the inputs and the outputs, the computational approach, the treatment of associativity, and the rounding and assumptions that impact accuracy. All of the models differ in some of the features, both compared with our model and compared among themselves.

5.2   Related Model Evaluation

Existing research also differs in how the modeling accuracy is evaluated, so much so that this basically makes the

---

[4]The issue of rounding is not discussed explicitly but the illustrations suggest it is likely done.

accuracy results incomparable. We explain some of the reasons by looking at how the model inputs are obtained and how the experimental conditions are controlled.

As far as the model inputs are concerned, the evaluations in [8, 9, 10] rely on simulators to obtain the workload profiles.[5] The use of simulators typically gives precise workload profiles, however, simulators often introduce overhead that is not acceptable in realistic settings, where the models would therefore work with potentially less precise inputs.

The evaluation in [13] determines the workload profiles that form the model inputs using experimental measurements on real hardware. The experimental measurements still carry some overhead, and the workload profiles are constructed from the measurements with some approximations.

Our evaluation is closer to [13] than the other reviewed evaluations since it also obtains model inputs using experimental measurements on real hardware.

Once the required inputs are available, the evaluation proceeds by independently modeling and measuring the effects of cache sharing on selected workload combinations. The results of modeling and measurement are compared to determine the modeling accuracy.

The workload combinations are almost always limited to pairs of workloads, except for [9], which uses up to 32 workloads of up to 4 different types. The workloads are almost always selected from the SPEC CPU benchmark suite, but the benchmark version and the configured input size varies. Typically, about tens of different workload combinations are used. Our evaluation roughly fits these general parameters – the somewhat limited choice from the SPEC CPU benchmark suite is compensated with a larger choice of the configured input sizes and the addition of other benchmarks, the total number of workload combinations we use is higher.

For a particular workload combination, how the combination is executed also matters. The workloads are known to have multiple phases with different behavior, and details such as synchronization and repetition can influence what phases end up competing for the cache:

- The experiments in [8] run the workloads once and stop the measurement when the shorter workload finishes.

- The experiments in [9] run a block of 400 million instructions at the start of the workloads.

- The experiments in [13] are described too vaguely to determine how the workloads were executed. The text suggests that only a single phase was considered for each benchmark, however, it does not say how the phases were identified and synchronized.

- The experiments in [10] run a block of 100 million accesses a constant distance from the start of the workloads.

Our experiments separate the initialization and the calculation parts of the workloads and run the calculation parts (which can contain multiple phases) repeatedly without synchronization. Compared to the reviewed evaluations, this increases the opportunity for different combinations of phases

to compete for the cache, and reduces the risk of observing artefacts due to strict workload synchronization.

The evaluations in [8, 9, 10] measure the effects of cache sharing on a simulator. Only the evaluation in [9] complements these with measurements on comparable real hardware, the other two evaluations use simulator configurations that potentially limit realism – in [8], the simulator uses special set indexing to ensure uniform set utilization, in [10], the simulator uses in-order processing that can stabilize the miss penalty. Also, it is not clear whether the simulators implement the detailed behavior of the cache replacement policy, which can impact the modeling accuracy significantly.

Of the reviewed evaluations, only the one in [13] uses real hardware, as does our evaluation.

Finally, the reviewed evaluations differ in the way the modeling accuracy is reported. Using MR for miss rate and IPC for instruction throughput, and denoting isolated, modeled and measured values respectively with $isol$, $pred$ and $real$, we have:

- In [8], the error is defined as the miss rate prediction error scaled against the measured miss rate,

$$error = \frac{MR_{pred} - MR_{real}}{MR_{real}}$$

- In [9], both the miss rate prediction error and the instruction throughput prediction error are reported, but neither is defined. There are hints suggesting the calculation is similar to the previous case.

- In [13], both the miss rate prediction error and the instruction throughput prediction error are reported, but neither is defined and there are no hints suggesting what the calculation looks like.

- In [10], the instruction throughput prediction error scaled against the isolated instruction throughput is reported,

$$error = \frac{IPC_{pred} - IPC_{real}}{IPC_{isol}}$$

The problem with reporting the relative miss rate prediction error, also discussed in [10], is that in low miss rate workloads, a large relative error may translate into a small performance impact. When the ultimate purpose of modeling is assessing performance, the relative miss rate prediction error is therefore not a good metric. We believe that multiple error metrics should be used together to help highlight different accuracy aspects, as we do in our evaluation.

To summarize, we show that the accuracy results of the reviewed evaluations are mutually incomparable. Additionally, no reviewed evaluation is documented sufficiently for constructing a comparable evaluation of our model. Lacking the option to produce comparable evaluation results, we have decided to strive for realistic evaluation settings, which give practically relevant picture of the achievable accuracy. We also take care to publish complete documentation – not just this text, but also complete tool sources and complete data files – to permit comparable evaluations against our model.

---

[5]The evaluation in [10] also explores the option of profile sampling.

6. CONCLUSION

The paper makes multiple contributions to memory cache models, motivated by the aplication in software performance modeling, but also useful in other contexts. First, we have presented a new cache model from the family of models that take the stack distance profile of multiple workloads as input and estimate the cache miss ratio and the instruction throughput as output. Among the properties particular to our model is the ability to calculate the stack distance profile of a combination of workloads. Other properties of our model were contrasted with related work as well.

We pay a special attention to evaluating the modeling accuracy in realistic settings, in particular when the competing workloads execute on real hardware with no synchronization between execution phases. We demonstrate the achievable accuracy with a series of measurements that not only give the overall results, but also analyze the various accuracy factors. We show that in our model, the miss penalty prediction is somewhat less influential than the miss rate prediction. Among the important factors distorting the miss rate prediction are the workload profile stability and the differences between the assumed strict LRU policy and the implemented pseudo LRU policy.

To isolate the individual accuracy factors, we have developed a specialized workload that is capable of mimicking a given stack distance profile. We use the workload to demonstrate a subtle relationship between the tools used to collect the stack distance profiles and the modeling accuracy – to our knowledge, this relationship has not been identified in existing research.

Finally, we identify multiple issues that make the modeling accuracy evaluation results in existing research mutually incomparable. In our evaluation, we carefully avoid the identified issues and publish complete tool sources and complete data files to permit comparable evaluations against our model. The sources and the data files are available at http://d3s.mff.cuni.cz/benchmark.

7. ACKNOWLEDGMENTS

We would like to thank Peter F. Sweeney for comments that have helped us improve the final revision of this paper.

This work was partially supported by the Czech Science Foundation projects GACR P202/10/J042 and GACR 201/09/H057, and by the Charles University project SVV-2011-263312.

8. REFERENCES

[1] SPEC CPU2006. http://www.spec.org/cpu2006.

[2] V. Babka, L. Bulej, M. Děcký, J. Kraft, P. Libič, L. Marek, C. Seceleanu, and P. Tůma. Resource usage modeling, Q-ImPrESS deliverable 3.3. http://www.q-impress.eu, February 2009.

[3] V. Babka and L. Marek. Frameworks for measuring effects of resource sharing. http://d3s.mff.cuni.cz/benchmark, 2010.

[4] V. Babka, L. Marek, and P. Tůma. When misses differ: Investigating impact of cache misses on observed performance. In *Proceedings of ICPADS 2009*, pages 112–119, Shenzhen, China, December 2009. IEEE.

[5] V. Babka and P. Tůma. Investigating cache parameters of x86 family processors. In *Proceedings of the SPEC Benchmark Workshop 2009*, volume 5419 of *LNCS*, pages 77–96. Springer, January 2009.

[6] V. Babka and P. Tůma. Can linear approximation improve performance prediction? In *Proceedings of EPEW 2011*, volume 6977 of *LNCS*, pages 250–264. Springer, October 2011.

[7] S. Balsamo, A. D. Marco, P. Inverardi, and M. Simeoni. Model-based performance prediction in software development: a survey. *IEEE Trans. Soft. Eng.*, 30(5):295–310, 2004.

[8] D. Chandra, F. Guo, S. Kim, and Y. Solihin. Predicting inter-thread cache contention on a chip multi-processor architecture. In *Proceedings of HPCA 2005*, pages 340–351. IEEE, 2005.

[9] X. E. Chen and T. M. Aamodt. A first-order fine-grained multithreaded throughput model. In *Proceedings of HPCA 2009*, pages 329–340. IEEE, 2009.

[10] D. Eklov, D. Black-Schaffer, and E. Hagersten. Fast modeling of shared caches in multicore systems. In *Proceedings of HiPEAC 2011*, pages 147–157. ACM, 2011.

[11] C. M. Grinstead and J. L. Snell. *Introduction to Probability*. American Mathematical Society, 1997.

[12] J. Seward et al. Valgrind. http://www.valgrind.org. Version 3.6.1.

[13] C. Xu, X. Chen, R. P. Dick, and Z. M. Mao. Cache contention and application performance prediction for multi-core systems. In *Proceedings of ISPASS 2010*, pages 76–86. IEEE, 2010.

Systematic Adoption of Genetic Programming for Deriving Software Performance Curves

Michael Faber
Karlsruhe Institute of Technology (KIT)
Karlsruhe, Germany
mail.michael.faber@gmail.com

Jens Happe
SAP Research
Karlsruhe, Germany
jens.happe@sap.com

ABSTRACT

Measurement-based approaches to software performance engineering apply analysis methods (e.g., statistical inference or machine learning) on raw measurement data with the goal to build a mathematical model describing the performance-relevant behavior of a system under test (SUT). The main challenge for such approaches is to find a reasonable trade-off between minimizing the amount of necessary measurement data used to build the model and maximizing the model's accuracy. Most existing methods require prior knowledge about parameter dependencies or their models are limited to only linear correlations. In this paper, we investigate the applicability of genetic programming (GP) to derive a mathematical equation expressing the performance behavior of the measured system (software performance curve). We systematically optimized the parameters of the GP algorithm to derive accurate software performance curves and applied techniques to prevent overfitting. We conducted an evaluation with a representative MySQL database system. The results clearly show that the GP algorithm outperforms other analysis techniques like inverse distance weighting (IDW) and multivariate adaptive regression splines (MARS) in terms of model accuracy.

Categories and Subject Descriptors

D.2.11 [**Software Engineering**]: Software Architectures; C.4 [**Performance of Systems**]; I.6.5 [**Simulation and Modeling**]: Model Development

General Terms

Performance Analysis, Performance Prediction, Genetic programming, Measurement-based

Keywords

Software Performance Engineering, Model Inference, Machine Learning, Black-box Approach

1. INTRODUCTION

Software performance is an important quality attribute and directly influences the total cost of ownership (TCO), customer satisfaction and even the productivity of employees [23]. Thus, software performance is crucial in today's enterprise systems. Methods of software performance analysis help architects to detect bottlenecks and performance problems and to judge different design alternatives. For this purpose, software performance models are created to predict the behavior of software systems. Besides analytical, model-based and prototype-based approaches, the measurement-based approach takes measurement data and uses analysis methods, such as statistics or machine learning, to extract performance-relevant factors of the system under test (SUT). Those measurement-based approaches do not necessarily require an understanding of the system internals but often consider the SUT as a black box. This makes them well-suited for large enterprise systems that are historically grown and not implemented from scratch [24]. Moreover, they are often applied to existing systems, such as legacy systems or services provided by third parties, for which either no internals are known or no internals are to be modeled.

The main goal of this work is to apply machine-learning techniques in order to infer accurate performance models based on measurement data. Those models are hereafter referred to as *software performance curves*. They describe the performance behavior of a system in dependence of the system's configuration and the usage profile. As mentioned above, system performance depends on many factors, leading to a high dimensionality of the problem. This *curse of dimensionality* [11] leads to sparse measurements of the parameter space. To reduce the measurement errors and stabilize the observed metrics, all measurements have to be repeated sufficiently. Thus, meaningful measurement results are very expensive and only a very limited number of measurements are available for model inference. Analysis methods must find a reasonable trade-off between minimizing the amount of necessary measurement data used to build the model while maximizing the model's accuracy. Besides appropriate analysis methods, the process of efficiently selecting new measurement points is crucial for receiving accurate performance curves. This aspect is investigated in more detail in another work [28] of our research group.

Existing approaches use analysis methods such as MARS [5], piecewise polynomial regressions [15] or genetic optimization [10] to infer software performance curves. Problems of these techniques are the assumptions about the input/output parameter dependencies or the resulting model accuracies. Genetic optimization and polynomial regression assume predefined structures for the input/output parameter dependency, expressed as mathematical equations, and focus on optimizing the coefficients of the equation. As this structure is not always known in practice, MARS tries to overcome this issue by approximating the dependency through combinations of piecewise-defined linear functions. However, this approach has problems when approximating functions which contain higher-order powers [11].

In this paper, we examine the ability of a machine learning technique, genetic programming (GP), to infer software performance curves. In contrast to genetic optimization, where a structure is already fixed (e.g., linear), GP does not make any assumptions about the input/output parameter dependency and optimizes the structure of the equation simultaneously with the coefficients (symbolic regression). We employed the Goal/Question/Metric (GQM) approach to derive a systematic plan for the optimization of the configuration of the genetic algorithm. This optimization is important when applying genetic algorithms to a certain problem domain (here the derivation of software performance curves). Then, we followed a four-stepped process to answer each question of the GQM plan. This process consists of i) the experiment definition, ii) experiment execution, iii) experiment analysis and iv) decision. The analysis step includes the application of statistical tests (Kruskal-Wallis Rank Sum Test and Wilcoxon Rank Sum Test) to choose the best alternative. To increase model accuracy and convergence speed, we experimented with providing domain knowledge (such as hypothesis about parameter dependencies) to the GP algorithm. However, the experiments showed that using domain knowledge has no significant influence on the resulting models. To improve the generalization of the result models, we applied techniques to prevent overfitting.

The evaluation contains a synthetic function and representative measurements of a MySQL database system. We compared the models created by the GP algorithm with those created by MARS and IDW. As training sets, we used randomly-distributed and equidistantly-distributed subsets of different sizes. The results for this evaluation reveal that GP outperforms other analysis techniques like MARS and IDW, not only in terms of the average relative error but also the dispersion of relative errors among single predictions is smaller. The main contributions of this paper are i) a generic and systematic approach to optimize and apply GP to any specific problem domain, ii) the adaption and implementation of GP to derive software performance curves, and iii) an evaluation using a synthetic function and measurements of a MySQL database to demonstrate the potential of the GP approach in contrast to other analysis techniques (MARS and IDW).

The remainder of the paper is structured as follows. Section 2 presents an overview of related work about measurement-based performance analysis and GP approaches. In Section 3, we provide foundations about the Software Performance Cockpit (SoPeCo) and GP. Section 4 describes our approach to adopt GP for the derivation of software performance curves. In Section 5, we evaluate the approach using a synthetic function and measurement data from a MySQL database. Our approach is discussed in Section 6. Finally, Section 7 concludes this paper.

2. RELATED WORK

The work related to our approach can be classified in the main categories of software performance engineering and genetic programming. First, we present approaches concerning measurement-based software performance analysis and model derivation. Second, we describe relevant work in the area of genetic programming.

The approaches in software performance engineering can be coarsely divided (according to [29]) into model-based (see [2] and [13] for detailed surveys) and measurement-based approaches (e.g., [5, 14, 15, 21]). In most measurement-based approaches, statistical inference or machine learning techniques are applied to derive predictions based on the measurement data. Courtois and Woodside [5] apply regression splines such as MARS to derive models and introduce a metric to determine the accuracy of the models. This allows to iteratively choose new measurement point using repelling forces until a desired model accuracy is reached. Lee et al. [15] compare polynomial regression and artificial neural networks (ANN) and suggest methods such as hierarchical clustering and correlation analysis to select the most relevant inputs. Their experiments revealed that both techniques lead to models with similar accuracies but differ in terms of their assumptions and the model transparency. A similar result is shown by the comparison in [19]: Psichogios et al. compared MARS with neural networks and found that "MARS is often more accurate and always much faster than neural networks". For a fair comparison of GP and ANN the latter requires similar adjustments in tuning like GP which is beyond the scope of this work. Thus, we chose MARS instead of ANN for the evaluation in Section 5. Sharma et al. [21] apply a machine learning technique, namely independent component analysis (ICA), to categorize workload requests and to identify their resource demands using only high-level measurement results (e.g., CPU/network usage or overall request rate). Zheng et al. [30] employ Kalman Filter estimators to track parameters which cannot be measured directly by using easy observable data such as response times. Kraft et al. [14] estimate service demands by applying linear regression and the maximum likelihood technique using only response time measurements. This approach avoids detailed instrumentations to receive samples for service demands.

In this part, we present approaches about genetic programming which compare different alternatives for generating constants, fitness functions, crossover operators and preventing overfitting. We used these approaches as a basis for our optimizations of the GP algorithm. Ryan and Keijzer [20] investigate the effects of different constant mutation types in the problem domain of symbolic regression. They state that, for symbolic regression, constant mutation types must find a good balance between the effort needed for the mutation and the probability of rejecting the whole individual in future generations. Ryan and Keijzer compare four different mutation types and evaluate their influence on the overall performance of the GP algorithm. Their experiments reveal, that the decision which operator performs best depends on the complexity of the problem which should be approximated. We used this approach as a basis and reproduced the experiments for the domain of deriving software performance curves. Ferrucci et al. examine the influence of different fitness functions [8] and conclude that the choice of an appropriate fitness function is crucial as it leads the whole evaluation process. Our experiments also reveal significant differences when comparing different fitness functions. Gustafson et al. suggest a way to improve a GP approach for the symbolic regression domain in [9]. They investigate the dissimilarity and diversity of the solutions during the evolutionary process. Finally, they suggest to prevent crossovers between parents having the same fitness value. Their experiments showed significant improvements after applying this improvement. However, in our experiments, we saw no improvements for the adjusted crossover operator. Panait and Luke compare six alternatives on how to evolve robust programs with GP [18]. Robust programs are solutions which generalize correctly from the learning data. During their experiments, they identified three methods which perform significantly better than the others for the domain of symbolic regression. We applied one of these methods (random per generation) and combined it with a cross-validation approach to prevent the effects of overfitting.

3. FOUNDATIONS

This section places our work in the context of the Software Performance Cockpit and introduces the concepts of machine learning and genetic programming.

The Software Performance Cockpit (SoPeCo) [26, 27] is a framework with the goal to make measurement-based software performance engineering more practicable. Enterprise software systems are usually quite complex and their performance depends on a variety of influencing factors. Different parts and layers of the system (e.g., operating system or middleware) require detailed knowledge and mostly separate tools for instrumentation and monitoring. The SoPeCo handles this challenge through a plug-in-based architecture which allows the encapsulation of domain knowledge and implementations within adapters. Westermann et al. defined three different responsibilities and tasks: The *System, Benchmark and Tool Experts* develop adapters for generating load and connecting parts of the software systems such as middleware or monitoring tools with the SoPeCo. *Analysis Experts* provide adapters which enable various statistical analysis of measurement results. *Performance Analysts* model the test scenario using the configuration meta-model provided by the framework. This includes aspects such as the use of different adapters (e.g., workload driver, monitoring) and providing system information where the adapters are deployed. For further information about the SoPeCo, we recommend [26] and [27].

When executing the configuration model created by the Performance Analyst, the SoPeCo automatically triggers systematic measurements and collects the reported metrics such as response time. A subsequent analysis adapter derives a *software performance curve* [28] which describes dependencies between system's configuration, its workload and the performance expressed through timing behavior, throughput or resource utilization. A performance curve might be realized through mathematical equations expressing these dependencies: Assuming that x_1 and x_2 are two performance-relevant factors acting as independent variables (inputs) and *responseTime* the dependent variable (output). A random performance curve might then be defined as $\hat{f}(x_1, x_2) = 2 * x_1 + 0.1 * x_2^2$. Such curves can be derived through statistical or machine learning techniques. Within this work, we applied genetic programming, as a common

machine learning technique, for the derivation of software performance curves.

Machine learning (ML) in general refers to the process of deriving knowledge from given training data. ML techniques create prediction models which estimate the outcome for a given set of features. Depending on the training data, ML distinguishes supervised and unsupervised learning techniques. Unsupervised techniques only use the features and no outcome variables for the training. Mostly, these techniques are used to cluster data. Supervised techniques require pairs of features and outcome variables for the training. Features have different types such as quantitative, qualitative or ordered categorical. The prediction of a quantitative output is called regression, whereas the prediction of qualitative output is often referred to as classification [11]. Due to the quantitative nature of performance metrics, we focus on regression techniques.

One field of machine learning are *evolutionary algorithms* (EA) which are approaches to solve optimization or search problems. EAs use an iterative approach to approximate an optimal solution. During each iteration (*generation*), the *population*, consisting of a certain number of *individuals*, evolves. This evolution is performed by *reproducing, mutating* and *crossing-over* individuals of the previous generation. Each individual represents a candidate solution and has a *fitness* value expressing the quality of the solution. The aim of EAs is to maximize this fitness over many generations. The main principles mentioned above and the concept of "survival of the fittest" (as described by Charles Darwin) are copied from nature. For more information, we recommend [4] and [7]. *Genetic programming* (GP) is a special application of EA and aims at deriving computer programs or mathematical equations. The individuals in GP are usually represented as tree structures and recombinations are tree operations such as randomly exchanging subtrees between two trees [12].

4. APPROACH

In this section, we present our approach to meet the challenge of deriving accurate software performance curves from measurements. In Section 4.1, we depict the overall idea of applying GP for the derivation of software performance curves and provide a simple illustrative example. In Section 4.2, we describe the initial configuration of the GP algorithm, formalize the training set and provide three definitions describing the model error. Next, we present all investigated aspects to adopt the GP algorithm to the specific problem using GQM plans (Section 4.3) and describe a generic process for the adoption of GP algorithms (Section 4.4). Finally, we provide a detailed example to show how we applied the process to systematically fulfill all goals defined in the GQM plan (Section 4.5).

4.1 Overview and Idea

The aim of our approach is to derive accurate software performance curves using measurement data. Since the retrieval of measurement data is very expensive in terms of time and effort, it is desirable to have an algorithm which is capable of deriving accurate performance curves using a small amount of data. To derive the performance curve, we use genetic programming which does not make any assumptions about the input/output parameter dependency

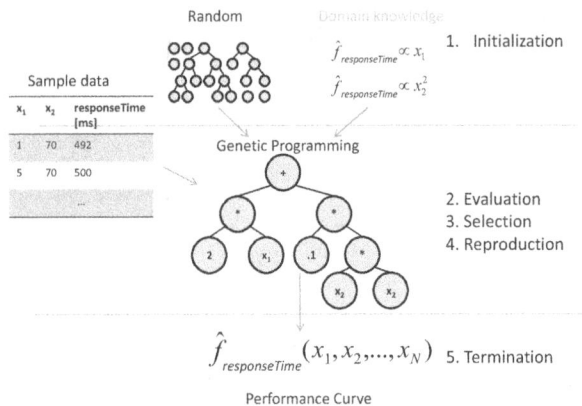

Figure 1: Overview of our approach

and optimizes the structure of the equation simultaneously with the coefficients (symbolic regression).

Figure 1 depicts the idea of our approach that applies genetic programming to software performance engineering. In the first step, GP is initialized with randomized data. The initialization may be improved by domain knowledge or prior statistic analyses. We investigated whether and how domain knowledge can be reused to improve the convergence speed and accuracy of our algorithm. However, our experiments inducting domain knowledge did not influence the results. Similarly, we evaluated the influence of prior statistical analyses that serve as input for the initialization. In our experiments, we did not observe any improvement in terms of convergence speed or model accuracy by these means. After the initialization, the genetic algorithm begins to evolve the individuals. The evolution starts with an evaluation of individuals by using the measurement data (Step 2). Then, the algorithm selects and reproduces fit individuals (Step 3 and 4) and repeats steps 2-4 for a given number of iterations (generations). Finally, the algorithm terminates (Step 5) when a given termination criteria, such as the desired accuracy level or runtime constraints, are fulfilled. The result of the algorithm is a software performance curve expressed through a mathematical equation.

Returning to the example provided in the previous section, we illustrate the genetic programming approach. The goal of the GP algorithm is to find the software performance curve $\hat{f}(x_1, x_2)$, which predicts the dependent variable *response-Time* using provided measurement data. Assume that the algorithm receives results of 50 independent response time measurements with different input configurations (values for x_1, x_2). To evaluate the fitness of each individual, the algorithm calculates the averaged relative error based on the provided training data (see Section 4.2). New individuals are created by recombining the genes (represented as trees) of two individuals. The trees comprise *operators* (e.g., +, -, *, /) serving as inner nodes and *constants* and *variables* (here x_1, x_2) serving as leaves. When the evolution of individuals finishes, the algorithm returns the fittest individual representing the software performance curve identified by the algorithm. The exemplary individual in the center of Figure 1 depicts one possible representation for the software performance curve ($\hat{f}(x_1, x_2) = 2 * x_1 + 0.1 * x_2^2$) in the internally-used tree representation.

4.2 Background

In this section, we present the initial setting of the GP algorithm which we used as a starting point for our optimizations. We also formalize the training set and introduce three definitions expressing the error of inferred models that we used as fitness functions and for judging the model quality.

The idea and concepts of evolutionary algorithms (e.g., GP) are very intuitive and general but its configuration is not. For example, the size of the population and amount of generations, the selection of parent individuals, probabilities for crossover and mutation, and the fitness function highly influence the efficiency of the algorithm (in terms of solution quality and convergence speed) and therefore must be chosen carefully. While some rules of thumb exist on how to set parameters for broad problem domains (e.g., in [12]), many systematic experiments are necessary to adjust the configuration towards a certain problem. We based the initial settings for the configuration parameters of the GP algorithm on the well-established suggestions by Koza [12] about applying GP to symbolic regression. The population had a size of $M = 1024$ and was evolved for $G = 51$ generations. The maximum tree depth was restricted during the run to $D_c = 17$ and during the initialization to $D_i = 6$. As function set we used arithmetic operations $(+, -, *, /)$. Probabilities for the crossover operator was set to $p_c = 0.9$ and for reproduction to $p_r = 0.1$. As a method for parent selection, we used the tournament selection with $k = 7$. In tournament selection, a group of k individuals is randomly selected and pair-wisely compared. The fittest individuals of two tournaments are chosen for the crossover. We used no structural mutation and selected inner nodes for crossovers with a probability of $p_{ip} = 0.8$.

The training set with N samples for a d-dimensional problem can be formulated as an $N \times (d+1)$-matrix $\mathbf{T}$, where the first d columns of each row represent the input parameters and the $d + 1$-th column contains the corresponding target metric (e.g., response time). Let $\vec{x_i}$ denote the transposed vector containing columns 1 to d of the i-th row of matrix $\mathbf{T}$ and thus representing the independent parameters for one tuple of training data. The sum of absolute residuals (SAR) based on the training set $\mathbf{T}$ can be used as a fitness measure and is defined as:

$$SAR_{\hat{f}}(\mathbf{T}) = \sum_{i=1}^{N} |\hat{f}(\vec{x_i}) - t_{i,d+1}| \quad . \tag{1}$$

with $\hat{f}$ being the prediction model, $\vec{x_i}$ the vector containing the input parameters and $t_{i,d+1}$ the corresponding target metric.

The relative error is defined as

$$RE(y, \hat{y}) = \begin{cases} |\frac{y - \hat{y}}{y}|, & \text{if } y \neq 0 \\ |y - \hat{y}|, & \text{otherwise} \end{cases} , \tag{2}$$

where y is the measured value and $\hat{y}$ is the predicted value. For the case that the measured value is 0, we used the absolute error as an approximation for the relative error.

We can now define the averaged relative error as

$$ARE_{\hat{f}}(\mathbf{T}) = \frac{\sum_{i=1}^{N} RE(t_{i,d+1}, \hat{f}(\vec{x_i}))}{N} , \tag{3}$$

where $\mathbf{T}$, $\vec{x_i}$, N and $\hat{f}$ are defined as above.

Part I: Parameter Optimizations
G1: Constants
G2: Fitness Function
G3: Multi-Dimensional Regression Problems
G4: Training Sets
G5: Extended Function Set
G6: Crossover
G7: Population Size and Number of Generations
Part II: Domain Knowledge
G8: Influence of One Domain Function
Part III: Overfitting
G9: Apply Efficient Technique to Prevent Overfitting

Table 1: Overview of all addressed goals

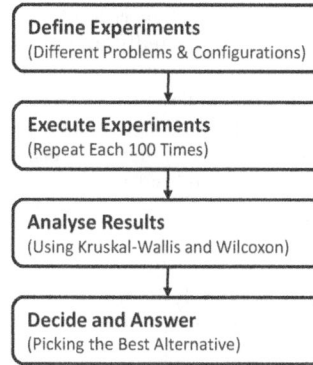

Figure 2: Process to answer questions through experiments

4.3 Examined Goals

In this section, we present the different aspects of the GP algorithm which we adapted and optimized. We used a Goal/Question/Metric plan for a systematic planning of all experiments.

The Goal/Question/Metric (GQM) [3] is a framework for systematic experimentation in software engineering. For this purpose, it defines a process of answering well-defined goals in a top-down fashion. The contribution of the framework is twofold: It helps to derive experiments in a goal-oriented manner and subsequently allows the systematic evaluation and interpretation of their results in order to answer the overall goals.

Table 1 depicts the goals we investigated within this work. The nine goals are organized in three groups: The first group summarizes all goals concerning parameter optimizations of the GP algorithm. To answer the question assigned to these goals, we used the process described in the Section 4.4. The second part investigates the introduction of domain knowledge. Overfitting, as a common problem in the machine learning domain, is addressed in part three.

The accuracy of performance curves highly depends on finding accurate coefficients. An appropriate generation and mutation of constants is addressed Goal G1. Furthermore, the fitness function is essential in genetic algorithms since it steers the whole evolutionary process. Goal G2 addresses the selection of an appropriate fitness function. Software performance is influenced by factors like the system's usage and configuration. Hence, Goal G3 investigates the ability of the algorithm to solve multi-dimensional regression problems. The training data is the only information for algorithm to build the performance models. Goal G4 investigates the influence of necessary preprocessing steps and the training set size. The expressiveness of the algorithm depends on the available operators (inner nodes) to build the models. Goal G5 was to extend the arithmetic function set $(+, -, *, /)$ with other functions such as `pow` or `log`. The crossover operator is responsible for building new individuals during the evolutionary process. Gustafson et al. improved the solution quality in symbolic regression domains by introducing constraints when picking the parent individuals for the crossover [9]. Goal G6 applies these algorithmic improvements to our approach. Goal G7, being the last goal concerning the parameter optimizations, investigates a reasonable population size and number of generations. After the adjustment of the GP algorithm, we enhanced it to use domain knowledge (Goal G8), such as parameter dependencies that are typical for software performance or queuing formulas. Overfitting is a common problem in all fields of machine learning which also needs to be addressed in our scenarios. Thus, we applied and evaluated different techniques to prevent overfitting (G9).

4.4 Generic Process for Adoption of GP Algorithms

In this section, we describe the systematic process which we used for answering the questions derived in the GQM plan. Even though the process is intuitive it is fundamental to describe the decision mechanism detailed since our adjustments of the GP algorithm and thus one of the main contribution of the paper are based on this process. The process is depicted in Figure 2 and described in the following.

Define Experiments.

The first step for answering a question about a reasonable parameter setting is the definition of experiments. The definition basically includes two parts. The first part is the selection of appropriate prediction problems and training sets. It is important, that the chosen prediction problems and training sets are representative for real problems in the target domain for which the GP algorithm should be optimized. The second part is the identification and implementation of different alternative configurations for the investigated question (e.g., different constant mutation types).

Execute Experiments.

The second step is the execution of the experiments. Since the GP approach is non-deterministic, we had to repeat all experiments for a sufficient number of times (n). This number is a trade-off between the execution time for the experiments and stabilized results. Using an initial experiment and the calculation of confidence bands we determined $n = 100$ as sufficient for our experiments. We observed that some evolutions lead to models with very high errors. Such outliers are common in symbolic regression. In order, to keep the experiment runtime to evaluate the effect of changes to the GP algorithm in a reasonable scope, we decided to remove the worst 10% of each 100 runs before analysing the results. When the GP algorithm is applied to a real problem, it will be executed repeatedly and thus removing the outliers during our experiments does not diesturb the results. All boxplots and statistical tests are based on the cleaned data. Due to the non-determinsm, we implemented the final analysis adapter such that it internally repeats the GP algorithm for x times and only returns the model of the best run.

Analyze Results.

The third step is the analysis of the experiment results. For this purpose, we use statistical tests to determine if the target metric (mostly the averaged relative error of the models) is significantly influenced by different configuration alternatives. The analysis results did not follow a normal distribution (also observed in [18]) and thus we used the Kruskal-Wallis Rank Sum Test and Wilcoxon Rank Sum Test [6]. They either lead to the decision that significant differences in the target metric exist or that the alternatives do not significantly influence the target metrics.

Decide and Answer.

The last step is the decision for one of the questioned alternatives based on the results of the statistical tests. After we answered one question, we picked the next from the GQM plan presented in the section above. We neglected mutual dependencies between configuration parameters of the GP algorithm and sequentially answered the questions.

We suggest this four-stepped process in combination with a GQM plan as a reasonable approach for optimizing the parameters of genetic programming algorithms in order to apply GP to a specific problem domain.

4.5 Detailed Investigation of One Question

In this section, we illustrate the process shown in Figure 2. We focus on Goal G1, which addresses the generation of constants. We derived five questions concerning the constant types, the ranges and their mutation types and probabilities:

- *Q1:* Which mutation type is the best for integer constants?

- *Q2:* Which mutation type is the best for float constants?

- *Q3:* How does the combination of both constant types (integer and float) perform?

- *Q4:* What is the optimal mutation rate?

- *Q5:* Are the constant intervals sufficient to generate big constants?

In the following, we address the first question of the list above to present the application of the process comprising experiment definition, experiment execution, result analysis and decision.

Concerning constant mutation, Koza [12] assumes that new constants are created during the evolution as combinations of other existing constants and functions. Thus, no mutation was considered, and all constant values remained unchanged after their initialization during the whole evolutionary process. Ryan and Keijzer on the other hand investigated the influence of different constant mutation types [20] (see Section 2). We based the three investigated mutation types on the ideas of Ryan and Keijzer.

Formula
$f_0(x_0) = 12 * x_0$
$f_1(x_0) = -41 * x_0$
$f_2(x_0) = 24 * x_0 + 3$
$f_3(x_0) = 54 * x_0^2 - 34 * x_0 + 7$
$f_4(x_0) = \frac{53}{97} * x_0^2$

Table 2: One-dimensional problems with focus on integer coefficients

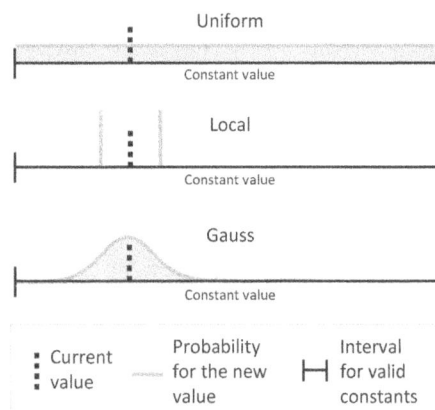

Figure 3: Investigated alternatives for the mutation of constants

4.5.1 Definition of Experiments

The experiment definition (see Section 4.4) includes the identification of representative problems and of different alternatives.

Problems.

We used the five problems listed in Table 2 for running this experiment. All of them have one independent parameter and contain only integer constants as coefficients. We intentionally used simple structures which we assumed likely to be found in early generations. This would mean, that the GP algorithm only has to find the correct coefficient, since the structure is already found. The training sets for each Problem k of Table 2 consist of 150 samples with the input parameters $\mathbf{X} = (0, 1, \ldots, 149)^T$. The i-th row of the 150×2-matrix $\mathbf{T_k}$ had the form $(x_i, f_k(x_i))$. The fact that the training data is distributed equidistantly over an interval (here $[0,149]$) is a realistic assumption, since systems are often measured in such a systematic way. We also consider the simple linear or quadratic structure of the problems as representative and common for dependencies in performance analysis.

Alternatives.

We compared four different alternatives against each other: no mutation (N), uniform mutation (U), local mutation (L) and Gaussian mutation (G). Figure 3 depicts all mutation types. The gray line illustrates the probability for a value after the mutation and the bold dashed line represents the constant value before the mutation. The uniform mutation generates a new random number with equal probabilities in the entire interval, independently of the current

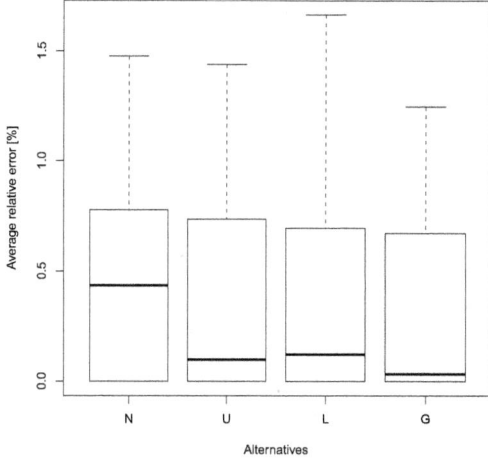

Figure 4: Boxplot with the model accuracies of Problem f_3

	Accuracy	Generation
Test	p-value	p-value
All (Kruskal-Wallis)	0.0007*	0.0012*
L-G (Wilcoxon)	0.6862	0.6111
N-G (Wilcoxon)	0.0022*	0.0022*
U-G (Wilcoxon)	0.0015*	0.0022*
N-L (Wilcoxon)	0.0086*	0.0109*
U-L (Wilcoxon)	0.0054*	0.0119*
U-N (Wilcoxon)	0.9841	0.9936

Table 3: Results of applied significance tests

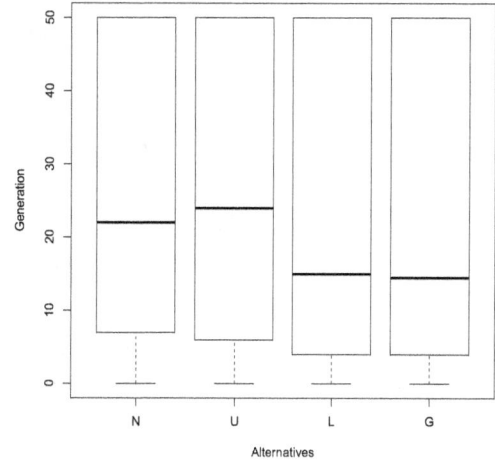

Figure 5: Boxplot with merged generations of Problems 0 to 4

constant value. The local mutation increases or decreases the current value (each with a probability of $p = 0.5$) using a fixed delta. The Gaussian mutation uses a Gaussian distribution as probability density function with the current constant value as mean value. For all alternatives, we used an interval for valid constants of $[-100, 100]$ and a probability for the constant mutations of $p_{cm} = 0.75$.

The number of alternatives (4) and problems (5) leads to a total number of 20 experiments. To get stabilized results, we repeated each experiment for 100 times (see Section 4.4) and thus issued 2000 independent evolutions for this experiment.

4.5.2 Analyzing the Results

In this section, we present our analysis of the results for this set of experiments and finally answer Question $Q1$. We used two metrics for the analysis: The averaged relative error (see Section 4.2) on the training data to express the quality of each solution and the generation at which a perfect fit was found as an indicator for the convergence speed.

For problems f_0, f_1 and f_2 nearly every run of all four alternatives generated the exact model leading to an averaged relative error of 0. The experiment runs for f_3 and f_4 lead to more variation in the model accuracies. Figure 4 shows a boxplot with the averaged relative errors for problem f_3 for all 90 runs (due to the outlier removal mentioned in Section 4.4). We omitted all values above the upper whisker in all boxplots to improve the illustration. The uniform (U) and local (L) mutation perform quiet similar, whereas no mutation (N) seems to perform slightly worse by having a median of 0.43% compared to 0.10% for uniform and 0.12% for local mutation. The Gaussian (G) mutation tends to perform best by having the lowest variance and the lowest median (0.03%).

To identify the best alternative, we merged the models of the 90 runs for each of the five problems. This lead to 450 models per alternative. We applied the Kruskal-Wallis Rank Sum test to identify if the differences among all four distributions are significant. The null hypothesis states that no differences among all tested groups exist. The test returned

a p-value of 0.0007 (see Table 3) implying significant differences between the groups. To identify between which groups the differences exist, we pair wisely applied the Wilcoxon test. The results are denoted in the column "Accuracy" of Table 3. The asterisk besides the value implies significant differences based on a significance level of $\alpha = 0.05$. This means, that local (L) and Gaussian (G) mutation perform significantly better than uniform (U) and no (N) mutation. Within both groups (L/G and U/N), no significant differences are testified.

The absolute differences in accuracy were quite small among all four alternatives. The medians of the merged accuracies for all alternatives are 0% and the largest difference of the third quartils is between N (0.183%) and G (0.000%). We further investigated the convergence speed, i.e., the generation at which the exact model was found. Figure 5 shows the boxplot containing the generations at which the exact models were found for each of the alternatives.

Local (L) and Gaussian (G) mutation perform similar and their medians are 15 (L) and 14.5 (G). The medians of uniform (U) and no (N) mutation are 24 (U) and 22 (N). The p-value of 0.0012 received by the Kruskal-Wallis test indicates that the null hypothesis can be rejected, meaning that significant differences among the alternatives exist. Thus, we performed a subsequent Wilcoxon test pair wisely for each alternative. The results of this test are depicted in the "Generation" column of Table 3. Again, an asterisk besides the p-value indicates an significant difference between the distributions on a significance level of $\alpha = 0.05$. The test reveals that Gaussian (G) and local (L) mutation has a significantly positive effect on the convergence speed compared to no mutation (N) and uniform mutation (U).

This analysis allowed us to answer the initial question, which mutation type performs best for integer constants. The statistical tests left us the choice between local (L) and Gaussian (G) mutation and we decided to use the Gaussian mutation (G) due to the better tendencies in accuracy (see Figure 4) and convergence speed (see Figure 5). We applied the same procedure to the remaining questions of all goals. In the next section, we briefly present the results for all goals.

4.6 Results of the Optimization and Final GP Settings

We conclude this section about the adaption of the GP algorithm with a summary of all results for each of the goals presented in Section 4.3.

Goal 1 addresses the constant mutation and our experiments reveal that the use of integer and float constants having the intervals [-100,100] and [0,1] is sufficient. The Gaussian mutation is applied to both constant types with a probability of $p_{cm} = 0.75$. A final experiment shows that this configuration is sufficient to generate constants with the desired accuracy. Goal 2 investigates the influence of different fitness functions and the experiments indicate that the use of relative errors leads to a faster convergence than using absolute residuals. Goal 3 investigates the ability of the GP algorithm to solve multi-dimensional problems. The experiment results show that simple problems such as linear combinations can be approximated accurately even if the dimensionality is high (up to 10 dimensions). Goal 4 addresses preprocessing of the training data. Corresponding experiments reveal that averaging measurement data with same input configurations (results of repeated measurements) leads to better results and to faster execution times. An appropriate size of the training set highly depends on the complexity of the underlying problem. It is crucial that the training set contains enough data to represent the problem otherwise the algorithm cannot build reasonable prediction models. Finding an appropriate function set is addressed in Goal 5. Based on our experiments, we decided to use two different function sets during independent runs of the algorithm: The "Basic" function set contains the arithmetic functions $(+, -, *, /)$. The "Extended" function set additionally contains the *exp*, *power*, *log* and *hinge* function. Driven by the work of Gustafson et al. [9], we investigated in Goal 6 the proposed algorithmic improvement of the parent selection process. However, the experiment reveals no significant improvement compared to tournament selection with $k = 7$. Goal 7 addresses the choice of an appropriate population size and a reasonable number of generations. Based on the experiments, we decided to evolve 2048 individuals for 102 generations per evolution.

Goal 8 investigates the influence of domain knowledge, but corresponding experiments indicate that the use of domain knowledge neither significantly influences the accuracy of the results nor convergence speed. Goal 9 copes with the problem of overfitting. The experiments persuades us to use a combination of two techniques: The first is a cross-validation which selects the best-of-run individual among all best-of-generation individuals based on a separate test set. The second technique uses only a subset of the available training data. The subset is changed randomly for each generation (see [18]). Experiments show that using these two techniques reduces the overfitting problem sufficiently for our purposes.

5. EVALUATION

In this section, we compare the accuracy of the models inferred by our GP algorithm with models derived by other analysis techniques. We start with applying the algorithms to a simple and synthetic function which allows the visualization of the results. The second and main part of the evaluation describes the application of the algorithm to real measurements of a MySQL database.

We automated the evaluation using the SoPeCo (see Section 3). As competitive analysis techniques, we used *inverse distance weighting* (IDW) and *multivariate adaptive regression splines* (MARS). As explained in Section 2, we used MARS instead of neural networks, since ANNs and other machine learning techniques would require similar adjustments as the GP algorithm which was beyond the scope of this work.

All analysis techniques are implemented as analysis adapter for the SoPeCo. In the following, we present all three techniques and explain the configuration parameters of the adapters besides the configuration of dependent and independent parameters.

IDW is a multivariate interpolation technique. Interpolation techniques estimate the value of unknown points as a combination of existing points. IDW uses a weight function for this combination, where the weight for each existing point is inverse to the distance between that point and the estimated point. IDW uses all surrounding points for the interpolation, meaning that all known points influence the estimation, but closer points with higher effects (see [22]). The IDW adapter has two additional configuration parameters: A strategy for calculating the distance between two points and an exponent for the distance metric to express their influence. We used the Euclidean norm as distance and a weight exponent of 2.

MARS is a non-parametric regression technique that creates models by combining piecewise linear basis functions. The algorithm creates the prediction model in two steps: First, it iteratively builds a model by combining the existing model with new basis functions. The second step uses backward deletion to prune the model. This reduces the model complexity and avoids an overfitting of the model (see [11]). The MARS analysis adapter does not implement the algorithm itself, but delegates the call to a corresponding module of the statistic tool R [1].

The GP analysis adapter implements the GP algorithm as presented in this work. The implementation is based on the ECJ framework [16]. The user must configure the function sets ("Basic" and/or "Extended') as described in Section 4.6. We used both function sets for this evaluation scenario. Since the GP algorithm is non-deterministic, the adapter implements an internal loop which repeats the evolution for a configurable number of times for each function set. After

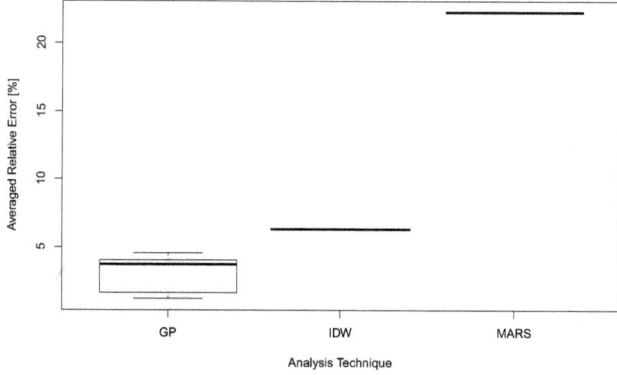

Figure 6: Model accuracies of the one-dimensional synthetic function

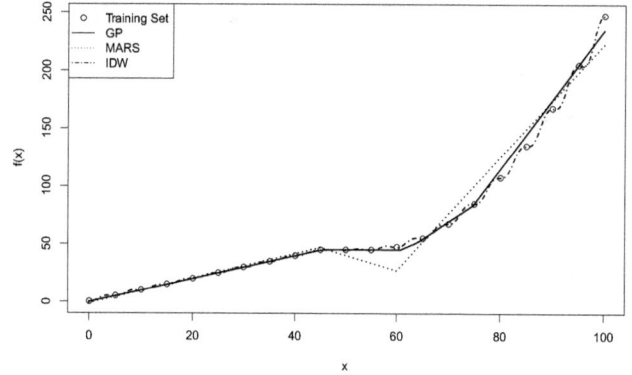

Figure 7: One-dimensional synthetic function illustrating the results of IDW, MARS and GP

all iterations, the adapter returns the best model based on the accuracy on internal test sets. We configured 5 iterations and thus one call of the adapter leads to 10 evolutions: 5 with the "Basic" function set and 5 with the "Extended" function set. Despite this mechanism, the results of the adapter are still non-deterministic. Thus, we called the GP analysis adapter 10 times for this evaluation.

In the following, we present the results of our twofold evaluation. The first part is based on a synthetic function and the second part uses realistic measurement results of a MySQL database system.

5.1 Synthetic Function

To illustrate the results of GP, IDW and MARS, we applied the different techniques to a synthetic function with only one independent parameter (one-dimensional). The target function is piece wisely defined as:

$$f(x) = \begin{cases} x, & \text{if } x \leq 45, \\ 45, & \text{if } 45 < x \leq 55, \\ 0.1 * (x-55)^2 + 45, & \text{if } x > 55. \end{cases} \quad (4)$$

The function is linear in the first part, constant in the middle part and quadratic in the last part. The training set for all three techniques contains 21 equally-distributed points with a distance of $\Delta x = 5$.

We used the averaged relative error (see Equation 3) as a metric to compare the three techniques. The averaged relative error is based on a validation set containing every value for x in the interval $[0, 100]$ with a step width of $\Delta x = 0.1$ and the corresponding $f(x)$. This leads to a total validation set size of 1001.

Figure 6 depicts the averaged relative errors of the results derived by the three different analysis techniques. We used a boxplot to illustrate the results from all 10 runs of the GP adapter. The results ranged from 1.20% up to 4.66%, with a median value of 3.72%. IDW lead to a model with 6.32% averaged relative error and MARS to a model with 22.66%. The worst model returned by the GP adapter is still 1.66% better than the result of IDW and 18% better than the MARS model.

Figure 7 shows the resulting functions of the IDW and MARS analysis and one result of the 10 GP runs. The

circles illustrate the training set containing 21 points. The dotted line represents the MARS result, which is composed of three linear functions. The first linear function perfectly fits the target function, whereas the second part approximates the constant part and the third the polynomial part. The dashed line shows the IDW result and the principle of IDW. Since IDW is an interpolation technique, every point of the training is intersected. The solid line depicts the third-best result of the GP analysis with an averaged relative error of 1.62%. This result is composed of 5 linear functions: One represents the linear part and one the constant part. The other three functions approximates the polynomial part of the target function.

5.2 Case Study: MySQL Database

In this part of the evaluation, we used measurements of a MySQL 5.5 [17] database to derive a software performance curve which describes the response times for different query types. We start the section with explaining the experiment setup for retrieving the measurements. Next, we explain two sampling methods (equidistant and random) which were used to retrieve points for the training set. Finally, we present and discuss the results of all three analysis techniques.

The MySQL 5.5 database was deployed on a machine having an Intel Core 2 Duo Processor with 2 × 2GHz, 2GB RAM and a SATA hard disk with 5400RPM and 8MB buffer (Hitachi-Travelstar). The database was accessed via LAN from a remote machine. The Software Performance Cockpit was used to automate the measurements. To receive stable results, each query was repeated for 50 times and the arithmetic average was used as training data.

The target metric is the response time and the input parameters were restricted to six parameters expressing the query type, the queue length and the queue structure. The first parameter (`AccessType`) differentiates between reading access (`Read`) and writing access (`Update`). The table size is fixed to 100,000 rows in this evaluation scenario. The second parameter (`NumberOfRequestedLines`) defines how many rows are accessed and is set to 1 (12,000) to approximate small (large) requests. The remaining four parame-

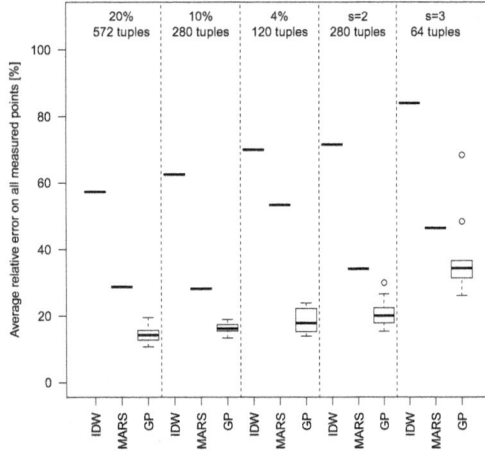

Figure 8: Model accuracies when using different analysis methods and training sets

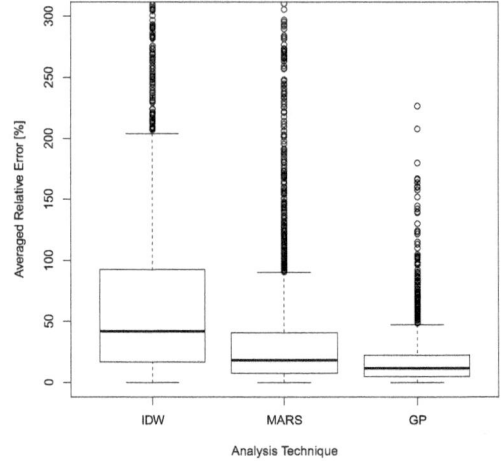

Figure 9: Relative errors of predictions for all points in the validation set using the 4% randomly-distributed training set

ters (`NumRead_1`, `NumRead_12000`, `NumUpdate_1` and `NumUpdate_12000`) describe the queue length and structure of the database. The value for each parameter indicates how many threads of the corresponding query type (Read/Update 1/12,000 lines) are currently in the queue. The domain for these parameters was defined by the interval [0,10]. The queue length can be derived by totaling all four parameters and was restricted to 10 in this scenario. The semantics of the parameters also imply that the thread counter for the current target query type must be larger than zero. For example, if we observe a small read job, $NumRead\_1$ must be larger than zero.

These parameter and domain definitions and the constraints, lead to 2,860 valid parameter combinations for this scenario. We measured all 2,860 points of the parameter space and used a subset as training set. The complete set was used as validation set to calculate the averaged relative error for all derived models. We used two different sampling types: random and equidistant. The former one randomly picks points among all valid points and adds them to the training set. These training sets were sampled once and then used as basis for all analysis techniques. The latter technique systematically creates all valid parameter combinations by varying all parameters using a minimum, maximum and a step width. This technique results in an equidistant distribution of points in the parameter space. We created three random training sets containing 20% (572 tuples), 10% (280 tuples) and 4% (120 tuples) of all 2,860 measurements and two equidistant training sets using a step width of $s = 2$ and $s = 3$ for all thread parameters, leading to 280 and 64 tuples.

Figure 8 depicts the model accuracies for different analysis methods and training sets. IDW returned the worst results with model accuracies between 57% and 84%. As expectd, the accuracy increases, when increasing the size of the training set. Surprisingly, it appears that randomly-sampled training sets lead to better model accuracies than equidistantly-sampled training sets (compare columns "10%" and "s=2" of Figure 8). The accuracies of the MARS results

are between IDW and GP and vary between 28% and 53%. The MARS results are also proportional to the training set size and random sampling performs better than equidistant sampling ("10%" and "s=2"). It is noticeable that the "s=3"-training set with 64 tuples leads to a better model than the 4%-training set with 120 tuples. The boxplots for GP represent the results of 10 independent runs of this analysis method (not to be mixed up with the internal repeats to receive one result). The models created with GP outperform the IDW and MARS models in most cases (except 2 models with the "s=3"-training set).

The GP analysis appears to be more stable towards the training set size. The medians of the model accuracies for all 10 runs vary between 14% and 21% for all training sets (except the "s=3"-training set with a median of 34%). The errors among all 10 calls using the same training set vary up to 10% for the randomly-sampled training sets. Due to the almost constant model accuracies, independent of the training set size (compare columns "20%", "10%" and "4%" of Figure 8), we assume that the remaining model errors are caused by measurement errors and are representing the noise and error in the training data. Higher accuracies are not desirable in this scenario as they would result in over fitting.

We compare the models created using the 4% randomly-distributed training set in more detail: The MARS model has an averaged relative error of 52.3% and IDW of 70.0%. The averaged relative error for all 10 GP models are between 14.0% and 23.0%. Besides the averaged relative error of a software performance curve, other metrics such as the variance of the relative errors among all predictions are meaningful. Instead of using the variance, we used a boxplot to visualize the quality for single predictions. Figure 9 depicts the relative errors for predictions of all points in the validation set. The model marked with "GP" is the median model (based on the averaged relative error for all predictions) among all 10 models created for this evaluation. The dispersion of the GP model is the lowest and 75%

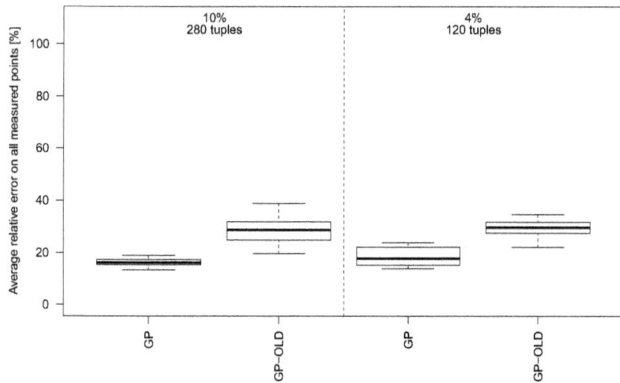

Figure 10: Differences of model accuracies between initial and optimized GP algorithm

of all predictions have a relative error smaller than 22.1%. The worst prediction has a relative error of 226.2%. For MARS (IDW), 75% of all predictions have relative errors below 40.7% (92.5%) and the error of the worst prediction is 1723% (706.7%).

5.3 Impact of the GP Optimization

In this section, we use the experiment setting described above to validate the influence of all parameter optimizations for the GP algorithm and all applied techniques to prevent overfitting. For this purpose, we built models using the GP algorithm without any techniques to prevent overfitting and the initial parameter settings (51 generations with a population size of 1024; no constant mutation; only arithmetic functions). Due to the non-determinism, we repeated the execution 10 times with the unmodified GP algorithm ("GP-Old") using the 10% and 4% training set.

Figure 10 depicts the results. The optimized GP algorithm, including the techniques to prevent overfitting, leads to more accurate models. The median runs have a difference of 12.6% (for the 10% training set) and 11.9% (for the 4% training set). This result shows, that the effort we put in optimizing the GP algorithm was justified. All optimizations, including the techniques to prevent overfitting, caused improvements of the derived software performance curves of about 12%.

6. DISCUSSION

The evaluation shows, that the models derived by GP are more accurate than the models created by MARS and IDW. The results also reveal that the algorithm performs well with only a few number of measurement samples. We integrated techniques to reduce the undesired effect of overfitting. The symbolic regression approach does not only find coefficients but simultaneously finds a structure for the model. Hence, the approach does not take any assumptions about the dependencies between the input and output parameters such as linearity in linear regression. The algorithm is capable of finding complex dependencies and might perform automatic parameter selection by using only variables which highly contribute to the model quality in terms of the fitness value. The experiments performed in the third goal (G3) reveal

that the algorithm also performs well for high-dimensional problems (tested up to ten dimensions).

The analysis method is, by nature, non-deterministic. Thus, it is necessary to repeat the analysis several times and finally select the best performance curve (based on a test set). To minimize this limitation, we integrated this loop including the selection step in our analysis adapter for the Software Performance Cockpit. The number of iterations can be configured by the user depending on the available time for the analysis step. However, the repeated execution of our algorithm leads to longer execution times compared to MARS and IDW. Another limitation of our approach is that the resulting formulas, representing the performance curve, are very complex and thus are not immediately comprehensible for the Performance Analyst. To overcome this lack of transparency, the Performance Analyst might simplify the resulting formula using tools such as MATLAB [25] in order to further analyze and interpret the formula manually.

7. CONCLUSION

In this paper, we examined the use of genetic programming as analysis method for deriving software performance curves. The concepts of evolutionary algorithms are very intuitive, but the adoption to a specific problem is not. We employed the GQM approach to systematically derive experiments for the optimization of the GP parameters. These optimizations include aspects such as constant mutations, population size and number of generations, function sets and techniques to prevent overfitting. In a final evaluation, we show that the optimized GP algorithm outperforms MARS and IDW in terms of model accuracy. A comparison of the optimized GP algorithm with the initial GP algorithm reveals an increase in the model accuracy of around 12%.

Our GP approach can be used by Performance Analysts to derive more accurate software performance curves. The complexity of the approach is hidden in an analysis adapter for the SoPeCo and thus the approach is easy-to-use just by configuration. We do not claim the GP approach fits for all analysis scenarios. Moreover, we see the approach as an additional analysis method which has its advantages in its flexibility. E.g., if a linear dependency between the parameters is known, MARS or a simple linear regression might be more appropriate. But especially if no parameter dependencies are known the GP approach might be an appropriate analysis method.

In our future work, we plan to apply this GP analysis also as a method to estimate parameter-dependent resource demands. Concerning the evaluation, we are currently working on a larger set of case studies comprising of standard benchmarks (e.g., SPECjvm2008) and SAP internal applications where we additionally compare multiple inference techniques such as CART and Kriging. Furthermore, more research is necessary to automatically identify the most influencing factors on the performance in order to reduce the number of measurements and to handle the curse of dimensionality. Concerning a further optimization of the GP algorithm, it is necessary to investigate the mutual dependencies between algorithm parameters (e.g., between mutation rate and number of generations). Additional improvements might be achieved by experimenting with other techniques to prevent overfitting and evaluate their efficiency using synthetic and realistic data.

8. REFERENCES

[1] The R Project for Statistical Computing. http://www.r-project.org, last visited: 05.09.2010, 2010.

[2] S. Balsamo, A. Di Marco, P. Inverardi, and M. Simeoni. Model-based performance prediction in software development: a survey. *Software Engineering, IEEE Transactions on*, 30(5):295 – 310, may 2004.

[3] V. R. Basili, G. Caldiera, and H. D. Rombach. The Goal Question Metric Approach. In J. J. Marciniak, editor, *Encyclopedia of Software Engineering - 2 Volume Set*, pages 528–532. John Wiley & Sons, 1994.

[4] D. Beasley, R. Martin, and D. Bull. An overview of genetic algorithms: Part 1. Fundamentals. *University computing*, 15:58–58, 1993.

[5] M. Courtois and M. Woodside. Using regression splines for software performance analysis. In *WOSP '00: Proceedings of the 2nd international workshop on Software and performance*, pages 105–114, New York, NY, USA, 2000. ACM.

[6] P. Dalgaard. *Introductory statistics with R*. Corr. print. edition, 2003.

[7] A. Eiben and J. Smith. *Introduction to evolutionary computing*. 2003.

[8] F. Ferrucci, C. Gravino, R. Oliveto, and F. Sarro. Genetic programming for effort estimation: An analysis of the impact of different fitness functions. *Search Based Software Engineering, International Symposium on*, 0:89–98, 2010.

[9] S. Gustafson, E. Burke, and N. Krasnogor. On improving genetic programming for symbolic regression. In *Evolutionary Computation, 2005. The 2005 IEEE Congress on*, volume 1, pages 912 –919 Vol.1, 2005.

[10] J. Happe, D. Westermann, K. Sachs, and L. Kapova. Statistical Inference of Software Performance Models for Parametric Performance Completions. In G. Heineman, J. Kofron, and F. Plasil, editors, *Research into Practice - Reality and Gaps (Proceedings of QoSA 2010)*, volume 6093 of *LNCS*, pages 20–35, 2010.

[11] T. J. Hastie, R. J. Tibshirani, and J. H. Friedman. *The elements of statistical learning : data mining, inference, and prediction*. Springer series in statistics. Springer-Verlag, Berlin, Germany, New York, NY, 2. ed. edition, 2009.

[12] J. R. Koza, editor. *Genetic programming*, volume [1, book]: On the programming of computers by means of natural selections. MIT Press, Cambridge, Mass., 3. print. edition, 1993.

[13] H. Koziolek. Performance evaluation of component-based software systems: A survey. *Perform. Eval.*, 67:634–658, August 2010.

[14] S. Kraft, S. Pacheco-Sanchez, G. Casale, and S. Dawson. Estimating service resource consumption from response time measurements. In *VALUETOOLS '09: Proceedings of the Fourth International ICST Conference on Performance Evaluation Methodologies and Tools*, pages 1–10, ICST, Brussels, Belgium, Belgium, 2009. ICST.

[15] B. C. Lee, D. M. Brooks, B. R. de Supinski, M. Schulz, K. Singh, and S. A. McKee. Methods of inference and learning for performance modeling of parallel applications. In *PPoPP '07: Proceedings of the 12th ACM SIGPLAN symposium on Principles and practice of parallel programming*, pages 249–258, New York, NY, USA, 2007. ACM.

[16] S. Luke. ECJ. http://cs.gmu.edu/~eclab/projects/ecj/, last visited: 16.01.2011.

[17] Oracle. Mysql 5.5. last visited 04.01.2011.

[18] L. Panait and S. Luke. Methods for evolving robust programs. In *Proceedings of the 2003 international conference on Genetic and evolutionary computation: PartII*, GECCO'03, pages 1740–1751, Berlin, Heidelberg, 2003. Springer-Verlag.

[19] D. C. Psichogios, R. D. De Veaux, and L. H. Ungar. Non-parametric system identification: A comparison of mars and neural networks. In *American Control Conference, 1992*, pages 1436 –1441, june 1992.

[20] C. Ryan and M. Keijzer. An analysis of diversity of constants of genetic programming. In *Proceedings of the 6th European conference on Genetic programming*, EuroGP'03, pages 404–413, Berlin, Heidelberg, 2003. Springer-Verlag.

[21] A. B. Sharma, R. Bhagwan, M. Choudhury, L. Golubchik, R. Govindan, and G. M. Voelker. Automatic request categorization in internet services. *SIGMETRICS Perform. Eval. Rev.*, 36(2):16–25, 2008.

[22] D. Shepard. A two-dimensional interpolation function for irregularly-spaced data. In *Proceedings of the 1968 23rd ACM national conference*, ACM '68, pages 517–524, New York, NY, USA, 1968. ACM.

[23] C. U. Smith. *Performance Engineering of Software Systems*. 1990.

[24] D. Thakkar, A. E. Hassan, G. Hamann, and P. Flora. A framework for measurement based performance modeling. In *WOSP '08: Proceedings of the 7th international workshop on Software and performance*, pages 55–66, New York, NY, USA, 2008. ACM.

[25] The MathWorks Inc. MATLAB, version 7.11, 2010.

[26] D. Westermann and J. Happe. Software Performance Cockpit. http://www.software-performance-cockpit.org/, September 2011.

[27] D. Westermann, J. Happe, M. Hauck, and C. Heupel. The performance cockpit approach: A framework for systematic performance evaluations. In *Proceedings of the 36th EUROMICRO Conference on Software Engineering and Advanced Applications (SEAA 2010)*, page To Appear. IEEE Computer Society, 2010.

[28] D. Westermann, R. Krebs, and J. Happe. Efficient experiment selection in automated software performance evaluations. In *Proceedings of 8th European Performance Engineering Workshop (EPEW)*, page To appear., 2011.

[29] M. Woodside, G. Franks, and D. C. Petriu. The future of software performance engineering. In *2007 Future of Software Engineering*, FOSE '07, pages 171–187, Washington, DC, USA, 2007. IEEE Computer Society.

[30] T. Zheng, C. Woodside, and M. Litoiu. Performance model estimation and tracking using optimal filters. *Software Engineering, IEEE Transactions on*, 34(3):391 –406, may-june 2008.

Fluid Limits of Queueing Networks with Batches

Luca Bortolussi
Department of Mathematics
and Computer Science
University of Trieste, Italy
luca@dmi.units.it

Mirco Tribastone
Institute of Informatics
Ludwig-Maximilians-Universität Munich,
Germany
tribastone@pst.ifi.lmu.de

ABSTRACT

This paper presents an analytical model for the performance prediction of queueing networks with batch services and batch arrivals, related to the fluid limit of a suitable single-parameter sequence of continuous-time Markov chains and interpreted as the deterministic approximation of the average behaviour of the stochastic process. Notably, the underlying system of ordinary differential equations exhibits discontinuities in the right-hand sides, which however are proven to yield a meaningful solution. A substantial numerical assessment is used to study the quality of the approximation and shows very good accuracy in networks with large job populations.

Categories and Subject Descriptors

I.6.5 [**Simulation and Modeling**]: Model Development—*Modeling methodologies*; D.2.8 [**Software Engineering**]: Metrics—*Performance measures*

General Terms

Performance

Keywords

queueing networks, batch services, fluid limits

1. INTRODUCTION

Batches are useful in the study of computer and communication systems for describing situations when an event gives rise to the simultaneous arrival of more than one element, or when servers accumulate a certain number of jobs before processing them so as to reduce, for instance, overheads in communication bandwidth [1].

There is a vast body of literature concerned with the analysis of batch systems, especially within queueing theory, with references which may be tracked as far back as the Twenties with Erlang's solution of the $M/E_k/1$ queue, which

may also be used to yield that of the $M^k/M/1$ queue. The book by Chaudhry and Templeton provides an exhaustive account of analyses of queueing systems with batch (or *bulk*) arrivals and service, both for transient and steady-state solutions [2].

The present paper considers queueing networks with open batch arrivals and batch services which can be described in terms of a continuous-time Markov chain (CTMC), with state descriptor characterised by a population vector which gives the job population in each station of the network. Models of this kind have been studied in the past, mostly with the aim of extending classical product-form solutions of ordinary queueing networks where jobs arrive at the network, transfer between nodes, and receive service *singly* [3, 4]. The works by Henderson and Taylor [5] and Henderson *et al.* [6] have provided product forms for a class of open and closed networks, respectively. Despite the considerable value from a theoretical viewpoint, these results present the drawback that in practical applications the computational cost of the normalising constant may be prohibitive, especially when analysing networks with large job populations.

The technique herein presented is instead based on an approximation in terms of a *fluid* model. In a classical setting, for a given network under study a sequence of CTMCs indexed by a single parameter, hereafter denoted by N, is suitably constructed so as to be shown to converge asymptotically to a system of ordinary differential equations (ODEs). The parameter is usually referred to as the network's size, e.g., the larger N the larger the initial population levels in the system. The limiting fluid behaviour is shown to be undistinguishable from a sample path of the CTMC for $N \to \infty$, thus justifying the ODE solution as an analytical approximate of the average behaviour of the network for large N. The framework is that of Kurtz, who has proven this form of convergence under relatively mild assumptions on the nature of the transitions in general CTMCs with a population-based state descriptor [7]. A brief overview of related work concerning fluid models, with applications to computer and communications systems, is provided in Section 2. This is followed by Section 3, where we present the relevant notation for the fluid framework considered in this paper.

The mathematics used to describe queueing networks with batches is discussed in Section 4 by means of a queueing system with Poisson batch arrivals at a station that serves singly. Two forms of scaling will be discussed which turn out to lead to different limit behaviours. The first — and perhaps the least surprising — case concerns a sequence of

CTMCs where the batch size is constant and the arrival intensity grows linearly with N (Section 4.1). This case belongs to the aforementioned standard framework of Kurtz. The other scaling considers the situation when the arrival rate is constant and the batch size is allowed to grow with N (Section 4.2). In this case, instead, the limit behaviour is a stochastic hybrid system (cf. [8]) which mixes continuous flows with Markovian jumps. However, also in this case a fluid ODE can be syntactically constructed, and its relationship with the hybrid limit will be discussed.

In Section 4.3, the running example is varied to analyse a queue with finite capacity. The (illustrative) purpose is to introduce another form of limit behaviour, namely that of an ODE with discontinuous right-hand side. To build some intuition as to how this arises from inherently discontinuities in the CTMC transitions rates, let c be the queue capacity and $b < c$ the arrival batch size. Then, the arrival rate will be some $\lambda > 0$ if the queue length is less than $c - b$ and 0 otherwise. Under these circumstances Kurtz's theorem cannot be applied, as it requires Lipschitz continuity of the ODE vector field. However, using recent developments concerned with non-smooth systems [9, 10], we show that such a fluid limit with discontinuities is meaningful. Clearly, an analogous form of discontinuity presents itself in the case of batch services. This situation is studied in detail in Section 5, which considers two forms of scaling that give rise to a deterministic limit and to a hybrid one.

Section 6 unifies these results in a general model of Markovian queueing networks with batch services and batch arrivals. The model is accompanied by a discussion in Section 6.2 concerning its applicability to practical situations, with emphasis on the impact of the forms of scaling studied in this paper. The natural question as to whether and under which conditions the deterministic trajectory may be used as an approximation to the expected behaviour of the stochastic process is investigated in Section 7 by means of a substantial numerical study. It confirms that the quality of the approximation improves with increasing population sizes, yielding accurate estimates for medium/large sized networks under a wide range of traffic conditions.

The paper ends in Section 8 with concluding remarks. In particular, we sketch a methodology to help the modeller choose between different analysis options—numerical solution of the underlying CTMC, stochastic simulation, or fluid approximations—according to the nature of the actual system under consideration.

2. RELATED WORK

Mean field and fluid approaches have a long-standing tradition in performance engineering and in queuing theory. Recently, general frameworks to apply mean-field asymptotic results, with limits defined in terms of ODEs, have been developed [11, 12, 13, 14, 10, 9]. Some of them deal with discrete-time Markov chain models, and show convergence under a suitable scaling of transition kernels and duration of a time step of the chain [11, 12]. Other deal with CTMC models [13, 14], possibly connecting the mean field approximation with high level formal languages to describe systems [13]. In all cases, Lipschitz continuity is required for the rates.

As discussed above, extensions of such frameworks to discontinuous rates and kernels, including new convergence results, have been proposed in [9, 10]. Our approach uses

these works to study approximations for queueing networks with batches. However, the contribution of this paper goes beyond a mere application of these results since we also consider non-fluid forms of scaling, giving rise to hybrid systems, which are not considered in all the aforementioned papers. To the best of these authors' knowledge, there has not been any application of fluid approximation to queue models with batches.

In the literature, many of the applications of mean-field limits for specific systems are concerned with models in which the assumption on Lipschitz continuity holds. Without pretending to be exhaustive, we recall recent work on the analysis of MAC protocols [12, 15], peer-to-peer protocols [16, 17], TCP protocols (with emphasis on data centers), [18, 19]), and load balancing policies [20, 21].

Similarly to us, [17] also studies a Piecewise Deterministic Markov Process [8]. However, the simple structure of their hybrid model, which permits to decouple stochastic dynamics from deterministic behaviour, enables analytical solutions. This is harder in our setting, due to the strong bidirectional coupling of the two dynamical regimes. This is why we focussed instead on approximate techniques, see Sections 4.2 and 8.

The authors of [18], instead, consider a fluid model based on delay differential equations which contain discontinuities in the right-hand side, induced by congestion control policies. However, contrary to queues with batches, such discontinuities have no dramatic impact on the dynamics (there is no sliding motion). In [19], instead, the focus is more on the control policy, studied from the point of view of control theory. Both [17] and [18] focus on the analysis of the fluid model and provide only experimental evidence of convergence of the pure stochastic system, without discussing the quality of approximation in detail.

The paper [12] considers a mean field approach that is different from the ones used in this paper. In particular, their limit result, proved in the paper, is concerned with Lipschitz continuous rates in a rapidly varying environment, that reaches instantaneously equilibrium in the limit. In [15], instead, the authors use a more classical mean field approach, with a limit in continuous times for Lipschitz continuous rates, and apply also a central limit result (i.e. a limit in terms of Stochastic Differential Equations with Gaussian noise). Papers [20, 21] use a classic mean field approach (i.e. with limits in continuous time and Lipschitz continuous rates) to study optimisation policies for load balancing. In particular, [21] exploits mean-field properties to compute performance measures at the level of single server or job.

3. NOTATION

In order to make the paper self-contained, in this section we fix the notation that will be used throughout the remainder. Additional background on fluid limits will be given in Section 4, while discussing an example of a queueing system with batch arrivals.

We will first introduce a simple language to describe network models as *population processes*, where the variables are the number of jobs at each station.

Formally, a CTMC representation for such models is the tuple $\mathcal{X} = (X, \mathcal{S}, x_0, \mathcal{T})$, where:

- $X = (X_1, \ldots, X_n)$ is a vector of *variables*, where n is the total number of stations in the network;

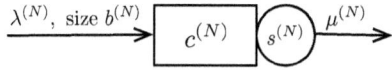

Figure 1: The queueing system with batch arrivals considered in Section 4.

- $\mathcal{S}$ is the (countable) *state space* of the CTMC;

- $x_0 \in \mathcal{S}$ is the *initial state* of the model;

- $\mathcal{T}$ is the set of *transitions*, where $\tau \in \mathcal{T}$ is in the form $\tau = (g_\tau(X), v_\tau, r_\tau(X))$; $g_\tau(X)$ is the *guard*, a conjunction of inequalities of the form $h(X) \geq 0$, for a suitably smooth function h (usually linear); $v_\tau \in \mathbb{R}^n$, is the *update vector*, i.e., a vector giving the net change on each variable caused by the transition (we require that $X + v_\tau \in \mathcal{S}$ whenever $g_\tau(X)$ is true); $r_\tau : \mathcal{S} \to \mathbb{R}_{\geq 0}$ is a Lipschitz continuous and bounded *rate function*, which specifies the rate of the transition as a function of the current state of the system.

Given a model $\mathcal{X}$, it is straightforward to obtain the infinitesimal generator matrix Q of the CTMC, which is given by the $|\mathcal{S}| \times |\mathcal{S}|$ matrix defined by

$$q_{x,x'} = \sum \{ r_\tau(x) \mid \tau \in \mathcal{T}, \ g_\tau(x) \ true, \ x' = x + v_\tau \}.$$

We indicate by $X(t)$ the state of such a CTMC at time t.

We will make our network models depend upon a parameter, N, which plays the role of the *system's size*; intuitively, the larger N, the larger the system, e.g., the more clients will request service. By varying N, we obtain a sequence $(\mathcal{X}^{(N)})_{N \in \mathbb{N}}$ of models, generating a sequence of CTMCs, denoted by $X^{(N)}(t)$. We aim at finding a fluid approximation of these models, for large N. In order to compare models of different size, we carry out the usual normalisation step, which consists in dividing all the populations by N, and rescaling transitions accordingly. This is essentially a change of variables from X to $\bar{X} = X/N$.

In general, given the CTMC model for level N, denoted by $\mathcal{X}^{(N)} = (X, \mathcal{S}^{(N)}, \mathcal{T}^{(N)}, x_0^{(N)})$, we denote its normalised version by $\bar{\mathcal{X}}^{(N)} = (\bar{X}, \bar{\mathcal{S}}^{(N)}, \bar{\mathcal{T}}^{(N)}, \bar{x}_0^{(N)})$, where $\bar{\mathcal{S}}^{(N)} = \mathcal{S}^{(N)}/N$, $\bar{x}_0^{(N)} = x_0^{(N)}/N$. The transitions $\bar{\tau} \in \bar{\mathcal{T}}^{(N)}$, with $\bar{\tau}$ defined as $(\bar{g}^{(N)}(\bar{X}), \bar{v}^{(N)}, \bar{r}^{(N)}(\bar{X}))$, are obtained from the corresponding transitions $\tau = (g^{(N)}(X), v^{(N)}, r^{(N)}(X))$ by setting $\bar{g}^{(N)}(\bar{X}) = g^{(N)}(X)$, $\bar{v}^{(N)} = v^{(N)}/N$, and $\bar{r}^{(N)}(\bar{X}) = r^{(N)}(X)$.

We introduce the following *indicator function* $I\{P(X)\}$, where $P(X)$ is a logical predicate on variables X, which is useful when describing rates with discontinuities.

$$I\{P(x)\} = \begin{cases} 1 & \text{if } P(x) \text{ true}, \\ 0 & \text{otherwise}. \end{cases}$$

4. FLUID APPROXIMATION OF BATCH ARRIVALS

In this section we discuss a simple multi-server queueing system with batch arrivals. In doing so, we present all fluid limit results that are needed in the paper. The queue has an exponentially distributed service rate $\mu^{(N)}$ and server multiplicity $s^{(N)}$. The batch arrivals have exponentially distributed interarrival times with rate $\lambda^{(N)}$ and batch sizes

$b^{(N)}$, where N is the scaling parameter for the CTMC sequence. The meaning of these parameters is summarised pictorially in Figure 1. The buffer is hereafter supposed to be unbounded. Then, Section 4.3 will study the case with finite capacity, indicated by $c^{(N)}$ in the figure.

The model may be formalised in the notation presented in the previous section. Its model $\mathcal{X}^{(N)}$ has a single variable, denoted by $X^{(N)}$ with domain $\mathbb{N}_0$, which counts the population of jobs in the buffer, and two transitions, τ_1 and τ_2. The arrival transition τ_1 has rate $\lambda_1^{(N)}$, no guard ($g_1 = true$), and update vector $v_1 = b^{(N)}$, while the service transition τ_2 has rate $\mu^{(N)} \min\{X^{(N)}, s^{(N)}\}$, no guard, and update vector $v_2 = -1$.

For given $\lambda, \mu > 0$ and $b, s \in \mathbb{N}$, we consider to scalings of the network parameters as follows.

S1 The batch size is constant, $b^{(N)} = b$, but the arrival rate of batches of clients increases with N, $\lambda^{(N)} = N\lambda$.

S2 Clients arrive at a constant rate $\lambda^{(N)} = \lambda$, but in batches of growing size, $b^{(N)} = Nb$.

In both cases, we need to increase the number of servers to keep up with the increased traffic, so that we always let $s^{(N)} = sN$. Notice that, in closed networks such as the one of Section 6, a natural interpretation for N is the total number of clients in the system.

4.1 Fluid Limit (S1)

The main idea behind *fluid* (or deterministic) approximations for a sequence of CTMCs $\bar{X}^{(N)}$ is that, if suitable scaling assumptions are satisfied by rates and update vectors, the sequence converges to a deterministic limit process, solution of an ordinary differential equation (ODE). Essentially, we have to require that rates increase with N and updates decrease as $1/N$ for all transitions. If this is the case, then as N gets larger and larger, the density of jumps increases while their magnitude decreases, hence jumps can be approximated as continuous derivatives in the limit.

To be more precise, the scaling conditions that we require are the following: for each transition $\tau^{(N)} \in \bar{\mathcal{T}}^{(N)}$ of the normalised model, the supremum of the rate $r_\tau^{(N)}$ must be of order N, i.e. $\sup_{x \in \bar{\mathcal{S}}^{(N)}} r_\tau^{(N)}(x) = \Theta(N)$, while the norm of the update vector $v_\tau^{(N)}$ must be of order $1/N$, i.e., $\|v_\tau^{(N)}\| = \Theta(1/N)$.

In order to construct the limit ODE, we need to define the *drift* of the model, i.e., the mean increment of variables at each step, which is

$$F^{(N)}(\bar{X}) = \sum_{\tau \in \bar{\mathcal{T}}} \bar{v}_\tau^{(N)} \ \bar{r}_\tau^{(N)}(\bar{X}).$$

Now, consider the smallest closed subset $E \subseteq \mathbb{R}^n$ containing all the state spaces $\bar{\mathcal{S}}$ of normalized models, that is $E = cl\left(\bigcup_{N \in \mathbb{N}} \bar{\mathcal{S}}^N \right)$, and assume that:

1. $F^{(N)}$ converges uniformly in E to a Lipschitz continuous function F;

2. the initial state of the CTMC sequence converges to a point in (the interior of) E, i.e. $\bar{x}_0^{(N)} \to x_0 \in E$;

3. $x(t)$ is the solution of the initial value problem $\frac{dx(t)}{dt} = F(x(t))$, $x(0) = x_0$.

Under such conditions, it is possible to prove the following theorem [7, 22, 23]:

THEOREM 1 (DETERMINISTIC APPROXIMATION). *Under the previous assumptions, for any $T < \infty$,*

$$\lim_{N \to \infty} \sup_{t \leq T} \|\bar{X}^{(N)}(t) - x(t)\| = 0 \quad \text{in probability.}$$

This theorem states that, for any finite time horizon T, the *trajectories* of the CTMC become indistinguishable from the solution of the fluid ODE $\frac{dx(t)}{dt} = F(x(t))$. Essentially, the sequence $\bar{X}^{(N)}(t)$ behaves as a deterministic process in the limit.

Of the two forms of scaling introduced at the beginning of Section 4, we observe that only S1, i.e., $\lambda^{(N)} = N\lambda$ and $b^{(N)} = b$, is amenable to fluid approximation. In S2, instead the arrival transition does not satisfy the scaling assumptions because the suprema of both the rate and the update vector are $\Theta(1)$.

Then, considering S1 and computing the drift, we obtain

$$F^{(N)}(x) = F(x) = k\lambda - \mu \min\{x, s\}, \qquad (1)$$

which is independent of N. Furthermore, assuming $\bar{x}_0^{(N)} = x_0 = 0$, the conditions of Theorem 1 are satisfied, and we can conclude that the sequence of CTMC converges uniformly to the solution of $\frac{dx(t)}{dt} = F(x(t))$ in any bounded time interval.

In this particular model, however, we can say something also about the steady-state behaviour of the sequence of CTMCs. In fact, it is easy to show that each CTMC in the sequence is irreducible and that the ODE has a unique globally attracting steady state, equal to $\frac{k\mu_1}{\mu_2}$, provided that $k\mu_1 < \mu_2 s$.[1] Under such conditions, it can be shown that

$$\lim_{N \to \infty} \lim_{t \to \infty} \|\bar{X}^N(t) - x(t)\| = 0$$

in probability [11, 24].

Finally, we point out that the equation $\frac{dx(t)}{dt} = F^{(N)}(x(t))$ has another interpretation, namely as an approximate equation for the average of the CTMC at level N [25, 26]. Using either a direct manipulation of the Chapman-Kolmogorov equations, or by Dynkin's formula in differential form [8], the exact equation for the derivative of the expected values of the CTMC reads

$$\frac{d\mathbb{E}[X]}{dt} = \mathbb{E}\left[F^{(N)}(X)\right].$$

By approximating $\mathbb{E}[\min\{x, y\}]$ with $\min\{E[x], E[y]\}$, one obtains

$$\frac{d\mathbb{E}[x]}{dt} = \mathbb{E}\left[F^{(N)}(x)\right] \approx F^{(N)}(\mathbb{E}[x]),$$

which is the fluid equation (using the level-N drift). In our example, however, as $F^N(x) = F(x)$, this is the proper fluid limit equation.

4.2 Hybrid Fluid Limit (S2)

Recalling that the scaling laws for case S2 are $\lambda^{(N)} = \lambda$ and $b^{(N)} = bN$, one observes that in this situation the temporal density of batch arrivals remains constant with respect to N, while the jump is constant in the normalised

---

[1] For $k\mu_1 = \mu_2 s$, the ODE has an infinite number of equilibria, namely all points $x \geq s$, while for $k\mu_1 > \mu_2 s$, the ODE goes to infinity.

variables, meaning that its magnitude increases in the unscaled model. Intuitively, the dynamics of such a transition maintains a similar structure for all N, always showing a stochastic behaviour. On the other hand, the service rate does enjoy a suitable scaling, hence this dynamics should intuitively become deterministic asymptotically. Therefore, we expect that, overall, this sequence of CTMCs still exhibits a limit behaviour, although not a purely deterministic one in the sense of Theorem 1, since its scaling conditions are not satisfied. Indeed, it turns out that the limit process is hybrid, mixing discrete/stochastic with continuous/deterministic evolution.

In order to put this intuition into a formal framework, we introduce Piecewise Deterministic Markov Processes, a model of stochastic hybrid systems interleaving periods of continuous evolution with discrete jumps [8]. Following [27], we consider a simple version with Markovian jumps (while in general also *instantaneous* jumps are allowed, happening as soon as their guard becomes true).

DEFINITION 1. *A simple Piecewise Deterministic Markov Process (PDMP) is a tuple $(D, X, \mathcal{D}, \varphi, \mathcal{T}, d_0, x_0)$, where:*

- *D is a vector of discrete variables, taking values in the finite set $\mathcal{D}$. An element $d \in \mathcal{D}$ is usually called a discrete mode. D can be the empty vector, and in this case $\mathcal{D}$ contains a single point;*

- *X is a vector of n continuous variables, taking values in (a subset of) $\mathbb{R}^n$;*

- *$\varphi : \mathcal{D} \times \mathbb{R}^n \to \mathbb{R}^n$ is a function that defines a Lipschitz continuous vector field for each mode $d \in \mathcal{D}$;*

- *$\mathcal{T}$ is a set of Markovian transitions in the form (r_i, R_i), where $r_i : \mathcal{D} \times \mathbb{R}^n \to \mathbb{R}_{\geq 0}$ is the rate of the transition, and $R_i : \mathcal{D} \times \mathbb{R}^n \to \mathcal{D} \times \mathbb{R}^n$ is the reset map.*

- *$(d_0, x_0) \in \mathcal{D} \times \mathbb{R}^n$ is the initial state.*

Intuitively, the dynamics of a simple PDMP is as follows. The process starts in the initial state (d_0, x_0) and the continuous variables evolve following the solution of the ODE $\frac{dX(t)}{dt} = \varphi(d_0, X(t))$, while the discrete variables remain constant. Such a continuous evolution is followed until a time T_1, when Markovian jump happens with rate

$$r(d_0, X) = \sum_{(r_i, R_i) \in \mathcal{T}} r_i(d_0, X).$$

A discrete transition i is chosen with probability proportional to its rate, i.e. $r_i(d_0, X(T_1))/r(d_0, X(T_1))$, and the system jumps to the new state $(d_1, x_1) = R_i(d_0, X(T_1))$. Then, the system starts again to evolve continuously from (d_1, x_1), until a new jump occurs. Applying this scheme iteratively yields the piecewise continuous trajectories of the PDMP.

We briefly sketch how to define the simple PDMP associated with a sequence of models $\bar{\mathcal{X}}^{(N)}$, referring to [27] for more details. The idea is to partition transitions of model $\bar{\mathcal{X}}^{(N)}$ into two classes, those amenable of continuous approximation (i.e., those satisfying the scaling conditions of Theorem 1), and those to be kept discrete (having rate and update vectors both independent of N in the normalised model). Then, variables not affected by continuous transitions will constitute the discrete variables of the PDMP,

Figure 2: Hybrid-automaton representation of the PDMP associated with the queueing system in Figure 1 to which scaling S2 is applied. There is one single mode and one single variable, x, subject to continuous evolution given by $\frac{dx}{dt} = -\mu \min\{x, s\}$ and to a stochastic jump happening with rate λ and changing the system from x to $x + b$.

while all other variables will become continuous variables. The vector field φ is defined like the drift, but restricting the summation to continuous transitions. Finally, Markovian transitions of the PDMP are obtained straightforwardly from the discrete transitions of the CTMC.

Applying this construction to the batch arrival example with the scaling S2, we obtain the following PDMP: it has one continuous variable ($\bar{X}$) and one discrete mode (there is no discrete variable), the vector field is $\varphi(\bar{X}) = -\mu \min\{\bar{X}, s\}$, and its unique Markovian transition has rate λ and reset map $R(\bar{X}) = \bar{X} + b$. A visual representation of this PDMP, in the usual style of hybrid automata, is shown in Figure 2.

Applying a result of [27], it can be shown that the sequence $\bar{X}^{(N)}(t)$ of CTMC converges in distribution to the PDMP $\bar{X}(t)$ obtained by the previously sketched construction, provided that the vector field is Lipschitz continuous (and rate functions are integrable).

The average behaviour of the limit PDMP can also be described by an ODE, using a more general version of the Dynkin Formula [8]. For any suitably smooth function f, it holds that

$$\frac{d\mathbb{E}[f(d,x)]}{dt} = \mathbb{E}\Big[\nabla f(d,x) \cdot \varphi(d,x) \\ + \sum_i r_i(d,x)\left(f(R_i(d,x)) - f(d,x)\right)\Big].$$

Let us now specialise the previous formula for the average $\mathbb{E}[d,x](t)$, and apply it to a PDMP obtained from a CTMC model described with the language of Section 3. For this, it holds that $R_i(d,x) = (d,x) + v_i$, therefore we obtain

$$\frac{d\mathbb{E}[d,x]}{dt} = \mathbb{E}\Big[\varphi(d,x) + \sum_i v_i r_i(d,x)\Big] = \mathbb{E}[F(d,x)],$$

where $F(d,x)$ is the (limit) drift of the CTMC model.

If we compute the equation of the average for the PDMP in Figure 2, we obtain

$$\frac{d\mathbb{E}[x]}{dt} = \lambda k - \mu \mathbb{E}[\min\{x,s\}],$$

which, given the approximation $\mathbb{E}[\min\{x,s\}] \approx \min\{\mathbb{E}[x], s\}$, is exactly the fluid differential equation (1) we obtained for the scaling S1.

4.3 Discontinuity in Rates

All the convergence results presented in the previous section require Lipschitz continuity of the drift or of the PDMP vector field. This is needed to ensure existence and uniqueness of the solutions of the fluid ODEs. Unfortunately, the

presence of guards in the CTMC transitions may introduce discontinuities in these functions, thus preventing an application of classical deterministic approximation results.

As an example, consider again the batch arrival model, with scaling S1, but additionally assume that the queue of the service station has bounded capacity $c^{(N)}$. Furthermore, we assume that the batch arrival is suspended whenever an arrival will overcome the capacity $c^{(N)}$. If we let $c^{(N)} = c_0^{(N)} + b^{(N)}$, then arrivals are suspended whenever $X > c_0^{(N)}$. Such a modification is easily accounted for by adding the guard $X \leq c_0^{(N)}$ to the batch arrival transition. In computing the drift for this modified model, we have to take into account the suspension policy, multiplying the arrival rate by the indicator function $I\{X \leq c_0^{(N)}\}$, so that the drift becomes

$$F^{(N)}(x) = F(x) = k\lambda I\{x \leq c_0\} - \mu \min\{x,s\}.$$

As $F(x)$ is discontinuous, the associated fluid equation $\frac{dx(t)}{dt} = F(x(t))$ is not an ODE, but rather a Piecewise Smooth dynamical system (PWS) [28].

PWS have continuous trajectories showing in general more complex behaviour than ODE solutions, even if in many circumstances the solutions of the initial value problems associated to a PWS exist and are unique.

Intuitively, the dynamics of a PWS within a continuity region of the vector field behaves like that of the solution of the corresponding ODE. However, differences arise in the proximity of a discontinuity surface. To fix the notation, suppose that a discontinuity surface $\mathcal{H}$ is defined as the set of zeros of a (sufficiently) smooth function $h : \mathbb{R}^n \to \mathbb{R}$, i.e., $\mathcal{H} = \{x \mid h(x) = 0\}$. This surface separates $\mathbb{R}^n$ in two regions: $R_1 = \{x \in \mathbb{R}^n \mid h(x) < 0\}$ and $R_2 = \{x \in \mathbb{R}^n \mid h(x) > 0\}$. Denote the restriction of the vector field F to R_1 by F_1 and the restriction of F to R_2 by F_2.

In the example, there is a single discontinuity surface, defined by the equation $x = c_0$, which defines the two regions $R_1 = \{x < c_0\}$ and $R_2 = \{x > c_0\}$. The vector field in R_1 is $F_1(x) = k\lambda - \mu \min\{x,s\}$, while $F_2(x) = -\mu \min\{x,s\}$.

The behaviour of a trajectory of the PWS when it hits the surface $\mathcal{H}$ in a point x essentially depends on the relative orientation of F_1 and F_2 around x. If both vector fields point towards the same region, then the trajectory crosses $\mathcal{H}$, possibly with a discontinuity in its derivative (*transversal crossing*). Formally, this happens if the projections of the vector fields along the normal $\nabla h(x)$ to the surface $\mathcal{H}$ in x (assumed to be always different from zero), $F_1(x) \cdot \nabla h(x)$ and $F_2(x) \cdot \nabla h(x)$, have the same sign.

In our example, $\nabla h(x) = 1$ and $F_2(c_0) < 0$, hence transversal crossing happens whenever $F_1(c_0) < 0$. This corresponds to the condition $\lambda < \frac{\mu}{k}\min\{c_0, s\}$. Notice that $\mathcal{H}$ can be crossed only from R_2 to R_1, an unfeasible situation as the initial conditions are always in R_1.

On the other hand, if the vector fields point in opposite directions of the surface $\mathcal{H}$ (in particular, the vector field in R_1 points towards R_2 and vice versa, meaning that $F_1(x) \cdot \nabla h(x) > 0$ and $F_2(x) \cdot \nabla h(x) < 0$), then the trajectory is constrained to move along $\mathcal{H}$, a behaviour known as *sliding motion*. In fact, the PWS moves along $\mathcal{H}$ following the so called *sliding vector field* $G(x)$, which is obtained as the convex combination of $F_1(x)$ and $F_2(x)$ tangential to $\mathcal{H}$.[2]

---

[2]Formally, $G(x) = \alpha(x)F_1(x) + (1 - \alpha(x))F_2(x)$, where $\alpha(x)$ satisfies $G(x) \cdot \nabla h(x) = 0$.

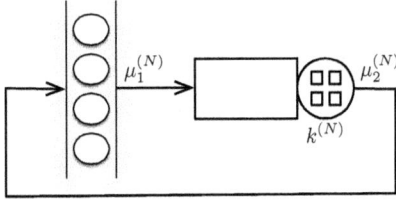

Figure 3: Closed queueing network with batch services (indicated by the small boxes within the service centre) studied in Section 5.

In our example, sliding motion happens whenever $F_1(c_0) > 0$, i.e. whenever $\lambda > \frac{\mu}{k}\min\{c_0, s\}$. In this case, the sliding vector field is $G(x) = 0$, hence once a trajectory hits the surface $\mathcal{H}$, it remains there forever.

Existence and uniqueness of solutions of a PWS is guaranteed if in each point of the surface $\mathcal{H}$ either $F_1(x) \cdot \nabla h(x) > 0$ or $F_2(x) \cdot \nabla h(x) < 0$ holds (this is known as the Filippov condition). This condition is verified by the batch arrival with bounded capacity.

Starting from a sequence of CTMC with nontrivial guards (but defined by smooth functions, for instance linear functions), and computing the drift as in the fluid approximation, we therefore obtain a PWS. In [9, 10], the authors have shown that such a sequence of CTMC converges to the solution of the associated PWS,[3] provided that such solution exists and is unique (and additionally it crosses a finite number of times discontinuity surfaces in any finite amount of time). This allows the use of fluid approximation also in these situations, once the regularity conditions on the PWS are proved.

For the batch arrival with bounded capacity, these regularity conditions hold hence the sequence of CTMC converges to the limit PWS.

5. BATCH SERVICES

We study suitable scalings for queues with batch services by considering the closed tandem network in Figure 3, which is also convenient to highlight the form of scaling to which the job population is subjected. Let the population vector be denoted by $X^{(N)} = (X_1^{(N)}, X_2^{(N)})$, where $X_1^{(N)}$ and $X_2^{(N)}$ represent the queue length at the delay station and at the batch service station, respectively. Let $X_0^{(N)} = (X_{1,0}^{(N)}, X_{2,0}^{(N)})$ be the initial condition, with $X_{1,0}^{(N)} + X_{2,0}^{(N)} = N$, i.e., the population grows with N. Let $k^{(N)}$ be the batch service size and $\mu_1^{(N)}$ and $\mu_2^{(N)}$ be the service rates at the delay station and at the queue with batches, respectively. The model is described by two transitions: τ_1 (service at the delay station) has rate $\mu_1^{(N)}$, no guard ($g_1 = true$), and update vector $v_1 = (-1, 1)$; τ_2 (batch service) has rate $\mu_2^{(N)}$, guard $X_2^{(N)} \geq k^{(N)}$, and update vector $v_2 = (k^{(N)}, -k^{(N)})$.

As in the case of batch arrivals, we consider two different scalings, for given $k \in \text{`}N$, $\mu_1, \mu_2 > 0$, and $X_0 \in \mathbb{N}^2$.

S3 $k^{(N)} = k$, $\mu_1^{(N)} = \mu_1$, $\mu_2^{(N)} = N\mu_2$, $X_0^{(N)} = NX_0$, i.e., the batch size is kept constant but the service rates

---
[3]Convergence is uniform in probability for any finite time horizon, as for Theorem 1.

Figure 4: HA-like representation of the limit PDMP for the example of Section 5.2.

grow with N, to keep up with increasing population sizes.

S4 $k^{(N)} = Nk$, $\mu_1^{(N)} = \mu_1$, $\mu_2^{(N)} = \mu_2$, $X_0^{(N)} = NX_0$, i.e., the batch grows but the service rates are maintained constant. Population sizes are increased as in S3.

In either case, the rate at the delay station is not varied.

5.1 Constant batch sizes, increasing rates (S3)

Classical limit theorems are not applicable under these circumstances because of the guard $X_2^{(N)} \geq k^{(N)}$, which in the N-th normalised model becomes $\bar{X}_2 \geq k^{(N)}/N$. This will give rise to a service rate which may be written in the form $\mu_2 I\{\bar{X}_2 \geq k/N\}$. The drift $F^{(N)}$ of the normalised CTMC at level N is therefore

$$F^{(N)}(x_1, x_2) = (-1, 1)\mu_1 x_1 + (k, -k)\mu_2 I\{x_2 \geq k/N\},$$

which converges to the limit drift

$$F(x_1, x_2) = (-1, 1)\mu_1 x_1 + (k, -k)\mu_2 I\{x_2 \geq 0\},$$

thus defining the limit PWS $\frac{dx(t)}{dt} = F(x(t))$. Although the presence of discontinuities prevents the use of classical limit theorems, the results discussed in Section 4.3 allow us to derive the convergence to F for this sequence of CTMCs.

5.2 Increasing batch sizes, constant rates (S4)

Under scaling S4, in the normalised model the update vector as well as the rates of the CTMC transitions are $\Theta(1)$. This independence from N is the characteristic scaling of the hybrid fluid limit introduced in Section 4.2. More specifically, the batch service will remain discrete and stochastic in the limit PDMP model, which is shown in Figure 4.

However, also in this case we can compute the drift and construct the fluid equation, which is now interpreted as a first-order approximation to the average behaviour of the limit PDMP. The drift of the CTMC at level N is

$$\begin{aligned}
F^{(N)}(x_1, x_2) &= F(x_1, x_2) \\
&= (-1, 1)\mu_1 x_1 + (k, -k)\mu_2 I\{x_2 \geq k\},
\end{aligned}$$

which is independent from N and gives rise to the ODE (with discontinuous right hand side) $\frac{dx(t)}{dt} = F(x(t))$.

5.3 Properties of the fluid equation

The fluid equation $\frac{dx(t)}{dt} = F^{(N)}(x(t))$, constructed using the N-dependent drift, is an approximation of the average behaviour both for scaling S3 and S4. In general, this equation is

$$\frac{dx(t)}{dt} = (-1, 1)\mu_1 x_1 + \left(\frac{k^{(N)}}{N}, -\frac{k^{(N)}}{N}\right)\mu_2^{(N)} I\left\{x_2 \geq \frac{k^{(N)}}{N}\right\},$$

where $\mu_2^{(N)}$ and $k^{(N)}$ scale either as S3 or as S4. It can be proved that this PWS system has a unique solution for any possible initial state $x \in [0,1]^2$, $x_1 + x_2 = 1$. Furthermore, there is a unique globally attracting steady state, which is

$$\left(\frac{k^{(N)}\mu_2^{(N)}}{N\mu_1}, 1 - \frac{k^{(N)}\mu_2^{(N)}}{N\mu_1} \right) \quad \text{if } \mu_2^{(N)} \leq \mu_1 \left(\frac{N}{k^{(N)}} - 1 \right),$$

$$\left(1 - \frac{k^{(N)}}{N}, \frac{k^{(N)}}{N} \right) \qquad \text{otherwise.}$$

The latter case corresponds to sliding motion along the discontinuity surface $x_2 = \frac{k^{(N)}}{N}$, and the equilibrium is reached in a finite amount of time.

The existence and uniqueness of solutions for any initial conditions and the presence of a global attractor bring us to conjecture that the results about limit behaviour holding for Lipschitz continuous fluid limits with a single globally attractive steady state extend also to this PWS system, allowing the use of the fluid equation to estimate the steady state behaviour. A formal proof of this result is current ongoing work.

6. NETWORKS WITH BATCHES

We are now ready to define fluid limits for a general class of queueing networks with batch services and arrivals. The general model is provided in Section 6.1, which also introduces two forms of scaling which combine those already discussed in Sections 4 and 5.

6.1 General model

Using standard notation and terminology, we consider an open network of n stations with exponential services and arrivals. In the following, let J_b and J_s be a partition of the set $\{1, 2, \ldots, n\}$, where J_b denotes the batch service stations and J_s denotes the single-job multi-server stations. The model is characterised by the following parameters.

- $\lambda = (\lambda_1, \ldots, \lambda_n)$ is the vector of the (Poisson) intensities of the exogenous arrivals at each station;

- $b = (b_1, \ldots, b_n)$ is the vector of the sizes of the batch arrivals;

- $P = (p_{ij})_{1 \leq i,j \leq n}$ is the routing probability matrix of size $n \times n$. Upon service at station i, jobs leave the network with probability $1 - \sum_{j=1}^{n} p_{ij}$;

- $\{k_i \mid i \in J_b\}$ is the set of batch service sizes;

- $\{s_i \mid i \in J_s\}$ is the set of server multiplicities at single-job stations. Let $s_i = \infty$ define an infinite-server (i.e., a delay) station;

- $\mu = (\mu_1, \ldots, \mu_n)$ is the vector of service rates. For single-job stations, it is the rate for each server in that station;

- $X = (X_1, \ldots, X_n)$ is a reachable state of the CTMC that defines the network, with X_i being the queue length at station i, including the jobs in service or currently accumulated in the batch;

- $X_0 = (X_{1,0}, \ldots, X_{n,0})$ is the initial state of the CTMC.

In order to define the family $\mathcal{X}^{(N)}$ of CTMCs, let $\lambda^{(N)}$, $b^{(N)}$, ... be the network configuration of the N-th CTMC of the sequence. We assume that the routing probabilities do not scale with N, i.e., $P^{(N)} = P$ for all N. Now, let e_i be a vector of length n of all zeros except the i-th element which

is set to 1. For all $1 \leq i, j \leq n$, the transitions of the N-th CTMC $\mathcal{X}^{(N)}$ are as follows.

batch arrival: $(\cdot, b_i^{(N)} e_i, \lambda_i^{(N)})$;

batch service: if $i \in J_b$,
$(X_i^{(N)} \geq k_i^{(N)}, -k_i^{(N)} e_i + k_i^{(N)} e_j, p_{ij}\mu_i^{(N)})$;

batch service (leaving network): if $i \in J_b$,
$(X_i^{(N)} \geq k_i^{(N)}, -k_i^{(N)} e_i, (1 - \sum_{j=1}^{n} p_{ij})\mu_i^{(N)})$;

single job service: if $i \in J_s$,
$(\cdot, -e_i + e_j, p_{ij}\mu_i^{(N)} \min\{X_i^{(N)}, s_i^{(N)}\})$

single job service (leaving network): if $i \in J_s$,
$(\cdot, -e_i, (1 - \sum_{j=1}^{n} p_{ij})\mu_i^{(N)} \min\{X_i^{(N)}, s_i^{(N)}\})$

In the remainder of this section, we study two distinct forms of scaling:

S5 $\lambda_i^{(N)} = N\lambda_i$, $b_i^{(N)} = b_i$, and $X_0^{(N)} = NX_0$. Furthermore, $\mu_i^{(N)} = N\mu_i$, $k_i^{(N)} = k_i$ for $i \in J_b$, i.e., for all batch service stations, while $\mu_j^{(N)} = \mu_j$ and $s_j^{(N)} = s_j N$ for $j \in J_s$, i.e., for stations that serve singly. This essentially corresponds to combining scaling S1 (for arrivals) and S3 (for batch services). The initial job populations scale as in the case of the closed network analysed in Section 5, whereas multiplicity levels at ordinary stations have the scaling as in Section 4.

S6 $\lambda_i^{(N)} = \lambda_i$, $b_i^{(N)} = b_i N$, and $X_0^{(N)} = NX_0$. Moreover, $\mu_i^{(N)} = \mu_i$, $k_i^{(N)} = k_i N$, for $i \in J_b$, while $\mu_j^{(N)} = \mu_j$ and $s_j^{(N)} = s_j N$ for $j \in J_s$. Giving the same dependence upon N to initial job populations and to server multiplicities, this scaling considers S2 for arrivals and S4 for batch services.

Similarly to the limit results presented in Sections 4 and 5, also in this general case the scaling will determine the kind of limit process. Scaling S5 results in a sequence of CTMCs having a fluid limit in terms of a PWS, due to the presence of discontinuities in the rate functions induced by batches. Also in the general case, we can invoke the results of [9, 10] to conclude convergence of the sequence of CTMCs to this limit. However, care has to be taken to ensure that the PWS has the regularity properties requested by the limit theorems (essentially, existence and uniqueness of the solutions everywhere). At the moment we still do not have a general result for the class of PWS models considered, hence we need to check all generated PWS for satisfaction of regularity properties. However, all the examples we studied enjoyed the requested properties, and we are currently working on a proof for the general case, or for reasonably large subsets.

On the other hand, if we consider scaling S6, we are in a situation leading to a stochastic hybrid limit, where all batch arrivals and services remain stochastic, and all other transitions are approximated by deterministic flows. In any case, we can always derive a fluid equation also for this scaling, using the drift of the CTMC at level N, to be interpreted as an approximation of the average of the stochastic process, or of the limit stochastic hybrid system.

Specifically, we can derive the following set of differential equations, that are a PWS: For all $i = 1, \ldots, n$, let

$$\frac{dx_i}{dt} = \lambda_i b_i + \sum_{j \in J_b} p_{ji} k_j \mu_j I\left\{x_j \geq \kappa_j^{(N)}\right\}$$
$$+ \sum_{j \in J_s} p_{ji} \mu_j \min(x_j, s_j) - \mu_i \min(x_i, s_i), \quad \text{if } i \in J_s,$$

$$\frac{dx_i}{dt} = \lambda_i b_i + \sum_{j \in J_b} p_{ji} k_j \mu_j I\left\{x_j \geq \kappa_i^{(N)}\right\}$$
$$+ \sum_{j \in J_s} p_{ji} \mu_j \min(x_j, s_j) - k_i \mu_i I\left\{x_i \geq \kappa_i^{(N)}\right\}, \text{if } i \in J_b,$$

where

$$\kappa_z^{(N)} = \begin{cases} k_z/N & \text{for scaling S5,} \\ k_z & \text{for scaling S6.} \end{cases}$$

6.2 Discussion

Mixing scalings.

In assuming S5 or S6, we are requesting that all batch transitions scale in the same way, i.e. with constant batch size and increasing rate (S5) or with increasing batch size and constant rate (S6). However, it is possible to consider a mixed scaling, in which some batch arrivals or services scale as S5 and some scale as S6. These models give rise to a limit PDMP, in which only transitions with increasing batch sizes are kept discrete. Therefore, the PDMP may exhibit discontinuous rates, unlike the previous cases. However, we conjecture that the limit results of [9, 27] can be combined so that convergence still holds, provided the PWS system has a sufficiently regular structure (existence and uniqueness of solutions for any initial condition).

Practical considerations.

In real applications, we generally do not have a sequence of CTMCs, but rather a specific model, with a given set of parameter values. Furthermore, it may not be known how the parameters are to scale with respect to N. This suggests to adopt the following policy. Construct the fluid limit equation, using the drift at level N, and approximate the average behaviour of the system by the solution of such an equation. Under the proper scaling conditions, as discussed above, then this equation also gives the limit behaviour of the model. However, for a fixed set of parameters, we wish to assess the accuracy error, i.e., how close the solution of the fluid PWS system is to the real average. This is problematic from a theoretical viewpoint as currently known error bounds are shown to grow doubly exponentially with the time horizon [23].

As a rule of thumb, we expect that if the population/scaling factor is large and the batch sizes are small (compared to the population/scaling factor), the behaviour is close to S5, hence the fluid equation will perform better. On the other hand, for relatively large batch sizes, the behaviour is close to the hybrid limit and the fluid equation may perform worse.

Indeed, let us consider again the example of Section 5. Applying the Dynkin formula to the generic drift $F^{(N)}$, we can see that the real average of the system follows the equa-

tion

$$\frac{d\mathbb{E}[x]}{dt} = (-1, 1)\mu_1 \mathbb{E}[x_1]$$
$$+ (k/N, -k/N)\,\mu_2^{(N)} \mathbb{E}\left[I\{x_2 \geq k^{(N)}/N\}\right],$$

from which we obtain the limit fluid equation by the approximation

$$\mathbb{P}\left\{\bar{X}_2 \geq k^{(N)}/N\right\} = \mathbb{E}\left[I\{x_2 \geq k^{(N)}/N\}\right]$$
$$\approx I\{\mathbb{E}[x_2] \geq k^{(N)}/N\}.$$

This can be quite crude, especially for values of the probability $\mathbb{P}\left\{\bar{X}_2 \geq k^{(N)}/N\right\}$ far from 0 or 1. In fact, with the considered approximation, we are just checking if the (approximate) average of the stochastic process is above or below the threshold $k^{(N)}/N\}$. Now, if the average is far away from such a threshold, we can expect that the probability $p = \mathbb{P}\left\{\bar{X}_2 \geq k^{(N)}/N\right\}$ to be close to 0 or 1, hence the approximation is good. However, when the average is close to the threshold, then p will have an intermediate value between 0 and 1, hence we expect the approximation to be worse. This phenomenon is less severe for large N (and small batch sizes), as we can assume S5 scaling, for which there is convergence to the solution of the fluid equation. On the other hand, for small N or large batch sizes (relatively to N), we expect large errors, because we are "closer" to scaling S6, for which the fluid equation is only an approximation of the average of the limit PDMP.

In the following section we provide numerical evidence showing that this fluid approach works quite well in many cases, but may introduce large errors, expecially for large batch sizes and when the limit PWS system shows sliding motion, i.e., when the process remains close to the switching threshold of the indicator function.

7. NUMERICAL EVALUATION

The quality of the accuracy provided by the approximate deterministic models was assessed by a numerical evaluation over a large parameter space. In studies of this kind two major routes may be taken. One is to carry out tests on a randomly generated validation dataset; the other approach is to perform an exhaustive exploration of a relatively small parameter space to subject the network under consideration to a wide variety of operating conditions. The numerical evaluation herein presented is based on the latter method and is inspired by early literature which deals with accuracy estimation in queueing networks [29, 30, 31].

7.1 Set-up and metrics

The simple tandem network presented in Figure 3 was used in this study. A summary of the parameter ranges is provided in Table 1. The job population sizes were kept purposely small across all tests. Hardly do these networks need to be subjected to approximate solution techniques since the state spaces of their underlying Markov chains is only of a few hundred states, which can be even easily dealt with by ordinary numerical CTMC solvers. These conditions are particularly problematic for deterministic approximations, thus the intent of this section is to stress this technique under its most unfavourable circumstances.

Case	k	Range of μ_1	μ_2	Range of job population
A1	5	$[0.005, 0.500]$	1.0	$15, \ldots, 80$
A2	5	$[0.005, 0.500]$	5.0	$75, \ldots, 400$
B1	10	$[0.010, 1.000]$	1.0	$15, \ldots, 80$
B2	10	$[0.010, 1.000]$	5.0	$75, \ldots, 400$
C1	15	$[0.020, 2.000]$	1.0	$15, \ldots, 80$
C2	15	$[0.020, 2.000]$	5.0	$75, \ldots, 400$

Table 1: Network parameters used for the assessment of the approximation accuracy. The labels in the first column are referred to in Section 7.2. For each dataset 700 equally spaced points in the parameter space were considered.

In each validation dataset, denoted by A1, A2, and so forth, the value of μ_2 was kept fixed whereas μ_1 and the job populations were changed so as to obtain different utilisation levels for the batch queue. This utilisation is here measured as the fraction of the network's steady-state throughput divided by the maximum attainable throughput at the batch queue, which is given by $k\mu_2$. To study the speed of convergence to the deterministic approximation, each configuration in the validation datasets labelled with 1 was scaled up according to the scaling laws S5. For instance, the model with $\mu_1 = 0.005$, $\mu_2 = 1.0$, $N = 15$ in A1 has the same fluid limit as that in A2 with $\mu_1 = 0.005$, $\mu_2 = 5 \times 1.0 = 5.0$, and $N = 5 \times 15 = 75$. Different batch sizes were also tested. In order to roughly maintain the same spectrum of network utilisations across all batch sizes, the ranges of μ_1 where adjusted in each validation dataset.

The approximation accuracy was measured as the percentage relative error of the throughput with respect to its statistical expectation, as computed by stochastic simulation with 95% confidence intervals below 1% radius. The fluid estimate was computed by standard numerical integration of the ODE, enhanced with an *event-detection* mechanism to check for sliding motion and to alter the vector field accordingly. This information was also used to test the hypothesis whether the ODE solutions that undergo sliding motion are generally less accurate than those that do not cross discontinuity regions.

7.2 Results

The results for the case A1 are shown as a contour plot in Figure 5a, where the levels are labelled with the relative error of the throughput for each network configuration. The axes are organised in such a way that points in the bottom-left part represent situations with light loads, as they are characterised by relatively low rates at the delay station and/or small population levels. Conversely, the points in the top-right part are related to high loads. The graph shows that the fluid model is particularly accurate in the latter situation (cf. absence of contours) whereas it suffers large errors in the former. This is perhaps not surprising since fluid models are generally not usable for networks with small population levels. Notably, a region where the approximation does not behave well is found in the middle of the chart; this corresponds to mid- to high-utilisation conditions for the batch queue of around 70–80% (cf. Figure 5d, which shows the utilisations for case A1). The error plots for cases B1 and C1, shown in Figures 5b and 5c, respectively, show

similar trends. For the sake of conciseness, the figures regarding the remaining cases are not provided.

The dotted curve in the error plots divides the N-μ_1 plane into two regions according to the behaviour of the ODE solutions. Parameters lying below the curve give rise to solutions that undergo sliding motion, whereas those above the curve do not cross discontinuity surfaces. In order to quantify the differences in accuracy between these two cases, let us consider the aggregated error statistics for all cases, collectively reported in Table 2. Aggregating the statistics according to these two regions of the parameter space sustains the hypothesis that such discontinuities do have a negative impact on the quality of the approximation. These results also indicate that the accuracy tends to degrade with increasing batch sizes (compare, e.g., A1, B1, and C1). However, the errors in the cases without sliding motion tend to be comparable across all cases, whereas significant differences may be noted in the cases exhibiting sliding motion.

Finally, the table clearly shows how the quality of the approximation improves with increasing population sizes — compare, for instance, the error statistics of A1 and A2. Let us remark that the accuracy is already satisfactory for most practical purposes for all configurations in A2, B2, and C2, although, as discussed above, those cases are not intended to be served by deterministic approximations given their excellent computational tractability. It is therefore not unreasonable to except very good accuracy in the case of large-scale models, where explicit enumeration is unfeasible and stochastic simulation costly.

8. CONCLUSION

Summary of contributions.

This paper has discussed deterministic approximations for queueing networks with batch arrivals and batch services. In some cases it is possible to straightforwardly apply classical limit theorems and interpret the solution to the resulting ODE system as the sample-path trajectory of a suitable sequence of CTMCs, thus justifying, for instance, its practical application as an estimate of the stochastic behaviour for large-scale models. However, for other network configurations, it turns out that the limit behaviour is an ODE with discontinuous right-hand side, or that it is not a deterministic process but rather a stochastic hybrid one.

In the former case, by appealing to recently established results we have been able to show that the discontinuous ODE model is still a meaningful limit trajectory in the sense of an extension of Kurtz's theory (which is originally valid for smooth ODEs). In the latter situation, instead, we have derived an approximating ODE system which may be interpreted as a first-order approximation to the limit hybrid automaton. A numerical study has highlighted that the quality of the approximation increases quite rapidly with larger populations of the network under consideration, with errors less than 3% on average even for networks of moderate size (i.e., a few hundred jobs).

Practical implications.

There are two main assumptions in our models. The first, which is common to all analyses based on CTMCs, is that every activity in the system under study can be reasonably considered as being distributed exponentially. The second,

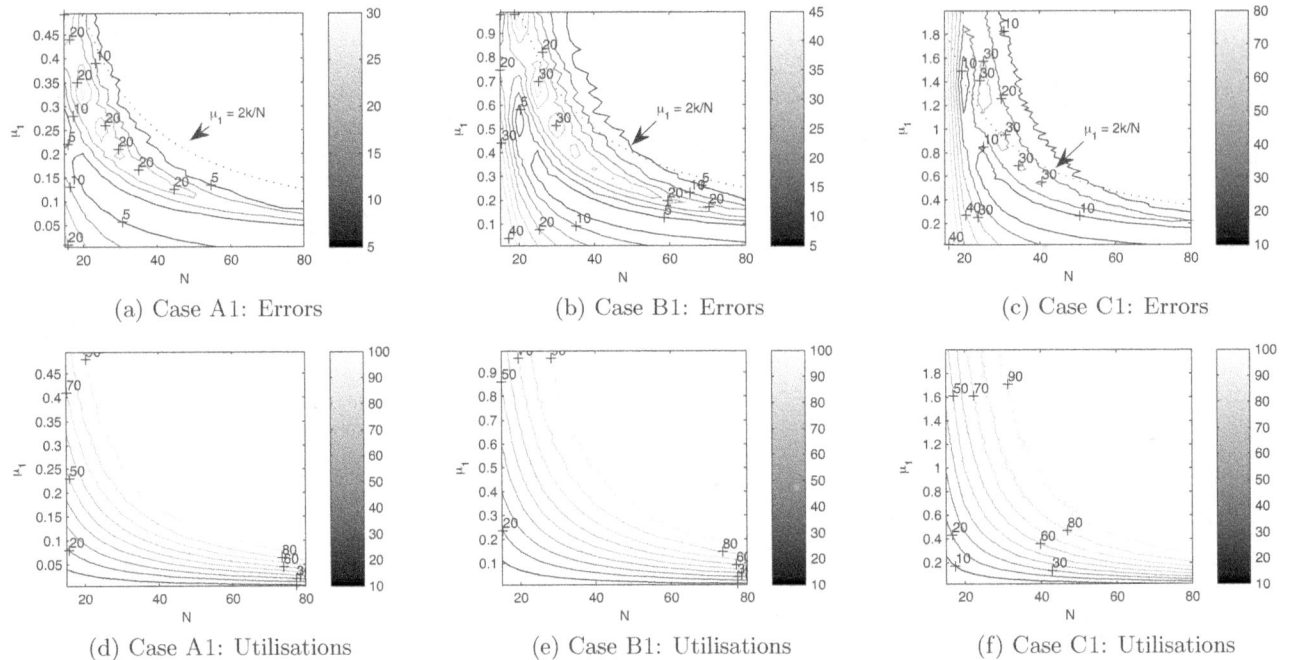

(a) Case A1: Errors   (b) Case B1: Errors   (c) Case C1: Errors

(d) Case A1: Utilisations   (e) Case B1: Utilisations   (f) Case C1: Utilisations

Figure 5: Contour plots of the percentage relative errors and the utilisations of the batch queue for the validation datasets in Table 1. The dotted line in the error plots divides the plane into two regions characterised by network parameters which lead to ODE solutions with sliding motion (below) and without discontinuities (above).

which is specific to our approach, is that of deterministic batch sizes. Under those assumptions, the techniques herein discussed are readily usable for the analysis of batch networks with general topologies. Taken together, the theoretical results and the numerical assessment suggest the following strategy for the performance evaluation of systems exhibiting batch behaviour.

- If the system is sufficiently small, the traditional numerical routes to transient or steady-analysis of the underlying CTMC may be taken [32]. In this case, the computational cost tends to be dominated by the population sizes of the jobs more than by the number of queues in the network.

- Larger models are typically more difficult to solve numerically due to the size of the generator matrix. In this case, stochastic simulation appears to be a viable option; stringent enough confidence interval give performance estimates which are usable for all practical purposes.

- The deterministic approximations presented in this paper could be used for massive systems: the numerical investigation suggests excellent accuracy for networks with thousands of jobs and more under all situations of traffic conditions and all parameter configurations (cf. last four columns for cases C1 and C2 in Table 2).

- Differential equations may still be preferred for systems of medium size in virtue of the low computational cost of the solution. This is particularly appealing for parameter sweeps over large configuration spaces during early-stage capacity planning, when the modeller

may be willing to trade accuracy for speed. Practically useful error bounds are not available, however the numerical results suggest some heuristic approaches to assessing the quality of the approximation. For instance, situations of sliding motion, which can be easily checked with a simple routine integrated with the numerical ODE solver, may flag potential inaccuracies.

Future work.

Though this paper was concerned with batch processing, there are other forms of service in queueing networks which may enjoy similar results in terms of nonstandard fluid limits. Ongoing work is being devoted to studying the case of multiclass networks with priorities.

Another interesting research line could be to study the hybrid limits further. Here, they have been approximated with deterministic equations. However, a hybrid automaton may be considered *per se* as an approximate representation. This raises the question whether it is possible to provide exact solutions; in any case, its simulation may be seen as an intermediate approach which is expected to be faster than the simulation of the overall CTMC, and more accurate than the deterministic approximation. The authors have been recently involved in (numerical) studies of this kind which confirm this behaviour, although in a different context [33]. Along this direction, a promising approach which we wish to investigate is that of using suitable moment-closure techniques [34] in order to improve the approximation of the expected behaviour of the hybrid automaton.

	With Sliding Motion				Without Sliding Motion					Overall			
Case	%	5th	Avg.	50th	95th	%	5th	Avg.	50th	95th	5th	Avg.	50th	95th
A1	33	0.74	8.63	6.80	21.41	67	0.11	3.14	1.13	15.04	0.15	4.96	1.87	18.92
A2	73	0.14	2.59	1.44	9.06	27	0.03	0.94	0.41	4.04	0.04	1.40	0.52	6.81
B1	38	1.21	15.23	12.56	38.08	62	0.15	5.22	1.71	21.54	0.23	9.16	4.57	30.12
B2	29	0.25	4.12	2.77	12.83	71	0.04	1.45	0.44	8.84	0.05	2.21	0.63	10.63
C1	34	1.86	28.28	18.29	79.80	66	0.15	5.22	1.84	26.51	0.19	13.80	5.27	73.79
C2	23	0.31	5.52	3.80	15.86	77	0.05	1.65	0.43	10.11	0.06	2.53	0.59	12.30

Table 2: Error statistics (5th quantile, average, median, and 95th quantile) for the validation sets in Table 1. The overall results (cf. last four columns) are disaggregated into two groups according to the nature of the ODE solution (with/without sliding motion). The first column for each group gives the fraction of models considered.

Acknowledgement

The authors thank the anonymous reviewers for constructive comments which helped improve the quality of this paper.

This work has been partially sponsored by the EU project ASCENS, 257414.

9. REFERENCES

[1] V.O.K. Li, Wanjiun Liao, Xiaoxin Qiu, and E.W.M. Wong. Performance model of interactive video-on-demand systems. *Selected Areas in Communications, IEEE Journal on*, 14(6):1099–1109, aug 1996.

[2] M.L. Chaudhry and J.G.C. Templeton. *A First Course in Bulk Queues*. John Wiley and Sons, 1983.

[3] F.P. Kelly. *Reversibility and Stochastic Networks*. Cambridge University Press, 2011.

[4] Forest Baskett, K. Mani Chandy, Richard R. Muntz, and Fernando G. Palacios. Open, closed, and mixed networks of queues with different classes of customers. *J. ACM*, 22(2):248–260, 1975.

[5] W. Henderson and P. Taylor. Product form in networks of queues with batch arrivals and batch services. *Queueing Systems*, 6:71–87, 1990. 10.1007/BF02411466.

[6] W. Henderson, C. Pearce, P. Taylor, and N. van Dijk. Closed queueing networks with batch services. *Queueing Systems*, 6:59–70, 1990. 10.1007/BF02411465.

[7] T. G. Kurtz. Solutions of ordinary differential equations as limits of pure Markov processes. *J. Appl. Prob.*, 7(1):49–58, April 1970.

[8] M.H.A. Davis. *Markov Models and Optimization*. Chapman & Hall, 1993.

[9] Luca Bortolussi. Hybrid limits of continuous time Markov chains. In *Proceedings of Eighth International Conference on the Quantitative Evaluation of Systems, QEST 2011*, pages 3–12. IEEE Computer Society, 2011.

[10] N. Gast and B. Gaujal. Mean field limit of non-smooth systems and differential inclusions. *SIGMETRICS Perform. Eval. Rev.*, 38:30–32, October 2010.

[11] M. Benaïm and J.Y. Le Boudec. A class of mean field interaction models for computer and communication systems. *Perform. Eval.*, 65(11-12):823–838, 2008.

[12] C. Bordenave, D. McDonald, and A. Proutiére. A particle system in interaction with a rapidly varying environment: Mean field limits and applications. *NHM*, 5(1):31–62, 2010.

[13] M. Tribastone, S. Gilmore, and J. Hillston. Scalable Differential Analysis of Process Algebra Models. *IEEE Transactions on Software Engineering*, 2010.

[14] A. Bobbio, M. Gribaudo, and M. Telek. Analysis of large scale interacting systems by mean field method. In *Proceedings of Fifth International Conference on the Quantitative Evaluaiton of Systems (QEST 2008)*, pages 215–224, 2008.

[15] G. Sharma, A.J. Ganesh, and P.B. Key. Performance analysis of contention based medium access control protocols. *IEEE Transactions on Information Theory*, 55(4):1665–1682, 2009.

[16] D. Qiu and R. Srikant. Modeling and performance analysis of bittorrent-like peer-to-peer networks. In *Proceedings of ACM SIGCOMM 2004*, pages 367–378, 2004.

[17] F. Clévenot and P. Nain. A simple model for the analysis of squirrel. In *Proceedings of INFOCOM 2004*, 2004.

[18] Mohammad Alizadeh, Adel Javanmard, and Balaji Prabhakar. Analysis of dctcp: stability, convergence, and fairness. In *Proceedings of ACM SIGMETRICS 2011*, pages 73–84, 2011.

[19] M. Alizadeh, A. Kabbani, B. Atikoglu, and B. Prabhakar. Stability analysis of qcn: the averaging principle. In *Proceedings of ACM SIGMETRICS 2011*, pages 49–60, 2011.

[20] A. Ganesh, S. Lilienthal, D. Manjunath, A. Proutiere, and F. Simatos. Load balancing via random local search in closed and open systems. In *Proceedings of ACM SIGMETRICS 2010*, pages 287–298, 2010.

[21] N. Gast and B. Gaujal. A mean field model of work stealing in large-scale systems. In *Proceedings of ACM SIGMETRICS 2010*, pages 13–24, 2010.

[22] R.W.R. Darling. Fluid limits of pure jump Markov processes: A practical guide. *arXiv. org*, 2002.

[23] R.W.R. Darling and J.R. Norris. Differential equation approximations for Markov chains. *Probability Surveys*, 5, 2008.

[24] M. Benaïm and J. Weibull. Deterministic

approximation of stochastic evolution in games. *Econometrica*, 2003.

[25] R. Hayden and J. T. Bradley. A fluid analysis framework for a Markovian process algebra. *Theoretical Computer Science*, 2010.

[26] L. Bortolussi. A master equation approach to differential approximations of stochastic concurrent constraint programming. In *Proceedings of the Sixth Workshop on Quantitative Aspects of Programming Languages (QAPL 2008)*, volume 220 of *ENTCS*, pages 163–180, 2008.

[27] L. Bortolussi. Limit behavior of the hybrid approximation of stochastic process algebras. In *Proceedings of 17th International Conference on Analytical and Stochastic Modeling Techniques and Applications, ASMTA 2010*, volume 6148 of *Lecture Notes in Computer Science*, pages 367–381. Springer, 2010.

[28] J. Cortes. Discontinuous dynamical systems: A tutorial on solutions, nonsmooth analysis, and stability. *IEEE Control Systems Magazine*, pages 36–73, 2008.

[29] Raymond M. Bryant, Anthony E. Krzesinski, and Peter Teunissen. The MVA pre-empt resume priority approximation. In *Proceedings of the 1983 ACM SIGMETRICS conference on Measurement and modeling of computer systems*, SIGMETRICS '83, pages 12–27, New York, NY, USA, 1983. ACM.

[30] Raymond M. Bryant, Anthony E. Krzesinski, M. Seetha Lakshmi, and K. Mani Chandy. The MVA priority approximation. *ACM Trans. Comput. Syst.*, 2:335–359, November 1984.

[31] Derek L. Eager and John N. Lipscomb. The AMVA priority approximation. *Performance Evaluation*, 8(3):173–193, 1988.

[32] William Stewart. *Introduction to the Numerical Solution of Markov Chains*. Princeton University Press, 1994.

[33] Luca Bortolussi, Vashti Galpin, Jane Hillston, and Mirco Tribastone. Hybrid semantics for pepa. In *QEST 2010, Seventh International Conference on the Quantitative Evaluation of Systems*, pages 181–190, Williamsburg, Virginia, USA, September 2010. IEEE Computer Society.

[34] A. Singh and J.P. Hespanha. Lognormal moment closures for biochemical reactions. In *Proceedings of 45th IEEE Conference on Decision and Control*, 2006.

An Approximate Solution for *Ph/Ph/1* and *Ph/Ph/1/N* Queues

Alexandre Brandwajn
Baskin School of Engineering
University of California Santa Cruz
USA
alexb@soe.ucsc.edu

Thomas Begin
LIP UMR CNRS - ENS Lyon -
UCB Lyon 1 - INRIA 5668
France
thomas.begin@ens-lyon.fr

ABSTRACT

We propose a simple approximation to assess the steady-state probabilities of the number of customers in *Ph/Ph/1* and *Ph/Ph/1/N* queues, as well as probabilities found on arrival, including the probability of buffer overflow for the *Ph/Ph/1/N* queue. The phase-type distributions considered are assumed to be acyclic. Our method involves iteration between solutions of an *M/Ph/1* queue with state-dependent arrival rate and a *Ph/M/1* queue with state-dependent service rate. We solve these queues using simple and efficient recurrences. By iterating between these two simpler models our approximation divides the state space, and is thus able to easily handle phase-type distributions with large numbers of stages (which might cause problems for classical numerical solutions). The proposed method converges typically within a few tens of iterations, and is asymptotically exact for queues with unrestricted queueing room. Its overall accuracy is good: generally within a few percent of the exact values, except when both the inter-arrival and the service time distributions exhibit low variability. In the latter case, especially under moderate loads, the use of our method is not recommended.

Categories and Subject Descriptors

G.3 [**Probability and Statistics**]: Queueing theory; D.4.8 [**Performance**]: Queueing theory

Keywords

Ph/Ph/1 and *Ph/Ph/1/N* queue, steady-state probabilities, buffer overflow probability, large number of phases, approximate solution, numerical stability.

1.   INTRODUCTION

Despite the recent proliferation of multi-server facilities in numerous application areas, e.g. [GAN03, GEP06], many situations remain where the processing of requests (customers) is performed by a single server. This is the case, for instance, for packets at a network interface [BOL93] or requests at a database

lock. Clearly, the distributions of the times between customer arrivals, as well as of the request service times are dependent on the particular application and, in general, need not be close to the exponential distribution. In many cases, there may be a high variability, in both the inter-arrival and service times. We use acyclic phase-type distributions (e.g. [BOB05]) to represent the time between arrivals and the service time so that the resulting model is a *Ph/Ph/1* queue. As is well known, any distribution can be approximated arbitrarily closely by a phase-type distribution [OCI90]. Since in all human-made systems the queueing room is finite, the unrestricted *Ph/Ph/1* queue may not be an adequate model for higher traffic intensity as the buffer overflow probability becomes of interest in many applications. Hence, we also explicitly consider a queue in which the total number of customers cannot exceed a given value N, i.e. the *Ph/Ph/1/N* queue.

Although there is a considerable body of literature devoted to the single-server queue, e.g. [CHAU92, COH82, OTT87, JAG88, ABA93], no explicit easily usable solution exists in the general case, not even for the average number of customers with unrestricted queueing room [BOL05, page 265]. There are established numerical methods to solve *Ph/Ph/1* queues (e.g. matrix-geometric methods [LAT99, BIN05]), however, due to the cardinality of the resulting state space, they may not scale well for large numbers of phases needed to adequately represent empirical distributions.

A number of approximations exist for the mean waiting time [BUZ93, KIM91, KUE79, SHA80, BOL05, RAO99], however, with few exceptions [WHI89], they are limited to the first two moments of the service and inter-arrival times, and none seems readily applicable to the evaluation of buffer overflow probabilities.

Recently, a simple numerically stable recurrent solution has been proposed to compute the steady-state probabilities for the number of customers in the *M/Ph/1* queue with state-dependent arrivals [BRA08], and an analogous recurrent approach to the computation of the steady-state probabilities in a *Ph/M/c* queue with state-dependent service [BRA12]. We propose to use these recurrent solutions to obtain an approximation for the steady-state distribution of the number of customers in the *Ph/Ph/1* and the *Ph/Ph/1/N* queues. The resulting approximation has the advantage of taking into account the actual form (as opposed to only the first two moments) of the service and inter-arrival distributions. The knowledge of the stationary probability for the number of customers in the system allows us to assess the state of

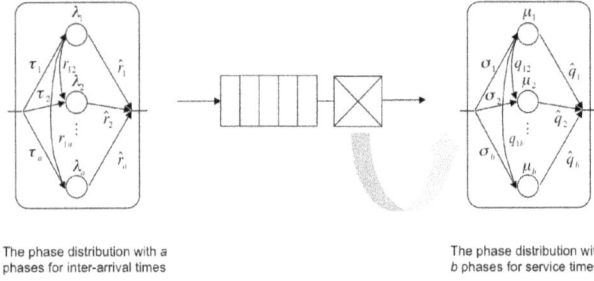

Figure 1. *Ph/Ph/1* queue.

the queue found by arriving requests, including the probabilities of buffer overflow.

In the following section, we derive our approximation. Section 3 gives numerical examples to illustrate the typical performance of this approximation. Section 4 concludes this paper.

2. APPROXIMATION

As stated before, we assume that the times between arrivals and the service times are represented as acyclic phase-type distributions [OCI90]. Figure 1 shows the corresponding *Ph/Ph/1* queue. We denote by a the number of phases in the distribution of the times between arrivals, and by b the number of phases in the distribution of the service times. The total current number of requests in the system is denoted by n. The steady-state of this queue can be described by the current phase of the arrival process j, the current phase of the service process (if the queue is nonempty) i, and by the total number of requests in the system, viz. (j,i,n). In the case of a finite queueing room, we consider that the arrival process continues unperturbed when the buffer is full and arriving customers are then simply lost. Other assumptions on the arrival process (e.g. blocking of the request source) are possible. Table 1 summarizes the notation used in our paper.

If we consider a marginal state description (i,n), our queue can be represented as Queue 1 in Figure 2 where the state-dependent rate of customer arrivals $\alpha(n,i)$ is given by

$$\alpha(n,i) = \sum_{j=1}^{a} \lambda_j \hat{r}_j \, p(j \mid n,i) \qquad (1)$$

Analogously, if we consider the marginal state description (j,n), our queue can be represented as Queue 2 shown in Figure 2 where the state-dependent rate of service $u(n,j)$ is given by

$$u(n,j) = \sum_{i=1}^{b} \mu_i \hat{q}_i \, p(i \mid n,j) \qquad (2)$$

To derive our approximation, we assume that $p(j \mid n,i) \approx p(j \mid n)$ and $p(i \mid n,j) \approx p(i \mid n)$. Consequently, we have $\alpha(n,i) \approx \alpha(n)$ and $u(n,j) \approx u(n)$. Queue 1 in Figure 2 then becomes an *M/Ph/1* queue with a state-dependent arrival rate $\alpha(n)$, and Queue 2 becomes a *Ph/M/1* queue with a state-dependent service rate $u(n)$. A simple recurrence can be used to obtain an efficient and numerically stable solution of the *M/Ph/1* queue [BRA08] yielding the state-dependent service rate $u(n)$. Similarly, an analogous simple recurrence can be used to obtain the state-dependent arrival rate $\alpha(n)$ [BRA12]. Hence, the obvious idea

Table 1. Principal notation used in this paper

τ_j	Probability that arrival process starts in phase j, $j = 1,...,a$
λ_j	Completion rate for phase j of arrival process
r_{jl}	Probability that arrival process continues in phase l upon completion of phase j, $j,l = 1,...,a$, $l > j$
$\hat{r}_j$	Probability that arrival process ends (new request generated) upon completion of phase j, $j = 1,...,a$
σ_i	Probability that service of a request starts in phase i, $i = 1,...,b$
μ_i	Completion rate for phase i of service process
q_{ih}	Probability that service process continues in phase h upon completion of phase i, $i,h = 1,...,b$, $h > i$
$\hat{q}_i$	Probability that service process ends (request departs the system) upon completion of phase i, $i = 1,...,b$
$p(i \mid n,j)$	Conditional probability that the service stage is i given that the number in the system is n and the current arrival stage is j
$p(j \mid n,i)$	Conditional probability that the arrival stage is j given that the number in the system is n and the current stage of the service process is i

to iterate between the solutions of these two queues until a fixed point is reached for the arrival and service rates.

Having obtained the arrival and service rates $\alpha(n)$ and $u(n)$, we can compute the steady-state probability for the number of customers in the system $p(n)$ as

$$p(n) \approx \frac{1}{G} \prod_{m=1}^{n} \alpha(m-1)/u(m), \; n = 0,1,... \qquad (3)$$

G is a normalization constant chosen so that $\sum_n p(n) = 1$. The mean number of customers in the system is $\bar{n} = \sum_n np(n)$. The probability that an arriving customer finds n customers already present in the system, $P_A(n)$, can be expressed as

$$P_A(n) \approx \frac{\alpha(n)p(n)}{\sum_{i \geq 0} \alpha(i)p(i)}, \qquad n = 0,1,... \qquad (4)$$

The proposed approximate solution can be described as follows (superscripts denote the iteration number)

(a) Set the initial value of the arrival rate $\alpha^0(n)$ to the inverse of the mean time between arrivals for all values of $n = 0,1,...$

(b) Solve the simple recurrence for the *M/Ph/1* queue [BRA08] with arrival rate $\alpha^{k-1}(n)$ ($k = 1,2,...$ is the iteration number) to produce the state-dependent service rate $u^k(n)$ for $n = 1,...,n^k_{max}$. With a finite buffer, n^k_{max} is the maximum number of customers in the system N, and with unrestricted buffer, it is the value of the number of customers n for which the rate $u^k(n)$ is close enough to its asymptotic value (cf. [BRA08].) Compute also the expected number of customers in the system $\bar{n}^k_a$ from the *M/Ph/1* model.

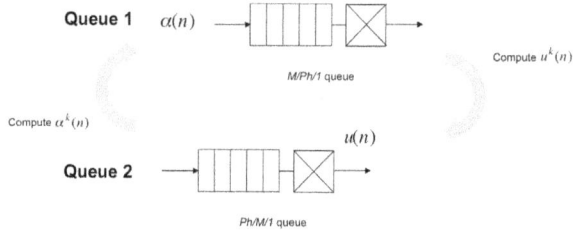

Figure 2. Iterations between *M/Ph/1* and *Ph/M/1* queues.

(c) Solve the *Ph/M/1* queue with the service rate $u^k(n)$ from Step (b), using the simple recurrence given in [BRA12], to produce the state-dependent arrival rate $\alpha^k(n)$ for $n = n^k_{max},...,0$. Compute also the expected number of customers in the system $\bar{n}^k_b$ from the *Ph/M/1* model.

(d) If $\left|1 - \bar{n}^k_a / \bar{n}^k_b\right| < \varepsilon$, where ε is the desired convergence stringency, go to Step (e), otherwise perform another step of the iteration, i.e., go to Step (b).

(e) Compute $p(n)$ and $P_A(n)$ from formulae (3) and (4), respectively.

In the next section we discuss the accuracy and speed of convergence of the proposed approximate solution.

3. ACCURACY AND SPEED OF CONVERGENCE

We performed a large number of tests of the proposed approximation comparing its results to those of an exact numeric solution. In addition to the mean number of customers in the system the test quantities included the probability that a customer has to wait before service, as well as the general shape of the steady-state probability distribution $p(n)$. It is interesting to note that our approximation produces the correct server utilization in the case of an unrestricted queueing room. For queues with restricted queueing room, we examined also the server utilization and the probability of buffer overflow. The typical accuracy tends to be good, within a few percent of the exact values. In virtually all cases a low number of iterations (a few tens) is sufficient to attain a fixed-point convergence of our approximate solution (in all examples, we used $\varepsilon = 10^{-7}$).

Four examples illustrate the behavior of the proposed method.

Example A: Small coefficients of variation (less than 1) for arrivals and service

We start by the case when the times between arrivals and the service times both exhibit low variability, viz., we consider an unrestricted $E_k/E_k/1$ queue with the same number of stages in the arrival and service distributions. In Figure 3 we show the relative error in the mean number of customers in such a system as a function of the server utilization for the number of stages varying from 2 to 10 , i.e., the squared coefficient of variation varying from 0.5 to 0.1. The approximation is, of course, exact for the *M/M/1* queue. We notice that the largest relative errors tend to occur in the range of moderate to moderately high server utilizations (say, 0.6 to 0.9). In this range, the accuracy of the approximation tends to degrade with the number of stages in the Erlang distribution, and exceeds 20% with 7 or more stages.

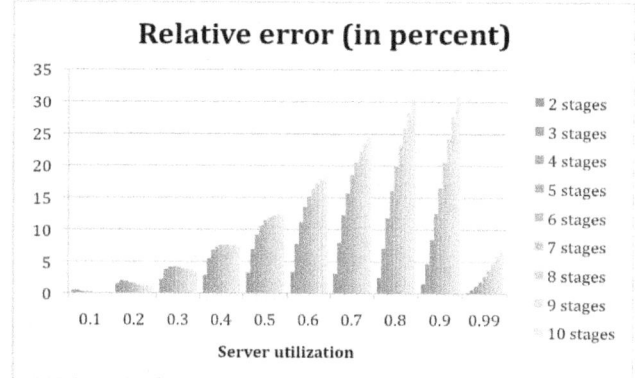

Figure 3. Relative error for mean number in system for a range of numbers of stages in arrival and service Erlang distributions (same number of stages for both) in Example A.

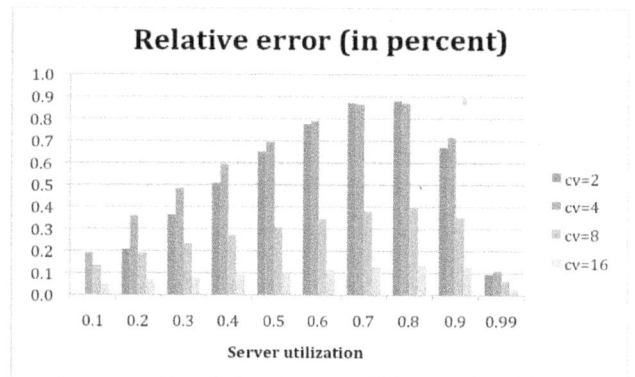

Figure 4. Relative error for mean number in system for a range of coefficients of variation in Example B.

Interestingly, as the server approaches saturation, the approximation accuracy improves. In fact, one can show that our approximation is asymptotically exact as $n \rightarrow \infty$ (see Appendix A.) This explains the improved accuracy near server saturation seen in Figure 3.

Intuitively, the lower accuracy when both arrivals and service exhibit high regularity, appears to be due to the fact that with hypo-exponential distributions, when the number of customers in the system is low (especially, just one user), the knowledge of the current stage of the service distribution provides non-negligible information on the possible stage of the arrival process (and vice versa). In particular, when there is a single user in the system and it is in its first stage of service, it is very likely that the arrival process is also in its first stage. This knowledge is lost in our approximation. Because the method tends to be inaccurate when both the time between arrivals and the service times exhibit low variability (say, coefficients of variation less than 0.3), especially for moderate loads, our approximation is not recommended in this case.

Example B: Coefficients of variation greater than 1

In our second example, we consider an unrestricted queue with times between arrivals represented by a two-phase hyper-exponential distribution (H$_2$). The service times are represented by a different two-phase H$_2$ distribution with mean 1 and the same coefficient of variation as the distribution of the times between

Table 2. Accuracy and convergence of speed in Example C

Server utilization	Mean number in the system		No wait probability		Number of iterations
	Exact	Appr.	Exact	Appr.	
0.1	0.1079	0.1079	0.8834	0.8834	3
0.2	0.2365	0.2365	0.7669	0.7669	3
0.3	0.3968	0.3968	0.6503	0.6503	3
0.4	0.6097	0.6097	0.5337	0.5337	3
0.5	0.9191	0.9191	0.4172	0.4172	4
0.6	1.4374	1.4373	0.3007	0.3007	4
0.7	2.5600	2.5599	0.1842	0.1843	4
0.8	7.3596	7.3590	0.0682	0.0682	5
0.9	173.623	173.861	0.0001	0.0001	15

arrivals (see Appendix.) Figure 4 shows the relative error for the mean number of users in the system for a range of traffic intensities and for coefficients of variation ranging from 2 to 16.

We observe that, in this example, the relative errors of the proposed approximation are small, on the order of a percent, and remain below 1% even for a traffic intensity of 0.99 and coefficients of variation of 16.

Example C: Large coefficient of variation for time between arrivals and small coefficient of variation for service

Our next example is a queue with a finite queueing room of 200 ($N = 200$). The time between arrivals is represented by a two-phase hyper-exponential distribution with a coefficient of variation of 20, and the service time is represented by an Erlang-5 distribution (squared coefficient of variation of 0.2). We show in Table 2 the results obtained for this example, including the number of iterations needed to achieve the convergence, for a range of server utilization values.

We observe that the relative errors of the proposed approximation remain below one percent despite the small coefficient of variation of the service time distribution. We also observe that only a few iterations are required to attain convergence. In our next example we take a closer look at the convergence pattern of our approximation in the context of a larger total number of phases.

Example D: Pareto-like distribution of the time between arrivals with 16 phases and four-phase service time distribution

In our last example, we consider a $Ph/Ph/1/N$ queue with a buffer size of $N = 15$. The arrival process is represented by a Pareto-like distribution with a total of 16 phases, 10 of which are used in the heavy-tail part of the distribution [BRA11]. The service time is represented as a mixture of two Erlang-2 distributions with overall mean 1 and coefficient of variation 3. The rate of a single stage in the first Erlang-2 distribution is 4.4064 and this distribution is selected with probability 0.95. With probability 0.05 the second Erlang-2 distribution is selected. The rate of a single stage for this distribution is 0.1758.

Figure 5 illustrates the convergence pattern of our approximation to its fixed-point solution for this example. We observe the evolution of the relative difference in mean number of customers between the $M/Ph/1$ and $Ph/M/1$ models as the iteration progresses for server utilizations of 0.5, 0.8 and 0.9. In all three

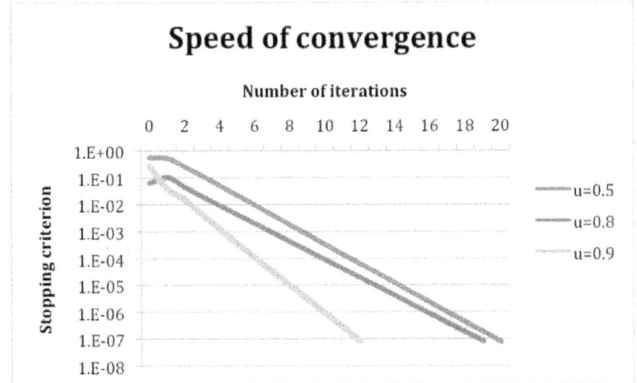

Figure 5. Speed of convergence of proposed approximation for various levels of server utilization for Example D.

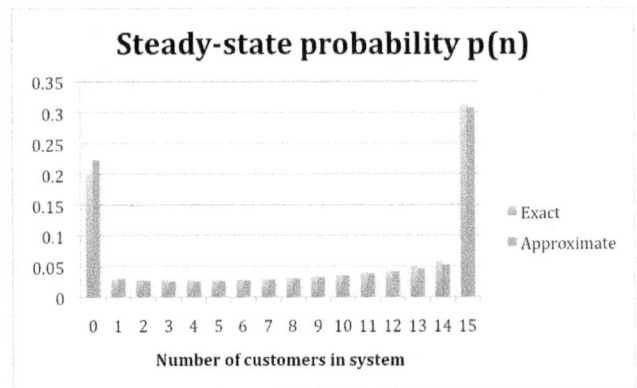

Figure 6. Exact and approximate probabilities for server utilization of 0.8 in Example D.

cases, the decrease in the relative difference appears to be geometric after the first few iterations. Such a geometric decrease seems typical for the convergence of the proposed method.

Figure 6 illustrates the ability of our approximation to reproduce the shape of the steady-state distribution of the number of customers in the system $p(n)$ (for server utilization of 0.8). We observe that the general shape of the steady-state distribution is well represented and the relative errors for individual state probabilities are moderate.

Summary discussion of empirical results

In the last three examples, the relative errors of the proposed approximation tend to be within just a few percent of the exact values and the method converges within a limited number of iterations. Loss probabilities (not reported in this paper) similarly tend to be with a few percent of the exact values. The above behavior appears typical for the method. As shown by example A, the proposed method tends to be less accurate when both the time between arrivals and the service times exhibit low variability (say, coefficients of variation less than 0.3), especially for moderate loads. Therefore, our approximation is not recommended in this case. Note that, as illustrated by example C, if only one of the inter-arrival or service time distributions exhibits low variability the method's accuracy does not seem affected.

Overall, the accuracy of the proposed approximation varies somewhat with the shape of the inter-arrival and service distributions (not just their first two moments). It tends to be particularly good when these distributions are skewed (e.g. unbalanced hyper-exponentials). Highly skewed distributions tend to be characteristic of the traffic in computer networks. It is important to note that these cases happen to be most difficult for some numerical methods [CHAU92] and discrete-event simulation alike [ASM00]. As illustrated by examples B and C, our method can easily handle problems with very large coefficients of variation.

It is worthwhile noting that the speed and numerical stability advantage of the proposed approximation over an exact numerical solution is particularly glaring with higher numbers of stages in the phase distributions. In our experimentation, the method easily handled distributions with hundred phases.

4. CONCLUSIONS

We have proposed an approximation to obtain steady-state probabilities of the number of customers in $Ph/Ph/1$ and $Ph/Ph/1/N$ queues, as well as related probabilities "seen" by an arriving customer, including the probability of buffer overflow in the case of the $Ph/Ph/1/N$ queue. The phase-type distributions considered are assumed to be acyclic. Our method iterates between solutions of an $M/Ph/1$ queue with state-dependent arrival rate and a $Ph/M/1$ queue with state-dependent service rate. Each of these queues is solved using an efficient numerically stable recurrence. The resulting method is simple and easy to implement.

Although we don't have a theoretical proof of convergence of our method, in practice it converges typically within a few tens of iterations. The results produced by our approximation tend to be within a few percent of the exact values, except when both the inter-arrival and the service time distributions exhibit low variability. In the latter case, especially under moderate loads, the use of our method is not recommended.

Compared to an exact numerical solution of a $Ph/Ph/1$ queue, by dividing the state space (through the iteration between the $M/Ph/1$ and $Ph/M/1$ queues) the proposed method affords a significant reduction in computational complexity. The resulting speed advantage is particularly significant with a larger number of phases possibly needed to represent empirical distributions. Additionally, numerical problems due to floating point underflow issues for very small state probabilities are reduced owing to the partitioning of the state space into normalized subsets.

Future work includes the extension of the proposed method to the $Ph/Ph/c$ queue.

5. REFERENCES

[ABA93] Abate, J., Choudhury, G. L. and Whitt, W. 1993. Calculation of the *GI/G/1* waiting time distribution and its cumulants from Pollaczek's formulas. *Arch. Elektr. Uebertragung 47*, 311-321.

[ASM00] Asmussen, K., Binswanger, K. and Hojgaard B. 2000. *Rare events simulation for heavy-tailed distributions.* Bernoulli. 6, 2, 303-322.

[BIN05] Bini, D. A., Latouche, G., Meini, B., 2005. *Numerical Methods for Structured Markov Chains.* Oxford University Press, Inc.

[BOB05] Bobbio, A., Horváth, A. and Telek, M. 2005. Matching Three Moments with Minimal Acyclic Phase Type Distributions. *Stochastic Models*. 21, 2, 303-326.

[BOL93] Bolot, J. 1993. End-to-end packet delay and loss behavior in the Internet. *In SIGCOMM Computer Communication Review*. 23, 4 (Oct. 1993), 289-298.

[BOL05] Bolch, G., Greiner, S., Meer, H. d. and Trivedi, K. S. 2005. *Queueing Networks and Markov Chains.* Second Edition, Wiley-Interscience.

[BUZ93] Buzacott, J.A. and Shanthikumar, J.G. 1993. *Stochastic models of manufacturing systems.* Prentice Hall, Englewood Cliffs.

[BRA08] Brandwajn, A. and Wang, H. 2008. A conditional probability approach to *M/G/1*-like queues. Performance Evaluation. 65, 5 (May. 2008), 366-381.

[BRA11] Brandwajn, A. and Begin, T. 2011. Performance evaluation of a single node with general arrivals and service. *In ASMTA 2011*.

[BRA12] Brandwajn, A. and Begin, T. 2012. A Recurrent Solution of *Ph/M/c/N*-like and *Ph/M/c*-like Queues. In INRIA Research Report 7321. (June 2010). To appear in J. of App. Probability. 49, 1 (March 2012).

[CHAU92] Chaudhry, M. L., Agarwal, M. and Templeton, J. G. 1992. Exact and approximate numerical solutions of steady-state distributions arising in the queue *GI/G/1*. *Queueing Systems Theory Applications*. 10, 1-2 (Jan. 1992), 105-152.

[COH82] Cohen, J.W. 1982. *The single server queue.* North- Holland (second edition).

[GAN03] Gans, N., Koole, G. and Mandelbaum, A. 2003. Telephone call centers: tutorial, review, and research prospects. *Manufacturing and Service Operations Management*, 5, 79-141.

[GEP06] Gepner, P. and Kowalik, M. F. 2006. Multi-Core Processors: New Way to Achieve High System Performance. *In Proceedings of PARELEC* (September 13 - 17, 2006). Washington, DC, 9-13.

[JAG88] Jagerman, D. 1988. Approximations for waiting time in *GI/G/1* systems. *Queueing Systems Theory Applications*. 2, 4 (Feb. 1988), 351-361.

[KIM91] Kimura, T. 1991. Approximating the Mean Waiting Time in the *GI/G/s* Queue. *The Journal of the Operational Research Society*. 42, 11 (Nov. 1991), 959- 970.

[LAT99] Latouche , G., Ramaswami, V., 1999. *Introduction to Matrix Analytic Methods in Stochastic Modeling*, ASA, 1999.

[OCI90] O'Cinneide, C.A. 1990. Characterization of phase-type distributions. *Communications in Statistics: Stochastic Models*. 6, 1, 1-57.

[OTT87] Ott, T.J. 1987. On the Stationary Waiting-Time Distribution in the *GI/G/1* Queue, I: Transform Methods and Almost-Phase-Type Distributions. *Advances in Applied Probability*. 19, 1 (Mar. 1987), 240-265.

[RAO99] Rao, B. V. and Feldman, R. M. 1999. Numerical approximations for the steady-state waiting times in a *GI/G/1* queue. *Queueing Systems Theory Applications*. 31, 1/2 (Jan. 1999), 25-42.

[SHA80] Shanthikumar, J.G. and Buzacott, J.A. 1980. On the approximations of the single-server queue. *International Journal Production Research*. 18 (1980), 761-773.

[WHI89] Whitt, W. 1989. An Interpolation Approximation for the Mean Workload in a *GI/G/1* Queue. *Operations Research*. 37, 6 (Nov. - Dec. 1989), 936-952.

APPENDIX

A. Solution asymptotically exact

We will now show that our method produces results that are asymptotically exact as $n \rightarrow \infty$ in the case of unrestricted queueing room.

Consider the original *Ph/Ph/1* queue described in Section 2. In steady state, the queue can be described by the probability $p(j,i,n)$ where j ($j = 1,...,a$) is the current phase of the arrival process, i ($i = 1,...,b$) is the current phase of the service process, and n is the current number of customers in the system. It is easy to show that $p(n)$, the marginal steady-state probability for the number of customers in the system, can be expressed as

$$p(n) = \frac{1}{H} \prod_{m=1}^{n} \beta(m-1)/\nu(m) \tag{5}$$

where

$$\beta(n) = \sum_{i=1}^{b}\sum_{j=1}^{a} \lambda_j \hat{r}_j p(j,i \mid n), \tag{6}$$

$$\nu(n) = \sum_{i=1}^{b}\sum_{j=1}^{a} \mu_i \hat{q}_i p(j,i \mid n), \tag{7}$$

H is a normalization constant chosen so that $\sum_n p(n) = 1$, and $p(j,i \mid n)$ denotes the steady-state conditional probability of the current arrival and service phases given the number in system. Using the identity $p(j,i,n) = p(j,i \mid n)p(n)$ in the balance equations we obtain explicit equations for $p(j,i \mid n)$. Letting $n \rightarrow \infty$, and denoting by $\tilde{p}(j,i)$ the limit of $p(j,i \mid n)$ as $n \rightarrow \infty$ in these equations, we get the following equations for the asymptotic probability $\tilde{p}(j,i)$

$$\tilde{p}(j,i)[\lambda_j + \mu_i] = \sum_{l=1}^{j-1} \lambda_l r_{lj} \tilde{p}(l,i) + \tau_j \tilde{\nu} \sum_{l=1}^{a} \lambda_l \hat{r}_l \tilde{p}(l,i)/\tilde{\beta}$$
$$+ \sum_{l=1}^{i-1} \mu_l q_{li} \tilde{p}(j,l) + \sigma_i \tilde{\beta} \sum_{l=1}^{b} \mu_l \hat{q}_l \tilde{p}(j,l)/\tilde{\nu} \tag{8}$$

where

$$\tilde{\beta} = \sum_{i=1}^{b}\sum_{j=1}^{a} \lambda_j \hat{r}_j \tilde{p}(j,i) \tag{9}$$

and

$$\tilde{\nu} = \sum_{i=1}^{b}\sum_{j=1}^{a} \mu_i \hat{q}_i \tilde{p}(j,i). \tag{10}$$

Note that there is no approximation involved in the above derivation.

Consider now the particular case of an $E_a/E_b/1$ queue. As discussed in Section 3, because of the sequential nature of the Erlang distribution, when there is just one customer and its service is in its first phase, it is very likely that the arrival process is also in its first stage. However, as the number of customers in the queue increases, there is less and less link between the current stage of service and process.

Hence, it is intuitively clear that, for an arbitrary *Ph/Ph/1* queue, as $n \rightarrow \infty$, the knowledge of the current phase of the service process provides less and less information on the current phase of the arrival process (and vice versa). Therefore, the probabilities of the current phases of arrival and service processes must become independent in the limit so that

$$\tilde{p}(j,i) = \tilde{f}(j)\tilde{g}(i) \tag{11}$$

where $\tilde{f}(j)$ is the limiting probability that phase of the arrival process is j, and $\tilde{g}(i)$ is the limiting probability that the phase of the service process is i.

Using the product form of the asymptotic probabilities $\tilde{p}(j,i)$ in (8), (9) and (10), and summing over all values of the current phase of the arrival process j ($j = 1,...,a$), we readily obtain after simple manipulation

$$\tilde{g}(i)[\mu_i + \tilde{\beta}] = \tilde{g}(i)\tilde{\nu} + \sum_{l=1}^{i-1} \mu_l q_{li} \tilde{g}(l) + \sigma_i \tilde{\beta}, \tag{12}$$

for $i = 1,...,b$.

Similarly, summing over all values of the current phase of the service process i ($i = 1,...,b$), we obtain after simple manipulation

$$\tilde{f}(j)[\lambda_j + \tilde{\nu}] = \tilde{f}(j)\tilde{\beta} + \sum_{l=1}^{j-1} \lambda_l r_{lj} \tilde{f}(l) + \tau_j \tilde{\nu}, \tag{13}$$

for $j = 1,...,a$.

Equation (12) turns out to be identical to the asymptotic equation for the *M/Ph/1* queue, and equation (13) is identical to the asymptotic equation for the *Ph/1/M* queue. Thus, by iterating between the solutions of these two queues, we are in effect solving iteratively the exact asymptotic equations for the *Ph/Ph/1* queue.

B. H2 distributions used in Examples B and C in Section 3

The mean service time is kept at 1. The parameters of the H_2 distributions for the service time are given in the following table.

Table 3. Parameters of the service time distributions in Example B

cv	μ_1	μ_2	σ_1	$\sigma_2 = 1 - \sigma_1$
2	8.00e-002	1.150e+000	1.121e-002	9.8879e-01
4	2.353e-002	1.2206e+000	4.340e-003	9.9566e-01
8	6.150e-003	1.2313e+000	1.206e-003	9.9879e-01
16	1.556e-003	1.2480e+000	3.097e-004	9.9969e-01

For a mean time between arrivals of 1, the parameters of the H_2 distribution for the inter-arrival time are given in Table 4.

Table 4. Parameters of the arrival distributions in Examples B and C

cv	λ_1	λ_2	τ_1	$\tau_2 = 1 - \tau_1$
2	5.714e-002	1.11e+000	5.480e-003	9.9452e-01
4	1.681e-002	1.1471e+000	2.187e-003	9.9781e-01
8	4.396e-003	1.1615e+000	6.136e-004	9.9939e-01
16	1.112e-003	1.16537e+000	1.579e-004	9.9984e-01
20	7.125e-004	1.16584e+000	1.014e-004	9.9990e-01

For higher times between arrivals, the rates λ_1, λ_2 are scaled down proportionately, e.g., for a mean time between arrivals of 2, these rates are doubled. Other parameters, such as τ_1, τ_2, remain unchanged.

A Class of Tractable Models for Run-Time Performance Evaluation

Giuliano Casale   Peter Harrison*
Department of Computing
Imperial College London
London SW7 2AZ, U.K.
{g.casale,pgh}@imperial.ac.uk

ABSTRACT

Run-time resource allocation requires the availability of system performance models that are both accurate and inexpensive to solve. We here propose a new methodology for run-time performance evaluation based on a class of closed queueing networks. Compared to exponential product-form models, the proposed queueing networks also support the inclusion of resources having first-come first-served scheduling under non-exponential service times. Motivated by the lack of an exact solution for these networks, we propose a fixed-point algorithm that approximates performance indexes in linear time and linear space with respect to the number of requests considered in the model. Numerical evaluation shows that, compared to simulation, the proposed models solved by fixed-point iteration have errors of about $1\% - 6\%$, while, on the same test cases, exponential product-form models suffer errors even in excess of 100%. Execution times on commodity hardware are of the order of a few seconds or less, making the proposed methodology practical for run-time decision-making.

Categories and Subject Descriptors

C.4 [**Performance of Systems**]: Modeling Techniques

General Terms

Performance, Algorithms

Keywords

Run-time prediction, analytical modeling, general distributions, closed queueing networks

*The work of G. Casale was supported by an Imperial College Junior Research Fellowship. The work of P. G. Harrison was supported in part by the Engineering and Physical Sciences Research Council of the United Kingdom, research grant number EP/D061717/1.

1. INTRODUCTION

Run-time management of software systems often requires the prediction, in a short amount of time, of the performance arising from the interaction of multiple requests, resources, and software components. Run-time operation often requires low computational costs, thus leading to the use of simplified performance models which assume exponentially distributed service times. However, this is not a realistic assumption for several software systems. For example, web service workloads exhibit different degrees of variability in their service times [17]. As a result of this, exponential models ignoring this variance tend to suffer high prediction errors, especially when first-come first-served scheduling policies are used at resources. Still, first-come first-serve policies are often used in software performance evaluation, for example to describe admission controls limiting the maximum threading level.

In this paper, we tackle the run-time prediction problem by introducing a fast approximation technique for the analysis of a quite general class of queueing network models that overcomes this issue. Queueing networks are often useful in studying complex resource allocation problems, where either hardware, software or network devices may become a performance bottleneck. The class of queueing networks we consider has the advantage of being better able to represent actual, empirical, distributions of resource service times than models that impose exponential assumptions. The proposed approach leverages on realistic parameterization intervals for the skewness of service time. Motivated by the analysis of a recent public dataset of 15000 web service invocations [28], we find that when the skewness lies in the same range seen in the real world trace, queueing systems parameterized with phase-type (PH) service distributions [20] exhibit regularities in the solution that we exploit to define an efficient, approximate solution method. In particular, the main technical contribution of the paper is a fixed point algorithm that accurately approximates the model in $O(N)$ time as the number of requests N issued to the resources grows. This provides a major advantage over existing methods for generally-distributed workloads which require polynomial time (typically, cubic or quadratic) and hence are often too slow for application in run-time service management. A case study related to connection pooling is provided later in the paper, which illustrates a possible application of the proposed methodology in practice.

The analysis of queueing models with non-exponential workloads has traditionally focused on approximate methods. Several techniques exist to analyze isolated queues [4], but a relatively small number of results have been obtained for networks of queues. First, in [22], Reiser develops an approximation technique based on the mean value analysis (MVA) equations [4]. The method is enhanced in [11], using a local iterative approximation approach. Diffusion approximation is also an important approximation for networks in heavy-load [15, 12]. Zahorjan *et. al.* develop an approximate technique based on Markov chain decomposition methods [27, 10]. A general methodology based on approximation to $G/G/1$-queues leads to the queueing network analysis proposed by Whitt [26]. More recently, work has been done in approximating networks in which arrival- or service-processes are represented by correlated Markov-modulated processes [13, 25, 7, 9, 8]. Such methods are able to evaluate more expressive models than are studied here, but typically their computational requirements are much larger than the ones we propose[1]. For example, methods based on flow equivalent techniques, such as [8], require computational costs that grow polynomially in the number of requests N. This makes it prohibitive to solve models with more than a few tens of requests. In contrast, using the proposed approach, we were easily able to solve models with several hundreds of requests in just a few seconds.

The rest of the paper is organized as follows. In Section 2 we give background about PH distributions and the workload models used throughout the paper. Section 3 provides motivation for this work by showing unexpected properties of queueing-based solutions when PH distributions are parameterized with a limited range for the skewness. Section 4 develops an approximate scalar expression to characterize $M/PH/1$ and $PH/PH/1$ queues that is accurate under such parameterizations. A fixed-point algorithm for solving the closed PH queueing networks is introduced in Section 5 and validated in Section 6. Section 7 applies our method to a connection pooling problem. Finally, Section 8 concludes the paper.

2. BACKGROUND

2.1 PH Distributions

Phase-type (PH) distributions generalize probability distributions such as exponential, hyper-exponential, Erlang and Coxian [20, 4]. Compared to these models, PH distributions are more flexible in approximating the heavy-tailed distributions that are common in computer workloads [18]. PH models are able in theory to fit any empirical distribution if their order is sufficiently large [1].

Formally, a PH distribution of order K, denoted PH(K), is a continuous-time Markov chain (CTMC) with K transient states and one absorbing state. The transient states are called *phases*. The initial state probability mass function for the CTMC is specified by a row vector $\boldsymbol{\alpha}$, where $\boldsymbol{\alpha}\mathbf{1} = 1$, $\mathbf{1}$ being a column vector of ones of the same length as $\boldsymbol{\alpha}$. The infinitesimal generator matrix for the CTMC is

$$\boldsymbol{Q} = \begin{bmatrix} \boldsymbol{T} & \boldsymbol{t} \\ \mathbf{0} & 0 \end{bmatrix}, \quad \boldsymbol{t} = -\boldsymbol{T}\mathbf{1},$$

where the $\boldsymbol{T}$ block is called the PH *subgenerator*. A sub-

---

[1]It should be noted that the method in [9] is extremely fast; however, it is not currently applicable to models with more than a single non-exponential queue.

generator $\boldsymbol{T}$ is defined similarly to an ordinary infinitesimal generator except that it satisfies $\boldsymbol{t} \geq 0$, $\boldsymbol{t}^T\mathbf{1} > 0$, where the column vector $\boldsymbol{t} = -\boldsymbol{T}\mathbf{1}$ is called an *exit vector* and represents the rate of jumping to the absorbing state from each of the K transient states of the PH distribution.

Conceptually, PH distributions model inter-arrival times of events as a time to absorption in a CTMC. Let X be the random variable for the time that the CTMC takes to reach the absorbing state after initialization. X can model either job inter-arrival times or service times, making PH distributions a flexible tool to describe the input parameters of a queueing model. In particular, with the above parameterization, it can be shown that the distribution modeled by the PH is

$$\Pr[X \leq x] = 1 - \boldsymbol{\alpha}e^{\boldsymbol{T}x}\mathbf{1}, \quad e^{\boldsymbol{T}x} = \sum_{k=0}^{\infty} \frac{(\boldsymbol{T}x)^k}{k!},$$

Many techniques for fitting PH distributions to empirical datasets have been proposed in the literature, using methods such as the EM algorithm [24] or moment matching [14]. *Examples.* An exponential distribution with rate μ has

$$\boldsymbol{\alpha} = \begin{bmatrix} 1 \end{bmatrix}, \quad \boldsymbol{T} = \begin{bmatrix} -\mu \end{bmatrix},$$

An Erlang-2 process is represented as

$$\boldsymbol{\alpha} = \begin{bmatrix} 1 & 0 \end{bmatrix}, \quad \boldsymbol{T} = \begin{bmatrix} -\mu & \mu \\ 0 & -\mu \end{bmatrix},$$

A two-phase hyper-exponential distribution with phase-1 selection probability p is defined as

$$\boldsymbol{\alpha} = \begin{bmatrix} p & 1-p \end{bmatrix}, \quad \boldsymbol{T} = \begin{bmatrix} -\mu_1 & 0 \\ 0 & -\mu_2 \end{bmatrix},$$

A Coxian distribution with K states has PH representation

$$\boldsymbol{\alpha} = \begin{bmatrix} 1 & 0 & \dots & 0 \end{bmatrix}, \quad \boldsymbol{T} = \begin{bmatrix} -\mu_1 & p_1\mu_1 & 0 & 0 \\ 0 & -\mu_2 & p_2\mu_2 & 0 \\ \vdots & \ddots & \ddots & \ddots \\ 0 & 0 & 0 & -\mu_K \end{bmatrix}.$$

PH renewal process. A sequence of independent and identically distributed (i.i.d.) samples $\{X_1, X_2, \dots\}$ is called a PH renewal process $(\boldsymbol{\alpha}, \boldsymbol{T})$ if the common distribution of the samples is PH with initial state probability mass function $\boldsymbol{\alpha}$ and subgenerator $\boldsymbol{T}$. A queueing system in which arrivals are Poisson and service times constitute a PH renewal process is called a $M/PH/1$ queue. If inter-arrival times also form a PH renewal process, the model is a $PH/PH/1$ queue.

2.2 Closed Queueing Networks

Throughout this paper, we study closed queueing networks as a tool to drive resource allocation decisions. A closed queueing network is populated by a fixed number N of circulating requests that visit a set of M resources. Requests may represent, for instance, a finite pool of N software threads issuing requests to resources. It is established in the literature that, as the population N grows, a closed model accurately approximates an open one [21]. This makes closed networks quite flexible provided that the computational costs of their solution techniques grow slowly with N.

In the models considered here, a request places a demand of X_k processing units when visiting resource k. Such processing units are assumed to include only the actual processing and thus disregard the overhead due to contention from other requests. Upon completion, the request is then routed to another resource. We assume that service times X_k belong to a PH renewal process $(\boldsymbol{\alpha}_k, \boldsymbol{T}_k)$ for all resources $1 \leq k \leq M$ and we call the resulting model a closed PH queueing network[2]. In such a network, the average service time at resource k is

$$S_k = \boldsymbol{\alpha}_k(-\boldsymbol{T}_k)^{-1}\boldsymbol{1},$$

which follows from known expressions for the moments of a PH distribution [20].

Upon completing service at resource j, a request is routed to resource k with probability $p_{j,k}$. The routing matrix

$$\boldsymbol{P} = \begin{bmatrix} p_{1,1} & p_{1,2} & \dots & p_{1,M} \\ p_{2,1} & p_{2,2} & \dots & p_{2,M} \\ \vdots & \vdots & \ddots & \vdots \\ p_{M,1} & p_{M,2} & \dots & p_{M,M} \end{bmatrix}$$

defines a discrete-time Markov chain, which we assume to be irreducible. The visit ratio to the different resources at steady-state is given by the row vector $\boldsymbol{v}$ satisfying $\boldsymbol{vP} = \boldsymbol{v}$, where $\boldsymbol{v1} = 1$. Thus, v_k is the fraction of times that a job is routed to resource k at steady-state. Using the convention that a job is completed upon passage through resource M, we define the average number of visits by a job to resource k prior to its completion by $V_k = v_k/v_M$, so that $V_M = 1$.

Finally, let $X(N)$ be the *throughput* of completed requests (as observed at station M) and let $R_k(N)$ be the mean *response time* at resource k, accumulated over V_k visits. The following output performance metrics of the queueing network model are considered throughout the paper for all resources $k = 1, \dots, M$:

- $\rho_k(N) = X(N)V_kS_k$ – the *utilization* of resource k

- $Q_k(N) = X(N)R_k(N)$ – the mean *queue-length* (i.e., backlog) at resource k, including the job in service

- $\pi_k(n)$ – the probability of observing n jobs at resource k

All the above metrics refer to the behavior of the system at steady state. Notice that since, by definition, $Q_k(N) = \sum_{n=1}^{N} n\pi_k(n)$, computing $X(N)$ and $\pi_k(n)$ provides full information also about the response times $R_k(N)$ at each resource. From these, it is easy to compute the system response time as $R(N) = \sum_{k=1}^{K} R_k(N)$, which is the mean time taken to complete a route through the resources before completion. In sections 4 and 5, we discuss the approximate computation of $X(N)$ and $\pi_k(n)$ for all resources $1 \leq k \leq M$.

2.3 Matrix Geometric Method

We briefly discuss the $M/PH/1$ queue where inter-arrival times are Poisson with rate λ and service times form a PH renewal process $(\boldsymbol{\alpha}, \boldsymbol{T})$ of order K. The $M/PH/1$ queue with first-come-first-served scheduling can be modeled as a structured CTMC called a quasi-birth-death (QBD) process. The CTMC state is a tuple (n, k), where n is the population

[2]Notice that a closed PH queueing network might be seen as a specialization of the recently proposed MAP queueing networks [7], which additionally offer the ability to consider service times that are correlated as described by a Markovian arrival process (MAP). However, such models are harder to solve and thus are less appealing for run-time applications.

of requests in the queue, including any job in service, and k is the currently active phase, out of K, of the PH service process. The QBD infinitesimal generator matrix then has block-tridiagonal form

$$\boldsymbol{Q} = \begin{bmatrix} -\lambda & \lambda\boldsymbol{\alpha} & 0 & 0 & 0 & \dots \\ \boldsymbol{t} & \boldsymbol{T} & \lambda\boldsymbol{I}_K & 0 & 0 & \dots \\ 0 & \boldsymbol{t\alpha} & \boldsymbol{T} & \lambda\boldsymbol{I}_K & 0 & \dots \\ 0 & 0 & \boldsymbol{t\alpha} & \boldsymbol{T} & \lambda\boldsymbol{I}_K & \dots \\ \vdots & \vdots & \vdots & \vdots & \vdots & \ddots \end{bmatrix}$$

where $\boldsymbol{t} = -\boldsymbol{Te}$, $\boldsymbol{t\alpha}$ is a rank-1 matrix and $\boldsymbol{I}_K$ is the identity matrix of order K. The steady-state probability distribution of the CTMC is the set of vectors $\boldsymbol{\pi}(n), n \geq 0$ such that $\boldsymbol{\pi}(n)_k$ is the probability that the state is (n, k) at equilibrium. Thus, $\boldsymbol{\pi}(n) = \sum_{k=1}^{K} \boldsymbol{\pi}(n)_k$ is the marginal queue-length probability mass function.

The steady state distribution $\boldsymbol{\pi}(n)$ is the unique solution of the global balanced equations $\boldsymbol{\pi Q} = 0$, $\boldsymbol{\pi 1} = 1$. An established result of matrix-geometric theory is that such solution may be expressed as a *rate matrix* $\boldsymbol{R}$ such that

$$\boldsymbol{\pi}(n+1) = \boldsymbol{\pi}(n)\boldsymbol{R}, \quad n \geq 1$$

and also $\boldsymbol{\pi}(0)$ can be obtained as a function of $\boldsymbol{R}$ [20]. Since the last expression is similar to one defining a geometric sequence, where the scalar geometric rate is replaced by the matrix $\boldsymbol{R}$, the solution for queueing models parameterized by PH distributions is often referred to as a *matrix-geometric solution*. Finally, we point out that a rich literature is available on the computation of the rate matrix $\boldsymbol{R}$, see [20, 4] and references therein. Publicly available tools for computing $\boldsymbol{R}$ in languages such as C++ and MATLAB have appeared in [23, 3] and are free for download.

3. A MOTIVATING EXAMPLE

We first provide motivation for the approximation developed in the next sections. Let us begin by illustrating the quality of the matrix geometric method when the service times of a $M/PH/1$ queue are parameterized using a real trace from the software domain. To this end, we consider the wsdream dataset recently presented in [28]. This dataset consists of a collection of 15000 response time traces spanning 150 invocation sequences for a set of 100 public web services. Each web service is called several times using different clients deployed on the PlanetLab infrastructure. As a model, we consider a $M/PH/1$ queueing system, where the service time random variable X follows a PH distribution fitted to a trace of the wsdream dataset. This case study may be representative of the performance of a software system that processes requests in first-come first-served order by calling a remote web service every time a request is admitted to service.

Let us first motivate the need for methods that consider non-exponential workloads. The *squared coefficient of variation* (SCV) of a random variable X is defined as the ratio between variance and squared mean: $SCV = Var[X]/E[X]^2$. Further, let $SKEW$ denote the skewness of X, which describes the asymmetry in its probability distribution function. Figure 1(a) illustrates typical values of SCV for the wsdream dataset. The empirical distribution plot shows that both high-variability (i.e., $SCV > 1$) and low-variability ($SCV < 1$) traces are frequent in the dataset, with the median value being $SCV = 0.5294$, close to an Erlang-2 dis-

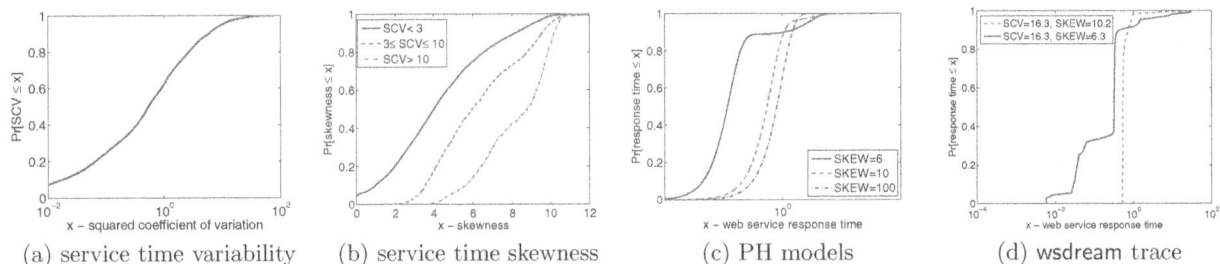

| (a) service time variability | (b) service time skewness | (c) PH models | (d) wsdream trace |

Figure 1: Characterization results for the wsdream trace [28]

tribution ($SCV = 0.50$). The fraction of traces with variability greater than an exponential ($SCV > 1$) is significant and represents 37.4% of the total. Such traces correspond to cases where approximating the trace by an exponential distribution results in the largest errors in the prediction of performance metrics by queueing models. Figure 1(b) further illustrates the distribution of $SKEW$ for increasing SCV values, showing that $SKEW$ is typically positive and reaches its maximum value around $SKEW \approx 12$.

Let us now examine the qualitative properties of skewness. For illustration purposes, we first consider PH distributions having same mean and variance but different skewness and we assume these PH models to represent response times for web services. Figure 1(c) illustrates the effects of skewness on the cumulative distribution function for three PH(2) models with mean $E[X] = 1$, $SCV = 16$ and $SKEW \in \{6, 10, 100\}$, where only the first two skewness values are representative of actual values seen in the wsdream trace. As we can see from the figure, for low skewness values, more probability mass is concentrated on small response times. This results in a bimodal (hyper-exponential) distribution, where a significant probability exists of sampling large values. Conversely, as the skewness increases, there is an increasing probability of sampling huge values, but the distribution is unimodal due to the low overall probability mass placed on the tail. As suggested by Figure 1(b), low skewness values are more frequent in web service traces, where it is indeed quite common to observe multi-modal distributions[3]. Figure 1(d) illustrates two distributions taken from the wsdream trace that illustrate such a property in real-world data. Similarly to the PH(2) models shown in Figure 1(c), low skewness values are associated with multimodal behavior.

3.1 Impact on Queueing Performance

Let us now compare the performance for $M/PH(2)/1$ queueing systems, where service times are parameterized to follow the same distributions used in Figure 1(c). The utilization of the queue is set to 80%. The marginal queue-length probability distributions obtained by the matrix geometric method are plotted in Figure 2(a). Although the high-variability makes these probabilities very different from those of a $M/M/1$ queue, the two cases for low skewness follow a regular geometric decay in the queue-length distribution like in a $M/M/1$, apart for some perturbations around the lowest queue-length sizes. Conversely, the model with $SKEW = 100$ shows a sharp change in the decay rate

around $n = 12$ jobs. This behavior can also be observed in other parameterizations, with the differences being more clearly visible at high load and for large SCV. Figure 2(b) shows simulation results for a $M/Trace/1$ queue, where the service time distributions are parameterized empirically using the two traces shown in Figure 1(d). Note that the maximum observed queue-length for the simulation experiment is limited by the simulation length that was set to 10^5 samples. The decay behavior of the two traces is consistent with the one seen in Figure 2(a), as can be seen from the early convergence to a geometric decay in the rate at a queue-length of around $n = 4$.

In order to show that such property is driven by skewness, Figure 3(a) and Figure 3(b) report experiments we performed with the $M/PH(2)/1$ queue to establish at which queue-length n the decay rate of the marginal distribution converges to the asymptotic one η within a 1% tolerance. That is, we seek the value n^* such that

$$n^* = \min_n \left| \frac{\pi_{n+1}}{\pi_n} - \eta \right| < 10^{-2} \qquad (1)$$

where π_n is the marginal equilibrium probability of observing n jobs in the queue (including any in service) and

$$\eta = \lim_{n \to +\infty} \frac{\pi_{n+1}}{\pi_n}$$

is called the *caudal characteristic* and represents the asymptotic geometric decay of the queue-length distribution. The results in Figure 3(a) and Figure 3(b) indicate that as the skewness varies within the range observed in the wsdream trace ($SKEW \leq 12$), there is early convergence to the asymptotic decay rate typically for small populations $n^* \leq 10 - 15$. This property does not hold when we consider a larger skewness values outside the range observed for the wsdream trace[4].

Summarizing, real-world software workloads can be characterized by large variability, due to the significant probability of observing large response times, and low skewness arising, in the cases we have found, in connection to multi-modal behavior. Parameterizing the service times of the $M/PH/1$ queue with low skewness values yields marginal queue-length probabilities that decay geometrically with good approximation. Motivated by this important observation, in the

---

[3]Manual examination of the wsdream traces is sufficient to verify the significant frequency of multi-modal traces.

[4]Notice that the experiment for $SCV = 1$ uses $SCV = 1+\epsilon$, where $\epsilon = 0.01$, so that we have the ability to control $SKEW$ without significantly deviating from the variability of an exponential distribution. In these experiments, it is clear that the geometric decay rate is constant from population $n = 1$ and thus the system always behaves similarly to an $M/M/1$ queue.

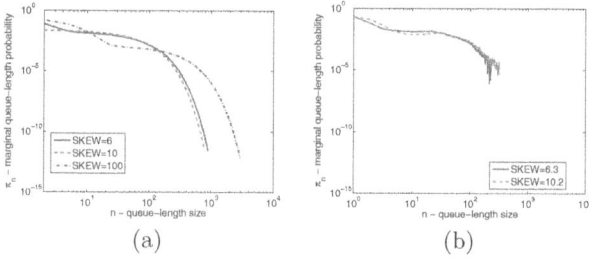

(a)   (b)

Figure 2: Queueing analysis of the two wsdream traces shown in Figure 1(d).

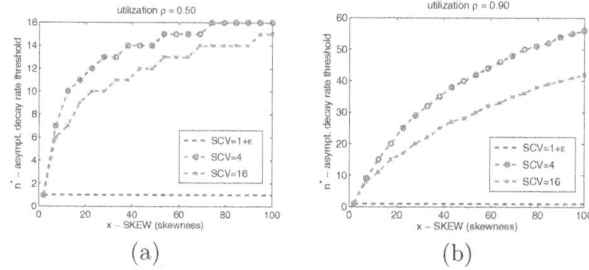

(a)   (b)

Figure 3: Asymptotic decay rate threshold, eq. (1)

next section we derive an approximation for $M/PH/1$ and $PH/PH/1$ queues that is later exploited to define a tractable class of PH queueing network models.

4. PH QUEUE APPROXIMATION

Based on the observations in the previous section, we now seek to obtain new approximate scalar expression for the steady-state distribution of queues with PH service. Let us consider first the asymptotic behavior of the steady-state distribution $\pi(n)$. The *caudal characteristic* η is the spectral radius of the rate matrix R, i.e., $\eta = \max_{1 \leq k \leq K} |\eta_k|$, where the quantities η_k are the eigenvalues of R. Let ℓ and r be the left and right unit-eigenvectors corresponding to eigenvalue η such that the rank-1 matrix $\Pi = r\ell$ is called the spectral *projector* for η. Neuts has shown that asymptotically $\pi(n + k) = \pi(n)\eta^k\Pi + o(\eta^k)$ as $n \to \infty$ for $k \geq 1$, which follows from the fact that, for irreducible, non-negative matrices R,

$$R^n = \eta^n\Pi + o(\eta^n) \qquad (2)$$

at large n [19]. Therefore the dynamics of a $M/PH/1$ queue when the number of jobs n is large is determined by the eigenvalue η and its projector Π only. The result holds also for the $PH/PH/1$ queue, which is considered in the remainder of the paper [20].

The approximation technique that we develop for queueing networks in this paper is based on the following assumptions:

A1. The steady-state solution of a queue with PH service times is entirely determined by the eigenvalue η and its projector Π. That is, we assume that (2) is valid at all populations $n \geq 1$, not only asymptoticly. Equivalently, this might be seen as studying a model where all non-dominating eigenvalues of R are set to 0, so that $R = \eta\Pi$.

A2. The conditional distribution of phases is identical at each population $n \geq 1$, i.e.

$$\widetilde{\theta} = \frac{\widetilde{\pi}(n)}{\widetilde{\pi}(n)\mathbf{1}}$$

so that $\widetilde{\theta}\mathbf{1} = 1$, where $\widetilde{\pi}(n)$ is the approximate probability distribution as opposed to the exact one $\pi(n)$. We take this conditional distribution to be the exact asymptotic one, i.e., $\widetilde{\theta} = \theta$, where θ is a left unit eigenvector of R, such $\theta\Pi = \eta\theta$, see Appendix A for details.

From the above approximating assumptions, we have, for all $n \geq 1$, that

$$\widetilde{\pi}(n + 1) = \widetilde{\pi}(n + 1)\mathbf{1} = \eta\widetilde{\pi}(n)\theta\Pi\mathbf{1} = \eta\widetilde{\pi}(n), \qquad (3)$$

Note that the utilization of the queue, ρ, must be $\rho = \sum_{n \geq 1} \widetilde{\pi}(n) = \widetilde{\pi}(1)(1 - \eta)^{-1}$, which combined with (3) yields the main result of this section:

$$\widetilde{\pi}(n) = \rho(1 - \eta)\eta^{n-1}, \qquad \widetilde{\pi}(0) = 1 - \rho, \qquad (4)$$

which provides an elegant scalar approximation for the matrix-geometric solution. The phase information is correspondingly approximated as

$$\widetilde{\pi}(n) = \widetilde{\pi}(n)\theta, \qquad \theta = \theta\Pi.$$

Notice that the above expressions require knowledge of Π and η, which follow from *exact* calculation of the matrix geometric solution R. This may suggest that the above approximation does not provide any computational advantage over an exact solution. However, as we show in the next section, the proposed approximation becomes valuable in the context of closed queueing networks, where the scalar nature of the equations suggest a simple iterative algorithm to compute the probability distribution of the network state at equilibrium. This iterative algorithm is detailed later in Proposition 1.

5. CLOSED PH QUEUEING NETWORKS

This section introduces a technique for the approximate analysis of closed queueing networks with PH service. We begin with a brief review of product-form networks with exponentially-distributed service times.

5.1 Exponential networks

In a closed queueing network with exponential servers, the joint probability mass function of network states may be written as:

$$\Pr[\boldsymbol{n}] = \frac{\prod_{k=1}^{M}(1 - \rho_k)\rho_k^{n_k}}{C(M, N)} \qquad (5)$$

where n_k is the number of requests at station k, the state is $\boldsymbol{n} = (n_1, n_2, \ldots, n_M)$, including the one in service (if any), $C(M, N)$ is a normalizing constant ensuring that $\sum_{\boldsymbol{n} \in S} \Pr[\boldsymbol{n}] = 1$, the state space of the network is the set

$$S = \left\{ (n_1, n_2, \ldots, n_M) : \sum_{k=1}^{M} n_k = N, n_k \geq 0, n_k \in \mathbb{N}_0 \right\},$$

and $\rho_k = X(N)S_kV_k$ is the utilization of station (or resource) k. Notice also that (5) is often rewritten as

$$\Pr[\boldsymbol{n}] = \frac{\prod_{k=1}^{M}(V_kS_k)^{n_k}}{G(M, N)}, \qquad (6)$$

where S_k is the mean service time of station k and $G(M,N) = C(M,N)/\prod_{k=1}^{M}(1-\rho_k)/(X(N))^M$. The two expressions are equivalent, but (6) does not require *a priori* knowledge of the throughput $X(N)$, which becomes an output quantity obtained by solving the model.

Buzen showed that an exponential network can be solved by the convolution algorithm [5], which recursively evaluates

$$G(M,N) = G(M-1,N) + V_M S_M\, G(M,N-1)$$

subject to initial conditions $G(0,N) = 0$ and $G(M,0) = 1$, where $G(M-1,N)$ (resp. $G(M,N-1)$) is the normalizing constant in a model with station M (resp. with a job) removed from the network. Using the normalizing constant, one can immediately find the joint probability mass function (6). This then provides mean performance metrics which are computed as:

$$X(N) = \frac{G(M,N-1)}{G(M,N)},$$

$$\pi_k(n_k) = \frac{(V_k S_k)^{n_k} G(M_k, N-n_k)}{G(M,N)},$$

where $G(M_k, N-n_k)$ is the normalizing constant of a network with station k removed and $N-n_k$ circulating jobs. Utilizations are $U_k(N) = X(N)V_k S_k = \sum_{n=1}^{N} \pi_k(n)$; mean queue-lengths are $Q_k(N) = \sum_{n=1}^{N} n\pi_k(n)$; mean response times follow by Little's law as $R_k(N) = Q_k(N)/X(N)$, for stations $1 \le k \le M$.

5.2 Cyclic PH networks

We first consider the analysis of cyclic PH networks where resources are arranged in series, so that $p_{M,1} = 1$ and $p_{i,i+1} = 1$, for $1 \le i \le M-1$. Assume initially that the network throughput $X(N)$ is known, so that the utilization of each resource i, $\rho_i = X(N)V_i S_i$, is easily determined. Also, let j denote the resource sending jobs to resource k, so here, $k = j+1 \mod M$.

In order to determine the joint probability mass function for the network state, we first study each resource k as a $PH/PH/1$ first-come-first-served queue in isolation. Both the service and arrival processes for such a queue are PH renewal processes $(\boldsymbol{\alpha}_k, \boldsymbol{T}_k)$ and $(\boldsymbol{\alpha}_j, \rho_j \boldsymbol{T}_j)$ respectively. The latter process is defined by assuming approximately that the inter-departure time between jobs at resource j has a PH distribution which is a scaled version of the service process $(\boldsymbol{\alpha}_j, \boldsymbol{T}_j)$; the mean inter-departure rate is adjusted to be $X(N)$ using the scaling factor ρ_j multiplying $\boldsymbol{T}_j$. The set of $PH/PH/1$ queues defined by the above approach can then be solved by the matrix geometric method to obtain the caudal characteristic η_k for each resource $1 \le k \le K$.

Based on our analysis of Section 4, we approximate the joint probability mass function for the state of the whole network by

$$\Pr[\boldsymbol{n}|X(N)] = \frac{\sum_{\boldsymbol{n} \in S} \prod_{k=1}^{M} F_k(n_k)}{G(M,N)} \quad (7)$$

where

$$F_k(n_k) = \begin{cases} 1 - \rho_k & \text{if } n_k = 0 \\ \rho_k(1-\eta_k)\eta_k^{n_k-1} & \text{if } n_k > 0 \end{cases}$$

We do not need to re-normalize the marginal probability to sum to unity for $n_k \le N$ since such a normalizing constant

is included in $G(M,N)$. From expression (7), it is possible to derive all the usual performance metrics for the queueing network model if the values of $G(M,N)$ and $X(N)$ are known; we discuss below the computation of these terms. Finally, observe that, once the model is solved, phase information for each queue can easily be retrieved using the relation $\boldsymbol{\pi}_k(n) = \pi_k(n)\boldsymbol{\theta}_k$ proposed as an asymptotically correct approximation in Section 4.

5.2.1 Normalizing Constant

We first note that (7) may be written as

$$\Pr[n_1,\ldots,n_M|X(N)] = \frac{\sum_S \prod_{k=1}^{M} q_k(1-\eta_k)\eta_k^{n_k-1}}{H(M,N)}, \quad (8)$$

where $H(M,N) = \prod_{k=1}^{M}(1-\rho_k)G(M,N)$, $q_k = \rho_k(1-\rho_k)^{-1}$. Expression (8) may be interpreted as the joint probability mass function at equilibrium of a Markovian queueing network with load-dependent service rates, where resource k serves jobs with rate

$$\mu_k(n_k) = \begin{cases} q_k^{-1}(1-\eta_k)^{-1}, & n_k = 1 \\ \eta_k^{-1}, & n_k > 1 \end{cases}$$

This enables direct computation of the normalizing constant $H(M,N)$ by the load-dependent convolution algorithm [5]. However, since load-dependent convolution is numerically unstable and existing stabilization techniques become expensive for models with several queues [6], we introduce a specialized method for computing the normalizing constant in (7). This determines efficiently the normalizing constant in $O(MN)$ time and $O(M)$ space.

PROPOSITION 1. *The normalizing constant $G(M,N)$ in (7) can be computed recursively by*

$$G(M,N) = (1-\rho_M)G(M-1,N) + \rho_M G^{aux}(M,N-1)$$
$$G^{aux}(M,N) = (1-\eta_M)G(M-1,N) + \eta_M G^{aux}(M,N-1)$$

with termination conditions

$$G(0,n) = 0, \qquad\qquad\qquad 1 \le n \le N \quad (9)$$
$$G^{aux}(m,0) = (1-\eta_m)\prod_{i=1}^{m-1}(1-\rho_i), \quad 1 \le m \le M, \quad (10)$$

where $G^{aux}(M,N)$ is the normalizing constant of an auxiliary model in which ρ_M is replaced in (7) by η_M.

Proof of the proposition is given in the final appendix. MATLAB code for computing the normalizing constant is reported in Algorithm 1.

5.2.2 Solving the Model

We wish to obtain the throughput $X(N)$ of the PH network by searching for a fixed point of the system of equations defined by (7), with the consistency constraints

$$\rho_k = 1 - \sum_{n:n_k=0} \Pr[n_1,\ldots,n_M|X(N)]$$
$$= 1 - \frac{(1-\rho_k)G(M_k,N)}{G(M,N)}, \quad (11)$$

for $1 \le k \le M$. The key observation that motivates this approach is that (11) is not, in general, satisfied for all guesses of $X(N)$ and thus of $\rho_k = X(N)V_k S_k$. This is because our analysis is approximate and so (7) does not guarantee a consistent description of the steady-state for all values of the

Algorithm 1 *MATLAB code for computing* $G(M,N)$.

Input: M, N, $rho(k) = \rho_k$, $eta(k) = \eta_k$, for $1 \leq k \leq M$
Output: $G(M,N)$
$resource\_indexes = 1 : M;$
$g = zeros(M+1, N+1);$
$gaux = zeros(M+1, N+1);$
for $k = resource\_indexes$ **do**
   $gaux(1+k, 1+n) = prod(1-rho(1:k-1))*(1-eta(k));$
end for
for $k = resource\_indexes$ **do**
   for $n = 1 : N$ **do**
      $gaux(1+k, 1+n) = max(0, 1-eta(k))*g(1+k-1, 1+n) + eta(k)*gaux(1+k, 1+n-1);$
      $g(1+k, 1+n) = max(0, 1-rho(k))*g(1+k-1, 1+n) + rho(k)*gaux(1+k, 1+n-1);$
   end for
end for
return $g(1+M, 1+N)$

---

input parameter $X(N)$. The proposed approximation leverages the heuristic hypothesis that, by guessing a suitable initial value for $X(N)$, a fixed point algorithm that seeks to minimize the violation of (11), while satisfying (7), will terminate with an estimate for $X(N)$ that is close to exact.

Since it is difficult to provide theoretical guarantees on the returned estimate due to the lack of characterizations of the exact solution of a PH queueing network, we first build confidence in the effectiveness of the approach by considering a small case study. The details of the particular fixed point algorithm are deferred to the next subsection. We consider here $M = 2$ resources, each having mean service time $E[X_1] = E[X_2] = 1$, arranged in a cyclic network topology. The population is $N = 10$ requests. Resource 1 has exponentially distributed service times, while resource 2's *SCV* and *SKEW* are chosen as follows. We progressively increase *SCV* from 1 to 64 by powers of 2, while simultaneously setting *SKEW* to the minimum possible value supported by a $PH(2)$ distribution with the specified SCV[5]. As a result of this parametrization, *SKEW* grows from 2 to 12, thus remaining representative of the web service traces studied in Section 3. Figure 4 illustrates experimental results. Figure 4(a) shows the exact throughput (exact) computed by numerical solution of the underlying CTMC and the product-form solution of an exponential queueing network (pfexp), solved by the convolution algorithm. As expected, the increase in *SCV* results in a change of the system throughput that is not reflected in the exponential queueing network solution. Conversely, fp-exact and fp-pfexp are the solutions returned by the fixed point approach described above when the exact and pfexp throughput estimates are used to set up the initial throughput value used by the algorithm. It is found that, regardless of the initial point chosen, the fixed-point method converges to the same solution, which follows the exact trend with a very small approximation error (average 1.85%, maximum 3.56%). Figure 4(b) illustrates the additional time needed to converge to the fixed

---

[5]Minimum skewness for a PH(2) distribution may be obtained by imposing $E[X^3] = 6E[X]^3(h_2^2 + h_3)$, where $h_2 = (E[X^2]/2 - E[X]^2)/E[X]^2$ and $h_3 = h_2(1 - h_2 - 2\sqrt{-h_2})$ [14].

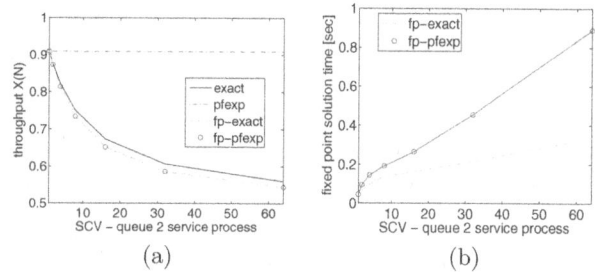

(a)   (b)

Figure 4: Fixed point algorithm result for a tandem model with $M = 2$ queues. Queue 1 has exponential service times. Population is $N = 10$.

point as a function of the initial throughput value. In all cases a fixed point is found and the execution time in MATLAB is less than 1 second on a laptop PC. For $N = 1000$ jobs, the execution time remains less than 4 seconds.

5.2.3 Fixed-Point Algorithm

The fixed-point algorithm comprises the following steps:
Step 0a. Initialize the iteration number to $i = 0$, set $I \geq 1$ as the maximum number of iterations and $\epsilon_{tol} > 0$ as the tolerance level for acceptable convergence.
Step 0b. Determine an initial throughput guess $X^{(0)}(N)$ by solving a corresponding queueing network model where all stations have exponential service times (with the same mean value) instead of PH. This can be done easily using the convolution algorithm or the mean value analysis (MVA) algorithm [5, 16].
Step 1. Increase the iteration number by setting $i := i + 1$.
Step 2. Compute $\rho_k^{(i-1)} = X^{(i-1)}(N)V_k S_k$, for $1 \leq k \leq M$.
Step 3. Determine the caudal characteristics $\eta_k^{(i)}$ for iteration i by application of the matrix geometric method to the $PH/PH/1$ queues with PH arrival process given by $(\boldsymbol{\alpha}_j, \rho_j^{(i-1)}\boldsymbol{T}_j)$ and PH service process given by $(\boldsymbol{\alpha}_k, \boldsymbol{T}_k)$, for all resources $1 \leq k \leq M$.
Step 4. Solve the PH network parameterized by $X^{(i-1)}(N)$ by computing its normalizing constant using Proposition 1. Then obtain the new utilization estimates

$$\widetilde{\rho}_k^{(i)} = 1 - \frac{(1 - \rho_k^{(i-1)})G(M_k, N)}{G(M, N)}$$

for all resources $1 \leq k \leq M$.
Step 5. Obtain a new throughput estimate $X^{(i)}(N)$ using the average of the throughputs predicted at the resources as follows:

$$X^{(i)}(N) = \sum_{k=1}^{M} \frac{1}{M} \left(\frac{\widetilde{\rho}_k^{(i-1)}}{V_k S_k} \right)$$

Step 6. If $|X^{(i)}(N) - X^{(i-1)}(N)| \leq \epsilon_{tol}$, the algorithm has converged adequately to a fixed point. Terminate, returning the estimate $X(N) = X^{(i)}(N)$. Conversely, if $|X^{(i)}(N) - X^{(i-1)}(N)| > \epsilon_{tol}$, go to Step 1 if $i \leq I$; go to Step 7 otherwise.
Step 7. The algorithm has not converged to a fixed point; terminate returning the sequence average $\sum_{i=1}^{I} X^{(i)}(N)/I$, together with an error message.

5.3 Generalizations

We now develop generalizations of the class of PH queueing networks considered in the previous subsection.

5.3.1 Infinite-server scheduling

Our first generalization involves the integration of $-/G/\infty$ queues, where requests can always be served in parallel thanks to the presence of an ample number of servers. Such resource models are commonly used in queueing networks to describe constant delays on the end-to-end path of a request or to model user think times. In the rest of the paper, we refer to infinite server stations as *delay stations* or simply *delays*.

We integrate delays in (7) as follows. Assume station indices are labeled such that $k = 1, \ldots, D$ are delay stations while $k = D + 1, \ldots, D + M$ are PH queues. Then $Z = \sum_{k=1}^{D} V_k S_k$ represents the cumulative mean service time spent by each request in delay stations prior to completing at the reference resource M. We propose to replace the first D delay stations by a single resource with index $k = 0$ having mean service time Z and $V_0 = 1$ visits, and to rename all the station indexes in order to range between 0 and M. Then $\rho_0 = ZX(N)$ is the mean number of requests in the delay stations at steady-state.

We can account for the state of the delays in (7) using the $M/G/\infty$ marginal queue-length distribution. That is, we revise (7) as follows:

$$\Pr[\boldsymbol{n}] = \frac{\sum_{(n_0, n_1, \ldots, n_M) \in S_0} D(n_0) \prod_{k=1}^{M} F_k(n_k)}{G(M, N)},$$

where the state space is now

$$S_0 = \left\{ (n_0, n_1, \ldots, n_M) : \sum_{k=0}^{M} n_k = N, n_k \geq 0, n_k \in \mathbb{N}_0 \right\},$$

and the factor for the delay is

$$D(n_0) = \frac{\rho_0^{n_0}}{n_0!},$$

where the local normalizing term $e^{-\rho_0}$ is factored into the network's normalizing constant. The computation of the normalizing constant now follows as before, the only difference being that (9) is replaced by the condition $G(0, n) = D(n)$, for $1 \leq n \leq N$. The fixed-point algorithm is modified according to the assumption that, for the delay station, the inter-arrival time and inter-departure time distributions are identical. This assumption is exact in the limiting case of a deterministic delay. Thus, if station k is fed by a delay station j, which in turn is fed by resource v, we assume that the distribution of arrivals at k is the inter-departure distribution of v. We have observed that in models where the flow was assumed to be Poisson, the throughput approximation errors were about 5-10 times larger than according to the above approximation.

5.3.2 Processor-sharing scheduling

The analysis of processor-sharing resources is simple thanks to the equivalence at steady-state between the queue length metrics of the $M/G/1$ processor-sharing queue and of the corresponding $M/M/1$ first-come-first-served queue with same utilization. We assume that this result remains valid when queues are embedded in PH queueing networks. This is, in general, an approximation since the input process at a resource may not be Poisson anymore.

Stemming from this idea, the product-form factor in (7) for a processor-sharing queue is defined to be

$$F_k(n_k) = (1 - \rho_k)\rho_k^{n_k}, \quad n_k \geq 0,$$

which is the marginal queue-length distribution of a $M/M/1$ first-come-first-served queue with utilization ρ_k. Note that it is sufficient to set $\eta_k = \rho_k$ to use the same implementation of both the normalizing constant algorithm and the fixed-point iteration for both first-come-first-served and processor-sharing queues.

5.3.3 General non-cyclic topologies

General topologies introduce complications relating to the splitting and joining of request flows. Consider two queues i and j that feed queue k and assume that they have utilizations ρ_i and ρ_j respectively, such that their departure flows may be approximated as PH renewal processes $(\boldsymbol{\pi}_i, \rho_i \boldsymbol{T}_i)$ and $(\boldsymbol{\pi}_j, \rho_j \boldsymbol{T}_j)$. Further, let $p_{i,k}$ and $p_{j,k}$ be the routing probabilities to queue k for jobs departing from queues i and j, respectively. Then the joined flow seen as input to queue k is *not* in general i.i.d. For example, the joined flow is negatively correlated when the distributions of the PH renewal processes are Erlang.

The problem can be addressed by revising the definition of the block matrices in the QBD for queue k. Let $\otimes$ and $\oplus$ be the Kronecker product and sum operators respectively and let U, V and K be the numbers of phases of the PH service processes of queues i, j and k, respectively. Then the QBD may be written as

$$\boldsymbol{Q}_k = \begin{bmatrix} \boldsymbol{L}_0 & \boldsymbol{F} & 0 & 0 & 0 & \cdots \\ \boldsymbol{B} & \boldsymbol{L} & \boldsymbol{F} & 0 & 0 & \cdots \\ 0 & \boldsymbol{B} & \boldsymbol{L} & \boldsymbol{F} & 0 & \cdots \\ 0 & 0 & \boldsymbol{B} & \boldsymbol{L} & \boldsymbol{F} & \cdots \\ \vdots & \vdots & \vdots & \vdots & \vdots & \ddots \end{bmatrix}$$

where

$$\boldsymbol{L}_0 = (\rho_i \boldsymbol{T}_i \oplus \rho_j \boldsymbol{T}_j) \otimes \boldsymbol{I}_K$$
$$\boldsymbol{L} = \rho_i \boldsymbol{T}_i \oplus \rho_j \boldsymbol{T}_j \oplus \boldsymbol{T}_k$$
$$\boldsymbol{F} = (p_{i,k}\rho_i \boldsymbol{t}_i \boldsymbol{\alpha}_i \oplus p_{j,k}\rho_j \boldsymbol{t}_j \boldsymbol{\alpha}_j) \otimes \boldsymbol{I}_K$$
$$\boldsymbol{B} = \boldsymbol{I}_{U \cdot V} \otimes \boldsymbol{t}_k \boldsymbol{\alpha}_k$$

in which $\boldsymbol{I}_n$ is the identity matrix of order n and $\boldsymbol{t}_u = -\boldsymbol{T}_u \boldsymbol{1}$. Solving for the caudal characteristic η provides an immediate generalization of the approach used for a cyclic PH network to a general network topology.

6. VALIDATION

In this section, we study the accuracy of the proposed approximations for networks with increasing size and different service time distributions.

6.1 $M = 2$ resources

We first investigate the accuracy of the proposed approximation method on a network with $M = 2$ resources. We perform experiments similar to the ones depicted in Figure 4, but for different parameterizations of the model. Figure 5(a) and Figure 5(b) illustrate the throughput error when the rates of the two stations are unbalanced. The mean service rate is shown at the top of both figures. The results indicate that for low SCV values the approximation is excellent, whereas at high SCV, there is some deviation between the

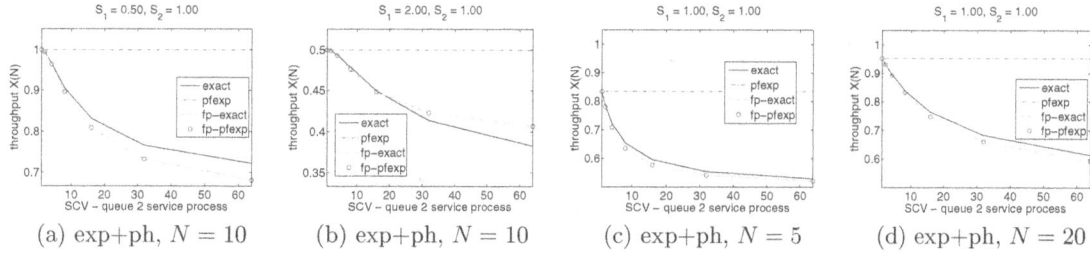

(a) exp+ph, $N = 10$ (b) exp+ph, $N = 10$ (c) exp+ph, $N = 5$ (d) exp+ph, $N = 20$

Figure 5: Sensitivity to values of mean service time and to population size; the model has $M = 2$ queues.

exact results and the approximations. The initial throughput value used for the fixed point algorithm is unimportant since fp-exact and fp-pfexp yield identical results. This was also observed in all the other experiments in this section. Quantitatively, the deviation at $SCV = 64$ is just 5.74% in Figure 5(a) and 6.35% in Figure 5(b). Once again, the results for corresponding product-form exponential networks are much worse, with an error of 38.41% in Figure 5(a) and 30.66% in Figure 5(b).

Notice that in all experiments, the maximum resource utilization is $U_{max} = \max_k S_k X(N)$, and Figure 5(a) and Figure 5(b) span a utilization range for the bottleneck queue from 0.70 to 1.00. Figure 5(c) and Figure 5(d) illustrate sensitivity to the network load by altering the number of requests N to $N = 5$ and $N = 20$, respectively. The results indicate that the accuracy of the method is quite insensitive to such changes in the job populations.

Figure 6(a) and Figure 6(b) illustrate the sensitivity of models when resource 1 is set, respectively, to have either an Erlang-2 distribution or a PH distribution identical to the one used in resource 2. Notice that for $SCV = 1$ the exact result no longer matches the exponential case, the first resource no longer being exponential. The former case is indeed very important for web services due to our observation in Section 3 that about 50% of recorded experiments have $SCV < 0.52$. The results in the two figures suggest again that the accuracy of the method is quite insensitive to the change in SCV.

Figure 7(a) shows how the accuracy of the method is affected by the skewness of the distribution. It is clear that, as the skewness raises above the $SKEW \leq 12$ boundary that we considered in Section 3, the scalar approximation we have proposed for the $PH/PH/1$ queue is no longer valid. It is still interesting to note, however, that most of the experiments with large skewness show a good agreement with the product-form exponential solution. This suggests that resources with high-skewness might be approximated as exponential resources without incurring major errors.

Figure 7(b) shows instead the growth of computational costs as the number of phases increases. For simplicity of parameterization, we consider an Erlang-n process at resource n and explore the values $n = 1, 2, 4, 8, 16, 32$. It is found that a parsimonious PH description with up to 8 states provides execution times that are less than 1 second. For $n = 16$ the time grows to 1.28 seconds and for $n = 32$ it grows to 6.80 seconds. Closer examination of execution traces reveals that the dominating component of the execution time is the matrix-geometric solution used to compute η_k for all resources.

Figure 8 shows sensitivity results for the case where a

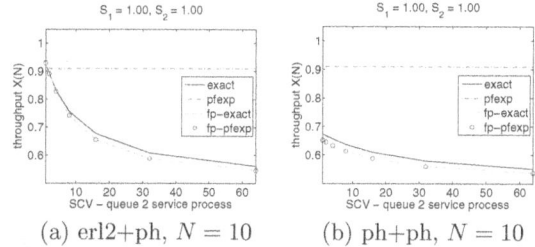

(a) erl2+ph, $N = 10$ (b) ph+ph, $N = 10$

Figure 6: Sensitivity to choice of distribution at resource 1; the model has $M = 2$ queues.

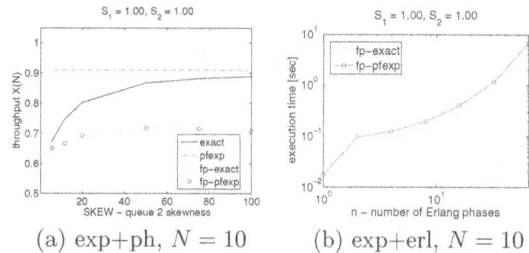

(a) exp+ph, $N = 10$ (b) exp+erl, $N = 10$

Figure 7: Sensitivity to skewness of distribution and to number of phases; the model has $M = 2$ queues.

delay station is added to the cyclic network, placed after resource 2. The population is $N = 10$. The two cases consider average delays $Z = 2$ and $Z = 10$, respectively resulting in worst-case approximation errors of 3.4% and 11.8%, which are much better than the corresponding errors in product-form models of 59.0% and 40.0%.

The execution times for fp-exact and fp-pfexp in all experiments in this subsection were less than 1 second on MATLAB. Memory requirement was negligible as well – of the order of kilobytes.

6.2 $M = 3$ resources

We next assessed the sensitivity of the results against the size of the network. Figure 9(a) and Figure 9(b) illustrate two cyclic networks with one or two resources having PH distributed service times. Notice that the range of maximum utilization is larger than in the previous experiments, especially in Figure 9(b), where it is between 0.4 and 1.00. We see that increasing the number of resources results in more accuracy in Figure 9(a), where the maximum error is just 2.84% for the fixed point method against 60.0% for the exponential product-form solution. In Figure 9(b), the errors grow to 6.13% for the fixed point and 109.1% for the

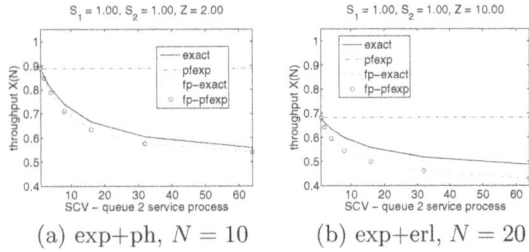

(a) exp+ph, $N = 10$ (b) exp+erl, $N = 20$

Figure 8: Sensitivity to delay stations; the model has $M = 2$ queues and a delay station.

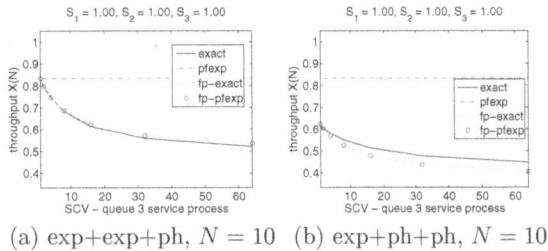

(a) exp+exp+ph, $N = 10$ (b) exp+ph+ph, $N = 10$

Figure 9: Sensitivity to choice of distribution at resource 1; the model has $M = 3$ queues.

exponential product-form solution. Such a difference from the case in Figure 9(a) may be explained by observing that, when more queues are PH, the request-flows between resources tend to deviate more markedly from a Poisson process. Such a situation cannot be handled by exponential networks[6], whereas our fixed-point method accounts for it effectively, thanks to the scaled input processes $(\boldsymbol{\alpha}_j, \rho_j \boldsymbol{T}_j)$. To test this conjecture, we repeated the experiment in Figure 9(b), replacing the scaled input processes $(\boldsymbol{\alpha}_j, \rho_j \boldsymbol{T}_j)$ by an exponential inter-arrival time with the same mean. Thus, the caudal characteristics η_k are for $M/PH/1$ queues rather than $PH/PH/1$ queues. It is found that the fixed point solution error grows to 37.69% for $SCV = 64$, so it is about 600% larger than with the $PH/PH/1$ approach. For the model in Figure 9(a), the degradation is similar, at 32.9%. These additional experiments provide robust evidence that the proposed approach is effective in describing the distribution of inter-departure times from resources.

Finally, Figure 10 shows sensitivity experiments similar to the ones developed in Figure 5. As before, no major deviations from the exact solution are observed. As with the cases of $M = 2$ resources, for $M = 3$, the execution times for fp-exact and fp-pfexp in all experiments were less than 1 second.

6.3 Large intractable models

We now illustrate the accuracy and scalability of the fixed-point method on models that are intractable by direct solution of the Markov chain. Figure 11(a) shows results for a model with $N = 100$ requests and $M = 10$ resources. The number of states in the underlying Markov process is 4.366×10^{15}, which is clearly intractable. All service times at the queueing resources follow an identical PH(2) distri-

---

[6]Notice that in closed exponential networks the flows are not Poisson either. However, empirical observations suggest that their variability is usually not too far from $SCV = 1$.

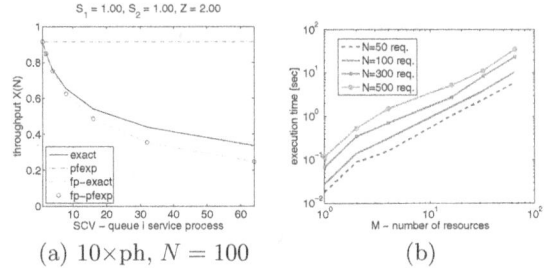

(a) $10\times$ph, $N = 100$ (b)

Figure 11: Sensitivity to model size.

bution with the specified SCV. The exact solution is computed by simulation, using the Java Modelling Tools suite simulator [2], configured with the independent replication method and 95% confidence intervals. Notice that utilization is identical for all resources and equal to the throughput since $S_k = 1$, for $1 \leq k \leq M$. Results indicate that the method is very accurate for $SCV \leq 10$ when the network is more heavily-loaded, whilst it gives slightly larger errors than in the previous examples at large $SCVs$. Overall, the trend is captured fairly well, especially when compared to the pfexp method. We have performed additional experiments and observed that as the bottleneck load grows, performance appears to be captured better at large SCV. Thus, it appears that the proposed approximation tends to perform better at medium/high loads. This is consistent with the discussion in Section 3, since under light load, the different decay rate at queue-length 1 (i.e., $\rho(1 - \eta)/(1 - \rho)$ as opposed to η) may reasonably become dominant.

Figure 11(b) shows computation times for large models with N up to 500 requests and networks of increasing size, M. In all cases, the fixed-point method can solve the model in a few seconds on a laptop computer. In particular, the execution times scale very efficiently with the population N, thanks to the $O(N)$ complexity of the normalizing constant computation.

7. SERVICE MANAGEMENT EXAMPLE

Finally, we introduce a case study of practical interest for the proposed class of performance models. Consider an application that defines a set of enterprise Java beans (EJBs) to deal with the business logic. Each EJB acquires data from a pool of C connection objects that represent entry-points for web services and database resources, collectively referred to as *data sources*. Assume that there are D data sources and there exist one or more dedicated connection objects for each data source. Thus $C \geq D$ and we denote by C_d the number of connection objects for data source d, $1 \leq d \leq D$. Assume also that queueing delays for outstanding calls at data sources are negligible and that each connection object stores the pending calls it will serve in a first-in-first-out buffer.

We consider the problem of allocating residual bandwidth at run-time by instantiation of new connection objects. Indeed, as the number of connection objects grows, more data can be fetched in parallel per unit of time from data sources and thus increase the application throughput if data acquisition is the performance bottleneck. However, a physical bandwidth limit exists which calls for deciding which data source to prioritize. For simplicity, we focus here on identify-

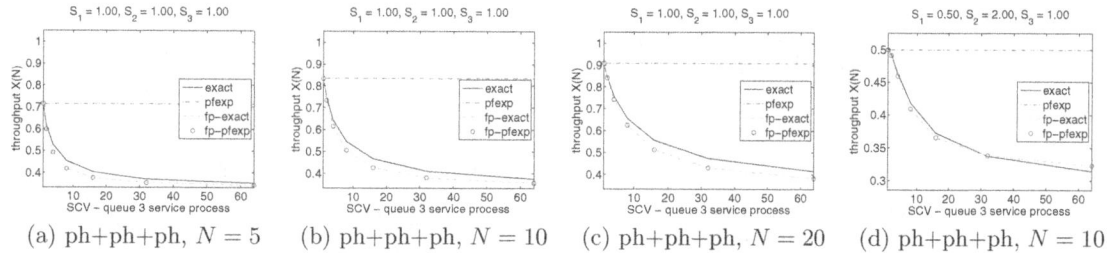

Figure 10: Sensitivity to values of mean service time and to the population size; the model has $M = 3$ queues.

ing the data source d^* that would be able to exploit best the greatest portion of the residual bandwidth, and thus acquire more data per time unit.

The decision problem may be tackled by studying a closed queueing network with N circulating requests representing the number of calls issued by EJBs to the connection objects. Define Z_d to be the average time that elapses between completion of a call to data source d and the successive arrival of a new call to that data source. Such a delay may be due to several factors, such as gaps in the arrival stream of requests, time taken by EJBs to process the business logic, level of parallelism for software worker threads used by the application. We model the system as a cyclic network with a first-come-first-served queue, representing the new connection object, a processor-sharing queue, representing available bandwidth, and a delay server with exponential rate Z_d^{-1}. Let R_d be the random variable for the response time of data source d and let $E[B_d]$ be the average data size in bits of a response from data source d over the network. Further, denote by μ the network bandwidth in bits per second and by $\rho_{net,d}$ the current network utilization due to calls to data source d. The average time to transfer data from source d may be estimated as $S_{net,d} = E[B_d]\mu^{-1}$. Since we consider single class models and the network utilization is available at run-time, we consider the scaled quantity $S^*_{net,d} = ((C_d + 1)/C_d)S_{net,d}(1 - \sum_{i \neq d} \rho_{net,i})^{-1}$. Here the utilization scaling factor accounts for the delay due to shared network bandwidth under the assumption that class d will not affect the bandwidth allocated to class $i \neq d$. Instead, the factor $((C_d + 1)/C_d)$ estimates the extra demand placed on the network by a new connection for source d. The example is based on two web service time-traces from the wsdream dataset, having respectively $E[R_1] = 412.43ms$, $SCV[R_1] = 22.35$, $SKEW[R_1] = 9.96$ and $E[R_2] = 661.00ms$, $SCV[R_2] = 0.50$, $SKEW[R_2] = 9.30$, which are fitted by PH(2)s. Thus, data source 1 has high-variability in its response while data source 2 has low variability. The other parameters used in the experiments are given in Table 1.

Notice that source $d = 1$ has the highest demand on network bandwidth and the smallest delay Z_d; thus the choice $d^* = 1$ seems natural. However, we find that low variability makes the choice $d^* = 2$ a better one. Simulation and analytical results are shown in Figure 12. Execution time for the fixed-point algorithm is just $4ms$ per experiment, as opposed to simulation that takes about $10s$ to converge. As we can see, the exponential network model pfexp, which cannot represent high-variability, predicts that an additional connection object would roughly provide the same bandwidth utilization for both data sources, with a slight preference for

$D = 2$	$C_1 = 1$	$C_2 = 1$
d	1	2
N	10	10
Z	$400ms$	$430ms$
$S_{net,d}$	$250ms$	$100ms$
$\rho_{net,d}$	0.5242	0.1518

Table 1: Model parameters.

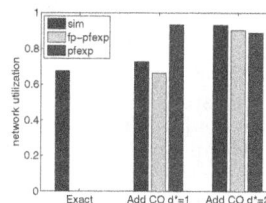

Figure 12: Application example results.

$d = 1$. Conversely fp-pfexp, the fixed-point algorithm initialized with the pfexp solution, correctly predicts that a benefit can be achieved only if the additional connection object is for data source $d = 2$. This is because the high variance of data source 1 would often block the line of requests queueing at the connection object buffer.

Summarizing, this small, but realistic, example shows that the proposed class of models may return surprising – but correct – decisions compared to those suggested by commonly used exponential models. Such predictions are obtained in negligible time and so are compatible with application to run-time decision problems of far greater complexity than that of this exemple.

8. CONCLUSION

We have presented a class of product-form expressions that approximate a diverse range of closed queueing networks with resources having generally distributed processing times. When the skewness of the distribution is not too large (e.g., $SKEW \leq 12$), it was found that the accuracy of the approximation is excellent at all levels of variability, as characterized by the second moment. A fixed-point algorithm that obtains such approximate solutions cheaply in terms of both time and space requirements has been implemented and its application to run-time service management has been illustrated. Future work will focus on the generalization of the proposed method to multi-class workloads as well as load-dependent and multi-server resources.

9. REFERENCES

[1] S. Asmussen and F. Koole. Marked point processes as limits of Markovian arrival streams. *J. Appl. Prob.*, 30:365–372, 1993.

[2] M. Bertoli, G. Casale, and G. Serazzi. User-friendly approach to capacity planning studies with Java Modelling Tools. In *Proc. of SIMUTools 2009*, pages 1–9. ACM, 2009.

[3] D. Bini, B. Meini, S. Steffé, and B. Van Houdt. Structured Markov chains solver: software tools. In *Proc. of SMCTOOLS Workshop*. ACM, 2006, http://win.ua.ac.be/~vanhoudt/.

[4] G. Bolch, S. Greiner, H. de Meer, and K. S. Trivedi. *Queueing Networks and Markov Chains.* 2nd ed., Wiley and Sons, 2006.

[5] J. P. Buzen. Computational algorithms for closed queueing networks with exponential servers. *Comm. of the ACM*, 16(9):527–531, 1973.

[6] G. Casale. A note on stable flow-equivalent aggregation in closed networks. *Queueing Systems*, 60(3-4):193–202, 2008.

[7] G. Casale, N. Mi, and E. Smirni. Bound analysis of closed queueing networks with workload burstiness. In *Proc. of ACM SIGMETRICS 2008*, pp. 13–24. ACM Press, 2008.

[8] G. Casale, N. Mi, L. Cherkasova, and E. Smirni. Dealing with burstiness in multi-tier applications: new models and their parameterization. *IEEE Trans. Software Eng.*, to appears.

[9] G. Casale, M. Tribastone. Fluid Analysis of Queueing in Two-Stage Random Environments. in *Proc. of QEST*, Aachen, Germany, Sep 2011.

[10] P. Courtois. Decomposability, instabilities, and saturation in multiprogramming systems. *Comm. of the ACM*, 18(7):371–377, 1975.

[11] D. L. Eager, D. Sorin, and M. K. Vernon. AMVA techniques for high service time variability. In *Proc. of ACM SIGMETRICS*, pages 217–228. ACM Press, 2000.

[12] E. Gelenbe and I. Mitrani. *Analysis and Synthesis of Computer Systems.* Academic Press, London, 1980.

[13] A. Heindl. *Traffic-Based Decomposition of General Queueing Networks with Correlated Input Processes.* Ph.D. Thesis, Shaker Verlag, Aachen, 2001.

[14] A. Heindl, G. Horvath, and K.Gross. Explicit Inverse Characterizations of Acyclic MAPs of Second Order. Proc. of *EPEW*, Springer LNCS 4054, 108–122, 2006.

[15] H. Kobayashi. Application of the diffusion approximation to queueing networks I: equilibrium queue distributions. *Journal of the ACM*, 21(2):316–328, 1974.

[16] E. D. Lazowska, J. Zahorjan, G. S. Graham, and K. C. Sevcik. *Quantitative System Performance.* Prentice-Hall, 1984.

[17] T. Marian, M. Balakrishnan, K. Birman, and R. van Renesse. Tempest: Soft state replication in the service tier. In *DSN*, pages 227–236. IEEE Computer Society, 2008.

[18] N. Mi, Q. Zhang, A. Riska, E. Smirni, and E. Riedel. Performance impacts of autocorrelated flows in multi-tiered systems. *Perform. Eval.*, 64(9-12):1082–1101, 2007.

[19] M. F. Neuts. The caudal characteristic curve of queues. *Adv. Appl. Prob.*, 18:221–254, 1986.

[20] M. F. Neuts. *Structured Stochastic Matrices of M/G/1 Type and Their Applications.* Marcel Dekker, New York, 1989.

[21] B. Pittel. Closed exponential networks of queues with saturation: the Jackson-type stationary distribution and its asymptotic analysis. *Math. Oper. Res.*, 4:357–378, 1979.

[22] M. Reiser. A queueing network analysis of computer communication networks with window flow control. *IEEE Trans. on Communications*, 27(8):1199–1209, 1979.

[23] A. Riska and E. Smirni. MAMsolver: A matrix analytic methods tool. In *Proc. of TOOLS, pp. 205–211.* Springer-Verlag, 2002, http://www.cs.wm.edu/MAMSolver/.

[24] A. Riska, V. Diev, and E. Smirni. An EM-based technique for approximating long-tailed data sets with PH distributions. *Perform. Eval.*, 55(1-2):147–164, Jan. 2004.

[25] R. Sadre and B. R. Haverkort. Fifiqueues: Fixed-point analysis of queueing networks with finite-buffer stations. In *Proc. of MMB*, pages 77–80, 1999.

[26] W. Whitt. The queueing network analyzer. *The bell system tech. journal*, 62(9):2779–2815, Nov. 1983.

[27] J. Zahorjan, E. D. Lazowska, and R. L. Garner. A decomposition approach to modelling high service time variability. *Perform. Eval.*, 3:35–54, 1983.

[28] Z. Zheng and M. R. Lyu. Collaborative reliability prediction of service-oriented systems. In *Proc. of ACM ICSE*, pp. 35–44, May 2010.

APPENDIX

A. ASYMPTOTIC DISTRIBUTIONS

The exact asymptotic distribution of the conditional distribution in a $PH/PH/1$ queue is known to exist from equation (2), i.e.,

$$
\begin{aligned}
\widetilde{\boldsymbol{\theta}} = \boldsymbol{\theta} &= \lim_{n\to\infty} \frac{\boldsymbol{\pi}(n)}{\boldsymbol{\pi}(n)\mathbf{1}} \\
&= \lim_{n\to\infty} \frac{\boldsymbol{\pi}(1)\boldsymbol{R}^{n-1}}{\boldsymbol{\pi}(1)\boldsymbol{R}^{n-1}\mathbf{1}} \\
&= \lim_{n\to\infty} \frac{\boldsymbol{\pi}(1)\eta^{n-1}\boldsymbol{\Pi}}{\boldsymbol{\pi}(1)\eta^{n-1}\mathbf{1}} \\
&= \frac{\boldsymbol{\pi}(1)\boldsymbol{r}}{\boldsymbol{\pi}(1)\mathbf{1}}\boldsymbol{\ell}
\end{aligned}
$$

Thus, $\boldsymbol{\theta}$ is a left-Perron-eigenvector of $\boldsymbol{R}$ (parallel to $\boldsymbol{\ell}$) and so, by the previous assumption, $\boldsymbol{\theta R} = \boldsymbol{\theta}\eta\boldsymbol{\Pi} = \eta\boldsymbol{\theta}$. Thus $\boldsymbol{\theta\Pi} = \boldsymbol{\theta}$. Notice that $\boldsymbol{\Pi}$ is the spectral projector for the $\boldsymbol{R}$ matrix associated with the *exact* solution $\boldsymbol{\pi}(n)$.

B. PROOF OF PROPOSITION 1

The normalizing constant may be written as

$$
G(M,N) = \sum_S \prod_{i=1}^{M} [(1-\rho_i)(1-\delta(n_i)) + \rho_i(1-\eta_i)\eta_i^{n_i-1}\delta(n_i)]
$$

where $\delta(n_i) = 1$ if $n_i \geq 1$, 0 otherwise. Observe now that

$$
\begin{aligned}
G(M,N) &= \sum_{(n_1,\ldots,n_M):n_M=0} (1-\rho_M)\prod_{i=1}^{M-1} x_i(n_i) \\
&+ \sum_{(n_1,\ldots,n_M):n_M\geq 1} \rho_M(1-\eta_M)\eta_M^{n_M-1}\prod_{i=1}^{M-1} x_i(n_i) \quad (12)
\end{aligned}
$$

where $x_i(n_i) = (1-\rho_i)(1-\delta(n_i)) + \rho_i(1-\eta_i)\eta_i^{n_i-1}$. Factoring out of the two summations $(1-\rho_M)$ and ρ_M, respectively, the right-hand side terms are, by definition, $G(M-1,N)$ and $G^{aux}(M,N-1)$, respectively. The terminations conditions also follow immediately by definition of G and G^{aux}. $\square$

Analysis of Bursty Workload-aware Self-adaptive Systems

Diego Perez-Palacin
Dpt. de Informática e
Ingeniería de Sistemas
Universidad de Zaragoza
Zaragoza, Spain
diegop@unizar.es

José Merseguer
Dpt. de Informática e
Ingeniería de Sistemas
Universidad de Zaragoza
Zaragoza, Spain
jmerse@unizar.es

Raffaela Mirandola
Dip. di Elettronica e
Informazione
Politecnico di Milano
Milano, Italy
mirandola@elet.polimi.it

ABSTRACT

Software is often embedded in dynamic contexts where it is subjected to high variable, non-stable, and usually bursty workloads. A key requirement for a software system is to be able to self-react to workload changes by adapting its behavior dynamically, to ensure both the correct functionalities and the required performance. Research on fitting variable workload traces into formal models has been carried out using Markovian Modulated Poisson Processes (MMPP). These works concentrate on modeling stable workload states, but accurate modeling of transient times still deserves attention since they are critical moments for the self-adaptation. In this work, we build on research in the area of MMPP trace fitting and we propose a Petri net fine-grained model for highly variable workloads that also accounts for transient times. We analyze differences between models of adaptive software that accurately represent workload state changes and models that do not. We evaluate their performance and availability and compare the results.

Categories and Subject Descriptors

C.4 [**Performance of Systems**]: [Modeling Techniques]; D.2.2 [**Software Engineering**]: Design Tools and Techniques—*Petri nets*

General Terms

Design, Performance

Keywords

Self-adaptive software, Bursty workload, Markovian models

1. INTRODUCTION

Software is often embedded in dynamic contexts where it is subjected to changes in its execution environment, workload or requirements. Self-adaptive software allows capabilities to detect context changes and to react to them, managing its processing resources autonomously and allocating or releasing them dynamically. Among the multiple sources of change, in this work we deal with changes in the workload.

The workload, for some kind of systems, is far from being stable but it presents high variability and shows *burstiness*, i.e., irregular spikes of congestion. This is a fact for example in networked and service-based systems, but not only [10]. If the workload model does not account for the existing *burstiness*, then the model analysis can lead to optimistic results; e.g., it declares a fair resource utilizations and probability of congestion, while in the real setting they would not be guaranteed.

Some formal methods that can model workloads considering the *burstiness* in the arrival rate are the Markov Arrival Processes (MAP) and a concrete subtype of them, the Markov Modulated Poisson Process (MMPP) [5]. Research on workload and network traffic fitting using MAPs and MMPPs have been already done and their results show an accurate modeling of the workload variability.

In particular, work on fitting MMPP and MAP parameters from workload traces with *burstiness* is very useful for the analysis of properties, such as performance or availability, of a wide range of systems. However, when we observe self-adaptive systems carefully, we realize that their optimal configurations are different depending on the workload they are receiving. These systems should adapt (e.g., provisioning or release of resources) during the *transient periods*, i.e., when the workload is becoming *bursty* and when the burst of arrivals is finishing. Usually there is no need for a software to change its context during stable periods of workload, it should have been adequately provisioned before, in fact during these transient periods.

Therefore, to properly analyze the performance or availability of self-adaptive systems, we need an accurate model of the workload. This model should include the transient times, even when they correspond to a small percentage of the total time (the rates normal and burst can last for hours while the change between them lasts just some minutes). Otherwise, results from model-based system analysis can be far away from results of the real working system. The reason is that the system starts the adaptation when anticipates the workload is close to be *bursty*. In this way, when the burst of requests arrive, the system is already in its optimal configuration. However, a system model whose workload does not care about transient times is not able to anticipate any workload change, and it will start its adaptations when the bursts of requests are already arriving. This can lead to too pessimistic performance and availability results from the model analysis.

In this work, we propose a model to take into account these transient periods. We exploit the research already done for two-state MMPP fitting and we aggregate to this MMPP a submodel of the transient times between normal arrival rate and bursty rates. Using the aggregation of models, we are able to analyze more accurately the non functional properties (NFP) of the software. To this end we build on the work done in [6, 2] for MMPP and MAP parameter fitting and we extend the generated models to be able to deal with self-adaptation.

Related Work.

The parameter fitting of Markovian models such as MMPPs and MAPs is a promising research field. For example, works [7, 8, 11, 6, 15, 3, 2] propose MAP and MMPP parameter fitting techiques starting from traffic traces. Some of these fitting works also deal with the modeling of burstiness characteristic and use the index of dispersion as burstiness estimator.

In our work we build on the results obtained in [6, 2] to choose the estimators of the workload trace and fit a two-sate MMPP that models the same characteristics as the workload trace for these estimators. However, to the best of our knowledge, our work is the first one modeling the transient times between workload states and using them when evaluating workload-aware self-adaptive systems.

Paper Organization.

The paper is organized as follows: Section 2 describes MAPs, MMPPs and their parameter fitting from a workload trace. Section 3 explains the meaning of the *transient* time and proposes a model for its representation. In Section 4 we put together the MMPPs model and the new model for the transient time and we present the complete workload model of their aggregation. Section 5 presents an experimental analysis that shows the difference between considering or not the transient time in the workload model by evaluating the performance and availability requirements of a self-adaptive system. Section 6 concludes the paper.

2. MMPP'S AND MAP'S

Accurate characterization of real workload traces is a need to devise a proper workload model. For some kind of systems, e.g. networked ones, such characterization should capture the high variability of the requests as well as the fact that they *burst* in on the system sometimes [10].

MMPPs are suitable to model variability and autocorrelation for event generation. An MMPP is a stochastic process that has been extensively used to model event arrivals processes and network traffic [5, 6, 7], which is able to represent high variability and temporal dependencies in the arrivals. In an MMPP, the arrival rate at each moment is determined by the state of a continuous-time Markov chain (CTMC). So, when the chain is in state i, the arrival process is a Poisson process with rate λ_i. An MMPP with N states is defined by a NxN matrix Σ representing the CTMC and a vector Λ of N components representing the arrival rates in each state.

$$\Sigma = \begin{pmatrix} -\sigma_{11} & \sigma_{12} & ... & \sigma_{1N} \\ \sigma_{21} & -\sigma_{22} & ... & \sigma_{2N} \\ & & ... & \\ \sigma_{N1} & \sigma_{N2} & ... & -\sigma_{NN} \end{pmatrix}, \Lambda = (\lambda_1, ..., \lambda_N),$$

where $\forall\, i, j, \quad \sigma_{ij} \geq 0, \quad \lambda_i \geq 0$ and $\forall\, i, \sum_{j:j\neq i} \sigma_{ij} = \sigma_{ii}$.

In this work, we consider MMPPs with two states. One of the states will represent the normal arrival rate (and we call it *normal*) and the other will represent the bursty arrival rate (and we call it *bursty*). A graphical representation of this two-state MMPP is given in Figure 1. λ_1, the *normal* arrival rate, and λ_2, the *bursty* arrival rate, are supposed to be much higher than transitions rates σ_{12} and σ_{21}.

A two-state MAP, Figure 2, can be seen as a continuous time Markov chain of two states, and the active state defines the arrival

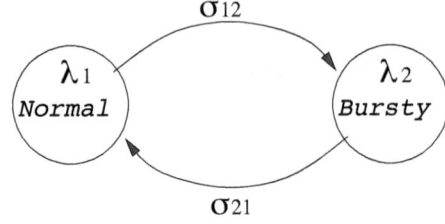

Figure 1: A two states MMPP

rate. In the chain, there can be transitions associated with the arrival of an event (called *completion* transitions, λ_{ij}, darker in the figure) and transitions that are not associated with event arrival (called *background* transitions, σ_{ij}). Moreover, when the chain is in state i, it can also generate arrivals with rate λ_{ii} without changing its state, modeled as a self-transition, λ_{ii}.

Formally, a MAP can be defined by two squared matrices D0 and D1, where $D0_{ij}, i \neq j$ represents the *background* transition rates from state i to j, $D1_{ij}$ describes *completion* transition rates, and $D0_{ii} = -(\sum_{j:j\neq i} D0_{ij} + \sum_j D1_{ij})$. Thus, $Q = D0 + D1$ is the infinitesimal generator matrix of the chain.

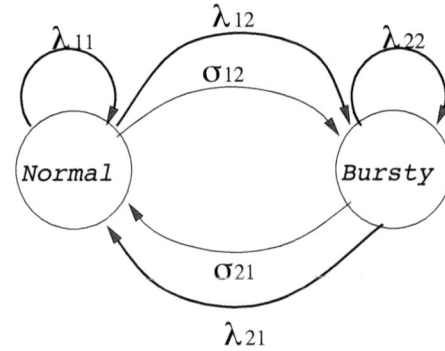

Figure 2: A two states MAP

An MMPP is a MAP that do not admit completion transitions that change the CTMC state, i.e., the elements not in the diagonal of $D1$ must be zero. Then, a two-state MMPP can be seen as a MAP whose matrices D0 and D1 are:

$$D0 = \begin{pmatrix} -(\sigma_{12} + \lambda_1) & \sigma_{12} \\ \sigma_{21} & -(\sigma_{21} + \lambda_2) \end{pmatrix}, D1 = diag(\Lambda)$$

2.1 MMPP fitting from a workload trace

Finding the characterizing values of a trace.

To fit a real workload trace to a two-state MMPP we just need to set its four parameters: $\lambda_1, \lambda_2, \sigma_{12}, \sigma_{21}$. To this end, we will use four characterizing values from the workload trace.

The first value is the *index of dispersion for counts* (IDC) of the trace. The IDC is frequently used as an estimator of the *burstiness* in a trace. The higher IDC value is, the more *burstiness* the trace has. In [6, 7] it is calculated as

$$IDC_t = \frac{var(N_t)}{E(N_t)}$$

where N_t is the number of arrival in an interval of t time units. So, the IDC is the variance in the number of arrivals in t time units divided by the mean number of arrivals in t time units. Since we are interested in the index of dispersion of arrivals in the steady state, we calculate

$$\lim_{t \to +\infty} IDC_t$$

To calculate the IDC we use the algorithm presented in [9, 2]. This algorithm is able to estimate the index of dispersion $IDC_{t \to +\infty}$ of a single workload trace.

For the rest of the characterizing values we take advantage of the work in [2], that indeed fits workload traces to MAP caring about the burstiness. Besides the IDC, these values are: the mean inter-arrival time of requests (m), the 50th percentile (i.e, the median) and the 95th percentile. Since in that work the authors are characterizing the burstiness of service times, the burstiness happens for high values of these service times, then making important to know the value for which the 95% of service times are lower. However, we are dealing with inter-arrival times, and the burstiness happens when the values of inter-arrival times are low. So, we prefer to know the value for which the 95% of times the inter-arrival time is higher than. For this reason, we use the 5th percentile instead of their 95th.

Experiment proposed.

As example of workload trace, we have used the monitored arrival times of requests to the FIFA 1998 World Cup site [16]. This has been the most complete example of workload trace we have been able to find. The timestamps are provided with granularity of one second and we have just used the requests that arrived to the Paris server region. Figure 3 shows the count of requests received by this region per minute. Since the workload was very low when the system was started and also the last days after the world cup, we have just concentrated in the middle days. We have used the arrivals of 34.7 consecutive days, then from minute 60,000 until minute 110,000. The arrivals in these 50,000 minutes have been considered in groups of 10 seconds and they are depicted in Figure 4. It is easy to see that the shape of the graph depicts a quite bursty workload. The selection of this time interval is not a restriction just to make the fitting algorithm work better but it exemplifies the kind of workloads we are really interested in. Since we are dealing with systems that are intended to continue working in the long term, we assume that the workload should not start and finish being low (as it happened to the World Cup website), but be always in the normal regime. So, we consider the first and last minutes as the system warm up and cool down, and we consider only the world cup days where the system was most used.

Fitting MMPP parameters.

The characterizing values of the trace are the following. The number of requests that we have dealt with is 140,998,569. The mean inter-arrival time of requests is 0.021276 seconds (i.e, close to 47 requests per second), calculated as the number of received requests divided by $3 \cdot 10^6$ (the amount of seconds in 50,000 minutes). The median (percentile 50th) of the inter-arrival times is 0.0159744408 and the 5th percentile is 0.00367 (this is, the inter-arrival time of the 95% of requests was higher than this value). The IDC is 686,200, we admitted a tolerance of $1 \cdot 10^{-7}$ for its calculation using the algorithm in [2]. The amount of time that the

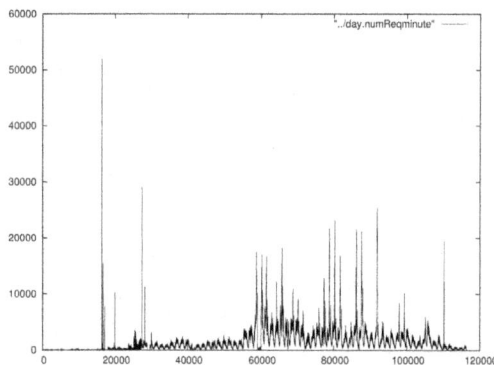

Figure 3: Requests per minute received in Paris region

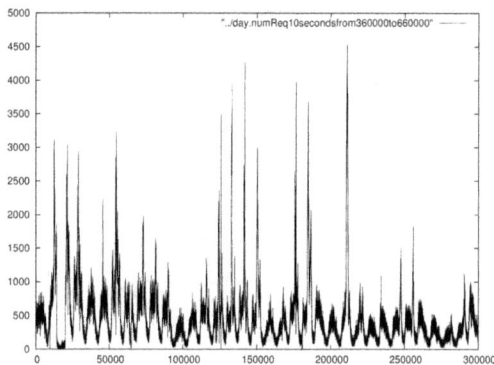

Figure 4: Requests every 10 seconds

algorithm considered approximate to infinite and for which the algorithm stopped was 45,140 seconds.

From these characterizing values, we fitted the MMPP. To fit the mean, 50th and 5th percentiles we have used the same equations as [2]. To fit the ICD, we have used the equation in [6, 7] that concretely deal with two-state MMPP parameters[1].

The results are:

$$\sigma_{11} = \sigma_{12} = 0.0000001314169$$

$$\sigma_{22} = \sigma_{21} = 0.0000273058047$$

$$\lambda_1 = 45.5395329586$$

$$\lambda_2 = 350.195877$$

As expected, we can see that the mean sojourn time in each state, $\sigma_{12}^{-1}, \sigma_{21}^{-1}$, is orders of magnitude higher than the mean requests inter-arrival times, $\lambda_1^{-1}, \lambda_2^{-1}$.

---

[1]This equation is $IDC_{t \to +\infty} = 1 + \frac{2\sigma_{12}\sigma_{21}(\lambda_1 - \lambda_2)^2}{(\sigma_{12} + \sigma_{21})^2(\lambda_1\sigma_{21} + \lambda_2\sigma_{12})}$

2.2 GSPN workload model

An accurate workload model with burstiness, as the one proposed by the MMPP, is a necessary and very useful tool for the eventual analysis of systems that execute under such conditions.

GSPNs [1] are broadly used to model the behavior and workload of systems and also as analyzable models to predict properties of software systems. GSPNs have already been used to analyze some properties of self-adaptive software systems, such as performance and energy [13, 12, 14]. Since our workload model should represent the injection of requests in the system in the same language as the behavioral system model, we pursue the proposed MMPP workload model but in terms of GSPN.

Since both GSPNs and MMPPs represent markovian processes, we can get a GSPN with the same behavior as the MMPP in a quite straightforward manner. This GSPN, the one in Fig. 5 representing the two state MMPP in Fig. 1, has as many places as states the MMPP, in this case P_1 and P_2 (for *normal* and *bursty*, respectively). Another place, $P_{arrivals}$, will mean the injection of requests in the system, i.e. injection of tokens in the GSPN that represents the behavior of the self-adaptive system. The time transitions T_{12} and T_{21} represent the MMPP change of state, then their firing rates are σ_{12} and σ_{21} obviously. The last two transitions, $T_{arrival1}$ and $T_{arrival2}$, represent the arrival rates in the MMPP, therefore their firing rates are λ_1 and λ_2 and they feed the $P_{arrivals}$ place.

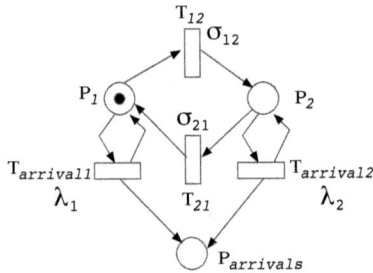

Figure 5: GSPN for the two states MMPP

3. MODELING TRANSIENT TIME BETWEEN STATES

3.1 Problem statement

As declared in the Introduction, a self-adaptive system needs some time to perform corrective actions (e.g., provisioning or release of resources) to fit into the new execution context. In systems whose adaptations depend on the workload variations, such adaptations should happen when the system changes from *normal* to *bursty* or vice versa, i.e., the system adapts to the environment during the transient times between states.

When looking at the real workload trace in Figure 6 we observe that such transient time, although fast, is not immediate, it lasts for around 41.6 minutes, starting around 850 and ending around 1100 ($\frac{1100-850}{6} = 41.6$). The figure shows a period of 250 minutes which corresponds to the zoom in the range from 209,500 to 211,000 in Figure 4. The transient time is assumed to be fast w.r.t. the mean sojourn time in each stable state that last for many hours. Our workload model should reflect the transient time accurately since in this period the self-adaptive system:

- perceives that the workload is leaving the normal state and the burst of arrivals are near to arrive, and

- performs its adaptations to change its configuration to a new one able to withstand the burst of requests.

In a two-state MMPP the transient time is not modeled as we can see in Figure 7. This figure represents a workload trace generated by the fitted MMPP in Section 2 and we observe that the change from *normal* state (arrival rate around 455 requests each 10 seconds) to *bursty* state (around 3500 requests during 10 seconds) is abrupt, no transient time is perceived.

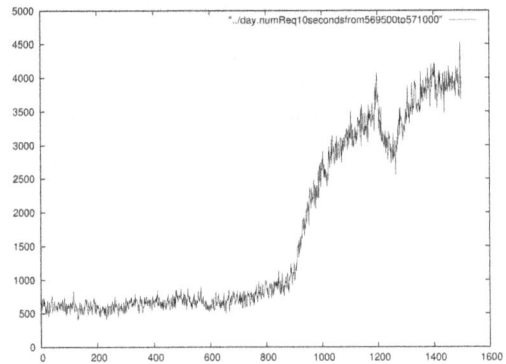

Figure 6: Real workload trace: focus on the increment

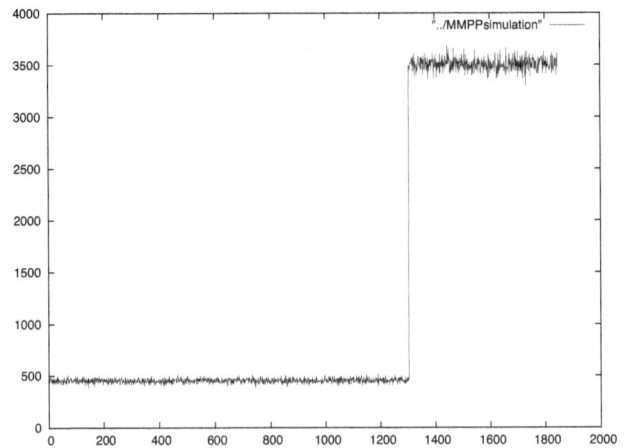

Figure 7: Workload trace modeled by the MMPP

3.2 Setting parameters of workload model

We pursue a GSPN to model the transient times in the real workload trace, i.e., the increments and decrements in the arrival rates of the requests. The zones of increment or decrement can be characterized by three parameters:

- the well-known λ_1 and λ_2,

- the amplitude of the zone, we call it mt_{inc} or mt_{dec}, they are measured in seconds, and they represent the mean amount of time that the workload is increasing from *normal* state to *bursty* state or decreasing from *bursty* to *normal* respectively,

- and additionally, from these parameters we can also calculate the acceleration of the curve in the zone, mr_{inc} or mr_{dec}, in $requests \cdot seconds^{-2}$.

In the following we describe how these parameters can be obtained from a real workload trace. Algorithm 1 shows the case of the calculation of the mean amount of time that the workload is increasing.

First (line 1 in Algorithm 1), we apply the technique presented in Section 2.1 to get λ_1 and λ_2.

Second (line 2), we go all over the counts[2] in the workload trace. Let us call $count_j$ the number of requests received by the count in position j. We find each j such that $count_{j-1} < \lambda_1 \leq count_j$, we call it $candidate_j$. That is, the candidates are the counts where the arrival rate has changed from being under the mean for the *normal* state to be over the mean.

Third (lines 3..9), for the first $candidate_j$ we find the first k, $k > j$, such that $(\lambda_1 > count_k) \vee (count_k > \lambda_2)$.

- If the first condition holds, we can discard $candidate_j$ since it means that the workload is not incrementing, but it had just exceeded the mean for a while and it has returned under the mean again (this is the usual behavior when the workload is in a stable state).

- If the second condition holds, we keep $candidate_j$ since we could have found a period of increment in the workload from *normal* to *bursty* arrival rates, this period is $[j, k]$.

Fourth (lines 10..17), for each $[j, k]$ period we have to discover whether it can be considered as a real workload increment or not. We assume that a real increment happens when the counts between $[j, k]$ increase constantly in a *coarse-grained* view of the workload.

As *coarse-grained* we mean that we zoom-out the counts in order to mask the short-term variability. To create the *coarse-grained* view, we reduce the $k - j$ monitored counts to N values, where each $N_n, 0 \leq n < N < (k - j)$, counts the number of arrivals in a period of length L. L is a choice and represents how much coarse will be the study. A too low L will not avoid the short-term variability (and then we will not realize that the workload is truly increasing), and a too big L will recognize as periods of constant increment some that should not be. Once L value is chosen, N is calculated as the largest value for which $N \cdot L \leq (k - j)$, i.e, $(k - j) < (N + 1) \cdot L$. If $N \cdot L \neq (k - j)$, we obviate in the study the last values $k - j - N \cdot L$ of the interval, that is, the interval to work changes from $[j, k]$ to $[j, j + N \cdot L]$. Now, we sum up in N_n the values of each group of L counts. Therefore, $N_n = \sum_{i=0}^{L-1} (count_{n \cdot L + j + i})$.

To finish the fourth step, we decide that $[j, k]$ is a real constant increment. Ideally, a constant increment happens if the number of counts N_n are increasing values, i.e, if $\forall n \in \{1..N-1\}$, $N_{n-1} < N_n$. However, we found that in every increment interval in the trace, there is at least one unexpected count of arrivals that is very different from its neighbor counts (too less or too much) that are also visible in the coarse-grained view. This unexpected count prevents satisfying the *for all* in the previous condition. To solve it, we add a percentage of tolerance $tol \in \mathbb{R}$, $0 \leq tol \leq 1$. Then, the amount of counts N_n, $n \in \{1..N-1\}$ that must satisfy the

condition $N_{n-1} < N_n$ is reduced from $N - 1$ (i.e, all counts) to $(1 - tol)(N - 1)$.

Fifth, if it has been decided that the interval represents a constant increment in the coarse-grained view, we get a parameter to characterize the interval $[j, k]$: the amplitude $t_{inc} = k - j$. Besides, we can derive more parameters from the interval such as the acceleration r_{inc} in the request arrival, calculated from λ_1, λ_2 and t_{inc} as $r_{inc} = \frac{\lambda_2 - \lambda_1}{t_{inc}}$.

Sixth, we repeat the third, fourth and fifth steps for all $candidate_j$.

Finally, using the discovered t_{inc} and derived r_{inc} in each iteration, we get the values of mt_{inc} and mr_{inc} as the mean of them (lines 18..23).

Algorithm 1 Parameter estimation

Require: Workload trace with the *count* of arrivals
Ensure: mt_{inc}
1: $(\lambda_1, \lambda_2) \leftarrow$ MMPPfitting($count$);
2: $candidates \leftarrow$ findCandidates($count, \lambda_1$);
3: $intervals \leftarrow \emptyset$;
4: **for all** $candidate \in candidates$ **do**
5:    $k \leftarrow$ getFirstCrossingValue($count, candidate, \lambda_1, \lambda_2$);
6:    **if** $count_k > \lambda_2$ **then**
7:       $intervals \leftarrow$ addInterval($intervals$, [$candidate, k$]);
8:    **end if**
9: **end for**
10: $L \leftarrow$ chooseL(); $tol \leftarrow$ chooseTol();
11: **for all** $interval \in intervals$ **do**
12:    $N \leftarrow$ calculateN($L, interval$);
13:    $subtrace \leftarrow$ makeCoarse($trace, interval, N$);
14:    **if not** isContinuousIncrement($subtrace, tol$) **then**
15:       $intervals \leftarrow$ discardInterval($intervals, interval$);
16:    **end if**
17: **end for**
18: $numberOfIntervals \leftarrow 0$; $incrTime \leftarrow 0$;
19: **for all** $interval \in intervals$ **do**
20:    $incrTime \leftarrow incrTime + interval.amplitude$;
21:    $numberOfIntervals \leftarrow numberOfIntervals + 1$;
22: **end for**
23: $mt_{inc} \leftarrow \frac{incrTime}{numberOfIntervals}$;
24: **return** mt_{inc}

We perform the same steps to discover the periods of time where the workload is decreasing. Using these periods, we will obtain mt_{dec} and mr_{dec}.

Note that mr_{inc} and mr_{dec} are real positive values ($\mathbb{R}^+$). So, we are assuming a constant acceleration and deceleration in the workload during transient time. On the one hand, this linear increment in the arrival rate is more accurate than the previously assumed immediate increment. Besides, the linearity in the increment/decrement corresponds to the long-term view of the increment, since we are still modeling the variability in the short-term. On the other hand, we are approximating to be linear any workload increment/decrement between states. Other possible representations of the workload increment/decrement are possible, but the identification of the kind of increment in the coarse-grained view is more complicated since we would also come into the field of curve fitting.

3.3 GSPN model for the transient time

The GSPNs in Figure 8 (a) and (b) model the transient time from *normal* to *burst* (increment in the arrival rate of requests) and from *burst* to *normal* (decrement in the arrival rate of requests), respectively.

---

[2]Remember that a count means the number of requests received in 10 seconds.

GSPN model: from normal to burst.

A key point is that, during the transient period, the arrival of requests are modeled as tokens created in place $P_{arrivals}$ at a variable rate. This rate will be $\lambda_1 + \lambda_{inc} \cdot \#P_{inc2}$ since transitions $T_{arrival1'}$ and $T_{arrivalInc}$ provide the tokens[3]. The former transition generates the workload of the *normal* state, λ_1, while the latter transition generates the increment of requests[4].

A token in P_{inc1} means that the system enters in the transient state so leaving the *normal* one. Then, every σ_{inc} units of time a new token is set in P_{inc2} to precisely generate the increment of requests. When the number of tokens in P_{inc2} is w_1, it means that the transient time has completed and the system enters in the *bursty* state P_2 by firing transition t_{inc2}.

Although not yet observed in the figure, transition t_{12} will fire when the normal arrival rate of request in the system has finished, hence to start this transient period.

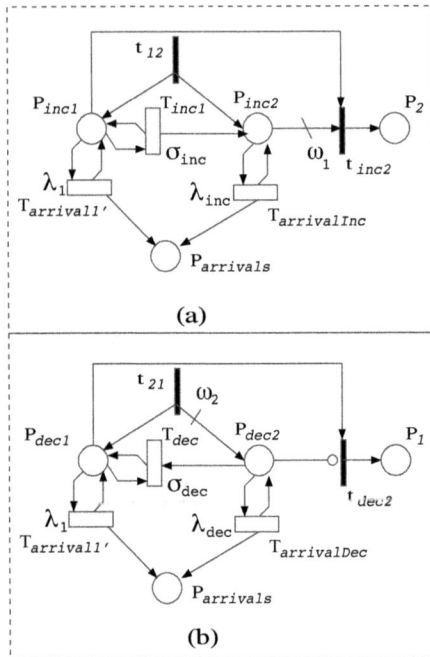

Figure 8: GSPNs: (a)increasing and (b)decreasing arrival rates of requests

Fitting GSPN parameters.

We use the four parameters computed in the previous subsection, λ_1, λ_2, mr_{inc} and mt_{inc}, to set the parameters of the GSPN, $w_1, \lambda_{inc}, \sigma_{inc}$.

First, note that the modeling of transient times increases the state space for the analysis. Fortunately, we can decide the amount of increment we allow. For the transient time that models the change from *normal* to *bursty*, the state space grows linearly with parameter $w_1 \geq 1$, and we can freely decide its value. The rationale is that w_1 corresponds with the amount of token variability in P_{inc2}. Then, observe that P_{inc2} can have tangible markings in the interval $[0, w_1 - 1]$, while markings where $\#P_{inc2} = w_1$ are vanishing

---

[3] $\#P_i$ is the number of tokens in place P_i.

[4] It is worth noting that we are considering *infinite server* semantic for all transitions

and do not affect for the state space analysis. This allowed variability entails that we model $w_1 - 1$ increments in the workload between λ_1 and λ_2. So, each token will increase the arrival rate in $inc = \frac{\lambda_2 - \lambda_1}{w_1}$ units. This inc is the value of λ_{inc}. Finally, we calculate how fast are created the tokens in P_{inc2}, this is, we calculate σ_{inc} of T_{inc1}. This transition fires $w_1 - 1$ times for each transient period, and it should fire in mt_{inc} time units. So its firing rate $\sigma_{inc} = \frac{w_1 - 1}{mt_{inc}}$.

Now it can be easily seen that we preserve the short term variability in the workload increment since the arrival rate is still based on stochastic processes exponentially distributed.

GSPN model: from burst to normal.

The differences between this model, in Figure 8 (b), and the previous one are:

- t_{21} starts this transient state by setting w_2 tokens in P_{dec2}. Again, parameter w_2 represents the amount of complexity we can afford to model the decrementing period in the workload. The size of the state space will be $w_2 + 1$ times the state space of the workload model without decrementing period.

- Tokens in P_{dec2} decrease at rate σ_{dec}, when P_{dec2} is empty the system enters in the *normal* state P_2. The σ_{dec} firing rate is $\frac{w_2}{mt_{dec}}$.

- The transient state generates requests at rate

$$\lambda_1 + \lambda_{dec} \cdot \#P_{dec2}.$$

Where λ_{dec} is $\frac{\lambda_2 - \lambda_1}{w_1}$.

4. COMPREHENSIVE WORKLOAD MODEL

So far we have proposed GSPN models separately, one model for the two characteristic states, in Figure 5, and two for the transient times, the increment of the workload in Figure 8(a) and the decrement in Figure 8(b). Our challenge now is to merge these three GSPN models to get a single one that cares for burstiness and transient times as required by self-adaptive systems.

Before merging the GSPNs we need to slightly modify the net of Figure 5: we remove the arc from T_{12} to P_2 and the arc from T_{21} to P_1. The rationale behind this modification is that we want to avoid the immediate change between *normal*, P_1, and *burst*, P_2, and vice versa.

The resulting GSPN is the one in Figure 9. We have used the composition operator for GSPNs formally defined in [4]. The essence of the operator is easy to understand, it overlaps the transitions (places) with the same name. For example, the place $P_{arrivals}$ appears in the three nets, however in the resulting net it appears only once, having as input arcs all the input arcs of the three original places.

The expert reader can argue that the GSPN in Figure 9 can be equivalent to a M-state MMPP where $M = 1 + w_1 + w_2$. In that case, the parameters of that M-state MMPP with the same characteristics as our workload model would be:

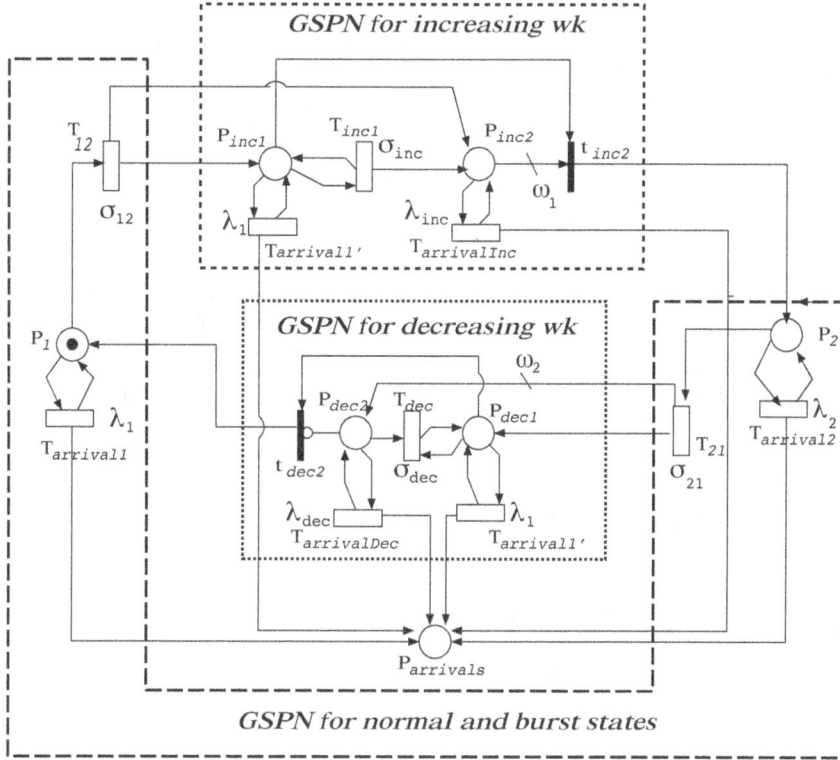

Figure 9: Complete workload model

$$\Sigma = \begin{pmatrix} -\sigma_{11} & \sigma_{12} & 0 & ... & & & 0 \\ 0 & -\sigma_{inc} & \sigma_{inc} & 0 & ... & & 0 \\ & & ... & & ... & & ... \\ 0... & 0 & -\sigma_{22} & \sigma_{22} & 0 & ... & 0 \\ 0... & & 0 & -\sigma_{dec} & \sigma_{dec} & 0 & ... & 0 \\ & & ... & & ... & & ... \\ 0... & & & & 0 & -\sigma_{dec} & \sigma_{dec} \\ \sigma_{dec} & 0... & & & & 0 & -\sigma_{dec} \end{pmatrix}$$

$$\Lambda = (\ \lambda_1, \lambda_1 + \lambda_{inc}, ..., \lambda_1 + (w_1 - 1)\lambda_{inc}, \lambda_2, \lambda_1 + w_2 \lambda_{dec}, ..., \lambda_1 + \lambda_{dec})$$

Then, a question arise: could that M-state MMPP be directly obtained from the workload trace using the technique presented in Section 2 for two-state MMPP?

The answer is yes. Nevertheless, there are some restrictive challenges to obtain the characterizing values of a M-state MMPP. These are: the algorithm to fit parameters of a M-state MMPP is much more time consuming and the estimation of its parameters are much more prone to inaccuracies. Moreover the current techniques to fit MMPP parameters do not directly deal with our problem (gaining accuracy in the transient times models).

5. EXPERIMENTAL ANALYSIS

In this section, we illustrate the results obtained in our experimentation. To this end we have considered a very simple sys-

tem with different workload models: first MMPPs and second our GSPN model, that includes the transient time between workload states. A third experiment is used as a benchmark for comparing the accuracy of the obtained results, it is a system simulation having a real workload trace, the one in Figure 4.

The system we use in this experimentation is a very simple software made of only one activity that requires on average 3ms of processing time [5]. There is a single processor executing a maximum of ten concurrent requests, queueing and serving them following a FIFO policy. Requests above ten are rejected.

We assume that requirements to architect the system are:

- R1- availability: *at least 99% of requests must be served, and*

- R2- performance: *the mean response time should be lower than 1 second.*

Note that the response time is not a critical requirement, since the maximum length of queue of requests to be served is nine, and they are served in a mean of 3ms. On the contrary, requirement R1 is the critical one.

When we analyzed the system considering a workload model without burstiness (i.e., taking into account the mean inter-arrival time derived from the real trace), the requirements were satisfied.

On the contrary, when taking into account the arrival in bursts, the analysis of the system showed that R1 cannot be guaranteed.

---

[5]To be able to compare approaches without including more variables that can distort results, we assume that the mentioned processing time is exponentially distributed with mean 3ms

A possible solution passes through the addition of a second processing resource. Now, having two processing resources, the system is able to satisfy both R1 and R2 also during bursty periods. However, the second processing resource has been added just to allow the requirements satisfaction during the periods of burstiness, which represents the worst-case scenario for the system. So, during the normal arrival rate periods, there is a wasting of resources.

We can use the model proposed in Section 3 to take into account the workload variability. To this end, we consider a system enhanced with a monitoring component. The monitor is a passive observer that measures the system workload. Then, the monitor notifies to a separate component, which acts as a controller, when the workload is changing and when to add a second processing resource. In the same way, it also decides to switch off one of the processing resources when the workload decreases. So, the system deployment is no longer static but it is dynamically adaptable.

We have set the following parameters for the self-adaptive system:

- The maximum arrival rate of requests that can be served by only one processing resource is the 80% of its maximum capacity. In other words, the controller decides to add a new processing resource when the workload goes above $\frac{1}{3ms}$ · $0.8 \approx 266$ requests per second.

- The maximum arrival rate of requests that can be served using both processing resources is 40 requests per second. When the workload rate is under this value, the second processing resource is shut down.

- Booting and shutting down times of the processing resources is one minute.

In the following, we explain the set-up of each experiment and the obtained results. After, we compare and discuss results.

MMPP workload model.
As MMPP workload we used the one already calculated in Section 2. We composed the MMPP model, in GSPN terms, with the GSPN that models the behavior of the described system. We analyzed the resulting GSPN and obtained the following results:
The percentage of requests rejected is 1.43%, so the availability is 98.56%; and the mean response time is 5.3ms.
Then, R2 is satisfied while R1 cannot be guaranteed.

MMPP with transient times workload model.
Using the MMPP parameters already calculated in Section 2 we applied the process described in Section 3 to identify in the trace in Figure 4 periods of coarse-grained-constantly-increasing workload.

The parameters L and tol have been set to 5 minutes and to 0.2, respectively. Then, the workload parameters mt_{inc}, mr_{inc}, mt_{dec} and mr_{dec} are:

$$mt_{inc} = 5192s \quad mr_{inc} = 0.58 requests \cdot s^{-2}$$

$$mt_{dec} = 3770s \quad mr_{dec} = -0.8081 requests \cdot s^{-2}$$

Following the procedure described in Section 3 we defined the structure of the GSPN models for the transient times. We then used the previous results as parameters of these GSPN models.

To complete the model definition, we decided the amount of affordable increment in the state space as $w_1 = 10, w_2 = 9$. Using these values, the remaining GSPNs parameters $w_1, \lambda_{inc}, \sigma_{inc}, w_2, \lambda_{dec}$ and σ_{dec} have been derived.

The GSPN modeling the workload has been obtained as described in Section 4 by composing the MMPP part with the GSPN derived for the transient times. Next, we composed the GSPN workload model with the GSPN that represents the behavior of the system. We analyzed this GSPN and we obtained the following results:
The percentage of requests rejected is 0.56%, so the availability is 99.44%; and the mean response time is 5ms.
Hence, R1 and R2 are satisfied.

Real workload trace execution.
For validation purpose, we have implemented a simulator of the system described in the example. We run the simulator and we injected the requests following the real workload trace.

We have obtained the following results:
The percentage of requests rejected is 0.05%, so the availability is 99.95%; and the mean response time is 3.7ms.
With the simulation and the real workload both requirements are satisfied.

	MMPP	MMPP with transient times	Real trace
Availability	98.56%	99.44%	99.95%
Performance	5.3ms	5ms	3.7ms

Table 1: Evaluation results with different input workload

5.1 Results discussion

Looking at Table 1 we can observe that the results obtained with both the MMPP model and MMPP with explicit transient time workload model are pessimistic with respect to the real ones. Indeed, the analysis of the models produced results showing lower availability and higher average response time with respect to the results obtained by the system simulation using the real workload trace. However, the results obtained with the MMPP including the transient time model are better than the ones obtained with the simple MMPP and closer to the system simulation results.

Actually, in this simple example we can see that the expected rejection probability of requests from model analysis with MMPP is $\frac{1.43}{0.05} = 28.6$ times higher than the calculated by simulating the real trace. Adding the transient times to the MMPP model, we have reduced this error to be $\frac{0.56}{0.05} = 11.2$ times higher; so, we have brought the result a 60% closer to the real one. Besides, the conclusion from the analysis of the model with MMPP workload would be that the proposed adaptive solution for the system does not satisfy availability requirement. This decision would be wrong because the actual system satisfies it.

Regarding the mean response time, adding the transient times to the MMPP model, we have just reduced the error of the results from being 1.43 times the real ones to be 1.35 times.

Note that, although all the experiments regarding requirement R1 seem to produce very similar results, this is not the case since availability is used to be measured as the "number of nines". In other words, if we compare a system with 99% of availability and another one with 99.9%, the latter is not just 0.9% more available than the first one but it is ten times more available. In our experiments, the availability obtained with the MMPP workload model without transient times resulted 28.6 times lower than the availability of the system with the real workload. Adding the transient time between states to the workload model we have been able to reduce the error of around the 60%, of course this is still not enough to guarantee results very close to the real ones.

6. CONCLUSION

Modern techniques to model high variable workloads and burstiness are based on Markovian models such as Markov Arrival Processes and Markov-Modulated Poisson Processes. They offer a powerful theory to model workload. Moreover, since they are based on Markovian processes, they can be easily included into the rest of the system model if it is also Markovian, such as the broadly used Markovian queueing networks or stochastic Petri nets. In this work we have identified a gap in the workload modeling for self-adaptive systems when using the MMPPs that makes inaccurate the analysis results. This gap refers to the modeling of the transient time between workload states.

This transient time is not modeled in MMPPs, because they focus on modeling stable workload states. Although these transient times may not be important for static systems, they are crucial when analyzing worklod-aware self-adaptive systems. To solve this challenge we have exploited previous results on MMPP fitting and we have proposed a model based on Petri Net taking into account the arrivals during the transient time between states. The obtained model has then been integrated in a Petri net describing the MMPP, so allowing a more complete representation of the workload.

A first experimentation comparing the results obtained with the proposed model and the classical MMPP models tested against a real trace workload, showed an increment in the analysis accuracy when the transient time are taken into account.

Besides, form our experimentation it is evident that, although we have reduced the errors in the analysis results, there is still a gap between model analysis results and real simulation ones.

At present, we are working on the implementation of our methodology on a real testbed, to assess its effectiveness through a more comprehensive set of real experiments. Another direction that deserves further investigation is the representation of the workload transient times when there are more than two stable states. Since the addition of the transient time models increases the state space of the model to analyze, if the MMPP that models the stable states has more than two states, it may not be possible to create the incrementing and decrementing transient time model between any two states. Contrarily, we should search which state transitions deserve attention to model their transient times and which ones do not deserve it.

Acknowledgments

This work has been partially supported by the European Community's Seventh Framework Programme under project DISC (Grant Agreement n. INFSO-ICT-224498), by CICYT DPI2010-20413, by Fundación Aragón I+D and by the IDEAS-ERC Project 227977-SMScom.

7. REFERENCES

[1] M. Ajmone Marsan, G. Balbo, G. Conte, S. Donatelli, and G. Franceschinis. *Modelling with Generalized Stochastic Petri Nets*. John Wiley Series in Parallel Computing - Chichester, 1995.

[2] G. Casale, N. Mi, L. Cherkasova, and E. Smirni. Dealing with burstiness in multi-tier applications: Models and their parameterization. *IEEE Trans. Software Eng. To appear*, 2012.

[3] G. Casale, E. Z. Zhang, and E. Smirni. Kpc-toolbox: Best recipes for automatic trace fitting using markovian arrival processes. *Perform. Eval.*, 67:873–896, September 2010.

[4] S. Donatelli and G. Franceschinis. PSR Methodology: integrating hardware and software models. In *ICATPN*, volume 1091 of *LNCS*, pages 133–152, 1996.

[5] W. Fischer and K. Meier-Hellstern. The Markov-modulated Poisson process (MMPP) cookbook. *Perform. Eval.*, 18:149–171, September 1993.

[6] R. Gusella. Characterizing the variability of arrival processes with indexes of dispersion. *Selected Areas in Communications, IEEE Journal on*, 9(2):203 –211, feb 1991.

[7] H. Heffes and D. Lucantoni. A markov modulated characterization of packetized voice and data traffic and related statistical multiplexer performance. *Selected Areas in Communications, IEEE Journal on*, 4(6):856 – 868, sep 1986.

[8] A. Horváth and M. Telek. Markovian modeling of real data traffic: Heuristic phase type and map fitting of heavy tailed and fractal like samples. In M. Calzarossa and S. Tucci, editors, *Performance Evaluation of Complex Systems: Techniques and Tools*, volume 2459 of *Lecture Notes in Computer Science*, pages 267–282. Springer Berlin / Heidelberg, 2002. 10.1007/3-540-45798-4_17.

[9] N. Mi, G. Casale, L. Cherkasova, and E. Smirni. Burstiness in multi-tier applications: symptoms, causes, and new models. In *Proceedings of the 9th ACM/IFIP/USENIX International Conference on Middleware*, Middleware '08, pages 265–286, New York, NY, USA, 2008. Springer-Verlag New York, Inc.

[10] N. Mi, Q. Zhang, A. Riska, E. Smirni, and E. Riedel. Performance impacts of autocorrelated flows in multi-tiered systems. *Perform. Eval.*, 64:1082–1101, October 2007.

[11] H. Okamura and T. Dohi. Faster maximum likelihood estimation algorithms for markovian arrival processes. In *Quantitative Evaluation of Systems, 2009. QEST '09. Sixth International Conference on the*, pages 73 –82, sept. 2009.

[12] D. Perez-Palacin and J. Merseguer. Performance sensitive self-adaptive service-oriented software using hidden markov models. In *Proceedings of WOSP/SIPEW '11*, pages 201–206, 2011.

[13] D. Perez-Palacin, J. Merseguer, and S. Bernardi. Performance aware open-world software in a 3-layer architecture. In *WOSP/SIPEW '10*, pages 49–56, New York, NY, USA, 2010. ACM.

[14] D. Perez-Palacin, R. Mirandola, and J. Merseguer. Enhancing a qos-based self-adaptive framework with energy management capabilities. In *Proceedings of the joint ACM SIGSOFT conference – QoSA and ACM SIGSOFT symposium – ISARCS on Quality of software architectures – QoSA and architecting critical systems – ISARCS*, QoSA-ISARCS '11, pages 165–170, New York, NY, USA, 2011. ACM.

[15] T. Rydén. An em algorithm for estimation in markov-modulated poisson processes. *Comput. Stat. Data Anal.*, 21:431–447, April 1996.

[16] World Cup 1998 Access logs. http://ita.ee.lbl.gov/html/contrib/WorldCup.html. 1998.

How A Consumer Can Measure Elasticity for Cloud Platforms

Sadeka Islam
National ICT Australia,
University of New South Wales
sadeka.islam@nicta.com.au

Kevin Lee
National ICT Australia,
University of New South Wales
kevin.lee@nicta.com.au

Alan Fekete
University of Sydney,
National ICT Australia
alan.fekete@sydney.edu.au

Anna Liu
National ICT Australia,
University of New South Wales
anna.liu@nicta.com.au

ABSTRACT

One major benefit claimed for cloud computing is elasticity: the cost to a consumer of computation can grow or shrink with the workload. This paper offers improved ways to quantify the elasticity concept, using data available to the consumer. We define a measure that reflects the financial penalty to a particular consumer, from under-provisioning (leading to unacceptable latency or unmet demand) or over-provisioning (paying more than necessary for the resources needed to support a workload). We have applied several workloads to a public cloud; from our experiments we extract insights into the characteristics of a platform that influence its elasticity. We explore the impact of the rules used to increase or decrease capacity.

Categories and Subject Descriptors

C.4 [**Computer Systems Organization**]: PERFORMANCE OF SYSTEMS—*Measurement techniques, Modeling techniques*; D.2.8 [**SOFTWARE ENGINEERING**]: Metrics—*Complexity measures, Performance measures*

Keywords

Cloud Computing, Elasticity, Performance Measures

1. INTRODUCTION

Cloud computing platforms are already used extensively by some companies with huge and rapidly growing computational needs, and traditional enterprises are looking closely at the cloud as an addition or even an alternative to running their own IT infrastructure. Many features of cloud platforms are attractive; e.g., cloud platforms may be low-cost and they may achieve high availability. One feature that is commonly a powerful selling point for cloud platforms is the claim that they are *elastic*; the user can pay only for what they need at a given time. The (US) National Institute of Standards and Technology (NIST)[1] defines elasticity:

> Capabilities can be rapidly and elastically provisioned, in some cases automatically, to quickly scale out, and rapidly released to quickly scale in. To the consumer, the capabilities available for provisioning often appear to be unlimited and can be purchased in any quantity at any time.

We note here two fundamental elements of elasticity: (1) Time (e.g., a platform is more elastic if resources are available sooner after a request is made), and (2) Cost (e.g., a platform charging on a per-hour basis is less elastic than one charging on a per-second basis).

Elasticity is a desirable property for many businesses. A startup facing rapid growth wishes that its costs start small, and grow as and when the income arrives to match. In contrast, traditional data processing requires a large up-front capital expenditure to buy and install IT systems. Traditionally, the cost must cover enough processing for the anticipated and the hoped-for growth; this leaves the company bearing much risk from uncertainty in the rate of growth. If growth is slower than expected, the revenue won't be available to pay for the infrastructure, while if growth is too fast, the systems may reach capacity and then a very expensive upgrade or expansion is needed. Also, it is common in web-based companies for demand to be periodic or bursty (e.g., the Slashdot effect). The workload may grow very rapidly when the idea is "hot", but fads are fickle and demand can then shrink back to a previous level. Traditional infrastructure must try to provision for the peak, and so it risks wasting resources after the peak has passed. In summary, elasticity can remove risk from a startup or an enterprise, by allowing "pay-as-you-grow" computing infrastructure where the costs adjust smoothly to rising (and perhaps falling) workload.

While all cloud offerings claim elasticity as a virtue that they possess, we can be sure that none are perfect in letting a customer pay for exactly what they need, and no more. There may be a minimum charge (e.g., 1 instance), there may be delays in adapting the platform to sudden increase in workload, and so on. Thus we would want to know

[1]See http://csrc.nist.gov/publications/drafts/800-145/Draft-SP-800-145_cloud-definition.pdf

how elastic is each system. As yet, the literature does not contain any explicit measurement to quantify the amount of elasticity in a platform. This is the gap that our paper addresses. We are *not* proposing a mechanism for minimising resource usage. Rather, we are proposing elasticity as a *property* of a platform with time and cost as its essential elements, and we demonstrate how elasticity can be measured with respect to applications with certain Quality of Service (QoS) requirements. We envisage that different mechanisms for minimising resource usage can be evaluated using our elasticity measure.

Just as with traditional IT infrastructure, the company seeking to use a cloud platform needs a basis for comparing different offerings, and choosing the one that will be best for its needs. The usual approach is to follow a benchmark, which includes a standardised workload, and defines exactly how to measure the behavior of any system when subjected to this workload. The benchmark gives one (or a few) summary numbers that represent the value to the chooser of the system; it is then reasonable to select the system with best benchmark results. Organisations like TPC and SPEC have a range of benchmarks for hardware and/or software systems. This paper is part of an effort in the research community to define appropriate measures that will allow comparing the desirableness of competing cloud platforms.

We draw attention to the difference between elasticity and scalability, since the two notions are often mixed up. Scalability is defined as the ability of a system to meet a larger workload requirement by adding a proportional amount of resources. It means that the system must be able to handle a high workload in a graceful manner (i.e., maintaining its performance). However, scalability is a time-free notion and it does not capture how long it takes for the system to achieve the desired performance level. In contrast, time is a central aspect in elasticity, which depends on the speed of response to changed workload.

One important feature of our work is that we regard benchmarking as a process done by the consumer of cloud services. We limit ourselves to running a benchmark as a consumer - this includes considering her application and workload profile, incorporating the business objectives, and taking observations that are available to the consumer through the platform's API or inside the user's application code. This makes our task harder, since we do not have access to arbitrary measurements of the infrastructure itself, but this viewpoint is necessary for our work to give the consumer a reasonable basis for choosing between competing platforms. In contrast, the provider's viewpoint of elasticity can be completely different because they have access to the measurements from the underlying physical infrastructure (hardware configuration and specification) and virtualisation environment. This enables them to do performance modelling and looking at interactions between components to deduce the performance outcome for a class of applications. For the consumer's viewpoint, we try to understand the elasticity behavior of the platform from its response to a suite of workload patterns.

A key idea in our proposal is to come up with a number that measures elasticity as a property of a cloud platform (though the actual figure-of-merit will vary depending on the application's business model, workloads, etc). To achieve this, we use workloads that vary over time in different ways. Some workloads will rise and fall repeatedly,

others will rise rapidly and then fall back slowly, etc. For each workload, we examine the way a platform responds to this, and we quantify the effect on the consumer's finances. That is, we use a cost measure in cents per hour, with a component that captures how much is wasted by paying for resources that are not needed at the time for the workload (overprovisioning), and a component to see how much the consumer suffers (opportunity cost) when the system is underprovisioned, that is, the platform is not providing enough resource for a recent surge in workload.

From our measurements, we have discovered several characteristics of a cloud platform that are important influences on the extent of elasticity. Some of these (such as the speed of responding to a request for increased provisioning) have already been discussed by practitioners, but others seem to have escaped attention. For example, we find in Amazon EC2 that there is a large improvement of elasticity from relatively simple changes in the set of rules that the system uses to control provisioning and deprovisioning. There is a set of rules (based on recent utilisation rates) that is widely followed, perhaps because it is done that way in tutorial examples. We find that this leads to rapid deprovisioning when load decreases, which leaves the system underprovisioned if a future upswing occurs. Because the financial impact from poor QoS (when demand can't be handled) is generally much more severe than the cost of running some extra resources for a while, this is a poor strategy. What is worse, on typical platforms one pays for an instance in quanta that represent a significant period of time (say 1 hour), so eagerness to deprovision can leave the consumer paying for a resource without the ability to use it.

The key contributions that this paper makes are (i) a novel framework for measuring elasticity, that can be run by a consumer and which takes account of the consumer's particular business situation (ii) a specific set of case studies, using one set of workload patterns and financial assumptions, to show that this approach can be carried out in practice, (iii) insights that we gained from the case studies, especially concerning the main internal characteristics of a platform that impact on the elasticity experience of a consumer.

This paper is structured as follows: Section 2 identifies relevant work on elasticity and cloud performance measurements. Section 3 presents our proposed benchmark for measuring elasticity, first as a general framework based on penalties that are expressed in monetary units, and then with specific choices for penalty functions, workload curves etc. Section 4 describes the details of the experimental setup, including the tools and specific cloud technologies used in our case studies. Section 5 presents empirical case studies that show the elasticity of particular platforms, given by different choices of rulesets that control provisioning decisions in a widely-used public cloud. We close the paper with a discussion of the lessons learnt and a conclusion.

2. RELATED WORK

The main objective of this paper is to provide a way for a consumer to measure how well (or not) each cloud platform delivers the elasticity property. The most relevant prior research is concerned with understanding the elasticity concept, and with measuring cloud platform performance. This work has appeared in formal academic forums, and/or in trade press or practitioner blogs.

2.1 Elasticity : Definition and Characteristics

It is important to get common usage of marketable terms such as "elastic". Several efforts explain the meaning of terms that are used about cloud platforms, and along with explanation, they point to aspects of the platform's performance that can be important for elasticity. Unlike our work, these studies do not give explicit measurement proposals.

Armbrust et al. [1] discuss relevant use cases and potential benefits for cloud platforms. Among their points, they draw attention to the value of cloud elasticity as compared to the conventional client-server model in the context of perceived risks due to over- and under- provisioning.

The prestigious National Institute of Standards and Technology (NIST) has pointed out rapidity in resource provisioning and de-provisioning as an important aspect of elasticity. Two other discussions from David Chiu[2] and Ricky Ho[3] have pointed to an additional important factor of elastic behavior, that of the granularity of usage accounting. That means that elasticity when load declines is not only a function of the speed to decommission a resource, but also it depends on whether charging for that resource is stopped immediately on decommissioning, or instead is delayed for a while (say till the end of a charging quantum of time).

2.2 Cloud Performance and Benchmarks

Recent research efforts have conducted in-depth performance analysis on the virtual machine instances offered by public cloud providers. For example, Stantchev et al. [14] introduce a generic benchmark to evaluate the nonfunctional properties (e.g., response time) of individual cloud offerings for web services from cost-benefit perspective. Dejun et al. [5] and Schad et al. [11] examine the performance stability and homogeneity aspects of VM instances over time. These studies are useful to understand the underlying performance characteristics of the cloud infrastructure, however they do not consider the responsiveness of the platform during scaling with the variation in workload demand. A group at HP Labs [2] has defined provider-done measurements for a range of quality features of cloud platforms, focusing on environmental factors such as energy use.

Cloud service providers adopt dynamic VM migration strategies to balance application workloads among different physical machines. Several groups [13, 6] have presented benchmarking solutions to quantify the comparison of live VM migration techniques for data center scenarios. We evaluate cloud platform's elasticity from the consumers' viewpoint, whereas their work takes the service providers' perspective. They define a set of performance measures for assessing the overheads associated with dynamic VM migration techniques. In contrast, we consider the impact of imperfect elasticity based on consumers' business situation.

Several performance benchmarks have been proposed to quantify many important cloud performance metrics, among them the resource spin-up (spin-down) delay. Yigitbasi et al. [16] present a framework to determine the performance overheads associated with the scaling latency of the virtual machine (VM) instances in the cloud. Li et al. [9] developed CloudCmp to analyse customer perceived performance and cost effectiveness (e.g., scaling latency, cost per operation) of

public cloud offerings. However, they do not combine their discrete performance metrics into a macroscopic overview of the platform's adaptability behavior. We propose a single summary measure for elasticity, which is influenced by several factors that were used in these earlier studies.

Yahoo! Cloud Serving Benchmark (YCSB) [4] evaluates performance of cloud databases (e.g., Cassandra, HBase) under load for a variety of workload scenarios as well as scale-up and elastic speed-up measures (that is, they consider workloads that grow and grow). Their work is valuable when seeking to analyse the performance implications of large database-intensive applications in the cloud; however, we also consider de-provisioning and resource granularity aspects. Furthermore, our elasticity model captures the financial implications as well as traditional performance.

Donald Kossmann's group at ETHZ has a research project on benchmarking cloud platforms. An initial workshop discussion [3] proposed that it would be useful to take the ratio of the throughput achieved by operations with acceptable response time, to the rate of requests, in workloads with successive peaks and troughs. The later conference paper [7] presents an extensive evaluation of the end-to-end scalability aspect of existing cloud database architectures for OLTP workloads. Here they define a set of performance and cost metrics to compare the throughput, performance/cost ratio and cost predictability of existing cloud database systems for larger and larger loads. They look at a much wider variety of measures than we do, but they omit to look at the speed of responding to change in workloads, nor do they consider workloads that can shrink as well as grow.

2.3 Elasticity Measurement Model

Weinman has proposed a numeric measurement of elasticity [15] using a conceptual model: consider a resource (e.g., computational capacity), then there is a demand curve $D(t)$ that indicates, as a function of time, how much resource is needed for the application to work properly. A function $R(t)$ shows how much resource is allocated to the application at each time. Perfect elasticity would be shown if $R(t) = D(t)$ for all t. Weinman identifies the situation where $R(t) > D(t)$ as "excess resource" (we say "overprovisioning"), and assigns it a cost which (in the simplest case) is linear in the quantity of resource that is allocated above that needed. Similarly, he considers "unserved demand" (which we call "underprovisioning") when $D(t) < R(t)$, and measures this by opportunity cost, linear in the difference. The constant of proportionality is much higher for unserved demand than for excess resource. Figure 1 illustrates this for a resource of CPU capacity; the curves show a hypothetical situation with a sine wave variation in demand (solid blue line), and linearly increasing supply (dotted black line). A value of 150% for demand indicates that the application could use one-and-a-half times the capability of the standard instance, and 150% as the supply indicates that the application has been allocated instruction execution from cycles that were one-and-a-half as frequent as those on a standard instance. Weinman's measure is a weighted combination of the areas between the curves (with higher weight for the areas of under-provisioning).

We propose improvements over Weinman's model in several respects. First, we design our workload suite to resemble complex real-world scenarios, while his workload types (e.g., constant one) are limited to theoretical analysis only. Sec-

---

[2]See Crossroads, Vol. 16, No. 3. (2010), pp. 3-4.
[3]See `http://horicky.blogspot.com/2009/07/between-elasticity-and-scalability.html`

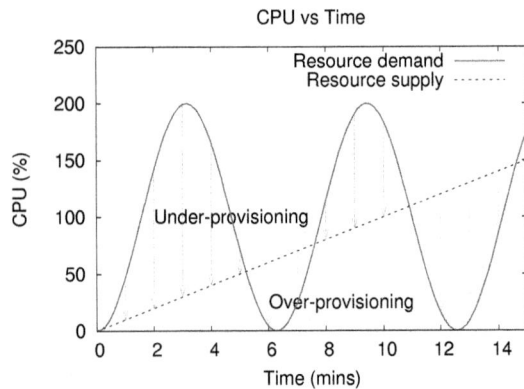

Figure 1: Elasticity Explained

ond, Weinman's area-based under-provisioning model can only accommodate unmet demand and is not able to include penalties resulting from unsatisfactory performance (e.g., high latency). We propose shifting our focus to a QoS-based under-provisioning model. Our under-provisioning model allows industry-typical SLAs, where, for example, the opportunity cost from high latency is not linear in the delay, but rather depends on whether the latency has breached a threshold, and furthermore we allow a small number of requests to see excessive latency. Also, we distinguish between the resources that are allocated, and those that are charged to the consumer (as we will see, the difference between these can be significant). In addition, we define a unified metric to summarize the financial penalties of a set of workload demands for a particular platform. Finally, we consider pragmatic issues needed to produce a figure-of-merit for a platform, by choosing explicit workloads and carrying out measurements, while Weinman's paper is entirely theoretical. Unlike Weinman, we explore the impact of the scaling rules used in the platform, to provision or deprovision resources.

3. ELASTICITY MEASUREMENT

This section defines our proposal, to determine a figure that expresses "how elastic is a given cloud platform". We explain a general framework to measure the cost of imperfect elasticity when running a given workload, with penalties for overprovisioning and underprovisioning; the sum of these is the penalty measurement for the workload. By considering a suite of workloads, and combining penalties calculated for each, we can define a figure-of-merit for a cloud platform. Next we discuss choices that we have made for an explicit measurement - that is, taking concrete decisions on the Service-Level Agreement (SLA) aspects that are evaluated, charging rates, and the particular suite of workloads.

3.1 Penalty model

We present our approach to measuring imperfections in elasticity for a given workload in monetary units. We assume that the system involves a variety of resource types. For example, the capacity of an EC2 instance can be measured by looking at its CPU, memory, network bandwidth, etc. We assume that each resource type can be allocated in units. We assume that the user can learn what level of resourcing is allocated and the relevant QoS metrics for their requests

(such as distribution of latency). Amazon CloudWatch[4] is an example of the monitoring functionality we expect.

Our elasticity model combines penalties for over-provisioning and for under-provisioning. The former captures the cost of *provisioned* but *unutilised* resources, while the latter measures opportunity cost from the performance degradation that arises with under-provisioning.

3.1.1 Penalty for Over-Provisioning

In existing cloud platforms, it is usual that resources are temporarily allocated to a consumer from a start time (when the consumer requests the resource based on observed or predicted needs, or when the system proactively allocates the resource) until a finish time. This is represented by a function we call available supply and denote by $R_i(t)$ for each resource i. In current platforms it can also happen that a resource may be charged to a consumer even without being available. For example, in Amazon EC2, an instance is charged from the time that provisioning is requested (even though there is a delay of several minutes before the instance is actually running for the consumer to utilise). Similarly, charging for an instance is done in one-hour blocks, so even after an instance is deprovisioned, the consumer may continue to be charged for it for a while. Thus we need another function $M_i(t)$ that represents the *chargeable supply* curve; this is what the consumer is actually paying for. These curves can be compared to the demand curve $D_i(t)$.

The basis of our penalty model is that the consumer's detriment in overprovisioning (when $R(t) > D(t)$) is essentially given by the difference between chargeable supply and demand; as well, we charge a penalty even in underprovisioned periods whenever a resource is charged for but not available (and hence not used). These penalties are computed with a constant of proportionality c_i that indicates what the consumer must pay for each resource unit. In real systems, resources of different types are often bundled, and only available in collections (e.g., an EC2 instance has CPU, bandwidth, storage etc.). We assume that some weighting is used to partition the actual monetary charge for the bundle between its contained resources.

Formally, we define the overprovision penalty $P_o(t_s, t_e)$ for a period starting at t_s and ending at t_e. We assume a set of resources indexed by i, and we use functions $D_i(t)$, $R_i(t)$, and $M_i(t)$ for the demand, available supply, and charged supply, respectively, of resource i at time t. Our definition aggregates the penalties from each resource, and for each resource we integrate over time.

Definition 1.

$$P_o(t_s, t_e) = \sum_i P_{o,i}(t_s, t_e)$$

$$P_{o,i}(t_s, t_e) = \int_{t_s}^{t_e} c_i \times d_i(t) dt$$

$$d_i(t) = \begin{cases} M_i(t) - D_i(t) & \text{if } R_i(t) > D_i(t), \\ M_i(t) - R_i(t) & \text{if } M_i(t) > R_i(t) \\ & \text{and } D_i(t) \geq R_i(t), \\ 0 & \text{otherwise.} \end{cases}$$

---

[4]See http://aws.amazon.com/cloudwatch/

3.1.2 Penalty for Under-Provisioning

Next, we turn to the penalty model for under-provisioning, when resources are insufficient and performance is poor. We measure the opportunity cost to the consumer, using SLAs that capture how service matters to them.

We assume that the consumer has used their business environment to determine a set of performance or Quality of Service (QoS) objectives, and that each is the foundation for an SLA-style quantification of unsatisfactory behavior. For example, the platform's failure to meet the objective of availability can be quantified by counting the percentage of requests that are rejected by the system. In many cases, such SLA quantification might reflect a wide variety of causes, not only those that arise from underprovisioning, but also some from e.g., network outage. We assume that the customer also knows how to convert each measurement into an expected financial impact. For example, there might be a dollar value of lost income for each percent of rejected requests. In many cases, the financial impact may be proportional to the measurement, but sometimes there are step functions or other nonlinear effects (for example, word-of-mouth may give a quadratic growth of the damage from inaccurate responses). To provide a proper baseline for the penalties, we also consider the ideal value that occurs when resources are unlimited (in practice, we measure with such a large amount of overprovision that any additional allocation would not change the SLA measurement).

Formally, we let Q be a non-empty set of QoS measures, and for each $q \in Q$, we consider a function $p_q(t)$ that reflects the amount of unsatisfactory behavior observed on the platform at time t. The consumer provides also, for each QoS aspect q, a function f_q that takes the observed measurement of unsatisfactory behavior and maps this to the financial impact on the consumer. Let $p_q^{opt}(t)$ denote the limit (as $K \leftarrow \infty$) of the amount of unsatisfactory behavior observed in a system that is statically allocated with K resources.

Thus we define the underprovision penalty $P_u(t_s, t_e)$ for a period starting at t_s and ending at t_e

Definition 2.

$$P_u(t_s, t_e) = \sum_{q \in Q} P_{u,q}(t_s, t_e)$$

$$P_{u,q}(t_s, t_e) = \int_{t_s}^{t_e} (f_q(p_q(t)) - f_q(p_q^{opt}(t)))dt$$

3.1.3 Total Penalty Rate for an Execution

We calculate the overall penalty score $P(t_s, t_e)$ accrued during an execution from t_s till t_e, by taking the sum of the penalties from both over- and under-provisioning; note that both are expressed in units of cents. We then calculate the total penalty rate P in cents per hour. A lower score for P indicates a more elastic response to the given workload.

Definition 3. The penalty score over a time interval $[t_s, t_e]$ is defined as follows:

$$P(t_s, t_e) = P_o(t_s, t_e) + P_u(t_s, t_e)$$

$$P = \frac{P(t_s, t_e)}{t_e - t_s}$$

3.2 Single Figure of Merit for Elasticity

The definitions above measure the elasticity of the system's response to a single demand workload. Different features of the workload may make elastic response easier or harder to achieve; for example, if the workload grows steadily and slowly, a system may adjust the allocation to match the demand, but a workload with unexpected bursts of activity may lead to more extensive under-provisioning. Thus, we consider a suite of different workloads, and determine the penalty rate for each of these.

In order to draw simple conclusion about the worthiness of one platform's elasticity over another, we wish to summarize the penalty rates for the entire workload collection into a single score, as usual in benchmarks. To combine measured penalty rates from several workloads into a single summary number, we follow the approach used by the SPEC family of benchmarks. That is, we choose a reference platform, and measure each workload on that platform as well as on the platform of interest. We take the ratio of the penalty rate on the platform we are measuring, to the rate of the same workload on the reference platform, and then we combine the ratios for the different workloads by the geometric mean. That is, if $P_{x,w}$ is the penalty rate for workload w on platform x, and we have n workloads in our suite, then we measure the elasticity of platform x relative to reference platform x_0 by

$$E = \sqrt[n]{\prod_{i=1}^{n} (P_{x,w_i}/P_{x_0,w_i})}$$

3.3 Choices for an Elasticity Benchmark

The approach to elasticity described above is flexible, and could be adapted to the needs of each consumer, through the choices available. We can set particular SLA objectives and metrics that reflect the business situation, workloads that are representative of that consumer's patterns of load variation, etc. To actually determine an elasticity score, we need to make one set of choices for all these parameters. For the purpose of this paper, we use the following. Our workload consists of requests that follow the TPC-W application design.

To calculate the overprovisioning penalty, we deal with a single resource (CPU capacity, relative to a standard small EC2 instance) and measure the financial charge as \$0.085 per hour per instance. This reflects the current charging policy of AWS. To calculate the underprovisioning penalty, we set the QoS constraints based on the existing user behavior studies in usability engineering literature [10]. In particular, each user in our workload pattern lands on the homepage first and then searches for newly released books. We expect at least 95% of these requests generated by the users will see a response within 2 seconds. So we have used the following two QoS aspects with associated penalties over an hourly evaluation period. The cost penalty for latency violation is a simplified version of the cost function mentioned in [8]. As e-commerce websites lose more revenue when latency is slow than for application down-time[5], we associate a lower cost penalty for unserved requests.

- (Latency) In each hour of measuring, there is no penalty as long as 95% of requests have response time up to 2 seconds; otherwise, a cost penalty, 12.5¢ will apply for each 1% of additional requests (beyond the allowed 5%) that exceed the 2 seconds latency.

---

[5]See http://blog.alertsite.com/2011/02/online-performance-is-business-performance/

- (Availability) Cost penalty of 10¢ per hour will apply for each 1% of requests that fail completely (they are rejected or timed out).

Note that the penalty for unmet demand is very high compared to the cost of provisioning; this is accurate for real consumers. As Weinman [15] points out, the cost of resources should be much less than the expected gain from using them (and the latter is what determines the opportunity cost of unmet demand).

The appropriate SLAs and their penalties may vary largely based on the business situation of the consumer of cloud services. In this paper we use a penalty corresponding to a rather small business (the penalty is only $10 in case the service is completely unavailable for an hour, when all requests are rejected). For a large e-commerce business application (e.g., e-bay), the appropriate penalty for down-time might be much higher[6], say $2000/second, and similarly the appropriate workloads would be much greater. The SLA penalty specified here should be considered as an illustration, to be adjusted based on the application's business context.

We have developed a workload suite to explore the platform's elasticity behavior for a range of patterns of demand change. We consider various workload characteristics (e.g., periodicity, growth and decay rate, randomness) to understand how the platform's elastic response varies across the workload space. In our measurements, we use a set of 10 different workloads, which grow and shrink in a variety of shapes, though (to make benchmarking manageable) all are fairly small, peaking with less than 10 instances, and lasting across 3 hours. Across time, some workloads show recurring cycles of growth and decrease, such as an hourly news cycle. Others have a single burst, such as when news breaks or during a marketing campaign[7]. We explore some trends as the length of cycles changes, etc., however work is still needed to consider the behavior with longer cycles such as daily ones, or longer-lasting one-off events. Further research is also needed on whether conclusions from small loads will be valid for much larger ones, as expected by large customers.

- Sinusoidal Workloads: These loads can be expressed as $D(t) = A(sin(2\pi t/T + \phi) + 1) + B$, where A is the amplitude, B is the base level, T is the period and ϕ is the phase shift. For the benchmark suite, we use three different examples, whose periods are 30 minutes, 60 minutes and 90 minutes, respectively. All have peak demand of 450 req/sec, and trough at 50 req/sec. A load of 150 req/sec is about what one VM instance can support.

- Sinusoidal Workload with Plateau: This workload type modifies the sinusoidal waveform, by introducing a level (unchanging) demand for a certain time, at each peak and trough. Thus the graph has the upswings and downswings, with flat plateau sections spacing them out. In the suite we have three workloads like this, each starting from the sinewave with period of 30 minutes; in one case the plateau at each peak lasts 10 minutes, in another it lasts 40 minutes, and in the last of this

type, the peak plateaus last 70 minutes each. In all cases, the plateaus at troughs last 45 minutes (and there is always a 10 minutes plateau at the start of the experiment and also at the end).

- Exponentially Bursting Workload: This workload type exhibits extremely rapid buildup in demand (rising U-fold each hour), followed by a decay (declining D-fold each hour). We provide two workloads of this type, one with $U = 18$ and $D = 2.25$; the other has $U = 24$ and $D = 3$ (so this rises and falls more quickly).

- Linearly Growing Workload: This workload represents a website whose popularity rises consistently. It can be stated as $D(t) = mt + c$, where m is the slope of the straight line and c is the y-axis intercept. We have one example of this type, with workload that starts at 50 requests/second (and stays here for 10 minutes to warm the system up), then the load rises steadily for 3 hours, each hour increasing the rate by an extra 240 requests/second. Thus we end up with 770 requests/second.

- Random Workload: The generation of requests is ongoing and independent. We have one example of this type, with requests produced by a Poisson process.

We note that the demand curves described above are expressed in terms of the rate requests are generated; in practice, performance variation in identical instances means that this does not cause the utilisation of CPU resources to track the desired demand pattern exactly.

4. IMPLEMENTATION

In this section, we illustrate the implementation details of our elasticity measurement environment. We first describe the architectural components of our experimental testbed and then outline the key steps to configure the testbed to fit the consumer-specific scenarios.

4.1 Experimental Setup

In the high level view, the architecture of our experimental setup can be seen as a client-server model. The client side is a workload generator implemented using JMeter[8], which is a Java workload generator used for load testing and measuring performance. The sole purpose of JMeter in this experiment is to generate workload based on our predefined workload patterns.

We chose TPC-W [12] as the application in all our suite of workloads, because it has easy-to-obtain code examples and it is most often used in the literature. It can be substituted with other applications if desired. TPC-W emulates user interactions of a complex e-commerce application (such as an online retail store). In our experiment, we adopt the online bookshop implementation of TPC-W application and deploy it into EC2 small instances. Instead of having the TPC-W workload generator at the client side, we use JMeter to specify our pre-defined workload patterns.

The server side is considered to be the System Under Test (SUT), which consists of a single load-balancer facing the client side, and a number of EC2 instances behind the load-balancer. We hosted the web server, application server

---

[6]See `http://www.raritan.com/resources/case-studies/ebay.pdf`

[7]See `ecn.channel9.msdn.com/o9/pdc09/ppt/SVC54.pptx`, `http://www.mediabistro.com/alltwitter/osama-bin-laden-twitter-record_b8019`

[8]See `http://jakarta.apache.org/jmeter/`

and database on the same EC2 m1.small instance at US-East Virginia region (the cost of each instance is 8.5¢ per hour, matching the penalty we apply for overprovisioning); as some of the database queries consumed more CPU, we had to restrict the processing rate for TPC-W server to 150 requests/second to achieve satisfactory performance. The number of instances is not fixed, but rather it is controlled by an autoscaling engine which dynamically increases and decreases the number of instances based on the amount of workload. The behavior of an autoscaling engine follows a set of rules that must be defined. Each ruleset produces a different "platform" for experimental evaluation, with different elasticity behavior.

An autoscaling rule has the form of pair consisting of an antecedent and a consequence. The antecedent is the condition to trigger the rule (e.g., CPU utilisation is greater than 80%) and a consequence is the action to trigger when the antecedent is satisfied (e.g., create one extra instance). In our experiments we consider three platforms, because we run with three different rulesets. The detailed configurations of the autoscaling engine (configured via AutoScaling[9] library) is shown in Table 1.

We have here explored rulesets that scale-out and -in by changing the number of instances, all of the same power. Some cloud platforms, including EC2, also allow one to provision instances of different capacity, vary bandwidth, etc.; how such rules alter the elasticity measures is an issue for further research, although our definitions will still apply.

We measure available supply $R(t)$ by using the reports from CloudWatch showing the number of instances that are allocated to our experiment; we treat k instances as $R(t) = 100 \times k\%$ of supply, so this function moves in discrete jumps. Chargeable supply $M(t)$ is determined from the launch time and termination time of the allocated EC2 instances, given by AWS EC2 API tools. For demand, our generator is defined to produce a given number of requests, rather than in the measure of CPU capacity, that is needed for our measurements. Thus we use an approximation: we graph $D(t)$ from what CloudWatch reports as the sum of the utilisation rates for all the allocated instances. As will be seen in the graphs in Section 5, this is quite distorted from the intended shape of the demand function. One distortion is that measured $D(t)$ is capped at the available supply, so under-provisioning does not show up as $D(t) > R(t)$. This inaccuracy is not serious for our measurement of elasticity, since the use of $D(t)$ in measurement is only for cases of over-provisioning; during under-provisioning, the penalty is based on QoS measures of latency and lost requests, and these do reveal the growth of true demand. Another inaccuracy is from the system architecture, where requests that arrive in a peak period may be delayed long enough that they lead to work being done at a later period (and thus measured $D(t)$ may be shifted rightwards from the true peak). As well, there is considerable variation in the performance of the supplied instances [5], so a given rate of request generation with 450 req/s can vary from 350% to 450% when we see the measured demand. Future work will find ways to more accurately measure demand in units of CPU capacity.

4.2 Configuration and Measurement Procedure

Here is the procedure for setting up the elasticity measurement environment. First, a VM image is prepared by installing necessary components for the target application (e.g., TPC-W). Then the load-balancer is launched and autoscaling configuration for the dynamically scalable server farm is set up. A monitoring agent (e.g., CloudWatch) is also configured to measure utilisation and performance data for each workload run.

Next, the scripts for all workload demands are distributed to the client-side load generator (e.g., JMeter). Each workload demand is applied to a fresh set-up of the server farm. At the end of each workload run, utilisation and performance data are collected from the monitoring agent and load generator respectively. The penalty rate for each workload demand is computed with the help of the penalty model, described in Section 3.1. Same procedure is repeated to measure the penalty rate for other workload demands. Finally a single elasticity score is derived by taking the geometric mean of the penalty rates of all workload demands in the collection.

5. CASE STUDIES

We describe in some detail the observations made when we run our workloads against Amazon EC2. These case studies serve two purposes. (1) As a means of sanity checking the elasticity model in Section 3. That is, we can see that the numerical scores, based on our elasticity model, do in fact align with what is observed in over- or underprovisioning. For example, in reducing the steepness of a workload increase we shall observe that supply tracks more closely to demand, and the penalty calculated is lower. (2) We demonstrate the usefulness of our elasticity benchmark in exposing situations where elasticity fails to occur as expected, and other interesting phenomena can be observed.

5.1 Explore Workload Patterns

To begin, we applied each of the 10 workload patterns from our elasticity benchmark, in EC2 with a fixed scaling ruleset 1 as defined in Table 1. This ruleset is common in tutorial examples, and it seems widespread in practice[10]. With this ruleset, the number of instances increases by one when average CPU utilisation exceeds 70%, and one instance is deprovisioned when CPU utilisation drops below 30%.

We illustrate first how to derive the penalty rate from the raw measurement data. For each workload demand, we compute over-provisioning amount by taking the difference between the charged resource supply and used-up resource demand for the entire workload duration (e.g., 110 minutes interval for sine workload with 30 minutes period). For these case studies, we consider only CPU resource and assume that its pricing is equal to that of an EC2 instance (i.e., 8.5¢/hour). Thus we calculate the unit price for CPU resource, assuming that each hour consists of 60 time units (i.e., 60 minutes) and supplied CPU at each time unit is $k \times 100\%$, where k is the number of charged VM instances. We work out the over-provisioning penalty by multiplying the unit CPU price with the over-provisioned quantity. For the under-provisioning penalty, we measure the percentage of latency violations and dropped requests and evaluate the opportunity cost of the degraded performance based on the SLA definition, described in Section 3.3. Finally, we aggregate the penalty values for over- and under-provisioning and

---

[9]See http://aws.amazon.com/autoscaling/

[10]See http://mtehrani30.blogspot.com/2011/05/amazon-auto-scaling.html

Table 1: AutoScaling Engine Configuration

Ruleset	Monitoring Interval	Upper Breach Duration	Lower Breach Duration	Upper Threshold	Lower Threshold	VM Increment	VM Decrement	Scale-out Cool down Period	Scale-in Cool down Period
1	1 min	2 mins	2 mins	70% CPU Average	30% CPU Average	1	1	2 mins	2 mins
2	1 min	2 mins	15 mins	70% CPU Average	20% CPU Average	2	2	2 mins	10 mins
3	1 min	4 mins	10 mins	1.5 sec Maximum Latency	20% CPU Average	1	1	2 mins	5 mins

normalise it to compute the penalty rate per hour, giving the penalty rate for a particular workload demand.

5.1.1 Effect of Over- and Under-provisioning

Figure 2 shows behavior of the platform in response to an input sinusoidal workload with a period of 30 minutes. The CPU graph shows the available supply, chargeable supply and demand curves over a 110-minute interval. Initially, there was only one instance available to serve the incoming requests. As workload demand increases (after 15 minutes), the rule triggers provisioning a new instance, but we observed a delay of about 6 minutes until that is available (however it is charged as soon as the launch begins). As workload generation is rising fast during this delay, the system experiences severe effects of under-provisioning: latency spikes and penalties accrue at about 20¢/min. In our implementation, demand is measured on the instances and so the curve shown is capped at the available supply, rather than showing the full upswing of the sinewave. The lag between charging for the instance and it being available, is reflected in a penalty for over-provisioning of about 0.14¢/min during this period.

Between timepoints 50 and 55, we see high penalties for both over-provisioning and under-provisioning. This may sound counter-intuitive as one might wonder how "excess resource" and "insufficient resource" co-exist at the same time. Looking at the CPU graph, we find significant difference between charged and available supply during that interval; the consumer continues paying for 3 extra unusable instances (2 de-provisioned instances from the previous cycle and 1 yet-to-be-provisioned instance in the current cycle) which contribute to over-provisioning penalty. Also, the available instance supply (i.e., 2 instances) is not enough to meet the increasing demand for that duration, thus resulting in high under-provisioning penalty.

5.1.2 Deprovisioning of Resources

Our work's inclusion of cases where workload declines is different from most previous proposals for cloud benchmarks. These situations show interesting phenomena. We saw situations where a lag in releasing resources was actually helpful for the consumer. In Figure 2 we see, on the downswing of the demand curve, that most of the resources claimed on the upswing were kept; this means that the next upswing could utilise these instances, and so the latency problems (and underprovisioning penalty) were much less severe than in the first cycle.

We also observe in downswings that the difference between chargeable supply and available supply is significant, with a deprovisioned instance continuing to attract charge till the end of the hour-long quantum. We see in the CPU graph of Figure 2 that the chargeable supply is simply not following the demand curve at all, and indeed there are extensive periods when the consumer is paying for 4 instances, even though they never have more than 2 available for use.

Considering the evolution of the supply led us to discover an unexpected inelasticity phenomenon, where the cloud-hosted application is never able to cut back to its initial state after a temporary workload burst. The average utilisation may not drop below 30% which triggers deprovisioning, even though several instances are not needed. To demonstrate this fact, we ran a sinusoidal workload pattern with peak at 670 req/s and trough at 270 req/s, and 40 minutes plateau at each peak and trough; the resultant graphs are shown in Figure 3. The peak workload triggered the creation of 6 instances. The long-lasting trough workload (about 136% CPU) could easily be served by 2 instances, however, the number of VM instances remained at 4.

5.1.3 Trends In Elasticity Scores

Looking at the penalty scores in Table 2, we can see how the calculated penalty varies with the type of workload. In all workloads (except the linear one), the overall penalty is dominated by the loss in revenue due to under-provisioning. This is appropriate to business customers as the opportunity cost, from unmet requests or unsatisfactory response that may annoy users, is much more than the cost of resources.

For pure sinusoidal workload patterns, the overall penalty declines with the increase in waveperiod. This demonstrates that, with these rulesets, the EC2 platform is better at adapting to changes that are less steep. Here underprovisioning penalties will be less severe as the demand will not have increased too much in the delay from triggering a new instance, until it is available to serve the load.

The sinusoidal workload with plateaus has higher overall penalty compared to the basic sinusoidal workload where the cycles are sharper. We attribute this to the insertion of a 45 minutes plateau at the trough which wipes out the resource-reuse phenomenon in subsequent cycles. With a trough plateau, the system has time to deprovision and return to its initial state before the next cycle; therefore, each cycle could not take advantage of the resources created in the previous cycle and it pays a similar underprovisioning penalty. As the length of the plateau at the peak increases (from 10 minutes to 70 minutes), overall penalty gradually

Table 2: Penalty for Benchmarking Workloads - Ruleset 1

Workload	$P_o(t_s, t_e)/hr$	$P_u(t_s, t_e)/hr$	$P(t_s, t_e)/hr$
sine_30	27.51¢	374.88¢	402.39¢
sine_60	28.84¢	133.65¢	162.49¢
sine_90	22.17¢	52.82¢	74.99¢
sine_plateau_10	22.08¢	554.44¢	576.52¢
sine_plateau_40	18.52¢	292.96¢	311.48¢
sine_plateau_70	23.81¢	174.19¢	198.0¢
exp_18_2.25	24.83¢	528.61¢	553.44¢
exp_24_3.0	17.65¢	1093.05¢	1110.7¢
linear_240	35.01¢	0.0¢	35.01¢
random	29.31¢	129.14¢	158.45¢

moves down. The system has time to adapt to the peak demand, and serve it effectively for longer.

For the exponential burst workloads, we observe large penalty values in Table 2. In general, under-provisioning penalty tends to rise as the growth rate increases; that means, the underlying cloud platform is not elastic enough to grow rapidly with these fast-paced workloads, thus resulting in sluggish performance as they head towards the peak. Figure 4 explains the performance implications of an exponential workload with growth 24-fold per hour and decay 3-fold per hour. The high under-provisioning cost in the penalty graph also confirms EC2 platform's inelasticity in coping up with this fast-paced workload pattern. The under-provisioning penalties incurred were much higher than in the sinusoidal workloads, indicating that EC2 platform is not so adaptive to traffic surges with high acceleration rate. Again, looking at the over-provisioning penalty graph, we observe large over-provisioning cost (around 0.43¢/min) right after the peak is over; as some of the VM instances launched during the peak load were available at the off-peak period, they just accrued more penalty due to over-provisioning with no significant reduction to under-provisioning penalty.

Unlike the above workloads, linear workload yields less overall penalty. This suggests that EC2 platform can easily cope up with workloads with lower and consistent growth. This is not surprising as slowly growing workload pattern is not affected by the provisioning delay of the underlying platform and therefore incur less under-provisioning penalty. However, we expect that as the slope becomes steeper, the overall penalty will show a rising trend, as the resources are not provisioned rapidly enough.

5.2 Explore Impact of Scaling Rules

In our experiments with the widely-used ruleset 1, under-provisioning penalty dominates the overall score. Sometimes the system took too long in adjusting to rapid growth in demand. When demand drops, there is a tradeoff: slow response increases the duration of overprovisioning charges, but it can help if an upswing follows that might reuse the retained resources. To improve the elasticity, one can try changing the scaling rules so that they are aggressive in provisioning extra resources and conservative enough in deprovisioning those resources. The initial (Ruleset 1) and adjusted (Rulesets 2 and 3) scaling rulesets are shown in Table 1. Ruleset 3 is distinctive by making scale-out decisions based on the monitored values of the application level

performance metric (response time) instead of considering a resource utilisation metric. This performance-based approach has been adopted by some practitioners for autoscaling cloud applications[11]. Ruleset 3 explores the tradeoffs in these different approaches to scaling.

Ruleset 2 performed markedly better than ruleset 1. Two major factors contribute to this improvement in ruleset 2: adding multiple instances at each trigger in the upswing and lazy deprovisioning in the downswing. The ruleset 1 is less responsive to the rapidly increasing sinusoidal and exponential workloads because it only adds one instance at each rule trigger and there is a cooling period which stops it from immediately creating another instance (even if the condition is again met). On the other hand, ruleset 2 increases two instances at each trigger thus it responds quicker to sharp workload increase.

On the downswing, ruleset 1 responds much quicker to the drop of demand by deprovisioning its resources. Though the trend of available supply follows closely with the demand, the chargeable supply does not follow as well: resources are being charged but not used. In contrast, as we intended, ruleset 2 (with an increased lower breach duration of 15 minutes and scale-in cool-down period of 10 minutes) keeps the resources from the previous upswing so that they are reused in the subsequent cycles of the workload demand.

This benefit from resource reuse holds as long as workloads come in periodic bursts and the inter-arrival time of bursts are short enough to retain some resources from the previous ones; otherwise, subsequent bursts will not be able to enjoy the resource reuse phenomenon as the resources are likely to be released by that time. For this reason, sine-plateau workloads could not make use of the resources from the previous cycle because of their long plateau at the trough (45 minutes). Same holds for exponential workload with growth rate 18 and decay rate 2.25 per hour; it could not improve that much with ruleset 2 as the duration between the bursts is long enough to set the number of instances back to the initial state (1 EC2 instance).

Results for all workloads of our suite are shown in Table 3, which should be compared to Table 2. One clear disadvantage of ruleset 2 is that it is likely to overprovision too much in the case where workload does not increase quickly. This is reflected in the experiment with the linear workload pattern. The modest pace of growth in demand here means that ruleset 1 was sufficient to align the resource supply with its resource demand. Ruleset 2 rather worsened the overall penalty by increasing the over-provisioning cost.

We observe a lower penalty score for ruleset 3 than for ruleset 1. Since the under-provisioning penalty is mostly dominated by high latency, we designed this ruleset to add an extra instance when the maximum latency goes beyond 75% of the allowed threshold. This ruleset triggers an instance provisioning request as soon as the observed latency starts rising due to request-buffering at the server. The results show that this ruleset ensures higher SLA conformance and hence lower under-provisioning penalty for most of the workloads. An increased lower-breach duration and scale-in cool-down period in the deprovisioning rule also promote resource reuse from previous cycles and thus contribute to the improvement in the penalty score.

The only short-coming of ruleset 3 is that it sometimes

---

[11]See http://blog.tonns.org/2011/01/autoscaling-revisited.html

Table 3: Penalty for Benchmarking Workloads - Ruleset 2

Workload	$P_o(t_s, t_e)/hr$	$P_u(t_s, t_e)/hr$	$P(t_s, t_e)/hr$	Ratio to Rule 1
sine_30	40.33¢	127.50¢	167.83¢	0.41
sine_60	38.49¢	1.98¢	40.47¢	0.24
sine_90	38.03¢	1.24¢	39.27¢	0.52
sine_plateau_10	33.94¢	335.56¢	369.5¢	0.64
sine_plateau_40	32.27¢	138.86¢	171.13¢	0.54
sine_plateau_70	33.24¢	44.52¢	77.76¢	0.39
exp_18_2.25	33.27¢	428.09¢	461.36¢	0.83
exp_24_3.0	60.62¢	416.47¢	477.09¢	0.42
linear_240	39.83¢	0.0¢	39.83¢	1.13
random	61.35¢	35.13¢	96.48¢	0.60
Geometric Mean	N/A	N/A	N/A	0.52

Table 4: Penalty for Benchmarking Workloads - Ruleset 3

Workload	$P_o(t_s, t_e)/hr$	$P_u(t_s, t_e)/hr$	$P(t_s, t_e)/hr$	Ratio to Rule 1
sine_30	25.22¢	181.29¢	206.51¢	0.51
sine_60	33.78¢	106.28¢	140.06¢	0.86
sine_90	60.23¢	0.0¢	60.23¢	0.80
sine_plateau_10	22.68¢	408.92¢	431.6¢	0.74
sine_plateau_40	20.93¢	223.88¢	244.81¢	0.78
sine_plateau_70	21.97¢	173.92¢	195.89¢	0.98
exp_18_2.25	27.0¢	538.42¢	565.42¢	1.02
exp_24_3.0	37.76¢	577.52¢	615.28¢	0.55
linear_240	15.68¢	11.19¢	26.87¢	0.76
random	36.63¢	108.75¢	145.38¢	0.91
Geometric Mean	N/A	N/A	N/A	0.77

results in excessive over-provisioning because of "rippling effect". This ruleset assumes resource bottleneck as the only cause for latency violation and therefore provisions extra instances to improve the observed latency. However, there might be several other reasons for high latency even after an instance is available, for example, the warm-up period of the newly provisioned instance, request-queuing in other instances or problems in third party web service calls[12]. If the rule sets too small a "cool-down" period (how long after a rule is triggered till it can be triggered again), then provisioning requests for new instances might be triggered repeatedly based on latency violation information that has not yet reflected the earlier provisionings. Figure 5 demonstrates this rippling phenomenon for one workload.

We computed a single figure of merit based on the SPEC family of benchmarks as defined in Section 3.2. We used the platform with ruleset 1 as the reference when evaluating ruleset 2 and 3. The last column in Table 3 and 4 shows the ratio of the total penalties for the two rulesets with respect to ruleset 1 for each of the 10 workload patterns. All but one of these ratios are smaller than one, indicating that both ruleset 2 and 3 are generally more elastic than ruleset 1 for the benchmark workload patterns. We calculated the geometric mean of these ratios (0.52 for ruleset 2 and 0.77 for ruleset 3), which quantifies the improvement in elasticity. Thus we demonstrated that our single figure for elasticity can be effectively used to compare different rule configura-

tions. It can also used to detect variation in elasticity level between platforms from different cloud providers, as well as variation over time within a cloud provider due to the consistently evolving underlying infrastructures of cloud.

6. DISCUSSION

Our case studies have given us insights into how a cloud platform can be better or worse at elasticity when following a varying workload. Identifying the importance of these characteristics should be of independent value to consumers who want to choose a platform, and they may also help a cloud provider to offer better elasticity in his platform.

It is well understood that the granularity of instances is important in elasticity. If a substantial PC-like (virtual) machine is the smallest unit of increased resource, this is less elastic than a platform which can allow each customer to have whatever percentage of the cycles that they need, as in the case of GAE[13]. Similarly, the time delay between a request for provisioning, until one can actually run on the new instance, can be significant. We observed that this delay varies unpredictably, but can be over 10 minutes. If the workload is increasing fast enough, by the time 10 minutes have elapsed, the previous configuration may have become badly overloaded. Ongoing changes in implementation by platform providers may lessen the provisioning delay, and thus improve observed elasticity. Finally, the delay to decommission an instance is also important. Being too slow to

[12]See http://aws-musings.com/choosing-the-right-metrics-for-autoscaling-your-ec2-cluster/

[13]See http://code.google.com/appengine

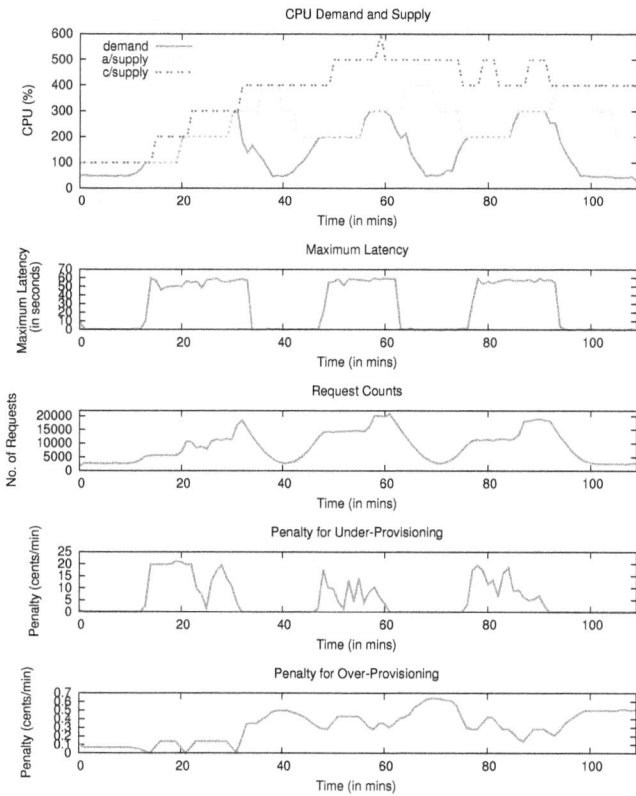

Figure 2: Results of Sinusoidal Workload with 30 Minutes Period

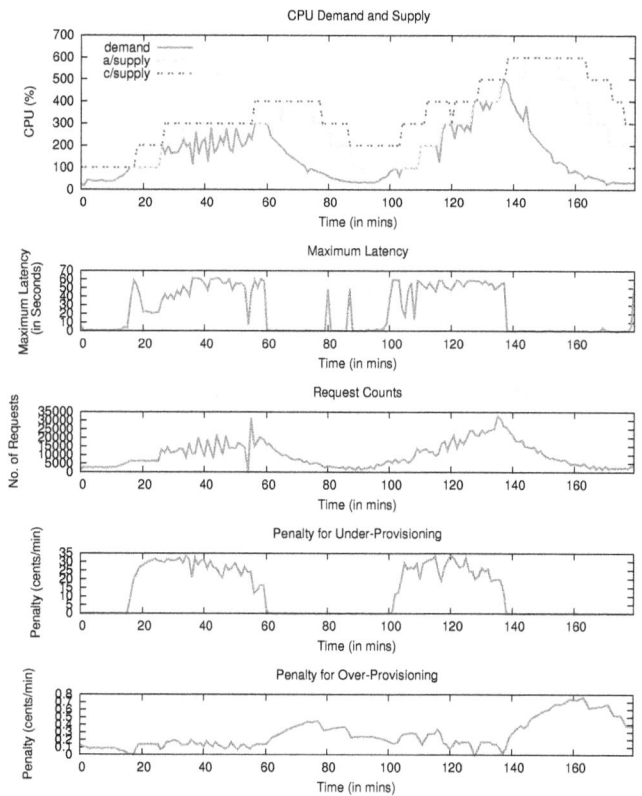

Figure 4: Results for Exponential Workload with Growth 24/hour and Decay 3/hour

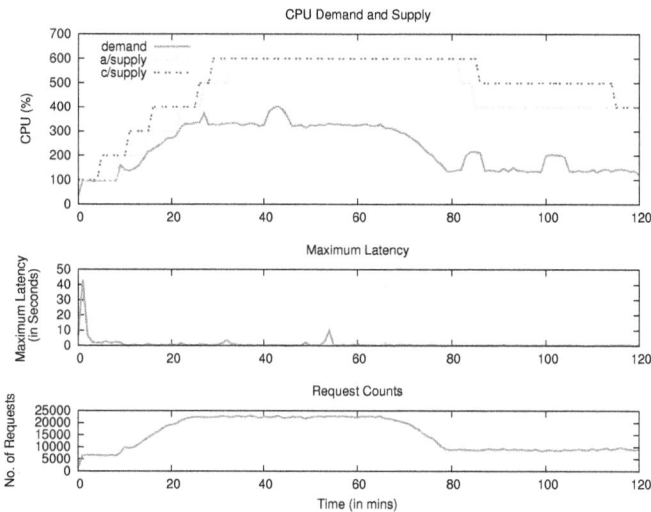

Figure 3: Results for the Trapping Scenario

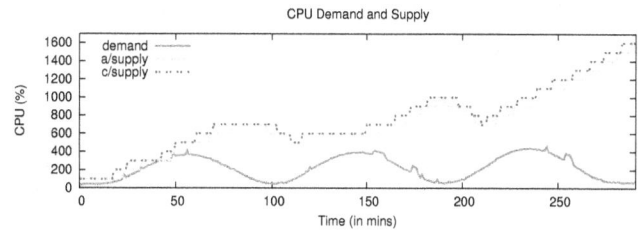

Figure 5: Rippling Effect for Sinusoidal Workload with 90 Minutes Period

give up resources is wasteful, but being too eager can leave the consumer without resources if/when workload recovers to previous levels.

We have seen how important it is to understand the way the consumer is charged for resources, We have seen that this can be quite different from the actual access to those resources, and the difference is important for the consumer's perception of elastic behavior. When charging runs till the end of a substantial quantum (e.g., an hour, for EC2), we can see financial losses from too rapid response to changed load. In particular, if the fluctuating load leads a consumer to give up an instance, and then they need to request it back, they may end up paying for it twice over.

Our experiments have shown how changes to the provisioning and deprovisioning rules can alter the elasticity of the platform. This seems to deserve much more attention from consumers, and we haven't found useful guidelines in research or tutorial literature. In particular, many applications seem to follow sample code, and use a default policy where instances are created or given up based on utilisation levels holding for a fairly short time (e.g., 2 minutes). By being less eager to deprovision, we saw a different ruleset gave significant improvement (about 50% for ruleset 2) in the elasticity measure. We also observed better SLA conformance for rules based on QoS (i.e., latency-based ruleset 3) as compared to the utilisation-based one (CPU-based ruleset 1); however, ruleset 3 is less reliable for autoscaling as it causes excessive over-provisioning when a QoS threshold is breached because of external factors (e.g., latency spike in other tiers or web services) instead of resource scarcity.

Running our benchmark has been informative for us. We now reflect directly on the advantages and disadvantages of the decisions we made in proposing this benchmark, that is, how exactly we decided to measure elasticity.

Having workloads with diverse patterns of growth and decline in demand is clearly essential. Those that rise rapidly (that is, fast compared to the provisioning delay in the platform) reveal many cases of poor elasticity. When demand declines and rises again, we see effects of charging quanta.

We followed the SPEC approach to combine information from several workloads into one number. It gives consistent relative scores no matter which platform is the reference. It is very robust in that it does not change depending on subtle choice of weights, nor on the scale chosen for each workload.

Our calculated penalty for overprovisioning is based on the charged level of resources, rather than on the resources that are actually allocated (as in Weinman's discussion of elasticity [15]). We have seen that there can be a considerable difference between these quantities. By this decision, we properly give a worse score for a system if it keeps charging over a longer quantum. Our penalty calculation for underprovision is based on observed QoS, and using consumer-supplied functions to convert each observation into the opportunity cost. We do not assume a constant impact of each unmet request. This clearly fits with widespread practice, where SLAs with penalty clauses are enshrined in contracts.

Overall, our approach fits the decision-making of a consumer selecting a suitable cloud platform for their needs.

7. CONCLUSION

Small and medium enterprises are heading towards the cloud for many reasons, including varying workload. To choose appropriately between platforms, a consumer of cloud services needs a way to measure the features that are important, one of which is the amount of elasticity of each platform. This paper offers a concrete proposal giving a numeric score for elasticity. We suggested specific new ways to use SLAs to determine penalties for underprovisioning. We have defined a suite of workloads that show a range of patterns over time. We carried out a case study showing that our approach is feasible, and that it leads to helpful insights into the elasticity properties of the platform. In particular, we have shown that one gets poor elasticity when following a widespread ruleset for provisioning and deprovisioning.

In future, we will extend our measurements to other platforms with a wider range of features. We hope to consider workloads that grow much further than our current set (which peak at demand for about half-a-dozen instances). We also will try examples with a greater range of SLAs and opportunity cost functions. We would like to make the benchmark running as automatic as possible. We see this paper as an important step towards allowing consumers to make informed choices between cloud platforms.

Acknowledgement

NICTA is funded by the Australian Government as represented by the Department of Broadband, Communications and the Digital Economy and the Australian Research Council through the ICT Centre of Excellence program. A grant from Amazon provided access to AWS.

8. REFERENCES

[1] M. Armbrust, A. Fox, R. Griffith, A. Joseph, R. Katz, A. Konwinski, G. Lee, D. Patterson, A. Rabkin, I. Stoica, and M. Zaharia. A view of cloud computing. *Communications of the ACM*, 53(4):50–58, 2010.

[2] C. Bash, T. Cader, Y. Chen, D. Gmach, R. Kaufman, D. Milojicic, A. Shah, and P. Sharma. HPL-2011-148: Cloud Sustainability Dashboard, Dynamically Assessing Sustainability of Data Centers and Clouds. Technical report, Hewlett-Packard Labs, 2011.

[3] C. Binnig, D. Kossmann, T. Kraska, and S. Loesing. How is the weather tomorrow?: towards a benchmark for the cloud. In *Proc DBTest'09*, 2009.

[4] B. Cooper, A. Silberstein, E. Tam, R. Ramakrishnan, and R. Sears. Benchmarking cloud serving systems with YCSB. In *Proc SoCC'10*, pages 143–154, 2010.

[5] J. Dejun, G. Pierre, and C. Chi. EC2 performance analysis for resource provisioning of service-oriented applications. In *ICSOC Workshops (Springer LNCS 6275)*, pages 197–207, 2009.

[6] D. Huang, D. Ye, Q. He, J. Chen, and K. Ye. Virt-LM: a benchmark for live migration of virtual machine. In *Proc ICPE'11*, pages 307–316, 2011.

[7] D. Kossmann, T. Kraska, and S. Loesing. An evaluation of alternative architectures for transaction processing in the cloud. In *Proc SIGMOD'10*, pages 579–590, 2010.

[8] S. Krompass, D. Gmach, A. Scholz, S. Seltzsam, and A. Kemper. Quality of service enabled database applications. In *ICSOC*, pages 215–226, 2006.

[9] A. Li, X. Yang, S. Kandula, and M. Zhang. CloudCmp: comparing public cloud providers. In *Proc IMC'10*, pages 1–14, 2010.

[10] F. Nah. A study on tolerable waiting time: how long are web users willing to wait? *Behaviour & Information Technology*, 23(3):153–163, 2004.

[11] J. Schad, J. Dittrich, and J.-A. Quiané-Ruiz. Runtime measurements in the cloud: Observing, analyzing, and reducing variance. *PVLDB*, 3(1):460–471, 2010.

[12] W. Smith. TPC-W: Benchmarking an ecommerce solution. White paper, Transaction Processing Performance Council, 2000.

[13] K. Srinivasan, S. Yuuw, and T. Adelmeyer. Dynamic VM migration: assessing its risks & rewards using a benchmark. In *Proc ICPE'11*, pages 317–322, 2011.

[14] V. Stantchev. Performance evaluation of cloud computing offerings. In *Proc IEEE AdvComp'09*, pages 187–192, 2009.

[15] J. Weinman. Time is Money: The Value of "On-Demand". www.joeweinman.com/Resources/Joe_Weinman_Time_Is_Money.pdf, Jan. 2011.

[16] N. Yigitbasi, A. Iosup, D. Epema, and S. Ostermann. C-meter: A framework for performance analysis of computing clouds. In *Proc CCGrid'09*, pages 472–477, 2009.

Statistical Detection of QoS Violations Based on CUSUM Control Charts

Ayman Amin
Faculty of Information and
Communication Technologies
Swinburne University of
Technology
Hawthorn, VIC 3122, Australia
aabdellah@swin.edu.au

Alan Colman
Faculty of Information and
Communication Technologies
Swinburne University of
Technology
Hawthorn, VIC 3122, Australia
acolman@swin.edu.au

Lars Grunske
Software Engineering: AG
AQUA
University of Kaiserslautern
Kaiserslautern,67653,
Germany
grunske@cs.uni-kl.de

ABSTRACT

Currently software systems operate in highly dynamic contexts, and consequently they have to adapt their behavior in response to changes in their contexts or/and requirements. Existing approaches trigger adaptations after detecting violations in quality of service (QoS) requirements by just comparing observed QoS values to predefined thresholds without any statistical confidence or certainty. These threshold-based adaptation approaches may perform unnecessary adaptations, which can lead to severe shortcomings such as follow-up failures or increased costs. In this paper we introduce a statistical approach based on CUSUM control charts called AuDeQAV - Automated Detection of QoS Attributes Violations. This approach estimates at runtime a current status of the running system, and monitors its QoS attributes and provides early detection of violations in its requirements with a defined level of confidence. This enables timely intervention preventing undesired consequences from the violation or from inappropriate remediation. We validated our approach using a series of experiments and response time datasets from real-world web services.

Categories and Subject Descriptors

D.2 [**Software Engineering**]: Subjects—*Software configuration management*

General Terms

Algorithms, Performance

Keywords

Quality of Service (QoS), Runtime Monitoring, QoS Violation, Runtime Adaptation, CUSUM Control Charts

1. INTRODUCTION

Software systems are being ever-increasingly used in our daily life and have become a crucial part of various critical and non-critical applications. Consequently, there is an increasing need for software systems that are more reliable, with higher performance, and support more users [4]. At runtime, software systems may suffer from changes in their operational environment or/and requirements specification, so they need to be adapted to satisfy the changed environment or/and specifications [28, 6, 3]. The research community has developed a number of approaches to building adaptive systems that respond to such changes, for example Rainbow [10], MUSIC [26], and StarMX [2], QoSMOS [3], just to name a few.

Currently, several approaches have been proposed either to monitor QoS attributes at runtime with the goal of detecting QoS violations in order to trigger adaptations (e.g. [13, 19, 23, 32, 33, 35, 37]), or to verify whether QoS values meet the desired level to detect violations of Service Level Agreements (SLAs) (e.g. [18, 27, 29, 14]). These approaches detect violations of QoS requirements by observing the running system and determining QoS values. If these values exceed a predefined threshold, they are considered to be QoS violations. These approaches have two important drawbacks.

- First, the approaches rely on detecting QoS violations based on an observation or sample. If there is a background volatility in measured values, there is no indication of statistical confidence that the sample in fact indicates a systemic problem. Consequently, unnecessary adaptations maybe performed leading to failures or increased costs associated with adaptation.

- Second, a running software system's typical performance capability is not characterized, so any unusual deviations from that behavior cannot be detected other than gross violations of QoS requirements. As a result we use a capability estimation technique that characterizes the current status of the software system behavior, which may help to improve detecting violations.

In our previous work [1] addressing these limitations we have proposed CREQA approach based on Shewhart and CUSUM control charts for the runtime evaluation of the software system's behavior to detect out-of-control situations, where the system's behavior has significantly changed.

However, the CREQA approach evaluates the software system's behavior *without* assuming any predefined QoS requirements. This approach may be useful in some cases but in most of the real cases there are predefined QoS requirements that need to be monitored and evaluated at runtime.

To address the drawbacks of the existing approaches and the limitation of our previous work, we propose a statistical approach called AuDeQAV (Automated Detection of QoS Attributes Violations) based on CUSUM control charts for the runtime detection of QoS attributes violations. This approach consists of four phases: (1) Estimating the running software system capability in terms of descriptive statistics, i.e. mean, standard deviation, and confidence interval of QoS attributes, in order to describe the current normal behavior; (2) Building a CUSUM control chart using the given QoS requirements; (3) After getting each new QoS observation, updating the CUSUM chart statistic and checking for statistically significant violations; (4) In case of detecting violations, providing warning signals to the management layer to take the required adaptation actions.

The main contributions of this paper include:

1. We propose an approach based on CUSUM control charts that characterizes a software system's capability and then monitors QoS attributes to detect QoS requirement violations before they lead to undesired consequences.

2. We use a case study and perform experiments to evaluate the accuracy and performance of the approach. In addition, we compare the approach with the threshold based method to highlight the former's advantages.

3. We apply the proposed approach to QoS response time data sets of real web services [5] to evaluate the applicability of the proposed approach.

The rest of the paper is organized as follows. Section 2 describes the research problem through a presentation of a motivating scenario and a discussion of related work. Section 3 provides some background on statistical control charts. The proposed approach AuDeQAV is discussed in Section 4. Evaluation of the proposed approach is reported in Section 5. Section 6 concludes the paper and outlines directions for future work.

2. RESEARCH PROBLEM

In this section we first present a scenario that illustrates QoS requirements of a real application. We then investigate the extent to which solutions presented in the literature can meet these requirements. The identified shortcomings are used to motivate our work.

2.1 Motivating Scenario

Scenario: A hospital has elderly patients who return home after a treatment but still need a daily follow up to complete the treatment course. The patients live in remote areas, and it is inconvenient for both the doctors and the patients to interact directly. To address this problem, the hospital will develop a Patient Assistance (PA) system [36, 12], which is a software- and telecommunication-based service, to enable the patients and the doctors to communicate in a timely manner. The patients' situations have different criticality levels. As such, there is a need to define a limit on the PA system's response time as QoS attribute based on the urgency of a patient's need. For example, when the patient's criticality level is high, the PA system should respond within two seconds to each request with a probability of 95% or higher.

Scenario Analysis: To assure the QoS requirements of the PA system, the hospital needs a management framework that monitors the PA system's QoS metrics. Then, based on the monitored QoS data, the management framework determines violations of the above requirements and gives warning signals to trigger the required adaptation actions, e.g. allocating more resources. This needs to be achieved before the violations lead to undesired consequences, e.g. putting a patient life in danger.

Consequently, to get a software system that is able to adapt itself in order to avoid QoS requirement violations its management framework must be able to monitor QoS attributes and detect in a timely manner QoS violations before they lead to undesired consequences. This can be achieved by continuously monitoring and collecting QoS values of the running system, and then using the collected data to infer unwanted systemic behavior.

2.2 Related Work

The above scenario shows that in order to fulfil the application requirements, the management framework needs the ability to monitor QoS attributes. In this subsection we investigate the literature and discuss how existing techniques/frameworks address the problem.

The Rainbow framework [10, 8], which has been developed to dynamically monitor and adapt a running software system, uses monitoring techniques to detect QoS violations after they have occurred by simply comparing the collected QoS values with the predefined threshold. It then uses condition-action scenarios (tactics) to fix these QoS violations. Other approaches [7, 9] that build on the Rainbow framework use the same mechanism to detect and address QoS violations.

The work in [31] proposes DySOA (Dynamic Service Oriented Architecture) that uses monitoring to track and collect information regarding a set of predefined QoS parameters (e.g. response time and failure rates), infrastructure characteristics (e.g. processor load and network bandwidth), and even context information (e.g. user GPS coordinates). The collected QoS information is directly compared to the QoS requirements; and in case of a deviation, the reconfiguration of the application is triggered.

In [16], a middleware architecture is proposed to enable SLA-driven clustering of QoS-aware application servers. This middleware consists of three components: The Configuration Service is responsible for managing the QoS-aware cluster, the Monitoring Service observes at runtime the application and verifies whether the QoS values meet the desired level to detect violations of SLAs, and the Load Balancing Service intercepts client requests to balance them among different cluster nodes. If the QoS values delivered by the cluster deviate from the desired level (e.g., the response time breaches the predefined threshold), the middleware reconfigures that cluster by adding clustered nodes.

Michlmayr et al. [18] have presented a framework that observes the QoS values and checks whether they meet the required levels to detect possible violations of SLAs. Once an SLA violation is detected, adaptive behavior can be triggered such as the hosting of new service instances. Also, in [27] a QoS requirements satisfaction is analyzed in terms of the SLA fulfillment, which is considered as the main quality criterion of a service.

Recent studies [19, 35] propose autonomic frameworks to monitor QoS attributes and dynamically adapt service-based systems in an automated manner in response to requirements violations. In [19], Mirandola and Potena propose a framework that dynamically adapts a service based system while minimizing the adaptation costs and guaranteeing a required level of QoS. This framework triggers adaptation actions automatically in response to runtime violation of system QoS constraints, or the availability/non-availability of services in the environment. Thongtra and Aagesen [35] present a framework for service configuration that has *goals*, which express required performance and income measures, and *policies*, which define actions in states with unwanted performance and income measures. This framework monitors quality attributes constraints and in the case of violations it triggers pre-defined policies.

All these approaches detect QoS violations by just comparing observed QoS values to predefined thresholds. Using such an approach has critical limitations:

- First, the current approaches collect QoS attribute values of a running system at specific times or periodically, i.e. second, minute, or hour; and if one (or more) of these collected values exceeds a predefined threshold they are considered to be QoS violations of the running system. However, in that sense these collected QoS values are considered to be samples, rather than a collection of all the experienced QoS values. This implies that false classifications are likely, and to correctly and significantly generalize to the running system over time one needs to either: (1) Collect all the experienced QoS values, which is inapplicable in most real-world cases, or (2) Use a statistical method that can generalize the behavior with a specified confidence level, e.g. 95%.

- Second, a software system capability, in terms of its different QoS attributes, can not be estimated. Where, it just verifies whether the QoS values exceed the given threshold and does not provide any information about the software system current status (e.g. the average and variance of the system response time). This updated capability estimation can help software system engineers to continuously obtain the current status of software system behavior, which enables them to detect a change or deviation in that behavior before undesired events occur.

The proposed AuDeQAV approach addresses these drawbacks. It uses collected QoS values to estimate the capability of the software system, and uses the predefined QoS requirements to build CUSUM chart to detect significant violations in these requirements with a specified confidence level.

3. CONTROL CHARTS BACKGROUND

Statistical control charts are an efficient quality control technique for online monitoring and detecting of changes and violations in a given statistical process [20, 11, 34, 15]. Control charts are constructed by taking sample readings of the variable to be controlled from the process, then plotting values of the quality characteristic of interest in time order on a chart. This chart contains a center line (CL), which represents the average value of the quality characteristic, and two other horizontal lines called the upper control limit (UCL) and the lower control limit (LCL). These control limits are chosen such that if the process is in-control, which means there is no change or shift in the process, nearly all of the sample points will fall between them. In general, if the values plot within the control limits, the process is assumed to be in-control, and no action is necessary. However, a value that falls outside of the control limits is taken as a signal that a change has occurred, the process is out-of-control, and investigation and corrective action are required.

The general model for a control chart proposed first by Shewhart [30] can be given as follows. Let X be a sample statistic that measures some quality characteristic of interest, and suppose that μ_X and σ_X are the mean and the standard deviation of X, respectively. Then chart parameters become:

$$UCL = \mu_X + D \cdot \sigma_X, \ CL = \mu_X, \ LCL = \mu_X - D \cdot \sigma_X \ (1)$$

where D is the distance expressed in standard deviation units of the control limits from the center line. Usually D is chosen in practice to be 3 standard deviations to give a statistical confidence level of about 99.7%. Thus, this control chart is called three sigma (3-σ) chart.

In the cases that the quality characteristic of interest is in the form of required probability, i.e. proportion, the Shewhart chart is called P-chart and its parameters become:

$$UCL = P_0 + D \cdot \sigma_{P_0}, \ CL = P_0, \ LCL = P_0 - D \cdot \sigma_{P_0} \ (2)$$

where P_0 is the required proportion to be monitored and its standard deviation σ_{P_0} is computed as $\sigma_{P_0} = \sqrt{(P_0(1 - P_0)/n)}$.

Example ▷ For the sake of illustrating how a P-chart can be used to monitor QoS requirement and detect violations, suppose that there is a running software system and the requirement is "No more than 2 seconds response time for 95% of the requests". In other words, the requirement is that the proportion of response time that is greater than 2 seconds is 0.05. To use a P-chart to monitor this software system performance the following steps are required: First, samples of size n (e.g. $n = 30$) from the system response time are taken. Second, a variable called rt is created, and it takes the value 1 if the response time is greater than 2 seconds and 0 otherwise. Third, the proportion of the response time (P_{rt}) that is greater than 2 seconds is computed, and the 3-σ control limits of P-chart are constructed using equation (2) and response time requirement as follows: UCL = 0.05 + 3($\sqrt{(0.05 * 0.95/30)}$) = 0.17, CL = 0.05, and LCL = 445 - 3(($\sqrt{(0.05 * 0.95/30)}$)) = -0.17. Fourth, the values of computed proportions P_{rt} are checked and compared to the control limits; and if there is any value that falls outside of these control limits, it is taken as a warning signal that a violation in the response time requirement has occurred. ◁

P-charts have a critical limitation when used at runtime because they wait until all the n sample observations are collected before computing the proportion. This process implies late detection of violations. Therefore, our proposed approach adopts advanced control charts that continuously monitor response time observations, and once the value is obtained it is checked and compared to the built chart limits. These control charts and their performance measures are discussed in detail in the following subsections.

3.1 CUSUM Control Charts

Page [22] has proposed CUSUM control charts as an effective alternative to the Shewhart control charts. These charts compute and plot the cumulative deviations sum of the sample values from a target (required) value. For example, suppose that samples of size $n = 1$ are collected, and X_j is the value of the jth sample. Then, the CUSUM control chart is formed by plotting the quantity $C_i = \sum_{j=1}^{i}(X_j - \mu_0)$ against the sample number, where μ_0 is the target value for the quality characteristic of interest. Because the CUSUM charts combine information from several samples, they are more effective than Shewhart charts for detecting small process shifts. Furthermore, they are a good candidate for situations where an automatic measurement of the quality characteristic is economically feasible as they are particularly effective with samples of size $n = 1$ [15].

If the cumulative sum statistic C_i fluctuates around zero, it indicates that the process remains in-control at the target value. However, if it has a positive (or negative) drift, it signals that the quality characteristic values have shifted upward (or downward). Therefore, if the CUSUM has either positive or negative trend in the plotted points, this should be considered as a signal that the quality characteristic values have deviated from the target and required value.

Particularly, if the quality characteristic of interest is proportion (P) and samples observations (X_t) are binary data (0 and 1 values), the CUSUM statistic is called Bernoulli CUSUM. This statistic, to be used to detect an increase in P, is computed using a tabular procedure as follows:

$$B_t = max[0,\ B_{t-1} + X_t - K], \quad t = 1, 2, \ldots, \quad (3)$$

where the starting value is $B_0 = 0$. The parameter K is called the reference value for the CUSUM chart. For the value of K to be determined, it is necessary to specify the values P_0 and P_1, where P_0 represents the target or required value (in our work, it is a QoS requirement) and $P_1 > P_0$ is an out-of-control (violation) value of P that is required to be quickly detected. In other words, $(P_1 - P_0)$ represents the violation size in P that is required to be quickly detected. After specifying P_0 and P_1, K can be computed as follows:

$$K = r_1 / r_2, \quad (4)$$

where, r_1 and r_2 are constants computed based on likelihood ratio test [15] as follows:

$$r_1 = -\ln\left[\frac{1 - P_1}{1 - P_0}\right]\ and\ r_2 = \ln\left[\frac{P_1(1 - P_0)}{P_0(1 - P_1)}\right] \quad (5)$$

The lower and upper control limits of CUSUM are computed as follows [25]:

$$LCL = -\frac{\ln\frac{(1-\alpha)}{\beta}}{2\ln\frac{P_1(1-P_0)}{P_0(1-P_1)}}\ and\ UCL = \frac{\ln\frac{(1-\beta)}{\alpha}}{2\ln\frac{P_1(1-P_0)}{P_0(1-P_1)}} \quad (6)$$

where α is an upper bound for an acceptable type I error (or a false positive) which means that the CUSUM chart decides that there is a violation in the QoS requirements of the running system even when the system is at the required level and does not have any violation, and β is an upper bound for an acceptable type II error (or a false negative) which means that the chart decides that there is no violation when the system has indeed violated its requirements. To improve the performance of CUSUM control charts, some researchers [17] have proposed the fast initial response (FIR) feature which permits a more rapid response to an initial out-of-control, especially at start-up or after the CUSUM chart has given an out-of-control signal.

In practice when the monitored proportion is small the LCL will be negative, and that means the lower limit is ineffective [24]. Consequently, our approach concentrates only on the upper limit (UCL), which in literature is normally called the decision interval H. It is clear from equation 6 that the value of this decision interval is determined by P_0, P_1, and the required α and β values. It is worth mentioning that statistically in practice $(1 - \alpha)$ and $(1 - \beta)$ refer to the statistical confidence and power levels of the chart, respectively.

3.2 Control Charts performance

The control chart performance is measured by the ability of the chart to detect changes in the process. The average run length (ARL), which is defined as the average number of samples that must be plotted on the chart before a sample indicates an out-of-control condition, is a commonly used measure for the performance of a control chart.

In the case of Shewhart chats, the ARL can be calculated from the mean of a geometric random variable [20]. For illustration, suppose that p is the probability that any point falls outside of the control limits, then, the ARL is computed as the inverse of that probability, $ARL = 1/p$. In the case of three sigma limits and an in-control process, we have $p = 0.0027$ based on the normal distribution and the in-control ARL (ARL_0) = 370. That means on the average a false alarm will be generated every 370 data points. In the case of out-of-control, to compute the out-of-control ARL (ARL_1); the probability p of a point falls outside of the control limits is needed and it depends on the shift size. Suppose the actual mean of process shifts by three standard deviations, then it is straightforward to show that $p = 0.5$ and $ARL_1 = 1/0.5 = 2$.

The ARL for the CUSUM chart depends on the decision interval H, which determines the width of control limits, and on the selected reference value K. Several authors investigated the optimal values of K and H, and they concluded that a CUSUM chart with smaller K is more sensitive to small shifts and violations [15]. Practically, it is advisable to choose the decision interval H that corresponds to an in-control ARL of roughly 740, which is equivalent to a 3σ Shewhart chart [15].

4. THE AUDEQAV APPROACH

The AuDeQAV is a statistical approach we introduce for the automated detection of QoS attributes violations. This approach uses CUSUM control charts. It has mainly two tasks. First, it uses collected QoS data to estimate at run-time the capability of a running system. This capability estimation is to obtain the current status of the software system's behavior. The capability is represented in terms of mean, standard deviation, and confidence interval of QoS attributes. Second, the AuDeQAV uses predefined QoS requirements and the software system capability estimates to construct a CUSUM model for monitoring the QoS values and detecting violations in their requirements.

To achieve these tasks, the AuDeQAV approach has four steps as depicted in Figure 1. In the following, we explain in detail these steps and illustrate the procedure based on the response time data of the Patient Assistance (PA) system.

Phase 1 (P1): Estimating Capability

In the first phase, the software system's capability is estimated in terms of descriptive statistics of specific QoS attributes. This estimation is performed after the software system has started, and it can be updated in different schedules:

1. After an adaptation has been triggered.

2. Every specific predefined period of time (including after an adaptation has been triggered), e.g. after every one day and also after any adaptation action has been triggered.

3. After getting each new QoS attribute value.

Basically, the main task of the approach in that phase is to use collected QoS values to estimate mean and standard deviation of the given QoS attributes, and then it uses these estimates to build QoS confidence interval, i.e. 95% confidence interval. In cases where the software system engineers do not have precise QoS requirements, they can use these QoS estimates and confidence intervals to update and refine these requirements. On the other hand, if there are precise requirements, the approach can initially estimate how these requirements are fulfilled from the collected QoS data. This initial estimation of requirements fulfilment can help the software system engineers later, when they have requirement violations, in triggering adaptation actions, e.g. by how much they need to increase the resources, or in refining the QoS requirements.

There is an important issue related to this phase: how many samples are needed to be used to accurately estimate the system capability? To address this issue, we use a sequential estimation method based on sampling theory. According to parametric estimation methods [21], the absolute relative error of estimating a population mean is less than a specified amount which can be evaluated as follows:

$$E = \frac{Z_{\alpha/2}\sigma}{\bar{x}\sqrt{n}} \quad (7)$$

where n, $\bar{x}$ and σ are the sample size, mean and standard deviation respectively. $Z_{\alpha/2}$ is a coefficient of the confidence level $100(1-\alpha)\%$, and it is computed from the standard normal distribution. This equation can be used only when $\bar{x}$ is normally distributed. To address this normality issue we use the central limit theorem [21], which simply reports that a mean of sample of size at least 30 observations driven from any distributed population can be approximated to be normally distributed.

Therefore, our sequential estimation method works as follows:

1. Specify the maximum absolute relative error (E_{req}) that is required to estimate the software system's capability. The required confidence level is also specified, e.g. 95%, to compute the coefficient $Z_{\alpha/2}$.

2. Once 30 QoS observations are obtained, the approach computes QoS mean and standard deviation, $\bar{x}$ and σ, and then computes E as in equation 7.

3. The inequality $E_{req} \leq E$ is evaluated. If it is satisfied, use these estimates; otherwise wait until new QoS observation are received and repeat 2 and 3 until capability estimates with a required accuracy are obtained.

Example ▷ Suppose that the proposed approach is being used to monitor the PA system's response time values (referred as PA(RT)) and to detect a violation in its requirement which is: *"No response time is more than 2 seconds for 95% of the requests"*. We specify the confidence level = 95% (accordingly, $Z_{\alpha/2} = 1.96$) and $E_{req} = 0.01$ to estimate the capability of PA system. Once the approach gets 30 response time observations, it computes mean (= 1621.6) and standard deviation (= 172.1), and then computes E (= 0.038). The approach concludes that $E_{req} < E$ and then estimates the capability in terms of mean, standard deviation, and 95% confidence interval of PA(RT). In addition, as we have assumed that we have a precise response time requirement (i.e. PA(RT) $\leq$ 2 seconds with 95%), the approach can initially estimate the fulfilment of this requirement (*ReqFul (%)*) by computing the proportion of response time values that are equal to or less than 2 seconds. These results are depicted in Table 1. These estimates in practice can be updated after getting each new response time observation. ◁

Metric (in ms)	Mean	Std. Dev.	Lower 95% limit	Upper 95% limit	ReqFul (%)
Value	1621.6	172.1	1468.9	1782.5	96.7

Table 1: **Response time capability estimates of PA system**

Phase 2 (P2): Building CUSUM Control Charts

After estimating software capability and getting the predefined QoS requirements, the approach builds the CUSUM control chart model to monitor QoS values and directly detect violations. This building of control chart is achieved by using the methodology of CUSUM control charts that are explained and discussed in Section 3. However, some additional issues need to be addressed in order to build CUSUM charts at runtime.

These issues are as follows. Initially, there are some parameters that need to be specified as discussed in Section 3. These parameters are P_0, P_1 and H. P_0 can be easily computed from the QoS requirement or from the capability estimates. However, software system engineers need to specify the other two parameters P_1 and H. As H and P_1 determine the violation size that needs to be quickly detected and the control chart limits, the performance of CUSUM charts is dominated by the specified values of these parameters. Therefore, software system engineers need to carefully specify these parameters values to design and build a control chart with much better performance to detect the preferred violation size with smaller false alarms. In the evaluation section we investigate in detail how to specify the parameters of CUSUM charts to help engineers to design control charts with better performance and fewer false alarms.

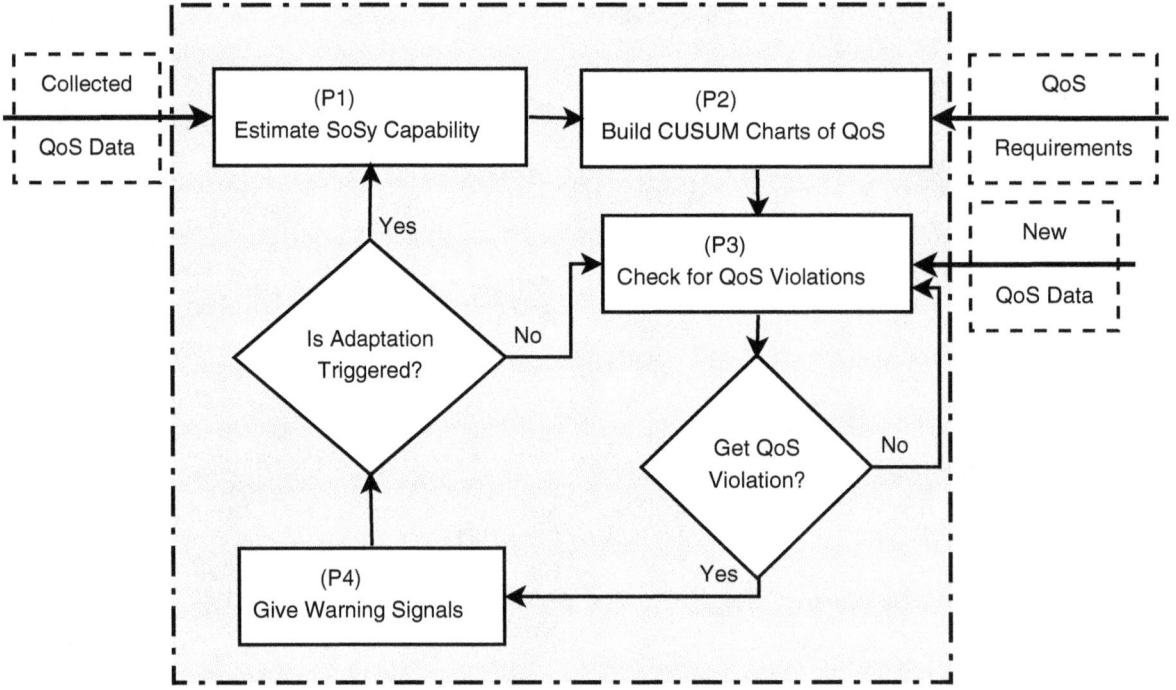

Figure 1: AuDeQAV approach process

Example ▷ To build a CUSUM chart for PA(RT), we first create a dummy variable X_t that takes the value 1 if the response time is greater than 2 seconds and 0 otherwise. Based on the response time requirement, it can be verified that $P_0 = 0.05$. In addition, we specify $P_1 = 0.10$, which means the violation size that we need to quickly detect is 0.05. Using P_0 and P_1 values and equations (4) and (5), K parameter value is computed ($= 0.0724$) and CUSUM statistic is rewritten as:

$$B_t = max[0, B_{t-1} + X_t - 0.0724], \quad t = 1, 2, \ldots, \quad (8)$$

where $B_0 = 0$. In addition, we set the statistical confidence and power of the chart to be 99%, which means that $\alpha = 0.01$ and $\beta = 0.01$. H value is computed using equation (6) as follows:

$$H = \frac{\ln \frac{(1-\beta)}{\alpha}}{2 \ln \frac{P_1(1-P_0)}{P_0(1-P_1)}} = \frac{\ln \frac{(1-0.01)}{0.01}}{2 \ln \frac{0.10(1-0.05)}{0.05(1-0.10)}} \approx 3.0 \quad (9)$$

▷

Phases 3 and 4 (P3&P4): Detecting QoS Violations and Giving Warning Signals

After building the CUSUM chart model (in P2) and getting each new QoS observation, the CUSUM statistic is recomputed; and once its value exceeds the decision interval H it is considered to be a requirement violation. Consequently a warning signal is sent to the management layer to trigger the necessary corrective adaptation.

Example ▷ For each new value of PA(RT), the approach continuously updates CUSUM statistic and checks for violations. Once it gets one value that exceeds $H = 3$, it gives a warning signal. To illustrate, we compute the sequential proportions of the response time values that are greater than

two seconds and the corresponding CUSUM statics and visualize this process in Figure 2. From this Figure, we can see that the approach detects violation of the response time requirement at sample 291, and this result is consistent with the sequentially computed proportion. ▷

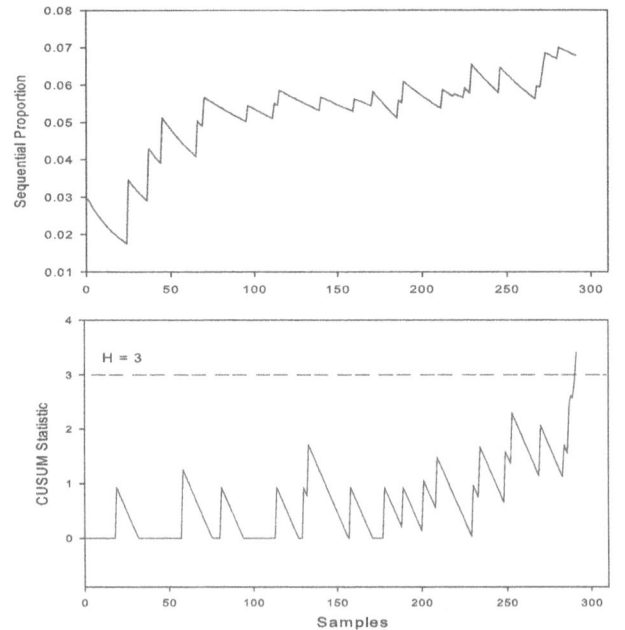

Figure 2: Applying AuDeQAV to monitor response time of PA system

5. EVALUATION

This section investigates various accuracy, performance, and applicability aspects of the proposed approach. First, the accuracy and performance of the approach are evaluated based on a series of experiments. Then, this approach is applied to datasets of response times from real-world web services in order to evaluate its applicability to analyzing and evaluating real situations. Finally, we discuss threats to the validity of our work.

5.1 Evaluating Accuracy and Performance

To investigate the performance and accuracy aspects of the proposed approach, it has been applied to the PA system case study. Based on this case study, a series of experiments have been performed in order to answer two basic research questions.

RQ1: How many samples are required for the approach to detect a violation in the QoS requirements, with respect to different violation sizes? And how many false alarms does the approach give?

RQ2: What is the real advantage of using the proposed approach over a simple threshold-based method to detect QoS violations?

RQ1: The number of samples required to detect a violation in the QoS requirements and the false alarm rate:

As discussed in the previous section, in order to apply the approach to monitor QoS attributes and detect violations in their requirements, the values of P_0, P_1, and H parameters need to be specified, and their specified values determine the values of ARL_0 and ARL_1. These ARL_0 and ARL_1 values refer to the expected false alarm rate and the expected number of samples to detect real occurred violations, respectively. Consequently, in our experiments we have a range of values for these parameters to analyze their effect on the performance of the proposed approach. These parameters and their specified values are discussed as follows:

- Response time requirement: To evaluate the performance of the approach in monitoring different requirements, we have five settings, i.e. that *no response time is more than 2 seconds for 99%, 95%, 90%, 85%, and 80% of the requests*. These requirements are expressed into required proportions of response times that are greater than 2 seconds (P_0 values) as inputs for CUSUM charts, i.e. 0.01, .05, 0.10, 0.15, and 0.20 respectively.

- Required violation size to be quickly detected ($[P_0-P_1]$ values): In our experiments we specify four violation sizes; 0.050, 0.075, 0.100, and 0.150.

- Decision interval (H): Its value is determined by the required statistical confidence ($1-\alpha$) and power ($1-\beta$). Therefore, we specify different values for H that vary from one to ten with an increment of one to represent different levels of α and β. It is worth noting that an increasing value of H provides increasing values of statistical confidence and power levels.

To explain in detail one scenario of these experiments, suppose we specify $P_0 = 0.05$, $P_1 = 0.10$, and $H = 4$. After that, a violation has been systematically injected with a predefined violation size into the case study's response time. Then the case study has been invoked, the AuDeQAV was run until it signaled a violation condition, and the number of samples (i.e. run lengths) was computed. Simply, the ARL was computed as the average of the run lengths of all the experiments with specific injected violation.

The results of this scenario are depicted (in italic) in the fourth column of data in Table 3(1). These results tell us that if our requirement is that *"the proportion of response times that are greater than 2 seconds is 0.05"* and the required violation size to be quickly detected is 0.05, then the approach (with statistical confidence and power level of about 99.75%) requires about 109 samples to detect a violation of size 0.05, about 70 samples to detect a violation of size 0.08, and about 10 samples to detect a violation of size 0.45. However, it gives a false alarm at about every 1188 samples (i.e. where the violation size = 0).

For more investigation, all the results for the requirement *"the proportion of response times that are greater than 2 seconds is 0.05"* with respect to different violation sizes and decision interval (H) values are depicted in Table 3. From this Table we can conclude the following:

1. Given the other parameters are fixed, an increasing value of the decision interval decreases the false alarm rate; however, at the same time it increases the required number of samples to detect a violation in the requirements. A similar result is concluded for the required violation size to be detected.

2. The larger the size of occurred violation, the smaller the number of samples required to detect this violation with the other parameters are fixed.

3. These results imply that there is a trade-off between decreasing the false alarm rate and decreasing the number of samples required to detect violations in the QoS requirements. In other words, increasing the statistical confidence and power levels will increase the number of samples and make the detection late. As a result, it is very important to choose reasonable values (not very high) for the chart confidence and power to enable the approach to provide better performance. Additionally, this confirms the common understanding based on [20, 34, 15].

We have obtained similar results by applying this approach to the other response time requirements, and consequently we can generalize that these parameters make the approach extensible for various preferences and requirements of software system engineers. They need only to decide a priori the maximum required false alarm rate and violation size required to be detected. Deciding the maximum required false alarm rate is very important as high false alarm rate may lead to perform unnecessary adaptations which cause severe shortcomings such as follow-up failures or increased costs. Currently, our approach uses default values for these two parameters as initial values and they can be changed according to software engineers' preferences. The default false alarm rate is a value that corresponds to statistical confidence and power levels of 99%, and the violation size equals to the required proportion to be monitored, i.e. $P_1 - P_0 = P_0$. However, it is worth mentioning that the optimal design of the proposed approach is the subject of our

(1) Required violation size ($P_1 - P_0$) to be detected = 0.05										
δP_0^* ⋱ H	1	2	3	4	5	6	7	8	9	10
0.00**	60.87	181.99	473.22	*1187.67*	2736.28	5889.48	12767.20	30567.20	38211.75	47037.67
0.05	23.60	45.86	76.38	*109.20*	142.57	179.11	214.39	246.88	279.47	320.33
0.08	18.22	33.19	51.19	*70.31*	89.97	109.33	129.89	147.43	168.02	187.88
0.10	14.34	24.68	36.85	*49.76*	61.98	75.06	87.74	100.38	113.32	126.06
0.15	10.33	16.73	23.95	*31.72*	39.52	47.23	55.07	62.84	70.58	78.30
0.25	6.72	10.34	14.30	*18.65*	23.18	27.58	32.01	36.40	40.80	45.18
0.35	4.99	7.54	10.20	*13.08*	16.13	19.22	22.39	25.38	28.42	31.40
0.45	3.99	5.99	8.00	*10.10*	12.34	14.69	17.15	19.57	21.92	24.18
0.70	2.66	3.99	5.33	*6.66*	7.99	9.34	10.73	12.18	13.78	15.46
0.95	2.00	3.00	4.00	*5.00*	6.00	7.00	8.00	9.00	10.00	11.00

(2) Required violation size ($P_1 - P_0$) to be detected = 0.075										
δP_0 ⋱ H	1	2	3	4	5	6	7	8	9	10
0.00	64.94	221.07	786.57	2672.81	9855.55	60011.67	180063.00	180064.00	185324.15	189271.31
0.05	24.63	51.97	91.92	139.79	191.78	243.06	300.44	362.53	411.80	469.63
0.08	18.48	35.16	56.75	80.18	103.33	127.40	150.39	174.55	198.06	222.64
0.10	14.56	25.81	39.91	54.80	69.08	83.95	98.61	113.24	127.67	142.45
0.15	10.47	17.28	25.32	33.83	42.55	51.20	59.57	68.23	76.61	85.01
0.25	6.70	10.40	14.46	18.99	23.59	28.24	32.84	37.51	41.99	46.57
0.35	4.99	7.58	10.31	13.29	16.45	19.72	22.90	26.04	29.18	32.40
0.45	4.01	6.04	8.08	10.24	12.59	15.05	17.57	20.08	22.41	24.76
0.70	2.67	4.01	5.34	6.67	8.02	9.39	10.83	12.38	14.06	15.75
0.95	2.00	3.00	4.00	5.00	6.00	7.00	8.00	9.00	10.00	11.00

(3) Required violation size ($P_1 - P_0$) to be detected = 0.10										
δP_0 ⋱ H	1	2	3	4	5	6	7	8	9	10
0.00	74.19	296.51	1234.18	4905.31	17396.91	26686.80	27528.20	28421.58	29751.91	30785.23
0.05	26.53	59.49	112.48	179.42	252.63	341.57	440.14	541.17	628.56	735.62
0.08	19.43	39.13	65.23	93.61	121.63	153.00	182.08	213.92	244.88	274.64
0.10	15.29	28.38	44.23	61.59	78.09	95.34	112.80	130.03	146.76	164.85
0.15	10.75	18.37	27.30	36.48	45.60	54.88	64.03	73.36	82.00	91.72
0.25	6.83	10.74	15.26	20.13	24.90	29.77	34.51	39.32	44.09	48.87
0.35	5.04	7.69	10.63	13.87	17.21	20.52	23.78	26.96	30.25	33.45
0.45	4.01	6.05	8.19	10.53	13.05	15.61	18.09	20.52	22.91	25.39
0.70	2.67	4.00	5.34	6.68	8.07	9.58	11.21	12.95	14.59	16.03
0.95	2.00	3.00	4.00	5.00	6.00	7.00	8.00	9.00	10.00	12.00

(4) Required violation size ($P_1 - P_0$) to be detected = 0.15										
δP_0 ⋱ H	1	2	3	4	5	6	7	8	9	10
0.00	75.48	353.64	1568.22	6698.72	27758.43	145364.00	151218.12	159851.52	165578.56	171582.45
0.05	27.78	70.37	154.52	281.10	465.03	710.50	1037.37	1444.22	1935.81	2585.88
0.08	20.33	44.71	83.49	131.01	184.50	245.46	309.68	365.37	438.64	511.03
0.10	15.92	32.22	53.96	78.27	103.81	129.02	156.26	180.92	207.17	233.84
0.15	10.96	19.45	29.94	41.33	52.44	63.72	74.86	85.98	96.82	107.88
0.25	6.88	11.08	16.03	21.36	26.65	31.96	37.17	42.57	47.87	53.25
0.35	5.04	7.80	10.93	14.34	17.91	21.45	24.90	28.30	31.80	35.24
0.45	3.99	6.05	8.26	10.74	13.38	16.01	18.58	21.12	23.68	26.25
0.70	2.67	4.00	5.34	6.70	8.15	9.76	11.53	13.23	14.72	16.14
0.95	2.00	3.00	4.00	5.00	6.00	7.00	8.00	9.00	11.00	12.00

* refers to occurred violation size

** refers to ARL_0 values

Table 2: ARL performance of AuDeQav approach

on-going research, as we need to develop an optimization-based method that helps in providing the optimal values of the approach parameters.

RQ2: Real advantages of using the proposed approach over a threshold-based method:

To emphasize the real advantages of using our proposed approach to detect QoS violations over a simple threshold-based method, we have applied the same experimental setup (in RQ1), and then we used our approach and the threshold-based method to detect violations.

In particular, the results of applying the threshold based method and our approach (with $P_1 = 0.10$ and $H = 3, 4, 5,$ and 6) for the requirement that *"the proportion of response times that are greater than 2 seconds is 0.05"* are depicted in Table 4. Initially, it is clear that the threshold based method does not require any parameters other than the QoS requirement (P_0 value); in contrast, our approach requires two other parameters P_1 and H to be specified. Thus the approach can cater for different preferences and requirements. To compare the performance in terms of the false alarm rate and the required samples to detect a violation, we compute a metric δARL that measures the change in ARL values of our approach comparing to threshold based method. This metric can be computed as:

$$\delta ARL = \frac{(ARL_{AuDeQAV} - ARL_{Threshold})}{ARL_{Threshold}} \quad (10)$$

where $ARL_{AuDeQAV}$ and $ARL_{Threshold}$ are ARL values of our proposed approach and threshold based method, respectively. This metric indicates that how many times the proposed approach duplicates the ARL values of the threshold based method. Based on this metric, if our approach duplicates ARL_0 more than its duplication for ARL_1 values, it implies its performance is better and gives smaller false alarm rate; and otherwise the threshold based method is better.

From Table 4, we can see that the performance of threshold based method is slightly better than our approach's with $H = 3$; however, our approach's performance is better with all other values of H. This result confirms that specifying the value of decision interval is very important in determining the proposed approach performance. Additionally, we can notice that the larger H value, the larger duplication of ARL_0 than ARL_1.

Generally, based on our experiments we can conclude the real advantages of our approach over the threshold based methods as follows:

1. First, our approach can estimate the current status of the running system through the capability estimation phase, and in some cases this can help the software system engineers to refine and update the QoS requirements. In contrast, the threshold based method only monitors the requirements by only comparing observed QoS values to predefined thresholds.

2. Second, in our approach statistical confidence and power levels can be specified a priori to represent the level of certainty in the taken decisions. On the other hand, threshold based method does not provide any confidence or certainty to generalize to the running system over time.

3. Third, as a way to enable a trade-off between the criticality of the QoS requirements and the cost-effectiveness of triggering adaptations, our approach provides the ability for the software system engineers to a priori specify the size of the required violation that is to be monitored and detected. Using a threshold based method does not provide this ability and gives all the violation sizes the same importance to be detected.

5.2 Evaluating Applicability

To further demonstrate the applicability of the proposed approach, we have selected five real-world web services' response time datasets. These response time datasets are collected by Cavallo et al. [5] by invoking the web services every hour for about four months. The description and response time requirements of these web services is reported in Table 5.

AuDeQAV approach can be applied at runtime to estimate these five web services' performance capability and detect violations in their requirements as follows:

1. The AuDeQAV uses the first 30 observations of the datasets to estimate the web services capability. The results are presented in the five left-most side columns of data of Table 6, and we can say initially that the response time requirements are fulfilled.

2. To continuously ensure that the performance of these web services is at the required level, the AuDeQAV uses the response time requirements and runs CUSUM chart (with $H = 3$ to give statistical confidence and power levels of about 99%) to monitor the web services response times and detect violations in their requirements. The results are depicted in the two right-most side columns of Table 6. To illustrate, the sequentially computed proportions of the response time values that are greater than 5.5 seconds for WS_4 and 7.5 seconds for WS_5 and their corresponding CUSUM statistics are depicted in Figures 3(1-4). Where the upper Figures 3(1) and 3(2) illustrate all the computed sequential proportions which provide the whole view of the behavior of WS_4 and WS_5 during about four months. The inner plots in Figures 3(3) and 3(4) visualize the approach behavior until the violation is detected. On the other hand, the outer plots in Figures 3(3) and 3(4) explain how the approach behaves over time to monitor WS_4 and WS_5, and they verify that this behavior is consistent with the corresponding sequential proportions.

3. After detecting changes in the response times of these web services, AuDeQAV gives warning signals to the management layer which in turn may trigger some adaptations, e.g. increasing the allocated resources for the web service application if the service provider is doing the monitoring or selecting a new service if the client is doing the monitoring.

4. If an adaptation is triggered, the web services' capability would need to be recalculated as in Step 1 above while the approach continues monitoring their experienced response time values.

It is worth mentioning that in our above example external web services are being invoked by a client, so little remedial action available to the client other than selecting another service. However, the AuDeQAV approach could also be used by service providers as part of a feedback loop to control provisioning levels for services in response to detected violations wrt their QoS requirements.

5.3 Threats to Validity

The threats to *internal validity* of the conducted experiments include the way we collect and measure QoS values

δP_0^*	Threshold Method	AuDeQAV $(H=3)$	δARL	AuDeQAV $(H=4)$	δARL	AuDeQAV $(H=5)$	δARL	AuDeQAV $(H=6)$	δARL
0.00**	107.05	473.22	3.42	1187.67	10.09	2736.28	24.56	5889.48	54.02
0.05	10.89	76.38	6.01	109.20	9.03	142.57	12.09	179.11	15.44
0.08	7.56	51.19	5.77	70.31	8.30	89.97	10.90	109.33	13.46
0.10	5.98	36.85	5.16	49.76	7.32	61.98	9.36	75.06	11.54
0.15	4.24	23.95	4.65	31.72	6.49	39.52	8.33	47.23	10.15
0.25	2.59	14.30	4.51	18.65	6.19	23.18	7.94	27.58	9.63
0.35	1.93	10.20	4.28	13.08	5.78	16.13	7.36	19.22	8.96
0.45	1.51	8.00	4.31	10.10	5.71	12.34	7.20	14.69	8.76
0.70	1.08	5.33	3.94	6.66	5.17	7.99	6.41	9.34	7.65
0.95	1.08	4.00	2.71	5.00	3.63	6.00	4.56	7.00	5.49

* refers to occurred violation size

** refers to ARL_0 values

Table 3: ARL performance of AuDeQav approach comparing to threshold based method

WSid	WS Name	Description	URL	rt.Req(s) [%]*
WS_1	XML Daily Fact	Returns a daily fact with an emphasis on XML Web Services and the use of XML within the Microsoft .NET Framework	`http://www.xmlme.com/WSDailyXml.asmx`	2.0 [95%]
WS_2	GetJoke	Outputs a random joke	`http://www.interpressfact.net/webservices/getJoke.asmx`	3.5 [95%]
WS_3	BLiquidity	Provides information on liquidity in a banking system	`http://webservices.lb.lt/BLiquidity/BLiquidity.asmx`	5.0 [90%]
WS_4	Fast Weather	Reports weather info for a given city	`http://ws2.serviceobjects.net/fw/FastWeather.asmx`	5.5 [90%]
WS_5	Currency Converter	Performs a currency conversion using the current quotation	`http://www.webservicex.com/CurrencyConvertor.asmx`	7.5 [90%]

* refers to response time requirement in seconds (s) with probability [%]

Table 4: Characteristics and response time requirements of the real web services

	Capability Estimation (in ms)					Violation Detection	
WSid	Mean	Std. Dev.	Lower 95% limit	Upper 95% limit	ReqFul (%)	Sample Number	Value (in ms)
WS_1	1512.5	169.4	1449.3	1575.8	96.67	305	3948
WS_2	2326.0	616.0	2096.0	2557.0	96.67	50	3798
WS_3	2495.0	2197.0	1674.0	3315.0	90.00	142	5743
WS_4	3861.0	4291.0	2259.0	5464.0	90.00	172	6166
WS_5	4676.0	1112.0	4253.0	5098.0	93.33	295	7715

Table 5: Real web services' capability estimates and their requirements' violation detection

and the range of scenarios that are simulated. To reduce the impact of these threats we have simulated a significant number of scenarios of the Patient Assistance (PA) system with a large variety of violation sizes and measured response time as a performance metric. This is to simulate various scenarios in reality and evaluate the corresponding accuracy and performance of the proposed approach.

On the other hand, *external validity* is threatened ﬀ obtained results cannot be generalized. For more realistic scenarios, we have applied the approach for the response time datasets of five real-world web services belonging to different domains. However, further applications to other web services are desirable. Additionally, we focus only on response time as a performance metric, the generalizations to other QoS attributes should be considered in future studies.

6. CONCLUSION AND FUTURE WORK

In this paper we have proposed a statistical approach AuDeQAV for runtime automated detection of violations in the QoS attributes requirements. This approach basically has two main tasks. First, it uses the collected QoS data to estimate the capability of the running software system in terms of descriptive statistics, i.e. mean, standard devia-

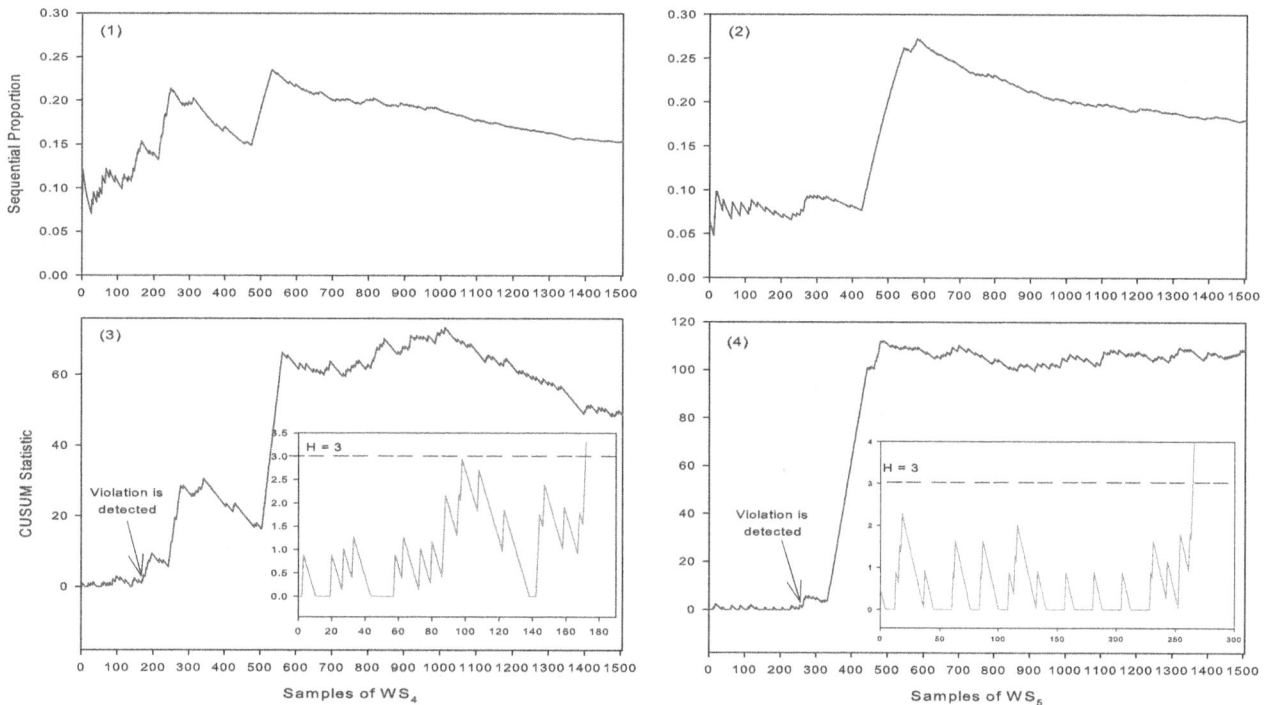

Figure 3: Applying AuDeQAV to monitor response time of WS_4 and WS_5

tion, and confidence interval of QoS attributes, in order to provide the current status of the system. Second, it uses the given QoS requirements to build the CUSUM chart model to monitor QoS attributes and directly detect violations wrt their requirements before undesired consequences occur.

The proposed approach was applied to experimental and real-world QoS datasets, especially response times; and the results demonstrate its accuracy in estimating the running software system capability and in monitoring and detecting QoS violations. Comparing the proposed approach with the threshold based method, we established the main advantages of our approach are: (1) Estimating the running system capability; (2) Providing statistical confidence and power levels which represent the level of certainty in the decisions taken; (3) Specifying the size of violation that is required to be quickly detected. Also, the results illustrate how the proposed approach might be applied to real-world software systems. The AuDeQAV approach therefore can be integrated into the existing software system management frameworks to support and advance dynamic runtime adaptation procedures.

We are planning to generalize this approach to add more QoS attributes, such as reliability and availability. The overhead of the proposed approach also needs to be carefully evaluated, especially for time-critical software systems. Similarly, to reduce the consumed memory a sliding window approach for the observed QoS attributes values needs to be investigated.

7. REFERENCES

[1] A. Amin, A. Colman, and L. Grunske. Using Automated Control Charts for the Runtime Evaluation of QoS Attributes. In *Proceedings of the 13ht IEEE International High Assurance Systems Engineering Symposium*. IEEE Computer Society, 2011.

[2] R. Asadollahi, M. Salehie, and L. Tahvildari. Starmx: A framework for developing self-managing java-based systems. In *ICSE Workshop on Software Engineering for Adaptive and Self-Managing Systems*, pages 58–67. IEEE Computer Society, 2009.

[3] R. Calinescu, L. Grunske, M. Z. Kwiatkowska, R. Mirandola, and G. Tamburrelli. Dynamic qos management and optimization in service-based systems. *IEEE Trans. Software Eng.*, 37(3):387–409, 2011.

[4] R. Calinescu and M. Kwiatkowska. Using quantitative analysis to implement autonomic IT systems. In *Proceedings of the 31st International Conference on Software Engineering*, pages 100–110. IEEE Computer Society, 2009.

[5] B. Cavallo, M. D. Penta, and G. Canfora. An empirical comparison of methods to support QoS-aware service selection. In *Proceedings of the 2nd International Workshop on Principles of Engineering Service-Oriented Systems*, pages 64–70. ACM, 2010.

[6] B. Cheng, R. de Lemos, H. Giese, P. Inverardi, J. Magee, J. Andersson, B. Becker, N. Bencomo, Y. Brun, B. Cukic, et al. Software engineering for self-adaptive systems: A research roadmap. *Software Engineering for Self-Adaptive Systems*, pages 1–26, 2009.

[7] S.-W. Cheng, A.-C. Huang, D. Garlan, B. Schmerl, and P. Steenkiste. An architecture for coordinating

multiple self-management systems. In *Proceedings of the 4th Working IEEE/IFIP Conference on Software Architecture*, pages 243–252. IEEE, 2004.

[8] S.-W. Cheng, A.-C. Huang, D. Garlan, B. Schmerl, and P. Steenkiste. Rainbow: Architecture-based self-adaptation with reusable infrastructure. In *Proceedings of the First International Conference on Autonomic Computing*, pages 276–277. IEEE Computer Society, 2004.

[9] A. cheng Huang and P. Steenkiste. Building self-adapting services using service-specific knowledge. In *Proceedings of IEEE High Performance Distributed Computing*, pages 34–43. IEEE, 2005.

[10] D. Garlan, S.-W. Cheng, A.-C. Huang, B. Schmerl, and P. Steenkiste. Rainbow: Architecture-based self-adaptation with reusable infrastructure. *Computer*, 37(10):46–54, 2004.

[11] R. D. Gibbons. Use of combined shewhart-cusum control charts for ground water monitoring applications. *Ground water*, 37(5):682–691, 1999.

[12] L. Grunske. An effective sequential statistical test for probabilistic monitoring. *Information and Software Technology*, 53(3):190 – 199, 2011.

[13] L. Grunske and P. Zhang. Monitoring probabilistic properties. In H. van Vliet and V. Issarny, editors, *Proceedings of the 7th joint meeting of the European Software Engineering Conference and the International Symposium on Foundations of Software Engineering*, pages 183–192. ACM, 2009.

[14] B. Halima, M. Guennoun, K. Drira, and M. Jmaiel. Providing Predictive Self-Healing for Web Services: A QoS Monitoring and Analysis-based Approach. *Journal of Information Assurance and Security*, 3(3):175–184, 2008.

[15] D. Hawkins and D. Olwell. *Cumulative sum charts and charting for quality improvement*. Springer Verlag, 1998.

[16] G. Lodi, F. Panzieri, D. Rossi, and E. Turrini. SLA-driven clustering of QoS-aware application servers. *IEEE Transactions on Software Engineering*, pages 186–197, 2007.

[17] A. Luceno and A. Cofino. The random intrinsic fast initial response of two-sided cusum charts. *An Official Journal of the Spanish Society of Statistics and Operations Research*, 15(2):505–524, 2006.

[18] A. Michlmayr, F. Rosenberg, P. Leitner, and S. Dustdar. Comprehensive QoS monitoring of Web services and event-based SLA violation detection. In *Proceedings of the 4th International Workshop on Middleware for Service Oriented Computing*, pages 1–6. ACM, 2009.

[19] R. Mirandola and P. Potena. A qos-based framework for the adaptation of service-based systems. *Scalable Computing: Practice and Experience*, 12(1), 2011.

[20] D. C. Montgomery. *Introduction to statistical quality control*. Wiley-India, 2007.

[21] D. C. Montgomery and G. C. Runger. *Applied statistics and probability for engineers*. New York; John Wiley, 2003.

[22] E. Page. Continuous inspection schemes. *Biometrika*, 41(1-2):100–115, 1954.

[23] F. Raimondi, J. Skene, and W. Emmerich. Efficient online monitoring of web-service SLAs. In *Proceedings of the 16th ACM SIGSOFT International Symposium on Foundations of software engineering*, pages 170–180, New York, NY, USA, 2008. ACM Press.

[24] M. Reynolds and Z. Stoumbos. A general approach to modeling cusum charts for a proportion. *IIE Transactions*, 32(6):515–535, 2000.

[25] M. Reynolds Jr and Z. Stoumbos. A cusum chart for monitoring a proportion when inspecting continuously. *Journal of Quality Technology*, 31(1):87–108, 1999.

[26] R. Rouvoy, P. Barone, Y. Ding, F. Eliassen, S. Hallsteinsen, J. Lorenzo, A. Mamelli, and U. Scholz. Music: Middleware support for self-adaptation in ubiquitous and service-oriented environments. *Software Engineering for Self-Adaptive Systems*, pages 164–182, 2009.

[27] D. Rud, A. Schmietendorf, and R. Dumke. Resource metrics for service-oriented infrastructures. *Proc. SEMSOA 2007*, pages 90–98, 2007.

[28] M. Salehie and L. Tahvildari. Self-adaptive software: Landscape and research challenges. *ACM Transactions on Autonomous and Adaptive Systems (TAAS)*, 4(2):1–42, 2009.

[29] F. Schulz. Towards Measuring the Degree of Fulfillment of Service Level Agreements. In *Third International Conference on Information and Computing*, pages 273–276. IEEE, 2010.

[30] W. A. Shewhart. Economic control of quality of manufactured product. *New York: Van Nostrand*, 1931.

[31] J. Siljee, I. Bosloper, J. Nijhuis, and D. Hammer. Dysoa: making service systems self-adaptive. In *ICSOC*, pages 255–268. Springer, 2005.

[32] J. Simmonds, Y. Gan, M. Chechik, S. Nejati, B. O'Farrell, E. Litani, and J. Waterhouse. Runtime monitoring of web service conversations. *IEEE T. Services Computing*, 2(3):223–244, 2009.

[33] J. Skene, A. Skene, J. Crampton, and W. Emmerich. The monitorability of service-level agreements for application-service provision. In V. Cortellessa, S. Uchitel, and D. Yankelevich, editors, *Proceedings of the 6th International Workshop on Software and Performance*, pages 3–14. ACM, 2007.

[34] Z. G. Stoumbos, M. R. Reynolds, T. P. Ryan, and W. H.Woodall. The state of statistical process control as we proceed into the 21st century. *Journal of the American Statistical Association*, 95(451):992–998, 2000.

[35] P. Thongtra and F. A. Aagesen. An autonomic framework for service configuration. In *Proceedings of the Sixth International Multi-Conference on Computing in the Global Information Technology*, pages 116–124, 2011.

[36] P. Zhang, B. Li, and L. Grunske. Timed property sequence chart. *Journal of Systems and Software*, 83(3):371–390, 2010.

[37] P. Zhang, W. Li, D. Wan, and L. Grunske. Monitoring of probabilistic timed property sequence charts. *Softw, Pract. Exper*, 41(7):841–866, 2011.

User-Friendly Approach for Handling Performance Parameters during Predictive Software Performance Engineering

Rasha Tawhid
School of Computer Science
Carleton University, Ottawa, ON, Canada
e-mail: rtawhid@connect.carleton.ca

Dorina Petriu
Dept. of Systems and Computer Engineering
Carleton University, Ottawa, ON, Canada
e-mail: petriu@sce.carleton.ca

ABSTRACT

A Software Product Line (SPL) is a set of similar software systems that share a common set of features. Instead of building each product from scratch, SPL development takes advantage of the reusability of the core assets shared among the SPL members. In this work, we integrate performance analysis in the early phases of SPL development process, applying the same reusability concept to the performance annotations. Instead of annotating from scratch the UML model of every derived product, we propose to annotate the SPL model once with generic performance annotations. After deriving the model of a product from the family model by an automatic transformation, the generic performance annotations need to be bound to concrete product-specific values provided by the developer. Dealing manually with a large number of performance annotations, by asking the developer to inspect every diagram in the generated model and to extract these annotations is an error-prone process. In this paper we propose to automate the collection of all generic parameters from the product model and to present them to the developer in a user-friendly format (e.g., a spreadsheet per diagram, indicating each generic parameter together with guiding information that helps the user in providing concrete binding values). There are two kinds of generic parametric annotations handled by our approach: product-specific (corresponding to the set of features selected for the product) and platform-specific (such as device choices, network connections, middleware, and runtime environment). The following model transformations for (a) generating a product model with generic annotations from the SPL model, (b) building the spreadsheet with generic parameters and guiding information, and (c) performing the actual binding are all realized in the Atlas Transformation Language (ATL).

Categories and Subject Descriptors

C.4 [**Performance of Systems**]: *modeling techniques, performance attributes*. D.2.4 [**Software/Program Verification**]: *model checking*

General Terms

Performance, Design

Keywords

Model-driven development, performance model, Performance Completion, ATL, MARTE, SPL, UML.

1. INTRODUCTION

A Software Product Line (SPL) is a set of similar software systems built from a shared set of assets, which are realizing a common set of features satisfying a particular domain. Experience shows that by adopting a SPL development approach, organizations achieve increased quality and significant reductions in cost and time to market [9].

An emerging trend apparent in the recent literature is that the SPL development moves toward adopting a Model-Driven Development (MDD) paradigm. This means that models are increasingly used to represent SPL artifacts, which are building blocks for many different products with all kind of options and alternatives. In previous research [22][23][24] the authors of the paper proposed to integrate performance analysis in the early phases of the model-driven development process for Software Product Lines (SPL), with the goal of evaluating the performance characteristic of different products by generating and analyzing quantitative performance models. Our starting point was the so-called SPL model, a multi-view UML model of the core family assets representing the commonality and variability between different products. We added another dimension to the SPL model, annotating it with generic performance specifications (i.e., using parameters instead of actual values) expressed in the standard UML profile MARTE [18]. Such parameters appear as variables and expression in the MARTE stereotype attributes.

In order to analyze the performance of a specific product running on a given platform, we need to generate a performance model for that product by model transformations from the SPL model with generic performance annotations. In our research, this is done in three big steps: a) instantiating a product model with generic performance parameters from the SPL model; b) binding the generic parameters to concrete values provided by the user and c) generating a performance model for the product from the model obtained in the previous step. The model transformation (a) was developed in our previous work [22][23]; step (b) represents the contribution of this paper; and the PUMA transformation (c) for generating performance models from annotated UML models has been developed previously in our research group [27].

Since step (b) requires input from the user, it is implemented by two transformations, as shown in Fig. 1: the first collects all the generic parameters that need to be bound to concrete values from the automatically generated product model and presents them to the developer in a user-friendly spreadsheet format, while the

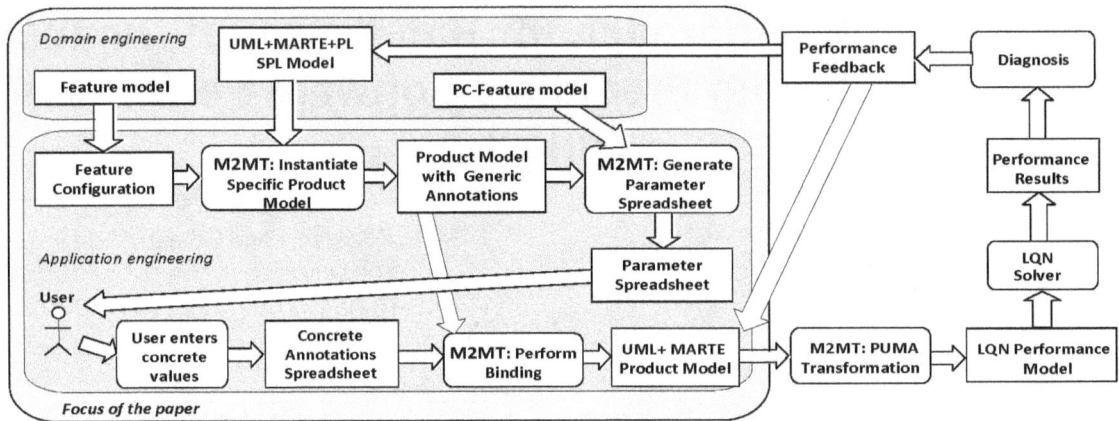

Figure 1. Approach for deriving a product performance model.

second performs the actual binding to concrete values provided by the developer. The list of annotation parameters presented to the developer contains not only the parameter name and the model elements it belongs to, but also some guiding information to help the user in providing concrete values, as explained in more detail in section 3.2.

Performance is a runtime property of the deployed system and depends on two types of factors: some are contained in the design model of the product (generated from the SPL model) while others characterize the underlying platforms and runtime environment. Performance models need to reflect both types of factors. Woodside et al. proposed the concept of performance completions to close the gap between abstract design models and external platform factors [26]. Performance completions provide a means to extend the modeling constructs of a system by including the influence of the underlying platforms and execution environments in performance evaluation models. Since our goal is to automate the derivation of a performance model for a specific product from the SPL model, we propose to deal with performance completions in the early phases of the SPL development process by using a so-called Performance Completion feature (PC-feature) model similar to [13]. The PC-feature model explicitly captures the variability in platform choices, execution environments, different types of communication realizations, and other external factors that have an impact on performance, such as different protocols for secure communication channels and represents the dependencies and relationships between them [23]. Therefore, our approach uses two feature models for a SPL: 1) a regular feature model for expressing the variability between member products (as described in Section 2.1), and 2) a PC-feature model introduced for performance analysis reasons to capture platform-specific variability (as described in Section 2.3).

We propose to include the performance impact of underlying platforms into the UML+MARTE model of a product as aggregated platform overheads, expressed in MARTE annotations attached to existing processing and communication resources in the generated product model. This will keep the model simple and still allow us to generate a performance model containing the performance effects of both the product and the platforms. Every possible PC-feature choice is mapped to certain MARTE annotations corresponding to UML model elements in the product model. This mapping is realized by the transformation generating the parameter spreadsheets, which is providing the user with

mapping information in order to put the annotation parameters needing to be bound to concrete values into context, as described in Section 3.2.

Dealing manually with a large number of performance parameters and with their mapping, by asking the developer to inspect every diagram in the model, to extract these annotations and to attach them to the corresponding PC-features, is an error-prone process. This paper proposes a model transformation approach to automate the collection of all the generic parameters that need to be bound to concrete variables from the annotated product model, presenting them to the user in a user-friendly format.

We claim that the proposed technique for handling annotation parameters is user-friendly after comparing it with another approach used in earlier phases of our research, where the binding information was given as a set of couples {<generic_parameter>, <concrete_value>} created manually by the developer, after careful inspection of the generated UML model to extract all the parameters. The older approach required a lot of work from the developer and was error prone. The parameter file produced by hand contained no context information and no guidelines.

The proposed technique is illustrated with an e-commerce case study. The e-commerce SPL can generate a distributed application that can handle either business-to-business (B2B) or business-to-consumer (B2C) systems.

The paper is organized as follows: section 2 presents the domain engineering process where the SPL model, the regular feature model and the PC-feature model are constructed; section 3 presents the model transformations for generating a product model with concrete performance specifications; related work is discussed in section 4; and section 5 presents the conclusions.

2. DOMAIN ENGINEERING PROCESS

The SPL development process is separated into two major phases: 1) *domain engineering* for creating and maintaining a set of reusable artifacts and introducing variability in these software artifacts, so that the next phase can make a specific decision according to the product's requirements; and 2) *application engineering* for building family member products from reusable artifacts created in the first phase instead of starting from scratch.

The SPL assets created by the domain engineering process of interest for our research are represented by a multi-view UML design model of the family, called the SPL model, which

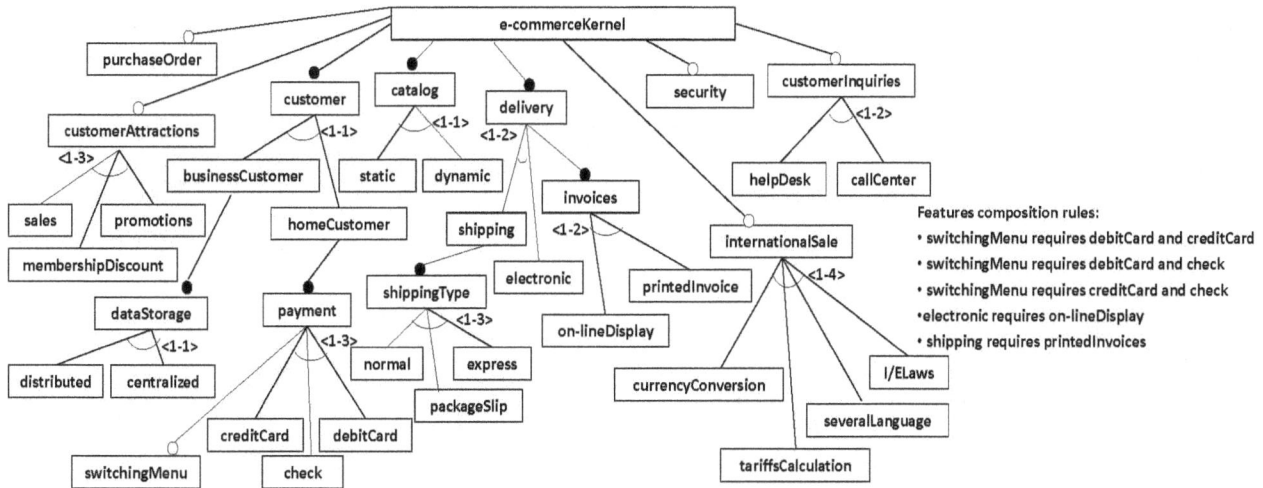

Figure 2. Feature model of the e-commerce SPL.

represents a superimposition of all variant products [22][23]. The creation of the SPL model employs two separate profiles: a product line profile introduced by Gomaa [12] for specifying the commonality and variability between products, and the MARTE profile for performance annotations. Another important outcome of the domain engineering process is the feature model used to represent commonalities and variabilities between family members in a concise taxonomic form. Additionally, we create a PC-feature model to represent the variability space of performance completions.

2.1 Feature Model

The feature models are used in our approach to represent two different variability spaces. This section describes the regular feature model representing functional variabilities between products. An example of feature model of an e-commerce SPL is represented in Fig. 2 in the extended FODA notation, Cardinality-Based Feature Model (CBFM) [11]. Since the FODA notation is not part of UML, the feature diagram is represented in the source model taken as input by our ATL transformation as an extended UML class diagram, where the features and feature groups are modeled as stereotyped classes and the dependencies and constraints between features as stereotyped associations. For instance, the two alternative features *Static* and *Dynamic* are mutually exclusive and so they are grouped into an *exactly-one-of* feature group called *Catalog*. In addition to functional features, we add to the diagram another type of features characterizing design decisions that have an impact on the non-functional requirements or properties. For example, the architectural decision related to the location of the data storage (centralized or distributed) affects performance, reliability and security, and is represented in the diagram by two mutually exclusive quality features. This type of feature related to a design decision is part of the design model, not just an additional PC-feature required only for performance analysis.

This feature model represents the set of all possible combinations of features for the products of the family. It describes the way features can be combined within this SPL. A specific product is configured by selecting a valid feature combination from the feature model, producing a so-called *feature configuration* based on the product's requirements. To enable the automatic derivation

of a given product model from the SPL model, the mapping between the features contained in the feature model and their realizations in a reusable SPL model needs to be specified, as shown in the next section. Also, each stereotyped class in the feature model has a tagged value indicating whether it is selected in a given feature configuration or not.

2.2 SPL Model

The SPL model should contain, among other assets, structural and behavioural views which are essential for the derivation of performance models. It consists of: 1) structural description of the software showing the high-level classes or components, especially if they are distributed and/or concurrent; 2) deployment of software to hardware devices; 3) a set of key performance scenarios defining the main system functions frequently executed.

Note that since the SPL model is generic, covering many products and containing variation points with variants, the MARTE annotations need to be generic as well. We use MARTE variables as a means of parameterizing the SPL performance annotations; such variables (parameters) will be assigned (bound to) concrete values during the product derivation process.

The functional requirements of the SPL are modeled as use cases. Use cases required by all family members are stereotyped as *«kernel»*. The variability distinguishing the members of a family from each other is explicitly modeled by use cases stereotyped as *«optional»* or *«alternative»*; such use cases are also annotated with the name of the feature(s) requiring them (given as stereotype attributes). This is an example of mapping between features and the model elements realizing them. The structural view of the SPL is presented as a class diagram and variabilities are modeled in the same manner as the use case diagram (i.e., stereotyped as *kernel*, *optional* or *alternative*). For more details about the SPL use case and class diagrams see [22][24].

The behavioural SPL view is modeled as sequence diagrams for each scenario of each use case of interest. Fig. 3 illustrates the kernel scenario *BrowseCatalog*. *«GaAnalysisContext»* is a MARTE stereotype indicating that the entire interaction diagram is to be considered for performance analysis. Its tag indicates a list of annotation variables representing context analysis parameters:

{contextParams = $N1, $Z1, $ReqT, $FSize, $Blocks}

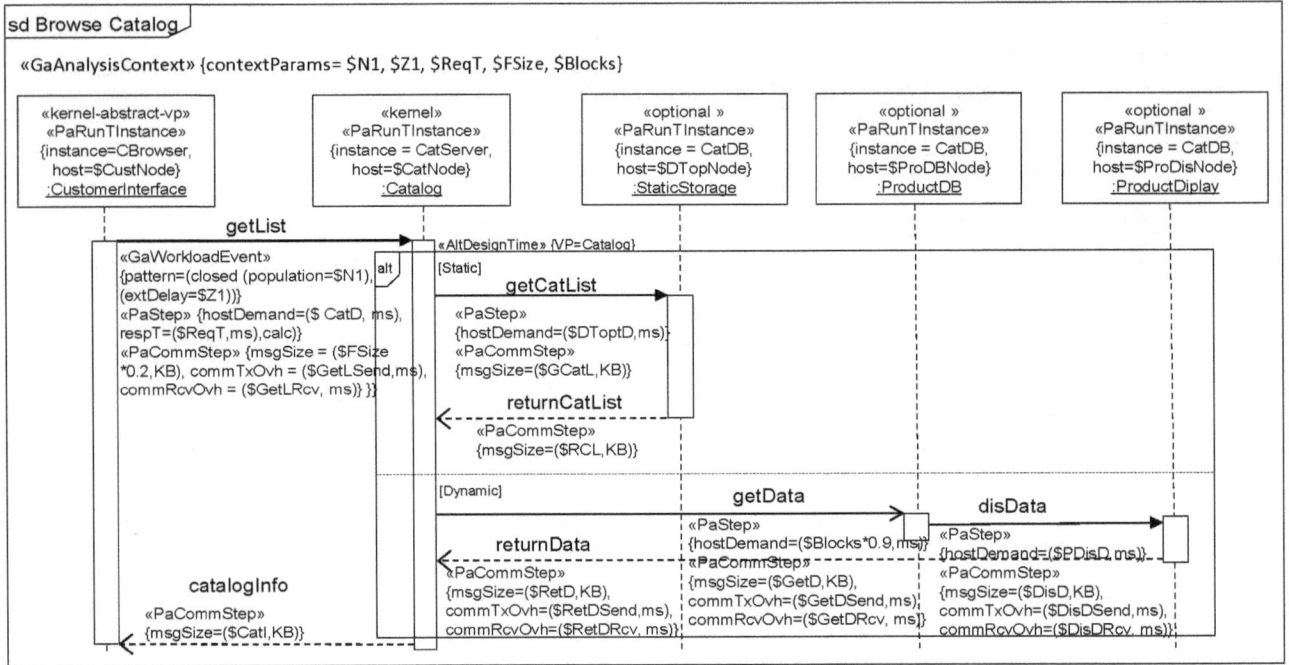

Figure 3. SPL Scenario Browse Catalog.

By convention, we use names starting with '$' for all MARTE variables to distinguish them from other identifiers and names.

The workload of a scenario is defined as a stream of events driving the system; a workload may be open or closed.

$$\text{«GaWorkloadEvent» } \{pattern=\$Patt\}$$

Sequence diagram variability that distinguishes between the behaviour of different features is expressed by extending the *alt* and *opt* fragments with the stereotypes *«AltDesignTime»* *«OptDesignTime»*, respectively. For example, the *alt* fragment stereotyped with *«AltDesignTime»* *{VP=Catalog}* gives two choices based on the value of the *Catalog* feature (*Static* or *Dynamic*); more specifically, each one of its *Interaction Operand* has a guard denoting the feature *Static* or *Dynamic*. An *alternative* feature that is rather complex and is represented as an extending use case, can be also modeled as an extended *alt* operator that contains an *Interaction Use* referring to an *Interaction* representing the extending use case. Note that regular *alt* and *opt* fragments that are not stereotyped represent choices to be made at runtime, as defined in UML.

Each lifeline whose role is an active object is stereotyped as *«PaRunTInstance»*, providing an explicit link at the annotation level between a role in a behavior definition (a lifeline) and the runtime instance of a process or thread (active object). For example, the tag *{instance=CBrowser}* indicates the name of runtime instance of a process executing the lifeline role, while the tag *{host=$CustNode}* indicates the physical node from the deployment diagram on which the instance is running. In this case, the *host* is given by the generic parameter *$CustNode*, which will be bound later to a concrete host name.

Conceptually, a scenario represented by a UML sequence diagram is composed of units of execution named steps. MARTE defines two kinds of steps for performance analysis: execution step (stereotyped *«PaStep»*) and communication step (stereotyped

«PaCommStep»). *«PaStep»* may be applied to an Execution Occurrence (represented as a thin rectangle on the lifeline) or to the message that triggers it. For instance, in Fig. 3, the message *getList* is stereotyped as an execution step:

$$\text{«PaStep» } \{hostDemand = (\$CatD, ms), \\ respT = ((\$ReqT, ms), calc)\}$$

where *hostDemand* indicates the execution time required by the step, given by the variable *$CatD* in time units of milliseconds. The attribute *respT* corresponds to the response time of the scenario starting with this step; the variable *$ReqT* will save the calculated response time in milliseconds. The same message *getList* is also stereotyped as a communication step:

$$\text{«PaCommStep» } \{ msgSize = (\$MReq, KB), \\ commTxOvh = (\$GetLSend, ms), \\ commRcvOvh = (\$GetLRcv, ms)\}\}$$

where the message size is the variable *$GetL* in KiloBytes. The overheads for sending and receiving this particular message are the variables *$GetLSend* and *$GetLRcv*, respectively, in milliseconds. We propose to annotate each communication step (which corresponds to a logical communication channel) with the CPU overheads for transferring the respective message: *commTxOvh* for transmitting (sending) the message and *commRcvOvh* for receiving it. Eventually, these overheads will be added in the performance model to the execution demands of the two execution hosts involved in the communication (one for sending and the other for receiving the respective message).

Since performance analysis depends on the software to hardware allocation, another structure diagram, which is not usually represented in the SPL models, has to be created in our approach.

2.3 SPL Performance Completion
In SPL, different members may vary from each other in terms of their functional requirements, quality attributes, platform choices,

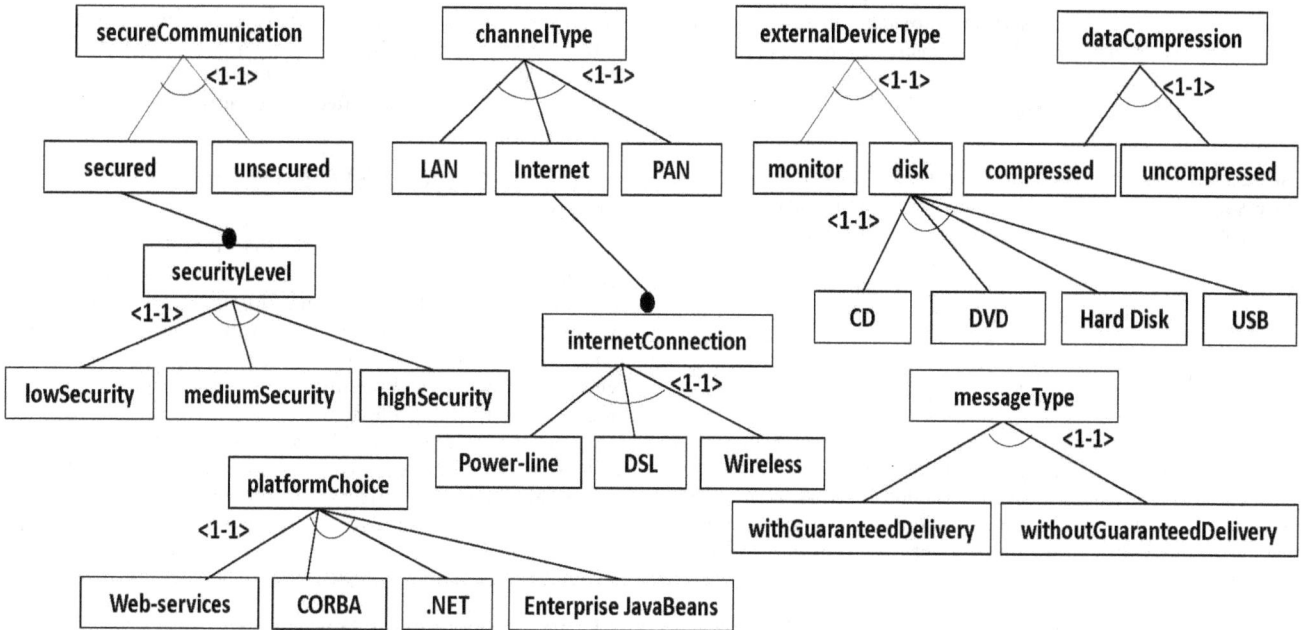

Figure 4. Part of the Performance-Completion feature model of the e-commerce SPL.

network connections, physical configurations, and middleware. Many details contained in the system that are not part of its design model but of the underlying platforms and environment, do affect the run-time performance and need to be represented in the performance model. *Performance completions*, as proposed by Woodside [26], are a manner to close the gap between the high-level design model and its different implementations. Performance completions provide a general concept to include low-level details of execution environment/platform in performance models.

This subsection covers the variability space of the performance completions and represents it through a Performance Completion feature model (PC-feature model) similar to [13]. Each feature from the PC-feature model shown in Fig. 4 may affect one or more performance attributes. For instance, data compression reduces the message size and at the same time increases the processor communication overhead for compressing and decompressing the data. Thus, it is mapped to the performance attributes message size and communication overhead through the MARTE attributes *msgSize*, *commTxOvh* and *commRcvOvh*, respectively. The mapping here is between a PC-feature and the performance attribute(s) affected by it, which are represented as MARTE stereotype attributes associated to different model elements. Table 1 illustrates this type of mapping between PC-features and the design model, set up through the MARTE stereotypes attached to model elements.

Fig. 4 illustrates a part of the PC-feature model for our case study. Adding security solutions requires more resources and longer execution times, which in turn has a significant impact on system performance. We introduce a PC-feature group called *secureCommunication* that contains two alternative features *secured* and *unsecured*. The *secured* feature offers three security level alternatives depending on the size of the key used in the handshake phase and on the strength of the encryption and message digest algorithms used in the data transfer phase, as proposed in [15]. Each security level requires different overheads for sending and receiving secure messages. These overheads are

mapped to the communication overheads through the attributes *commRcvOvh* and *commTxOvh*, which represent the host demand overheads for receiving and sending messages, respectively. Since not all the messages exchanged in a product need to have the same communication overheads, we propose to annotate each individual message stereotyped as «PaCommStep» with the processing overheads for the respective message: *commTxOvh* for transmitting (sending) it and *commRcvOvh* for receiving it. In fact, these overheads correspond to the logical communication channel that conveys the respective message. Eventually, the logical channel will be allocated to a physical communication channel (e.g., network or bus) and to two execution hosts, the sender and the receiver. The *commTxOvh* overhead will be eventually added in the performance model to the execution demands of the sender host and *commRcvOvh* to that of the receiver host.

Each type of physical communication channel stereotyped «GaCommHost» has different capacity for the amount of information that can be transmitted over it. As the channel's capacity increases, the latency time for transmitting data over this

Table 1. Mapping of PC-features to affected performance attributes

PC-feature	Affected Performance Attribute	MARTE Stereotype	MARTE Attribute
secureCommunication	Comm. overhead	PaCommStep	commRcvOvh commTxOvh
channelType	Channel Capacity Channel Latency	GaCommHost	capacity blockT
dataCompression	Message size Comm. overhead	PaCommStep	msgSize commRcvOvh commTxOvh
externalDeviceType	Service Time	PaStep	extOpDemand
messageType	Comm. overhead	PaCommStep	commTxOvh

channel decreases. Our example provides three different communication channels with three alternative connections for the Internet. The capacity and latency for each physical channel type are mapped to the attributes *capacity* and *blockT* of the stereotype «*GaCommHost*».

Data compression requires extra operations that increase the processing time, but at the same time compression helps reducing the use of resources, such as hard disk space or communication channel bandwidth. Data compression/decompression is adding an overhead when sending and receiving a message, which is mapped to the attributes *commTxOvh* and *commRcvOvh*, respectively. However, compression also reduces the amount of data to be transferred and thus decreases the delivery time (e.g., a compression algorithm may reduce the size of data to 60% [13]).

Thus, the amount of compressed data transmitted over a physical channel is mapped to the attribute *msgSize*. Another communication mechanism that affects the delivery time of a message is whether the communication is with or without guaranteed delivery [13]; the effect is mapped to the *commTxOverhead* attribute.

The PC-feature group *platformChoice* includes different types of middleware such as CORBA, Web-services, etc., which will affect also the communication overheads. We may either map their effect to the *commTxOvh* and *commRcvOvh* attributes, or may use MARTE external operations described below.

MARTE provides specifically the concept of "external operation calls" to represent resource operations that are not explicitly modeled within the UML design model, but may have an impact on performance. The stereotype «*PaStep*» has two attributes: a) *extOpDemands*, an ordered set of identifiers for operations by external services which are demanded by this Step, in a form understood by the performance environment, and b) *extOpCount*, an ordered set of number of requests made for each external operation during one execution of the Step, listed in the same order as the demands. Examples of such external calls are middleware operations or disk operations hidden in database calls. Different types of external devices are represented in the PC-feature model by the feature *externalDeviceType*. Each device offers different operations times with different execution times. The invocation of such operations is represented by the attributes *extOpDemands* and *extOpCount* of an execution step.

It is important to note that the MARTE annotation contain both performance-affecting attributes of the product we want to analyze, as well as environment/platform characteristics. For instance, the CPU execution times of different scenario steps are indicated by the attributes *hostDemand* of «*PaStep*». The size of a message from a sequence diagram represented by the attribute *msgSize* is a property of the software product, which may be modified by properties of the communication channel, such as compression/decompression. The product model obtained by the transformation presented in the next section includes both the performance attribute contained directly in the design model and the platform/environment factors corresponding to PC-features.

In order to automate the process of generating a user-friendly representation of the generic MARTE parameters that need to be bound to concrete values, the mapping between the PC-features and the performance attributes they affect needs to be specified, as

shown in the next section. Also, each stereotyped class representing a feature in the PC-feature model has a tagged value indicating the list of the attributes it affects. For instance, the PC-feature *DataCompression* affects the attribute list {*msgSize*, *commTxOvh*, *commRcvOvh*}.

3. MODEL TRANSFORMATION APPROACH

The derivation of a specific UML product model with concrete performance annotations from the SPL model with generic annotations requires three model transformations: a) transforming the SPL model to a product model with generic performance annotations, b) generating spreadsheets for the user containing generic parameters and guiding information for the specific product, c) performing the actual binding by using the concrete values provided by the user. We have implemented these model transformations in the Atlas Transformation Language (ATL). We handle two kind of generic parametric annotations: a) product-specific (due to the variability expressed in the SPL model) and platform-specific (due to device choices, network connections, middleware, and runtime environment).

3.1 Product Model Derivation

This subsection describes briefly the first model transformation for generating a product model with generic performance annotations from the SPL model, which was developed by the authors in previous work [22][23][24].

Our derivation approach uses the mapping technique previously proposed in [24] to set up the mapping between a functional feature from the feature model and the model element(s) realizing the feature in the SPL model (both in the structural and behavioural views).

The derivation process is initiated by specifying a given product through its feature configuration (i.e., the legal combination of features characterizing the product). The second step in the derivation process is to select the use cases realizing the chosen features. The product class diagram is derived in the third step in a similar way to the use case diagram. The final step of the product derivation is to generate the sequence diagrams corresponding to different scenarios of the chosen use cases. Each such scenario is modeled as a sequence diagram, which has to be selected from the SPL model and copied to the product one. The PL variability stereotypes are eliminated after binding the generic roles associated to the lifelines of each selected sequence diagram to specific roles corresponding to the chosen features. For instance, the sequence diagram *BrowseCatalog* has the generic alternate role *CustomerInterface* which has to be bound to a concrete role, either *B2BInterface* or *B2CInterface* to realize the features *BusinessCustomer* or *HomeCustomer*, respectively. However, the selection of the optional roles is based on the corresponding features. For instance, the generic optional role *StaticStorage* is selected if the feature *Static Catalog* is chosen. More details about the derivation approach and the mapping of functional features to model elements are presented in our previous work [24].

The outcome of this model transformation is a product model where the variability related to SPL has been resolved based on the chosen feature configuration. However, the performance annotations are still generic and need to be bound to concrete values.

3.2 Generating User-Friendly Representation

The generic parameters of a product model derived from the SPL model are related to different kind of information: a) product-specific resource demands (such as execution times, number of repetitions and probabilities of different steps); b) software-to-hardware allocation (such as component instances to processors); and c) platform/environment-specific performance details (also called performance completions). The user (i.e., performance analyst) needs to provide concrete values for all generic parameters; this will transform the generic product model into a platform-specific model describing the run-time behaviour of the product for a specific run-time environment.

Choosing concrete values to be assigned to the generic performance parameters of type (a) is not a simple problem. In general, it is difficult to estimate quantitative resource demands for each step in the design phase, when an implementation does not exist and cannot be measured yet. Several approaches are used by performance analysts to come up with reasonable estimates in the early design stages: expert experience with previous versions or with similar software, understanding of the algorithm complexity, measurements of reused software, measurements of existing libraries, or using time budgets. As the project advances, early estimates can be replaced with measured values for the most critical parts. Therefore, it is helpful for the user of our approach to keep a clearly organized record for the concrete values used for binding in different stages of the project. For this reason, we proposed to automate the collection of the generic parameters from the model on spreadsheets, which will be provided to the user.

The parameters of type (b) are related to the allocation of software components to processors available for the application. For example, Fig. 5 shows a part of the deployment diagram to be used for the scenario *BrowseCatalog*. The user has to decide for a product what is the actual hardware configuration and how to allocate the software to processing nodes. The MARTE stereotype *«RunTInstance»* annotating a lifeline in a sequence diagram provides an explicit connection between a role in the behaviour model and the corresponding runtime instance of a component. The attribute *host* of this stereotype indicates on which physical node from the deployment diagram the instance is running. Using parameters for the attribute *host* enable us to allocate each role (a software component) to an actual hardware resource. The transformation collects all these hardware resources and associates their list to each lifeline in the spreadsheets. The user decides on the actual allocation by choosing a processor from this list. For instance, the user may decide to allocate the role *ProductDisplay* to the actual processing node *CatalogNode*.

The performance effects of variations in the platform/environment factors (such as network connections, middleware, operating system and platform choices) are included into our model by aggregating the overheads caused by each factor and by attaching them via MARTE annotations to the affected model elements. As already mentioned, the variations in platform/environment factors are represented in our approach through the PC-feature model (as explained in the previous section). A specific run-time instance of a product is configured by selecting a valid PC-feature combination from the PC-feature model. We define a PC-feature configuration as a complete set of choices of PC-features for a specific model element. For instance, a PC-feature configuration for a given message could be {*MediumSecurity, Compressed, CORBA, withoutGuaranteedDelivery*}.

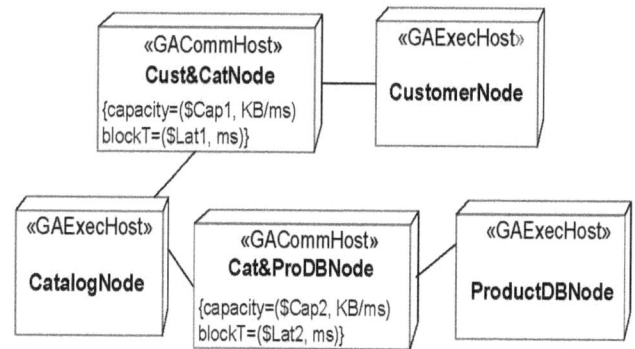

Figure 5. Part of a product deployment diagram.

It is interesting to note that a PC-feature has impact on a subset of model elements in the model, but not necessarily on all model elements of the same type. For instance, the PC-feature *securedCommunication* affects only certain communication channels in a product model, not all of them. Hence, a PC-feature needs to be associated to certain model element(s), not to the entire product. This mapping is set up through the MARTE performance specifications annotating the affected model elements in the product model, as described in section 2.3.

Dealing manually with a huge number of performance annotations by asking the developer to inspect every diagram in the generated product model, to extract the generic parameters and to match them with the PC-features is an error-prone process. We propose to automate the process of collecting all generic parameters that need to be bound to concrete values from the product model and to associate each PC-feature to the model element(s) it may affect, then present the information to the developer in a user-friendly format. We generate a spreadsheet per diagram, indicating for each generic parameter some guiding information that helps the user in providing concrete binding values.

An example of such guiding information is the different overheads for sending and receiving secure messages. For instance, in [15] overhead data is provided for three security levels (low, medium and high): the handshake overhead is (10.2ms, 23.8 ms, 48.0 ms), and the data transfer overhead per KB of data is (0.104 ms, 0.268 ms, 0.609 ms). For instance, we used this data as guiding information in Fig. 6. For instance, the overhead for sending a message with low security level is $(5.1+0.052*msgsize)$ and for receiving is $(5.1+0.052*msgsize)$. For a given SPL, the performance analyst may tailor the guiding information to the platform and environment intended for performance analysis.

The process of generating the spreadsheets takes place after a specific product model is derived from the SPL model. Due to the large semantic gap between the source and target models of the transformation, we follow the example "Microsoft Office Excel Extractor" [7] from the Eclipse/ATL website, which applies the principle of separation of concerns and breaks the transformation into a series of simpler transformations. This transformation series enables us to get some control over the order in which to navigate the ATL source models. The process is composed of four different model transformations:

a) From a specific UML product model into a Table model that contains several tables, one for each sequence diagram; each parametric performance annotation is represented as a table row;

Element Type	Element Name	Stereotype Name	AttributeName	PC-Feature Group Name	PC-Feature Name	Guideline for Value	Generic Parameter	Concrete Value
Context Analysis Parameters {$N1, $Z1, $ReqT, $FSize, $Blocks}								
Message	getList	PaStep	hostDemand	application-annotation			$CatD (ms)	
		PaCommStep	msgSize	«exactly-one-of feature» dataCompression	compressed / uncompressed	reduce by 10% ...30% / No effect	$FSize *0.2 (KB)	
			commTxOverhead	«exactly-one-of feature» secureCommunication	unsecured / secured	No effect		
				«exactly-one-of feature» securityLevel	lowSecurity / mediumSecurity / highSecurity	add (5.1+0.052*msgsize) / add (11.9+0.134*msgsize) / add (24.0+0.305*msgsize)		
				«exactly-one-of feature» dataCompression	compressed / uncompressed	increase by 2% ...5% / No effect	$GetLSend (ms)	
			commRcvOverhead	«exactly-one-of feature» secureCommunication	unsecured / secured	No effect		
				«exactly-one-of feature» securityLevel	lowSecurity / mediumSecurity / highSecurity	add (5.1+0.052*msgsize) / add (11.9+0.134*msgsize) / add (24.0+0.305*msgsize)		
				«exactly-one-of feature» dataCompression	compressed / uncompressed	increase by 2% ...5% / No effect	$GetLRcv (ms)	

Figure 6. Part of the generated Spreadsheet for the scenario Browse Catalog.

b) From the Table model into a SpreadsheetMLSimplified model that represents (as the name says) a simplified subset of the spreadsheetML XML used by Microsoft to import/export Excel workbook's data from/to XML;

c) From the SpreadsheetMLSimplified into an XML model;

d) The XML model created in the previous step is re-written as an XML file which can be directly opened by Microsoft Excel.

The mapping between PC-features and the corresponding performance attributes takes place during the transformation (a). Each MARTE attribute gets the name of the PC-features that have an impact on this attribute attached to it. For instance, the attribute *msgSize* is associated with the PC-feature *Data Compressed*. Another association is between the MARTE attribute *host* annotating a model element of type lifeline and the list of all available deployment nodes from the deployment diagram. After the user selects a PC-feature combination for each model element, he/she can delete the remaining unselected PC-features from the spreadsheet, ending up with a small set of rows containing annotations that need to be bound to concrete values.

The transformation handles differently the context analysis parameters, which are usually defined by the modeler to be carried without binding throughout the entire transformation process, from the SPL model to the performance model for a product. These parameters can be used to explore the performance analysis space. A list of the context analysis parameters are provided to the user, who will decide whether to bind them now to concrete values, or to use them unbound in MARTE expressions.

The four transformations are implemented in the Atlas Transformation Language (ATL) [1]. An ATL transformation is composed of a set of rules and helpers. The rules define the mapping between the source and target model, while the helpers are methods that can be called from different points in the ATL

transformation. The rules of the first transformation handle the generation of the Table model from the UML product model. A few examples of helpers and rules of this transformation are given in the Appendix, with extensive comments in natural language.

A part of the generated spreadsheet for the scenario *BrowseCatalog* is shown in Fig. 5. For instance, the PC-feature *dataCompression* is mapped to the MARTE attribute *msgSize* annotating a model element of type message. As the value of the attribute *msgSize* is an expression $FSize*0.2 in function of the context analysis parameter $FSize, it is the user's choice to bind it at this level or keep it as a parameter in the output it produces. The column titled *Concrete Value* is designated for the user to enter appropriate concrete value for each generic parameter, while the column *Guideline for Value* provides a typical range of values to guide the user. For instance, if the PC-selection features chosen are "secured" with "low security level", the concrete value entered by the user is obtained by evaluating the expression (5.1+0.052*msgSize), assuming that the user follows the provided guideline. Assuming that the choice for the PC-feature *dataCompression* is "compressed", the user may decide to increase by 4% the existing overhead due to security features. In general, the guidelines can be adjusted by the performance analyst for a given SPL and a known execution environment. The generated spreadsheet presents a user-friendly format for the users of the transformation who have to provide appropriate concrete values for binding the generic performance annotations. Being automatically generated, they capture all the parameters that need to be bound and reduce the incidence of errors.

3.3 Performing the Actual Binding

After the user selects an actual processor for each lifeline role provided in the spreadsheets and enters concrete values for all the generic performance parameters, the next model transformation takes as input these spreadsheets along with its corresponding product model, and binds all the generic parameters to the actual values provided by the user. The outcome of the transformation is a specific product model with concrete performance annotations, which can be further transformed into a performance model.

In order to automate the actual binding process, the generated spreadsheets with concrete values are given as a mark model to the binding transformation. The mark model concept has been introduced in the OMG MDA guide [19] as a means of providing concrete parameter values to a transformation. This capability of allowing transformation parameterization through mark model instances makes the transformation generic and more reusable in different contexts.

To consider the spreadsheets as a mark model for the transformation, we apply the same principle of separation of concerns and break the transformation into a series of simpler transformations as in [7]. Three extra model transformations have to be done before performing the actual binding: a) from the spreadsheets (XML file) to an XML model; b) from XML model to the required syntax in Ecore-based format; c) which is further extracted as an XML file that can be accepted by ATL. The main transformation to perform the actual binding takes place now, after the mark model is ready to be injected into the model transformation as an XML file with the required syntax. As an example, the helper called by different rules to get the value of an attribute is shown in the Appendix.

4. RELATED WORK

This section surveys briefly work from literature related to software performance engineering in the context of Model-Driven Architecture, where the concepts of platform-independent and platform-specific models were introduced. Special attention is given to work focused on software product lines.

The Model-Driven Architecture approach is extended in [10] with non-functional modeling and analysis concepts by adding new models and transformations for validation activities. The concepts of platform independent and platform specific are used through the new type of models to obtain an accurate validation.

The concept of performance completions was proposed in [26] to close the gap between application design models and external platform factors. Performance completions provide a means to extend the modeling constructs of a system by including the influence of the underlying platforms and execution environments in performance evaluation models.

A model transformation framework is proposed in [25] for automatically including the impact of middleware on the architecture and the performance of distributed systems. The middleware descriptions are presented as a library in the framework. Using this library, designers can model the system with different types of middleware and then obtain a platform-specific model. A LQN model build by hand is used for performance evaluation.

An approach for performance prediction of component-base software systems in proposed in [2]. The approach based on operational analysis of QN models where performance bounds are computed without deriving a QN model from the software specification. Performance bounds such as system throughput and response time are used to answer several performance-related and what-if questions such as the bottleneck resource if the platform configuration is changed.

A method for designing parametric performance completions that are independent of a specific platform is proposed in [13]. The

variability in the platforms is described by using a feature model. The completions can be instantiated for different environments by explicitly coupling the transformations to performance models and implementation to add the necessary details to both.

A queueing model for the performance of Web servers is presented in [14]. The model includes the impacts of workloads, hardware/software configurations, communication protocols, and interconnect topologies. It is implemented in a simulation tool and the results are validated with results from a test lab environment.

A literature survey on approaches that address non-functional requirements (NFRs) is presented in [8]. The classification is based on software variability, requirements analysis, elicitation, reusability, and traceability as well as aspect-oriented development. Variability related to SPL is also discussed.

In the context of SPL, to the best of our knowledge, no work has been done to evaluate and predict the performance of a given product by generating a formal performance model. Most of the work aims to model non-functional requirements (NFRs) in the same way as functional requirements. Some of the works are concerned with the interactions between selected features and the NFRs and propose different techniques to represent these interactions and dependencies.

In [4], the MARTE profile is analyzed to identify the variability mechanisms of the profile in order to model variability in embedded SPL models. Although MARTE was not defined for product lines, the paper proposes to combine it with existing mechanisms for representing variability, but it does not explain how this can be achieved. A model analysis process for embedded SPL is presented in [5] to validate and verify quality attributes variability. The concept of multilevel and staged feature model is applied by introducing more than one feature models that represent different information at different abstraction levels; however, the traceability links between the multilevel models and the design model are not explained.

In [3], the authors propose an integrated tool-supported approach that considers both qualitative and quantitative quality attributes without imposing hierarchical structural constraints. The integration of SPL quality attributes is addressed by assigning quality attributes to software elements in the solution domain and linking these elements to features. An aggregation function is used to collect the quality attributes depending on the selected features for a given product.

A literature survey on approaches that analyze and design non-functional requirements in a systematic way for SPL is presented in [16]. The main concepts of the surveyed approaches are based on the interactions between the functional and non-functional features.

An approach called Svamp is proposed to model functional and quality variability at the architectural level of the SPL [20]. The approach integrates several models: a Kumbang model to represent the functional and structural variability in the architecture and to define components that are used by other models; a quality attribute model to specify the quality properties and a quality variability model for expressing variability within these quality attributes.

Reference [6] extends the feature model with so-called extra-functional features representing non-functional features. Constraint programming is used to reason on this extended feature model to answer some questions such as how many potential products the feature model contains.

The Product Line UML-Based Software Engineering (PLUS) method is extended in [21] to specify performance requirements by introducing several stereotypes specific to model performance requirements such as «optional» and «alternative performance feature».

Reference [17] handles one of the problems of human interaction in the context of SPL; the decision-making process that requires humans to answer questions to configure a specific product. They propose an approach for automatically optimizing the order of questions with every answer. The optimization is done in an incremental way and in real-time.

To the best of our knowledge, ours is the first approach to generate automatically a performance model of a product from the software model of the family by a chain of model transformations. We handle the variability and commonality between the products of a family and the variability of the underlying platforms. We propose to address the performance impact of the underlying platforms as aggregated platform overheads expressed in MARTE annotations attached to the affected model elements. This will keep the model simple and still allow us to generate a performance model containing the performance effects of the platforms.

5. CONCLUSIONS

This paper is an integral part of a larger research effort to integrate performance analysis in the early phases of the development process of software product lines. Our goal is to generate automatically a performance model for a given product, which can be used to analyze its performance. Through performance analysis we can gain insight into the run-time performance characteristics and thus provide guidance for design choices early in the system development.

SPL development takes advantage of the reusability of the core assets shared among the SPL members. When integrating performance analysis in the early phases of SPL development, we take advantage of the reusability concept applied to performance annotations. Instead of annotating from scratch the UML model of every automatically derived product, we propose to annotate the SPL model once with generic performance annotations. After deriving the model of a product from the family model by an automatic transformation, the generic performance annotations need to be bound to concrete product-specific values provided by the developer.

To the best of our knowledge, our research is the first to tackle this problem. Dealing manually with a large number of performance parameters and with their mapping to each model elements, by asking the developer to inspect every diagram in the model, to extract these annotations and to attach them to the corresponding PC-features, is an error-prone process. Automating the entire process of extracting this information from a product model, generating spreadsheets, and performing the actual binding make the process of providing concrete values for performance variables more user-friendly and less error-prone. It is also more efficient and easier to repeat this process every time a new generic product model is derived from the SPL model or changes to the execution environment happen. The performance characteristics of different platforms can be measured and reused for many products executed on a variety of runtime environments. Future work will use Aspect-Oriented Modeling for including the impacts of underlying platforms by presenting each PC-feature in the PC-feature model as a generic aspect model that can be reused with different applications.

6. ACKNOWLEDGMENTS

This research was partially supported by the Natural Sciences and Engineering Research Council of Canada (NSERC) and by the Centre of Excellence for Research in Adaptive Systems (CERAS).

7. REFERENCES

[1] Atlas Transformation Language (ATL), www.eclipse.org/m2m/atl

[2] Balsamo, S., Marzolla, M., and Mirandola, R., "Efficient Performance Models in Component-Based Software Engineering", Proc. of the 32nd EUROMICRO Conference on Software Engineering and Advanced, 2006.

[3] Bartholdt, J., Medak, M. and Oberhauser, R, "Integrating Quality Modeling with Feature Modeling in Software Product Lines", Proc. of the 4th Int Conference on Software Engineering Advances (ICSEA2009), pp.365-370, 2009.

[4] Belategi, L., Sagardui, G., Etxeberria, L., "MARTE mechanisms to model variability when analyzing embedded software product Lines", Proc. Of the 14th Int Conference on Software Product Line (SPLC'10), pp.466-470, 2010.

[5] Belategi, L., Sagardui, G. and Etxeberria, L., "Model based analysis process for embedded software product lines", Proc of the 2011 Int Conference on Software and Systems Process (ICSSP '11), 2011.

[6] Benavides, D., Trinidad, P., and Ruiz-Cort'es, A., "Automated Reasoning on Feature Models", Proc. of 17th Int. Conference on Advanced Information Systems Engineering (CAiSE), 2005.

[7] Brunelière, H., ATL Transformation Example: Microsoft Office Excel Extractor, http://www.eclipse.org/m2m/atl/atlTransformations/MSOffic eExcelExtractor/ExampleMicrosoftOfficeExcelExtractor[v00 .01].pdf

[8] Chung, L., Leite, J.C. sampaio do prado, "On Non-Functional Requirements in Software Engineering", Conceptual Modeling: Foundations and Applications, pp. 363-379, 2009.

[9] Clements, P. C. and Northrop, L. M. (2001). "Software Product Lines: Practice and Patterns", p.608, Addison-Wesley, 2001.

[10] Cortellessa, V., Di Marco, A. & Inverardi, P., "Non-Functional Modeling and Validation in Model-Driven Architecture", Proc of the 6th Working IEEE/IFIP Conference on Software Architecture (WICSA07), pp. 25, Mumbai, 2007.

[11] Czarnecki, K., Helsen, S., and Eisenecker, U., "Formalizing cardinality-based feature models and their specialization", Software Process Improvement and Practice, pp. 7–29, 2005.

[12] Gomaa, H., "Designing Software Product Lines with UML: From Use Cases to Pattern-based Software Architectures", Addison-Wesley Object Technology Series, July 2005.

[13] Happe, J., Becker, S., Rathfelder C., Friedrich, H., and Reussner, R., "Parametric performance completions for model-driven performance prediction", Performance Evaluation, Vol.67, No.8, pp.694-716, 2010.

[14] Mei, R. D. van der, Hariharan, R., Reeser, P.K., "Web Server Performance Modeling. Telecommunication Systems (TELSYS) 16(3-4), pp. 361-378, 2001.

[15] Menasce, D., Almeida, V., and Dowdy, L., "Performance by Design: Computer Capacity Planning by Example", Prentice Hall PTR, Upper Saddle River, NJ 07458, 2004.

[16] Nguyen, Q.,"Non-Functional Requirements Analysis Modeling for Software Product Lines", Proc. of Modeling in Software Engineering (MISE'09), ICSE workshop, pp. 56-61, 2009.

[17] Nohrer, A. and Egyed, A., "Optimizing User Guidance during Decision-Making", Proc. of the 15th Int Conference on Software Product Line (SPLC'11), Munich, Germany, 2011.

[18] Object Management Group, "UML Profile for Modeling and Analysis of Real-Time and Embedded Systems (MARTE)", Version 1.1, OMG document formal/2011-06-02, 2011.

[19] Object Management Group, "MDA Guide Version 1.0.1", omg/03-06-01, 2003.

[20] Raatikainen, M., Niemelä, E., Myllärniemi, V., and Männistö, T., "Svamp - An Integrated Approach for Modeling Functional and Quality Variability", 2nd Int Workshop on Variability Modeling of Software-intensive Systems (VaMoS), 2008.

[21] Street, J. and Gomaa, H.,"An Approach to Performance Modeling of Software Product Lines", Workshop on Modeling and Analysis of Real-Time and Embedded Systems, Genova, Italy, October 2006.

[22] Tawhid, R. and Petriu, D.C., "Towards Automatic Derivation of a Product Performance Model from a UML Software Product Line Model", Proc. of the 2008 ACM Int. Workshop on Software Performance (WOSP08), pp. 91-102, 2008.

[23] Tawhid, R. and Petriu, D.C., "Automatic Derivation of a Product Performance Model from a Software Product Line Model", Proc. of the 15th Int Conference on Software Product Line (SPLC'11), Munich, Germany, 2011.

[24] Tawhid, R. and Petriu, D.C., "Integrating Performance Analysis in Software Product Line Development Process", book chapter in Software Product Lines - The Automated Analysis, InTech - Open Access Publisher, 2011 (in press).

[25] Verdickt, T., Dhoedt, B., Gielen, F., and Demeester, P., "Automatic Inclusion of Middleware Performance Attributes into Architectural UML Software Models", IEEE Trans. on Software Engineering, Vol. 31, No. 8, 2005.

[26] Woodside, M., Petriu, D. C., and Siddiqui. K. H., "Performance-related Completions for Software Specifications". Proc. of the 22rd Int Conference on Software Engineering, ICSE 2002, pp. 22-32, Orlando, Florida, USA, 2002.

[27] Woodside, M., Petriu, D. C, Petriu, D. B., Shen, H., Israr, T., and Merseguer, J., "Performance by Unified Model Analysis (PUMA)", Proc. of the 5th ACM Int.Workshop on Software and Performance WOSP'2005, pp. 1-12, Palma, Spain, 2005.

Appendix

Examples of ATL rules and helpers to transform a UML product model into a Table model:

```
-- Rule Interaction2Table transforms each SD
-- in UML model to a table in Table model
rule Interaction2Table {
        from     interaction : UML!Interaction
                 (interaction.hasStereotype('GaAnalysisContext'))

-- Define the headers' names
        using { titles_name : Sequence(String) =
                Sequence{'Element_Type','Stereotype_Name',
                'Attribute_Name','Element_Name',
                'PC-feature_Name','Guideline for Value',
                'Generic_Parameter', 'Concrete_Value'}; }
        to       table : Table!Table(
                 name <- interaction.name,
                 rows <- Sequence{title_row, blank_row,

-- create a row for each attribute
                 Sequence{UML!Message.allInstances()->
                    collect(e |thisModule.resolveTemp
                    (e,'hostDemand_row'))},
                 Sequence{UML!Message.allInstances()->
                 collect(e | thisModule.resolveTemp
                    (e,'msgSize_row')) },
                 Sequence{UML!Message.allInstances()->
                    collect(e | thisModule.resolveTemp
                    (e,'commTxOvh_row')) },
                 Sequence{UML!Message.allInstances()->
                    collect(e | thisModule.resolveTemp
                    (e,'commRcvOvh_row')) }} ),
-- create the title row
             title_row : Table!Row(
             cells <- Sequence{ title_cols }),
             title_cols : distinct Table!Cell
             foreach(name in titles_name)
             (content <- name),
```

```
-- create a blank row
        blank_row : Table!Row(
        cells <- Sequence{ blank_cols }),
        blank_cols : Table!Cell(
        content <- " ") }

-- Rule Message2Rows collects all the generic tagged values
-- of the stereotypes «PaStep» or «PaCommStep» extending
-- model elements of type message and transforms them to a
-- row in a table
rule Message2Rows {
        from     message : UML!Message
        using { hostDemand_name : Sequence(String)=
             Sequence{'Message','PaStep','hostDemand',
             message.name,'Application-Annotation',
             message.getTagValues('PaStep','hostDemand')};
             msgSize_name : Sequence(String) =
             Sequence{'Message','PaCommStep','msgSize',
             message.name,

-- call helper "pcFeatureName" to get PC-feature
-- affects attribute msgSize
             message.pcFeatureName('PaCommStep','msgSize'),

-- call helper "getTagValues" to get the generic attribute value
             message.getTagValues('PaCommStep','msgSize')};
             commTxOvh_name : Sequence(String) =
             Sequence{'Message','PaCommStep','commTxOvh',
             message.name,
             message.pcFeatureName('PaCommStep','commTxOvh'),
             message.getTagValues('PaCommStep','commTxOvh')};
             commRcvOvh_name : Sequence(String) =
             Sequence{'Message','PaCommStep','commRcvOvh',
             message.name},
             message.pcFeatureName('PaCommStep','commRcvOvh'),
             message.getTagValues('PaCommStep','commRcvOvh')};}
        to   hostDemand_row : Table!Row(
                     cells <- Sequence{hostDemand_cols}),
```

```
hostDemand_cols : distinct Table!Cell
        foreach(name in hostDemand_name)
        content <- name),
msgSize_row : Table!Row(
        cells <- Sequence{ msgSize_cols }),
msgSize_cols : distinct Table!Cell
        foreach(name in msgSize_name) (
        content <- name),
commTxOvh_row : Table!Row(
        cells <- Sequence{ commTxOvh_cols}),
commTxOvh_cols : distinct Table!Cell
        foreach(name in commTxOvh_name) (
        content <- name),
commRcvOvh_row : Table!Row(
        cells <- Sequence{ commRcvOvh_cols}),
commRcvOvh_cols : distinct Table!Cell
        foreach(name in commRcvOvh_name) (
        content <- name)}
```

```
-- This helper returns the tagged value of the
-- stereotype's attribute; both stereotype and
-- attribute name are given as parameters
    helper context UML!Element def :
        getTagValues(stereotype:String,tag:String) :
        UML!Element =
    if      self.getAppliedStereotypes()->
        select(e | e.name =stereotype)->notEmpty()
    then self.getValue(self.getAppliedStereotypes()
        ->select(e|e.name=stereotype )->first(),tag)
        ->first()
    else "    endif;
```

```
-- This helper returns "true" if the respective model element is
-- stereotyped with the stereotype name given as a parameter
    helper context UML!Element  def:
        hasStereotype(stereotype:String) :
        Boolean =  self.getAppliedStereotypes()
        -> exists(c|c.name.startsWith(stereotype));
```

```
-- This helper returns the PC-feature name affecting the
-- respective attribute;both stereotype and attribute name are
-- given as parameters
    helper context UML!Element def :
        pcFeatureName(stereotype:String, name:String):
        String =
    if    self.getAppliedStereotypes() ->
        select(e | e.name = stereotype)->notEmpty()
    then UML!Class.allInstances() ->
        select(class|class.getTagValues
        ('pc-feature','AttList')=name) ->
        collect(c|c.name)->first()
    else "      endif;
```

An Example of a helper from the transformation performing the actual binding:

```
-- This helper returns the value of the attribute 'value' and gets
-- as a parameter the value of the attribute 'name' by checking
-- all elements in mark model 'parameters'
    helper def : getParameter (variable : String) : String =
        XML!Element.allInstancesFrom
        ('parameters')->select(m|m.name = 'Row')->
        select(a|a.getStringAttrValue('name')= variable)
        ->first().getStringAttrValue('value');
```

```
-- This helper is called by the previous one to return the value
-- of a string attribute. It returns an empty string if the attribute
-- doesn't exist.
    helper context XML!Element def:
        getStringAttrValue(attrName : String) : String =
    let  attX :Sequence(XML!Attribute)= self.children
        ->select(a|a.oclIsTypeOf(XML!Attribute) and
        a.name = attrName)->asSequence()  in
    if      attX -> notEmpty()
    then    attX ->first().value
    else "              endif;
```

Architecture-Level Reliability Prediction of Concurrent Systems

†Leslie Cheung, *Ivo Krka, *Leana Golubchik, *Nenad Medvidovic
†NetApp, 495 E Java Dr, Sunnyvale, CA 94089
*Computer Science Department, Univ of Southern California, Los Angeles, CA 90089
leslie.cheung@netapp.com, {krka, leana, neno}@usc.edu

ABSTRACT

Stringent requirements on modern software systems dictate evaluation of dependability qualities, such as reliability, as early as possible in a system's life cycle. A primary shortcoming of the existing design-time reliability prediction approaches is their lack of support for modeling and analyzing concurrency in a scalable way. To address the scalability challenge, we propose SHARP, an architecture-level reliability prediction framework that analyzes a hierarchical scenario-based specification of system behavior. It achieves scalability by utilizing the scenario relations embodied in this hierarchy. SHARP first constructs and solves models of basic scenarios, and combines the obtained results based on the defined scenario dependencies; the dependencies we handle are sequential and parallel execution of multiple scenarios. This process iteratively continues through the scenario hierarchy until finally obtaining the system reliability estimate. Our evaluations performed on real-world specifications indicate that SHARP is (a) almost as accurate as a traditional non-hierarchical method, and (b) more scalable than other existing techniques.

Categories and Subject Descriptors

D.2.4 [**Software Engineering**]: Software/Program Verification—
Reliability

Keywords

Scalability, Concurrent Systems, Hierarchical Approach

1. INTRODUCTION

The success of most software systems is directly related to their dependability. One of the challenges in developing dependable software is that problems discovered during system implementation or operation can be prohibitively costly to address [2]: the principal design decisions that critically affect system dependability are made long before [26]. This suggests that analyzing a system's dependability at design time is of critical importance. In this paper, we focus on estimating the reliability of a system under design, and propose SHARP, a Scalable, Hierarchical, Architecture-level,

ICPE'12, April 22-25, 2012, Boston, Massachusetts, USA
Copyright 2012 ACM 978-1-4503-1202-8/12/04 ...$10.00.

Reliability Prediction framework, which improves upon the current state-of-the-art. To motivate the need for SHARP, we first highlight the shortcomings of the existing approaches.

A number of existing approaches quantify the reliability of a system by analyzing its architectural models (recently surveyed in [8, 12, 13, 15]). These existing techniques generate a stochastic reliability model from software architectural models, and most of them assume a sequential system for which a reliability model only needs to keep track of the currently running component. This is inadequate when modeling realistic systems in which many components are running and communicating concurrently. A straightforward approach to predicting the reliability of a concurrent system is to build a model that keeps track of the internal states of all system components. Such an approach is taken, e.g., in [7, 22, 28]; in this paper we refer to a model produced using such approaches as a "flat model". Flat-model approaches suffer from scalability (i.e., "state explosion") problems: generating and solving the reliability models is prohibitively costly, and even infeasible, with growing system sizes.

By contrast, the framework we propose in this paper, SHARP, explicitly focuses on predicting reliability of concurrent software systems in a scalable and accurate manner. At a high level, we generate continuous-time Markov chain (CTMC)-based reliability models from software architectural models — each describing a different part of the system's behavior. Reliability can then be computed by appropriately combining the results of the models. The improved scalability is achieved through an iterative hierarchical approach that takes advantage of the popular scenario-based behavioral specifications. For example, SHARP can assess reliability of a system whose behavior is described using high-level Message Sequence Charts (hMSCs) [27], Interaction Overview Diagrams (IODs) [29], or UML Sequence Diagrams with fragments [19]. Note that these specification languages allow an engineer to specify how smaller behavioral sequences form more complex behaviors. To ensure the accuracy of the reliability estimates, SHARP takes into account the contention for system resources while combining different parts of a system's behavioral description.

To use SHARP, an engineer needs to provide a system's behavioral specification, help to define the failure states, and specify the operational profile. Our previous work [3, 15] provides an in-depth treatment of the information sources from which these inputs are derivable; note that SHARP does not require more input information than other existing techniques. Based on the inputs, SHARP produces a system reliability estimate, as well as the reliability estimates for the smaller scenario sequences.

The input behavioral specification should consist of a system-level scenario-based specification (e.g., hMSC or IOD) and compo-

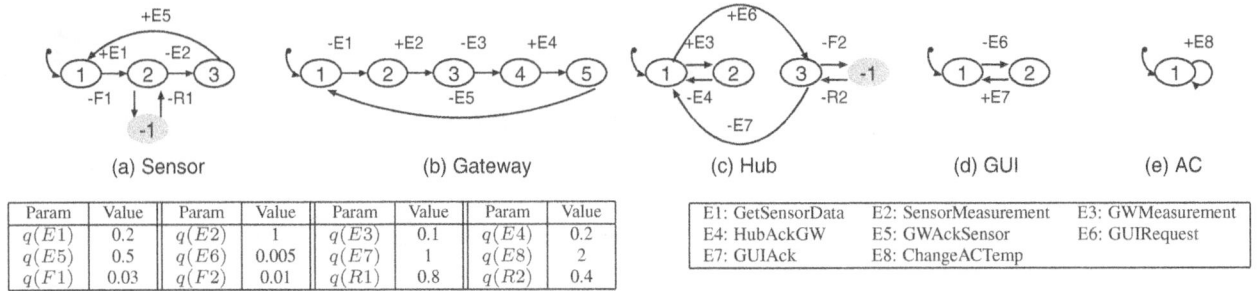

Figure 1: Components' state diagrams

Param	Value	Param	Value	Param	Value	Param	Value
$q(E1)$	0.2	$q(E2)$	1	$q(E3)$	0.1	$q(E4)$	0.2
$q(E5)$	0.5	$q(E6)$	0.005	$q(E7)$	1	$q(E8)$	2
$q(F1)$	0.03	$q(F2)$	0.01	$q(R1)$	0.8	$q(R2)$	0.4

E1: GetSensorData	E2: SensorMeasurement	E3: GWMeasurement
E4: HubAckGW	E5: GWAckSensor	E6: GUIRequest
E7: GUIAck	E8: ChangeACTemp	

nent-level state machine behavior models.[1] The scenario specification has two parts: (a) the description of the desirable event sequences (basic scenarios) and (b) the characterization of how different scenarios relate to one another (complex scenarios). SHARP accounts for different types of scenario dependencies: sequential (scenario A is followed by scenario B), conditional (scenario A is followed by scenario B or scenario C), and concurrent (scenario A and scenario B run concurrently). The expected operational profile should define the frequencies of event occurrence, the probabilities of the conditional scenario continuations, and the number of scenario instances that can be running concurrently. In our work, we identify failure states by analyzing architectural defects using our previously published technique [3, 24]; note that SHARP is not dependent on these specific techniques and any other existing technique can be used to obtain the failure information.

The main idea behind SHARP is that rather than considering a concurrent system as having simultaneously running components (e.g., [22]), we view it as having different *scenarios* executing concurrently. To generate a system model, SHARP first generates and solves reliability models of the basic scenarios, and then incorporates these results into higher-level models according to the defined inter-scenario relationships. We have developed efficient algorithms for (a) estimating the reliability of a complex scenario comprising a sequence of dependent lower-level scenarios and (b) estimating the reliability of a complex scenario comprising multiple concurrently running lower-level scenarios. SHARP iteratively goes through the behavioral specification until finally calculating the reliability of the highest-level scenario. Intuitively, a model of a basic scenario is expected to be relatively small, and solving a number of smaller submodels (rather than one very large, possibly intractable model) while intelligently combining them results in both space and computational savings.

As mentioned above, an important consideration distinguishing SHARP from related approaches is that software components in a concurrent system share and compete for resources such as services provided by other components. To ensure that the reliability estimates are accurate although submodels are analyzed separately, SHARP analyzes the contention between software components and incorporates the results into the reliability models.

We evaluate SHARP's scalability and accuracy on a set of real-world system specifications. Since SHARP is an approximation of the "flat model" used in other techniques, we examine the extent to which SHARP's scalability benefits are achieved at the cost of prediction accuracy. Our results demonstrate that SHARP provides accurate estimates when compared to the "flat model", while significantly reducing computational cost in practice.

In Section 2, we describe a running example used in this pa-

per, and discuss additional background of the presented work. We overview the different parts of the SHARP framework in Section 3 and describe the specifics of the reliability computation algorithms in Section 4. We follow with our evaluations in Section 5, and describe other architecture-based reliability estimation techniques related to SHARP in Section 6. Finally, we conclude in Section 7.

2. BACKGROUND

In this section we introduce the running example (Section 2.1), summarize our prior work used to populate the initial software models with reliability related information (Section 2.2).

2.1 Running Example

The running example we use in this paper is a version of MIDAS, a sensor network application [17]. The application monitors the room temperature and controls the air conditioner (AC). MIDAS consists of five different types of components: a *Sensor* measures temperature and sends the measured data to a *Gateway*. The *Gateway* aggregates and translates the data and sends it to a *Hub*, which determines whether it should turn the *AC* unit on or off. Users can view the current temperature and change the thresholds using a *GUI* component, which then sends an update to the *Hub*.

The state diagrams depicted in Figure 1 capture the behavior of the MIDAS components. In a component state diagram, an event E is either a sending event or a receiving event. Sending and receiving events is represented by "−" and "+", respectively. In SHARP, an event needs to have a specification of its arrival rate in states in which that event is enabled. Some of the state machines in Figure 1 include failure states (labeled with −1) that represent erroneous behavior triggered by a failure event F. Below, we outline how we derive a system's operational profile and the component failure states in our evaluations.

The system-level behavior of MIDAS is captured using five basic scenarios shown in Figure 2:

- the *SensorGW* scenario processes measurements from a *Sensor* by a *Gateway* (Figure 2(a));
- the *GWHub* scenario processes aggregated measurements from a *Gateway* to the *Hub* (Figure 2(b));
- the *GWAck* scenario acknowledges the *Sensor*'s measurement (Figure 2(c));
- the *GUIRequest* scenario updates the temperature readings and changes thresholds (Figure 2(d)); and
- the *ChangeACTemp* scenario turns *AC* on or off according to the temperature readings (Figure 2(e)).

The five basic scenarios are in turn combined to describe the overall system behavior as shown in Figure 3. This higher-level behavioral description consists of relations between basic and complex scenarios that together form a scenario hierarchy. The scenar-

---

[1] These can be automatically obtained from a scenario specification using existing techniques (e.g., [14, 29]).

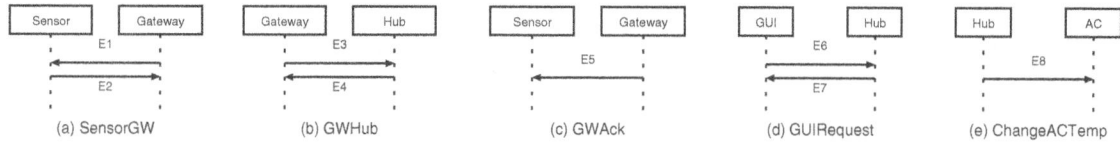

Figure 2: Sequence diagrams

ios can run concurrently or sequentially one after the other. In MIDAS, complex scenario *Sensors_PAR* represents the parallel execution of multiple *Sensors* running the *SensorGW* scenario (Figure 3 describes a system variant with two gateways, each connects to two sensors). Furthermore, the complex scenario *SensorMeasurement* specifies a longer sequence that summarizes how a sensor measurement is propagated from *Sensors* to *Gateway* to *Hub* and back. In SHARP, an application engineer also needs to annotate the scenario hierarchy with (1) branching probabilities when one scenario can be sequentially followed by multiple other scenarios, and (2) the number of scenario instances that run in parallel.

2.2 Prior Work

The focus of our previous research has been on (1) classifying and discovering *architectural defects* [24] and (2) analyzing and extracting *operational profile* information from various information sources [3, 15]. In SHARP, we analyze the impact of the discovered architectural defects (e.g., mismatches between components' operation protocols) on the system's reliability and enrich the initial component and scenario models with the extracted operational profile information. While we utilize our prior techniques to obtain the SHARP inputs, SHARP is in no way dependent on those techniques. In principle, any other existing technique can be used to extract the failure and operational profile operation. Note that defects that are introduced beyond the design stage, such as coding errors, are not considered in architecture-level reliability analysis, as our goal here is to evaluate the impact of different design decisions, rather than ensuring that system reliability meets certain requirements (e.g., five 9's rule). In the remainder of this section, we discuss how the failure and operational profile information is incorporated into the initial software models.

2.2.1 Failure information

To determine the possible system failure states, we first analyze the system components' architectural models by applying a defect classification technique [24]. The example defects detected using the technique in [24] include interface mismatches, specification incompleteness, and behavioral inconsistencies. Once defects are identified, we add a failure transition from each state in which a defect may be triggered. For example, applying the defect classifi-

cation technique on MIDAS, we determine that a *Sensor* is unable to notify the *Gateway* when it is running out of battery. This defect was discovered as a mismatch between the two components' interaction protocols.[2] Failures caused by this defect are represented as the failure state -1 in Figure 1(a). As in most existing approaches [8, 12, 13, 15], we assume that time between failures is exponentially distributed.

In addition to modeling failures, SHARP supports modeling the recovery from a failure. For example, *Sensor* returns to State 2 as the *Sensor* recovers from the interaction protocol mismatch via a reset. In general, a component can return to any state designated by the system designer during defect analysis. In this paper, the running example and the evaluation systems have recoverable failures, and hence we apply steady state analysis (see Section 2.2.3 for details). However, SHARP can be adapted to apply transient analysis to handle irrecoverable failures with minimal modifications.

2.2.2 Operational profile

To parametrize the initial software models with operational profile information, we build on our previous work [3, 15] that estimates the parameters in component-level reliability models from the available information sources: domain knowledge, requirements documentation, system simulation, and execution logs of functionally similar systems. The specific value of the technique we introduced in [3] is that it allows an engineer to assess the quality of the different available information sources. For example, we can rely on domain knowledge to estimate the transition rates, but we have shown in [3] that such an estimate may be subjective and inaccurate for complex systems. Utilizing execution logs of an existing system is useful in predicting the operational profiles while designing a new version, but such information would be unavailable for estimating operational profiles regarding any new feature that is not present in the existing version.

The operational profile information is mapped into the model as transition rates for the desired behaviors as well as failure and recovery transition rates. For example, the event *GetSensorData* ($E1$) from Figure 1 is determined to occur every 5 seconds (rate of 0.2 events per second). At the system level, SHARP requires

---

[2]Note that the component models resulting in this interaction protocol mismatch [3] are elided for brevity.

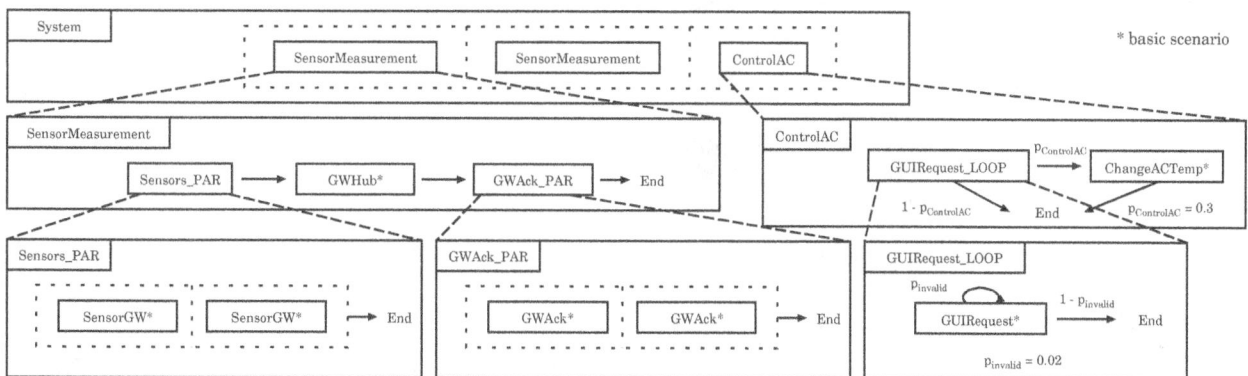

Figure 3: MIDAS scenarios organized in a hierarchy

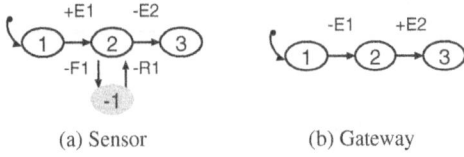

(a) Sensor   (b) Gateway

Figure 4: Component submodels of *SensorGW*

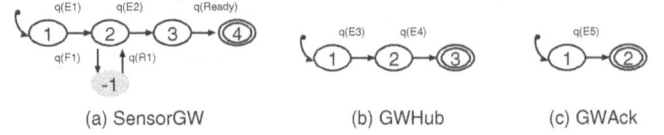

(a) SensorGW   (b) GWHub   (c) GWAck

Figure 5: Example SBMs of MIDAS basic scenarios

transition rates for the events in a scenario sequence, which are directly extrapolated from the component models. Furthermore, the initial scenario-level model is enriched in SHARP with information about the possible concurrently running scenario instances.

2.2.3 Generating Reliability Models of Basic Scenarios

We described how we generate a CTMC-based reliability model that we refer to as a scenario-based reliability model (SBM for short) in [4], and provide this information here for completeness.

To generate the SBM for a scenario, we first generate a component submodel for each component in each scenario, and then apply parallel composition, as in [22]. A component submodel of Component $Comp_c$ in Scenario $Scen_i$, $Comp_c\_Scen_i$, is a state machine model describing the behavior of $Comp_c$ in $Scen_i$, in which a state transition represents the occurrence of an event in the corresponding sequence diagram. In our MIDAS example, the component submodels for the *SensorGW* scenario (recall Figure 2) are depicted in Figure 4.

The next step is to add failure states to each component submodel. by leveraging the component model as described in Section 2.2.1. For example, to model the defect in the *Sensor*, represented by the failure state -1 in Figure 1(a), we add a failure state, State -1, in Figure 4, a failure transition from State 2 to State -1, and a recovery transition from State -1 to State 2.

We then generate an SBM for each basic scenario $Scen_i$ by applying parallel composition [16] to the component submodels $Comp_c\_Scen_i$ for all $Comp_c$. Examples SBMs for the basic MIDAS scenarios as depicted in Figure 5. In our example, applying parallel composition to the component submodels in Figure 4 would result in the SBM for the *SensorGW* scenario depicted in Figure 5(a). (Note that State 3 in the *SensorGW* scenario (Figure 5(a)) corresponds to contention modeling, which we describe in Section 4.1).

Finally, we determine the transition rate between the states based on the operational profile estimated using the techniques described in Section 2.2.2. Formally, let Q_i be the transition rate matrix for $Scen_i$'s SBM. If the transition from State j to State k corresponds to the event E, the transition rate $Q_i(j, k) = q(E)$, where $q(E)$ is the rate that event E occurs. To complete the SBM, according to [25], we set the diagonal entries $Q(j, j)$ such that each row in Q sums to zeros.[3]

To solve for scenario reliability r_i, we redistribute the rate going to the SBM's End state to the Start state to analyze the system's long-term execution; the assumption here is that the particular scenario will eventually execute again. Once we have completed this step, we compute r_i by computing the probability of not being in the failure state when the system is in steady state. i.e., $r_i = 1 - \sum_{f \in F_i} \pi_i(f)$, where F_i is a set of failure states in

$Scen_i$, and $\vec{\pi}_i$ is the steady state probability vector, which can be computed using standard methods [25].

3. AN OVERVIEW OF SHARP

In this section, we outline the envisioned benefits that motivated us to develop SHARP and provide a high-level description of the technical steps that comprise SHARP.

SHARP estimates reliability of a system based on (a) a non-probabilistic behavioral specification consisting of component-level state-based models and system-level scenario-based models, (b) the operational profile, and (c) the definition of failure states. At a high level, SHARP partitions the system behavior into smaller analyzable parts according to the scenario specification, generates a CTMC-based reliability model for each part, and computes system reliability by combining the results of the reliability models using a hierarchical approach we develop. With SHARP, we address two crucial obstacles that prevent the application of architecture-based reliability estimation techniques to complex, concurrent systems:

1. Efficiently solving a reliability model that captures complex system behaviors consisting of elaborate multi-scenario sequences.
2. Efficiently estimating system reliability when a system consists of a large number of concurrently running components and scenarios.

The first obstacle corresponds to the ability to deal with sequential scenario combinations without having to solve the corresponding non-scalable "flat" model used by other approaches [22]. The second obstacle relates to the need to handle multiple scenario instances running concurrently. For example, we want to be able to efficiently solve the *Sensors_PAR* scenario from Figure 3 even in situations when we have many concurrently running *Sensor*s. SHARP resolves these obstacles by first generating and solving the reliability models of smaller scenarios and then incorporating the results into reliability models of the complex scenarios; this is done in a bottom-up way throughout the specified scenario hierarchy.

SHARP consists of activities that determine (1) the reliability and completion times for the basic scenarios, and (2) the reliability and completion times for the complex, sequential (SEQ) and parallel (PAR) scenarios based exclusively on the reliability and completion times of the scenarios they reference. As an example, Figure 6 illustrates the steps that SHARP performs to analyze the reliability of the *SensorMeasurement* scenario from Figure 3. The process for obtaining the reliability information for *GWHub* and *GWAck_PAR* is identical to the process for *SensorGW* and *SensorsPAR* and is not shown. Intuitively, SHARP first analyzes the low-level, basic scenarios and incrementally incorporates the lower-level analysis results in the higher-level SEQ and PAR scenario models. As shown in Figure 6, analyzing a higher-level scenario model in SHARP involves reusing the results from the lower level without the need to recalculate or refine the calculations.

For a basic scenario, we generate a SBM as described in Section 2.2.3. The unique aspect of our approach is that we slice the component reliability models according to the basic scenario in order to determine the possible failure states related to that scenario's

---

[3]Note that self-loops in a component model (i.e., an event that causes a transition from a state to itself) have been implicitly accounted for here. Since self-loops do not cause any state transitions, they do not affect the probability distribution of being in a state in a CTMC, and are therefore dropped in an SBM.

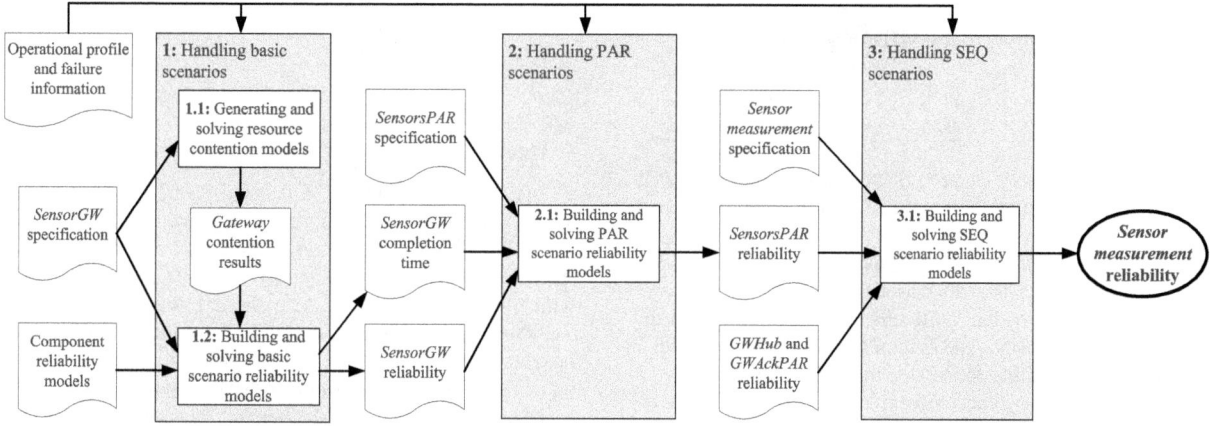

Figure 6: An illustration of SHARP applied on the complex *SensorMeasurement* scenario

execution. By doing so, we reuse information about architectural defects, thus making the reliability analysis more meaningful as opposed to having an engineer "guess" the failure states.

A software architect can choose to augment the SBM to model resource contention with special "queueing" states. Intuitively, a queueing state simulates a situation when an event may not be processed immediately because of resource constraints. For example, while a single-threaded *Gateway* is processing data from one *Sensor*, it may receive data from another; consequently, we augment the SBM by adding a state to represent queueing of the *Sensor*'s request (State 3 in the *SensorGW* SBM from Figure 5). In Section 4.1, we describe how we obtain the contention-related parameters using queueing networks (QNs) [25]. The basic scenario SBMs are finally solved for scenario reliability and completion time using standard methods. Note that completion times are necessary for SHARP to handle PAR scenarios.

To solve for the reliability of a complex scenario with sequential dependencies (e.g., the *SensorMeasurement* from Figure 3) in which a number of basic scenarios may be running one after another, we propose a technique based on stochastic complementation [18]. Stochastic complementation is a standard technique for solving large Markov chains that relies on partitioning a large model into smaller analyzable parts. Our application of stochastic complementation utilizes the partitioning that is intrinsically present in a SEQ scenario where each sub-scenario has only one entry point. For example, when analyzing the MIDAS scenario hierarchy (Figure 3) SHARP utilizes the SEQ relations in the *SensorMeasurement* scenario to solve *Sensors_PAR*, *GWHub*, and *GWAck_PAR* first, and then incorporate the obtained results into a small, high-level *SensorMeasurement* model with only three states. Technically, this corresponds to lumping the states of each sub-scenario into one state, and then solving one "flat" CTMC that represents the three sub-scenarios. Note that stochastic complementation does not result in a less accurate solution than a "flat" model — the computational savings come for free. SHARP attains additional computational savings by computing the reliability of lower-level scenarios only once and then reusing the results in multiple SEQ scenarios that reference them.

Using the existing state-of-the-art, computing the reliability of a complex parallel (PAR) scenario would require keeping track of the internal states of all components during system execution. As discussed earlier, this approach is intractable for larger concurrent systems. To this end, we propose symbolic representation of the system execution state that utilizes a CTMC to keep track of the number of the currently running scenario instances. To abstract a

Table 1: Definition of Variables used in SHARP

$Q(i,j)$	Transition rate from State i to State j in an SBM
$q(E)$	Avg rate that event E occurs
$C_i = (c_1, c_2, \ldots)$	A combination with c_j instances of $Scen_j$
$P_j(c_j)$	Probability of having c_j instances of $Scen_j$
I_j	Max number of instances of $Scen_j$
$\mathbf{I}$	$max_j(I_j)$
d_j	Avg delay caused by $Scen_k, k \neq j$
$P(C_i)$	Probability that Combination C_i occurs
$R(C_i)$	Reliability of Combination C_i
r_i	Reliability of $Scen_i$
t_j	Completion time of $Scen_j$
$\mathbf{S}$	Total num of unique scenarios
H_j	Num of child scenarios of $Scen_j$

scenario's execution state to either running or completed, SHARP uses the completion times that are calculated for the child scenarios. Each state of a PAR scenario SBM can be described as a *combination* of child scenarios. For example, we aggregate the overall behavior of *Sensors_PAR* from Figure 3 with an SBM depicted in Figure 9 that tracks whether there are zero, one, or two concurrently running instances of *SensorGW*. In Section 4.3, we detail the steps involved in solving a PAR scenario's reliability and we evaluate the accuracy of the obtained results obtained in Section 5.

4. DETAILS OF SHARP

For space reasons, we cannot provide a detailed treatment of every step in SHARP. Instead, we choose to "dive into" the parts of SHARP that are novel; we omit details of the parts that are computationally straightforward and identical to other existing approaches [3, 22, 30] (e.g., computation of reliability and completion times for a CTMC). Namely, we present the details of *contention modeling and analysis* at the level of basic scenarios (Section 4.1), *combining scenarios with sequential dependencies* (Section 4.2), and *scalable concurrent behavior modeling and analysis* (Section 4.3). A list of variables that would be used in this section are summarized in Table 1.

4.1 Contention Modeling

In Section 2.2.3, we discussed the comparatively straightforward steps taken to devise a scenario's corresponding CTMC. We solve

Table 2: r_i and t_i of the MIDAS scenarios

Scenario	r_i	t_i	Scenario	r_i	t_i
SensorMeasurement	0.9867	27.394	GUIRequest	0.9999	201.03
ChangeACTemp	1	0.5	GUI_LOOP	0.9999	205.13
ControlAC	0.9999	205.28	System	0.9940	287.46

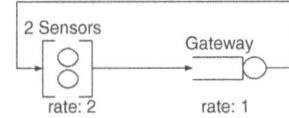

Figure 7: QN model of the *SensorMeasurement* scenario

these CTMCs for reliability and completion times using standard techniques [25]. For completeness, we provide the computed results for the MIDAS scenarios in Table 2.

When several components (callers) request services from a servicing component (callee), the callee needs to allocate its resources appropriately to serve a caller, while other callers would need to wait to obtain service.[4] Since the system behavior may be different when a request is waiting for service than when it is being processed, we add a *queueing* state to represent that a caller's request is queued. Formally, let E be an event with an arrival rate of $q(E)$ that triggers a transition from State j to State k in an SBM. If there is a component that may be servicing other requests upon receiving E, we add a queueing state q into the SBM, such that $Q(j, \text{q}) = q(E)$, and $Q(\text{q}, k) = q(Ready)$. *Ready* is an event indicating that the callee is ready to process the request of the caller of interest, and hence $q(Ready)$ corresponds to the time waiting for the callee's service. Note that $q(Ready)$ excludes the callee's service time, as the service time has been accounted for in the caller's SBM.[5] As an example, in the *SensorMeasurement* scenario, the *Gateway* could be servicing a *Sensor*'s request when another *Sensor* sends a request. Therefore, we insert State 3 between States 2 and 4 to represent queueing, as in Figure 5(a). Any other points of contention would be modeled in a similar manner.

The next step is to determine $q(Ready)$, the outgoing rate of the queueing state. We define $q(Ready) = \frac{1}{T_{wait}}$, where T_{wait} is the average time a caller waits to receive service. To compute T_{wait}, we solve a *queueing network* (QN) [25], which describes the queueing behavior of the callers' requests. Here, we model the callee component as a single server in the QN. Since information about how a component is implemented and deployed may be unavailable during design, it is unclear how to incorporate other resources (e.g., CPU and memory) into the QN. Therefore, we model the callee component as a black box. This QN can be refined if such information is available.

To build such a QN, we utilize the following information: (a) the number of different types of callers (i.e., the different types of components where each type can request different services with different processing times), and the maximum number of each type of caller that may request a service; (b) how often a caller requests a service (arrival rate); (c) how long the callee takes to serve a request (service rate);[6] and (d) the callee's queueing discipline. Note that (a) is derivable from the system's requirements and architectural models; (b) is available from the operational profile (i.e., the rate of an event E); and (c) is the total rate leaving a state k also derivable from the operational profile. The operational profile information and the other model parameters can be determined using

our previous technique [3]. Lastly, (d) can be available from the system's requirements pertaining to architectural constraints (e.g., using a middleware that serves requests in a round-robin fashion). The constructed QN is finally solved for the average waiting time in the queue using standard methods [25]. Since (a)-(c) are readily available, once the contention points have been identified and (d) the queueing discipline has been specified, the process of generating and solving the QN for $q(Ready)$ can be automated.

The QN for the *SensorMeasurement* scenario is depicted in Figure 7. As an example, we are modeling the case when a *Sensor* sends measurements to the *Gateway* while the *Gateway* is processing another *Sensor* request. Hence, we have one class of callers: two *Sensors* may send measurements to the *Gateway* with the arrival rate of $2 \times q(E2) = 2$, processing rate of $q(E3) = 1$, and the *Gateway* is a FCFS callee. After solving the QN for the average waiting time at *Gateway*'s queue in Figure 7, the resulting rate of leaving the queueing state (state 3) in Figure 5(a) is estimated to be 5. Other points of contention in the SBMs are treated analogously.

4.2 Combining Scenarios with Sequential Dependencies

To analyze a complex scenarios with sequential dependencies, we apply stochastic complementation to generate a SEQ scenario's SBM by combining the SBMs of the child scenarios (Step 2.1). This is a novel use of an advanced stochastic method for analyzing a software system's quality attribute, and comprises an important contribution of this paper. Intuitively, stochastic complementation breaks a large Markov model into a number of submodels, solves the submodels separately, and reconstructs results of the original model. The special structure required for an efficient solution using stochastic complementation is that each submodel has only one start state. Notably, the generated basic scenario SBMs satisfy this requirement as they have a single starting state. We solve the resulting SEQ scenario SBM for scenario reliability (Step 2.2) in a similar manner to existing approaches [6, 22, 30].

4.2.1 Step 2.1: Generating SBM

We generate an SBM for a SEQ scenario as follows: we first generate the states of the model, and then compute the transition rates with respect to the applied stochastic complementation [18]. The states in a SEQ scenario's SBM correspond to the child scenarios. We determine the transitions according to the dependencies between the child scenarios. If a SEQ scenario $Scen_i$ has a child scenario $Scen_k$ executing after another child scenario $Scen_j$, we add a transition from state j to state k in $Scen_i$'s SBM. For example, the SBMs of the SEQ scenarios in MIDAS are depicted in Figure 8.[7]

The transition rates for each transition determined above are calculated as follows [18]:

$$Q_i(j, k) = (p_i(j, k))out_j \qquad (1)$$

where $p_i(j, k)$ is the probability that $Scen_k$ executes after the execution of $Scen_j$, and out_j is defined in a similar manner to [18]:

---

[4] As the flat model results in callees serving the callers on a FCFS basis, we also use FCFS in our exposition. However, SHARP allows other queueing disciplines.

[5] By plugging $q(Ready)$ into a component's SBM (a CTMC), we are essentially assuming that the waiting time is exponentially distributed, which may not be the case in general. We make this approximation for modeling convenience.

[6] For ease of exposition, we assume both the inter-arrival time and service time are exponentially distributed in this paper. In general, these assumptions can be removed, but it may be computationally costly to solve for $q(Ready)$ if the resulting QN is not in product-form [1].

[7] Note that the self-loop in State 1 of the *GUI_LOOP* scenario (depicted as dotted arrow in Figure 8), representing that the user's input is invalid, has been dropped, because a CTMC implicitly accounts for self-loops.

126

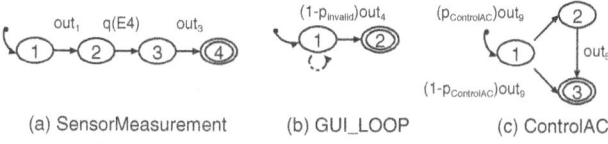

(a) SensorMeasurement   (b) GUI_LOOP   (c) ControlAC

Figure 8: SBMs of the SEQ scenarios

$$out_j = \sum_{s \in S_j} (\pi_j(s)) Q_j(s, End) \qquad (2)$$

where S_j is a set of states in $Scen_j$, $\pi_j(s)$ is the steady state probability of being in State s in the $Scen_j$'s model, and $Q_j(s, End)$ is the transition rate going from State s to the End state in $Scen_j$'s model. For example, in *GUI_LOOP* (Figure 8(b)), let $Scen_i = GUI\_LOOP$ and $Scen_j = GUIRequest$, the transition rate from State 1 to State 2 in $Scen_i$ is

$$
\begin{aligned}
Q_i(1,2) &= p_i(1,2)(\sum_{s \in S_j} \pi_j(s) Q_j(s, End)) \\
&= (1 - p_{invalid})(\pi_j(2))(q(E7)) \\
&= (0.98)(0.005)(1) = 0.0049
\end{aligned}
$$

Furthermore, when we move up a level in the hierarchy to *ControlAC* (Figure 3) the transition rate going from State 1 to 2 in *ControlAC*'s SBM in (Figure 8(c)) becomes

$$
\begin{aligned}
Q_i(1,2) &= p_i(1,2) \sum_{s \in S_j} \pi_j(s) Q_j(s, End) \\
&= (p_{ControlAC})(1) Q_j(s, End) \\
&= (0.3)(1)(0.0049) = 0.0015
\end{aligned}
$$

4.2.2 Step 2.2: Computing Scenario Reliability

To solve for a sequential scenario's reliability, we redistribute the rate going to the End state of a SEQ scenario SBM and solve the model for its steady state probability vector $\vec{\pi}_i$, as in Section 2.2.3. Once we have computed $\vec{\pi}_i$ and r_j for all child scenarios $Scen_j$, we solve the scenario reliability using the equation

$$r_i = 1 - \sum_j \pi_i(j) r_j \qquad (3)$$

Continuing with our example, to solve for $\vec{\pi}_i$ using the SBM of the *ControlAC* scenario, after redistributing the rate going to the End state, we have the following rate matrix:

$$
\begin{bmatrix}
-0.0015 & 0.0015 \\
2 & -2
\end{bmatrix} \qquad (4)
$$

Solving this model gives us $\vec{\pi}_i = [0.9993, 0.0007]$. The reliability of the *ChangeACTemp* is 1, as there is no defect identified in that scenario. Hence, the reliability of the *ControlAC* scenario is $r_i = (0.9993)(0.9999) + (0.0007)(1) = 0.9999$. The reliabilities of other scenarios, and are depicted in Table 2, are similarly computed.

4.3 Scalable Concurrency Modeling

This section describes the SHARP steps that are performed when calculating the reliability of a complex PAR scenario. Note that we refer to the symbolic model discussed in Section 3 as the concurrency-level model. SHARP first determines the feasible scenario combinations (Step 3.1), and constructs the concurrency-level model (Step 3.2). Next, SHARP calculates the probabilities (Step 3.4)

Table 3: Values of $P(C_k)$ and $R(C_k)$ in the *System* scenario

C_i	$P(C_i)$	$R(C_i)$	C_i	$P(C_i)$	$R(C_i)$
(0,0)	0.0420	0.9605	(1,0)	0.0630	0.9735
(2,0)	0.1260	0.9866	(3,0)	0.7266	0.9999
(0,1)	0.0077	0.9606	(1,1)	0.0116	0.9736
(2,1)	0.0231	0.9867			

and the reliabilities (Step 3.5) of the different scenario combinations. SHARP ultimately uses the obtained information to compute the overall PAR scenario reliability (Step 3.6). Noting that the concurrency model can get intractable when dealing with very large systems for which concurrent scenario instances may number in the thousands, SHARP employs model truncation [25] (Step 3.3).

4.3.1 Step 3.1: Determining Scenario Combinations

Determining the possible combinations is the first step in solving for reliability and completion time of a PAR scenario. A combination, C_i, is defined as $C_i = (c_1, c_2, \ldots, c_{H_j})$, where c_j is the number of completed instances of $Scen_j$, and H_j is the number of child scenarios.[8] We also define I_j to be the number of instances of $Scen_j$ that needs to be completed, and $\mathbf{I} = max(I_j)$ to be the largest number of possible instances among all $Scen_j$. The execution of a PAR scenario is completed only when all child scenarios have completed their execution.

In order to find scenario reliability, we need to compute the distribution of the possible combinations. Since, in general, not all combinations of scenarios in a system may be possible, we allow a system architect to specify the combinations that are not possible (or allowed). For instance, in MIDAS, such a restriction exists to avoid exhausting the resources of the *Hub* by allowing no more than three *Hub* requests. Hence, in the *System* scenario from Figure 3, if we set $I_1 = 3$ and $I_2 = 1$, and include the restriction that $I_1 + I_2 \leq 3$, then the possible scenario combinations are those depicted in Table 3. Note that the I's are small in our example as we try to keep it simple.

4.3.2 Step 3.2: Concurrency-Level Model Generation

To compute the probability $P_j(c_j)$ that c_j instances of a child scenario $Scen_j$ have completed, we generate a concurrency-level model for each child scenario. A concurrency-level model is a CTMC, whose states correspond to the number of completed instances of $Scen_j$. We use the concurrency-level model to compute the probabilities $P_j(c_j)$, where c_j denotes the number of completed $Scen_j$ instances. The determination of the final state in a concurrency-level model depends on the number of concurrently running child scenarios.

When there is one child scenario, completing I_j instances of $Scen_j$ represents the completion of the whole PAR scenario. For example, the concurrency-level models corresponding to *Sensors_PAR* and *GWAck_PAR* in MIDAS are depicted in Figures 9(a) and (b), respectively. The final state in these models is state 2 because there can be two concurrently running instances of *Sensors_PAR* and *GWAck_PAR*.

When there is more than one child scenario, completing I_j instances of $Scen_j$ means that the execution of all instances has been completed. $Scen_j$ can only execute again when all other scenarios have been completed, and the parent scenario executes again. We

---

[8]We assume that the probability that more than one scenario completes in the exact same instant in time is negligible. This is a standard assumption in Markov chain models which makes them more tractable without a significant loss in what is expressible with such models.

127

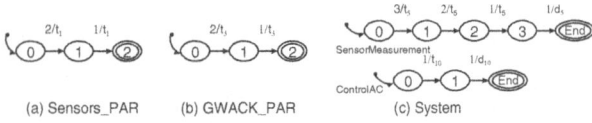

Figure 9: SBMs of the PAR scenarios

Table 4: Values of $P_j(c_j)$ in the *System* scenario

SensorMeasurement				ControlAC	
Parameter	Value	Parameter	Value	Parameter	Value
$P_1(0)$	0.0305	$P_1(2)$	0.0916	$P_2(0)$	0.8949
$P_1(1)$	0.0458	$P_1(3)$	0.8321	$P_2(1)$	0.1051

add a state End to model this behavior, and define State End to be the final state of each concurrency-level model. We also add a transition from state I_j, which corresponds to completing all instances of $Scen_j$, to State E. For example, the concurrency-level models corresponding to the *System* scenario are depicted in Figure 9(c).

The transition rate from state c_j ($c_j < I_j$), representing c_j completed instances of $Scen_j$, to state $c_j + 1$ is $(I_j - c_j)(1/t_j)$, where t_j is completion time of $Scen_j$, which is assumed to be exponentially distributed. The transition rate corresponds to the rate an instance of $Scen_j$ completes, when there are c_j completed instances. t_j can be computed using standard techniques, which involves solving for the average passage time from State 1 to any End state in the SBM using $Q'_j \vec{T}_j = -e$ [25], where Q'_j is the matrix after eliminating the row and column corresponds to the End state in Q_j, $-e$ is a column vector of -1 with the appropriate dimension, and $T_j(k)$ is the average passage time from State k to the End state. i.e., $t_j = T_j(1)$.

The transition from state I_j to state End has a rate of $1/d_j$, where d_j is the average of the total delay caused by other scenarios $Scen_k$, $k \neq j$. We set $d_j = \sum_{k \neq j} I_k t_k$.[9]

4.3.3 Step 3.3: Performing Model Truncation

To further reduce the computational cost, we eliminate the combinations in a PAR scenario that are rarely visited according to a model truncation technique from [25].

The steady probability distribution of c_j, the number of completed instances of $Scen_j$, depends on the values of t_j (scenario completion time), as well as the completion time of other scenarios t_k, $Scen_k \neq Scen_j$. $P_j(c_j)$ can be obtained by solving a concurrency-level model using standard techniques. As an illustration, we depict the steady-state probability distribution of c_j in Figure 10. We assume the completion rate of other scenarios are fixed, and $d_j = 1$. Also, we set $\mathbf{I} = 50$, and varied t_j at different values. For instance, when $t_j = 100$, 29 (out of 51) possible values of $P_j(c_j)$ become smaller than 1%.

In generating the scenario combinations, we can elide the values of the completed scenario instances c_j that occur rarely. Specifically, we consider x as a relevant value of c_j if $P_j(c_j = x)$ is larger than a threshold ϵ (thus, the case without using truncation has $\epsilon = 0$). For example, if $\epsilon = 0.01$ (depicted as a dotted line in Figure 10), when $t = 100$, $d_j = 1$, and $\mathbf{I} = 50$, we only consider 22 out of the 51 state in the concurrency-level model.

Note that there is a tradeoff between the number of states we elide and the loss in accuracy when applying model truncation. We evaluate this tradeoff in Section 5.2.

---

[9]Note that d_j is an approximation, which assumes that the average time to complete an instance of $Scen_k$, given that $Scen_j$ has completed, is still t_k. An exact computation of d_j involves transient analysis, which is computationally more expensive [25].

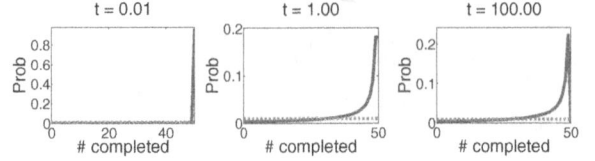

Figure 10: Probability distribution of the number of completed instances

4.3.4 Step 3.4: Computing Combination Probability

SHARP solves the concurrency-level model for the probability distribution of each combination. We define $P(C_i)$ to be the probability that C_i occurs, i.e., $P(C_i) = P(c_1, c_2, \ldots, c_{H_j})$ is the probability that there are c_j completed instances of $Scen_j$ for each $j = 1 \ldots H_j$. Since we assume that all instances of all child scenarios run independently, $P(C_i) \simeq (\prod_j P_j(c_j))/W$, where $P_j(c_j)$ is the probability that c_j instances of $Scen_j$ have completed, and $W = \sum_j P(C_j)$ is a normalization factor[10] that ensures that $P(C_j)$ sum to 1. In the *System* scenario from Figure 3, $P(c_1, c_2)$ is the probability that there are c_1 and c_2 completed instances of *SensorMeasurement* and *ControlAC*, respectively. Hence, $P(c_1, c_2) \simeq (P_1(c_1) \times P_2(c_2))/W$.

Assuming that once the whole PAR scenario has completed its execution it will be executed again, we merge the final state F and the initial state 0. We solve the resulting model for $P_j(c_j)$ using standard techniques [25]. Table 4 gives the probability distribution of $P_j(c_j)$ in the two PAR scenarios of our MIDAS example; these are computed using the concurrency-level models from Figure 9. Furthermore, Table 3 gives the *System* scenario combination probabilities, computed using the data from Table 4. Since the computation of the distribution of different scenario combinations is done in an approximate manner, in Section 5 we evaluate the accuracy of this approximation, as well as the reduction in computational cost.

At the level of the entire system, the assumption that a PAR scenario is completed only when all child scenarios have finished executing may be restrictive. In some systems that continuously run, child scenarios start and complete independently. For example, after the *Sensors* finish taking measurements, they do not necessarily have to wait for the *GUI* to update the data before taking additional measurements. In [4], we handle these independent concurrent scenarios with a modified concurrency-level model. Specifically, this model has additional transitions that represent the spawning of new scenario instances and are directed opposite to those depicted in Figure 9.

4.3.5 Step 3.5: Computing Combination Reliability

Here, we make a simplifying assumption that the system fails if any scenario instance has failed. SHARP can accommodate more complex failure conditions as discussed in [4]. Given this assumption, the reliability of a combination C_i is $R(C_i) = \prod_{j=1}^{H_j} r_j^{(I_j - c_j)}$. We repeat this calculation for each combination. Table 3 gives reliabilities of all scenario combinations for MIDAS.

4.3.6 Step 3.6: Computing Scenario Reliability

We compute scenario reliability by combining the results of the previous steps. Reliability of a PAR scenario is defined as the sum of the scenario combinations' reliabilities, weighted by the probability that the combination occurs, i.e., $r_i = \sum_k P(C_k)R(C_k)$.

In our running example, the reliability of the *System* scenario, and hence system reliability, is 0.9940, which, in this case, is within

---

[10]The normalization factor is needed because, in general, not all combinations of scenarios may be allowed.

Table 5: Definition of Variables used in Complexity Analysis

$\mathbf{U}$	Total num of unique components
$\mathbf{C}$	Total num of components
$\mathbf{E}$	Total num of events
$\mathbf{S}$	Total num of unique scenarios
$\mathbf{S_B}$	Total num of basic scenarios
$\mathbf{S_I}$	Total num of intermediary scenarios
I_j	Max number of instances of $Scen_j$
$\mathbf{I}$	$max_j(I_j)$
M_j	Max number of states in $Comp_j$
$\mathbf{M}$	$max_j(M_j)$

0.05% of the ground truth of 0.9935, obtained by solving the "flat model", as detailed below.

5. EVALUATION

We evaluate SHARP along two dimensions: *complexity* of generating and solving concurrent systems' reliability models as compared to those derived from existing techniques (Section 5.1), and *accuracy* (Section 5.2). We compare SHARP against a flat model, which is used as the "ground-truth". Flat model is essentially used by Rodrigues et al. [22], where a system reliability model is generated by applying parallel composition to component models.[11]

We applied SHARP to a variety of systems, with different numbers of components, scenarios, and numbers of scenario instances. Note that the system we used in evaluating SHARP is relatively simple, because the flat models of larger systems quickly become too large to solve, and we would lack an objective baseline for comparison. We show representative results obtained from the following systems:

1. An instantiation of MIDAS with twelve *Sensors*, six *Gateways*, one *Hub*, one *GUI*, and one *AC*.

2. A GPS system with route guidance, audio player, and bluetooth phone capabilities. This system has five major components. The system's behavior is captured with 21 basic scenarios. The GPS system has limited concurrency due to the system's purpose. For example, it typically makes little sense to have two instances of a route guidance scenario to perform the same route guidance service.

   To evaluate SHARP in a controlled manner, we injected the following defects into this GPS system: (a) a defect in the *EnergyMonitor (EM)* component which may lead to failure to notify other system components when the battery is low, and (b) a defect in the *RouteGuidance (RG)* component which may lead to failure in updating a user's location accurately.

3. A client-server system (CS) with possibly many clients and a single server that provides remote file access. The system behavior is described with one basic scenario. The server processes the client requests in a FCFS fashion with an assumption of infinite buffer space. We primarily leverage CS to illustrate the effect of contention modeling when there are many clients competing for the same resource. We consider a defect in the server that may lead to failure to reply to the client when a requested file cannot be retrieved.

---

[11] [22] assumes irrecoverable failures. As we discussed earlier, SHARP can model irrecoverable failures with minor modifications.

Table 6: Worst-case complexity

Complexity	SHARP	Flat Model
Time	$O(\mathbf{S_I} \max(\mathbf{S^3}, \mathbf{SI^3} + (\mathbf{S+2})\mathbf{I^S}) +$ $\mathbf{S_B}(\mathbf{M^{3C}} + \mathbf{M^C EI^E}))$	$O(\mathbf{M^{3C}})$
Space	$O(\mathbf{S} + \max(\mathbf{M^{2C}}, \mathbf{S^2}, \mathbf{SI}))$	$O(\mathbf{M^{2C}})$

5.1 Complexity Analysis

We now explore the complexity of SHARP as compared to the flat model. We first describe the theoretical worst-case complexity of each approach in Section 5.1.1, and then discuss the computational cost that is likely to arise in practice in Section 5.1.2.

5.1.1 Worst Case Complexity

Let $\mathbf{U}$ be the number of unique components, $\mathbf{C}$ be the total number of components, $\mathbf{E}$ be the number of events, $\mathbf{S}$ be the number of scenarios (basic and intermediary), $\mathbf{S_B}$ be the number of basic scenarios, $\mathbf{S_I}$ be the number of intermediary scenarios (i.e., $\mathbf{S} = \mathbf{S_B} + \mathbf{S_I}$), I_j be the number of instances of $Scen_j$, $\mathbf{I} = max(I_j)$ for all $Scen_j$, M_j be the number of states of $Comp_j$, and $\mathbf{M} = max(M_j)$ for all $Comp_j$. These definitions are summarized in Table 5, and the resulting complexities are summarized in Table 6. Let us first analyze the complexity of SHARP:

Basic scenarios: In the worst case, every state in every component participate in a basic scenario, and hence the SBM may have as many as $O(\mathbf{M^C})$ states. Once we have determined the states in the SBM, we need to determine the transitions between each pair of states. Therefore, the complexity of the generation of a SBM is $O(\mathbf{M^{2C}})$. The complexity of solving a SBM [12] is $O(\mathbf{M^{3C}})$. Thus, the time complexity of generating and solving the SBM for a basic scenario is $O((\mathbf{M^{2C}} + \mathbf{M^{3C}})) = O(\mathbf{M^{3C}})$. The space complexity of generating and solving a basic scenario's SBM is $O(\mathbf{M^{2C}})$ — once we have solved a SBM, we can reuse its space as we generate SBMs one at a time.

Contention Modeling: In the worst case, there is contention in every state in the SBM of a basic scenario. If, as a result, we add a queueing state corresponding to each state, we double the size of every SBM of each basic scenarios, which does not affect the worst case complexity of solving it ($O((2\mathbf{M^C})^3 = O(8\mathbf{M^{3C}}) = O(\mathbf{M^{3C}}))$. Thus, in the worst case, we have $O(\mathbf{M^C})$ QNs to solve. Since we assume product-form QN, the worst case complexity of solving one such QN is $O(\mathbf{EI^E})$ [20]. Thus, the worst case time complexity of solving all QNs would be $O(\mathbf{M^C EI^E})$.

SEQ scenarios: Since there are at most $\mathbf{S}$ scenarios in the system, there are at most $\mathbf{S}$ states in the SBM of a SEQ scenario, because each scenario is represented by a state in the SBM of a SEQ scenario. Therefore, the complexities of generating and solving the SBM of a SEQ scenario are $O(\mathbf{S^2})$ and $O(\mathbf{S^3})$, respectively, and the space complexity is $O(\mathbf{S^2})$, as discussed above.

PAR scenarios: In the worst case, all $\mathbf{S}$ scenarios run in parallel. In Step 2.2, since each concurrency-level model has at most $O(\mathbf{I})$ states, the complexity of solving for all $\mathbf{S}$ of them is $O(\mathbf{SI^3})$. Step 2.4 requires computing $P(C_j)$ for each $Comb_j$, therefore the complexity is $O(\mathbf{I^S})$ as we have I^S combinations. In computing the reliability of a combination in Step 2.5, we need to multiply the reliabilities for each child scenario $Scen_i$, and hence the complexity of this step is $O(\mathbf{SI^S})$. Finally, in Step 2.6, we compute scenario reliability by multiplying $R(C_j)$ and $P(C_j)$ for each scenario, so the complexity is $O(\mathbf{I^S})$. Therefore, the complexity of solving for reliability of a PAR scenario is $O(\mathbf{S_I}(\mathbf{SI^3} + 2\mathbf{I^S} + \mathbf{SI^S})) = O(\mathbf{S_I}(\mathbf{SI^3} + (\mathbf{S+2})\mathbf{I^S}))$. The space complexity of solving the

---

[12] The time complexity of solving a Markov chain with $\mathbf{N}$ states is $O(\mathbf{N^3})$, and the space complexity for storing the corresponding rate matrix is $\mathbf{N^2}$.

Table 7: Summary of computational costs in practice

	U	C	M	S_B	I	E	Flat Model	SHARP
MIDAS	5	12	5	5	6	8	1.52×10^{12}	692
GPS	5	5	17	21	1	43	1.17×10^{11}	1331
CS	2	9	2	1	8	2	1.34×10^{8}	737

PAR scenarios is $O(\mathbf{SI})$, as we need to store the results of the concurrency-level models.

Note that we have not considered the computational cost savings of model truncation (Step 2.3) in this complexity analysis, as model truncation does not reduce the worst-case complexity.

Overall Complexity: First, since there are $\mathbf{S_B}$ basic scenarios, the complexity of generating and solving all $\mathbf{S_B}$ SBMs of the basic scenarios is $O(\mathbf{S_B}(\mathbf{M^{3C}} + \mathbf{M^C EI^E}))$. There are $\mathbf{S_I}$ intermediary scenarios, which each of them could either be s SEQ or PAR scenario. As we do not know which of SEQ or PAR scenario is more expensive to solve in the worst case (it depends on the values of $\mathbf{S}$ and $\mathbf{I}$), we describe the complexity of solve an intermediary scenario to be $O(max(\mathbf{S^3}, \mathbf{SI^3} + (\mathbf{S}+2)\mathbf{I^S}))$. Therefore, the overall time complexity is $O(\mathbf{S_B}(\mathbf{M^{3C}} + \mathbf{M^C EI^E})) + \mathbf{S_I} max(\mathbf{S^3}, \mathbf{SI^3} + (\mathbf{S}+2)\mathbf{I^S})$.

In analyzing the overall space complexity, we need to consider the space needed to store the results of the scenarios that have been processed, in addition to the space needed to store the SBM of the scenario that is being processed. Since we store the r_i and t_i of each $\mathbf{S}$ scenario in the worst case, the space needed to store the results of $\mathbf{S}$ scenarios is $O(2\mathbf{S})$. The "last" scenario could be a basic, SEQ, or a PAR scenario, so the space complexity is the maximum space needed among the three types of scenarios. Thus, the overall space complexity is $O(\mathbf{S} + max(\mathbf{M^{2C}}, \mathbf{S^2}, \mathbf{SI}))$.

In the flat model, we first apply parallel composition using all components, for which the complexity is $O(\mathbf{M^{2C}})$. The time complexity of solving the flat model is $O(\mathbf{M^{3C}})$. Therefore, the overall time complexity of the flat model approach is $O(\mathbf{M^{2C}} + \mathbf{M^{3C}}) = O(\mathbf{M^{3C}})$. Since the flat model has as many as $O(\mathbf{M^C})$ states, its space complexity is $O(\mathbf{M^{2C}})$.

5.1.2 Computational Cost Analysis

Table 7 summarizes the computational costs to solve for system reliability using the flat model and SHARP. We denote the number of unique components with $\mathbf{U}$; $\mathbf{C}$ is the total number of components; $\mathbf{S_B}$ is the number of basic scenarios; and $\mathbf{M} = max(\mathbf{M}_j)$, where $\mathbf{M}_j$ is the number of states of $Comp_j$. Additionally, $\mathbf{I}_i$ is the number of instances of $Scen_i$, and $\mathbf{I} = max(\mathbf{I}_i)$ for all $Scen_i$. The computational cost savings using SHARP are significant for all three systems' evaluation.

Comparing the computational costs of the three systems yields some interesting observations. We noticed that it is more expensive to solve the GPS system model than the MIDAS model, since the GPS system is modeled with 21 basic scenarios and we generate and solve an SBM for each scenario. Although systems with more basic scenarios are more expensive to solve in SHARP, the computational costs in practice are still significantly lower as compared to the flat model. While CS is simpler than MIDAS, it costs more to solve it for reliability. This is because the number of parallel scenario instances is larger in CS ($\mathbf{I} = 8$) than MIDAS ($\mathbf{I} = 3$), which results in a larger PAR scenario model.

Since SBMs are likely to be smaller than the flat model, we argue that SHARP in practice requires significantly less space than the flat model. The savings are also due to the fact that we can generate and solve SBMs one at a time, and thus reuse the space. Fur-

thermore, given that SHARP takes the approach of solving many smaller models rather than one large model, it is possible to solve the different branches of the hierarchy in parallel. The results discussed above were confirmed by a number of other example systems.

5.2 Accuracy

Our goal is to provide evidence that SHARP is sufficiently accurate to be used in making design decisions. Therefore, we compare the *sensitivities* of SHARP and the corresponding flat model: if the differences in the changes of reliability estimates are reasonably small when the same parameter is varied in the two models, then SHARP can be considered accurate.

5.2.1 Sensitivity Analysis

First, we compared the sensitivities of SHARP and the flat model when model parameters change. We vary a parameter within a range (to be specified below), and observe how system reliability changes. Here, we present results corresponding to varying failure-related parameters in the MIDAS and GPS systems. We performed similar experiments by varying other parameters and using other systems' models. The results were qualitatively similar.

The inaccuracies in our estimates come from the solution of the PAR scenarios, because of the approximations we made (recall Section 4.3). We generate the SBM of the basic scenarios using the same technique as in existing work, therefore the results are the same. The solution of the SEQ scenarios is exact: the steady state probability using our stochastic complementation-based approach is the same as if solved directly (with a flat model) [18].

Next, we study how the inaccuracies propagate to the system level. In Figures 11(a) - (d), we vary the failure rates of the *Sensor* and *Hub* components in MIDAS, and the *EM* and *RG* components in GPS between 0.1 and 0.5. In Figures 11(f) - (i), we vary the recovery rates of *Sensor* and *Hub* in MIDAS, and *EM* and *RG* in GPS between 0.2 and 0.8. We observe that results obtained from SHARP closely follow the flat model in these experiments.

We also illustrate that SHARP is useful in highlighting components that are more critical to a system's reliability. For instance, in Figure 11, when we vary the failure rates of *Sensor* and *Hub* between 0.1 and 0.5, system reliabilities obtained from SHARP change by 4% and 0.4%, suggesting that under these conditions *Sensor* is the more critical component. This is corroborated by the flat model.

5.2.2 Effect of Contention Modeling

To illustrate the importance of modeling contention in SHARP, we use CS with a single scenario. By increasing the number of clients, we can model a highly-contended system. For example, our results with one server and 8 clients are depicted in Figures 11(e) and (j), where we present the results of using SHARP without contention modeling, SHARP with contention modeling, as well as results from the flat model (which includes contention) as a baseline for comparison. The differences between the results obtained from SHARP without contention modeling and the flat model can be as large as 12% (when the failure rate is 0.2), while the results with contention modeling are much more accurate (the error is generally about 2%, and no larger than 5%, when the failure rate is 0.2). This occurs because, without contention modeling SHARP includes the time spent waiting to be served as processing time, thus overestimating the processing time. In turn, this lowers the reliability because processing a request may trigger a defect in the server that waiting for service does not. Results obtained using other systems are qualitatively similar, and are omitted for brevity.

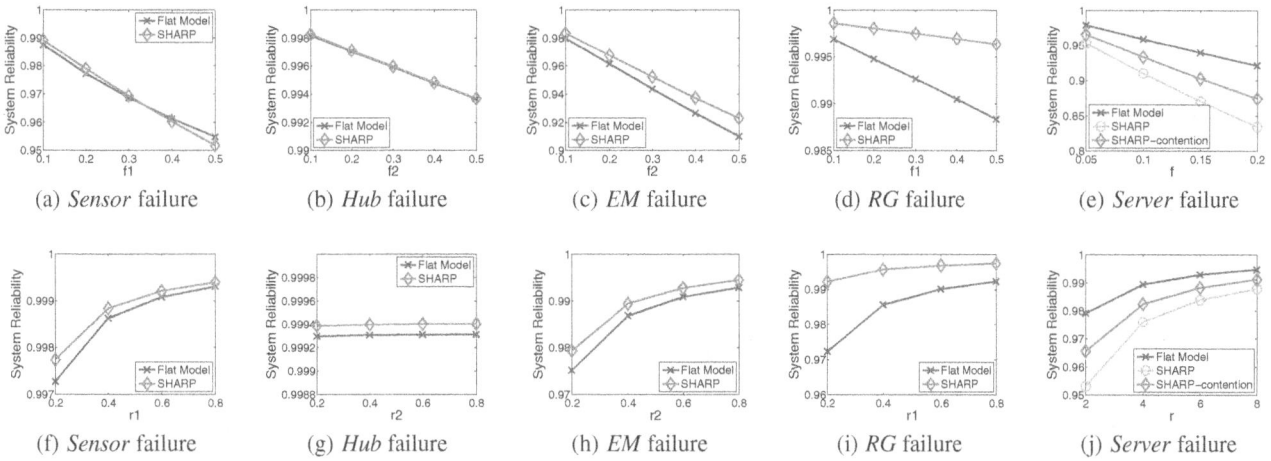

(a) *Sensor* failure   (b) *Hub* failure   (c) *EM* failure   (d) *RG* failure   (e) *Server* failure

(f) *Sensor* failure   (g) *Hub* failure   (h) *EM* failure   (i) *RG* failure   (j) *Server* failure

Figure 11: Sensitivity analysis at the system level

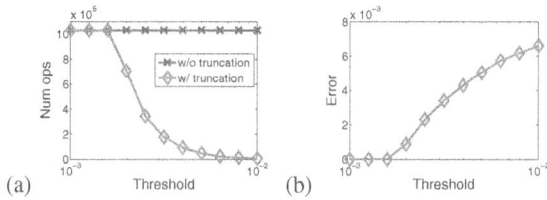

Figure 12: (a) Computational cost of SHARP with and without truncation, (b) Errors caused by model truncation

5.2.3 Effect of Model Truncation

In evaluating the effect of truncation (recall Section 4.3.3), we first study the computational cost savings. As a representative illustration, in Figure 12(a), we plot the number of operations needed to solve for the reliability of MIDAS with one *GUI*, *AC*, and *Hub*, and 100 *Gateways*, with each *Gateways* connects to two *Sensors*. i.e., there are 100 instances of the *SensorMeasurement* scenario. In Figure 12(a), we varied the threshold (x-axis, plotted in log-scale), and plotted the number of operations needed to solve SHARP with truncation. We fixed the scenario reliability of *SensorMeasurement* at 0.99, and the completion time at 1. The cost without truncation is our baseline, and can be considered as having a threshold of 0. As we can see from Figure 12(a), the computational cost savings can be significant.

Next, we study the error in reliability estimates when truncation is used. The results are depicted in Figure 12(b). We varied the threshold in the x-axis, and plotted the error in reliability estimates as compared to the results without truncation (y-axis). The error is expectedly smaller for smaller thresholds, The largest error is 0.8% for the threshold of 10^{-2}. Our experiments with model truncation suggest it as an effective way of reducing the analysis space for concurrent systems with minimal losses in accuracy.

6. RELATED WORK

Current literature includes a number of software reliability prediction techniques that are applicable at the architectural level [5, 7, 9, 10, 11, 21, 22, 23, 28, 30]. A comprehensive treatment of these is given in several surveys on the topic [15, 8, 12, 13]. Many of these approaches are influenced by [5], which is one of the earliest works on reliability prediction that considers a system's internal structure using Markov chains. In [5], the states in the reliability model represent components, while the transitions represent transfer of control between components. These transitions are assumed

to follow the Markov property (i.e., a transition to the next state is determined only by the current state). The work in [5] assumes a sequential system, and most existing approaches, with the notable exception of [7, 22, 28], make the same assumption. Since our work focuses on *concurrent* systems, we restrict the remaining discussion mostly to works that address concurrency. We also comment on approaches that make use of scenario-based models, as well as approaches based on formalisms other than Markov chains.

As noted earlier, in modeling a concurrent system one typically needs to keep track of the status of all components. [7, 22, 28] have taken this approach, in which a state S in a model of a concurrent system is described by $\mathbf{C}$ variables, where $\mathbf{C}$ is the number of components in the system, i.e., $S = (S^1, S^2, \ldots, S^{\mathbf{C}})$. In [7, 28], components are modeled as black-boxes, which are either active or idle, i.e., $S^i = 0$ when $Comp_i$ is idle and $S^i = 1$ when $Comp_i$ is active. In addition to scalability problems, this is also a shortcoming since representing the internal structure of components facilitates more accurate models. For example, some defects may only be triggered when the component performs certain functions. To address this, instead of modeling the status of a component as either active or idle, one can use a finer-granularity component model; this would result in the type of model used in [22], where S^i represents the state of $Comp_i$. Specifically, [22] generates component models from scenario models and then generates a system model by combining the component models using parallel composition.

In our earlier work in [4], we estimate the reliability of concurrency systems, modeled as independent scenarios running in parallel. The major differences between this paper and our earlier work are (1) we model the dependencies between scenarios in this paper, while in [4] we assume scenarios are independent; (2) we allow scenarios that are running in parallel synchronize (recall Section 4.3.4); and (3) we explore contention modeling in details (Section 2.2.3), which is first hypothesized as future direction in [4].

Existing approaches are also inflexible with respect to different notions of system failure, e.g., in [5, 10, 11, 21, 28], failures are represented by transitions to a failure state in the (Markov-chain based) reliability model. In these models (which assume a single-threaded system), being in state S_i indicates that $Comp_i$ is active, while all other components are idle. A transition from a state S_i to a failure state indicates that $Comp_i$ has failed. This means that if any active component has failed, the entire system is considered to have failed. This is also the case in [22], where the system transitions to a failure state when any active component fails. The work in [7, 9] does not include failure states explicitly; rather essentially a reward is assigned to each state (with the value of the reward representing the probability of the system failing in that state), where the system's reliability is computed as a Markov reward function [25]. However, the system failure description is still limited, assuming that the system fails when any (active) component fails. [28] provides a somewhat richer description of system failures, where a reliability model includes backup components that can provide services when the primary component fails; the system fails when the primary component and all backup components fail. However, this approach is not capable (without significant changes) of describing other notions of system failure, e.g., an OR-type relationship (the system fails when $Comp_A$ or $Comp_B$ fails). Such notions of system failure can be described within SHARP, by changing the way we compute combination reliability in Section 4.3.5.

Some existing approaches make use of scenario models [10, 22, 30], but they assume a sequential system, with the exception of [22] as described above. For example, in [30] system reliability is defined as the weighted sum of scenario reliabilities. The weights represent the probabilities that each scenario occurs, with the assumption that one scenario is active at a time. This is not the case in our work: in a concurrent system, it is possible to have concurrency within a scenario, as well as multiple scenarios and/or multiple instances of the same scenario running simultaneously. Moreover, [30] assumes that the probabilities of each scenario occurring are known, which is also not the case in our work.

7. CONCLUSIONS

We presented SHARP, a scalable framework for predicting reliability of concurrent systems. SHARP models concurrency by allowing multiple instances of system scenarios to run simultaneously. We overcame inherent scalability problems by leveraging scenario models and using an approximate hierarchical technique that allowed generation and solution of smaller parts of the overall model at a given time. Our experimental evaluation showed that SHARP's scalability, which is missing from existing techniques, is achieved without significant degradation in the prediction accuracy.

8. ACKNOWLEDGEMENTS

This work is supported by the NSF (award numbers 0509539, 0920612, and 0905665).

9. REFERENCES

[1] F. Baskett et al. Open, closed, and mixed networks of queues with different classes of customers. *J. ACM*, 22(2), 1975.

[2] B. Boehm. Software engineering economics. *IEEE TSE*, 10(1), 1984.

[3] L. Cheung et al. Early prediction of software component reliability. In *ICSE'08*.

[4] L. Cheung et al. SHARP: A scalable approach to architecture-level reliability prediction of concurrent systems. In *QUOVADIS'10*.

[5] R.C. Cheung. A user-oriented software reliability model. *IEEE TSE*, 6(2), 1980.

[6] V. Cortellessa et al. Early reliability assessment of uml based software models. In *WOSP'02*.

[7] R. El-Kharboutly et al. UML-based methodology for reliability analysis of concurrent software applications. *I. J. Comput. Appl.*, 14(4), 2007.

[8] S. Gokhale. Architecture-based software reliability analysis: Overview and limitations. *IEEE TDSC*, 4(1), 2007.

[9] S. Gokhale and K. Trivedi. Reliability prediction and sensitivity analysis based on software architecture. In *ISSRE 2002*.

[10] K. Goseva-Popstojanova et al. Architectural-level risk analysis using UML. *IEEE TSE*, 29(3), 2003.

[11] K. Goseva-Popstojanova and S. Kamavaram. Software reliability estimation under uncertainty: Generalization of the method of moments. In *HASE 2004*.

[12] K. Goseva-Popstojanova and K. Trivedi. Architecture-based approaches to software reliability prediction. *Intl J. Computer & Mathematics with Applications*, 46(7), 2003.

[13] A. Immonen and E. Niemela. Survey of reliability and availability prediction methods from the viewpoint of software architecture. *Software and Systems Modeling*, Jan 2007.

[14] I. Krka et al. Synthesizing partial component-level behavior models from system specifications. In *ESEC/FSE 2009*.

[15] I. Krka et al. A comprehensive exploration of challenges in architecture-based reliability estimation. *Architecting Dependable Systems*, 6, 2009.

[16] J. Magee and J. Kramer. *Concurrency: State Models And Java Programs*. John Wiley & Sons, 2006.

[17] S. Malek et al. Reconceptualizing a family of heterogeneous embedded systems via explicit architectural support. In *ICSE'07*.

[18] C. D. Meyer. Stochastic complementation, uncoupling Markov chains, and the theory of nearly reducible systems. *SIAM Review*, 31(2), 1989.

[19] OMG. UML 2.2 specification, 2009.

[20] M. Reiser and S. S. Lavenberg. Mean value analysis of closed multichain queueing networks. *J. ACM*, 27(2), 1980.

[21] R. Reussner et al. Reliability prediction for component-based software architectures. *J. of Systems and Software*, 66(3), 2003.

[22] G. Rodrigues et al. Using scenarios to predict the reliability of concurrent component-based software systems. In *FASE 2005*.

[23] R. Roshandel et al. A Bayesian model for predicting reliability of software systems at the architectural level. In *QoSA 2007*.

[24] R. Roshandel, B. Schmerl N. Medvidovic, D. Garlan, and D. Zhang. Understanding tradeoffs among different architectural modeling approaches. In *WICSA 2004*.

[25] W. Stewart. *Probability, Markov Chains, Queues, and Simulation*. Princeton University Press, 2009.

[26] R. Taylor, N. Medvidovic, and E. Dashofy. *Software Architecture: Foundations, Theory, and Practice*. Wiley, 2009.

[27] S. Uchitel et al. Incremental elaboration of scenario-based specifications and behavior models using implied scenarios. *ACM TOSEM*, 13(1), 2004.

[28] W. Wang et al. Architecture-based software reliability modeling. *J. of Systems and Software*, 79(1), 2006.

[29] J. Whittle and P.K. Jayaraman. Synthesizing hierarchical state machines from expressive scenario descriptions. *ACM TOSEM*, 19(3), 2010.

[30] S. Yacoub et al. Scenario-based reliability analysis of component-based software. In *ISSRE'99*.

The Implementation of the Server Efficiency Rating Tool

Mike G. Tricker
Microsoft Corporation

mike.tricker@microsoft.com

Klaus-Dieter Lange
Hewlett-Packard Company

klaus.lange@hp.com

Jeremy A. Arnold
IBM Corporation

arnoldje@us.ibm.com

Hansfried Block
Fujitsu Technology Solutions GmbH

hansfried.block@ts.fujitsu.com

Christian Koopmann
University of Paderborn

koop-chris@hotmail.de

ABSTRACT

The Server Efficiency Rating Tool (SERT) [1] has been developed by Standard Performance Evaluation Corporation (SPEC) [2] at the request of the US Environmental Protection Agency (EPA) [3], prompted by concerns that US datacenters consumed almost 3% of all energy in 2010. Since the majority was consumed by servers and their associated heat dissipation systems the EPA launched the ENERGY STAR Computer Server [4] program, focusing on providing projected power consumption information to aid potential server users and purchasers. This program has now been extended to a world-wide audience.

This paper expands upon the one published in 2011 [6], which described the initial design and early development phases of the SERT. Since that publication, the SERT has continued to evolve and has entered the first Beta phase in October 2011 with the goal of being released in 2012. This paper describes more of the details of how the SERT is structured. This includes how components interrelate, how the underlying system capabilities are discovered, and how the various hardware subsystems are measured individually using dedicated worklets.

Categories and Subject Descriptors

H.3.4 [**Systems and Software**]: Performance evaluation (efficiency and effectiveness)

General Terms

Design, Experimentation, Measurement, Performance, Reliability, Standardization

Keywords

SPEC, SERT, Rating Tool, Benchmark, Energy Efficiency, Power, Server, Storage, Datacenter, ENERGY STAR, Environmental Protection Agency, EPA

1. INTRODUCTION

SPEC was founded in 1988 as a nonprofit organization dedicated to the creation of industry standards for measuring the performance of various aspects of computers and their associated software. It now includes representatives from more than 80 member companies and organizations and has released more than 30 industry-standard benchmarks, which have been used to create more than 20,000 peer-reviewed published performance reports.

SPEC is composed of four major groups: the Open Systems Group (OSG), the High Performance Group (HPG), the Graphics and Workstation Performance Group (GPWG) and most recently the newly created Research Group (RG). The OSG comprises groups covering the major areas of desktop, workstation and server benchmarking and performance evaluation. These groups are responsible for benchmarks characterizing CPU, Java, SFS, Virtualization, and Power. The latter is specifically addressed by the SPECpower Committee, which is responsible for creating and updating the SPECpower_ssj2008 benchmark (ssj2008) [7]. This industry standards committee is currently developing the SERT for the EPA's next generation of ENERGY STAR for Servers program.

Ssj2008 was developed as the first industry-standard cross-platform benchmark for evaluating the combined power and performance characteristics of volume and multi-node server systems. It is based on primarily transactional server-side Java workloads, which exploit many aspects of commercially available Java implementations while exercising processors (CPUs), memory hierarchies (including caches), and the general Symmetric Multiprocessing (SMP) scalability of the systems under test.

The EPA has been tracking the growth in computer (and more specifically server) energy consumption for several years, hosting the Conference on Enterprise Servers and Data Center: Opportunities for Energy Savings in January 2006. Later that year the EPA announced its intention to develop an ENERGY STAR for Enterprise Computer Servers program with broad industry participation and support. This resulted in the ENERGY STAR Computer Server specification launched in May 2009, which recommended the use of ssj2008 to provide the data required to complete the EPA Power and Performance Data Sheet [8].

The SERT has been developed specifically to address the EPA requirements for Version 2 of the ENERGY STAR server [5] program. Unlike most SPEC products, it is not a benchmark having a single score model for use in comparison or marketing.

Instead, it is an evaluation tool that produces detailed information regarding the influence of CPU, memory, and storage IO configurations on overall server power consumption. This resulting information is intended to educate and enable informed purchasing decisions across a broad spectrum of potential customer types and technical backgrounds.

To provide an example of potential usage patterns the Storage IO worklets included in the SERT have been used for an extensive series of experiments on various storage device configurations, including different numbers and models of SATA and SAS HDD and SSD storage devices. The tests were executed on two different computer server models with different maximal storage device capacities under the Microsoft Windows Server 2008 R2 operating system. A modified version of SPEC PTDaemon was employed for the power measurements of total system power in parallel with RAID controller power and storage device power.

This paper also outlines some of the thoughts on how to best describe these subsystem capabilities in ways usable by the broadest range of potential consumers. The authors also intend to provide a follow-up paper with the experimental evaluation once a stable set of SERT worklets is finalized.

2. MOVING BEYOND SSJ2008

When the EPA began to develop Version 2 of the ENERGY STAR for Computer Servers program, they decided that more detailed information regarding the relationship between power consumption and performance for servers was needed. This decision in turn led to the initial requirements for the SERT, which differs from previous SPEC projects in a number of significant ways.

The first and most important difference is that the SERT is not intended to be a benchmark, a fact reflected by the "Rating Tool" aspect of its name. Benchmarks relating to performance and energy efficiency typically focus on the capabilities of servers in addressing specific application areas or business models, often by simulating typical workloads such as Web, File & Print or Database Servers. In contrast, the SERT focuses on providing a first order approximation of energy efficiency across a broad range of application environments.

Unlike most benchmarks, there is no single absolute score as the final outcome of a measurement sequence. This is combined with the EPA requirement for the SERT to be run in an "as shipped" or "out of the box" system configuration, with minimal configuration changes allowed to the system firmware/BIOS, operating system (OS) or middleware such as the Java Virtual Machine (JVM) of the System Under Test (SUT). This deliberate lack of opportunity for optimization is intended to move the focus onto delivering results for the major power-drawing subsystems within a server (CPU, memory, network and storage IO) that will be of use to prospective purchasers and users of servers who need to support multiple workloads with differing performance and IO characteristics.

The distribution of SERT will be similar to that of existing SPEC Benchmarks and the Full Disclosure Report (FDR) produced by each SERT test run will include all setup and tuning details sufficient to enable others to re-create the result(s). The goal is to present the customer the real raw data without a company's marketing "spin", which may unduly benefit companies with greater resources to draw from. It is also intended (in agreement with the EPA) that absolute scores may not be used in marketing

materials. The aim is to increase participation from smaller companies in the program, specifically looking beyond the traditional multi-national Original Equipment Manufacturers (OEMs), such as smaller Value Added Resellers (VARs) and local system integrators who may manufacture their owns systems from widely available motherboards and components and are a critical part of worldwide emerging markets.

3. AN OVERVIEW OF THE SERT

The SERT is designed to be scalable to a maximum of 64 nodes (limited to a set of homogenous servers or blade servers) and to support multiple power analyzers and temperature sensors. The simplest SERT hardware measurement configuration requires four main hardware components; one **Power Analyzer**, one **Temperature sensor,** a **SUT** and the **Controller**.

The SERT is composed of several elements, starting with the test harness, named **Chauffeur,** which handles the logistical side of measuring and recording the power consumption and inlet temperature of the SUT. It also controls the software installed on both the SUT and Controller, communicating via the TCP/IP transport protocol.

Chauffeur communicates with the **Director**, which instructs the SUT to execute the **suite**, comprising a set of workloads. The **workload** comprises a set of worklets, which exercise the SUT while Chauffeur collects the power and temperature data. The **worklets** are the actual code designed to stress a specific system resource or resources, such as the CPU, memory or storage IO.

The temperature sensor must be placed no more than 50mm in front of (upwind of) the main airflow inlet of the SUT. The SERT will measure the inlet temperature of the SUT and marks the results "valid" only if the temperature measured is 20°C or higher, in order to discourage the "gaming" of the test environment. A stable temperature value is not required during warm-up or measurement phases.

The power analyzer must be located between the AC Line Voltage Source and the SUT. Both are connected to the Controller via their device specific interfaces, as shown in Figure 1. Each analyzer and sensor interacts with its dedicated instance of the **SPEC PTDaemon**, which gathers their readings while the worklets are executed.

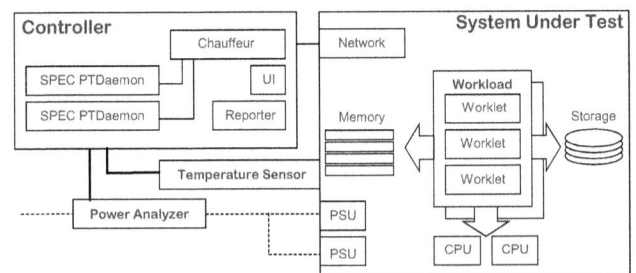

Figure 1. The SERT Overview

The **Reporter**, executed after all measurements phases are completed, compiles all of the environmental, power, and performance data for a complete test run into an easy to read report. The output format will be HTML, plain text, extensible markup language (XML), and comma-separated values (CSV); the HTML report includes a graphical visualization of the results.

4. ARCHITECTURAL CONSIDERATIONS

When the SERT was being designed, a number of decisions were made to produce a comprehensive (and extensible) test in a timely manner to meet the EPA's ENERGY STAR requirements. As SPEC is primarily a volunteer organization that relies on the resources made available by the participating members, it imposes constraints on the development phases.

Consequently, the SERT is currently targeted at 64-bit hardware and OSs only, as this limits the amount of integration testing that is required. Likewise, the majority of code has been developed in Java, partly to ease the cross-platform porting and also reflecting the expertise of SPECpower as ssj2008 was developed in Java. Some C code for certain low-level operations is implemented, as this is also relatively easy to port across platforms.

The SERT goes beyond the hardware goals of Version 2 of the ENERGY STAR server program and is intended to support servers with up to eight processors (also referred to as sockets) and up to 64 nodes, which may be blades or a set of homogeneous multi-node servers. Multi-node servers are defined as having shared infrastructure such as power supplies or backplanes that prevent the servers from operating independently. For example, blade servers are installed in a common enclosure, which usually includes shared power supplies, fans, storage devices, and IO infrastructure such as a backplane or switch.

A primary design goal for the SERT was to scale system performance in proportion to the system configuration. As more components are added (CPU, memory and storage) to a server, the workloads included in the SERT needed to use those resources efficiently, resulting in higher performance when compared against the same basic server design with a less rich hardware configuration. Likewise, if faster components are used instead of the default ones, then the performance needs also increase to reflect that change. This is very important, as adding more or faster components will typically increase the power consumed by a server, affecting the overall efficiency reported. The SERT also supports multiple workload levels (currently idle, 33%, 67% and 100%) that show the overall power/performance characteristics for the server under varying degrees of load, as typically observed in data centers across varying workloads and usage scenarios.

It is also important that the SERT not unnecessarily penalize servers that are not designed to be expandable, but at the same time credits those with greater expandability. Many higher-end servers include highly desirable reliability features such as redundant power supplies and fans, so it is important that such servers not be unduly penalized by the SERT. To ensure that all sorts of server vendors could afford to use the SERT it was agreed with the EPA that the only hardware to be tested will be included within the primary server enclosure. This eliminates the need for complex and expensive external storage devices and network hardware, which greatly simplifies the configuration and use of the SERT. At the same time it includes the server components that draw the most power, including storage devices such as solid state disks or rotating media.

5. SERT: DEFINITION AND EXECUTION

The SERT is composed of a suite of worklets, each of which exercises the SUT in a specific way. For example, the XmlValidate worklet performs validation on a randomly generated XML document, while the Sequential IO worklet performs sequential IO operations on all storage devices included in the SUT. These worklets are grouped into workloads according to the component of the SUT that they are intended to stress: CPU, memory, and storage IO. In addition, a Combined workload consists of application-focused worklets that stress the components of the SUT in a more balanced manner. Figure 2 shows the relationship between the overall suite, workloads, and worklets.

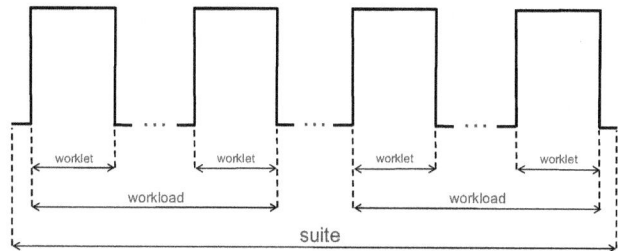

Figure 2. Suite Overview

During a SERT run, each of the worklets is executed consecutively. Each worklet is run in its own set of JVMs or processes in order to minimize interactions between different worklets. Chauffeur automatically launches these client JVMs and coordinates the work among them. Most worklets use multiple client JVMs on the SUT and Chauffeur automatically uses operating system-specific affinity commands to pin each JVM to specific processors in order to avoid artificial limits to scaling. In this context, "client JVM" refers to the client side of a client-server communication pattern and is the JVM that does all of the real work. JVM command-line options are set by Chauffeur (with configurable overrides), allowing for self-tuning of heap sizes and ensuring that the command-line options are reported accurately.

The use of multiple JVMs for running a single worklet is primarily to avoid software bottlenecks (whether in the JVM implementation or in the SERT worklets) from limiting scalability since SERT is intended primarily for measuring the energy efficiency of the hardware and not the software stack. SERT is quite capable of running each worklet in a single JVM, but performance results are likely to be better when using multiple JVMs, e.g., each JVM can be affinitized to a specific processor and therefore all memory accesses will be local to that processor.

Worklets designed for concurrent execution may also be combined into a co-mingled worklet where the individual component worklets run simultaneously rather than consecutively. This introduces more realistic task switching, which is especially useful for IO load simulation. In the current implementation, there is no direct support for the parallel composition of worklets. Instead, a co-mingled worklet can be implemented by creating a new worklet that consists of transactions taken from other worklets, e.g., a processor-intensive transaction and a disk access transaction. As in any other worklet, these transactions could be specified to execute in whatever ratios are desired, e.g., 70% processor intensive, 20% disk reads, 10% disk writes. A future version of SERT/Chauffeur may include support for directly running multiple worklets in parallel.

Most worklets use a "Graduated Measurement" execution sequence (Figure 3). These worklets begin by executing a short warm-up phase (30 sec.), and then run two calibration phases (120 sec.) to automatically determine the maximum throughput each worklet can run on the SUT. Then the worklet runs at multiple load levels, such as 100%, 67%, and 33% of the maximum throughput, generating independent scores for each load level. Each interval of execution includes a pre-measurement (15 sec.) and post-measurement (15 sec.) period in addition to the actual measurement period; each of these periods run for a fixed amount of time. Between each load level a sleep phase (10 sec.) is observed.

Performance and power are reported for the measurement phase (120 sec.) only. This ensures that the worklet is running at steady-state in all client JVMs at the time performance and power are measured.

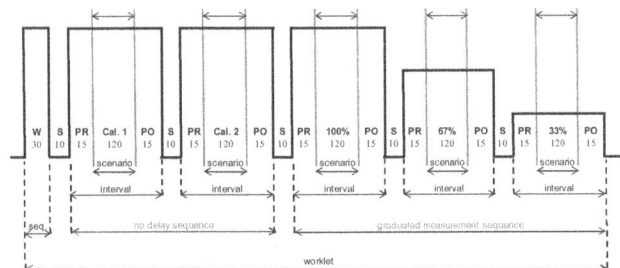

Figure 3. Phases of a Graduated Measurement Sequence

An alternative "Fixed Iteration" execution sequence (Figure 4) is used for worklets that do not support multiple load levels. These worklets run a fixed number of test iterations rather than for a fixed period of time. They optionally include some number of pre- and post-measurement iterations, similar to the pre- and post-measurement periods in a Graduated Measurement sequence.

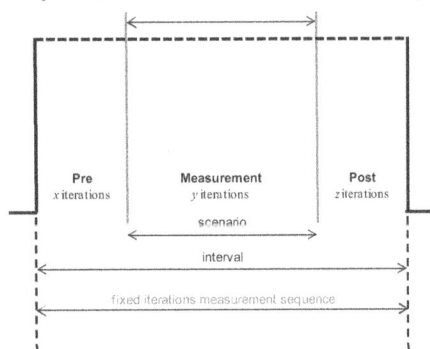

Figure 4. Phases of a Fixed Iteration Sequence

All of the time intervals are configurable in Chauffeur (though the SERT run rules will probably disallow users from changing the interval lengths) and the interval lengths can be adjusted separately for each worklet. The current SERT builds use a two minute warm-up period for the Storage IO worklets since testing has shown that a longer warm-up provides more consistent results for these worklets. Warm-up intervals of 30 seconds are working well for most other worklets, but additional adjustments to the interval lengths will be made if necessary as the SERT is finalized. While a 30 second interval may be needlessly long for some worklets, this constitutes less than 5% of the total worklet run time, so it is unlikely that the warm-up periods will be shortened.

One challenging design goal was that the SERT should thoroughly test the SUT, but at the same time not take so long to complete a test pass that multiple runs in a normal working day became impossible. A complete pass is currently taking between four and five hours depending on SUT hardware configuration and this will be further tuned during the Beta program.

The results from individual worklets are reported individually and can also be combined into higher-level metrics at the workload level to summarize the performance for a particular subcomponent.

5.1 Target Load Levels

Since servers frequently run at less than 100% utilization, it is important for the SERT to assess energy efficiency at multiple load levels. The Chauffer test harness runs each worklet in a calibration mode to determine the maximum transaction rate that the worklet can achieve on the SUT. For each Target Load Level (100%, 67%, 33%), Chauffeur calculates the target transaction rate and the corresponding mean time from the start of one transaction to the start of the next transaction. During the measurement interval, randomized delays are inserted into the worklet execution; these delays follow an exponential distribution that statistically converges to the desired transaction rate. As a result, lower target loads consist of short bursts of activity separated by periods of inactivity. Figure 5 shows a 67% and 33% target load distributions.

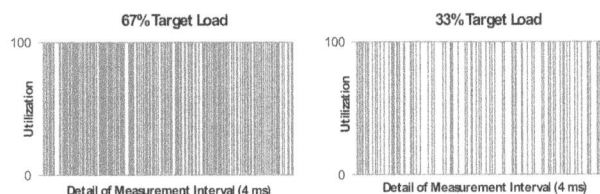

Figure 5. Load Distribution at different Target Loads

6. WORKLET CANDIDATES

SERT worklets were designed under a set of public guidelines [10] to ensure consistent results across a broad spectrum of technologies. For example, each workload must automatically calibrate itself to report the maximum performance available in that specific hardware configuration, and must then be adjustable to target load levels from 100-0% of the maximum performance. Each worklet also needs to scale with the available hardware resources which the execution model deemed "important", e.g., a CPU worklet needs to scale with the number of processors, cores, hardware threads and the clock frequency.

The SERT Design Document [1] offers a detailed breakdown of what each worklet does and how it works. Currently 16 worklets are under evaluation and categorized in Table 1.

The workloads can be summarized as:

CPU: Data compression, encryption/decryption, complex number arithmetic, matrix factorization, floating point array manipulation, sorting algorithm, string manipulation, and XML document validation;

Memory: XML document manipulation and validation using pre-computed and cached data lookup, and array manipulation with read/write operations across four major classes of data transformation;

Storage IO: Four individual transaction pairs combining sequential/random read/write and a mixed transaction which combines all four;

Combined: The concept of CSSJ is derived from ssj2008, which simulated an on-line Transaction Processing workload in which customers order and pay for goods from warehouses that handle delivery and stock replenishment;

Active Idle: A steady state in which the server is ready to execute any worklet but is not actually doing so, leading to a measure of efficiency for a fully functional but otherwise idle state.

Table 1. Worklet Candidates

Workload	Worklet	Sequence Execution	Metric
CPU	Compress	Graduated	Transactions/sec
	CryptoAES	Graduated	Transactions/sec
	SOR	Graduated	Transactions/sec
	SORT	Graduated	Transactions/sec
	SHA256	Graduated	Transactions/sec
	FFT	Graduated	Transactions/sec
	LU	Graduated	Transactions/sec
	XmlValidate	Graduated	Transactions/sec
Memory	XmlValidate1	Graduated	Transactions/sec*cache size*cache scaling factor
	XmlValidate2	Graduated	Transactions/sec*cache size*cache scaling factor
	Flood	Fixed	Memory bandwidth (GB/sec)*memory size (GB)
Storage IO	Random	Graduated	Transactions/sec
	Sequential	Graduated	Transactions/sec
	Mixed	Graduated	Transactions/sec
Combined	CSSJ	Graduated	Transactions/sec
Idle	Active Idle	N/A	N/A

There are no worklets related to **Network IO**, which will be handled by a "configuration modifier" that simulates the steady state efficiency of a network device. After testing a variety of network interface cards (NICs) across a range of workloads it was observed that the power consumption of the actual devices approximated very closely to a constant (including in the case of NICs that perform offloading from the host processor), with CPU and memory power consumption being the biggest factors influencing overall system efficiency. Combined with the extensive set of external hardware required to effectively test network bandwidth and performance, it was agreed with the EPA that a modifier would be applied to simulate the network IO contribution to overall server efficiency.

7. STORAGE IO WORKLETS

The Storage IO worklets developed for SERT generate synthetic loads on server storage devices mimicking basic access patterns from real world usage models. The tests described in this paper were performed to check the suitability of the implementation for the designed purpose, especially testing whether the design goals given in the SERT Design Document section 2.6.1 [1] are met.

7.1 Test Configurations

The experiments described in this paper are based on prerelease versions of SERT. The results may not be representative for the final release.

In order to show the scaling capabilities of the Storage IO worklets the tests were executed on two different server models:

1.) Fujitsu PRIMERGY TX300 S6 tower server with up to 20 internal 2.5" disk drive bays was selected for showing scale out properties using many devices;

2.) the rack server model PRIMERGY RX300 S6 with up to 12 internal 2.5" disk drive bays was used for the experiments with different device technologies and for separate measurements of the controller and storage device power.

7.1.1 Power Measurement Set-Up

Each controller and each storage device backplane requires its own power analyzer for the internal measurements. The high end configuration in the tower server includes up to two controllers and two backplanes, which exceeded the limits of available power analyzers. Therefore internal measurements were performed for the rack server experiments only.

Temperature sensors were used in all test scenarios to measure the ambient temperature and ensure that it always stays above the required minimum of 20°C, which has been selected as a realistic data center temperature and ensures that testing is not "gamed" by the use of artificially low temperatures. The temperature sensors are omitted in the following configuration pictures for better readability.

7.1.1.1 Tower Server Measurement Set-Up

For this test series the server Power Supply Unit (PSU) was connected to a ZES LMG450 multichannel power analyzer as shown in Figure 6. The default version of SPEC PTDaemon as included in the SERT Beta 1 kit was used for this configuration.

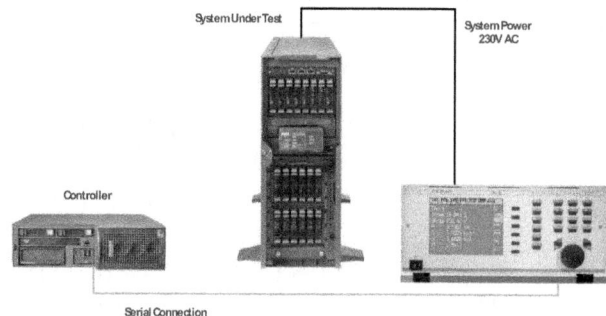

Figure 6. Tower Server Measurement Set-Up

7.1.1.2 Rack Server Measurement Set-Up

Besides an Infratek 107A-1 power analyzer measuring the overall server power consumption at the system's PSU (230V AC), two high precision ZES LMG95 single phase power analyzers were added for measuring the RAID controller and storage device power (12V DC). One of these was connected to a PCI Express (PCIe) adapter card inserted between the PCIe main board slot and the RAID controller. The other one was connected to the storage device backplane. Figure 7 shows the general set-up.

The RAID controller requires two voltages: 3.3V for standby and 12V for active mode. Separate measurements have shown that the standby power does not change with the load. Therefore, only the 12V power was measured for these tests. A fixed amount of 2.1W standby power was added to all controller power measurements for result evaluation. The storage device backplane includes a

SAS expander in order to support 12 device ports using two SAS 4x connectors provided by the RAID controller. The expander power is included in the device power measurements.

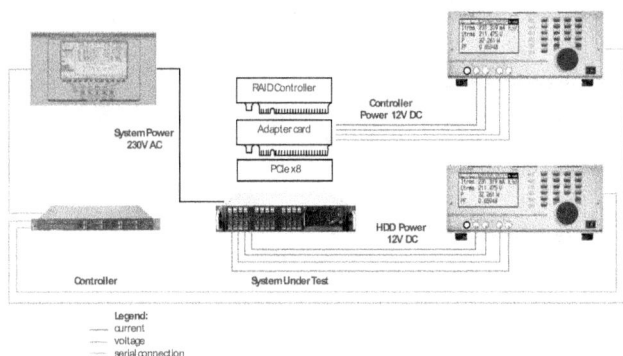

Figure 7. Rack Server Measurement Set-Up

A modified version of SPEC PTDaemon, which supports DC measurements, was implemented for the test series. The uncertainties of DC measurements are significantly higher than those of AC measurements, specifically with lower voltages. In order to stay below the 1% uncertainty threshold required for SPEC power measurements, high precision power analyzers had to be used. This special version of PTDaemon is for internal use only. Currently there are no plans to release this version with the final SERT kit.

7.1.2 The SERT Storage IO Worklets

The SERT includes three Storage IO worklets implementing the basic storage access patterns (sequential, random and mixed) using the characteristics given in Table 2.

Table 2. Storage Worklet Characteristics

Worklet	Access Pattern	Block Size	Read / Write Ratio
Sequential	100% Seq.	128kB	9 / 1
Mixed	50% Seq.	128kB	9 / 1
	50% Rand.	8kB	7 / 3
Random	100% Rand.	8kB	2 / 1

The code requires the storage test devices being formatted to a standard file system, e.g., NTFS (Windows), ext4 (Linux). For optimal performance this file system should store no other files but the test files created by the storage worklets. SERT starts one client instance per storage device, each running four user threads in parallel. Each user thread creates two test files of 1GB size, i.e., there are eight 1GB test files per device. These test files are generated consecutively per device in order to ensure largely sequential layout on the physical storage media. Existing test files will be reused for subsequent tests and will not be recreated for every test run. Because of the four parallel users per device, the sequential access is not completely sequential on the physical media. However, the four user threads are required to guarantee sufficient outstanding IO operations in the device queue to keep them constantly busy, even for high performance storage devices, e.g., SSDs.

Table 3 shows the test files and their corresponding users. The file name format is: <Client-ID>-<User-ID>-<File_Number>.dat; where Client-ID uniquely identifies the storage device.

All storage worklets share the same basic code. The default access pattern and test file definitions shown above are specified in

configuration files and can be modified for research purposes without changing the code, but must be used unchanged for valid SERT results.

Table 3. Test Files

File Name	User	Size
001-0001-001.dat	1	1GB
001-0001-002.dat	1	1GB
:	:	:
001-0004-002.dat	4	1GB

As specified in the SERT Design Document [1] the Storage IO worklets should give credit to higher performance storage devices independently of any controller or main memory caching features. In order to achieve this goal the storage worklet code uses basic OS File IO routines configured to provide unbuffered access to the physical devices circumventing any caching mechanisms. This kind of IO routines is not directly available via integrated Java classes. Instead, the Java Native Access (JNA) interface is used to call the native OS File IO routines from within the SERT Java code.

Finally, it should be mentioned that the sequential code completely walks through one test file per user before changing to the next one. The random code switches position randomly between the two test files and within these files.

7.1.3 The Tested Configurations

The basic configuration of the two test systems as described below was nearly identical for most of the test cases:

- CPU: 2 x Intel Xeon X5675
- RAM: 12 x 2GB (Rack Server) / 8GB (Tower Server) PC3-10600R DIMMs
- RAID Controller: 1 x LSI 2108 SAS
- PSU: 1 x 800W
- OS: Microsoft Windows Server 2008 R2
- File System: NTFS
- JVM: Oracle HotSpot 1.6.0_27-b07 (Rack Server) Oracle HotSpot 1.7.0_02-b13 (Tower Server)
- Storage Devices: different types and numbers (see below)

The tower server was tested with 146GB 2.5" SAS 10krpm HDDs only, which were used as boot devices on both servers, too.

A second partition was created on these boot devices and used for some of the storage worklet test cases.

The tower server test cases are described using the following notation: **OS + (x, y)**. Where x denotes the number of disks connected to the first RAID controller in addition to the OS boot device (maximum eight included OS) and y denotes the device count for the second RAID controller (maximum 12). The following configurations have been tested:
OS + (7, 0), OS + (4, 0), OS + (2, 0), OS + (1, 0), OS + (0, 0), OS + (7, 12), OS + (7, 9), OS + (6, 6), OS + (4, 4), OS + (3, 4)

As the rack server includes a single RAID controller only, the description is given as OS + x, x = number of storage devices (maximum 12 including OS).

The rack server test configurations:

OS + 8, OS + 4, OS + 2, OS + 1, OS + 0 (= 2nd boot dev. partition)

138

This sequence of test configurations was executed using the following storage devices from different manufacturers (all 2.5" form factor):

- 120GB SATA 5.4krpm
- 500GB SATA 7.2krpm
- 146GB SAS 10krpm
- 146GB SAS 15krpm
- 64GB SATA SSD

SATA and SAS disks have significant price/performance differences. One of the key differences relates to their respective densities, with SAS offering significantly better performance; while SATA offers much better density. It is not the intention of this paper to analyze the respective benefits of the competing technologies, but to make use of the different storage access attributes across varying devices speeds.

Each of these configurations on both servers was tested with five consecutive SERT runs in order to examine the run to run variations. The SERT test configuration file (config-all.xml) was modified to execute the Storage IO and Idle worklets only, resulting in a reduced execution time of about one hour per test run.

7.2 Tower Server Test Results

This section presents the results of the experiments executed on the tower server with up to 19 tested storage devices: detailed description of the Storage IO worklet scaling capabilities, comparison of the power consumption of the three worklets, and results of the hardware configuration changes.

After finishing the first set of tests using the SERT Beta 1 kit, problems with the seeding of the Random Number Generator in the worklet code were detected. These problems have been fixed in a subsequent internal SERT release. The results presented below are from a second test series using this internal release.

7.2.1 Storage Device Scaling - Sequential Access

Table 4 and Table 5 show the throughput and power results of the sequential access worklet for an increasing number of devices at all three load levels, starting with a second partition on the OS boot device up to 19 additional SAS 10krpm HDDs.

Observations:

- Throughput for the second partition on the boot device is close to a single separate device.

- Throughput scales almost linearly with the number of storage devices.

- Throughput for the two configurations with seven HDDs is about the same. Power consumption for the OS + (3,4) configuration is higher because a second RAID controller was added and the 12 HDD backplane includes a SAS expander, which consumes additional power. The basic power difference is clearly visible looking at Idle power values.

- The three non-zero load levels get to the expected throughput. Power difference between 33% and 67% is higher than between 67% and 100% due to active power management at lower load levels.

- Processor time as shown in Table 4 and 5 is very low and scales with the number of storage devices, except for the low

end configurations with one to four devices, which all cause a similar base load on the CPU.

Table 4. Storage Device Scaling Results – Part 1

Devices SAS 10krpm	OS+ (0,0)	OS+ (1,0)	OS+ (2,0)	OS+ (4,0)	OS+ (7,0)
100% seq. (MB/s)	40.9	44.2	88.3	175.0	303.8
67% seq. (MB/s)	27.6	29.6	58.9	117.3	203.8
33% seq. (MB/s)	13.7	14.8	29.5	58.8	101.6
100% seq. (W)	120.6	126.3	140.4	162.4	195.5
67% seq. (W)	118.8	124.5	137.5	157.1	188.3
33% seq. (W)	115.7	121.5	131.8	148.4	176.1
Idle (W)	109.3	115.3	121.4	132.5	154.8
% Processor Time	0.7%	0.5%	0.4%	0.7%	1.4%

Table 5. Storage Device Scaling Results – Part 2

Devices SAS 10krpm	OS+ (3,4)	OS+ (4,4)	OS+ (6,6)	OS+ (7,9)	OS+ (7,12)
100% seq. (MB/s)	305.0	349.7	523.9	692.9	823.3
67% seq. (MB/s)	204.7	234.4	351.6	464.8	552.5
33% seq. (MB/s)	102.4	117.1	175.6	232.2	276.3
100% seq. (W)	211.2	223.5	258.3	298.0	323.6
67% seq. (W)	204.9	216.6	250.4	287.9	311.8
33% seq. (W)	192.0	202.7	233.5	268.9	291.9
Idle (W)	172.5	180.5	204.7	230.9	255.0
% Processor Time	1.2%	1.4%	2.1%	2.6%	3.0%

7.2.2 Worklet Power Comparison

The power and performance differences for all three worklets and all tower server test configurations are shown in Table 6 and 7. For this comparison only the results of the 100% load level are shown.

Mixed access throughput is roughly 85% and random throughput is about 75% of pure sequential throughput for most configurations.

There are only minor differences in power consumption between the three worklets with sequential at the top and random at the bottom.

Table 6. Storage IO Power Comparison Results – Part 1

Devices SAS 10krpm	OS + (0, 0)	OS + (1, 0)	OS + (2, 0)	OS + (4, 0)	OS + (7, 0)
100% Seq. (MB/s)	40.9	44.2	88.3	175.0	303.8
100% Mix. (MB/s)	19.2	20.3	39.2	79.2	137.0
100% Rnd. (MB/s)	2.1	2.1	4.1	8.2	14.3
100% Seq. (W)	120.6	126.3	140.4	162.4	195.5
100% Mix. (W)	118.8	123.4	136.4	158.3	190.6
100% Rnd. (W)	116.7	120.5	133.3	153.0	184.2
Idle (W)	109.3	115.3	121.4	132.5	154.8

Table 7. Storage IO Power Comparison Results – Part 2

Devices SAS 10krpm	OS + (3, 4)	OS + (4, 4)	OS + (6, 6)	OS + (7, 9)	OS + (7, 12)
100% Seq. (MB/s)	305.0	349.7	523.9	692.9	823.3
100% Mix. (MB/s)	137.4	157.6	235.7	313.2	371.9
100% Rnd. (MB/s)	14.3	16.4	24.6	32.7	38.9

Devices SAS 10krpm	OS + (3, 4)	OS + (4, 4)	OS + (6, 6)	OS + (7, 9)	OS + (7, 12)
100% Seq. (W)	211.2	223.5	258.3	298.0	323.6
100% Mix. (W)	207.2	218.7	253.3	291.9	316.5
100% Rnd. (W)	199.5	212.0	247.2	285.8	310.4
Idle (W)	172.5	180.5	204.7	230.9	255.0

7.2.3 JVM Comparison

For some selected configurations a second sequence of tests was executed using IBM J9 JVM instead of Oracle HotSpot. The results presented in Table 8 show that there are virtually no power or performance differences between these JVMs.

This is the desired behavior of all SERT worklets and specifically of the Storage worklets.

Table 8. Oracle HotSpot versus IBM J9 - Results

Devices @ 100% load	OS+ (1,0)	OS+ (4,0)	OS+ (3,4)	OS+ (7,12)
Seq. HotSpot (MB/s)	44.2	303.8	523.9	823.3
Seq. J9 (MB/s)	44.4	305.0	523.7	822.4
Rnd. HotSpot (MB/s)	2.1	14.3	24.6	38.9
Rnd. J9 (MB/s)	2.2	14.4	24.7	39.0
Seq. HotSpot (W)	126.3	195.5	258.3	323.6
Seq. J9 (W)	125.5	193.6	260.4	328.8
Rnd. HotSpot (W)	120.5	184.2	247.2	310.4
Rnd. J9 (W)	122.9	182.2	248.5	313.6
Idle (W)	115.3	154.8	204.7	255.0

7.2.4 RAM Comparison

Another experiment compares power consumption for two main memory configurations: 12 x 8GB and 6 x 1GB. The DIMM technology for both configurations was the same.

Both configurations perform about the same, i.e., the smaller memory capacity is still sufficient to exercise the full number of HDDs unrestricted. Previous tests have shown that each Storage IO client instance requires less than 256MB of heap space, so even much smaller memory configurations are able to support the Storage IO worklets.

Table 9. 96GB versus 6GB - Results

Devices @ 100% load	OS+ (1,0)	OS+ (7,12)
Seq. 96GB (MB/s)	44.2	823.3
Seq. 24GB (MB/s)	44.1	823.3
Rnd. 96GB (MB/s)	2.1	38.9
Rnd. 24GB (MB/s)	2.1	38.9
Seq. 96GB (W)	126.3	323.6
Seq. 24GB (W)	118.8	313.8
Rnd. 96GB (W)	120.5	310.4
Rnd. 24GB (W)	113.3	302.5
Idle 96GB (W)	115.3	255.0
Idle 24GB (W)	107.5	253.3

Although the number and capacity of DIMMs was cut by half, the system power was only reduced slightly as shown in Table 9. The base difference can be inferred comparing the Idle rows. Memory power is only a minor part of the overall power, which is

dominated by the storage device power at Idle and by CPU power at 100% load.

7.2.5 PSU Comparison

For the following test series in the tower server a second PSU was added. This is a typical configuration for many data centers which require PSU redundancy. As expected this has no influence on the IO performance. However, there is a significant rise in power, mainly because PSU efficiency is very poor below 20% of nominal power, e.g., below 20% of 2 x 800W = 320W.

Table 10. 1 PSU versus 2 PSUs - Results

Devices @ 100% load	OS+ (1,0)	OS+ (7,12)
Seq. 1PSU (MB/s)	44.1	823.3
Seq. 2PSUs (MB/s)	44.0	823.4
Rnd. 1PSU (MB/s)	2.1	38.9
Rnd. 2PSUs (MB/s)	2.1	38.9
Seq. 1PSU (W)	118.8	313.8
Seq. 2PSUs (W)	137.1	321.4
Rnd. 1PSU (W)	113.3	302.5
Rnd. 2PSUs (W)	132.7	309.7
Idle 1PSU (W)	107.5	253.3
Idle 2PSUs (W)	126.4	261.0

7.2.6 CPU Comparison

For the final test series in the tower server the tests were repeated using different CPU models: a top bin high performance unit and a low voltage model with significantly reduced performance. These experiments were executed on two storage configurations only with the minimal and maximal number of storage devices.

The CPU properties of the standard processor used for the majority of the experiments and the new ones added for this comparison are given in Table 11.

Table 11. Storage IO CPU Properties

CPU	Freq. (GHz)	Cores	Threads	Cache (MB)	TDP (W)
X5690	3.46	6	12	12	130
X5675	3.06	6	12	12	130
L5609	1.86	4	4	12	40

The throughput and power results of these experiments are presented in Table 12. All results are for the sequential access worklet at 100% load.

Table 12. Storage IO CPU Comparison - Results

Devices @ 100% load	OS+ (1,0)	OS+ (7,12)
Seq. X5690 (MB/s)	44.3	822.0
Seq. X5675 (MB/s)	44.2	823.3
Seq. L5609 (MB/s)	44.2	822.7
Seq. X5690 (W)	127.5	327.0
Seq. X5675 (W)	126.3	323.6
Seq. L5609 (W)	116.4	307.1
Idle X5690 (W)	114.4	258.5
Idle X5675 (W)	115.3	255.0
Idle L5609 (W)	103.7	243.8

The performance results confirm that the storage device throughput does not depend on the CPU capabilities. Even the low end processor is capable of saturating the highest number of storage devices. The two 130W CPUs only show minor power differences, whereas the low voltage CPU consumes significantly less power. This is the desired behavior and conforms to the SERT design goals.

7.3 Rack Server Test Results

The extended measurement set-up of the rack server gives a more detailed view of the server power consumption, especially showing the power drawn by the main Storage IO components, the RAID controller, and the storage devices themselves. All the test results presented below are from tests using the Beta 1 SERT release.

7.3.1 System-, Disk-, and Controller-Power

Table 13 displays the performance and power usage for one to eight SATA 5.4krpm HDDs using the sequential access pattern. Different from the previous tables, the power for the storage devices and the RAID controller are shown instead of overall system power.

Table 13. Storage IO Component Power - Results

Devices SATA 5.4krpm	Idle	100%	67%	33%
1 HDD (MB/s)	N/A	14.8	9.9	5.0
2 HDDs (MB/s)	N/A	29.9	20.1	10.0
4 HDDs (MB/s)	N/A	60.6	40.4	20.2
8 HDDs (MB/s)	N/A	120.2	80.5	40.3
1 HDD Disk (W)	13.8	15.8	15.5	15.3
2 HDDs Disk (W)	14.6	18.6	18.0	17.5
4 HDDs Disk (W)	16.1	24.0	22.7	21.6
8 HDDs Disk (W)	19.5	34.7	32.4	30.3
1 HDD Ctr. (W)	8.3	8.3	8.3	8.3
8 HDD Ctr. (W)	8.3	8.3	8.3	8.3

Same as with the previously described tower tests, the performance scales almost linearly with the number of HDDs and the three load levels are matched closely. The device power for the load levels however does not change much. Significant differences can be observed for higher device counts and between Idle and 100% only.

The controller power is completely independent of any load or the number of connected storage devices; it stayed at a constant level for all these experiments.

Another view showing the minimal and maximal configurations of these tests is presented in Table 14, emphasizing the difference between overall system power and component power.

The overall system power increase is much higher than the power increase of the Storage IO components, especially for higher number of devices. The two Delta rows in Table 14 confirm this observation. System power usage is dominated by CPU power, which significantly increases with higher throughput. The device power however is less dependent on the load. Particularly for rotating media, it is mainly determined by the basic power for spinning the platters.

Table 14. System Power versus IO Device Power - Results

Devices SATA 5.4rpm	Idle	100%	67%	33%
1 HDD Sys. (W)	137.7	154.6	147.1	142.9
8 HDDs Sys. (W)	144.0	213.6	200.7	183.9
Delta	6.3	58.9	53.7	41.0
1 HDD Disk (W)	13.8	15.8	15.5	15.3
8 HDDs Disk (W)	19.5	34.7	32.4	30.3
Delta	5.7	18.8	16.8	15.0
1 HDD Ctr. (W)	8.3	8.3	8.3	8.3
8 HDD Ctr. (W)	8.3	8.3	8.3	8.3

7.3.2 Comparing Storage Technologies

A global overview covering all types of storage devices included in the tests is given in Table 15.

The displayed scaling does not exactly match the real differences between the technologies due to a problem with the Storage IO worklet code. The SATA 5.4k, SAS 10k, and SSD tests were performed with code, which did include some unwanted debug code. This code generated an excessive number of log messages on the OS device, which effectively limited the throughput of these configurations. The other configurations have been tested using new binaries without the debug code. Due to the high number of tests, there was no time left to repeat the measurements. Some comparison tests indicate that the difference is less than 5%.

Remarks:

- The 8 SSD configuration is limited by the available bandwidth of the SATA connectors.
- System power increases with the number of devices and the rotational speed, where SSD technology shows the expected lower System power, especially in Idle mode.
- System power in 1 HDD configurations is dominated by CPU power, causing the irregular SSD behavior for this configuration.

Table 15. Storage Technology Comparison - Results

Devices @ 100% Seq.	SATA 5.4k	SATA 7.2k	SAS 10k	SAS 15k	SATA SSD
1 HDD (MB/s)	14.8	41.0	34.0	76.1	177.0
2 HDDs (MB/s)	29.9	61.0	66.7	151.0	365.5
4 HDDs (MB/s)	60.6	124.2	135.0	302.0	723.2
8 HDDs (MB/s)	120.2	252.7	270.9	588.0	844.7
1 HDD (W)	154.6	174.3	176.1	184.0	193.8
2 HDDs (W)	173.0	176.6	191.3	201.7	200.4
4 HDDs (W)	189.3	201.6	214.1	224.4	212.8
8 HDDs (W)	213.6	226.9	255.2	263.6	218.2
Idle 1 HDD (W)	137.7	145.9	147.8	150.4	145.9
Idle 8HDDs	144.0	169.0	189.3	197.5	147.1

Table 16 displays power consumption, adding power measured internally for the different devices. This data show that SSD device power is actually below device power for the other four technologies, even for the one device configuration. SSD system power for one device is higher though due to the increased CPU power caused by the higher SSD throughput.

Table 16. System-, Controller-, and Device-Power - Results

Devices @ 100% Seq.	SATA 5.4k	SATA 7.2k	SAS 10k	SAS 15k	SATA SSD
1 HDD Sys. (W)	154.6	174.3	176.1	184.0	193.8
2 HDDs Sys. (W)	173.0	176.6	191.3	201.7	200.4
4 HDDs Sys. (W)	189.3	201.6	214.1	224.4	212.8
8 HDDs Sys. (W)	213.6	226.9	255.2	263.6	218.2
1 HDD Dev. (W)	15.8	17.5	19.9	19.8	15.4
2 HDDs Dev. (W)	18.6	20.8	26.5	26.6	17.8
4 HDDs Dev. (W)	24.0	28.7	40.5	39.8	22.2
8 HDDs Dev. (W)	34.7	44.4	68.3	66.8	26.4
1 HDD Ctr. (W)	8.3	8.3	8.4	8.4	8.4
8 HDDs Ctr. (W)	8.3	8.5	8.5	8.7	8.6

7.4 Problems Observed

This paper primarily presents the results from the sequential access worklet. The reason is that the other two worklets, mixed and random access, have shown inconsistent results in several configurations, specifically with one or two storage devices only. This problem was caused by setting bad seeds for the random number generators in the storage worklet code of the Beta 1 kit. It has been fixed in a later internal SERT release, which was used for the repeated tower server test results presented above. There was no time left to repeat the rack server tests with this new SERT kit. However, the tower server experiments have shown that the sequential access worklet results of the Beta 1 kit are accurate.

In the critical configurations, observed are very high run to run variations for the Beta 1 test sequences, characterized by a Coefficient of Variation (CV) between 10% and 30%. The acceptable CV limit for SERT tests is defined as 3%. Most of the configurations typically show very low variations, e.g., CV < 0.5% for the five consecutive test runs in our experiments.

Also for the critical configurations in the Beta 1 kit the 100% load point was missed regularly, in some cases less than 70% of the calibrated throughput has been achieved.

8. SERT UI

Users may configure the SERT by manually editing the various configuration files or utilize the newly designed SERT User Interface (SERT UI) in order to manage the behavior of each component.

During **Host Discovery** (Figure 8), the detailed hardware and software configuration of the SUT are gathered automatically by a remote task that uses the industry standard Common Information Model (CIM) definitions that are widely supported across hardware and OS platforms.

The SERT UI provides a graphical interface for gathering all the SUT hardware and software configuration data, configuring and running the SERT, as well as archiving the measured results and log files. It also supports the ability to save and re-import complete configurations to simplify repeated testing.

The default mode executes the entire SERT suite (all worklets) in sequence, each worklet in a new instance of the local JVM, in order to create an EPA compliant test record. The SERT UI also offers an advanced research mode allowing the selective execution of a subset of workloads and worklets.

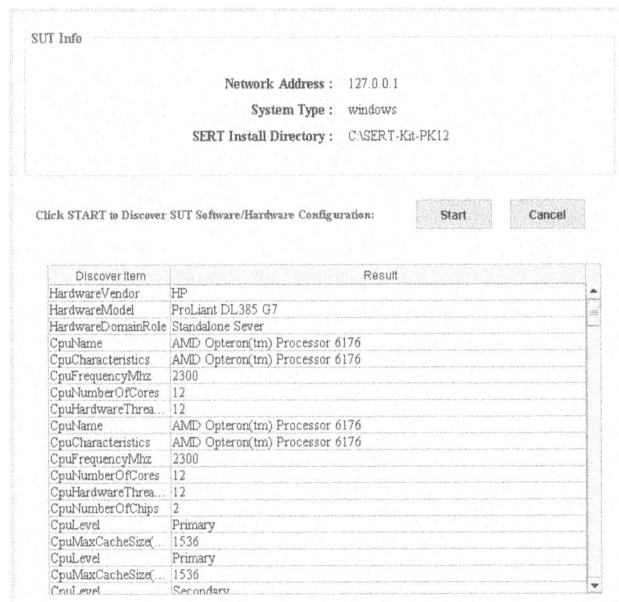

Figure 8. SERT UI: Host Discovery

At the **Launch Test** (Figure 9) the progress of the entire suite can be observed, as well as the status of the currently executing worklet.

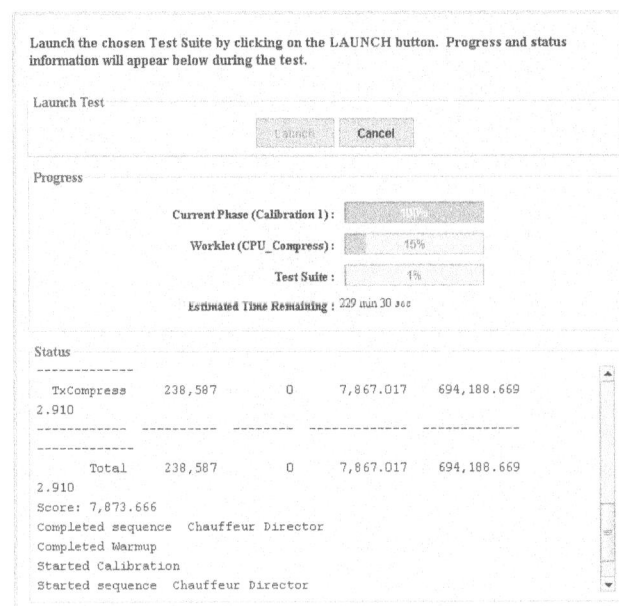

Figure 9. SERT UI: Suite Launch Menu

9. CONCLUSIONS

At the time of writing, the first Beta of the SERT has been delivered, with a second to follow soon, and a Release Candidate is targeted for the first half of 2012. The expectation is that the SERT will be released, together with Version 2 of the ENERGY STAR Computer Server program, in the first half of 2012.

By building on the knowledge gained during the development and on-going support of ssj2008, SPECpower was able to develop a tool that is easier to configure and use while offering a broader set of tests focusing on the major sub-components of servers. It provides the ability to support large systems with a high number of processors and server nodes, and with unlimited memory and on-board storage devices. The design is fundamentally extensible so that as new hardware types emerge additional worklets can easily be added.

With the growing worldwide interest in increasing server and data center efficiency it is anticipated that the SERT will be even more widely used than ssj2008. There are already plans in consideration for future enhancements that the highly modular architecture supporting various forms of serial and parallel test execution is designed to support. Additional platforms and architectures may be supported as industry resources are made available for test and development.

The results presented here demonstrate that the Storage IO worklets included in the SPEC SERT largely meet the intended design goals. They can be used for reliable measurements of storage device efficiency, extending the capabilities of currently available computer server efficiency benchmarks.

Experiments have shown that total system power increases significantly in proportion to the number of storage devices and the load levels, whereas the storage device power increases only marginal at higher load levels. The RAID controller power was almost stable under all test conditions.

Further experiments are planned comparing additional hardware configurations, other operating systems plus different JVM versions and parameters. A comparison of the most important RAID configurations is intended for testing the applicability of the Storage IO worklets to these device configurations.

By offering a detailed breakdown of subsystem efficiency, the SERT enables potential server purchasers to evaluate and compare aspects of different servers that relate most closely to a broad range of potential workloads. This range can include any environment, from small office users combining all their applications onto a handful of servers up to enterprise data centers supporting many tens of thousands of users and thousands of different workloads. It is anticipated that the SERT will be the first of a new class of system evaluation tools that will be widely used across the world in the years to come.

10. ACKNOWLEDGMENTS

The authors want to acknowledge the additional members of the SPECpower Committee who have contributed to the design, development, testing, and overall success of the SERT: Paul Muehr, Van Smith, Greg Darnell, John Beckett, Karl Huppler, Sanjay Sharma, and David Ott.

The authors would also like to acknowledge Karin Wulf for providing a modified version of SPEC PTDaemon supporting DC power measurements and Peter Klassen for executing numerous measurements for this paper.

The name SPEC together with the tool and benchmark names SERT, PTDaemon, and SPECpower_ssj2008 are registered trademarks of the Standard Performance Evaluation Corporation (SPEC).

11. REFERENCES

[1] Server Efficiency Rating Tool public Design Document (latest version): http://www.spec.org/sert/docs/SERT-Design_Doc.pdf

[2] Standard Performance Evaluation Corporation home page: http://www.spec.org

[3] US EPA ENERGY STAR Enterprise Servers home page: http://www.energystar.gov/index.cfm?c=archives.enterprise_servers

[4] US EPA ENERGY STAR Computer Specification Version 1.0: http://www.energystar.gov/ia/partners/product_specs/program_reqs/computer_server_prog_req.pdf

[5] US EPA ENERGY STAR Computer Servers Draft 1 Version 2.0: http://www.energystar.gov/ia/partners/prod_development/revisions/downloads/computer_servers/Draft1Version2ComputerServers.pdf

[6] K.-D. Lange and M. G. Tricker. The design and development of the server energy efficiency rating tool (SERT). In International Conference on Performance Engineering (Mar. 2011), 145-150. DOI= http://doi.acm.org/10.1145/1958746.1958769

[7] K.-D. Lange. Identifying Shades of Green: The SPECpower Benchmarks, IEEE Computer, V42 #3 2009, 95-97, DOI= http://dx.doi.org/10.1109/MC.2009.84

[8] US EPA ENERGY STAR Computer Servers Draft 1 Version 2.0 - http://www.energystar.gov/ia/partners/prod_development/revisions/downloads/computer_servers/Draft1Version2PowerPerformanceDatasheet.pdf

[9] Server Efficiency Rating Tool home page: http://www.spec.org/sert/

Busy Bee: How to Use Traffic Information for Better Scheduling of Background Tasks

Feng Yan
College of William and Mary
Williamsburg, VA, USA
fyan@cs.wm.edu

Alma Riska
EMC Corporation
Cambridge, MA, USA
alma.riska@emc.com

Evgenia Smirni
College of William and Mary
Williamsburg, VA, USA
esmirni@cs.wm.edu

ABSTRACT

Computer systems, in general, and storage systems, in particular, rely on meeting their performance, reliability, and availability targets via scheduling of management and maintenance activities as background tasks. Such tasks may cause significant delays to user workload if scheduled extemporaneously. Here, we propose a scheduling policy for background tasks that is based on the statistical characteristics of the system's busy periods and that aims at completing background work expediently. Extensive trace-driven simulations show that the scheduling policy is robust and that it succeeds in completing background work faster than common practices while impacting user performance minimally.

Categories and Subject Descriptors

C.4 [**Computer Systems Organization**]: Performance of Systems

General Terms

Performance, Algorithms

Keywords

performance, workload characterization, busy periods, background tasks, asynchronous tasks, user traffic, storage systems

1. INTRODUCTION

Systems that support emerging computing paradigms such as cloud computing are growing distinctively larger and more complex. In order to meet the ever increasing user needs for high availability, reliability, performance, and cost-effectiveness [13, 20, 12, 3], systems are built by integrating off-the-shelf components that are managed and maintained *asynchronously*, i.e., outside the critical path of user requests. While the amount and criticality of asynchronous management is commensurate with system complexity, the expectation for such work is to remain transparent from the system

users. Examples of tasks that complete asynchronously in the system, i.e., in the background, include logging of monitored resources, garbage collection, data synchronization, and data verification. Within the storage component, a significant amount of work is completed asynchronously in the background, especially because storage tasks are not instantaneously preemptable [14, 19].

While background work in storage systems may be associated with performance improvement, e.g., moving data from the low performing tier of SATA drives to the high performing tier of SSD drives [8], it mostly targets enhancement of data availability and reliability, e.g., verification of data consistency for protection against bit-rots and replication of data in multiple storage devices or systems for added redundancy. The goal is to strike a balance between meeting user service level objectives while completing the background work as fast as possible. This goal is particularly important for background tasks that are time sensitive. Examples of time sensitive background tasks include geographically distributed data centers where data consistency is achieved only *eventually* by distributing the redundant new data asynchronously, in the background [22].

Judicious selection of scheduling *asynchronous work* vs. *user traffic* is not an easy task. The challenge lies in the fact that future user workload characteristics are seldom known a priori. If the background tasks are scheduled without consideration for user traffic, the impact on user performance may be severe.

Common practices use simplistic measures, such as average utilization, to guide background task scheduling. Such metrics cannot describe accurately current system conditions and often yield unstable solutions because the workload, particularly in storage systems, can be fairly dynamic over short time scales. To limit the impact of background work on user performance, there exist elaborate techniques that focus on idle waiting before starting background work [5, 7]. There are techniques that even provide guarantees on the performance impact caused to user performance [15]. While some techniques that are used to schedule background work operate on fixed parameters that restrict their adaptivity to a changing workload [5, 7], others rely on monitoring a variety of complex processes, such as system idleness, delays caused by the background tasks, and user performance [15].

In this paper, we present a simple yet adaptive solution to the problem of scheduling tasks in the background by proposing a quantitative framework that aims at monitoring, learning, and making scheduling decisions based on a few, easy to monitor metrics. The monitored metrics capture sufficient details on the current foreground workload and the resulting available idle capacity that allow the proposed scheduling policy to complete the background work as fast as possible but with minimal impact on user performance. All scheduling decisions are based *only* on the stochastic characteristics of the length of *user busy periods* in the system. The goal is to schedule as much as possible background work when the impact on performance of user traffic is anticipated to be small (because upcoming busy periods are short) and limit delays on foreground traffic when busy periods are anticipated to be long.

Results from extensive experimentation via trace-driven simulations show that the proposed scheduling policy can maintain the same foreground performance while completing the asynchronous work up to 50% faster. The benefits of the proposed scheduling policy are particularly high when it matters most, i.e., when foreground performance imposes stringent limitations on the tolerance toward additional delays due to background work. The proposed scheduling policy enables the system to sustain its performance in the presence of background tasks, even where there are changes in the user traffic characteristics, by adapting the background scheduling parameters to current foreground characteristics. The robustness and resilience of the scheduling policy is evident especially under swift changes in user workload.

This paper is organized as follows. In Section 2, we give an overview of related work. In Section 3, we provide a detailed characterization of a set of enterprise traces and show how this characterization can be used to develop the new scheduling strategy. In Section 4, we propose a dynamic scheduling framework aiming at improving the performance of background work while maintaining foreground performance. Section 5 presents an extensive set of trace-driven experiments that demonstrates the effectiveness and robustness of the proposed scheduling technique. We conclude and discuss future directions in Section 6.

2. STATE OF THE ART AND MOTIVATION

Today's systems complete most of their resource management and maintenance tasks in the background. In storage systems there is a plethora of activities that are executed asynchronously as background tasks [1, 21] aiming at improving performance, reliability, and availability [11, 2, 24, 12]. In addition, a large body of literature points out the existence of idle periods that are interleaved with periods of high utilization [7, 18, 5]. These idle periods offer an opportunity to serve tasks of low priority, such as data synchronization, but may lead to performance degradation if a foreground task arrives while a background task is in service. This is the case especially in storage systems, because tasks are not instantaneously preemptable. As a result, the foreground requests could be unavoidably delayed when the system executes background tasks.

Conventionally, scheduling of background tasks is done using a non-work-conserving approach by delaying the execution of an outstanding background job with a fixed time when the system becomes idle of foreground workload [5]. This technique avoids using short idle intervals to serve long background jobs and averts severe degradation in foreground performance. Approaches for adaptively determining the amount of time that the system should stay idle, while there is background work to be completed, are proposed for power saving in mobile devices by spinning-down their disks [4,

10]. pClock is a framework that allows multiple workloads to share storage while achieves performance isolation via scheduling [9]. This approach may be also used to allocate spare system capacity to background jobs. Storage performance insulation has been achieved by co-scheduling time slices for each workload type [23].

In [15, 16], the authors propose a framework to estimate when and for how long to utilize idle periods in a system for processing low priority background tasks without violating pre-defined foreground performance targets. This is achieved by extending the non-work-conserving nature of background scheduling as first suggested in [7, 5]. The histogram of past idle intervals can be used to determine: (1) the amount of idle wait till a background task can start and (2) the amount of the expected idle time to be used for scheduling background tasks. The consequence is that the system may remain idle while background tasks are still outstanding after the estimated time to utilize an idle interval for background scheduling elapses. Key to the methodology developed in [15, 16] are the statistical characteristics of idle times which are used for effective background task scheduling.

Systems today have to support a wide range of background tasks. These tasks should be served transparently from foreground tasks but should not starve. Avoiding starvation is the primary target to be met. In addition, if the background tasks are time-sensitive, as it is often the case in storage systems, then they should complete as soon as possible. There is an ever increasing number of time-sensitive asynchronous tasks in storage systems that are served in the background. Examples of such tasks include the asynchronous data updates in geographically distributed data centers. The data in such systems resides in multiple devices, nodes, and locations for purposes of availability and performance. New data is committed asynchronously to all designated nodes in order to avoid network and other delays that may severely impact user perceived performance. As a result the consistency of data across the distributed system is achieved *eventually* as data is committed to its destinations as a background process [22]. Note that for as long as the data is not consistent across *all* of its assigned nodes, data integrity is compromised. This is a clear case where completion of background tasks is time sensitive.

In this paper, we strive to achieve two goals: first to complete the background work while avoiding starvation at all costs and second to reduce its response time as much as possible to better serve time sensitive tasks. Our aim is to maintain the performance of foreground tasks at the same level as common practices, e.g., the approach in [5], while serving background tasks faster. Background tasks in storage systems have similar service demands as foreground requests. This means that if a foreground request arrives to find the system serving a background task, then the delay expectation is approximately two times the average service demand of a foreground request (i.e., accounting for the background work to complete and the storage system to get ready - positioning - to serve the next request). We consider such a delay to be "tolerable". This means that controlling foreground delay due to background work is effectively done by delaying *only* the start of a background busy period.

Deploying any "wait period" before background tasks start execution [5, 15] would result in non-work-conserving scheduling of the background tasks with low degradation on fore-

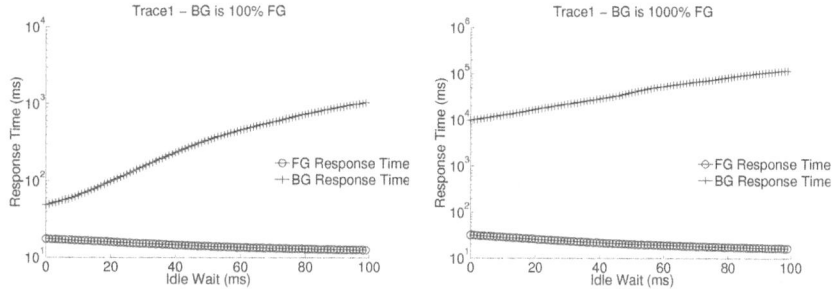

Figure 1: Performance comparison in terms of mean response time between the foreground and background tasks for a disk-level trace under conservative scheduling with fixed waiting ranging from 1ms to 100ms. The results of aggressive scheduling are also shown in the graph, i.e., the point corresponding to idle wait = 0. The response times are in log scale.

ground performance. Such non-work-conserving scheduling we denote as "conservative". A zero "wait period" would result in work-conserving scheduling of the background tasks and better utilization of the available idleness. We denote this policy as "aggressive". To gain intuition on the simultaneous effect on the performance of both foreground and background jobs, we evaluate the aggressive and the conservative scheduling policies via a set of trace-driven simulations. We consider constant idle wait times as in [5] ranging from 0 to 100 ms. Details on the disk drive traces that are used are provided in Section 3. Here we simply want to highlight the advantages and disadvantages of aggressive versus conservative scheduling.

As already discussed, background tasks in a system are commonly a function of the current workload (e.g., data synchronization). Therefore, it is reasonable to assume that multiple asynchronous features generate background work out of the incoming user workload. We explore here two scenarios where the background work (BG) is 100% and 1000% of the foreground work (FG). Results are shown in Figure 1. From the graphs, we can see that aggressive scheduling gives the worst foreground performance while achieving the best background performance. With conservative scheduling, the foreground performance improves as the fixed idle wait (see x-axis) increases, which confirms the need to protect foreground performance via idle waiting. However, we also observe that background performance decreases much faster when compared with the degradation caused to foreground performance. For large periods of idle waiting, foreground response time improves slightly while the performance of the background tasks degrades by orders of magnitude when compared to shorter or zero idle waiting. Since these two scheduling policies are complementary to each other, we are motivated to design a new scheduling algorithm to improve the response time of background work while preserving foreground performance.

Recall that performance degradation of foreground work comes from the fact that the system needs some time to switch from serving background work before it can serve foreground requests. The *entire set* of foreground requests in the following busy period is delayed. Our key observation here is that the impact of background tasks on foreground performance is larger if the delayed foreground busy periods are long (i.e., measured in number of requests) than if they are short.

We stress that in prior work, all efforts focused on incor-

porating characteristics of the arrival process, service process, or idleness of the system into the scheduling of background tasks. In this paper, we design an intelligent scheduling mechanism by exploring and taking advantage of the stochastic characteristics of busy periods *only*.

3. WORKLOAD CHARACTERIZATION

In this section, we analyze the enterprise disk-level traces used in the evaluation of the scheduling policy that is devised in this paper. We give general information about the traces but also focus on the stochastic characteristics of their busy periods.

3.1 Overview of Traces

We use three enterprise traces measured at the disk level from servers running enterprise-grade applications [18]. Although the storage subsystem of the servers consists of multiple RAID groups, we use here the user traffic seen by three individual disks located in different RAID groups. The traces are twelve hours long. Each trace contains the following information for each request: the arrival time, the departure time, the type of request (i.e., read or write), the request length in bytes, and its location on the disk.

In Table 1 we show a set of metrics that provide some general information on the availability of idle time at the disk level and the characteristics of foreground busy periods. The data in Table 1 shows that the disks are clearly underutilized and they have good potential to serve background work. The large coefficient of variation (C.V.), which is a normalized measure of the dispersion defined as the ratio of the standard deviation to the mean, and the large maximum length of idle intervals imply significant variability in the length of idle periods. This concurs with the discussion in the previous section: if the purpose is to serve background work timely, then limiting the time where background work can be served is not a good strategy. For busy period lengths, the moderate C.V. values coupled with the large value of the maximum length, suggest that there is also variability in the length of busy periods, albeit at a less degree than in idle periods. The impact on foreground performance due to interleaving foreground with background work may be quite different from one busy period to the next.

3.2 Characteristics of Busy Periods

Because the impact of the background tasks is strongly related to the length of the upcoming foreground busy period,

Trace	Util	Idle Periods in *ms*			Busy Periods in *IOs*		
	(%)	Mean	Maximum	C.V.	Mean	Maximum	C.V.
Trace1	5.6	192.6	325589	8.4	2.16	240	2.1
Trace2	1.7	767.5	186817	2.3	2.84	110	1.3
Trace3	0.7	2000.2	364876	3.8	2.39	190	2.4

Table 1: General busy period and idle period characteristics of our traces.

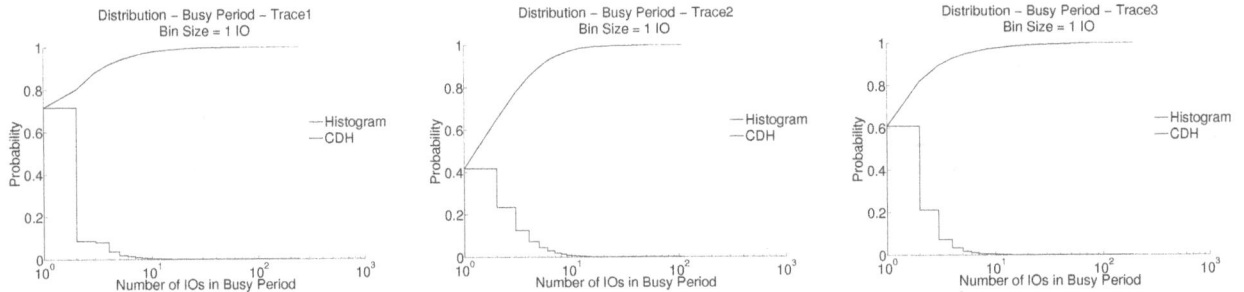

Figure 2: The distribution of the busy periods measured by number of requests.

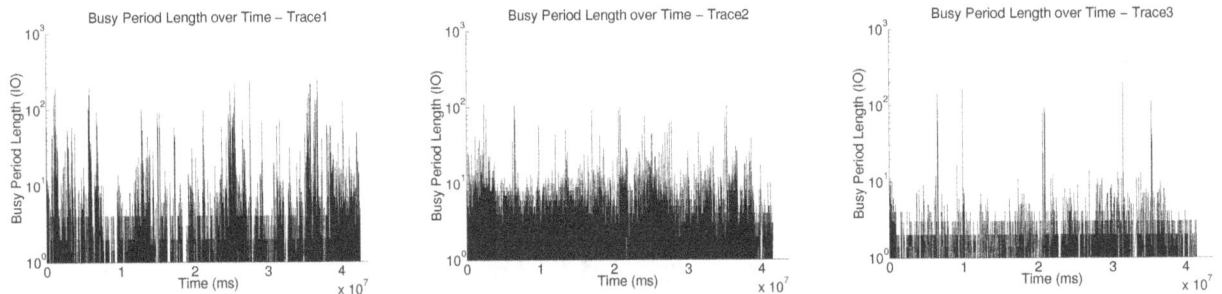

Figure 3: The across time plots of busy periods length measured by number of requests.

we now focus on the statistical features of foreground busy periods. In Figure 2 we plot the CDH (Cumulative Distribution Histogram) and relative frequencies using a bin size of one request. Note the log scale for the x-axis. The shape of the plots implies long tails for busy periods across all workloads, i.e., most of the busy periods are short while a few of them are quite long. One can see that across all workloads, 90% of busy periods are less or equal to 4 requests per busy period. This implies that if the background work delays a busy period, then it is with high probability that there are up to four requests to be delayed. Yet, there is also a sizable percentage of the workload with long busy periods (i.e., more than 4 requests) where the performance degradation of foreground work is going to be noticeable. The argument here is that *if* we can anticipate when these long busy periods arrive, then the performance can be improved significantly by avoiding to serve background jobs during those time intervals.

Next, we plot the length of every busy period across time, measured in number of requests, see Figure 3. The plots show a clear repetitive cluster behavior in the sequence of long busy periods (i.e., greater than 4 requests) for Trace1 and Trace2. The graphs show that the majority of busy periods are 4 to 6 requests. We conclude that this number can be used as a threshold that distinguishes busy periods as short or long.

In addition, the "clustering" of long busy periods shown in

Figure 3 suggests that there is a consistent behavior across time. If we understand better how such clustering occurs, then we can use it to detect the upcoming clusters of busy periods. Once such a cluster is detected, then it would be beneficial to foreground performance if the background work is scheduled "conservatively" (i.e., the system idle waits before starting the background tasks). Once the system predicts that the upcoming busy periods are not expected to be long, then it resumes a more "aggressive" scheduling of background tasks (i.e., schedule them immediately after the system becomes idle of foreground requests). These observations are the basic premises for the design of a scheduling policy that dynamically adapts to a changing workload.

4. DYNAMIC SCHEDULING POLICY

In this section, we propose a dynamic scheduling policy that interleaves background tasks with foreground tasks efficiently. The goal here is to improve the performance of background work, measured via its response time, while preserving foreground performance, also measured via its response time. The dynamic policy that we propose alternates between scheduling background tasks aggressively or conservatively, based on the statistical characteristics of foreground busy periods and their recent history. As future busy periods are not known a priori, the algorithm cannot always make the best decision, but it can reach to a well-informed decision based on statistics of recent workload history. The policy parameters are extracted from the most recent history of foreground busy periods.

```
1. if in characterization state do
   a. update busy period length trace
   b. calculate the Threshold of long busy period based on
      90th percentile
   c. calculate the Cluster Window Size (CWS) based on
      Eqs. 1
2. if system in decision making state do
   a. initialize:
      i.   system state (sys_state) = idle
      ii.  busy period state (BP_state) = short
      iii. cluster count (cluster_count) = 0
      iv.  busy period length (BP_length) = 0
      v.   queue length (QL) = 0
   b. if sys_state = idle
      i. if BP_state = long and cluster_count > 0
         for no FG IO arrive do
            use aggressive scheduling to schedule BG work
            cluster_count − −
      ii. else
         for no FG IO arrive do
            use conservative scheduling to schedule BG work
   c. upon FG IO arrive
      i.   sys_state = busy;
      ii.  QL ++
      iii. BP_length ++
      iv.  if BP_length >= Threshold and (BP_state) = short
           BP_state = long
           cluster_count = CWS
      v.   go to Step 2.b
   d. upon FG IO depart
      i.   QL ++
      ii.  if QL == 0
           sys_state = idle
           BP_length = 0
      iii. go to Step 2.b
```

Figure 4: Algorithm of dynamic scheduling.

Aggressive scheduling may result in foreground performance degradation, because if short idle periods are utilized for background work, then with high probability, it delays all requests in the upcoming foreground busy period. The idle wait ensures that only long idle periods are used for background work. For a thorough discussion on the impact of idle wait on the performance of both foreground and background work, we direct the reader to [5, 15]. If there is a large amount of background work that is time critical, then the background tasks would have to continue to run as long as the system is idle, endangering the performance of upcoming foreground tasks. We argue that rather than limiting the amount of background work during idle periods as in [15], we limit the potential degradation on foreground performance:

- by selecting a fixed large idle wait for the periods when the system is experiencing a sequence of long foreground busy periods, with the expectation that such idle waiting would forbear the system from serving background work, and

- by canceling idle waiting if it is detected that the system is experiencing short foreground busy periods. This action would give the system the opportunity to serve a large amount of background work while delaying only a small portion of the foreground requests.

The algorithm first categorizes busy periods as long or short. Within a predefined time window, we log the information of busy period lengths and update their histogram, a process that is inexpensive, both computationally and space-wise. At the end of the time window, the count of requests that corresponds to the 90th percentile of the busy period histogram defines a *Threshold* whose value distinguishes busy periods as long or short. A new histogram is build for the next time window, which allows the algorithm to adapt well the *Threshold* parameter to changing workloads.

After categorizing the busy periods, the next step is to predict the incoming busy period length. To this end and according to the analysis in Section 3, we explore the clustered pattern of busy periods within each time window. This suggests that after an elapsed long busy period and based on recent history, we may be able to predict with accuracy whether the upcoming busy periods are long or short. To achieve this, we observe the conditional probability that two subsequent busy periods are long, i.e., if they are separated by one idle period with lag equal to one, as well as the conditional probabilities of busy periods that are separated by two or more idle periods, i.e., with lags equal to two or more. We define the *Cluster Window Size* (*CWS*) as the average number of consecutive long busy periods occurring with a given high probability value. Let P_{lag} be the conditional probability that the *lag*th busy period is long given that the current busy period is long (we could use any sufficiently large number here instead of twenty so that we capture enough probability mass). We define *CWS* as the smallest *lag* such that the sum of P_{lag} is equal or over 0.8:

$$CWS = min\{lag| \sum_{lag=1}^{20} P_{lag} >= 0.8\} \qquad (1)$$

After a long busy period is detected, then *CWS* gives the number of upcoming busy periods that are expected to be long. During the intermittent idle intervals within those periods (which may be long or short), background work is served conservatively, i.e., deploying an idle wait period. After this number expires, background tasks are served aggressively, i.e., without any idle waiting, till the next long busy period is detected and conservative scheduling gets activated again. Note that the calculation of *CWS* is done once for every time window, in order to reflect well changes in the process of the foreground busy periods.

Note that, according to Equation (1), the stronger the clustering in the foreground busy period lengths, the shorter the *CWS*, and the longer the system serves background tasks aggressively. If the long foreground busy periods in the system are distributed randomly, i.e., there is no clustering, then *CWS* is long and the system schedules background tasks conservatively. Hence, the dynamic scheduling policy we propose here extracts the stochastic characteristics of foreground busy period lengths and reduces to the common practice of conservatively scheduling depending on the predicted foreground arrivals. Figure 4 gives the pseudo-code of the dynamic background scheduling policy.

In Figure 5 we give an example of how the aggressive, conservative, and dynamic algorithms work. We assume that there are several background tasks outstanding and the system currently operates under short foreground busy periods (the first three user busy periods marked with "S" in the fig-

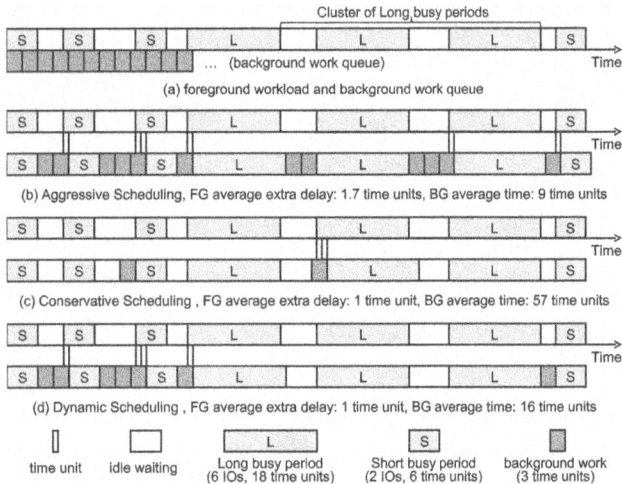

Figure 5: Example on the behavior of the three different background scheduling algorithm, aggressive, conservative, and dynamic.

ure) that are then followed by long user busy periods. After detecting the first long busy period (the fourth busy period), the next busy period (the fifth busy period) is marked as part of the next cluster of long busy periods. We assume that the estimations from previous observations have converged on a cluster size of 2 (i.e., the value of CWS) and that the threshold to differentiate busy period lengths is 4 requests. We assume in the example that the short busy periods are 2 requests long and that the long busy periods are 6 requests long. We assume that each user request is 3 time units, with one time unit being 2 ms. The six idle intervals in the depicted scenario are 5, 8, 4, 7, 8 and 3 time units long, respectively.

Based on the discussion in this section:

- Idle waiting for the dynamic scheduling is larger than the value selected by common practices for the conservative scheduling (i.e., two times of user service demands). In the example we assume that idle wait for dynamic scheduling is 1.5 times longer than the idle time for conservative scheduling.

- Aggressive scheduling does not idle wait and serves the background tasks the fastest (i.e., uses 9 time units on the average) with the largest extra delay (e.g., 1.7 time units) per user request.

- Conservative scheduling serves the background work the slowest (i.e., 57 time units on the average) with an average extra delay per user request of 1 time unit.

- Dynamic scheduling works best because it strikes a good balance between the performance of background tasks (i.e., 16 time units on the average) and an average added delay per user request of 1 time unit only.

This high-level example shows that dynamic scheduling is expected to behave like conservative scheduling with regard to foreground performance, and like aggressive scheduling with regard to background work performance. In the following section we evaluate these scheduling polices in detail.

5. EXPERIMENTAL EVALUATION

In this section, we evaluate the dynamic algorithm illustrated in Figure 4. The goal is to demonstrate that our algorithm can (1) effectively use the learned foreground busy period characteristics to schedule background tasks and (2) swiftly adapt its background scheduling to changing foreground traffic patterns such that both foreground and background tasks sustain the best possible performance. We evaluate two scenarios. In the first scenario, the system operates under a "stable" workload, while in the second one, the system operates under a workload that changes swiftly half-way through the experiment.

5.1 Experimental Setting

Our experimental evaluation is trace driven. The traces described in Section 3, are used as our foreground traffic. We use Trace1, Trace2, and Trace3 as representative of a stable operating environment. The scenario with the "swiftly changing" workload is achieved by concatenating Trace2 and Trace1, in this order.

As discussed in previous sections, our framework can be applied for scheduling of asynchronous tasks that when new data arrives into a geographically distributed storage system and need to be replicated across nodes for redundancy. In such systems, the redundancy is in the form of replication (e.g., the Google File System [6] replicates data 3 times) or erasure coding (e.g., the data is split into N fragments, encoded into N+M fragments, and distributed into N+M different disks/nodes) [17]. The asynchronous tasks in such scenarios consist of reading the recently updated data, computing the codes for the case of erasure coding, and sending them to their destination via the network. Consistent with this behavior, in our evaluation the background tasks have similar demands as the foreground ones and their intensity is a function of the WRITE foreground traffic, which varies by system. The results hold across a wide range of amount of background work but here we show only two representative cases: (1) the background work is equal to the amount of foreground work (i.e., common scenario, 100% of foreground work) and (2) the background work is 10 times the amount of foreground work (i.e., an extreme scenario, 1000% of foreground work).

Switching from serving background tasks to serving user requests is not instantaneous. Upon arrival of a new user IO which finds the system serving a background task, the system must first complete the background work before repositioning the disk head back to the location of the new request. In our evaluation, we assume that the penalty experienced by foreground requests due to background tasks is about two times the average service time of foreground requests. Note that because both foreground and background tasks have service and response times at the millisecond (ms) level, all our metrics of interest are measured in ms. Although replicating a large file or set of files may take overall more time, they are considered tasks that are generally split into multiple smaller tasks. Serving the smaller tasks faster is the goal of our framework.

Our dynamic algorithm uses short-term history (i.e., observations during a time window to calculate the *Threshold* and *CWS*. During each time window, we build the histogram of busy periods and based on this histogram we calculate the *Threshold* and *CWS* parameters, which are used to schedule the background tasks during the next time win-

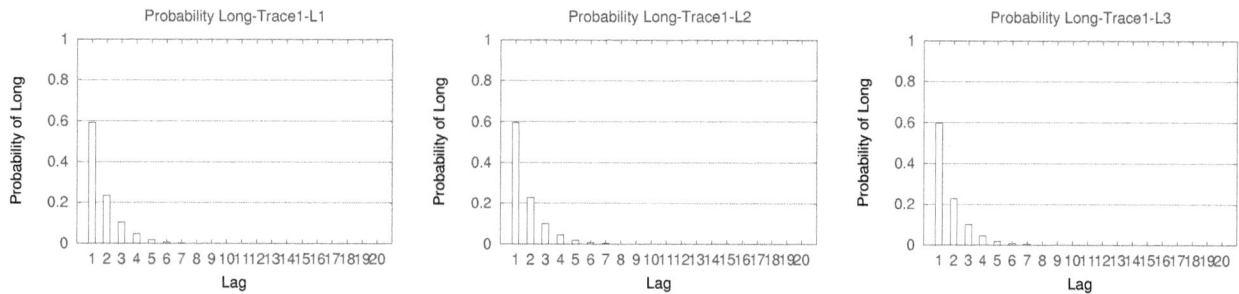

Figure 6: Probability plots that a long busy period is followed by a similar long one for lag 1 to lag 20 for different portions of Trace1. Three windows are considered: $Start = 0.5$ *hour* (left graph), $Start = 1$ *hour* (center graph), and $Start = 1.5 hour$ (right graph).

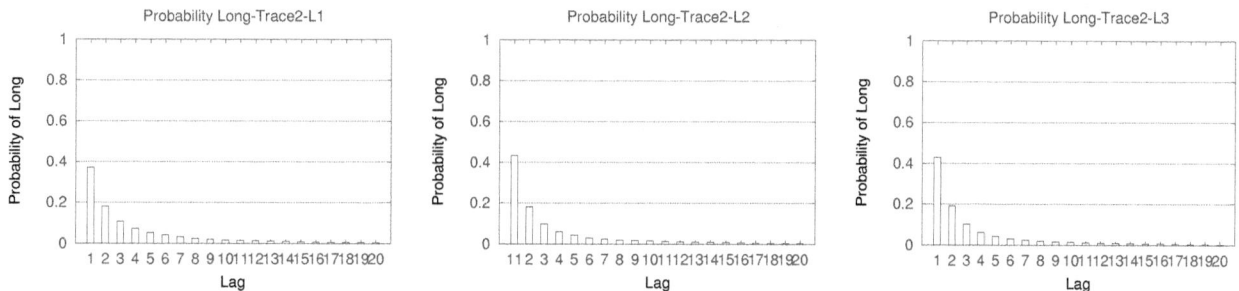

Figure 7: Probability plots that a long busy period is followed by a similar long one for lag 1 to lag 20 for different portions of Trace2. Three windows are considered: $Start = 0.5$ *hour* (left graph), $Start = 1$ *hour* (center graph), and $Start = 1.5$ *hour* (right graph).

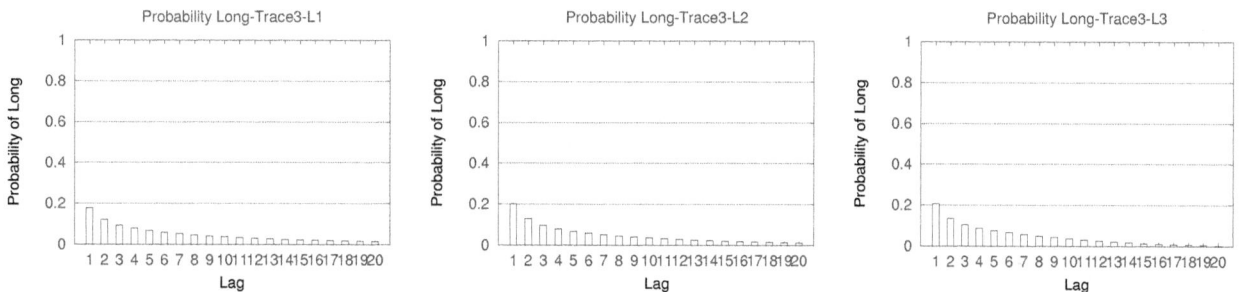

Figure 8: Probability plots that a long busy period is followed by a similar long one for lag 1 to lag 20 for different portions of Trace3. Three windows are considered: $Start = 0.5$ *hour* (left graph), $Start = 1$ *hour* (center graph), and $Start = 1.5$ *hour* (right graph).

dow. The moment the *Threshold* and *CWS* parameters are computed, the histogram is discarded. During the next window where background scheduling is enabled, we collect data to construct a new histogram which is then used to calculate the *Threshold* and *CWS* parameters for the next scheduling window. Note that for Trace1, Trace2, and Trace3, we specifically focus on a 5-hour window, i.e., we collect the histogram during a window defined by $[Start, Start + 5)$ and apply the policy during $[Start + 5, Start + 10)$. To show the robustness of the policy irrespective of the *Start* value, we show results for three different sequences of 10-hour periods.

In our experiments, the amount of idle wait before starting the asynchronous tasks determines the aggressiveness of background scheduling. As idle wait increases, the impact on the response time of foreground requests decreases and the response time of background tasks increases. Here, we evaluate the entire range of idle wait values from 0 to 100 ms. Zero idle wait corresponds to the most aggressive background scheduling.

5.2 Evaluation Scenario One: Stable Workload

We drive our simulation using the three traces described in Table 1. Each trace has characteristics that change gradually over the course of its 12 hours span. Since changes are not dramatic, we consider such traces to represent stable operating environments, where our framework is expected to capture gradual changes effectively.

During the first time window, our scheduling framework

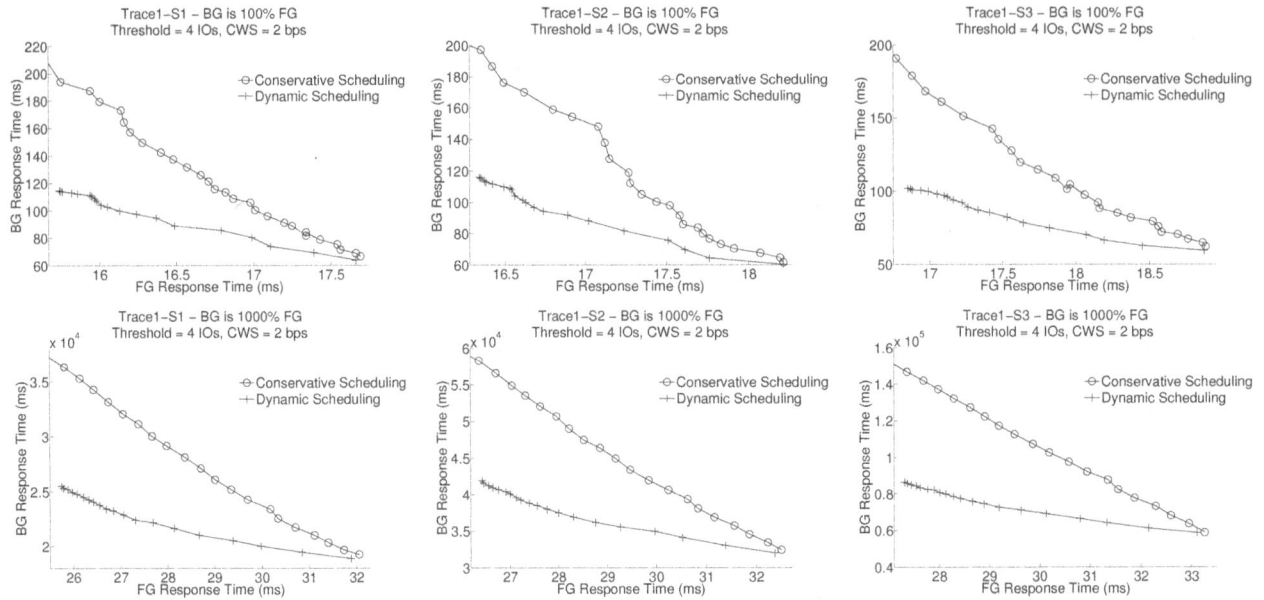

Figure 10: Scheduling comparison between dynamic and conservative scheduling for Trace1, scheduling results use the three respective periods given in Figure 6 (left, center, right columns) to schedule in the next 5 hours.

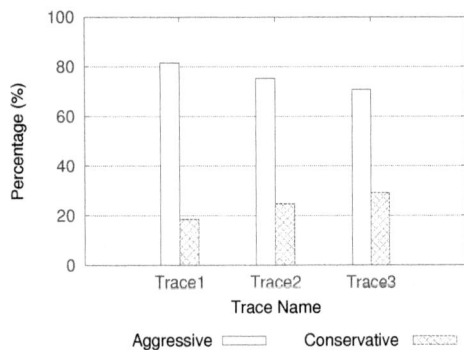

Figure 9: The percentage of time in aggressive mode and conservative mode under dynamic scheduling.

monitors the system busy periods, builds their histogram, and once the time window elapses, computes the *Threshold* and *CWS* values. Recall that *Threshold* corresponds to the value of the 90th percentile of busy periods, while the *CWS* is computed based on the values of the conditional probability P_{lag} that two busy periods separated by *lag* idle intervals are both long. As different histograms are collected over different windows, the changes in the workload are captured by *Threshold* and *CWS*. Figures 6, 7, and 8 show the values of the conditional probabilities of long busy periods over three different 5-hour windows.

The dynamic algorithm strives to exploit any relationship that exists in the sequence of foreground busy periods. If the clustering across time is weak, as in Trace3 (see Figure 8), then the expectation is for the dynamic algorithm to operate more often in the conservative mode (i.e., applying some idle wait). If the clustering is non-existent, then the proposed algorithm should *always* operate in the conservative mode.

Figures 6, 7, and 8 clearly show a stable behavior across

time within each trace. Across traces, we notice that Trace1 has long busy periods clustered together because its conditional probability values are highest among the three traces. Clustering reduces for Trace2, while Trace3 depicts the least clustering. This means that the dependence structure weakens from Trace1 to Trace3. Therefore the computed *CWS* values increase as the dependence of long busy periods reduces from Trace1 to Trace3.

Figure 9 shows how long (in percentage of time) the dynamic algorithm operates in the conservative mode and how long in the aggressive mode. As expected from the discussion on the results in Figures 6, 7, and 8, Trace1 spends the most time in the aggressive mode because the long busy periods in this trace are well clustered, allowing the algorithm to predict well their occurrence.

Because of the overhead to switch from a background task to a foreground task, the more background work served, the higher the impact on foreground performance. The goal is to serve faster the outstanding background work, while sustaining foreground performance. Here we evaluate the effectiveness and robustness of the proposed dynamic scheduling by comparing the background mean response time for the *same* foreground mean response time under both the dynamic and conservative scheduling policies.

Figures 10, 11, and 12 show the average performance of background work for Trace1, Trace2 and Trace3, respectively, as a function of the achieved foreground response time. The figures are organized in a 2 by 3 grid, where each column corresponds to the performance achieved in a given window (the same ones depicted in Figures 6 through 8), and each row corresponds to the amount of background work generated in the system (i.e., 100% and 1000% of foreground work).

Recall that foreground response time is generally increased by the execution of asynchronous tasks because they arrive stochastically and the switch between asynchronous and

152

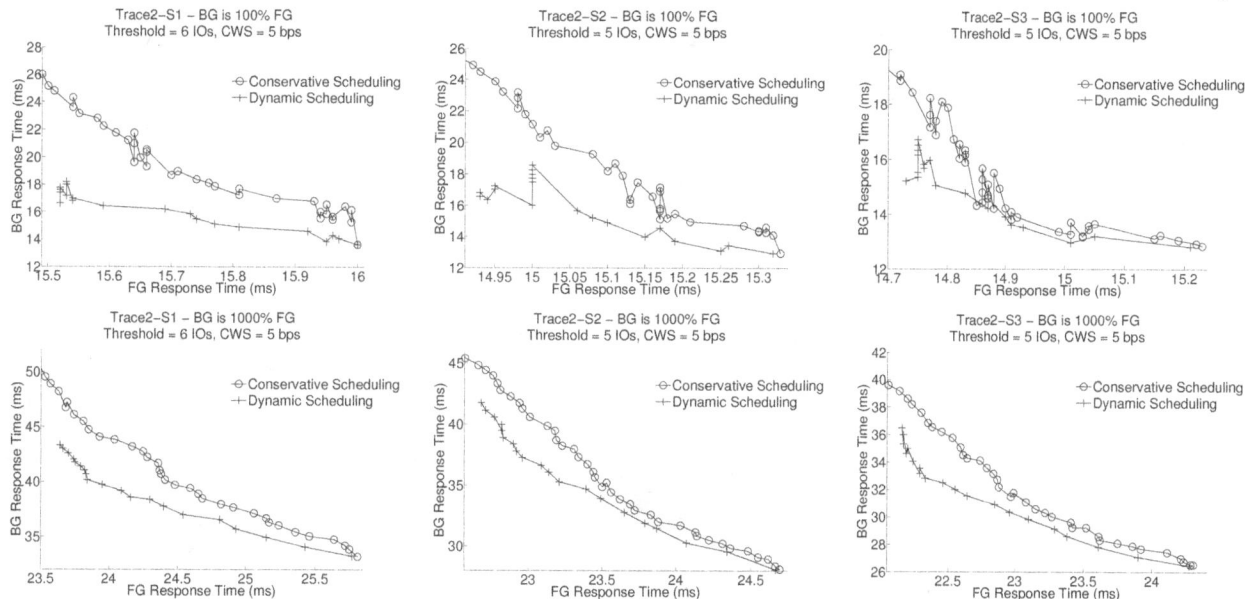

Figure 11: Scheduling comparison between dynamic and conservative scheduling for Trace2, scheduling results use the three respective periods given in Figure 7 (left, center, right columns) to schedule in the next 5 hours.

foreground tasks is not instantaneous. This means that as long as the idle wait value is smaller than the maximum idle interval length, there may be degradation in foreground performance. Idle wait is a way to control and limit performance degradation but not avoid it [16]. Our goal is to make sure we do not violate any foreground performance targets in the system. As expected, the foreground response time increases as the value of the idle wait decreases. For an idle wait of zero (i.e., corresponding to the aggressive scheduling policy), there is almost no distinction between the foreground and background work, because the background work starts executing as soon as the system becomes idle. Our scheduling always converges to this case in all plots (see the rightmost points in Figures 10, 11, and 12). Across all graphs, the more the background work (see the differences between the rows of plots), the higher the foreground degradation and background response time. Results can be summarized as follows:

- **Trace1:** Figure 10 clearly indicates that there are consistent gains across all time periods and for all amounts of background work. The dynamic scheduling can often speed up background work by as much as 50 percent.

- **Trace2:** Figure 11 shows that the gains of dynamic scheduling reduce when compared with the results of Trace1 because the probabilities of a long busy period being followed by another long busy period within a certain lag reduce (compare Figure 6 with Figure 7). However, dynamic scheduling consistently outperforms conservative scheduling, particularly for large idle waits that are captured by the leftmost part of the plots.

- **Trace3:** Figure 12 shows that Trace3 behaves similarly to Trace2. Note that the dynamic scheduling is more robust than the conservative one, which causes

fluctuation on performance of background work. This is a result of variability in both idle and busy periods.

One of the most important observations is that for longer idle wait times (left portion of each plot) where foreground performance is degraded less, the dynamic scheduling consistently outperforms the conservative one. As a result, in cases when there are stringent performance targets for foreground requests, the performance advantage of dynamic scheduling is clear. If the foreground work is less sensitive to delays, then conservative scheduling with short idle waits results to a simple and good solution. In general, aggressive scheduling is not a good practical choice because it may cause severe or unbounded delays to foreground performance.

Another characteristic of the dynamic scheduling policy that sets it apart from the conservative one, is its resilience with regard to changes in the workload and scheduling parameters. In all evaluated scenarios in Figures 10, 11, and 12 the results from the dynamic scheduling are gradually reflecting the change, i.e., there are no oscillations on performance as it is often the case for the conservative scheduling. This is a direct outcome of the fact that our dynamic scheduling adapts its parameters to the changes in workload characteristics while the conservative or aggressive policies are oblivious to the workload characteristics. Such gradual changing behavior as characteristics change is desirable in systems because it allows applications to run smoothly.

Of particular importance is the sensitivity of the scheduling policies toward the chosen idle wait value. Figures 10, 11, and 12 show that the performance of both foreground and background work under the proposed dynamic scheduling policy varies but in a significantly narrower range than under the conservative scheduling policy. This implies that for the dynamic scheduling policy, identifying the optimal idle wait value is not critical. Applying the common practices that suggest to select an idle wait as a function of foreground service demands would yield satisfactory results.

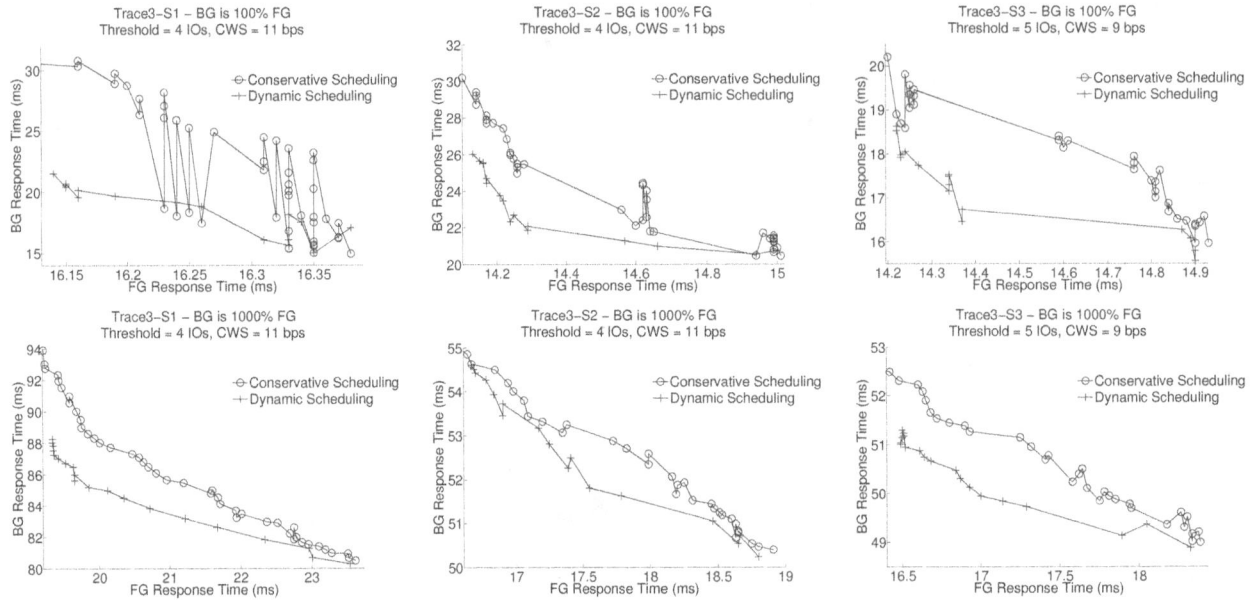

Figure 12: Scheduling comparison between dynamic and conservative scheduling for Trace3, scheduling results use the three respective periods given in Figure 8 (left, center, right columns) to schedule in the next 5 hours.

Overall, we conclude that the dynamic scheduling policy is robust and consistently achieves fast service of asynchronous tasks while sustaining foreground performance.

5.3 Evaluation Scenario Two: Swiftly Changing Workload

We concatenate Trace2 and Trace1 to obtain a new trace which we name Trace4. Trace4 is used to evaluate the adaptivity of the proposed scheduling policy as the workload changes swiftly. The new trace has a 24-hour span. Because Trace2 and Trace1 have different characteristics (e.g., Threshold and CWS), we expect a significant change around the 12th hour in the characteristics of Trace4. In order to capture the behavior of the dynamic scheduling policy, we chose to show here the following three learning windows from the 24-hour duration of Trace4.

- Period 1: learning window from the beginning up to the 8th hour; scheduling decisions apply from the start of the 9th hour through the 16th hour (i.e., learning happens before the workload change and applies during the workload change).

- Period 2: learning window from the 6th hour to the 14th hour; scheduling decisions apply from the start of the 15th hour through the 22nd hour (i.e., learning includes only a small portion of changed workload and applies over the period after the workload change).

- Period 3: learning window from the 8th hour to the 16th hour; scheduling decisions apply from the start of the 17th hour through the 24th hour (i.e., learning has equal portion before and after the workload change and applies over the period after the workload change).

Figure 13 shows the conditional probabilities for the three time windows and reflects the workload changes. We note

also that Threshold changes gradually from 6 in the leftmost plot to 4 in the rightmost plot as the observed amount of Trace1 increases.

We present the scheduling results in Figure 14. We observe that the dynamic scheduling policy is robust and consistently performs well, even during the workload transition periods. Performance improves as the learning window includes more of Trace1 (e.g., note the differences in the foreground and the background performance in the center and rightmost columns). Overall, we conclude that the learning process incorporated in the dynamic scheduling algorithm, enables the scheduling policy to adapt well even to swift changes in workload characteristics.

6. CONCLUSIONS

In this paper, we propose a dynamic framework for scheduling background tasks, often associated with eventual consistency in geographically distributed storage systems. The framework ensures that the performance of foreground traffic is sustained while data consistency is achieved as fast as possible. We define a metric that measures the likelihood that busy periods of similar length arrive in a clustered way. This metric allows us to identify patterns in the length of busy periods and their probabilistic arrival. The reasoning behind the proposed scheduling framework is that if there is a cluster of short busy periods, then the system schedules aggressively the background work without much impact on foreground performance. If the cluster of long busy periods is detected, then scheduling of background tasks is done conservatively during the anticipated duration of long busy periods, i.e., only long idle intervals are used for serving background work. Extensive trace-driven experimentation shows that the framework is effective and robust. It achieves better response time for the background work without degrading performance of foreground traffic.

In the future, we plan to extend the work presented here

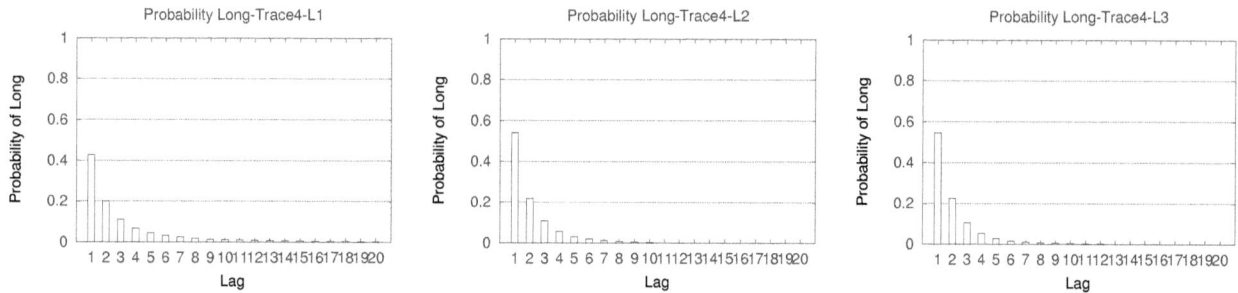

Figure 13: Probability plots that a long busy period is followed by a similar long one for lag 1 to lag 20 for different portions of Trace4. Three windows are considered: $Start = 0$, i.e., starting at the beginning of the trace (left graph), $Start = 6$ hour (center graph), and $Start = 8$ hour (right graph).

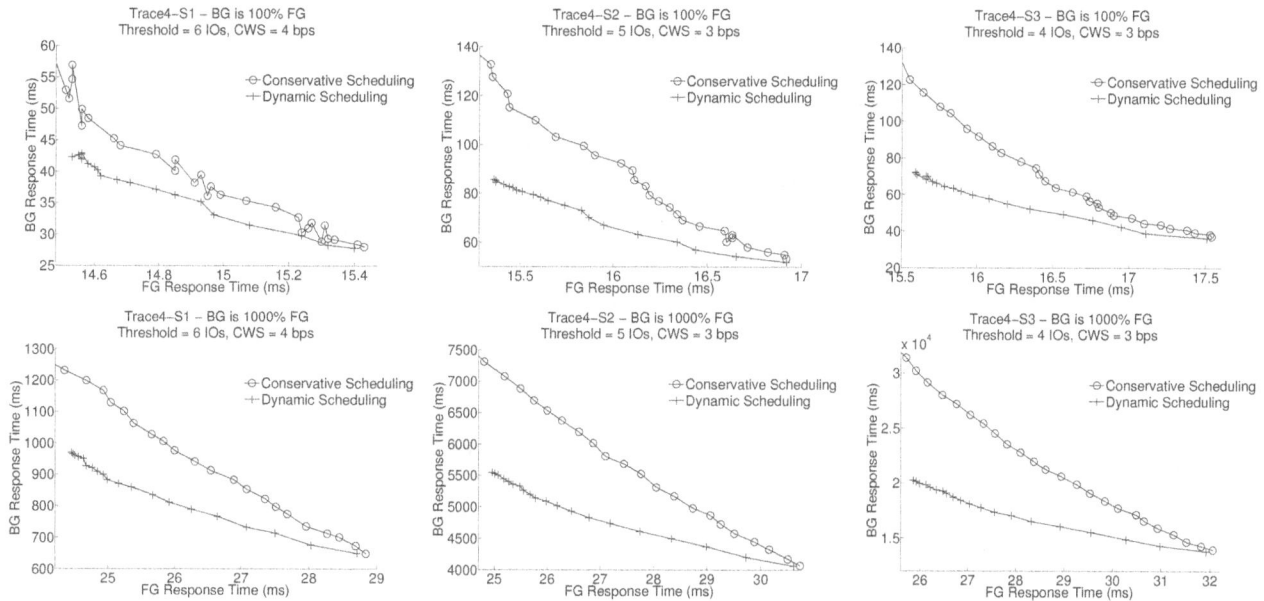

Figure 14: Scheduling comparison between dynamic and conservative scheduling for Trace4, scheduling results use the three respective windows given in Figure 13 (left, center, right columns) to schedule in the next 8 hours.

to learn and detect the length of the cluster of both busy and idle periods, aiming for the best outcome on scheduling time sensitive background work. We are also planning to use this framework to schedule work with different but close priorities, where foreground work can be delayed more than background work, at least for some periods of time.

7. ACKNOWLEDGMENTS

This work is supported by NSF grants CCF-0811417 and CCF-0937925. The authors thank Seagate Technology for providing the enterprise traces used for this work. We thank our shepherd J. Nelson Amaral for his assistance in improving the presentation of this paper.

8. REFERENCES

[1] E. Bachmat and J. Schindler. Analysis of methods for scheduling low priority disk drive tasks. In *SIGMETRICS*, pages 55–65, 2002.

[2] L. N. Bairavasundaram, G. R. Goodson, S. Pasupathy, and J. Schindler. An analysis of latent sector errors in disk drives. In *SIGMETRICS*, pages 289–300, 2007.

[3] J. L. Bruno, J. C. Brustoloni, E. Gabber, B. Özden, and A. Silberschatz. Disk scheduling with quality of service guarantees. In *ICMCS, Vol. 2*, pages 400–405, 1999.

[4] F. Douglis and P. Krishnan. Adaptive disk spin-down policies for mobile computers. *Computing Systems*, 8(4):381–413, 1995.

[5] L. Eggert and J. D. Touch. Idletime scheduling with preemption intervals. In *SOSP*, pages 249–262, 2005.

[6] S. Ghemawat, H. Gobioff, and S.-T. Leung. The google file system. In *SOSP*, pages 29–43, 2003.

[7] R. A. Golding, P. B. II, C. Staelin, T. Sullivan, and J. Wilkes. Idleness is not sloth. In *USENIX Winter*, pages 201–212, 1995.

[8] J. Guerra, H. Pucha, J. S. Glider, W. Belluomini, and

R. Rangaswami. Cost effective storage using extent based dynamic tiering. In *FAST*, pages 273–286, 2011.

[9] A. Gulati, A. Merchant, and P. J. Varman. pclock: an arrival curve based approach for qos guarantees in shared storage systems. In *SIGMETRICS*, pages 13–24, 2007.

[10] D. P. Helmbold, D. D. E. Long, T. L. Sconyers, and B. Sherrod. Adaptive disk spin-down for mobile computers. *MONET*, 5(4):285–297, 2000.

[11] H. Huang, W. Hung, and K. G. Shin. Fs2: dynamic data replication in free disk space for improving disk performance and energy consumption. In *SOSP*, pages 263–276, 2005.

[12] I. Iliadis, R. Haas, X.-Y. Hu, and E. Eleftheriou. Disk scrubbing versus intra-disk redundancy for high-reliability raid storage systems. In *SIGMETRICS*, pages 241–252, 2008.

[13] C. R. Lumb, A. Merchant, and G. A. Alvarez. Façade: Virtual storage devices with performance guarantees. In *FAST*, pages 131–144, 2003.

[14] M. K. McKusick and G. R. Ganger. Soft updates: A technique for eliminating most synchronous writes in the fast filesystem. In *USENIX Annual Technical Conference, FREENIX Track*, pages 1–17, 1999.

[15] N. Mi, A. Riska, X. Li, E. Smirni, and E. Riedel. Restrained utilization of idleness for transparent scheduling of background tasks. In *SIGMETRICS/Performance*, pages 205–216, 2009.

[16] N. Mi, A. Riska, Q. Zhang, E. Smirni, and E. Riedel. Efficient management of idleness in storage systems. *TOS*, 5(2), 2009.

[17] J. S. Plank, J. Luo, C. D. Schuman, L. Xu, and Z. Wilcox-O'Hearn. A performance evaluation and examination of open-source erasure coding libraries for storage. In *FAST*, pages 253–265, 2009.

[18] A. Riska and E. Riedel. Disk drive level workload characterization. In *USENIX Annual Technical Conference, General Track*, pages 97–102, 2006.

[19] M. I. Seltzer, G. R. Ganger, M. K. McKusick, K. A. Smith, C. A. N. Soules, and C. A. Stein. Journaling versus soft updates: Asynchronous meta-data protection in file systems. In *USENIX Annual Technical Conference, General Track*, pages 71–84, 2000.

[20] M. Sivathanu, V. Prabhakaran, A. C. Arpaci-Dusseau, and R. H. Arpaci-Dusseau. Improving storage system availability with d-graid. *TOS*, 1(2):133–170, 2005.

[21] E. Thereska, J. Schindler, J. S. Bucy, B. Salmon, C. R. Lumb, and G. R. Ganger. A framework for building unobtrusive disk maintenance applications. In *FAST*, pages 213–226, 2004.

[22] W. Vogels. Eventually consistent. *ACM Queue*, 6(6):14–19, 2008.

[23] M. Wachs and G. R. Ganger. Co-scheduling of disk head time in cluster-based storage. In *SRDS*, pages 278–287, 2009.

[24] F. Yan, X. Mountrouidou, A. Riska, and E. Smirni. Copy rate synchronization with performance guarantees for work consolidation in storage clusters. In *GreenMetrics 2011 Workshop*, San Jose, CA, USA, 2011.

Towards Efficient Supercomputing:
Searching for the Right Efficiency Metric

Chung-Hsing Hsu, Jeffery A. Kuehn, and Stephen W. Poole
Computer Science and Mathematics Division
Oak Ridge National Laboratory
Oak Ridge, Tennessee, USA
{hsuc,kuehn,spoole}@ornl.gov

ABSTRACT

Efficiency in supercomputing has traditionally focused on execution time. In early 2000's, the concept of total cost of ownership was re-introduced, with the introduction of efficiency measure to include aspects such as energy and space. Yet the supercomputing community has never agreed upon a metric that can cover these aspects completely and also provide a fair basis for comparison. This paper examines the metrics that have been proposed in the past decade, and proposes a vector-valued metric for efficient supercomputing. Using this metric, the paper presents a study of where the supercomputing industry has been and where it stands today with respect to efficient supercomputing.

Categories and Subject Descriptors

C.4 [**Computer Systems Organization**]: Performance of Systems—*measurement techniques, performance attributes*; D.2.8 [**Software Engineering**]: Metrics—*performance measures*

General Terms

Design, Measurement, Performance, Standardization

Keywords

Energy efficiency, TOP500, Green500, SPECpower

1. INTRODUCTION

Efficiency in supercomputing has traditionally focused on definitions based on execution time and is often conflated with performance. It is commonly measured in terms of a calculation rate such as floating point operations per second (FLOPS) or instructions per second. In fact, this type of metric is conveniently used to define a supercomputer [36]. For example, the TOP500 project [39] ranks computers by how quickly each can solve the LINPACK benchmark [6]; the first 500 are called "supercomputers". The LINPACK benchmark has a fixed number of algorithmic steps to take for a given problem size, thus the quoted MFLOPS metric is a reference to number of such steps per second.

In early 2000's, the concept of total cost of ownership (TCO) was re-introduced into the supercomputing community, with the introduction of efficiency measure to include aspects such as energy, space, reliability, and availability. All of these had been considered before, but were seemingly of less importance prior to this. There was a concern that we were designing new supercomputers with little consideration for the overall TCO. Many of the current leaders in the current TOP500 list consume multiple megawatts to just run the LINPACK benchmark, costing agencies like U.S. Department of Energy one million U.S. dollars per megawatt per year. As a result, there has been a substantial increase in the interest in pursuing efficient supercomputing.

An immediate question is how to quantify efficiency in supercomputing [16]. One possible metric is the performance-power ratio. For example, the Green500 project [13] re-ranks TOP500 supercomputers by LINPACK performance per watt (or equivalently, algorithmic steps per joule), referred to as FLOPS/W. However, this "miles per gallon" type of metric is criticized as being inappropriate for ranking supercomputers, due to its inability to track machines by size which may or may not reflect the total capability [36].

Today, the supercomputing community is still searching for an appropriate metric that can cover all major aspects of efficiency, while providing a fair basis for comparison [7]. This paper presents our journey in this search, focused on including both time and energy into the metric. We noticed that the struggle is not strictly limited to the supercomputing community. The enterprise server industry, for example, is also searching for a similar metric [8]. As a result, new metrics have been proposed. We observed a trend shared by many new metrics: shifting from a scalar-valued metric to a vector-valued metric, which inspired our work in this paper.

The contribution of this paper is a vector-valued metric for efficient supercomputing. The metric consists of two scalars, one for performance and the other for energy efficiency, in order to reflect the view that energy is as important as performance. Using the metric, the paper presents a study of where the supercomputing industry has been and where it stands today with respect to efficient supercomputing. In fact, the paper is more concerned about the *dimensionality* of the metric space, trying to make a case for vector metric. It is less concerned about the measurement rules for acquiring each scalar value. As we will see later, this decoupling allows us to plug into the real measurement results from various sources to conduct the analysis.

The rest of the paper is organized as follows. We first present an overview of the metrics proposed in the past decade and analyze their trends in Section 2. We then present a vector-valued metric, focusing on performance and energy efficiency in Section 3. We delay the introduction of the new metric until we provide a historical basis and enough groundwork to enable the the reader to judge the improvements offered. Following that, we discuss in details the use of the metric to study the historical trend of computer systems with respect to efficient supercomputing in Section 3.2. As an illustration, we compare the new ranking produce by the metric with the TOP500 list and the Green500 list. Finally, we conclude the paper in Section 4.

2. RELATED WORK

This section presents an overview of the performance and energy metrics proposed from the supercomputing community to the circuit design community. The emphasis will be on the *type* of metric and on the *trend* of shifting from a scalar-valued metric to a vector-valued metric. To start with, we give a general definition of efficiency: efficiency describes the extent to which effort or resource is *well* spent for the intended task. It is a measurable concept, quantitatively determined by the ratio of output to input.

2.1 Performance Benchmarks

Performance measurement of computer systems has been a focus of much standardization effort. Multiple industry consortia formed by competing vendors participate to improve the quality and ease of comparison for a particular audience [5], e.g., the Transaction Processing Performance Council (TPC) and the Standard Performance Evaluation Corporation (SPEC). Each consortium addresses a different audience or type of application. For example, TPC addresses on-line transaction processing and has two active benchmarks that measure the computer system performance in terms of transactions per second (TPS).

For supercomputer vendors, the performance on the LIN-PACK benchmark is currently the de facto standard. The benchmark solves a dense linear algebra problem. However, it is criticized as not being representative enough for typical supercomputer workload. As a result, there emerge efforts to add other supercomputing relevant benchmarks. For example, Graph 500 [11] measures the performance of graph search in edge traversals per second. SPEC MPI2007 [25] composes 13 benchmarks from several application domains. HPCC [15] consists of 7 tests for various system features.

Most standard benchmarks measure performance in terms of services per unit of time, although the definition of service is different. SPEC MPI2007 is an exception. It uses the speedup with respect to a reference machine as the metric for each benchmark. The final rating, a scalar value, is given by the geometric mean of these speedups. Of late there has been a trend towards using suites of benchmarks which report multiple performance values.

2.2 Energy Benchmarks

Standard energy benchmarks are also emerging. TPC, for example, augmented all its performance benchmarks with methods to measure and report energy consumption as joules per transaction (W/TPS). SPEC currently releases three benchmarks of this kind. One of them, SPECpower_ssj2008, measures transactions per joule at eleven different load levels [12]. JouleSort [30] represents an academic effort, which measures the energy required to sort a fixed number of ran-domly permuted records, reporting it as sorted records per joule. Poess et al. has a survey [29] comparing energy benchmarks from major industry consortia.

The proceeding benchmarks are generally service oriented. There are advocates for hardware oriented benchmarks because energy consumption strongly depends on workload [14], system configuration [28] and load level [33]. SWEEP [3] is one such example. It is an academic attempt to evaluate the energy efficiency of a server across the workload space through synthetic workload generation. Molka et al. [23] have a similar effort but for parallel workload generation. SERT [18] developed by SPEC is yet another example, and it targets server-class computer systems.

Most benchmarks measure energy efficiency in terms of services per unit of energy (i.e., the performance-power ratio). In terms of the trend, both performance and energy efficiency are reported, although some benchmarks distinguish between the primary metric and the secondary ones. The drive to hardware oriented benchmark will require multiple energy values to be reported.

For supercomputer vendors, the choices of energy benchmarks are limited. There is the Green500 project [13] that uses the LINPACK benchmark to rank supercomputers by their performance-power ratios starting from November 2007. This power data was also added to the TOP500 list in June 2008. The performance-power ratio is criticized, because it is an intensive metric and thus cannot be used to rank supercomputers by size; however, the ratio is useful for ranking technologies [36].

2.3 Energy Efficiency Metrics

Besides the performance-power ratio (i.e., services per joule), there are other useful types of energy metrics. One metric is the average power (i.e., joules per second). Another metric is the ratio of the energy consumption on the target machine relative to the reference machine [3], similar to the way the performance is defined in SPEC MPI2007.

A third metric is PUE (Power Usage Effectiveness) [37]. PUE measures how much of the total electricity used by a data center goes to the IT equipment, as opposed to being used on cooling systems and the power infrastructure. PUE was developed by an IT industry group, The Green Grid (TGG), in 2007, and is now widely uses. PUE is a percentage metric, with both input and output measured in the same dimension, energy.

PUE can be viewed as a measure for energy proportionality [1]. Energy proportionality is originally a design principle to ensure the energy consumption is proportional to the executed workload. This paper interprets it as the extent to which energy is *well* spent to the services delivered. In this sense, PUE considers energy to be well spent when it is consumed by the IT equipment, not by other equipments or lost during transmission or conversion.

There exist measures to quantify the energy proportionality of a server. For example, Varsamopoulos and Gupta [40] proposed the IPR metric to measure the power range and the LDR metric to measure the linearity. Ryckbosch et al. [31] proposed the EP metric to measure how closely the actual system approaches the ideal case (i.e., the power consumption is linear to the rate of service). SPECpower_ssj2008 includes some notion of energy proportionality, but does not explicitly quantify it [31].

For supercomputers, a task force from TOP500, Green500,

TGG and the EE HPC Working Group [7] have been formed to develop a stronger set of energy efficiency metric(s). PUE is taken as an external constraint and held as an independent variable. The metric of interest is currently workloads per unit of energy where workloads are to leverage well established benchmarks. PUE is considered insufficient because it only compares energy use relative to the support infrastructure. As a result, an energy inefficient system may still have an excellent PUE value if its support infrastructure provides efficient power delivery and cooling. Some argue that an absolute metric, such as the performance-power ratio, should be reported as well [26]. Furthermore, while PUE is meant for tracking datacenter progress over time, it is now mis-used as a comparison tool between different data centers [38].

2.4 Composite Metrics

A composite metric in this case is the end product of trying to combine both performance and energy efficiency into a scalar-valued measure. They generally take the multiplicative form of

$$(\text{performance})^{\alpha} \cdot (\text{energy efficiency})^{\beta}$$

with parameters α and β. It is the choice of the parameter values that make composite metrics seem artificial.

For example, the low-power circuit design community typically uses a single index to guide design tradeoffs and faces a similar challenge to simultaneously optimize performance and power. As a result, researchers have proposed several metrics. Some of the popular metrics are in the form of ED^n [27] where E is the energy, D is the circuit delay, and n is a nonnegative integer; for example, the power-delay product (PDP, $n=0$), the energy-delay product (EDP, $n=1$) [10], and the energy-delay-squared product (ED2P, $n=2$) [20]. The larger the n, the more emphasis on performance.

The ED^n metric is also used for high-end computer systems. We see suggestions on using PDP for workstations, and EDP for servers [4] and supercomputers [32]. Ge et al. [9] proposed to generalize ED2P as $E^{(1-\gamma)}D^{2(1+\gamma)}$, $-1 \leq \gamma \leq 1$, for computer clusters. Bekas and Curioni [2] argued that D should be replaced by an application dependent function of D. Clearly, there is no consensus on the choices for α and β, if we interpret E and D as the reciprocal of energy efficiency and performance, respectively.

What may be agreed upon is the value of the multiplicative form. This can be seen from a figure of merit for mobile devices [19] to the SWaP metric for single servers [22] to a parameterized utility metric for supercomputers [36]. The construction principle is to multiply all desired quantities (such as performance) and divide them by undesired quantities (such as power and size).

3. A VECTOR-VALUED METRIC

This section presents the proposed vector-valued metric for efficient supercomputing. It starts with the definition of the metric, followed by illustrations on how the metric can be used. The trend of efficient supercomputing is analyzed and a new ranking induced by the metric is compared with the TOP500 list and the Green500 list. After that, the desired properties of the metric are listed and discussed.

3.1 The Metric

We view performance and energy efficiency as two separate dimensions of the efficiency metric. In other words,

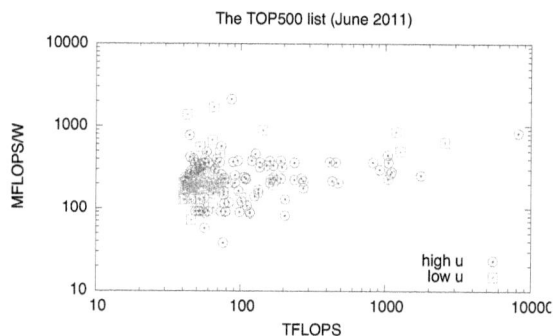

Figure 1: TOP500 in June 2011.

the metric is represented by a two-dimensional vector. We feel that any composite metric is biased one way or another. Transparency preserves the context of the data and enables end users to assess the relevance of the results to their specific application environments [18].

Performance and energy efficiency are defined in the typical way. They are measured in algorithmic steps per second and per joule, respectively. The metric can be visualized as a scatter plot, with the x-axis representing performance and the y-axis representing energy efficiency. The x-axis can also be viewed as the timeline as performance increases over time. A similar plot has been used elsewhere [3].

Note that the vector-valued metric assumes that energy is as important as performance. Furthermore, the two dimensions are separate but not independent. There have been several studies on characterizing the energy-time tradeoffs of a supercomputing application. Finally, although the metric cannot be used to create a total order of the computer systems, it can help generate a *partial* order.

3.2 The Use of the Metric

As an illustration of the value of the new metric, we first take the subset of TOP500 systems which have the power consumption data, and visualize the distribution of their metric values. The data is from the TOP500 list released in June 2011 with 186 unique metric values. Figure 1 shows the distribution of these values. We see that fastest machines have slightly better energy efficiency in general. As a result, these machines still remain at the top ranks in the Green500 list. This may ease the concern that energy efficiency is an intensive quantity, and ranking based on it would favor smaller-scale (and thus slower) systems. On the other hand, these systems do not have the highest energy efficiency. In fact, the energy efficiency of the TOP500 supercomputers are more similar than different, indicating that many of them are built with similar technologies.

The figure also shows that there is no clear winner in two competing designs for an advanced supercomputer. The CPU-based design achieves over 70% of the computational capability whereas the GPU-based design only achieves 50% utilization. GPU-based machines are typically advertised for their potential energy efficiency, but the low utilization of the computational capability leads them to have only comparable efficiency with CPU-based machines. (Note that the low utilization for the less powerful systems is due to the use of slower interconnect.) In the same spirit, there is an ongoing debate in the processor design community as to whether

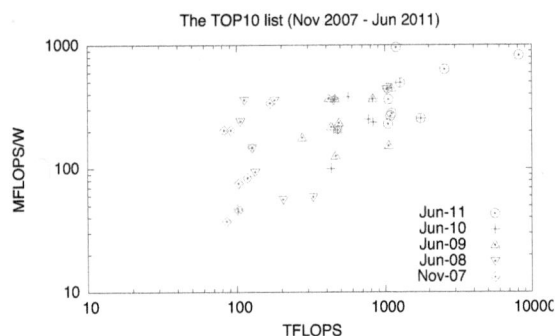

Figure 2: TOP10 over time.

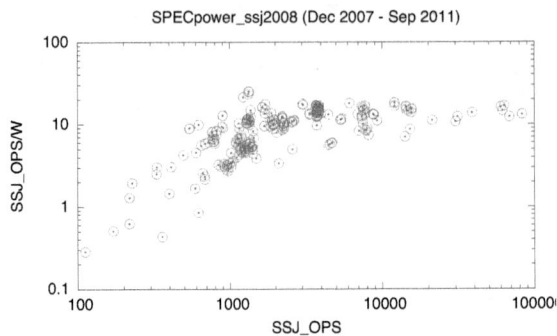

Figure 4: SPECpower_ssj2008 @ 100% over time.

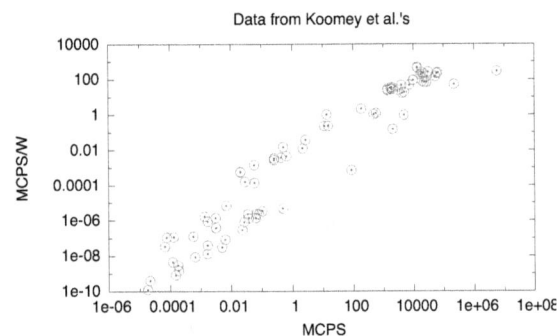

Figure 3: Koomey et al.'s data [17].

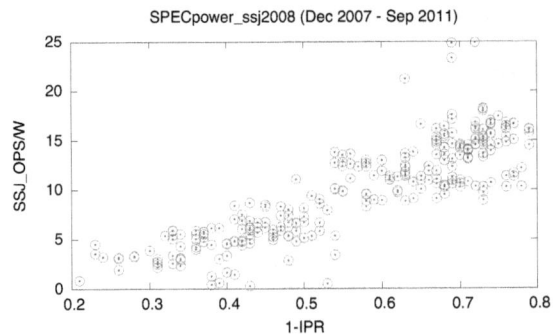

Figure 5: The correlation between energy efficiency and energy proportionality.

slower but more energy efficient "wimpy" processors, aggregated in large numbers, beat "brawny" processors [21, 24].

Figure 2 shows the metric values for the TOP10 supercomputers over different time periods from November 2007 until June 2011. We can see that both performance and energy efficiency are improved over the years. A similar observation can be made for the 10 most energy efficient supercomputers. The multi-dimensional improvement is most likely due to the combined effects of smaller transistor sizes, custom interconnects and more processing elements [34]. The figure also seems to suggest that performance and energy efficiency are improved at similar rates. This observation matches well with Koomey's Law [17] described below.

Koomey and his colleagues recently published a study showing that both performance and energy efficiency tracks very well with Moore's Law [17]. Specifically, they found that the energy efficiency of computation has doubled every 1.57 years from 1946 onward. This rate of improvement is slightly slower than that for personal computers (PCs), which saw efficiency double every 1.52 years from 1975 to 2009. Performance for PCs is doubled every 1.5 years during that time period. For comparison, we plot Koomey et al.'s data [17] as shown in Figure 3. The figure shows a linear correlation, meaning that both performance and energy efficiency are improved at steady rates. This correlation is quite different from what we see in Figure 1.

In order to make more sense out of the results above, we plot the metric values of individual servers benchmarked through SPECpower_ssj2008 at the 100% load-level. The data is from the public records [35] released between December 2007 and September 2011 with 270 unique metric

values. Figure 4 shows the result. This figures is similar to Figure 1 in that systems with higher performance have similar energy efficiency. The figure also shows that the improvement over energy efficiency becomes much slower in recent years.

Further examination indicates that the energy efficiency of servers improves at a steady pace but slower than the performance improvement. A major driving force for the improvement of energy efficiency is the improvement of energy proportionality. Figure 5 shows the correlation between energy efficiency and energy proportionality using the SPECpower_ssj2008 data. We use 1-IPR as the measure for energy efficiency where IPR is the ratio of the idle power to the peak power. The figure shows that a more energy proportional server tends to have a higher energy efficiency.

Unfortunately, we cannot conduct similar analysis to the TOP500 supercomputers since the list does not report the idle power of each supercomputer. We conjecture that supercomputers have relatively lower (but more similar) energy proportionality, and therefore the variation of their energy efficiency is not as significant.

Finally, we want to comment on how the proposed metric can help create a ranking among supercomputers. Although the metric is vector-valued and thus cannot create a total order, it can generate a partial order. We define the partial order in the typical, mathematical manner. Specifically, system A is better than system B if both of its performance and energy efficiency are higher; otherwise, they are incomparable, meaning each system has different advantages. The partial order among all systems creates a directed acyclic graph

Table 1: The 10 most efficient supercomputers.

Rank	η_T	η_E	$\eta_T \cdot \eta_E$	(η_T, η_E)
1	M1	M109	M1	{M1,M5,M109}
2	M2	M165	M2	
3	M3	M430	M5	
4	M4	M5	M4	{M2,M22,M54,M165}
5	M5	M54	M10	
6	M6	M1	M3	
7	M7	M406	M8	
8	M8	M407	M6	{M3,M4,M430}
9	M9	M408	M12	
10	M10	M22	M7	

which can be converted into a layered graph. The layers in the graph enable us to create a ranking, one rank for each layer. Table 1 shows this new ranking with respect to other rankings. The notation Mn means the nth supercomputer in the TOP500 list. Notations η_T and η_E represent performance and energy efficiency respectively. Notation $\{A, B\}$ means systems A and B are incomparable.

We see multiple supercomputers at the same rank, meaning that none of them dominates the other in terms of efficiency. For example, there are three systems M1, M5 and M109 at rank 1. Both M1 and M109 aggregate many low-power processors whereas M5 uses energy efficient accelerators. M1 delivers the highest performance; M5 and M109 are more energy efficient. M5 is GPU-based, consisting of 73,278 cores. In contrast, M109 is Cell-based with 8,192 cores. In other words, although M109 is more energy efficient than M5, M5 is larger in size and provides higher performance.

One novel aspect of the new ranking is that it identifies new "middle" classes. Consider Figure 1, a scatter plot of the TOP500 list with performance as the x-axis and energy efficiency as the y-axis. System M1 is the rightmost point in the plot whereas system M109 is the topmost point. System M5 represents a new class: machine that computes faster than M109 (the most energy-efficient supercomputer) and consumes less energy than M1 (the best-performance supercomputer). Ideally, the multi-dimensional space also provides a natural mechanism to capture some sense of distance, for example, the Euclidean distance which can then be used to cluster systems.

3.3 Further Discussion

In the following we list and briefly discuss a set of desired properties for a good efficiency metric.

1. *Higher is better*: This property looks for a "normalized" metric such that it represents efficiency, not inefficiency. There may or may not exist an upper bound for the metric value.

2. *Capture energy proportionality*: A consensus in the community is to define energy efficiency as the *useful* IT work per joule where how to measure the usefulness is not yet agreed upon.

3. *Not utilization based*: There is an expectation that the usefulness is not closely dependent on how the computer system is utilized. The 100% system utilization does not necessarily imply that the progress of the intended task is also at the full speed.

4. *Not biased*: The hope is to induce a fair comparison. However, this property is rather subjective. For example, some suggest not to favor large-scale machines [16] whereas others want this favoritism [36].

5. *Insightful*: A good metric not only identifies the best system but also finds the distance between two systems so as to help driving design decisions between two drastically different design directions.

4. CONCLUSIONS

This paper has examined the metrics to quantify efficient supercomputing in terms of performance and energy efficiency. Some metrics are driven by industry consortia while others are borrowed from the low-power circuit design community. Although there is not yet a consensus in the supercomputing community on what the right efficiency metric is, there is a trend of shifting from a scalar-valued metric to a vector-valued metric. We follow the same trend and propose a vector-valued metric for efficient supercomputing. Using the metric, the paper presented a study of historical data and current state of the art with respect to efficient supercomputing.

5. ACKNOWLEDGMENTS

This work was partially supported by the Extreme Scale Systems Center at Oak Ridge National Laboratory. The submitted manuscript has been authored by a contractor of the U.S. Government under Contract No. DE-AC05-00OR22725. Accordingly, the U.S. Government retains a non-exclusive, royalty-free license to publish or reproduce the published form of this contribution, or allow others to do so, for U.S. Government purposes. We wish to thank the anonymous reviewers for their valuable comments.

6. REFERENCES

[1] L. Barroso and U. Hölzle. The case for energy-proportional computing. *IEEE Computer*, 40(12):33–37, Dec. 2007.

[2] C. Bekas and A. Curioni. A new energy aware performance metric. In *International Conference on Energy-Aware High Performance Computing*, Sept. 2010.

[3] K. D. Bois, T. Schaeps, S. Polfliet, F. Ryckbosch, and L. Eeckhout. SWEEP: Evaluating computer system energy efficiency using synthetic workloads. In *International Conference on High Performance Embedded Architectures and Compilers*, Jan. 2011.

[4] D. Brooks, P. Bose, S. Schuster, H. Jacobson, P. Kudva, A.Buyuktosunoglu, J.-D. Wellman, V. Zyuban, M. Gupta, and P. Cook. Power-aware microarchitecture: Design and modeling challenges for the next generation microprocessors. *IEEE Micro*, 20(6):26–44, November/December 2000.

[5] T. Conte and W. Hwu. Advances in benchmarking techniques: New standards and quantitative metrics. *Advances in Computers*, 41:231–253, 1995.

[6] J. Dongarra, P. Luszczek, and A. Petitet. The LINPACK benchmark: Past, present, and future. *Concurrency and Computation: Practice and Experience*, 15(9):803–820, Aug. 2003.

[7] Energy Efficient High Performance Computing Working Group. http://eehpcwg.lbl.gov.

[8] A. Fanara, E. Haines, and A. Howard. The state of energy and performance benchmarking for enterprise servers. In *TPC Technology Conference on Performance Evaluation and Benchmarking*, Aug. 2009.

[9] R. Ge, X. Feng, and K. Cameron. Improvement of power-performance efficiency for high-end computing. In *Workshop on High-Performance, Power-Aware Computing*, Apr. 2005.

[10] R. Gonzalez and M. Horowitz. Energy dissipation in general purpose microprocessors. *IEEE Journal of Solid-State Circuits*, 31(9):1277–1284, Sept. 1996.

[11] The Graph 500 list. http://www.graph500.org.

[12] L. Gray, A. Kumar, and H. Li. Workload characterization of the SPECpower_ssj2008 benchmark. In *SPEC International Performance Evaluation Workshop*, June 2008.

[13] The Green500 list: Environmentally responsible supercomputing. http://www.green500.org.

[14] D. Hackenberg, R. Schöne, D. Molka, M. Müller, and A. Knüpfer. Quantifying power consumption variations of HPC systems using SPEC MPI benchmarks. In *International Conference on Energy-Aware High Performance Computing*, Sept. 2010.

[15] HPC Challenge benchmark. http://icl.cs.utk.edu/hpcc/.

[16] C. Hsu, W. Feng, and J. Archuleta. Towards efficient supercomputing: A quest for the right metric. In *Workshop on High-Performance, Power-Aware Computing*, Apr. 2005.

[17] J. Koomey, S. Berard, M. Sanchez, and H. Wong. Implications of historical trends in the electrical efficiency of computing. *IEEE Annals of the History of Computing*, 33(3):46–54, July-September 2011.

[18] K.-D. Lange and M. Tricker. The design and development of the server efficiency rating tool (SERT). In *International Conference on Performance Engineering*, Mar. 2011.

[19] T. Makimoto, K. Eguchi, and M. Yoneyama. The cooler the better: New directions in the nomadic age. *IEEE Computer*, 34(4):38–42, Apr. 2001.

[20] A. Martin. Towards an energy complexity of computation. *Information Processing Letters*, 77:181–187, Feb. 2001.

[21] D. Meisner and T. Wenisch. Does low-power design imply energy efficiency for data centers. In *International Symposium on Low Power Electronics and Design*, Aug. 2011.

[22] S. Microsystems. The SWaP (Space, Watts and Performance) metric, 2007.

[23] D. Molka, D. Hackenberg, R. Schöne, T. Minartz, and W. Nagel. Flexible workload generation for HPC cluster efficiency benchmarking. In *International Conference on Energy-Aware High Performance Computing*, Sept. 2011.

[24] T. Mudge and U. Hölzle. Challenges and opportunities for extremely energy-efficient processors. *IEEE Micro*, 30(4):20–24, July/August 2010.

[25] M. Müller, M. van Waveren, R. Lieberman, B. Whitney, H. Saito, K. Kumaran, J. Baron, W. Brantley, C. Parrott, T. Elken, H. Feng, and C. Ponder. SPEC MPI2007:an application benchmark suite for parallel systems using MPI. *Concurrency and Computation: Practice and Experience*, 22(2):191–205, Feb. 2010.

[26] V. Pel. Energy efficiency aspects in Cray supercomputers. In *International Conference on Energy-Aware High Performance Computing*, Sept. 2010.

[27] P. Pénzes and A. Martin. Energy-delay efficiency of VLSI computations. In *ACM Great Lakes Symposium on VLSI*, Apr. 2002.

[28] M. Poess, R. Nambiar, and K. Vaid. Optimizing benchmark configurations for energy efficiency. In *International Conference on Performance Engineering*, Mar. 2011.

[29] M. Poess, R. Nambiar, K. Vaid, J. J.M. Stephens, K. Huppler, and E. Haines. Energy benchmarks: A detailed analysis. In *International Conference on Energy-Efficient Computing and Networking*, Apr. 2010.

[30] S. Rivoire, M. Shah, P. Ranganathan, and C. Kozyrakis. JouleSort: A balanced energy-efficiency benchmark. In *International Conference on Management of Data*, June 2007.

[31] F. Ryckbosch, S. Polfliet, and L. Eeckhout. Trend in server energy-proportionality. *IEEE Computer*, 44(9):69–72, Sept. 2011.

[32] V. Sarkar. ExaScale software study: Software challenges in extreme scale systems. DARPA IPTO Report, Sept. 2009.

[33] D. Schall, V. Hoefner, and M. Kern. Towards an enhanced benchmark advocating energy-efficient systems. In *TPC Technology Conference on Performance Evaluation & Benchmarking*, Aug. 2011.

[34] T. Scogland, B. Subramaniam, and W. Feng. Emerging trends on the evolving Green500: Year three. In *Workshop on High-Performance, Power-Aware Computing*, May 2011.

[35] SPECpower_ssj2008 Results. http://www.spec.org/power_ssj2008/results/.

[36] E. Strohmaier. Generalized utility metrics for supercomputers. June 2009.

[37] The Green Grid. The Green Grid power efficiency metrics: PUE and DCiE, 2007.

[38] The Green Grid. Recommendations for measuring and reporting overall data center efficiency (version 2), May 2011.

[39] TOP500 supercomputing sites. http://www.top500.org.

[40] G. Varsamopoulos and S. Gupta. Energy proportionality and the future: Metrics and directions. In *International Workshop on Green Computing*, Sept. 2010.

Keynote Talk

New Challenges in Performance Engineering

Amnon Naamad
EMC
Hopkinton Mass. USA
amnon.naamad@emc.com

Abstract

Recent new technologies and paradigm shifts in the IT business make the role of performance engineers significantly more challenging than any other time in the past. Flash technology, virtualization, and Cloud computing provide new options for performance optimization; however, materializing the potential of these technologies in a predictable and cost effective manner is a challenge. New performance management software and planning tools that are based on scientific research and analysis are required to meet the new expectations that users have.

The presentation will discuss some of the new technologies, their potential impact on IT, the tools that are being developed to exploit the technologies and some of the open questions still remaining.

In particular, the presentation will focus on the subjects of Tiered Storage, Performance in Cloud environments, and proactive performance management.

Categories & Subject Descriptors: Computer Systems Organization: Performance of Systems

Subjects: Modeling technique, Performance Attributes, Design Studies

General Terms: Algorithms, Management, Performance

Bio

Amnon Naamad is an EMC Fellow serving as the manager of the Innovation and Systems Engineering team and as the CTO of the Enterprise Storage Division (ESD). Amnon is responsible for generating, collecting, analyzing, and promoting innovative ideas to enhance EMC Symmetrix functionality and performance, and assisting with the translation of these ideas into products and solutions.

Amnon joined EMC in 1997, and shortly thereafter became the Manager of Symmetrix Performance Engineering. In April 2006, he was promoted to lead the Innovation and Systems Engineering Group within Symmetrix Engineering.

Prior to EMC, Amnon was the CTO of I-Logix, where he led the development of the simulation, analysis, and automatic code generators of Statemate. Amnon along with colleagues at I-Logix received the ACM Software Systems Award for 2007, ACM SIGSOFT Impact Paper Award for 2008, and the ICSE Most Influential Paper Award for 1998.

Previous to I-Logix, Amnon held a variety of positions in the high-tech industry as a lead developer. This includes development of software for processing images taken from CAT scanners and software for Optical Character Readers. He also worked in academia teaching Computer Science classes at Tel Aviv University and a class at Brandeis University. He also served four years of active military service in the Israeli Defense Forces.

Amnon holds B.S. and M.S. degrees in Mathematics from Tel Aviv University, and a Ph.D. in Computer Science from Northwestern University. His areas of research included the Design and Analysis of Algorithms, Graph Theory, Computational Geometry and Software Engineering.

Workload Generation for Microprocessor Performance Evaluation

SPEC PhD Award (Invited Abstract)

Luk Van Ertvelde
Ghent University, Belgium
lvertvel@elis.ugent.be

Thesis Supervisor: Lieven Eeckhout
Ghent University, Belgium
leeckhou@elis.ugent.be

ABSTRACT

This PhD thesis [1], awarded with the SPEC Distinguished Dissertation Award 2011, proposes and studies three workload generation and reduction techniques for microprocessor performance evaluation. (1) The thesis proposes code mutation, a novel methodology for hiding proprietary information from computer programs while maintaining representative behavior; code mutation enables dissemination of proprietary applications as benchmarks to third parties in both academia and industry. (2) It contributes to sampled simulation by proposing NSL-BLRL, a novel warm-up technique that reduces simulation time by an order of magnitude over state-of-the-art. (3) It presents a benchmark synthesis framework for generating synthetic benchmarks from a set of desired program statistics. The benchmarks are generated in a high-level programming language, which enables both compiler and hardware exploration.

Categories and Subject Descriptors

C.0 [**Computer Systems Organization**]: Modeling of computer architecture; C.4 [**Computer Systems Organization**]: Performance of Systems—*Modeling Techniques*

General Terms

Design, Performance, Measurement, Experimentation

Keywords

Workload Characterization, Workload Generation, Sampled Simulation

1. INTRODUCTION

Microprocessors have drastically advanced over the years, from scalar in-order execution processors to complex superscalar out-of-order and multi-core processors. The ever-increasing microarchitectural complexity necessitates benchmark programs to evaluate the performance of a new microprocessor, hence, organizations such as SPEC, EEMBC, etc., released standardized benchmark suites. Although this has streamlined the process of performance evaluation, computer architects and engineers still face several important benchmarking challenges.

1. Benchmarks should be representative for the (future) applications that are expected to run on the target computer sys-

tem; however, it is not always possible to select a representative benchmark suite for at least three reasons. For one, standardized benchmark suites are typically derived from open-source programs because industry hesitates to share proprietary applications, and open-source programs have the advantage that they are portable across different platforms. The limitation though is that these benchmarks may not be representative for the real-world applications of interest. Secondly, existing benchmark suites are often outdated because the application space is constantly evolving and developing new benchmark suites is extremely time-consuming and costly. Finally, benchmarks are modeled after existing applications that may be less relevant by the time the product hits the market.

2. Coming up with a benchmark that is short-running yet representative is another major challenge. Contemporary application benchmark suites like SPEC CPU2006 execute trillions of instructions in order to stress contemporary and future processors in a meaningful way. If we also take into account that during microarchitectural research a multitude of design alternatives need to be evaluated, we easily end up with months or even years of simulation time. This may stretch the time-to-market of newly designed microprocessors. Hence, it is infeasible to simulate entire application benchmarks using detailed cycle-accurate simulators.

3. Finally, a benchmark should enable both (micro)architecture and compiler research and development. Although existing benchmarks satisfy this requirement, this is typically not the case for workload generation techniques that reduce the dynamic instruction count in order to address the simulation challenge. These techniques often operate on binaries which eliminates their utility for compiler exploration and instruction-set architecture exploration.

2. CONTRIBUTIONS

This dissertation [1] proposes three novel benchmark generation and reduction techniques to address the aforementioned challenges. In particular, code mutation addresses the proprietary nature of application codes; sampled simulation using NSL-BLRL reduces the long simulation times of contemporary benchmarks; finally, benchmark synthesis reduces simulation time and hides proprietary information in the reduced workloads.

2.1 Code Mutation

We first propose code mutation [2, 4] to stimulate sharing of proprietary applications between third parties in academia and industry. Code mutation is a novel methodology that mutates a proprietary application to complicate reverse engineering so that it can be distributed as an application benchmark among several parties. These benchmark mutants hide the functional semantics of proprietary applications while exhibiting similar performance characteristics. We therefore exploit two observations: (i) miss events have a dominant impact on performance on contemporary microprocessors, and (ii) many variables of contemporary applications exhibit invariant behavior at run time. More specifically, we compute program slices for memory access operations and/or control flow operations trimmed through constant value and branch profiles. Subsequently, we mutate the instructions not appearing in these slices through binary rewriting. The end result is a benchmark mutant that can serve as a proxy for the proprietary application during benchmarking experiments by third parties.

Our experimental results using SPEC CPU2000 and MiBench benchmarks show that code mutation is an effective approach that mutates (i) up to 90% of the binary, (ii) up to 50% of the dynamically executed instructions, and (iii) up to 35% of the at-run-time-exposed inter-operation data dependencies. In addition, the performance characteristics of the mutant are very similar to those of the proprietary application across a wide range of microarchitectures and hardware implementations.

Code mutation will mostly benefit companies that develop (embedded) microarchitectures and companies that offer (in-house built) services to remote customers. Such companies are reluctant to distribute their proprietary software. As an alternative, they can use mutated benchmarks as proxies for their proprietary software to help drive performance evaluation by third parties as well as guide purchasing decisions of hardware infrastructure. Being able to generate representative benchmark mutants without revealing proprietary information can also be an encouragement for industry to collaborate more closely with academia, i.e., it would make performance evaluation in academia more realistic and therefore more relevant for industry. Eventually, this may lead to more valuable research directions. In addition, developing benchmarks is both hard and time-consuming to do in academia, for which code mutation may be a solution.

2.2 Sampled Simulation: NSL-BLRL

Code mutation conceals the intellectual property of an application, but it does not lend itself to the generation of short-running benchmarks. Sampled simulation on the other hand reduces the simulation time of an application significantly. The key idea of sampled simulation is to simulate only a small sample from a complete benchmark execution in a detailed manner (a sample consists of one or more sampling units). The performance bottleneck in sampled simulation is the establishment of the microarchitecture state (caches, branch predictor, etc.) at the beginning of each sampling unit. The unknown microarchitecture starting image at the beginning of a sampling unit is often referred to as the cold-start problem.

We address the cold-start problem by proposing a new cache warmup method, namely NSL-BLRL [5, 6] which builds on No-State-Loss (NSL) and Boundary Line Reuse Latency (BLRL) for minimizing the cost associated with cycle-accurate processor cache hierarchy simulation in sampled simulation. The idea of NSL-BLRL is to establish the cache state at the beginning of a sampling unit using a checkpoint that stores a truncated NSL stream. NSL scans the pre-sampling unit and records the last reference to each unique memory location. This is called the least-recently used (LRU) stream. This stream is then truncated to form the NSL-BLRL warmup checkpoint by inspecting the sampling unit for de-termining how far in the pre-sampling unit one needs to go back to accurately warm up the cache state for the given sampling unit.

This approach yields several benefits over prior work: substantial simulation speedups compared to BLRL (up to 1.4× under fast-forwarding and up to 14.9× under checkpointing) and significant reductions in disk space requirements compared to NSL (on average 30%), for a selection of SPEC CPU2000 benchmarks.

2.3 HLL Benchmark Synthesis

Although code mutation can be used in combination with sampled simulation to generate short-running workloads that can be distributed to third parties without revealing intellectual property, there are a number of limitations. The most important limitation is that this approach operates at the assembly level, and as a result, it cannot be used for compiler exploration and ISA exploration purposes. We therefore propose a novel benchmark synthesis framework that generates synthetic benchmarks in a high-level programming language.

The benchmark synthesis framework [3, 4] aims at generating small but representative benchmarks that can serve as proxies for other applications without revealing proprietary information; and because the benchmarks are generated in a high-level language, they can be used to explore the architecture and compiler space. The methodology to generate these benchmarks comprises two key steps: (i) profiling a real-world (proprietary) application (that is compiled at a low optimization level) to measure its execution characteristics, and (ii) modeling these characteristics into a synthetic benchmark clone. To capture a program's control flow behavior in a statistical way, we introduce a new structure: the Statistical Flow Graph with Loop information (SFGL).

We demonstrate good correspondence between the synthetic and original applications across instruction-set architectures, microarchitectures and compiler optimizations, and we point out the major sources of error in the benchmark synthesis process. We verified using software plagiarism detection tools that the synthetic benchmark clones indeed hide proprietary information from the original applications.

We argue that our framework can be used for several applications: distributing synthetic benchmarks as proxies for proprietary applications, drive architecture and compiler research and development, speed up simulation, model emerging and hard-to-setup workloads, and benchmark consolidation.

3. REFERENCES

[1] L. Van Ertvelde. *Workload Generation for Microprocessor Performance Evaluation*. PhD thesis, Ghent University, Belgium, 2010.

[2] L. Van Ertvelde and L. Eeckhout. Dispersing proprietary applications as benchmarks through code mutation. In *The International Conference on Architectural Support for Programming Languages and Operating Systems (ASPLOS)*, pages 201–210, 2008.

[3] L. Van Ertvelde and L. Eeckhout. Benchmark synthesis for architecture and compiler exploration. In *Proceedings of the IEEE International Symposium on Workload Characterization (IISWC)*, pages 106–116, 2010.

[4] L. Van Ertvelde and L. Eeckhout. Workload reduction and generation techniques. *IEEE Micro*, 30(6):57–65, 2010.

[5] L. Van Ertvelde, F. Hellebaut, and L. Eeckhout. Accurate and efficient cache warmup for sampled processor simulation through NSL-BLRL. *The Computer Journal*, 51(2):192–206, 2008.

[6] L. Van Ertvelde, F. Hellebaut, L. Eeckhout, and K. De Bosschere. NSL-BLRL: Efficient cache warmup for sampled processor simulation. In *Proceedings of the Annual Simulation Symposium (ANSS)*, pages 168–177, 2006.

Performance Evaluation and Benchmarking of Event-Based Systems

SPEC Distinguished Dissertation Award 2011 (Invited Abstract)

Kai Sachs
SAP AG, Germany
kai.sachs@sap.com
Thesis Supervisor:
Alejandro Buchmann, TU Darmstadt, Germany
buchmann@dvs.tu-darmstadt.de

Categories and Subject Descriptors

C.4 [**Computer Systems Organization**]: Performance of Systems—*Modeling techniques, Design studies, Measurement techniques*

Keywords

Benchmark, Event-based systems, Message-oriented middleware, SPECjms2007

Event-based systems (EBS) are increasingly used as underlying technology in many mission critical areas and large-scale environments, such as environmental monitoring and location-based services [3]. Moreover, novel event-based applications are typically highly distributed and data intensive with stringent requirements for performance and scalability. Since their reliability is crucial for the whole IT infrastructure, a certain Quality-of-Service (QoS) level has to be ensured. The motivation for our work was to support the development and maintenance of EBS that meet their QoS requirements. Given that EBS differ from traditional software in fundamental aspects such as their underlying communications paradigm, specific solutions and concepts are needed. System architects and deployers need tools and methodologies, which allow them to evaluate and forecast system performance and behavior in certain situations to identify potential performance problems and bottlenecks. Common approaches are benchmarking and performance modeling. However, no general performance modeling methodologies focusing on EBS had been published. Furthermore, there was a lack of test harnesses and benchmarks using representative workloads for EBS. Consequently, we focused on the development of a performance modeling methodology of EBS as well as on approaches to benchmark them. We summarize now our main contributions and proposed approaches.

To comprehend our contributions, an understanding of the fundamental ideas of EBS is essential. Generally, EBS are software systems in which an observed event triggers a reaction. For more details and definitions of events and related concepts refer to [3]. We evaluated the variety of underlying technologies with a focus on distributed EBS and message-orientend middlewares (MOMs) and provided a survey of products and standards [7]. In our review of existing work, we identified a lack of benchmarks and performance modeling approaches for EBS [5]. To support a structural evaluation of benchmarks, we introduced five categories of requirements [9]: (i) *Representativeness:* the benchmark has to be based on a representative workload. (ii) *Comprehensiveness:* exercise all platform features typically used in applications. (iii) *Focus:* place the emphasis on the technology server and minimize the impact of other services, e.g., databases. (iv) *Configurability:* provide a configurable tool for performance analysis. (v) *Scalability:* provide ways to scale the workload in a flexible manner.

None of the existing benchmarks met all our requirements. Therefore, we saw a strong need for independent and standardized benchmarks for EBS fulfilling the requirements. To address this need we developed the first industry standard benchmark for EBS jointly with the SPEC (Standard Performance Evaluation Corporation). As underlying technology platform we chose Java Message Service (JMS). This was motivated by the fact that MOMs are widely used in industry and the quasi-standard for MOMs is JMS. Our efforts resulted in the *SPECjms2007* standard benchmark [9]. Its main contributions were twofold: based on the feedback of industrial partners, we specified a comprehensive standardized workload with different scaling options and implemented the benchmark using a newly developed complex and flexible framework.

Using the SPECjms2007 benchmark we introduced a methodology for performance evaluation of message-oriented middleware platforms and showed how the workload can be tailored to evaluate selected performance aspects [10]. We demonstrated our methodology in a case study of a leading JMS platform and conducted in-depth performance analyses of the platform for a number of different workload and configuration scenarios.

The SPECjms2007 business scenario was specified independently from the underlying technology. Therefore, its usage is not limited to a specific type of EBS. We illustrated how the standardized workload can be applied to other EBS using the example of *jms2009-PS*, a benchmark for publish/subscribe-based communication [8]. This benchmark provides a flexible framework for performance analysis with a strong focus on research. The proposed benchmarks are now the de facto standard benchmarks for evaluating

ICPE'12, April 22–25, 2012, Boston, Massachusetts, USA
ACM 978-1-4503-1202-8/12/04.

messaging platforms and have already been used successfully by several industrial and research organizations as a basis for further research on performance analysis of EBS.

To the best of our knowledge, no work introducing a general methodology for modeling EBS had been published. As a consequence, we investigated whether and how traditional performance modeling approaches are suitable to model the specifica of EBS. We introduced a formal definition of EBS and their performance aspects, which allows us, e.g., to describe workload properties and routing behavior in a structured way [6]. Resulting from our analysis of existing modeling techniques, we proposed an approach to characterize the workload and to model the performance aspects of EBS. We used operational analysis techniques to describe the system traffic and derived an approximation for the mean event delivery latency. We then showed how more detailed performance models based on queueing Petri nets (QPNs) [1] could be built and used to provide more accurate performance prediction. We chose QPNs as performance modeling technique because of their modeling power and expressiveness. Our approach allows evaluating and predicting the performance of an EBS and provides detailed system models. It can be used for an in-depth performance analysis and to identify potential bottlenecks. A further contribution is a terminology for performance modeling patterns targeting common aspects of event-based applications using QPNs [7, 11].

To additionally improve the modeling power of QPNs, we suggested several extensions of the standard QPNs, which allow building models in a more flexible and general way and address several limitations of QPNs [7]. By introducing a level of abstraction, it is possible to distinguish between logical and physical layers in our models. This enables to flexibly map logical to physical resources and thus makes it easy to customize the model to a specific deployment. The different layers allow reusing one logical model in several physical models or to map several logical models to one physical model. Furthermore, we addressed two limiting aspects of standard QPNs: constant cardinalities and the lack of transition priorities. By introducing non-constant cardinalities of transitions we increased the modeling flexibility and minimized the number of transition modes. The missing support of transition priorities in standard QPNs limits the control of the transition firing order. We addressed this restriction by incorporating priorities for transitions into QPNs and discussed several ways to implement them. Our extensions were integrated in the QPME / SimQPN software tools [4] or are planned for the upcoming release.

Finally, we validated the approach in two case studies. We applied our methodology to model EBS and predicted their performance and system behavior under load successfully. As part of the first case study we extended SIENA, a well-known distributed EBS [2], with a runtime measurement framework and predicted the runtime behavior including delivery latency for a basic workload [6] with a single event type. In the second case study, we developed a comprehensive model of the complete SPECjms2007 workload including the persistent layer, point-to-point and publish/subscribe communication [11]. To model the workload we applied our performance modeling patterns as well as our proposed QPN extensions.

We evaluated its accuracy in a commercial middleware environment. To validate our modeling technique we investigated deployments of the benchmark in representative environments comparing the model predictions against measurements on the real systems. A number of different scenarios with varying workload intensity (up to 30,000 messages / 4,500 transaction per second) and interaction mixes were taken into account. By means of the proposed models we were able to predict the performance accurately. No models of realistic systems of the size and complexity of the one considered in this case study exist in the literature.

Both case studies demonstrated the effectiveness and practicality of the proposed modeling and prediction methodology in the context of a real-world scenario. The advantage of the approach is that it is both practical and general, and it can be readily applied for performance evaluation of distributed EBS and MOM. The technique can be exploited as a powerful tool for performance prediction and capacity planning during the software engineering lifecycle of message-oriented event-driven systems.

Our results open up new avenues of research in the area of event-based systems. Our performance modeling methodology can be used to build self-adaptive EBS using automatic model extraction techniques. Such systems could dynamically adjust their configuration to ensure that QoS requirements are continuously met.

1. REFERENCES

[1] F. Bause. QN + PN = QPN - Combining Queueing Networks and Petri Nets. Tech. report no.461, Dept. of CS, University of Dortmund, Germany, 1993.

[2] A. Carzaniga, D. S. Rosenblum, and A. Wolf. Design and Evaluation of a Wide-Area Event Notification Service. *ACM Trans. Comput. Syst.*, 19(3), 2001.

[3] A. Hinze, K. Sachs, and A. Buchmann. Event-based applications and enabling technologies. In *Proc. of the ACM DEBS*, 2009.

[4] S. Kounev and C. Dutz. QPME - A Performance Modeling Tool Based on Queueing Petri Nets. *ACM SIGMETRICS PER*, 36(4):46 51, 2009.

[5] S. Kounev and K. Sachs. Benchmarking and performance modeling of event-based systems. *it - Information Technology*, 51(5):262–269, 2009.

[6] S. Kounev, K. Sachs, J. Bacon, and A. P. Buchmann. A methodology for performance modeling of distributed Event-Based systems. In *Proc. of the IEEE ISORC*, 2008.

[7] K. Sachs. *Performance Modeling and Benchmarking of Event-Based Systems*. PhD thesis, TU Darmstadt, 2010.

[8] K. Sachs, S. Appel, S. Kounev, and A. Buchmann. Benchmarking publish/subscribe-based messaging systems. In *DASFAA 2010 - Int. Workshops: BenchmarX'10*, LNCS. Springer, 2010.

[9] K. Sachs, S. Kounev, J. Bacon, and A. Buchmann. Workload characterization of the SPECjms2007 benchmark. In *Proc. of EPEW*, LNCS. Springer, 2007.

[10] K. Sachs, S. Kounev, J. Bacon, and A. Buchmann. Performance evaluation of message-oriented middleware using the SPECjms2007 benchmark. *Performance Evaluation*, 66(8):410–434, 2009.

[11] K. Sachs, S. Kounev, and A. Buchmann. Performance modeling and analysis of message-oriented event-driven systems. *Software and Systems Modeling*, 2012. DOI: 10.1007/s10270-012-0228-1.

Efficient Update Data Generation for DBMS Benchmarks

Michael Frank
University of Passau
Faculty of Computer Science
and Mathematics
Passau, Germany
frank@fim.uni-passau.de

Meikel Poess
Oracle Corporation
500 Oracle Parkway
Redwood Shores, CA-94404
meikel.poess@oracle.com

Tilmann Rabl
University of Toronto
Department of Electrical and
Computer Engineering
Toronto, ON, Canada
tilmann.rabl@utoronto.ca

ABSTRACT

It is without doubt that industry standard benchmarks have been proven to be crucial to the innovation and productivity of the computing industry. They are important to the fair and standardized assessment of performance across different vendors, different system versions from the same vendor and across different architectures. Good benchmarks are even meant to drive industry and technology forward. Since at some point, after all reasonable advances have been made using a particular benchmark even good benchmarks become obsolete over time. This is why standard consortia periodically overhaul their existing benchmarks or develop new benchmarks. An extremely time and resource consuming task in the creation of new benchmarks is the development of benchmark generators, especially because benchmarks tend to become more and more complex. The first version of the Parallel Data Generation Framework (PDGF), a generic data generator, was capable of generating data for the initial load of arbitrary relational schemas. It was, however, not able to generate data for the actual workload, i.e. input data for transactions (insert, delete and update), incremental load etc., mainly because it did not understand the notion of updates. Updates are data changes that occur over time, e.g. a customer changes address, switches job, gets married or has children. Many benchmarks, need to reflect these changes during their workloads. In this paper we present PDGF Version 2, which contains extensions enabling the generation of update data.

Categories and Subject Descriptors

K.6.2 [**Management of Computing and Information Systems**]: Installation Management—*benchmark, performance and usage measurement*

General Terms

Measurement

Keywords

Benchmark, Data Generation

1. INTRODUCTION

Over the years industry standard benchmarks have proven to be crucial to the innovation and productivity of the computing industry. They are important to the fair and standardized assessment of performance across different vendors, different system versions from the same vendor and across different architectures. Hence, they are used by system and software vendors as much as they are used by customers during their purchase decisions. Vendors use them to differentiate their systems' performance from those of other vendors, while they use them internally to monitor systems' performance across releases and, in case of software, even across daily builds. Customers use industry standard benchmarks to cost effectively compare the performance of systems. Without benchmarks they would need to invest in the performance analysis of different systems.

In the last 25 years many industry standard benchmarks were developed by benchmark consortia. Among these consortia are, most notably, the Standard Performance Evaluation Corporation (SPEC), the Transaction Processing Performance Council (TPC) and the Storage Performance Council (SPC). While focusing on slightly different aspects of system performance, they all follow a common goal, namely to develop fair and verifiable standard benchmarks, and to police and publish results on a large number of systems. In this paper we focus on those benchmarks that measure performance of database management systems (DBMS).

While the fundamental steps in a DBMS benchmark have remained the same over the years, namely to load the initial database and then to run a workload, e.g. transactions or queries, the complexities of the benchmarks have increased enormously [11]. For instance, TPC-A, TPC's first OLTP benchmark specification, counted 43 pages and used a single, simple, update-intensive transaction to emulate update-intensive database environments. The transaction access a schema with four tables, all with 1:n relationships. In comparison TPC-E, TPC's latest OLTP benchmark specification counts 286 pages and consists of 10 transactions emulating the complex operation of a brokerage firm. Its transactions access a schema with 9 tables and complex relationships.

Each benchmark requires tools to generate datasets for the initial load and the subsequent workload. In [21] we have analyzed data generation requirement of today's complex DBMS environments. While the data dependencies in

TPC-A were restricted to foreign-key/primary key relation-ships and data volumes were in the gigabyes, TPC-E's data dependencies are more complex. For the initial load of a DBMS we have identified three classes of data dependen-cies: i) intra row dependencies, e.g. the city and zip code of an address table, ii) intra table dependencies, e.g. the n:1 relation-ships of normalized schemas and iii) inter table de-pendencies, e.g. Foreign key, primary key relationships. In [21] we have shown how the Parallel Data Generation Frame-work (PDGF) can be configured to generate the above data.

Since then we have been working on PDGF based data generators for TPC-H and a new extract, transform and load (ETL) benchmark [25] of the Transaction Processing Performance Council (TPC). This work has revealed that the above data dependencies also exists in the data sets. Consider the two tables of a customer management system:

$$Customer = \{C_1, C_2, ..., C_n\} \quad (1)$$

$$CustomerAddress = \{CA_1, CA_2, ..., CA_n\} \quad (2)$$

with the primary keys C_1 and CA_1 and the foreign key CA_2 to join to C_1 of the customer table. Now consider the fol-lowing workload: For a random customer find his address and update each field C_i with a likelihood of L_i. In case the customer address key range is dense and static finding an existing customer and his address is trivial. But what if the keys are not dense, or we add customers as part of the workload. Then the key range evolves over time making it more difficult to pick valid keys, especially in parallel data generation.

The above scenario is very common in ETL systems as their main workload is to load data, especially incremental data that can contain updates to pre-existing data. The ETL benchmark, currently under development by the TPC, defines two sets of schemas, one to emulate the source tables and one to define the target tables. The workload is defined in terms of transformation that map the input data of the source tables to the output data of the target tables. As a result writing a data generator for an ETL benchmark is very challenging. The update data needs to be generated deterministically, i.e. for each table one needs to be able to set the number of new, updated and deleted records.

In this paper we present our extensions to PDGF that en-able the deterministic generation of intra-table dependencies and updates for database benchmarking, which were devel-oped specifically to support TPC's ETL benchmark devel-opment. Our main contributions are:

- the principle of a growing permutation, that is basis for our update generation strategy,

- an extension of our data generation approach to gen-erate intra-table dependencies,

- the development of a framework for transparent, con-sistent and repeatable generation of inserts, updates, and deletes for generated data.

The remainder of this paper is organized as follows: In the next section we discuss related work, especially data generators that try to solve similar problems. In Section 3 we briefly review the architecture and design goals of the PDGF. Section 4, the main contribution of this paper, de-tails the basic principles of our approach for generating up-dates and how it is integrated in PDGF. We present some performance numbers in Section 5, before concluding in Sec-tion 6.

2. RELATED WORK

Data generation for performance evaluation is part of the daily business of researchers and DB administrators. Most of their data generators are special purpose implementations for a single dataset. The active demand for generic data gen-eration tools feeds a lively industry in this niche that sells their generators for hundreds to thousands of dollars. Exam-ples of commercial tools are Red Gate SQL Data Generator [22], DTM Data Generator [6], and GS DataGenerator [8]. But still new companies are entering this segment, e.g. Log-icBlox with their TestBlox software.

There has been quite a lot of research on data genera-tion for performance benchmarking purposes. An impor-tant milestone was the paper by Gray et al. [7], the authors showed how to generate data sets with different distributions and dense unique sequences in linear time and in parallel. Fast, parallel generation of data with special distribution characteristics is the foundation of our data generation ap-proach.

Most scientific data generators have been built for a single benchmark as well. Examples of simple data sets (i.e. that only consists of single tables or or unrelated tables) are Set-Query [15], TeraSort, MalGen [1], YCSB [5], the Wisconsin database [2], and Bristlecone [4]. To generate data intra-and inter-table dependencies – as specified in [21] – the data generators have to be more sophisticated. For large data sets two solutions are common: either to re-read the generated data or to use a per user simulation for the generation. An examples for the former approach is dbgen [24], the data gen-erator provided by the TPC for the TPC-H benchmark[17], another approach was presented by Bruno and Chaudhuri [3]: it largely relies on scanning a given database to gener-ate various distributions and interdependencies. Two fur-ther tools that offer similar capabilities are MUDD [23] and PSDG [9]. Both feature description languages for the defi-nition of the data layout and advanced distributions. The later approach is often realized by graph based models as presented by Houkjær et al. [10] and Lin et al. [12].

All of these data generators consider the benchmarking as a two phased procedure, first the data has to be loaded and then a workload must be processed. Therefore, they generate a historical load and rely on a workload generator for queries and updates. However, in some cases the histor-ical workload also reflects the stream of updates, e.g. in an history-keeping dimension [14]. This cannot be generated by either of the generators above.

3. PARALLEL DATA GENERATION FRAMEWORK

The Parallel Data Generation Framework (PDGF), devel-oped at the University of Passau, is a generic data generator for relational data [19]. It was designed to take advantage of today's multi-core processors and large clusters of com-puters to generate exabytes of synthetic data very quickly. It was originally built for the generation of large, relational data sets stored as flat files. Since the release of PDGF Version 1.0 major parts have been extended and many new functionality has been added.

The most important improvement in *PDGF 2.0* is the

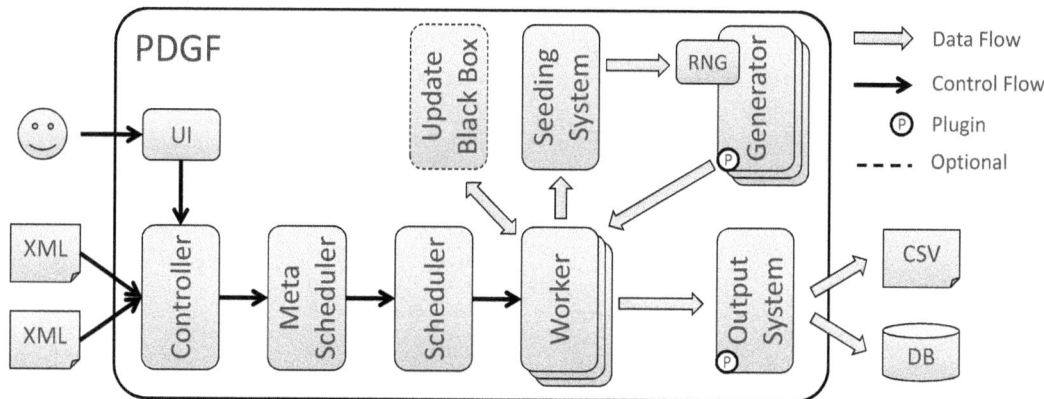

Figure 1: PDGF Architecture

ability to represent and generate data changes over time. *PDGF 2.0* is capable of performing multiple updates throughout a benchmark run, like adding, changing and deleting tuples. This allows the simulation of the natural growth of a data set over time. Changed data can be generated as a changed data capture file (CDC file), containing all the transactions and changes in a specific time interval, or as a snapshot of the entire table at a specific point in time. The high data generation speed is achieved by exploiting multi-core processors running in large clusters using the parallelism in pseudo random numbers. PDGF uses a fully computational approach and is a pure Java implementation which makes it very portable.

At its core PDGF consists of a set of functions that maps virtual IDs to row values using hierarchically seeded random number generators. Currently, PDGF uses 8 Byte integers for seeds and random numbers.

Each table, each column of a table and each row of a table have their own deterministic seeds, seeding a corresponding random number generator with a period of $2^{64} - 1$, long enough to generate petabytes of data. The seeded random number generators are then used to compute the row values. This unique seeding approach enables PDGF to quickly generate any row value for each field of a table independently and deterministically. Even for large relational schemas with hundreds of tables, and thousands of columns per table the total number of seeds for tables and columns is manageable and can be cached in PDGF. For instance, 1000 tables with 1000 columns each requires a cache of only 7.6 Megabytes. Dependencies of columns, i.e. intra-row (e.g. ZIP->city), intra-table (e.g. surrogate key sequence) and inter-table (e.g. referential integrity) can be resolved without caching all values or re-reading previously generated data back in. We extended the seeding strategy to reflect time-related dependencies and will give further details in Section 4.1.

Since the first publication of PDGF we have added many features and replaced or extended about 80% of its code base. The result, *PDGF 2.0*, will be presented in detail in the following section.

3.1 Architectural Overview

PDGF is designed as a generic data generator for benchmarking relational database systems. It was built with the intention to enable a fast generation of non-trivial datasets as used in TPC-H [18]. As such PDGF was designed with the following four goals in mind:

- Configurability: PDGF is configurable to generate any type of schema. The description of the data schema and the generation output are described by two separate XML files.

- Extensibility: PDGF can be extended to allow for the implementation of future requirements. Nearly every aspect of PDGF is exchangeable and expandable through plugins, enabling a broad band of applications.

- Scalability: This is achieved by parallelizing data generation in threads across processor cores, processors and machines without many thread dependencies to avoid costly inter-thread communication.

- Efficiency: PDGF efficiently uses all available system resources while scaling linearly.

Figure 1 presents a high-level overview of PDGF's architecture. The controller, depicted on the left side, is the interface to the user by means of input files and a user interface (UI), which can be either a graphical user interface, an interactive shell, or a command line interface. The controller reads meta-data about the schema to be generated, i.e. table definitions, value distributions, output formats and system configurations, from two XML files and initiates the meta scheduler. The meta scheduler organizes the data generation across multiple machines. It also instantiates the scheduler that spawns multiple worker threads (by default one for each core). The scheduler divides the work and assigns equal sized, continuous portions of the data to each worker. The actual data generation is done by so called generators, which are executed in the worker threads. The workers use the seeding system to give a correctly instantiated random number generator to the data generators. These generate the actual values. To generate non-uniform data the system features various distributions that can be applied to the random numbers. If updates have to be generated, the worker use the optional update black box to retrieve the correct update ID (see section 4.6). The values are then written to the output system that writes them to files or any other target. The output system can further manipulate the data, e.g. splitting or grouping the generated data into multiple files

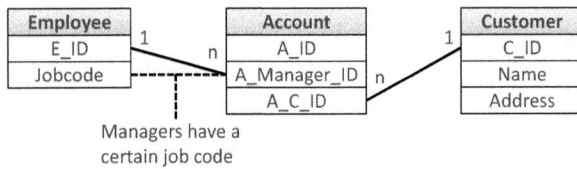

Figure 2: Example schema

and apply further formatting. As indicated, data generators and output modules can be replaced or extended by user defined plugins. The workflow of a data generation process is as follows:

- Initialization: The controller, guided by the user, loads and parses the configuration files to determine the schema and value distributions, and instantiates the schedulers.

- Partitioning: The meta scheduler determines, which data has to be generated by a particular PDGF instance. The scheduler partitions the workload further and assigns work units to worker threads,

- Data Generation: For each column the worker invokes the appropriate data generator that generates the actual value and forwards the data to the output.

- Data Output: PDGF supports many different output formats. The output system formats the generated data as specified in the configuration and writes it to the specified target, e.g. a file.

The following sections discuss our approaches to meet our design goals, i.e. configurability, extensibility, scalability, and efficiency.

3.2 Configurability

PDGF can be controlled by command line parameters, via the built-in interactive shell or through external components like a GUI. The data generation in PDGF 2.0 is controlled by two XML based configuration files: i) the *Schema XML* file and ii) the *Generation XML* file.

The schema XML file describes the schema of the data set to be generated, how values for a certain table columns should be generated, the relationship between table columns and the distributions of table values.

Listing 1 shows the schema configuration file for the schema introduced in Figure 2. It starts with the definition of three properties prop, i.e. SF, Size_Emp and SizeAcc. Support for multiple properties was added in PDGF 2.0 for an easier adaption of table sizes and in order to express non-linear growth between tables. However, properties can be deployed to parameterize the configuration. After the properties are defined the project seed is set. This seed is the *root* seed. By changing it the complete data set will change. After the seed the default random number generator is specified. It is possible to specify different random number generator implementations for different parts of the generated data. The definition of the schema follows. It defines three relations: employee, account and customer. Each relation is represented by a table tag. Within each table tag single attributes are defined using field tags. They define generators, distributions and references.

```
1  <schema name="mySchema">
2  <prop name="SF"        type="long">10</prop>
3  <prop name="Size_Emp" type="long">50</prop>
4  <prop name="Size_Acc" type="long">200*SF</prop>
5  <seed>1234567890</seed>
6  <rng name="PdgfDefaultRandom"/>
7  <table name="employee">
8   <size>SF * Size_Emp</size>
9   <field name="e_id" type="INTEGER">
10   <generator name="pdgf.generator.IdGenerator"/>
11   </field>
12   <field name="jobcode" type="INTEGER">
13    <size>20</size>
14    <generator name="pdgf.generator.PermuteJobID"/>
15   </field>
16  </table>
17  <table name="account">
18   <size>Size_Acc</size>
19   <field name="a_id" type="INTEGER">
20    <generator name="IdGenerator"/>
21   </field>
22   <field name="a_manager_id" type="INTEGER">
23    <generator name="pdgf.generator.PermuteJobID">
24     <reference>
25      <table>employee</table><field>jobcode</field>
26     </reference>
27    </generator>
28   </field>
29   <field name="a_c_id" type="INTEGER">
30    <generator name="DefaultReferenceGenerator">
31     <reference>
32      <table>customer</table><field>cust_id</field>
33     </reference>
34    </generator>
35   </field>
36  </table>
37  <table name="customer" type="update">
38   <size>SF*100</size> <!--initial table size-->
39   <newPercentage>20</newPercentage>
40   <updatePercentage>75</updatePercentage>
41   <deletePercentage>5</deletePercentage>
42   <!--size of each update batch-->
43   <UpdateSize>50 * SF</UpdateSize>
44   <updateFirstID>1</updateFirstID>
45   <updateLastID>3</updateLastID>
46   <field name="c_id" type="INTEGER">
47    <updatePercentage>0</updatePercentage>
48    <generator name="pdgf.generator.IdGenerator"/>
49   </field>
50   <field name="name" type="INTEGER">
51    <updatePercentage>0</updatePercentage>
52    <generator name="pdgf.generator.DictList">
53     <file>dicts/Given-Names.dict</file>
54    </generator>
55   </field>
56   <field name="address" type="INTEGER">
57    <updatePercentage>0.25 * 100</updatePercentage>
58    ...</field>
59  </table>
60  </schema>
```

Listing 1: Schema Configuration File

To enable the specification of complex relations between tables and virtual tables, we have added a second XML configuration file, the Generation XML file. Virtual tables are not generated, but used for referencing instead. The generation XML file defines how data structures are defined, what scheduler strategy to use, and how to perform the final processing before the generated data is either directly stored in a database, written to flat files or XML files. See Listing 2 for an example of a Generation XML file for the example of Figure 2. Flat files can be specified using a template, which is in-line Java code and compiled at runtime. For examples see Listing 2 line 9 and 20.

172

```
1  <project>
2    <scheduler name="DefaultScheduler"></scheduler>
3    <output name="CSVRowOutput">
4      <sortByRowID>true</sortByRowID>
5      <delimiter>|</delimiter><!--file field separator>
6      <outputDir>output/</outputDir>
7      <fileEnding>.txt</fileEnding>
8      <fileTemplate>table.getName() +
         fileEnding</fileTemplate>
9    </output>
10   <schema name="mySchema">
11     <table name="account">
12       <scheduler name="UpdateScheduler"/>
13       <output name="CSVRowOutput">
14            <sortByRowID>true</sortByRowID>
15       <delimiter>|</delimiter>
16       <outputDir>output/</outputDir>
17       <fileEnding>.txt</fileEnding>
18       <fileTemplate>"Batch"+(updateID+1)
19       +"/"+table.getName()+fileEnding</fileTemplate>
20       </output>
21     </table>
22   </schema>
23  </project>
```

Listing 2: Generation Configuration File

```
1   public class MyOwnGenerator extends Generator {
2    private String myOwnNodeValue;
3    boolean required=false, used=true;
4    public MyOwnGenerator() {
5     super("My first generator");
6    }
7
8    public void nextValue(AbstractPDGFRandom rng,
         GenerationContext gc,
9      FieldValueDTO fv) {
10    fv.setValue(myOwnNodeValue);
11   }
12
13   protected void initStage0_configParsers(){
14    addNodeParser(new Parser(required, used,
         "myOwnNode", this, "someDescription" ) {
15     protected void parse(Node node){
16      myOwnNodeValue=node.getTextContent();
17      if(myOwnNodeValue.isEmpty())
18       error("must not be empty!");
19    }});
20  }}
```

Listing 3: Example of Simple Generator Implementation

PDGF's template approach is very flexible. PDGF 2.0 features a *TemplateOutput* plugin, allowing the specification of the exact formating of generated information within the XML file using plain Java code. Despite the mixture of XML and Java code this approach has many benefits for the configuration file writers. They do not require a Java SDK or an integrated development environment (IDE) to be installed to create a new or adapt an output plugin. This is especially useful if PDGF is running on a server and is controlled remotely using e.g. a terminal session. Using the *TemplateOutput*, PDGFs output formating can be quickly and easily adapted by using any available text editor. During runtime the Java code is extracted from XML, compiled and loaded entirely in memory using the Javassist framework, which is itself written entirely in Java. As real bytecode is generated, there is no performance penalty using this approach instead of writing a dedicated output plugin class. The Java in XML template concept can also be applied to generators, speeding up their testing and development. However, writing a dedicated plugin class is still the preferred way of extending PDGF, as such a class can be reused and they offer better configurability and better access to PDGF's internal APIs.

Both XML files are validated by the framework on a modular basis. This means that XML subtrees are parsed directly by the modules that need the information. Plugin writers can easily extend the XML node parser for their components. An example can be seen in in Listing 3.

PDGF's internal seeding strategy, parallelization, and reference generation is encapsulated in what we refer to as a black box. The plugin API and the configuration files hide the internals and make it therefore relatively simple to write a custom plugin. While PDGF abstracts from parallelization details as much as possible for certain plugin types, some parallelization details have to be considered. This is for example the case for scheduling and output plugins since these are synchronization points within the framework.

3.3 Extensibility

Since we aimed to built a generic data generator, extensibility is a paramount design goal. Therefore, our implemen-

tation allows for all major parts of PDGF to be extended and replaced by custom plugins. For each module a corresponding superclass within the pdgf.plugin package exists. To implement a custom plugin this superclass can be extended. PDGF automatically imports all plugins that are stored in its plugin folder. Alternatively, plugins can be loaded with command line arguments and during runtime. To use a custom plugin in the schema configuration file, its fully qualified class name needs to be specified. This can be seen in Listing 1 line 10.

Every plugin is part of a parent/child(s) structure, which resembles the XML Document Object Model tree. This makes accessing and navigating the internal data structure very easy and intuitive. A properties API allows for variable assignment and simple arithmetic calculations within the XML file. This can be seen in Listing 1. PDGF supports long, double and date values, non-nested brackets and the four basic operations $\{+, -, *, /\}$. Properties can be nested as shown in Listing 1, where the value of property *Size_Acc* is dependent of property *SF* multiplied by 200.

3.4 Scalability

Traditionally the generation of synthetic data scales very nicely as long as there are no synchronization points between processes/threads. Hence, the goal for PDGF was to reduce synchronization between processes/threads to an absolute minimum. However, some synchronization is still required. The most notable synchronization points are those to shared resources like the hard disk. All synchronization critical data structures are cloned for each thread. PDGF's computational approach of data generation in general provides for a synchronization, cache and disk/network read access free way of generating data. PDGF does not rely on an underlying database management system or other caching facilities to store intermediate values or resolving data interdependencies. This allows linear scalability across processor cores and systems, as every worker thread and instance of PDGF generates its own data partition without the need of waiting for intermediate results of other parts or control communication between them. This is especially important in shared nothing architectures where the exchange of data between nodes is very expensive.

3.5 Efficiency

The same strategies that enable the scalability are responsible for the efficiency of the framework. Every complex data structure is an organization of the relations between its entities. To generate a relation, one must know the value of the related entity. With an computational approach disk and network access can be avoided by computing values. When comparing the amount of CPU cycles required e.g. for hard disk access to the amount of cycles required to (re-)calculate the value on demand in nearly all cases the (re-)calculation is much cheaper. The same is true for in memory cache structures. The costs for maintaining e.g. a LRU cache data structure outweighed its benefits of avoiding (re-)calculation. This may not be true for every data set one wishes to generated, but for most cases this is true. The only value caching strategy of PDGF is to cache the last generated value of each generator for intra tuple dependencies. PDGF's ability to utilize all available compute resources and avoiding idle times due to synchronization are providing it with an outstanding efficiency.

4. COMPUTATIONAL APPROACH TO DATA GENERATION

As long as there are no dependencies between data values, PDGF can compute each data value completely independent. Even in the presence of data dependencies there is no need to scan for values or cache referenced values, as each value can be recalculated by reseeding the random number generators. The underlying principle is a series of mapping steps. Each data value in the data set has a virtual unique key similar to an virtual address in a database system. With this key the data value can be addressed. The addressing in a table can be done the same way as in a 2 dimensional matrix, each cell can be identified with the table's columns and rows. The complete key K of a value consists of three identifiers:

$$K : (table\ ID,\ column\ ID,\ row\ ID)$$

To track changes of the values over time PDGF 2.0 uses an additional attribute, the *update ID*. The resulting key consists of four identifiers:

$$K : (table\ ID,\ column\ ID,\ update\ ID,\ row\ ID)$$

The update ID addresses an abstract time unit. If the time component is not required the update ID is always set to zero. Otherwise the range of legitimate update IDs is specified in the schema configuration file (an example can be seen in Listing 1, line 45-46). All values addressed by a key are usually derived from a random number that is generated by a permutation or a random number generator (RNG). Both, the permutation and the RNG require an initial value, i.e. a *seed*, to initialize their internal state. PDGFs data generation approach requires the permutation or random number generator to deterministically generate the random number for a given seed and key. Based on this key a value generator deterministically generates the concrete value. That means that a repeated computation of a

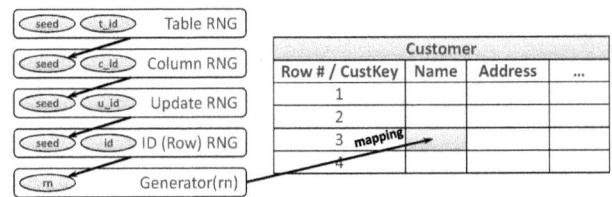

Figure 3: PDGF's Seeding Strategy

value will always lead to the same result. Since the values are derived from a random number, the RNG or permutation must always start from the same internal state, i.e. from the same seed. This assures that the generation uses the same stream of random numbers for a repeated generation of the same values. PDGF uses the following steps to deterministically generate a value for a certain key K:

1 generate a unique seed S for K, $S \rightarrow K$,

2 seed a random number generator with S

3 pass the seeded RNG to the value generator which is responsible to generate the actual value

4 the generator uses the provided RNG to generate the required amount of random numbers and calculates the concrete value

The seed is generated using the deterministic seeding strategy which will be discussed in detail in the next section. The value generator uses the generated random numbers to deterministically generate a value, a very common generator is a dictionary lookup: the line number is calculated by computing the modulo of the random number. This is also used in the example in Listing 1, line 53 (the DictList generator).

4.1 Seeding Strategy

In PDGF the mapping of a key to the corresponding seed is realized by a hierarchical seeding strategy. Basically, multiple random number generators are chained. In Figure 3 this hierarchical organization can be seen. To generate the random number of a certain field in the data set the seed for the relevant field has to be calculated. Starting from a single master seed (see listing 1 line 5) for the complete data set (project) the table RNG generates a series of seeds one for every table. Each table seed seeds a new RNG which is used to generate seeds for every column. With the column seed the update RNG is seeded which in turn seeds the row RNG. The row RNG then generates a seed for every field, which is used to seed the value generator which deterministically generates the final value.

This strategy is very efficient since most of the seeds can easily be cached. The number of tables and columns which is also the number of their seeds is usually relatively small and does not change during the generation process. Therefore, these seeds can be cached. The update ID also changes only periodically and can therefore be cached as well. Only the row changes very frequently. Since the seeds are organized hierarchically it is only necessary to retrieve the lowest cached seed. With this seed the row RNG is seeded. These operations are computationally inexpensive. With the seeded row RNG the random number that is basis for

```
void skip(long step){
        seed += step;
}

long next() {
 ++seed;
 long x = seed;
 x = x ^ (x >>> 15);           //XOR1
 x = x ^ (x << 35);            //XOR1
 x = x ^ (x >>> 4);            //XOR1
 x = 4768777513237032739L * x; //MWCG
 x = x ^ (x << 17);            //XOR2
 x = x ^ (x >>> 31);           //XOR2
 x = x ^ (x << 8);             //XOR2
 return x;
}
```

Listing 4: Counter-PRNG Hash Function

the value generation can be generated. A problem arises during reference computation. If a reference must retrieve the value from row 1000, a normal RNG had to be seeded and called 1000 times to retrieve the 1000th random number in the random number stream. This would be to costly. The problem can be solved if the RNG is capable to jump to the n-th random number in the random number stream without calculating all n-1 values before. The function to directly jump to a certain position in the random number stream is called skip ahead. The random number generator algorithm has to directly support this function.

4.2 PRNG

The deterministic generation of data relies largely on the properties of pseudo random number generators. To be more precise, a qualifying random number generator has to satisfy the following properties:

i) It must be very fast, i.e. computationally inexpensive; ii) It must be able to generate random values for all number primitives of Java; iii) It must have a sufficiently long period, to be able to generate petabytes of data; iv) It must be statistically sound in its value distribution; and v) It must support a computationally inexpensive skip ahead function.

Java's default random number generator does not satisfy these requirements because of its short period, poor distribution of values, lack of speed and most of all, the missing skip ahead functionality.

The PRNG used in PDGF generates random numbers by hashing successive counter values where a seed serves as the initial counter value. This approach makes skipping ahead an arbitrary number of values inexpensive as it is only a single add operation of two long primitives. The algorithm itself, as shown in listing 4, is a combined generator consisting of two XOR-shift-generators surrounding a multiply-with-carry-generator. The design of the algorithm was inspired by the works of Marsaglia [13] and Panneton and L'Ecuyer [16].

This above default PRNG can be exchanged with any other PRNG as long as all of the above requirements are met. In addition it is possible to specify a different PRNG for each generator.

4.3 Permutations

Pseudo random numbers are not sufficient to generate all types of complex data. Three examples of data that cannot be generated by a PRNG presented above are:

1 Streams of unique numbers in a predefined range (for example for sampling without replacement),

2 Streams of random numbers with exact distributions (for example generate 100 random values with exactly 20 times value "2" and 80 times with value "6" without a counter), and

3 Inverted random numbers, i.e. generate the position in the stream of a random number.

A PRNG is a injective mapping function, that means it maps distinct elements of its domain to distinct element of its codomain. In general and specifically in the case of our PRNG, this mapping cannot be reversed, so it is not possible to map a random number back to its seed.

Unless all generated random numbers are cached, PRNGs cannot be used for sampling without replacement. However, permutations can be used for sampling without replacement. The simplest way of generating a random permutation of values in a range [0, n] is shuffling an array containing the numbers 1 to n. This approach is time and memory consuming. The later is a big problem if billions of random numbers need to be generated. Allocating a sufficiently big array is inefficient and in some cases even impossible due to memory or programing language restrictions (in Java the maximum array size is $2^{31} - 1$. Storing long values in such an array requires 16 gigabyte). A permutation algorithm suitable to be used in a parallel data generation environment must meet the following criteria. The permutation function: i) Must be a computational approach to do the mapping, ii) Must be reasonable fast (computationally inexpensive), iii) Must be randomizeable by means of a seed, and iv) Should be bijective.

A permutation can be used in more complex ways than just for sampling without replacement if the permutation is a bijective function. Consider the following example from listing 1: An employee table E with primary key $E_{e_I D}$ contains records for all employees of a company. Employee job types are identified by a numerical field $E_{JobCode}$ within this table. An account table A has a foreign key $A_{a_{manager_i} d}$ referencing employees in E through their $E_{e_I D}$. However, only employees are referenced with a specific job type, e.g. $E_{JobCode}$=315 representing *account managers*. Using the seeding strategy described in 4.1 the $E_{JobCode}$ of an employee can be easily recomputed if the employee's $A_{a_{manager_i} d}$ is known. During the generation of data for the *Accounts* table we need to generate employee $A_{a_{manager_i} d}$ that correspond only to employees that are account managers. One approach would be to pick a random $E_{e_I D}$ and see whether this employee is an account manager. If yes, this $E_{e_I D}$ is picked. If not, a new $E_{e_I D}$ is picked. Besides being inefficient, this approach is not deterministic, especially in parallel data generation. Another approach is to cache the employee table or generate it completely every time. For large employee tables, this is either very memory intensive or a computational nightmare.

A computational solution is to use a bijective mapping function as shown in Figure 4. If the left side in Figure 4 represents the employee IDs ($E_{e_I D}$) then the right side is grouped into blocks of job codes ($E_{JobCode}$). To determine if a specific employee, identified with his ID $E_{e_I D}$ is an *account manager*, we compute the permutation for the ID in the

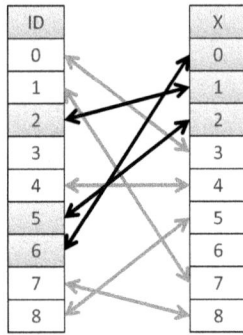

Figure 4: Bijective permutation with offset

following way:

$$X = perm(e_I D) \tag{3}$$

If the permutation result X is within a certain block e.g let the first block $[0,2]$ represent *account managers*, it is assigned the $E_{JobCode}$=315, i.e. the employee job code for account manager. In Figure 4 this is the case if X is within $[0,2]$ on the right side of the permutation. To get the $E_{e_I D}$ for a random *account manager*, we select a random number R from the block of account manages, which is between $[0,2]$ on the right side and compute the reverse permutation:

$$e_I D = inversePerm(R) \tag{4}$$

Let R be 2, then the inverse permutation for the example in Figure 4 is 5. Now we know, that the employee with employee ID ($E_{e_I D} = 5$) is an account manager. This way it is possible to pick (compute) a random employee from the set of account managers without caching, precalculating or storing any other information than the total amount of existing account managers within the employee table. In the next section we will explain how to compute a bijective permutation.

4.4 Bijective Permutation

PDGFs implementation of an bijective permutation is based on a linear permutation polynomial. It fulfills all the above required criteria. It is a special case of quadratic permutation polynomials $g(x) = ax^2 + bx + c$ for the ring $\mathbb{Z}/p^k\mathbb{Z}$, with $k = 1$. In the case $k = 1$ a must be 0 and $b \neq 0$. The linear permutation polynomial is therefore defined as $g(x) = bx + c$; $\mathbb{Z}/p\mathbb{Z}$; $b \neq 0$ and the inverse permutation as $g^{-1}(y) = (x - c) \cdot b^{-1}$, where b^{-1} is the inverse element of b in $\mathbb{Z}/p\mathbb{Z}$. This implies that $b^{-1} \cdot b \bmod p = 1$. The value for p is the number of elements in the permutation. To define different permutations polynomial we have to determine different values for b b^{-1} and c using a seed similar to a PRNG. In fact our implementation uses the seed to seed a PRNG to generate random values. For c we choose a positive random number. Obviously, p is not necessarily a prime number. If p is not prime, there might not be an inverse element for every possible b in $\mathbb{Z}/p\mathbb{Z}$. Hence, suitable values for b and b^{-1} must be found. To find a suitable b, b is chosen randomly until it satisfies the condition $b^{-1} \cdot b \bmod p = 1$. Without such a pair of b's the permutation does not work.

Once valid values are found the algorithm is very simple as can be seen in Listing 5. There are two important implementation details. First, Java's % operator is not a real modulo

```
perm(x){
 y = (x * b + c) mod p
 return y;
}

invperm(y){
 x=((y - c) * b_inv) mod p
 return x;
}
```

Listing 5: Bijective permutation

but a remainder and cannot be used. Second, the limited range of values: as PDGF is intended to generate billions of rows/ID, the multiplication of x and b using long primitive may overflow resulting in a erroneous calculation. Our implementation, therefore, tests if the values could overflow and if true uses `BigIntegers` instead of primitives supporting numbers greater than `Long.MAX_VALUE`.

4.5 Growing Offset Permutation

The simple permutations described in Section 4.3 work if the number of elements is static. However, if the number of elements varies as, for example for updates in a table, a more involved approach is needed. Consider the following variation of the example illustrated in Section 4.3: Let's assume we want to add or remove entries in the customer table from listing 1 due to common actions such as gaining new customers, removing old customers. These actions change the number of elements in the permutation which is not supported by a general permutation.

To solve this problem we have developed a permutation with flexible number of elements, i.e. a permutation with a mechanism to add and remove elements without destroying the existing permutation. We call this permutation *growing offset permutation*. The name indicates that our permutation can grow and be reduced by a certain offset. The offset concept is the same as used in Section 4.3 to identify employees which are *account managers*. We define a mapping of ID's on one side to continuous groups of offsets on the other side of the permutation. The offsets are used to determine the amount of IDs added and removed from the permutation. Basis of the growing offset permutation are multiple instances of bijective permutations. The instances are organized in a hierarchical structure as shown in Figure 5.

There are practical limitations to the depth of such a hierarchy of bijective permutations. To keep the size manageable we introduced the notion of an abstract time unit T, which we call **generation**. During every generation elements can be removed and added. If the likelihood of removing elements from the permutation is higher than the likelihood of adding elements the growing offset permutation eventually runs out of elements, i.e. we will have an empty generation against which no updates are possible. Otherwise if the likelihood of adding an element is higher the number of elements will grow. If both, adding and removing, have equal probability the size will be constant. A generation T can be seen as a snapshot containing the state of the table during the time period of length T. The period of a generations can be specified, e.g. seconds, minutes, days or years, depending on the desired granularity.

Each generation requires its own instance of a bijective

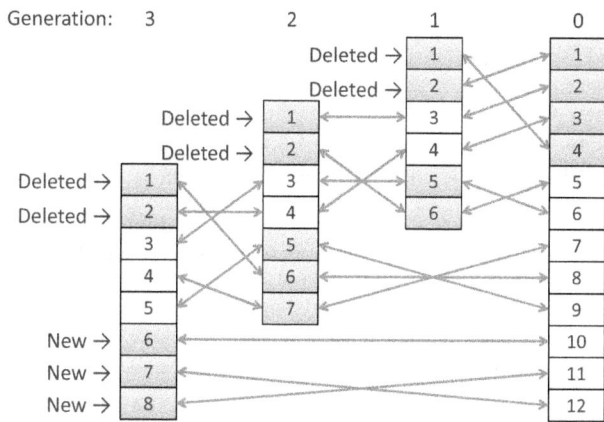

Figure 5: Growing Offset Permutation

permutation. The first generation behaves exactly as a normal permutation as depicted in Figure 4. On the right hand side the primary keys of the table can be seen, e.g. employee identifiers. In generation 0 there are four initial elements. In the first generation two elements are deleted, two are changed and two are added. For generation 1, we define three ranges Delete[1, 2], Change[3,4] and New[5,6]. The change part will be important later in Section 4.6 and will be excluded for now. All IDs selected by the permutation from left to right in the range Delete[1,2] are deleted in generation 1. In our example these are the IDs {4,1}.

The permutation for generation 2 maps to generation 1 and not directly to the ID range. It also adds an offset, as the values [1,2] in generation 1 are no longer available since they were deleted. In Figure 5 generation 2 maps $1 \rightarrow 1$ and $2 \rightarrow 4$ but two elements where removed at generation 1. To address this fact an offset is added to the mapping, the correct elements in generation 1 are: $1 \rightarrow (1 + 2) = 3$ and $2 \rightarrow (4 + 2) = 6$. To find the real values for 3 and 6 we have to use the first generation's permutation to the real ID. As result, ID 2 and 5 are determined to be deleted in generation 2. The mapping chain for generation 2 is: $1 \rightarrow 1 + 2 = 3 \rightarrow 2$ and $2 \rightarrow 4 + 2 = 6 \rightarrow 5$. For generation 3 it is $1 \rightarrow 4 + 2 = 6 \rightarrow 8$ and $2 \rightarrow 2 + 2 = 4 \rightarrow 2 + 2 = 4 \rightarrow 3$. Notice that in the chain for 1 in generation 3 we skip generation 1, as 1 in generation 3 maps to 6 in generation 2 and 6 is new in generation 2. Therefore it cannot have a mapping to generation 1 as this ID has not yet existed in generation 1. This schema guarantees that deleted ID are not picked again (e.g. for updates) and it makes it possible to grow permutations in each generation by adding an arbitrary amount of new elements.

4.6 Update Black Box

In order to encapsulate the evolution of the data over time PDGF 2.0 features an *update black box*. The update black box implements the previously described time-sliced based data evolution based on the Growing Offset Permutation. Each abstract time slice is identified by an ID, in the following called *updateID*. Consider the generation of data for a table containing *cutomers* records, e.g. *c_ID, name, address*. The attribute ID uniquely identifies a customer. There can be three different update *actions*: *new, change, delete*. New

customers are inserted into this table with a given likelihood in a *new* action. Customers are updated in a *change* action that occurs with a certain likelihood. For every *change* action one or more values in the customers tuple change, e.g the address. Obviously, not all values change always at the same time. For example the ID will never change and the name is very unlikely to change, while a fictitious field *last change* would change every time. The end of the lifecycle of a customer record is marked by *delete* action. When the record is deleted no more changes can happen to a customer record and the ID will not be reused again. The update black box models and manages the lifecycle of all IDs in one table. For an ID the cycle is: $new \rightarrow new_{0...n} \rightarrow delete$. As mentioned above, the time granularity is defined by the length of one time slice that is identified by a *update ID*. The time slice is the abstract minimum length of time and can have an arbitrary fixed-sized duration. In every time slice a given number of records - identified by their IDs - are affected by one of the three update actions. For each actions the correct number of records will be added, changed, or deleted in each cycle depending on the actions likelihood. The update black box can calculate the state of every ID for every time slice. It can therefore decide if a certain ID exists, is inserted, deleted or updated in this time slice. Furthermore, the update black box can calculate in which time slice a record was inserted, deleted or updated. This is necessary to retrieve the current state of a record.

The described update black box is integrated in PDGF 2.0 but can be exchanged/extended through plugins. Key feature of its implementation is the growing offset permutation presented before.

4.7 Generation Workflow

In this section we will give a complete overview of the data generation procedure. In an initial load phase PDGF parses the XML file, builds its internal representation, validates and initializes all modules. In the next step the scheduler selects the next table to generate. The scheduler is responsible to split the workload among the threads, e.g. in a round robin fashion. To allow for different scheduling schemes, PDGF 2.0 features a meta scheduler that enables a specific scheduler per table. The threads receive work units from the scheduler. These work units are the description of the next generation task of a thread. In the most basic example this is a table ID, the first and the last row of the data partition that the thread has to generate. Based on this information the worker constructs the key for the next field, uses the seeding strategy to obtain the seed, and seeds the generator's RNG. Then the thread requests the next value from the generator. The generator usually uses the provided RNG to calculate the value. The thread requests all values within a row from the specified generators and passes them to the responsible output system. The output system formats the row and writes it in a file. This is done for all rows in the partition. After that the thread requests the next work unit until all data is generated.

4.8 Some Performance Considerations

As mentioned in Section 3.1 scalability and efficiency are important design goals for PDGF. Hence, during the implementation of PDGF we constantly watched out for pitfalls that might cause bad performance. For example, object allocation and deallocation can be a serious bottleneck, es-

177

pecially in systems automatic garbage collection. We use reusable data transfer objects for communication between components, thereby, minimizing allocation and deallocation overhead.

One problem in parallel data generators is the generation of ordered output, as the arrival time and thus the order of generated data for individual threads is not always deterministic. Sorting or synchronizing the write operations of generated data can easily become a serious bottleneck. One approach is to block all threads that generated data that arrives too "'early"' until the right element arrives. This is very inefficient. In some cases caching can alleviate the inefficiency, because it allows fast threads to proceed and sort within the cache. PDGF features an ordering cache based on a lock free concurrent SkipListMap data structure. One is used as a value store for the generated data. A second SkipListMap is used to build a custom PriorityLock. The SkipListMap in the PriorityLock is used as a ordered wait list to put threads into sleep state when they are ahead of the current sliding window. A housekeeper thread drains the cache and notifies the thread at the head of the wait list each time an element is removed from the sorted value cache. Using this caching and locking schema we can a assure a high throughput.

5. PERFORMANCE EVALUATION

High data generation speed is of paramount importance for PDGF 2.0. The data sets that are required for TPC benchmarks can reach 100 terabytes. They are typically generated on multi-core systems and in some cases on clusters of multi-core systems. Hence, PDGF 2.0 is required to scale both up and out with various systems.

High data generation speed is particularly important if data sets are generated right before benchmark execution. This helps in implementing an ad-hoc benchmark, because only the data set characteristics (min, max values, distributions etc.) are known a-prior, but not the data itself.

We evaluate PDGF 2.0 on a 24 core enterprise level SMP server. This server has four X5670 Intel Xeon CPUs with six cores and twelve megabytes cache each. They are clocked at 2.93 GHz. The server has a total of 140 gigabytes main memory. Because we do not have access to a sufficiently fast storage array (24 cores would require about 600 MB/s write speed), we write all data to \dev\null.

We generate data for an ETL scenario, similar to the benchmark proposed by Wyatt et. al [25], which is based on the data model of TPC-E. Specifically, we generate a Trading table consisting of six columns: i) LastTradeDate, the date of last completed trading day, ii) SecuritySymbol, symbol of the security, iii) ClosingPrice, closing price of the security on LastTradeDate, iv) HighPrice, highest price for the security on LastTradeDate, v) LowPrice, lowest price for the security on LastTradeDate and vi) Volume, trading volume for the security on LastTradeDate. It models daily trading information of securities on exchanges for multiple years. The table is sorted by its first column, LastTradeDate. SecuritySymbol is a reference (foreign key) to a table holding securities. However, only references to certain securities qualify. The securities table does not need to be generated in order to choose qualifying security references. ClosingPrice and HighPrice are random numbers with a specific distribution in different ranges and LowPrice and Volume are intra-column references to ClosingPrice.

For the above table we generate the initial data and 3 update sets, each representing data for one trading day. The update sets contain two additional fields, because they represent data from a change data capture (CDC) system. The first field denotes whether the data is an insert, update or delete. The second represents a database sequence number, basically an incrementally increasing ID. The historical data set includes one record per active security per day between a start date and end date. Each incremental data sets contains one record per active security. The number of active securities depend on a scale factor. The abstract schema can be seen in the table below:

Field	Comment
CDC ID	1,2,3,... (update only)
CDC Flag	i, u, or d (update only)
Date	Sort order
Reference	To other table
Number	Real with predefined distribution
Number	Integer with predefined distribution
Reference	Intra-table reference * random number
Reference	Intra-table reference * random number

We conduct two experiments. The first tests how well PDGF scales with the number of processor cores on a given system. This is tested by generating the data sets for a ficed scale factor of 1.000.000, which results in a total data set of 18 gigabytes. Starting with a single thread we incrementally double the number of threads to a maximum of 32. Obviously, PDGF can only use as many cores as the given number of threads. Therefore, PDGF is not able to fully utilize the system with less than 24 threads. Figure 6 shows the generation time (solid line) and the throughput (dotted line) for this test. The generation speed scales nicely with the number of threads up to 8 threads. Starting with 16 threads scalability flattens out. The maximum throughput of nearly 180 MB/s is achieved with 16 threads. At 32 threads, which is 8 threads more than the number of physical cores, the throughput starts decreasing. The sublinear speedup is due to the synchronization overhead as well as the competition of generation threads with controlling threads. The update black box in PDGF 2.0 follows a producer-consumer pattern, which contains inherent synchronization points and there are several other threads that contain synchronization points. If these threads have to compete with the generation threads the overall throughput can decrease.

To get so some more insights on the synchronization overhead, we run the same test on a SPARC T3-4 server. This system has 4 T3 CPUs with 16 cores, each clocked at 1.65 GHz with a cache size of 6 MB. Each core has 8 threads resulting in a total of 512 threads, i.e. virtual processors. The system had 512 gigabytes of RAM. On this system we chose a scale factor of 100.000 resulting in 1.8 gigabytes of data. The result of this test are depicted in Figure 7. On the first impression the results are surprising. The data generation scales well up to 32 threads and then slows down dramatically. However, these results verify our previous findings. As soon as the generation threads compete with the control threads the generation speed decreases. An interesting side effect is the better performance of 512 threads. We assume that the thread scheduling works more effective if all hardware threads are utilized.

In our second experiment we generated three different data set sizes with 32 threads. We used scale factors 1.000.000,

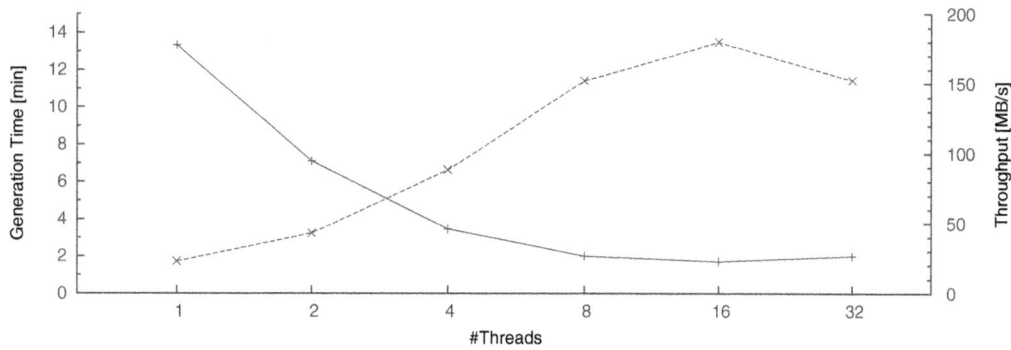

Figure 6: Generating 18 Gigabytes with Different Numbers of Threads

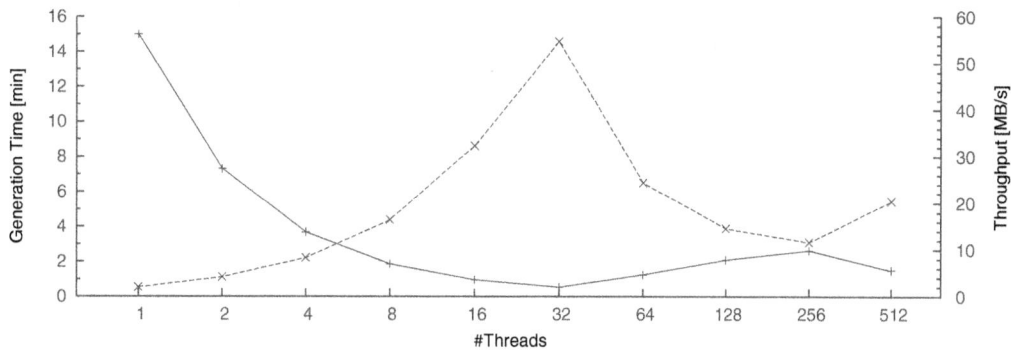

Figure 7: Generating 1.8 Gigabytes with Different Numbers of Threads

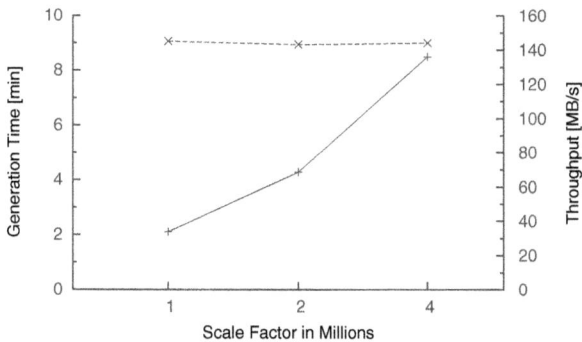

Figure 8: Generating 18-72 Gigabytes with 32 Threads

2.000.000, and 4.000.000; resulting in 18, 36, and 72 gigabytes of data. In Figure 8 the generation time (solid line) and the throughput (dotted line) can be seen for each run. The throughput is fairly constant at 144 MB/s, consequently the generation time is directly dependent to the scale factor. This indicates that it is possible to generate arbitrary large data sets without decreasing throughput. With 144 MB/s it would take less than 2 hours to generate data sets of one terabyte.

In general, these results present the good scalability of our system. For large SMP systems like our test system the synchronization overhead is reasonable, but it decreases the overall speedup at high thread counts. However, this is an example of a fairly complex relation. Most tables are less complicated to generate and will therefore have much better throughput and scalability.

6. CONCLUSIONS

In this paper we have presented our approach to data generation that makes it possible to generate consistent updates and change data captures. Our approach is based on the parallel data generation framework, PDGF, Version 1.0. The new version is PDGF 2.0. Basis of our method is the exploitation of determinism in random number generation. To generate unique references to we use invertible permutations. To generate consistent updates we have introduced the concept of a growing offset permutation which enables us to keep track of the changes in the database when we generate update, inserts and deletes. Our experiments show that the generation scales perfectly with the problem size and that we can achieve good speedups on large enterprise class server systems.

For future work we will further extend this concept to generate verifiable query workloads. For this we will generate queries using our data generator as references to the base tables. This way we will be able to pre-compute the query results and therefore also test the correctness of the system under test. For this we will combine the deterministic data generation with our workload generation concept [20].

7. ACKNOWLEDGEMENTS

The authors would like to thank Manuel Danisch for his help with the implementation of PDGF 2.0. Furthermore, we thank the anonymous reviewers for their valuable input that helped to improve the quality of the paper.

8. REFERENCES

[1] C. Bennett, R. Grossman, and J. Seidman. MalStone: A Benchmark for Data Intensive Computing. Technical report, Open Cloud Consortium, 2009.

[2] D. Bitton, D. J. DeWitt, and C. Turbyfill. Benchmarking Database Systems: A Systematic Approach. In *VLDB '83: Proceedings of the 9th International Conference on Very Large Data Bases*, pages 8–19, San Francisco, CA, USA, November 1983. ACM, Morgan Kaufmann Publishers Inc.

[3] N. Bruno and S. Chaudhuri. Flexible Database Generators. In *VLDB '05: Proceedings of the 31st International Conference on Very Large Databases*, pages 1097–1107. VLDB Endowment, 2005.

[4] Continuent. Bristlecone. https://bristlecone.svn.sourceforge.net/svnroot/-bristlecone/trunk/bristlecone/.

[5] B. F. Cooper, A. Silberstein, E. Tam, R. Ramakrishnan, and R. Sears. Benchmarking Cloud Serving Systems with YCSB. In *SoCC '10: Proceedings of the 1st ACM Symposium on Cloud Computing*, pages 143–154, New York, NY, USA, 2010. ACM.

[6] DTM Database Tools. Dtm data generator. http://www.sqledit.com/dg/.

[7] J. Gray, P. Sundaresan, S. Englert, K. Baclawski, and P. J. Weinberger. Quickly Generating Billion-Record Synthetic Databases. In *SIGMOD '94: Proceedings of the 1994 ACM SIGMOD International Conference on Management of Data*, pages 243–252, New York, NY, USA, 1994. ACM.

[8] GSApps. Gs data generator. http://www.gsapps.com/products/datagenerator/.

[9] J. E. Hoag and C. W. Thompson. A Parallel General-Purpose Synthetic Data Generator. *SIGMOD Record*, 36(1):19–24, 2007.

[10] K. Houkjær, K. Torp, and R. Wind. Simple and Realistic Data Generation. In *VLDB '06: Proceedings of the 32nd international conference on Very large data bases*, pages 1243–1246. VLDB Endowment, 2006.

[11] K. Huppler. The Art of Building a Good Benchmark. In *TPCTC '09: First TPC Technology Conference on Performance Evaluation and Benchmarking*, pages 18–30, 2009.

[12] P. J. Lin, B. Samadi, A. Cipolone, D. R. Jeske, S. Cox, C. Rendón, D. Holt, and R. Xiao. Development of a Synthetic Data Set Generator for Building and Testing Information Discovery Systems. In *ITNG '06: Proceedings of the Third International Conference on Information Technology: New Generations*, pages 707–712, Washington, DC, USA, 2006. IEEE Computer Society.

[13] G. Marsaglia. Xorshift RNGs. *Journal Of Statistical Software*, 8(14):1–6, 2003.

[14] R. O. Nambiar and M. Poess. The Making of TPC-DS. In *VLDB '06: Proceedings of the 32nd International Conference on Very Large Data Bases*, pages 1049–1058, 2006.

[15] P. E. O'Neil. The Set Query Benchmark. In J. Gray, editor, *The Benchmark Handbook for Database and Transaction Systems (2nd Edition)*. Morgan Kaufmann Publishers, 1993.

[16] F. Panneton and P. L'ecuyer. On the Xorshift Random Number Generators. *ACM Transactions on Modeling and Computer Simulation*, 15(4):346–361, 2005.

[17] M. Poess and C. Floyd. New TPC Benchmarks for Decision Support and Web Commerce. *SIGMOD Record*, 29(4):64–71, 2000.

[18] M. Poess, T. Rabl, M. Frank, and M. Danisch. A PDGF Implementation for TPC-H. In *TPCTC '11: Third TPC Technology Conference on Performance Evaluation and Benchmarking*, 2011.

[19] T. Rabl, M. Frank, H. M. Sergieh, and H. Kosch. A Data Generator for Cloud-Scale Benchmarking. In *TPCTC '10:Proceedings of the Second TPC Technology Conference on Performance Evaluation, Measurement and Characterization of Complex Systems*, pages 41–56, 2010.

[20] T. Rabl, A. Lang, T. Hackl, B. Sick, and H. Kosch. Generating Shifting Workloads to Benchmark Adaptability in Relational Database Systems. In R. O. Nambiar and M. Poess, editors, *TPCTC '09: First TPC Technology Conference on Performance Evaluation and Benchmarking*, volume 5895 of *Lecture Notes in Computer Science*, pages 116–131. Springer, 2009.

[21] T. Rabl and M. Poess. Parallel Data Generation for Performance Analysis of Large, Complex RDBMS. In *DBTest '11: Proceedings of the 4th International Workshop on Testing Database Systems*, page 5, 2011.

[22] Red Gate. Sql data generator 2.0. http://www.red-gate.com/products/sql-development/sql-data-generator/.

[23] J. M. Stephens and M. Poess. MUDD: a multi-dimensional data generator. In *WOSP '04: Proceedings of the 4th International Workshop on Software and Performance*, pages 104–109, New York, NY, USA, 2004. ACM.

[24] The Transaction Performance Processing Council. Dbgen. http://www.tpc.org/tpch/.

[25] L. Wyatt, B. Caufield, and D. Pol. Principles for an ETL Benchmark. In *TPC TC '09: First TPC Technology Conference on Performance Evaluation and Benchmarking*, pages 183–198, 2009.

Studying Hardware and Software Trade-Offs for a Real-Life Web 2.0 Workload

Stijn Polfliet   Frederick Ryckbosch   Lieven Eeckhout

ELIS Department, Ghent University
Sint-Pietersnieuwstraat 41, B-9000 Gent, Belgium
{stijn.polfliet, frederick.ryckbosch, lieven.eeckhout}@elis.UGent.be

ABSTRACT

Designing data centers for Web 2.0 social networking applications is a major challenge because of the large number of users, the large scale of the data centers, the distributed application base, and the cost sensitivity of a data center facility. Optimizing the data center for performance per dollar is far from trivial.

In this paper, we present a case study characterizing and evaluating hardware/software design choices for a real-life Web 2.0 workload. We sample the Web 2.0 workload both in space and in time to obtain a reduced workload that can be replayed, driven by input data captured from a real data center. The reduced workload captures the important services (and their interactions) and allows for evaluating how hardware choices affect end-user experience (as measured by response times).

We consider the Netlog workload, a popular and commercially deployed social networking site with a large user base, and we explore hardware trade-offs in terms of core count, clock frequency, traditional hard disks versus solid-state disks, etc., for the different servers, and we obtain several interesting insights. Further, we present two use cases illustrating how our characterization method can be used for guiding hardware purchasing decisions as well as software optimizations.

Categories and Subject Descriptors

C.0 [**Computer Systems Organization**]: Modeling of computer architecture; C.4 [**Computer Systems Organization**]: Performance of Systems—*Modeling Techniques*

General Terms

Design, Performance, Measurement, Experimentation

Keywords

Data center, Web 2.0, performance analysis

1. INTRODUCTION

Internet usage has grown by 480% over the past ten years worldwide according to a recent study by Internet World Stats[1]. This fast increase is due to various novel Internet services that are being offered, along with ubiquitous Internet access possibilities through various devices including mobile devices such as smartphones, tablets and netbooks. Online social networking in particular has been booming over the past few years, and has been attracting an increasing number of customers. Facebook, for example, has more than 800 million active users as of January 2012[2], and 50% of these users log on to Facebook at least once a day. Twitter generates 140 million tweet messages per day as of February 2011[3]. LinkedIn has more than 135 million professionals around the world as of November 2011[4]. Netlog, a social networking site where users can keep in touch with and extend their social network, is currently available in 40 languages and has more than 94 million users throughout Europe as of January 2012[5]. Clearly, social networking communities have become an important part of digital life.

Designing the servers and data centers to support social networking is challenging, for a number of reasons. As mentioned above, social networks have millions of users, which requires distributed applications running in large data centers [2]. The ensemble of servers is often referred to as a warehouse-scale computer [3] and scaling out to this large a scale clearly is a major design challenge. Because of their scale, data centers are very much cost driven — optimizing the cost per server even by only a couple tens of dollars results in substantial cost savings and proportional increases in profit. There are various factors affecting the cost of a data center, such as the hardware infrastructure (servers, racks and switches), power and cooling infrastructure, operating expenditure, and real estate. Hence, data centers are very cost-sensitive and need to be optimized for the ensemble. As a result, operators drive their data center design decisions towards a sweet spot that optimizes performance per dollar.

A key question when installing a new data center obviously is which new hardware infrastructure, i.e., which servers, to buy. This is a non-trivial question given the many constraints. On the one hand, the hardware should be a good fit for the workloads that are going to run in the data center. The workloads themselves

---

[1]http://internetworldstats.com/stats.htm
[2]http://www.facebook.com/press/info.php?statistics
[3]http://blog.kissmetrics.com/twitter-statistics/
[4]http://press.linkedin.com/about
[5]http://en.netlog.com/go/about

could be very diverse — some workloads are interactive, others are batch-style workloads and thus throughput-sensitive and not latency-critical; some workloads are memory-intensive while others are primarily compute-intensive or I/O-intensive. Hence, some compromise middle-of-the-road architecture may need to be chosen to satisfy the opposing demands; alternatively, one may opt for a heterogeneous system where different workloads run on different types of hardware. Further, one needs to anticipate what new workloads might emerge in the coming years, and how existing workloads are likely to evolve over time. On the other hand, given how cost-sensitive a data center is, it is of utmost importance that the correct hardware is purchased for the correct task. High-end hardware is expensive and consumes significant amounts of power, which leads to a substantial total cost of ownership. This may be the correct choice if the workloads need this high level of performance. If not, less expensive and less power-hungry hardware may be a much better choice.

It is exactly this purchasing question that motivated this work: Can we come up with a way of guiding service operators and owners of data centers to what hardware to purchase for a given workload? Although this might be a simple question to answer when considering a single workload that runs on a single server, answering this question is quite complicated when it comes to a Web 2.0 social networking workload. A social networking workload consists of multiple services that run on multiple servers in a distributed way in a data center, e.g., Web servers, database servers, memcached servers, etc. The fundamental difficulty that a Web 2.0 workload imposes is that the performance of the ensemble can only be measured by modeling and evaluating the ensemble, because of the complex interplay between the various servers and services. In other words, performance as perceived by the end-user, i.e., the response times observed by the end user, is a result of the performance of the individual servers as well as the overall interaction among the servers. Put differently, optimizing the performance of an individual server may not necessarily be beneficial for the ensemble and may not necessarily have impact on end-user experience, nor may it have impact on the total cost of ownership.

In this paper, we present a case study in which we characterize a real-life Web 2.0 workload and evaluate hardware and software design choices. We sample the Web 2.0 workload both in space and in time to obtain a reduced workload that can be replayed, driven by real input data. The reduced workload captures the important services (and their interactions) and allows for evaluating how hardware choices affect end-user experience.

We consider Netlog's commercially used Web 2.0 social networking workload, and we evaluate how hardware design choices such as number of cores, CPU clock frequency, hard-disk drive (HDD) versus solid-state drive (SSD), etc. affect overall end-user perceived performance. We conclude that the number of cores per node is not important for the Web servers in our workload, hence the hardware choice should be driven by cost per core; further, we find that the end-user response time is inversely proportional to Web server CPU frequency. SSDs reduce the longest response times by around 30% over HDDs in the database servers, which may or may not be justifiable given the significantly higher cost for SSD compared to HDD. Finally, the memcached servers show low levels of CPU utilization while being memory-bound, hence the

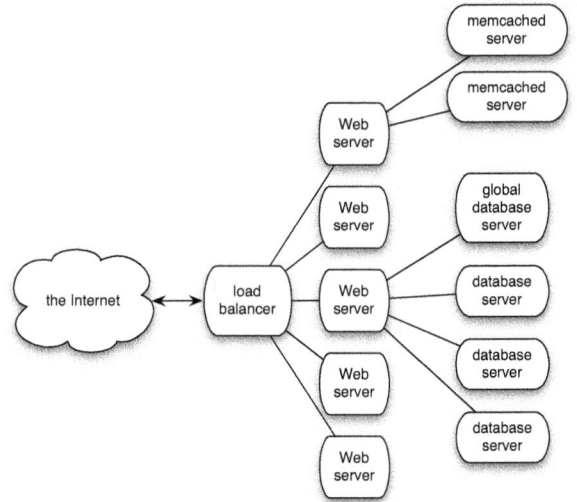

Figure 1: Netlog's architecture.

hardware choice should be driven by the cost of integrating more main memory in the server.

We believe that this approach is not only useful to service providers and data center owners, but also to architects, system builders, and integrators to understand Web 2.0 workloads and how hardware choices affect user-perceived performance, server throughput, and utilization. Further, software developers and data center system administrators may find the approach useful to identify and solve performance bottlenecks in the software and experiment with alternative software implementations. To demonstrate the potential usage of the characterization, we present two uses cases illustrating how it can be leveraged for guiding hardware purchasing decisions and software optimizations.

This paper is organized as follows. We first describe the Web 2.0 workload used in this study (Section 2). We then set the goals for this paper (Section 3) and describe our methodology in more detail (Section 4). We detail our experimental setup (Section 5) and then present our results (Section 6). We focus on two important use cases for this work (Section 7). Finally, we discuss related work (Section 8) and conclude (Section 9).

2. NETLOG WEB 2.0 WORKLOAD

As mentioned in the introduction, we use Netlog's software infrastructure as a representative Web 2.0 workload. Netlog hosts a social networking site that is targeted at bringing people together. As of January 2012, Netlog is currently available in 40 languages and has more than 94 million members throughout Europe. According to ComScore[6], Netlog is the pageview market leader in Belgium, Italy, Austria, Switserland, Romania and Turkey; and it is the second market leader in the Netherlands, Germany, France and Portugal. Netlog has around 100 million viewers per month, leading to over two billion pageviews per month. Netlog users can chat with other friends, share pictures, write blog entries, watch movies and listen to music.

Netlog's architecture is illustrated in Figure 1. A load balancer

---

[6]http://www.comscore.com/

distributes the incoming requests among the Web servers. The Web servers process the requests and assemble a response by fetching recently accessed data from the memcached servers. If the requested data is not present in one of the memcached servers, the Web server communicates with one of the database servers. There is one global database that holds general information with user data (like nickname and passwords). All other user data is spread among multiple database servers using a technique called 'sharding'[7]. Each of the servers run on a physical machine. The relative fraction of servers is as follows: 54% of Netlog's servers are Web servers, 16% are memcached servers and 30% are database servers. The Netlog data center hosts more than 1,500 servers.

Netlog's data center is partitioned among the languages that it supports, i.e., servers are devoted to one particular language. The largest language is Dutch, followed by German, Italian, Arabic, English, and others. Interestingly, usage patterns are similar across languages, hence, the same relative occurrence of Web, caching and database servers is maintained across all the languages.

In terms of software, the Web servers run the Apache HTTP server[8]; the caching servers run Memcached[9]; and the database servers run MySQL[10]. For more information, please refer to Section 5.

3. CASE STUDY GOALS

Before describing our case study in great detail, we first need to set out its goals. First, we want to be able to characterize and evaluate end-user perceived performance of a Web 2.0 system. This implies that a representative part of the workload needs to be duplicated in the experimental environment which enables evaluating overall end-to-end performance. This in turn implies that a set of machines needs to be engaged with each machine running part of the workload — some run Web servers, some run database servers, others run memcached servers. Collectively, this set of machines runs the entire workload. This experimental environment, when supplied with real user requests, will act like a real data center running the real workload. This enables measuring user-perceived response times as well as server-side throughput and utilization.

Second, the experimental environment by itself will not provide useful measurement data. It also needs a method to feed real-life user requests into the experimental environment. In other words, real user requests need to be captured and recorded in a real data center and then need to be replayed in our experimental environment. This will enable us to measure how design choices in the hardware and the software affect user-perceived performance as well as server throughput and utilization.

Third, in addition to being able to faithfully replay real-life user requests, it is useful to be able to stress the setup through experiments in which user requests are submitted at a fixed rate. This allows for gaining insight into the system's limits and how the system

will react in case of high loads. For example, it allows for learning about how user-perceived response time is affected by server load. Or, it allows for understanding the maximum allowable server load before seeing degradations in user response times.

Finally, we need the ability to run reproducible experiments, or in other words, we want to draw similar performance figures when running the same experiment multiple times. This allow us to measure how changes in system configuration parameters affect performance. In the end, we want to use the experimental environment and change both hardware and software settings to understand how hardware and software design choices affect user-perceived performance as well as server-level throughput and utilization. This not only enables service providers and data center owners to purchase, provision and configure their hardware and software, it also enables architects, system builders and integrators, software developers, etc. where to focus when optimizing overall system performance.

4. METHODOLOGY

Our methodology has a number of important features in order to make the experimental environment both efficient and effective for carrying out our case study.

- **Sampling in space.** It is obviously prohibitively costly to duplicate an entire Web 2.0 workload with possibly hundreds, if not thousands, of servers in the experimental environment. We therefore sample the workload in space and we select a reduced but representative portion of the workload as the basis for the experimental framework. For the Netlog workload, we select one language out of the many languages that Netlog's workload supports; this language is representative for the other languages and for the Netlog workload at large. Sampling in space allows us to evaluate a commercial Web 2.0 workload with hundreds of servers in real operation with only 10 servers in our experimental environment.

- **Sampling in time.** Replaying a Web 2.0 workload using real-life user input, as we will describe next, can be very time-consuming, especially if one wants to replay multiple days of real-life operation in the data center. Moreover, in order to understand performance trends across hardware and software design changes, one may need to explore many configurations and hence run the workload multiple times. This may make the experimental setup impractical to use. Hence, we analyze the time-varying behavior of the workload and we identify representative phases in the execution, which we sample from, and which we can accurately extrapolate performance numbers to the entire workload. Sampling in time allows to analyze only a few hours of real time while being representative for a workload that runs for days.

- **Workload warm-up.** Sampling in time implies that we evaluate only a small fraction of the total run time. A potential pitfall with this approach is that system state might be very different when replaying under sampling than if one were to replay a workload for days of execution. This is referred to as the cold-start problem. In other words, the system needs to be warmed up when employing sampling in time

---

[7]Sharding is a horizontal partitioning database design principle whereby rows of a database table are held separately, rather than splitting by columns. Each partition forms part of a shard, which may in turn be located on a separate database server or physical location.

[8]http://httpd.apache.org/

[9]http://memcached.org/

[10]http://www.mysql.com/

so that the performance characteristics during the evaluation are representative for as if we were to run the entire workload. Our methodology uses a statistics-based approach to gauge whether the system is warmed up sufficiently.

- **Replaying empirical user request streams.** As mentioned before, we capture and replay real-life user requests. The user request file that we store on disk and that we use as input to the experimental environment contains sufficient information for faithfully replaying real-life users requests. In other words, the input served to the load balancer of the Netlog workload is identical under replay as when we captured it during real-life operation.

We now discuss the various steps of our methodology in more detail.

4.1 Sampling in space

As part of this study we duplicated Netlog's workload. Because it is infeasible to duplicate Netlog's entire workload, we chose to duplicate a small part only, namely the part associated with the Slovene language. This is feasible to do, and leads to a representative workload. Netlog organizes its servers such that there are a number of physical servers per language domain. Hence, by selecting a language domain and by only duplicating that language domain, we sample in space while being representative for the entire workload. The Slovene part is representative for Netlog's entire workload because it exhibits the same partitioning of servers as the rest of Netlog's workload. Also, we observe similar degree of activity and access behavior (access to profiles, photos, videos, etc.) for the Slovene language as for the other languages.

Duplicating the Slovene language part of Netlog's workload can be done with a reasonable number of servers. Our setup includes 6 Web servers, 1 memcached server and 2 database servers; this distribution across server types is identical to what is observed for the entire Netlog workload, across all the languages. Further, our setup includes the entire Slovene database and all of its records. The data present in our duplicate copy is anonymized. This is done through hashing while maintaining the length of the records.

4.2 Validating the setup

Duplicating a Web 2.0 workload is a significant effort and involves fine-tuning various software settings and configurations that necessitates proper validation. We validated our experimental framework both functionally and with respect to behavior and timing. In particular, we automatically verified whether the file sizes returned by the duplicated workload match the file sizes observed in the real workload. The reason for doing so is that some of the Web pages returned by the Web 2.0 workload are composed semi-randomly, and hence its content may not be perfectly identical when requesting the same page multiple times. In our experimental environment, we found that 99.3% of the responses fall within a 5% error bound with respect to file size compared to the real workload environment, as shown in Figure 2.

4.3 Replaying user requests

An important aspect of the experimental environment is the replay of user requests. In order to do so, we collect user requests

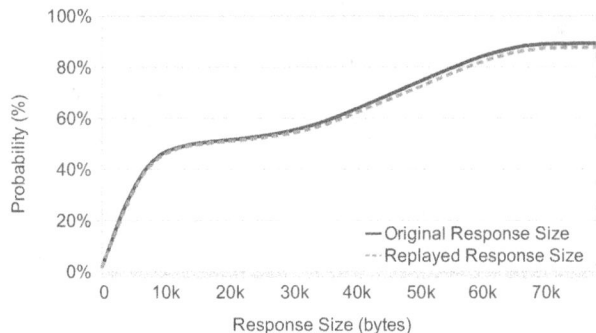

Figure 2: Distribution of response sizes when comparing real versus replayed requests.

as observed at the load balancer. The information collected by the user input recorder consists of the following items — recall that the data is anonymized:

- **Header information.** All HTTP header information is recorded so the same request can be reconstructed. This includes the requested URL, browser information, supported encoding formats, etc.

- **Timing information.** The date and time the request was submitted is recorded (at microsecond resolution). This allows for maintaining precise timing information when replaying the user request file. This is important to model bursty behavior in user requests.

- **User data.** The input recorder captures all POST data that is sent to the Web servers. Note that GET data is already captured as part of the URL in the header. All HTTP cookies are saved as well, and are used to do automated login.

The file that contains these user requests is fairly large and contains 24 GB of data per day on average. Our user input recorder uses `tcpdump`[11] to log the network traffic to a file in `pcap`[12] format. `pcap` defines an API for capturing network traffic. On Linux/Unix systems, this is implemented in the `libpcap` library which most network tools like tcpdump, Wireshark, etc. implement. A limitation of `tcpdump/pcap` is that it may drop packets; however, packet loss rate was less than 0.002% for a 1 Gbps network in our setup.

The replayer reads the user request file and replays the requests one by one. This means that the replayer picks the first request, sends the request to the Web 2.0 workload at the time specified in the request file. It then picks the next request and sends it at its time, etc. The replayer does not wait for the response to come back to determine the next request; all the requests are available in the user request file.

Implementing the user request replayer is a challenge in itself. The reason is that the user request file is huge in size, and the requests need to be submitted to the workload at a fine time granularity. Reading the request file from disk, and submitting requests in real-time is too slow. On the other hand, it is impractical to store

---

[11]http://www.tcpdump.org/
[12]http://www.winpcap.org/ntar/draft/PCAP-DumpFileFormat.html

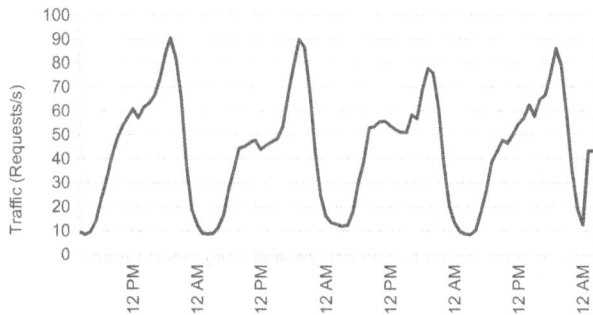

Figure 3: Netlog traffic profile for four days to the Slovene language domain.

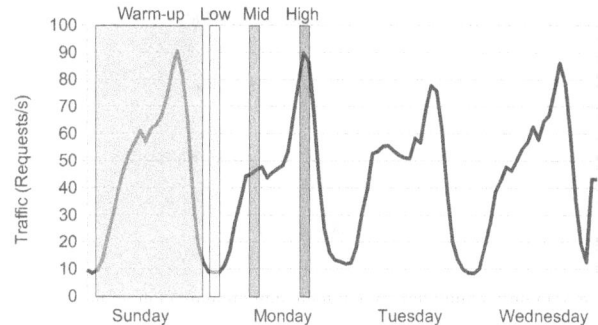

Figure 4: Identifying representative samples based on traffic intensity.

the entire request file in main memory. We therefore developed a two-thread replayer. The first thread reads the `pcap` file and fills in the requests in the request pool in memory. The second thread then reads from the request pool and submits the requests to the workload using `libcurl`[13], which is a client-side URL transfer library that supports sending requests using the HTTP protocol to a remote Web server.

4.4 Sampling in time

We recorded four days (March 13–16, 2011) of user activity to the Slovene language domain of the Netlog workload. This was done by capturing all the user requests (and their timing) at the load balancer. Replaying these four days of activity in real time would require four days of experimentation time. Although this is doable if one were to evaluate a single design point, exploring trade-offs by varying hardware and/or software parameters, quickly leads to impractically long experimentation times. We therefore employ sampling in time to evaluate only parts of the workload activity while being representative for the entire workload.

Figure 3 shows traffic over a four day period in number of requests per second. Clearly, we observe cyclic behavior in which there is much more activity in the evening than during the day. Traffic increases steeply in the morning between 6am and 9am, and remains somewhat stable or increases more slowly between 9 am and 5pm. Once past 5pm, traffic increases steeply until 8pm. We observe a sharp decrease in the number of requests past 9pm. This traffic pattern suggests that sampling in time is a sensible idea, i.e., by picking samples that represent different traffic patterns, one can significantly reduce the load that needs to be replayed, which will lead to significant improvements in experimentation speed, while reproducing a representative workload.

We set ourselves a number of goals for how to sample in time. We want the samples to be representative in a number of ways: we want the samples to represent diverse traffic intensity as well as the sort of activity that the samples cover, i.e., as mentioned before, Netlog offers various sorts of services ranging from chatting to watching videos, etc., hence the samples should cover these different types of activity well. Further, we prefer having a few long representative samples over having many small samples. The reason is that small samples require more precise warmup of the system than longer samples in order to be accurate.

We therefore employ the following two-step sampling proce-

---

[13]http://curl.haxx.se/

dure. We first aim at finding a number of time periods with different traffic intensity. We employ k-means clustering as our classification method [5]. The input to the clustering algorithm is a time series representing the number of requests per minute. The clustering algorithm then aims at classifying this time series in a number of clusters N. It initially picks N cluster centroids in a random fashion, and assigns all data elements in the time series to its closest cluster. In the next iteration, the algorithm recomputes the cluster centroid, and subsequently reassigns all data elements to clusters. This iterative process is repeated until convergence, or until a maximum number of iterations is done. An important question is how many clusters N should one pick. We use the Bayesian Information Criterion (BIC) [9], which is a measure for how well the clustering matches the data. Using a maximum value of $N_{max} = 6$ — recall we aim for a limited number of samples — we obtain the result that $N = 3$ yields the optimum BIC score. Hence, we obtain three samples. These are shown in Figure 4. Intuitively, these three samples correspond to low-intensity, medium-intensity and high-intensity traffic, respectively.

The next question is how long the samples should be in these low, medium and high-intensity traffic regions. We therefore rely on our second requirement: we want the samples to cover diverse behavior in terms of the type of traffic. We identify 30 major types of traffic including messages, photos, videos, friends, music, etc. This yields a 30-dimensional time series: each data element in the time series consists of 30 values, namely the number of requests per minute for each type of traffic. We then apply k-means clustering on this 30-dimensional time series which yields the optimum number of four clusters using the BIC score. These four clusters represent the predominant traffic rates observed at a given point in time. Figure 5 illustrates how the time series of ten hours of the second day is distributed across these four clusters. Interestingly, some traffic rates are more predominant during some periods of time, and traffic rate predominance varies fairly quickly. However, if we take a long enough snapshot, e.g., two hours, the sample contains all traffic rates. The end result for sampling in time, thus is that we pick three samples of two hours of activity from the low, medium and high-intensity regions.

4.5 Warmup

With sampling in time, an important issue is how to start from a warmed-up system state so that the performance numbers that we obtain from our experiments are representative for the real work-

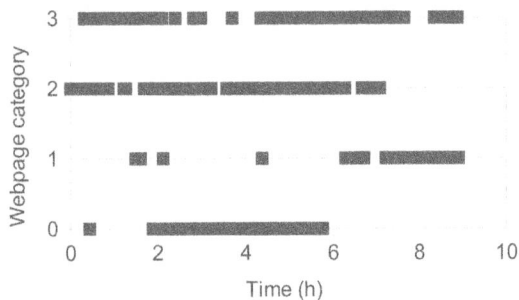

Figure 5: Traffic classified by its type.

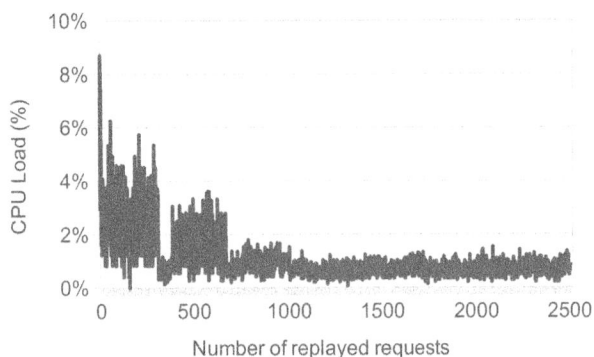

Figure 6: Quantifying PHP cache warmup behavior. Replay speed is set to a fixed rate of 10 requests/s.

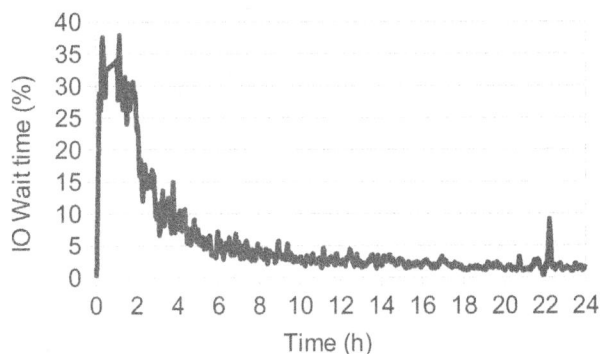

Figure 7: Quantifying how long one needs to warmup the database and memcached servers: I/O wait time on the database server is shown as a function of time when replaying the first day.

load. Clearly, starting from a cold state is not going to be accurate because the performance of the workload will be very different from what one would observe in a real (and warmed-up) environment. Warmup of a Web 2.0 workload involves a number of issues. First, as mentioned before, the Web servers run PHP code, and hence they rely on an opcode cache that caches the bytecodes; the PHP engine does not need to interpret cached bytecodes again, and hence it achieves better performance. This implies that the performance of the PHP engine is relatively low initially, but then improves gradually as more and more code gets cached and optimized; this is obviously reflected in the Web server response times observed by the end user. In other words, in the context of this work, it is important that we measure the performance of the PHP engine in steady-state modus, in which it executes highly optimized code as opposed to interpreting the PHP code. As shown in Figure 6, the CPU load is higher when the PHP engine is first initialized. In this stage, the PHP engine still has to compile all PHP code. After 1,000 requests most PHP pages are compiled and loaded into the cache, hence, we conclude that the PHP cache is warmed up in the order of a couple seconds.

Second, and more importantly, we also need to warm up the memcached and database servers. Initially, in a cold system, all the requests will go to the database server because the memcached server does not cache any data yet; further, the database server will need to read from disk to access the database. Hence, we will observe a significant fraction of time spent waiting for I/O both over the network and for accessing disks. Indeed, gigabytes of data need to be read in the database and transferred from the database servers to a memcached server. This requires a large number of user re-

quests being sent to the system to warmup the database and memcached servers. Figure 7 illustrates the fraction I/O wait time on the database server starting from a cold state as a function of time. We observe that the fraction I/O wait time, which is proportional to how often one needs to access the database on disk and transfer data to the memcached server, decreases as a function of time. Although there is a steep decrease in I/O wait time in the first few hours, it takes close to an entire day before I/O wait time drops below a few percent which represents a fully warmed up system.

In order to get more confidence in this finding we employ the Kolmogorov-Smirnov statistical test to verify whether the system is sufficiently warmed up. The Kolmogorov-Smirnov test is a non-parametric test for the equality of continuous, one-dimensional probability distributions. It basically measures whether two distributions are equal or not; the exact form of the distribution is not important, hence it is labeled a non-parametric test. In this work, we compare the distribution of user response times starting from a cold versus a warmed-up system. This is done in steps of 5,000 user requests, see Figure 8. The P-value reported by the Kolmogorov-Smirnov test gives an estimate for how good the correspondence is between starting from no-warmup versus a fully warmed up system; the P-value is a higher-is-better metric. We observe that the P-value saturates after approximately six hours of warmup, and reaches its highest score after 18 to 20 hours of warmup. Based on these observations we decided to warm up our experimental system with one full day of load.

Note that, in our experimental environment, it does not take a full day to actually warmup the entire system. During warmup, we quickly submit an entire day's user requests to the Netlog workload, as fast as possible. This takes approximately two hours in our setup. Once the system is warmed up, we then submit user requests for the sample of interest at the time stamps as stored in the user request file, as explained before.

5. EXPERIMENTAL SETUP

As mentioned before, we duplicated the Slovene language domain of the Netlog workload to our experimental environment. Our infrastructure consists of 10 dual AMD Opteron 6168 servers, with each server having 24 cores in total or 12 cores per CPU. Each

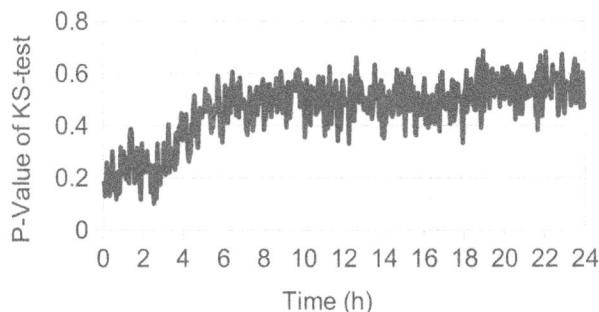

Figure 8: Using the Kolmogorov-Smirnov test to verify whether the system is sufficiently warmed up by comparing the distribution of response times under full versus no warmup.

server has at least 64 GB of main memory, and is equipped with both a regular HDD (1 TB Seagate SATA 7200 rpm) as well as an SSD (128 GB ATP Velocity MII). We configure the machines as 6 Web servers, 1 memcached server, and 2 database servers. The tenth server is used to generate workload traffic and inject user requests to the system under test.

Our baseline configuration runs all the cores at 1.9 GHz. We provision the Web servers as well as the database servers with 64 GB of main memory. The memcached server is equipped with 128 GB of RAM. Further, we assume a HDD drive in each of the servers — we consider SSD in the database servers in one of the experiments.

Our infrastructure uses Ubuntu 10.04[14]. The Web server is configured with Apache 2.2[15] and runs PHP 5.2[16]. The database software used is a MySQL derivative, Percona 5.1. We use the standard Memcached 1.4.2[17] version as our caching mechanism.

6. RESULTS AND DISCUSSION

Using our experimental environment, we now focus on gaining insights in how hardware trade-offs affect user-perceived performance (response times) for the end-to-end workload. We first consider user requests submitted at the rate as measured in the real-life workload, and we look at hardware trade-offs for the Web server, memcached server and database server, respectively. Subsequently, we consider fixed-rate experiments in order to stress the system.

6.1 Web server

We evaluate two hardware trade-offs for the Web server, namely CPU clock frequency and the number of cores per node. Figure 9 shows the distribution of the user response times while changing the Web server's CPU frequency in three steps: 1.9 GHz, 1.3 GHz and 800 MHz. The distribution of response times is skewed, i.e., there is a peak in the response time distribution around 0.04 seconds at 1.9 GHz, and the distribution has a fairly long and heavy tail for longer response times. We observe similarly skewed distributions at lower CPU clock frequencies, yet the distributions shift towards the right with decreasing frequencies, i.e., user response time increases with lower clock frequencies. This is perhaps intuitive, as

---

[14]http://www.ubuntu.com

[15]http://www.apache.org/

[16]http://www.php.net

[17]http://www.memcached.org/

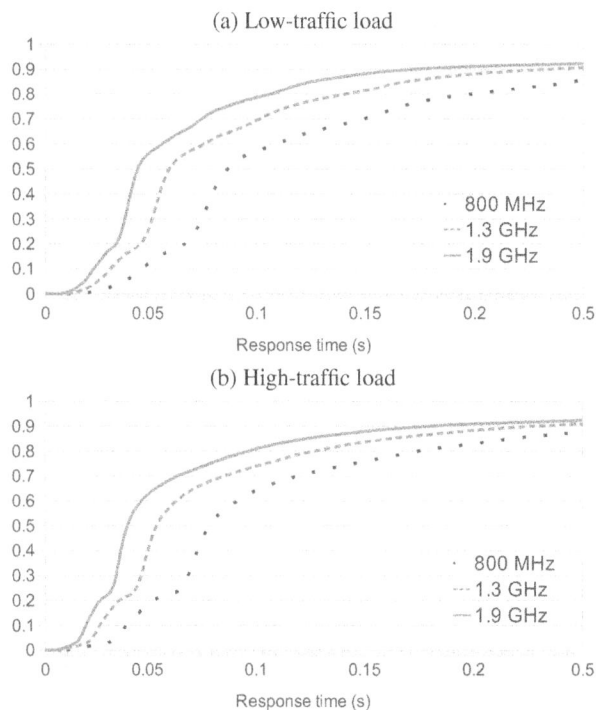

Figure 9: Distribution of user response times while changing the Web server's CPU frequency under (a) low-traffic load and (b) high-traffic load.

the CPU gets more work done per unit of time at higher clock frequencies. It is interesting to observe though that Web server clock frequency has a significant impact on user response times (even at low CPU loads, as we will see next). In conclusion, user response time is sensitive to Web server clock frequency. Hence, the Web server should have a sufficiently high clock frequency in order not to exceed particular bounds on user response time.

An important point of concern in provisioning servers for a Web 2.0 workload is to have sufficient leeway to accommodate bursty traffic behavior and sudden high peaks of load. For gauging the amount of leeway on a server, we use CPU load. If the CPU load is sufficiently low, this means that the server can accommodate additional work. Figure 10 quantifies Web server CPU load as a function of clock frequency. Clearly, CPU load increases with lower CPU frequencies.

As alluded to before, the response time distribution has a fairly long and heavy tail. A heavy-tailed response time distribution is a significant issue in Web 2.0 workloads because it implies that some users are experiencing an unusually long response time. Given the large number of concurrent users of Web 2.0 workloads, and although the number is small in terms of percentages, still a significant number of users will be experiencing very long response times. Very long and unpredictable response times quickly irritate end users, which may have a significant impact on company revenue if users sign off because of the slow response times. Because of this, companies such as Google and others heavily focus on the 99% percentile of the user response times when optimizing overall system performance. Figure 11 shows the percentile response times as a function of Web server CPU clock frequency. For exam-

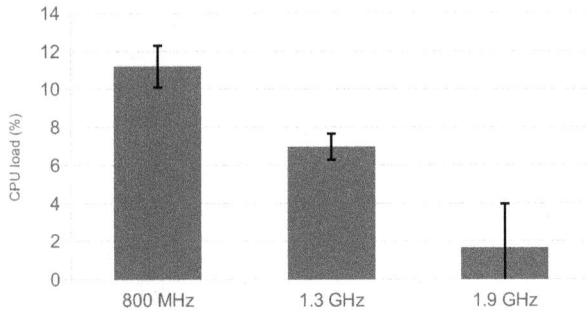

Figure 10: Web server CPU load as a function of CPU clock frequency for the high-traffic load scenario.

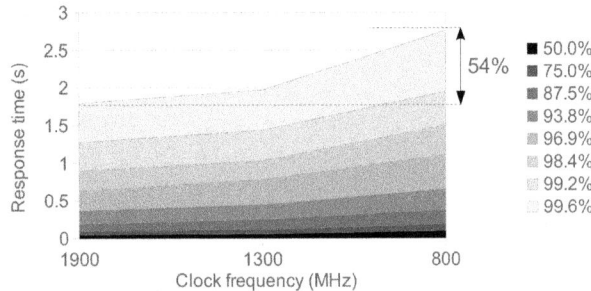

Figure 11: Percentile response times as a function of Web server CPU clock frequency.

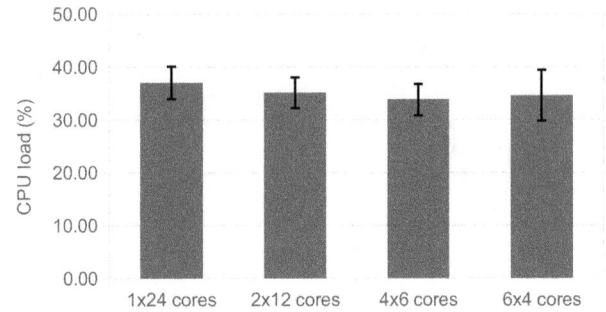

Figure 12: Web server CPU load as a function of the number of nodes and cores per node: $m \times n$ means m nodes and n cores per node.

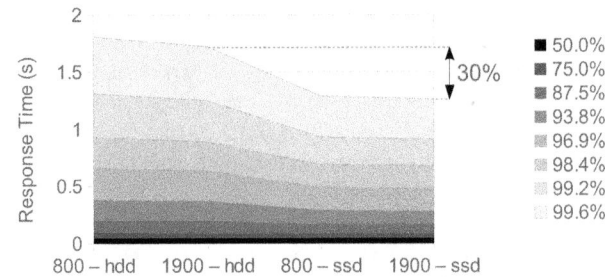

Figure 13: Trading off HDD versus SSD and CPU clock frequency for the database servers.

ple, this graph shows that, see the top left, 99.6% of the response times are below 1.8 seconds at 1.9GHz. The 99.6% percentile goes up to 2.8 seconds at 800MHz, see the top right. The interesting observation is that long-latency response times increase sub-linearly with decreasing Web server clock frequency. The 99.6% percentile response time increases by 54% only, while decreasing clock frequency from 1.9GHz to 800MHz, or increasing cycle time by 138% from 0.53ns to 1.25ns.

The second hardware trade-off that we study relates to the number of cores per node one should have for the Web server. The reason why this is an interesting trade-off is that systems with more sockets per node are more expensive, i.e., a four-socket system is typically more than twice as expensive as a two-socket system. Similarly, the number of cores per CPU also directly relates to cost. Figure 12 quantifies Web server CPU load as a function of the number of nodes and the number of cores per node. (Recall that CPU load is a good proxy for user response time as observed.) We vary from one Web server node with 24 cores enabled, to 2 nodes and 12 cores each, to 4 nodes and 6 cores each, to 6 nodes and 4 cores each. Clearly, CPU load (and response time) is not affected much by node and core count (as long as the total number of cores is constant). This suggests that the Web server is a workload that scales well with core count, even across nodes. In conclusion, when purchasing Web server hardware, although total core count is important, core count per node is not. This is an important insight to take into account when determining how many servers to buy with how many cores each. Determining the best buy (number of servers and number of cores per server) depends on many factors such as performance, power cost, real estate cost, reliability, availability, etc.,

however, this case study shows that the number of cores per server is a parameter one can tweak to optimize Web server performance per dollar.

6.2 Database server

As mentioned before, the database servers generate substantial disk I/O activity. We therefore focus on a hardware trade-off that involves HDDs versus SSDs in the database servers. We also vary CPU clock frequency. Figure 13 quantifies the percentile response times for the four hardware design points that result from changing clock frequency and hard drives. We observe that, while short response times are not greatly affected by replacing the HDD with an SSD, the 99.6% percentile response time decreases by 30% when trading an HDD for an SSD. Although this is a significant reduction in the longest response times observed, it may not justify the significantly higher cost of SSD versus HDD.

6.3 Memcached server

The memcached server has a very low typical CPU load, and is primarily memory and network-bound. The average CPU load for the memcached server is typically below 5% when stressed with 6 Web servers. Figure 14 shows CPU time versus network time for a memcached experiment in which we generate memcached GET requests of varying size, more specifically, the responses of the GET requests are of varying size. This clearly shows that memcached performance is mainly determined by the network. Hence, CPU performance for the memcached servers is not critical, and one could for example deploy relatively inexpensive servers. It is

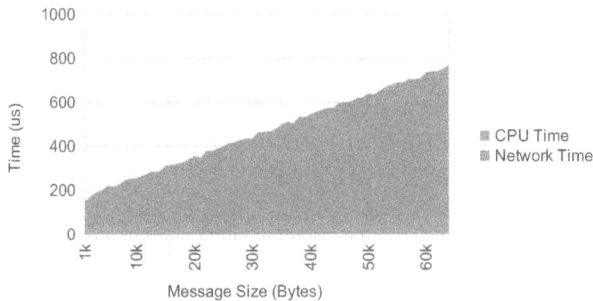

Figure 14: CPU time versus network time for memcached requests of different size.

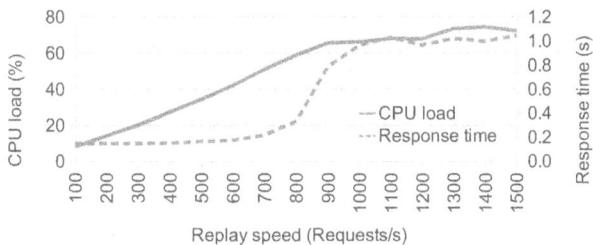

Figure 15: CPU load and average response time as a function of the number of requests per second under a fixed-rate experiment.

important for the memcached servers to have sufficient amount of memory though.

6.4 Fixed-rate experiments

The experiments done so far involved replaying the user requests as recorded in the real-life workload, i.e., the requests are submitted at a rate determined by the users. We now consider experiments in which we submit requests at a fixed rate. The reason for doing so is to stress the system under high levels of request rates in order to understand how CPU load and user response times are affected by the load imposed on the entire workload. Figure 15 quantifies CPU load of the Web servers (left axis) and the average response time (right axis) as a function of the number of requests per second submitted to the system. Interestingly, the response time remains low and CPU load increases linearly with request rate, up until a request rate of 700 requests per second. Beyond 800 requests per second, CPU load saturates around 65 to 75 percent, and response time increases substantially from 0.2 seconds to approximately 1 second. The reason why response time saturates beyond 1,000 requests per second is that requests get dropped once the Web server's CPU load gets too high as it runs out of resources and is unable to process all incoming requests. Note that handling a request is more than just generating static content: every Web server request typically initiates several memcached and database requests.

7. USE CASES

The approach we have followed can be applied to numerous use cases. For example, data center owners and service providers can use the approach to guide purchasing decisions. Similarly, system architects, integrators and implementors can use the approach to gain insight in how fundamental design decisions of the data center

architecture affect user perceived performance. Finally, software architects and system administrators can use the approach to drive software design decisions, identify and address performance bottlenecks and evaluate alternative software implementations.

In this section, we present two use cases to illustrate the potential of the approach for making hardware and software design choices.

7.1 Hardware purchasing

The first use case that we present relates to hardware design choices, and more specifically to data center owners and service providers who wish to understand which hardware to purchase for a given workload. As mentioned earlier, this is a challenging question because of the many constraints one needs to deal with, ranging from purchasing cost, energy/power cost, cooling cost, performance, throughput, density, etc. In this use case, we look at two of the most important factors, namely performance and purchasing cost, for guiding the purchasing decisions. We also consider the implications on a third factor, namely power consumption.

Data center owners and service providers who wish to upgrade their hardware infrastructure face a challenging problem, and their decisions are mostly guided by experience and advice given by the hardware vendor(s). We now describe a scenario in which a hardware vendor would make a recommendation on which hardware to purchase. This scenario is hypothetical — we did not actually ask a hardware vendor for making a suggestion for a specific configuration for the given Web 2.0 workload. However, the suggested configuration is based on rules of thumb, and therefore we believe it is realistic. The hardware prices are based on real cost numbers of a large online hardware vendor. We now describe the suggested hardware configuration.

- **Web server**: It is well-known that Web servers are performance-hungry. Therefore, a hardware vendor might, for example, suggest a high-performance system with an Intel Xeon X3480 (3.06 GHz, 8MB LLC Cache, 4 cores, Hyper-Threading), 8 GB RAM and a typical HDD. The price for this web server is $1,795.

- **Memcached server**: Because memory is an important factor in a memcached server, the vendor might suggest including more memory, leading to an Intel Xeon X3480, with 16 GB RAM and a typical HDD. The price for this system is $2,015.

- **Database server**: Finally, because the hard disk is often a bottleneck on a database server, a hardware vendor might suggest to replace the HDD with an SSD, leading to a system with an Intel Xeon X3480, 16 GB RAM and an SSD. The price for this database server is $2,915.

The total cost of this configuration, including 6 Web servers, 1 memcached server and 2 database servers — recall the 6-1-2 ratio of web, memcached and database servers in the Netlog configuration as described earlier — equals $18,615.

Now, given the insight obtained from this study as described in Section 6, we can make the following alternative recommendations for a hardware configuration.

- **Suggestion #1: Low-cost memcached and database server**

  As previously reported, a memcached server does not need a high-performance CPU. We therefore suggest a CPU of

189

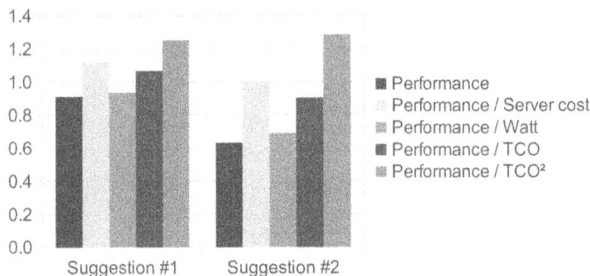

Figure 16: Several performance trade-offs for different hardware suggestions compared to the hardware vendor suggestion.

the same class as proposed by the hardware vendor, but at a lower clock frequency (e.g., Intel Xeon X3440 at 2.53 GHz). The same is true for the database server. On top of that we suggest not to consider an SSD, because of its high cost and relatively low performance gain over HDD for this particular workload.

The lower price for the CPU makes the memcached and database server cost $1,445 each. The total price of our suggested configuration now equals $15,105. This means a purchasing cost reduction of 18.9%.

Using the results presented in Figure 13, we conclude that, using this configuration, 50% of all requests will not experience any extra latency. For the other 50% of the requests, response times would increase from 11% for the 75% percentile to 39% for the 99.6% percentile. In summary, performance as perceived by the end user would be reduced by 9.1% on average. It is then up to the service provider to balance the purchase cost against the loss in performance for a small fraction of the user requests.

- **Suggestion #2: Low-frequency Web server**

  We can go one step further and use a CPU at lower clock frequency for the Web servers as well (Intel Xeon X3440 at 2.53 GHz). The price of the Web server is now $1,225. This could mean a total purchasing cost reduction of 37.2% over the hardware vendor suggested configuration.

  User requests would now observe a latency increase by 29% for the 50% percentile, and up to 56% for the 99.6% percentile. On average, end-user performance would be reduced by 36.9%. Again, it is up to the service provider to determine whether this loss in performance is worth the reduction in cost.

So far, when computing the cost reduction, we only focused on purchasing cost and we did not account for savings due to lower power consumption, leading to reduction in cost for powering and cooling the servers. Power consumption is a significant cost factor in today's servers and data centers [3], hence it should be taken into account when computing cost savings. In Figure 16, we show different metrics to help the service provider determine which platform should be chosen; the reason for considering multiple metrics is that different criteria might be appropriate for different scenarios. All metrics are higher-is-better metrics, and all values are normal-

ized against the suggestion by the hardware vendor; a value greater than one thus is in favor of one of our suggestions.

- **Performance:** As mentioned before, raw performance drops by 9.1% for suggestion #1 and 36.9% for suggestion #2. This metric does not take any cost factor into account.

- **Performance per server cost:** Suggestion #1 reduces cost without dramatically reducing performance. When using server hardware costs in our metric, the benefit for suggestion #1 is 12.0%. The benefit for suggestion #2 is almost zero because of the extra decrease in performance, i.e., cost saving is offset by performance decrease.

- **Performance per Watt:** In the above case study, we considered two server configurations, one at 3.06 GHz and one at 2.53 GHz, which corresponds to a 17.3% reduction in clock frequency. Dynamic power consumption is proportional to clock frequency, so CPU dynamic power consumption will be lowered by 17.3% as well. The Intel X3480 has a Thermal Design Point (TDP) of 95 Watts and we assume other components (motherboard, disk, memory, etc.) to consume 100 Watts in total. The reduce in wattage is low compared to the performance decrease, resulting in a net decrease in performance per Watt for the two suggestions compared to the hardware vendor's suggestion. However, this metric only considers power consumption and does not take electricity costs into account.

- **Performance per TCO:** As mentioned before, data center facilities and online services are cost-sensitive, and hence, a metric for the data center should include some notion of total cost of ownership (TCO). TCO includes server purchasing cost plus electricity cost for powering and cooling the servers. We assume electricity cost to be $0.07/kWh and we assume a three-year depreciation cycle. For the cooling cost, we assume there is need for 1 Watt of cooling power for each Watt of consumed power. The three-year total cost of ownership (TCO) for 6 Web servers, 1 memcached server and 2 databaser servers consists of hardware cost, power cost and cooling cost; this makes $24,887 for the hardware vendor's suggestion, $21,201 for suggestion #1 and $17,428 for suggestion #2. This means a reduction in TCO of 14.8% and 30.0% for suggestions #1 and #2, respectively. The performance per TCO metric leads to a gain of 6.7% for suggestion #1 and a loss of 10.0% for suggestion #2.

- **Performance per TCO^2 :** If total cost of ownership is more important than performance, performance per TCO-squared might be an appropriate metric. Using this metric, it is clear that there is a big benefit in using our two suggestions compared to the hardware vendor's suggestion, with a respective gain of 25.2% and 28.5%.

Note that total (both static and dynamic) power consumption is likely to be reduced even more because of reduced operating temperature which reduces leakage power consumption. In other words, the reduced cost factors mentioned above are pessimistic cost savings; actual savings in power consumption and total cost of ownership will be higher.

In summary, this case study illustrated evaluating hardware design choices in the data center, enabling service providers, data center owners, as well as system architects to make trade-offs taking into account end-user performance of a Web 2.0 workload.

7.2 Software optimizations

Whereas the first use case considered a hardware design trade-off, our second use case illustrates the potential for driving software trade-offs and analyses. The reason why this is valuable is that setting up such experiments in a live data center is considered to be too risky because it might interrupt normal operation. Our approach on the other hand allows for setting up such experiments in a controlled environment while being able to apply real-life user requests.

In this case study, we analyze the performance for an alternative Web server software package. As mentioned before, Netlog uses the Apache Web server software to process all user requests on the Web servers. Another well-known web server software package is called NGINX[18]. In Figure 17, we show the percentage increase in the number of requests that were handled under 300 ms, the chosen metric for this case study. We compare different NGINX configurations to the standard Netlog Apache configuration. On the horizontal axis we distinguish several NGINX configurations, starting with the default configuration on the left side.

We observe that replacing Apache by a default NGINX setup increases the number of requests handled under 300 ms by 7.5%. This number gets up to 13.5% when tuning the number of connections per worker thread. We also disabled the HTTP keepalive feature[19], but conclude that there is no performance difference in disabling this feature.

NGINX reduces response times as perceived by the end user, thereby increasing customer satisfaction. This will lead to more users visiting the social network site, leading to an increase in company profit. System engineers and software developers can easily study other software tweaks or parameter tuning for maximizing performance in the data center by using the proposed method.

8. RELATED WORK

8.1 Data center workloads

A number of studies have been conducted recently to understand what hardware platform is best suited for a given data center workload. In all of these setups, a single server is considered — the study focuses on leaf-node performance — and/or microbenchmarks with specific behavior are employed. In contrast, this paper considers a setup involving multiple physical servers running real workloads, and we focus on end-user performance.

Kozyrakis et al. [6] consider three Microsoft online services, Hotmail, Cosmos (framework for distributed storage and analytics) and the Bing search engine, and their goal is to understand how online services and technology trends affect design decisions in the data center. They collect performance data from production servers subject to real user input, and in addition, they set up

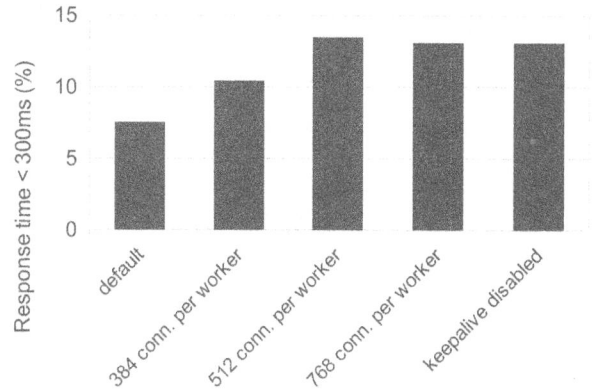

Figure 17: Increase in number of requests handled under 300 ms for different NGINX configurations, compared to the Apache Web server.

a slightly modified version of the software in a lab setup in order to perform stress tests for evaluating individual server performance under peak load. Our work differs from the Kozyrakis et al. work in two important ways: (i) we consider a different workload (Web 2.0 social networking), and (ii) our methodology is very different: our lab setup includes multiple servers, running unmodified production software supplied with real-life user input; in addition, we focus on end-user perceived performance.

Lim et al. [7] consider four Internet-sector benchmarks, namely Web search (search a very large dataset within sub-seconds), webmail (interactive sessions of reading, composing and sending emails), YouTube (media servers servicing requests for video files), and mapreduce (series of map and reduce functions performed on key/value pairs in a distributed file system). These benchmarks are network-intensive (webmail), I/O-bound (YouTube) or exhibit mixed CPU and I/O activity (Web search and mapreduce). Lim et al. reach the conclusion that lower-end consumer platforms are more performance-cost efficient — leading to a $2\times$ improvement relative to high-end servers. Low-end embedded servers have the potential to offer even more cost savings at the same performance.

Andersen et al. [1] propose the Fast Array of Wimpy Nodes (FAWN) data center architecture with low-power embedded servers coupled with flash memory for random read I/O-intensive workloads. Vasudevan et al. [10] evaluate under what workloads the FAWN architecture performs well while considering a broad set of microbenchmarks ranging from I/O-bound workloads to CPU- and memory-intensive benchmarks. They conclude that low-end nodes are more energy-efficient than high-end CPUs, except for problems that cannot be parallelized or whose working set cannot be split to fit in the cache or memory available to the smaller nodes — wimpy cores are too low-end for these workloads.

Reddi et al. [8] evaluate the Microsoft Bing Web search engine on Intel Xeon and Atom processors. They conclude that this Web search engine is more computationally demanding than traditional enterprise workloads such as file servers, mail servers, Web servers, etc. Hence, they conclude that embedded mobile-space processors are beneficial in terms of their power efficiency, however, these processors would benefit from better performance to achieve better service-level agreements and quality-of-service.

---

[18]http://www.nginx.net/ – High performance Web server with low memory footprint.

[19]The 'keepalive' feature is used for actively maintaining a connection between a client and a server.

8.2 Sampling

Sampling is not a novel method in performance analysis. Some of the prior work mentioned above focuses on leaf-node performance, an example of sampling in space. Sampling in time is heavily used in architectural simulation. Current benchmarks execute hundreds of billions, if not trillions, of instructions, and detailed cycle-accurate simulation is too slow to efficiently simulate these workloads in a reasonable amount of time. This problem is further exacerbated given the surge of multi-core processor architectures, i.e., multiple cores and their interactions need to simulated, which is challenging given that most cycle-accurate simulators are single-threaded.

Sampled simulation takes a number of samples from the dynamic instruction stream and only simulates these samples in great detail. Conte et al. [4] were the first to use sampling for processor simulation. They select samples randomly and use statistics theory to build confidence bounds. Further, they quantify what fraction of the sampling error comes from the sampling itself (sampling bias) versus the fraction of the error due to imperfect state at the beginning of each sample (non-sampling bias or cold-start problem). Wunderlich et al. [11] employ periodic sampling and very small samples while keeping the cache and predictor structures 'warm', i.e., cache and predictor state is simulated, while fast-forwarding between samples.

Whereas both the Conte et al. as well as the Wunderlich et al. approaches select a large number of samples and rely on statistics to evaluate the representativeness of the samples, Sherwood et al. [9] employ knowledge about program structure and its execution to determine representative samples. They collect program statistics, e.g., basic block vectors (BBVs), during a profiling run, and they then rely on clustering to determine a set of representative samples. The approach taken in this paper is similar to Sherwood et al. although we take different workload statistics as input to the sample selection algorithm, while considering server workloads rather than CPU workloads.

9. CONCLUSION

In this paper, we presented a case study in which we characterized a real-life Web 2.0 workload and evaluated hardware and software design choices in the data center. Our methodology samples the Web 2.0 workload both in space and in time to obtain a reduced workload that can be replayed, driven by input data captured from a real data center. The reduced workload captures the important services (and their interactions) and allows for evaluating how hardware and software choices affect end-user experience (response times).

The real-life Web 2.0 workload used in this work is Netlog, a popular and commercially deployed social networking site with a large user base in Europe. We explored hardware trade-offs in terms of core count, clock frequency, HDD versus SSD, etc., for the Web, memcached and database servers, and we obtain several interesting insights, such as the Web servers scale well with core count, and end-user response times are inversely proportional to Web server CPU frequency; an SSD reduces the longest response times by around 30% over an HDD in the database servers, which may or may not be justifiable given the significantly higher cost for SSD versus; memcached servers show low levels of CPU utilization, and are both memory and network-bound, hence, hardware choice should be driven by the cost of integrating more main memory in the server. Further, we presented two case studies illustrating how the method can be used for guiding hardware purchasing decisions as well as software optimizations.

Acknowledgements

We thank the anonymous reviewers for their constructive and insightful feedback. Stijn Polfliet is supported through a doctoral fellowship by the Agency for Innovation by Science and Technology (IWT). Frederick Ryckbosch is supported through a doctoral fellowship by the Research Foundation–Flanders (FWO). Additional support is provided by the FWO projects G.0255.08, and G.0179.10, the UGent-BOF projects 01J14407 and 01Z04109, and the European Research Council under the European Community's Seventh Framework Programme (FP7/2007-2013) / ERC Grant agreement no. 259295.

10. REFERENCES

[1] D. G. Andersen, J. Franklin, M. Kaminsky, A. Phanishayee, L. Tan, and V. Vasudevan. FAWN: A fast array of wimpy nodes. In *Proceedings of the International ACM Symposium on Operating Systems Principles (SOSP)*, pages 1–14, Oct. 2009.

[2] L. A. Barroso, J. Dean, and U. Hölzle. Web search for a planet: The google cluster architecture. *IEEE Micro*, 23(2):22–28, Mar. 2003.

[3] L. A. Barroso and U. Hölzle. *The Datacenter as a Computer: An Introduction to the Design of Warehouse-Scale Machines*. Synthesis Lectures on Computer Architecture. Morgan and Claypool Publishers, 2009.

[4] T. M. Conte, M. A. Hirsch, and K. N. Menezes. Reducing state loss for effective trace sampling of superscalar processors. In *Proceedings of the International Conference on Computer Design (ICCD)*, pages 468–477, Oct. 1996.

[5] R. A. Johnson and D. W. Wichern. *Applied Multivariate Statistical Analysis*. Prentice Hall, fifth edition, 2002.

[6] C. Kozyrakis, A. Kansal, S. Sankar, and K. Vaid. Server engineering insights for large-scale online services. *IEEE Micro*, 30:8–19, July/August 2010.

[7] K. Lim, P. Ranganathan, J. Chang, C. Patel, T. Mudge, and S. Reinhardt. Understanding and designing new server architectures for emerging warehouse-computing environments. In *Proceedings of the International Symposium on Computer Architecture (ISCA)*, pages 315–326, June 2008.

[8] V. J. Reddi, B. C. Lee, T. Chilimbi, and K. Vaid. Web search using mobile cores: Quantifying and mitigating the price of efficiency. In *Proceedings of the International Symposium on Computer Architecture (ISCA)*, pages 26–36, June 2010.

[9] T. Sherwood, E. Perelman, G. Hamerly, and B. Calder. Automatically characterizing large scale program behavior. In *Proceedings of the International Conference on Architectural Support for Programming Languages and Operating Systems (ASPLOS)*, pages 45–57, Oct. 2002.

[10] V. Vasudevan, D. Andersen, M. Kaminsky, L. Tan, J. Franklin, and I. Moraru. Energy-efficient cluster computing with FAWN: Workloads and implications. In *Proceedings of the 1st International Conference on Energy-Efficient Computing and Networking (e-Energy)*, pages 195–204, Apr. 2010.

[11] R. E. Wunderlich, T. F. Wenisch, B. Falsafi, and J. C. Hoe. SMARTS: Accelerating microarchitecture simulation via rigorous statistical sampling. In *Proceedings of the Annual International Symposium on Computer Architecture (ISCA)*, pages 84–95, June 2003.

Benchmarking Decentralized Monitoring Mechanisms in Peer-to-Peer Systems

Dominik Stingl, Christian Gross,
Sebastian Kaune, Ralf Steinmetz
Multimedia Communications Lab
TU Darmstadt
Darmstadt, Germany
{stingl,chrgross,kaune,
steinmetz}@kom.tu-darmstadt.de

Karsten Saller
Real Time Systems Lab
TU Darmstadt
Darmstadt, Germany
karsten.saller@es.tu-darmstadt.de

ABSTRACT

Decentralized monitoring mechanisms enable obtaining a global view on different attributes and the state of Peer-to-Peer systems. Therefore, such mechanisms are essential for managing and optimizing Peer-to-Peer systems. Nonetheless, when deciding on an appropriate mechanism, system designers are faced with a major challenge. Comparing different existing monitoring mechanisms is complex because evaluation methodologies differ widely. To overcome this challenge and to achieve a fair evaluation and comparison, we present a set of dedicated benchmarks for monitoring mechanisms. These benchmarks evaluate relevant functional and non-functional requirements of monitoring mechanisms using appropriate workloads and metrics. We demonstrate the feasibility and expressiveness of our benchmarks by evaluating and comparing three different monitoring mechanisms and highlighting their performance and overhead.

Categories and Subject Descriptors

C.2.4 [**Computer-Communication Networks**]: Distributed Systems; C.4.1 [**Performance of Systems**]: Performance attributes

General Terms

Performance, Standardization

Keywords

Benchmarking, Decentralized Monitoring Mechanisms, Peer-to-Peer Systems, Performance Comparison

1. INTRODUCTION

In the last decade, monitoring of Peer-to-Peer (P2P) systems has gained much research interest resulting in a plethora of different monitoring approaches, each providing different performance characteristics. All approaches have in common, that they reveal general insights about the network and application [24], or summarize the characteristics of the participants [7].

Given the multitude of existing solutions, a fair comparison between several solutions is hard to achieve, if not impossible. This lack of comparability results from the widely differing evaluation methodology for decentralized monitoring mechanisms: (i) although designed for the same purpose with similar functionality, the addressed non-functional requirements vary, (ii) the applied workloads to evaluate the quality of a mechanism differ widely in their composition, and (iii) different metrics are used to quantify the quality of the system.

To overcome this lack of comparability, we present the following contributions:

(i) We identify the relevant non-functional requirements for decentralized monitoring mechanisms for P2P systems, such as scalability and robustness. Given these requirements, we propose a set of benchmarks that investigate how decentralized monitoring mechanisms meet these non-functional requirements. Therefore, each developed benchmark consists of one or several workloads, which evaluate a specific non-functional requirement by a predefined set of appropriate metrics. Based on the provided benchmarks, the quality of decentralized monitoring mechanisms can be evaluated and compared in a reproducible and unbiased way. Furthermore, our benchmarks can be applied to tune the parameter setting of a system to identify an optimal configuration for a particular workload scenario.

(ii) To exemplify our methodology, we present a case study and discuss the benchmarking results of three monitoring approaches (a gossip-based and tree-based approach as well as a simple centralized approach as reference). Thus, we are not interested in declaring one approach "better" or "worse" than another as denoted by Rhea et al. [19], but in showing the applicability and expressiveness of our presented benchmarks.

The rest of this paper is structured as follows: Section 2 provides the background on decentralized P2P monitoring mechanisms followed by Section 3 presenting our benchmarking methodology. The benchmarking results are presented in Section 4. Subsequently, we discuss related work in Section 5, summarize this paper in Section 6 and give an outlook on future work.

2. DECENTRALIZED MONITORING MECHANISMS

In this section, we give a brief overview on decentralized monitoring mechanisms highlighting their offered functionality and composition. For the design of benchmarks, it is indispensable to understand, which functionality is provided by the considered class of mechanisms, because it influences the identification of the relevant non-functional requirements for this class. Based on these requirements, the different benchmarks can be defined, as outlined in Subsection 3.1. Moreover, the offered functionality serves to design an interface for the class of mechanisms to access and execute the relevant operations during a benchmark.

2.1 Functional Description

A decentralized monitoring mechanism [12,16,23,24] gathers different types of data from the whole system to assess and calculate the *global state* of the system and its participants. The information to collect is represented by a set of *attributes*, measured by every participating peer. Depending on the focus of a monitoring mechanism, the gathered attributes range from the transmitted traffic [18], over application-related information [23], to the user and its utilized communication device [7].

Due to the large number of users, the transmission of the measured attributes and its subsequent collection at one or several data sinks results in a high amount of data, consuming a considerable amount of bandwidth resources in the system. Existing approaches, therefore, apply aggregation of the monitored attributes to compress the size of the data and to save the bandwidth of the participating peers. Using this aggregation, a monitoring mechanism calculates the so-called *global view* of a monitored attribute, which can be subsequently used to deduce the aforementioned global state of the whole system. Typical aggregates that are used for the calculation of a global view cover functions, such as minimum, maximum, sum, average, or standard deviation [3,16]. After the computation of a global view for a set of aggregates, each participating peer in a P2P system can retrieve the newly created information.

2.2 Architectural Description

In the following, we present the architecture of a decentralized monitoring mechanism, which provides the previously mentioned functionality. We sketch how a decentralized monitoring mechanism is composed and integrated into a P2P system. In contrast to the functional description, the information about a mechanism's composition is not mandatory for the design of benchmarks, because we evaluate the whole mechanism and do not study the impact of internal components on the overall behavior. The overview, however, justifies the choice of a tree- and gossip-based approach for the case study in Section 4, because it becomes apparent that the topology mainly influences the behavior of the monitoring mechanism. In the following, we present the three basic components, every monitoring mechanism can be reduced to.

Topology Construction and Maintenance.

In literature, *trees* [16,24] and *meshes* [11,12] constitute the two prominent topologies for a decentralized monitoring mechanism. Within a tree topology, information is only exchanged between children and parents. Within a mesh topology, one or several neighbors are randomly chosen to exchange monitored information [5]. This results in *gossip-based* communication, which is often used as a synonym when describing the communication within mesh-based monitoring mechanisms. Furthermore, there are several hybrid approaches, combining gossip-based aggregation in trees [23] or creating trees of mesh-based networks [2,18].

The topology maintenance depends on the network environment and its network topology. Monitoring approaches that are deployed in static and structured environments, such as in the area of grid computing [18], heavily differ from approaches for autonomous systems with highly dynamic users. The herein considered mechanisms for P2P systems must actively maintain the monitoring topology and additionally manage the arrival and departure of peers [1,2]. Therefore, they rely on additional mechanisms, such as Distributed Hash Tables (DHT) or membership protocols [10].

Data Collection.

This component sketches how monitored data is exchanged. Typically, gossip-based monitoring approaches actively send data to neighboring peers [12], also denoted as *push*. If the message sent triggers the transmission of an answer at the receiver, the gossip-based approach applies *push-pull*-based data collection [11]. Tree-based approaches can decide to either *push* data [7] or to alternatively *pull* data from neighbors [16,18]. To trigger the collection of measured data, monitoring mechanisms rely on a periodic or event-based collection. For the latter case, the activating event may be, for example, (i) a newly measured value of an attribute at a peer, (ii) a query for the global view of an attribute, (iii) or the attempt of the system to generate a snapshot of an attribute at a certain point in time.

Result Dissemination.

This component highlights the possibilities to disseminate the global view of the monitored attributes. The existing strategies comprise *proactive* and *reactive* result dissemination. While proactive dissemination transmits the created global view to all or only a subset of peers, reactive dissemination sends the global view of attributes only to requesting peers. Tree-based monitoring approaches allow choosing between the different dissemination strategies, whereas proactive dissemination is implicitly integrated in gossip-based monitoring, due to the push-based collection of data.

3. BENCHMARKING DECENTRALIZED MONITORING MECHANISMS

In this section, we describe the design of our benchmarks, which will be used for the comparison of the different monitoring mechanisms in our case study. The designing process for a particular benchmark consists of the following three aspects: (i) The system specification provides the basis for the definition of benchmarks (Section 3.1). It illustrates the functional and non-functional requirements, each system has to fulfill. (ii) Given the requirements, appropriate workload schemes to benchmark a system are identified (Section 3.2). (iii) To quantify the obtained results of an applied workload, a set of metrics is created (Section 3.3). Finally, Section 3.4 outlines the combination of the three mandatory aspects in one or several benchmarks.

3.1 System Specification

Our system under test (SUT) consists of a decentralized monitoring mechanism, which is set up on top of a P2P system. To benchmark the SUT, it provides an interface to apply different workloads on the system and to measure the produced results. In case that the class of mechanisms being benchmarked does not provide a predefined interface, it must be derived based on the functional requirements of that class. To cover a wide range of existing approaches, the common functionality must be carefully analyzed and merged in a set of methods within the interface.

Due to the fact that neither an interface nor the provided functionality of a decentralized monitoring mechanism is specified, we examined existing approaches to highlight the key aspects. As outlined in Section 2, a decentralized monitoring mechanism calculates and provides the global view for a set of attributes. For that reason, each participant locally measures and stores the specified attributes for the overall collection. When the collection process is finished, the global view of attributes can be retrieved by the participating peers. Based on this description, the common functionality of a decentralized monitoring mechanism can be defined within the following interface.

- `setLocalValue(String name, double value)` stores a locally measured value of an attribute for the latter collection.

- `getGlobalViewOfAttributes()` returns the global view of all monitored attributes.

Every monitoring approach, applying our benchmarks, must provide this functionality and implement the specified interface in order to be evaluated or compared to another solution. Thus to apply the different workloads and to measure the produced results, the resulting interface of the SUT is located at each peer, which participates and monitors the system.

Besides the architecture and the design of the interface, the system specification also outlines the non-functional requirements of a system. Therefore, we identified the following *quality aspects*, representing the relevant non-functional requirements of decentralized monitoring mechanisms. These requirements build the basis for the subsequent identification of workloads and metrics.

- **Performance** characterizes the quality of the provided functionality of a mechanism. In the context of monitoring, we divide performance into *validity* and *timeliness*. With validity, we address the accuracy of the delivered results, which can be characterized through the difference between the measured and the actual global view of an attribute. Since the provisioning of correct information is the primary function of a decentralized monitoring mechanism, validity represents a central aspect. Besides the delivery of correct results, timeliness covers the aspect how fast the monitoring mechanism captures the global view and how fast it can deliver or distribute this view in the system.

- **Costs** comprise the communication or computation overhead produced by the monitoring mechanism to perform its task with a certain performance.

- **Fairness** can be evaluated with respect to performance and costs. On the one hand, a fair system should offer the same access to the provided services and avoid starving peers. On the other hand, a fair system should distribute the operational costs that peers are not overloaded.

- **Scalability** refers to the ability of a monitoring mechanism to preserve its performance at reasonable costs, while increasing the number of participating nodes or monitored attributes. A threshold for acceptable performance or costs must be defined by the application scenario.

- **Robustness** deals with the behavior of the whole P2P system in the presence of external and unpredictable events. These events mainly comprise massive fluctuations of participants due to, e.g., a network collapse or flash crowd behavior.

- **Stability** characterizes the ability of a decentralized monitoring mechanism to deal with the random behavior of autonomous peers in a P2P system. We consider the random behavior in terms of churn, which describes the varying frequency of arriving and leaving peers.

The identified non-functional requirements can be divided into two classes of quality aspects. On the one hand, there are quality aspects, such as performance, costs, and fairness, which can be quantified by metrics. Based on these metrics, it is possible to estimate if a mechanism meets these requirements. In contrast, the second class of quality aspects cannot directly be assessed by individual metrics, but is quantifiable by metrics, which are related to the first class of quality aspects. Instead, the second class of quality aspects characterizes the properties of a workload.

3.2 Workloads

For benchmarking decentralized monitoring mechanisms, we elaborated several workloads to address the identified quality aspects. These workloads are applied on the SUT, while the participating peers perform their tasks and measure a set of predefined attributes. Using the captured attributes, the monitoring mechanism calculates the global view for each attribute, as described in Section 2.1. Afterwards, this global view is disseminated to the peers. To examine validity of a monitoring mechanism under the specified workloads, the measured global view is compared to the so-called *correct global view*. In contrast to the global view obtained by the monitoring mechanism, the correct global view of an attribute is calculated based on a snapshot of the system at a certain point in time. Except for the peer count of a monitoring mechanism, we do not measure common system attributes (e.g., network traffic or number of messages) nor domain-specific attributes (e.g., lookup-rates or file-downloads for file-sharing systems) to evaluate validity. Instead, the peers in our benchmark obtain their monitored values from a *value generator*, as presented by Graffi [6]. This generator calculates a new value for each monitoring peer based on the current time and on the defined function. Afterwards, the calculated global view is compared with the actual value retrieved from the value generator to assess the validity of the monitoring mechanism.

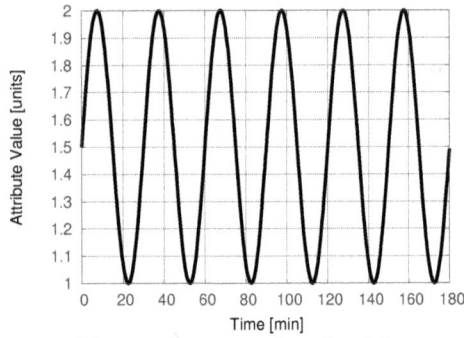

Figure 1: Sine reference signal with a period of 30min.

The value generator facilitates a more detailed analysis, because we can define functions with differing complexity, which refer to constant or highly varying attributes. It is possible to design individual functions that exhibit desired characteristics, such as steep slopes or periodicity, in order to estimate to which extent a monitoring mechanism is able to capture a varying signal. For example, it is easier to capture the values of a slightly increasing linear function than of a sine or a rectangular function. Moreover, the value generator improves the comparability of results in terms of validity. The monitored values of a function are independent from the enclosing P2P system (e.g., P2P file-sharing application) and current workload scenario (e.g., churn), thus, the values are not biased. In order to evaluate validity within our benchmarks, we implement a sine function, as displayed in Figure 1.

Besides this function for the value generator, we propose a set of workloads. These workloads are not application-related but synthetic workloads. They are domain-specific and model typical scenarios that are common for P2P system, such as churn or an increasing number of peers. We decided to apply synthetic workloads (i) to provide application-independent results and (ii) to stress a system regarding a particular, isolated quality aspect.

Baseline.

The baseline workload represents idealized conditions and provides insights on the behavior of the monitoring mechanism under these conditions. In contrast to the remaining workloads, this workload does neither include message loss, which is enabled for the rest of workloads, nor consider churn, which is addressed in a separate workload. Moreover, other workload parameters, such as the number of peers or the amount of monitored attributes, are fixed during this workload. This results in a static workload scenario with a fixed number of peers and perfect network conditions.

Churn.

In this workload scenario, we evaluate stability of a monitoring mechanism in the presence of churn. As underlying model, we employ an exponential churn model, which assumes an exponentially distributed mean session time per peer. The workload consists of several runs, which model the peers with different mean session times per run.

Massive join/crash.

The massive join workload consists of one run. During this run, we assume that a predefined fraction of new peers

Symbol	Description
T	The set of time samples
$P(t)$	The set of online peers at time $t \in T$
$A(t)$	The set of attributes being monitored at time t
$X_m(a,t,p)$	The *measured* global aggregate X of an attribute $a \in A(t)$ at time $t \in T$ available at a peer $p \in P(t)$
$X_c(a,t)$	The *correct* global aggregate X of an attribute $a \in A(t)$, which is calculated based on a snapshot of the system at time $t \in T$
$\tau_{\min}(X(a,t,p))$	The time of the oldest sample being included into an aggregate
$\tau_{\max}(X(a,t,p))$	The time of the most recent sample being included into an aggregate
$\Delta t_{\mathrm{agg}}(X(a,t,p))$	The aggregation time considers all included values for a global view and is calculated as $\Delta t_{\mathrm{agg}}(X(a,t,p)) = \tau_{\max} - \tau_{\min}$
$\Delta t_{\mathrm{prop}}(X(a,t,p))$	The propagation time for a global aggregate from a data sink to a peer
$\Delta t_{\mathrm{req}}(X(a,t,p))$	The time to answer a request for a global aggregate

Table 1: List of mathematical symbols

simultaneously joins the system. Within the context of a massive crash, the workload consists of a single run as well and covers the ungraceful departure of a predefined fraction of peers. These workloads evaluate the robustness of a decentralized monitoring mechanism, since it has to deal with a sudden change in the system state as well as in the amount of peers. For both workloads, one has to differentiate between a collapse of the monitoring mechanism due to the breakdown of the whole P2P system or due to the inability of the monitoring mechanism to reorganize itself.

Increasing number of attributes.

In this workload scenario, we investigate scalability of a monitoring mechanism by scaling the amount of transmitted and processed data. We denote this type of scalability as *vertical scalability*. The workload consists of several runs. For each run, we increase the number of monitored attributes, which results in a higher amount of transmitted and processed data.

Increasing number of peers.

With the linear increase of peers in the system, this workload investigates another type of scalability of a monitoring mechanism, which we denote as *horizontal scalability*. In contrast to the previously described workload, which addresses vertical scalability, this workload increases the number of peers to an upper bound during one run and not during several runs.

3.3 Metrics

In this subsection, we introduce the metrics being measured to evaluate a decentralized monitoring mechanism. In order to describe the metrics below, we use the set of symbols shown in Table 1.

3.3.1 Per peer metrics

The following metrics are measured on a per peer basis for each participant of the P2P system. They can be mapped onto the quality aspects performance and costs.

Performance Metrics:

- $t_{\text{stale}}(X(a,t,p))$ denotes the staleness or age of an aggregate in seconds, observed at peer $p \in P(t)$ and is calculated as

$$t_{\text{stale}}(X(a,t,p)) = \Delta t_{\text{agg}} + \Delta t_{\text{prop}} + \Delta t_{\text{req}}$$

- $\epsilon_X(a,t,p)$ represents the relative monitoring error in percent for an aggregate X of on attribute $a \in A(t)$ at peer $p \in P(t)$ at time $t \in T$ and is defined as:

$$\epsilon_X(a,t,p) = \frac{|X_m(a,t,p) - X_c(a,t)|}{X_c(a,t)} * 100\%$$

Cost Metric:

- $l(t,p)$ represents the total traffic in $\frac{\text{kB}}{\text{s}}$ at peer $p \in P(t)$ at time $t \in T$. It comprises the up- and download traffic and is calculated as follows:

$$l(t,p) = l_{\text{up}}(t,p) + l_{\text{down}}(t,p)$$

3.3.2 Global Metrics

Based on the per peer metrics the following global metrics can be calculated:

- The mean of a metric x over the set of peers at time $t \in T$:

$$\overline{x}(t) = \frac{1}{|P|} \sum_{p \in P} x(p,t).$$

- The mean of a metric x over the set of time samples per peer $p \in P$:

$$\widetilde{x}(p) = \frac{1}{|T|} \sum_{t \in T} x(p,t).$$

- The total mean of a metric x:

$$\widehat{x} = \frac{1}{|T||P|} \sum_{t \in T} \sum_{p \in P} x(p,t).$$

3.4 Benchmark Implementation

Having introduced the system specification, workloads, and metrics, we present the benchmark implementation. This implementation combines the three components and creates the different benchmarks to evaluate the SUT. We have derived four different benchmarks that investigate and evaluate the system in a baseline, robustness, stability, and scalability benchmark. Before presenting all benchmarks, we describe the basis for each benchmark, which consists of three different phases as shown in Figure 2: (i) the setup phase of 60min in which 1,000 peers join the system, (ii) the stabilization phase of additional 20min, which ensures that the whole P2P system is set up correctly and stable, and (iii) a workload and measurement phase of 180min, where the different workload schemes are applied and where the benchmarking metrics are captured.

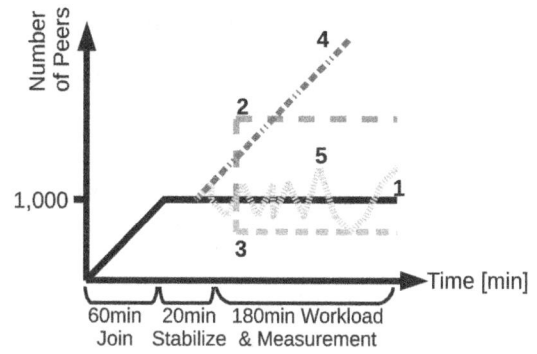

Figure 2: Schematic drawing of the schemes for varying the number of peers: (1) constant number of peers, (2) massive join, (3) massive leave, (4) linear increase, and (5) regular churn.

Baseline Benchmark.

The baseline benchmark provides insights on performance and costs in an idealized environment without message loss or peer churn. Using the *baseline* workload, this benchmark represents a reference for the remaining benchmarks regarding (i) the examined quality aspects of a particular monitoring mechanism as well as (ii) the comparison between the different monitoring mechanisms.

Scalability Benchmark.

To examine the scalability of a decentralized monitoring mechanism, we divide scalability into horizontal and vertical scalability. Horizontal scalability is benchmarked by the workload with an *increasing number of peers*. Within this workload the number of peers is linearly increased from 1,000 to 10,000 peers during the workload and measurement phase. In contrast, the workload with an *increasing number of attributes* benchmarks vertical scalability. The workload consists of three runs and covers scenarios with 10, 100, and 1,000 attributes, which are monitored by the system.

Stability Benchmark.

For investigating the stability of the system, we apply the workload for *churn*. The workload consists of three runs, which model peers with a mean session time of 60, 30, and 15min. With the increasing frequency of arriving and leaving peers per run, this workload examines the stability of a decentralized monitoring mechanism.

Robustness Benchmark.

In the robustness benchmark, we investigate the system behavior in two different scenarios defined by the *massive join* and *massive crash* workloads. We look at the system behavior when (i) 50% of the peers simultaneously leave and (ii) 100% new peers simultaneously join the system. We consider a system to be robust if these metrics reach predefined levels after a crash or a massive join. While the levels must be defined by the application scenario in which the particular monitoring approach should be used, we restrict the evaluation of robustness to a comparison of the three different systems.

4. BENCHMARKING RESULTS

In order to evaluate our benchmarks, we chose three different monitoring mechanisms and implemented them in the P2P simulation framework PeerfactSim.KOM [21]. We benchmarked all three systems using the previously defined benchmarks. Before presenting the results for each benchmark and outlining the most important conclusions, Subsection 4.1 summarizes the simulation setup and details the three chosen monitoring mechanisms.

4.1 Simulation Setup

We simulate each of the three monitoring mechanisms on top of a Chord overlay [22], since the tree-based approach requires a DHT to build its monitoring topology. Out of the four presented benchmarks, each benchmark is simulated with its corresponding workloads and metrics. During the workload phase, which lasts 180min (cf. Subsection 3.4), we periodically measure the produced data of the simulation with an interval of a minute. The data comprises the produced results of the monitoring mechanism and the traffic of the whole system, including the overlay as well. After sketching the basis for our simulations, we detail our selected monitoring mechanisms and briefly justify our choice.

Based on the description of decentralized monitoring mechanisms in Section 2, it becomes apparent that the selection of the topology heavily influences the decisions for the remaining two components of a monitoring mechanism. Thus, the topology constitutes the main decision criterion for a monitoring mechanism, as outlined by Makhloufi et al. [17]. Therefore, we select two decentralized monitoring approaches, which rely on different topologies, while their mechanisms for data collection and result dissemination are similar. Data collection and result dissemination are part of the discussion for future work (cf. Section 6). For the benchmark, we selected (i) a tree-based approach, (ii) a gossip-based approach, and (iii) a centralized monitoring solution as reference, which are detailed in the following.

4.1.1 A Tree-Based Monitoring Mechanism

The monitoring mechanism, introduced by Graffi et al. [7], relies on the lookup-functionality of the underlying DHT to build its tree topology based on the given peer IDs. Using the created topology, every participating peer, either leaf or inner node of the tree, periodically sends its set of attributes towards the root, which calculates the global view of all monitored attributes. This results in a push-based data collection mechanism. Simultaneously, the root regularly sends the information down the tree to every inner node and leaf, leading to a proactive result dissemination. We set both update intervals to 60s as proposed by Graffi et al. [7].

4.1.2 A Mesh-Based Monitoring Mechanism

To evaluate our benchmark on mesh-based systems, this subsection details the approach by Jelasity et al. [11], which relies on gossip-based communication to monitor the P2P system. For this type of communication, the underlying overlay network must only allow for the retrieval of neighbors to periodically communicate with a randomly chosen subset of them. The mesh-based monitoring mechanism divides the time into *epochs*, which in turn consist of a predefined amount of *cycles* to calculate the global view of the monitored attributes. We set the amount of cycles per epoch

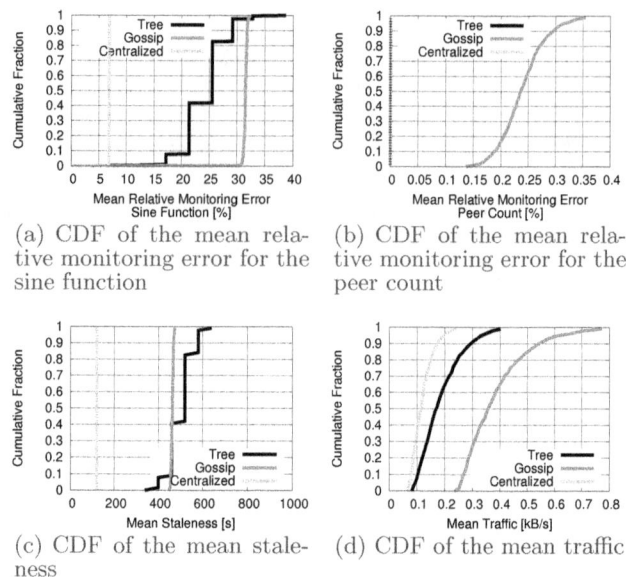

(a) CDF of the mean relative monitoring error for the sine function

(b) CDF of the mean relative monitoring error for the peer count

(c) CDF of the mean staleness

(d) CDF of the mean traffic

Figure 3: Per peer results for performance and costs, measured during the baseline workload.

to 30 with a cycle length of 10s, which correspond to the values indicated by Jelasity et al. [11]. In the beginning of a new epoch, every participating peer measures its attributes and periodically sends the current values to a randomly chosen neighbor. Through the aggregation of the measured attributes at each peer, the values converge to the average at the end of an epoch. Besides periodically pushing the own data to a neighbor, every peer that receives such a message, replies to this message with its own data. Thus, the system implements a *push-pull-based* data propagation.

4.1.3 A Centralized Monitoring Approach

In order to have a reference for decentralized monitoring mechanisms, we implemented a centralized monitoring approach, which is set up on top of the overlay. All participating peers of the centralized monitoring mechanism periodically push their measured attributes to a central server, which calculates the global view of the monitored attributes. Afterwards, the server proactively disseminates the computed global view to all peers in the system, resulting in a proactive result dissemination. Similar to the tree-based approach, we set both update intervals to 60s. In the following evaluation, the statistics of the centralized approach represent an optimal monitoring solution and serve as reference. Therefore, we mainly detail the comparison of the decentralized solutions and only refer to the centralized approach where appropriate.

4.2 Baseline Benchmark

We first study the performance and costs of the different approaches under idealized conditions within the baseline benchmark. Starting with performance in terms of validity, Figure 3(a) and 3(b) show the cumulative fraction of the mean relative monitoring error per peer averaged over a simulation denoted as $\epsilon_{avg}(a, t, p)$. Both plots outline that the tree-based approach outperforms the gossip-based approach and in terms of the relative error for the peer count even catches up with the centralized approach. Although, each mechanism is able to capture the total amount of peers, the

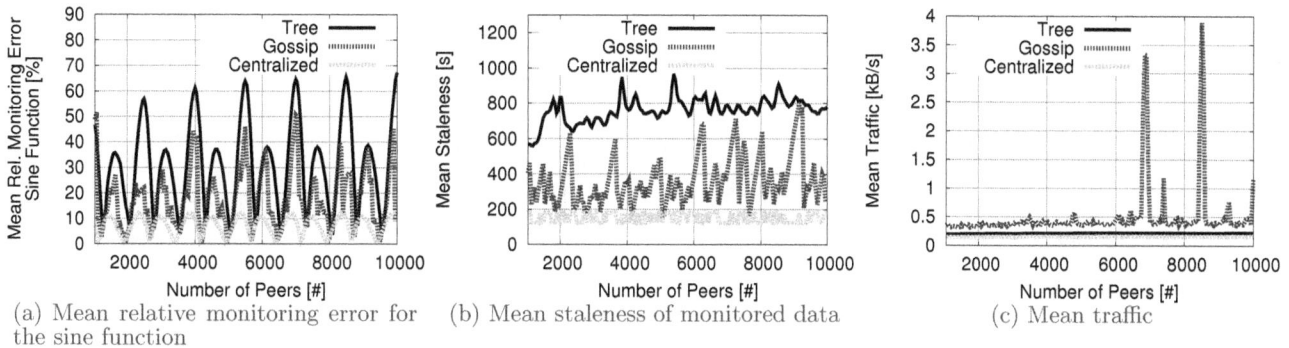

(a) Mean relative monitoring error for the sine function

(b) Mean staleness of monitored data

(c) Mean traffic

Figure 4: Per peer results for performance and costs, measured during the horizontal scalability workload. The x-axes show the actual number of peers in the system, which increases from 1,000 to 10,000 peers over an interval of 180min.

gossip-based approach exhibits a small deviation. Dealing with fairness, every participating peer of the gossip-based approach is provided with a similar monitoring error. Contrary to this, the error of the tree-based approach is spread over a larger interval, due to its hierarchical topology and the stepwise data propagation down the tree.

Considering the mean staleness per peer $t_{\text{stale}}(\widetilde{X(a,t,p)})$, as displayed in Figure 3(c), we observe that the tree-based approach only partially outperforms the gossip-based approach, because a larger fraction of peers obtains older results in contrast to the gossip-based approach. This results in a mean staleness of 462s for the gossip-based and 501s for the tree-based approach. The obtained results for staleness lead to the interesting finding that the provided validity of the tree-based approach is slightly higher than of the gossip-based approach, whereas the staleness does not support this trend. Dealing with the distribution of staleness among the peers, the same characteristics as for the previously presented error distribution in Figure 3(a) can be observed.

Considering the costs of a peer in terms of the mean total traffic $\widetilde{l(t,p)}$ (Figure 3(d)), the produced communication overhead of the tree-based approach nearly reaches the minimum overhead of the centralized approach. In contrast, the tree-based approach does not evenly balance the load among the peers. The gossip-based approach produces the highest traffic due to a shorter update frequency of the mechanism. Compared to the other monitoring approaches, the distribution of costs is even worse, because the traffic depends on the amount of neighbors in the network, which differs among the peers and is not limited as for the tree-based and centralized approach.

4.3 Scalability Benchmark

At first, we study performance and costs of the considered monitoring mechanisms during the *horizontal scalability workload*. Looking at validity, displayed in Figure 4(a), we notice that the tree-based monitoring mechanism produces a higher mean error $\epsilon_{avg}(a,t,p)$ than the gossip-based approach. This results from the fact that the dynamic and growing system has a higher impact on the tree than on the mesh topology. Due to the arrival of new peers, the continuous reorganization of the monitoring tree delays the result calculation and dissemination, because the data remains longer in tree. In contrast, we observe a smaller impact on the mesh topology, because the arrival of new peers does not

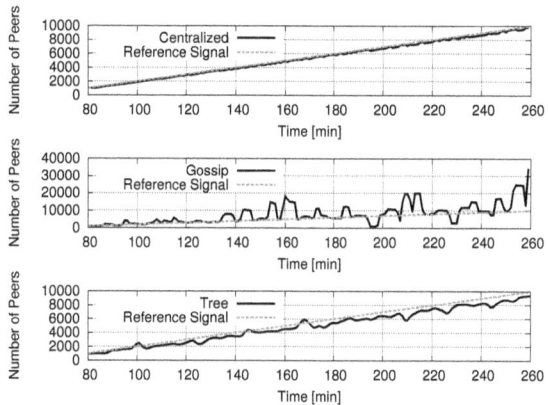

Figure 5: Actual vs. monitored number of peers over time during the horizontal scalability workload.

require a reorganization of the underlying topology. Instead, new peers can be inserted anywhere into the mesh.

Figure 4(b) outlines the results for the mean staleness $\overline{t_{\text{stale}}(X(a,t,p))}$ and confirms the previous statements regarding the mean monitoring error for the reference signal. Due to the reorganization and the resulting delay, the tree-based approach exhibits a higher mean staleness of results with values up to 967s, whereas the gossip-based approach performs better, but exhibits highly fluctuating values, which vary between 146s and 805s.

In contrast to the results for the mean error of the monitored function, the drawn conclusion does not hold for the monitored number of peers. Figure 5 shows that the tree-based approach outperforms the gossip-based approach, which exhibits considerable outliers. The opposed outcome in terms of the peer count originates from the underlying peer counting procedure of the considered gossip-based approach. Contrary to the measurement of other attributes, e.g., the reference signal, peer counting is more susceptible to the dynamic of the system.

Dealing with the mean total traffic $\overline{l(t,p)}$ (Figure 4(c)), we observe a similar trend as for the baseline benchmark. While the tree-based approach nearly produces as less traffic as the centralized approach, the gossip-based approach causes the highest amount of traffic. However, it becomes apparent that both decentralized monitoring approaches scale well with the increasing number of peers.

Next, we study the results for the *vertical scalability workload*. The plots show the truncated mean after discard-

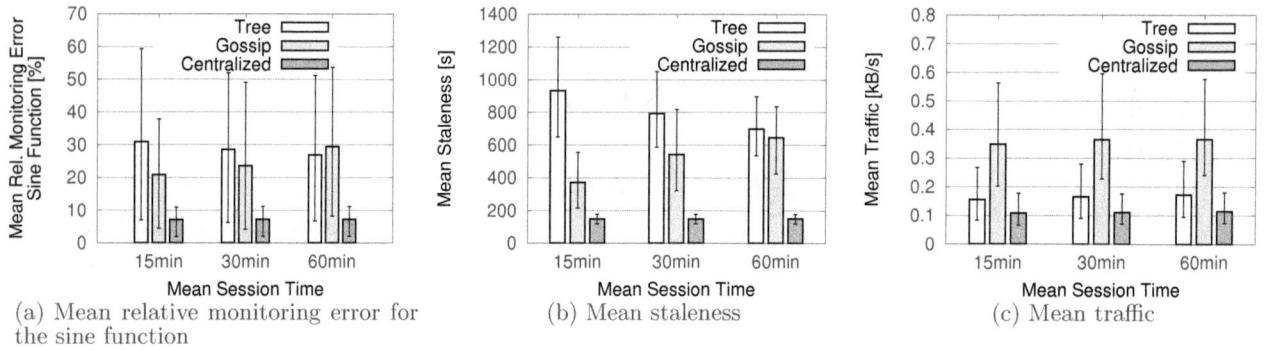

(a) Mean relative monitoring error for the sine function

(b) Mean staleness

(c) Mean traffic

Figure 6: Per peer results for performance and costs, measured during the churn workload.

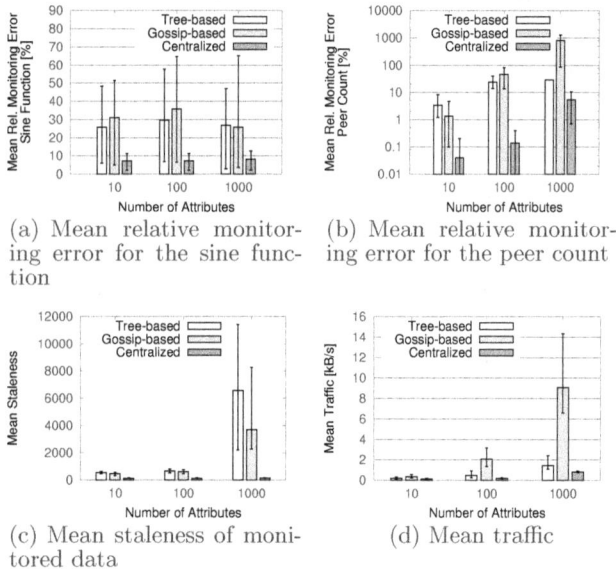

(a) Mean relative monitoring error for the sine function

(b) Mean relative monitoring error for the peer count

(c) Mean staleness of monitored data

(d) Mean traffic

Figure 7: Per peer results for performance and costs, measured during the vertical scalability workload.

ing the values, which are below the 10- and above the 90-percentile. For each mechanism, Figure 7(d) shows that the total traffic per peer increases with the growing number of monitored attributes. While the mean relative monitoring error for the sine function in Figure 7(a) still indicates that the decentralized alternatives are able to handle the increased traffic, the mean relative error for the peer count (cf. Figure 7(b)) as well as the mean staleness of the provided results (cf. Figure 7(c)) outline contrary results. In terms of the peer count error, the underlying procedure for the peer count of the gossip-based approach reveals again its weakness in the presence of dynamic and unreliable environments. Although there are several paths between two peers inside a mesh, whereby bottlenecks, such as overloaded or slow peers, can be bypassed, the peer count procedure does not benefit from the mesh topology. Dealing with staleness, the age of the provided results of the tree-based approach significantly increases with a growing number of attributes. The reason for the degrading performance in terms of timeliness originates from the underlying tree-topology: If a path from the root to a sub-tree, or the other way round, is congested, the information cannot be forwarded. It resides at an inner node, leading to a bottleneck in the tree topology.

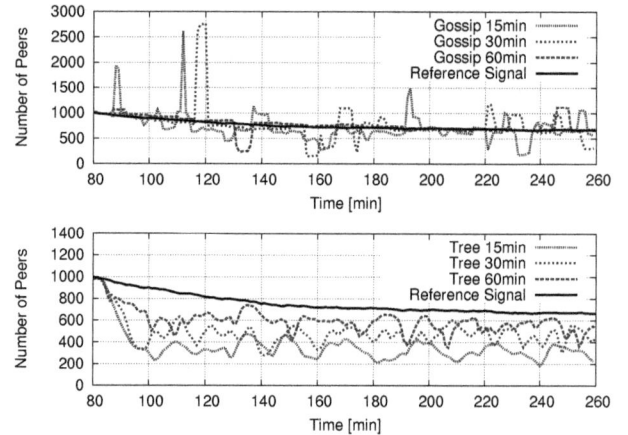

Figure 8: Actual vs. monitored number of peers over time with a mean peer session time of 15, 30, and 60 minutes.

4.4 Stability Benchmark

Examining the different monitoring approaches with respect to stability, we start with the evaluation of performance. Figure 8 shows the monitored number of peers averaged over all currently participating peers in the system. We omit the outcome of the centralized approach, since the results are accurate and do not significantly differ for the different mean session lengths. Instead, we plot the results for the two decentralized approaches dependent on the mean session time. Based on the displayed results, it becomes apparent that the tree-based approach suffers from the increasing peer fluctuations, because it cannot handle the resulting dynamic of the P2P system and degrades in terms of the provided performance. In contrast, the gossip-based approach manages the increasing dynamic of the system in a better way. Although exhibiting some outliers, whose occurrences increase with a decreasing mean session time, the gossip-based approach is capable of monitoring the current number of peers in the system.

A similar trend can also be observed, when looking at performance of the tree-based approach in terms of validity and timeliness. Figure 6(a) and 6(b) show an increase of the mean relative monitoring error $\widehat{\epsilon_{avg}(a, t, p)}$ as well as of the mean staleness of results $t_{\text{stale}}\widehat{(X(a, t, p))}$, whereas the gossip-based approach outperforms the tree-based approach in terms of validity and reduces the age of monitored results.

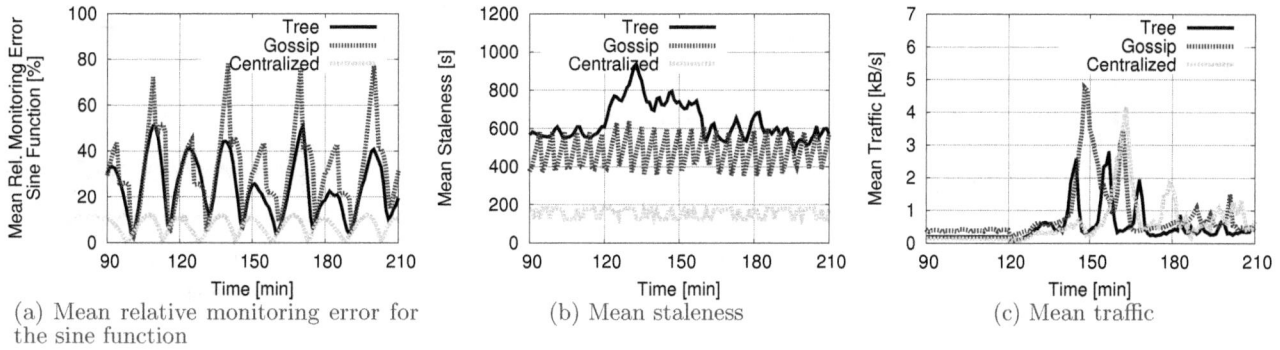

(a) Mean relative monitoring error for the sine function

(b) Mean staleness

(c) Mean traffic

Figure 9: Per peer results for performance and costs over time, measured during the massive crash workload.

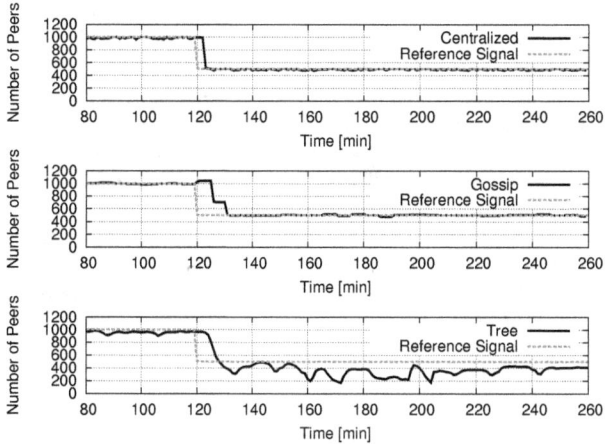

Figure 10: Actual vs. monitored number of peers over time during the massive crash workload.

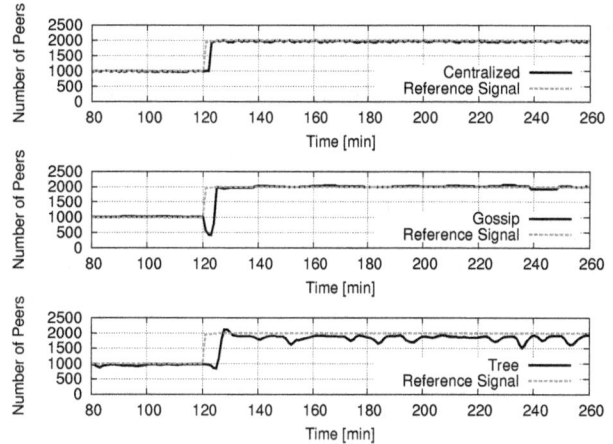

Figure 11: Actual vs. monitored number of peers over time during the massive join workload.

Dealing with costs, as displayed in Figure 6(c), the increasing churn rate shows little effect on the mean total traffic $\overline{l(t, p)}$ of the decentralized monitoring mechanisms.

4.5 Robustness Benchmark

Starting with the *massive crash workload*, Figure 10 displays the peer count to examine validity for the considered monitoring mechanisms during this workload. The gossip-based approach handles the sudden change in the system, settles down after 10min at the correct number of peers, and delivers stable results over time. Figure 9(b) and 9(a) reveal as well the robust behavior of the gossip-based approach. Irregardless of the sudden change in the system, the mean staleness $\overline{t_{stale}(X(a, t, p))}$ oscillates around 481s, while the mean relative monitoring error for the sine function $\epsilon_{avg}(a, t, p)$ retains its characteristic oscillation. In contrast, the tree-based approach is not able to recover from the crash and delivers incorrect and fluctuating results, especially in terms of the mean error for the peer count. The reason for this failure originates from the collapse of the underlying Chord overlay. The monitoring topology cannot be created and maintained without the lookup-functionality of the overlay.

Examining the costs during and after the crash, Figure 9(c) displays a highly varying mean traffic $\overline{l(t, p)}$ for each approach. The highly fluctuating traffic from Chord's maintenance mechanisms, which react on the departure of peers and calm down after a certain amount of time.

For the *massive join workload*, Figure 11 displays the pro-

vided results of the three alternatives in terms of the monitored number of peers. Contrary to the previously discussed results of the massive crash workload, each mechanism manages the sudden increase of peers in the system and returns to its normal state after a period of time. This trend can also be observed, when looking at other metrics that quantify the performance of our alternatives: (i) In terms of validity, Figure 12(a) outlines that all mechanisms recover and provide similar results. (ii) Figure 12(b) shows that the mean staleness $\overline{t_{stale}(X(a, t, p))}$ of the provided results does not degrade due to the massive join and the sudden increase in the system size. Dealing with costs, Figure 12(c) shows that the mean total traffic does not change and levels off after short fluctuations.

4.6 Discussion of Results

Having presented the benchmark of the different monitoring approaches, this section summarizes the obtained results. Subsequently, we discuss and compare the initial performance evaluation of the respective papers that introduced the herein utilized monitoring mechanisms.

Under idealized conditions, the tree-based monitoring approach outperforms the gossip-based approach in terms of validity, while producing less traffic, which is balanced more regularly among the peers. Regarding the mean monitoring error for the peer count, the tree-based approach even catches up with the centralized approach. In contrast, the hierarchical structure results in a biased distribution of results, because leaves or distant nodes from the root obtain

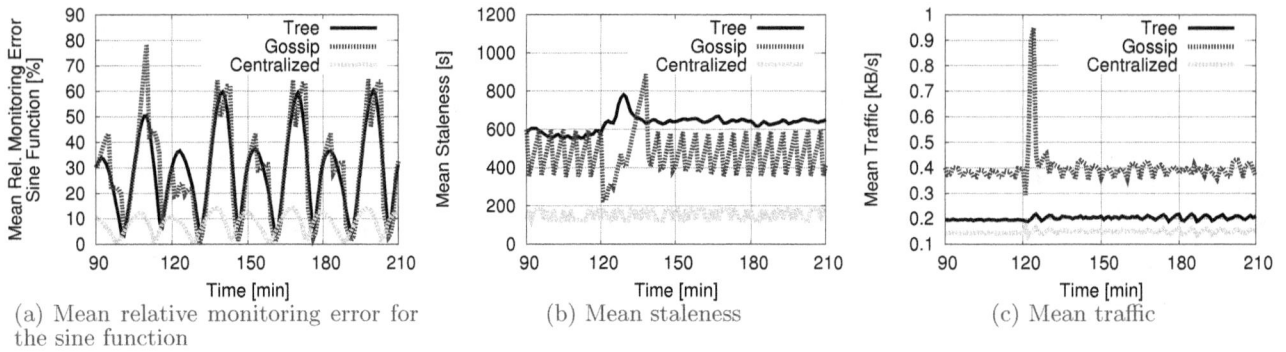

(a) Mean relative monitoring error for the sine function

(b) Mean staleness

(c) Mean traffic

Figure 12: Per peer results for performance and costs over time, measured during the massive join workload.

inaccurate and old results. In the presence of churn, the performance of the tree-based approach significantly decreases dependent on the mean session time of the peers in the system. On the contrary, the underlying mesh topology of the gossip-based approach exhibits a better stability and is capable of handling the increasing dynamic in the system, still providing valid and fresh results. Nevertheless, the peer count procedure shows its susceptibility to the altering mesh topology. In terms of extreme peer fluctuations, which characterize the robustness of a mechanism, the corresponding benchmark outlines that the gossip-based approach is robust enough to handle sudden changes in the system and even provide results on top of a crashed overlay. Due to the intensive application of the lookup functionality of the overlay by the tree-based approach, the monitoring mechanism collapses during the crash. Although, it is capable of handling a sudden increase of peers in the P2P system. Dealing with scalability of a decentralized monitoring mechanism, the horizontal workload outlines that the decentralized mechanisms scale with a growing number of peers. The increased amount of peers has only a negligible influence on performance and costs, except for the underlying peer count procedure of the gossip-based approach, which exhibits considerable outliers. Dealing with the vertical scalability workload, the resulting traffic of both decentralized monitoring mechanisms increases and leads to a decreasing validity and increasing staleness of the monitored attributes. We observe that the tree-based approach already suffers from a smaller increase in traffic regarding its performance, while the participants in the gossip-based approach must handle a considerable amount of traffic.

In the following, we discuss and compare the initial performance evaluation for the gossip- and subsequently the tree-based approach. Jelasity et al. [11] evaluate their approach with respect to scalability, robustness, and stability. In terms of scalability, the paper only addresses horizontal scalability, which is evaluated based on mathematical analysis. The paper omits an evaluation in terms of vertical scalability. While the authors rely on validity, or accuracy as denoted by the authors, to characterize the performance of the presented approach, costs are not considered during the simulative and experimental evaluation. Consequently, the drawn conclusions in terms of scalability, stability, and robustness cover only performance. Using our presented methodology, we have shown in Section 4.3 and 4.5 that the resulting costs in terms of traffic are not influenced by peer-related workloads, e.g., horizontal scalability, massive crash or join. Instead, we could show in Section 4.5, that a grow-

ing amount of monitored attributes results in a considerable increase of traffic and that the produced traffic influences the provided results (cf. Section 4.2). In terms of accuracy, Jelasity et al. only consider the peer count as measurable attribute in their evaluation, because it represents a "worst-case" due to its sensitivity to failures. The assessment of accuracy based on "normal" attributes, such as modeled by our value generator, is omitted. Based on our methodology, we showed the increased susceptibility of the peer counting procedure in contrast to the robust calculation of "normal" attributes (cf. Section 4.3 and 4.4). Dealing with the experiments on stability and robustness, Jelasity et al. present an exhaustive evaluation, which examines the effect of peer crashes, different message loss rates and churn on the performance of the mechanism. Within these experiments, the authors only concentrate on one epoch of the protocol, while long-term effects are ignored. Thus, out of the presented results, it is not obvious if the presented approach can recover and how long this might take.

In contrast to the previous and our methodology, the tree-based approach [6,7] is just evaluated in terms of scalability and stability, but set up on two different overlays. With respect to stability, the corresponding workload consists of different churn levels, which are applied on the system during one run. In terms of scalability, the decentralized monitoring mechanism was evaluated under a varying amount of peers in separate runs. Similar to our methodology, Graffi et al. evaluate the performance of the presented approach in terms of validity and timeliness, which they denote as precision and freshness. On the contrary, they evaluate validity and timeliness of the obtained results only at the root, while dissemination of results back to the remaining peers is not taken into account. Dealing with validity, they look at the peer count and other attributes, which are either measured by the peers or modeled by their implemented value generator. While examining the resulting costs and their distribution among the peers, they do not evaluate how validity of the obtained results differs among the peers. In this regard, Section 4.2 outlines that the topology of the tree heavily influences validity and timeliness. Moreover, we showed that the tree-based approach provides a similar performance as the centralized approach under idealized conditions. On the contrary, Section 4.3 outlines that the approach suffers from an increasing amount of attributes, while it cannot handle massive crashes, in contrast to massive joins (cf. Section 4.5), and that performance degrades if peer fluctuation increases (cf. Section 4.4).

Based on the two examples of performance evaluation, it

becomes apparent that there is no standardized way for the evaluation of decentralized monitoring mechanisms. Moreover, the examples outline that a comparison of several mechanisms based on the differing initial evaluations is hard to achieve. The presented evaluations only agree on a fraction of quality aspects, such as validity, costs, or scalability, which are examined. On the contrary, other important aspects, e.g., robustness, or fairness are neglected. The resulting workloads, evaluation scenarios, and setups differ widely and cannot be compared. Besides a standardized set of quality aspects or workloads, a unified approach must be established to capture the measurements for the evaluation. As shown by the examples, measurements can be taken at all peers, while other evaluations rely on measurements at single peers, such as the root. ⸲

5. RELATED WORK

The related work in the area of benchmarks for decentralized systems details the methodology and aspects as well as existing implementations for the performance evaluation. The considered implementations range from distributed hash tables (DHT) [15], over networked virtual environments [8, 13], to decentralized monitoring mechanisms [3, 4].

Haeberlen et al. [9] discuss the general benefits of a benchmark for decentralized systems, leading to an improved comparability between different approaches and a better classification of the obtained results. In addition to the positive features of a standardized methodology, their paper also highlights common dangers of a benchmark, which might originate from inappropriate or false standardization, incomplete tests or ossification of a standard. Besides this general description of benchmarks in decentralized systems, we already focus on a benchmarking methodology in the area of P2P systems in our previous work [14]. We outline the specifics for the design of a P2P benchmark and give a concrete definition for benchmarking search overlays and overlays for networked virtual environments.

Apart from the description of the benchmarking methodology, several approaches exist that present the implementation of a benchmark for a P2P system. Li et al. [15] develop a methodology to evaluate the efficiency of different DHTs by examining the trade-off between performance and cost. Therefore, they define different types of workloads to test the overlays under varying conditions and to investigate overlays with different parameter settings. Kovacevic et al. evaluate in [13] the suitability of DHTs in networked virtual environments. They develop a dedicated benchmark that addresses the investigation of relevant quality aspects for these environments by defining appropriate metrics. An extended version of the benchmark has been proposed by Gross et al. [8], which allows for the comparison of arbitrary overlays for networked virtual environments implementing a certain interface definition.

Regarding the benchmark for decentralized monitoring mechanisms, Bawa et al. [3] present a benchmark for three different aggregation approaches ranging from a tree-based over a gossip-based to a hybrid topology to monitor a P2P network. Given the made assumptions for the benchmark (e.g., network topology, distributed state, and communication failures), the paper compares the three approaches regarding different quality aspects, covering flexibility, generality, termination, and correctness. Our presented benchmarks extend the work by Bawa et al. concerning the ex-

amination of the identified non-functional requirements. For the evaluation of accuracy, we define a detailed analysis for a monitoring mechanism and its produced monitoring error based on reference signals of the value generator, besides peer count. Moreover, we identified different workloads to stress the monitoring mechanisms under different conditions for the examination of quality aspects, such as robustness. In [4], Cappos and Hartman compare their developed tree-based monitoring mechanism with another tree-based approach [24] and a centralized solution, using analytical models, simulations, and experiments. We extend the extensive evaluation in their work by including the examination of accuracy for decentralized monitoring mechanisms. In addition, we add the investigation of robustness for decentralized monitoring mechanisms by massive join/crash workloads.

The problem of missing comparability becomes even more clear in a survey of decentralized aggregation mechanisms by Makhloufi et al. [17]. While giving a good overview about different schemes for aggregation protocols, highlighting the different design decisions, the concluding table, which lists the performance of the considered approaches, does not enable a fair comparison between them. This results from the fact that the summary only summarizes the results of the respective papers.

6. FUTURE WORK

In this paper, we have presented our approach for a set of benchmarks, which establishes a standardized evaluation of decentralized monitoring mechanisms to facilitate comparability of results. For the standardized evaluation, we (i) defined a common interface for a unified access of the provided functionality, (ii) identified relevant non-functional requirements of the considered class of mechanisms, and (iii) designed a set of workloads and metrics to evaluate and quantify the non-functional requirements. We presented the implementation of four different benchmarks (baseline, stability, robustness, scalability) for evaluating performance and costs of decentralized monitoring mechanisms. Thereby, we identified characteristic performance and cost profiles as well as monitoring capabilities for two decentralized monitoring mechanisms (a gossip-based and a tree-based approach) as well as for a centralized approach, which served as a reference.

We plan to apply our benchmarks on different decentralized monitoring mechanisms, since the presented application of benchmarks only considered monitoring approaches with push-based data collection and proactive result dissemination. Therefore, we intend to benchmark pull-based and reactive monitoring mechanisms as well, in order to determine the trade-off between push- and pull-based data aggregation, or proactive and reactive result dissemination, as already analyzed in our previous work [20].

In the future we plan to exchange the underlying overlay with other well known overlays in order to investigate the interdependencies in terms of performance and costs between monitoring mechanisms and underlying overlays. Besides, we will not only focus on the communicational overhead caused by a decentralized monitoring mechanism, but also consider the computational overhead, such as the resulting I/O- or CPU-usage. Moreover, we plan to execute our benchmarks in larger simulations, which exceed the capabilities of typical testbeds, such as PlanetLab.

7. ACKNOWLEDGMENTS

This work has been supported by the German Research Foundation (DFG), Research Group 733, "QuaP2P: Quality Improvement of Peer-to-Peer Systems".

8. REFERENCES

[1] K. Albrecht, R. Arnold, M. Gahwiler, and R. Wattenhofer. Aggregating Information in Peer-to-Peer Systems for Improved Join and Leave. In *Proc. of the 4th Internat. Conf. on Peer-to-Peer Computing*, pages 227–234, 2004.

[2] M. S. Artigas, P. García, and A. F. G. Skarmeta. DECA: A Hierarchical Framework for DECentralized Aggregation in DHTs. In *Large Scale Management of Distributed Systems*, volume 4269, pages 246–257. Springer, 2006.

[3] M. Bawa, H. Garcia-Molina, A. Gionis, and R. Motwani. Estimating Aggregates on a Peer-to-Peer Network. Tech. Rep. 2003-24, Stanford InfoLab, 2003.

[4] J. Cappos and J. H. Hartman. San Fermín: Aggregating Large Data Sets Using a Binomial Swap Forest. In *Proc. of the 5th USENIX Symposium on Networked Systems Design and Implementation*, pages 147–160, 2008.

[5] P. T. Eugster, R. Guerraoui, A.-M. Kermarrec, and L. Massoulié. Epidemic Information Dissemination in Distributed Systems. *IEEE Computer*, 37(5):60–67, 2004.

[6] K. Graffi. *Monitoring and Management of Peer-to-Peer Systems*. PhD thesis, Technische Universtiät Darmstadt, 2010.

[7] K. Graffi, D. Stingl, J. Rueckert, A. Kovacevic, and R. Steinmetz. Monitoring and Management of Structured Peer-to-Peer Systems. In *Proc. of the 9th Internat. Conf. on Peer-to-Peer Computing*, pages 311–320, 2009.

[8] C. Gross, M. Lehn, C. Münker, A. Buchmann, and R. Steinmetz. Towards a Comparative Performance Evaluation of Overlays for Networked Virtual Environments. In *Proc. of the 11th Internat. Conf. on Peer-to-Peer Computing*, pages 34–43, 2011.

[9] A. Haeberlen, A. Mislove, A. Post, and P. Druschel. Fallacies in Evaluating Decentralized Systems. In *Proc. of the 5th Internat. Workshop on Peer-to-Peer Systems*, 2006.

[10] M. Jelasity, R. Guerraoui, A.-M. Kermarrec, and M. van Steen. The Peer Sampling Service: Experimental Evaluation of Unstructured Gossip-Based Implementations. In *Proc. of the 5th ACM/IFIP/USENIX Internat. Conf. on Middleware*, pages 79–98, 2004.

[11] M. Jelasity, A. Montresor, and O. Babaoglu. Gossip-Based Aggregation in Large Dynamic Networks. *ACM Transactions on Computer Systems*, 23(3):219–252, 2005.

[12] D. Kempe, A. Dobra, and J. Gehrke. Gossip-based computation of aggregate information. In *Proc. of the 44th Annual IEEE Symposium on Foundations of Computer Science*, pages 482–491, 2003.

[13] A. Kovacevic, K. Graffi, S. Kaune, C. Leng, and R. Steinmetz. Towards Benchmarking of Structured Peer-to-Peer Overlays for Network Virtual Environments. In *Proc. of the 14th Internat. Conf. on Parallel and Distributed Systems*, pages 799–804, 2008.

[14] M. Lehn, T. Triebel, C. Gross, D. Stingl, K. Saller, W. Effelsberg, A. Kovacevic, and R. Steinmetz. Designing Benchmarks for P2P Systems. In *From Active Data Management to Event-Based Systems and More*, volume 6462, pages 209–229. Springer, 2010.

[15] J. Li, J. Stribling, R. Morris, M. F. Kaashoek, and T. M. Gil. A Performance vs. Cost Framework for Evaluating DHT Design Tradeoffs Under Churn. In *Proc. of the 24th Annual Joint Conf. of the IEEE Computer and Communications Societies*, pages 225–236, 2005.

[16] S. Madden, M. J. Franklin, J. M. Hellerstein, and W. Hong. Tag: A Tiny AGgregation Service for Ad-hoc Sensor Networks. In *ACM SIGOPS Operating Systems Review*, volume 36, pages 131–146, 2002.

[17] R. Makhloufi, G. Bonnet, G. Doyen, and D. Gaiti. Decentralized Aggregation Protocols in Peer-to-Peer Networks : A Survey. In *Modelling Autonomic Communications Environments*, volume 5844, pages 111–116. Springer, 2009.

[18] M. L. Massie, B. N. Chun, and D. E. Culler. The Ganglia Distributed Monitoring System: Design, Implementation, and Experience. *Parallel Computing*, 30(7):817–840, 2004.

[19] S. Rhea, T. Roscoe, and J. Kubiatowicz. Structured Peer-to-Peer Overlays Need Application-Driven Benchmarks. In *Peer-to-Peer Systems II*, pages 56–67. Springer, 2003.

[20] K. Saller, D. Stingl, and A. Schürr. D^4M, a Self-Adapting Decentralized Derived Data Collection and Monitoring Framework. In *Workshops der wissenschaftlichen Konferenz Kommunikation in Verteilten Systemen*, pages 245–256, 2011.

[21] D. Stingl, C. Gross, J. Rückert, L. Nobach, A. Kovacevic, and R. Steinmetz. PeerfactSim.KOM: A Simulation Framework for Peer-to-Peer Systems. In *Proc. of the Internat. Conf. on High Performance Computing and Simulation*, pages 577–584, 2011.

[22] I. Stoica, R. Morris, D. Karger, M. F. Kaashoek, and H. Balakrishnan. Chord: A Scalable Peer-to-Peer Lookup Service for Internet Applications. In *Proc. of the Conf. on Applications, Technologies, Architectures, and Protocols for Computer Communications*, pages 149–160, 2001.

[23] R. Van Renesse, K. P. Birman, and W. Vogels. Astrolabe: A Robust and Scalable Technology for Distributed System Monitoring, Management, and Data Mining. *ACM Transactions on Computer Systems*, 21(2):164–206, 2003.

[24] P. Yalagandula and M. Dahlin. A Scalable Distributed Information Management System. *ACM SIGCOMM Computer Communication Review*, 34(4):379–390, 2004.

An Industrial Case Study of Performance and Cost Design Space Exploration

Thijmen de Gooijer
ABB Corporate Research
Industrial Software Systems
Västerås, Sweden
thijmen@acm.org

Anton Jansen
ABB Corporate Research
Industrial Software Systems
Västerås, Sweden
anton.jansen@se.abb.com

Heiko Koziolek
ABB Corporate Research
Industrial Software Systems
Ladenburg, Germany
heiko.koziolek@de.abb.com

Anne Koziolek
Department of Informatics,
University of Zurich
Zurich, Switzerland
koziolek@ifi.uzh.ch

ABSTRACT

Determining the trade-off between performance and costs of a distributed software system is important as it enables fulfilling performance requirements in a cost-efficient way. The large amount of design alternatives for such systems often leads software architects to select a suboptimal solution, which may either waste resources or cannot cope with future workloads. Recently, several approaches have appeared to assist software architects with this design task. In this paper, we present a case study applying one of these approaches, i.e. PerOpteryx, to explore the design space of an existing industrial distributed software system from ABB. To facilitate the design exploration, we created a highly detailed performance and cost model, which was instrumental in determining a cost-efficient architecture solution using an evolutionary algorithm. The case study demonstrates the capabilities of various modern performance modeling tools and a design space exploration tool in an industrial setting, provides lessons learned, and helps other software architects in solving similar problems.

Categories and Subject Descriptors

C.4 [**Performance of Systems**]: [modeling techniques]; D.2.8 [**Software Engineering**]: Metrics—*performance measures*; D.2.11 [**Software Engineering**]: Software Architectures

1. INTRODUCTION

Evolving a software intensive system is typically far from trivial. One of the first steps in this process is to create a common shared vision among the system stakeholders for the future of the system. Once this vision has been established, a system road-map can be created that outlines the steps and time-schedule in which the system should evolve. However, creating a reasonable vision and associated road-map proves to be complicated in practice. Often, the trade-offs among the quality attributes are not understood well enough to make an informed decision. One way to improve this understanding is by performing design space exploration. In such an exploration, quantitative analysis models are created that evaluate various architectural alternatives with respect to the system's relevant quality attributes. In turn, this activity creates a deeper understanding of the trade-offs among the quality attributes, thereby enabling more informed decision making.

A challenge for the aforementioned approach is that its associated methods and tools are largely untested in an industrial setting outside the academic research groups they originated from. This creates uncertainty about whether these methods and tools are fit for purpose and actually deliver the value they promise. This in turn stands in the way of popularization, i.e. the ability of an approach to gain wide spread industrial acceptance [38].

The main contribution of this paper is therefore a case study presenting the application of various academic tools and methods for design space exploration in an industrial setting. Our case study presents how we explore component re-allocation, replication, and hardware changes and their performance and cost implications. To the best of our knowledge, this combination of explored changes has not been automatically explored for performance in other works yet. We present the selection criteria for the used methods and tools, the application of them, and the results they delivered. Finally, we present lessons learned and provide pointers for future research directions.

The rest of this paper is organized as follows. Section 2 introduces the system under study, the performance and costs goals of the case study, and the overall approach followed. Next, Section 3 presents the performance measurements, which are used in Section 4 to build a performance model. Section 5 reports on our manual exploration of the design space with the aforementioned performance model, the formalization of our cost model, and how we used both to automatically explore the degrees of freedom in our design space. Lessons learned and pointers for future research directions are presented in Section 6. The paper concludes with related work in Section 7 and with conclusions and future work in Section 8.

2. CASE STUDY OVERVIEW

2.1 System under study

The system studied in this paper is one of ABB's remote diagnostic solutions (RDS). The RDS is a 150 kLOC system used for service activities on thousands of industrial devices and records device status information, failures, and other data. We note that throughout the paper certain details of the system are intentionally changed to protect ABB's intellectual property.

During normal operation the industrial devices periodically contact the RDS to upload diagnostic status information. In cases of abnormal behavior, the devices upload error information to the RDS for future analysis. Customers can track the status of their devices on a website and can generate reports, for example, showing device failures over the last year. Service engineers can troubleshoot device problems either on-site or remotely by sending commands to the device through the RDS.

Part of the RDS is illustrated in Fig. 2. The devices run device specific software that connects to the 'RDS Connection Point', which runs in ABB's DMZ (perimeter network for security reasons). Here the data enters ABB's internal network and is send onward to the core components on the application server.

The system core components handle both the processing and storing of the uploaded data, as well as the publishing of data and interaction with external systems. Data that is received from devices is processed and then stored in the database. Certain data uploads are mined in the 'Data Mining and Prediction Computation' component, for example, to predict the wear of parts. The customer website is hosted outside the RDS back-end and gets data from the RDS web services via a proxy (not shown). The website for service engineers is hosted within the same environment as the RDS web services. Both websites offer access to reports that are created by a separate reporting component, which is not shown in the model.

The RDS is connected to various other systems. One example is shown in the diagram in Fig. 2: the 'ABB customer and device database' interface, which represents a Microsoft SQL Server (MS-SQL) plug-in that synchronizes the RDS database against a central ABB database recording information on which customers have what service contracts for which devices. This synchronization scheme reduces the latency for look-up of this information when a human user or device connects to the system.

2.2 Performance and Cost Goal

ABB wants to improve the performance of RDS by re-architecting, because its back-end is operating at its performance and scalability limits. Performance tuning or short term fixes (e.g., faster CPUs) will not sustainably solve the problems in the long term for three reasons. Firstly, the architecture was conceived in a setting where time-to-market took priority over performance and scalability requirements. Hence, the current architecture has not been designed with performance and scalability in mind. Secondly, the number of devices connected to the back-end is expected to grow by

an order of magnitude within the coming years. Finally, the amount of data that has to be processed for each device, is expected to increase by an order of magnitude in the same period. Together, these dimensions of growth will significantly increase the demands on computational power and storage capacity.

The performance metric of main interest to the system stakeholders is the device upload throughput, i.e., the number of uploads the system can handle per second. It was decided that the system resource on average must not be utilized more than 50% to be able to cope with workload peaks. Considering that the speed of the target hardware resources will grow significantly in the next years, the performance goal for the system was specified as: "The system resources must not be utilized more than 50 percent for a ten times higher arrival rate of device uploads".

The architectural redesign should manage to fulfill the performance goal while controlling cost at the same time. It is not feasible to identify the best design option by prototyping or measurements. Changes to the existing system would be required to take measurements, but the cost and effort required to alter the system solely for performance tests are too high because of its complexity. Furthermore, the capacity predicted by a performance model can be combined with the business growth scenario to get a time-line on the architectural road-map. Thereby, we can avoid the risk of starting work too late and experiencing capacity problems, or being too early and making unnecessary investments. Therefore, ABB decided to create a performance model and cost model to aid architectural and business decision making, to conduct capacity planning and to search the design space for architectural solutions that can fulfill the performance goal in a cost effective manner.

2.3 Case Study Activities

Our case study consisted of three major activities: performance measurement (Section 3), performance modeling (Section 4), and design space exploration (Section 5). Fig. 1 provides an overview of the steps performed for the case study. The following sections will detail each step.

3. PERFORMANCE MEASUREMENT

Measurements are needed to create an accurate performance model. To accurately measure the performance of the RDS, a number of steps needs to be performed. First, tools have to be selected (Section 3.1). Second, a model should be created of the system workload (Section 3.2). Finally, measurements have to be performed (Section 3.3).

3.1 Measurement Tool Selection

The first step entails finding the appropriate tools needed to measure the performance of the system. In short, this consists of:

- A load generator tool to simulate stimuli to the systems in a controlled way.
- An Application Performance Management (APM) tool, which can measure the response time of different stimuli (called business transactions) to the system.
- A (distributed) profiler, which can tell us how the response time of the different stimuli is distributed. This information is vital, as we would like to understand how the performance is build up to focus our re-architecting efforts.

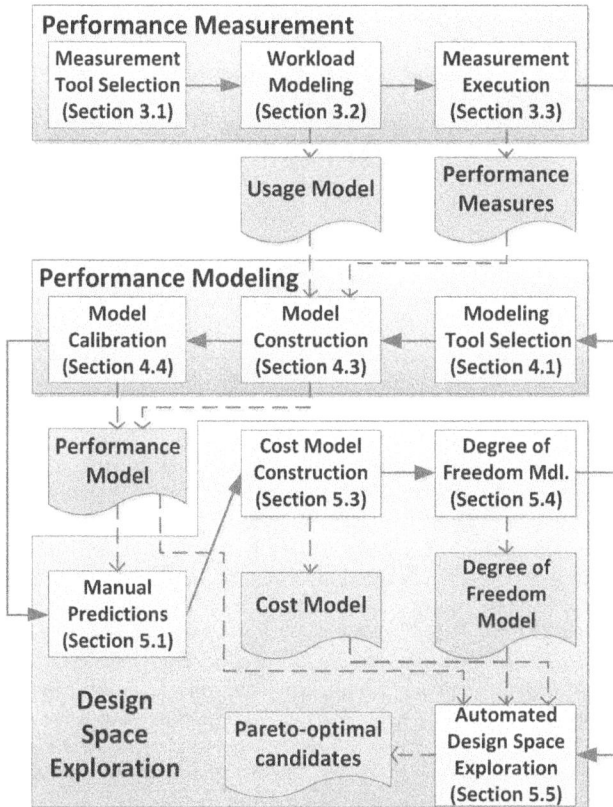

Figure 1: Case Study Approach

We created an initial list of 58 different tools that could fulfill some of this functionality. After removing the alternatives that were no longer maintained or lacked feature completeness the list shrunk to 17 tools. For each of these 17 tools, we classified their functionality and costs by attending online sales presentations of the various tool vendors. In the end, we settled on using the NeoLoad load generator tool [17] in combination with the dynaTrace APM tool [16], because the tools integrate nicely, dynaTrace makes instrumentation of .Net applications easy and NeoLoad supports MS Silverlight.

The dynaTrace tool offers normal performance measurement functionality and distributed profiling functionality. DynaTrace traces requests through all tiers in a distributed application and stores measurements on each individual request in so-called PurePaths. DynaTrace instruments the .NET application code in the CLR layer, thus allowing PurePaths to show timings (i.e., CPU time, execution time, latency) as deep as at the method-level. The recorded measurements can be summarized and viewed in several ways. For example, dynaTrace can create sequence diagrams of PurePaths or show a break-down of how much time was spent in various APIs.

3.2 Workload Modeling

The second step deals with the issue of finding out what the typical workload on the system is. Firstly, we organized a workshop with the developers to find out the actors on the system and their main use cases. Secondly, we turned on the logging facilities of the IIS containers to record the stimuli to the system for a month in production. Using the Sawmill log analysis tool [18], we determined the most frequent used

use cases: the periodic uploading of diagnostic/error information by devices and the interaction of Service Engineers (SE) with the system. Surprisingly enough, the customer related use cases were relatively low in frequency. Most likely this is due to customers being only interested in interacting with the system when the devices have considerable issues, which is not often the case.

The RDS thus executes two performance-critical usage scenarios during production: periodic uploading of diagnostic status information from devices and the interaction of service engineers (SE) with the system. We approximated the uploads with an open workload having an arrival rate of 78.6 requests per minute. Furthermore, we characterized the SE interactions with a closed workload with a user population of 39.3 and a think time of 15 seconds. All values were derived from the production logs of the system.

We decided to run load tests with the system on three different workload intensities: low, medium, and high. The workloads are specified in Table 1 as the number of sustained uploads received from the devices per minute, and the number of concurrent service engineers requesting internal web pages from the system.

The medium workload approximates the current production load on RDS. The low workload was used as an initial calibration point for the performance model and is approximately half the production load. The advantage of the low workload is that the system behavior is more stable and consistent, making it easier to study. The high workload represents a step towards the target capacity and enables us to study how the resource demands change at increasing loads.

workload	uploads/min	SE requests/min
low	41.0	20.5
medium	78.6	39.3
high	187.9	93.9

Table 1: The model calibration workloads used. (data is altered to protect ABB's intellectual property)

3.3 Measurement Execution

The third and final step, performing the measurements, has to deal with an important constraint to the case study: the need to minimize the impact of the study on ongoing development and operation activities of the system. To address this issue, we built a separate "experimental" copy of the system in the ABB Corporate Research labs. This copy consisted of a recently released version of the RDS, which is deployed on a large server running virtualization software. This deployment in virtual servers allows us to easily test out different deployments of the system with varying hardware resources. For the virtualization software we choose to go with VMWare ESX, as we have local in-house IT expertise to manage such servers.

The experimental copy of the RDS runs on three virtual machines. The NeoLoad load generator runs on a separate physical machine to emulate industrial devices uploading data and service engineers generating requests to the RDS. DynaTrace data collection agents were installed on the DMZ and application server. Information on the performance of the database server was recorded by subscribing dynaTrace to its Windows performance monitor counters, as dynaTrace cannot instrument the Microsoft SQL Server (MS-SQL).

During the first load tests on our system, we verified the consistency of the performance measurements and we gained sufficient confidence in dynaTrace's instrumentation to run all our measurements for 30 minutes. In the next tests, we stressed the system to observe its behavior under peak loads and to find its bottlenecks and capacity limits. Both test phases needed several iterations to adjust dynaTrace's instrumentation, so that requests were traced through all tiers correctly. During the stress tests we varied the hardware configuration of the virtual machines to explore the sensitivity of the application to the amount of CPU cores and memory and several concurrency settings of the ASP.Net container.

Finally, we performed two types of structured measurements to support the performance modeling. First, we ran load tests matching our workload model, which later could be compared to model predictions to calibrate the model. We used average values from these load tests to instatiate our model. Second, we measured just a single request to get a clear picture of runtime system behavior to base the behavioral part of the performance model upon. When recreating the workload model in NeoLoad, we needed several iterations until the generated workload matched the model.

Some data we could not gather using dynaTrace. First of all, some metrics were not easily recorded or isolated. For example, network latency measurements were more easily obtained using a ping tool and MS-SQL's performance counters were better studied with the MS-SQL profiler tool. Second, it was difficult to interpret results. For example, significant differences between CPU and execution time were difficult to account for, because the instrumentation of the ASP.Net container itself was insufficient.

4. PERFORMANCE MODEL

To construct a performance model for the ABB RDS, we first selected an appropriate modeling notation (Section 4.1), which turned out to be the Palladio Component Model (Section 4.2). Based on the performance measurements results, the workload model, and additional analyses, we constructed a Palladio model for the ABB RDS (Section 4.3), which we calibrated (Section 4.4) until it reflected the performance of the system under study well.

4.1 Method and Tool Selection

We conducted a survey of performance modeling tools [23] and selected initial candidates based on three criteria: (i) support for performance modeling of software architectures, (ii) available recent tooling, (iii) tool maturity and stability. Most mature tools do not meet the first criterion, while prototypical academic tools often fail on the latter two as described in the following.

The low-level Petri Net modeling tools GreatSPN [15] and ORIS [7] as well as the SHARPE [12] tool do not reflect software architectures naturally. This problem also applies to PRISM [10]. The ArgoSPE [1], and TwoTowers [14] tools are not actively updated anymore. Intermediate modeling languages, such as KlaperSuite [4] or CSM [2], were discarded due to their still instable transformation from UML models.

The commercial Hyperformix tool [35] is expensive, while from publicly available information it is difficult to judge whether the tool offers major benefits in our use case. The PEPA tools [9] use a powerful process algebra, but the pro-

totypical mapping from UML models to PEPA has not been maintained for several years.

Six tools appeared mature enough and promising to fit our architectural modeling problem: Java Modeling Tools (JMT) [3], the Layered Queuing Network Solver (LQNS) [5], Palladio workbench [8], QPME [11], SPE-ED [13], and Möbius [6].

Based on our requirements, we analyzed the different tools. Some of Möbius' formalisms do not target at software architecture performance modeling. The SPE-ED tool specifically targets architecture modeling, but it is no longer actively updated. Furthermore, both Möbius and SPE-ED are subject to license fees for commercial use. While their price is reasonable, the acquisition of commercial software within a corporation considerably delays work. Therefore both tools were rejected.

For QPME, we lacked a release of the stable version 2.0, thus we could not use the improvements made in this version. While both LQNS and Palladio workbench offer modeling concepts that are easily mapped onto software modeling concepts, we decided to start modeling using JMT, which feature more intuitive user interfaces and the best documentation. JMT's simplicity in modeling and ability to be directly downloaded contributed to this decision.

Unfortunately, JMT quickly proved not expressive enough. For example, asynchronous behavior could not be directly expressed. Also, the semantic gap between our software design concepts (components interacting by web service calls) and the QNM formalism were an obstacle.

Finally, we opted to use the Palladio workbench, because it supports the simulation of architectural models and because its 'UML-like' interface makes it easier to construct models and communicate them with the stakeholders than LQNS. The ability to re-use models and components was another useful feature [23]. Moreover, the Palladio workbench has been used in industrial case studies before [27, 33], thus we assume that it is mature and sufficiently stable. Palladio's drawbacks lie in its more laborious model creation due to the complex meta model and its weaker user documentation.

4.2 Palladio Component Model

The PCM is based on the component-based software engineering philosophy and distinguishes four developer roles, each modeling part of a system: component developer, software architect, system deployer, and domain expert. Once the model parts from each role have been assembled, the combined model is transformed into a simulation or analysis model to derive the desired performance metrics. Next, we discuss each role's modeling tasks and illustrate the use of the PCM with the ABB RDS model (Fig. 2).

The *component developer role* is responsible for modeling and implementing software components. She puts models of her components and their interfaces in a `Component Repository`, a distinct model container in the PCM. When a developer creates the model of a component she specifies its resource demands for each provided service as well as calls to other components in a so-called `Service Effect Specification` (SEFF).

As an example consider the `SEFF` on the right of Fig. 2. It shows an internal action that requires 100 ms of CPU time and an external call to insert data into the database. Besides mean values, the PCM meta model supports arbitrary

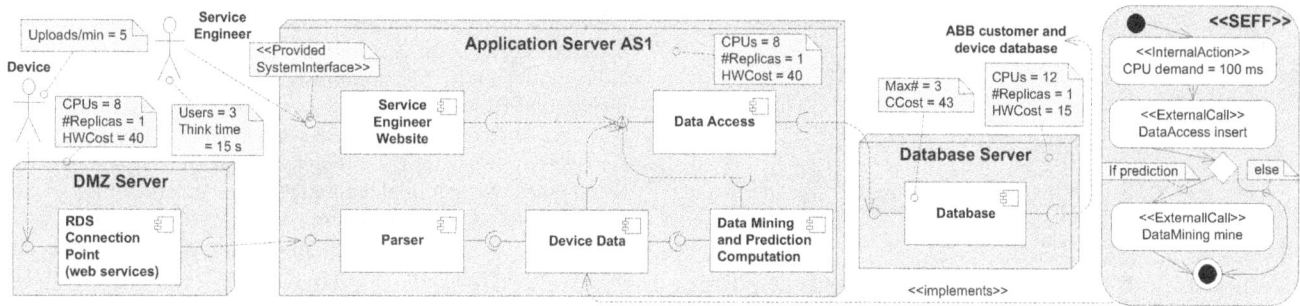

Figure 2: Palladio Component Model of the ABB remote diagnostic system (in UML notation)

probability distributions as resource demands. Other supported resource demands are, for example, the number of threads required from a thread pool or hard disk accesses. The component developer role can also specify component cost (CCost), for example, our database component has cost 10 (CCost = 43) (cf. Section 5.3).

The *software architect role* specifies a `System Model` by selecting components from the component repository and connecting required interfaces to matching provided interfaces. The *system deployer role* specifies a `Resource Environment` containing concrete hardware resources, such as CPU, hard disks, and network connections. These resources can be annotated with hardware costs. For example, application server AS1 in Fig. 2 has 8 CPU cores (CPUs = 8), costs 40 units (HWCost = 40, cf. Section 5.3), and is not replicated (#Replicas = 1).

Finally, the *domain expert role* specifies the usage of the system in a `Usage Model`, which contains scenarios of calls as well as an open or closed workload for each scenario.

The Palladio workbench tool currently provides two performance solvers: SimuCom and PCM2LQN. We chose PCM2LQN in combination with the LQNS analytical solver, because it is usually much faster than SimuCom. Automatic design space exploration requires to evaluate many candidates, so runtime is important. PCM2LQN maps the Palladio models to a layered queueing network (LQN). This does not contradict our former decision against LQNS, since here the LQN models remained transparent to the stakeholders and were only used for model solution. The LQN's analytic solver [26] is restricted compared to SimuCom, since it only provides mean value performance metrics and does not support arbitrary passive resources such as semaphores.

4.3 Model Construction

To model the RDS like in the experimental setup as a Palladio model, we studied its structure and behavior by analyzing the available documentation, talking to its developers, analyzing the source code and performing different load tests. Then, we constructed the model as follows:

Component Repository: Using the existing architectural descriptions to create the component repository formed a major challenge, because these documents were limited in detail and only provided a component level logical view and a deployment view. We used these views to select the components to include in our PCM component repository. Initially, the RDS repository consisted of seven components, seven interfaces, and 27 component services.

SEFFs: To specify the SEFFs for each component service *(step 2)*, we used dynaTrace to analyze the system behav-

ior. We created single stimulus measurements (e.g., a single upload) and analyzed them in depth using the method-level performance information for each transaction in dynaTrace PurePaths [16]. The method level turned out to be far too detailed for a useful behavioral model.

Therefore, we opted to model system behavior at the level of web service calls between the tiers. In some cases, we added more detail to capture differences between use cases. For example, the data mining component needed to be modeled in some detail to get accurate predictions for each type of upload, because the component is quite complex and resource intensive. We further used various overviews of dynaTrace to ensure that we included the most frequent and demanding parts of the software. While we used the aforementioned server log analysis results to limited the SEFFs in our model to represent only the most frequent use cases.

One of the more complex SEFFs is depicted as an example in Fig. 3. While heavily abstracting from the actual source code, it still shows a complex control flow with several resource demands to CPU and hard disk as well as several calls to other components and web services.

While log analyses also revealed that the uploads were not uniformly spread over time, we assumed that the upload rate will be flattened due to easily implementable changes to the system. Since ABB can control the upload schedule to a great extent this is a reasonable assumption. However, we do reserve capacity for (limited) peaks. The reporting functionality of RDS was not included despite its significant performance impact, because there are concrete plans to migrate this functionality to a dedicated server.

Several aspects of the application infrastructure were not considered in the performance model. First of all, the RDS interacts with ABB internal and external 3rd party systems. Our model assumed that the response times of the services offered by these systems do not increase as the load within RDS increases, because we could not easily obtain information about the scalability of these systems.

Second, the Microsoft SQL Server (MS-SQL) database replication/duplication mechanisms were not modeled in detail. The exact behavior of the MS-SQL in these cases is hardly known, and it was not feasible to conduct experiments to prototype the behavior. As a result the database scalability figures and resource requirements are expected to be slightly optimistic.

System Model: From the resulting Palladio component repository, we created a system model instantiating and connecting the components. It contained 7 component instances and 7 connectors. In this case, creating the connections of the components was straightforward.

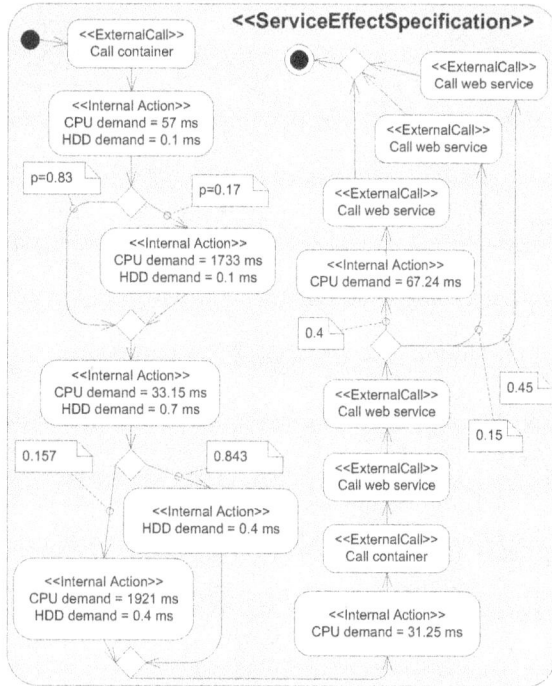

Figure 3: An example service effect specification (SEFF) from the RDS Palladio model showing the inner behavior of one component service in terms of resource demands and calls to other components

Resource Environment: In our case, this model is made up of three servers, each with a CPU and hard disk. The network capacity is assumed to always be sufficient and scaled up by the IT provider as required. The first reason for this assumption is that we expect our IT provider to actually be able to provide the capacity and latency required. The second reason is the limited detail offered by Palladio's network simulator and the subsequent difficulty of specifying the network subsystem in detail. One would have to determine, for a complex system running in .NET, how much latency network messages are issued in each layer.

Allocation Model: We mapped the seven component instances to the three servers in the resource environment according to the allocation in our experimental setup (Fig. 2).

Usage Model: Our usage model reflects the upload service and the service engineering interaction with the system. The former was a periodic request to the system modeled with an open workload and three differently weighted upload types. The latter comprised a more complex user interaction with different branches, loops, and user think times and a closed workload.

4.4 Model Calibration

Calibration of performance models is important to ensure that the resource demands in the model accurately reflect the resource demands in the real system. For calibration of the RDS model, we executed the Palladio performance solvers and compared the predicted utilization for each resource with the utilizations measured by their respective windows performance counters. We conducted this comparison for each of the three workloads introduced in Section 3.3 to assure that the model was robust against different workload intensities.

Despite using the detailed resource demands measured by dynaTrace, the utilizations derived from the initial RDS Palladio model showed a moderate deviation from the actually measured utilizations. Thus, we ran additional experiments and performed code reviews to get a better understanding of the system and why the prediction was off. We focused on those parts of the model where it showed errors of more than 20 % compared to the measurement results. This led to useful insight, either to refine the model or to learn more about the RDS architecture, the system behavior, and bottlenecks in the system. The utilizations derived in each calibration step were recorded in an Excel sheet to track the model accuracy and the effect of changes made to the model.

After calibration the model gives values up to 30% too low for the DMZ server CPU utilization. That means that for a 25% CPU utilization the actual CPU utilization could be 32.5%. The application server utilization figures are off by a maximum of 10% and the database server CPU utilization results are at most 30% too high. Three quarter of the response times for both internal and external calls are within 30% of the measured value.

We report the errors for our high load scenario, because this is most representative of our target workload. The errors for the other two workloads are lower. Overall, the error percentages are reasonable, but not desirably small. However, both our measurements in the experimental setup and our experience during earlier work [23] showed that the application server, for which our model most accurately predicts utilization, would be the most likely bottleneck. There are two main reasons it was not economical to further improve the accuracy of the model. First, the complex behavior of the ASP.Net container especially with our asynchronous application could not be understood within reasonable time. Second, the application behavior was complex, because of its size and the way it was written.

5. DESIGN SPACE EXPLORATION

Based on the created performance model, we want to find cost-efficient architectures to cope with the expected increased workload (cf. Section 3.2). We consider three workload scenarios: Scenario 1 considers a higher workload scenario due to more connected devices. Scenarios 2 and 3 additionally consider an eightfold (scen. 2) and fourfold (scen. 3) increase of processed data per device. For each scenario, we want to determine the architecture that fulfills our main performance goal (50% utilization maximum) at the lowest cost. We first ran several manual predictions using the calibrated model (Section 5.1). Because of the large design space, we applied the automated design space exploration tool 'PerOpteryx' (Section 5.2). As a prerequisite we created a formal PerOpteryx cost model (Section 5.3) and a degree of freedom model (Section 5.4). Finally, we ran several predictions and created an architectural road-map (Section 5.5).

5.1 Manual Exploration

Initially, we partially explored the design space by manually modifying the baseline model [23]. First, we used the AFK scale cube theory, which explains scalability in three fundamental dimensions, the axes of the cube. Scalability can be increased by moving the design along these axes by cloning, performing task-based splits or performing request-based splits. We created three architectural alternatives, each exploring one axis of the AFK scale cube [19]. Second, we combined several scalability strategies and our knowledge about hardware costs to create further alternatives to cost-effectively meet our capacity goal. Finally, we reflected several updates of the operational software in our model, because the development continued during our study.

The first of our AFK-scale cube inspired alternatives, scales the system by assigning each component to its own server. This complies to the Y-axis in the AFK scale cube. However, some components put higher demands on system resources than others. Therefore, it is inefficient to put each component on its own server. The maximum capacity of this model variant shows that network communication would become a bottleneck.

A move along the X-axis of the AFK scale cube increases replication in a system (e.g., double the number of application servers). All replicas should be identical, which requires database replication. We achieved this by having three databases for two pipelines in the system: one shared-write database and two read-only databases. This scheme is interesting because read-only databases do not have to be updated in real-time.

The AFK scale cube Z-axis also uses replication, but additionally partitions the data. Partitions are based on the data or the sender of a request. For example, processing in the RDS could be split on warning versus diagnostic messages, or the physical location, or owner of the sending device.

All alternatives did not consider operational cost. Therefore, we also developed an informal cost model with hardware cost, software licensing cost and hosting cost. Hardware and hosting costs are provided by ABB's IT provider. A spreadsheet cost model created by the IT provider captures these costs. For software licensing an internal software license price list was integrated with the IT provider's spreadsheet to complete our informal cost model.

We further refined the alternatives with replication after finding a configuration with a balanced utilization of the hardware across all tiers. In the end, we settled on a configuration with one DMZ server running the connection point and parser component, one application server running the other components and one database server only hosting the database, i.e., a 1:1:1 configuration.

To scale up for the expected high workload (scen. 1), we first replicated the application server with an X-split (i.e., two load-balanced application servers, a 1:2:1 configuration). For further workload increase (scen. 2+3), this configuration could be replicated in its entirety for additional capacity (i.e., a 2:4:2 configuration). This resulting architecture should be able to cope with the load, yet it is conservative. For example, no tiers were introduced or removed, and there was no separation based on the request type to different pipelines (i.e., z-split).

The potential design space for the system is prohibitively large and cannot be explored by hand. Thus, both to confirm our results and to find even better solutions, we conducted an automatic exploration of the design space with PerOpteryx, as described in the following.

5.2 PerOpteryx: Automated Exploration

The PerOpteryx tool was designed as an automatic design space exploration tool for PCM models [34, 30]. We selected PerOpteryx because of its ability to explore many degrees of freedom, which sets it apart from similar tools.

Additionally, its implementation can directly process PCM models. PerOpteryx applies a meta-heuristic search process on a given PCM model to find new architectural candidates with improved performance or costs. Fig. 4 shows a high-level overview of PerOpteryx's search process:

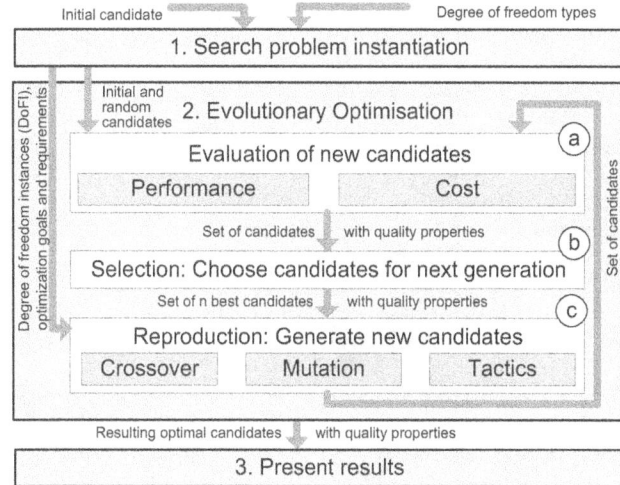

Figure 4: PerOpteryx process model (from [30])

As a prerequisite for applying PerOpteryx, the *degree of freedom types* to consider for optimizing the architecture need to be defined. These types describe how an architecture model may be changed to improve its quality properties [31]. For example, the degree of freedom type "component allocation" describes how components may be re-allocated to different servers that provide the required resources.

In **step 1**, we manually model the search space as a set of *degrees of freedom instances* to explore. Each degree of freedom instance has a set of design options (e.g., a set of CPU clock frequencies between 2 and 4 GHz, or a set of servers a component may be allocated to). Each possible architectural candidate in the search space can be represented relative to the initial PCM model as a set of decisions. This set of decisions—one for each degree instance—is called the genome of the candidate. Furthermore, the *optimization goal and requirements* are modeled in step 1. For example, we can define that the response time of a certain system service and the costs should be optimized, while a given minimum throughput requirement and a given maximum utilization requirement must be fulfilled.

If multiple quality metrics should be optimized, PerOpteryx searches for Pareto-optimal candidates: A candidate is Pareto optimal if there exists no other candidate that is better in all quality metrics. The result of such an optimization is a Pareto front: A set of candidates that are Pareto optimal with respect to other candidates evaluated so far, and which should approximate the set of globally Pareto-optimal candidates well. If only a single quality metric should be optimized, the minimum or maximum value (depending on the metric) is searched.

In **step 2** PerOpteryx applies evolutionary optimization based on the genomes. This step is fully automated. It uses the NSGA-II algorithm [24], which is one of the advanced elitist multi-objective evolutionary algorithms. In addition to the initial PCM model genome, PerOpteryx generates several candidate genomes randomly based on the degree of

211

freedom instances as the starting population. Then, iteratively, the main steps of evaluation (step 2a), selection (step 2b), and reproduction (step 2c) are applied.

First, each candidate is evaluated by generating the PCM model from the genome and then applying the LQN and costs solvers (**2a**). The most promising candidates (i.e. close to the current Pareto front, fulfilling the requirements, and well spread) are selected for further manipulation, while the least promising candidates are discarded (**2b**). During reproduction (**2c**), PerOpteryx manipulates the selected candidate genomes using crossover, mutation, or tactics (cf. [30]), and creates a number of new candidates.

From the results (**step 3**), the software architect can identify interesting solutions in the Pareto front fulfilling the user requirements and make well-informed trade-off decisions. To be able to apply PerOpteryx on the RDS Palladio model, we first created a formal PerOpteryx cost model (Section 5.3) and a degree of freedom instances model (Section 5.4) as described in the following two subsections.

5.3 Formal RDS Cost Model

The PerOpteryx cost model allows to annotate both hardware resources and software components with the total cost of ownership, so that the overall costs can be derived by summing up all annotations. For our case study, we model the total costs for a multiple year period, which is reasonable since the hosting contract has a minimum duration of several years. In total our cost model contained 7 hardware resource and 6 software component cost annotations. The hardware resource costs were a function depending on the number of cores used.

However, the cost prediction cannot be fully accurate. First, prices are re-negotiated every year. Second, we can only coarsely approximate the future disk storage demands. Finally, we do not have access to price information for strategic global hosting options, which means that we cannot explore the viability of replicating the RDS in various geographical locations to lower cost and latency.

Furthermore, we are unable to express between different types of leases. The IT provider offers both physical and virtual machines for lease to ABB. The two main differences are that virtual machines have a much shorter minimum lease duration and that the price for the same computational power will drop more significantly over time than for physical servers. While these aspects are not of major impact on what is the best trade-off between price and performance, it has to be kept in mind that a longer lease for physical machines that have constant capacity and price (whereas virtual machines will become cheaper for constant capacity) reduces flexibility and may hurdle future expansion.

5.4 Degrees of Freedom and Goal

For the ABB RDS system, we identified and modeled three relevant degree of freedom types:

Component allocation may be altered by shifting components from one resources container to another. However, there are restriction to not deploy all components on the DMZ servers and to deploy database components on specific configurations recommended by the IT provider. With four additional resource containers as potential application servers in the model, PerOpteryx can explore a Y-axis split with one dedicated application server per component.

Resource container replication clones a resource container including all contained components. In our model, all resource containers may be replicated. We defined the upper limits for replication based on the experience from our manual exploration [23]. If database components are replicated, an additional overhead occurs between them to communicate their state. This is supported by our degree of freedom concept, as it allows to change multiple elements of the architecture model together [31]. Thus, we reflected this synchronization overhead by modeling different database component versions, one for each replication level.

Number of (CPU) cores can be varied to increase or decrease the capacity of a resource container. To support this degree of freedom type, the cost model describes hardware cost of a resource container relative to the number of cores. The resulting design space has 18 degree of freedom instances:

- 5 *component allocation* choices for the five components initially allocated to application server AS1: They may be allocated to any of the five application servers and to either the DMZ server or the database server, depending on security and compatibility considerations.
- 6 *number of (CPU) cores* choices for the five available application servers and the DMZ server, each instance allows to use 1, 2, 3, 4, 6, or 8 cores as offered by our IT provider.
- 7 *resource container replication* choices for the five application servers (1 to 8 replicas), the DMZ server (1 to 8 replicas), and the database server (1 to 3 replicas). The *resource container replication* degree of freedom instance for the database server also changes the used version of the database component to reflect the synchronization overhead of different replication levels.

The size of this design space is the combination of choices within these instances and thus is 3.67×10^{15} possible architecture candidates.

The degree of freedom types "Resource container replication" and "Number of cores" have been newly defined for this work. As such, the combined optimization of software architectures along all three degree of freedom types has not been presented before and shows the extensibility of PerOpteryx. Furthermore, the possibility to model the changing database behavior (due to synchronization) for different number of replicas shows the flexibility of PerOpteryx' degree of freedom concept.

The goal of the design space exploration for a given workload is to find an architectural candidate that minimizes costs while fulfilling performance requirements. Three performance requirements are relevant: First, the response time of service engineers when calling a system service should be below a given threshold. Second, the response time of the upload service called by the devices should be below a given threshold to ensure the timeliness of the data. Finally, the CPU utilization of all used servers should be below 50%.

5.5 Automated Exploration Results

In the following, we present the exploration results for the three scenarios. As I/O activity is not modeled in the RDS performance model, PerOpteryx cannot take it into account. This assumption has to be validated in future work.

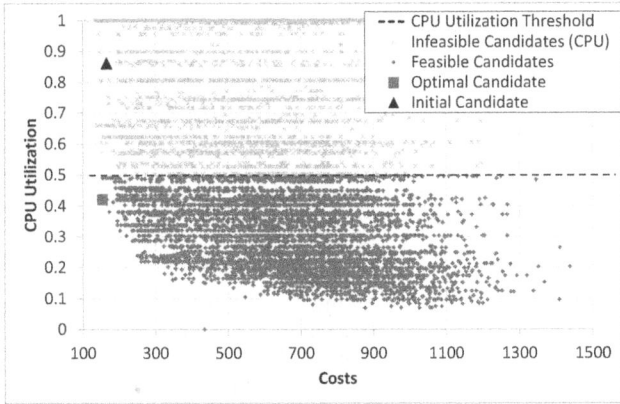

Figure 5: Evaluated Architecture Candidates for High Workload Scenario (Scenario 1). The line at 50% CPU utilization separates feasible candidates (below) from infeasible ones (above).

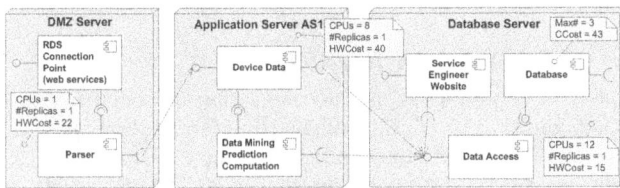

Figure 6: Found Optimal Architecture for High Workload (Scenario 1)

5.5.1 Scenario 1: Higher Workload

For the higher workload scenario, we first ran 3 PerOpteryx explorations of the full design space in parallel on a quad-core machine. Each run took approx. 8 hours. Analyzing the results, we found that the system does not need many servers to cope with the load. Thus, to refine the results, we reduced the design space to use only up to three application servers, and ran another 3 PerOpteryx explorations. Altogether, 17,857 architectural candidates were evaluated.

Fig. 5 shows all architecture candidates evaluated during the design space exploration. They are plotted for their costs and the maximum CPU utilization, which is the highest utilized server among all used servers.

Candidates marked with a cross ($\times$) have a too high CPU utilization (above the threshold of 50%). Overloaded candidates are plotted as having a CPU utilization of 1. The response time requirements are fulfilled by all architecture candidates that fulfill the utilization requirement.

Many candidates fulfilling all requirements have been found, with varying costs. The optimal candidate (i.e. the candidate with the lowest costs) is marked by a square. This optimal candidate uses three servers (DMZ server, DB server, and one application server) and distributes the components to them as shown in Fig. 6. Some components are moved to the DMZ and DB server, compared to the initial candidate. No replication has to be introduced, which would lead to unnecessarily high costs. Furthermore, the number of cores of the DMZ server are reduced in the optimal candidate to save additional costs.

Note, that we did not consider the potentially increased reliability of the system due to replication. A reliability model could be added to reflect this, so that PerOpteryx

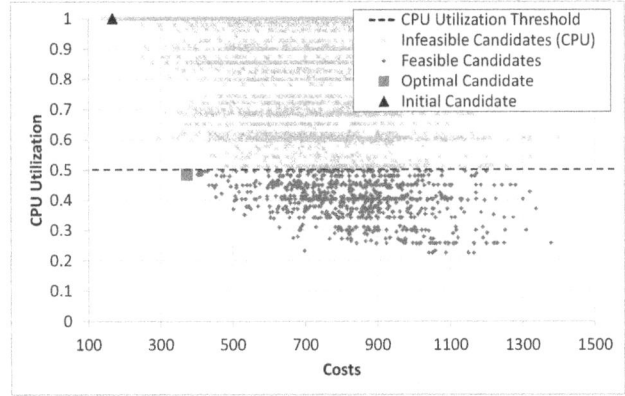

Figure 7: Evaluated Architecture Candidates for High Workload and Information Growth 8 (Scenario 2)

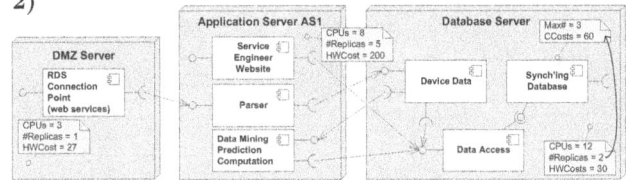

Figure 8: Found Optimal Architecture for High Workload and Information Growth 8 (Scenario 2)

could also explore this quality dimension (as for example done in [34]).

5.5.2 Scenario 2: Higher Workload and Information Growth

If each device sends more data for processing, this leads to an increased demand of some of the components per device request. Thus, the overall load of the system increases further. In this scenario 2, we assume an increase of device information by a factor 8, which leads to higher resource demands in some components where the computation is dependent on the amount of processed data. The new demands were modeled by adding a scalar to the original demands. We defined the scalars based on the theoretical complexity of the operation. For example, a database write scales linearly with the amount of data to be written.

8436 candidates have been evaluated for this scenario in 3 parallel PerOpteryx runs, each running for approx. 8 hours. Fig. 7 shows the evaluated candidates. Compared to the previous scenario, fewer candidates have been evaluated because only the full design space has been explored. More of the evaluated candidates are infeasible or even overloaded and the feasible candidates have higher costs, as expected for the increased workload. The initial candidate as shown in Fig. 2 and the optimal candidate found for the previous scenario 1 are overloaded in this workload situation.

The found optimal candidate is shown in Fig. 8. The components are allocated differently to the servers. Additionally, five replicas of the application server and 2 replicas of the database server are used. This also leads to higher component costs for the database, as two instances have to be paid for. Still PerOpteryx found it beneficial to use the database server as well and even add components to it, because the (physical) database server is less expensive relative to computing power (recall Section 5.3).

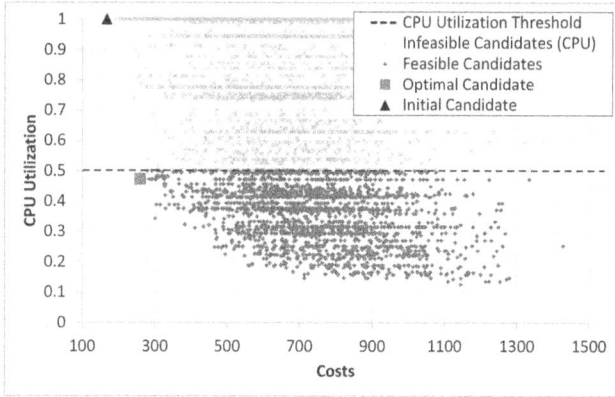

Figure 9: Evaluated Architecture Candidates for High Workload and Information Growth 4 (Scenario 3)

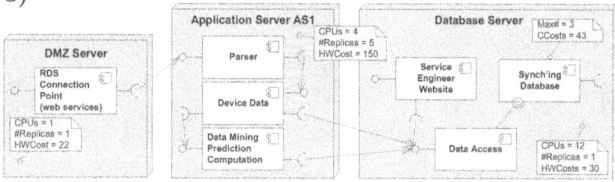

Figure 10: Found Optimal Architecture for High Workload and Information Growth 4 (Scenario 3)

5.5.3 Scenario 3: Higher Workload and Intermediate Information Growth

As a migration step from scenario 1 to scenario 2 with information growth, we additionally analyzed an intermediate information growth of a factor 4. The PerOpteryx setup and run statistics are comparable to scenario 2. Fig. 9 shows the evaluated candidates. As expected, the cloud of evaluated candidates lies in between the results of scenario 1 and 2. For example, there are fewer feasible candidates than in scenario 1, but more than in scenario 2.

Fig. 10 shows the resulting optimal candidate. Compared to the optimal candidate from scenario 1 (Fig. 6), PerOpteryx has moved the Parser component to the application server as well, to be able to use only one DMZ server. The database server is unchanged. The application server has been strengthened to cope with the increased load and the additional Parser component.

However, additional manual exploration shows that the candidate is not truly optimal: PerOpteryx chose to use 5 replicas with 4 cores each here. After inspecting PerOpteryx' optimal candidates, we found that an application server with 3 replicas and 8 cores each would actually be even slightly faster and cheaper (only costs of 120 instead of 150). Thus, a longer exploration run would be required here for a truly optimal solution. Alternatively, we could devise additional PerOpteryx tactics that first analyze the costs for replication of cores and servers and then adjust the model to achieve the cheapest configuration with equivalent processing power. Note, however, that PerOpteryx' automation still is beneficial, as it would be laborious or even impossible to come to these conclusions with manual exploration only.

5.5.4 Summary and Recommendations

Based on these results, we can recommend a road-map for scaling the RDS. First, to cope with the expected work-load increase (scenario 1), the system should be configured in a three tier configuration as shown in Fig. 6. During our manual exploration we made a similar conclusion with regards to the DMZ server. However, we did not know which components to off-load from the application server to the database server. We did consider to place both the data access and data mining predictions on the database server but this overloaded the database server. Hence, the optimal solution for scenario 1 is a partial surprise, but is still valid.

If the workload becomes higher (e.g. due to information growth, scenario 3), the application server should host more components and should be replicated as shown in Fig. 10. Finally, a further increased workload due to more information growth (scenario 2) requires to replicate all three tiers as shown in Fig. 8, while at the same time the allocation of components to application server and database server is slightly adjusted to make optimal use of the processing power. Based one these findings, we formulated a 5 year road-map for the future development of the system. We plan to validate our evaluation after 2 years, as the first steps in the road-map have been realized.

6. LESSONS LEARNED

In this section we share the lessons that we took from our study and that we consider of value to other industry practitioners. Researchers may find ideas on how to improve their performance modeling techniques to meet industry needs.

Performance modeling increases understanding.

The performance modeling proved useful in itself, because it forced us to understand the system's (performance) behavior and identify the bottlenecks. It helped us to ask the right questions about the system and gave us insight that was potentially just as valuable as capacity predictions. For example, model calibration helped us to find oddities in the system behavior. The model represents a polished version of the system that should match its average behavior, but under varying loads measurements and predictions occasionally diverge. One of the things we learned during calibration was that a lock statement was put in the code to limit the amount of concurrently running data mining processes, as to free resources for the internal website that was running on the same server.

Predictions shift stakeholder discussion.

The discussion about the architectural road-map with our stakeholders changed once we introduced the model predictions. The data shifted the conversation from discussion towards a situation where we explained the modeling/evaluation results and the road-map was more or less taken for granted. There was no longer discussion about what the way forward should be. This means that the credibility of our study was high, despite or maybe due to the fact that we presented our stakeholders with a detailed overview of the assumptions underlying the model, their effect on accuracy, and a list of things we did to ensure accuracy.

Economic benefit must exist.

The cost of measuring and modeling are quite high. One has to consider the cost for load generator and measurement tools, training, an experimental copy of the system, and human resources. The latter include the strain on developers and product owners, in addition to the cost for the performance study team. Our study took approximately four full-time employees six months. Adding everything up, one can conclude this type of projects are too expensive for small systems. Short-term fixes may turn-out to be cheaper, despite their inefficiency. We are therefore not surprised that performance fire-fighting is still common practice. More support for performance modelers would be required to decrease the needed effort, e.g. by automatically creating initial performance models based on log data.

Corporate processes may stall license agreements.

It is important to take into account the time required to reach license agreements with vendors. We encountered two problems. First, the license model of software vendors may not fit multi-national companies that have the need to migrate their licenses between machines in different countries. Second, academic software owners do not realize how tedious corporate processes are and how even their simple license hurdles corporate use of their software. For example, due to the need for non-standard licenses to be reviewed by legal experts. This is unfortunate because corporations can often afford to be early adaptors of new technology due to the expertise and money they have available to experiment.

Performance of performance modeling tools limited.

Even for modestly sized systems such as the RDS the performance of the performance modeling tools may be a problem. In our earlier study, we could not use the standard distribution of Palladio workbench, because it ran out of memory [23]. In this study, we reverted to the LQNS to limit the runtime of our design space exploration. The scalability of the modeling formalism also proved to be important. We could comfortably model the RDS and various architectural variations, but we think that the model complexity will be significant for systems that are two times bigger.

It pays off to invest in good tools.

It is difficult to overemphasize the convenience of having the right tools. The combination of dynaTrace and NeoLoad enabled us to take an enormous amount of measurements, and to navigate these easily. In practice, this meant that we could easily study the effect of different software and hardware configurations on performance. The changing of hardware configurations was enabled by using virtual machines in our experimental setup. The repository of performance measurements, which included over 100 load test runs, was frequently consulted during model construction.

7. RELATED WORK

Our work uses the foundations of software performance engineering [39, 21, 32] and multi-objective meta-heuristic optimization [22]. We compare our approach to (i) recent industrial case studies on performance prediction and (ii) recent design space exploration approaches in the software performance domain.

Most recent industrial case studies on performance modeling are restricted to a limited number of evaluated design alternatives. Liu and Gorton [36] constructed a queueing network for an EJB application and conducted a capacity planning study, predicting the throughput for a growing number of database connections. Kounev [29] built a queuing Petri net for the specJAppServer2004. The author measured the system for different workloads and analyzed the impact of a higher number of application server nodes (i.e., 2,4,6,8) for various performance metrics.

Jin et al. [28] modeled the performance of a meter-data system for utilities with a layered queuing network model.

They constructed a very large LQN with more than 20 processors and over 100 tasks. After benchmarking the system, they analyzed the throughput of the system for massively higher workloads. Huber et al. [27] built a Palladio Component Model instance for a storage virtualization system from IBM. They measured performance of the system and analyzed the performance for a synchronous and asynchronous re-design using the model. All of the listed case studies analyze only a single degree of freedom and/or changing workload and do not explicitly address the performance and costs trade-offs for different alternatives.

Concerning design space exploration approaches in the performance domain, three main classes can be distinguished: *Rule-based approaches* improve the architecture by applying predefined actions under certain conditions. *Specialized optimization approaches* have been suggested for certain problem formulations, but they are limited to one or few degree of freedom types at a time. *Meta-heuristic approaches* apply general, often stochastic search strategies to improve the architecture. They use limited knowledge about the search problem itself.

Two recent rule-based approaches are Performance-Booster and ArchE. With PerformanceBooster, Xu et al. [40] present a semi-automated approach to find configuration and design improvements on the model level. Based on a LQN model, performance problems (e.g., bottlenecks, long paths) are identified in a first step. Then, mitigation rules are applied. Diaz-Pace et al. [25] have developed the ArchE framework. ArchE assists the software architect during the design to create architectures that meet quality requirements. It provides the evaluation tools for modifiability or performance analysis, and suggests modifiability improvements. Rule-based approaches share the two limitations of being restricted to the pre-defined improvement rules and the potential of getting stuck in local optima.

Two recent meta-heuristic approaches are ArcheOpteryx and SASSY. Aleti et al.[20] use ArcheOpteryx to optimize architectural models with evolutionary algorithms for multiple arbitrary quality attributes. As a single degree of freedom, they vary the deployment of components to hardware nodes. Menascé et al. [37] generate service-oriented architectures using SASSY that satisfy quality requirements, using service selection and architectural patterns. They use random-restart hill-climbing. All meta-heuristic-based approaches to software architecture improvement explore only one or few degrees of freedom of the architectural model. The combination of component allocation, replication, and hardware changes as supported by PerOpteryx is not supported by the other approaches, and furthermore PerOpteryx is extensible by plugging in additional model transformations [31].

In addition, the other approaches target to mitigate existing performance problems or improve quality properties, while our study targets to optimize costs while maintaining acceptable performance (still, other quality properties can also be optimized with our approach, if reasonable in setting at hand).

8. CONCLUSIONS

This paper has demonstrated how to construct a component-based performance model using state of the art tools for measuring and modeling. We applied the automatic design space exploration tool PerOpteryx on this model and evaluated more than 33,000 architectural candidates for an optimal trade-off between performance and costs in three scenarios. Our case study resulted in a migration road-map for a cost-effective evolution of the existing system.

Our approach enables ABB to comply with future performance requirements (thus helping in sales) and to avoid poor architectural solutions (thus improving development efficiency). It also helps in better understanding the performance impacts on the system and is thus instrumental in performance tuning. Other practitioners can draw from our experiences. For researchers, we have demonstrated that automated design space exploration is feasible for a complex industrial system albeit incurring significant costs. We have created a detailed performance models and found pointers for future research.

Performance measurement and modeling should become more tightly integrated (e.g., by creating Palladio models automatically from dynaTrace results). Network modeling was rather abstract in our study due to the lack of support in the Palladio model. More detailed modeling of the network could lead to even more accurate prediction results. There is potential to automatically draw feasible migration road-maps from the PerOpteryx results for different workloads by highlighting compatible candidates. This should be investigated in future research in more detail.

9. REFERENCES

[1] ArgoSPE plug-in for ArgoUML. argospe.tigris.org/.
[2] Core Scenario Model. www.sce.carleton.ca/rads/puma/.
[3] Java Modelling Tools. jmt.sourceforge.net/.
[4] KlaperSuite. klaper.sourceforge.net/.
[5] Layered Queueing Network Solver software package. www.sce.carleton.ca/rads/lqns/.
[6] Möbius tool. www.mobius.illinois.edu/.
[7] Oris Tool. www.stlab.dsi.unifi.it/oris/.
[8] Palladio Software Architecture Simulator. www.palladio-simulator.com/.
[9] PEPA Tools. www.dcs.ed.ac.uk/pepa/tools/.
[10] PRISM probabilistic model checker. www.prismmodelchecker.org/.
[11] QPME – Queueing Petri net Modeling Environment. descartes.ipd.kit.edu/projects/qpme/.
[12] SHARPE. people.ee.duke.edu/~kst/software_packages.html.
[13] SPE-ED Performance Modeling Tool. www.perfeng.com/sped.htm.
[14] TwoTowers tool. www.sti.uniurb.it/bernardo/twotowers/.
[15] GreatSPN – GRaphical Editor and Analyzer for Timed and Stochastic Petri Nets. www.di.unito.it/~greatspn, 2008.
[16] Dynatrace – Application Performance Management and Monitoring. www.dynatrace.com, 2011.
[17] Neotys Neoload Load Testing Tool. www.neotys.com/product/overview-neoload.html, 2011.
[18] Sawmill – Universal log file analysis tool. www.sawmill.net, 2011.
[19] M. L. Abbott and M. T. Fisher. *The art of scalability.* Addison–Wesley, 2009.
[20] A. Aleti, S. Bjornander, L. Grunske, and I. Meedeniya. Archeopterix: An extendable tool for architecture optimization of AADL models. *Proc. of the ICSE Workshop on MOMPES*, pages 61–71, 2009.
[21] S. Balsamo, A. Di Marco, P. Inverardi, and M. Simeoni. Model-based performance prediction in software development: a survey. *IEEE Trans. on SE*, 30(5):295–310, May 2004.
[22] C. A. Coello Coello, C. Dhaenens, and L. Jourdan. Multi-objective combinatorial optimization: Problematic and context. In *Advances in Multi-Objective Nature Inspired Computing*, volume 272 of *Studies in Computational Intelligence*, pages 1–21. Springer, 2010.
[23] T. de Gooijer. Performance Modeling of ASP.Net Web Service Applications: an Industrial Case Study. Master's thesis, Mälardalen University, Västerås, Sweden, 2011.
[24] K. Deb, S. Agrawal, A. Pratap, and T. Meyarivan. A fast elitist non-dominated sorting genetic algorithm for multi-objective optimization: NSGA-II. In *Parallel Problem Solving from Nature PPSN VI*, volume 1917/2000, pages 849–858. Springer, 2000.
[25] A. Díaz Pace, H. Kim, L. Bass, P. Bianco, and F. Bachmann. Integrating quality-attribute reasoning frameworks in the archE design assistant. In *Proc. 4th Int. Conf. on the Quality of Software-Architectures (QoSA 2008)*, volume 5281, pages 171–188, 2008.
[26] G. Franks, T. Omari, C. M. Woodside, O. Das, and S. Derisavi. Enhanced modeling and solution of layered queueing networks. *IEEE Trans. on SE*, 35(2):148–161, 2009.
[27] N. Huber, S. Becker, C. Rathfelder, J. Schweflinghaus, and R. Reussner. Performance modeling in industry: a case study on storage virtualization. In *Proc. of ICSE'10*, pages 1–10. ACM, 2010.
[28] Y. Jin, A. Tang, J. Han, and Y. Liu. Performance Evaluation and Prediction for Legacy Information Systems. In *Proc. of ICSE'07*, pages 540–549. Ieee, May 2007.
[29] S. Kounev. Performance Modeling and Evaluation of Distributed Component-Based Systems Using Queueing Petri Nets. *IEEE Trans. on SE*, 32(7):486–502, July 2006.
[30] A. Koziolek, H. Koziolek, and R. Reussner. PerOpteryx: Automated Application of Tactics in Multi-Objective Software Architecture Optimization. In *Proc. 7th Int. Conf. on the Quality of Software Architectures (QoSA'11)*, pages 33–42. ACM, 2011.
[31] A. Koziolek and R. Reussner. Towards a generic quality optimisation framework for component-based system models. In *Proc. 14th Int. ACM Sigsoft Symposium on Component-based Software Engineering (CBSE'11)*, pages 103–108. ACM, June 2011.
[32] H. Koziolek. Performance evaluation of component-based software systems: A survey. *Performance Evaluation*, 67(8):634–658, Aug. 2010.
[33] H. Koziolek, B. Schlich, C. Bilich, R. Weiss, S. Becker, K. Krogmann, M. Trifu, R. Mirandola, and A. Koziolek. An Industrial Case Study on Quality Impact Prediction for Evolving Service-Oriented Software. In *Proc. of ICSE'11, SEIP Track*. ACM, May 2011.
[34] A. Koziolek (Martens), H. Koziolek, S. Becker, and R. Reussner. Automatically improve software architecture models for performance, reliability, and cost using evolutionary algorithms. *Proceedings of ICPE'10*, pages 105–116, January 2010.
[35] C. Letner and R. Gimarc. A Methodology for Predicting the Scalability of Distributed Production Systems. In *CMG Conference*, volume 1, page 223. Computer Measurement Group; 1997, 2005.
[36] V. Liu, I. Gorton, and A. Fekete. Design-level performance prediction of component-based applications. *IEEE Trans. on SE*, 31(11):928–941, Nov. 2005.
[37] D. A. Menascé, J. M. Ewing, H. Gomaa, S. Malex, and J. a. P. Sousa. A framework for utility-based service oriented design in SASSY. In *Proceedings of ICPE'10*, pages 27–36. ACM, 2010.
[38] S. T. Redwine JR and W. E. Riddle. Software Technology Maturation. In *Proc. of ICSE'85*, pages 189–200. IEEE, 1985.
[39] C. U. Smith and L. G. Williams. *Performance Solutions*. Addison-Wesley, 2002.
[40] J. Xu. Rule-based automatic software performance diagnosis and improvement. *Performance Evaluation*, 67(8):585–611, Aug. 2010.

Using Computer Simulation to Predict the Performance of Multithreaded Programs

Alexander Tarvo
Brown University
Providence, RI
alexta@cs.brown.edu

Steven P. Reiss
Brown University
Providence, RI
spr@cs.brown.edu

ABSTRACT

Predicting the performance of a computer program facilitates its efficient design, deployment, and problem detection. However, predicting performance of multithreaded programs is complicated by complex locking behavior and concurrent usage of computational resources. Existing performance models either require running the program in many different configurations or impose restrictions on the types of programs that can be modeled.

This paper presents our approach towards building performance models that do not require vast amounts of training data. Our models are built using a combination of queuing networks and probabilistic call graphs. All necessary information is collected using static and dynamic analyses of a single run of the program. In our experiments these models were able to accurately predict performance of different types of multithreaded programs and detected those configurations that result in the programs' high performance.

Categories and Subject Descriptors

C.4 [**Computer Systems Organization**]: Performance of systems—*Modeling techniques*; D.2.9 [**Software Engineering**]: Management—*Software configuration management*; I.6 [**Computing Methodologies**]: Simulation and Modeling

General Terms

Performance

Keywords

Simulation, performance, modeling, configuration

1. INTRODUCTION

Performance is an important characteristic of any software system. It depends on various factors, such as the architecture of the program, properties of the underlying hardware, and characteristics of the system's workload. The performance is also strongly influenced by values of configuration options of the program. Examples of such options can be the size of the internal cache for input-output (I/O) operations or the number of working threads.

Proper understanding of how the configuration of the system affects its performance is essential for many applications. Usually this requires building a *performance prediction model* of the system. This model should be able to predict performance characteristics of the system for different configurations, which include variations in workload, configuration options, and characteristics of the hardware.

Performance prediction models can be useful in various scenarios. During the program's development, such models can estimate the program's performance characteristics and thus help detecting potential problems early [11]. Once the program is deployed, performance models can discover configurations of the system that result in its high performance on a particular platform. Similarly, models may be used for answering "what-if" questions, such as "how will the throughput change if I doubled the number of working threads?"

Performance models become a central component in building self-configuring and autonomic systems [15]. Here prediction results are used to dynamically reconfigure the system to achieve a higher performance. Performance prediction can be used to schedule tasks on high-performance computer systems [12] and large clusters [7]. This allows for both reducing the running time of the program and increasing utilization of the computation resources. Finally, the performance model can be useful in detecting run-time problems with the application. A large discrepancy between predicted and actual performance measurements may be a sign of an anomalous behavior of the system.

Building models of multithreaded programs is not easy. It requires carefully modeling the complex locking behavior of the application and concurrent usage of various computational resources such as the CPU and the I/O subsystem. As a result, existing performance models either impose restrictions on the types of programs that can be modeled or require collecting vast amounts of data about the performance of the system in different configurations. Such limitations often make these models impractical.

Our work attempts to overcome these limitations. We develop an innovative technique that *requires less data to build the model and allows modeling of a wider range of applications*. These models can predict performance of multithreaded programs running in various configurations under the established workload. Our models also predict performance of individual program components and utilization of computational resources, which facilitates performance analysis of the system and bottleneck detection.

In our research we use a combination of static and dynamic analyses to collect information about the program. We analyze the program, instrument it at the key points, and run it in a certain configuration to collect the necessary data.

We use a the discrete event approach to simulate computer programs. At the high level we represent a program using a queuing model whose queues correspond to queues and buffers in the program, and whose servers correspond to the program's threads. Each thread is simulated using a probabilistic call graph whose vertices correspond to fragments of the program's code.

For modeling purposes we split the program into fragments; each fragment performing an elementary operation such as CPU-bound computations, I/O operations, synchronizations, buffering, etc. These fragments correspond to appropriate components in the model. This approach contrasts with less generic models, where the program is viewed as a combination of high level constructs specific to the kind of the program being simulated, for example an MPI call.

As a result, our models allow simulating almost any multithreaded program. To further increase flexibility of the modeling, components that simulate underlying OS and hardware are independent of the model of the program. To verify feasibility of our approach we have built models of the simple scientific computing application and the web server running under the Linux OS.

Our work extends the existing state of the art in the area of performance modeling in several aspects:

- our modeling framework is not restricted to simulation of a single class of multithreaded applications and can be used to simulate a wider range of programs;

- we propose a simple yet powerful technique to model I/O operations in the program, including simulation of both hardware and software components of the I/O subsystem;

- we pay strong attention to the proper simulation of the concurrent usage of computation resources.

The remainder of this paper is organized as follows. Section 2 surveys the related work in the area. Section 3 outlines the general approach towards building the model. Section 4 describes the model itself. Section 5 focuses on data collection. Section 6 presents experimental results. Section 7 concludes and outlines directions for future work.

2. RELATED WORK

Existing performance models can be divided into three main classes according to the method they use: analytical models, black-box models, and simulation models. Despite implementation differences, at the high level all of them represent the system as a function $y = f(x)$. Here x are metrics describing system's configuration and workload, and y is some measure of the system's performance.

Analytical models explicitly specify the function $f(x)$ using a set of formulas. N. Bennani and A. Menasce [15] used analytical model in the controller for the autonomic data center. E. Thereska and D. Narayanan [23], [16] used such models to predict performance of the DBMS depending on the size of the buffer pool. These studies report relative error $\varepsilon \leq 0.1$ for predicting throughput and $\varepsilon \in (0.33, 0.68)$ for predicting response time. However, it is not clear if the presented methodology can be easily applied to other applications or if it can incorporate other parameters.

Analytical models are compact and expressive; however, their development requires considerable mathematical skills and deep understanding of the system. Moreover, complex behavior is difficult to describe with analytical models.

Black-box or statistical models are used to alleviate these problems. They utilize no information about the internal structure of the system and do not formulate the function $y = f(x)$ explicitly. Instead, the program is executed in different configurations and its performance is measured. Then some machine learning technique is used to learn the $y = f(x)$ dependency from the data.

In particular, B. Lee et al. [14] used linear regression and neural networks to predict performance of the linear equation solver running on the grid; they report $\varepsilon \in (0.02, 0.11)$. A. Ganapathi et al. [7] used a technique based on the k-NN method to predict performance of the Hadoop queries. They achieved high correlation ($R^2 = 0.87-0.93$) between predicted and actual running times. Their work [8] uses machine learning techniques to predict the execution time of queries in the DBMS.

Disadvantages of the black-box models are the need for large amount of data to train the model and the lack of flexibility. The system must be run in many different configurations in order to collect sufficient amount of training data. Any change to the software or hardware of the system requires re-training the whole model [20]. Furthermore, these models can predict only high-level performance metrics and cannot give an insight into details of the system's performance.

There are attempts to work around these limitations. In particular, large amounts of data can be available directly from a user base [21] or from a large number of runs [19]. Unfortunately, these solution works only for very popular applications and can raise privacy concerns. Chun et al. [6] uses internal program features instead of configuration metrics x to build performance models of CPU-bound programs. This allows reducing the amount of training data for the model, but requires complex program analysis.

Simulation is another popular approach towards performance modeling. The structure of simulation models follows the structure of the system, where components of the system directly correspond to the components of the model. Building these models doesn't require as much data as black-box models, but requires an expert knowledge of the system.

An example of a simulation model is the PACE framework [18] that predicts performance of CPU-bound applications running on a high-performance computer system. PACE was used to predict the execution time of the **nreg** image processing application with the $\varepsilon <= 0.1$ [12]. However, PACE is limited to simulation of MPI-based programs.

One traditional tool used for simulation is Petri networks. Nguen and Apon [17] rely on Petri nets to predict throughput of Linux file system with $\varepsilon \in (0.12, 0.34)$. Gilmore et al. [9] use PEPA networks, a combination of Petri network and PEPA algebra, to build a model of a secure Web service.

Another well-established simulation methodology is queuing networks, which are extensively used for performance modeling of computer networks. However, van der Mei et al.

[24] used queuing network to study impact of networking parameters at the performance of the web server. IRONModel [22] simulates performance of the experimental cluster-based storage system using the combination of queuing model, black-box, and analytical models.

Layered Queue Networks (LQN) extend the queuing networks by introducing the hierarchy of the model components. Xu et al. [27] uses LQN to build a model of a distributed JavaBeans application with $\varepsilon = (0.02, 0.25)$. Israr et al. [11] attempts to automatically build LQN models of commercial message-passing programs from their traces.

Petri nets, queuing models, and LQN are successful in predicting performance of computer networks and distributed programs at the high level. Unfortunately, these models in their classical form fail to properly simulate complex synchronization operations and concurrent usage of computational resources such as CPU and hard drives by multiple threads [26]. Consequently, their applicability to modeling multithreaded applications is limited. In our work we attempt to overcome these limitations.

3. MODEL DEFINITION

For the purpose of simulation we represent computations performed by the program as request processing. We denote a *request* as something the program has to react to. The program processes the request by performing certain operations. The performance of the request processing system can be described by various metrics, such as the response time R (an overall delay between request arrival and its completion), throughput T (the number of requests served in the unit of time), or the number of requests dropped.

This approach naturally allows simulating reactive systems which constitute a majority of modern computer programs. For example, in the web server, the request corresponds to an incoming HTTP connection. The processing of the request includes reading a web-page from the disk and sending it to the user. In the model of the UI application, e.g. a text editor, the request corresponds to a keystroke or a mouse move. The response of the application includes updating its UI and underlying data. Scientific applications can be also simulated in this way. Here, the request can correspond to the object or set of objects in the program. The program responds to the request by performing computations and sending the request to the next component in the system.

We employ a two-tier simulation of computer programs. At the high level, we simulate the program using a queuing network model [13]. At the low level, we simulate threads as probabilistic call graphs. Both types of models are built using discrete-event principles, where the simulation time is advanced by discrete steps and the state of the system does not change between time advances.

The high-level model explicitly simulates the flow of the request as it is being processed by the program, from its arrival to completion. It is a queuing network model where queues correspond to program's queues and buffers, and servers correspond to the program's threads.

Our model differs from the classical queuing networks. First, it does not restrict the structure and properties of the model, such as the number of service nodes n or parameters of the arrival process λ. Second, the server nodes are models on their own that simulate the program's threads. Finally, the high-level model does not explicitly define service de-

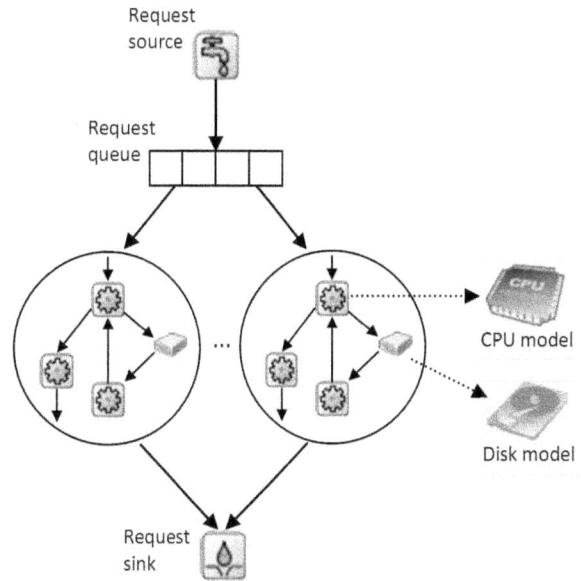

Figure 1: A high-level model for a web server

mand for requests; these are simulated by the lower-level thread models. Nevertheless, the high-level model is capable of collecting the same performance measures as queuing models, such as R, T, or the number of requests in the system N.

Figure 1 provides a (somewhat simplified) example of a high-level model for a multithreaded web server. The server works as follows: when the incoming HTTP request arrives, the server calls `accept()` to open a socket for communicating with the client. The request is placed into the queue for incoming connections. Once one of the working threads becomes available, it fetches the request for processing from that queue. The thread verifies that the requested page exists, reads it from the disk and sends it back to the client. When processing of the request is complete, the thread closes a connection and fetches another request from the queue.

The elements of the high-level model reflect basic stages of processing the request by the web server. The request itself corresponds to the socket ID. It is created by a request source, which corresponds to the `accept()` call in the server's code. Correspondingly, the server node (depicted as a circle) denotes a working thread. The server node itself is implemented as a lower-level thread model. Once the processing is over, the request is sent to the sink, which corresponds to closing the client socket by the server.

Lower-level thread models simulate delays that occur in threads when they process requests. Thread models are implemented as probabilistic call graphs, whose vertices S correspond to the pieces of the thread's code – *code fragments*. A special vertex $s_0 \in S$ is a starting code fragment, which is executed upon the thread start. Edges of the graph represent a possible transition of control flow between the code fragments. Probabilities of these transitions are defined with a mapping $\delta : S \to P(S)$.

We distinguish three basic types of code fragments: computation, I/O, and synchronization fragments. These fragments are represented with vertices of the corresponding type in the call graph. Furthermore, we define special vertices s_{in} and s_{out} to communicate with the higher-level queuing model. The input vertices s_{in} fetch requests from the queues of the high-level queuing model. Output vertices s_{out} generate requests and send them to the queuing model.

Execution of each code fragment results in the delay τ. Whereas the call graph structure $< S, s_0, \delta >$ does not generally change in time, *execution times for code fragments depend on various factors, such as the degree of parallelism of the program and characteristics of the underlying hardware*. For example, consider multiple threads that perform equal amount of CPU-intense computations. If the number of threads is bigger than the number of CPUs, the amount of time required for each thread to finish computations will be higher than if that thread was running alone. The same logic applies to I/O operations: the amount of time required for an I/O operation to complete strongly depends on the number and properties of other I/O operations occurring at the same time.

As a result, instead of specifying the exact time τ required for each code fragment to finish, we rather define a set of parameters Π of that code fragment. In turn, Π will be used to calculate τ during the model's runtime.

This necessitates modeling of the underlying hardware and the Operating System (OS). This model will track $Q(t)$ – the state of the whole simulation at each moment of time t. Thread models use this OS/hardware model to compute τ as a function $\tau = f(\Pi, Q(t))$. We have developed models of the CPU/OS thread scheduler and the disk I/O subsystem that compute τ for computation fragments and disk I/O fragments correspondingly.

Different types of code fragments are described by different sets of parameters. A computation fragment is described by a parameter set $\Pi_{cpu} = \{\tau_{cpu}\}$, where τ_{cpu} is the *CPU time* for that fragment. The CPU time is the time necessary to execute the code fragment if it was running on the CPU uninterrupted. A disk I/O fragment is described by $\Pi_{disk} = \{dio_1, ..., dio_k\}$, where $\{dio_1, ..., dio_k\}$ are low-level disk I/O requests spawned by the OS for that I/O fragment.

4. MODEL BUILDING

Using the methodology described above, we have developed a framework to simulate multithreaded programs written in general-purpose programming languages such as C, C++, or Java. We do not restrict ourselves to modeling programs developed using a certain framework (e.g. MPI). We rather develop a generic approach that can be extended, if necessary, to support different frameworks for parallel programming. Nevertheless we pose several important assumptions on the systems we can simulate. First, we do not predict performance characteristics for each individual request. Instead, we predict average performance of the program for a given workload, which can be a mix of requests with different characteristics. Second, we assume that transition probabilities δ remain unchanged across the configuration space of the program. This, in turn, might imply that properties of incoming requests must also remain unchanged in time.

Furthermore, there are limitations caused by the simulation framework in its current state. First, we assume there is no other significant computation or I/O activity in the system, except the program being simulated. Second, currently

we can simulate programs running only on the commodity hardware, such as a desktop PC or a general-purpose server. However, these limitations can be alleviated by improving our framework.

We rely on the OMNET [1] simulation framework to build our models. OMNET model consists of interconnected *blocks* communicating using messages. Internally, blocks and messages are implemented as C++ classes. Although OMNET provides general framework for developing those entities, it is a responsibility of the model developer to implement desired functionality in blocks and messages.

High-level and low-level models contain different types of blocks. High-level models contain blocks that represent request sources, sinks, queues, threads, and program-wide locks (barriers, critical sections etc). The high-level model also contains blocks simulating the I/O subsystem and the thread scheduler. Low-level (thread) models consist of computation blocks, I/O blocks, blocks that simulate calls to locks, blocks that read/write data from the high-level model, and dispatch blocks that implement transition probabilities δ.

Each block has a set of parameters that generally represents properties of the corresponding program structures. Values of the block parameters are obtained during the data collection stage. Since values of parameters for a block representing a code fragment can fluctuate across different executions of that code fragment, we treat them as a distributions $\mathbb{P}^{\Pi}$.

The high-level model creates requests, queues them, and sends them to low-level thread models for processing. The request itself is represented as a *request message* flowing from one block to another. The request normally corresponds to some data item in the real-life program, such as a file descriptor, socket ID, a class instance, or a handle. In the high-level model threads appear as "black boxes" without any notion of their internal structure. Each thread is represented as a separate block, such that, if the program has 8 working threads, it has 8 such blocks.

The Figure 2 shows the high-level model for the Galaxy – a simple scientific application. Here requests correspond to Java objects, and arrows depict how requests flow between the model's blocks. The model contains two working threads that interact through two queues, and one main thread.

Details of the thread are simulated by the lower-level thread models. Here the thread is represented as a group of blocks that corresponds to the vertices S of its probabilistic call graph. Execution flow in a thread is also simulated by the message passing. When the model of the program is started, the *computation flow message* (CFM) is created for every thread and is sent to its initial block s_0. Then the computation flow message starts traveling through the call graph of the thread, which simulates the execution of the actual thread. Flow of the message is controlled by the dispatch blocks that reroute the message to other blocks in the model according to the probabilities δ.

The Figure 3 shows thread models for the Galaxy. Here arrows depict flow of the CFM between the threads' code blocks. The CFMs are created using the `sourceOnce` blocks. It must be noted that in addition to blocks that represent fragments of the program's code, thread models also contain service blocks used to control simulation and collect results. In particular, the `setTimer/readTimer` blocks measure the time necessary for the CFM to travel between those, which allows predicting execution time for fragments of the program. The `stopper` block stops the simulation after receiving the predefined number of CFMs.

To pass the request message in and out of the thread we rely on a special group of blocks in the thread model – reader and writer blocks that implement s_{in}, s_{out} actions of our formal model. Once the CFM reaches the reader block, that block fetches the request message from the queue or from other source in the high-level model. If no request is available, the reader either delays the CFM until the request becomes available, thus effectively blocking the execution of the thread (which might correspond to a locking behavior in the producer-consumer pattern), or just reroutes the CFM. Correspondingly, when the CFM reaches the writer block, the block outputs the request message to the high-level model. The thread model shown at the Figure 3 (right) has a pair of reader/writer blocks that access a queue in the high-level model.

4.1 Simulating Delays in Thread Execution

As the CFM travels through the thread model, various blocks can delay its passage, thus simulating delays τ that occur during the thread execution. These delays occur because of CPU-intense computations, I/O activities, or when execution of the thread is blocked by synchronization mechanisms such as critical sections or semaphores.

To simulate these delays, we employ two groups of blocks: *caller blocks* and *central blocks*. Different types of caller and central blocks are used to simulate different types of delays. However, all of them interact according to the same principle.

Caller blocks are parts of the thread model. When the caller block receives a CFM, it delays that message and notifies the corresponding central block using a separate message. The exact type of that message depends on the type of the caller/central block pair. The parameters of the message are sampled from the $\mathbb{P}^{\Pi}$ – distribution of parameters for the caller block.

The central block is a part of a high-level model. Once it receives the message from the caller block, it updates the internal state of the model $Q(t)$. Then, it uses message parameters and the $Q(t)$ to simulate the delay τ. Once the delay has passed, the central block sends the message back the caller block. The caller block in turn sends the original CFM to the next block in the thread model.

4.1.1 Simulating synchronization delays

To simulate high-level synchronization primitives in the program the modeling framework employs a wide range of different block types. Every lock in the program is represented by a corresponding central block. Parameters of the central block correspond to properties of the lock. For example, the barrier block has one parameter – the capacity of the barrier. Correspondingly, caller blocks represent calls to these locks. Every type of synchronization primitive is represented by different centra/caller block pair. For example, the barrier is represented by a SyncBarrier central block; calls to that barrier are represented by SyncBarrier_await caller blocks.

These blocks explicitly simulate the functioning of the lock. When the caller block sends the *synchronization message* to the central block, the central block updates its internal state accordingly and makes a decision if the calling thread should block or not. If the thread should not block, the central block sends the synchronization message back to the caller immediately. However, if the central block decides that the calling thread must wait, it delays sending the synchronization message back until the caller can be unblocked.

The high-level model shown at the Figure 2 contains four central blocks that represent barriers and one central block that represents the critical section. Correspondingly, the thread models at the Figure 3 contain caller blocks that call these central blocks.

4.1.2 Simulating Computations

To simulate delays that occur due to CPU-intense computations the model uses a combination of computation blocks (caller blocks) and a CPU/Scheduler block (a central block). In addition to simulating delays, the CPU/Scheduler also predicts CPU utilization by the program.

When the computation block sends the *computation message* to the CPU/Scheduler block, it passes a τ_{cpu} as a parameter of that message. τ_{cpu} is sampled from the $\mathbb{P}^{\Pi}_{cpu}$ for the corresponding code fragment. The CPU/Scheduler block simulates the CPU with the given number of cores and the round-robin OS thread scheduler with equal priority of all the threads. Once the CPU/Scheduler receives a message from the computation block, it puts that message into the queue of "ready" threads. When one of the computation cores of the simulated CPU frees, the CPU/Scheduler takes the first message out of the "ready" queue and simulates computations by introducing a delay whose length is equal to $min(\tau_{cpu}, OS\ time\ quantum)$. After the delay is expired, the CPU/Scheduler either sends the message back to the origin block (in case computations are complete) or places it back into the "ready" queue, where it awaits another time quantum. The length of the time quantum is sampled from the distribution that represents quantum length of the actual Linux thread scheduler.

In our example the high-level model contains the `cpuScheduler` block, which implements the model of the CPU/ Scheduler. Each of thread models contain one computation block that call `cpuScheduler`.

4.1.3 Simulating Disk I/O

To simulate delays that occur because of the disk I/O the model uses a combination of DiskIOOperation (caller block) and DiskIOModule (central block). DiskIOModule simulates the disk I/O subsystem of a computer and also predicts disk utilization.

DiskIOOperation represents a disk I/O fragment. When the DiskIOOperation block receives the CFM, it retrieves the number k and parameters of the low-level I/O messages $\{dio_1, ..., dio_k\}$ from the distribution $\mathbb{P}^{\Pi}_{disk}$. In the case of the cache hit the $k = 0$, and the DiskIOOperation immediately sends the CFM to the next block. Otherwise the DiskIOOperation sends k *disk I/O messages* to the DiskIOModule block. Each message represents a low-level I/O request $dio_i, i \in (1, ..., k)$. These messages are sent to the DiskIOModule sequentially. If the message represents a synchronous operation, the DiskIOModule waits for its completion before sending the next disk I/O message. Otherwise it sends the next disk I/O message to the DiskIOModule immediately.

The DiskIOModule combines models of the I/O scheduler and the hard drive. The disk I/O message is initially sent to the model of the I/O scheduler. If the hard drive is idle at the moment, the I/O scheduler model sends the request directly to the hard drive model. Otherwise, the disk I/O message is placed in the queue that simulates the request queue of the actual I/O scheduler. When the hard drive model becomes available, it fetches the next request to be processed from that queue. The real I/O scheduler orders requests according to the index of the disk block they are accessing, but since this information is not known to the model, the hard drive model fetches requests from the random positions of the queue.

The model of the hard drive calculates the disk processing time τ_{disk} for the request and delays the request for that time. However, τ_{disk} depends on parameters of the request, such as the amount of data transferred, locality of the operation (how close are disk sectors accessed by different requests etc), and other factors. To account for those, the model treats τ_{disk} as conditional distribution $P(\tau_{disk}|x_{dio})$, where x_{dio} are parameters of the I/O request. As for now we use the type of the request (synchronous read, metadata read, read-ahead) as a parameter, since it implicitly represents the locality of the I/O operation. In particular, read-ahead requests usually do not require the disk seek operation and, thus, have significantly shorter τ_{disk}. Currently, we are working on incorporating other request parameters to increase the overall accuracy of simulation.

4.2 Simulating OS limits

OS can impose a variety of limits on the program such as the maximum number of open file descriptors. These limits can severely affect the program's behavior and can be viewed as additional parameters of the system.

To simulate OS limits we have also implemented a combination of a central block and caller blocks. A code fragment that attempts to acquire some resource (such as a call to accept() or open() functions that acquire a file descriptor) is represented by a caller block. When the CFM arrives to the caller block, the block calls an OSLimits central block and requests to allocate an instance of corresponding resource. OSLimits updates the state of the system and notifies the caller if the resource was granted or not. The result of the call is logged by the caller block for the further analysis. Moreover, it can be used to reroute the CFM if the request was denied, thus simulating the behavior of the real program.

5. DATA COLLECTION

Building models of the multithreaded program requires collecting following information about the program itself as well as the underlying OS and the hardware:

- information on thread interaction in the program, including synchronization mechanisms and request queues;

- probabilistic call graphs $< S, s_0, \delta >$ for all the threads;

- parameters Π of individual code fragments;

- performance characteristics of the underlying OS and hardware.

To collect this data we analyze the system, instrument it, and run it in *one specific configuration*. This is a major advantage over the black-box methods, which require running the program in a large number of configurations.

We utilize a mixed approach towards program analysis. We manually analyze the program at the high-level to establish its structure and use automated solutions to obtain the rest of the data.

During the manual analysis we determine the general sequence of operations that happen during the request processing. First we identify synchronization mechanisms and working threads. Then we analyze the threads' code to detect code fragments and determine their types. Next, we instrument the program by inserting probes at the borders of individual code fragments. Each probe is identified by the unique ID, thus each code fragment can be uniquely identified by the pair of IDs of surrounding probes. Program instrumentation completes manual analysis of the program. The rest of the data collection is performed automatically.

To collect information on code fragments we run the instrumented program in one representative configuration. When the probe is hit during the program's execution, we record CPU time τ_{cpu} and wallclock time τ for the code fragment. Our instrumentation is very lightweight: every probe slows the execution of the program in average by 1-2 microseconds. To further decrease instrumentation overhead, we rely on statistical sampling [10].

Once execution of the program has finished, the instrumentation log is analyzed automatically and the following information is retrieved:

- τ_{cpu} for all code fragments, which forms $\mathbb{P}_{cpu}^{\Pi}$;

- transition probabilities δ for each thread;

- τ for all code fragments;

- performance metrics of the program, such as the response time R, throughput T etc.

τ and performance metrics (R, T) are used solely for analyzing simulation results and model debugging.

Unfortunately, the user-mode log does not include information on I/O operations and page cache usage. To capture this data we instrument following places of the Linux kernel using the SystemTap framework [2]:

- start and end of the system call routines that can initiate I/O requests, such as sys_read() or sys_stat();

- the generic_make_request() function, which inserts the request for the low-level I/O operation into the queue of the I/O scheduler;

- the blk_start_request() function, which is called when the I/O scheduler passes a request to the physical device (a hard drive);

- I/O completion routines.

This instrumentation yields the following measurements:

- the number k and properties of I/O requests $\{dio_1, ..., dio_k\}$ issued by the system call. Properties of the request include type of the request (synchronous read, metadata read, read-ahead), and amount of data transferred. Altogether this data comprise the distribution of parameters $\mathbb{P}_{disk}^{\Pi}$ for the corresponding disk I/O fragment;

- τ_{disk}: the amount of time required to process the I/O request by the hard drive. τ_{disk} is calculated as the time difference between the call to the `blk_start_request()` and the completion routine. τ_{disk} is used to build the model of the I/O subsystem;

- τ_{io}: total time required for I/O request to complete, which is the sum of the time spent in the I/O scheduler queue and τ_{disk}. τ_{io} is calculated as the time difference between the call to the `generic_make_request()` and the completion routine. τ_{io} is used to verify the model of the I/O subsystem.

The number of I/O requests k is an important parameter of an I/O code fragment, as it implicitly represents the probability of hitting the OS page cache. As the value of k varies for different requests, it should be considered a random variable.

It has been shown [25] that the cache of a constant size can be represented as a birth-death process. If there are no changes in parameters of the incoming requests, such a process converges to the equilibrium state, where the probability of a cache hit remains constant. Unfortunately, in the general case the size of the OS page cache can vary. But if our initial assumptions (absence of other significant activity in the system and no rapid changes in the workload) hold, the size of the OS page cache should not change. As a result, the probability of cache hit should also remain the same.

To validate this claim we conducted a series of experiments with the web server that uses `stat()` and `read()` functions to access data on the hard drive. These experiments confirmed that, after serving a large number of requests, the system reaches an equilibrium state and the distribution of k does not change. This is an important observation as it allows us to easily simulate the OS page cache. To bring a system into an equilibrium state we issue a large number (around 10^5) of "warm-up" requests prior to taking actual measurements of k.

6. MODEL VERIFICATION

To test our approach for performance prediction we built models of two multithreaded programs. These programs are very different in their purpose, architecture, behavior, and programming languages and thus can be representative for a larger class of applications. The first program is Galaxy, a CPU-bound scientific computing application. The second program is tinyhttpd, a disk I/O-bound web server. Instrumented source code and models for these programs can be downloaded from [3]. We have created other models which are not presented here due to space constraints.

To estimate accuracy of the model we ran the program in different configurations and recorded actual performance of the program for each configuration. Afterwards we simulate the program in same configurations and record predicted performance. Then we calculate relative error ε between measured and predicted performance metrics as

$$\varepsilon = \frac{|measured - predicted|}{measured}$$

The higher is the relative error the worse is the accuracy of prediction. For the ideal model that predicts the program's performance without any errors $\varepsilon \to 0$.

All our experiments were conducted on a PC equipped with an Intel Q6600 quad-core 2.4 GHz CPU, 4 GB RAM and 160 GB hard drive running under the Ubuntu Linux 10.04 OS.

6.1 Galaxy: the n-body simulator

Galaxy is a simple Java scientific computing application that simulates the gravitational interaction of multiple celestial bodies. Although mostly used as an educational example, this program employs a variety of synchronization techniques and is a good representative of a multithreaded scientific application.

Galaxy uses a conventional approach to the problem of n-bodies simulation. It discretizes time into small steps and calculates movement of objects during the each such step. To achieve good performance, the Galaxy implements the Barnes-Hut [5] algorithm, which involves building an octree. A single iteration of the Galaxy algorithm involves three major actions in a strict order: calculating forces acting on bodies and updating bodies' positions; rebuilding the octree; and checking bodies for collisions. The length of iteration can be viewed as a response time R and thus represents the most important performance metric of the Galaxy.

Galaxy uses multiple thread pools to speed up computations. The first thread pool ("force threads") calculates forces and updates positions of the bodies, while the second thread pool ("collision threads") detects body collisions. Thread pools communicate through synchronized queues. The ordering of operations is enforced by the main thread of the program, which uses barriers to synchronize threads in thread pools. The main thread is also responsible for rebuilding the octree.

Configuration options of the Galaxy include two parameters that directly influence performance of the program: the number of force threads and the number of collision threads. To cover all the configurations that are adequate for our hardware we experimented with 1,2,4,6,8,12 and 16 force threads and collision threads. Overall configuration space included 49 configurations, which includes all possible combinations of the number of force and collision threads.

We ran Galaxy in all 49 configurations. In every configuration Galaxy was used to simulate 10000 bodies for 1000 iterations (in all the experiments we assume that our test workloads are representative). To get reliable measurements of the program's performance three runs were performed in each configuration. Iteration lengths R were recorded during each run; their mean value $\overline{R}$ was used as an *actual* value of $R_{measured}$ for each configuration of the Galaxy.

One noteworthy finding is that the Galaxy iteration length depends mostly on the number of force threads, and only slightly on the number of collision threads. This can be explained by the fact that force calculations are significantly more expensive than the collision checks. However, the overall performance of the Galaxy highly depends on the number of collisions. As simulation time advances, many objects are getting merged during the collisions, so the Galaxy must perform less computations. This observation is important since the model must accurately simulate such a complex behavior.

We manually built both high-level and thread models of the Galaxy. The high-level model is shown at the Figure 2. Upon model initialization requests are created by the `fillBodies` block, which sends them to the `positionsQueue`. `positionsQueue` and `forcesQueue` are queue blocks that represent synchronized queues in the program. `galaxy_forces-`

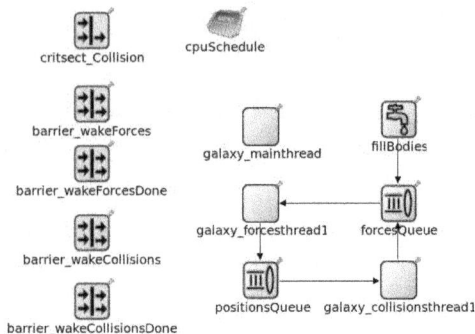

Figure 2: OMNET model of the Galaxy (high-level)

`thread` and `galaxy_collisionthread` blocks represent the force thread and the collision thread, while the `galaxy_mainthread` block represents the main thread of the program.

Low-level thread models for the Galaxy are shown at the Figure 3 (the model of the collision thread is not shown due to the lack of space). The model of the main thread contains four blocks that call corresponding barrier blocks of the high-level model. `wakeForces_await` and `wakeForcesDone_await` blocks are used to wake up/suspend force threads, while `wakeCollisions_await` and `wakeCollisionsDone_await` do same for the collision threads. The `octreeBuild` computation block simulates rebuilding the octree.

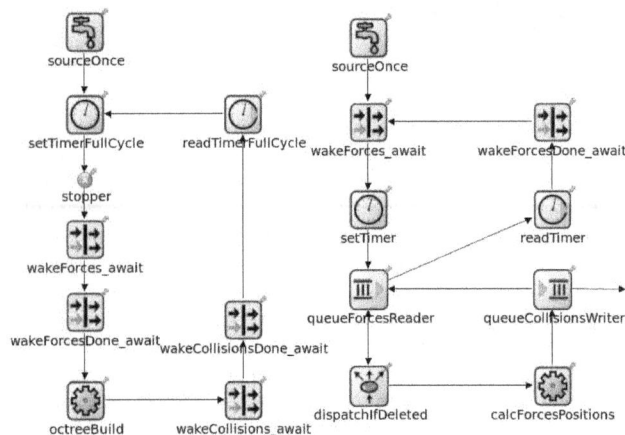

Figure 3: OMNET models of Galaxy threads: main thread and force thread

The model of the force thread uses the `queueForces-Reader` reader block to fetch requests from the `forcesQueue`. Then the `dispatchIfDeleted` dispatch block simulates a check if the body has been marked as collided with another body. If the collision has occured, the corresponding request is deleted and the CFM is sent back to the `queueForces-Reader`. Otherwise the CFM is sent to the `calcForcesPositions` computation block that simulates calcuation of the net force acting on the body. Next, the model outputs the request to the `positionsQueue` using the `queueCollisionsWriter` writer block and attempts to fetch a new request from the `forcesQueue`. Once all the requests in the `forcesQueue` have been processed, the thread uses the `wakeForcesDone_await` caller block to notify the main thread.

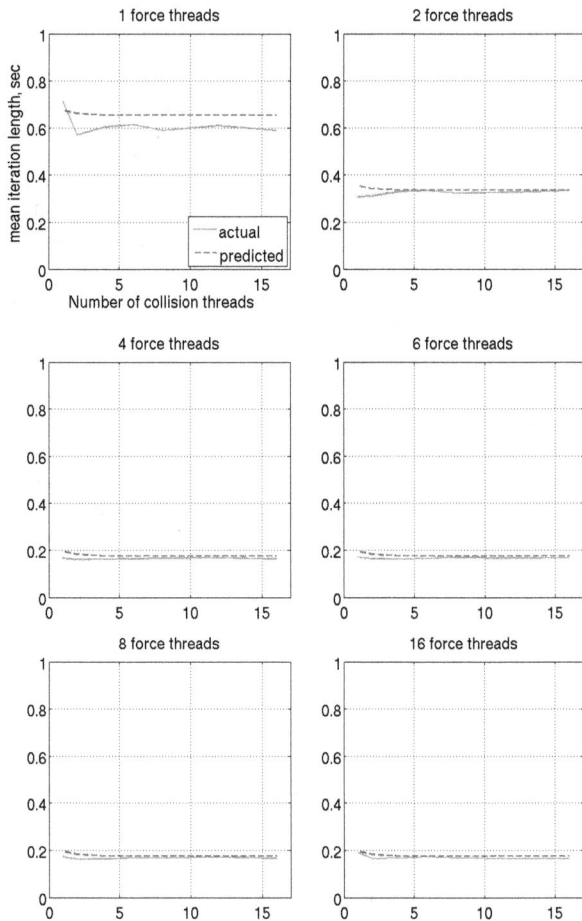

Figure 4: Experimental results for the Galaxy

Finally, `wakeForces_await` block suspends the thread until it is waken up by the the central thread during the next iteration.

To define parameters for the low-level thread models we instrumented Galaxy code with 29 probes and ran it in the configuration with 2 force threads and 2 collision threads. In these experiments the probability of collision was 1.01×10^{-5}, the mean value of $\overline{\tau}_{cpu}$ (`octreeBuild`) $= 5.40 \times 10^{-3}$ sec, and $\overline{\tau}_{cpu}$ (`calcForcesPositions`) $= 4.33 \times 10^{-5}$ sec.

We used the model to predict the iteration length of the Galaxy in each configuration. Similarly, the model was ran three times in each configuration and the average iteration lengths was used as a predicted value $R_{predicted}$. The comparison of actual and predicted iteration lengths is shown at the Figure 4.

The relative error varies in $\varepsilon \in (0.002, 0.179)$ depending on the program configuration. The average error measured across all the configurations is $\overline{\varepsilon} = 0.073$, which is comparable to statistical prediction models [14], [6]. Relative errors for all the configurations are listed in the Table 1.

These results convince us that the model predicts iteration length of Galaxy with reasonable accuracy. Furthermore, the model locates those configurations that result in the high performance of the program. In particular, it cor-

Table 1: Relative errors for predicting the Galaxy iteration length

Num. collision threads	The number of force threads						
	1	2	4	6	8	12	16
1	0.054	0.161	0.084	0.067	0.110	0.074	0.111
2	0.155	0.102	0.018	0.007	0.038	0.028	0.005
4	0.179	0.132	0.086	0.072	0.056	0.048	0.076
6	0.151	0.115	0.090	0.067	0.042	0.059	0.054
8	0.143	0.126	0.075	0.051	0.050	0.036	0.062
12	0.174	0.122	0.069	0.057	0.036	0.058	0.054
16	0.033	0.105	0.052	0.014	0.053	0.069	0.070

Table 2: Predicted average CPU utilization for the Galaxy, %

Num. collision threads	The number of force threads						
	1	2	4	6	8	12	16
1	100.0	102.1	103.1	103.1	103.1	103.1	103.1
2	189.5	197.0	201.0	201.0	201.0	201.0	201.0
4	342.9	368.3	382.4	382.4	382.6	382.4	382.5
6	343.0	368.2	382.5	382.4	382.5	382.4	382.5
8	342.9	368.3	382.4	382.4	382.4	382.4	382.4
12	342.7	368.2	382.3	382.2	382.3	382.1	382.2
16	342.6	367.9	382.1	382.1	382.0	382.1	382.1

rectly points that the number of force processing threads must be $>= 4$, while the number of collision threads has no significant impact on Galaxy performance.

Table 2 provides the predicted CPU utilization values for the Galaxy on the test system *averaged over the whole run* (value of 100% denotes a full utilization of a single CPU core). Note that *on average* Galaxy never fully utilizes all four CPU cores. Although force calculations and collision detections are prefectly parallelizable and can utilize all the CPU cores, rebuilding the octree is not a parallelizable operation. It is executed only by a main thread, which can use only a single CPU core at a time. Information on CPU utilization can be used to improve the Galaxy algorithm and further tune configuration options of the program.

6.2 tinyhttpd: the web server

Predicting performance of the web server is a more complex task since it involves simulating not only computations, but also I/O operations. In our work we built the model of a tinyhttpd multithreaded web server [4]. tinyhttpd is written on C programming language. It is simple and compact, which facilitates its analysis, but at the same time it is representative for a large class of server applications.

When the tinyhttpd receives an incoming request, it puts the request into the queue until one of its working threads becomes available. The working thread then picks the request from the queue, retrieves the local path to the requested file, and verifies its existence using a stat() function. If the file exists, the thread opens it for reading. If the file was opened successfully, the thread reads the file in 1024-bytes chunks and sends them to the client. Otherwise it sends the "Internal Server Error" response. Once data transfer is complete, the working thread closes the connection and picks up the next incoming request from the queue.

In our experiments we used the tinyhttpd to host 200000 static web pages from the Wikipedia archive. According to the common practice, atime functionality was disabled to

improve performance of the server. We used the http_load software [6] to simulate client connections to our web server. httpd_load is running on a client computer (Intel 2.4 GHz dual-core CPU, 4 GB RAM, 250 GB HDD) connected to the server with a 100 MBit Ethernet LAN.

The main metric we used to measure the performance of a web server was the response time R. We define R as a time difference between accepting the incoming connection and sending the response (more accurately – closing the communication socket). In addition to R we also measured the total throughput T and the number of error responses.

The configuration space of the web server includes two parameters: the incoming request rate (IRR) and the number of working threads of the web server. By varying the IRR we simulate behavior of the web server under the different load. In our experiments we vary IRR from 10 requests per second (rps) to 130 rps with the step of 10 rps. The number of working threads is the only configuration parameter of the web server itself that affects its performance. We run the web server with 2, 4, 6 and 8 working threads.

As a result, the total number of different experimental configurations is 13*4=52, which includes all the possible combinations of the number of threads and incoming request rates. For each configuration we ran both the actual program and its model and record average values of performance metrics. During each run 10,000 requests were issued; every run was repeated six times to get averaged results for each configuration.

Depending on the values of IRR the web server has two distinct states of operation (see Figure 5). For IRR ≤ 50 rps the I/O subsystem is not fully utilized and the R is minimal ($R \in$ (10-20 ms)). IRR $\geq$ 60-70 rps result in the overload of the I/O subsystem. Processing the request takes longer time, and incoming connections start accumulating in the web server queue. As a result, the web server is brought to the point of the saturation, where it exceeds the OS-imposed limit of 1024 open file descriptors (remember, each connection requires an open file descriptor). The server is unable to open files on the disk for reading, and the number of error responses increases. At this point the R reaches 14-17 sec. and remains steady. The total throughput T, however, continues to grow as it does not distinguish between requests that fail or return successfully.

One interesting observation is that the number of working threads has a relatively small influence on R. This is explained by the fact that the performance of the web server is largely determined by the performance of the I/O system, and the I/O system (hard drive) can effectively carry out only a single I/O operation at a time. As a result, the increase in the number of parallel operations is negated by a proportional increase in the average execution time for each individual I/O operation. We believe this example illustrates necessity for the proper simulation of I/O operations, as they often becoming a determining factor in the program's performance.

To build the model of the tinyhttpd, we instrumented its code with 21 probes and ran it in the configuration with 4 threads and IRR=70 rps. Our model predicts the R for stationary states reasonably well ($\varepsilon \leq 0.30$), but its accuracy decreases at the point of transition (see Table 3). But since the size of the transitional region is small, the average error across all the configurations $\bar{\varepsilon} = 0.203$. The total throughput T is predicted highly accurately ($\varepsilon \leq 0.021$), but in

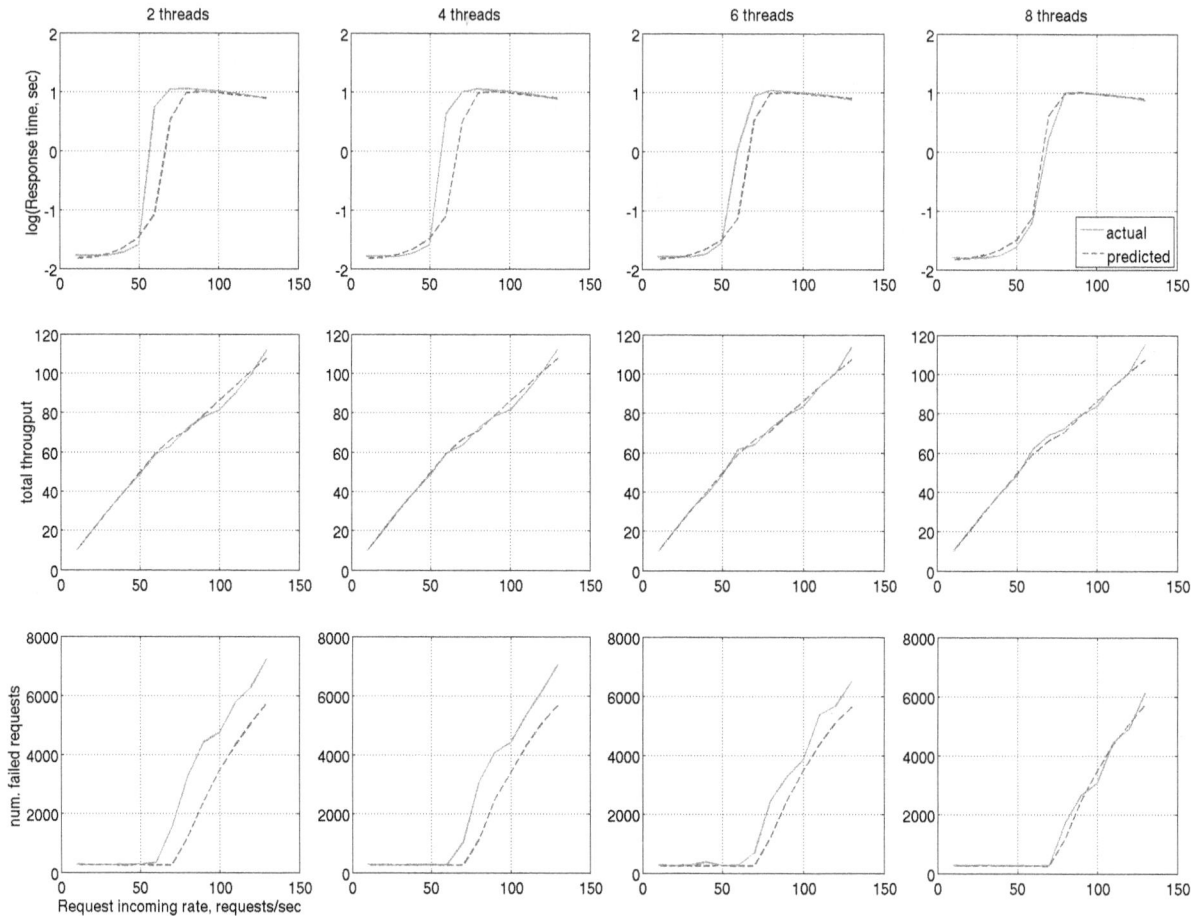

Figure 5: Experimental results for the tinyhttpd. top row: the response time R (logarithmic scale); middle row: the throughput T; bottom row: the number of error responses

order to correctly interpret T, one has to take into account the number of error responses. Unfortunately, the model predicts this metric with somewhat lower accuracy: at the transition point $\varepsilon = 1$ and average error $\overline{\varepsilon} = 0.214$. However, the number of failures in the transition region is small ($\leq 10\%$ of all the requests), so even the slight variation in the actual number of failed requests significantly affects prediction accuracy. We expect to further improve accuracy by developing a more sophisticated I/O model. Nevertheless, even with the current simple model our results are comparable to those obtained from a more refined model of the Linux I/O subsystem [17].

Furthermore, the *model accurately predicts values of configuration parameters where the transitional behavior occurs*. This result is important, since usually the goal of performance models is not just to predict performance of the program across all the possible configurations, but to find those configurations that result in high performance.

The output of the model is not limited to the high-level performance metrics such as R and T. It can predict execution time for individual code fragments or groups of code fragments. In particular, for tinyhttpd it also predicts the overall time required for the working thread to process the request ($\varepsilon \in (0.001, 0.340)$, $\overline{\varepsilon} = 0.074$), time necessary to complete for `stat()` ($\varepsilon \in (0.044, 0.456)$, $\overline{\varepsilon} = 0.212$) and `read()` ($\varepsilon \in (0.001, 0.539)$, $\overline{\varepsilon} = 0.151$) calls. This enables

us to use the model for finding unobvious bottlenecks in the program. For example in our case it was discovered that a single `stat()` call can take as much time as reading the whole file in 1kb blocks. Furthermore, the model produces readings of hardware resource usage, such as average CPU or hard drive load. Unfortunately, space limitations do not allow us providing elaborated results for these metrics.

7. CONCLUSIONS AND FUTURE WORK

In this paper we presented our approach for modeling performance of the multithreaded computer programs. We pay special attention to simulating concurrent usage of the underlying OS and hardware by multiple threads. As a result, our models do not require extensive amounts of training data and do not pose significant restrictions on the types of programs that can be modeled.

We implemented our methodology in practice by developing an extensive end-to-end framework for simulating multithreaded programs, which includes tools for data collection and model building. Finally, we verified our approach by building models of both CPU- and I/O-bound multithreaded programs.

Our model accurately predicts the performance of multithreaded programs with a high degree of accuracy. The model also allows predicting performance of individual pro-

Table 3: Relative errors for predicting the tinyhttpd performance metrics

Response time R

Num. threads	Incoming request rate												
	10	20	30	40	50	60	70	80	90	100	110	120	130
2	0.098	0.073	0.083	0.184	0.448	0.981	0.570	0.115	0.059	0.070	0.050	0.018	0.037
4	0.081	0.050	0.092	0.182	0.366	0.981	0.543	0.118	0.046	0.068	0.042	0.013	0.038
6	0.080	0.033	0.093	0.233	0.145	0.927	0.448	0.083	0.025	0.041	0.011	0.007	0.063
8	0.068	0.010	0.126	0.275	0.415	0.550	1.555	0.005	0.000	0.011	0.011	0.005	0.078

Total throughput (including error responses) T

Num. threads	Incoming request rate												
	10	20	30	40	50	60	70	80	90	100	110	120	130
2	0.003	0.003	0.015	0.004	0.022	0.013	0.051	0.016	0.009	0.061	0.043	0.018	0.039
4	0.004	0.003	0.016	0.004	0.022	0.003	0.051	0.020	0.002	0.056	0.034	0.005	0.045
6	0.004	0.003	0.016	0.034	0.020	0.034	0.042	0.023	0.002	0.032	0.002	0.002	0.057
8	0.004	0.003	0.015	0.003	0.023	0.040	0.045	0.023	0.008	0.031	0.004	0.000	0.071

Number of error responses

Num. threads	Incoming request rate												
	10	20	30	40	50	60	70	80	90	100	110	120	130
2	0.000	0.000	0.000	0.000	0.000	1.000	1.000	0.684	0.482	0.281	0.263	0.199	0.214
4	0.000	0.000	0.000	0.000	0.000	1.000	1.000	0.690	0.411	0.249	0.202	0.180	0.203
6	0.000	0.000	0.000	0.000	0.000	0.000	1.000	0.566	0.265	0.104	0.199	0.102	0.136
8	0.000	0.000	0.000	0.000	0.000	0.000	0.000	0.366	0.068	0.159	0.011	0.037	0.066

gram components and usage of computation resources. More importantly, *our models accurately predict those configurations of the program that result in its high performance.*

These results encourage us to continue working on simulation of computer programs. Most importantly, we plan automate building the models of programs. This would allow us building models of complex applications such as industrial web and DBMS servers, search servers and crowlers. As a first step, we plan developing tools for automatic discovery of I/O and synchronization routines in the program. This would allow instrumenting the program's code and building probabilistic graphs of the working threads without human intervention. As a more distant prospective, we plan to automate building high-level queuing models of the program.

Moreover, we investigate different approaches towards I/O modeling. We plan developing a purely statistical model of the disk I/O. This model should allow simulating various types of the hardware, such as RAID arrays, and provide higher accuracy. Similarly, we plan developing a model for network I/O since, in certain scenarios, network delays can become determinant of the program's performance.

8. REFERENCES

[1] http://www.omnetpp.org/.
[2] http://sourceware.org/systemtap/.
[3] http://cs.brown.edu/~alexta/PERSIK.html.
[4] http://sourceforge.net/projects/tinyhttpd/.
[5] J. Barnes and P. Hut. A hierarchical o(n log n) force-calculation algorithm. *Nature*, 324:446–449, 1986.
[6] B.-G. Chun, L. Huang, S. Lee, P. Maniatis, and M. Naik. Mantis: Predicting system performance through program analysis and modeling. *CoRR*, abs/1010.0019, 2010.
[7] A. Ganapathi, Y. Chen, A. Fox, R. Katz, and D. Patterson. Statistics-driven workload modeling for the cloud. In *Proc. of International Conference on Data Engineering Workshops (ICDEW)*, pages 87 –92, march 2010.
[8] A. Ganapathi, H. Kuno, U. Dayal, J. L. Wiener, A. Fox, M. Jordan, and D. Patterson. Predicting multiple metrics for queries: Better decisions enabled by machine learning. In *Proc. of International Conference on Data Engineering*, pages 592–603, Washington, DC, USA, 2009. IEEE Computer Society.
[9] S. Gilmore, J. Hillston, L. Kloul, and M. Ribaudo. Software performance modelling using pepa nets. In *Proc. of of international workshop on Software and performance*, WOSP '04, pages 13–23, New York, NY, USA, 2004. ACM.
[10] M. Hauswirth and T. M. Chilimbi. Low-overhead memory leak detection using adaptive statistical profiling. In *Proc. of International Conference on Architectural support for programming languages and operating systems*, ASPLOS-XI, pages 156–164, New York, NY, USA, 2004. ACM.
[11] T. A. Israr, D. H. Lau, G. Franks, and M. Woodside. Automatic generation of layered queuing software performance models from commonly available traces. In *Proc. of International Workshop on Software and Performance*, WOSP '05, pages 147–158, New York, NY, USA, 2005. ACM.
[12] S. A. Jarvis, B. P. Foley, P. J. Isitt, D. P. Spooner, D. Rueckert, and G. R. Nudd. Performance prediction for a code with data-dependent runtimes. *Concurr. Comput. : Pract. Exper.*, 20:195–206, March 2008.
[13] E. D. Lazowska, J. Zahorjan, G. S. Graham, and K. C. Sevcik. *Quantitative System Performance, Computer System Analysis Using Queuing Network Models.* Prentice Hall, 1984.
[14] B. C. Lee, D. M. Brooks, B. R. de Supinski, M. Schulz, K. Singh, and S. A. McKee. Methods of inference and learning for performance modeling of parallel applications. In *Proc. of SIGPLAN symposium on Principles and practice of parallel programming*, PPoPP '07, pages 249–258, New York, NY, USA, 2007. ACM.
[15] M. N. Bennani and D. A. Menasce. Resource allocation for autonomic data centers using analytic performance models. pages 229–240, 2005.

[16] D. Narayanan, E. Thereska, and A. Ailamaki. Continuous resource monitoring for self-predicting dbms. In *Proc. of International Symposium on Modeling, Analysis, and Simulation of Computer and Telecommunication Systems*, pages 239–248, Washington, DC, USA, 2005. IEEE Computer Society.

[17] H. Q. Nguyen and A. Apon. Hierarchical performance measurement and modeling of the linux file system. In *Proc. of International Conference on Performance Engineering*, ICPE '11, pages 73–84, New York, NY, USA, 2011. ACM.

[18] G. R. Nudd, D. J. Kerbyson, E. Papaefstathiou, S. C. Perry, J. S. Harper, and D. V. Wilcox. Pace–a toolset for the performance prediction of parallel and distributed systems. *Int. J. High Perform. Comput. Appl.*, 14:228–251, August 2000.

[19] K. Singh, E. İpek, S. A. McKee, B. R. de Supinski, M. Schulz, and R. Caruana. Predicting parallel application performance via machine learning approaches: Research articles. volume 19, pages 2219–2235, Chichester, UK, December 2007. John Wiley and Sons Ltd.

[20] D. Thakkar, A. E. Hassan, G. Hamann, and P. Flora. A framework for measurement based performance modeling. In *Proc. of International Workshop on Software and Performance*, WOSP '08, pages 55–66, New York, NY, USA, 2008. ACM.

[21] E. Thereska, B. Doebel, A. X. Zheng, and P. Nobel. Practical performance models for complex, popular applications. In *Proc. of SIGMETRICS International Conference on Measurement and Modeling of Computer Systems*, SIGMETRICS '10, pages 1–12, New York, NY, USA, 2010. ACM.

[22] E. Thereska and G. R. Ganger. Ironmodel: robust performance models in the wild. In *Pro. of SIGMETRICS International Conference on Measurement and Modeling of Computer Systems*, SIGMETRICS '08, pages 253–264, New York, NY, USA, 2008. ACM.

[23] E. Thereska, D. Narayanan, and G. R. Ganger. Towards self-predicting systems: What if you could ask "what-if"? *Knowl. Eng. Rev.*, 21:261–267, September 2006.

[24] R. van der Mei, R. Hariharan, and P. Reeser. Web server performance modeling. *Telecommunication Systems*, 16:361–378, 2001. 10.1023/A:1016667027983.

[25] Y. Z. Wenying Feng. A birthâĂŞdeath model for web cache systems: Numerical solutions and simulation. *Nonlinear Analysis: Hybrid Systems*, 2:272–284, 2008.

[26] X. Wu and M. Woodside. Performance modeling from software components. In *Proc. of International Workshop on Software and Performance*, WOSP '04, pages 290–301, New York, NY, USA, 2004. ACM.

[27] J. Xu, A. Oufimtsev, M. Woodside, and L. Murphy. Performance modeling and prediction of enterprise javabeans with layered queuing network templates. In *Proc. of Conference on Specification and Verification of Component-based Systems*, SAVCBS '05, New York, NY, USA, 2005. ACM.

Parallel File System Measurement and Modeling Using Colored Petri Nets

Hai Nguyen
University of Arkansas
Fayetteville, Arkansas, USA
1-501-342-2932
hqn01@uark.edu

Amy Apon
Clemson University
Clemson, South Carolina, USA
1-864-656-5769
aapon@clemson.edu

ABSTRACT

Parallel file systems are significant challenges for high performance data-intensive system designers due to their complexity. Being able to study features and designs before building the actual system is an advantage that a simulation model can offer. This paper presents a detailed simulation-based performance model of the PVFS parallel file system. The model is developed using Colored Petri Nets. The goal of the simulation model is to provide a tool to examine end-to-end performance of a parallel file system and to build a foundation that can be easily expanded upon in the future to model many different types of parallel file systems. The performance evaluation results of the model demonstrate that the model performance behavior is close to the expected behavior of the real PVFS file system.

Categories and Subject Descriptors

C.4 [**Computer Systems Organization**]: Performance of Systems
– *Modeling techniques.*

D.2.2 [**Software Engineering**]: Design Tools and Techniques –
Petri nets.

D.4.3 [**Operating Systems**]: File System Managements.

General Terms

Design, Experimentation, Measurement, Performance.

Keywords

Colored Petri Net, parallel file system modeling, parallel file system simulation, PVFS.

1. INTRODUCTION AND MOTIVATION

New processor and clustering technologies allow modern high-performance computing environments to achieve very high data processing power. As a consequence, the I/O workloads of high-performance computing systems are very specialized and very different from normal desktop environments [7]. High-performance scientific and business applications tend to access

data in very large blocks and they also tend to access storage cooperatively to achieve better overall throughput.

Due to such high demand on storage systems, large-scale cluster-based storage systems [2, 13] are often utilized in high performance data-intensive computing environments [5, 17]. These cluster-based parallel storage systems are usually composed of multiple individual storage devices such as direct-attached storage devices or Storage Area Network (SAN) devices. These individual storage devices together provide the high I/O data rates needed by the computing environments but they also add to the complexity of the environment and the overhead of environment management. This paper describes a simulation modeling environment that could allow researchers to fine tune both the performance and the management aspects of a parallel storage architecture.

The PVFS file system is chosen to be the candidate for this study. PVFS, jointly developed by Clemson University and Argonne National Laboratory, is a well-established parallel file system. The parallel I/O mechanism utilized by PVFS is also used by many other popular parallel file systems. Although lacking some advanced features implemented by later-developed parallel file systems, PVFS provides a solid foundation to study and understand parallel I/O. The PVFS simulation model can be extended in future research to provide more advanced features. This research utilizes a local file system simulator developed by Nguyen and Apon in [10] to simulate the local file system of the I/O servers.

In this research, the well known Petri Nets formalism is utilized to simulate and evaluate complex data services in a parallel file system. A Colored Petri Net [8] is a graphical oriented language for design, specification, simulation and verification of systems. This language is particularly well-suited to illustrate and simulate systems in which communication and synchronization between components and resource sharing are primary concerns [9]. This makes it a very good tool for modeling file systems. CPNTools [12] is utilized for simulation and analysis.

The rest of this paper is organized as follows. Section 2 discusses related work in the parallel file system simulation research area. Section 3 provides a quick overview of the PVFS file system. Section 4 presents an I/O workload and performance study of the PVFS file system. Section 5 discusses the implementation of the simulation model using Colored Petri Nets. Multiple design decisions and assumptions are also described in this section. Section 6 presents the model performance validation against the performance of real file systems. Section 7 concludes the paper.

2. RELATED WORK

Cope et al. [4] develop a simulation toolkit called CODES to help system designers with design constraints of exascale storage systems. The authors present the capabilities of the simulator that assist systems designers in designing and assessing exascale storage systems. They also demonstrate the use of CODES to evaluate a potentially exascale storage network model and storage system. Wang and Kaeli in [14] present ParIOSim, a validated execution-driven parallel I/O simulator for network storage systems. ParIOSim provides an environment for users to test and evaluate different storage architectures and applications. They have compared simulator accuracy against measurements on different platforms using both synthetic and system-level I/O benchmarks. ParIOSim can also be utilized to optimize storage system at the application level. Bagrodia et al. [1] describe a simulator that can be used to predict the performance of MPI-IO programs. Their simulator can be utilized by MPI-IO programs as a function of architectural characteristics, caching algorithms, and alternative implementations of collective I/O operations. In [6], Gaonkar et al. present a multi-formalism model of a Lustre-like file system. The model is developed using Mobius, which is a multi-paradigm multi-solution comprehensive framework for model-based dependability and performance evaluation of systems. The authors also analyze the model's detailed behavior and present the results obtained from a simulation study.

Zhaobin et al. [16] show that Stochastic Petri Net (SPN) models can be used to analyze the performance of hybrid I/O Data Grid storage systems. The authors discuss their implementation of a typical storage system SPN model. Based on aggregate I/O, they also simplify the complexity of the model. Their work can be used to study complex and irregular I/O patterns of Data Grid applications. Although the primary goal of their research is not building a parallel file system simulator, the authors develop the model to support their research. Similar in this respect, to investigate server-to-server communication in parallel file systems, Carns et al. [3] develop a parallel file system simulator using the OMNeT++ simulation framework. Their simulator provides a representative model of how the modified version of PVFS performs with the proposed improvements.

3. OVERVIEW OF THE PVFS FILE SYSTEM

PVFS file system is designed to be a robust, scalable, and easy-to-deploy and use parallel file system for Linux cluster. The file system provides high bandwidth for concurrent read/write operations from multiple processes to a common file. PVFS was also designed to function with standard Unix/Linux file system commands. Applications utilizing the standard Unix/Linux I/O library can access the PVFS file system without modification and recompiling. The PVFS file system is distributed using an open source license. These features make PVFS a popular choice for researchers at academic institutions and national labs, as well as companies.

PVFS is designed as a client-server system with multiple servers called I/O daemons. Although there is no restriction, I/O daemons typically run on separate nodes in the cluster. These nodes are called I/O nodes and have disks attached to them. Each PVFS file is striped across the disks on the I/O nodes. PVFS also has a manager daemon that handles only metadata operations such as

permission checking for file creation, open, close, and remove operations. Metadata, in this case, refers to information describing the characteristics of a file, such as permissions, file owner and group, time stamps, and in the case of parallel file system, the distribution of the file data in the cluster. When a client accesses a file, the manager provides the locations of the I/O nodes on which file data are located. The client uses this information to communicate directly with I/O nodes to retrieve the needed data. The PVFS manager does not participate in the read/write operations.

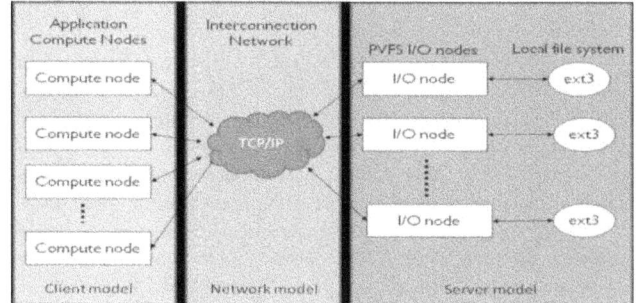

Figure 1: PVFS file system and typical cluster architecture

PVFS uses local file systems instead of raw devices to store both its file data and metadata. As a result of this design, PVFS file data, after being distributed across several I/O nodes, are stored as local files within the I/O nodes' local file system.

4. PERFORMANCE MEASUREMENT STUDY

The objective of the performance measurement study is to analyze the behavior of the PVFS file system. By studying the PVFS file system performance we can better understand the level of detail needed for the simulation model.

4.1 Experimental setup

Performance measurement experiments are executed on a PVFS cluster, as shown in Figure 1, with the I/O servers (Dell PowerEdge 1850) configured as shown in Table 1. The I/O servers are set up to have 5 drives with a RAID 5 configuration. The PVFS cluster is located in an isolated environment with dedicated resources to minimize extra factors that affect performance study. The primary I/O testing suite used in the following experiments is iozone [11].

Table 1: Experimental test bed configuration

Processors	Dual Intel Xeon processors at 2.8GHz
Front side bus	533MHz
Cache	512KB L2 cache
Chipset	ServerWorks GC LE
Memory	4GB DDR-2 400 SDRAM
Drive controller	Embedded dual channel Ultra320 SCSI
RAID controller	PERC 4/Di
Hard drives	Fujitsu MAT3147NC 147GB 10,000 rpm
	Seagate ST3146707LC 146GB 10,000 rpm

The cluster has a total of 4 I/O servers with a total capacity of approximately 2 Tbytes. The test PVFS cluster provides adequate space for testing and enough I/O servers to run a performance validation study.

4.2 I/O Workload study

Designed to achieve massive performance by parallelizing I/O accesses, PVFS, like any other parallel file system, works best with large files, using sequential access with large block size. Knowing this, applications running on PVFS file systems are configured to take advantage of this behavior as much as possible. Using a very large I/O buffer, an application sequentially accesses the file system with large block sizes of up to 100 Mbytes. Observations were made of I/O workloads on multiple PVFS file systems in a shared production environment with about 276 Tbytes of total capacity. The breakdown of I/O workload percentage is shown in Table 2. Pure random I/O in Table 2 includes I/O accesses that are less than 10Kbytes in size and have random access pattern. Large block size sequential I/O includes I/O accesses that are bigger than 1Mbytes in size and have sequential access pattern. Sequential I/O accesses with size smaller than 1Mbytes and I/O accesses with mix pattern are presented in the second category.

Table 2: Workload breakdown in a Production environment

Pure random I/O	0.00028%
Mix random I/O and sequential I/O	2.047%
Large block size sequential I/O	97.952%

From the real-world workload breakdown, it is clear that pure random I/O occupies a very small amount of workload on the parallel file system. Sequential workloads with very large block size occupy a majority of the total workload. PVFS and other parallel file systems are designed for this type of workload. Of course, the I/O access pattern on a file system depends on the user of the file system. However, if one should choose to use PVFS for pure small files and a random access workload, the performance of the parallel file system will degrade. Sequential I/O workloads and mixed workloads are selected for study and evaluation in the simulation model.

4.3 I/O performance study with different file sizes and block sizes

This measurement study is to observe the I/O behavior of the PVFS file system when the file size and block size change. First, sequential I/O write performance is examined using a set of small to large size files (from 4Kbytes to 1Gbytes). The results for the sequential I/O write measurement experiments are presented in Figure 2. The I/O write throughput at small file sizes is less than I/O throughput at larger file sizes. This observation shows that the I/O performance is not at peak level until file size is equal to or greater than 2Mbytes. There are multiple factors contributing to this behavior. The first factor is the nature of PVFS. PVFS is a parallel file system. Files stored in a PVFS file system are divided into multiple stripes using a default stripe size of 64Kbytes and are distributed across multiple I/O servers. By striping file

contents across multiple servers, a client machine can access several pieces of file data at the same time. For a small file, this mechanism creates some overhead which causes the I/O performance to become lower until the file size is large enough to obtain the full advantage of the workload parallelization as shown in Figure 2. In these experiments, the smallest file that uses all I/O servers is 4*64K, or 256Kbytes. A second factor is the file system synchronization. PVFS synchronizes the local file system in the I/O nodes when it closes the file, forcing data to be written to disk. For a small file, the delay-write mechanism utilized by Linux provides little benefit and thus the I/O performance is affected until the file size is large enough to obtain the full advantage of the delay-write mechanism. The file size where the I/O performance becomes stable is a function of a numerous other factors including the local file system buffer size, the local file system dirty page ratio threshold, and the PVFS stripe size. For this particular testing PVFS cluster, that file size is approximately 2Mbytes.

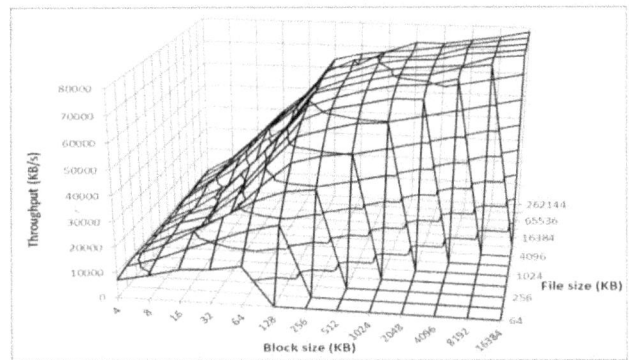

Figure 2: Sequential write performance experiment

The results for the sequential I/O read measurement experiments are presented in Figure 3. The read experiments use a similar set of files, and the block sizes vary the same way as with write experiments. However, these measurements show that for a fixed block size and a sequential workload the I/O read performance is not directly affected by file size. Unlike writes, reads in PVFS are implemented as read operations on the local file system in the I/O nodes and utilize the Linux buffer cache. For sequential workloads, fetching of whole blocks of the local file system and the buffer cache causes whole blocks to be loaded into memory from disk independently of the read request size. The throughput is then limited by the transfer of data across the network.

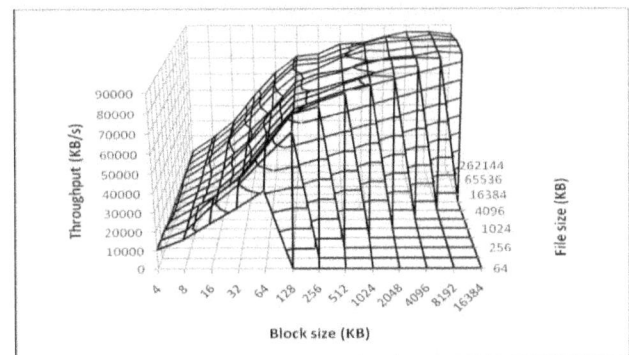

Figure 3: Sequential read performance experiment

According to the read and write measurement results, after the file size becomes large enough, the PVFS I/O performance does not change. After reaching this stable file size, the I/O performance is then affected by the block size of the I/O operations. However, the I/O performance drops sharply when the file size reaches the physical memory capacity of the machine. This behavior is caused by memory reclaiming and swapping, which in turn causes disk thrashing, leading to I/O performance degradation.

Based on these performance characteristics, 512Mbytes is selected to be the standard file size for all models in the performance study. It is large enough to have stable performance but smaller than the physical memory capacity of the test machines.

5. IMPLEMENTATION OF THE SIMULATION MODEL

The first and foremost goal for a parallel file system is to achieve massive I/O throughput. This is done by providing access to multiple I/O resources in parallel. PVFS as well as many other parallel file systems implements this by utilizing multiple connected local file systems as foundation. The simulation model for the parallel file system is developed using a similar concept. It utilizes multiple connected local file system simulation models as its foundation. It interfaces with higher level applications and provides them the response time associated with each I/O request. The implementation of the simulation model is presented in a top down fashion, from application level down to the local file system level, and each level is described using Colored Petri Nets.

5.1 Assumptions and model limitations

Similar to the local file system simulation model, the parallel simulation is also divided into an I/O read model and an I/O write model. Read operations and write operations are simulated separately to simplify the complexity of simulating a parallel file system.

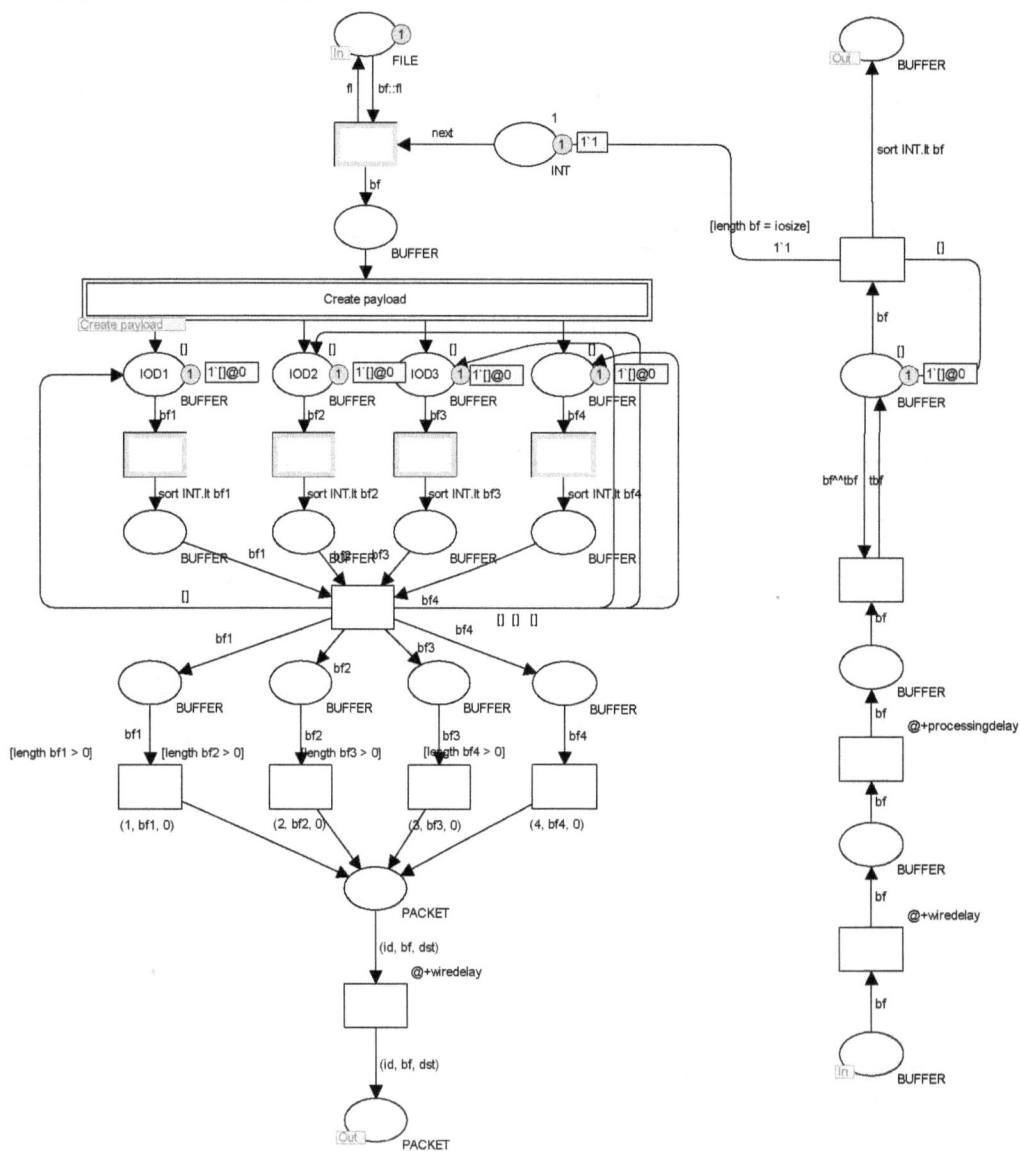

Figure 4: PVFS read - client model

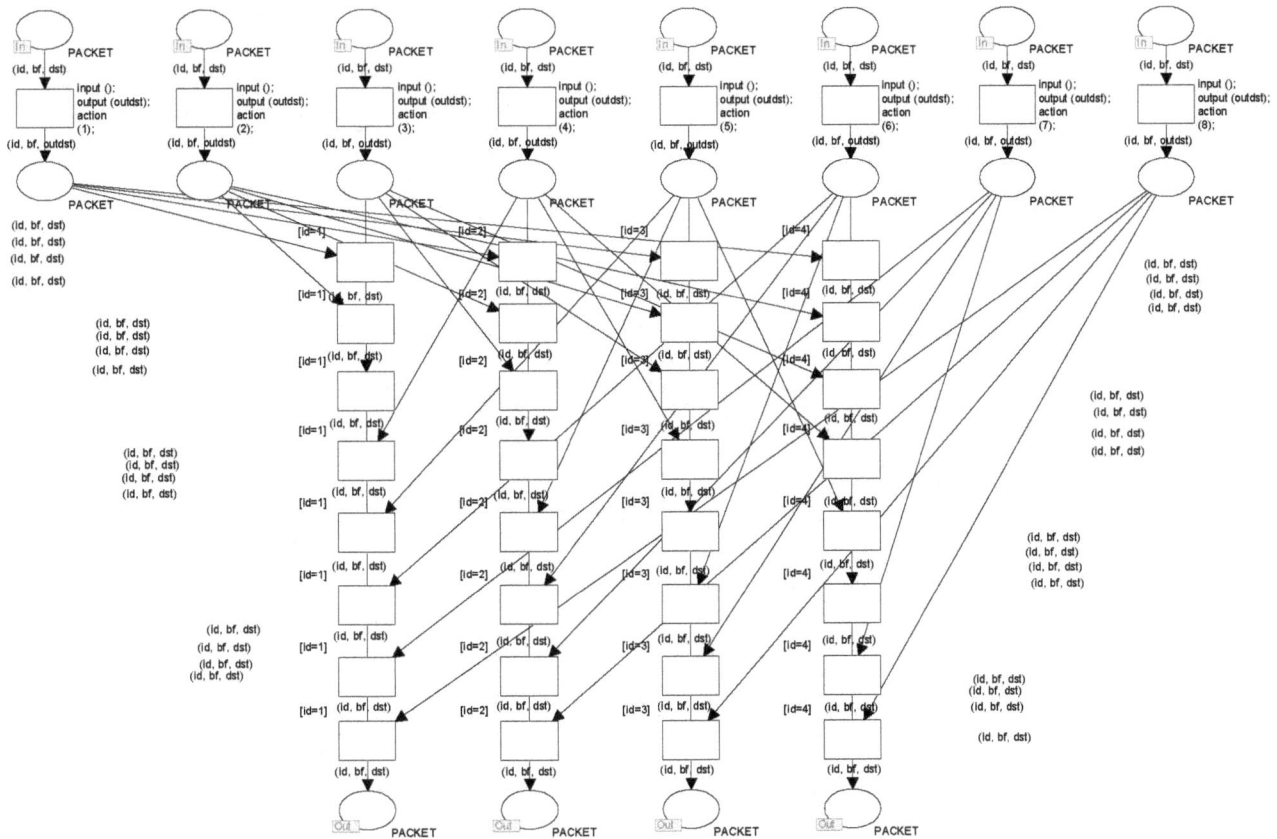

Figure 5: PVFS read - network transmission model

A key difference between a parallel file system and a local file system is the network component. Since parallel file systems use the network to simultaneously access multiple local file system at the same time, a parallel file system simulation model must contain a network model. Although the network simulation model is an important component in the parallel file system simulation model, it only serves as a transport from the client model to the server model. The network model does not need to model every network operation in detail [15]. A single-server queuing model is used to simulate network end-to-end performance.

The number of I/O servers in a PVFS cluster is determined at the time the cluster is built. After the cluster goes into production, the number of I/O servers is generally fixed. Although, under some circumstances, I/O servers can be added or removed from the cluster, this procedure usually causes the original data on the cluster to be destroyed. For the simulation model, the PVFS cluster has four I/O servers.

5.2 File read model implementation

From the application standpoint, reading a file basically divides the file into smaller manageable blocks and reads them into memory. Reading a file from a parallel file system is a straightforward extension of reading a file from a local file system. The operation is divided into three main components: the client component, the network component and the server component.

5.2.1 File read model client component

At the application level, the model is simple. A loop breaks the needed file into multiple blocks of read requests and passes the list of these blocks to the client simulation component. The client component processes the data, and then passes the data requests to the network component. The result of the read operation is an array of data passed back from the network model. The Petri net for the application level is simple and not shown.

The implementation of the client component could be described as dividing the block of read requests into a list of payloads and passing this list to the network component to send over the network to the server component. The number of payloads depends on the number of I/O servers in the file system. The Petri net implementation of the client component with four I/O servers is presented in Figure 4. Payloads are created by striping request data into multiple chunks according to the file system's stripe size parameter. The stripe size in PVFS usually is 64 Kbytes. The default distribution of data chunks in a payload is done using a round-robin mechanism.

After the payloads are created, the client component prepares the packets before sending them to the network component. This process represents the network stack on the client computer. While this process could be considered a part of the network component, it uses physical resources on the client machine and thus is more closely related to the client component. In taking the payloads and building network packets around them, the client component adds the network identifications of the I/O servers to the network packets. The network component will later use this

233

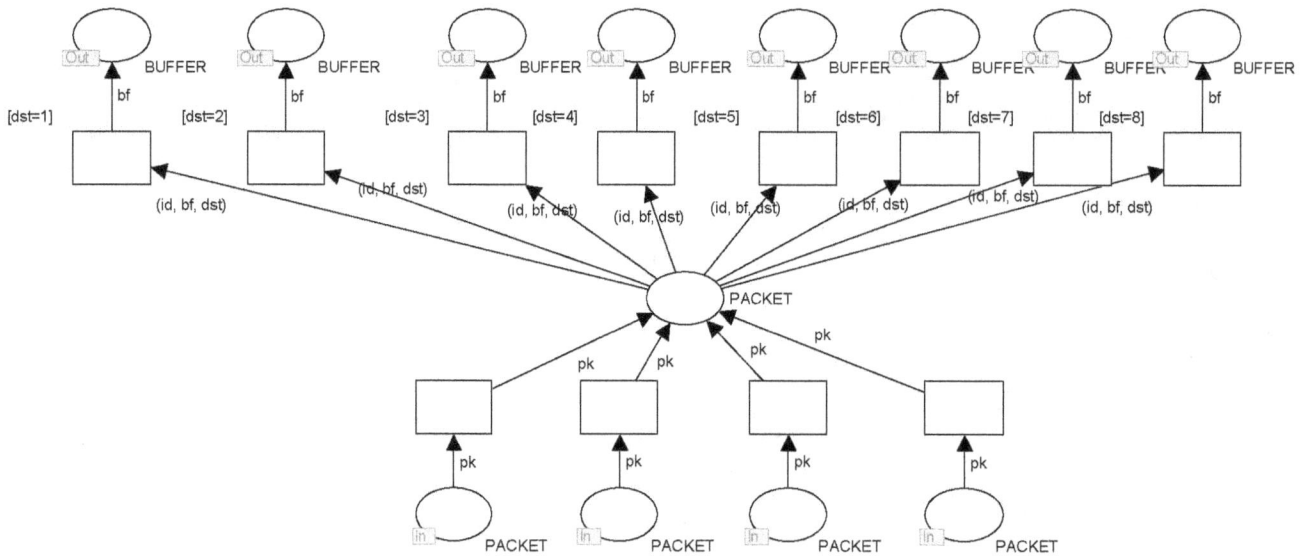

Figure 6: PVFS read - network receiving model

information to deliver the packets to the correct I/O servers. For an I/O read operation, the client component only sends read requests to the servers. Read requests are very small and will not need to be broken down into smaller fragments. After the network packets are created, they are sent to the network device buffer.

In addition to sending read requests to the I/O servers, the client component also receives data being sent back from the I/O servers. From the network device receiving buffer, the client component gathers the network packets. It assembles the data from these network packets received from different I/O servers into the requested result and sends it back to the application.

5.2.2 File read model network component

The network component provides the transportation for the data packets from the client to the I/O servers. Since only end-to-end performance characteristics of the network component are needed, the network component does not model switches and routers in

detail. Instead, the network component is designed using a multiplexer model. The client packets are examined and routed to the correct I/O servers.

When the result data are sent back to the clients, a similar mechanism is used. The server component, depending on the origin of the data, will send data packets back to the original requested client. The network component examines the packets and routes them to the correct clients. The Petri Net models of the sending and the receiving network components for PVFS file read operation are presented in Figure 5 and Figure 6.

5.2.3 File read model server component

I/O servers are where the actual I/O operations are performed. Each PVFS file system has multiple I/O servers that work independently in parallel to provide large I/O bandwidth that a single local file system could never achieve.

Each I/O server, similar to the client side, has a network layer to

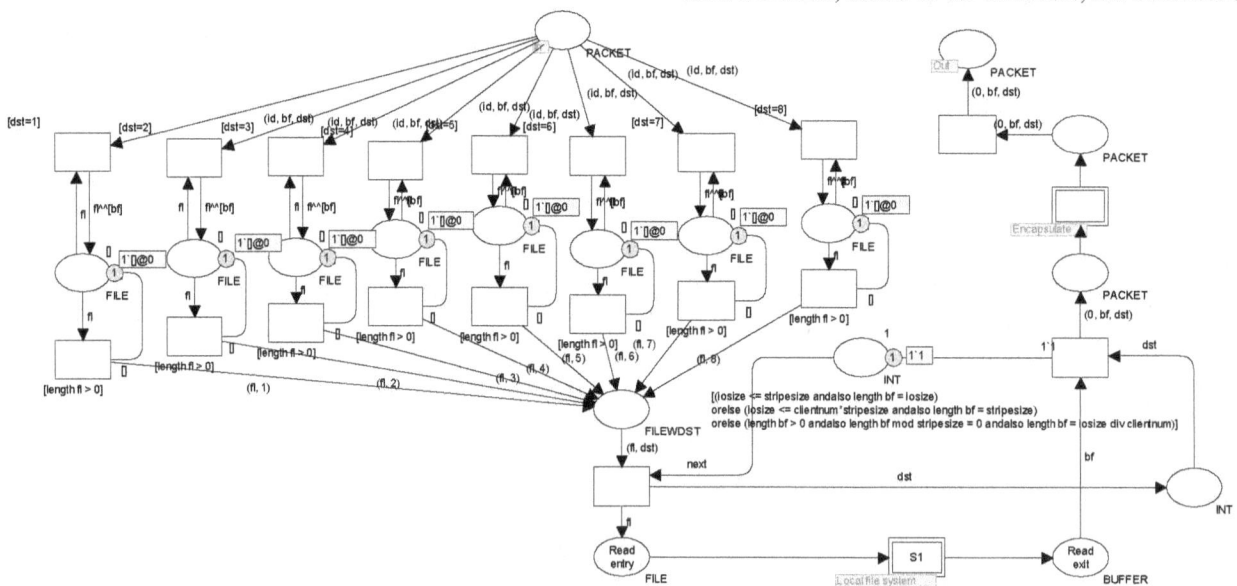

Figure 7: PVFS read - server model

process network packets from the network component. A network packet, after arriving at the I/O server, is examined and categorized into different receive buffers, using a first-come-first-served (FCFS) mechanism. This process is designed following the same implementation in the real system. Each client has its own receive buffer.

The server component, following a FCFS order, takes read requests from the receive buffers and sends them to the local file system model [10]. The requests are sent in chunks of 64 Kbytes by default. If the PVFS file system is built with a different stripe size, this chunk size is changed. The local file system on the I/O server performs a sequential read operation. Since the I/O server component takes a read request from the receive buffers using FCFS order, the read request chunks are mixed together. The next chunk of read requests may not be from the same client as the chunk before it. Two different clients rarely try to read the same file at the same location. This causes the read requests stream sent to the local file system to have a distinctive pattern of multiple interleaved streams of sequential read requests. Each stream may start at a random location. The Petri Net model for the server component for PVFS file read operation with eight clients is presented in Figure 7.

After the read requests pass through the local file system component, this component returns the result. At this step, the I/O

server component sends these data through a network packet creation process that is similar to the client component. When the client component sends the read requests over the network, the size of these read requests are relatively small and can fit within a standard frame. The result data, however, do not. They need to be divided into multiple segments along with attached headers and network addresses. The segment size of a packet is limited by the MTU of the network. Usually, in a Gigabit Ethernet network, the MTU is set to 1500. This means that a network packet maximum size is 1500 bytes.

5.3 File write model implementation

From the application standpoint, writing a file to a parallel file system is an extension of writing a file to a local file system. The application level model is very similar to the I/O read model. The operation is divided into three main components: the client component, the network component and the server component. The Petri Net implementation of the application level model is simple and is not presented due to space limitations.

5.3.1 File write model client component

The top level of the file write model client component is simple. The file data to be written to disk are broken into multiple blocks of write requests. These write requests are passed to the client simulation component. The client component processes the data,

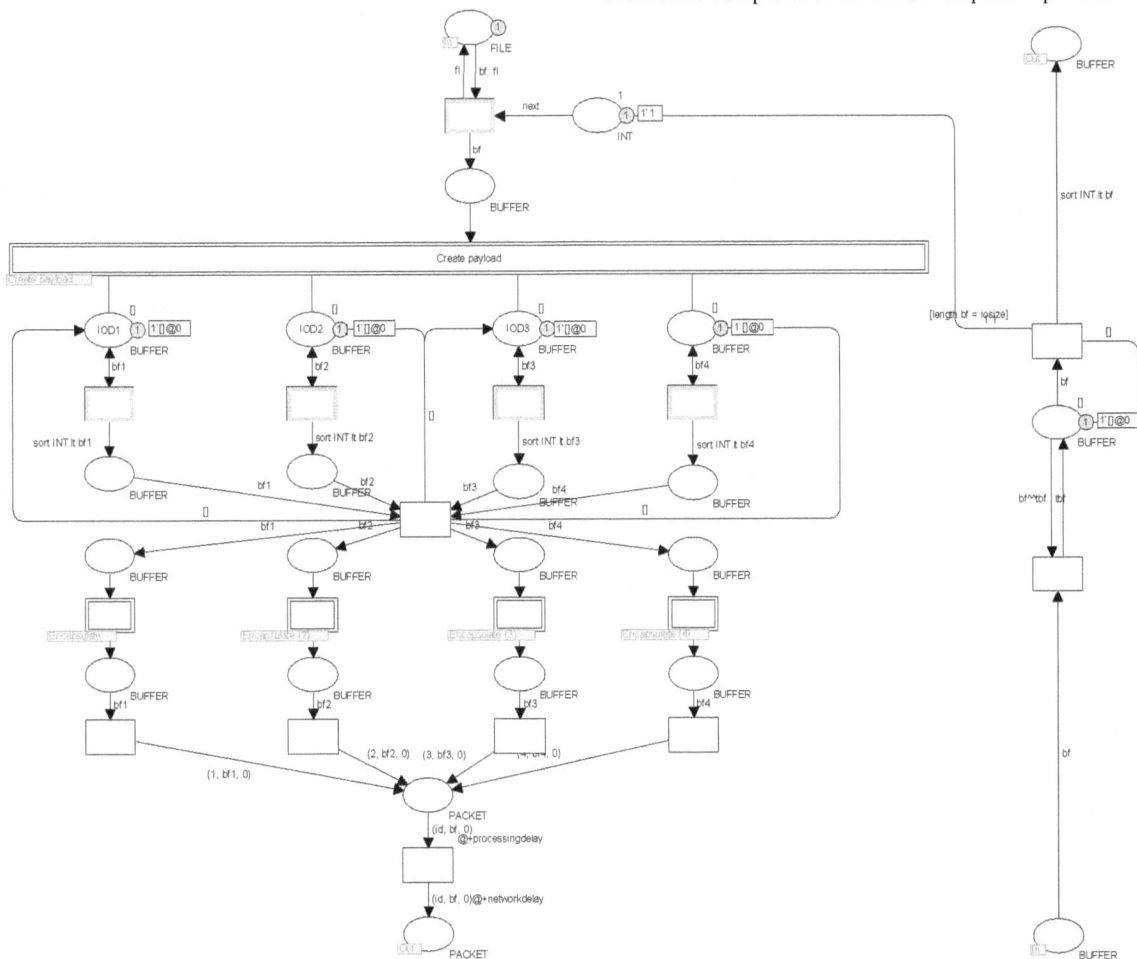

Figure 8: PVFS write - client model

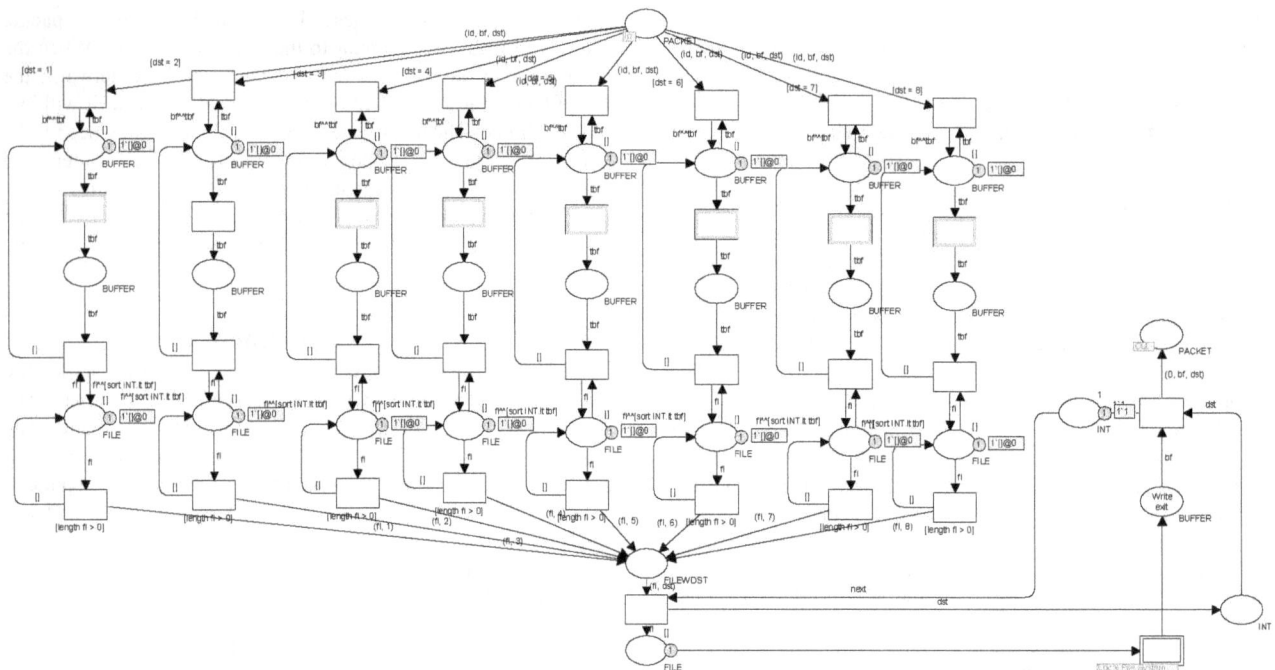

Figure 9: PVFS write - server model

and then sends the packaged data to the network component. The result of the write operation is a series of return codes received from the network model.

The implementation of the client component for the file write operation is quite similar to the client component of the file read operation. However, write requests not only contain requests to write data to disk but also contain the actual data needed to be written. The client component needs to divide these blocks of data into multiple payloads. The number of actual payloads is determined by the number of I/O servers in the system. The Petri Net model for the PVFS client component is presented in Figure 8. Payloads are created by striping request data into multiple chunks according to the file system's stripe depth parameter. The distribution of data chunks in a payload is done using a round-robin mechanism.

After creating the payloads, the client component attaches network addresses and control information to the payloads to create network packets. Since the packet size depends on the MTU of the network, the client component has to split the payloads into multiple segments. The packet size for data sending from clients to I/O servers is also at the maximum size of 1500 bytes.

5.3.2 File write model network component

The network component model in the file write operation is very similar to the network component model in the file read operation. There are only some slight differences in the model due to the data flow of the operation being different. The network packets from the client component are examined, the destination addresses are checked, and the packets are routed to the correct receiver. The network component provides the transportation for the packets and also simulates the wire-delay on the network medium. The Petri Net model for the sending and the receiving network component for PVFS file write are similar to the network model

utilized in PVFS file read described in section 5.2.2 and are not presented due to space limitation.

5.3.3 File write model server component

The file write server component is built upon the local write model. A network packet, after arriving at the I/O server, is processed and sent to the local file write model. The server creates a receive buffer for each client sending in requests. It also examines the network packets and moves the request data into the correct buffers using FCFS mechanism. This process is designed to follow the same implementation as in the real system.

Since each packet is limited by the maximum segmentation size of the network, the server component combines multiple packet data into the original request sent by the client. Unlike the file read server model, the file write server model does not attempt to combine the original request into 64Kbytes chunk. Instead it combines the fragmented data into the original request and sends it to the local file write model [10]. Because of this, the block sizes of the write requests sent to the local file write model are not fixed. PVFS relies on the delay write mechanism of the local file system to combine multiple different small write requests into big and sequential write requests. The local file system on the I/O server performs the write operation. Since the server model sends the write requests to the local file system model as it receives in a FCFS order, the block size of the write requests are quite random. Even though, the write requests could be in sequential order, the block sizes of the requests are not. This creates a distinctive I/O access pattern. The Petri Net model for PVFS file write server model is presented in Figure 9. After read requests pass through the local file system component, it returns the result data read from disk.

6. PARALLEL FILE SYSTEM SIMULATION MODEL PERFORMANCE VALIDATION

This section presents the performance validation of the simulation model for a PVFS file system. Because PVFS is a parallel file system, the number of clients accessing the file system at the same time is important. The file system is designed to provide a massive I/O bandwidth and throughput by allowing multiple I/O servers to work with multiple clients at the same time.

6.1 Validation setup

In order to validate the entire Petri Net file system model against real-world data, the model hardware parameters, such as memory delay, execution speed, function overhead, and disk speed, are measured using kernel traces directly from the machines on which the experiments are executed. The performance parameters of the network stack on the client and server machines are also measured using kernel traces. Network performance parameters on the wire are recorded using network monitoring tools, including ping, traceroute and packet sniffer. The PVFS file system model is implemented with four I/O servers. The performance validations are executed starting with one client accessing the file system. The number of clients is increased until the number of clients equals eight. The number of clients is determined from observing the real file system under the validation workload. By using from one to eight clients (double the number of servers) accessing the file system simultaneously, the file system level of stress is enough to demonstrate many interesting aspects of the file system performance. We present the performance results of one, four, and eight clients experiments in this paper.

6.2 Sequential workload performance validation

Simulations are run several times, and the average results are used to compare with iozone benchmark results running on the test system. The simulation experiments are run using synthetic I/O requests simulating sequential I/O. The I/O requests are grouped into similar block-size configurations of the iozone benchmark.

6.2.1 Single client performance experiment

In this performance measurement, one client reads and writes to the PVFS file system. The result of the I/O read performance in the experiment is presented in Figure 10. The error bars are set at 20%.

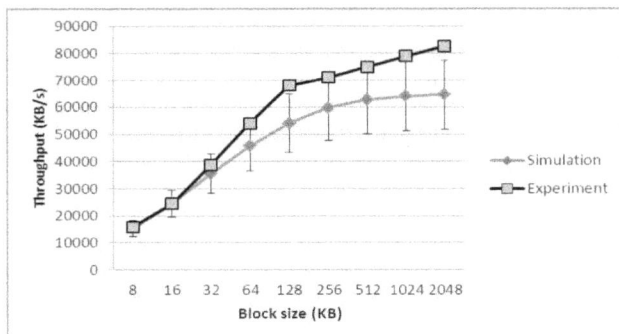

Figure 10: Single client read performance

All points, except the last one, are within or very close to 20% of the real-world measurement. Even though the last data point is farther away than other data points, it is still a very good result. The simulation data points are consistently lower than real-world data. The result of the I/O write performance in the experiment is presented in Figure 11. The error bars are set at 20%.

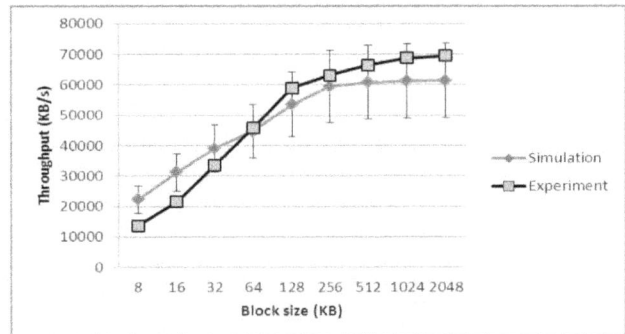

Figure 11: Single client write performance

Like the I/O read result, the I/O write result is also very good. The majority of data points are within 20% of the real system measurement. Simulation data in this experiment are not consistently lower than real-world data as is observed in the I/O read result. At small block size, the simulation results are higher than real-world data, but at bigger block sizes, the simulation results become lower.

The reason for this model behavior comes from the buffer design of the I/O server model. The I/O server has a receive buffer for every client sending requests to the server. Data are taken out of the buffers using a first-come-first-served (FCFS) order. The receive buffers in the real server are implemented using a linked-list data structure. The larger the buffer, the slower an item in the buffer can be accessed. Currently, the buffers of the simulation model are implemented to have a fixed operating cost. This means that the time it takes to access an item in the buffer stays the same, regardless of the size of the buffer. The number of write requests needed to write a file when using a small block size is much larger than the number of write requests when using a large block size. In the simulation model, this does not change the time it takes to de-queue requests. This causes the simulation model to run faster than the real system at the small block sizes and slower than the real system at the large block sizes. Adding this level to detail to the model is an area of future research.

6.2.2 Four clients performance experiment

In this experiment, four clients read and write to the PVFS model. The result of the I/O read performance in the experiment is presented in Figure 12. The error bars are set at 20%.

With four clients accessing the PVFS file system at the same time, we start to notice variations within the data points, especially in the real-world data. The simulation data, however, are still very consistent. This is because the simulation model has fewer factors that affect the result. As more clients access the PVFS file system, more outside factors are introduced to the real-world data. For example, with four clients the requests at each I/O server are interleaved, creating a highly random and non-sequential access pattern. The access pattern affects the response time of the I/O servers. Active management of the access pattern at the I/O servers is an interesting area of further research.

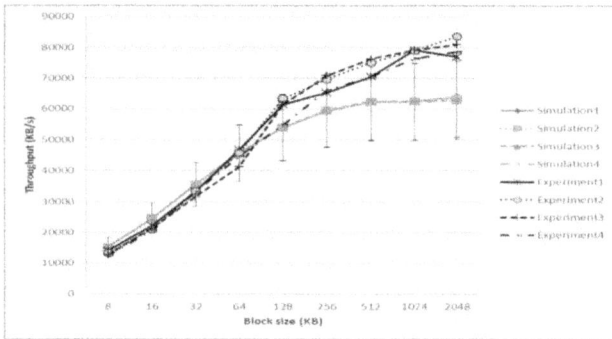

Figure 12: Four clients read performance

Even with the increasing variation of the data points, the experimental result is still good. The performance behavior is similar to what we have observed in previous experiments. The last two data points are not within 20% of the real-world data, but are still very close. The result of the I/O write performance in the experiment is presented in Figure 13. The error bars are set at 20%.

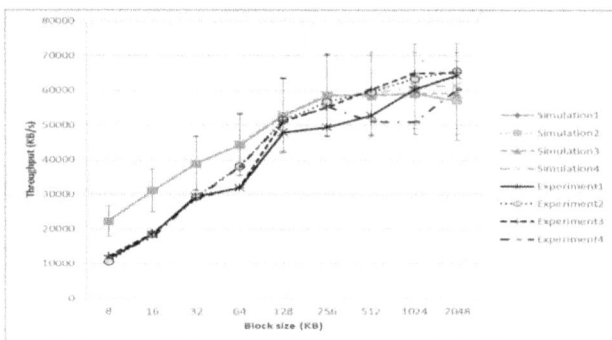

Figure 13: Four clients write performance

The I/O write experiment result also has variations. The amount of variations is slightly more than in the I/O read experiment. In general, the performance behavior is slightly different to what we have previously observed. The simulation data points are higher than the real-world data points at small block sizes. The simulation data points are lower than the real-world data points at larger block sizes.

The simulation data points are still within 20% of the real-world data points or close to them. The two data points at smallest block sizes are somewhat farther away from the real-world data points.

6.2.3 Eight clients performance experiment
In this experiment, eight clients read and write to the PVFS model. The result of the I/O read performance in the experiment is presented in Figure 14. The error bars are set at 20%.

When the number of clients simultaneously reading the PVFS file system reaches eight clients, we expect the stress level of the file system to be very high, and the experiment supports that expectation. At this level of stress, even the middle block sizes data points, which have stayed very stable until now, start to show variations and distortions. The high level of random and non-sequential reads due to eight interleaved request causes many data

points to vary and fall well outside of the 20% error range. The biggest changes are at the big block sizes. As the number of client increases, the errors at the big block sizes also increase, especially at the largest block size.

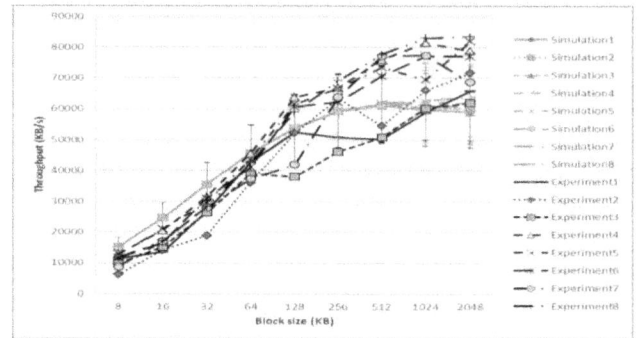

Figure 14: Eight clients read performance

As stated in the previous experiment, simulation data points show much less variations and distortions. This makes sense, as the simulation model has fewer outside factors and does not model the interleaved access pattern at the I/O nodes. Simulation experiments are also performed under well-controlled and precise conditions. The result of the I/O write performance in the experiment is presented in Figure 15. The error bars are set at 20%.

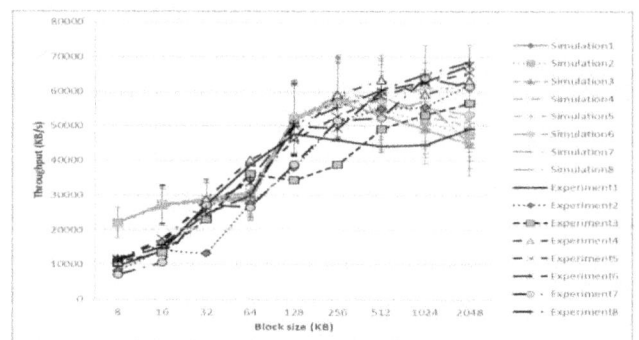

Figure 15: Eight clients write performance

Even when eight clients write to the PVFS file system at the same time, with the only exception at the 64Kbytes block size, the simulation performance behavior is still quite consistent with what was observed previously. In this experiment, many data points fall outside of the 20% error range; however, simulation data points still group together very well, especially for small block sizes. Even though there are variations among simulation data points, the magnitude of errors for small block sizes are relatively the same as earlier results. The magnitude of errors for large block sizes, however, increases when the number of clients simultaneously writing to the PVFS file system increases.

6.3 Hybrid workload performance validation

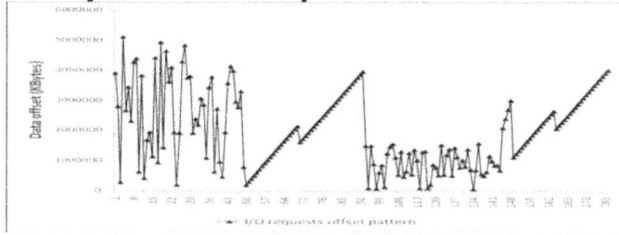

Figure 16: Hybrid workload I/O pattern

The simulation experiments are run using sets of I/O requests traces captured from the real systems. These traces are mix of random I/Os and sequential I/Os. Figure 16 shows a portion of the I/O request traces. There are several other traces captured from multiple client machines but are not shown here.

6.3.1 Single clients performance experiment

In this performance measurement, one client reads and writes to the PVFS file system. The simulation result is within 20% of the real-world measurement. The result of the I/O read and I/O write performance in the experiment are presented in Figure 17. The write performance result is also within 20% of the real-world measurement.

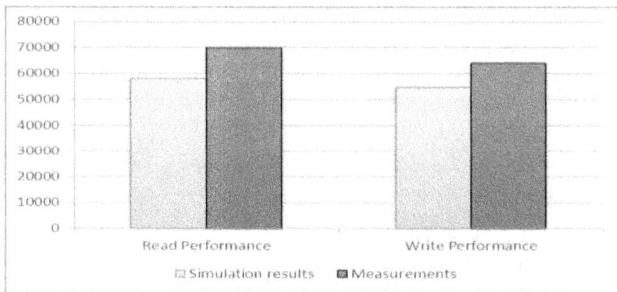

Figure 17: Single client read and write performance

6.3.2 Four clients performance experiment

In this performance measurement, four clients simultaneously read and write to the PVFS file system. The result of the I/O read performance in the experiment is presented in Figure 18.

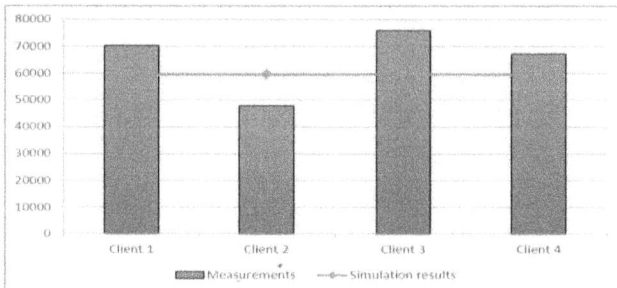

Figure 18: Four clients read performance

With four clients accessing the PVFS file system simultaneously, we start to notice variations within the data points, similar to the results using a sequential workload. Even with the increasing variation of the data points, the experiment results are still within 25% of the real-world data but are significantly larger than the errors in the two clients experiment. The result of the I/O write performance in the experiment is presented in Figure 19.

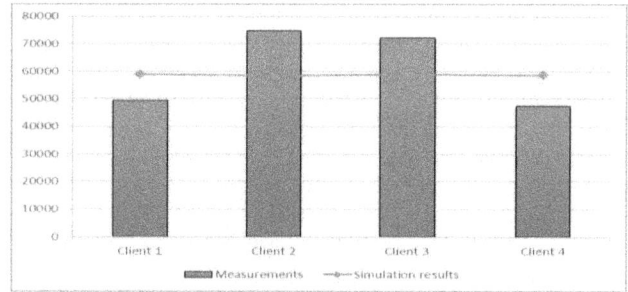

Figure 19: Four clients write performance

6.3.3 Eight clients performance experiment

In this performance measurement, eight clients read and write to the PVFS file system. The result of the I/O read performance in the experiment is presented in Figure 20.

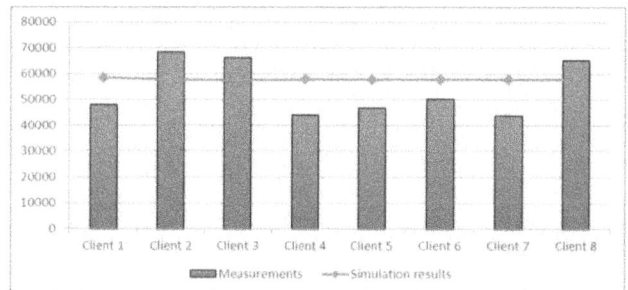

Figure 20: Eight clients read performance

When the number of clients simultaneously accessing the PVFS file system reaches eight clients, the stress level of the file system reaches an expected high level. Similar to the sequential experiments, data points show variations and distortions. Many data points have more than 40% errors. The result of the I/O write performance in the experiment is presented in Figure 21

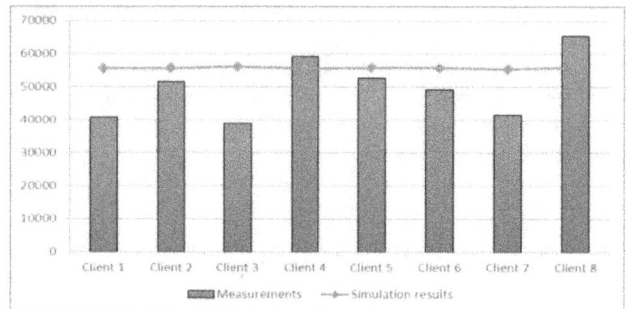

Figure 21: Eight clients write performance

6.4 Validation summary

In this section, detailed performance validation experiments of the simulation model of the PVFS file system are presented. The performance validation utilizes synthetic sequential I/O workload and traces of real-world data to study the simulation model. Performance validations are set up with several separate experiments using different numbers of clients accessing the PVFS file system. By increasing the number of clients from small to large, we observe the behavior of the simulation model when the stress level of the file system increases. For the single client experiment, the simulation performances are within 20% of the real file system. When the number of clients increases the errors and variations start to become larger since the stress level on the file system increases. When the numbers of clients become equal to or larger than four clients, the variations and distortions become visible. The simulation data points group together better than the real-world data points because the affecting factors are much less in the simulation environment. In general, the performance behavior is consistent throughout the performance validation process. The performance validation results are good, considering that this is a very complex environment, involving a parallel file system and multiple clients accessing simultaneously.

7. CONCLUSION

This paper presents a set of detailed and hierarchical performance models of the PVFS file system using Colored Petri Nets. PVFS read operation and PVFS write operation are studied and their models are built. Each operation is divided into sub-components: client, network and server. The models of these components are presented. The current PVFS model is set up to have eight clients and four servers. This is equal to a small production file system. The model can be extended to have more clients and servers. The model currently uses TCP/IP protocol over a Gigabit Ethernet network. It can also be modified to simulate a different network protocol and different network hardware in future research. The model can also be easily modified in a future work to model a different parallel file system using the foundation built in this research such as PVFS2 or GPFS. The network component model can be improved to the model network buffer more accurately as well, and can be extended to model different type of network hardware.

The ability to evaluate end-to-end parallel file system performance allows many applications for the simulation model. A proof of concept study can be performed for a business or scientific application using I/O traces with the simulation model. The results can be used to determine if the file system is suitable for the application. The model can also be used to perform bottle-neck analysis for a parallel file system. Studying the flow of I/O requests from the client to the server and back to the client could show which component in a complex parallel file system needs to be upgraded to improve performance or does not need to be upgraded to avoid cost.

8. ACKNOWLEDGMENTS

This research is based upon work supported by the National Science Foundation under Grant No. 0421099 and Grant No. 0722625.

9. REFERENCES

[1] Bagrodia, R., Docy, S., and Kahn, A. 1997. Parallel Simulation of Parallel File Systems and I/O Programs. In *Proceedings of the 1997 ACM/IEEE conference on Supercomputing (CDROM)*, San Jose, CA, 1997, pp. 1-17.

[2] Carns, P.H., Ligon, III, W.B., Ross, R.B., and Thakur, R. 2000. Pvfs: A Parallel File System for Linux Clusters. In *Proceedings of the 4th annual Linux Showcase & Conference - Volume 4*, Atlanta, Georgia, 2000, pp. 28-28.

[3] Carns, P.H., Settlemyer, B.W., Ligon, III, W.B. 2008. Using Server-to-Server Communication in Parallel File Systems to Simplify Consistency and Improve Performance. In *Proceedings of the 2008 ACM/IEEE conference on Supercomputing*, Austin, Texas, 2008, pp. 1-8.

[4] Cope, J., et al. 2011. Codes: Enabling Co-Design of Multilayer Exascale Storage Architectures. In *Proceedings of the Workshop on Emerging Supercomputing Technologies 2011*, Tucson, AZ, 2011.

[5] CERN (Conseil Européen pour la Recherche Nucléaire). 2011. http://www.cern.ch

[6] Gaonkar, S., et al. 2009. Performance and Dependability Modeling with Mobius. *SIGMETRICS Perform. Eval. Rev.*, 36:16-21, 2009.

[7] Gorton, I., Greenfield, P., Szalay, A., and Williams, R. 2008. Data-intensive computing in the 21st century. *Computer*, 41:30–32, 2008.

[8] Jensen, K. 1996. *Coloured Petri nets (2nd ed.): basic concepts, analysis methods and practical use: volume 1.* Springer-Verlag, London, UK, 1996.

[9] Kristensen, L.M., Christensen, S., and Jensen, K. 1998. The practitioner's guide to coloured petri nets. *International Journal on Software Tools for Technology Transfer*, 2:98–132, 1998.

[10] Nguyen, H.Q. and Apon, A. 2011. Hierarchical Performance Measurement and Modeling of the Linux File System. In *Proceeding of the second joint WOSP/SIPEW international conference on Performance engineering*, Karlsruhe, Germany, 2011, pp. 73-84.

[11] Norcott, W.D. and Capps, D. 2011. Iozone Filesystem Benchmark. 2011. http://www.iozone.org

[12] Ratzer, A.V. et al. 2003. CPN Tools for editing, simulating, and analyzing coloured petri nets. In *ICATPN'03: Proceedings of the 24th international conference on Applications and theory of Petri nets*, pages 450–462, Berlin, Heidelberg, 2003. Springer-Verlag.

[13] Schmuck, F. and Haskin, R. 2002. GPFS: A Shared-Disk File System for Large Computing Clusters. In *Proceedings of the 1st USENIX Conference on File and Storage Technologies*, Monterey, CA, 2002, p. 19.

[14] Wang, Y. and Kaeli, D. 2004. Execution-driven simulation of network storage systems. In *Proceedings of the 12th IEEE International Symposium on Modeling, Analysis, and Simulation of Computer and Telecommunications Systems (MASCOTS'04)*, pages 604–611, Los Alamitos, CA, USA, 2004. IEEE Computer Society.

[15] Zaitsev, D.A. and Shmeleva, T.R. 2011. A Parametric Colored Petri Net Model of a Switched Network. *International Journal of Communications, Network and System Sciences*, vol. 04, pp. 65-76, 2011.

[16] Zhaobin, L. and Haitao, L. 2007. Modeling and Performance Evaluation of Hybrid Storage I/O in Data Grid. In *Network and Parallel Computing Workshops*, 2007. NPC Workshops. IFIP International Conference on, 2007, pp. 624-629.

[17] Wellcome Trust Sanger Institute. 2011. http://www.sanger.ac.

Apache Hadoop Performance-Tuning Methodologies and Best Practices

Shrinivas B. Joshi
Advanced Micro Devices, Inc.
7171 Southwest Pkwy
Austin, TX 78735 USA
shrinivas.joshi@amd.com

ABSTRACT
Apache Hadoop is a Java based distributed computing framework built for applications implemented using MapReduce programming model. In recent years, Hadoop technology has experienced an unprecedented growth in its adoption. From single-node clusters to clusters with well over thousands of nodes, Hadoop technology is being used to perform myriad of functions – search optimizations, data mining, click stream analytics, machine learning to name a few. Although setting up Hadoop clusters and building applications for Hadoop is a well understood area, tuning Hadoop clusters for optimal performance is still a black art. In this demo paper, we will attempt to provide the audience with a holistic approach of Hadoop performance tuning methodologies and best practices. We discuss hardware as well as software tuning techniques including BIOS, OS, JVM and Hadoop configuration parameters tuning.

Categories and Subject Descriptors
C.4 [**Computer Systems Organization**]: Performance of systems

General Terms
Performance

Keywords
Performance tuning, Apache Hadoop, Map-Reduce

1. INTRODUCTION
Users who have deployed and tried tuning their Hadoop [1] clusters for the first time will certainly attest to the fact that optimizing Hadoop clusters is a daunting task. Apart from the nature and implementation of Hadoop jobs, hardware, network infrastructure, OS, JVM, and Hadoop configuration properties all have a significant impact on performance and scalability. Using *TeraSort* as a reference workload, this demo paper attempts to educate the audience on challenges involved in performance-tuning of Hadoop setup, tuning best practices, empirical data on effect of various tunings on performance, and some future directions.

2. CHALLENGES
Hadoop is a large, complex framework involving a number of entities interacting with each other across multiple hardware systems. Performance of Hadoop jobs is sensitive to every

component of the cluster stack - Hadoop configuration, JVM, OS, network infrastructure, underlying hardware, and possibly BIOS settings. Hadoop supports a large number of configuration properties and a good chunk of these can potentially impact performance. As with any large software system, diagnosing performance issues is a complicated task.

3. EXPERIMENT SETUP
For the purpose of this study we used two different Hadoop cluster configurations.

3.1 Cluster A
The first cluster, Cluster A, has following configuration:

- 7 data nodes, 1 name node: 2 chips/6 cores per chip, AMD Opteron[TM][1]2435 @2.6GHz
- 16GB DDR2 800 RAM per node
- 6 x 1TB Samsung SpinpointF3 7200 rpm disks
- Ubuntu 11.04 Server x64, Oracle JDK6 update 25 x64
- TeraSort dataset size – 64 GB

3.2 Cluster B
The second cluster, Cluster B, has following configuration:

- 5 data nodes: 2 chips/4 cores per chip, AMD Opteron[TM] 2356 @2.3GHz
- 1 name node: 4 chips/4 cores per chip: AMD Opteron[TM] 8356 @2.6GHz
- 64GB DDR2 667 and DDR2 800 RAM
- 6 x 1TB Samsung SpinpointF3 7200 rpm disks
- Ubuntu 11.04 Server x64, Oracle JDK6 update 25 x64
- TeraSort dataset size – 1 TB

While presenting empirical data we highlight performance improvements on the cluster that demonstrated bigger gains amongst the two clusters.

4. PERFORMANCE TUNING
4.1 Hadoop Configuration Tuning
This section contains guidelines on Hadoop configuration parameters tuning procedure.

Using maximum possible map and reduce slots, identify the optimal number of disks that maximizes I/O bandwidth. On Cluster A, we noticed more than 50% performance improvement while using 5 hard disks as compared to using only 1 hard disk. Experiment with different HDFS block sizes. You may have to re-evaluate optimal block size after other tunings mentioned in subsequent sections. Identify Java heap usage and garbage collections characteristics (GC) of Hadoop framework processes and tune their JVM settings accordingly. On the Hadoop configuration parameter tuning side, start with biggest payoff properties such map output compression and JVM reuse policy. In our experience, enabling map output compression using LZO codec has shown better performance. On Cluster B, we saw close to 30% performance improvement by enabling LZO based map compression as compared to no compression. If you have short running map tasks, enable JVM reuse policy. If memory is not a bottleneck, try to eliminate map-side spills by tuning io.sort.mb Hadoop property. At the least, try to reduce the number of spills. In case there are no spills, tune io.sort.spill.percent Hadoop property. On Cluster B, we noticed close to 20% improvement in performance by avoiding map-side spills and tuning io.sort.factor property. Try to avoid or eliminate intermediate disk I/O operations on reduce side by tuning Java heap sizes. If the reduce functionality is not heap-heavy, try to tune reduce buffer size. Tuning reduce-side configuration properties offered 6% improvement in performance on Cluster B. Tune framework-related resources such as task tracker threads, data node, and name node handler count.

4.2 JVM Configuration Tuning

In this section we discuss different JVM command-line switches and their potential impact on performance of Hadoop workloads.

On 64-bit Oracle JDK6 update 25 JVM, compressed pointers are enabled by default. If you are using an older version of JDK and compressed pointers are disabled, experiment with enabling them. Compressed pointers reduce memory footprint. We saw more than 3% improvement in performance by enabling compressed pointers on Cluster A. Biased-locking feature in Oracle HotSpot JDK improves performance in situations with un-contended locks. Given the architecture of Hadoop framework, biased locking should generally improve performance. On Cluster A, we noticed more than 5% improvement by enabling biased locking. Oracle JVM optimizations enabled by command-line flags such as AggressiveOpts, UseCompressedStrings, and UseStringCache can have an impact on Hadoop performance. Try experimenting with these flags. We, however, noticed 2% degradation in performance by enabling AggressiveOpts flag on Cluster A. Verify whether the JVM is running out-of-code cache. Increase code cache size if necessary. Experiment with UseNUMA and UseLargePages JVM flags. Perform detailed GC log analysis and tuning of the map and reduce JVM processes. We noticed a 3% improvement in performance by tuning GC flags on Cluster A.

4.3 OS Configuration Tuning

This section presents information about impact of tuning Linux OS properties on Hadoop performance.

Certain Linux distributions support EXT4 as the default file-system type. If you are using another type of file system, experiment with EXT4 file system. We noticed 9% performance improvements by using EXT4 file-system over EXT3 on Cluster

A. By default, every file read operation triggers a disk write operation for maintaining last access time of the file. Disable this logging using noatime, nodirtaime FS attributes. Experiment with other FS tuning attributes such as extent, flex_bg, barrier etc. On Cluster B, we noticed 15% improvement in performance by using noatime FS attribute. Linux kernels support 4 different types of I/O schedulers – CFQ, deadline, no-op, and anticipatory. Experiment with different choices of I/O scheduler, especially CFQ and deadline. On Cluster B, CFQ scheduler performed 15% better than deadline scheduler. Linux OS limits such as max open file descriptors and epoll limits can have an effect on performance, experiment with these limits. We, however, saw regression of 1% by increasing open fd limit to 16K from its default value of 1K on Cluster A.

4.4 BIOS Configuration Tuning

In this section we discuss some of the BIOS parameters that could potentially impact Hadoop performance.

Native command queuing (NCQ) feature of modern hard drives helps improve I/O performance by optimizing drive head movement. Experiment with AHCI option in BIOS, which can be used to enable NCQ mode. When all the CPU cores on the hardware are not fully utilized, the processor could be downgrading CPU frequency and other resources such as HyperTransport^{TM} links. Experiment with ACPI and other power-related BIOS options. We noticed 1% performance improvement by disabling power saving mode in the BIOS. This observation was made on Cluster A. On some AMD processor-based systems, NorthBridge frequency and width are dynamically tuned to reduce power consumption. If memory bandwidth is a bottleneck, experiment with options that can be used to modify NorthBridge frequency and width settings. On Cluster A, we noticed 2% improvement in performance by tuning NorthBridge settings. Modern AMD processors support a feature called HT assists (a.k.a. probe filters). This feature reduces traffic on memory interconnects at the expense of some portion of L3 cache. Experiment with HT assists settings; disable it if your job is sensitive to L3 cache size.

5. CONCLUSIONS AND FUTURE WORK

This demo paper discussed some of the best practices in tuning different components of the software and the hardware stack running Apache Hadoop framework. We were able to achieve speed-up factor of 4.2x on Cluster A and 2.1x on Cluster B running TeraSort workload. Configuration tuning of all the components of Hadoop stack is an important exercise and can offer a huge performance payoff. Different Hadoop workloads will have different characteristics, so it is important to experiment with different tuning options. We want to perform a similar study in multi-tenant environments and in the cloud environment. We want to explore JVM and JDK optimizations targeting peculiar characteristics of Hadoop framework and the jobs running on top of it.

6. REFERENCES

[1] Apache Hadoop. http://hadoop.apache.org/

Find Your Best Match:
Predicting Performance of Consolidated Workloads

Danilo Ansaloni
University of Lugano
Lugano, Switzerland
danilo.ansaloni@usi.ch

Lydia Y. Chen
IBM Research Zürich
Laboratory
Rüschlikon, Switzerland
yic@zurich.ibm.com

Evgenia Smirni
College of William and Mary
Virginia, USA
esmirni@cs.wm.edu

Akira Yokokawa
University of Lugano
Lugano, Switzerland
akira.yokokawa@usi.ch

Walter Binder
University of Lugano
Lugano, Switzerland
walter.binder@usi.ch

ABSTRACT

Modern multicore platforms allow system administrators to reduce the costs of the IT infrastructure by consolidating heterogeneous workloads on the same physical machine. To this end, it is important to develop efficient profiling techniques and accurate performance predictions to avoid violating service-level objectives. In this work we present Tresa, a novel tool to automatically characterize workloads and accurately estimate the execution time of different consolidations. These results can be used to optimize consolidations depending on service-level objectives.

Categories and Subject Descriptors

D.4.8 [**Operating Systems**]: Performance—*Modeling and Prediction*

General Terms

Management, Measurement, Performance

Keywords

Workload consolidation, performance modeling

1. INTRODUCTION

Administrators of large data centers and cloud computing platforms often struggle to consolidate sets of heterogeneous workloads on the same physical machine in order to maximize resource utilization without violating service-level objectives, such as maximum execution time. This problem is often challenging because performance interference between consolidated workloads may significantly affect their execution time [1].

In this work we present Tresa, a tool that helps system administrators choosing how to consolidate workloads by providing precise predictions of their execution time. The novel scientific contributions are:

1. a workload characterization technique based on standard, low-overhead tools (i.e., `iostat`, `mpstat`, `sar`, and `vmstat`) available on prevailing UNIX-like systems;

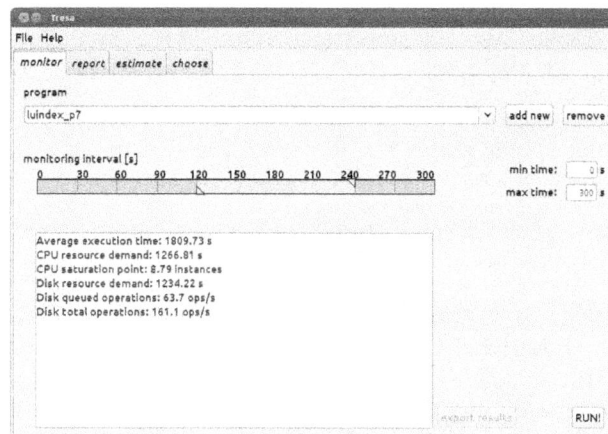

Figure 1: Screenshot of Tresa: interface of the black-box profiler.

2. a mathematical model based on queueing theory, solved using mean-value analysis;

3. a tool to automate workload characterization and to predict the average execution time of different consolidations.

2. TRESA

The graphical interface of Tresa presents 4 tabs (i.e., `monitor`, `report`, `estimate`, and `choose`) that allow users to characterize workloads and to choose consolidations that optimize throughput without exceeding a given maximum execution time.

Figure 1 shows the `monitor` tab, which provides an interface to our black-box profiler. Users have to specify how to start the workload and choose the duration of the warm-up phase and of the observation interval. Tresa profiles the execution of a single instance of the specified program and stores all relevant runtime metrics.

In the `report` tab, users can visualize all collected values and derived metrics. This data is internally used by Tresa to compute the *resource demands* of a single program, which are the inputs to our queueing network model. Tresa uses

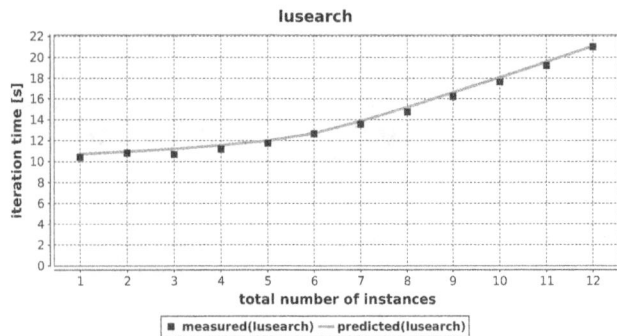

(a) Homogeneous consolidations of multiple instances of `lusearch`

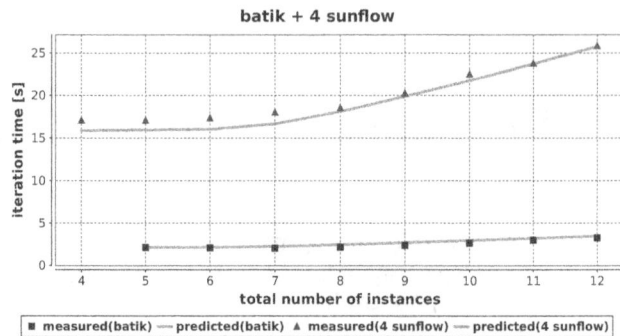

(b) Heterogeneous consolidations of 4 instances of `sunflow` with multiple instances of `batik`

Figure 2: Measured and predicted iteration time of consolidations of DaCapo benchmarks.

mean-value analysis to precisely predict the execution time of consolidations of various workloads.

The `estimate` tab generates detailed charts (used in Section 3) of the predicted execution time for homogeneous and heterogeneous consolidations, that is, consolidations involving a single class, respectively multiple classes, of workloads.

Finally, the `choose` tab provides a high-level view of all predictions, organized in a table format. By selecting a maximum execution time, it is possible to highlight the consolidations that lead to the highest throughput without violating the constraint on execution time.

3. EVALUATION

We evaluate our predictions on an IBM Power 750 Express server, with a single processor board hosting 8 cores running at 3.00GHz and 64GB of RAM. The system runs AIX 6.1 (64 bit) and IBM J9 JVM SR8-FP1 (64 bit). The observed applications are benchmarks from the DaCapo 9.12[1] suite, executed in a loop within the same JVM process and with external concurrency set to 1. The warm-up phase has a duration of 2 minutes and the profiling interval is 3 minutes.

Figure 2(a) reports the average iteration time of homogeneous consolidations of an increasing number of instances of `lusearch`. As predicted by our tool, consolidations of up to 5 instances of `lusearch` do not noticeably affect the iteration time. After 5 instances, the iteration time starts increasing because all cores are used most of the time (i.e., the CPU utilization is close to 100%).

Figure 2(b) illustrates the average iteration time of heterogeneous consolidations of 4 instances of `sunflow` with an increasing number of instances of `batik`. In this case, up to 3 instances of `batik` can be consolidated with 4 instances of `sunflow` without significantly affecting the iteration time. For both benchmarks, our predictions closely match the measured iteration time, with a maximum error of 8.1%.

To evaluate the overall quality of our predictions, we conducted an exhaustive set of experiments of homogeneous and heterogeneous consolidations. Across 160 considered homogeneous consolidations, the average prediction error is only 6.0%, while it is 8.4% across 400 considered heterogeneous consolidations.

4. RELATED WORK

Wood et al. developed Sandpiper [5], which implements two profiling approaches, (1) a black-box approach (i.e., fully OS- and application-agnostic), and (2) a gray-box approach exploiting OS- and application-level statistics. Moreover, in [4] the authors use a regression-based model to profile and predict application resource requirements in a virtualized environment. Lu et al. [2] developed a profiling methodology that viewed the problem of physical resource utilization as the source of a separation problem in digital signal processing, and designed a directed factor graph (DFG) to successfully model the dependence relationships among different resources (CPU, memory, disk, network) across virtual and physical layers.

In general, little is known about prediction of execution time for consolidations of multiple classes of workloads. To the best of our knowledge, the only theoretical methodology that focuses on this problem is the one presented in [3]. We depart from prior work by applying the theoretical methodology in [3] to solve the difficult problem of predicting performance in a multicore system where multiple programs are consolidated.

5. REFERENCES

[1] Y. Koh, R. C. Knauerhase, P. Brett, M. Bowman, Z. Wen, and C. Pu. An Analysis of Performance Interference Effects in Virtual Environments. In *Proceedings of the 2007 IEEE International Symposium on Performance Analysis of Systems & Software*, ISPASS 2007, pages 200–209, 2007.

[2] L. Lu, H. Zhang, G. Jiang, H. Chen, K. Yoshihira, and E. Smirni. Untangling Mixed Information to Calibrate Resource Utilization in Virtual Machines. In *Proceedings of the 8th ACM International Conference on Autonomic Computing*, ICAC 2011, pages 151–160, 2011.

[3] E. Rosti, F. Schiavoni, and G. Serazzi. Queueing Network Models with Two Classes of Customers. In *Proceedings of the Fifth International Symposium on Modeling, Analysis, and Simulation of Computer and Telecommunication Systems*, MASCOTS 1997, pages 229–234, 1997.

[4] T. Wood, L. Cherkasova, K. Ozonat, and P. Shenoy. Profiling and Modeling Resource Usage of Virtualized Applications. In *Proceedings of the 9th ACM/IFIP/USENIX International Conference on Middleware*, Middleware 2008, pages 366–387, 2008.

[5] T. Wood, P. Shenoy, A. Venkataramani, and M. Yousif. *Black-box and Gray-box Strategies for Virtual Machine Migration*. In *Proceedings of the 4th USENIX Symposium on Networked Systems Design & Implementation*, NSDI 2007, pages 229–242, 2007.

---

[1]Website: `http://dacapobench.org/`

Importing PMIF Models into PIPE2 using M2M Transformation

Pere Bonet
Computing and Maths Department
Universitat de les Illes Balears
07071 Palma de Mallorca, Spain

p.bonet@uib.cat

Catalina M. Lladó
Computing and Maths Department
Universitat de les Illes Balears
07071 Palma de Mallorca, Spain

cllado@uib.cat

ABSTRACT

Model-to-model (M2M) transformation is a key aspect of model-driven development (MDD), where importing and exporting models fits very well. A queueing network based metamodel (PMIF) and a Petri net metamodel are specified using the Eclipse Modelling Framework. The transformation from PMIF models to Petri net models is then build using ATL. This paper presents such a transformation and its integration into PIPE2, a Petri net modelling tool. It also illustrates the transformation by a simple example.

Categories and Subject Descriptors

B.8.2 [**Performance and Reliability**]: Performance Analysis and Design Aids

Keywords

M2M (model-to-model transformation), Performance models, Petri Nets, PMIF, Queueing networks

1. INTRODUCTION

Interchange formats have been defined for the interchange of queueing network models, Petri nets models, and others. However, there is still scope to extend their application to multiple formalisms, in particular interchanging models that can be a Petri net or a queueing network. This way a tool that analyses Petri nets can import, for example, a queueing network model and vice-versa.

Model-to-model (M2M) transformation can be done in many different ways. The advantages of using a transformation language instead of java-based transformations are discussed in [4]. Yet still, it has not been much used in performance engineering.

We present a Queueing Network (QN) based metamodel (PMIF, Performance Model Interchange Format) and a Petri net (PN) metamodel that are specified using Eclipse's EMF (Eclipse Modeling Framework) and its M2M transformation using ATL, which is part of EMF and provides a completely automated process for model to model transformations. This process needs the source model (which in our case the PMIF metamodel), the target model (in our case the PN one), and a transformation code expressed in ATL language (described by rules).

A different approach to multiformalism is offered by Mobius, OsMoSys and SIMTHESys [3]. All of them aim to provide a methodology and tool support for multi-formalism models' design and evaluation, and consider model composition and multiple solution methods.

2. M2M TRANSFORMATION

Our transformation's input is a PMIF [5] model, a common representation for system performance model that follows the QN paradigm. The PMIF metamodel espeficied in Eclipse is shown in Fig 1. On the other hand the output transformation is a PN model that follows the EMF metamodel shown in Fig 2.

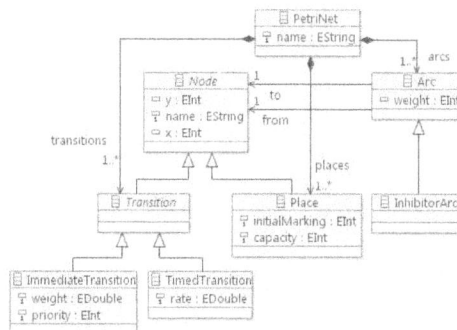

Figure 2: Petri net metamodel

The ATL transformation specifies how a PMIF model is transformed into a PN model. Each element in the QN has its correspondent element(s) in the PN. The most important elements and their counterparts are described next: (1) PMIF Servers and WorkUnitServers are nodes that provide some processing service for one or more Workloads. Its PN counterpart is a structure composed by a place, which represents the server queue, a timed transition whose firing rate is the inverse of the service time of the node, a place which represents the job exiting the node after having received its service and the necessary arcs to keep places and transitions connected. If there is more than one workload in the system (see below), this needs to be replicated as many times as workloads are served by one Server or WorkUnitServer since tokens are not distinguishable in a PN. This information is found in the ServiceRequest elements. (2) A PMIF OpenWorkload represents a workload with a potentially infinite population where transactions or jobs arrive from the

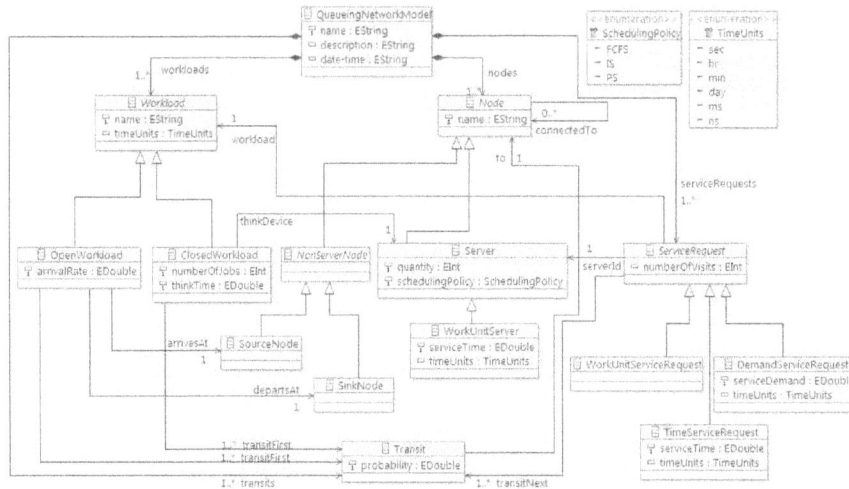

Figure 1: PMIF metamodel

outside world, receive service, and exit. The PN representation of this element consists of a timed transition whose firing rate is equal to the open workload arrival rate, a place that represents the arrival of the jobs and an arc connecting the transition and the place. (3) A PMIF ClosedWorkload represents a workload with a fixed population that circulates among the Servers, so it is represented in the PN has a place with the population as its initial marking. A closed workload has a ThinkDevice or independent delay node (for example, to model finite collections of users) characterized by its ThinkTime (average interval of time that elapses between the completion of a transaction or job and the submission of the next transaction or job). The ThinkDevice counterpart is as the server nodes.

Once the ATL transformation is done and we have a PN model, an XSLT transformation is applied, so the model is specified with PIPE2's [1] format, which is a pseudo PNML [2]. The original intention was to use a model to text transformation. However, all the ones we could find would possibly work in the Eclipse environment but could not be exported to be build as part as an existing application as PIPE2. This way, using PIPE2 we can open a PMIF model, as shown in Fig. 3. Clearly PIPE2 has been updated so it allows for the importing option and the transformation process.

3. CASE STUDY AND CONCLUSIONS

As a case study we use the Oracle example described in [6], with 3 servers (CPU, UserThink and Delay). Its PMIF model is imported into PIPE2 and the PN seen for this example in as shown in Fig. 3, only with some transitions and places moved a little bit so the drawing is clearer (the transformation output leaves some arcs crossed). In fact, improving the automatic drawing of the nets is part of our future work as well as the import of more complex QN models, for example, allowing for different scheduling policies. Performance indexes obtained for this example are exactly as shown in [6], so it demostrates the correct transformation of our tool.

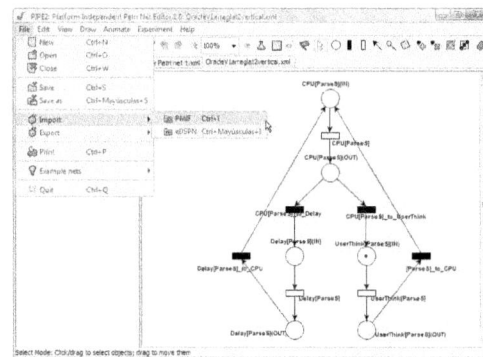

Figure 3: Oracle case study

Acknowledgments

This work is partially funded by the TIN2010-16345 EIGER project of the *Ministerio de Educacion y Ciencia*, Spain.

4. REFERENCES

[1] Platform Independent Petri net Editor 2. http://pipe2.sourceforge.net/.

[2] PNML, Petri Net Markup Language. www.pnml.org.

[3] E. Barbierato, M. Gribaudo, and M. Iacono. Exploiting multiformalism models for testing and performance evaluation in simthesys. In *Valuetools*, 2011.

[4] V. Cortellessa, S. Di Gregorio, and A. Di Marco. Using atl for transformations in software performance engineering: a step ahead of java-based transformations? In *Proc. of the 7th Int. Workshop on Software and Performance*, pages 127–132. ACM, 2008.

[5] C. U. Smith, C. M. Lladó, and R. Puigjaner. Performance Model Interchange Format (PMIF 2): A Comprehensive Approach to Queueing Network Model Interoperability. *Performance Evaluation*, 67(7):548 – 568, 2010.

[6] C.U. Smith and C. Milsap. Software performance engineering for Oracle applications: Measurements and models. In *Proc. Computer Measurement Group*, Las Vegas, NV, USA, 7-12 December 2008.

Kieker: A Framework for Application Performance Monitoring and Dynamic Software Analysis
— Invited Demo Paper —

André van Hoorn, Jan Waller, and Wilhelm Hasselbring

Software Engineering Group, Christian-Albrechts-University Kiel, 24098 Kiel, Germany

{avh,jwa,wha}@informatik.uni-kiel.de

ABSTRACT

Kieker is an extensible framework for monitoring and analyzing the runtime behavior of concurrent or distributed software systems. It provides measurement probes for application performance monitoring and control-flow tracing. Analysis plugins extract and visualize architectural models, augmented by quantitative observations. Configurable readers and writers allow Kieker to be used for online and offline analysis. This paper reviews the Kieker framework focusing on its features, its provided extension points for custom components, as well the imposed monitoring overhead.

Categories and Subject Descriptors

D.2.5 [**Software Engineering**]: Testing and Debugging—*Monitors, Tracing*; D.2.8 [**Software Engineering**]: Metrics—*Performance measures*

1. INTRODUCTION

Application-level monitoring and dynamic analysis of software systems are a basis for various quality-of-service evaluation and reverse-engineering tasks. Example use cases include the diagnosis of SLO violations, online capacity management, as well as performance model extraction and calibration. The Kieker framework provides monitoring, analysis, and visualization support for these purposes.

Kieker development started in 2006 as a small tool for monitoring response times of Java software operations. Since then, Kieker has evolved into a powerful and extensible dynamic analysis framework for Java-based systems, including, e.g., model extraction and visualization support for dependency graphs, sequence diagrams etc. [1]. Kieker has been been used for dynamic analysis of production systems in industry [1, 2]. Recently, monitoring adapters for additional platforms, such as .NET and COM, have been added. In 2011, Kieker was reviewed, accepted, and published as a recommended tool by the SPEC Research Group. Since then, the tool is also distributed as part of SPEC RG's tool repository at http://research.spec.org/projects/tools.html.

2. FRAMEWORK AND CORE FEATURES

The Kieker framework is structured into a monitoring and an analysis part [1]. On the monitoring side, *monitoring probes* collect measurements represented as *monitoring records*, which a *monitoring writer* passes to a configured *monitoring log or stream*. On the analysis side, *monitoring readers* import monitoring records of interest from the monitoring log/stream and pass them to a configurable pipe-and-filter architecture of *analysis plugins*. For the mentioned components, Kieker already includes a number of implementations, summarized below. Given the framework's extensibility, custom components can be developed easily, if required.

Focusing on application-level monitoring, Kieker includes monitoring probes for collecting timing and trace information from distributed executions of software operations. Additionally, probes for sampling system-level measures, e.g., CPU utilization and memory usage, are included. Kieker supports monitoring logs and streams utilizing file systems, databases, as well as JMS and JMX queues. A number of plugins for reconstructing, analyzing, and visualizing software architectural models such as calling-dependency graphs, call trees, and sequence diagrams are included.

3. DYNAMIC ANALYSIS WORKFLOW

Running a dynamic analysis with Kieker requires the instrumentation of the software system, as well as the specification of the monitoring and analysis configuration. Fig. 1 illustrates a typical dynamic analysis workflow with Kieker.

Components of the software system need to be instrumented with *monitoring probes*. Usually, existing monitoring probes and record types are sufficient, but depending on the required measurement data and involved technologies, custom monitoring probes and monitoring record types may be implemented.

In most cases, it is not necessary to implement custom monitoring writers and readers. File system (with comma-separated files) or database writers enable direct access to the *monitoring log/stream* and collected *monitoring records* can be analyzed using standard spread-sheet or statistics tools. Additionally, collected or queued records can be transferred to an *analysis configuration*.

On the analysis side, a configuration of monitoring readers and analysis plugins needs to be defined, using the included pipe-and-filter framework. Once defined, these configurations can be executed with Kieker to analyze previously collected (offline) or incoming (online) monitoring records and to produce textual output or graphical visualizations.

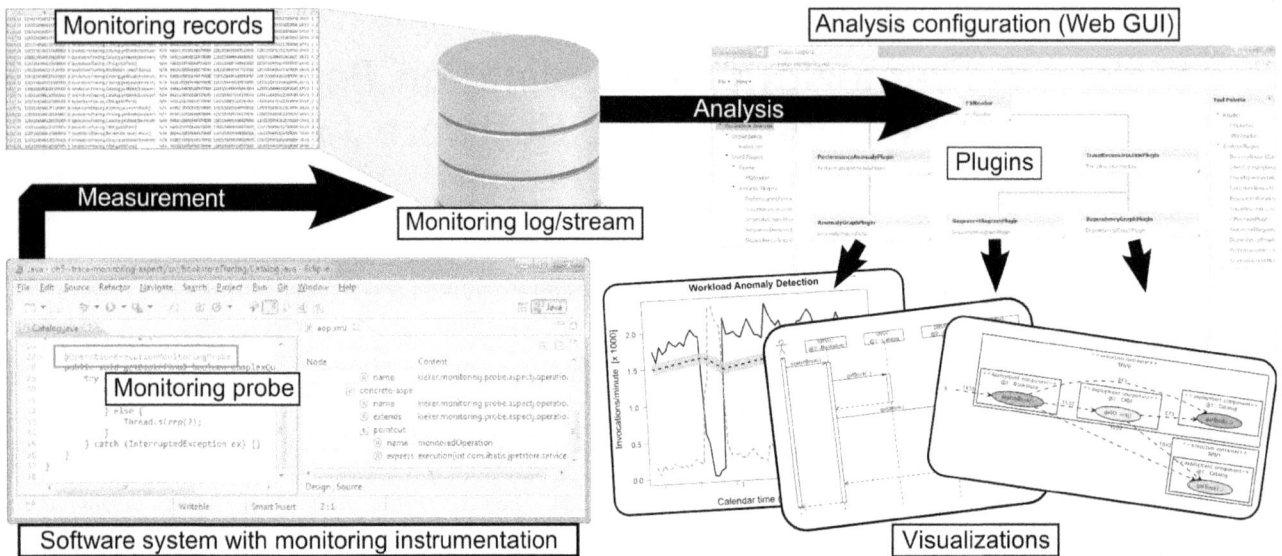

Figure 1: Illustration of a typical dynamic analysis workflow utilizing Kieker

4. MONITORING OVERHEAD

Monitoring of software systems imposes a performance overhead. We performed extensive micro- and macro-benchmarks to quantify this impact on Java applications. In Fig. 2, we present the results of such a micro-benchmark to determine the three portions of the monitoring overhead [1] and of such a macro-benchmark to quantify the overhead of monitoring a typical enterprise system, represented by the SPECjEnterprise™ 2010 industry benchmark.[1]

On a typical enterprise server machine, our micro-benchmarks for a single method call reveal a median overhead of $0.1\,\mu s$ for instrumentation, $1.0\,\mu s$ to collect performance data, and $2.7\,\mu s$ to write the collected data to a file system (Fig. 2 (a)). These results scale linearly with additional monitored method calls. The macro-benchmark simulates a typical Java EE application with 40 instrumented classes and 138 instrumented methods, accessed by approximately 260 concurrent threads. A comparison of the average response times without and with active Kieker monitoring reveals the average overhead at below 10% (Fig. 2 (b)).

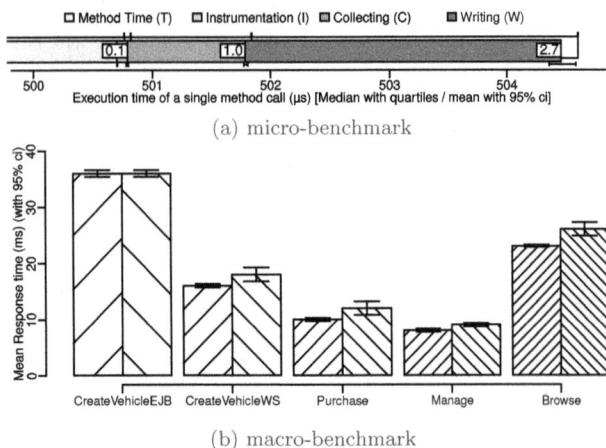

(a) micro-benchmark

(b) macro-benchmark

Figure 2: Summary of monitoring overhead results

5. CONCLUSION & FUTURE WORK

Kieker is developed and employed for various purposes in research, teaching, and practice. Application areas include: performance evaluation, self-adaptation control (e.g., online capacity management), problem localization, simulation (replaying workload traces for driving simulations; measurement and logging of simulation data; analysis of simulation results), and software reverse engineering (e.g., extraction of architectural and usage models). In these contexts, our future work includes the development of additional analysis plugins, e.g., improved support for analyzing concurrent behavior. In addition to Java, .NET, and COM, we are working on monitoring support for other platforms, such as COBOL. Currently, we are developing a Web-based user interface for configuring and running dynamic analyses with Kieker. A road map is provided on the Kieker home page [3]: http://www.kieker-monitoring.net

References

[1] A. van Hoorn, M. Rohr, W. Hasselbring, J. Waller, J. Ehlers, S. Frey, and D. Kieselhorst. Continuous monitoring of software services: Design and application of the Kieker framework. TR-0921, Dept. of Computer Science, Univ. of Kiel, Germany, 2009.

[2] M. Rohr, A. van Hoorn, W. Hasselbring, M. Lübcke, and S. Alekseev. Workload-intensity-sensitive timing behavior analysis for distributed multi-user software systems. In *Proc. Joint WOSP/SIPEW Int. Conf. on Perf. Eng. (WOSP/SIPEW '10)*, pages 87–92. ACM, 2010.

[3] Kieker home page. http://www.kieker-monitoring.net.

This work is partly funded by the German Federal Ministry of Education and Research (BMBF) under grant number 01IS10051.

[1] SPECjEnterprise is a trademark of the Standard Performance Evaluation Corp. (SPEC). The SPECjEnterprise2010 results or findings in this publication have not been reviewed or accepted by SPEC, therefore no comparison nor performance inference can be made against any published SPEC result. The official web site for SPECjEnterprise2010 is located at http://www.spec.org/jEnterprise2010/.

SPEC - Driving Better Benchmarks

Walter Bays
Oracle Corporation
walter.bays@oracle.com

Klaus-Dieter Lange
Hewlett-Packard Company
klaus.lange@hp.com

ABSTRACT
The driving philosophy for the Standard Performance Evaluation Corporation (SPEC) is to ensure that the marketplace has a fair and useful set of metrics to differentiate systems is by providing standardized benchmark suites. This paper gives an overview of SPEC and its continuous drive for better benchmarks.

Categories and Subject Descriptors
H.3.4 [**Systems and Software**]: Performance evaluation (efficiency and effectiveness)

General Terms
Design, Experimentation, Measurement, Performance, Reliability, Standardization

Keywords
SPEC, SERT, Rating Tool, Benchmark, Energy Efficiency, Power, Server, Storage, Datacenter, EPA

1. IN A NUTSHELL
SPEC [1] was formed from the instigation and sponsorship of Electronic Engineering Times (E.E. Times), and by the cooperative development work of Hewlett-Packard Corp., Sun Microsystems Inc., Apollo Computer Inc., and MIPS Computer Systems Inc. Their effort to develop a benchmark standardizing activity was converted into a non-profit Corporation of the state of California, on November 14, 1988. Its mission is to ensure that the marketplace has a fair and useful set of metrics to differentiate the newest generation of a range of platforms from symmetric multiprocessing (SMP) and Non-Uniform Memory Architecture (NUMA) to clustered multiprocessing server systems.

SPEC has grown to become one of the most successful performance standardization bodies. SPEC's community has developed more than 30 industry-standard benchmarks for system performance evaluation in a variety of application areas and provided thousands of benchmark licenses globally. SPEC publishes several hundred different performance results each quarter spanning a variety of system performance disciplines.

SPEC reviews all submitted results and allows publication of benchmark results only if the results are found to in compliance with run rules. Members closely monitor the public usage of SPEC results to ensure accordance with SPEC's General Availability and Fair Use rules.

The SPEC membership is open to any interested company or entity and currently includes computer hardware and software companies, educational institutions, and government agencies..

2. ORGANIZATION OVERVIEW
The Corporation is comprised of a Board of Directors (BoD), officers, president, and a staff (SPEC Headquarters) to carry out the business of SPEC. The BoD has established several SPEC Board Committees to handle specific task and supports several benchmark development groups under SPEC's umbrella. Each of the groups can support subcommittees, working groups, or project groups on their own.

SPEC has established four of those groups: the Open Systems Group (OSG) [2], the High Performance Group (HPG) [3], the Graphics and Workstation Performance Group (GPWG) [4] and most recently, the newly created Research Group (RG) [5]. These groups covering the major areas of desktop, workstation, handheld devices, and server benchmarking and performance evaluation. Individual committees are responsible for benchmarks characterizing CPU, Cloud Computing, Graphic, JAVA, File System, Session Initiation Protocol (SIP), Virtualization, and Energy Efficiency.

2.1 Open System Group
The OSG is organized into several committees and working groups focusing on the development of component-, and systems-level benchmarks for desktop, workstations, handheld devices and servers running open operating system environments (e.g.,SPEC CPU2006, SPECjEnterprise2010, SPECjbb2005, SPECjms2007, SPECjvm2008, SPECsip_Infrastructure2011, SPEC SFS2008, SPECpower_ssj2008, SPECvirt_sc2010).

2.2 High Performance Group
The HPG develops benchmarks that represent large, real applications, in scientific and technical computing supporting industry standard parallel application programming interfaces (APIs), OpenMP and MPI. HPG benchmarks are designed to run on several data sets sizes (from a few minutes to days of execution time).

2.3 Graphics and Workstation Performance Group
The GWPG entertains two Project Group for developing consistent, repeatable graphics and workstation performance benchmarks that reflect user experiences with popular applications.

2.3.1 SPECapc
The Application Performance Characterization (SPECapc) group was formed in 1997 to provide a broad-ranging set of standardized benchmarks for graphics and workstation

applications. The group's current benchmarks span popular CAD/CAM, digital content creation, and visualization applications.

2.3.1 SPECgpc

The Graphics Performance Characterization (SPECgpc) group, began in 1993, establishes performance benchmarks for graphics systems running under OpenGL and other application programming interfaces (APIs). The group's SPECviewperf benchmark is the most popular standardized software for evaluating performance based on popular graphics applications.

2.4 Research Group

The RG is the newest group established to serve as a platform for collaborative research efforts in the area of quantitative system evaluation and analysis, fostering the interaction between industry and academia in the field.

The scope of the group includes computer benchmarking, performance evaluation, and experimental system analysis considering both classical performance metrics such as response time, throughput, scalability and efficiency, as well as other non-functional system properties included under the term dependability, e.g., availability, reliability, and security.

The conducted research efforts span the design of metrics for system evaluation as well as the development of methodologies, techniques and tools for measurement, load testing, profiling, workload characterization, dependability and efficiency evaluation of computing systems.

3. BENCHMARK DEVELOPMENT

The benchmark development is driven by the interest of the members who provide engineering resources to design and implement a new benchmark or workload. In each SPEC group there are formal and informal processes by which consensus is built and tasks are distributed. In general one or more members request establishing a working group to investigate the new area of interest. This working group will create a specific proposal and after approval, a subcommittee or project group tackles implementation (design, code, docs, and rules). When the benchmark is complete it begins general membership review (GMR), the release materials are polished and members run benchmarks for the first round of submissions, which are generally concurrent with the final release. The BoD approves product pricing and any related releases. Once released, the benchmark will be maintained and enter normal submission, review, and publication cycle.

4. RESULT PUBLICATION

SPEC publishes a large set of benchmark results on its web site. Measurements are most often performed and submitted to SPEC by hardware and software vendors testing their own system, nevertheless non-vendors publish results as well. Prior to publication, the results undergo peer review. During this typically two weeks review, the full disclosure report (FDR) is examined by members of the benchmark committee including competitors of the submitting vendors. Questions regarding any aspect of run rule compliance may be raised and answered before the result is accepted for publication. Additionally, those FDRs document all the configuration details and tuning parameters required for an independent party to duplicate the result on the same system.

5. CONCLUSIONS

Two major advantages of SPEC development methods are low cost and open review. Cost is lowered by shared development, common test methodology, and applicability to a range of platforms from single processor systems to clusters. Confidence in results is increased by public availability of the benchmark code, drivers, and detailed run and reporting rules, peer review, and ability of independent third parties to reproduce test results. Further advantages are that benchmarks are retired and replaced every three to five years to keep pace with technology and new benchmarks can be created whenever there is sufficient interest (influential members can have a strong guidance on its direction and space)

6. ACKNOWLEDGMENTS

The authors want to acknowledge all the participants from member organizations and the SPEC HQ who have contributed to the overall success of SPEC.

The name SPEC together with its tool, benchmark and service names are registered trademarks of the Standard Performance Evaluation Corporation (SPEC).

7. REFERENCES

[1] Standard Performance Evaluation Corporation: http://www.spec.org

[2] SPEC OSG: http://www.spec.org/osg/

[3] SPEC HPG: http://www.spec.org/hpg/

[4] SPEC GWPG: http://www.spec.org/gwpg/

[5] SPEC Research: http://research.spec.org/

SPECvirt_sc2010 - Driving Virtualization Innovation

David L. Schmidt
Hewlett-Packard Company
d.schmidt@hp.com

Andrew Bond
Red Hat, Inc.
abond@redhat.com

Lisa Roderick
VMware, Inc.
lroderic@vmware.com

Klaus-Dieter Lange
Hewlett-Packard Company
klaus.lange@hp.com

ABSTRACT

Overview and future outlook of the #1 industry standard virtualization benchmark, SPECvirt_sc2010.

Categories and Subject Descriptors

H.3.4 [**Systems and Software**]: Performance evaluation (efficiency and effectiveness)

General Terms

Design, Experimentation, Measurement, Performance, Reliability, Standardization

Keywords

ACM 978-1-4503-1202-8/12/04.ACM 978-1-4503-1202-8/12/04.SPEC, Virtualization, Benchmark, Energy Efficiency, Server, Storage, Datacenter

1. SPECvirt_sc2010 OVERVIEW

SPECvirt_sc2010 [1] is designed to be a standard method for measuring a virtualization platform's ability to manage a server consolidation scenario in the datacenter and for comparing performance between virtualized environments. It is intended to measure the performance of the hardware, software, and application layers in a virtualized environment. This includes both hardware and virtualization software and is intended to be run by hardware vendors, virtualization software vendors, application software vendors, academic researchers, and datacenter managers. The benchmark is designed to scale across a wide range of systems and is comprised of a set of component workloads representing common application categories typical of virtualized environments.

Rather than offering a single benchmark workload that attempts to approximate the breadth of consolidated virtualized server characteristics found today, SPECvirt_sc2010 uses a three-workload benchmark design: a webserver, Java application server, and a mail server workload. The three workloads SPECvirt_sc2010 utilizes are derived from SPECweb2005, SPECjAppServer2004, and SPECmail2008.

All three workloads drive pre-defined loads against sets of virtualized servers. The SPECvirt_sc2010 harness running on the client side controls the workloads. Each workload must maintain a quality of service (QoS) criteria in order to be considered valid.

The benchmark utilizes the concept of a "tile" as a mechanism to increase the stress on the system under test (SUT). Each tile contains six virtual machines that are used to drive the three workloads of the benchmark (Figure 1). Two of the virtual machines are used for the web server workload, the web server VM and the infrastructure server VM which houses the data store for the webserver.

The application server workload utilizes a virtual machine that runs the application server software and a database VM. The mail server workload runs on a single virtual machine. One virtual machine is kept idle to represent VMs in a typical user environment which are not running at full capacity. Stress on the SUT is increased by adding more tiles.

All tiles must be identically configured and operate independently of each other – i.e. they each have their own unique workload dataset. Peak performance is the point at which the addition of another tile either fails the QoS criteria or fails to improve the overall metric.

The benchmark allows the freedom to select the virtualization implementation, the software applications that run within the VMs, and the hardware configuration as long as the benchmark's run rules are followed. SPECvirt_sc2010 also implements the SPECpower methodology [2] for power measurement.

The benchmarker has the option of running with power monitoring enabled and can submit results to any of three categories:

performance only – (SPECvirt_sc2010)

performance/power for the SUT – (SPECvirt_sc2010_PPW)

performance/power for the Server only – (SPECvirt_sc2010_ServerPPW)

As with all SPEC benchmarks, an extensive set of run rules govern SPECvirt_sc2010 disclosures to ensure fairness of results. SPECvirt_sc2010 results are not intended for use in sizing or capacity planning. The benchmark does not address multiple host performance or application virtualization.

2. Future Design Considerations

As hardware and software technologies continue to progress and marketplace virtualization trends evolve, The SPEC Virtualization committee continues to work on updates and future benchmarks

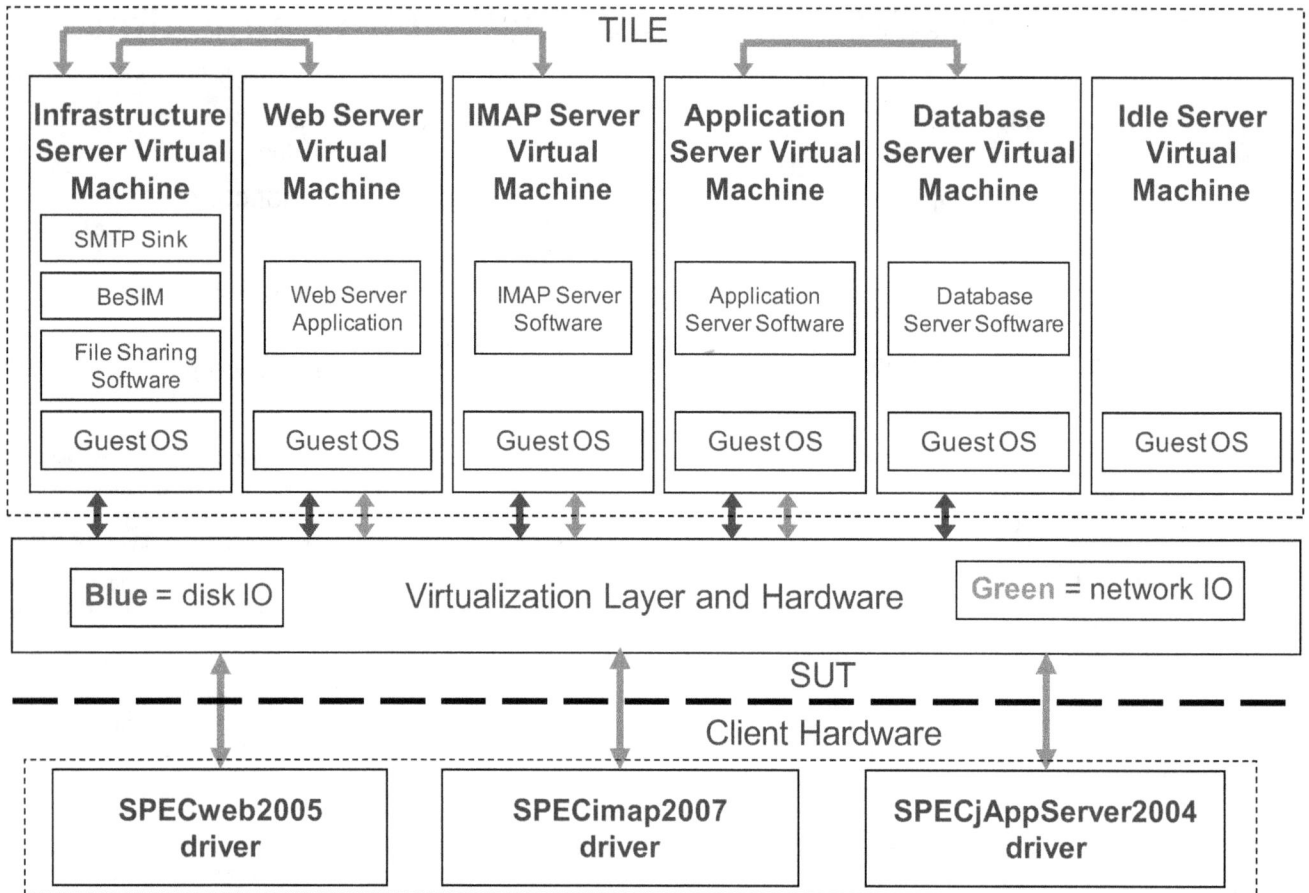

Figure 1: SPECvirt_sc2010 Benchmark Single Tile Design

to provide meaningful tools to measure these technologies. Several future design considerations for new workload models, including enterprise-class server consolidation and data center virtualization (such as VM provisioning and VM migration), are currently being discussed and developed for future benchmark releases.

3. ACKNOWLEDGMENTS

The authors want to acknowledge the additional members of the SPEC Virtualization Subcommittee who have contributed to the design, development, testing, and overall success of SPECvirt_sc2010.

The name SPEC together with its tool and benchmark names are registered trademarks of the Standard Performance Evaluation Corporation (SPEC) [3].

4. REFERENCES

[1] SPECvirt_sc2010 home page: http://www.spec.org/virt_sc2010/

[2] Standard Performance Evaluation Corporation home page: http://www.spec.org

[3] SPEC Benchmark Methodology: http://www.spec.org/power/docs/SPEC-Power_and_Performance_Methodology.pdf

SPECpower_ssj2008 - Driving Server Energy Efficiency

Mike G. Tricker
Microsoft Corporation

mike.tricker@microsoft.com

Klaus-Dieter Lange
Hewlett-Packard Company

klaus.lange@hp.com

Jeremy A. Arnold
IBM Corporation

arnoldje@us.ibm.com

Hansfried Block
Fujitsu Technology Solutions GmbH

hansfried.block@ts.fujitsu.com

Sanjay Sharma
Intel Corporation

sanjay.sharma@intel.com

ABSTRACT

SPECpower_ssj2008 [1] is the first industry-standard SPEC [2] benchmark that evaluates the power and performance characteristics of volume server-class and multi-node class computers. This poster-paper gives an overview of the benchmark that defines the server power measurement standards [8] in the same way SPEC have done for performance.

Categories and Subject Descriptors

H.3.4 [**Systems and Software**]: Performance evaluation (efficiency and effectiveness)

General Terms

Design, Experimentation, Measurement, Performance, Reliability, Standardization

Keywords

SPEC, SPECpower, Rating Tool, Benchmark, Energy Efficiency, Power, Server, Storage, Datacenter, ENERGY STAR, Environmental Protection Agency, EPA

1. SPECPOWER_SSJ2008

The general approach [3] is to compare measured performance with measured power consumption. An initial requirement was to include power measurement data of a system running at different target load levels to reflect the fact that data center server systems run at different target loads relative to maximum throughput.

2. CONFIGURATION OVERVIEW

The simplest SPECpower_ssj2008 hardware measurement configuration [7] requires four main hardware components: one **Power Analyzer**, one **Temperature sensor,** a **SUT** and the **Controller**. SPECpower_ssj2008 is composed of several elements; with the first is the test Control and Collect System (**CCS**) [4]**,** which handles the logistical side of measuring and recording the power consumption and inlet temperature of the

SUT. It also controls the software installed on both the SUT and Controller, communicating via the TCP/IP transport protocol.

CCS communicates with the **Director**, which instructs the SUT to execute the **workload** [5] while CCS collects the power and temperature data.

The temperature sensor must be placed no more than 50mm in front of (upwind of) the main airflow inlet of the SUT. SPECpower_ssj2008 will measure the inlet temperature of the SUT and marks the results "valid" only if the temperature measured is 20°C or higher, in order to discourage the "gaming" of the test environment. A stable temperature value is not required during warm-up or measurement phases.

The power analyzer must be located between the AC Line Voltage Source and the SUT. Both are connected to the Controller via their device specific interfaces, as shown in Figure 1. Each analyzer and sensor interacts with its dedicated instance of the **SPEC PTDaemon** [6]**,** which gathers their readings while the worklets are executed.

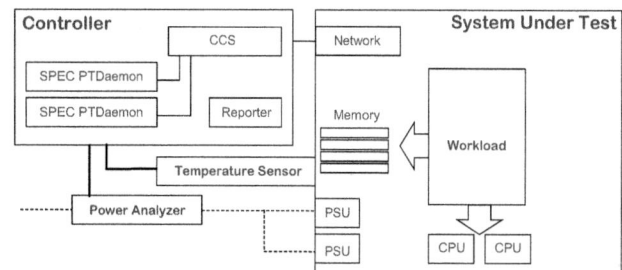

Figure 1. SPECpower_ssj2008 Overview

The **Reporter**, executed after all measurements phases are completed, compiles all of the environmental, power, and performance data for a complete test run into an easy to read report. The output format will be HTML and plain text. The HTML report includes a graphical visualization of the results.

3. WORKLOAD

SPEC recognized that many servers include technologies to reduce the power consumption when the system is running at low utilizations. Since most systems spend much of their time running at less than full capacity, SPEC developed a methodology which advocated measuring performance and power consumption at a variety of system loads.

3.1 Load Levels

An SSJ run consists of two main phases: Calibration and running at a series of Target Loads. The calibration phase is used to determine the maximum throughput that a system is capable of sustaining. Once this calibrated throughput is established, the system runs at a series of target loads. Each load runs at some percentage of the calibrated throughput. For compliant runs, the sequence of load levels decreases from 100% to 0% in increments of 10% (Figure 2). Measuring the points in decreasing order limits the change in load to 10% at each level, resulting in a more stable power measurement. Using increasing order would have resulted in a jump from 100% to 10% moving from the final calibration interval to the first target load and another jump from 100% to Active Idle at the end of the run.

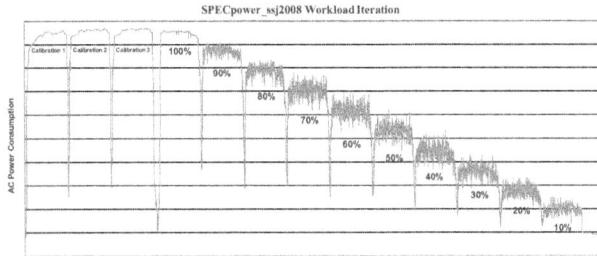

Figure 2. Load Levels

4. Driving Server Energy Efficiency

The game changing innovations, flexible design, cross-platform implementation, and automatic power measurement harness made SPECpower_ssj2008 the first industry standard benchmark to measure the power and performance characteristics of volume server-class compute-equipment.

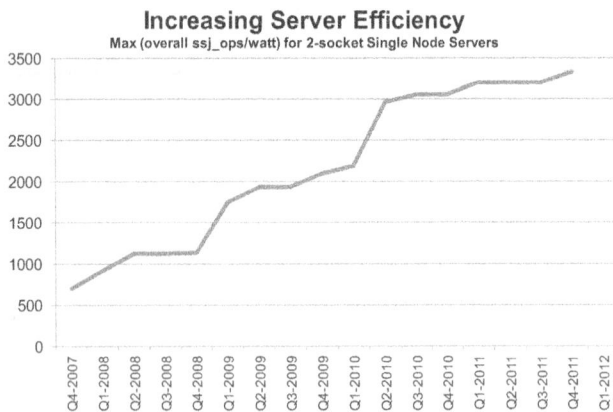

Figure 3. Dual Server Efficiency Trend

SPECpower_ssj2008 was first released in December 2007, most recently updated in 2011, and continues to drive innovations in server efficiency (Figure 3). Rather than trying to approximate all the typical workloads used across organizations SPECpower_ssj2008 is focused on transactional server-side Java workloads that simulate a warehouse-based customer ordering, supply and replenishment model. This synthetic workload exercises many aspects of commercially-available Java implementations, together with the underlying server hardware including processors (with support for multiple cores per processor), memory hierarchies (including caches) and the system Symmetric Multiprocessing (SMP) scalability.

5. ACKNOWLEDGMENTS

The authors want to acknowledge the additional members of the SPECpower Committee who have contributed to the design, development, testing, and overall success of the SPECpower_ssj2008: Paul Muehr, Van Smith, Greg Darnell, John Beckett, Karl Huppler, and David Ott.

The name SPEC together with its tool and benchmark names are registered trademarks of the Standard Performance Evaluation Corporation (SPEC).

6. REFERENCES

[1] SPECpower_ssj2008 web site:
http://www.spec.org/power_ssj2008/

[2] Standard Performance Evaluation Corporation home page:
http://www.spec.org

[3] SPECpower_ssj2008 Design Document – Overview:
http://www.spec.org/power/docs/SPECpower_ssj2008-Design_ssj.pdf

[4] SPECpower_ssj2008 Design Document – CCS:
http://www.spec.org/power/docs/SPECpower_ssj2008-Design_ccs.pdf

[5] SPECpower_ssj2008 Design Document – SSJ Workload:
http://www.spec.org/power/docs/SPECpower_ssj2008-Design_ssj.pdf

[6] SPEC PTDaemon Design Document:
http://www.spec.org/power/docs/SPEC-PTDaemon_Design.pdf

[7] Power and Temperature Measurement Setup Guide:
http://www.spec.org/power/docs/SPEC-Power_Measurement_Setup_Guide.pdf

[8] Benchmark Methodology:
http://www.spec.org/power/docs/SPEC-Power_and_Performance_Methodology.pdf

Server Efficiency Rating Tool (SERT)

Mike G. Tricker
Microsoft Corporation
mike.tricker@microsoft.com

Klaus-Dieter Lange
Hewlett-Packard Company
klaus.lange@hp.com

Jeremy A. Arnold
IBM Corporation
arnoldje@us.ibm.com

Hansfried Block
Fujitsu Technology Solutions GmbH
hansfried.block@ts.fujitsu.com

Sanjay Sharma
Intel Corporation
sanjay.sharma@intel.com

ABSTRACT

The Server Efficiency Rating Tool (SERT) [1] has been developed by Standard Performance Evaluation Corporation (SPEC) [2] at the request of the US Environmental Protection Agency (EPA) [3], prompted by concerns that US datacenters consumed almost 3% of all energy in 2010. This poster-paper gives an overview of the SERT

Categories and Subject Descriptors

H.3.4 [**Systems and Software**]: Performance evaluation (efficiency and effectiveness)

General Terms

Design, Experimentation, Measurement, Performance, Reliability, Standardization

Keywords

SPEC, SERT, Rating Tool, Benchmark, Energy Efficiency, Power, Server, Storage, Datacenter, ENERGY STAR, Environmental Protection Agency, EPA

1. AN OVERVIEW OF THE SERT

The SERT is designed to be scalable to a maximum of 64 nodes (limited to a set of homogenous servers or blade servers) and to support multiple power analyzers and temperature sensors. The simplest SERT hardware measurement configuration requires four main hardware components: one **Power Analyzer**, one **Temperature sensor,** a **SUT** and the **Controller**.

The SERT is composed of several elements, starting with the test harness, named **Chauffeur,** which handles the logistical side of measuring and recording the power consumption and inlet temperature of the SUT. It also controls the software installed on both the SUT and Controller, communicating via the TCP/IP transport protocol.

Chauffeur communicates with the **Director**, which instructs the SUT to execute the **suite**, comprising a set of workloads. The **workload** comprises a set of worklets, which exercise the SUT

while Chauffeur collects the power and temperature data. The **worklets** are the actual code designed to stress a specific system resource or resources, such as the CPU, memory or storage IO.

The temperature sensor must be placed no more than 50mm in front of (upwind of) the main airflow inlet of the SUT. The SERT will measure the inlet temperature of the SUT and marks the results "valid" only if the temperature measured is 20°C or higher, in order to discourage the "gaming" of the test environment. A stable temperature value is not required during warm-up or measurement phases.

The power analyzer must be located between the AC Line Voltage Source and the SUT. Both are connected to the Controller via their device specific interfaces, as shown in Figure 1. Each analyzer and sensor interacts with its dedicated instance of the **SPEC PTDaemon,** which gathers their readings while the worklets are executed.

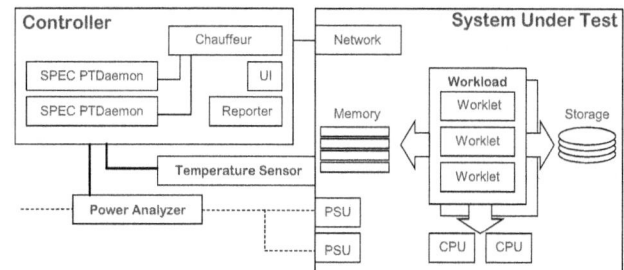

Figure 1. The SERT Overview

The **Reporter**, executed after all measurements phases are completed, compiles all of the environmental, power, and performance data for a complete test run into an easy to read report. The output format will be HTML, plain text, extensible markup language (XML), and comma-separated values (CSV); the HTML report includes a graphical visualization of the results.

2. WORKLET CANDIDATES

SERT worklets were designed under a set of public guidelines [1] to ensure consistent results across a broad spectrum of technologies. For example, each workload must automatically calibrate itself to report the maximum performance available in that specific hardware configuration, and must then be adjustable to target load levels from 100-0% of the maximum performance. Each worklet also needs to scale with the available hardware resources which the execution model deemed "important", e.g., a

CPU worklet needs to scale with the number of processors, cores, hardware threads, and the clock frequency.

The SERT Design Document [1] offers a detailed breakdown of what each worklet does and how it works. Currently a total of 16 worklets is under evaluation, which can be summarized as:

CPU: Data compression, encryption/decryption, complex number arithmetic, matrix factorization, floating point array manipulation, sorting algorithm, string manipulation, and XML document validation;

Memory: XML document manipulation and validation using pre-computed and cached data lookup, and array manipulation with read/write operations across four major classes of data transformation;

Storage IO: Four individual transaction pairs combining sequential/random read/write and a mixed transaction, which combines all four;

Combined: The concept of CSSJ is derived from ssj2008, which simulated an on-line Transaction Processing workload in which customers order and pay for goods from warehouses that handle delivery and stock replenishment;

Active Idle: A steady state in which the server is ready to execute any worklet but is not actually doing so, leading to a measure of efficiency for a fully functional but otherwise idle state.

There are no worklets related to **Network IO**, which will be handled by a "configuration modifier" that simulates the steady state efficiency of a network device. After testing a variety of network interface cards (NICs) across a range of workloads it was observed that the power consumption of the actual devices approximated very closely to a constant (including in the case of NICs that perform offloading from the host processor), with CPU and memory power consumption being the biggest factors influencing overall system efficiency. Combined with the extensive set of external hardware required to effectively test network bandwidth and performance, it was agreed with the EPA that a modifier would be applied to simulate the network IO contribution to overall server efficiency.

3. SERT UI

Users may configure the SERT by manually editing the various configuration files or utilizing the newly designed SERT User Interface (SERT UI) in order to manage the behavior of each component.

During **Host Discovery,** the detailed hardware and software configuration of the SUT are gathered automatically by a remote task that uses the industry standard Common Information Model (CIM) definitions that are widely supported across hardware and OS platforms.

The SERT UI provides a graphical interface for gathering all the SUT hardware and software configuration data, configuring and running the SERT, as well as archiving the measured results and log files. It also supports the ability to save and re-import complete configurations to simplify repeated testing.

The default mode executes the entire SERT suite (all worklets) in sequence, with each worklet in a new instance of the local Java Virtuel Machine (JVM), in order to create an EPA compliant test record. The SERT UI also offers an advanced research mode allowing the selective execution of a subset of workloads and worklets.

At the **Launch Test** (Figure 2) the progress of the entire suite can be observed, as well as the status of the currently executing worklet.

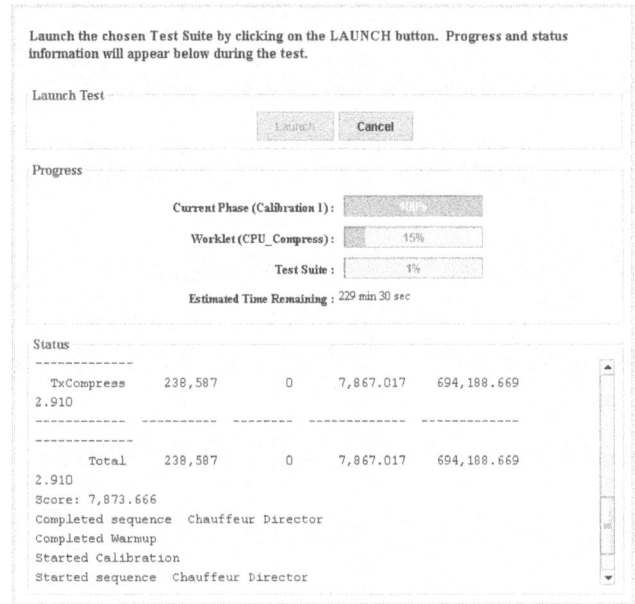

Figure 2. SERT UI: Suite Launch Menu

4. CONCLUSIONS

At the time of writing, the first Beta of the SERT has been delivered, with a second to follow soon, and a Release Candidate is targeted for the first half of 2012. The expectation is that the SERT will be released, together with Version 2 of the ENERGY STAR Computer Server program, in the first half of 2012.

5. ACKNOWLEDGMENTS

The authors want to acknowledge the additional members of the SPECpower Committee who have contributed to the design, development, testing, and overall success of the SERT: Paul Muehr, Van Smith, Greg Darnell, John Beckett, Karl Huppler, Nathan Totura and David Ott.

The name SPEC together with its tool and benchmark names are registered trademarks of the Standard Performance Evaluation Corporation (SPEC).

6. REFERENCES

[1] Server Efficiency Rating Tool public Design Document (latest version): http://www.spec.org/sert/docs/SERT-Design_Doc.pdf

[2] Standard Performance Evaluation Corporation home page: http://www.spec.org

[3] US EPA ENERGY STAR Enterprise Servers home page: http://www.energystar.gov/index.cfm?c=archives.enterprise_servers

SPEC - Enabling Efficiency Measurement

Karl Huppler
IBM Corporation

huppler@us.ibm.com

Klaus-Dieter Lange
Hewlett-Packard Company

klaus.lange@hp.com

John Beckett
Dell, Inc.

john_beckett@dell.com

ABSTRACT

An overview of the SPEC PTDaemon and SPEC's Benchmark Methodology.

Categories and Subject Descriptors

H.3.4 [**Systems and Software**]: Performance evaluation (efficiency and effectiveness)

General Terms

Design, Experimentation, Measurement, Performance, Reliability, Standardization

Keywords

SPEC, SERT, Rating Tool, Benchmark, Energy Efficiency, Power, Server, Storage, Datacenter, EPA

1. INTRODUCTION

Over the years, computing solutions have become less expensive to purchase and maintain delivering more and more computing capacity at lower and lower equipment and operational costs. At the same time, the cost of energy has continued to rise. In some areas the amount of power that is available can no longer grow with the demand. In order to create benchmarks including an efficiency aspect SPEC [1] created fundamental guidelines [3] and an interface [4] to measure the power consumption during benchmark measurements.

2. BENCHMARK METHODOLOGY

SPEC's Benchmark Methodology is intended for performance benchmark designers and implementers who want to integrate a power component into their benchmark. This document also serves as an introduction to those who need to understand the relationship between power and performance metrics in computer systems benchmarks.

The assumption is that the business model and benchmark application are already selected and may already be implemented. Guidance is provided for including power metrics in existing benchmarks, as well as altering existing benchmarks and designing new ones to provide a more complete view of energy consumption.

SPEC Benchmark Methodology covers the flowering topics:

- Defining Power components within Performance Benchmarks
- System Under Test (SUT)

- Power Measurement
- Environmental considerations
- Performance/Power metrics
- Reporting
- Automation and Validation

It also includes a comprehensive appendix about energy terminology.

3. SPEC PTDaemon

SPEC's Power/Temperature Daemon (also known as PTDaemon, PTD or ptd) is used by benchmarks to offload the work of controlling a power analyzer or temperature sensor during measurement intervals to a system other than the SUT. It hides the details of different power analyzer interface protocols and behaviors from the benchmark software, presenting a common TCP/IP-based interface that can be readily integrated into different benchmark harnesses.

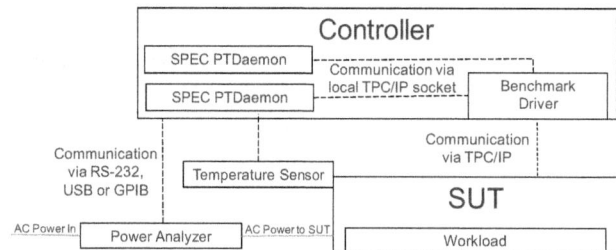

Figure 1 – SPEC PTDaemon Setup

The benchmark harness connects to PTDaemon (Figure 1) by opening a TCP port and using a proprietary protocol to control devices and retrieve measurement data. For larger configurations, multiple IP/port combinations can be used to control multiple devices.

PTDaemon can connect to multiple analyzer and sensor types via protocols and interfaces specific to each device type. The device type is specified by a parameter passed locally on the command line on initial invocation of the daemon.

The communication protocol between the SUT and PTDaemon does not change regardless of device type. This allows the benchmark to be developed independently of the measurement types to be supported.

3.1 Code Structure

PTDaemon is implemented using a main process that controls initialization and the network command interface, with a separate thread that manages the power analyzer or temperature sensor. Some analyzers that do not operate with a standard command/response structure also require an additional thread to receive asynchronous data from the device. Upon startup the main process performs the following steps:

- Parses command-line arguments and checks for validity
- Initializes the analyzer interface
- Connects to the analyzer and checks for valid responses
- Initializes the network connection and opens a socket in listen mode
- Optionally sets ampere and voltage ranges

At this point, the main process goes into a command-handling loop, where it receives commands, parses them, performs any necessary actions, and sends a response back across the network.

The device thread is started any time a measurement interval is begun. It consists of a timed loop that calls the analyzer read function, logs the values, and then sleeps any remaining time before the next scheduled sample. The device thread ends when either the benchmark harness requests an end to measurements or a network error occurred.

The device thread will not disconnect when the network connection is closed cleanly by the remote end. This allows measurements to continue without an active network connection, allowing the possibility of measuring power during arbitrary periods including reboots or low power modes without the necessity of any third-party software control.

3.2 Power Analyzer Support for PTDaemon

To support different power analyzers, each device needs its own module in PTDaemon. PTDaemon is periodically updated to support new power analyzers, temperature sensors, and additional device features. SPEC members and licensees can use the Power Analyzer Acceptance Process [5] to add software support for new devices and submit tests to SPEC for review and possible inclusion in later PTDaemon releases.

When support for a new device is requested by a SPEC licensee or device vendor, a volunteer sponsor from within SPEC will work on the software implementation. Complimentary binary licenses for PTDaemon can also be provided to third parties to assist with testing of the new device.

Once the initial software support has been added, the new analyzer is compared against a previously accepted power analyzer by running both with SPECpower_ssj2008 simultaneously while connected in series. Then, the order of the analyzers is reversed to negate any measurement differences due to voltage drops or power consumption of the analyzers themselves. The results of this test are scrutinized to determine whether the averaged power values from the two devices differ more than the sum of tolerances of each power analyzer device.

Another part of the SPEC Power Analyzer Acceptance Test uses an internal tool to generate power pulses of specific durations, which are used to examine the sampling windows of the power analyzer under test. The measured power values are compared to the corresponding to the pulse widths generated by the tool, as well as other criteria such as duplicate and missing sample limits are used to judge the new analyzer. Additionally, there are separate criteria for Multi-channel Power Analyzers that differ from Single-channel Power Analyzers.

Once the results of this testing have been submitted to SPEC, all relevant compliance requirements from the SPECpower_ssj2008 power analyzer device Run Rules are reviewed to determine if all requirements are met. If all criteria are satisfied, SPEC will accept the device for compliant benchmark testing and add support to a later release of PTDaemon.

4. CONCLUSION

The ground breaking work from the SPECpower Committee [2] created a path for easy implementation of an energy metric as utilized by TPC-Energy, the Server Efficiency Rating Tool (SERT - the upcoming EPA Energy Star for Servers v2.0 from SPEC), and many of the SPEC benchmarks such as SPECpower_ssj2008, SPECvirt_sc2010, and SPECweb2009.

In addition, SPEC is licensing PTDaemon for both non-profit and commercial entities, so the work that SPEC has done to refine power collection methodology and hide the details of different power analyzers behind the PTDaemon interface will help ease the process of other organizations to develop meaningful power efficiency workloads.

5. ACKNOWLEDGMENTS

The authors want to acknowledge the additional members of the SPECpower Committee who have contributed to the design, development, testing, and overall success of the Power Methodology and PTDaemon: Paul Muehr, Van Smith, Greg Darnell, Hansfried Block, Jeremy Arnold, Sanjay Sharma, David Ott, and Mike Tricker.

The name SPEC together with its tool, benchmark and service names are registered trademarks of the Standard Performance Evaluation Corporation (SPEC).

6. REFERENCES

[1] Standard Performance Evaluation Corporation: http://www.spec.org

[2] SPECpower: http://www.spec.org/power/

[3] SPEC Benchmark Methodology: http://www.spec.org/power/docs/SPEC-Power_and_Performance_Methodology.pdf

[4] SPEC PTDaemon: http://www.spec.org/power/docs/SPEC-PTDaemon_Design.pdf

[5] SPEC Power Analyzer Acceptance Process: http://www.spec.org/power/docs/SPEC-Power_Analyzer_Acceptance_Process.pdf

Understanding Performance Modeling for Modular Mobile-Cloud Applications

Ioana Giurgiu
Systems Group, Dept. of Computer Science, ETH Zurich
igiurgiu@inf.ethz.ch

ABSTRACT

Mobile devices are becoming the main entry points to the growing number of cloud applications and services. Unlike traditional approaches, we pursue a flexible architectural model where cloud hosted applications are distributed between mobile devices and the cloud in a bid to improve interaction performance. Given the increasing variety of mobile platforms or virtual instances, in this paper we approach the problem of estimating performance for such applications in two steps. First, we identify the factors that impact interaction response times, such as the application distribution schemes, workload sizes and intensities, or the resource variations of the mobile-cloud setup. Second, we attempt to find correlations between these factors and to understand how to build a unified and generic performance estimation model.

Categories and Subject Descriptors

C.4 [**Performance of Systems**]: Modeling Techniques

Keywords

Mobile cloud applications, performance models

1. INTRODUCTION

Mobile devices are becoming the main entry points to the growing number of cloud applications and services. The predominant architecture for offering such services to users are browser-based applications, where most, if not all, of the application software is hosted in the cloud. In such scenarios, performance depends only on the available bandwidth and connection latency between the mobile device and the cloud instance. To alleviate the network problem, we explore an alternative model for cloud applications, where the cloud instance dynamically migrates part of the application to the mobile device to improve user experience, by minimizing data transfers and overall interaction times. Our model uses *modularization* [7] to allow flexible distributed deployments of applications, from keeping only the user interface on the device to hosting the whole application locally.

Given the increasing variety of mobile platforms and cloud instances, we cannot aasume to always have access to accurate measurements in all scenarios, by running the applications a-priori. Therefore, in this paper we address the following question: *"What is the best performance of an application, when distributed between a mobile device MD and a cloud virtual instance VI, with workload Y?"*. The *mobile device* MD and *virtual instance* VI represent the setup to estimate the application's response time for, without actually running it. With the diversity of mobile devices, each with different resource capabilities, the application performance will vary accordingly. For an image processing application, one would experience higher response times on a Motorola Droid (i.e. 600MHz CPU) compared to an HTC Desire (i.e. 1GHz CPU), when using the same distribution scheme and cloud instance. Similar changes in response time are observed when different virtual instances are used.

Best performance is correlated with the application *distribution scheme* that achieves the lowest response time in the setup (MD, VI). In practice, it is hardly the case that the distribution with best response time for a specific (MD, VI) setup will be optimal for other setups, as well. For the image processing example, offloading less computational parts on the Motorola Droid results in better interaction times, because its CPU capability is lower. In addition, the type of *workload* a user inputs to such an application will impact performance dramatically. Imagine how the response time varies for a panorama application, where instead of submitting 3 images of 100kB each, a user sends 6 images of 500kB each. Both times spent in executing image processing algorithms and transferring data remotely become much higher.

To summarize, we identify relevant factors that impact the performance estimation of a modular mobile-cloud application in an (MD, VI) setup: (a) the application distribution scheme, (b) the workload size and intensity, and (c) the resource variations observed between (MD, VI) and *logged* setups for which the application was previously run. Given the variability of these factors, the problem becomes complex and requires one to understand what are the application demands for a specific resource and how they are impacted by workload types. In addition, one must find correlations between application demands and the resource variations of the (MD, VI) setup compared to logged setups, to understand which distribution scheme would indeed provide the best response time. We discuss the relevant factors and their correlations in Section 3, after introducing the current state of the art in Section 1.1 and modular mobile-cloud applications in Section 2. We conclude in Section 4.

1.1 State of the art

Performance modeling and estimation is studied especially for distributed and multi-tier applications. A preferred approach is based on queuing models of complex networked services. Stewart and Shen [9] predict throughput and mean response time based on performance profiles and M/G/1 queuing expressions. Urgaonkar et al. [10] describe a complex queuing network model for multi-tier applications. Their approach requires extensive calibration, but can be used for dynamic capacity provisioning, performance prediction, bottleneck identification and admission control. In [11], the authors look into performance modeling of virtualized resource allocation, based on probabilistic relationships between virtualized CPU allocation and application response time.

Another direction focuses on workload modeling. In Magpie [1], the authors exploit knowledge of application architecture to determine the resource demands of different transaction types. Stewart et al. [8] propose a model for performance prediction based on the nonstationarity character of transactions types, by relying solely on lightweight passive measurements. Rolia et al. [4] proposes a resource demand modeling approach, while others attempt to diagnose performance changes by comparing request flows from two executions [5], or to estimate performance for embedded systems based on discrete event simulations [3].

Some work has also been done in modeling and estimating performance in the context of mobile devices. In [6], the authors introduce a method based on linear regression and clustering to predict performance requirements of mobile devices tasks using hardware resource utilizations and input data. However, to the best of our knowledge all the existing performance models for mobile devices address only scenarios where applications are entirely run locally. Instead, we are tackling the performance estimation problem for distributed applications between mobile devices and cloud instances.

2. MOBILE-CLOUD APPLICATIONS

Mobile-cloud applications are cloud applications enabled to run on mobile platforms, by distributing their components between virtual instances and a mobile device. As with mobile applications, the user requires spontaneous and faster interactions for mobile-cloud applications, as well. Since applications are different in their resource demands, there is no unique distribution scheme that maximizes performance for all. Therefore, to add flexibility in how applications are distributed, we propose an architectural model that applies the modularity principle [7]. According to it, applications are organized as sets of processing modules that communicate with each other, each module encompassing a logical functionality or a set of highly cohesive functionalities.

Let us assume an application is composed of N modules, $\mathbb{M} = \{M_i | i = 1, 2, ..., N\}$, as in Figure 1a. M_1 represents the entry point in the application and the minimal code that needs to be installed on the mobile device that allows the user to start an interaction. Typically, M_1 implements the application user interface, while the remaining modules implement main logical functionalities. The communication between modules is modeled as a *directed acyclic graph* (DAG), where a module M_i issues requests to all the

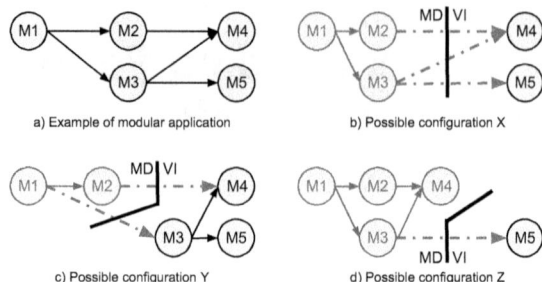

a) Example of modular application   b) Possible configuration X

c) Possible configuration Y   d) Possible configuration Z

Figure 1: Abstract example of modular application and possible distribution partitionings between MD and VI.

modules M_j it logically depends on, $i \neq j$, until it reaches the last module M_N. In the simplest case, each such request is processed exactly once and the result is sent in reverse order until it reaches M_1, which then returns it to the user. More complex processing is possible when a request can visit a module *multiple* times. As an example, consider a keyword search which triggers queries on different tables in a database. In the sequential case, each request is issued once the processing of the previous request has finished. The more complex parallel case is not currently addressed.

Given the DAG representation of a modular application, we define a partitioning between the mobile device MD and the virtual instance VI as two non-overlapping sets of modules that cover all application modules, P_{MD} and P_{VI}, respectively. Therefore, $P_{MD} \cup P_{VI} = \mathbb{M}$ and $P_{MD} \cap P_{VI} = \emptyset$. Examples of possible partitionings are shown in Figures 1b–d. In [2] we have investigated how distribution partitionings impact application performance, especially when user inputs and number of requests per module change over time. This confirms the need to understand the performance modeling problem for mobile-cloud applications.

3. HOW TO MODEL PERFORMANCE OF MOBILE-CLOUD APPLICATIONS?

In the context of modular mobile-cloud applications, we define a *distribution setup* as a (MD_x, VI_y) pair, such that $MD_x \in \mathbb{MD} = \{MD_x | x = 1, 2, ..., X\}$ and $VI_y \in \mathbb{VI} = \{VI_y | y = 1, 2, ..., Y\}$, where $\mathbb{MD}$ and $\mathbb{VI}$ represent sets of diverse mobile devices and cloud instances, respectively. Our goal is to identify and model relevant application and infrastructure parameters, in order to accurately estimate the application's response time in a specific such setup.

First, we account for logged measurements of application executions in different setups (e.g. (MD_1, VI_2) = (HTC Desire, Amazon EC2-Small)) and distributions (e.g. $M_{1,2,3}$ on the mobile device and the remaining modules remote), to identify the application demands for the underlying resources. Second, we need to characterize how the new setup (e.g. (MD_2, VI_3) = (Motorola Droid, Amazon EC2-Large)) differs from the logged setups in terms of resources. Third, it is important to characterize workload size and intensity, and to understand how these factors can be correlated in a unified model.

3.1 Identifying application demands for underlying resources

To understand how resource demanding a modular application is, we represent it as a network of M queues $Q_1, ...,$

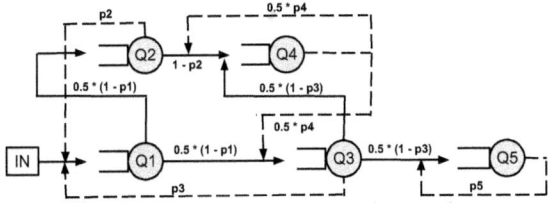

Figure 2: Modeling the example modular application using a network of queues.

Q_M. Each queue represents a specific application module and the underlying platform it runs on. When a request arrives at module M_i, it triggers one or more requests to modules M_j it depends on; recall the example of a keyword search that triggers multiple queries at different database tables. In our queueing model, we capture this by allowing a request to make multiple *visits* to a queue during its overall execution, and by introducing a transition from each queue to its predecessor. Figure 2 represents the queue model for the application in Figure 1a. After processing at queue Q_j, a request follows one of two paths based on the application communication model. Either it returns to one of the b queues from which it received the request, Q_i, with probability $\frac{p_j}{b}$, or it proceeds to one of the c queues to which it depends on, Q_k, with probability $\frac{1-p_i}{c}$. In practice, we cannot associate exact values to these probabilities, since application dataflows for different inputs or factors can be different. However, with enough collected measurements, we can compute aggregated medians of request visits per module and assign their values to the corresponding probabilities.

Let S_i denote the service time of a request at Q_i, $1 \le i \le M$, and W_i the waiting time from Q_i to one of the c queues it depends on. By using these basic queue properties and logged measurements from previous runs, we can model and identify the application demands for specific underlying resources. The service time at Q_i represents the execution time of module M_i, which is a measure of the CPU demand per module. The waiting time from Q_i is equivalent with the time required to transfer data to a subsequent queue, thus an expression of the network demand. By comparing the total service time with the total waiting time, we can understand how much of the total response time is spent performing computational tasks and transferring data, respectively.

Open problems. The queue network naturally models CPU and bandwidth resources. However, especially on mobile platforms, memory is a scarce resource that needs to be accounted for. One possible model extension is to assign to each application module a network of queues, where each queue corresponds to a specific resource. This way, by estimating the utilizations at the queues, we can understand how memory impacts application performance.

3.2 Application workload modeling

In mobile-cloud applications, the following observations about workload hold: (a) workload consists of *request-reply* interactions; (b) interactions have a limited number of *types* (e.g. browsing, online payment, printing for a ticket machine application); (c) interaction types influence resource demands; (d) interaction mix is *nonstationary*, meaning it changes over time. Nonstationary processes can be used to model workloads, but do not address the complementary problem of workload forecasting. However, as shown in [8] if

accurate forecasts are available, they can be mapped to accurate performance predictions. Therefore, we make the following assumptions prior to formulating a workload model: (a) all previous application interactions are logged, (b) the modules CPU utilization and the bandwidth utilization between them are extracted from the measured execution and data transfer times.

To capture the application behavior for a specific workload, we observe a number of sequential interactions performed by a user over windows of fixed length T. Assuming that the application can process S interaction types, we denote by S_i the number of interactions of the i-th type, where $1 \le i \le S$. U_{r,M_j} is the average utilization of resource r at module M_j during the monitoring window. This representation is natural for CPU, because its utilization corresponds to execution times measured at module level. Instead, for network resources the average utilization is a property of all the incoming communication links to module M_j. Therefore, we define D_{i,M_j} as the average service time of interactions of type i at module M_j, while for network resources, we need to replace the *service* time with the summed *waiting* time on all incoming links to M_j. Based on the utilization law, for each monitoring window and resource r we obtain:

$$\sum_i S_i D_{i,M_j} = U_{r,M_j} T \qquad (1)$$

In practice, it is infeasible to obtain accurate service or waiting times D_{i,M_j}. Thus, we consider the approximated costs of D_{i,M_j} for resource r (i.e. CPU or bandwidth) and denote it by C_{i,M_j}. An approximated utilization U'_{r,M_j} and the corresponding amount of time when resource r is used by specific application operations, can be computed as

$$U'_{r,M_j} = \frac{\sum_i S_i C_{i,M_j}}{T} \qquad T'_{r,M_j} = \sum_i S_i C_{i,M_j} \qquad (2)$$

To solve the equation for the approximated costs C_{i,M_j}, several regression methods can be used. Typically, the goal is either to minimize the absolute error between U'_{r,M_j} and U_{r,M_j}, or their squared error over each monitoring window.

Open problems. It is worth investigating which regression methods are most suitable to be used for the application types we are targeting. Furthermore, an open question is how the monitoring window size and workload intensities impact the accuracy of the regression solution.

3.3 Inter- and intra- variations for mobile devices and virtual instances

Further we quantify how different is the current setup, for which we estimate the application's response time, from logged setups, in terms of resources capacities and usages.

Let us denote the current setup $S_{current} = (MD_c, VI_c)$ and the logged setup $S_{logged} = (MD_l, VI_l)$. For simplicity reasons, at this stage we only consider a single logged setup. In comparing $S_{current}$ and S_{logged}, two types of resource variations are used between MD_c and MD_l, as well as VI_c and VI_l, respectively. We denote by *inter-type variation*, the difference between the resources capacities when comparing distinct mobile devices and EC2 instances, respectively. An example is given in Table 1, where we want to compute the resources variation of the (Motorola Droid, EC2-Large) setup relative to the logged (HTC Desire, EC2-Small) setup.

In practice, the *inter-type variation* does not accurately reflect the difference between two distinct mobile devices or

Table 1: Resource-based comparison between two setups

Resources	LOGGED		CURRENT	
	HTC	EC2-S	Motorola	EC2-L
CPU	1 GHz	1 CU	600 MHz	4 CU
3G HSDPA	7.2 Mbps	–	10.2 Mbps	–
3G HSUPA	2 Mbps	–	5.76 Mbps	–
WiFi	802.11 b/g	–	802.11 b/g	–

virtual instances. For example, a mobile device usually runs several applications simultaneously, which means it cannot allocate 100% of the CPU or network capacities for an incoming application. Therefore, we define the *intra-type* variation to account for the actual resources usages on the underlying infrastructure. It only applies to compare mobile devices, since in real scenarios a third party has no access to information about the current resources usages in the cloud.

For instance, let us consider the HTC Desire in Table 1 has 70% CPU usage, while the Motorola Droid has 20% CPU usage. For a computational intensive application, it is possible that even though HTC Desire has a larger CPU capacity, its higher usage compared to the Droid would impact the application performance, making it slower in practice. We combine the inter- and intra- type variations to quantify how much faster or slower would the current mobile device be relative to the logged device, while executing computational modules or transferring data as follows:

$$C_r = \frac{r_{AB}(MD_c) * r_{USED}(MD_c)}{r_{AB}(MD_l) * r_{USED}(MD_l)} \quad (3)$$

where r_{AB} is the absolute capacity of the resource r (i.e. CPU and WiFi / 3G) and r_{USED} represents how much of r_{AB} in percentages is already used by other applications. If $C_r < 1$, then for the application parts that demand resource r, MD_c would require a longer execution time. The opposite applies for $C_r > 1$.

Open problems. In quantifying the inter- and intra- variations, we made the simplifying assumption that there is only one logged setup to compare against. In practice, this is hardly the case and therefore it is important to identify the logged setup that is closest to the current setup in terms of its resource capacities and usages. One possible direction is to treat resources as independent variables and apply regression-based methods.

3.4 Discussion

Finally, we want to correlate and combine all three factors discussed (Sections 3.1–3.3) in a unified estimation model. The queuing model proposed to identify application demands for underlying resources and the workload model based on nonstationary interactions combine naturally. In fact, the workload representation is an extension of the queuing model. Assuming that an interaction of type j lasts for k windows, we estimate the time required to execute operations that demand a specific resource r (i.e. computational steps require CPU, data transfers require bandwidth) over all N application modules, by combining the expressions from Eq. (2)

and (3) as follows:

$$RT_r = \sum_{t=1}^{k} C_r^t \sum_{j=1}^{N} T_{r,M_j}^{'t} \quad RT = RT_{CPU} + RT_{bandwidth} \quad (4)$$

In our current model that only considers CPU and bandwidth resources, it is easy to estimate the overall response time (RT) of an interaction by summing the times required to perform computational steps at module level (RT_{CPU}) and to transfer data between modules ($RT_{bandwidth}$). However, it requires further study to understand how to encompass additional resources, such as memory.

4. CONCLUSIONS

Modular mobile-cloud applications provide an alternative architectural model to flexibly distribute applications parts between a mobile device and a virtual instance to improve interaction response times. In this paper, we address the complex problem of estimating what would be the best response times for such applications in the case of specific workloads and mobile-cloud setups, without actually running them. We discuss how to model the impact of the application distribution scheme, as well as the workload size and intensity, and how they can be correlated with the resource variations of the given setups against logged setups. Future work will focus on finalizing a unified and generic model that encompasses all the above factors and evaluating its accuracy in real scenarios.

5. REFERENCES

[1] BARHAM, P., DONNELLY, A., ISAACS, R., AND MORTIER, R. Using magpie for request extraction and workload modelling. In *Proc. of the 6th Conference on Symposium on Operating Systems Design and Implementation* (2004).

[2] GIURGIU, I., RIVA, O., JURIC, D., KRIVULEV, I., AND ALONSO, G. Calling the cloud: Enabling mobile phones as interfaces to cloud applications. In *Proc. of the 10th International Conference on Middleware* (2009).

[3] MADL, G., DUTT, M., AND ABDELWAHED, S. Performance estimation of distributed real-time embedded systems by discrete events simulations. In *Proc. of the International Conference on Embedded Software* (2007).

[4] ROLIA, J., KALBASI, A., KRISHNAMURTHY, D., AND DAWSON, S. Resource demand modeling for multi-tier services. In *Proc. of the 1st International Conference on Performance Engineering* (2010).

[5] SAMBASIVAN, R. R., ZHENG, A. X., DE ROSA, M., KREVAT, E., WHITMAN, S., STROUCKEN, M., WANG, W., XU, L., AND GANGER, G. R. Diagnosing performance changes by comparing request flows. In *Proc. of the 8th USENIX Symposium on Networked Systems Design and Implementation* (2011).

[6] SCHWARZER, S., PESCHLOW, P., PUSTINA, L., AND MARTINI, P. Automatic estimation of performance requirements for software tasks of mobile devices. In *Proc. of the 2nd International Conference on Performance Engineering* (2011).

[7] STEVENS, W., MYERS, G., AND CONSTANTINE, L. Structured design. In *IBM Systems Journal, 13(2)* (1974).

[8] STEWART, C., KELLY, T., AND ZHANG, A. Exploiting nonstationarity for performance prediction. In *Proc. of the European Conference on Computer Systems* (2007).

[9] STEWART, C., AND SHEN, K. Performance modelling and system management for multi-component online services. In *Proc. of the 2nd Conference on Networked Systems Design and Implementation* (2005).

[10] URGAONKAR, B., PACIFICI, G., SHENOY, P., SPREITZER, M., AND TANTAWI, A. An analyical model for multi-tier internet services and its applications. In *Proc. of the International Conference on Measurement and Modeling of Computer Systems* (2005).

[11] WATSON, B. J., MARWAH, M., GMACH, D., DN MARTIN ARLITT, Y. C., AND WANG, Z. Probabilistic performance modelling of virtualized resource allocation. In *Proc. of the 7th International Conference on Autonomic Computing* (2010).

Is your Cloud Elastic Enough?
Performance Modeling the Elasticity of Infrastructure as a Service (IaaS) Cloud Applications

Paul Brebner
NICTA/ANU
Canberra
Australia
Paul.Brebner@nicta.com.au

ABSTRACT

Elasticity, the ability to rapidly scale resources up and down on demand, is an essential feature of public cloud platforms. However, it is difficult to understand the elasticity requirements of a given application and workload, and if the elasticity provided by a cloud provider will meet those requirements. We introduce the elasticity mechanisms of a typical Infrastructure as a Service (IaaS) cloud platform (inspired by Amazon EC2). We have enhanced our Service Oriented Performance Modeling method and tool to model and predict the elasticity characteristics of three realistic applications and workloads on this cloud platform. We compare the pay-as-you-go instance costs and end-user response time service level agreements for different elasticity scenarios. The model is also able to predict the elasticity requirements (in terms of the maximum instance spin-up time) for the three applications. We conclude with an analysis of the results.

Categories and Subject Descriptors

C.4 [Performance of Systems]: Modeling Techniques

General Terms

Performance

Keywords

Cloud, IaaS, Elasticity

1. Cloud Elasticity

"My biggest problem is elasticity. VM spin-up time... Ten to 20 minutes is just too long to handle a spike in Yahoo's traffic when big news breaks such as the Japan tsunami or the death of Osama bin Laden or Michael Jackson." Todd Papaioannou, Vice President of Yahoo's cloud architecture, quoted in [1].

Not everyone is running an enterprise on the scale of Yahoo, but in order to take advantage of the opportunities provided by cloud computing it is vital to understand the elasticity characteristics of applications, workloads and cloud platforms. Intrinsic to the definition of cloud computing is that resources are dynamically increased and decreased on demand, and that charging is consumption based.

Permission to make digital or hard copies of all or part of this work for personal or classroom use is granted without fee provided that copies are not made or distributed for profit or commercial advantage and that copies bear this notice and the full citation on the first page. To copy otherwise, or republish, to post on servers or to redistribute to lists, requires prior specific permission and/or a fee.
ICPE'12, April 22–25, 2012, Boston, Massachusetts, USA.
Copyright 2012 ACM 978-1-4503-1202-8/12/04...$10.00.

Ideally a cloud platform is infinitely and instantaneously elastic. An application could be scaled out indefinitely with increasing load, and this could happen as fast as the load increases with no degradation of response times. Resources would be available instantly and the application would be immediately deployed and available for use. A perfectly elastic cloud platform would be ideal for hosting interactive applications with strict response time requirements, and with spiky unpredictable workloads. These are difficult to host on traditional fixed and finite infrastructures as the quantity of resources is not known in advance, and the cost of keeping the resources available for occasional extreme load events is prohibitive.

However, real clouds are not perfectly elastic. There will inevitably be a delay between when resources are requested, and when the application is running and available on it. The resource provisioning speed may depend on a number of factors including: the type of cloud platform (e.g. Infrastructure vs. Platform as a Service); the type, cost model, number, size, or speed of resources requested; the availability of spare resources in the requested region and the demand on the cloud platform from other users; the rate of increase (acceleration) of the workload; and any quotas or limits imposed by the cloud platform or the contract with them.

On a typical (e.g. Amazon EC2) IaaS (Infrastructure as a Service) cloud platform the elasticity infrastructure enables auto-scaling of instances for an application with user customised rules which periodically fire to check metric values, make decisions, and request an action in response (e.g. increasing or decreasing instances by a specified amount). There are typically a number of steps involved in auto-scaling:

- Periodically fire the rules (e.g. every 5 minutes):
  - Depending on the metric and threshold (e.g. server utilisation > 80%) and
  - The statistic and time period (e.g. average over the last 10 minutes)
  - Then execute the resource request actions (e.g. increase instances by 1).

The cloud infrastructure cannot instantly respond to this request as it has to first find and reserve an available server, create a new virtual machine instance on it, deploy the application code and other data onto the new virtual machine, start the application, and include the new instance in a load balancer so it can be accessed externally (e.g. the Amazon Elastic Load Balancer). The time taken for all these steps is often referred to as the instance "spin-up" time. It may also be possible to suspend the rules from firing for some period of time once a rule has fired to allow the requested actions to be completed, to prevent premature rule firing. For the remaining discussion we assume "on-demand" instance types, with a typical (constant) instance spin-up time of 10 minutes. In practice, spin-up time depends on the particular cloud provider and can vary considerably. Consequently, most cloud providers do not have a Service Level Agreement (SLA) for spin-up time.

1.1 Cloud Elasticity Modeling

Our research since 2007 has focused on the performance modeling of Service Oriented Architectures. We have developed a tool and method for SOA performance modeling which has been trialed and validated on a large number of government and non-government enterprise SOAs at different stages of the software development lifecycle. From these engagements we have selected three example applications and workloads that are particularly relevant for evaluating cloud elasticity.

The three example applications are: (1) BigCo, an enterprise application that has a variety of different user types (internal, external business partners, and web and mobile customers), with a workload which gradually increases and then decreases over a 24 hour period (2) Lunch&COB, a whole of government SOA application which is distributed over four zones (separate applications deployed on distinct Virtual Machines), with 2 different workloads, one longer but lower peak at lunch time and another higher but shorter peak near close of business, and (3) FlashCrowd, a web site which typically has a low background load, and then occasionally exhibits a very large spike in demand over a 1 hour period (representative of a "Flash Crowd").

We have previously modeled and validated these applications and loads for fixed resources to explore the impact of different workloads, for capacity planning, to assist with developing SLAs, and to investigate architectural alternatives and evolution [10][11][12][13][14]. From these experiments we know that these three applications are CPU rather than network or database limited. We have also modeled different resourcing models including virtualisation and cloud platforms (e.g. Amazon EC2, Google AppEngine, Microsoft Azure) to predict performance, scalability, cost, and power consumption [8][9]. Other related research has explored related cloud elasticity issues including cloud modeling prediction, and cloud elasticity architecture [2][3][4][5][6][7]. Our tool is model driven and supports a meta-model of the service oriented performance model and GUI-based editing, viewing and animation. To predict the metrics from it, a transformation is made to a run-time version of the model which is simulated dynamically using a discrete event simulator. Complex dynamic resourcing models can be built and solved at run-time with this approach, making it ideal for investigating cloud elasticity which intrinsically has time as a variable. Cost is a secondary metric which is computed from knowledge of the cloud cost model, resource usage, and instance start and stop times.

We have constructed models of these three applications on a generic elastic cloud platform (inspired by Amazon EC2), focusing solely on the CPU resource requirements, SLAs and costs. Figure 1 shows the main components of an elastic compute cloud that are included in our cloud elasticity models: incoming load, elastic load balancer, virtual machines with deployed application, and elasticity mechanisms (monitoring, rules, instance requests, instance provisioning, etc) contributing to the spin-up time.

1.2 Elasticity Scenarios

We explore the following elasticity scenarios for the examples.

Default (10 minute spin-up time). To illustrate the impact of "typical" elasticity characteristics we assume the following default settings for the cloud platform auto-scaling rules and instance spin-up behaviour: Rule check every minute, increase request threshold of 80% average server utilisation computed over 1 minute, instance decrease threshold of 30% server utilisation over 10 minutes, 1 instance increase/decrease at a time, and a rule suspension time equal to the instance spin-up time, which is set to 10 minutes by default.

Worst case elasticity has no elasticity mechanism and instead relies on fixed over-provisioning of resources for the 24 hour period. Only if the maximum load is known in advance can sufficient fixed resources can be made available in advance to prevent SLA violations. Depending on the workload, the cost is likely to be higher than using elasticity to manage resources dynamically. If the workload is higher than predicted then the fixed resources will be saturated and the SLA will be violated.

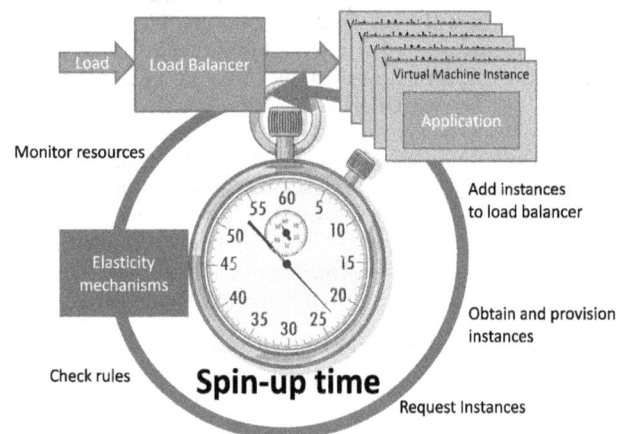

Figure 1 Cloud Elasticity Architecture

Best case elasticity attempts to predict the most elasticity that can be achieved given the constraints of a cloud platform, but assuming zero spin-up time. The minimum rule check period is 1 minute, and that the charging model is hourly. Increase threshold is increased to 95% Utilisation and decrease threshold is increased to 50% Utilisation. Higher thresholds can be used and still satisfy the SLA as less headroom is needed due to instances being available instantly.

To be **perfectly elastic** the resources exactly match the demand (no more or less), there is no time delay between detecting load changes and changing resourcing levels (resourcing is instantaneous), and you only pay for what you consume (charging is fine-grain consumption based). Even though it is unlikely that any cloud platforms are perfectly elastic, we can model it by assuming a perfectly elastic cloud platform and an extremely fine-grained cost model which only charges for resources that are actually consumed, by the CPU Millisecond, at a rate pro rata to the default cost model. Table 1 summarizes the elasticity scenarios (columns) in terms of the resources (fixed or elastic), spin-up times, and charging settings.

We also predict the **Elasticity Break point.** In order to find the breaking point (where the platform is not elastic enough) the spin-up time is increased until the SLA is violated (or decreased if 10 minutes is too long).

Table 1 Elasticity Scenarios

	Worst	10 min	Best	Perfect
Resources	Fixed	Elastic	Elastic	Elastic
Spin-up	In advance	10 min	0 min	0 min
Charging	Hourly	Hourly	Hourly	Millisecond

2. Examples Elasticity Predictions

2.1 Example 1: BigCo

The workload for the first application, BigCo, runs for 24 hours and represents an observed extreme case of a typical day (Figure 2). During the 24 period the load ranges from a low of 300TPH (Transactions Per Hour) to a high of 27,000 TPH.

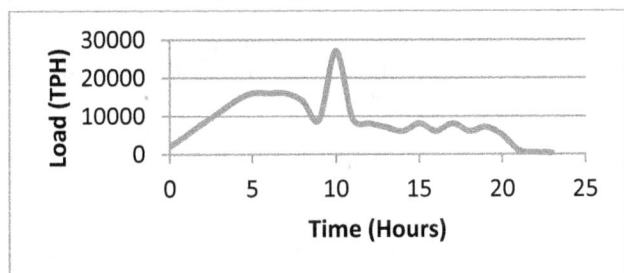

Figure 2 BigCo Workload

All three examples are user facing interactive applications with strict response time requirements of a few seconds at most. The SLA is 99% of transactions taking less than 10 seconds. IaaS cloud platforms typically offer a variety of instance sizes, from partial cores (multi-tenancy on shared servers) to multiple cores (single-tenancy on large servers). Due to the minimum application requirements for core speed and other resources (e.g. memory and network bandwidth), we selected a single-tenancy 4 core (approx 2.4GHz Intel core speed) instance type with a cost of 40 cents an hour or part thereof. We ran the model with the 24 hour workload for all the elasticity scenarios. Figure 5 shows the total running cost, and Figure 6 shows the elasticity breaking point (50 minutes). A 10 minute spin-up results in a cost saving of 32% compared with the worst case, increasing to 54% as spin-up time approaches zero, while perfect elasticity is 71% cheaper.

2.2 Example 2: Lunch&COB

Our second example is modeled on a government Service Oriented Architecture (SOA) application supporting multiple user types including government, business, and citizens. This example was originally modeled and validated on dedicated hardware, and we have since modeled it on various cloud platforms. It is a distributed application consisting of four distinct application zones which are deployed on separate virtual machines. The workloads occur during business hours (12 hours). Two peaks are expected, one around lunchtime with a peak of 10,000TPH and the highest with a peak of 20,000TPH at close of business (COB) as shown in Figure 4. The workloads impose different demands on each of the application zones, so the resources for each zone must be scaled at different rates.

The breaking point is 20 minutes when the SLA is violated (Figure 6). The Lunch&COB example is more demanding than BigCo and there is little room for an increase in the cloud platform spin-up time before the SLA is violated. Figure 5 shows

the cost for 12 hours for the scenarios. The 10 minute and best case elasticity costs are very similar and represent a cost saving compared with the worst case of up to 50%. The fact that they are very similar indicates that the elasticity is close to breaking point. However, perfect elasticity is 89% cheaper, suggesting that there is even more room for improvement in the elasticity of cloud platforms for more elastically demanding applications and workloads such as Lunch&COB.

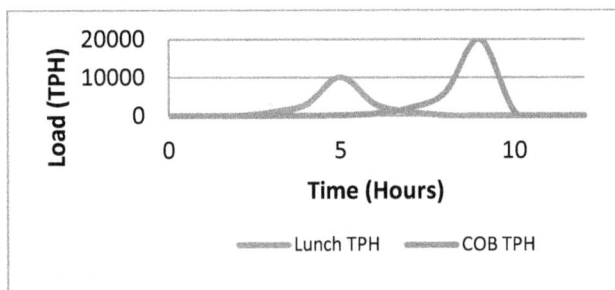

Figure 3 Lunch&COB Workloads

2.3 Example 3: FlashCrowd

The 3rd example is modeled on an emergency web service application which was designed for infrequent use when the main web site was in danger of overloading due to an exceptional load spike caused by an emergency situation. The workload is expected to increase within 30 minutes from the normal peak load of 5TPS to a maximum of 470TPS (a factor of 92), and then drop back to normal very quickly, the load spike lasting for 1 hour. The complete workload runs for 2 hours with over 1.25 million service calls in this period (Figure 4).

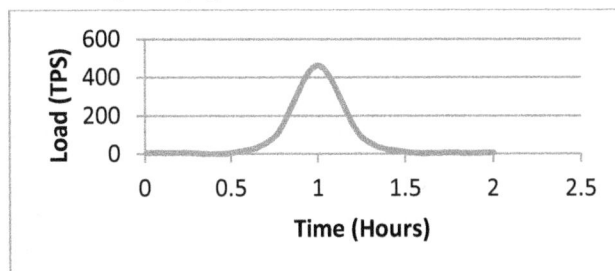

Figure 4 FlashCrowd Workload

FlashCrowd has more demanding elasticity requirements than the previous examples, as a 10-minute spin-up time cannot provision CPUs fast enough, and the system saturates and catastrophically fails the SLA. In fact, the model predicts that 5 minutes is the longest possible spin-up time. However, in order to achieve the SLA with 5 minutes spin up it is necessary to request *30 instances* at a time, rather than just 1 at a time. Unlike the 10 minute default spin-up time scenario, the worst, perfect and best case elasticity scenarios all satisfy the SLA. Figure 5 shows total costs for 2 hours for scenarios, with the default case using a 5 minute spin-up time. Figure 6 compares the elasticity breaking points for all the examples.

3. Observations

More cores are needed for the peak loads using elasticity compared with fixed resources. For example, for FlashCrowd 356 cores were needed with 5 minute spin-up compared with 272 for fixed. This is significantly higher, and will impose more demand on the shared cloud infrastructure, and potentially more cost for the user, particularly if the elasticity rules result in significantly more instances being requested than actually needed.

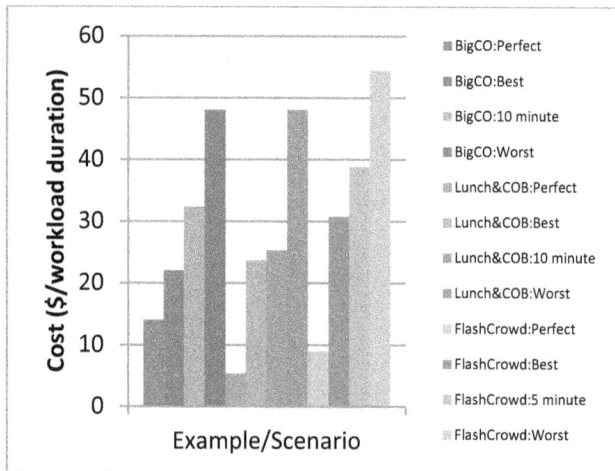

Figure 5 Example/Scenario costs ($/workload duration)

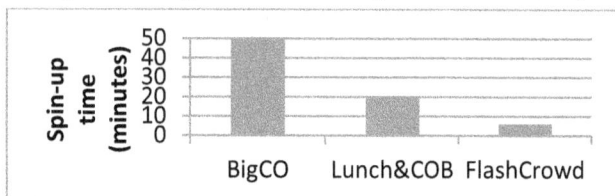

Figure 6 Elasticity Breaking points

The approach of predicting both cost and response time SLAs for applications deployed on cloud platforms allows for both comparison of different elasticity scenarios, and determining if the platform is elastic enough.

Using perfect elasticity as the base line, the best case scenarios were 1.5 to 4.5 times more expensive, the 10/5 minute spin-up scenarios were 2 to 5 times more expensive, and the worst case (fixed) scenarios were 3 to 10 times more expensive. This indicates that dynamic resourcing shows consistent cost advantages over fixed resourcing, realistic (10/5 minute) spin-up times were not significantly more than best case (zero minute), and that reducing spin-up times to zero (best case) without also reducing the granularity of the charging model (perfect case) will not significantly reduce costs. However, all the cloud elasticity options, even the fixed instance scenarios, are relatively cheap.

A 10 minute spin-up time was sufficiently elastic for 2 out of the 3 example applications, but the 3rd example required a spin-up time of 5 minutes and knowledge of the workload so that a larger number of instances could be requested. This suggests that for many applications the current elasticity (spin-up times and elasticity mechanisms) may be adequate, but for more demanding applications improvements in cloud elasticity technology are needed. Computing the SLAs for given elasticity settings enables us to determine if the SLA is satisfied, and to find the longest spin-up time that satisfies the SLA, thereby answering the question "Is a cloud platform elastic enough for a given application and workload?" Modeling elasticity prior to deployment enables cloud platforms to be evaluated before investing the effort porting the application to a selected platform, with increased confidence in cost and performance.

4. ACKNOWLEDGMENTS

NICTA is funded by the Australian Government as represented by the Department of Broadband, Communications and the Digital Economy and the Australian Research Council through the ICT Centre of Excellence program.

5. REFERENCES

[1] Julie Bort, "Yahoo builds ultimate private cloud", Network World, July 19, 2011.

[2] Amy Spellmann, Richard Gimarc, Mark Preston, "Leveraging the Cloud for Green IT: Predicting the Energy, Cost and Performance of Cloud Computing" , CMG '09 Conference

[3] Urszula Herman-Izycka, "Flash Crowd Prediction", Master's Thesis, Vrije Universiteit, Amsterdam, The Netherlands, 2006

[4] Nilabja Roy, Abhishek Dubey, Aniruddha Gokhale, "Efficient Autoscaling in the Cloud Using Predictive Models for Workload Forecasting," IEEE 4th International Conference on Cloud Computing 2011, 500-507.

[5] Clovis Chapman, Wolfgang Emmerich, Fermín Galán Márquez, Stuart Clayman, Alex Galis: "Software architecture definition for on-demand cloud provisioning", HPDC '10. ACM, New York, NY, USA, 61-72.

[6] Rodrigo N. Calheiros, Rajiv Ranjan, Anton Beloglazov, César A. F. De Rose, Rajkumar Buyya: "CloudSim: a toolkit for modeling and simulation of cloud computing environments", Softw., Pract. Exper. 41(1): 23-50 (2011)

[7] Luis M. Vaquero, Luis Rodero-Merino, and Rajkumar Buyya. "Dynamically scaling applications in the cloud", SIGCOMM Comput. Commun. Rev. Volume 41, Issue 1, 2011, 45-52.

[8] Brebner, P., O'Brien, L, Gray, J., "Performance modeling power consumption and carbon emissions for Server Virtualization of Service Oriented Architectures (SOAs)". EDOCW 2009. 13th. 92-99.

[9] Paul Brebner, Anna Liu: "Performance and Cost Assessment of Cloud Services", ICSOC Workshops 2010: 39-50.

[10] Brebner, P. C. 2008. "Performance modeling for service oriented architectures", ICSE Companion '08. ACM, New York, NY, 953-954.

[11] Paul Brebner, Liam O'Brien, Jon Gray. "Performance Modeling for e-Government Service Oriented Architectures (SOAs)", ASWEC Conference Proceedings (Perth, March, 2008), 130-138.

[12] Brebner, P. 2009. "Service-Oriented Performance Modeling the MULE Enterprise Service Bus (ESB) Loan Broker Application", SEAA 2009. IEEE Computer Society, Washington, DC, 404-411.

[13] Paul Brebner, Liam O'Brien, Jon Gray: "Performance modeling evolving Enterprise Service Oriented Architectures", WICSA/ECSA 2009: 71-80.

[14] Paul C. Brebner. "Real-world performance modeling of enterprise service oriented architectures: delivering business value with complexity and constraints". ICPE '11. ACM, New York, NY, USA, 85-96.

Clock Driven Programming: A Programming Paradigm which Enables Machine-independent Performance Design

Kenjiro Yamanaka
NTT DATA Corpration
3-3-9 Toyosu, Koto-ku
Tokyo, Japan
yamanakaknj@nttdata.co.jp

ABSTRACT

Cloud computing provides more efficient resource utilization and reduced costs for software systems. However, performance assurance of these systems is difficult because the execution environment cannot be precisely specified and can change dynamically. This paper presents a new programming paradigm, in which software performance is independent from execution environments. The paradigm is called clock driven programming (CDP). The main idea is to introduce the notion of a periodic timer, i.e., clock, for synchronizing program execution timing, just like a clock signal is used in synchronous circuit design. This paper defines CDP and derives the theoretical throughput formula of a CDP program. A CDP program shows the same throughput, even if it runs on different execution environments when its timer period is the same. Therefore, using the CDP enables performance assurance in cloud.

Categories and Subject Descriptors

C.4 [**Performance of Systems**]: Performance attributes; D.2.8 [**Software Engineering**]: Metrics—*Performance measures*; D.1.0 [**Programming Techniques**]: General

1. INTRODUCTION

Cloud computing provides dynamic system environments. Using a cloud service like Amazon EC2, system resources can be procured quickly. The pay-as-you-go model can result in more efficient resource utilization and reduced costs. Dynamic system environments make performance assurance difficult. Virtual machine performance varies as a result of other VMs in the same physical machine. There are variations in machines provided in the cloud, even if the same instance type is used. Users cannot specify the exact machine. This is because this restriction enables rapid provisioning and the pay-as-you-go model. As software performance depends on execution environments, system performance can vary.

Performance engineering has been providing performance prediction methods using a model-based approach. If a precise model of the system is available, we can estimate an execution environment which meets performance demand. However, these methods are not suitable for dynamic system environments. In cloud, we cannot obtain some performance parameters required by the performance model. To handle dynamic system environments, we need new approaches. Open-world software [2] seems to be one of such new approaches.

We present a new approach to assure system performance in dynamic system environments. If software performance does not depend on execution environments, system performance assurance in dynamic system environments can be resolved. We present a programming paradigm in which software performance is independent from execution environments. We call it clock driven programming because its model is clock driven, i.e. synchronous, circuit design. In the synchronous design, performance of circuits does not depend on the device technology but on the clock frequency. This feature makes performance assurance easy. Clock driven programming, as presented here, is a transplantation of synchronous circuit design to software. In CDP, a program is driven by just one periodic timer. If the execution time of the program is less than the timer period, software performance is determined not by the execution environment but by the timer period. This is the principle that CDP enables machine-independent performance design.

In Section 2, the definition of clock driven programming is presented. In Section 3, we will consider performance of CDP programs. In Section 4, we present related works and conclusion.

2. CLOCK DRIVEN PROGRAMMING

Clock driven programming is a subset of event driven programming (EDP). Here, C language is used for sample codes, but any programming languages and operating systems that support EDP can be used to implement CDP. In CDP, we write a program in the same procedure as project planning. 1) We list tasks, and then describe each one. 2) We derive a precedence relation between tasks and create a PERT chart. 3) We create a schedule that satisfy the precedence constraints. CDP is explained in this order.

2.1 Task

A task is a state machine which performs the task repeatedly. A task is driven by a periodic timer and the execution time of the task needs to be less than the timer period. This requirement can be divided into the following two requirements.

Requirement 1. A task has an upper bound of execution steps. □

Requirement 2. Each statement in a task has an upper bound of execution time. □

To fulfill these requirements, we define a task as follows.

Definition 1. (Task) A task is a software module that has the following elements.
1) Internal variables: One or more variables holding values. 2) Interface functions: Zero or more global functions for other tasks to refer to and update internal variables. 3) A reset function: A global function for initializing internal variables. 4) A task's main function: A global function called from within the timer event handler.

All functions consist of statements composed by sequence (;) and selection (if then else). □

The task's main function satisfies Requirement 1 because it does not include repetition. To satisfy Requirement 2, we do not use blocking I/O in tasks. Execution of **read()** is blocked by OS until data become available. This means there is no upper bound of the execution time of **read()**. Instead, we use non-blocking I/O in tasks.

Although a task does not include repetition, the computability of a task is equivalent to usual programs. The following theorem assures this property.

THEOREM 1. *(Normal Form Theorem [3] [1])*
Every flowchart is equivalent to a while-program with **one** *occurrence of while-do, provided additional variables are allowed.* □

The normal form theorem is similar to the famous structure theorem. The difference is number of occurrences of while-do: whereas the structure theorem allows any number, the normal form theorem allows just one. In CDP, just one while-do is expressed by a periodic timer execution, and additional variables are expressed as an internal variable, which usually named 'state'. Practically, **for** statements which have a fixed upper bound of iteration count can be used. This type of repetition is considered to be an abbreviation of the combination of sequence and selection.

Listing 1 shows an example of a task description.

Listing 1: Sample task (TaskA)

```
1  typedef enum {free, calc1, calc2, fin} taskA_state_t;
2  typedef struct {
3    taskA_state_t state; int x, y, result;
4  } taskA_data_t;
5  static taskA_data_t taskA_data;
6
7  #define LIMIT (100)
8  const int busy = -1;
9  const int param_err = -2;
10
11 extern int F (int);
12
13 int calc (int x, int y) {
14   int ret = busy;
15   if (y > 0) {
16     if (taskA_data.state == free) {
```

---

[1]There is no well-known name of this theorem. Harel [3] investigated this theorem and pointed out that its ancestor was Kleene's 1936 normal form theorem for partial recursive functions. Therefore, we call it normal form theorem.

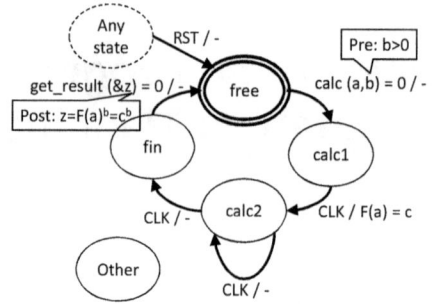

Figure 1: State diagram of TaskA.

```
17       taskA_data.state = calc1;
18       taskA_data.x = x;
19       taskA_data.y = y;
20       ret = 0;
21     }
22   } else {
23     ret = param_err;
24   }
25   return (ret);
26 }
27
28 int get_result (int* y) {
29   int ret = busy;
30   if (taskA_data.state == fin) {
31     *y = taskA_data.result;
32     taskA_data.state = free;
33     ret = 0;
34   }
35   return (ret);
36 }
37
38 void taskA_RST () {
39   taskA_data.state = free;
40 }
41
42 void taskA_CLK () {
43   int i, c;
44
45   switch (taskA_data.state) {
46   case calc1:
47     taskA_data.x = F (taskA_data.x);
48     taskA_data.result = taskA_data.x;
49     taskA_data.y--;
50     taskA_data.state = calc2;
51     break;
52   case calc2:
53     if (taskA_data.y > LIMIT) {
54       c = LIMIT;
55       taskA_data.y -= LIMIT;
56     } else {
57       c = taskA_data.y;
58       taskA_data.y = 0;
59     }
60     for (i = 0; i < c && i < LIMIT; i++) {
61       taskA_data.result *= taskA_data.x;
62     }
63     if (taskA_data.y == 0) {
64       taskA_data.state = fin;
65     }
66     break;
67   default:
68     break;
69   }
70 }
```

TaskA computes $F(x)^y$ repeatedly. Internal variable is defined on Line 5. Two interface functions, **calc()** for requesting a calculation and **get_result()** for getting the result are defined on Line 13 and 28. The reset function which is denoted by name with **_RST** and the main function with **_CLK** are defined on Line 38 and 42.

A state diagram gives a clear view of the task's behavior. A state diagram of taskA is shown in Figure 1. Let S be the whole set of assignment of values to internal variables in a task, and $S_1, \ldots, S_n$ be a finite partition of S. We call each S_i ($1 \leq i \leq n$) a state, and denote it as node. In Figure 1, S is divided in five states by the value of **taskA_data.state**.

A transition $S_i \xrightarrow{f/g} S_j$ means that when the function f is executed in the state S_i, f executes an external function g, and the result state becomes S_j. We omit transitions from node S_i to S_i unless the omission leads misunderstanding. A state that includes the result of the reset function is called an accepting state, and denoted by a double line circle. In Figure 1, the state 'free' is the accepting state. On this state, the machine waits for a new request and accepts it. The machine executes the requested task, and returns to an accepting state. In other states, the state machine rejects the new one, so the requester needs to wait.

Listing 2 shows a task (taskB), which uses taskA.

Listing 2: Sample task (TaskB)

```
1  void taskB_CLK()
2  {
3      switch (taskB_data.state) {
4      ...
5      case state_10:
6          if (calc (taskB_data.a, taskB_data.b) == 0) {
7              taskB_data.state = state_11;
8          }
9          break;
10     case state_11:
11         if (get_result (&taskB_data.z) == 0) {
12             taskB_data.state = state_12;
13         }
14         break;
15     case state_12:
16     ...
17     }
18 }
```

Listing 2 describes a part of taskB's main function, to show how to use taskA. TaskB requests taskA to calculate $F(a)^b$ at state_10. If the request is accepted, taskB's state is changed to state_11. At state_11, taskB waits the result by calling get_result(). If taskB gets the result, taskB's state is changed to state_12.

When taskA is working for taskB, another task should wait for until taskA become free. If there are multiple tasks with the same features, we can handle multiple requests simultaneously. In CDP, we represent multiple tasks with the same features using arrayed task. An arrayed task has internal variables as an array. Each global function of an arrayed task has an additional parameter to select internal variables in the array.

2.2 Creating a PERT Chart

After describing tasks, we derive the precedence relation between tasks. A task's main function calls an interface function of other task to get a processing result. For example, taskB calls get_result() to get $F(a)^b$. TaskB can get the result after the execution of taskA_CLK(), because processing is performed taskA_CLK(). Therefore, taskA_CLK() must be executed earlier than taskB_CLK(). This means that the precedence relation between tasks can be determined by caller-callee relation of task's interface functions. We can create a PERT chart of a CDP program by reversing arrows in the static call-graph of the program. This procedure is shown in Figure 2. A PERT chart must be a directed acyclic graph (DAG). To keep the created chart DAG, we need to meet the following requirement.

Requirement 3. A call-graph of a CDP program must be acyclic.

The parallel execution of a task's main function and interface function may cause data hazard. If this happens, the

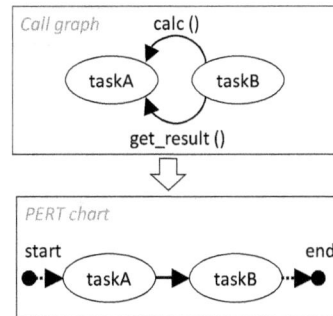

Figure 2: Conversion from call graph to PERT chart

assignment of values to internal variables may change non-deterministically. Data hazard between them can be prevented by using the precedence relation. If scheduling is carried out by using this, the task's main function and interface function are not executed in parallel. There is another source of data hazard. This is parallel execution of the task's interface functions. To prevent this hazard, CDP requires the following.

Requirement 4. If interface functions of a task can be executed in parallel, these functions satisfy Bernstein's conditions.

We can determine the parallel executability of interface functions using the following procedure. Let graph $G = <V, A>$ be a PERT chart derived from a CDP program, and $G^+ = <V, A^+>$ be the transitive closure of G. If two tasks u, w satisfy $<u, w> \notin A^+$ and $<w, u> \notin A^+$, u and w are likely to be scheduled in parallel. If there exists a task v such that $<v, u> \in A, <v, w> \in A$, interface functions of v called in u and ones called in w can be executed in parallel.

THEOREM 2. *(Bernstein's conditions[1])*
Let $R(f)$ be a set of internal variables which are referred in function f, and $W(f)$ be a set of internal variables which are updated in function f.
$$R(f) \cap W(g) = \phi, \ R(g) \cap W(f) = \phi, \ W(f) \cap W(g) = \phi.$$
If these three conditions are upheld, parallel execution of functions f and g does not cause any data hazard. □

If a program does not satisfy Requirement 3 and 4, the program has static semantic errors. A CDP program has the following property.

PROPERTY 1. *A CDP program is data hazard free if tasks in the program are scheduled to satisfy the precedence constraint given by the PERT chart of the program.* □

This is obvious because module scope rule protects illegal access to internal variables. In CDP, data hazard is prevented by static semantics checks. This is possible because there is no repetition in tasks.

2.3 Scheduling

The last step of CDP is making the schedule of tasks that satisfy precedence constraints. A PERT chart used explaining the scheduling method is shown in Figure 3.

To represent a schedule, we usually assign start times of tasks. If execution times of tasks are known and constant, this method is easy to understand. However, execution times of tasks are neither fixed nor known because these

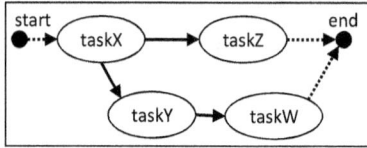

Figure 3: Sample PERT chart

varies with execution environments. In CDP, we represent a schedule using sequential composition. To create a sequential schedule, we use the topological sort of the PERT chart. We can create three schedules from Figure 3.

```
S1 = taskX_CLK(); taskY_CLK(); taskW_CLK(); taskZ_CLK();
S2 = taskX_CLK(); taskY_CLK(); taskZ_CLK(); taskW_CLK();
S3 = taskX_CLK(); taskZ_CLK(); taskY_CLK(); taskW_CLK();
```

The selection of schedules does not affect execution result of the program because of Property 1. Listing 3 shows the timer event handler and the main function. This sample assumes Windows OS. `OnTimer()` is the timer handler that executes the schedule S1 (Line 3). In the main function, we initialize tasks (Line 13, 14), then start timer (Line 19). In this program, the timer period is 100 ms (Line 10, 19). This program terminate when the event **end** is set (Line 20).

Listing 3: Timer handler and main function

```
1  static Handle end;
2
3  void OnTimer () {
4      /* Schedule S1 */
5      taskX_CLK (); taskY_CLK ();
6      taskW_CLK (); taskZ_CLK ();
7  }
8
9  int main () {
10     unsigned int period = 100; /* Unit: ms */
11     MSG msg;
12
13     taskX_RST (); taskY_RST ();
14     taskW_RST (); taskZ_RST ();
15
16     /* Create Events end */
17     end = CreateEvent (NULL, FALSE, FALSE, NULL);
18
19     SetTimer (NULL, 0, period, OnTimer);
20     while (WaitForSingleObject(end, 0) == WAIT_TIMEOUT) {
21         GetMessage (&msg, NULL, 0, 0);
22         DispatchMessage (&msg);
23     }
24 }
```

There is no precedence relation between `task_clk(i)` in an arrayed task. Therefore, we can make a schedule of `task_clk(i)` in any order.

Context switching of multitask OS may cause random delay to the task's execution. Such delay may cause a critical error if the schedule is represented based on time. However, our schedule representation does not depend on the task's execution time. Random delay extends the completion time of the schedule, but the precedence relation between tasks are kept. Therefore, a CDP program works well under multitask OS.

3. PERFORMANCE OF CDP PROGRAMS

This section defines the throughput of a task, and derives the theoretical throughput formula. In general, throughput is represented by transactions per sec. First, we define transaction for a task.

Definition 2. (Transaction) Transaction is a series of state transition which satisfy the following three conditions. First,

it starts a state transition from an accepting state to a non-accepting one. Second, it ends at a state transition from a non-accepting state to an accepting one. Third, it does not contain an accepting state in the middle. □

The following is a series of state transition of taskA in section 2. The series of state transition in boldface is a transaction.

$$free \xrightarrow{CLK/-} free \xrightarrow{calc(a,5)=0/-} \mathbf{calc1} \xrightarrow{CLK/F(a)=c} \mathbf{calc2}$$
$$\xrightarrow{CLK/-} \mathbf{fin} \xrightarrow{get\_result(\&z)=0/-} \mathbf{free} \xrightarrow{CLK/-} free$$

Definition 3. (Clocks per transaction: CPT) The CPT of a transaction is the number of `CLK` contained in the transaction. □

We derive the theoretical throughput formula. If all CLK belongs to transactions, the throughput of a task becomes the maximum. In this case, the throughput is denoted by $1/(cT)$, where c is the CPT and T is the time period. We can increase the throughput using arrayed task. If the number of elements of the array is m, the throughput becomes $m/(cT)$. In order to preserve the timer period, duty ratio D, the ratio of the task's execution time to the timer period, must be kept to less than 1. The reciprocal of T is the frequency f. From the above, the maximum throughput of a task P is obtained using the following formula.

$$P = \frac{m}{c}f \qquad (if\ D < 1) \qquad (1)$$

The performance variance of execution environments does not affect throughput of a CDP program. It affects duty ratio. The duty ratio is proportional to the frequency f. Therefore, if the frequency f is chosen appropriately, we can assure throughput of the program irrespective of execution environments.

4. RELATED WORKS AND CONCLUSION

The predecessor of the clock-driven programming is a programming method that has been used in real-time systems [4]. The main progress of CDP is introducing Requriment 4, Bernstein's conditions, to prevent non-determinism caused by schedule selection.

Clock driven programming was defined and the theoretical throughput formula was derived. A CDP program shows the same throughput even if it runs on different execution environments when its timer period is the same. On the other hand, an adaptation method is required in order to change performance according to environment. The dynamic control of timer period enables such adaptation, but needs to further study.

5. ACKNOWLEDGMENTS

This work was partially supported by Ministry of Internal Affairs and Communications of the Japanese Government.

6. REFERENCES

[1] A. Bernstein. Analysis of programs for parallel processing. *IEEE Trans. on Electronic Computers*, (5):757–763, 1966.

[2] C. Ghezzi. The challenges of open-world software. In *Proc. of WOSP '07*.

[3] D. Harel. On folk theorems. *CACM*, 23:379–389, July 1980.

[4] J. W. Liu. *Real-time systems*. Prentice Hall, 2000.

A Performance Modeling "Blending" Approach for Early Life-cycle Risk Mitigation

Paul Brebner
NICTA/ANU
Canberra Research Laboratory
7A London Circuit, Canberra
Paul.Brebner@nicta.com.au

ABSTRACT

In this paper we describe our first experiences of a performance modeling "blending" approach for early life-cycle risk mitigation in a large enterprise integration project. The goal was to use performance modeling to assist with defining the requirements for the system and to identify areas of architecture and technology risk which could be addressed in future phases of the project. We modified our Service Oriented Performance Modeling approach to enable useful models to be constructed by "blending" data from a variety of imprecise and incomplete information sources prior to the existence of concrete requirements or implementations. The approach iterated over two phases to ensure that deficiencies in method and information identified in the first phase were addressed in the second phase. Activities included scenario and workload modeling in phase 1, and software infrastructure, workload and "blended" modeling in phase 2. The resulting models enabled early exploration of critical assumptions and architectural alternatives. The results were enthusiastically received by the client and used by key decision makers and as inputs for future project phases. The "blending" approach to early life-cycle performance modeling raised the profile of architecture performance risk mitigation in the inception phase, so that performance is more likely be a feature of the subsequent development phases.

Categories and Subject Descriptors

C.4 [Performance of Systems]: Modeling Techniques

General Terms

Performance

Keywords

Blended performance modeling, Early life-cycle risk mitigation

1. INTRODUCTION

This paper describes our first experiences with using performance modeling for risk mitigation early in the life-cycle of a large-scale enterprise integration project. Typically performance modeling is used in later stages of a software development lifecycle when there is sufficient concrete information about the requirements and implementation of a system to build and parameterize models

with the required predictive accuracy. However, for systems that have undefined requirements and which have no implementation the value of building a performance model appears to be limited. Over the last 2 years we have been involved in risk mitigation for a large scale enterprise integration project. The goal was to use performance modeling to assist with defining the requirements for the system and to identify areas of architecture and technology risk which could be addressed in future phases of the project.

Our Service Oriented Performance Modeling approach [5-8] has been applied on many projects of different types and technologies. It is a method with tool support for performance modeling Service Oriented Architectures directly using SOA concepts. Service Oriented Performance Models consist of workloads, composite and simple services, and servers. Workloads capture the external use of the system and include aspects such as external consumers of services and the associated business processes (workflows consuming services). Composite services describe applications in terms of the externally visible service interfaces and the business processes (workflows) and dependencies on other services that implement them, simple services are atomic services for which no further decomposition is possible or required, and servers are the physical hardware resources available for the processing of service demands on simple services (e.g. servers and networks). See Figure 1.

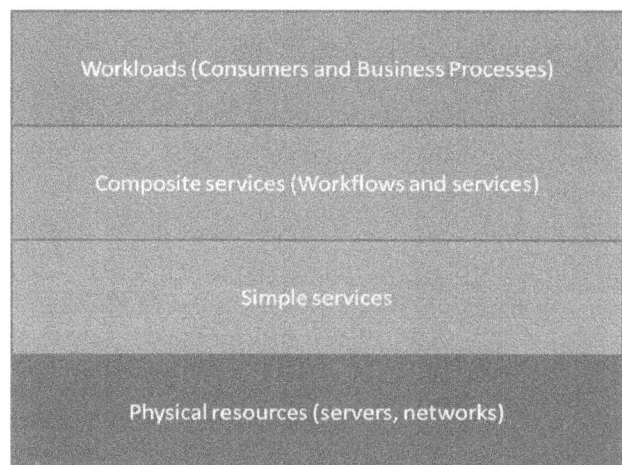

Figure 1 Modelling components

Our methodology for iteratively constructing and calibrating models with these component types from a variety of information and document sources has been adequate for modeling later in the lifecycle [5-8]. Typically we have sufficient concrete information to build a complete model with all component types identified, modeled and parameterized. This produces models of high predictive accuracy but limited benefit due to being built so late in the life-cycle and because they are only models of what actually "is". In other cases some parts of the system exist, and partial models are built of those parts allowing the rest of the system to be modeled in different ways to explore alternatives. For example, the software implementation is modeled "as is", but the unknown workloads and servers are modeled to explore the impact of different load types and sizes on capacity requirements. Or, the known workloads are modeled, but different architectures, designs, and resourcing approaches are modeled for as yet unknown software and hardware.

For this project the challenge was that nothing "concrete" was known at the start. In section 2 we briefly introduce the project context, and in section 3 the details of the phases and modeling activities are covered finishing with the "Blending" approach.

2. PROJECT CONTEXT

The project was an enterprise integration project with the following characteristics. The enterprise was geographically dispersed, with the majority of users located around Australia, but some located overseas. Existing and new applications were to be migrated and integrated using SOA, specifically using Enterprise Service Buses (ESBs). ESBs would be located around Australia and overseas where applications and users were collected. ESBs would be connected together in a federation to allow them to be managed independently, but accessed according to security policies from other ESBs. A variety of common services (e.g. registry, security, XML, etc) would be available on each ESB to allow the construction of new business processes and composite applications which would find, utilize, and extend the functionality of the existing and future applications. The applications would typically be made accessible via the ESBs, but would not be hosted by the ESBs directly. The project was time-bound with delivery milestones spaced regularly across approximately a two year period.

3. MODELING ACTIVITIES

We broke the modeling problem down into the following sub-activities split over two phases. See Figure 2.

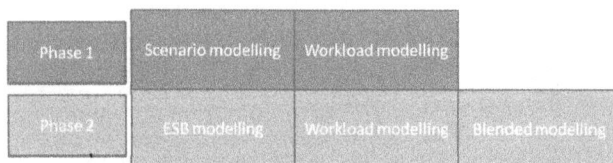

Figure 2 Phases and Modeling Activities

3.1 Scenario Modeling (Business process and composite service modeling)

The first phase of the project was dedicated to understanding how the system would be used. To facilitate this, the project client invested significant effort to develop a set of scenarios to capture the possible uses of the system from a variety of stakeholders. Scenarios included information about the different user roles, the common and application services used, data flows, and the business processes involved in achieving a single and complete end user goal. A single performance critical scenario was selected to focus on, and a partial implementation and initial performance model constructed to provide confidence that the modeling approach was suitable for the task. The implementation and modeling of the scenario was complicated by the fact that a

fair amount of interpretation was required in order to build it, that it was complicated and involved many different user roles, 10s of composite and simple services, 100s of business process steps, 5-10 ESB locations, and all of the application services had to be defined and implemented.

Given the project constraints (budget, staff, resources, and finances) only a representative subset of the scenario was implemented. However, we were able to model the entire scenario, and using performance data obtained from the partial implementation we were able to parameterize the complete model. The model was successfully validated against the partial implementation and could be used to predict the performance (e.g. response time) and capacity (e.g. servers and networks) of the complete scenario. We also learnt useful lessons about how best to obtain performance data from the type of ESB stacks and services involved. We also concluded that more information was needed about how the ESBs would be used in practice (the implementation of the scenario was simplistic (the implementation and target architectures were different, and the implementation only used a very small subset of ESB functionality), how ESBs would interact among themselves (e.g. if a target service was not available at a local ESB how would it be accessed remotely), about the workloads (number, location, and user loads).

3.2 Workload Modeling

Workload modeling was done in two phases. In the initial phase (concurrent with 3.1) the data from an organization wide survey of the user community was analyzed. We discovered that there were (a) a large number of communities, (b) that a few communities interacted with a large number of other communities, (c) the majority interacted with only a few other communities, (d) a large number of interactions were within the same user community, (e) no business process information was available (purely high-level data flow information), and (f) the survey was lacking critical information such as locations, load frequency and data volumes.

In the first phase we built a performance model based on the initial workload and ESB implementation information only. This model was designed to show what was assumed about the workloads mapped onto very simple ESB architecture alternatives. We had to make many assumptions to fill in the missing workload information (which just became variables that could be explored with the aid of the model). The main assumptions were that the each user community was located in a single unique location, and that the workload demands (frequency and data sizes) were proportional to the number of data types connected to other communities. The alternative ESB architectures reflected two extreme cases: (1) a single logical ESB backbone (a single logical ESB that all communications went through, but made up of multiple physical ESB resources), and (2) multiple ESBs, one per workload community. In practice, the actual architecture will be something in between (i.e. some user communities will be split over multiple locations; some user communities will be co-located with others at the same location). Being on a partial model of the system and with so many assumptions this type of model was only intended to explore some extreme architectural variants and the impact of changing workload demands, and to reveal gaps in the information available.

In phase 2 we planned to fill in the missing gaps in the second phase with a survey designed to elicit more specific performance information from a representative subset of the user communities. Part of the overall modeling strategy was to "blend" multiple sources of information together for the final model in phase 2. At the end of phase 1 we had partial models of the business processes/composite services and workloads. The focus of phase 2 was to better understand the ESB implementation and architecture issues and build a more complete model.

We eventually used two approaches to improve our knowledge of the workloads in phase 2. The first was the survey which due to changes in the project and budgets was far more limited than planned and therefore did not produce the desired results. We were able to obtain the type of information we needed (including number and location of user communities, amount of data sent and received within and to and from other user communities, and frequency of data transfers), but the sample size was too small to extrapolate in any sensible way. We therefore relied on a second approach which was to consult with several experts whose knowledge was both broader and deeper across the whole set of user communities. This approach resulted in capturing at least some knowledge about the majority of the user communities and gave us the following critical information: (1) number of user communities and their locations, and therefore the total number of ESB locations as well, (2) basic information about the number and type of workloads each community was involved with including relative frequency, data sizes, and the network of communities and locations involved in each. Several hundred distinct workloads were discovered. Some preprocessing in the way of aggregation of users in the same location was done before this data was used in the blended model in phase 2 (3.4).

3.3 ESB Modeling

The initial implementation of the "scenario" in 3.1 was done by the client on an in-house test-bed on a variety of vendor ESB stacks. For phase 2 we decided that we needed to understand ESB performance and architectural dimensions in a more controlled environment and we set up our own test-bed across a number of servers on an isolated network segment in our own laboratory. In order to do this quickly and to have the maximum control and understanding of the ESB technology and performance results we used an open source high-performance ESB technology. This was deployed and tuned on 4 servers so we could experiment with single ESB node performance, and multiple ESB node performance. One server was used to host the client and load generator, two servers hosted the ESB stack and ESB composite service implementation, and the fourth server hosted the target business service (accessible via the ESBs, but not hosted on them so as to simplify modeling and performance data capture but also to reflect the anticipated architecture of the eventual system).

Further investigation found that there were a number of critical core ESB services that were relevant to the performance of the system. These were: Authentication and Authorization, Encryption, XML Transformation, Registry Lookup, Composite Services & Business Process, and support for multiple transports (e.g. HTTP, JMS).

We designed, implemented and deployed a representative composite application that utilized these ESB services in the way expected, and conducted extensive performance tests on two main architectures. The first architecture was a single node ESB. This example represents the case that a service consumer accesses an ESB and requests a specific service. All of the ESB services are involved in determining if the user can access the service, the service is found to be located on the local ESB, and is then

invoked and the response routed back to the consumer. The second architecture involved two ESBs with identical code. See Figure 3.

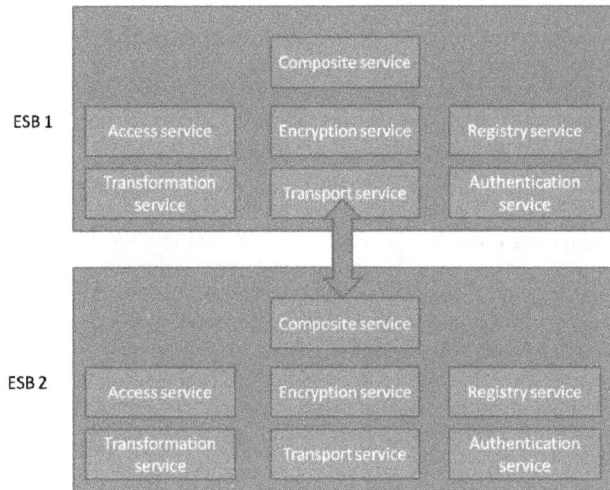

Figure 3 Two ESB node architecture

This example represents the case where the service is not available on the first ESB, so the request is redirected to the second ESB which handles it in the same way that the first one did, eventually finding the service locally and managing the call/response back to the first ESB. This process could be recursive across more than two ESB nodes and represents the case where multiple ESB "domains" have to be navigated in order to use a target service that is located at a specific ESB. We also explored the impact of the message size on the times spent in each ESB service. Not surprisingly the times increase rapidly for some services with increasing data size, specifically encryption and transformation.

Upon completion of the performance testing we had sufficient information to be able to build a detailed model of single and multiple ESB node performance for representation composite applications with different data sizes and ESB services involved. Some of the findings from this work were that: (1) the resource demands of encryption and transformation are substantial and increase with message data size, (2) the resource demands of encryption are asymmetrical (the consumer consumes more resources than the provider).

3.4 Blended Model

Near the end of phase 2 we therefore had good understanding of the types and locations of workloads, the number and location of ESB nodes, and the performance of one representative ESB technology (implementation and architecture). Combined with the work previously done in phase 1 modeling the business process/composite service scenario, and with some assumptions, we had sufficient information to build "blended" models of possible systems.

The first critical concrete piece of information we used from the workload information was the number and location of ESB nodes. This gave us the ability to populate the model with a fixed number of ESB node instances (approximately 20). The location information was also used to determine network connectivity (number and speed of networks between each ESB node) as this was information that was available from another source. The workload information was preprocessed so that model parameterization was simplified. We ended up with 3 workload types for each ESB node location representing the aggregate workloads of each type for all the user communities at that location. The workload types represented a simple publication of data from one node to other nodes, a more complex business process involving the transfer of data of medium size and the involvement of a reasonable number of services, and a very complicated business process involving the transfer of large amounts of data and the involvement of many services.

The tricky bit of the modeling at this point was determining how to model the dependency on services at different nodes given the originating node. For simplicity we assumed that the probability of any given node being involved was proportional to the connectedness of the nodes from an analysis of the workload data. This resulted in the same probability distribution overall as in the workload data, but may not be true for any given interaction. The service demands on each ESB node were parameterized based on the ESB modeling results from 3.3, and varied depending on the number of ESB nodes involved in calling a target service.

Given that the resulting model was not intended to, and could never in practice, produce a single definitive and validated set of performance metrics for the target system, how was it used in practice? Firstly we used the model to determine which information was likely to be more critical to the performance of the system. We did this by conducting a single variable sensitivity analysis on the parameters related to the workloads, and the parameters related to the ESB resource usage. This clearly showed that the frequency and complexity of one type of workload was critical. Changing it by even a small amount resulted in large changes in performance characteristics of individual ESB nodes and across the whole system (number of CPU cores). It also showed that the ESB security overhead was critical. If either or both of these parameters are significantly higher than the "default" values assumed then the system rapidly becomes unusable and unbuildable, taking too long to process requests and requiring resources orders of magnitude higher than realistically available.

The model was also able to be used to explore some architectural alternatives. These included whether to transfer data via the ESB or use some out-of-band mechanism, and the impact of forcing all services to be available locally on each ESB compared with services having specific (possibly multiple) locations (the most extreme case being centralized only). Again the model was able to show the likely tradeoffs in terms of both performance (response times) and capacity requirements. It was obvious that even with optimistic assumptions about workload demands that transferring data larger than small messages over the ESBs would significantly impact performance and resource requirements. We also discovered that there were huge variations in resource requirements for individual ESB nodes depending on the assumptions made about service locations. Some nodes needed only several CPU cores, while others needed hundreds of cores. In practice this would be exacerbated with dynamic changes in workloads.

Apart from server capacity modeling, we also explored network capacity issues. We discovered that even optimistic assumptions resulted in some of the slower networks completely saturating, and even some of the faster networks were approaching maximum capacity.

4. SUMMARY

In conclusion, this experience has demonstrated that there is potential for earlier and more informative performance modeling of large scale enterprise transformation projects (e.g. migration, integration, etc) for the purpose of reducing risk [3] (rather than purely to give highly accurate performance predictions). The approach evolved from our earlier experiences modeling "concrete" SOA implementations [5], changes in SOAs [6], ESBs [7], and complex real-world modeling [8]. It is different in that the final performance models constructed represent an "abstract" future system (c.f. [1]).

The work has not been validated in the sense that model predictions can be compared to a final working system (which is only in the planning phases, as in [2]). It is a work-in-progress in that we have not yet turned this early life-cycle modeling experience into a complete method or proved it on similar projects. Both the process of modeling and the results have been enthusiastically received by our client and used by key decision makers and as inputs for a number of gateway reviews and future project phases. For this project, the "Blending" approach to early life-cycle performance modeling raised the profile of architecture performance risk mitigation in the inception phase [3], so that performance is more likely be a feature of the subsequent development phases [4].

5. ACKNOWLEDGMENTS

NICTA is funded by the Australian Government as represented by the Department of Broadband, Communications and the Digital Economy and the Australian Research Council through the ICT Centre of Excellence program.

6. REFERENCES

[1] Lloyd G. Williams and Connie U. Smith. 2002. PASA^{SM}: a method for the performance assessment of software architectures. In *Proceedings of the 3rd international workshop on Software and performance* (WOSP '02). ACM, New York, NY, USA, 179-189. DOI=10.1145/584369.584397 http://doi.acm.org/10.1145/584369.584397

[2] Woodside, M.; Franks, G.; Petriu, D.C.; The Future of Software Performance Engineering. In *Future of Software Engineering* (FOSE '07). May 2007, 171-187. 10.1109/FOSE.2007.32

[3] Wolfgang Emmerich. 2002. Distributed component technologies and their software engineering implications. In *Proceedings of the 24th International Conference on Software Engineering* (ICSE '02). ACM, New York, NY, USA, 537-546. DOI=10.1145/581339.581405 http://doi.acm.org/10.1145/581339.581405

[4] J.D. Meier, Srinath Vasireddy, Ashish Babbar, and Alex Mackman. Improving .NET Application Performance and Scalability. May 2004. Chapter 2 – Performance Modeling. http://msdn.microsoft.com/en-us/library/ff647767.aspx

[5] Paul Brebner: Performance modeling for service oriented architectures. ICSE Companion 2008: 953-954

[6] Paul Brebner, Liam O'Brien, Jon Gray: Performance modeling evolving Enterprise Service Oriented Architectures. WICSA/ECSA 2009: 71-80

[7] Paul Brebner: Service-Oriented Performance Modeling the MULE Enterprise Service Bus (ESB) Loan Broker Application. EUROMICRO-SEAA 2009: 404-411

[8] Paul Brebner: Real-world performance modeling of enterprise service oriented architectures: delivering business value with complexity and constraints. ICPE 2011: 85-96

Compositional Performance Abstractions of Software Connectors

Misha Strittmatter
Karlsruhe Institute of Technology
Am Fasanengarten 5
76131 Karlsruhe, Germany
misha.strittmatter@student.kit.edu

Lucia (Kapova) Happe
Karlsruhe Institute of Technology
Am Fasanengarten 5
76131 Karlsruhe, Germany
kapova@kit.edu

ABSTRACT

Typically, to provide accurate predictions, a performance model has to include low-level details such as used communication infrastructure, or connectors and influence of the underlying middleware platform. In order to profit from the research on inter-component communication and connector design, performance prediction approaches need to include models of different kinds of connectors. It is not always feasible to model complex connectors with all their details. The choice of suitable abstraction filter, which reduces the amount of detailed information needed with respect to the model purpose, is crucial to decrease modelling effort. We propose an approach by which an abstract connector model can be augmented with selected adaptations and enhancements using model completions to result in a more detailed connector model. As the purpose of our models is performance prediction, we designed a suitable abstraction filter based on the *Pipes & Filters* pattern to produce performance models of connectors. Thus, we need to characterize only a small set of compositional and reusable transformations. The selection of applied transformations is then based on the feature-oriented design of the connector's completion.

Categories and Subject Descriptors

C.4 [**Computer Systems Organization**]: Performance of Systems—*Modeling techniques*; D.2.8 [**Software Engineering**]: Metrics; D.2.11 [**Software Engineering**]: Software Architecture—*Patterns*

Keywords

Connectors, Model Completions, Performance Abstractions

1. INTRODUCTION

In Model-Driven Software Performance Engineering (MD-SPE), applications are composed from prefabricated components. The modelling of the system is done at a high abstraction level. Adding non-functional information to the compo-

nent specifications enables a system-wide analysis. This is the main intention of the Palladio Component Model (PCM) [2]. A design-time performance prediction using component-based models requires plenty of implementation details to be sufficiently accurate. Model Completions [5] are one possible approach to reduce model development effort and keep the model free from implementation details (especially in early development stages), by adding components with performance-relevant details to the model transparently for the user and automatically by model transformations.

The separation of concerns is essential to avoid construction of large and monolithic models, which are hard to maintain or reuse. Reusability of such models is limited especially because they are often designed for one purpose, and as such do not consider possible enhancements when the purpose of the model changes and new domain-specific details have to be introduced. For example, a component-based architecture model could be used to predict performance. However, the same model could be used to analyse reliability, as well. Both of these purposes require additional domain-specific details, i.e. performance or reliability specific implementation details.

Model Completions support the reuse of purpose-specific abstractions of specific implementation details, which could be configured and used for different purposes. Moreover because the integration of the completions is automated, they are also a technique of experimenting with different settings without having to adapt the whole model manually. The goal of this paper is to create a basis for the implementation of completions which insert connector models into PCM model instances. Although, we have used PCM as modelling language, the analysed connectors and their feature models are applicable for all component-based systems in general. This work introduces: i) compositional performance abstractions that define model transformations to enhance models of connectors; ii) feature models describing possible configuration variants of the connectors; and iii) descriptions on how the configurations of these features influence the system architecture and performance. Subjects of analysis are the connectors, such as procedure calls, messaging, streaming and blackboards analysed by [3]. We focus in this work on performance of the software systems and thus we provide only performance abstractions of the features in the feature models.

The paper is structured as follows. After discussing the foundations in Section 2, we provide a discussion on the suitable connector abstractions in Section 3. The result of this analysis is an architecture and feature-oriented design of an exemplary connector. Section 4 discusses the implementation of the completions. Section 5 gives an overview of work related to our approach. Finally, Section 6 concludes the paper, highlights future research directions, and additionally, we discuss the limitations and the validity of the approach.

2. FOUNDATIONS

Software performance engineering (SPE) enables an early performance evaluation of software systems. It allows software architects and developers to identify potential performance problems, such as bottlenecks, in their software systems during the design phase. For this purpose, SPE integrates performance predictions directly in the software development process.

MD-SPE [1] aims to improve the prediction quality of performance models while requiring little manual effort. Software architects describe their system in a language specific to their domain and annotate these models with configurations of performance abstractions (completions) or other performance-relevant information. *Completions* [5] are configurable transformations which add performance-relevant details about the implementation, execution environment etc. to the models. Executing all completions results in the refined model, which then can be transformed into a performance model. Typical models for performance analysis are queueing networks, stochastic Petri nets, or stochastic process algebras. Solving the performance models by analytical or simulation-based methods yields various performance metrics for the system under study. In practice, tools encapsulate the transformation and the solution of the models and hide their complexity.

A *Feature Diagram* is a tree with its nodes representing features (except the root). The connection between nodes carry annotations, which state rules on how features can be selected. E.g. there are optional or mandatory features, alternative (or) and mutually exclusive (xor) feature sets. A tree can be instantiated by selecting features (following the rules) and annotating additional data, where demanded. We use such instances as configuration for completions [5].

We apply our approach in the area of *Component-base Software Architecture*. The implementation of our approach is based on an architectural modelling language PCM [2]. It is specifically designed for performance prediction of component-based systems, with an automatic transformation into a discrete-event simulation of generalised queuing networks. Software *components* are the core entities of the PCM. Basic components contain an abstract behavioural specification called Resource Demanding-Service Effect Specification (RD-SEFF) for each provided service. RD-SEFFs describe how component services use resources and call required services using an annotated control flow graph. *AssemblyConnectors* connect required interfaces with provided interfaces. *Resource containers* model the hardware environment in the PCM. They represent nodes, e.g., servers or client computers, on which components can be allocated. They provide a set of processing resources, such as CPUs and hard disks, which can be utilized by the hosted components.

3. CONNECTOR ABSTRACTIONS

The purpose of our models is performance prediction, therefore we aim to model only performance abstractions of connectors, thus we can abstract from the functional details and concentrate on the performance-relevant dependencies. From a performance point of view, a connector is a chain of components producing load dependent on the size of data being sent through it (and sometimes on additional properties, e.g. entropy). In such a highly abstract connector model, we can simplify the basic building blocks of connectors to two types of activities: buffering of transferred data and computation or I/O activities involving the data. This is very similar to the *Pipes & Filters* pattern, which is an architecture pattern for data stream processing systems [4]. As we break down the connector's overall task into several independent incremental processing steps, we can use the Pipes & Filters pattern and consider filters as processing steps, which execute their subtask, while pipes connect adjacent filters and provide buffering, linking and transport. A filter is defined by the load it generates (dependent on the properties of data) and if and how it changes the properties of data (e.g. compression reduces bytesize, but increases entropy). The filters of a connector also form a chain of producer-consumer systems. A filter is a consumer with regard to his predecessor and a producer with regard to his successor, while the pipes are the bounded buffers in between. This internal mechanism is modelled in the RD-SEFFs of the filter and pipe components. Filters also have a definable amount of worker threads. One challenge we faced was to model the behaviour of these active components (opposed to reactive components, which just pass a call along) using the PCM. This was achieved by adding worker management interfaces, so that the pipe could acquire and release workers of adjacent pipes.

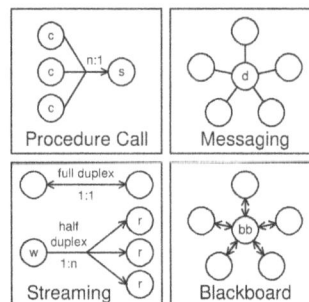

Figure 1: Connector Layout

The settings in which a particular connector can be used are determined by its topology. In the scope of this work we built several exemplary connectors (including their feature trees) with varying topology and arbitrary cardinality, whose underlying architectures were designed by [3]. These connectors are *Procedure Call*, *Messaging*, *Streaming* and *Blackboard*. Their layout is shown in Fig. 1. The Procedure Call and half duplex Streaming connectors feature unidirectional, while Full Duplex and Blackboard connectors feature bidirectional communication. Components connected to the Messaging connector can either be sender, receiver or both. Considering one direction of communication, a call can either be synchronous (i.e. caller will wait for response) or asynchronous (i.e. caller can resume as soon as the call was accepted by the first pipe).

Fig. 2 shows the sub feature tree which is used to configure the behavior of one generic filter. The declarations of the sizes of worker pool and buffer of the preceding pipe are

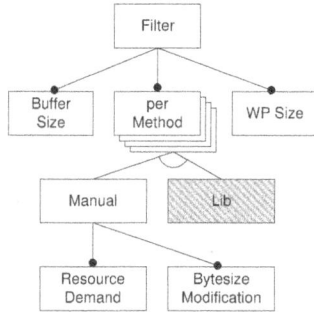

Figure 2: Filter (Sub) Feature Diagram

mandatory. For each method, which is contained in the signature of the interface on which the connector is being applied, one can either define the further behaviour of the filter manually or use predefined formulas.

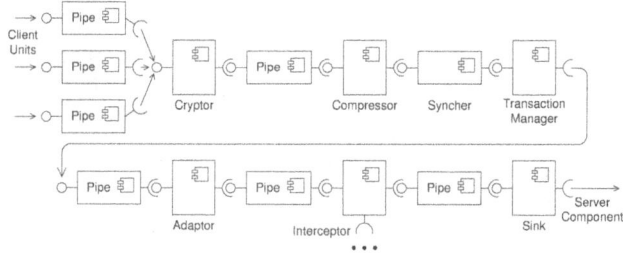

Figure 3: Procedure Call Connector Server Unit

A connector is composed of multiple units (a unit is nothing more than an assembly of components). The most simple 1:1 procedure call connector e.g. is composed of a client and a server unit. Should the two components (which are connected by the connector) be deployed on different resource containers, the client unit will be deployed on the client's container and vice versa. As an example of how the connector looks like when realized within the PCM, Fig. 3 shows the server unit of a procedure call connector (though in this case it has 3:1 cardinality). The unit is fully featured (all features which map to server side filters are selected). Most processing steps are realized as simple filters, while the interceptor can be linked to an external interface and the transaction manager may be inserted by another (nested) completion.

4. COMPLETION IMPLEMENTATION

To adapt models corresponding to the real system, we implemented a transformation realizing connector completions and composing them from basic elements. It is a model-to-model transformation using QVT Relational [7]. The tool used to run the transformation is the Medini QVT Engine. The transformation can be divided into a number of basic steps. As the first step of the transformation, the source model has to be copied completely into the target model, but without the annotated *AssemblyConnectors* (because it will be replaced by our connector abstraction). Then the *Connectors* have to be created. The creation of a *Connector* can be divided into the following steps: (a) find elements in the target model, (b) create new elements, (c) connect elements, (d) allocate elements, and (e) place elements. First,

the location (*pivot element*) and the elements that are directly connected to this location, where the *Connector* has to be inserted into the copied system, has to be identified. The new elements and their interconnections are defined by the feature diagram. For each completion, a completion transformation is generated. Second, this generated transformation is executed and all the new elements that are part of the connector are integrated. Then all the elements get allocated to hardware resources depending on the allocation in the source model. At the end all created elements have to be placed inside the system or the allocation element to be at the right place in the PCM model.

The resulting transformation then integrates the selected model primitives based on the configuration of the feature model (cf. Figure 4). Moreover, the transformation calibrates the feature model for a certain platform by adding the resource demands to the connector primitives modelled as filters (cf. Figure 4: Resource Demands (RD)).

In the performance abstractions of connectors, a feature is a discrete design element of connector and a model (i.e., transformation) primitive is a relation from an abstract connector to a more detailed connector. These transformation primitives operate on the connectors and their parameters. Each transformation primitive introduces a part of connector and their composition builds a whole valid connector. In order to achieve generality and flexibility, we have to achieve appropriate granularity of transformation primitives. However, in most of the approaches the additional effort that is required to compose a large number of these small parts is a problem. The means to implementing the primitives and derive the transformation were chosen with this concern in mind. Thus, we implement the primitives as relational transformation fragments (i.e., in QVT-R) with a very high compositionality. The Figure 4 illustrates a few simple compositional and reusable transformation primitives used to implement the procedure call connector.

5. RELATED WORK

Mehta et al. [6] present an approach to a taxonomy of connectors. They feature several levels of categories each of which provides a connector instance on the lowest levels. New connector instances can be composed by combining multiple features from the lowest levels. A technical report of Bures and Plasil [3] explains how connectors can be composed of elements and illustrates the connector generation process. In preparation to our work, we researched how other component systems treat connectors. While they are mainly not used for design time performance predictions, there are still important aspects for our work in these systems. As surveyed in [1], *ROBOCOP*, a component model with a performance prediction framework, has its application in the field of embedded systems. In addition, to passive components it also supports active and mixed-mode components. As an outcome of the active/passive consideration it also explicitly distinguishes between synchronous and asynchronous calls. *OLAN* is an environment for architecture description of distributed systems using middleware. It also features explicit synchronous and asynchronous calls. The *SOFA* component model, treats connectors as first class entities and they can be described by their architecture.

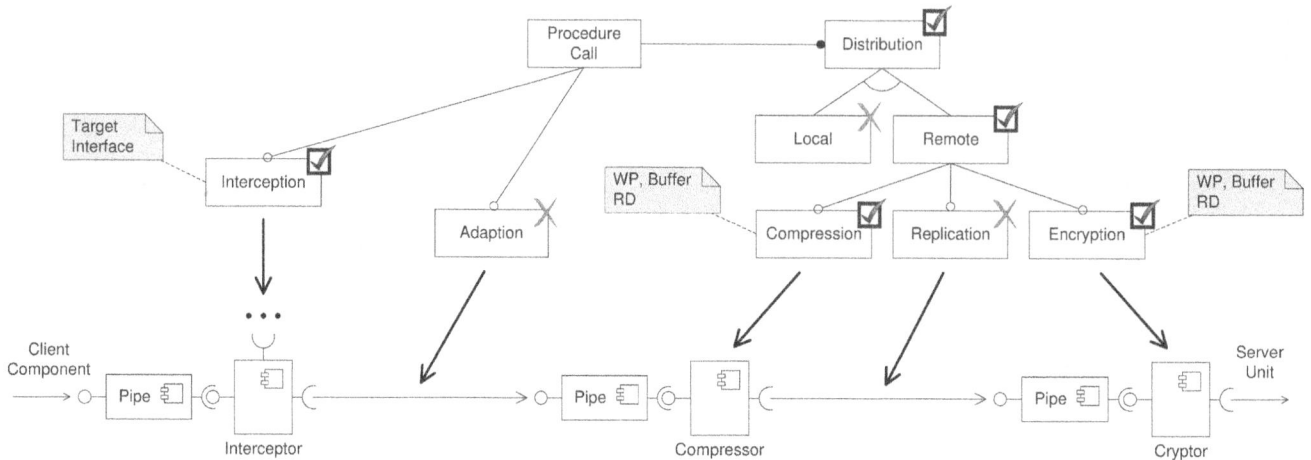

Figure 4: Resulting active fragments of transformation in the completion.

6. CONCLUSIONS AND VISIONS

In this work-in-progress paper a suitable performance abstraction for Procedure Call Connector, its design and performance impact, was analysed. As part of the definition, connector feature models summarizing the configuration options were identified and systematically analysed. An important aspect of this work was to examine the potential of the PCM regarding its ability to model connectors. As a conclusion, almost everything was possible to implement with the PCM's own means. The behaviour of active components can be emulated with passive resources representing threadpools. Buffering is done through the use of blocking on passive resources, asynchronous calls through forking. Connectors do not have to be considered as first class entities since they can be utilized using completions. Only the lack of an internal component state was a constraint (e.g. when considering GC effects). Without it, the blackboard connector cannot be used to communicate exact values. Instead it responds with statistical data. The resulting connector models were composed from reappearing and reusable parts, which consequently eased the development of the required model transformations. In this work, we showed that starting with general models and deciding about the purpose of models later in the model development is acceptable, when the models' purposes can be handled in isolation. In other words, an early usage of modelling abstractions designed for one specific purpose only mirrors in the later usage of models and the effort necessary to automate modelling actions.

As such this paper is a starting point for a wide variety of further work. A more comprehensive case study should be conducted to evaluate the effect of the whole concept and the whole set of possible features. The results can also be used to calibrate the architecture, its configuration as well as predefined values, formulas and libraries. Most valuable would be a complete integration of automated measurements and regressions benchmarks (e.g. Performance Cockpit [8]) to calibrate completions. Such approaches can provide multidimensional parametrised resource demands needed for completions with less-effort. Especially already developed completions (e.g. middleware completions) have to be coordinated or combined with the connector-completion.Finally, the matured completion can be included in a completion library or be directly integrated into the PCM IDE.

7. REFERENCES

[1] S. Balsamo, A. Di Marco, P. Inverardi, and M. Simeoni. Model-Based Performance Prediction in Software Development: A Survey. *Transactions on Software Engineering*, 30(5):295–310, May 2004.

[2] S. Becker, H. Koziolek, and R. Reussner. The Palladio component model for model-driven performance prediction. 82:3–22, 2009.

[3] T. Bures and F. Plasil. Composing connectors of elements. Technical Report 3, Dep. of SW Engineering, Charles University, Prague, May 2003.

[4] F. Buschmann. *Pattern-oriented software architecture*, volume 1: A system of patterns. Wiley, Chichester [u.a.], repr. edition, 2007.

[5] L. Kapova and T. Goldschmidt. Automated feature model-based generation of refinement transformations. In *Proceedings of the 35th EUROMICRO Conference on Software Engineering and Advanced Applications (SEAA)*. IEEE, 2009.

[6] N. R. Mehta, N. Medvidovic, and S. Phadke. Towards a taxonomy of software connectors. In *ICSE '00: Proceedings of the 22nd international conference on Software engineering*, pages 178–187, New York, NY, USA, 2000. ACM.

[7] Object Management Group. *MOF 2.0 Query/View/Transformation, version 1.0*, Apr. 2008.

[8] D. Westermann, J. Happe, M. Hauck, and C. Heupel. The performance cockpit approach: A framework for systematic performance evaluations. In *Proceedings of the 36th EUROMICRO Conference on Software Engineering and Advanced Applications (SEAA 2010)*. IEEE Computer Society, 2010.

Efficiency Improvements for Solving Layered Queueing Networks

Greg Franks
greg@sce.carleton.ca

Lianhua Li
lianhua@sce.carleton.ca

Department of Systems and Computer Engineering, Carleton University
Ottawa, ON Canada K1S 5B6

ABSTRACT

Layered Queueing Networks (LQN) have been successfully by numerous researchers to solve performance models of multi-tier client server systems. A common approach for solving a LQN is to split the model up into a set of submodels, then employ approximate mean value analysis (AMVA) on each of these submodels in an interactive fashion and using the results from the solution of one submodel as inputs to the others. This paper addresses the performance of the layered queueing network solver, LQNS, in terms of submodel construction and in terms of changes to Bard-Schweitzer and Linearizer AMVA, in order to improve performance. In some of the models described in this paper, there is a difference in four orders of magnitude between the fastest and slowest approaches.

Categories and Subject Descriptors

C.4 [**Performance of Systems**]: Modeling Techniques

General Terms

Performance

Keywords

Performance Analysis, Approximate Mean Value Analysis

1. INTRODUCTION

The Layered Queueing Network (LQN) model exploits a key property that a task may, during its service, stop while making a nested request to another server. This type of interaction, a remote procedure call, is very common in the software of today's distributed systems. Conventional product-form queueing networks cannot be used to solve these types of models because of the blocking. The call to the lower level server creates a form of simultaneous resource possession because the customer is occupying the client and it's server during the remote procedure call.

Figure 1 shows a *Layered Queueing Network* (LQN) using a condensed notation. The parallelograms in the figure represents *Tasks*. Tasks are concurrent entities and can make requests to other tasks in the model. Tasks in layer 1 in the figure are called *Reference Tasks* and are the customers in the model. Tasks at lower layers in the model, called *active servers*, can both accept requests and make requests to other tasks and are used to model actual tasks in the system, non-processor hardware devices such as disks, and passive resources such as critical sections. The circles in the figure represent *processors* and are *pure servers* are used to consume time. Both tasks and processors can be *multiservers*. For reference tasks, a multiserver represents a population of customers greater than one.

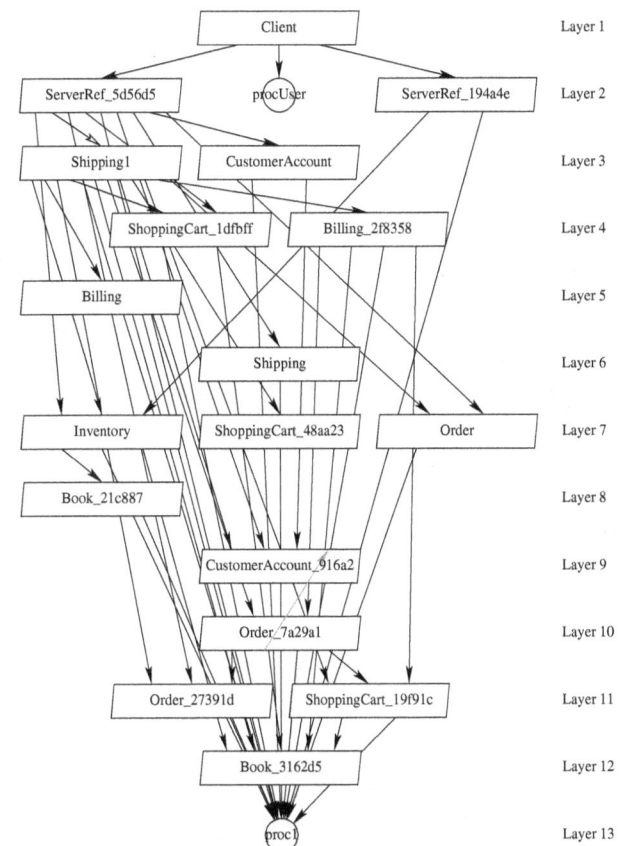

Figure 1: Bookstore model (from [4]).

Calls in Figure 1 are shown as directed arcs from one task to another. Calls can either be synchronous or asynchronous; replies from synchronous requests can be deferred to lower layer servers through forwarding. Layering arises from analyzing the call graph of the requests from the customers in layer one, to the servers (usually processors) at the deepest layer in the graph. A complete description of the model can be found in [3].

Fast analytic solutions for solving a Layered Queueing Network were developed in [9], with Stochastic Rendezvous Networks (SRVN), and in [7] with the Method of Layers (MOL). Stochastic Rendezvous Networks treated each server independently and used new approximations for calculating the residence times at servers. The Method of Layers introduced the important concept of grouping servers in "layer submodels", then solved the submodels using Linearizer approximate Mean Value Analysis (AMVA). Blocking delays caused by synchronous calls are treated as surrogate delays [5] and are imported from other submodels. The Layered Queueing Network (LQN) model is an extension of both MOL and SRVN and incorporates features found in important application systems [3].

Layer submodels can be constructed in a variety of different ways. This paper examines five different layering techniques, ranging from a single server per layer, like the SRVN method in [9], to the extreme opposite case where there is only one layer containing all of the servers in the model. Approximate MVA is used to solve each of the layer submodels so the approximate MVA algorithm was modified to reduce the amount of iteration. The modified algorithms are compared against the original implementation for improvements in performance and variations in the results.

2. LAYERING QUEUEING NETWORK SOLVER

The layered queueing network solver (LQNS) [3] is used in this work. Algorithm 1 lists the major steps used to solve a model. The algorithm iterates over each of the submodels and uses successive substitution to converge on a solution. The algorithm will terminates when the root of the sum of mean difference in utilizations of the entities in the model is less than a user-defined amount or some pre-defined iteration limit is reached.

Algorithm 1 LQNS Algorithm

1: Read input and create LQNS model.
2: Create S submodels based on layers.
3: **repeat**
4:    **for** $s \leftarrow 1$ to S **do**
5:       Solve submodel s using approximate MVA.
6:       Set waiting times for submodel s.
7:       Set think times for submodel $s + 1$.
8:    **end for**
9: **until** convergence or iteration limit
10: Save results.

2.1 Submodel Creation

Submodels are constructed by first finding a set of *servers* (starting from layer 2), then finding all of the callers to these servers regardless of layer and treating these entities as *clients*. A task or processor can appear as a *server* in ex-

actly one submodel. However, a task can appear as a *client* in multiple places.

Five submodel construction strategies are studied in this paper:

SRVN: Each submodel consists of exactly one server (see [9]).

Batched: Each submodel treats of all of the tasks and processors at a given layer as servers.

MOL: *Software* submodels are constructed by treating only the tasks at a given layer as servers. A single *hardware* submodel is constructed using all of the processors as servers (see [7]).

HwSw: Two submodels are used: a *software* submodel is constructed by treating all non-reference tasks as servers and a *hardware* submodel like MOL. A task may appear as both a client and a server with this approach.

Squashed Only one submodel is used where all non-reference tasks and processors are treated as servers. Non-reference tasks will appear as both a client and a server.

2.2 Submodel Solution

Submodels are solved by converting a submodel into an ordinary queueing network model then solving this model either Bard-Schweitzer proportionate estimation [1, 8] or Linearizer [2] AMVA. Inputs to the AMVA solver are think and service times. Outputs are waiting (or residence) times, throughputs and utilizations. The clients in a submodel map to the chains in the queueing model and represented using delay centers. The service time for a client in a submodel are found by summing up the residence times to all the client's servers, except for those servers that are in the same submodel. Think times, Z, for clients in a submodel are set using the input parameters for reference tasks, and derived from the throughputs, λ, and the utilizations, U, for non-reference tasks. The servers in the submodel make up the queueing centers in the queueing model. The queueing discipline of the center depends on the task or processor type in the input model.

Once the queueing network for a submodel has been solved, the waiting time components corresponding to the submodel are updated for all of the submodel's clients, and the throughputs and utilizations are updated for all the submodel's servers. This process is repeated over all the submodels in the model until the convergence criteria has been met.

3. APPROXIMATE MVA CHANGES

In solving a layered queueing network using Linearizer AMVA, there are three levels of loops: the outer iteration shown in Algorithm 1, the loops in Linearizer for running Bard-Schweitzer AMVA, and the iterations within Bard-Schweitzer AMVA itself. This section briefly describes Approximate MVA and the changes to Linearizer and Bard-Schweitzer AMVA to remove most of this looping.

3.1 One Step MVA

Algorithm 2 shows one step of the main algorithm for Mean Value Analysis. The function `wait(m, k, n)` is used to calculate the residence time at queueing station m for chain k for the population vector $\mathbf{n}$. The computational cost of one-step MVA is $O(MK)$ where M is the total number of stations in the queueing model and K is the total number of chains. Exact MVA recursively performs one-step MVA for all customer populations starting from zero, using the results from a previous solution with one customer removed from a chain j in the current iteration. It becomes prohibitively expensive for moderate numbers of chains and customers.

Algorithm 2 step(n)

1: **for** $m \leftarrow 1$ to M **do** {One-step MVA}
2:   **for** $k \leftarrow 1$ to K **do**
3:     $R_{mk} \leftarrow v_{mk} \times wait(m, k, \mathbf{n})$
4:   **end for**
5: **end for**
6: **for** $k \leftarrow 1$ to K **do**
7:   $\lambda_k \leftarrow \dfrac{n_k}{Z_k + \sum\limits_{m=1}^{M} R_{mk}}$

8:   **for** $m \leftarrow 1$ to M **do**
9:     $L_{mk}(\mathbf{n}) \leftarrow \lambda_k R_{mk}$
10:   **end for**
11: **end for**

3.2 Bard-Schweitzer AMVA

Bard-Schweitzer proportional estimation AMVA [8] breaks the recursion in Exact MVA by solving the network at $\mathbf{N}$ (the full customer population). It estimates the queue lengths L_{mk} at station m for each chain k with one customer removed from chain e_j, by assuming that $L_{mk}(\mathbf{N} - e_j)$ is proportional to $L_{mk}(\mathbf{N})$, i.e:

$$L_{mk}(\mathbf{N} - e_j) = \begin{cases} L_{mk}(\mathbf{N}) & \text{for } k \neq j \\ \frac{N_j - 1}{N_j} L_{mk}(\mathbf{N}) & \text{for } k = j \end{cases}$$

Algorithm 3 shows the Bard-Schweitzer AMVA algorithm as incorporated by Linearizer. $D_{mkj}(\mathbf{N}) = 0$ is a value used to adjust the proportion one customer contributes to the length of a queue. For pure Bard-Schweitzer AMVA, $D_{mkj}(\mathbf{N})) = 0$.

Algorithm 3 core(N)

1: **repeat**
2:   {Estimate L_{mk}}
3:   **for** $m \leftarrow 1$ to M **do**
4:     **for** $k \leftarrow 1$ to K **do**
5:       $F_{mk}(\mathbf{N}) = L_{mk}(\mathbf{N})/N_k$
6:       **for** $j \leftarrow 1$ to K **do**
7:         $L_{mk}(\mathbf{N}-e_j) \leftarrow (\mathbf{N}-e_j)_k \cdot (F_{mk}(\mathbf{N}) + D_{mkj}(\mathbf{N}))$
8:       **end for**
9:     **end for**
10:   **end for**
11:   step($\mathbf{N}$) {One-step MVA}
12:   {Termination test}
13: **until** $\max\limits_{m \in M, k \in K} \dfrac{|L_{mk}^I(\mathbf{N}) - L_{mk}^{I-1}(\mathbf{N})|}{N_k} \leq \dfrac{1}{4000 + 16|\mathbf{N}|}$

3.3 Linearizer AMVA

Bard-Schweitzer AMVA often has large errors because the queue length estimate $L_{mk}(\mathbf{N} - e_j)$ is not a simple ratio of

the customers in chain j. Linearizer [2] improves the accuracy of the Bard-Schweitzer approximation by calculating a scaling factor D_{mkj} to be used to find the populations of the queues with one customer removed. Linearizer finds the scaling factors by solving the queueing network using the Schweitzer approximation at both the full customer population $\mathbf{N}$, and $\mathbf{N} - e_j$ (i.e., one customer removed from chain j) for all K chains. Algorithm 4 shows the Linearizer algorithm.

Algorithm 4 linearizer(N)

1: Initialize $L, \forall m, k$
2: **for** $I \leftarrow 1$ to 2 **do**
3:   core($\mathbf{N}$) {Step 1}
4:   **for** $c \leftarrow 1$ to K **do** {Step 2}
5:     core($\mathbf{N} - \mathbf{e}_c$)
6:   **end for**
7:   **for** $m \leftarrow 1$ to M **do** {Step 3}
8:     **for** $k \leftarrow 1$ to K **do**
9:       $F_{mk}(\mathbf{N}) \leftarrow L_{mk}(\mathbf{N})/N_k$
10:       **for** $j \leftarrow 1$ to K **do**
11:         $F_{mk}(\mathbf{N} - \mathbf{e}_j) \leftarrow L_{mk}(\mathbf{N} - \mathbf{e}_j)/N_k$
12:         $D_{mkj}(\mathbf{N}) \leftarrow F_{mk}(\mathbf{N} - \mathbf{e}_j) - F_{mk}(\mathbf{N})$
13:       **end for**
14:     **end for**
15:   **end for**
16: **end for**
17: core($\mathbf{N}$) {Step 1}

3.4 AMVA Changes

Three changes have been incorporated into the LQNS solver to speed up MVA.

1. Restart MVA from previous solution [6]: After the first iteration of Algorithm 1, values exist for the queue lengths of all stations so the initialization step at line 1 in Algorithm 4 does not need to be run again.

2. Run core($\mathbf{N} - \mathbf{e}_c$) in Linearizer only once instead of twice: The Linearizer algorithm in [2] runs the Bard-Schweitzer core() three times at the full population $\mathbf{N}$, and twice with one customer removed from chain j for all K chains. After the first run of Linearizer, the invocation of core at line 3 in Algorithm 4 will generate the same results as the last iteration of core at line 17. Therefore, for the second and subsequent invocations of Linearizer for a submodel, omit the call to core at line 3.

   The second performance improvement to Linearizer is to reduce the number of iterations of the main loop at line 2 in Algorithm 4 from 2 to 1. In effect, the main loop of linearizer is now being performed by the main loop of Algorithm 1.

3. Don't iterated core: In Algorithm 3, remove the **repeat** ... **until** loop at lines 1 and 13. Again, the main loop of Algorithm 1 can perform this step.

4. TEST CASE

In the results that follow a model of a bookstore application [4] was solved using the five layering strategies described earlier in §2.1 and using Linearizer AMVA (LIN), One-Step

MVA	Layering Strategy				
Solver	Batched	HwSw	MOL	Squashed	SRVN
Number of outer iterations.					
LIN	13	17	25	22	14
OSL	17	21	16	27	21
BSC	20	17	48	22	14
OSM	34	41	31	47	40
Calls to `wait()` $\times 10^4$					
LIN	26117	40129	87852	70247	26900
OSL	632	1036	814	1824	655
BSC	99	133	519	264	99
OSM	3	4	7	5	3
Run times (in mm:ss.cc)					
LIN	00:37	00:56	01:47	01:41	00:38
OSL	00:10	00:14	00:11	00:28	00:10
BSC	00:03	00:04	00:17	00:07	00:03
OSM	00:02	00:02	00:06	00:03	00:02

Table 1: Results for the Bookstore model.

Linearizer (OSL), Bard-Schweitzer (BSC), and One-Step MVA (OSM). Table 4 shows the number of outer iterations of Algorithm 1, the number of calls to the `wait()` function and the overall run time for each approach.

This model has a software bottleneck at task **Server-Ref_5d56d5**. The throughput of the model is the same to four digits of precision regardless of the layering strategy or whether the one-step approximation was used (Linearizer and Bard-Schweitzer do produce different results, which is not unexpected). Using the One-Step Linearizer (OSL) approximation reduces the number of calls to `wait()` by up to two orders of magnitude and using One-Step MVA (OSM) improves the performance by four orders. Run times of the solver are also improved significantly from the worst to best case.

The one-step approximation increases the number of outer iterations of Algorithm 1 for all of the layering strategies excepting MOL. The MOL algorithm solves the software submodel to convergence prior to solving the hardware model. The extra precision at the early stages of the iteration are not beneficial so the one-step variant converges more quickly overall.

5. CONCLUSIONS

This paper has examined the performance effects on the solution speed of the Layered Queueing Network Solver from using five different layering strategies and from changes to the iterative structure of approximate MVA. A performance model is solved by iterating among a set of submodels, each of which is an ordinary queuing network. The layering strategies ranged from a set of submodels, each consisting of exactly one serving station, to the opposite extreme of exactly one submodel. The case study considered in this paper showed that the final result produced by the solver was relatively insensitive to the layering approach chosen. However, the approaches that created submodels with least number of customer chains (SRVN and batched) were the least costly.

This paper also looked at improvements to the iterative structure of the queueing model solution. Three changes were made. First, rather than re-initializing the MVA so-

lution from scratch each time a submodel was solved, the iteration was started from the previous solution of the submodel. Second, the number of iterations in Linearizer's main loop were reduced, partly because of the "warm start" introduced earlier, and partly because the outer iteration of the overall algorithm was going to run multiple times. Finally, the third change was to stop iterating the "core" Bard-Schweitzer algorithm at the heart of Linearizer. Much of the work obtaining "accurate" solutions during early iterations of the outer-most loop is wasted because the parameters for a given submodel are going to change anyway due to solutions to other submodels. Using One-Step Linearizer reduced the computational effort by about two orders of magnitude. Using One-Step MVA further reduced the cost by another two orders of magnitude.

The improvements to Approximate Mean Value Analysis described here are not limited to solutions to layered queueing networks. Rather, they can be incorporated into any solution that iterates between multiple queueing models.

Acknowledgments

This research was supported by a grant from NSERC, the Natural Sciences and Engineering Research Council of Canada.

6. REFERENCES

[1] Y. Bard. Some extensions to multiclass queueing network analysis. In M. Arato, A. Butrimenko, and E. Gelenbe, editors, *Performance of Computer Systems*. North-Holland, Amsterdam, 1979.

[2] K. M. Chandy and D. Neuse. Linearizer: A heuristic algorithm for queueing network models of computing systems. *Commun. ACM*, 25(2):126–134, Feb. 1982.

[3] G. Franks, T. Al-Omari, M. Woodside, O. Das, and S. Derisavi. Enhanced modeling and solution of layered queueing networks. *IEEE Trans. Softw. Eng.*, 35(2):148–161, Mar.–Apr. 2009.

[4] T. Israr, M. Woodside, and G. Franks. Interaction tree algorithms to extract effective architecture and layered performance models from traces. *J. Syst. and Soft.*, 80(4):474–492, Apr. 2007.

[5] P. A. Jacobson and E. D. Lazowska. Analyzing queueing networks with simultaneous resource possession. *Commun. ACM*, 25(2):142–151, Feb. 1982.

[6] M. Mroz and G. Franks. A performance experiment system supporting fast mapping of system issues. In 4th *International Conf. on Performance Evaluation Methodologies and Tools*, Pisa, Italy, Oct. 20–22 2009.

[7] J. A. Rolia and K. A. Sevcik. The method of layers. *IEEE Trans. Softw. Eng.*, 21(8):689–700, Aug. 1995.

[8] P. Schweitzer. Approximate analysis of multiclass closed networks of queues. In *Proc. International Conference on Stochastic Control and Optimization*, Amsterdam, 1979.

[9] C. M. Woodside, J. E. Neilson, D. C. Petriu, and S. Majumdar. The stochastic rendezvous network model for performance of synchronous client-server-like distributed software. *IEEE Trans. Comput.*, 44(8):20–34, Aug. 1995.

Integrating Software Performance Curves with the Palladio Component Model

Alexander Wert
SAP Research
Vincenz-Priessnitz-Str. 1
Karlsruhe, Germany
alexander.wert@sap.com

Jens Happe
SAP Research
Vincenz-Priessnitz-Str. 1
Karlsruhe, Germany
jens.happe@sap.com

Dennis Westermann
SAP Research
Vincenz-Priessnitz-Str. 1
Karlsruhe, Germany
dennis.westermann@sap.com

ABSTRACT

Software performance engineering for enterprise applications is becoming more and more challenging as the size and complexity of software landscapes increases. Systems are built on powerful middleware platforms, existing software components, and 3rd party services. The internal structure of such a software basis is often unknown especially if business and system boundaries are crossed. Existing model-driven performance engineering approaches realise a pure top down prediction approach. Software architects have to provide a complete model of their system in order to conduct performance analyses. Measurement-based approaches depend on the availability of the complete system under test. In this paper, we propose a concept for the combination of model-driven and measurement-based performance engineering. We integrate software performance curves with the Palladio Component Model (PCM) (an advanced model-based performance prediction approach) in order to enable the evaluation of enterprise applications which depend on a large software basis.

Categories and Subject Descriptors

C.4 [**Performance of Systems**]: Measurement techniques

1. INTRODUCTION

The performance (response time, throughput, and resource utilisation) of enterprise applications is crucial for their success. Performance directly influences the total cost of ownership (hardware and energy) as well as customer satisfaction. In order to develop performant applications, software architects need to evaluate the influence of different design alternatives on software performance, identify critical components, and plan capacities of their system early in the development cycle.

The increasing complexity of software systems makes design time performance analyses a difficult task that requires a high expertise in the system under study and performance engineering. Today's enterprise applications are built on a complex technology stack including powerful middleware platforms, different operating systems and virtualisation technologies. Furthermore, systems are placed in a software landscape with which they interact and on which they depend. The external systems largely contribute to the per-formance of an enterprise application and thus have to be considered for performance analyses. In most cases, no performance models are available for systems that have been developed over the past decades or are provided by 3rd parties. The necessary information to build performance models for these systems is not available or performance modelling is too much effort.

Model-driven performance engineering approaches [3] implement a pure top down approach and thus require performance models for all relevant parts of a system. This requirement can render their application impossible for software systems placed in a software landscape. Approaches for measurement-based performance evaluation (such as [19, 6]) require no (or at least no detailed) models of a system. However, they depend on the availability of large parts of the application and can only be applied later in the development cycle. During these stages, the evaluation of design decisions and the identification of critical components requires large and costly code changes and thus is inefficient. Other approaches combine performance prediction models with systematic measurements (such as [14, 12]) for resource demand estimation. However, these approaches still rely on knowledge about the internal structure of a system.

In this paper, we integrate model-driven and measurement-based performance prediction approaches. We introduce the concept of *software performance curves*, which describe the performance (response time, throughput, and resource utilisation) of a service or (sub-)system in dependence on its usage and configuration. Performance curves are inferred from systematic measurements using statistical methods and machine learning techniques. Performance curves characterise the response time, throughput, and resource utilisation of services which are available, but whose internal structure is unknown or too complex. To enable design-time performance analysis, we integrated performance curves into the Palladio Component Model (PCM) [4], an advanced approach for model-driven performance engineering. With the combination of model-driven and measurement-based performance analysis, software architects can evaluate design decisions, identify critical components, and plan capacities during early development stages including the effects of the system's environment.

The contribution of this paper is a concept for the integration of measurement-based and model-driven performance engineering approaches. Moreover, we introduce an interpreter of performance curves which extends the PCM model-to-text transformations that map a performance model to a discrete-event simulation.

This paper is structured as follows. Section 2 provides a brief overview of our approach. In Section 3, we present the concept of performance curves and provide an examples. Section 4 describes the integration of performance curves with the PCM. In Section 5, we describe related research. Finally, Section 6 concludes this paper.

2. OVERVIEW

In model-driven performance engineering (survey in [3] and [10]), architectural models of a software system are annotated with performance-relevant information such as resource demands and branching probabilities. These models are transformed to analytical models, such as stochastic Petri nets, stochastic process algebras, and queueing models (overview in [5]) or to discrete-event simulations [15, 13].

For the integration of model-driven and measurement-based performance analysis, we assume that some parts of the system are already available (for example, 3rd party services or software artefacts) and other parts are newly developed. The performance analysis follows the process shown in Figure 1.

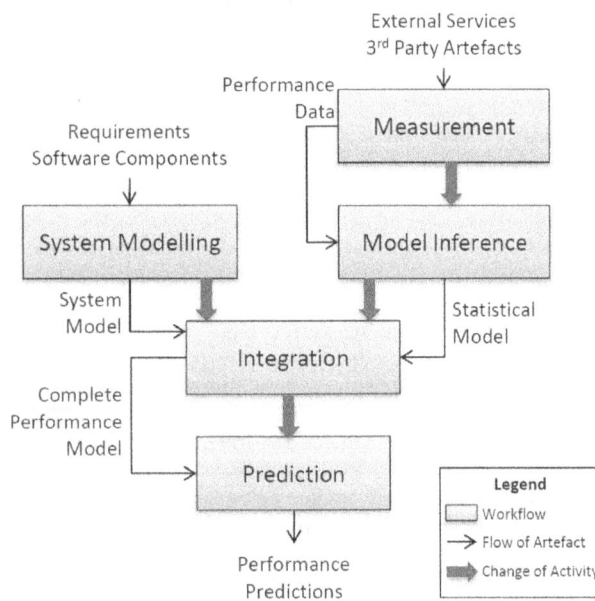

Figure 1: Overview of integrating model-driven and measurement-based performance analysis.

For the newly created parts, we can apply the standard approach for model-driven performance engineering [11]. Software architects specify the system's components, behaviour, deployment, and usage (*System Modelling*). This activity results in a *System Model* that describes the newly developed parts as well as its usage. In order to consider the effect of existing parts in performance analysis, we need to include them in the prediction model. However, modelling existing (sub-)systems can be difficult if the system has been developed by or is provided by a 3rd party. For in-house components, performance modelling can also become a difficult task due to the complexity and heterogeneity of systems. However, existing systems can be measured (*Measurement*) resulting in *Performance Data* of the system. Such data can be used for *Model Inference*. In this step, statistical methods

and machine learning techniques derive a model of the system that describes its performance properties on an abstract level. Such models can be either simple performance models (such as used in [12]) or arbitrary statistical models (such as used in [7]). To consider the effect of system external parts on performance, these models have to be integrated with or made available in model-driven prediction approaches (*Integration*). This step merges both model types and creates a common basis for further performance analysis (*Prediction*). Based on the *Performance Predictions*, software architects and performance analysts can decide about design alternatives, plan capacities, or identify critical components. In the following section, we introduce the concept of *performance curves* illustrating it on an example.

3. SOFTWARE PERFORMANCE CURVES

In most cases, the necessary information to build performance models for 3rd party software systems is not available. Thus, we propose to specify the timing behaviour of such systems by more abstract models called *performance curves*. A performance curve describes the performance metrics of interest (e.g., response time) in dependence on a set of input parameters (e.g. number of requested table rows).

Formally, a performance curve describes the performance $\mathcal{P}$ (response time, throughput, and resource utilisation) of a system in dependence on a set of input parameters $A_1, \ldots, A_n$ with $n \in \mathbb{N}$. It is a function $f: A_1 \times A_2 \times \ldots \times A_n \to \mathbb{R}$, where each input parameter A_i is a number ($\subset \mathbb{R}$), an enumeration, or a boolean value. The function's result represents the performance metric of interest. A performance curve is inferred from systematic measurement of a software system using statistical methods [8], such as symbolic regression or multidimensional interpolation techniques like Kriging.

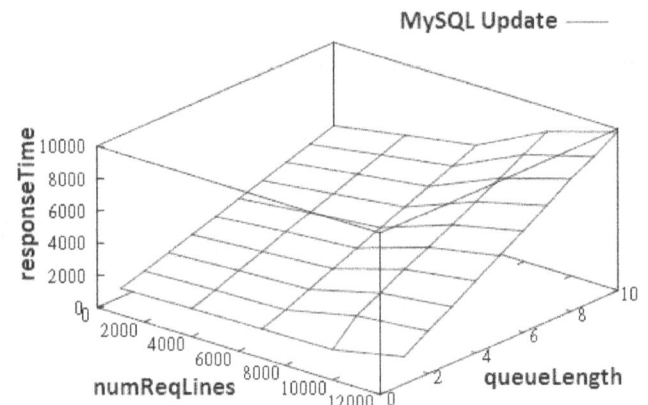

Figure 2: Performance curves for Apache Derby and MySQL.

In Figure 3, we depicted a simple example for a performance curve with two input parameters. Therefore, we measured the response time of a database systems' (MySQL 5.5 [1]) update operation in dependence of the queue length and the number of requested rows. We measured the response times for a queue length of 1 to 10 (step size 1) and for a number of requested rows between 1 and 12,000 (step size 3000). This example should only illustrate the idea behind performance curve. In most cases, accurate perfor-

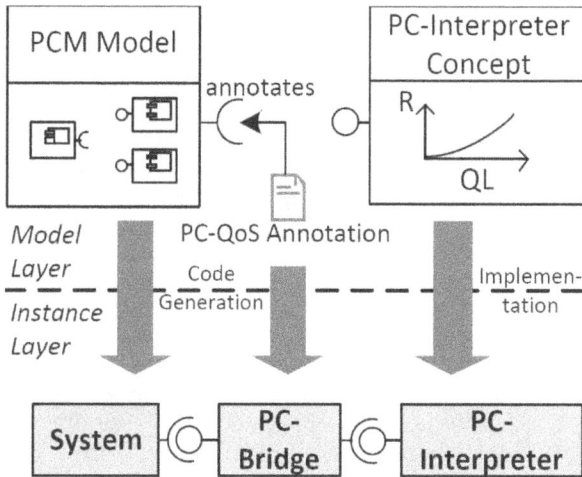

Figure 3: Integrating performance curves using QoSAnnotations.

mance curves of real software systems are much more complex and high dimensional. For the measurements, we used the *Software Performance Cockpit* [17, 16] applying the *FullExplorationStrategy*, which measures the performance of all combinations of possible parameter values. More sophisticated and efficient strategies have been presented in [18].

4. INTEGRATION CONCEPT

In the following, we introduce our concept for integrating performance curves with the Palladio Component Model and describe our extension of the transformations that map PCM-instances to a discrete-event simulation called SimuCom (for details about SimuCom see [4]).

We can integrate a performance curve into a component-based architecture using three different approaches: i) A performance curve models latencies and thus could be modelled as a specific kind of resource, ii) a performance curve describes the performance of a black-box component and thus could be specified as special components, and iii) performance curves model external services and components considering no further service dependencies and thus could specify the performance of system external calls. The first two approaches have significant drawbacks. Resources cannot provide the complex interfaces needed to capture the parameter dependencies of performance curves. Therefore, the first approach is not applicable. Furthermore, the performance of software components depends on their usage, deployment, and external services. Performance curves are currently not parametrised for arbitrary deployments or for the exchange of external services. Therefore, the second approach can lead to erroneous models and inaccurate predictions. In the following, we describe the integration of performance curves with model-driven prediction approaches as system external calls (iii).

Figure 3 gives an overview of the integration of performance curves into the PCM. At the model layer (top of Figure 3), PCM models with a system required role indicate their dependency on an external system. The external system is a black-box, whose internal structure and behaviour is unknown but a performance curve is available. To integrate a performance curve as an external system into the

PCM, we extend its quality of service annotations (*QoSAnnotations*). *QoSAnnotations* specify the performance of system external calls by annotating the *RequiredRoles* and corresponding signatures of the required interface. We introduce the new annotation type *PerformanceCurveQoSAnnotation* (called *PC-QoSAnnotation* in Figure 3) which references the *RequiredRole* to be annotated and a *PerformanceCurveSpecification* (in the following called PC-SPEC) which describes the performance curve. Thus, the *PerformanceCurveQoSAnnotation* contains the information necessary to link the required role of the system to the performance information captured by the performance curve.

We designed and implemented a performance curve interpreter concept (*PC-Interpreter Concept*) providing an interface which is linked to the PCM's simulation. A *PC-Interpreter* (bottom right in Figure 3) loads a performance curve, determines response times and simulates delays. Essentially, the *PC-Interpreter* contains the generic logic for performance curve integration. A bridge (*PC-Bridge*) implements the logic necessary for adapting the application specific interfaces to the interface of the *PC-Interpreter*. This is necessary since the simulation-code generated from PCM models requires different interfaces than the *PC-Interpreter* provides. The interface and signatures which the required role of the PCM model comprises vary from case to case. Therefore, the *PC-Bridge* is generated for each application of a performance curve. In order to generate the code of the *PC-Bridge*, the *PerformanceCurveQoSAnnotation* and the contained *PerformanceCurveSpecification* are transformed to simulation code.

In the PCM, the simulation-code generation creates a Java class for each component of a system. For each SEFF-action and provided interface signature a method is generated containing the corresponding simulation code. The *PC-Bridge* can be integrated into the generated method of the external call (in the following called M) in order to redirect the simulation control flow to the *PC-Interpreter*. Then, the *PC-Interpreter* loads the specified performance curve, calculates the response time for the passed parameter values and simulates a delay. After that, the *PC-Interpreter* returns the control flow to M. The simulation engine measures the time for the execution of M, which can be used later for performance analysis and prediction.

5. RELATED WORK

In this section, we discuss research work dealing with measurement-based performance prediction and its combination with model-based approaches.

Woodside et al. [19] introduced the idea of a workbench for automated measurement of resource demands. The results are derived by function fitting and the maintenance of resource functions is done by a repository. Woodside assumes an analytical approach of performance consideration rather than using simulations. Furthermore, Woodside briefly mentions the idea of combining measurement results with system models by considering resource functions as model parameters. However, the measurements are used to refine an existing model and do not completely abstract from the internal behaviour of the (sub-)system.

Babka [2] introduced an approach for integrating (external) resource models into performance models based on queuing Petri nets. Babka also applies discrete-event simulation for performance prediction. However, in contrast to this paper, Babka focuses on low-level hardware and software resources like CPU caches or locks, whereas in our approach it does not matter whether the resource is a low-level resource like a CPU or a complex legacy system. Another difference is our assumption that the considered resource might be a black-box, i. e. the internal behaviour is unknown. A similar approach by Liu et al. [14] builds a queuing network model whose input values are computed based on benchmarks. The goal of the queuing network model is to derive performance metrics for J2EE applications.

Jin et al. [9] introduce an approach called BMM that combines benchmarking, production system monitoring, and performance modelling. Their goal is to quantify the performance characteristics of real-world legacy systems under various load conditions. However, the measurements are driven by the upfront selection of a performance model (e.g layered queuing network) which is later on built based on the measurement results.

6. CONCLUSIONS

In this paper, we presented a combination of model-driven and measurement-based performance analysis. Our approach allows software architects to combine models of a software system with performance curves of existing (sub-)systems. The latter are derived by systematic measurements using the Software Performance Cockpit [17, 16]. We integrated the performance curves into the Palladio Component Model (PCM) [4]. For this purpose, we extended the discrete-event simulation (SimuCom) of the PCM with an interpreter and adapter for performance curves.

The integration of model-driven and measurement-based performance analysis allows software architects to evaluate design alternatives, plan capacities, and identify critical components of a software system even though the system depends on external services, 3rd party components or legacy systems. Having this integration in place, performance engineering becomes more applicable in practice reducing the manual effort necessary to build prediction models.

In our future work, we look into issues that arise for the measurement of complex systems. With an increasing number of parameters, the number of measurements grows exponentially ("curse of dimensionality" [8]). A first measure to reduce the complexity is to identify and focus on the relevant parameters only. For this purpose, we look into different screening techniques that rank parameters according to their influence. Moreover, the integration of performance curves into the PCM requires further extensions. For example, performance curves have to consider interaction effects with other components or performance curves that occur if they share common resources. Last but not least, we need to gather more experience applying our approach in more complex scenarios within SAP.

7. REFERENCES

[1] Mysql 5.5. last visited 04.01.2011.
[2] V. Babka. Resource Sharing in QPN-based Performance Models. In J. Safrankova and J. Pavlu, editors, In the Proceedings of WDS'08. Citeseer, 2008.
[3] S. Balsamo, A. Di Marco, P. Inverardi, and M. Simeoni. Model-Based Performance Prediction in Software Development: A Survey. IEEE Transactions on Software Engineering, 30(5):295–310, May 2004.
[4] S. Becker, H. Koziolek, and R. Reussner. The Palladio component model for model-driven performance prediction. Journal of Systems and Software, 2009.
[5] M. Bernardo and J. Hillston, editors. Formal Methods for Performance Evaluation (Int. School on Formal Methods for Design of Computer, Communication, and Software Systems, SFM2007). 2007.
[6] G. Denaro, A. Polini, and W. Emmerich. Early performance testing of distributed software applications. SIGSOFT Software Engineering Notes, 29(1):94–103, 2004.
[7] J. Happe, D. Westermann, K. Sachs, and L. Kapova. Statistical Inference of Software Performance Models for Parametric Performance Completions. In Proc. of QoSA 2010), LNCS. Springer, 2010.
[8] T. Hastie, R. Tibshirani, and J. Friedman. The Elements of Statistical Learning: Data mining, Inference ,and Prediction. Springer, 2009.
[9] Y. Jin, A. Tang, J. Han, and Y. Liu. Performance evaluation and prediction for legacy information systems. In Proceedings of 29th ICSE 2007, Washington, DC, USA, 2007. IEEE Computer Society.
[10] H. Koziolek. Performance evaluation of component-based software systems: A survey. Performance Evaluation, 2009.
[11] H. Koziolek, S. Becker, J. Happe, and R. Reussner. Life-Cycle Aware Modelling of Software Components. 5182, Oct. 2008.
[12] S. Kraft, S. Pacheco-Sanchez, G. Casale, and S. Dawson. Estimating service resource consumption from response time measurements. In Proceedings of Valuetools 2006, New York, NY, USA, 2006. ACM.
[13] P. L'Ecuyer and E. Buist. Simulation in Java with SSJ. In Proc. of the 37th Conf. on Winter Simulation, pages 611–620. WSC 2005, 2005.
[14] Y. Liu, A. Fekete, and I. Gorton. Design-Level Performance Prediction of Component-Based Applications. IEEE Transactions on Software Engineering, 31(11):928–941, 2005.
[15] B. Page and W. Kreutzer. The Java Simulation Handbook. Simulating Discrete Event Systems with UML and Java. 2005.
[16] D. Westermann and J. Happe. Software Performance Cockpit. http://www.sopeco.org/, 2011.
[17] D. Westermann, J. Happe, M. Hauck, and C. Heupel. The performance cockpit approach: A framework for systematic performance evaluations. In Proc. of the 36th EUROMICRO SEAA 2010). IEEE CS, 2010.
[18] D. Westermann, R. Krebs, and J. Happe. Efficient experiment selection in automated software performance evaluations. In EPEW '11: Proc. of the 8th European Performance Engineering Workshop, Berlin, Heidelberg, 2011. Springer.
[19] C. M. Woodside, V. Vetland, M. Courtois, and S. Bayarov. Resource function capture for performance aspects of software components and sub-systems. In Performance Engineering, State of the Art and Current Trends, London, UK, 2001. Springer-Verlag.

SPECjbb2012: Updated Metrics for a Business Benchmark

Aleksey Shipilev
Oracle Corporation
Saint-Petersburg, Russian Fed.
aleksey.shipilev@oracle.com

David Keenan
Oracle Corporation
Albany, NY, USA
david.keenan@oracle.com

ABSTRACT

SPEC [1] benchmarks have an excellent track record as useful tools for performance engineers. Many hardware vendors, software developers, and researchers continue to use SPEC benchmarks as reference workloads to characterize systems, test compiler optimizations, track performance regression tracking, and software quality.

SPECjbb2005 is the industry standard benchmark for evaluating the performance of servers running typical Java business applications. Modern customer requirements and use cases have shifted the focus of performance assessments from pure throughput to include throughput/response time and throughput/power considerations.

SPECjbb2012 is the new incarnation of SPECjbb2005, targeted to assess these new demands. This paper gives the highlights for new metrics in SPECjbb2012, the rationale behind them, and technical challenges faced in its implementation.

Categories and Subject Descriptors

D.2.8 [**Software Engineering**]: Metrics—*performance measures*

General Terms

Design, Measurement, Performance

Keywords

SPECjbb2005, SPECjbb2012, response time, max injection rate, critical injection rate

1. DESIGN CONSIDERATIONS

The design goal for SPECjbb2012 was to keep the simplicity of SPECjbb2005 [2], while addressing more requirements and use cases for the benchmark.

The classic metric in a business benchmark is *raw throughput*, which tells a lot about system capacity at its peak.

However, the emerging importance of power and response time requirements has pushed benchmark vendors to adopt new metrics.

The usual design for server-centric client/server benchmark is having one or multiple clients (*drivers*) to issue requests for one or multiple *Systems Under Test (SUT)* with some characteristic requested *injection rate (IR)*, and realistic think times delays and distributions.

The largest complication in this scheme is that clients do not have instant feedback on server utilization and capacity. Spefifically, queueing on the server side, communication latencies, delays in processing, etc. are causing delays in feedback to the client. Intelligent schemes for tuning IR, i.e. increasing IR when the server can process more, or decrease IR when the server can not, should take these considerations into account.

In the grand scheme of things, introducing an adaptive scheme into workload implies including a feedback loop, bringing the work into scope of control theory. In fact, we had experienced the predictions of control theory, when naive schemes for auto-tuning experienced semi-harmonic oscillations, or long transitional periods.

Because of that, most workloads are falling back to running at a stable, or *preset*, IR, and letting the user decide at which IR level to run. While SPECjbb2012 supports running at a preset IR to facilitate performance analysis and workload development, we considered getting maximum workload scores in this mode a tedious task for the user.

1.1 Settling Criteria

The key observation for automatic tuning of IR is that the Driver has quite a limited opportunity to infer the state of the SUT. The mere fact that the Driver's request was accepted does not imply it will get processed in a reasonable time, nor does the rejection of the Driver's request imply the SUT is unable to process more in the next time slot.

One of the naive feedback solutions to this problem is having a bounded acceptance queue on the SUT side, which will deny Driver requests from being accepted when the SUT is over-saturated. However, we observed the performance of the workload to be extremely sensitive to queue size across different JVMs, and different architectures, etc. Hence, we saw the need for a more vendor-neutral solution.

To address this, we instrumented the SUT to provide us with the actual *processing rate (PR)*, which tells us how many requests were actually processed. By comparing this with *requested IR (rIR)* we can deduce whether the SUT is capable of handling the IR we are injecting or not. Additionally, the Driver is instrumented to provide *actual IR (aIR)*, which tells how many actual requests were submitted to the system.

This enables us to change the IR dynamically, and observe whether the system had settled on new a IR by cross-comparing rIR, aIR, and PR. If those three match, then the system is running steadily on the requested IR. Discrepancies in either highlights a capacity problem with the Driver, or the SUT.

1.2 Saturating the SUT

One of the goals for SPECjbb2012 is to keep the Driver light enough so not to require large machines to feed the SUT with requests. The key observation is that once the Driver had to maintain the state for each outstanding request to the SUT, the overhead of maintaining this state grows with number of outstanding requests. Then, by Little's Law, the number of requests is growing as the product of throughput and response time.

From the implementation standpoint, this either calls for an asynchronous processing scheme with a small number of threads dealing with larger amount of clients, or a synchronous processing scheme with a huge number of threads, one per client. While asynchronous processing can solve resource problems, measuring response time requires precise timings, and waiting for someone to process asynchronous response will skew the response time measurement.

We solved this dilemma by clearly separating *probe* and *saturate* requests. Probe requests are synchronously waiting for a response, thus providing the means for measuring response time accurately. There's a bounded number of threads servicing probe requests. Saturate requests are submitted without waiting for a response; hence, the Driver threads are freed up once a saturate request is accepted, and can be recycled to submit another saturate request. Since there's no response time measurement, we are able to submit *batches* of saturate requests to further unload the Driver. There's a tradeoff between the accuracy of think time distributions maintained by Driver, and the impact of the Driver itself. Both probe and saturate requests share the same submission budget, which ensures that the Driver submission rate does not out-pace the requested IR. We have verified that this approach is able to inject several orders of magnitude more requests than the SUT had to process.

2. METRICS

2.1 Raw throughput metric: max IR

Given the mechanics above, we can gradually increase the IR within one run, and see if the system settles on it. There are some complications with warmup and steady state. The measurement is done in two phases: searching for a high-bound of maxIR (hbIR), and then searching for maxIR itself.

The schematics for hbIR searching is to grow IR exponentially, starting from some base IR:

$$IR(n) = IR_{base} + IR_{step} * \alpha^n, \alpha > 1, n \in N$$

Once we hit over-saturation, we set the base IR to the previous successful IR, and restart the search. Obviously, since base IR is always growing, and there exists the system limit on possible IR, this search converges. The mere fact we can't step upwards anymore means we had also completed warmup. Each step during this search takes a few seconds, hence hbIR is not measured in steady state.

The next phase is to measure maxIR during steady state. We have to try multiple IRs, each of those should be done in steady state, which will take some time to achieve. However, there's also the reasonable limit on run time. To fit these contradicting requirements, the workload slowly grows IR in a linear fashion, hoping for a smooth transition between steady states on consequent IRs:

$$IR(n) = IR_{hb} * \beta, \beta \in [0; 1]$$

In default mode, we are doing 1% steps with 30 sec measurement each. At some point the system will fail to settle, and the IR preceding that point will be counted as the actual maxIR. There are also retry mechanisms in place to tolerate inadvertent hiccups. We had found maxIR is within [75; 95]% of hbIR on most systems.

2.2 Response time metric: critical IR

We can reuse the data from maxIR measurement to infer response time metrics. Since probe requests are happening during search for maxIR, we are effectively gathering the response time samples on different levels of maxIR. In fact, we can build the *throughput – response time (TRT) curves*, which is the ultimate characteristic of the workload running on the system.

Point measures are still more useful as metrics, so we have to infer something from the TRT curve. In SPECjbb2012 we had settled on throughput-related metric named *critical IR*, which is defined as maximum IR, at which some service-level agreement for response time is still achieved.

By default, critical IR is measured at 100 ms response time target in the 99th percentile. However, since all response time samples are saved in the logs for the run, there are ways to post-mortem compute critical IR for different response time targets and percentile levels.

Additional methods for conditioning response time samples, like bootstrapping, are possible to provide more robust approximations for critical IR at high percentile levels.

2.3 Power metric: W/ops

Once we determine a precise maxIR, we can go for power measurement. Best practices for power measurement mandate measurement on different IR levels, going from peak IR down to essentially zero IR (so called *"active-idle state"*) [3]. This requirement does not allow us to do power measurement during TRT curve, which goes in an upward direction. However, we can dedicate another phase of the workload specifically for power measurement.

3. IMPLEMENTATION CONSIDERATIONS

3.1 Re-initialization

The major issue with changing the IR during the run is the risk of over-saturation, when the system is not able to handle the IR we are injecting. In the best case, this will grow the occupancy of the submission queues in the SUT. In the worst case, this over-saturation might impede normal operation of the SUT, knocking it off of steady state, or even drive it to an inconsistent state.

To clean up after over-saturation, the workload can invoke *re-initialization*, which will shutdown all parts of the workload except for a minimal infrastructure, ask for aggressive GCs, and then initialize the workload again. This effectively resets the system to a pristine state.

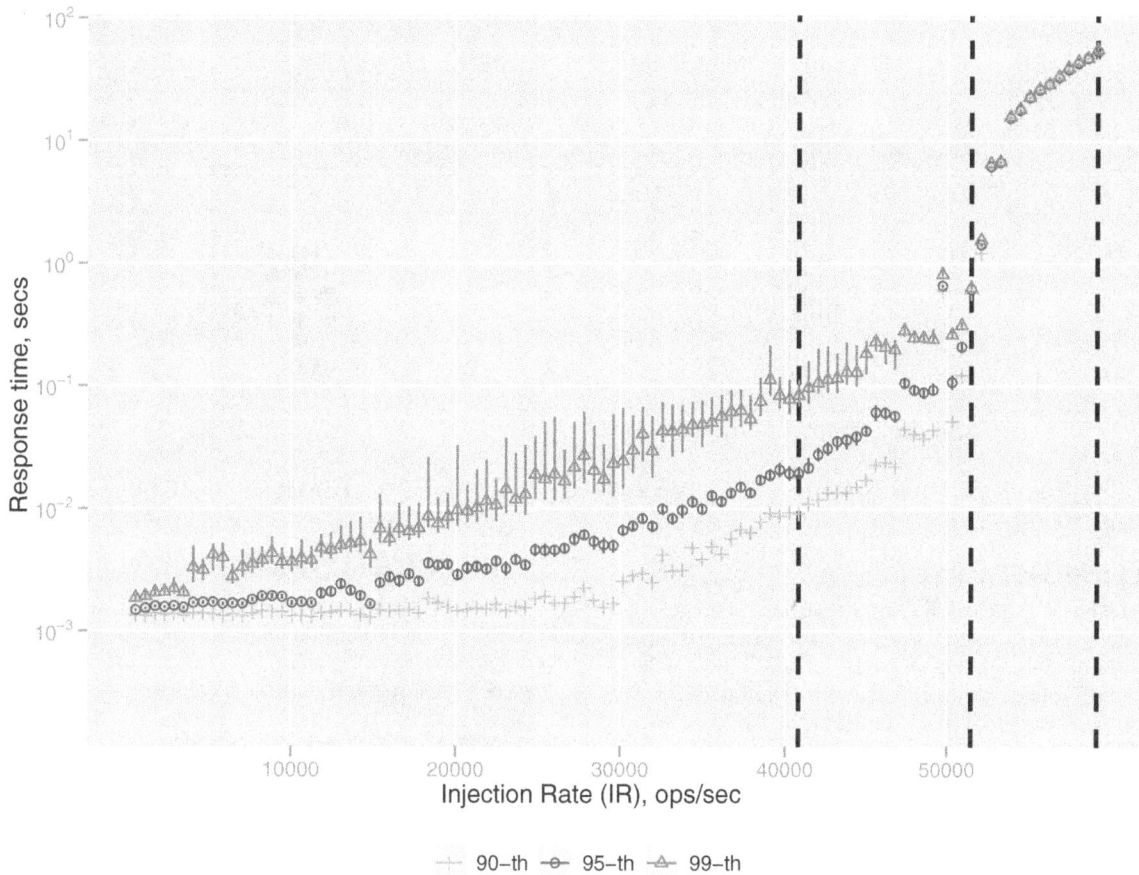

Figure 1: Typical throughput - response time curve

3.2 Snapshots

The problem with re-initialization is that it discards all the business data collected during the run, and starts over. Sometimes this is undesirable, because the data state is a part of the steady state. To account for that, the workload can *snapshot* its state at known good points during the workload lifetime, essentially serializing the state of all data structures to a binary blob, and storing it.

Given the concurrent nature of the workload, snapshots require quiescence; hence, acquiring a snapshot breaks the steady state. Combined with the cost of serializing, compressing, and writing out the snapshots, we can only afford that in several designated places in the workload.

Re-initialization uses the last available snapshot to restore the system state. Each subsequent snapshot is a better starting point should re-initialization be required.

3.3 Heartbeats

Sometimes over-saturation causes the system to go completely haywire. In these conditions, it may happen that remote communication is sometimes stalled, and the Controller's request to terminate the run might not be delivered to the JVM in question.

To address this, the *heartbeats (HB)* infrastructure is used. There are multiple HB watchdogs running in the JVMs, periodically polling each other. Once a HB watchdog fails to receive its pending heartbeats, it assumes the system has lost

control, and terminates the activity in the current JVM. It also shuts itself down, so other HB watchdogs can detect the failure. After HB failure occurs, the system can only recover with re-initialization.

While there are other ways to control the system, e.g. let the Controller reinforce the intent to run at a specific IR every once in a while, we had found the HB infrastructure to be useful in other failure modes, e.g. when one of the JVMs participating in the run crashes or suddenly dies.

4. EXPERIMENTAL STUDY

Empirical evaluation of the proposed metrics scheme is the current focus of SPECjbb2012 development. In this section, we highlight the results of one. The experimental setup was as follows:

- Intel Xeon X7560 (Nehalem-EX), 4 sockets, 10 cores per socket, 2 threads per core, running at 2.27 GHz.

- 16x 4Gb PC3-8500F DIMMs, 64 Gb total

- Oracle JDK 7 Update 2, RedHat AS 5 (64-bit)

- SPECjbb2012 beta (EOY 2011), transports disabled

- Java params: -d64 -Xmx8g -Xms8g -XX:+UseNUMA -XX:+UseConcMarkSweepGC -XX:-UseBiasedLocking

289

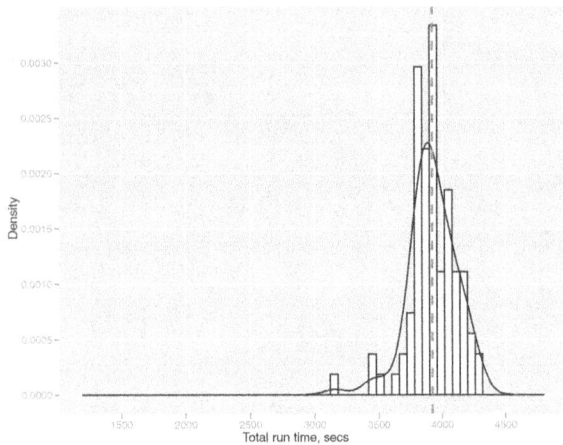

Figure 2: Total run time

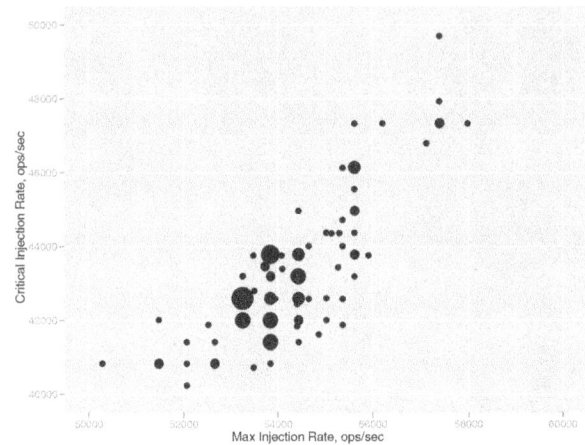

Figure 3: maxIR/criticalIR correlation

4.1 Typical TRT curve

Figure 1 shows typical TRT curve gathered during the run. Vertical dashed lines correspond to critical IR, max IR, and high-bound IR, respectively. The Y axis is log-scale, hence RT quantiles are growing at an exponential rate. Notice that the critical IR line intercepts the 99th percentile curve at 100ms target. The curve itself is rather monotonic to enable measurements on lower RT targets. Additional robust approximation schemes are suggested to remove the high-quantile jitter.

The max IR line clearly demarcates the start of over-saturation, where response times are getting orders of magnitude higher. Over-saturation is detected by failing to settle on requested IR, but the artifacts on TRT curve are visible as well.

4.2 Run time

Obviously, there's tradeoff between workload run time and accuracy. Longer workloads can afford more precise measurements, while shorter workloads provide a better user experience. SPECjbb2012 has sensible targets with regards to run times, to not exceed 2 hours, while aggressively pushing into a 1 hour envelope. Figure 2 gives the impression of usual run times for SPECjbb2012. The mean run time is close to 4.000 seconds, at least 3.600 of which takes building TRT curve.

4.3 Metrics variance

To estimate variance, we had executed 100 complete runs on the target hardware. These measurements include both intrinsic workload variance, as well as general run-to-run variance due to indeterminism in JVM behavior [4].

The results for maxIR and criticalIR are packed into Figure 3. With the default settings, maxIR is quantized in 100 levels, with the highest level equaling hbIR. Since hbIR is also variating, the number of possible values for maxIR is much larger than 100. Critical IR experiences quantization as well for the same reason.

The variance of the workload is much larger than quanta size; hence, finer steps in TRT curve seem unnecessary. We are currently investigating the reasons behind the workload variance, and what can be reasonably done in the workload to shun unwarranted sources of indeterminism.

5. FUTURE WORK

At the present moment, SPECjbb2012 development has reached the stabilization phase. More assessments are in progress, variance is being investigated, and general workload behavior on wide range of platforms is being researched.

6. ACKNOWLEDGMENTS

The authors want to acknowledge the additional members of the SPEC JAVA Subcommittee who have contributed to the design, development, testing, and overall success of SPEC benchmarks. The name SPEC together with its tool and benchmark names are registered trademarks of the Standard Performance Evaluation Corporation (SPEC).

7. REFERENCES

[1] Standard Performance Evaluation Corporation http://www.spec.org/
[2] A. Adamson, D. Dagastine, S. Sarne. SPECjbb2005 - A Year in the Life of a Benchmark.
[3] Standard Performance Evaluation Corporation. SPEC Power and Performance. Benchmark Methodology, V2.1.
[4] A. Georges, D. Buytaert, and L. Eeckhout. Statistically rigorous java performance evaluation. *SIGPLAN Not.*, 42:57–76, October 2007.

OpenCL and the 13 Dwarfs: A Work in Progress*

W. Feng, H. Lin, T. Scogland, and J. Zhang
Department of Computer Science
Virginia Tech
{feng, hlin2, njustn, zjing14}@cs.vt.edu

ABSTRACT

In the past, evaluating the architectural innovation of parallel computing devices relied on a benchmark suite based on existing programs, e.g., EEMBC or SPEC. However, with the growing ubiquity of parallel computing devices, we argue that it is unclear how best to express parallel computation, and hence, a need exists to identify a higher level of abstraction for reasoning about parallel application requirements. Therefore, the goal of this combination "Work-in-Progress and Vision" paper is to delineate application requirements in a manner that is not overly specific to individual applications or the optimizations used for certain hardware platforms, so that we can draw broader conclusions about hardware requirements. Our initial effort, dubbed "OpenCL and the 13 Dwarfs" or OCD for short, realizes Berkeley's 13 computational dwarfs of scientific computing in OpenCL, where each dwarf captures a pattern of computation and communication that is common to a class of important applications.

Categories and Subject Descriptors: *D.0 [General]; I.6.3 [Simulation & Modeling]: Applications; J.0 [General]*

General Terms: Algorithms, Benchmarking, Measurement, Experimentation.

Keywords: computational dwarfs, OpenCL, GPU, heterogeneous computing, portability.

1. INTRODUCTION

The increasing proliferation of heterogeneous computing platforms presents the parallel computing community with the challenge of evaluating the efficacy of such parallel architectures, particularly given the diversity of hardware architectures and their associated (non-interoperable) programming environments such as Cilk+ and CUDA. For instance, the graphics processing unit (GPU), which has become an increasingly popular processor, differs substantially from traditional CPU architectures. The GPU offers simpler SIMD-like processing elements to deliver extraordinary performance for data-parallel and task-parallel jobs. Its ability to support massive multi-threaded parallelism indicates its capability as a high-throughput processor versus the low-latency CPU, which is optimized for single-threaded performance.

Performance benchmark suites have been playing an important role in evaluating hardware design. However, traditional parallel benchmark suites have serious shortcomings when trying to evaluate evolving heterogeneous computing systems. First, such suites are written in programming models designed for CPUs and thus cannot be run directly on the emergent heterogeneous architectures. Second, such suites typically focus on concrete implementations of specific applications. Those applications are not necessarily sufficient for capturing future trends in parallel computing or for comprehensively exercising new heterogeneous architectures.

To address the above issues, we present *OpenCL and 13 Dwarfs* or OCD for short, a benchmark suite that aims to provide a "future-proofed" software methodology to enable the evaluation of hardware innovation across a gamut of architectures. We choose to use OpenCL because it is a standardized industry effort addressing the lack of interoperability in heterogeneous programming models. While it began as a programming model for programming GPUs, and optionally falling back on CPUs, the major processor vendors — including AMD, ARM, IBM, Intel, and NVIDIA — have either released or are developing OpenCL compilers and run-time systems. Using OpenCL as our programming model of choice will enable our benchmark suite to work well across a wide range of platforms today and into the future.

In addition, we seek to enable a fundamental re-thinking of both hardware and programming models by capturing application design via high-level computation and communication patterns. To this end, we select application kernels following computation and communication patterns from the *Berkeley 13 Dwarfs* [2]. We focus on these because they offer a diverse set of patterns, each of which is relevant across a variety of domains. For example, the n-body method is relevant across physics, chemistry, and a variety of other domains.

We are populating each dwarf with an application as a starting point. However, because no single application completely captures the breadth of a dwarf, our longer-term intent is to include multiple applications that present different aspects of a given dwarf as well as a synthetic benchmark that represents the dwarf alone (without other patterns included) to form a full application. In this way, we hope to create a set of implementations which may be used to make

---

*This work was supported in part by NSF I/UCRC IIP-0804155 (via NSF CHREC) and a DoD National Defense Science & Engineering Graduate Fellowship (NDSEG).

generalizations about the higher-level patterns and the effectiveness of a given platform for executing a given pattern.

The initial release of OCD is meant to provide functionally portable benchmarks in OpenCL and allow users to draw conclusions based on the performance of portable code. To accomplish this, we have made an effort to avoid optimizing any given benchmark specifically for a given underlying platform, and instead, focus on writing to the programming model.[1] The result is that more reasonable performance comparisons across different architectures are possible.

2. THE 13 DWARFS

Below is a brief description of each of the 13 Berkeley dwarfs, along with a description of our initial instantiation of the dwarf in OCD, if applicable.

Dense linear algebra consists of dense matrix and vector operations. It has a high ratio of math-to-load operations and a high degree of data interdependency between threads. We are finalizing a benchmark for this dwarf based on LU factorization, but for the time being, we include the k-means clustering algorithm, denoted as kmeans in OCD.

Sparse linear algebra solves the same problem as dense linear algebra but has matrices with few non-zero entries. To reduce space and computation, such algorithms store and operate on a list of values and indices rather than proper matrices, resulting in more indirect memory accesses. For OCD, we implement a pattern for matrix-vector multiplication that uses a *compressed spare row* format to store sparse matrices. As such, the implemented dwarf is denoted as csr.

Spectral methods transform data from/to either a spatial or temporal domain. The execution profile is typically characterized by multiple stages of processing, where dependencies within a stage form a "butterfly" pattern of computation. We capture this pattern via a FFT, i.e., clfft in OCD.

N-body methods calculate interactions between many discrete points and are characterized by large numbers of independent calculations within a timestep, followed by all-to-all communication between timesteps. Our GEM code [1], denoted as gemnoui in OCD, calculates the effect that all atoms have on the charge at each point along the surface of a molecule, leading to $O(M * N)$ complexity where N is atoms and M is points along the surface.

Structured grids organize data in a regular multidimensional grid, where computation proceeds as a series of grid updates. For each grid update, all points are updated using values from a small neighborhood around each point. The neighborhood is normally implicit in the data and determined by the algorithm. For OCD, we include srad, short for *speckle-reducing anisotropic diffusion*, a stencil-based pattern of computation and communication that reduces noise and enhances feature clarity in 2D images.

Unstructured grids possess data structures, e.g., linked list of pointers, that keep track of the location and 'neighborhood' of points which are used to update the location. Like sparse linear algebra, updates typically involve multiple levels of memory reference indirection, as an update to any point requires first determining a list of neighboring points, and then loading values from those neighboring points. For OCD, we include a pattern of computation and communication that is representative of an unstructured grid code for computational fluid dynamics, denoted as cfd in OCD.

MapReduce captures the repeated independent execution of a "map" function and results are aggregated at the end via a "reduce" function. No communication is required between processes in the map phase, but the reduce phase requires global communication. For OCD, we have a prototype dwarf that we dub StreamMR ("streamer").

Combinational logic exploits bit-level parallelism in order to achieve high throughput. Such a workload involves performing simple operations on very large amounts of data. For OCD, we include crc, short for cyclic redundancy check, which is used to generates hashes or signatures of files to verify their correct transfer over a network.

Graph traversal visits and evaluates a number of objects in a graph. Such algorithms typically involve a significant amount of random memory access for indirect lookups. The bottleneck is generally due to access latency rather than access bandwidth. For OCD, we include breadth-first search (bfs) and bitonic sort (bsort).

Dynamic programming solves a complex problem by solving a series of simpler subproblems. For OCD, we adopt the Needleman-Wunsch algorithm, i.e., needle in OCD. This algorithmic pattern calculates the optimal alignment of two strings by calculating scores based on all possible alignments in a matrix and backtracking along the highest scoring path.

Backtrack & branch-and-bound approaches generally search a very large search space to find a globally optimal solution. Because the search space is so large, an implicit method is needed to prune the search space to make this approach computationally tractable. For OCD, we capture the computation and communication pattern of the A* search algorithm (astar in OCD).

Graphical models map variables into nodes and conditional probabilities into edges, e.g., Bayesian networks. For OCD, we have captured this pattern of computation and communication via a hidden Markov model.

Finite state machines capture a system whose behavior is defined by states, transitions defined by inputs and the current state, and events associated with transitions or states. These dwarf algorithms are highly dependent on conditional operations and interdependent data, which are also commonly found in graph traversal. For OCD, we provide a "temporal data mining" algorithm, which discovers temporal correlations between EEG events from the brain.

3. EXPERIENCES WITH OCD

This section presents our experiences with *OpenCL and the 13 Dwarfs (OCD)* across a myriad of CPU and GPU computing platforms.

3.1 Experimental Setup

For all of our experiments, we ran OCD on a single test box consisting of two quad-core Intel Xeon E5405 CPUs, 4GB of DDR3 memory, and at any one time, a single GPU. We physically swapped between an AMD HD5450, AMD HD5870, NVIDIA GT520, and NVIDIA C2050 to ensure comparable results between the different GPU platforms. The software environment is x86_64 Ubuntu 10.04 with Linux kernel 2.6.32, using GCC 4.4.3 along with NVIDIA SDK 4.0, AMD APP SDK 2.5 RC2 and Intel OpenCL SDK 1.5. The drivers used are AMD Catalyst 11.11 and NVIDIA 290.10.

3.2 Runtime Diversity

In theory, OpenCL performance on a single piece of hardware ought to be consistent regardless of the runtime sys-

---

[1] Similarly, other benchmark suites write to MPI or a general CPU rather than to Intel SSE4 instructions, for example.

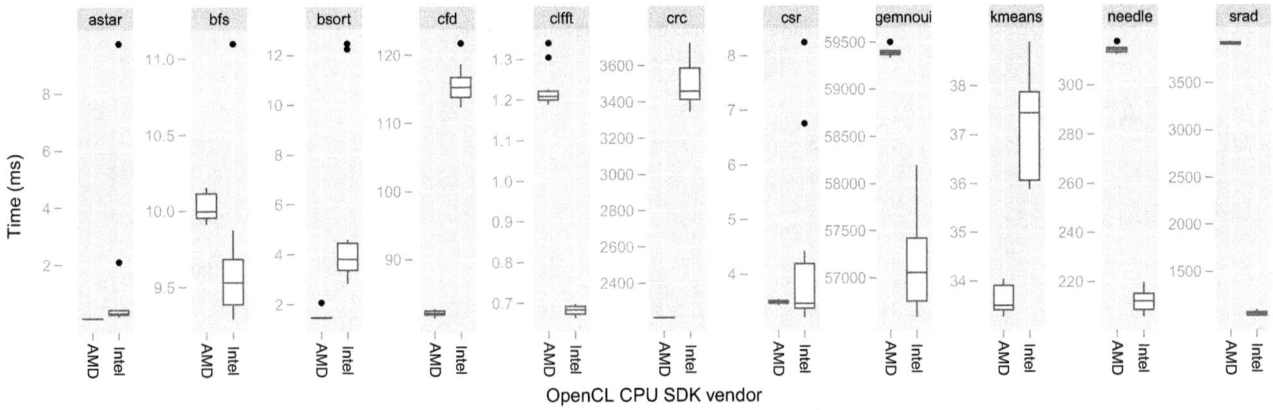

Figure 1: Time for each benchmark on two quad-core Intel Xeon CPUs across OpenCL CPU runtimes from AMD and Intel for all implemented dwarfs. Each box represents the interquartile range with a line at the median, whiskers reach to the data point closest to 1.5x the interquartile range outside of the middle 50 percent without going over, and dots are those points which fall past that mark.

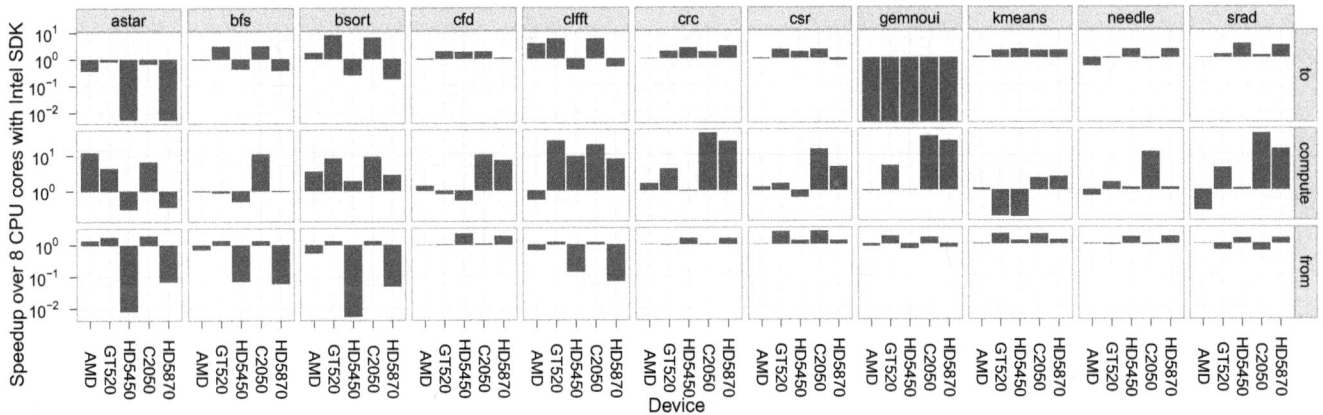

Figure 2: Speedup of the three segments of each application, i.e., data transfer to the device, computation on the device and data transfer back from it, over the Intel OpenCL SDK on eight Intel Xeon cores.

tem; but in practice, this is rarely the case. To illustrate this point, we compared the performance of our OCD across two different SDKs, namely the AMD OpenCL SDK and the new Intel OpenCL SDK, while running on *identical* hardware. Figure 1 shows the empirical results.

Since our experimental platform consisted of a pair of Intel Xeon CPUs, the initial expectation was that Intel's SDK would either match AMD's or outperform it for each case, but that was not the case. For example, the *combinational logic* dwarf performed approximately 50% faster on the AMD SDK than on the Intel SDK. In addition, the performance of the Intel SDK was much more erratic than with the AMD SDK. In some cases, like astar and csr, the performance range spanned an order of magnitude more than the range of the results using the AMD SDK. In general, the results show that the more compute-intensive applications performed better with the Intel SDK while the data-transfer-heavy applications perform better with AMD. Overall, what the above tells us is that the compiler and runtime of a system can have a significant effect on realized performance.

3.3 Architecture Diversity

For an ecosystem like OpenCL, which works across multiple architectures, there exists a wide diversity in the capabilities of the underlying architectures. To analyze the behavior of the dwarfs across such diverse platforms, we collected performance results across all the OCD benchmarks running on the aforementioned devices. Figure 2 presents the results as speedup over the Intel SDK CPU results, on a log_{10} scale. The devices in these plots are grouped by type — CPU, low-power GPUs, and high-power GPUs. The GT520 and C2050 are low-power and high-power NVIDIA GPUs, respectively, while the HD5450 and HD5870 are low-power and high-power AMD GPUs, respectively.

The results show that the performance profiles of OCD are quite diverse, not only with respect to the compute time, but also transfer times to and from the device. In fact, we were surprised by the spread of the results for data transfer times. For virtually all of the dwarfs, the data transfer time from the CPU to the GPU was actually shorter than the transfer from the CPU "to" the CPU; the same held true for pulling the data back. The notable exception to this was the Intel SDK version of GEM (i.e., gemnoui), the n-body dwarf from OCD. The code for data transfer in GEM uses the hinting available in OpenCL to specify that the host buffer supplied by the user should be used directly by the OpenCL runtime system, if possible, rather than treating it as a source for a copy. Only the Intel SDK, however, actually honors that

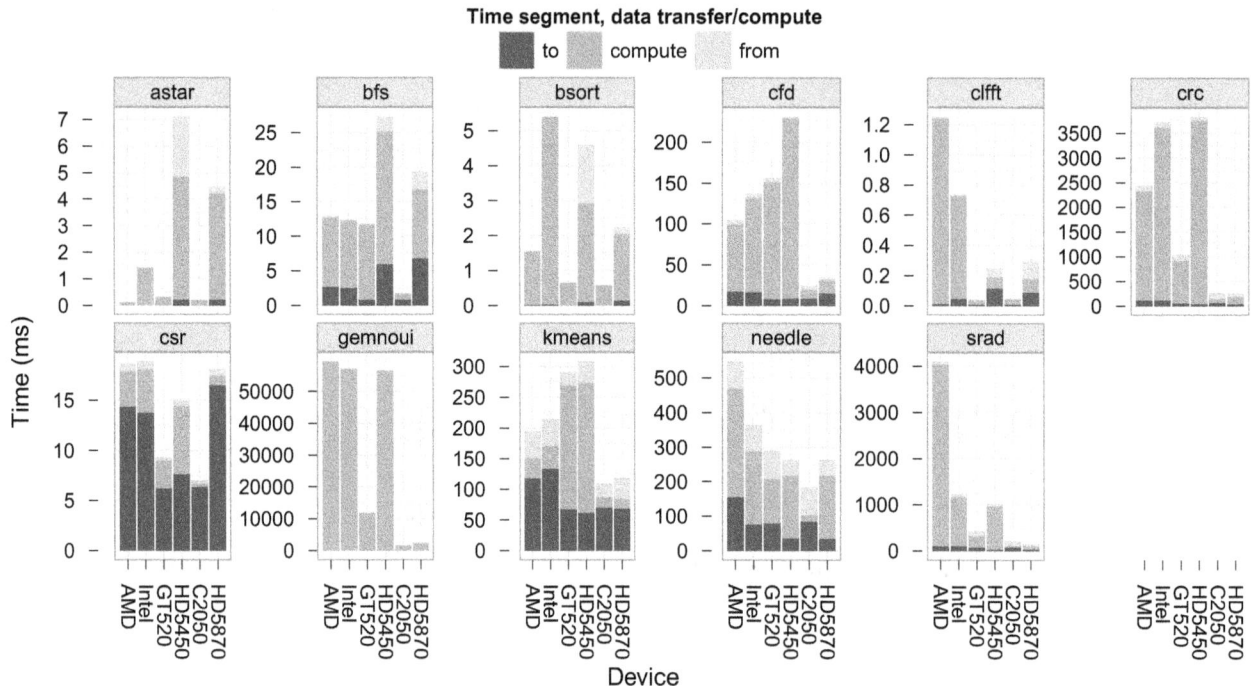

Figure 3: Absolute runtime for all implemented dwarfs across all platforms.

request; the end result is that the transfer time "to" the CPU is extraordinarily small. So, the question remains as to why the data transfer from CPU to GPU across PCIe is generally faster than from one location in CPU memory to another location in CPU memory, a subject of future work.

Relative to both compute time and transfer time, the GPUs from each vendor exhibit similar behavior for certain features, e.g., the performance of data transfer from AMD GPUs for astar, bfs, and bsort. Perhaps more surprising are the anomalies. For instance, the clfft dwarf is the only one for which using low-power GPUs is faster than the high-power GPUs. This particular implementation of FFT is written in such a way that it is highly dependent on the performance of a single processing unit on the GPU rather than the aggregated performance of all the processing units in a GPU. In turn, this seems to favor the smaller GPUs.

In addition to the normalized results, we also present the absolute results as a stack, as shown in Figure 3. While this represents the same data as in Figure 2, it encompasses more devices and allows one to more easily compare the distribution of the actual time spent on data movement and computation for each of the dwarfs. In this case, the times can range from well over 50% data transfer (csr) to over 99% computation (gemnoui). Also interesting is how the performance profile changes from platform to platform. For example, astar spends almost no time to transfer data to or from NVIDIA GPUs but spends significantly more time doing so on the AMD GPUs.

4. CONCLUSION AND FUTURE WORK

In writing and testing the OCD benchmarks, we have found the Berkeley dwarfs to be an effective way to select and classify benchmarks. Using OCD, we have found significant diversity in the applications, architectures, and runtime environments.

Overall, we believe that OpenCL and the 13 Dwarfs will provide a useful baseline for the evaluation of platforms and runtime systems across application domains. In the future, we will continue populating each dwarf with representative applications as well as investigate architecture-aware optimization techniques for the included benchmarks. We are also investigating the possibility of packaging a subset of the OCD to the SPEC High Performance Group (SPEC HPG).

5. AVAILABILITY

The initial release of OCD, currently being beta-tested by selected members of the NSF Center for High-Performance Reconfigurable Computing (CHREC), includes benchmarks representing 11 of the 13 patterns, with the rest to follow in the near future. It has been tested across a multitude of parallel computing architectures including multicore CPUs, graphics processing units (GPUs), accelerated processing units (APUs), i.e., AMD's fused CPU+GPU on a die, and soon, field-programmable gate arrays (FPGAs). It is slated for open-source deployment to the community in April 2012.

6. REFERENCES

[1] R. Anandakrishnan, T. Scogland, A. Fenley, J. Gordon, W. Feng, and A. Onufriev. Accelerating Electrostatic Surface Potential Calculation with Multi-Scale Approximation on Graphics Processing Units. *J. Molecular Graphics and Modelling*, June 2010.

[2] K. Asanovic, R. Bodik, B. Catanzaro, J. Gebis, P. Husbands, K. Keutzer, D. Patterson, W. Plishker, J. Shalf, S. Williams, and K. Yelick. The Landscape of Parallel Computing Research: A View from Berkeley. Technical Report UCB/EECS-2006-183, EECS Department, University of California, Dec. 2006.

Automatic NUMA Characterization using Cbench*

Ryan Braithwaite
Los Alamos National
Laboratory
Los Alamos, NM, USA
rkbrait@lanl.gov

Wu-chun Feng
Dept. of Computer Science
Virginia Tech
Blacksburg, VA, USA
feng@cs.vt.edu

Patrick McCormick
Los Alamos National
Laboratory
Los Alamos, NM, USA
pat@lanl.gov

ABSTRACT

Clusters of seemingly homogeneous compute nodes are increasingly heterogeneous within each node due to replication and distribution of node-level subsystems. This intra-node heterogeneity can adversely affect program execution performance by inflicting additional data-access costs when accessing non-local data. In this work-in-progress paper, we present extensions to the Cbench Scalable Testing Framework for analyzing main memory and PCIe data-access performance in modern NUMA architectures. The information provided by this tool will be of use for task scheduling, performance modeling, and evaluation of NUMA systems.

Categories and Subject Descriptors

C.1.2 [**Processor Architectures**]: Multiple Data Stream Architectures (Multiprocessors)

Keywords

NUMA, Benchmarking, System Analysis

1. INTRODUCTION

Non-uniform memory access (NUMA) architectures are the de facto standard for servers today. The wholesale shift toward the replication and distribution of system resources is driven by the need to increase memory and I/O bandwidth to satisfy more cores simultaneously accessing data. In NUMA systems, resources local to a processor exhibit the uniform access bandwidth and latency to which programs that are designed for uniform memory access (UMA) systems are accustomed. However, resources that are remote to a processor may be subject to significantly worse bandwidth and latency data-transfer characteristics. Differences in the designs of NUMA architectures may result in substantially different data-access performance for each architecture.

When non-local resources are accessed frequently, data-access latency and bandwidth in modern NUMA architectures can significantly affect program performance. For applications that are sen-

sitive to data-access performance, it may be critical for a system designer or application developer to understand the NUMA characteristics of the system in which the program is executed so as to avoid remote data accesses as much as possible.

We propose the use of empirical micro-benchmark data to provide data-access performance information to assist with NUMA system analysis. To run these tests in a deterministic and automated fashion, we present the addition of NUMA testing to the Cbench Scalable Testing Framework [1] [8].

The purpose of this paper is to present the characterization of data-access performance in modern NUMA server architectures using Cbench. The report generated by our new tool provides a straightforward method for comparing data-access attributes in NUMA systems. This knowledge may be used to improve application behavior in NUMA systems, improve system configurations, model the performance of applications in specific NUMA systems, and be used by run-time schedulers to improve program execution efficiency.

Our contributions are two-fold: *NUMA system characterization* and the initial implementation of *NUMA data-access performance extensions to the Cbench Scalable Testing Framework*. For the former, we present methods for data-access *bandwidth* characterization in modern NUMA architectures using open-source micro-benchmarks. This characterization analyzes CPU interconnect links and PCIe interconnect lanes to describe the bandwidth capabilities of a NUMA system. For the latter, we present the addition of our NUMA system characterization tests to the Cbench cluster testing framework in order to assist with the analysis of NUMA architectures.

This tool provides a straightforward method for analyzing and comparing data-access performance across thousands of nodes in a cluster or single stand-alone nodes, as necessary. While other NUMA tools analyze only the hierarchy of NUMA memory nodes in a system, our Cbench tool allows for analysis of the hierarchy, performance, and hardware design of a NUMA system.

2. RELATED WORK & BACKGROUND

The characterization of a NUMA system is typically thought of in terms of the hierarchy of memory nodes and the *distance* between nodes. The libnuma [4] and hwloc [2] projects describe NUMA systems in this manner, including the distance to additional hardware resources such as PCIe-based interfaces for networking and graphics.

Both tools rely on the Linux /proc and /sys kernel filesystems to determine NUMA hierarchy information for a system. The NUMA distance data reported by libnuma is derived by the kernel from the BIOS ACPI tables and may be wrong or incomplete. The hwloc project interrogates these kernel filesystems to provide the programmer with other architectural details of a system in addi-

---

* This work was supported in part by NSF I/UCRC IIP-0804155 via the NSF Center for High-Performance Reconfigurable Computing and Los Alamos National Laboratory via the Accelerated Strategic Computing program of the Department of Energy. Los Alamos National Laboratory is operated by Los Alamos National Security LLC for the US Department of Energy under contract DE-AC52-06NA25396.

tion to the ACPI-based NUMA distance information presented by `libnuma`. The notion of NUMA distance only takes into account which nodes are connected to each other. Modern NUMA designs, such as AMD's Magny-Cours and Interlagos architectures, have variable-width CPU interconnect links and therefore exhibit different bandwidth for links of the same NUMA distance.

To provide the *performance* details necessary to describe these newer systems, we build upon existing tools and libraries by measuring the performance for data-access operations between memory nodes and between memory nodes and PCIe devices, specifically GPUs. Our primary goal in characterizing NUMA systems is to quantify the data-access performance of each type of data access that is possible in a system so that the impact of the hierarchy on a system's performance is better understood.

As a case study, we examine the AMD Magny-Cours two-socket (2P) architecture shown in Figure 1. This system has two sources of

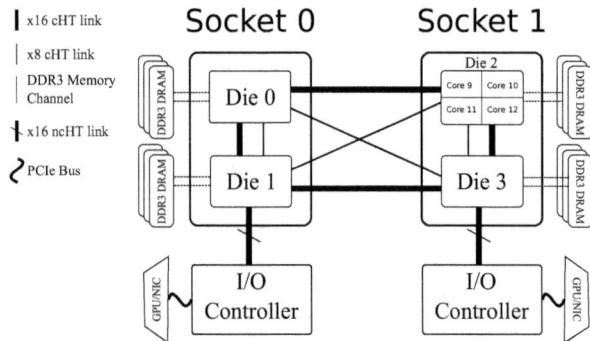

Figure 1: AMD Socket G34 2P Architecture

NUMA performance complexity: the CPU package, consisting of two CPU dies, three levels of cache, and wires in a socket; and the HyperTransport (HT) interconnect links between CPUs and other components. This increased complexity results in substantial data-access heterogeneity despite the fact that it is only a 2P design.

3. CBENCH AS A NUMA ANALYSIS TOOL

Cbench is a benchmark utility framework developed at Sandia National Laboratories and designed for HPC system integration engineers and analysts. The Cbench framework consists of a toolkit of Perl and Bash scripts that manage the building of supported open-source benchmarks from source code and the creation, submission, and analysis of benchmark jobs on Linux HPC clusters. In addition, Cbench provides basic statistical analysis to compare benchmark results for nodes in a cluster so that machines with substandard performance may be automatically identified. Running benchmark programs in Cbench provides a robust and straightforward method for executing identical tests on evaluation machines in order to compare performance.

Cbench is also used to evaluate new systems and architectures. The Cbench Single-Node-Benchmark (SNB) script runs node-level tests and produces a LaTeX report showing the baseline performance of a given system.

3.1 Previous Cbench Capabilities

The main focus of the Cbench framework is to run benchmark jobs across a large number of nodes in a Linux cluster to test various attributes of the system. Benchmark tests run within Cbench are generally divided into cluster-level MPI-based tests (e.g. `Linpack`, OSU Bandwidth Benchmarks, NAS Parallel Benchmarks) and node-level serial or parallel tests (e.g. `STREAM`, `memtester`, node-level `Linpack`). The NUMA data-access characterization effort

presented in this paper is focused on node-level data-access bandwidth, so we focus on the node-level portion of Cbench.

3.2 Integrating NUMA Testing and Analysis

Our goal is to enable comprehensive NUMA performance analysis using Cbench. As a starting point, we extended the Cbench framework to characterize the single-threaded data-access bandwidth of NUMA systems. This characterization is achieved by running benchmark programs using the possible data-access scenarios for a given system and partition the results into *bandwidth classes*, or equivalence classes of data-access bandwidth, based on the empirical results.

We automate these data-access characterization tests by adding the capability to run benchmarks in a NUMA-aware fashion (i.e., running benchmarks with CPU scheduler and memory allocation policies explicitly set) to the SNB script in Cbench. This included adding the ability to detect bandwidth equivalence classes from the data produced by these benchmark tests to the Cbench SNB scripts. Table 1 summarizes our additions to Cbench.

Table 1: Capabilities of Cbench Versions

	OLD CBENCH	NUMA CBENCH
MPI-level	✓	✓
Node-level	✓	✓
NUMA Memory		✓
NUMA PCIe+GPU BW		✓
NUMA BW Classes		✓

3.2.1 Data-Access Bandwidth Benchmarks

We use the STREAM [6] [7] benchmark to determine memory-access bandwidth between CPU cores and memory nodes, interconnect links, memory controller overhead, and memory technology (e.g., DDR3). STREAM executes four types of memory-access operations on a large data array: Add, Copy, Scale, and Triad. Triad is similar to operations found in many scientific applications, so we report only Triad results.

We use components of the Scalable HeterOgeneous Computing (SHOC) benchmark suite [3] to characterize PCIe data-access bandwidth. The data-access performance of a device connected by PCIe I/O links in a system such as that shown in Figure 1 is a function of traversing the PCIe links, the HT CPU interconnect links from CPUs to PCIe devices, controllers and chipsets along the CPU-to-PCIe path, and the specific PCIe device that contains the requested data. We present the analysis of high-performance GPUs transferring data across the PCIe interconnect to requesting processors in the system shown in Figure 1 and described in Table 3. The CPU-to-I/O controller affinity shown by these tests also applies to other PCIe devices, though the reported absolute bandwidth for other devices may differ.

Analysis of data transfers for a GPU connected by PCIe involves measuring the download rate (writing to GPU memory) and the readback rate (reading from GPU memory) when transferring data between the host CPU core and the GPU device. To measure these rates, we use the `BusSpeedDownload` and `BusSpeedReadback` tests in the SHOC benchmark suite. These tests measure the bandwidth of the link(s) between host processor and GPU device by transferring data payloads of varying size to (download) and from (readback) the GPU device. Systems configured with NVIDIA GPUs can run both CUDA and OpenCL code, and in some cases, the PCIe bandwidth reported by the CUDA and OpenCL versions of SHOC vary. Cbench is configured to run both versions, though we only report CUDA results in this paper.

3.2.2 Testing Data-Access Bandwidth

Benchmarking every data-access scenario in a NUMA system entails mapping benchmark processes and their memory in every possible configuration that a program might encounter during execution. For modern many-core systems, mapping processes to individual cores greatly expands the set of core-to-node combinations that must be tested. To test all processor-core-to-memory-node combinations, $p \times m$ tests must be executed, where p is the number of CPU cores and m is the number of memory nodes in a system and where $p >> n$. However, cores that are attached to the same memory node show virtually identical memory bandwidth when accessing data on a given memory node (see Table 2), so core-to-node testing is unnecessary. We therefore allow the process scheduler to choose to schedule a process on any core attached to a memory node (i.e. any core on the same die). Such a process-to-node mapping reduces the number of tests to $m \times m$ and is done at run-time using the `numactl` tool for both STREAM and SHOC benchmarks. This ensures that the host CPU process is executed on the appropriate cores and that its memory is bound to the appropriate memory node.

For PCIe tests, it is technically only necessary to characterize one set of core/memory node combinations because GPU memory transfers use pinned memory. This means that the location of the pinned memory, not the location of the host CPU process, is the determining factor in the data-access performance for GPU programs. Nevertheless, for completeness the download and readback rates for each of the node-to-device combinations in a system are gathered by Cbench and organized into bandwidth equivalence classes, similar to the results of the STREAM benchmarks.

3.2.3 Addition of NUMA Tests to Cbench

We extend the SNB script to characterize data accesses in NUMA systems by running a given program from all cores to all memory nodes or from all memory nodes to all memory nodes and binding CPU and memory affinity as described in Section 3.2.2. This solution has the benefit of providing NUMA characterization capability to any of the node-level tests already supported by Cbench. Cbench builds many varieties of the STREAM benchmark; using versions from different compilers only requires instructing Cbench to build the benchmarks with the appropriate compiler.

GPU benchmark support in Cbench is in the early stages of development, and the addition of the SHOC PCIe bandwidth tests to the Single-Node-Benchmark script provides the first complete GPU testing capability for Cbench. These SHOC tests facilitate PCIe data-access characterization similar to the STREAM tests discussed previously.

3.2.4 Automatic Bandwidth Class Detection

A critical component of our data-access bandwidth analysis is the synthesis of *bandwidth classes* from a system's benchmark results. We employ the `Algorithm::KMeans` Perl module implementation of K-Means clustering [5] to provide automatic bandwidth classification of the benchmark results gathered by Cbench. To prepare the data for K-Means analysis, we first process the results for all iterations of each STREAM or SHOC benchmark version that was executed by Cbench and use only the best result for each

data-access scenario. Pruning the data in this manner improves the accuracy of the K-Means algorithm by preventing cluster detection for results that are produced by poorly-optimized benchmark executables and not actual bandwidth classes. Once the data are pruned, the K-Means algorithm is used to determine the best clusters for the benchmark dataset.

There are two elements of the K-Means cluster algorithm that are of paramount concern: the number of clusters in the data (K) and the initial cluster center values. This algorithm automatically tries all values of K where $2 \leq K \leq \sqrt{\frac{N}{2}}$ and N is the number of data points for a given data set. The value of K with the best ratio of $\frac{avg.\ cluster\ radius}{avg.\ dist.\ btw.\ cluster\ centers}$ is returned as the number of clusters in the data. The upper bound for K was set by the module developer and has been sufficient for our purposes. The choice of the initial cluster center values for each K is the most critical aspect of proper bandwidth class detection using K-Means. The initial cluster centers are chosen using random data points, which means that the quality of the final classification is somewhat random. For a first effort at automating the process of data-access classification this randomness is acceptable, but we intend to improve the accuracy and determinism of the classification process.

3.3 Cbench NUMA Characterization Results

Cbench SNB NUMA Report. Tables 4 and 5 show the LATEX report for memory and PCIe data-access bandwidth results produced by the Cbench SNB script for the system described in Table 3. As noted previously, the best results for each type of data access are used to determine the bandwidth classes shown in Table 4. The tables generated by Cbench are useful for comparing versions of a benchmark, as well as for checking the configuration of the machine. For example, the PCIe results in Table 5 show that both GPU devices are local to memory nodes 0 and 1 (i.e. both GPUs are local to socket 0), meaning that both are accessed through the same I/O controller and that the system may be misconfigured.

4. CONCLUSION

Next Steps. The NUMA data-access performance characterization work in this paper focused on a two-socket AMD system. Systems with much more heterogeneous architectures are available today, and analyzing these systems is one of the primary focuses of our next development effort. Furthermore, other aspects of NUMA-related data-access performance such as data-access latency, network I/O, and disk I/O will be incorporated into Cbench to provide a more comprehensive analysis of data-access performance.

The work presented in this paper focused exclusively on single-threaded analysis of data-access bandwidth. We have the initial implementation of multi-threaded memory bandwidth tests using an MPI version of STREAM already in Cbench. The analysis of sharing data-access resources among multiple threads is key to predictive performance modeling in NUMA systems. As we further develop our multi-threaded testing ability, we are also working to develop data-access performance models using both single-threaded and multi-threaded system characterization data from Cbench to model the performance of applications in NUMA systems by taking into account a program's data-access profile and the performance

Table 2: Core-to-Memory-Node STREAM TRIAD Results
Test run 30 times from each core 0-3 to each memory node

To Mem. Node	Mean BW	Std. Dev.
0	8.1 GB/s	0.020
1	5.1 GB/s	0.013
2/3	3.0 GB/s	0.023

Table 3: Configuration of the AMD 2P Test System

CPU Model	Magny-Cours 6134
CPU Cores/Mem. Nodes	16/4
Motherboard	Supermicro H8DGG
GPUs (#)	Tesla C2050 (2)
Linux Kernel	2.6.18-194.17.4.el5

Table 4: **Data-Access Bandwidth Classes as determined by Cbench for AMD 2P NUMA System**

BW Class	STREAM Triad (GB/s)	BusSpeedDownload (GB/s)	BusSpeedReadback (GB/s)
0	$3.92 < BW \leq 6.44$	$5.32 < BW \leq 5.85$	$5.33 < BW \leq 6.58$
1	$2.18 < BW \leq 3.92$	$2.35 < BW \leq 5.32$	$2.32 < BW \leq 5.33$
2	≤ 2.18	≤ 2.35 GB/s	< 2.32

Table 5: **NUMA STREAM and SHOC Bandwidth Test Results**

STREAM Triad (GB/s) – best value in each column is highlighted									
	CPU: Node 0	CPU: Node 0	CPU: Node 0	CPU: Node 0	$\cdots$	CPU: Node 3	CPU: Node 3	CPU: Node 3	CPU: Node 3
	Mem: Node 0	Mem: Node 1	Mem: Node 2	Mem: Node 3	$\cdots$	Mem: Node 0	Mem: Node 1	Mem: Node 2	Mem: Node 3
stream-big-c	6.40	3.91	2.16	2.15	$\cdots$	2.13	2.14	3.92	6.32
stream-big-f	6.11	3.78	2.14	2.11	$\cdots$	2.11	2.10	3.79	6.11
stream-c	5.32	3.35	2.18	2.15	$\cdots$	2.15	2.13	3.88	5.34
stream-f	5.35	3.35	2.17	2.13	$\cdots$	2.15	2.12	3.90	5.37
stream-gcc-c	6.12	3.88	2.15	2.14	$\cdots$	2.14	2.15	3.89	6.28
stream-gcc2-c	6.38	3.91	2.15	2.12	$\cdots$	2.12	2.12	3.91	6.14

SHOC CUDA PCIe Bandwidth Tests (GB/s) – values colored according to BW class									
Device 0									
BusSpeedDownload	5.85	5.32	2.35	2.32	$\cdots$	5.81	5.32	2.35	2.30
BusSpeedReadback	6.58	5.32	2.31	2.28	$\cdots$	6.58	5.28	2.31	2.28
Device 1									
BusSpeedDownload	5.81	5.32	2.35	2.32	$\cdots$	5.81	5.32	2.35	2.30
BusSpeedReadback	6.58	5.30	2.31	2.29	$\cdots$	6.58	5.27	2.31	2.28

penalties associated with remote data accesses in a given system. Task scheduling may also be improved by maximizing data-access performance using the data we generated by Cbench.

Summary. By adding NUMA data-access bandwidth characterization, the Cbench Single-Node-Benchmark script is now a useful tool for analyzing NUMA data-access performance. We presented this promising and extensible tool using single-threaded memory and GPU benchmarks to characterize data-access bandwidth in modern NUMA systems and we will continue to develop additional characterization tests as we look at other factors affecting data-access performance.

5. REFERENCES

[1] Cbench. http://cbench.sourceforge.net, Aug. 2011.

[2] F. Broquedis, J. Clet-Ortega, S. Moreaud, N. Furmento, B. Goglin, G. Mercier, S. Thibault, and R. Namyst. hwloc: A Generic Framework for Managing Hardware Affinities in HPC Applications. In *18th Euromicro International Conference on Parallel, Distributed and Network-Based Processing (PDP)*, pages 180 –186, 2010.

[3] A. Danalis, G. Marin, C. McCurdy, J. S. Meredith, P. C. Roth, K. Spafford, V. Tipparaju, and J. S. Vetter. The Scalable Heterogeneous Computing (SHOC) Benchmark Suite. In *3rd Workshop on General-Purpose Computation on Graphics Processing Units*, GPGPU '10, pages 63–74, New York, NY, USA, 2010. ACM.

[4] A. Kleen. A NUMA API for Linux. Technical report, SUSE Labs, April 2005.

[5] S. Lloyd. Least Squares Quantization in PCM. *Information Theory, IEEE Transactions on*, 28(2):129–137, March 1982.

[6] J. D. McCalpin. STREAM: Sustainable Memory Bandwidth in High Performance Computers. Technical report, University of Virginia, Charlottesville, Virginia, 1991-2007. A continually updated technical report. http://www.cs.virginia.edu/stream/.

[7] J. D. McCalpin. Memory bandwidth and machine balance in current high performance computers. *IEEE Computer Society Technical Committee on Computer Architecture Newsletter*, pages 19–25, Dec. 1995.

[8] J. Ogden. Cbench: A Software Toolkit for Testing, Benchmarking, and Qualifying HPTC Linux Clusters. Technical report, Sandia National Laboratories, Accessed August 2011.

Automated Detection of Performance Regressions Using Statistical Process Control Techniques

Thanh H. D. Nguyen, Bram Adams,
Zhen Ming Jiang, Ahmed E. Hassan
Software Analysis and Intelligence Lab (SAIL)
School of Computing, Queen's University
Kingston, Ontario, Canada
{thanhnguyen,bram,zmjiang,ahmed}@cs.queensu.ca

Mohamed Nasser, Parminder Flora
Performance Engineering
Research In Motion (RIM)
Waterloo, Ontario, Canada

ABSTRACT

The goal of performance regression testing is to check for performance regressions in a new version of a software system. Performance regression testing is an important phase in the software development process. Performance regression testing is very time consuming yet there is usually little time assigned for it. A typical test run would output thousands of performance counters. Testers usually have to manually inspect these counters to identify performance regressions. In this paper, we propose an approach to analyze performance counters across test runs using a statistical process control technique called control charts. We evaluate our approach using historical data of a large software team as well as an open-source software project. The results show that our approach can accurately identify performance regressions in both software systems. Feedback from practitioners is very promising due to the simplicity and ease of explanation of the results.

Categories and Subject Descriptors

D.2 [**Software/Program Verification**]: Statistical methods; C.4 [**Performance of Systems**]: Measurement techniques; H.3 [**Systems and Software**]: Performance evaluation (efficiency and effectiveness)

General Terms

Performance engineering, load testing, statistical control technique

1. INTRODUCTION

Performance regression testing is an important task in the software engineering process. The main goal of performance regression testing is to detect performance regressions. A performance regression means that a new version of a software system has worse performance than prior versions. After a development iteration of bug fixes and new features, code changes might degrade the software's performance. Hence, performance engineers must perform regression tests to make sure that the software still performs as good as previous versions. Performance regression testing is very important to large software systems where a large number of field problems are performance related [19].

Performance regression testing is very time consuming yet there is usually little time allocated for it. A typical test run puts the software through a field-like load for an extended period of time, during which performance counters are collected. The number of counters is usually very large. One hour of a typical test run can produce millions of samples for hundreds of performance counters, which require a large amount of time to analyze. Unfortunately, performance regression testing is usually performed at the end of the development cycle, right before a tight release deadline; allowing very little time for performance engineers to conduct and analyze the tests.

Control charts is a statistical control technique that has been widely used in manufacturing processes [16] where quality control is essential. A manufacturing process has inputs, i.e., raw materials, and output, i.e., products. Control charts can detect deviations in the output due to variations in the process or inputs across different manufacturing runs. If there is a high deviation, an operator is alerted.

A software system is similar to a manufacturing process. There are data inputs, e.g., the load inputs, and data outputs, e.g., the performance counters. When performance regressions occur, the output performance counters deviate. A control chart can potentially be applied to compare performance regression tests where the process inputs are the load, e.g., page requests on a web server, and the process outputs are performance counters, e.g., CPU utilization or disk IO activities. Unfortunately, control charts have two assumptions about the data that are hard to meet in a performance regression test. First, control charts assume that the outputs, i.e., performance counters, have a uni-modal normal distribution, since deviations are defined from the mean of such a distribution. Second, control charts assume that the load inputs do not vary across runs. If the inputs are different, the counters would fluctuate according to the inputs. Since both assumptions do not hold for performance load tests, it seems that control charts cannot be applied to this domain as is.

In this paper, we propose an approach that customizes control charts to automatically detect performance regressions. It addresses the two issues with the assumptions mentioned above. To evaluate our approach, we conduct a case study on a large enterprise software system and an open-source software system. Feedback from practitioners indicates that the simplicity of our approach is a very important factor, which encourages adoption because it is easy to communicate the results to others.

The contributions of this paper are:

- We propose an approach based on control charts to identify performance regressions.

- We derive effective solutions to satisfy the two assumptions of control charts about non-varying load and normality of the performance counters.

- We show that our approach can automatically identify performance regressions by evaluating its accuracy on a large enterprise system and an open-source software system.

The paper is organized as follows. In the next section, we introduce control charts. Section 3 provides the background on performance regression testing and the challenges in practice. Section 4 describes our control charts based approach, which addresses the challenges. In Section 5, we present the two case studies, which evaluate our approach. Section 6 summarizes the related work and the feedback from practitioners on our approach. We conclude in Section 8.

2. CONTROL CHARTS

2.1 What Are Control Charts?

Control charts were first introduced by Shewhart [16] at Bell Labs, formerly known as Western Electric, in the early 1920s. The goal of control charts is to automatically determine if a deviation in a process is due to common causes, e.g., input fluctuation, or due to special causes, e.g., defects. Control charts were originally used to monitor deviation on telephone switches.

Control charts have since become a common tool in statistical quality control. Control charts are commonly used to detect problems in manufacturing processes where raw materials are inputs and the completed products are outputs. We note that, despite the name, control charts is not just a visualization technique. It is a statistical technique that outputs a measurement index called violation ratio.

Figure 1(a) and 1(b) show two example control charts. The x-axis represents time, e.g., minutes. The y-axis is the process output data. For this example, we monitor the response rate of a web server. The two solid lines are the Upper Control Limits (UCL) and Lower Control Limit (LCL) in between which the dashed line in the middle is the Centre Line (CL). Figure 1(a) is an example where a process output is within its control limits. This should be the normal operation of the web server. Figure 1(b), on the other hand, is an example where a process output is out-of-control. In this case, operators should be alerted for further investigation.

2.2 Construction of Control Charts

A control chart is typically built using two datasets: a baseline dataset and a target dataset.

The *baseline dataset* is used to create the control limits, i.e., LCL, CL, and UCL. In the example of Figure 1(a) and 1(b), the baseline set would be the response time of the web server

in the previous hour, previous day, or any past operation periods. The CL is the median of all samples in the baseline dataset during a particular period. The LCL is the lower limit of the normal behaviour range. The UCL is the upper limit. The LCL and the UCL can be defined in several ways. A common choice is three standard deviations from the CL. Another choice would be the 1th, 5th, or 10th percentiles for the LCL and 90th, 95th, or 99th percentiles for the UCL. For example: there are eleven response time readings of 3, 4, 5, 6, 7, 8, 9, 10, 11, 12, and 13 milliseconds in the baseline set. If we use the 10th and the 90th percentile as control limits, the LCL, CL, and UCL would be 4, 8, and 12 respectively.

The *target dataset* is then scored against the control limits of the baseline dataset. In Figure 1(a) and 1(b), the target data are the crosses. Those would be the response time of the current operating periods, e.g., the current hour or day.

The result of an analysis using control charts is the *violation ratio*. The violation ratio is the percentage of the target dataset that is outside the control limits. For example, if the LCL and the UCL is 4 and 12 respectively, and there are ten readings of 4, 2, 6, 2, 7, 9, 11, 13, 8, and 6, then the violation ratio is 30% (3/10). The violation ratio represents the degree to which the current operation is out-of-control. A threshold is chosen by the operator to indicate when an alert should be raised. A suitable threshold must be greater than the normally expected violation ratio. For example, if we choose the 10th and the 90th percentile as control limits, the expected violation ratio is 20%, because that is the violation ratio when scoring the baseline dataset against the control chart built using itself. So, the operator probably wants to set a threshold of 25% or 30%.

2.3 Assumptions of Control Charts

There are two basic assumptions of control charts:

Non-varying process input. Process output usually fluctuates with the process input. If the process input rate increases, the violation ratio will increase and an alert will be raised independent of how the system reacts to the fluctuation input. Such alert would be a false positive because it does not correspond to a problem. So, the first condition for applying control charts is the stability of the process input.

Normality of process output. Process output usually has a linear relationship with the process input. This linear relation leads to a normal distribution of the process output which is the main underlying statistical foundation of control charts. However, some manufacture processes take multiple types of input, each of which individually still output a normal distribution. However, the combination of these inputs would have a multi-modal distribution, which is impossible to compare using control charts.

In the following sections, we explain in details why these assumptions are hard to meet in performance regression testing. We will give examples for each assumption and propose solutions to adapt the performance counters such that we can apply control charts to detect performance regressions.

3. PERFORMANCE REGRESSION TESTING

Performance regression test is a kind of load test that aims to detect performance regressions in the new version of a software system. A performance regression means that the new version uses more resources or has less throughput than

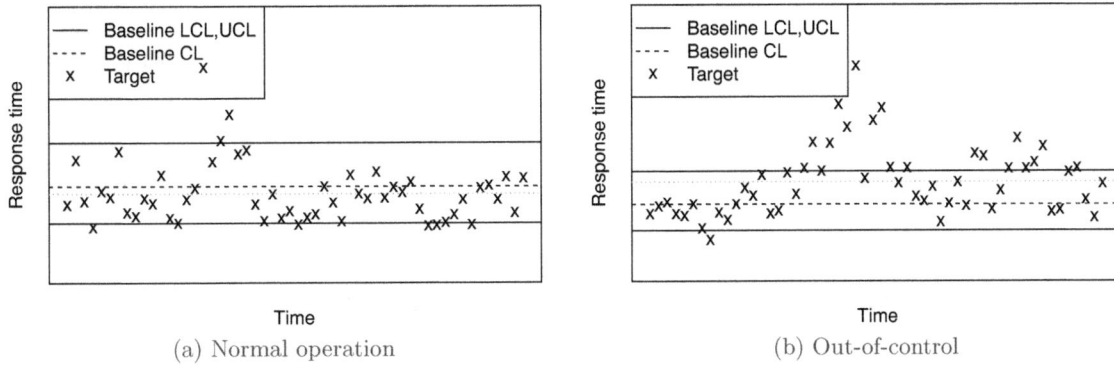

Figure 1: Example of a control chart, which detects deviation in process output.

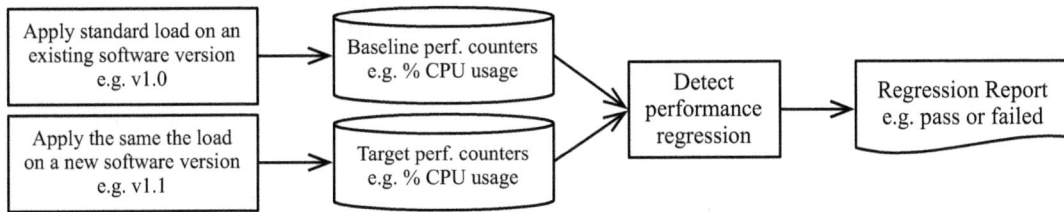

Figure 2: Conceptual diagram of performance regression testing.

prior versions. We note the difference between performance regression testing and stress testing (which is not the focus of this paper). The goal of stress testing is to benchmark the maximum load a software system can handle. The goal of a performance regression testing, on the other hand, is to determine if there is a performance regression between software versions at a normal field-like load. Figure 2 shows a conceptual diagram of a performance regression testing process which is very similar to other regression testing (e.g, functional regression testing).

Apply the load. Both the existing version and the new version are put through the same load input. The load input is usually called a load profile which describes the expected workload of the system once it is operational in the field [1]. A load profile consists of the use case scenarios and the rate of these scenarios. For example, a commercial website should process 100 page requests/sec. So the test engineers would use a load generator to create 100 pages requests/sec which are directed to the web server under test. This rate is maintained for several hours or even a few days. To mimic real life, the rate is applied using a randomizer instead of applying it in a constant fashion.

During the test, the application is monitored to record the execution logs and performance counters data. In our case, we are only interested in performance counters. A load test typically collects four main types of performance counters:

- CPU utilization: the percentage of utilized CPU per thread (in percentage).

- Memory utilization: the used memory (in megabytes).

- Network IO: the amount of network transfer (in and out - in megabytes).

- Disk IO: the amount of disk input and output.

Detect performance regressions. After the tests are done, the test engineers have to analyze the performance counters. They compare the counters of the new version with the existing version. The runs/counters of the existing version are called the baseline runs/counters. The runs/counters of the new version are called the target runs/counters. If the target counters are similar to the baseline counters, the test will pass, i.e., there is no performance regression. Otherwise, the test engineers will alert the developers about the potential of performance regression in the new version. For example, if the baseline run uses 40% of CPU on average and the target run uses 39% of CPU on average, the new version should be acceptable. However, if the target run uses 55% of CPU on average, there is likely a performance problem with the new version.

3.1 Challenges in Detecting Performance Regressions

There is already good commercial support for executing performance regression test and recording performance counters. HP has the LoadRunner software [9], which can automatically simulate the work load of many network protocols. Microsoft also has a load test tool, which can simulate load on web sites or web services. The tool is offered as part of the Visual Studio suite [14]. On the other hand, detecting performance regression is usually done manually.

Challenge 1: Many performance counters to analyze.

In large software systems, e.g., Google search engine or large web server farms, there are many components across several machines. The total number of counters are in the thousands with each counter being sampled at a high rate leading to millions of data samples to analyze. Comparing the counters to find performance regressions is very time consuming.

301

Challenge 2: Inconsistent performance counters across test runs.

A big assumption in performance regression testing, as conceptualized in Figure 2, is that the performance counters will be the same if the software does not change. Thus, if the baseline run uses X% of CPU and target run also uses X%, then there is no change in the performance, i.e., there are no performance regressions. On the opposite side, if the target run uses >X% of CPU, then there is likely a performance regression. The assumption here is that X% is a fixed number.

In a large software system, the output performance counters might be different due to the nondeterministic nature of the system. For example, a web server would cache the recently accessed web pages to improve performance. If there is a high burst of page requests at the beginning of a test run, the performance of the rest of the run will be remarkably better than if the high burst happens at the end of the run, because the cache would be filled faster in the former case. Hence, five different baseline runs can yield 57%, 65%, 62%, 56%, and 60% of CPU utilization. Although all the runs average at about 60%, it is not clear if 60% should be the baseline to compare against when a new version of the software is tested. If the new version's run yields a 65% CPU utilization, can we be certain that there is a performance regression? After all, there is one baseline run that uses 65% CPU.

To eliminate uncertainty, every time a new test run is performed, the testers usually have to rerun the old version test right after so they can compare between the two runs. The extra run is very time consuming.

4. A CONTROL CHARTS BASED APPROACH TO DETECT PERFORMANCE REGRESSIONS

A good approach to detect performance regressions should address the two aforementioned challenges from the previous section.

Trubin et al. [18] proposed the use of control charts for infield monitoring of software systems where performance counters fluctuate according to the input load. Control charts can automatically learn if the deviation is out of a control limit, at which time, the operator can be alerted. The use of control charts for monitoring inspires us to explore them for the study of performance counters in performance regression tests. A control chart from the counters of previous test runs, may be able to detect "out of control" behaviours, i.e., deviations, in the new test run. The difficulty though is that we want to detect deviations of the process, i.e., the software system, not the deviations of the input, i.e., the load.

Figure 3 shows a conceptual overview of our proposed control charts based approach. For each counter, we use the counters in all the baseline runs, i.e., the runs of prior versions, to determine the control limits for the control chart. Then, we score the target run using those limits. The resulted violation ratio is an indicator of performance regressions in the new software version. If the violation ratio is high, the chance of a regression is high as well. If the violation ratio is low, the chance of a regression is low.

An approach based on control charts would address the two challenges of performance regression testing. Control charts provide an automated and efficient way to use previous baseline runs to compare against a new test run without having to perform more baseline runs (i.e., with minimal human intervention).

However, to apply control charts to detect performance regressions, we have to satisfy the two assumptions of control charts explained in Section 2: non-varying process input and normality of the output. Unfortunately, these two assumptions are difficult to meet if we use the performance counters as is. Hence we propose two preprocessing steps on the counter data before constructing the control chart. These steps are represented as the Scale and Filter processing boxes in Figure 3). In the next two subsections, we describe in detail each of the proposed solutions and evaluate their effectiveness.

4.1 Satisfying the Non-Varying Input Assumption

In performance regression testing (Figure 2), the same load is applied to both the baseline and target version. For example if the load profile specifies a rate of 5,000 requests per hour, the load generator will aim for 5,000 requests per hour in total using a randomizer. The randomization of the load is essential to trigger possible race conditions and to ensure a realistic test run. However, the randomization leads to varying inputs throughout the different time periods of a test run. The impact of randomization on the input load and the output counters increases as the system becomes more complex with many subcomponents having their own processing threads and timers. Even in the Dell DVD Store system [5] (see Section 5), which is a relatively small and simple system, the load driver employs a randomizer. This randomizer makes it impossible to get two similar test runs with the same effective load input.

If the input load are different between runs, it is difficult to identify performance regressions since the difference in the counters can be caused by the different in the input load instead of performance related changes in the code. Figure 5 shows a performance counter of two different runs coming from two successive versions of a software system (see Section 5 for more details). We divide the runs into eight equal periods of time (x-axis). The y-axis shows the median of the performance counter during that period. The red line with round points is the baseline, which is from an earlier build. The blue line with triangular points is the target, which is from the new build. According to documentation, the fixes between the two builds should not affect the performance of the system. Hence, the performance counters should be very similar. Yet, it turns out that they are different because of the variation in the effective input load due to randomization of the load. The smallest difference is 2% in the eighth period. The highest difference is 30% in the first period. On average, the difference is about 20%. The actual load inputs are about 14% different between the two runs.

4.1.1 Proposed Solution

Our proposal is to scale the performance counter according to the load. Under normal load and for well designed systems, we can expect that performance counters are proportionally linear to the load intensity. The higher the load, the higher the performance counters are. Thus, the rela-

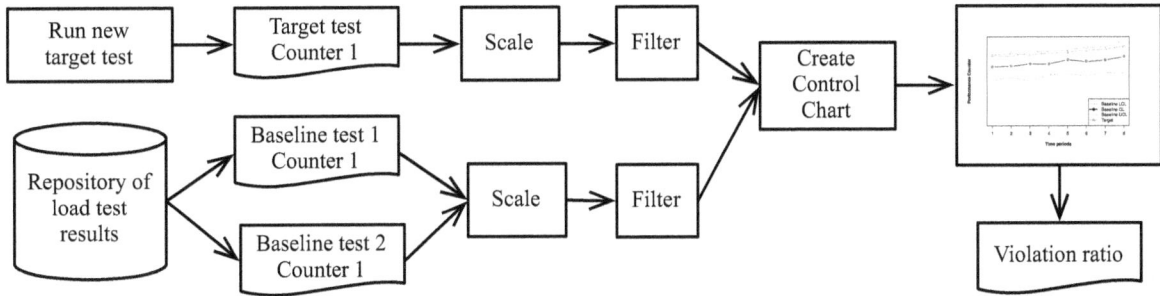

Figure 3: Outline of our approach to detect performance regression.

tionship between counter values and the input load can be described with the following linear equation:

$$c = \alpha * l + \beta \qquad (1)$$

In this equation, c is the average value of the performance counter samples in a particular period of a run. l is the actual input load in that period. α and β are the coefficients of the linear model.

To minimize the effect of load differences on the counters, we derive the following technique to scale each counter of the target run:

- We collect the counter samples (c_b) and corresponding loads (l_b) in the baseline runs. For example, in third minute the CPU utilization is 30% when the load is 4,000 requests per minute. In the next minute, the load increases to 4,100 so the CPU utilization increases to 32%.

- We determine α and β by fitting counter samples, e.g. the CPU utilization, and the corresponding load, e.g. the number of requests per second, into the linear model: $c_b = \alpha * l_b + \beta$ as in (1). The baseline runs usually have thousands of samples, which is enough to fit the linear model.

- Using the fitted α and β, we can then scale the corresponding counter of the target run (c_t) using the corresponding load value (l_t) as in (2).

$$c_t = c_b * \frac{\alpha * l_t + \beta}{\alpha * l_b + \beta} \qquad (2)$$

4.1.2 Evaluation

Evaluation Approach. The accuracy of the scaling technique depends on the accuracy of the linear model in (1). To evaluate the accuracy of the linear model, we need to use the test runs of a software system. Hence, we evaluate the accuracy on an industrial software system (see Section 5 for more information).

We run a set of controlled test runs to build the linear model as in (1). The control runs use the same stable version. We pick a different target load for each test. For example, if the first three runs have actual loads of 1,000, 1,200, and 1,000, we will aim for a load of 1,200 for the fourth run. This choice ensures that we have enough data samples for each load level, i.e., two runs with 1,000 and two runs with 1,200 in this example.

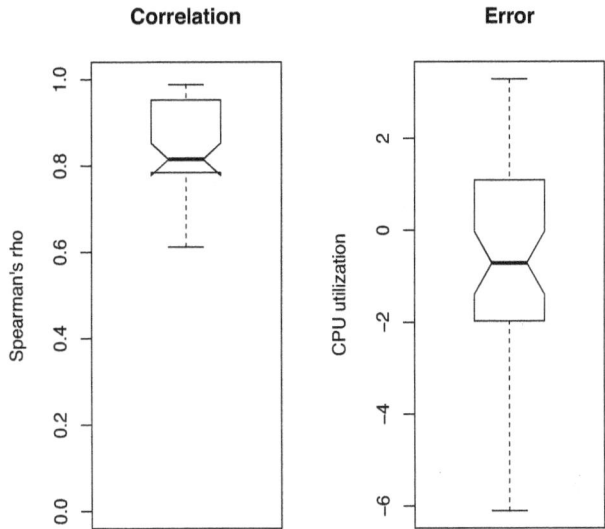

Figure 4: The accuracy of the linear model in (1). Left: The Spearman correlations between the predicted and actual performance counter values of 50 random splits. Right: The errors between the predict and actual value in percentage.

For each test run, we extract the total amount of load l and the mean performance counter c for each period of the runs. Then we train a linear model to determine α and β using part of the data. Then we can test the accuracy of the model using the rest of the data. This technique is used commonly to evaluate linear models. A common ratio for train and testing data is 2:1. We randomly sample two-thirds of the periods to train the linear model. Then we use the remaining one-third to test the model. We repeat this process 50 times to eliminate possible sampling bias.

Results. Figure 4 shows the result of our evaluation. The graph on the left is the box plot of the Spearman correlation between the predicted and the actual counter values. If the Spearman correlation nears zero, the model is a bad one. If the Spearman correlation nears one, then the model fits well. As we can see, all 50 random splits yield very high

303

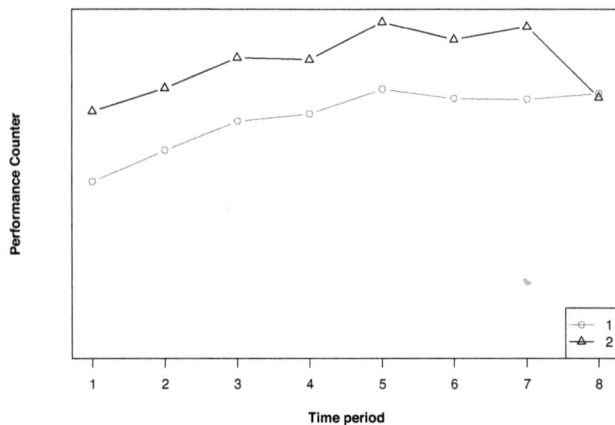

Figure 5: The performance counters of two test runs. The difference in performance is not a performance regression since both runs are of very similar builds. The difference (20% average) is due to differences in the actual load.

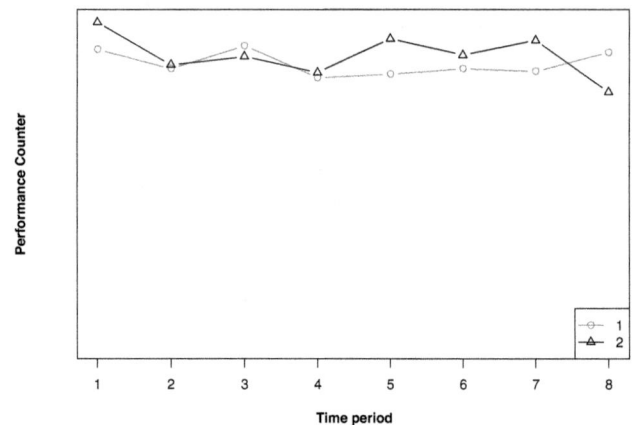

Figure 6: The scaled performance counters of two test runs in Figure 5. We scale the performance counter according to the load to minimize the effect of load differences between test runs. The average difference between the two runs is only 9% as compared to 20% before scaling.

correlations. The graph on the right is the box plot of the mean error between the predicted and the actual counter values. As we can see, the errors, which are less than 2% in most cases, are very small. These results show that the linear model used to scale the performance counters based on the actual load is very accurate.

Example. Figure 6 shows the performance counters of the two runs in Figure 5 after our scaling. The counters of the two tests are now very similar. As we can see, after scaling, the target runs fluctuate closer to the baseline test. The difference between the two runs is about 9% (between 2% to 15%) after scaling compared to 20% (between 2% to 30%) without scaling (Figure 5).

4.2 Satisfying the Normality of Output Assumption

Process output is usually proportional to the input. So the counter samples' distribution should be a uni-modal normal distribution (unless the load is pushed to the maximum, as in stress testing, the counter distribution will skew to the right).

However, the assumption here is that there is only one kind of effective load input. If there are many kinds of input, the distribution of counters would be multi-modal as we explained in Section 2.3. Figure 9 shows the normal QQ plot of a performance counter of a software under test (the Enterprise system in Section 5). If the counter is uni-modal, its samples should form a diagonal straight line. As we can see, the upper part of the data fluctuates around a diagonal straight line. However, the lower end does not. Unfortunately, the data points at the lower end are not outliers; they appear in all test runs of the software. As such, the overall distribution is not uni-modal. A Shapiro-Wilk normality test on the data confirms that with $p < 0.05$.

Figure 7 shows a density plot of a performance counter of two test runs of the same software under test. These two runs come from two successive versions. The green line

with round points is the baseline run, which is based on an older version. The red line with triangles is the target, which is from a new version. As we can see in the graph, the distribution of the performance counters resembles a normal distribution. However, the left tail of the distribution always stays up instead of decreasing to zero.

When the system is under a load, the performance counters respond to the according load in a normal distribution. However, in between periods of high load, the performance counter is zero since there is no load input. The first point on the density plot for both runs is about 4%. Hence, the performance counter is at zero for about 4% of the time during both test runs. The target run spent 5% of its time at semi-idle state (the second point from the left on the red curve). We discover that, when there is no load, the system performs book keeping tasks. These tasks require only small amounts of resources. We can consider these tasks as a different kind a load input. These secondary tasks create a second peak in the distribution curve, which explains the long tail in the QQ plot of Figure 9.

Unfortunately, this is a common behaviour. For example, on a web server, a web page would contain images. When a web page is requested by the client, the web server has to process and serve the page itself and the attached images. The CPU cycles required to process an image are almost minimal. Web pages, on the other hand, require much more processing since there might be server side scripts on them. Thus the distribution of the CPU utilization would be a bi-modal distribution. The main peak would correspond to processing the web pages. The secondary peak would correspond to processing the images.

In the software system we study, only 16% of the studied test runs are uni-modal. We confirm that these runs are, in fact, normal as confirmed by Shapiro-Wilk tests ($p > 0.05$). The majority of the runs, which is about 84%, have a bi-modal distribution similar to that of the target run in

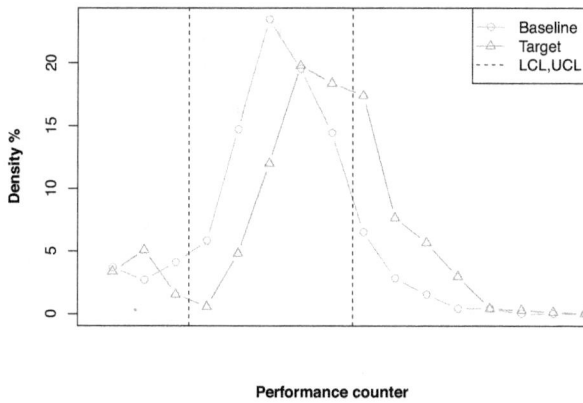

Figure 7: Density plot of two test runs.

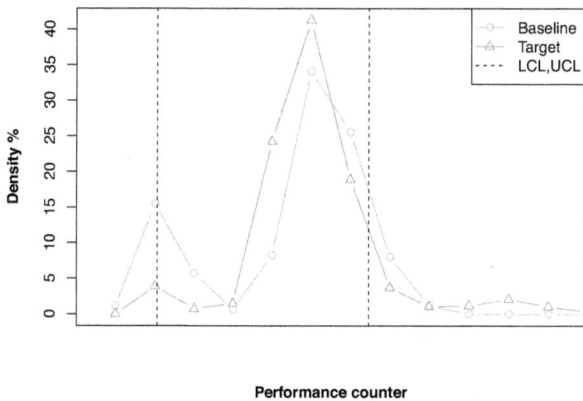

Figure 8: Density plot of another two different test runs. These two runs are on a better hardware system so the left peak is much higher than the two runs in Figure 7.

Figure 7. In the bi-modal runs, the left peak corresponds to the idle-time spent on book-keeping tasks. The right peak corresponds to the actual task of handling the load. The relative scale of the two peaks depends on how fast the hardware is. The faster the hardware, the more time the system idles, i.e., the left peak will be higher. The slower the hardware, the less time the system has to idle because it has to use more resource to process the load. The right peak will be higher and the left peak might not be there. The two runs shown in Figure 7 are on relatively standard equipment. Figure 8 shows another two test runs that are performed on better hardware configurations. As we can see, the left peaks in the density plots are more prominent in the runs with better hardware.

4.2.1 Proposed Solution

Our proposed solution is to filter out the counters' samples that correspond to the secondary task. The solution works because performance regression testing is interested in the performance of the system when it is under load, i.e., when performance counters record relatively high values. Small deviations are of no interest.

To implement the filtering solution, we derive a simple

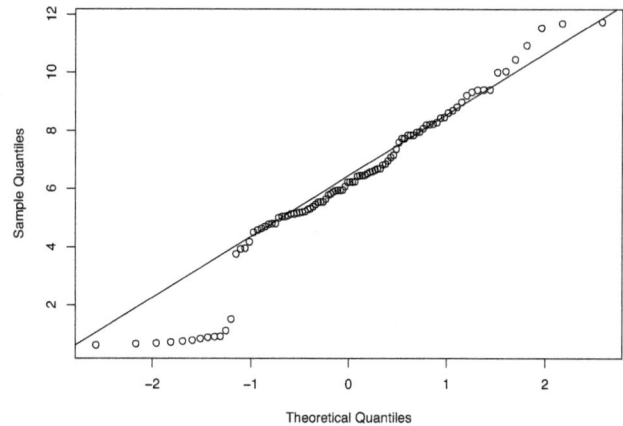

Figure 9: Normal QQ plot of CPU utilization counters. We show only 100 random samples of CPU utilization from the run to improve readability.

algorithm to detect the local minima, i.e., the lowest point between the two peaks of a bi-modal distribution. Then, we simply remove the data points on the left of the local minima. The algorithm is similar to a high pass filter in an audio system. For example, after the filtering is applied, the first three points on the target run's density plot in Figure 7 (the red line with triangles) would become zeros.

An alternative solution is to increase the load as the server hardware becomes more powerful. The increased load will make sure that the system spends less time idling and more time processing the load, thus, removing the left peak. However, artificially increase the load for the sake of normality defeats the purpose of performance regression testing and compromises the ability to compare new tests to old tests.

4.2.2 Evaluation

Evaluation Approach. To evaluate the effectiveness of our filtering technique, we pick three major versions of the software system (the Enterprise system in Section 5) that we are most familiar with. For each run of the three versions, we generate a QQ plot and run the Shapiro-Wilk normality test to determine if the runs' performance counters are normal. Then, we apply our filtering technique and check for normality again.

Results. We first manually inspect the density plots of each run in the three versions. About 88% of the runs have a bi-modal distribution. About 66% do not have a normal distribution, i.e., the Shapiro-Wilk tests on these runs return $p < 0.05$. If the left peak is small enough, it will pass the normality test. After filtering, 91% of the non-normal runs become normal. We believe this demonstrates the effectiveness of our filtering solution.

Example. Figure 10 shows the QQ plot of the same data as in Figure 9 after our filtering solution. As we can see, the data points are clustered more around the diagonal line. This means that the distribution is more normal. We perform the Shapiro-Wilk normality test on the data to confirm. The test confirms that the data is normal ($p > 0.05$). We can now use the counter data to build a control chart.

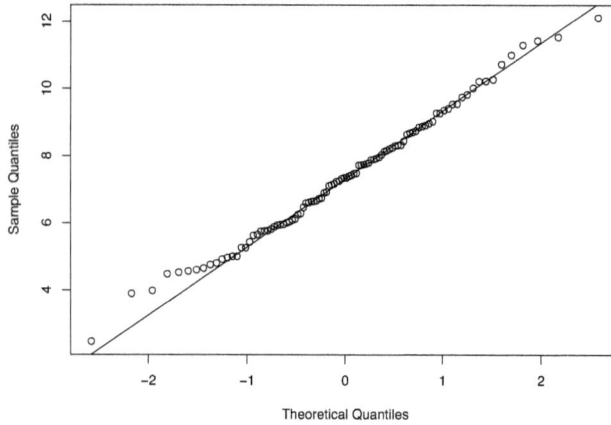

Figure 10: Normal QQ plot of the performance counters after our filtering process. The data is the same as in the QQ plot of Figure 9. After we remove the data that corresponds to the idle-time tasks, the distribution becomes normal.

5. CASE STUDIES

In this section, we describe the two case studies that we conduct to evaluate the effectiveness of our control charts based approach for detecting performance regressions.

5.1 Case Study Design

To measure the accuracy of our approach: **a)** We need to pick a software system with a repository of good and bad tests. **b)** For each test in the repository we use the rest of the tests in the repository as baseline tests. We build a control chart using these tests to create the control limits. These control limits are, then, used to score the picked test. **c)** We measure the violation ratio and determine whether a test has passed or failed. **d)** We measure the precision and recall of our approach using the following formulas by comparing against the correct classification of a test:

$$precision = \frac{|classified\ bad\ runs \cap actual\ bad\ runs|}{|classified\ bad\ runs|} \quad (3)$$

$$recall = \frac{|classified\ bad\ runs \cap actual\ bad\ runs|}{|actual\ bad\ runs|} \quad (4)$$

There are three criteria that we considered in picking the case studies. We pick two case studies that fit these criteria. The first case study is a large and complex enterprise software system (denoted as Enterprise system). The second one is a small and simple open-source software (denoted as DS2). Table 1 shows a summary of the differences between the two case studies.

Which performance counters should be analyzed? In the Enterprise system, the focus of the performance regression tests is to keep the CPU utilization low because the engineers already know that CPU is the most performance sensitive resource. On the other hand, the DS2 system is new. We do not know much about its performance characteristic. Thus, we have to analyze all performance counters.

Table 1: Properties of the two case studies

Factor	Enterprise	DS2
Functionality	Telecommunication	E-Commerce
Vendor's business model	Commercial	Open-source
Size	Large	Small
Complexity	Complex	Simple
Known counter to analyze	Yes, use CPU	No, use all
Determining kinds of performance	Unknown	Known
Source of performance regression	Real	Injection

What kind of performance regression problems can we detect? In the Enterprise system, the testers' classification of the test results is available. Hence, we can calculate the precision and recall of our approach on real-life performance problems. However, we do not know what kind of performance regression problems our approach can detect since we cannot access the code. On the other hand, we have the code for DS2. Thus, we inject performance problems, which are well known in practice [8], into the code of DS2 and run our own test runs.

What is the threshold for the violation ratio? For the enterprise system, we study the impact of different violation ratios. For the DS2 system, we show an automated technique to determine the threshold. The technique can be used for the enterprise system as well.

5.2 Case study 1: Enterprise system

The system is a typical multiple-tier server client architecture. The performance engineers perform performance regression tests at the end of each development iteration. The tests that we use in this study exercise load on multiple subsystems residing on different servers. The behaviour of the subsystems and the hardware servers is recorded during the test run. The test engineers then analyze the performance counters. After the runs are analyzed, they are saved to a repository so test engineers can compare future test runs with these runs.

We pick a few versions of the software that we are most familiar with for our case study. There are about 110 runs in total. These runs include past passed runs without performance regressions and failed runs with performance regressions. We note that we also used this dataset to evaluate the effectiveness of the scale and the filter processing in Section 4.1 and Section 4.2.

5.2.1 Evaluation Approach

We first establish the baseline for our comparison. We do this with the help of the engineers. For each test run, we ask the engineers to determine if the run contains performance regressions, i.e., it is a bad run, or not, i.e., it is a good run. We used the engineers' evaluation instead of ours because we lack domain knowledge and may be biased.

We compare our classifications with the engineers' classification and report the accuracy. However, we need to decide on a threshold, t, such that if the violation ratio $V_x > t$, run

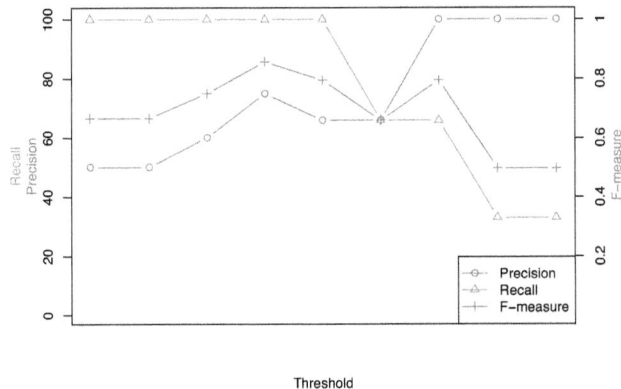

Figure 11: The accuracy of our automated approach compared the engineers' evaluation in the Enterprise case study.

x is marked as bad. For this study we explore a range of values for t, to understand the sensitivity of our approach to the choice of t.

5.2.2 Results

Figure 11 shows the precision, recall, and F-measure of our approach. The threshold increases from left to right. We hide the actual threshold values for confidentiality reasons. When the threshold increases, our classifier marks more runs as bad, in which case the precision (blue with circles) will increase but the recall (red with triangles) will decrease. The f-measure (brown with pluses) is maximized when both the precision and recall are at the optimum balance. The higher the f-measure, the better the accuracy. The f-measure is highest when the precision is 75% precision and the recall is 100%.

> *Our approach can identify test runs having performance regressions with 75% precision and 100% recall in a real software project.*

5.3 Case study 2: Dell DVD store

The Dell DVD store (DS2) is an open-source three-tier web application [5] that simulates an electronic commerce system. DS2 is typically used to benchmark new hardware system installations. We inject performance regressions into the DS2 code. Using the original code, we can produce good runs. Using the injected code, we can produce bad runs.

We set up DS2 in a lab environment and perform our own tests. The lab setup includes three Pentium III servers running Windows XP and Windows 2008 with 512MB of RAM. The first machine is the MySQL 5.5 database server [15], the second machine the Apache Tomcat web application server [17]. The third machine is used to run the load driver. All test runs use the same configuration as in Table 2. During each run, all performance counters associated with the Apache Tomcat and MySQL database processes are recorded.

Table 2: Dell DVD store configuration

Property	Value
Database size	Medium (1GB)
Number of threads	50
Ramp rate	25
Warm up time	1 minutes
Run duration	60 minutes
Customer think time	0 seconds
Percentage of new customers	20%
Average number of searches per order	3
Average number of items returned in each search	5
Average number of items purchased per order	5

Table 3: Common inefficient programming scenarios

Scenario	Good	Bad
Query limit	Limit the number of rows returned by the database to what will be displayed	Get everything then filter on the web server
System print	Remove unnecessary debug log printouts	Leave debug log printouts in the code
DB connection	Reuse database connections when possible	Create new connections for every query
Key index	Create database index for frequently used queries	Forget to create index for frequently used queries
Text index	Create full-text index for text columns	Forget to create full-text index for text columns

5.3.1 Evaluation Approach

Create data. We perform the baseline runs with the original code from Dell. We note, though, that one particular database connection was not closed properly in the original code. So we fix this bug before running the tests. Then, we perform the bad runs with injected problems. In each of these bad runs, we modify the JSP code to simulate common inefficient programming mistakes that are committed by junior developers [8]. Table 3 shows the scenarios we simulate. Each of these scenarios would cause a performance regression in a test run.

Procedure. We derive a procedure that use control charts to decide if a test run has performance regressions given the good baseline runs. The input of this procedure would be the counters of the new test runs and the counters of the baseline runs.

- **Step 1 - Determining violation ratio thresholds for each counter:** In this step, we only use the baseline runs to determine a suitable threshold for each counter. For each counter and for each baseline run, we create a control chart using the that run as a target test and the remaining runs as baseline. Then we measure the violation ratio of that counter on that run. We define the threshold for that counter as the maximum violation ratio for all baseline runs. For example, we have five baseline runs. The violation ratios of the

Table 4: Target run: System print, Baseline: Good runs 1, 2, 3, 4, and 5

Counter	Threshold	Violation Ratio
MySQL IO read bytes/s	8.3%	9.7%
Tomcat pool paged bytes	19.4%	83.3%
Tomcat IO data bytes/s	9.7%	98.6%
Tomcat IO write bytes/s	9.7%	98.6%
Tomcat IO data operations/s	8.3%	100%
Tomcat IO write operations/s	8.3%	100%

Tomcat's page faults per second counter of each run are 2.5%, 4.2%, 1.4%, 4.2%, and 12.5%. The threshold of the page faults counter of this baseline set is 12.5%.

- **Step 2 - Identifying out-of-control counters:** For each counter in the target test run, we calculate the violation ratio on the control chart built from the same counter in the baseline runs. If the violation ratio is higher than the threshold in Step 1, we record the counter and the violation ratio. For example, if the Tomcat's page faults per second counter's violation ratio is greater than 12.5%, we consider the page faults counter as out-of-control. We present the counters ordered in the amount of violation relative to the threshold.

The result of the procedure for each target run on a set of baseline runs is a list of out-of-control counters and the corresponding violation ratio. For example, Table 4 shows the result of the analysis where the target is one run with the system print problem (see Table 3) using five good runs as baseline. The first column is the counter name. The next column is the threshold. For example, the threshold for MySQL IO read bytes/s is 8.3% which means that the highest violation ratios among the five good runs is 8.3%. The last column is the violation ratio. As we can see, since the Tomcat process has to write more to the disk in the bad run, the top four out-of-control counters are Tomcat IO related.

5.3.2 Results

Table 5 shows the results of our test runs with the five inefficient programming scenarios as described in Table 3. We performed ten good runs and three runs for each scenario. Due to space constraints, we show the number of out-of-control counters and the average violation ratio for five good runs and one run for each scenario. We note that for the DS2 system, most of the performance counters are already normally distributed. So only scaling, as described in Section 4.1 is required.

As we can see from the first five rows of Table 5, when we use one of the good runs as the target against other good runs as baseline, the number of out-of-control counters and the average violation ratios are low. Two out of the five runs do not have any out-of-control counters. The other three runs have average violation ratios of 13.15%, 13.6%, and 27.7%. Since we pick the 5th and 95th percentiles as the lower and upper limits, a 10% violation is expected for any counter. Thus 13% violation ratio is considered low.

The bottom five rows of Table 5 show the results for the

Table 5: Analysis results for Dell DVD Store

Target run	Baseline runs	# out-of-control counters	Average violation ratio
GO 1	GO 2, 3, 4, 5	2	13.15%
GO 2	GO 1, 3, 4, 5	0	NA
GO 3	GO 1, 2, 4, 5	3	27.7%
GO 4	GO 1, 2, 3, 5	5	13.6%
GO 5	GO 1, 2, 3, 4	0	NA
QL	GO 1, 2, 3, 4, 5	14	81.2%
SP	GO 1, 2, 3, 4, 5	6	81.7%
DC	GO 1, 2, 3, 4, 5	2	12.5%
KI	GO 1, 2, 3, 4, 5	2	100%
TI	GO 1, 2, 3, 4, 5	17	71.2%

GO - Good, QL - Query limit, SP - System print, DC - DB connection, KI - Key index, TI - Text index (See Table 3 for description of the problematic test runs)

problematic runs using the good runs as baseline. The number of out-of-control counters and the average violation ratios are high except for the DB connection scenario (DC). In summary, our proposed approach can detect performance regressions in four out of the five scenarios.

We later find that, for the DC scenario, the new version of the MySQL client library has optimizations that automatically reuse existing connections instead of creating extra connections. So even though we injected extra connections to the JSP code, no new connection is created to the MySQL server. This false negative case further validates the accuracy of our approach.

> *Our approach can identify four out of five common inefficient programming scenarios.*

6. RELATED WORK

To the best of our knowledge, there are only three other approaches that aim to detect regressions in a load test. Foo et al. [7, 6] detect the change in behaviour among the performance counters using association rules. If the differences are higher than a threshold, the run is marked as a bad run for further analysis. Malik et al. [13] use a factor analysis technique called principal component analysis to transform all the counters into a small set of more distinct vectors. Then, they compare the pairwise correlations between the vectors in the new run with those of the baseline run. They were able to identify possible problems in the new run. Other approaches analyze the execution logs. For example, Jiang et al. [11, 12] introduced approaches to automatically detect anomalies in performance load tests by detecting out-of-order sequences in the software's execution logs produced during a test run. If the frequency of the out-of-order sequences is higher in a test run, the run is marked as bad.

Our evaluation shows that the accuracy of control charts based approach is comparable to previous studies that also automatically verify load tests. Foo et al. [7]'s association rules approach, which also uses performance counters, achieved 75% to 100% precision and 52% to 67% recall. Jiang et al. [11]'s approach, which uses execution logs,

Table 6: Practitioners' feedback on the three approaches

Approach	Strength	Weakness
Foo et al. [7]	Provide support for root cause analysis of bad runs	Complicated to explain
Malik et al. [13]	Compresses counters into a small number of important indices	Complicated to communicate findings due to the use of compressed counters
Control charts	Simple and easy to communicate	No support for root cause analysis

achieved around 77% precision. Our approach reaches comparable precision (75%) and recall (100%) on the Enterprise system. However, it is probably not wise to compare precision and recall across studies since the study settings and the evaluation methods are different.

There are also other approaches to detect anomalies during performance motoring of production systems. Many of these techniques could be modified to detect performance regressions. However, such work has not been done to date. For example, Cohen et al. [4] proposed the use of a supervised machine learning technique called Tree-Augmented Bayesian Networks to identify combinations of related metrics that are highly correlated with faults. This technique might be able to identify counters that are highly correlated with bad runs. Jiang et al. [10] used Normalized Mutual Information to cluster correlated metrics. Then, they used the Wilcoxon Rank-Sum test on the metrics to identify faulty components. This approach can be used to identify problematic subsystems during a load test. Chen et al. [2] also suggest an approach that analyzes the execution logs to identify problematic subsystems. Cherkasova et al. [3] develop regression-based transaction models from the counters. Then they use the model to identify runtime problems.

7. FEEDBACK FROM PRACTITIONERS

To better understand the differences and similarities between our, Foo et al. [7]'s, and Malik et al. [13]'s approach. We sought feedback from performance engineers who have used all three approaches.

The feedback is summarized in Table 6. In general, the strength of our approach compared to the other two approaches is the simplicity and intuitiveness. Control charts quantify the performance quality of a software into a measurable and easy to explain quantity, i.e., the violation ratio. Thus performance engineers can easily communicate the test results with others. It is much harder to convince the developers that some statistical model determined the failure of a test than to say that some counters have many more violations than before. Because of that, practitioners felt that our control charts approach has a high chance of adoption in practice.

The practitioners noted that a weakness of our approach is that it does not provide support for root cause analysis of the performance regressions. Foo et al. [7], through their association rules, can give a probable cause to the performance regressions. With that feedback, we are currently investigating the relationship between different performance

counters when a performance regression occurs. We conjecture that we can also use control charts to support root cause analysis.

The practitioners also noted that our approach to scale the load using a linear model might not work for systems with complex queuing. Instead, it might be worthwhile exploring the use of Queuing Network models to do the scaling for such systems. We are currently trying to find a software system that would exhibit such a queuing profile to better understand the negative impact of such a profile on our assumptions about the linear relation between load inputs and load outputs.

8. CONCLUSION

In this study, we propose an approach that uses control charts to automated detect performance regressions in software system. We suggest two techniques that overcome the two challenges of using control charts. We evaluate our approach using test runs of a large commercial software system and an open-source software system.

The results in both case studies are promising. The classification by our automated approach can achieve about 75% precision and 100% recall compared to the real evaluation in the Enterprise system. On the DS2 system, we can correctly identify four out of the five inefficient programming scenarios. This is especially good considered that the other scenario is actually a false negative.

We believe that our results warrant further studies to apply statistical process control techniques such as control charts, into software testing. For instance, the scaling technique that we suggested in Section 4.1 might not be suitable for other software systems where performance counters are not linearly proportional to the load. Similarly, the filtering technique in Section 4.2 might not be suitable for other software system where the secondary load should also be considered. Different scaling and filtering techniques should be derived for such cases.

Statistical process control has been used in many fields such as business and manufacturing. Hence, researchers in those fields already have a broad and solid knowledge on how to leverage these techniques in their operation. If we can leverage these statistical process control techniques into software testing we might be able to reduce the cost of running and analyzing tests and improve software quality overall.

9. ACKNOWLEDGEMENT

We would like to thank Research in Motion (RIM) for providing support and data access for this study. The findings and opinions expressed in this paper are those of the authors and do not necessarily represent or reflect those of RIM and/or its subsidiaries and affiliates. Moreover, our results do not in any way reflect the quality of RIM's products.

10. REFERENCES

[1] A. Avritzer and E. R. Weyuker. The automatic generation of load test suites and the assessment of the resulting software. *IEEE Transactions on Software Engineering (TSE)*, 21(9):705–716, 1995.

[2] M. Y. Chen, E. Kiciman, E. Fratkin, A. Fox, and E. Brewer. Pinpoint: Problem determination in large,

dynamic internet services. In *International Conference on Dependable Systems and Networks (DSN)*, pages 595–604, 2002.

[3] L. Cherkasova, K. Ozonat, M. Ningfang, J. Symons, and E. Smirni. Anomaly? application change? or workload change? towards automated detection of application performance anomaly and change. In *International Conference on Dependable Systems and Networks (DSN)*, pages 452–461, 2008.

[4] I. Cohen, M. Goldszmidt, T. Kelly, J. Symons, and J. S. Chase. Correlating instrumentation data to system states: a building block for automated diagnosis and control. In *Symposium on Opearting Systems Design Implementation*, pages 231–244, San Francisco, CA, 2004. USENIX Association.

[5] Dell Inc. DVD Store Test Application, 2010. Ver. 2.1.

[6] K. C. Foo. Automated discovery of performance regressions in enterprise applications. Master's thesis, 2011.

[7] K. C. Foo, J. Zhen Ming, B. Adams, A. E. Hassan, Z. Ying, and P. Flora. Mining performance regression testing repositories for automated performance analysis. In *International Conference on Quality Software (QSIC)*, pages 32–41, 2010.

[8] H. W. Gunther. Websphere application server development best practices for performance and scalability. *IBM WebSphere Application Server Standard and Advanced Editions - White paper*, 2000.

[9] Hewlett Packard. Loadrunner, 2010.

[10] M. Jiang, M. A. Munawar, T. Reidemeister, and P. A. S. Ward. Automatic fault detection and diagnosis in complex software systems by information-theoretic monitoring. In *International Conference on Dependable Systems Networks (DSN)*, pages 285–294, 2009.

[11] Z. M. Jiang, A. E. Hassan, G. Hamann, and P. Flora. Automatic identification of load testing problems. In *International Conference on Software Maintenance (ICSM)*, pages 307–316, 2008.

[12] Z. M. Jiang, A. E. Hassan, G. Hamann, and P. Flora. Automatic performance analysis of load tests. In *International Conference in Software Maintenance (ICSM)*, pages 125–134, Edmonton, 2009.

[13] H. Malik. A methodology to support load test analysis. In *International Conference on Software Engineering (ICSE)*, pages 421–424, Cape Town, South Africa, 2010. ACM.

[14] Microsoft Corp. Windows reliability and performance monitor, 2011.

[15] MySQL AB. Mysql community server, 2011. Ver. 5.5.

[16] W. Shewhart. *Economic Control of Quality of Manufactured Product*. American Society for Quality Control, 1931.

[17] The Apache Software Foundation. Tomcat, 2010. Ver. 5.5.

[18] I. Trubin. Capturing workload pathology by statistical exception detection system. In *Computer Measurement Group (CMG)*, 2005.

[19] E. J. Weyuker and F. I. Vokolos. Experience with performance testing of software systems: Issues, an approach, and case study. *IEEE Transactions on Software Engineering (TSE)*, 26(12):1147–1156, 2000.

Capturing Performance Assumptions using Stochastic Performance Logic

Lubomír Bulej[1,2]   Tomáš Bureš[1,2]   Jaroslav Keznikl[1,2]
Alena Koubková[1]   Andrej Podzimek[1,2]   Petr Tůma[1]

[1]Charles University in Prague
Faculty of Mathematics and Physics
Malostranské náměstí 25
118 00 Prague 1, Czech Republic

[2]Academy of Sciences of the Czech Republic
Institute of Computer Science
Pod Vodárenskou věží 2
182 07 Prague 8, Czech Republic

{bulej,bures,keznikl,koubkova,podzimek,tuma}@d3s.mff.cuni.cz

ABSTRACT

Compared to functional unit testing, automated performance testing is difficult, partially because correctness criteria are more difficult to express for performance than for functionality. Where existing approaches rely on absolute bounds on the execution time, we aim to express assertions on code performance in relative, hardware-independent terms. To this end, we introduce Stochastic Performance Logic (SPL), which allows making statements about relative method performance. Since SPL interpretation is based on statistical tests applied to performance measurements, it allows (for a special class of formulas) calculating the minimum probability at which a particular SPL formula holds. We prove basic properties of the logic and present an algorithm for SAT-solver-guided evaluation of SPL formulas, which allows optimizing the number of performance measurements that need to be made. Finally, we propose integration of SPL formulas with Java code using higher-level performance annotations, for performance testing and documentation purposes.

Categories and Subject Descriptors

D.2.4 [**Software/Program Verification**]: Assertion checkers; F.3.1 [**Specifying and Verifying and Reasoning about Programs**]: Assertions

General Terms

Algorithms, Theory

Keywords

performance testing, regression benchmarking

1. INTRODUCTION

Closing the gap between code and documentation is an important trend that can be found in modern software engineering approaches, such as test driven development [1] or design by contract [2]. In both cases, the project code is imbued with additional information, capturing developer assumptions or intended usage. Such information usually takes the form of assertions, unit tests, or preconditions and postconditions associated with individual methods. Besides enhancing the documentation, this information lends itself to automatic testing or formal verification, which can be easily incorporated into the development process. By using tools such as JUnit [3] or Google Test [4] for testing, and Java Modeling Language [5] or Microsoft Verifier for Concurrent C [6] for verification, the developers gain more freedom in exploring design choices and evolve existing design to meet new requirements. Should they make a mistake, an automatic safety net will promply inform them of assertion or contract violations, or newly introduced bugs.

However, the tools available today are mostly geared towards functional testing. We believe there is little doubt that similar support for performance testing – that is, being able to express performance-related developer assumptions or intended usage in code and test or verify them automatically – would be beneficial. Yet it is, unfortunately, more difficult to do – for multiple reasons:

- Except in special application domains, such as real-time systems, the boundary between sufficient and insufficient performance is not sharp. It is therefore more difficult to specify conditions that should be tested.

- Performance is typically platform-dependent, but the conditions that should be met need to be more general, lest their utility is severely limited.[1]

- Performance testing can be more difficult to configure and execute than functional testing.

In past work [7, 8, 9], we focused on the execution and evaluation aspects of performance testing. Here, we contribute to the ability to specify conditions that should be tested.

---

[1]Actually, test results are also platform-dependent and therefore of potentially limited utility. On the other hand, the fact that a test is only testing a particular execution on a particular platform is generally accepted, this issue is therefore not unique to performance.

To avoid expressing conditions in a platform-dependent manner, we have decided to rely on relative terms – we develop a special many-sorted first-order logic that allows us to express statements about relative performance of functions or methods in code. The logic, here called Stochastic Performance Logic (SPL), is interpreted using statistical hypothesis testing, which allows calculating the probability at which a particular SPL statement holds.

Besides introducing the logic and its interpretation, we also prove basic properties of the logic and present an algorithm for SAT-solver-guided evaluation of SPL formulas, which allows optimizing the number of performance measurements that need to be made. We also propose to integrate SPL formulas with Java code using annotations.

Among potential applications of our work, we see the possibility to document developer assumptions related to performance – for example, when the developer implements a user interface method with the assumption that caching a bitmap representation of a picture is faster than decoding the picture on each draw, that assumption can be represented in code and tested automatically. The assumptions can also be interpreted as a contract between code and external components and tested during integration, making the integration process more reliable. Another useful application is an aid in debugging, similar to traditional assertions.

The paper is structured as follows. We define the Stochastic Performance Logic (SPL) in Section 2, to provide a formal ground for statements about performance. To illustrate the semantics of SPL, we introduce a natural interpretation of the logic in Section 3, while for use with real-world performance data, we define sample-based SPL interpretation in Section 4. In Section 5 we discuss the issues related to statistical errors when evaluating SPL formulas and show that for a special group of practically relevant formulas, the probability of error can be bounded. The fitness of SPL for performance comparisons is discussed and evaluated in Section 6. For efficient evaluation of SPL formulas in performance unit testing, we introduce a SAT-solver-guided algorithm in Section 7, and outline the potential integration of SPL into Java programs in Section 8. In closing, we discuss related approaches in Section 9, and conclude the paper in Section 10.

2. STOCHASTIC PERFORMANCE LOGIC

To avoid platform dependency found in statements expressing that a method completes its operation in certain time bounds, we need to compare the performance of one method to performance of some other method. Thus even when the performance of both methods changes with the underlying platform, the relation between the two should hold and if it does not, it is certainly worth developer attention.

To achieve this, we formally define the performance of a method as a random variable representing the time it takes to execute the method with random input parameters. The nature of the random input is formally represented by *workload class* and *method workload*. The workload is parametrized by *workload parameters*, which capture the dimensions along which the workload can be varied, e.g. array size, matrix sparsity, numberof vertices in a graph, etc.

Definition 1. Workload class is a function $\mathfrak{L} : P^n \rightarrow (\Omega \rightarrow I)$, where for a given $\mathfrak{L}$, P is a set of *workload parameter* values, n is the number of parameters, Ω is a sample

space, and I is a set of objects (method input arguments) in a chosen programming language.

For later definitions we also require that there is a total ordering over P.

Definition 2. Method workload is a random variable $L^{p_1,\dots,p_n}$ such that $L^{p_1,\dots,p_n} = \mathfrak{L}(p_1,\dots,p_n)$ for a given workload class $\mathfrak{L}$ and parameters $p_1,\dots,p_n$.

Unlike conventional random variables that map observations to a real number, method workload is a random variable that maps observations to object instances, which serve as random input parameters for the method under test. If necessary, the developer may adjust the underlying stochastic process to obtain random input parameters representing domain-specific workloads, e.g., partially sorted arrays.

To demonstrate the above concepts, let us assume we want to measure the performance of a method S, which sorts an array of integers. The input parameters for the sort method S are characterized by workload class $\mathfrak{L}_S : \mathbb{N}^+ \rightarrow (\Omega_S \rightarrow I_S)$. Let us assume that the workload class $\mathfrak{L}_S$ represents an array of random integers, with a single parameter determining the size of the array. The method workload returned by the workload class is a random variable, whose observations are instances of random arrays of given size. For example, method inputs in form of random arrays of size 1000 will be obtained from observations of random variable $L_S^{1000} : \Omega_S \rightarrow I_S = \mathfrak{L}_S(1000)$.

Note that without loss of generality, we assume in the formalization that there is exactly one $\mathfrak{L}_M$ for a particular method M and that M has just one input argument.

With the formal representation of a workload in place, we now proceed to define the method performance.

Definition 3. Let $M(in)$ be a method in a chosen programming language and $in \in I$ its input argument. Then *method performance* $P_M : P^n \rightarrow (\Omega \rightarrow \mathbb{R})$ is a function that for given workload parameters $p_1,\dots,p_n$ returns a random variable, whose observations correspond to execution duration of method M with input parameters obtained from observations of $L_M^{p_1,\dots,p_n} = \mathfrak{L}_M(p_1,\dots,p_n)$, where $\mathfrak{L}_M$ is the workload class for method M.

We can now define the Stochastic Performance Logic (SPL) that will let us make comparative statements about method performance under a particular method workload. To facilitate comparison of method performance, SPL is based on regular arithmetics, in particular on axioms of equality and inequality adapted for the method performance domain.

Definition 4. SPL is a many-sorted first-order logic defined as follows:

- There is a set $FunPe$ of function symbols for method performances with arities $P^n \rightarrow (\Omega \rightarrow \mathbb{R})$ for $n \in \mathbb{N}^+$.

- There is a set $FunT$ of function symbols for performance observation transformation functions with arity $\mathbb{R} \rightarrow \mathbb{R}$.

- The logic has equality and inequality relations $=$, $\leq$ for arity $P \times P$.

- The logic has equality and inequality relations $\leq_{p(tl,tr)}$, $=_{p(tl,tr)}$ with arity $(\Omega \rightarrow \mathbb{R}) \times (\Omega \rightarrow \mathbb{R})$, where $tl, tr \in FunT$.

- Quantifiers (both universal and existential) are allowed only over finite subsets of P.

- For $x, y, z \in P$ and $P_M, P_N \in FunPe$, the logic has the following axioms:

$$x \leq x \tag{1}$$

$$(x \leq y \wedge y \leq x) \leftrightarrow x = y \tag{2}$$

$$(x \leq y \wedge y \leq z) \rightarrow x \leq z \tag{3}$$

For each pair $tl, tr \in FunT$ such that

$$\forall o \in \mathbb{R} : tl(o) \leq tr(o), \text{there is an axiom} \tag{4}$$

$$P_M(x_1, \ldots, x_m) \leq_{p(tl,tr)} P_M(x_1, \ldots, x_m)$$

$$(P_M(x_1, \ldots, x_m) \leq_{p(tm,tn)} P_N(y_1, \ldots, y_n) \wedge$$
$$P_N(y_1, \ldots, y_n) \leq_{p(tn,tm)} P_M(x_1, \ldots, x_m)) \leftrightarrow \tag{5}$$
$$P_M(x_1, \ldots, x_m) =_{p(tm,tn)} P_N(y_1, \ldots, y_n)$$

Axioms (1)–(3) come from arithmetics, since workload parameters (P) are essentially real or integer numbers. In analogy to (1)–(2), axiom (4) may be regarded as generalised reflexivity, and axiom (5) shows the correspondence between $=_p$ and $\leq_p$. An analogy of (3), i.e. transitivity, cannot be introduced for $=_p$ and $\leq_p$, because it does not hold for all interpretations of SPL (see Section 4).

Note that even though we currently do not make use of the axioms in our approach, they make the properties of the logic more obvious (in particular the performance relations $=_p$ and $\leq_p$). Specifically, the lack of transitivity for performance relations ensures that SPL formulas can only express statements that are consistent with hypothesis testing approaches used in the SPL interpretation.

Using the logic defined above, we would like to express assumptions about method performance in the spirit of the following examples:

Example 1. "On arrays of 100, 500, 1000, 5000, and 10000 elements, the sorting algorithm A is at most 5% faster and at most 5% slower than sorting algorithm B."

$$\forall n \in \{100, 500, 1000, 5000, 10000\} :$$
$$P_A(n) \geq_{p(id,\lambda x.0.95x)} P_B(n) \wedge P_A(n) \leq_{p(id,\lambda x.1.05x)} P_B(n)$$

Example 2. "On buffers of 256, 1024, 4096, 16384, and 65536 bytes, the Rijndael encryption algorithm is at least 10% faster than the Blowfish encryption algorithm and at most 200 times slower than array copy."

$$\forall n \in \{256, 1024, 4096, 16384, 65536\} :$$
$$P_{Rijndael}(n) \leq_{p(id,\lambda x.0.9x)} P_{Blowfish}(n) \wedge$$
$$P_{Rijndael}(n) \leq_{p(id,\lambda x.200x)} P_{ArrayCopy}(n)$$

For compact in-place representation of performance observation transformation functions, we use the lambda notation [10], with id as a shortcut for identity, $id = \lambda x.x$.

To ensure correspondence between SPL formulas in Examples 1 and 2 and their textual description, we need to define SPL semantics that provides the intended interpretation.

3. SPL INTERPRETATION

A natural way to compare random variables is to compare their expected values. Since method performance is a random variable, it is only natural to base SPL interpretation,

and particularly the interpretation of equality and inequality relations, on the expected value of method performance. Other (valid) interpretations are possible, but for simplicity, we first define the *expected-value-based interpretation* and prove its consistency with the SPL axioms.

Each function symbol $f_{Pe} \in FunPe$ is interpreted as a method performance, i.e. an n-ary function that for input parameter $p_1, \ldots, p_n$ returns a random variable $\Omega \rightarrow \mathbb{R}$, the observation of which corresponds to performance observation as defined in Definition 3.

Each function symbol $f_T \in FunT$ is interpreted as a performance observation transformation function, which is a function $\mathbb{R} \rightarrow \mathbb{R}$. In the context of equality and inequality relations between method performances, f_T represents transformation (e.g. scaling) of the observed performance – e.g., statement "*M is 2 times slower than N*" is expressed as $P_M =_{p(id,\lambda x.2x)} P_N$, where $f_{T_1} = id$ and $f_{T_2} = \lambda x.2x$.

The relational operators $\leq$ and $=$ for arity $P \times P$ are interpreted in the classic way, based on total ordering of P.

The interpretation of the relational operators $=_p$ and $\leq_p$ is defined as follows:

Definition 5. Let $tm, tn : \mathbb{R} \rightarrow \mathbb{R}$ be performance observation transformation functions, P_M and P_N be method performances, and $x_1, \ldots, x_m, y_1, \ldots, x_n$ be workload parameters. Then the relations $\leq_{p(tm,tn)}, =_{p(tm,tn)} : (\Omega \rightarrow \mathbb{R}) \times (\Omega \rightarrow \mathbb{R})$ are interpreted as follows:

$$P_M(x_1, \ldots, x_m) \leq_{p(tm,tn)} P_N(y_1, \ldots, y_n) \quad \text{iff}$$
$$E(tm(P_M(x_1, \ldots, x_m))) \leq E(tn(P_N(y_1, \ldots, y_n)));$$

$$P_M(x_1, \ldots, x_m) =_{p(tm,tn)} P_N(y_1, \ldots, y_n) \quad \text{iff}$$
$$E(tm(P_M(x_1, \ldots, x_m))) = E(tn(P_N(y_1, \ldots, y_n))),$$

where $E(X)$ denotes the expected value of the random variable X, and $tm(X)$ denotes a random variable derived from X by applying function tm on each observation of X.[2]

At this point, it is clear that the expected-value-based interpretation of SPL has the required semantics. However, we have yet to show that this interpretation is consistent with the SPL axioms.

The following lemma and theorem show that the interpretation of $=_p$ and $\leq_p$, as defined by Definition 5, is consistent with axioms (4) and (5). The consistency with other axioms trivially results from the assumption of total ordering on P.

LEMMA 1. *Let $X, Y : \Omega \rightarrow \mathbb{R}$ be random variables, and $tl, tr, tx, ty : \mathbb{R} \rightarrow \mathbb{R}$ be performance observation transformation functions. Then the following holds:*

$$(\forall o \in \mathbb{R} : tl(o) \leq tr(o)) \rightarrow E(tl(X)) \leq E(tr(X))$$

$$(E(tx(X)) \leq E(ty(Y)) \wedge E(ty(Y)) \leq E(tx(X))) \leftrightarrow$$
$$E(tx(X)) = E(ty(Y))$$

---

[2]Note that the effect of the performance observation transformation function on distribution parameters is potentially complex. We assume that in practical applications, the performance observation transformation functions will be limited to linear shift and scale.

PROOF. The validity of the first formula follows from the definition of the expected value. Let $f(x)$ be the probability density function of random variable X. Since $f(x) \geq 0$, it holds that

$$E(tl(X)) = \int_{-\infty}^{\infty} tl(x)f(x)dx \leq \int_{-\infty}^{\infty} tr(x)f(x)dx = E(tr(X))$$

The validity of the second formula follows naturally from the properties of total ordering on real numbers. $\square$

Note that we assumed M to be a continuous random variable. The proof would be the same for a discrete random variable, except with a sum in place of the integral.

THEOREM 1. *The interpretation of performance relations $\leq_p$ and $=_p$, as given by Definition 5, is consistent with axioms (4) and (5).*

PROOF. The proof of the theorem naturally follows from Lemma 1 by substituting $P_M(x_1, \ldots, x_m)$ for X and $P_N(y_1, \ldots, y_n)$ for Y. $\square$

While the above interpretation illustrates the idea behind SPL, it assumes that the expected value $E(tl(X))$ can be computed. Unfortunately, this assumption hardly ever holds, because the distribution function of X is typically unknown, and so is the expected value. While it is possible to measure durations of method invocations for the purpose of method performance comparison, the type of the distribution and its parameters remain unknown.

4. SAMPLE-BASED INTERPRETATION

To avoid the problem with unknown distribution function and the expected value of a random variable, we turn to sample based methods that work with parameter estimates derived from measurements. This leads us to a *sample-based interpretation* of SPL that relies solely on the observations of random variables. Due to limited applicability of the expected-value-based interpretation, we will only deal with the sample-based interpretation in the rest of the paper.

The basic idea is to replace the comparison of expected values in the interpretation of $\leq_p$ and $=_p$ by a statistical test. Given a set of observations of method performances (i.e. random variables), the test will allow us to determine whether the mean values of the observed method performances are in a particular relation (i.e., $\leq_p$ or $=_p$).

However, to formulate the sample-based interpretation, we first need to fix the set of observations for which the relations will be interpreted. We therefore define an *experiment*, denoted $\mathcal{E}$, as a finite set of observations of method performances under a particular method workload.

Definition 6. Experiment $\mathcal{E}$ is a collection of $\mathcal{O}_{P_M(p_1,\ldots,p_m)}$, where $\mathcal{O}_{P_M(p_1,\ldots,p_m)} = \{P_M^1(p_1,\ldots,p_m),\ldots,P_M^V(p_1,\ldots,p_m)\}$ is a set of V observations of method performance P_M subjected to workload $L_M^{p_1,\ldots,p_m}$, and where $P_M^i(p_1,\ldots,p_m)$ denotes i-th observation of performance of method M.

Having established the concept of an experiment, we can now define the sample-based interpretation of SPL (note that it depends on a particular experiment).

The interpretation is the same as given in Section 3, only Definition 7 is used to assign semantics to method performance relations.

Definition 7. Let $tm, tn : \mathbb{R} \to \mathbb{R}$ be performance observation transformation functions, P_M and P_N be method performances, $x_1,\ldots,x_m,y_1,\ldots,y_n$ be workload parameters, and $\alpha \in \langle 0, 0.5 \rangle$ be a fixed significance level.

For a given experiment $\mathcal{E}$, the relations $\leq_{p(tm,tn)}$ and $=_{p(tm,tn)}$ are interpreted as follows:

- $P_M(x_1,\ldots,x_m) \leq_{p(tm,tn)} P_N(y_1,\ldots,y_n)$ iff the null hypothesis

  $\mathrm{H}_0 : E(tm(P_M^i(x_1,\ldots,x_m))) \leq E(tn(P_N^j(y_1,\ldots,y_n)))$

  cannot be rejected by one-sided Welch's t-test [11] at significance level α based on the observations gathered in the experiment $\mathcal{E}$;

- $P_M(x_1,\ldots,x_m) =_{p(tm,tn)} P_N(y_1,\ldots,y_n)$ iff the null hypothesis

  $\mathrm{H}_0 : E(tm(P_M^i(x_1,\ldots,x_m))) = E(tn(P_N^j(y_1,\ldots,y_n)))$

  cannot be rejected by two-sided Welch's t-test at significance level 2α based on the observations gathered in the experiment $\mathcal{E}$;

where $E(tm(P_M^i(\ldots)))$ and $E(tn(P_N^j(\ldots)))$ denote the mean value of performance observations transformed by function tm or tn, respectively.

Briefly, the Welch's t-test rejects with significance level α the null hypothesis $\overline{X} = \overline{Y}$ against the alternative hypothesis $\overline{X} \neq \overline{Y}$ if

$$\left| \frac{\overline{X} - \overline{Y}}{\sqrt{\frac{S_X^2}{V_X} + \frac{S_Y^2}{V_Y}}} \right| > t_{\nu,\alpha/2}$$

and rejects with significance level α the null hypothesis $\overline{X} \leq \overline{Y}$ against the alternative hypothesis $\overline{X} > \overline{Y}$ if

$$\frac{\overline{X} - \overline{Y}}{\sqrt{\frac{S_X^2}{V_X} + \frac{S_Y^2}{V_Y}}} > t_{\nu,\alpha}$$

where V_i is the sample size, S_i^2 is the sample variance, $t_{\nu,\alpha}$ is the $(1 - \alpha)$-quantile of the Student's distribution with ν levels of freedom, with ν computed as follows:

$$\nu = \frac{\left(\frac{S_X^2}{V_X} + \frac{S_Y^2}{V_Y} \right)^2}{\frac{S_X^4}{V_X^2(V_X-1)} + \frac{S_Y^4}{V_Y^2(V_Y-1)}}$$

Although Welch's t-test formally requires normal distribution of X and Y, it is robust to violations of normality due to the Central Limit Theorem.

As in Section 3, we need to show that the sample-based interpretation of SPL is consistent with axioms (4) and (5).

THEOREM 2. *The interpretation of relations $\leq_p$, and $=_p$, as given by Definition 7, is consistent with axiom (4) for a given fixed experiment $\mathcal{E}$.*

PROOF. For sake of brevity, we will denote the sample mean $E(tl(P_M^i(x_1,\ldots,x_m)))$ as $\overline{X}_{tl}$ and the sample variance $\mathrm{Var}(tl(P_M^i(x_1,\ldots,x_m)))$ as S_{tl}^2; $\overline{X}_{tr}$ and S_{tr}^2 are defined in a similar way.

Assuming $\forall o \in \mathbb{R} : tl(o) \leq tr(o)$, we have to prove that the null-hypothesis $\mathrm{H}_0 : \overline{X}_{tl} \leq \overline{X}_{tr}$ cannot be rejected by the Welch's t-test.

Based on the formulation of the t-test, it means that the null-hypothesis can be rejected if

$$\frac{\overline{X}_{tl} - \overline{X}_{tr}}{\sqrt{\frac{S_{tl}^2}{V} + \frac{S_{tr}^2}{V}}} > t_{\nu,\alpha}$$

where V is the number of samples $P_M^i(x_1, \ldots, x_m)$ in the experiment $\mathcal{E}$.

Since the denominator is a positive number, the whole fraction is non-positive. However, the right hand side $t_{\nu,\alpha}$ is a non-negative number since we assumed that $\alpha \leq 0.5$. This means that the inequality never holds and thus the null-hypothesis cannot be rejected. $\square$

THEOREM 3. *The interpretation of relations $\leq_p$, and $=_p$, as given by Definition 7, is consistent with axiom (5) for a given fixed experiment $\mathcal{E}$.*

PROOF. For sake of brevity, we will denote the sample mean $E(tx(P_X^i(x_1, \ldots, x_m)))$ as $\overline{X}$ and the sample variance $\mathrm{Var}(tx(P_X^i(x_1, \ldots, x_m)))$ as S_X^2; $\overline{Y}$ and S_Y^2 are defined in a similar way.

By interpreting axiom (5) according to Definition 7, we get the following statements:

$$P_M(x_1, \ldots, x_m) \leq_{p(tm,tn)} P_N(y_1, \ldots, y_n)$$
$$\longleftrightarrow \frac{\overline{X} - \overline{Y}}{\sqrt{\frac{S_X^2}{V_X} + \frac{S_Y^2}{V_Y}}} \leq t_{\nu_{X,Y},\alpha}$$

$$P_N(y_1, \ldots, y_n) \leq_{p(tn,tm)} P_M(x_1, \ldots, x_m)$$
$$\longleftrightarrow \frac{\overline{Y} - \overline{X}}{\sqrt{\frac{S_Y^2}{V_Y} + \frac{S_X^2}{V_X}}} \leq t_{\nu_{Y,X},\alpha}$$

$$P_M(x_1, \ldots, x_m) =_{p(tm,tn)} P_N(y_1, \ldots, y_n)$$
$$\longleftrightarrow -t_{\nu_{X,Y},\alpha} \leq \frac{\overline{X} - \overline{Y}}{\sqrt{\frac{S_X^2}{V_X} + \frac{S_Y^2}{V_Y}}} \leq t_{\nu_{X,Y},\alpha}$$

Thus, we need to show that

$$\frac{\overline{X} - \overline{Y}}{\sqrt{\frac{S_X^2}{V_X} + \frac{S_Y^2}{V_Y}}} \leq t_{\nu_{X,Y},\alpha} \wedge \frac{\overline{Y} - \overline{X}}{\sqrt{\frac{S_Y^2}{V_Y} + \frac{S_X^2}{V_X}}} \leq t_{\nu_{Y,X},\alpha}$$
$$\longleftrightarrow -t_{\nu_{X,Y},\alpha} \leq \frac{\overline{X} - \overline{Y}}{\sqrt{\frac{S_X^2}{V_X} + \frac{S_Y^2}{V_Y}}} \leq t_{\nu_{X,Y},\alpha}$$

This holds, because $\nu_{X,Y} = \nu_{Y,X}$ and thus

$$\frac{\overline{Y} - \overline{X}}{\sqrt{\frac{S_Y^2}{V_Y} + \frac{S_X^2}{V_X}}} \leq t_{\nu_{Y,X},\alpha} \longleftrightarrow -t_{\nu_{X,Y},\alpha} \leq \frac{\overline{X} - \overline{Y}}{\sqrt{\frac{S_X^2}{V_X} + \frac{S_Y^2}{V_Y}}}$$

$\square$

Note that, as indicated in Section 2, the transitivity (i.e. $(P_X(\ldots) \leq_{p(tx,ty)} P_Y(\ldots) \wedge P_Y(\ldots) \leq_{p(ty,tz)} P_Z(\ldots)) \to P_X(\ldots) \leq_{p(tx,tz)} P_Z(\ldots))$ does not hold for the sample-based interpretation. This can be shown by considering the following observations and performing single-sided tests at significance level $\alpha = 0.05$: $\mathcal{O}_{P_X} = \{2, 4\}$, $\mathcal{O}_{P_Y} = \{-1, 1\}$, $\mathcal{O}_{P_Z} = \{-4, -2\}$.

5. CORRECTNESS OF EVALUATION

The valuation of the relations $=_p$ and $\leq_p$ in the sample-based interpretation of an SPL formula depends on the results of statistical tests applied to the samples of method performance collected during an experiment. Each statistical test performed to determine the valuation of a particular relation in the SPL formula may introduce either a Type I (true null hypothesis rejected) or Type II (false null hypothesis not rejected) error. As a consequence, the valuation of a formula in SPL with sample-based interpretation is correct only with some probability.

This probability could be estimated from the probabilities of introducing a Type I or Type II error in each test. For Type I error, the probability equals the test significance level and is 2α for $=_p$ and α for $\leq_p$. For Type II error, the probability is unknown and cannot be determined. It is therefore impossible, in general, to calculate the probability that the valuation of a formula is incorrect.

In some cases, for example when the valuation of a formula only depends on a rejection of a particular test, an estimate of Type I error based on the significance level can be made. However, when interested in the error potentially introduced by the evaluation of the whole formula, the cumulative nature of errors introduced by individual tests must be accounted for. For example, when the formula

$$P_M(10) \leq_{p(id,id)} P_N(10) \wedge P_M(50) \leq_{p(id,id)} P_N(50)$$

evaluates to "false", it is possible that the first, or the second, or both tests introduced a Type I error into the evaluation. Conversely, when the formula evaluates to "true", some of the tests may have introduced a Type II error. These two types of errors may also occur at the same time, for example when a formula contains terms with and without negation.

To bound the probability of incorrect evaluation, we define the set of relations needed for the formula evaluation:

Definition 8. A set of performance relations $\mathcal{R}$ is a set of all tuples $\langle \diamond, tm, tn, P_M(\dot{x}_1, \ldots, \dot{x}_m), P_N(\dot{y}_1, \ldots, \dot{y}_n) \rangle$, where $\diamond$ is either $=_p$ or $\leq_p$ and $\dot{x}_i, \dot{y}_j$ are particular fixed workload parameter values.

Definition 9. For a given formula F, we define the *evaluation skeleton* as a partial function $\mathcal{S}_F : \mathcal{R} \to \{True, False\}$, such that F can be evaluated using just the valuations given by $\mathcal{S}_F$. The skeleton is minimal in the sense that no relation can be removed from $\mathcal{S}_F$ without breaking the skeleton property of being sufficient to evaluate formula F.

Definition 10. For a given formula F, we define $\mathcal{S}_F^{True}$ as a set of all evaluation skeletons under which the formula evaluates to "true". Similarly $\mathcal{S}_F^{False}$ is a set of all evaluation skeletons under which the formula evaluates to "false".

The probability that a formula has been evaluated incorrectly can be then estimated using the idea behind Bonferroni correction [12]. For example, when a formula evaluates to "true", we can bound the probability $P(\text{F is "true"} \mid \text{F does not hold})$ by summing up α (i.e. Type I error probability) or β (i.e. Type II error probability) for all tests that may be needed for the evaluation.

Since only α is known, we can effectively bound the probability only for formulas that are evaluated solely as a result of test rejections. For example, if the formula $P_M(10) \leq_{p(id,id)}$

$P_N(10) \wedge P_M(50) \leq_{p(id,id)} P_N(50)$ is "false", we know that this valuation was based only on test rejections.

This is formalized by the following theorem.

THEOREM 4. *Let F be an SPL-formula. If every evaluation of formula F to "true" is based only on rejections (i.e. $\forall \mathcal{S}_F \in \mathcal{S}_F^{True} : range(\mathcal{S}_F) = \{False\}$), then*

$$P(F \text{ is "true"} \mid F \text{ does not hold}) \leq \sum_{\forall R \in \mathcal{R}_F^{True}} P_S(R)$$

where $\mathcal{R}_F^{True} = \bigcup_{\mathcal{S}_F \in \mathcal{S}_F^{True}} domain(\mathcal{S}_F)$ is the set of all relations that may be used for evaluating the formula to "true", and $P_S(R)$ is the significance level for a test, i.e. 2α for $=_p$, and α for $\leq_p$.
Similarly, if every evaluation of formula F to "false" is based only on rejections,

$$P(F \text{ is "false"} \mid F \text{ holds}) \leq \sum_{\forall R \in \mathcal{R}_F^{False}} P_S(R)$$

where $\mathcal{R}_F^{False} = \bigcup_{\mathcal{S}_F \in \mathcal{S}_F^{False}} domain(\mathcal{S}_F)$.

PROOF. The probability $P(F$ is "true" $\mid$ F does not hold), may be bounded by the probability that at least one of the tests from $\mathcal{R}_F^{True}$ gave an incorrect Type I result (the test rejected a true null hypothesis). This probability can bound using Boole's inequality as:

$$P\left(\bigcup_{R \in \mathcal{R}_F^{True}} Err(R)\right) \leq \sum_{R \in \mathcal{R}_F^{True}} P(Err(R))$$

where $Err(R)$ denotes an event "Type I error occurred in test for R". This inequality holds even for tests which are not statistically independent.

The bound for the probability $P(F$ is "false" $\mid$ F holds) can be proved in the same way. $\square$

Although Theorem 4 is only applicable to a special class of formulas, it appears sufficient for practical use. Expressing simple assumptions (along the lines presented in the examples) using SPL will result in formulas simple enough to allow calculating the probability of incorrect evaluation.

Considering Examples 1 and 2, when the formula evaluates to "false", we can calculate the probability of correct evaluation based solely on the knowledge of α. In fact, the probability is $(1 - 10\alpha)$ for both cases.

It is also possible to transform the formulas to similar dual formulas for which the probability of correctness can be determined when they evaluate to "true". This can be done by using strict inequalities instead of non-strict ones, which will reverse the null hypothesis, so the underlying test will need to reject the null hypothesis to be considered successful. Since the strict inequality is used as a "syntactic sugar" for the negation of the opposite non-strict inequality,

$$P_M <_{p(tm,tn)} P_N \leftrightarrow \neg(P_M \geq_{p(tm,tn)} P_N)$$
$$P_M >_{p(tm,tn)} P_N \leftrightarrow \neg(P_M \leq_{p(tm,tn)} P_N),$$

the formula with strict inequalities can be simply converted to the corresponding SPL formula which only uses the non-strict inequalities.

Examples 1 and 2 can be thus rewritten to Examples 3 and 4 (we only show the first step of the conversion) as follows:

Example 3. "On arrays of 100, 500, 1000, 5000, and 10000 elements, the sorting algorithm A less than 5% faster and less than 5% slower compared to sorting algorithm B"

$$\forall n \in \{100, 500, 1000, 5000, 10000\} :$$
$$P_A(n) >_{p(id,\lambda x.0.95x)} P_B(n) \wedge P_A(n) <_{p(id,\lambda x.1.05x)} P_B(n)$$

The formula above therefore corresponds to the following SPL formula:

$$\forall n \in \{100, 500, 1000, 5000, 10000\} :$$
$$\neg(P_A(n) \leq_{p(id,\lambda x.0.95x)} P_B(n) \vee P_A(n) \geq_{p(id,\lambda x.1.05x)} P_B(n))$$

Example 4. "On buffers of 256, 1024, 4096, 16384, and 65536 bytes, the Rijndael encryption algorithm is more than 10% faster than the Blowfish encryption algorithm and less than 200 times slower than array copy."

$$\forall n \in \{256, 1024, 4096, 16384, 65536\} :$$
$$P_{\text{Rijndael}}(n) <_{p(id,\lambda x.0.9x)} P_{\text{Blowfish}}(n) \wedge$$
$$P_{\text{Rijndael}}(n) <_{p(id,\lambda x.200x)} P_{\text{ArrayCopy}}(n)$$

6. FITNESS FOR PURPOSE

Before moving on to discuss the automated evaluation of SPL formulas, we need to answer an obvious question: for which kind of program methods is the SPL approach suitable? The answer clearly depends on the choice of SPL interpretation. So far, we have introduced interpretations that are based on comparing the mean value of method performance, i.e. the location estimator of the underlying distribution. Therefore, the SPL approach should be well-suited for methods whose performance can be reasonably described by a mean value, i.e. the underlying distribution is unimodal, without heavy tails. We expect such methods to be relatively small, often representing the computational kernel of an application, handling (bulk) data transformations and processing. We believe that for such methods, most developers will be able to intuitively understand the concept of method performance, identify factors influencing it, and possibly express performance assumptions by comparing it (in relative terms) to performance of other (similar) methods.

Although the mean value can be calculated even in the case of multi-modal and heavy-tailed distributions, it does not represent the essential characteristics of the distribution very well. Such performance data are difficult to interpret, and we are not confident that a developer will be able to intuitively understand the performance of a method with such complex behavior — let alone express performance assumptions by comparison with other methods.

To evaluate the fitness of SPL for performance comparisons, we have therefore conducted experiments with two sets of simple methods that fall into the (loose) category of computational kernels. One set implements two sort algorithms, and the other implements various encryption algorithms, including null encryption (memory copying). The experiments correspond to the examples introduced in Sections 2 and 5.

All experiments were run on a 64-bit platform[3], executing on a single core within Oracle JVM 7 on top of Fedora Linux[4], with all non-essential system services disabled. We

---

[3]Dell OptiPlex 780, Intel Core 2 Quad Q9550 CPU at 2.83 GHz, 4 GiB DDR3 RAM at 1066 MHz

[4]Fedora 15, Linux Kernel 2.6.40.4-5.fc15, GLIBC 2.14, JRE 1.7.0-b147

collected the durations of individual method invocations, with new random input generated before each invocation. The data from the first 15000 invocations were discarded, intended only to warm up the system and let the JIT compiler optimize the code. The next 100000 invocations provided samples of method performance for each method under test.

As per the sample-based SPL interpretation, all performance relations are evaluated using Welch's one-sided t-test. Results presented below show the evaluation of SPL formulas on experimental data with the underlying tests performed at significance level $\alpha = 0.01$.

6.1 "Similar performance" assumptions

The first set of experiments covers Examples 1 and 3, both assuming that the performance of two methods is similar, i.e. the performance difference is bounded.

We evaluate the SPL formula from Example 1 in two scenarios. In the first one, we compare (the performance of) two different methods with an identical implementation of the Insertion Sort algorithm, and expect the formula to evaluate to *true*. In the second case, we compare methods implementing the Insertion Sort and Dual Pivot Quick Sort algorithms, and expect the formula to evaluate to *false*.

$n = 100$	$n = 500$	$n = 1000$	$n = 5000$	$n = 10^4$	$\alpha = 0.01$
$P_{\text{Insertion}}(n) \geq_{p(id,\lambda x.0.95x)} P_{\text{Insertion}}(n)$					*true*
0.969	1	1	1	1	$\wedge$
$P_{\text{Insertion}}(n) \leq_{p(id,\lambda x.1.05x)} P_{\text{Insertion}}(n)$					*true*
0.999	1	1	1	1	
$P_{\text{Insertion}}(n) \geq_{p(id,\lambda x.0.95x)} P_{\text{DualPivot}}(n)$					*true*
1	1	1	1	1	$\wedge$
$P_{\text{Insertion}}(n) \leq_{p(id,\lambda x.1.05x)} P_{\text{DualPivot}}(n)$					*false*
0	0	0	0	0	

Table 1: Test results and p-values for Example 1

The results of the experiment are shown in Table 1. For each relation, the table presents the p-value of the t-test applied to observations of method performance under a particular workload. A performance relation will evaluate to *true* if none of the tests rejects the null hypothesis. Conversely, if any of the tests rejects the null hypothesis (p-value $< \alpha$), the relation evaluates to *false*. The final column combines the evaluation of individual relations into the final result.

In both cases, the results correspond to the expectation, but there is a problem with the *true* evaluation in the first case. When an expression written in standard logic holds, we are not used to question the result. In SPL with sample-based interpretation (i.e. statistical testing) and this particular formulation of assumptions, we have no indication as to how "strong" the *true* evaluation is — while the tests did not reject the null hypotheses, they did not confirm them.

As a remedy, in Section 5 the formula from Example 1 was rewritten to only evaluate to *true* if all the tests reject the null hypothesis. Formulated as in Example 3, it not only provides "stronger" answers, but also enables estimating the probability that the answer is wrong (Type I error).

The results of evaluating the modified SPL formula on the same data are shown in Table 2. Unlike in the previous case, a relation evaluates to *true* only if the null hypothesis is rejected for all workloads. While the result of comparison between Selection Sort and Dual Pivot Quick Sort did not change, the formula relating the performance of two identical implementations of Selection Sort now evaluates to *false*.

$n = 100$	$n = 500$	$n = 1000$	$n = 5000$	$n = 10^4$	$\alpha = 0.01$
$P_{\text{Insertion}}(n) > e_{p(id,\lambda x.0.95x)} P_{\text{Insertion}}(n)$					*false*
0.031	0	0	0	0	$\wedge$
$P_{\text{Insertion}}(n) <_{p(id,\lambda x.1.05x)} P_{\text{Insertion}}(n)$					*true*
5.555e-05	0	0	0	0	
$P_{\text{Insertion}}(n) >_{p(id,\lambda x.0.95x)} P_{\text{DualPivot}}(n)$					*true*
0	0	0	0	0	$\wedge$
$P_{\text{Insertion}}(n) <_{p(id,\lambda x.1.05x)} P_{\text{DualPivot}}(n)$					*false*
1	1	1	1	1	

Table 2: Test results and p-values for Example 3

The p-value of the failing test indicates that a true null hypothesis could be rejected with probability 0.031, which is too much for $\alpha = 0.01$, but would be sufficient for $\alpha = 0.05$. The test failed to reject the null hypothesis due to outliers in the data. Unfortunately, even though they are present in all measurements, they have bigger impact on shorter durations measured with smaller workloads.

At this point, even though the performance assumption had failed, the developer has obtained a more informative result and has several options. By analysing the cause of the failure, the developer can conclude that there is too much interference during measurement and either relax the significance level α, avoid measurements on small workloads, improve measurement accuracy [13], or filter the outliers from the measurement.

In this particular case, if the developer chose to avoid workloads with array of size 100, the formula would evaluate to *true* at significance level $\alpha = 0.01$ even if the interval for "considered similar" difference in performance was reduced to 1% from the current (liberal) 10%.

6.2 "Different performance" assumptions

The second set of experiments covers Examples 2 and 4, both making statements about relative performance of three methods.

As in the previous experiment, we first evaluate the SPL formula from Example 2, which assumes the Rijndael encryption algorithm to be at most 200× slower than array copy, but still at least 10% faster than the Blowfish encryption algorithm.[5]

$n = 2^8$	$n = 2^{10}$	$n = 2^{12}$	$n = 2^{14}$	$n = 2^{16}$	$\alpha = 0.01$
$P_{\text{Rijndael}}(n) \leq_{p(id,\lambda x.0.9x)} P_{\text{Blowfish}}(n)$					*true*
1	1	1	1	1	$\wedge$
$P_{\text{Rijndael}}(n) \leq_{p(id,\lambda x.200x)} P_{\text{ArrayCopy}}(n)$					*false*
1	1.444e-73	0	0	1	
$P_{\text{Rijndael}}(n) \leq_{p(id,\lambda x.275x)} P_{\text{ArrayCopy}}(n)$					*true*
1	1	1	1	1	

Table 3: Test results and p-values for Example 2

The results of the experiment are shown in Table 3. As in the experimental evaluation of Example 1, a relation evaluates to *true* if non of the tests rejects the null hypothesis.

The first part of the formula regarding the relative performance of the Rijndael and the Blowfish algorithms evaluates to *true*. The second part, regarding the relative performance of the Rijndael algorithm vs. array copy (null encryption), evaluates to *false*, because the underlying test rejects the null hypothesis in 3 out of 5 cases. To a developer, this

---

[5]Both algorithms operated in CBC mode, using 128-bit keys, and the implementation used was provided by the default (Oracle) provider of Java Cryptography Extensions.

would mean that he either overestimated the performance of the Rijndael encryption algorithm during formulation of the assumption, or that the formula does not hold on this particular platform.

Since we know that we have only guessed at the relative performance of Rijndael vs. array copy, we can use a more conservative estimate and assume that the Rindael algorithm is, say, at most 275× slower. Under this assumption, the second part of the formula will evaluate to *true* (double row at the bottom of Table 3), as will the whole formula.

However, like in the previous experiment, we have no indication as to "how true" is the *true* the formula evaluates to. Again, as a remedy, we rewrite the formula as per Example 4, to obtain a variant that will only evaluate to *true* if all the tests reject the null hypothesis.

$n = 2^8$	$n = 2^{10}$	$n = 2^{12}$	$n = 2^{14}$	$n = 2^{16}$	$\alpha = 0.01$
$P_{\text{Rijndael}}(n) <_{p(id,\lambda x.0.9x)} P_{\text{Blowfish}}(n)$					*true*
0	0	0	0	0	$\wedge$
$P_{\text{Rijndael}}(n) <_{p(id,\lambda x.275x)} P_{\text{ArrayCopy}}(n)$					*true*
0	0	1.988e-52	0	0	

Table 4: Test results and p-values for Example 4

The results of evaluating the modified SPL formula on the same data are shown in Table 4. Again, like in the experimental evaluation of Example 3, a relation evaluates to *true* only if the null hypothesis is rejected for all workloads.

Since we have only tested the more conservative assumption regarding the relative performance of the Rijndael algorithm and array copy, the entire formula evaluates to *true*. Unlike in the previous case though, we know that the resulting *true* is "fairly strong", because only one of the tests had non-zero p-value, and even that was practically zero.

7. EFFICIENT FORMULA EVALUATION

While writing SPL formulas is relatively easy, evaluating them requires collecting significant amount of performance data. In many cases, evaluating a single performance relation or a single test may decide the value of the whole formula, rendering other tests and relations irrelevant, and time put into collecting performance data wasted.

To enable efficient evaluation of SPL formulas in automated performance testing, we have applied the idea of SMT-solving [14, 15, 16] to solving SPL formulas. The basic idea is to solve the propositional part of a formula using a regular SAT solver, and delegate the non-propositional predicates to a specialized decision procedure. In case of SPL, the decision procedure is responsible for collecting performance data and applying the statistical tests to evaluate performance predicates. This approach allows to only collect performance data demanded by the solving algorithm and avoid measurements for predicates that do not influence the value of a formula.

Before describing the actual SPL-evaluation algorithm, we first need to define the concepts of a *propositional skeleton* and *satisfiability-irrelevant variable set*:

Definition 11. For a quantifier-free SPL formula F we define its *propositional skeleton* as a propositional-logic formula F_S, where each occurrence of a performance-relation predicate (i.e., $P_M(\dot{x}_1, \ldots, \dot{x}_m) \leq_{p(tn,tm)} P_N(\dot{y}_1, \ldots, \dot{y}_n)$ or $P_M(\dot{x}_1, \ldots, \dot{x}_m) =_{p(tn,tm)} P_N(\dot{y}_1, \ldots, \dot{y}_n)$) is replaced by a

variable $W_{P_M(\dot{x}_1,\ldots,\dot{x}_m) \leq_{p(tn,tm)} P_N(\dot{y}_1,\ldots,\dot{y}_n)}$, $W_{P_M(\dot{x}_1,\ldots,\dot{x}_m) =_{p(tn,tm)} P_N(\dot{y}_1,\ldots,\dot{y}_n)}$ respectively.

Note that since SPL only allows quantifiers over finite subsets of P, any SPL formula can be transformed to a quantifier-free SPL formula by expanding all quantifiers into finite conjuction (universal) or finite disjunction (existential).

The unsatisfiability of a propositional skeleton implies unsatisfiability of the associated SPL formula (the opposite does not hold). Additionally, the satisfiability of an SPL formula implies satisfiability of its propositional skeleton.

Definition 12. Having a propositional formula F and its satisfying partial valuation[6] V_P, then a *satisfiability-irrelevant* set R_{SI} is a subset of all propositional variables of F such that all the possible valuations of R_{SI} combined with V_P yield a satisfying valuation of F.

SPL-solving algorithm. For a given formula, the algorithm uses a SAT solver to obtain a valuation of its propositional skeleton and checks the feasibility of the skeleton valuation by evaluating the associated performance predicates. If the skeleton valuation is infeasible (i.e., the valuation of a performance predicate given by the decision procedure differs from the valuation of the associated skeleton variable), another valuation is obtained from the SAT solver. The results of the decision procedure are stored and taken into account in subsequent runs of the SAT solver, thus eliminating the infeasible valuations and "locking" the matching valuations. This is repeated either until the valuation of all performance predicates is validated, or until the skeleton, in combination with the stored results, becomes unsatisfiable.

In contrast to SMT-solving, the aim of SPL-solving is to (preferably) only evaluate performance predicates necessary for deciding the satisfiability of a formula (recall evaluation skeleton from Definition 9). Therefore, while checking the feasibility of a skeleton valuation, we identify the satisfiability-irrelevant set with respect to this valuation and consider only the relevant variables. This allows us to skip evaluation of a (potentially large) number of performance predicates. The satisfiability-irrelevant set is constructed incrementally. Before running the decision procedure for a particular skeleton variable, the variable is tested for inclusion in the current version of the satisfiability-irrelevant set. However, since the decision procedure can reject the current skeleton valuation, it is necessary to rebuild this set accordingly.

An outline of the SPL-solving algorithm is shown in Figure 1. Before going into detail, we first describe the notation. For a given SPL formula F, the *MakeSkeleton* function returns its propositional skeleton F_S and the set of all propositional variables substituted for performance predicates R. R_U is the set of all variables from R that have not yet been evaluated by the decision procedure and their valuations are thus undecided. R_{SI} is a satisfiability-irrelevant subset of variables from F_S. V_P is a partial valuation of F_S enforcing the results of the previous decision-procedure runs. The *SolveSAT* function provides a temporary valuation V_{temp} of F_S, based on the partial valuation V_P. The tuple (var, val) denotes a variable from R and its valuation

---

[6] A *satisfying partial valuation* is a partial valuation that can be extended to a complete satisfying valuation.

in V_{temp}. For a variable var, the $IsSatIr$ function decides whether $R_{SI} \cup \{var\}$ is satisfiability-irrelevant for formula F_S and partial valuation V_{SIP}. $MeasureAndTest$ is the decision procedure for performance predicates (as described in Section 4), and m is the result of the procedure (i.e., true or false).

```
 1: F_S, R ← MakeSkeleton(F)
 2: R_U ← R, R_SI ← ∅, V_P ← ∅
 3: V_temp ← SolveSAT(F_S, V_P)
 4: if V_temp = false then
 5:     return false
 6: end if
 7: for all (var, val) ∈ V_temp ∩ R_U do
 8:     V_SIP ← V_temp \ ({var} ∪ R_SI)
 9:     if IsSatIr(var, F_S, V_SIP, R_SI) then
10:         R_U ← R_U \ {var}
11:         R_SI ← R_SI ∪ {var}
12:     else
13:         m ← MeasureAndTest(var)
14:         V_P ← V_P ∪ {(var, m)}
15:         R_U ← R_U \ {var}
16:         if val ≠ m then
17:             R_U ← R_U ∪ R_SI, R_SI ← ∅
18:             goto line 3
19:         end if
20:     end if
21: end for
22: return true
```

Figure 1: SPL-solving algorithm

After the propositional skeleton F_S is created and the involved sets R_U, R_{SI}, as well as the partial valuation V_P are initialized (lines 1-2), a satisfying valuation of F_S combined with V_P is obtained from the SAT solver (line 3). If the SAT solver indicates that F_S combined with V_P is unsatisfiable, the algorithm returns "false" (lines 4-6), because it implies that the original SPL formula is unsatisfiable with respect to measurements dictating V_P. Otherwise, the algorithm sequentially processes valuations of all variables which were not yet checked by the decision procedure (line 7). Each variable is first tested for membership in the current version of R_{SI} with respect to the current skeleton valuation V_{temp} (lines 8-9). If the variable can be added into R_{SI}, then it is added (lines 10-11). Otherwise, it is necessary to call the decision procedure $MeasureAndTest$ (line 13). The result of the decision procedure is added to V_P to be enforced in the subsequent SAT solver runs (line 14). If the stored result conforms to the current skeleton valuation V_{temp}, the next variable is processed. Otherwise V_{temp} is infeasible with respect to the measurements and a new skeleton valuation has to be obtained from the SAT solver (lines 16-19). The new valuation also invalidates the current R_{SI} (line 17).

Correctness of the SPL-solving algorithm. The correctness of the algorithm results from the fact that the algorithm returns "false" only if the propositional skeleton itself is unsatisfiable or if enforcing the measurement-based valuations makes it unsatisfiable. Moreover, the algorithm returns "true" only in cases where the partial measurement-based valuation is satisfying and all the other variables form

a satisfiability-irrelevant set (including the case of empty partial valuation when the formula is a tautology).

Identification of a satisfiability-irrelevant set. During SPL-solving, the variables are sequentially tested for membership in the (incrementally constructed) satisfiability-irrelevant set. For this, we provide a simple algorithm transforming the problem of deciding whether a given set is satisfiability-irrelevant to a formula-satisfiability problem, subsequently solved by a SAT solver. In fact, the resulting SAT formula mimics the Definition 12.

For a formula F, its partial valuation V_P, and the tested (potentially satisfiability-irrelevant) set R_{SI} the transformation yields the following auxiliary formula (let V_T and V_F represent the positively and negatively valuated variables of V_P, respectively, and $r_1 \ldots r_n$ be the elements of R_{SI}):

$$(\wedge_{\forall x \in V_T} x) \wedge (\wedge_{\forall y \in V_F} \neg y) \wedge$$
$$F[r_1 \mapsto false, r_2 \mapsto false, \ldots r_n \mapsto false] \wedge$$
$$F[r_1 \mapsto true, r_2 \mapsto false, \ldots r_n \mapsto false] \wedge$$
$$F[r_1 \mapsto false, r_2 \mapsto true, \ldots r_n \mapsto false] \wedge$$
$$\vdots$$
$$F[r_1 \mapsto true, r_2 \mapsto true, \ldots r_n \mapsto true]$$

where $F[r_1 \mapsto val_1, \ldots, r_n \mapsto val_n]$ denotes a formula derived from F by substituting all occurrences of $r_1, \ldots, r_n$ by the associated boolean constants $val_1, \ldots, val_n$.

The first line of the auxiliary formula enforces the given partial valuation V_P, while the remaining lines capture all possible valuations of R_{SI}.

Decision procedure for performance predicates. Under the sample-based SPL interpretation (Section 4), the decision procedure evaluates performance predicates via statistical testing. For this it first effects collection of performance data from experiments in which the methods under test (two sides of a performance relation) are subjected to workload according to given performance parameters. The statistical test is applied to the performance data and the result of the test is returned as the result of the decision procedure.

7.1 Algorithm discussion

The above SPL-solving algorithm heuristically optimizes the number of evaluated performance predicates (and thus the number of performance measurements). This is important, since SPL formulas may have non-trivial Boolean structure, containing arbitrary combination of conjunctions and disjunctions. For example, if a method M uses two implementations A and B of a library function (selected according to environment settings), we may want to express that performance of M depends on performance of either A or B. This could be expressed by a formula similar to the following disjunction:

$$\left(P_M(\dot{n}) \geq_{p(id, \lambda x. c_{A1} x)} P_A(\dot{n}) \wedge P_M(\dot{n}) \leq_{p(id, \lambda x. c_{A2} x)} P_A(\dot{n})\right)$$

$$\vee$$

$$\left(P_M(\dot{n}) \geq_{p(id, \lambda x. c_{B1} x)} P_B(\dot{n}) \wedge P_M(\dot{n}) \leq_{p(id, \lambda x. c_{B2} x)} P_B(\dot{n})\right)$$

where the coefficients c_{A1}, c_{A2}, c_{B1}, and c_{B2} capture the level of dependency. Disjunctions will be also introduced when using implication or equivalence.

The results of the heuristic depend on the skeleton valuation given by the SAT solver and the order in which the predicates are evaluated. However, the heuristic can be further improved, especially by exploiting the fact that the cost of evaluation of performance predicates can differ depending on the methods under test and workload parameters — mainly because collection of performance data will take different time. For example, evaluating a predicate comparing sorting algorithms will be significantly faster for arrays of size 100 than arrays of size 10000. This leads to a slight modification of the initial problem — each performance predicate in an SPL formula F can be assigned a cost of its evaluation. While solving the propositional skeleton of F, identification of a satisfiability-irrelevant set containing expensive predicates may greatly reduce the run-time of the SPL-solving algorithm, since the most expensive performance predicates might not need to be evaluated.

This could be addressed by employing a SAT solver that provides the satisfiability-irrelevant set as a part of the satisfying valuation, and is able to return an optimal valuation with respect to a given valuation-cost function. For such a SAT solver, a cost function assigning to each positively or negatively-valuated skeleton variable the evaluation cost of the associated performance predicate, while assigning 0 to all the variables in the satisfiability-irrelevant set, would yield the desired valuation. Although optimizing SAT solvers do exist (for example MiniSAT [17]), the problem of returning a satisfiability-irrelevant set as a part of the result has not yet been satisfactorily addressed. Nevertheless, even the usage of a minimizing SAT solver does no guarantee the least total cost of the evaluated performance predicates, which provides room for further investigation.

8. INTEGRATION WITH JAVA

We aim to use SPL in a setting similar to unit testing with JUnit or similar framework. A developer wishing to capture and periodically test performance assumptions should be able to do so by performing steps similar to writing unit tests. Specifically, we target the following use-cases. (UC1) The author of a method makes an assumption about its performance and wants to capture this assumption along with the method definition (i.e., provided nonfunctional property). (UC2) In code using another method, the author of the code makes an assumption about the performance of the used method and wants to capture this assumption along with the code (i.e., required nonfunctional property). (UC3) A third-party developer/tester has additional performance assumptions to those captured in the code; it is therefore necessary to capture and test these assumptions separately.

For the scenario denoted as UC1, we propose encoding SPL formulas using Java annotations. Based on these annotation, automated performance testing software can carry out measurements needed by the algorithm presented in Section 7 to evaluate the SPL formula. The @SPL annotation can be used to specify a set of SPL formulas for each method.

A simple application of the @SPL annotation is shown in Figure 2. In this case, the SPL formula requires that the execution time of the annotated method (referenced by the SELF keyword) be lower or equal to the execution time of method g() in class Y for two different types of input. The variable n in the SPL formula is used as a parameter for an implicit *input generator*[7] related to the annotated method.

---

[7] Input generators are instances of `Iterable<Object[]>` that provide sequences of method inputs for performance measurements.

In straightforward cases like this one, input generators can be located using a naming conventions.

```
@SPL(formula = "for n {1,2} SELF(n) <= Y.g(n)")
int method(int[] parameter) { /* ... */ }
```

Figure 2: A simple application of @SPL.

Figure 3 illustrates how a custom input generator can be used (and reused). When an input generator is specified explicitly, the SPL evaluation framework will use the custom generator instead of the default one and use the supplied parameters to configure it. Each method can have multiple input generators.

```
@SPL(
    generators = "org.gen.Generator(parameter)",
    formula = "for n {1,2} SELF(n) <= Y.g(n)"
)
```

Figure 3: Defining a shared custom generator.

An advanced scenario with multiple generators is shown in Figure 4. Three different generators (with identifiers `gen[1-3]`) are defined and can be referenced within `formula`. The various forms of generator names provide the testing framework with information on creating generator instances.

```
@SPL(
    generators = {
        "gen1:gen.Gen1(parameter)",
        "gen2:gen.Gen2#factory(arg)",
        "gen3:gen.Gen3(parameter)#fact(arg)"
    },
    methods = {
        "methodX:pkg.AClass(parameter)#methodX",
        "methodY:pkg.JustStatic#methodY"
    },
    formula =
        "for j {1,2} k {1,2}" +
        "SELF[gen1](j) >= methodX[gen2](j) &" +
        "methodY[gen3](j,k) <=(x.10x,id)" +
            "SELF[gen3](j,k)"
)
```

Figure 4: A complex @SPL annotation example.

The example in Figure 4 also includes method references. When referencing non-static methods in other classes, these classes have to be instantiated first, which is the main purpose of the `method` parameter. Aliases defined in `methods` can be used instead of the fully qualified method names in `formula`.

As far as UC1 is concerned, performance annotations can be evaluated by a standalone SPL evaluation tool, which automatically evaluates all SPL-annotated methods in a given class or set of classes. UC2 can be addressed by taking an approach similar to UC1, i.e., by introducing SPL-annotated wrappers of the respective methods.

To address UC3, as well as complex cases of UC1 and UC2 (beyond the expressive power of annotations), we envision using an API inspired by JUnit, as shown in Figure 5.

```
void assertSPLOfMethod(
    Method method,
    Map<String, Entry<Object, Method>> methods,
    Map<String, InputGenerator> generators
);

void assertSPLFormula(
    String formula,
    Method method
);

void assertSPLFormula(
    String formula,
    Map<String, Entry<Object, Method>> methods,
    Map<String, InputGenerator> generators
);
```

Figure 5: SPL API based on JUnit.

The `assertSPLOfMethod()` method addresses the complex cases of UC1 and UC2 by evaluating the `@SPL` annotation of `method` in combination with the `methods` and `generators` parameters, which allows overriding the original method and generator definitions, and using locally initialized generators and method references. The `assertSPLFormula()` method family covers UC3, where the first version of `assertSPL-Formula()` evaluates the supplied SPL `formula` using method and generator references obtained from the `@SPL` annotation of `method` and the second version uses explicitly provided `methods` and `generators` for the evaluation.

9. RELATED WORK

Current performance specification methods focus on analysis of previously-measured or run-time performance data (with the goal to verify given performance assertions). In contrast, SPL is targeting repetitive performance testing by first stating a performance assertion and then using the SPL-solving algorithm to obtain the measurements needed to decide satisfiability of the assertions. The following related performance-specification methods share this property.

PSpec [18] is a language for expressing performance assertions which targets similar goals – regression testing and code documentation. It uses absolute performance metrics (e.g., execution time) to capture the expected performance, which makes the formulas either non-portable, or too liberal. The performance data is collected from application logs.

PIP [19] is a similar approach exploiting declarative performance expectations with the goal of debugging behavior and performance of distributed systems. In contrast to SPL, PIP includes description of system behavior and the expected performance is declared with respect to such behavioral specification. Similar to PSpec, PIP uses application logs to obtain performance measurements and uses absolute performance metrics (such as CPU time, message latency) in performance expectations.

Performance assertions based on the PA language are introduced in [20]. Similar to our approach, the assertions are part of the source code. The assertions are checked at run-time and support local behavior adaptations based on the results. However, the method is not suitable for automated performance testing. The PA language provides access to various performance metrics (both absolute and relative) as well as key features of the architecture and user parameters.

Complementary to our method, in [21] the system-level performance expectations are descibed imperatively, using programmatic tests of globally measured performance data. The measurements are performed at run-time via injected probes and the data is analyzed continuously.

Similarly, [22] employs the A language to express validation programs concerning both business logic and performance characteristics (balanced CPU load) of Internet services. The method focuses mainly on run-time validation of operator actions and static configuration.

JUnitPerf [8] is an extension to the JUnit [3] framework, based on ideas from [18], It provides accurate time measurements and tests in the scope of a unit test. Similar to SPL, JUnitPerf targets automated performance testing while stressing simple usage scenarios. However, the performance assertions are not portable.

While we do not address the creation of SPL assertions in this work, there are also methods concerning specification of performance requirements at design-time. A process for constructing a performance-annotation model for UML is described in [23], with annotations based on the UML Profile for Schedulability, Performance, and Time specification. Such UML models can be then transformed to performance-analysis models based for example on Petri Nets [24].

An evolutionary methodology for performance-requirements specification is presented in [25]. It is based on refinement of the performance requirements during development. Further approaches for performance assessment and modeling in context of software architecture are compared in [26].

An important part of this work is the SPL-solving algorithm based on the idea of SMT-solving. Similar to classic SMT-solving techniques [14, 15], employed for example in Z3 [16], our approach uses a SAT solver for solving the propositional skeleton of the input formula. However, since the SPL-solving algorithm determines the measurements needed for deciding a given performance assertion, the number of evaluated performance predicates can be optimized by identifying a satisfiability-irrelevant set of propositional variables. This is not supported by the state-of-the-art SMT solvers, since there is no need to optimize the number of invocations of the underlying predicate-logic decision procedure.

10. CONCLUSION AND FUTURE WORK

Performance assertions and their analysis is an extensively-studied topic, yet so far in most cases, the assertions can be only expressed in absolute terms. Our goal is to enable the developer to express performance assumptions in simple, intuitive terms. To this end, we have introduced a novel method for describing performance assertions using Stochastic Performance Logic (SPL), which allows making statements about relative method performance in a platform independent way. Developer input is required in matters such as choosing the workload sizes relevant for the assumption, but providing such input appears to be more intuitive than having to guess the duration of method execution.

---

[8] http://clarkware.com/software/JUnitPerf.html

Our approach relies on statistical testing, and unless different interpretation is defined, it is well suited for a specific class of methods (computational and data transformation kernels) with simple behavior (performance-wise). The performance of such methods can be represented by an uni-modal distribution of execution times for a given workload, and for which comparisons between location parameters such as mean value make sense. To facilitate efficient evaluation of SPL formulas in automated testing, we have presented an SPL solving algorithm that will drive the execution of experiments to collect performance data required to evaluate an SPL formula, possibly avoiding unnecessary measurements. To stress the practical impact of our approach, we have presented a set of annotations for the Java language that enable initial integration of SPL formulas with code.

We believe that these three components (the logic, the solving algorithm, and the annotation) provide a solid foundation for automated performance testing. Even though the foundations are solid, there is still a lot of room for improvement. In case of SPL, new theorems and axioms may be introduced, not only to show more complex properties of the logic, but also to guide the SAT solver in its search for satisfying valuations of SPL formulas. The SPL solving algorithm itself can be improved, provided a suitable optimizing SAT-solver can be found or developed. Finally, integration with code can be simplified by introducing more high-level annotations that will cover typical situations without the need to resorting to low-level SPL formulas.

11. ACKNOWLEDGMENTS

This work was partially supported by the Grant Agency of the Czech Republic project GACR P202/10/J042 and by the EU project ASCENS 257414.

12. REFERENCES

[1] K. Beck, *Test Driven Development: By Example*. 2002.
[2] B. Meyer, "Applying "Design by Contract"," *IEEE Computer*, vol. 25, 1992.
[3] P. Tahchiev, F. Leme, V. Massol, and G. Gregory, *JUnit in Action, 2nd Edition*. 2010.
[4] Google, "Googletest." http://code.google.com/p/googletest/.
[5] G. T. Leavens, C. Ruby, R. Leino, E. Poll, and B. Jacobs, "JML: Notations and Tools Supporting Detailed Design in Java," in *OOPSLA'00*, 2000.
[6] E. Cohen, W. Schulte, and S. Tobies, "A Practical Verification Methodology for Concurrent Programs," 2009.
[7] T. Kalibera and P. Tuma, "Precise Regression Benchmarking with Random Effects: Improving Mono Benchmark Results," in *Formal Methods and Stochastic Models for Performance Evaluation*, vol. 4054 of *LNCS*, Springer, 2006.
[8] T. Kalibera, J. Lehotsky, D. Majda, B. Repcek, M. Tomcanyi, A. Tomecek, P. Tuma, and J. Urban, "Automated Benchmarking and Analysis Tool," in *VALUETOOLS'06*, ACM, 2006.
[9] L. Bulej, T. Kalibera, and P. Tuma, "Repeated Results Analysis for Middleware Regression Benchmarking," *Perf. Evaluation*, vol. 60, 2005.
[10] H. P. Barendregt, *The Lambda Calculus, Its Syntax and Semantics*. North-Holland, Amsterdam, 1984.
[11] B. L. Welch, "The Generalization of 'Student's' Problem when Several Different Population Variances are Involved," *Biometrika*, vol. 34, 1947.
[12] L. Wasserman, *All of Statistics: A Concise Course in Statistical Inference*. Springer Texts in Statistics, Springer, 2003.
[13] T. Kalibera and P. Tuma, "Precise Regression Benchmarking with Random Effects: Improving Mono Benchmark Results," in *Formal Methods and Stochastic Models for Performance Evaluation*, vol. 4054 of *LNCS*, Springer, 2006.
[14] C. Barrett, D. Dill, and A. Stump, "Checking Satisfiability of First-Order Formulas by Incremental Translation to SAT," in *Computer Aided Verification*, vol. 2404 of *LNCS*, Springer, 2002.
[15] L. de Moura and N. Bjørner, "Satisfiability Modulo Theories: An Appetizer," in *Formal Methods: Foundations and Applications*, vol. 5902 of *LNCS*, Springer, 2009.
[16] L. de Moura and N. Bjorner, "Z3: An Efficient SMT Solver," in *Tools and Algorithms for the Construction and Analysis of Systems*, vol. 4963 of *LNCS*, Springer, 2008.
[17] N. E'en and N. Sorensson, "Translating Pseudo-boolean Constraints into SAT," *J. on Satisfiability, Boolean Modeling and Computation*, 2006.
[18] S. E. Perl and W. E. Weihl, "Performance assertion checking," *SIGOPS Oper. Syst. Rev.*, vol. 27, 1993.
[19] P. Reynolds, C. Killian, J. L. Wiener, J. C. Mogul, M. A. Shah, and A. Vahdat, "Pip: Detecting the Unexpected in Distributed Systems," in *NSDI'06*, USENIX, 2006.
[20] J. S. Vetter and P. H. Worley, "Asserting Performance Expectations," in *Proc. 2002 ACM/IEEE Conf. on Supercomputing*, Supercomputing '02, IEEE CS, 2002.
[21] X. Liu, Z. Guo, X. Wang, F. Chen, X. Lian, J. Tang, M. Wu, M. F. Kaashoek, and Z. Zhang, "D3S: Debugging Deployed Distributed Systems," in *NSDI'08*, USENIX, 2008.
[22] A. Tjang, F. Oliveira, R. Bianchini, R. Martin, and T. Nguyen, "Model-Based Validation for Internet Services," in *Proc. 28th IEEE Intl. Symp. on Reliable Distributed Systems*, 2009.
[23] H. Du, R. Gan, K. Liu, Z. Zhang, and D. Booy, "Method for Constructing Performance Annotation Model Based on Architecture Design of Information Systems," in *Research and Practical Issues of Enterprise Information Systems II*, vol. 255 of *IFIP*, Springer, 2008.
[24] S. Distefano, D. Paci, A. Puliafito, and M. Scarpa, "UML Design and Software Performance Modeling," in *Computer and Information Sciences - ISCIS 2004*, vol. 3280 of *LNCS*, Springer, 2004.
[25] C.-W. Ho and L. Williams, "Developing Software Performance with the Performance Refinement and Evolution Model," in *WOSP'07*, ACM, 2007.
[26] M. A. Isa and D. N. A. Jawawi, "Comparative Evaluation of Performance Assessment and Modeling Method for Software Architecture," in *Software Engineering and Computer Systems*, vol. 181 of *CCIS*, Springer, 2011.

Refactoring Access Control Policies for Performance Improvement

Donia El Kateb
Laboratory of Advanced
Software SYstems (LASSY)
University of Luxembourg
Luxembourg
donia.elkateb@uni.lu

Tejeddine Mouelhi
Security, Reliability and Trust
Interdisciplinary Research
Center, SnT
University of Luxembourg
Luxembourg
tejeddine.mouelhi@uni.lu

Yves Le Traon
Laboratory of Advanced
Software SYstems (LASSY) &
Security, Reliability and Trust
Interdisciplinary Research
Center, SnT
University of Luxembourg
Luxembourg
yves.letraon@uni.lu

JeeHyun Hwang
Dept. of Computer Science
North Carolina State
University
U.S.A
jhwang4@ncsu.edu

Tao Xie
Dept. of Computer Science
North Carolina State
University
U.S.A
xie@csc.ncsu.edu

ABSTRACT

In order to facilitate managing authorization, access control architectures are designed to separate the business logic from an access control policy. To determine whether a user can access which resources, a request is formulated from a component, called a Policy Enforcement Point (PEP) located in application code. Given a request, a Policy Decision Point (PDP) evaluates the request against an access control policy and returns its access decision (i.e., permit or deny) to the PEP. With the growth of sensitive information for protection in an application, an access control policy consists of a larger number of rules, which often cause a performance bottleneck. To address this issue, we propose to refactor access control policies for performance improvement by splitting a policy (handled by a single PDP) into its corresponding multiple policies with a smaller number of rules (handled by multiple PDPs). We define seven attribute-set-based splitting criteria to facilitate splitting a policy. We have conducted an evaluation on three subjects of real-life Java systems, each of which interacts with access control policies. Our evaluation results show that (1) our approach preserves the initial architectural model in terms of interaction between the business logic and its corresponding rules in a policy, and (2) our approach enables to substantially reduce request evaluation time for most splitting criteria.

Categories and Subject Descriptors

D.4.8 [**Performance**]: Measurements; C.4 [**Performance of systems**]: Performance attributes

General Terms

Performance, Design

Keywords

Access Control, Performance, Refactoring, Policy Enforcement Point, Policy Decision Point, eXtensible Access Control Markup Language

1. INTRODUCTION

Access control mechanisms regulate which users could perform which actions on what system resources based on access control policies. Access control policies (policies in short) are based on various access control models such as Role-Based Access Control (RBAC) [7], Mandatory Access Control (MAC) [6], Discretionary Access Control (DAC) [10], and Organization-Based Access Control (OrBAC) [9]. Access control policies are specified in various policy specification languages such as the eXtensible Access Control Markup Language (XACML) [3] and Enterprise Privacy Authorization Language (EPAL) [1]. A policy-based system allows policy authors to define rules that specify actions (e.g., read) that subjects (e.g., students) can take on resources (e.g., grades) in a policy. In the context of policy-based systems, an access control architecture is often designed with respect to a popular architectural concept that separates Policy Enforcement Points (PEPs) from a Policy Decision Point (PDP) [19]. More specifically, a PEP is located inside an application's code (i.e., business logic of the system). Business logic describes functional algorithms to govern information exchange between access control decision logic and a user interface (i.e., presentation). Given requests (e.g., student A requests to read her grade resource B) formulated by the PEP, the PDP evaluates the requests and returns their responses (e.g., permit or deny) by evaluating these requests against rules in a policy.

An important benefit of such architecture is to facilitate managing access rights in a fine-grained way by decoupling the business logic from the access control decision logic, which can be standardized and separately managed. However, this architecture may cause performance degradation especially when policy authors maintain a single policy with a large number of rules to regulate the whole system's resources. Consider that the policy is centralized with *only* one single PDP. The PDP evaluates requests (issued by PEPs) against the large number of rules in the policy in real-time. Such centralization can be a major factor for degrading performance as our previous work [13] showed that efficient request evaluation with a large number of rules is a challenging task. This performance bottleneck issue may impact service availability as well, especially when dealing with a huge number of requests within a short time.

In order to address this performance bottleneck issue, we propose an approach to refactor policies automatically to significantly reduce request evaluation time. As manual refactoring is tedious and error-prone, an important benefit of our automated approach is to reduce significant human efforts as well as improving performance. Our approach includes two techniques: (1) refactoring a policy (handled by single PDP) to its corresponding multiple policies each with a smaller number of rules (handled by multiple PDPs), and (2) preserving the architectural property stating that a single PDP is triggered by a given PEP at a time.

In the first technique, our approach takes a splitting criterion and an original global policy (i.e., a policy governing all of access rights in the system) as an input, and returns a set of corresponding subpolicies, each of which consists of a smaller number of rules. This refactoring involves grouping rules in the global policy into several subsets based on the splitting criterion. More specifically, we propose a set of splitting criteria to refactor the global policy to smaller policies. A splitting criterion selects and groups the rules handled by the overall PDP into specific PDPs. Each criterion-specific PDP encapsulates a sub-policy that represents a set of rules that share the same combination of attribute elements (Subject, Action, and/or Resource). In the second technique, our approach aims at preserving the architectural property that only a single PDP is triggered by a given PEP at a time. More specifically, given a request, each PEP should be mapped to a PDP loaded with a policy, which includes a set of rules to be applicable for the request. Therefore, our refactoring maintains the architectural property of centralized architectures in policy-based systems.

We collect three subjects of real-life Java systems. Each system interacts with access control policies, whose corresponding request evaluation faces performance degradation. The policies are specified in eXtensible Access Control Markup Language (XACML) [3]. XACML is an XML-based policy specification language popularly used for web-based applications and services.

While our subjects are based on XACML policies, our approach could be applicable to any software system that interacts with policies specified in other policy specification languages. We conduct an evaluation to show performance improvement achieved by our approach in terms of request evaluation time. We leverage two types of PDPs to measure request evaluation time. The first one is the Sun PDP implementation [2], which is a popular open source PDP, and the second one is XEngine [13], which transforms an original policy into its corresponding policy in a tree format by mapping attribute values with numerical values. Our evaluation results show that our approach preserves the policy behaviors of the centralized architectures and the architectural property. Our evaluation results also show that our approach enables reducing the request evaluation time substantially. This paper makes the following three main contributions:

- We propose an automated approach that refactors a single global policy to policies each with a smaller number of rules. This refactoring helps improve performance of request evaluation time.

- We propose a set of splitting criteria to help refactor a policy in a systematic way. Our proposed splitting criteria do not alter policy behaviors of the centralized architectures.

- We conduct an evaluation on three Java systems interacting with XACML policies. We measure performance in terms of request evaluation time. Our evaluation results show that our approach achieves substantially faster than that of the centralized architectures in terms of request evaluation time.

The remainder of this paper is organized as follows. Section 2 introduces concepts related to our research problem addressed in this paper. Section 3 presents the overall approach. Section 4 presents evaluation results and discusses the effectiveness of our approach. Section 5 discusses related work. Section 6 concludes this paper and discusses future research directions.

2. CONTEXT/PROBLEM STATEMENT

This section further details a centralized architecture, its two desirable features such as synergy and reconfigurability, and its induced penalty (performance bottlenecks). Managing access control policies is one of the most challenging issues faced by an organization due to frequent changes in a policy. For example, a policy-based system has to handle some specific requirements such as role swapping when employees are given temporary assignments, as well as changes in the policies and procedures, new assets, users and job positions in the organization.

2.1 Centralization of Architectures

To facilitate policy management, an access control policy is traditionally modeled, analyzed, and implemented as a separate component encapsulated in a PDP. This separation leads to the centralized architecture presented in Figure 1, in which one single PDP is responsible for granting/denying the accesses that are requested. This centralized architecture is a simple solution to easily handle changes in policy-based systems by enabling the policy author to directly change policies on the single PDP. The separation between the PEP and the PDP simplifies policy management across many heterogeneous systems and limits potential risks arising from incorrect policy implementation or maintenance when the policy is hardcoded inside the business logic.

2.2 Centralization: A Threat for Performance

In such a centralized system, when a service regulated by an access control policy requires an access to some resources in the system, the PEP calls the PDP to retrieve an authorization decision based on the policy encapsulated in the PDP. This authorization decision is made through the evaluation of rules in the policy. Subsequently, an authorization decision (permit/deny) is returned to the PEP. When a huge number of access requests are sent by the PEP to the PDP, two bottlenecks cause performance degradation:

- all the access requests have to be managed through the same input channel of the PDP.

- the centralized PDP computes an access request by searching which rule is applicable among all the rules that the encapsulated policy contains.

A request evaluation time is thus strongly related to

- the number of rules in the policy that the PDP contains [14].

- the workload (i.e., the number of requests) that have to be evaluated by the system.

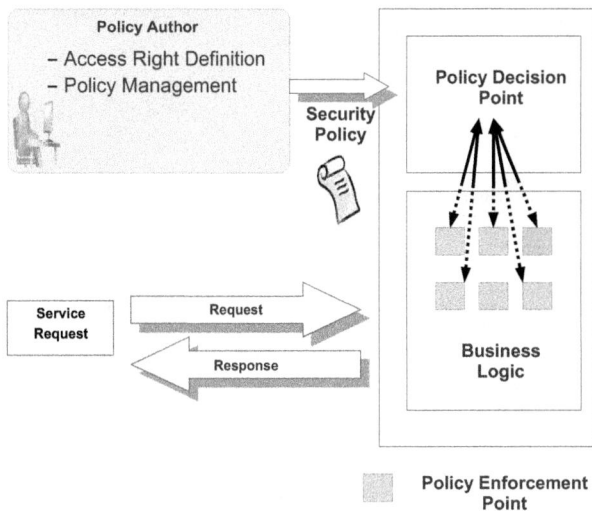

Figure 1: Access Control Request Evaluation

The request evaluation time depends on the size (number of rules) of the policy that the PDP encapsulates. For a given policy size, the evaluation time to evaluate requests increases linearly with the workload (i.e., the number of requests). Our *Hypothesis 1* is that the more rules a policy contains, the higher the slope of the evaluation time with an increasing workload. *Hypothesis 1* validity is discussed in Section 4. As a consequence, one possibility to improve performance consists in splitting the centralized PDP into PDPs with smaller policy sizes. We consider keeping the same input channel in the decentralized architecture. Therefore, we do not change the PEP code. Note that if a specific input channel is required for each PEP, developers are required to change the PEP code to map each PEP with its corresponding PDP.

2.3 Centralization: PEPs and PDP Synergy

Centralization offers a desirable feature by simplifying the routing of requests to the right PDP. Figure 2 illustrates the model of the access control architecture. In this model, a set of business processes, which comply to users' needs, is illustrated by the business logic, which is enforced by multiple PEPs. Conceptually, the decision is decoupled from the enforcement and involves a decision making process in which each PEP interacts with the same single PDP. The key point concerns the cardinality linking PEPs to the PDP. While a PDP is potentially linked to many PEPs, any PEP is strictly linked to exactly one PDP (which is unique in the centralized model). Since there is only one PDP, the requests are all routed to this unique PDP. No particular treatment is required to map a given PEP in the business logic to the corresponding PDP, embedding the requested rules. Another advantage of this many-to-one association is the clear traceability between what has been specified by the policy and the PEPs enforcing this policy at the business logic level. In such setting, when access control policies are updated or removed, the related PEPs can be easily located and updated or removed. Thus the application is updated synchronously with the policy changes. We call this desirable property *synergy* of the access control architecture: an access control architecture is said to be *synergic* if any PEP always sends its requests to the same

PDP. As a consequence, splitting the centralized PDP into PDPs of smaller policy sizes may break this synergy since calls issued by PEPs can be handled by several PDPs. In this work, we consider various splitting criteria to transform a centralized PDP into PDPs with smaller policy size. Our *Hypothesis 2* is with comparable PDP policy sizes, the evaluation time will be reduced when the architecture is synergic. This hypothesis is investigated in Section 4.

2.4 Tradeoff for Refactoring

The following facts are taken into account in our work:

- Access control architectures are centralized with a unique PDP.

- Centralization eases reconfiguration of an access control policy.

- Centralization threatens performance.

- Direct mapping from any PEP to only one PDP makes the access control architectures synergic.

- A synergic system facilitates PEP request routing and eases policy maintenance.

The goal of our work is to improve performance by refactoring the centralized model into its corresponding decentralized model with multiple PDPs. The resulting architecture must have an equivalent behavior and should not impact the desirable properties of the centralized model, namely reconfigurability and synergy. Automating the transformation from a centralized to a decentralized architecture is required to preserve reconfigurability. With automation, we can still reconfigure the centralized policy, and then automatically refactor the architecture. We propose automatic refactoring of a centralized model into its corresponding decentralized model while preserving high reconfigurability. However, refactoring the architecture by splitting the centralized PDP into smaller ones may break the initial synergy. This phenomenon is studied in the empirical study of Section 4 together with *Hypothesis 2*. In the next section, we give an overview of the XACML language since it is the standard language used in this paper to implement a PDP.

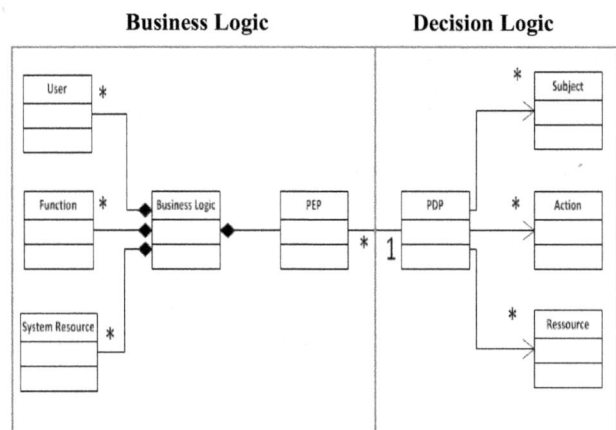

Figure 2: Access Control Model

2.5 XACML Policies and Performance Issues

In this paper, we focus on access control policies specified in the eXtensible Access Control Modeling Language (XACML) [3]. XACML is an XML-based standard policy specification language that defines a syntax of access control policies and requests/responses. XACML enables policy authors to externalize access control policies for the sake of interoperability since access control policies can be designed independently from the underlying programming language or platform. Such flexibility enables to easily update access control policies to comply with new requirements. An XACML policy is constructed as follows. A `policy set` element consists of a sequence of `policy` elements, a combining algorithm, and a `policy target` element. A `policy` element is expressed through a `target`, a set of `rules`, and a rule combining algorithm. A `target` element consists of the set of subjects, resources, and actions to which a policy or a rule is applicable. A `rule` consists of a `target` element, a `condition` element, and an `effect`. A `condition` element is a boolean expression that specifies the environmental context (e.g., time and location restrictions) in which the rule applies. Finally, an `effect` is the rule's authorization decision, which is either permit or deny. Given a request, a PDP evaluates the request against the `rules` in the policy by matching subjects, resources, and actions in the request. More specifically, an XACML request encapsulates attributes that define which subject requests to take action on which resource (e.g., subject Bob requests to borrow a book). Given a request that satisfies the `target` and `condition` elements in a rule, the rule's effect is taken as the decision. If the request does not satisfy the `target` and `condition` elements in any rule, its response yields the "NotApplicable" decision.

When more than one rule is applicable to a request, the combining algorithm helps determine which rule's effect can be finally given as the decision for the request. For example, given two rules that are applicable to the same request and provide different decisions, the permit-overrides algorithm prioritizes a permit decision over the other decisions. More precisely, when using the permit-overrides algorithm, the policy evaluation produces one of the following three decisions for a request:

- Permit if at least one permit rule is applicable for the request.

- Deny if no permit rule is applicable and at least one deny rule is applicable for the request.

- NotApplicable if no rule is applicable for the request.

A `policy target` element describes what the policy applies to by referring to attributes of subjects, resources, and actions. Figure 3 shows a simplified XACML policy that denies subject Bob to borrow a book.

XACML policies become more complex when handling increasing complexity of organizations in terms of structure, relationships, activities, and access control requirements. In such a situation, a policy often consists of a large number of rules to specify policy behaviors for various resources, users, and actions in the organizations. In policy-based systems, policy authors manage a centralized and a single PDP loaded with a single policy to govern all system resources. However, due to a large number of rules for evaluation, this centralization raises performance concerns related to request evaluation time for access control policies and may degrade the system efficiency and slow down the overall business processes.

We present the following three main factors that may cause to degrade XACML request evaluation performance:

- An XACML policy may contain various attribute elements including `target` elements. Retrieval of attribute values in

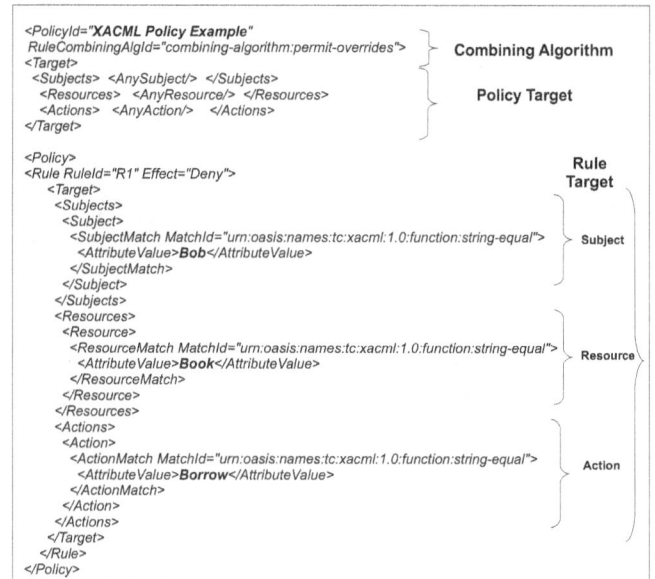

Figure 3: XACML Policy Example

the `target` elements for request evaluation may increase the evaluation time.

- A `policy set` consists of a set of policies. Given a request, a PDP determines the final authorization decision (i.e., effect) of the whole `policy set` after combining all the applicable rules' decisions for the request. Computing and combining applicable rules' decisions contribute to increasing the evaluation time.

- `Condition` elements in rules can be complex because these elements are built from an arbitrary nesting of boolean functions and attributes. In such a situation, evaluating `condition` elements may slow down request evaluation time.

3. POLICY REFACTORING

This section describes our approach of refactoring access control policies to improve performance by reducing the number of policy rules potentially applicable to a request. For refactoring policies in a systematic way, we propose seven policy splitting criteria based on attribute sets. Moreover, we explain how to select a splitting criterion that preserves the synergy in the access control architecture.

3.1 Policy Splitting Criteria

During the evaluation process, the attribute values in a given request are compared with the attribute values in the target of a rule. If there is a match between the request's attribute values and target's attribute values, the rule is then applicable to the request. In the decision making process, applicable rules contribute to determining the final authorization decision whereas non-applicable rules are not relevant in this process. For request evaluation, not all the rules are applicable to the request. In other words, only part of the rules (i.e, relevant rules) are applicable to the request and can contribute to determining the final decision.

We propose an approach to evaluate a request against only the relevant rules for the given request by refactoring the access control policies. Our approach aims at splitting a single global policy into multiple smaller policies based on attribute combination. For a given policy-based system, we transform its policy P into policies P_{SC_w} containing a smaller number of rules and conforming to a Splitting Criterion SC_w. An SC_w defines the set of attributes that are considered to classify all the rules into subsets each with the same attribute values and w denotes the number of attributes that have to be considered conjointly for aggregating rules based on specific attribute elements. Table 1 shows our proposed splitting criteria categorized according to attribute element combinations.

Table 1: Splitting Criteria

Categories	Splitting Criteria
SC_1	$\langle Subject \rangle$, $\langle Resource \rangle$, $\langle Action \rangle$
SC_2	$\langle Subject, Action \rangle$, $\langle Subject, Resource \rangle$ $\langle Resource, Action \rangle$
SC_3	$\langle Subject, Resource, Action \rangle$

To illustrate our approach, we present examples that take into consideration the XACML language features. In Figure 4, our approach refactors an XACML policy P according to the splitting criterion $SC_1 = \langle Subject \rangle$. Our refactoring results in two sub-policies Pa and Pb. Each sub-policy consists of relevant rules with regards to the same subject (Alice or Bob in this case).

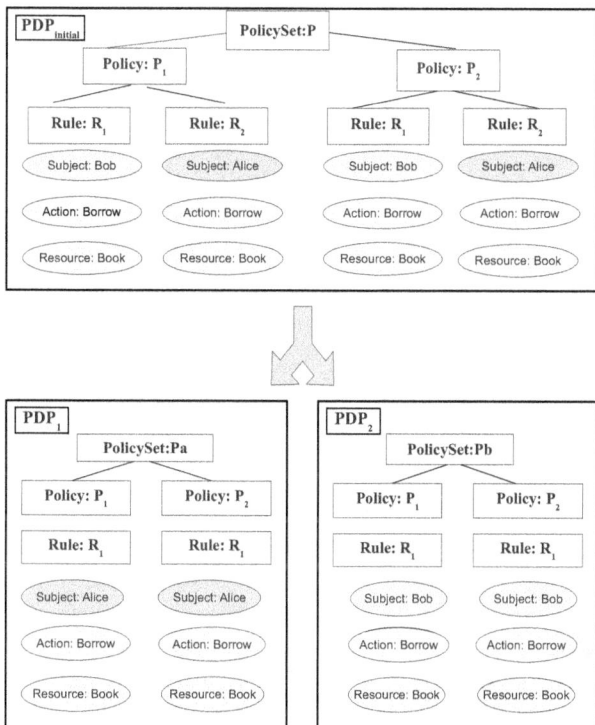

Figure 4: Refactoring a Policy According to $SC_1 = \langle Subject \rangle$

Technically, to split a given policy P according to $SC_1 = \langle Subject \rangle$, we start by parsing the global policy P and by collecting the overall subject attribute values in the policy. For each collected subject attribute value Sa, we consider the global policy and we delete the

---

Algorithm 1 Policy Splitting Algorithm for $SC_1 = \langle Subject \rangle$

Input: XACML Policy P, Splitting Criterion $SC_1 = \langle Subject \rangle$
Output: Sub-policies Set: S
SplitPolicy()
S=Ø
/* Collect all subjects in all the rules /*
for each Rule R_i in Policy P **do**
    /* Fetch all the targets to extract attribute collection based on SC */
    for each Target.Subject in R_i **do**
        SubjectCollection.add(SubjectElement.attribute)
    end for
end for
/* Build sub-policies based on subjects collected in SubjectCollection */
for int $i = 0$; $i <$ SubjectCollection.size(); $i++$ **do**
    /* Remove all the rules that do not contain SubjectCollection.at(i) in their Target */
    for each Rule R_i in Policy P **do**
        if $R_i.Target.SubjectElement$! $=$ AnySubject **then**
            if (Target.SubjectElement.attribute in R_i) ! $=$ SubjectCollection.at(i) **then**
                Remove R_i
            end if
        end if
    end for
    /* $P_{(SubjectCollection.at(i))}$ is a sub-policy with only rules where the subjectAttribute is equal to SubjectCollection.at(i) */
    /* Add the sub-policy to the set of sub-policies */
    $S = S \cup P_{(SubjectCollection.at(i))}$
end for

---

rules that do not contain Sa as a subject attribute value in the target element attributes. After all the successive deletions, the global policy is refactored to a policy that contains only the rules with Sa in their subject attribute values. Algorithm 1 describes the splitting process for $SC_1 = \langle Subject \rangle$.

Our algorithm is safe in the sense that it does not change the authorization behavior of the PDP. There are two important issues to be considered when reasoning about the safety of the algorithm:

- Can the splitting impact authorization results when a policy set includes multiple policies with different combining algorithms?

- When AnySubject, AnyAction or AnyResource are used as target element values, does the splitting change the behavior of the PDP?

The first issue is addressed by the way the algorithm operates. The first step of the algorithm goes through all the rules and extracts the set of target element values (the set of subjects, the set of actions, and/or the set of resources) based on the splitting criterion. Then, based on the extracted result, the splitting is performed by removing the rules with different splitting criterion values (such as a subject different from the splitting criterion subject). The rules that are kept are therefore not modified and their behavior is not altered. When there are several policies with different combining algorithms, the rules that are kept do not impact the evaluation behavior because they remain attached to the same combining algorithm. Moreover their order and their content are not modified.

The second issue is addressed by keeping all the rules that involve AnySubject, AnyAction, or AnyResource in all sub-policies because by definition during evaluation, these values are taken into consideration for evaluating all possible values of subjects, actions, and resources. It is worth mentioning this following consideration related to the refactoring process: XACML supports multi-valued attributes in policies and requests. In XACML policies, `target` elements define a set of attribute values, which match with the context element in an access control request. In Figure 5, the subject attribute includes two attributes (one is "role" and the other is "isEq-subjUserId-resUserId"). In order to match the subject with multi-valued attributes, a request should include at least `pc-member` and `true` for "role" and "isEq-subjUserId-resUserId", respectively. Our approach considers such a whole subject element as a single entity, which is not split by the policy splitter component.

```
<Subjects>
  <Subject>
    <SubjectMatch MatchId="urn:oasis:names:tc:xacml:1.0:function:string-equal">
      <AttributeValue>Administrator</AttributeValue>
    <SubjectAttributeDesignator AttributeId="role"/>
    </SubjectMatch>
    <SubjectMatch MatchId="urn:oasis:names:tc:xacml:1.0:function:string-equal">
      <AttributeValue >true</AttributeValue>
    <SubjectAttributeDesignator AttributeId="isEq-subjUserId-resUserId"/>
    </SubjectMatch>
  </Subject>
</Subjects>
```

Figure 5: Multi-attribute Values in `target` Element

After the splitting is performed, our approach creates one or more PDPs that comply with the splitting criterion. We use the Sun PDP [3] to evaluate a request against policies specified in XACML. During request evaluation, the Sun PDP checks the request against the policy and determines whether the decision is permit or deny. Given a request, our approach runs the Sun PDP loaded with the request's relevant policy, which is used during the decision making process. The PDP then retrieves the rules that are applicable to the request. Figure 6 presents our approach to handling request evaluation with multiple policies. During the evaluation process, given a request, our approach verifies the matching between the request's attribute value and the policy target elements attributes. Our approach then selects only the relevant policy among all the policies for a given request. After the selection of the relevant policy, all of its relevant rules for the decision making are evaluated. Figure 7 shows an overview of our approach. In our approach, the policy splitter component plays a role to refactor access control policies. Given a single PDP loaded with the initial global policy, the policy splitter component conducts automated refactoring by creating multiple PDPs loaded with XACML policies, which are split from the initial global policy based on the user-specified splitting criterion. If the initial global policy is changed, the policy splitter component is required to refactor the policy again to create PDPs with the most recent relevant policies. Our refactoring approach is safe in the sense that the approach does not impact existing security aspects in a given system.

3.2 Architecture Model Preservation: PEP-PDP Synergy

We propose to preserve the synergy property in the access control architecture by mapping a PEP and a PDP loaded with the relevant policy for a request dynamically at runtime. As shown in Section 3.1, given multiple PDPs after the policy refactoring, we consider (1) how PEPs are organized at the application level, and (2) how PEPs are linked to their corresponding PDPs. In the worst case, splitting the initial PDP into multiple PDPs may lead to a non-

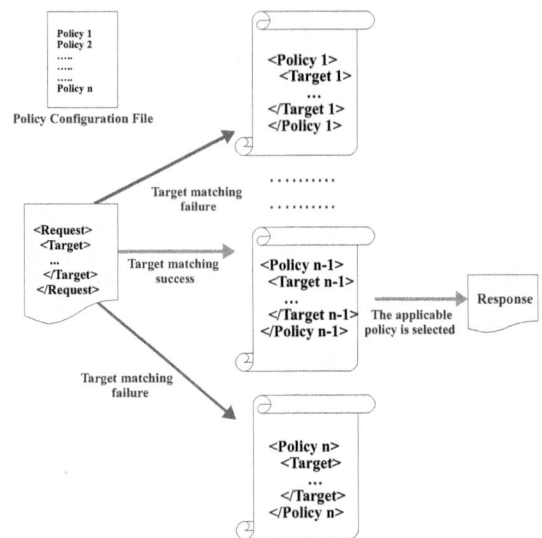

Figure 6: Applicable-Policy Selection

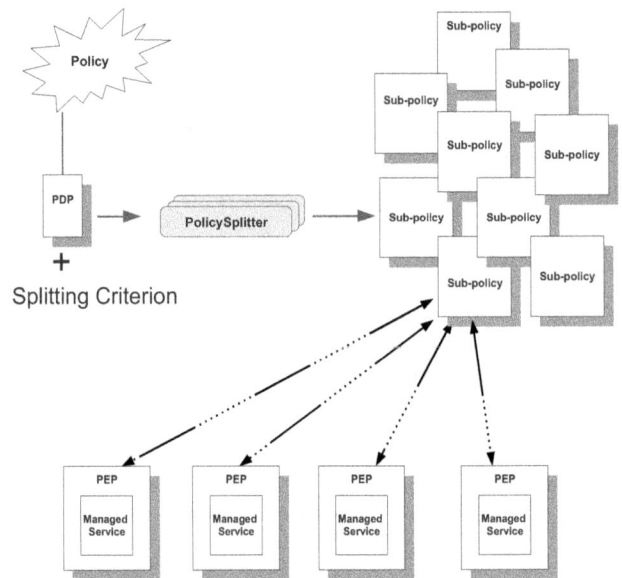

Figure 7: Overview of the Refactoring Process

synergic system: a PEP may send its requests to several PDPs. The PDP that handles a given request is only known at runtime. Such a resulting architecture breaks the PEP-PDP synergy and the conceptual simplicity of the initial architecture model. In the best case, the refactoring preserves the simplicity of the initial architecture by keeping a many-to-one association between PEPs to PDPs. Given a request, our approach maps a PEP to a PDP with relevant rules for the request. Therefore, different requests issued from a PEP should be handled by the same PDP. Operationally, the request evaluation involves one policy. In this case, our refactoring does not impact the conceptual architecture of the system.

Figure 8 presents a PDP encapsulating a global policy that has been refactored. The system that is presented on the left is resulted from a desirable refactoring whereas the one on the right is resulted from an undesirable refactoring.

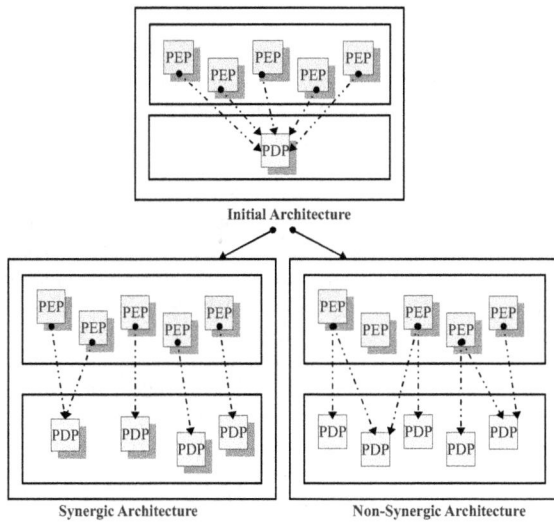

Figure 8: Synergic vs Non-synergic System

At the application level, a PEP is represented by a method call that triggers a decision making process. Figure 9 presents a sample PEP code snippet from our previous work [11]. This code snippet shows an example of a PEP represented by the method `checkSecurity`, which calls a method of the class `SecurityPolicyService`, which formulates a request to invoke the PDP component. The PEP represented by the method `ServiceUtils.checkSecurity` may issue requests that have subject "user" along fixed action and resource ("LibrarySecurityModel.BORROWBOOK_METHOD"), ("LibrarySecurityModel.BOOK_VIEW"). Consider that we refactor a policy using $SC_2 = \langle Resource, Action \rangle$, $SC_1 = \langle Action \rangle$, or $SC_1 = \langle Resource \rangle$. Given a request issued from the PEP, our approach runs a PDP loaded with a policy containing rules sharing the same action and resource attribute values. Thus the splitting process that preserves the mapping between the PEPs and the PDP is the one that considers the following splitting criteria: $SC_2 = \langle Resource, Action \rangle$, $SC_1 = \langle Action \rangle$, and $SC_1 = \langle Resource \rangle$ in this case. In the evaluation section, we investigate the impact of the synergy property on performance.

```
public void borrowBook(User user, Book book) throws
SecuritPolicyViolationException {

// call to the security service
        ServiceUtils.checkSecurity(user,
LibrarySecurityModel.BORROWBOOK\_METHOD,
LibrarySecurityModel.BOOK\_VIEW),
ContextManager.getTemporalContext());}

// call to business objects
// borrow the book for the user
book.execute(Book.BORROW, user);
// call the dao class to update the database
bookDAO.insertBorrow(userDTO, bookDTO);}
```

Figure 9: PEP Deployment Example

4. EVALUATION

We carried out our evaluation on a desktop PC running Ubuntu 10.04 with a Core i5, 2530 Mhz processor, and 4 GB of RAM. We have implemented a tool, called `PolicySplitter` to split policies according to a given splitting criterion automatically. The tool is implemented in Java and is available for download [4].

4.1 Objectives and Metrics

Our evaluation intends to answer the following research questions:

1. **RQ1.** How faster can request evaluation time of multiple Sun PDPs with policies split by our approach achieve compared to that of an existing single Sun PDP? This question helps show that our approach can improve performance in terms of request evaluation time. Moreover, we compare request evaluation time for different splitting criteria.

2. **RQ2.** With comparable PDP policy sizes, is request evaluation time of a system faster when its architecture is synergic? This research question investigates *Hypothesis 2* presented in Section 2.

3. **RQ3.** How faster can request evaluation time of multiple XEngines with policies split by our approach achieve compared to that of an existing single XEngine? This question helps show that our approach can improve performance in terms of request evaluation time for other advanced policy evaluation engines such as XEngine.

4. **RQ4.** How faster does request processing time of multiple XEngines with policies split by our approach achieve compared to that of the Sun PDP with policies split by our approach? This question aims at checking whether XEngine in combination with our approach performs better than the Sun PDP combined with our approach as well.

5. **RQ5.** For larger PDP policy size, do we observe higher slope of the evaluation time with an increasing workload? This research question investigates *Hypothesis 1* (presented in Section 2) on the impact of the number of rules in a given PDP on the evaluation time.

To address these research questions, we go through the following evaluation setup based on two different empirical studies:

- First, we evaluate the performance improvement regarding the decision making process by taking into consideration the whole system (PEPs and PDPs). We compared request evaluation time with a single global policy (handled by a single PDP) against request evaluation time with split policies. All the splitting criteria have been considered in our evaluation. `IA` denotes an "Initial Architecture", which uses the single global policy for request evaluation. This step allows studying the behavior of splitting criteria that preserve the synergy property in the access control architecture.

- Second, we apply our approach on the Sun PDP and XEngine [13], respectively, to investigate the effectiveness of our approach on various decision engines. We aim at showing that our approach is complementary to an existing decision engine, even an optimized one such as XEngine.

329

4.2 Subjects

The subjects include three real-life Java systems each of which interacts with access control policies. Full details on our subjects are available elsewhere [11, 17, 18]. We next describe our three subjects.

- The Library Management System (LMS) provides web services to manage books in a public library.

- The Virtual Meeting System (VMS) provides web conference services. VMS allows users to organize online meetings in a distributed platform.

- The Auction Sale Management System (ASMS) allows users to buy or sell items online. A seller initiates an auction by submitting a description of an item that she wants to sell with its expected minimum price. Users then participate in the bidding process by bidding the item. To bid on the item, user must have enough money in his/her account before bidding.

Our subjects are initially built upon the Sun PDP [3] as a decision engine, which is a popularly used PDP to evaluate requests. We started by a processing step, in which we have augmented the rules in the three original policies for these studies, as it would be difficult to observe performance improvement results with systems including few rules. In our evaluations, LMS policy contains 720 rules, VMS has 945 rules, and ASMS has 1760 rules. The rules that we added do not modify the system behavior as they are conform to the specifications. Moreover, to assess performance improvement over an existing advanced PDP, we adopt XEngine (instead of the Sun PDP) in our subjects to evaluate requests. XEngine is an advanced policy evaluation engine, which transforms the hierarchical tree structure of the XACML policy to a flat structure to reduce request evaluation time. XEngine also handles various combining algorithms supported by XACML.

4.3 Performance Improvement: Sun PDP

In order to answer **RQ1**, we generated the resulting sub-policies for all the splitting criteria defined in Section 3.1. For each splitting criterion, we have executed system tests to generate requests that trigger all the PEPs in the evaluation. The test generation step leads to the execution of all combinations of possible requests described in our previous work [18]. The process of test generation is repeated ten times to alleviate the impact of randomness. We applied this process for each splitting criterion and calculated evaluation time on average of a system under test. Figure 10 presents evaluation time for policies split based on each splitting criterion and the global policy of the subjects. We can make two observations:

- Compared to the evaluation time of IA, our approach improves performance for all of splitting criteria in terms of evaluation time. This observation is consistent with our expected results; the evaluation time against policies with a smaller number of rules (compared with the number of rules in IA) is faster than that against policies in IA.

- The splitting criterion $SC = \langle Action, Resource \rangle$ enables to show the fastest evaluation time. Such observation is due to the fact that the PEPs in our three subjects are organized based on $SC_2 = \langle Action, Resource \rangle$. This observation pleads in favor of applying a splitting criterion that takes into account the PEP-PDP synergy.

To identify the splitting criterion that generates the smallest number of PDPs, we have studied the number of policies generated by

Table 2: Splitting Criteria Classification

	S	A	R	SA	SR	AR	SAR	IA
Synergic		x	x			x		x
Not-Synergic	x			x	x		x	

the splitting. Figure 11 shows the results. We observed the number of policies based on our proposed three categories: (1) the SC_1 category leads to the smallest number N_1 of PDPs, (2) the SC_2 category leads to a medium number N_2 ($N_1 < N_2 < N_3$) of PDPs, and (3) SC_3 leads to the largest number N_3 of PDPs. While the SC_1 category leads to the smallest number of PDPs, each PDP encapsulates a relatively large number of rules in a policy (compared with that of SC_2 and SC_3, which leads to performance degradation). We have classified splitting criteria according to their preservation of the synergy property considering our subjects. The classification is shown in Table 2 where S denotes Subject, R denotes Resource, A denotes Action, and IA denotes Initial Architecture. For example, AR denotes SC=$< Action, Resource >$. AR, A, and R are synergic splitting criteria since all the PEPs in our considered three systems are organized as shown in Figure 9.

To answer **RQ2**, we have evaluated PDPs in the three systems and for the different splitting criteria. The results presented in Figure 12 show the average number of rules in each PDP, for each splitting criterion in the three systems. We can observe that the AR criterion produces comparable size of PDPs with the SR criterion; however, as shown in Figure 10, AR is the best splitting criterion in terms of evaluation time performance. Moreover, the number of PDPs produced with the splitting critera S and A is comparable; the criterion A, which is synergic, has evaluation time less than the one produced by the splitting criterion S, which is not synergic. This result supports our *Hypothesis 2*, which states that with comparable PDP sizes, the evaluation time would be reduced when the architecture is synergic.

4.4 Performance Improvement: XEngine

In order to answer **RQ3** and **RQ4**, we measure request evaluation time of multiple XEngines with policies split by our approach compared with that of an existing single XEngine and that of multiple Sun PDPs with policies split by our approach, respectively. The goal of this empirical study is to show the impact of combining XEngine with our splitting process. XEngine itself improves dramatically the performance of the Sun PDP mainly for three reasons:

- It uses a refactoring process that transforms the hierarchical structure of the XACML policy to a flat structure.

- It converts multiple combining algorithms to a single one.

- It relies on a tree structure that minimizes the request evaluation time.

We propose to use XEngine conjointly with the refactoring process presented in this work. We have evaluated our approach in two settings:

- Considering evaluation with decision engines based on XEngine with split policies and with the initial policy.

- Considering evaluation with decision engines based on the Sun PDP with split policies and with the initial policy.

In this step, we do not reason about the synergy, since we do not consider the application level for the three systems. We measure

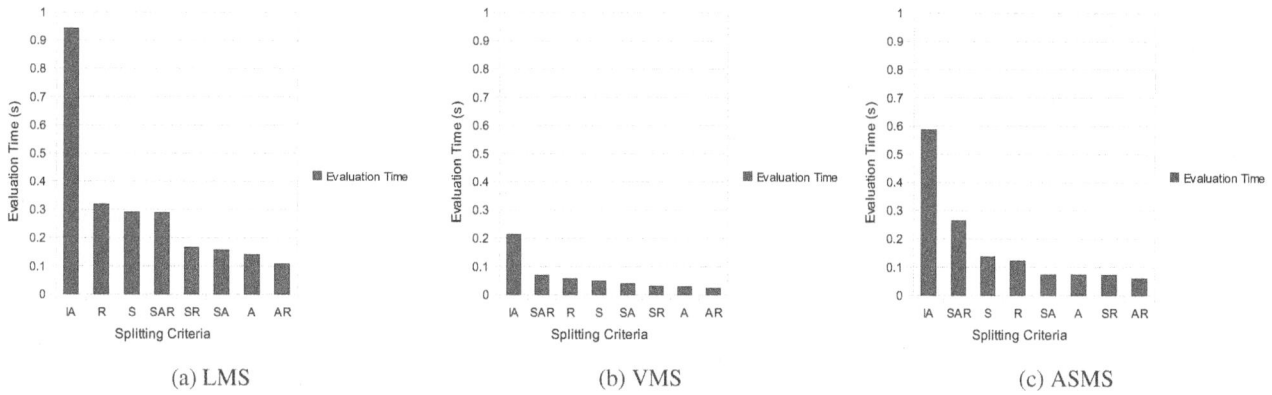

	(a) LMS	(b) VMS	(c) ASMS

Figure 10: Request Evaluation Time for the Three Subjects

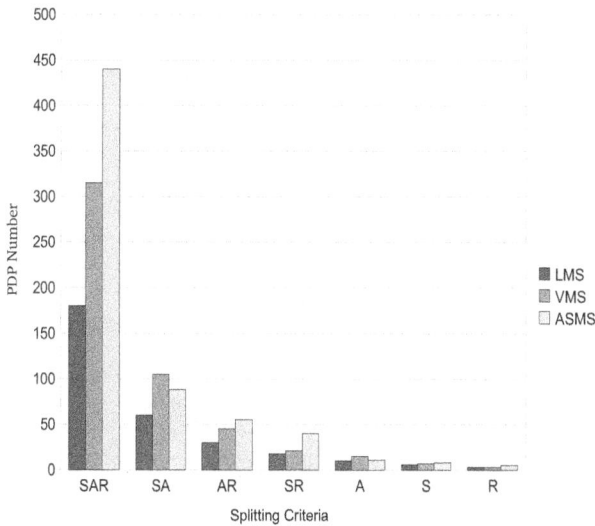

Figure 11: PDP Number Produced with Splitting Criteria

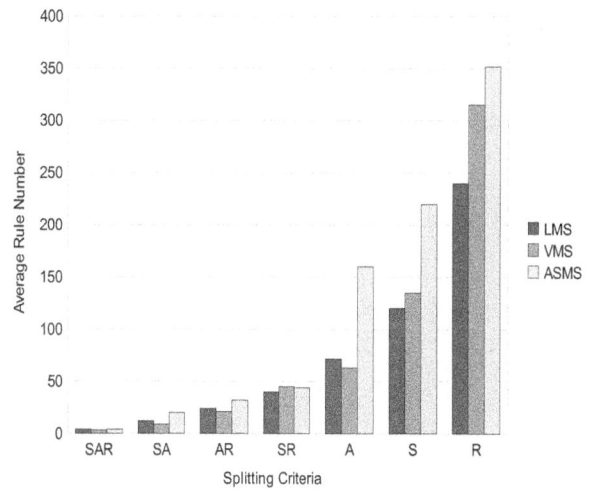

Figure 12: Average of Rule Numbers per PDP in the Three Systems

request evaluation time by evaluating a randomly generated set of 10,000 requests as proposed in our previous work [15]. The request evaluation time is evaluated for the three systems. The results are presented in Tables 3, 4, and 5.

In the three tables, the percentage of performance improvement denoted as "% PI" shows the reduction of request evaluation time (achieved by our approach) over the request evaluation with the initial architecture (IA).

Multiple XEngines with split policies, in most cases, enable to reduce the evaluation time compared to XEngine with a single policy. This result is shown in Table 5 for ASMS where the evaluation time is reduced about 33 times from 1639 ms in the initial architecture (IA) to 49 ms with the splittig criterion SAR. This empirical observation shows that our refactoring conjointly with XEngine enables to improve the performance of the evaluation process for most of the splitting criteria and thus answers **RQ3**.

As shown in the three tables, there are some splitting criteria that lead to decrease of performance such as the splitting criterion R in

VMS system, which leads to degrade the evaluation time to -44%. These results need to be investigated with further studies.

Through the three tables, we observe that, when our subjects are equipped with XEngine, our proposed approach substantially improves performance (compared to the results with the Sun PDP) for most of the splitting criteria. For the splitting criterion SC=$\langle Action \rangle$ abbreviated as A, in the LMS system, the evaluation time is reduced about 22 times: from 2703 ms to 120 ms with XEngine, this observation enables to answer **RQ4**.

4.5 Impact of Increasing Workload

To investigate **RQ5**, we have calculated request evaluation time according to the number of requests incoming to a system. For each policy in the three systems (ASMS, LMS, and VMS), we generated 5000, 10000, .., 50000 random requests to measure the evaluation time (ms). The results are shown in Figure 13. For the three systems, we observe that the evaluation time increases when the number of requests increases in a system. With an increasing system

Table 3: Evaluation Time (ms) in LMS

	SAR	AR	SA	SR	R	S	A	IA
Sun PDP	485	922	1453	1875	2578	2703	2703	2625
% PI Sun PDP	81.5	64.9	44.6	28.6	1.8	-3	-3	0
XEngine	26	47	67	95	190	164	120	613
% PI XEngine	95.7	92.3	89.0	84.5	69	73.2	80.4	0

Table 4: Evaluation Time (ms) in VMS

	SAR	AR	SA	SR	R	S	A	IA
Sun PDP	1281	2640	3422	3734	6078	5921	6781	5766
% PI Sun PDP	77.8	54.2	40.6	35.2	-5.4	-2.7	-17.6	0
XEngine	34	67	96	145	384	274	149	265
% PI XEngine	87.2	74.7	63.8	45.3	-44.9	-3.4	43.8	0

Table 5: Evaluation Time (ms) in ASMS

	SAR	AR	SA	SR	R	S	A	IA
Sun PDP	2280	2734	3625	8297	7750	8188	6859	7156
% PI Sun PDP	68.1	61.8	49.3	-15.9	-8.3	-14.4	4.1	0
XEngine	49	60	104	196	310	566	262	1639
% PI XEngine	97	96.3	93.65	88	81	65.5	84	0

load, the request evaluation time is considerably improved when using the splitting process compared to the initial architecture. The results shown in Figure 13 are interpreted by the average of PDP sizes presented in Figure 12. The results are consistent with *Hypothesis 1* (presented in Section 2), which states that the slope of evaluation time increases with PDP size in a system with an increasing workload.

To deploy our approach, we need to fetch the relevant PDP for a given request at runtime. Therefore, request processing time includes both fetching time and request evaluation time. Figure 14 shows percentage of fetching time over the global evaluation time for request evaluation in LMS. The fetching time increases according to the PDP size. The fetching time is relatively small in comparison with the total evaluation time and thus does not impact significantly the evaluation time.

4.6 Summary

We summarize the results of the evaluation:

- We have experimentally shown the effectiveness of the splitting in reducing the evaluation time. Our refactoring process improves both a typical PDP (the Sun PDP) and an advanced PDP (XEngine).

- When the sizes of PDPs are comparable, the splitting criteria that are synergic enable to have the best results in terms of evaluation time.

The evaluation of the synergy property on improving performance has to be strengthened by conducting other experiments on other evaluation subjects and by considering different organizations of PEPs at the application level.

4.7 Threats to Validity

The threats to external validity primarily include the degree to which subjects, policies, and test requests are representative of true practice. These threats could be reduced by further evaluation on a wider type and larger number of policies and a larger number of test requests in future work. In particular, our approach is based on only

seven proposed splitting criteria. We could develop additional splitting criteria to split policies and measure efficiency in terms of request evaluation time. In addition, our approach generates random test requests, which may induce bias or randomness in our results. To prevent such a bias, we conduct our evaluation for 10 times and measure an average value of evaluation results. The threats to internal validity are instrumentation effects that can bias our results such as faults in the Sun PDP, XEngine, `PolicySplitter`, measurement tool in terms of request evaluation, and random request generators.

5. RELATED WORK

There are several previous approaches about performance issues in security mechanisms. Ammons et al. [5] have presented techniques to reduce the overhead engendered from implementing a security model in IBM's WebSphere Application Server (WAS). Their approach identifies bottlencks through code instrumentation and focuses on two aspects: the temporal redundancy (when security checks are made frequently) and the spatial redundancy (using the same security techniques on the same code execution paths). For the first aspect, they use caching mechanisms to store checks results, so that the decision is retrieved from the cache. For the second aspect, they used a technique based on specialization, which consists in replacing an expensive check with a cheaper one for frequent paths. While this previous approach focuses on bottlencks in program code, in this paper, we propose a new approach to refactor access control policies by reducing the number of rules in each split policy.

Various approaches [8,12,14] have been proposed to address performance issues in systems interacting with access control policies. Jahid et al. [8] focus on XACML policy verification for database access control. They presented a model that converts attribute-based policies into access control lists. They implemented their approach called MyABDAC. While they measured performance of MyABDAC in terms of request evaluation, they did not show how much MyABDAC gains improvement over an existing PDP.

Marouf et al. [14] have proposed an approach for policy evaluation based on a clustering algorithm that reorders rules and policies within the policy set so that the access to applicable policies is faster. Their categorization is based on the subject target element. Their approach requires identifying the rules that are frequently used. Our approach follows a different strategy and does not require knowing which rules are used frequently. In addition, the rule reordering is tightly related to specific systems. If the PDP is shared between several systems, their approach could not be applicable since the most "used" rules may vary between systems.

Lin et al. [12] decomposed a global XACML policy into local policies related to collaborating parties, and the local policies are sent to corresponding PDPs. The request evaluation is based on local policies by considering the relationships among local policies. In their approach, the optimization is based on storing the effect of each rule and each local policy for a given request. Caching decision results is then used to optimize evaluation time for an incoming request. However, there were no experimental results for measuring the efficiency of their approach when compared to the traditional architecture. While the previous approaches have focused on the PDP component to optimize the request evaluation, Miseldine et al. [16] addressed this problem by analyzing rule location on XACML policies and requests at the design level so that the relevant rules for the request are accessed faster on evaluation time.

Our contribution in this paper brings new dimensions over our previous work on access control [13, 17, 18]. We have proposed

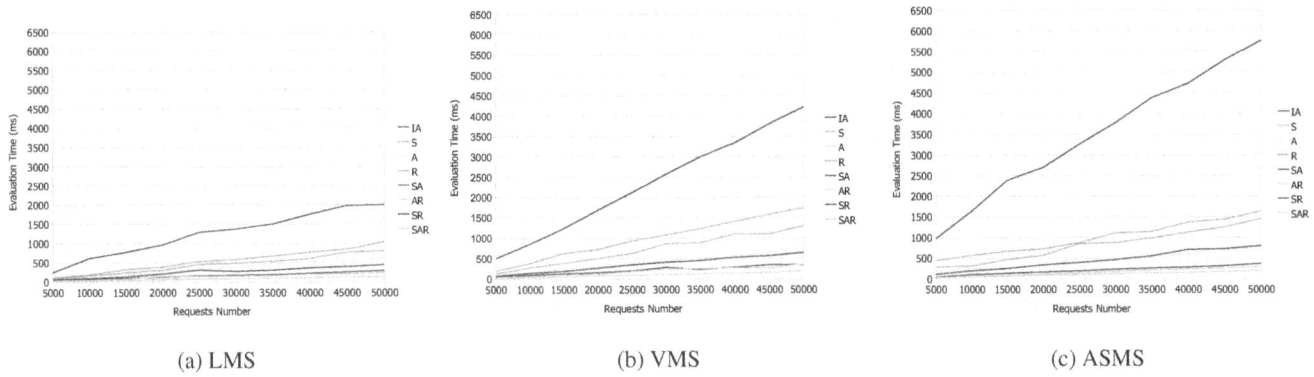

(a) LMS (b) VMS (c) ASMS

Figure 13: Evaluation Time for Our Subjects, LMS, VMS, and ASMS Depending on the Request Number

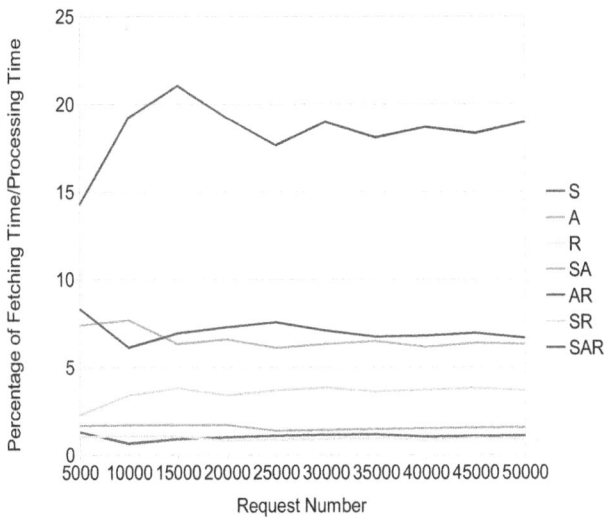

Figure 14: Percentage of Fetching Time

XEngine [13], which focuses particularly on performance issues addressed with XACML policy evaluation. XEngine proposes an alternative solution to brute force searching based on an XACML policy conversion to a tree structure to minimize the request evaluation time. It involves a refactoring process that transforms the global policy to a decision diagram that is then converted to forwarding tables. In our contribution in this paper, we introduce a new refactoring process that involves splitting the policy into smaller sub-policies. Our two refactoring processes are combined to decrease the evaluation time.

6. CONCLUSION AND FUTURE WORK

In this paper, we have tackled the performance issue in the decision making mechanism for access control and have proposed an automated refactoring process that enables to reduce request evaluation time substantially. All the reasonings about performance factors have not included hardware considerations. However, performance improvement at the software/logical level as done by our approach would complement performance improvement at the hard-

ware level to best improve the overall performance. Our approach has been applied to XACML policies and it can be generalized to policies in other policy specification languages (such as EPAL). To support and automate the refactoring process, we have designed and implemented the PolicySplitter tool, which transforms a given policy into small ones, according to a chosen splitting criterion. Most obtained results have shown a significant gain in evaluation time. The best gain in performance is reached by the criterion that respects the synergy property. This result pleads in favor of a refactoring process that takes into account the way PEPs are scattered inside the system business logic. In this work, we have easily identified the different PEPs since we know exactly how our system functionalities are implemented and thus how PEPs are organized inside the system. In future work, we plan to automatically identify the different PEPs of a given system. This technique is an important step complementary to our current approach, since this technique enables knowing how PEPs are organized in the system and thus allows to select automatically the most suitable splitting criterion for a given system.

7. ACKNOWLEDGMENTS

This work is supported in part by NSF grants CCF-0845272, CCF-0915400, CNS-0958235, an NIST grant, and ARO Grant No. W911NF-08-1-0443.

8. REFERENCES

[1] IBM, Enterprise Privacy Authorization Language (EPAL), Version 1.2 . http://www.w3.org/Submission/2003/SUBM-EPAL-20031110, 2003.

[2] OASIS eXtensible Access Control Markup Language (XACML). http://www.oasis-open.org/committees/xacml/, 2005.

[3] Sun's XACML implementation. http://sunxacml.sourceforge.net/, 2005.

[4] PolicySplitter Tool. http://www.mouelhi.com/policysplitter.html, 2011.

[5] G. Ammons, J. deok Choi, M. Gupta, and N. Swamy. Finding and removing performance bottlenecks in large systems. In *Proceedings of European Conference on Object-Oriented Programming*, pages 170–194, 2004.

[6] E. D. Bell and J. L. La Padula. Secure computer system: Unified exposition and multics interpretation. MITRE Corporation, 1976.

333

[7] D. F. Ferraiolo, R. S. Sandhu, S. I. Gavrila, D. R. Kuhn, and R. Chandramouli. Proposed NIST standard for role-based access control. *ACM Transactions on Information and System Security*, 4(3):224–274, 2001.

[8] S. Jahid, C. A. Gunter, I. Hoque, and H. Okhravi. MyABDAC: Compiling XACML Policies for Attribute-Based Database Access Control. In *Proceedings of the first ACM Conference on Data and Application Security and Privacy*, pages 97–108, 2011.

[9] A. A. E. Kalam, S. Benferhat, A. Miège, R. E. Baida, F. Cuppens, C. Saurel, P. Balbiani, Y. Deswarte, and G. Trouessin. Organization based access control. In *Proceedings of 10th IEEE International Conference on Policies for Distributed Systems and Networks*, pages 120–131, 2003.

[10] B. Lampson. Protection. In *Proceedings of the 5th Princeton Conference on Information Sciences and Systems*, 1971.

[11] Y. Le Traon, T. Mouelhi, A. Pretschner, and B. Baudry. Test-driven assessment of access control in legacy applications. In *Proceedings of the 2008 International Conference on Software Testing, Verification, and Validation*, pages 238–247, 2008.

[12] D. Lin, P. Rao, E. Bertino, N. Li, and J. Lobo. Policy decomposition for collaborative access control. In *Proceedings of the 13th ACM Symposium on Access Control Models and Technologies*, pages 103–112, 2008.

[13] A. X. Liu, F. Chen, J. Hwang, and T. Xie. XEngine: A fast and scalable XACML policy evaluation engine. In *Proceedings of International Conference on Measurement and Modeling of Computer Systems*, pages 265–276, 2008.

[14] S. Marouf, M. Shehab, A. Squicciarini, and S. Sundareswaran. Statistics & clustering based framework for efficient XACML policy evaluation. In *Proceedings of 10th IEEE International Conference on Policies for Distributed Systems and Networks*, pages 118–125, 2009.

[15] E. Martin, T. Xie, and T. Yu. Defining and measuring policy coverage in testing access control policies. In *Proceedings of 8th International Conference on Information and Communications Security*, pages 139–158, 2006.

[16] P. L. Miseldine. Automated XACML policy reconfiguration for evaluation optimisation. In *Proceedings of 4th International Workshop on Software Engineering for Secure Systems*, pages 1–8, 2008.

[17] T. Mouelhi, F. Fleurey, B. Baudry, and Y. Traon. A model-based framework for security policy specification, deployment and testing. In *Proceedings of 11th International Conference on Model Driven Engineering Languages and Systems*, pages 537–552, 2008.

[18] T. Mouelhi, Y. L. Traon, and B. Baudry. Transforming and selecting functional test cases for security policy testing. In *Proceedings of 2009 International Conference on Software Testing Verification and Validation*, pages 171–180, 2009.

[19] R. Yavatkar, D. Pendarakis, and R. Guerin. A framework for policy-based admission control. RFC Editor, 2000.

Hirundo: A Mechanism for Automated Production of Optimized Data Stream Graphs

Miyuru Dayarathna
Department of Computer Science
Tokyo Institute of Technology
2-12-1 Oookayama, Meguro-ku,
Tokyo 152-8552, Japan
dayarathna.m.aa@m.titech.ac.jp

Toyotaro Suzumura
Department of Computer Science
Tokyo Institute of Technology and
IBM Research - Tokyo
2-12-1 Oookayama, Meguro-ku,
Tokyo 152-8552, Japan
suzumura@cs.titech.ac.jp

ABSTRACT

Stream programs have to be crafted carefully to maximize the performance gain that can be obtained from stream processing environments. Manual fine tuning of a stream program is a very difficult process which requires considerable amount of programmer time and expertise. In this paper we present Hirundo, which is a mechanism for automatically generating optimized stream programs that are tailored for the environment they run. Hirundo analyzes, identifies the structure of a stream program, and transforms it to many different sample programs with same semantics using the notions of Tri-Operator Transformation, Transformer Blocks, and Operator Blocks Fusion. Then it uses empirical optimization information to identify a small subset of generated sample programs that could deliver high performance. It runs the selected sample programs in the run-time environment for a short period of time to obtain their performance information. Hirundo utilizes these information to output a ranked list of optimized stream programs that are tailored for a particular run-time environment. Hirundo has been developed using Python as a prototype application for optimizing SPADE programs, which run on System S stream processing run-time. Using three example real world stream processing applications we demonstrate effectiveness of our approach, and discuss how well it generalizes for automatic stream program performance optimization.

Categories and Subject Descriptors

I.2.2 [**Computing Methodologies**]: Automatic Programming—*Program transformation, Program synthesis*; H.3.4 [**Information Systems**]: Systems and Software—*Distributed systems*

General Terms

Performance, Design, Measurement, Algorithms

Keywords

Stream processing, performance optimization, fault tolerance, data-intensive computing, scalability

1. INTRODUCTION

Importance of high performance data stream processing has been emphasized more than ever before due to appearance of many online data stream sources. Until now there have been two dominant stream programming models called relational model [3] and operator-based model [18][10]. With the introduction of commercial stream processing systems such as IBM InfoSphere Streams [24] and open source initiatives like Yahoo S4 [21], it can be expected that operator-based stream processing systems may play a key role in future high performance stream computing undertakings.

As we pointed out in [10], High performance of a stream program is characterized not only by its structure, but also by the topology and performance characteristics of the stream processing system on which it runs. Nevertheless stream programs deployed on most of the stream processing systems may produce low performance while they continuously receive huge amounts of input data, and while there are abundant computational resources under utilized by the run-time environment.

One solution for this issue is to manually fine tune the program to consume unused system capacity. This will lead to faster processing of input data leading to a higher throughput [27]. However, this requires tremendous amount of programmer's time and expertise since there are various different ways an operator-based stream program can be written that gives the same semantics but widely different performance characteristics. Sometimes programmer needs to port the program to a different run-time environment that offers totally different performance characteristics. Furthermore, in production environments run-time topology may change quite frequently. E.g. Existing nodes of the run-time may be brought down for maintenance. Therefore, this approach costs a lot for organizations, and might not be practical in certain production environments.

Another solution for this problem is to conduct a profile driven optimization. Results from profiling can be used to characterize the run-time behavior of operators [32], and an optimization model can be created to come up with higher performing alternatives. However, we address the problem of performance optimization from the point of view of the programmer because source level design decisions could affect the entire application's performance even if profile driven optimization is used. Since we do not modify the compiler/scheduler during the optimization process, our approach can be generalized to different operator based stream processing systems easily.

Given an operator-based stream program, we describe a method for automatically identifying the best version of the program that is suited for a particular stream processing run-time environment. In achieving our goal, we first identify the structure of the stream program (i.e. input program). Then we transform the data flow graph of the program to a number of different data flow graphs (i.e. sample programs) preserving program semantics. Then we choose a subset of sample programs using the information gathered from previous similar performance optimization attempts (we call this performance prediction). Next, a subset of the chosen sample programs are run in the stream processing run-time, and their performance information are gathered. Based on the results of analyzing the performance information such as throughput, elapsed time, etc., a ranked subset of sample programs are identified as the output that provides better performance compared to input program. An optimization mechanism prototype based on System S was implemented using Python to evaluate the feasibility of our approach.

To the best of our knowledge this is the first such attempt made to automate the construction of optimized stream programs. Use of the term "Optimized" here means deriving efficient stream programs that can harness the full performance of stream processing environment they run on. Specifically, our contributions in this paper can be stated as follows,

- *Tri-Operator Transformation* : We introduce a novel method of transforming operator-based data flow graph of a stream program without violating its semantics.

- *Transformer Blocks* : We describe the use of collections of operators as transformation primitives during the optimization process.

- *Stream Program Performance Prediction* : Hirundo uses empirical data of similar optimization attempts to reduce the effort required for identifying optimized program versions.

- *Stream Program Performance Characterization* : Using K-means clustering on Hirundo's database, we describe a method of identifying common characteristics of high/low performing programs, which would benefit stream programmers in producing high performance stream programs.

- *Fault Tolerance* : Hirundo emphasizes the importance of fault detection in the run-time environment during the process of optimization in order to ensure accuracy of the results it produces.

The paper is structured as follows. We describe related work for Hirundo in Section 2 and provide an overview for SPADE language in Section 3. We describe the methodology in Section 4. The concepts of Tri-Operator Transformation, Operator Blocks Fusion, and Transformer Blocks are described in Sections 5, 6, and 7 respectively which forms the basis of our methodology. We describe how we narrow down the search space for optimized sample programs in Section 8. Measures taken to ensure the semantically correctness of the sample programs is described in Section 9. Fault tolerance of Hirundo is explained in Section 10. We give implementation details of Hirundo in Section 11. Evaluation details of our prototype system are given in Section 12. Next, we discuss the achievements of our objectives and limitations of our current prototype under the Section 13. Finally we present some further work and conclude in Section 14.

2. RELATED WORK

Optimization of data flow graphs has been widely addressed research issue.

Early efforts in automatic parallelization of sequential programs studied methods for automatic data partitioning and distribution of computations in distributed-memory multicomputer systems [8][22][6]. However, the distributed computing model handled by these works differ from stream computing model. Hirundo concentrates more on computations that are data-intensive, and does not conduct any static code optimizations like these works.

Automatic composition of workflows has been addressed by Quin *et al.* [23] and Liew *et al.* [19]. Compared to them, Hirundo concentrates on automatic optimization in the context of stream computing, and ensures the optimization process does not get affected by node failures. This issue has not been addressed by these works.

Hirundo introduces use of Transformer blocks during its data flow graph transformations in the context of stream computing. There has been similar use of recurring patterns for optimizing workflows by Liew *et al.* [29] and Hall *et al.* [13].

There has been works on performance prediction of parallel applications by partial execution [30] using skeletons [26] etc. Furthermore, recent relational data base servers use empirical cost information for producing optimized query plans [7][1][17]. Yet, Hirundo follows a different approach for identifying optimized sample programs by integrating results from partial execution of sample programs with empirical data.

Subquery optimization of relational database systems by Bellamkonda *et al.* [7] has similarity to what Hirundo does since both the approaches use code transformation as the means of optimization. Table partitioning in relational databases is a technique used for optimizing SQL query performance [14]. This technique is analogous to Hirundo's Tri-OP Transformation.

Stream graph partitioning [18][28] tackles the problem of stream program performance optimization at lower levels of stream processing environment compared with the approach followed by this work. Hirundo approaches the solution from the source program level of a stream application.

Recently there has been interest of automatically optimizing programs written for MapReduce systems [4]. Similarly compiler of DryadLINQ [31] system performs static optimizations which enables automatic synthesis of optimized

LINQ code. However, these systems do not perform high level code transformations like Hirundo does during the process of optimization. Hirundo outputs a ranked list of optimized sample programs, whereas these systems performs their optimizations in lower levels.

3. SPADE - AN OPERATOR-BASED STREAM PROCESSING LANGUAGE

Hirundo has been designed for optimizing operator-based data stream programs. Current implementation of Hirundo has been developed on top of System S [12] stream processing system and SPADE language [12][16].

Stream programs developed based on operator-based programming model are organized as data flow graphs consisting of operators and streams [18]. Operators are the smallest possible building blocks that are required to deliver the computation an application is supposed to deliver. Streams are directed edges that connect pairs of operators, and carries data from source to destination operators.

SPADE language (the latest version is referred to as Stream Processing Language (SPL) [15]) consists of two types of operators called composite and primitive operators [15]. A composite operator consists of a reusable stream subgraph that can be invoked to define streams. Primitive operators are basic building blocks of composite operators. Primitive operators can be further categorized in to built-in operators (BIOP), user-defined operators (UDOP), raw UDOPs, and user-defined built-in-operators (UBOP). In this paper we mainly concentrate on BIOPs since current Hirundo implementation supports a subset of BIOPs (Source, Functor, Aggregate, and Sink). Out of them, Source operator is used to create a stream from data flowing from an external source [16]. It is capable of parsing, creating tuples as well as interacting with external devices [16]. A Sink operator converts a stream of data from the program into a flow of tuples that can be used by external entities. Functor operator on the other hand, is used for performing tuple-level manipulations such as filtering, projection, mapping, attribute creation, and transformation etc. Aggregate operators are used for grouping and summarization of incoming tuples.

4. METHODOLOGY

Hirundo accepts a stream program and a sample data file as input. The input data file is segmented in to collections of sample input data files. Input program is analyzed to identify *Operator Blocks*. An operator block is simply a collection of operators (1 or more) that is identified by Hirundo's grammar. After Hirundo identifies all the operator blocks present within the input program it generates sample programs (S) (More details are given in next section). Based on current processing environment's profile information [11] and learnings from previous optimization runs, Hirundo selects a subset (U_1:$U_1 \subset S$;$|U_1|$=n) from the sample programs. The subset U_1 is compiled using parallel compiler of Hirundo, and the resulting programs are run in the stream processor environment for a time window W_t. A ranked list of programs R_1 (R_1:$R_1 \subset U_1$; $|R_1|$=m; m < n) is selected based on the performance results obtained by running the programs. R_1 is merged with a next best subset of programs U_2 from S (U_2:$U_2 \subset S$;$U_1 \cap U_2$=∅;$|U_2|$=n-m) to form U_3. All the pro-

grams in U_3 are run in the stream processing environment. Similar to previous case, a ranked list of R_2 (R_2:$R_2 \subset U_3$; $|R_2|$=m; m < n) is selected as the output. This process is shown in Figure 1.

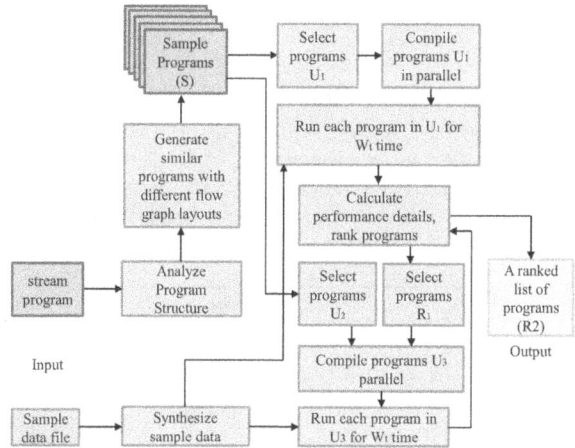

Figure 1: Methodology of Hirundo

5. TRI-OPERATOR TRANSFORMATION

As described in Section 1, we introduce a methodology for transforming a stream program to a variety of sample applications, which are used as sample programs for optimization process. Our method is based on *Parallel Streams* design pattern [5]. We term the algorithm that does this transformation as *Tri-Operator Transformation* (i.e. Tri-OP Transformation). The algorithm transforms data flow graphs by three operator blocks at a time.

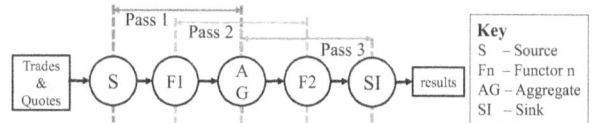

Figure 2: Data flow graph of Volume Weighted Average Price application and how it is traversed by GENERATE() procedure.

5.1 Concept

Lets consider three adjacent operator blocks (an operator block is a collection of operators) A, B, and C in a data flow graph (Shown in Figure 3(a)). From here onwards we will denote such operator block as A_B_C. Note that we use the term "operator block" to denote each A, B, and C as well as A_B_C because A_B_C itself is a collection of operators.

The aim of Hirundo's data flow graph transformation is to generate a variety of data flow graphs for a given stream program. We have chosen to transform 3 adjacent operator blocks at a time due to several reasons. First, while choosing more than 3 operator blocks would have enabled us to create more sophisticated data flow graphs, we decided to stick with 3 operator blocks due to simplicity of transformation logic involved with 3 operator blocks. Second, transformation logic should not increase number of operators exponentially. Changing the number of middle operator blocks (i.e. operator block B shown in Figure 3(a)) in a 3 operator blocks combination, we can achieve this feature easily. Furthermore, use of 3 operator blocks at a time allows us to generate higher variety of patterns than the variety of patterns that could be generated using only two operator blocks.

5.1.1 Transformer Patterns

In the rest of this paper we will use the notation i-j-k (i, j, k are positive integers including 0) to denote a transformation pattern. Pseudocode of `transform()` procedure in Algorithm 3 explains how an operator block A_B_C is transformed by an i-j-k pattern.

Algorithm 1 tri_op_transform(G, d)	Algorithm 2 generate(G, i, j, k)
1: oblist ← emptylist	1: m ← 0
2: **for** i ← 0 to d **do**	2: v ← getroot(G)
3: **for** j ← 0 to d **do**	3: **while** v has next **do**
4: **for** k ← 0 to d **do**	4: invarray ← getnextthreevertices(v)
5: outdictionary ← generate(G, i, j, k)	5: **if** length[inarray] = 3 **then**
6: oblist.add(outdictionary)	6: tvarray[m] ← transform(invarray, i, j, k)
7: **end for**	7: m ← m + 1
8: **end for**	8: v ← invarray[2]
9: **end for**	9: **end if**
10: weld(oblist, len(G))	10: **end while**
	11: **return** (tvarray)

Tri-OP transformation does not do any change to A_B_C operator blocks if it transforms using the pattern 1-1-1. The meaning of 1-1-1 can be described as follows. Keep one A, increase the number of Bs to 1×1, and map transformed B operator blocks to one C. Tri-OP transformation does not consider any other patterns having only 0s or 1s (e.g. 0-0-0, 0-0-1) other than the pattern 1-1-1 to avoid duplication. Transformation pattern 1-2-1 transforms A_B_C in to A_2B_C (See Figure 3(b)). This means that keep one A, increase the number of Bs to two, and map the two Bs to one C. This is an example for increase of middle operator blocks. Minimum number of middle operator blocks is 1.

Tri-OP transformation creates a single B when it finds j=0. E.g. When transformation pattern 2-0-2 is applied to A_B_C, it results in 2A_B_2C (Shown in Figure 3(d)). In this example two As are mapped to a single B. Then streams from B are mapped to two Cs. The value of j plays an important role in describing the structure of the resulting operator block. Lets take the scenario of applying 2-1-2 transformation to A_B_C. This is an example for i = k, j = 1 scenario in Line 13 of Algorithm 3. It will result in 2A_2B_2C, having two operator blocks from each category (shown Figure 3(c)). Furthermore, these operator blocks will be connected in parallel. Yet when transforming by 2-1-1 it will result in 2A_2B_C, which changes number of A and B operators to 2, and keeps single C operator. Similarly 2-2-2 (shown in Figure 3(e)) and 2-2-3 transformation patterns result in 2A_4B_2C and 2A_4B_3C transformed operator blocks respectively.

5.2 Algorithm

Lets consider how Tri-OP transformation is conducted on a real world example application of stream computing. We use Volume Weighted Average Price (*VWAP*) written using five operator blocks (Described more in the Evaluation Section) for this purpose. This program's data flow graph is shown in Figure 2.

After Hirundo accepts the input program it parses the program using Program Structure Analyzer (Described in sub section 11.1). Program Structure Analyzer identifies each operator block and creates a graph (G) that represents the structure of the input program. Graph G is fed to `tri_op_transform()` procedure (shown in Algorithm 1) along with a depth value d. Depth value d is a positive integer that determines to what extent input program will be transformed.

Initially an empty operator block list (oblist) is created. An operator block is represented as a dictionary object. The procedure traverses graph G in steps of 3 operator blocks. This can be observed from the three `for()` loops (Lines 2-4, Algorithm 1). Each pass generates an i-j-k pattern.

The `tri_op_transform()` procedure calls `generate()` procedure passing the graph G and the i, j and k values (Pseudocode of `generate()` is shown in Algorithm 2). Functionality of the `generate()` procedure can be visualized using Figure 2. First, `generate()` procedure moves to the root node of the graph (in the example it is the source operator (S)). Then it selects three adjacent operator blocks from root (S, F1, AG) by calling the procedure `getnextthreevertices()`, and applies the transformation of the i-j-k pattern by calling `transform()`. This is termed as the pass1 in Figure 2. Then `generate()` procedure moves to the neighbor of the root (that is F1), picks three operator blocks (F1, AG, F2) and applies the transformation of i-j-k pattern to them (pass2). Note that we chose the second operator block rather than the fourth operator block because to enable transformation of graphs with vertex counts not belonging to multipliers of three. Finally it applies transformation of i-j-k pattern to operator blocks AG, F2, SI (pass3). If there are n operator blocks present in a data flow graph, `generate()` procedure does the i-j-k pattern transformation n-2 times. The resulting n-2 operator blocks are saved in a dictionary. We call these operator blocks as *Transformed Operator Blocks*. The keys (i.e. labels) of the transformed operator blocks are created using i,j,k values and the input operator block names (i.e. A, B, and C). The dictionary gets saved in the oblist (See line 6 of Algorithm 1).

Finally `tri_op_transform()` procedure calls `weld()` procedure (shown in Algorithm 4) by passing the transformed operator blocks list (oblist) and the input program graph length (glen) to `weld()` (glen is 5 for the VWAP application shown in Figure 2). The `weld()` procedure selects matching operator blocks from oblist, and fuses them to create sample programs. (Concept of fusion is described with more details in Section 6.) As shown in Algorithm 4, `weld()` procedure traverses the list of transformed operator blocks that it received. If a particular operator block has one or more source operators (i.e. It is a source operator block), the procedure creates a matched operator blocks list (fList). Then it finds matching operator blocks for source operator block by calling `findoblist()` (Line 5 in Algorithm 4) and stores in another operator block list (tList). The pseudocode of `findoblist()` procedure is shown in Algorithm 6. If tList is not empty it means that there are matching operator blocks for source operator. In this case transformed operator blocks list received from `generate()` procedure (oblist), tList, fList, maximum depth of traversal (glen - 3) are fed to a recursive procedure called `getmatchob()` as shown in Line 7 of Algorithm 4.

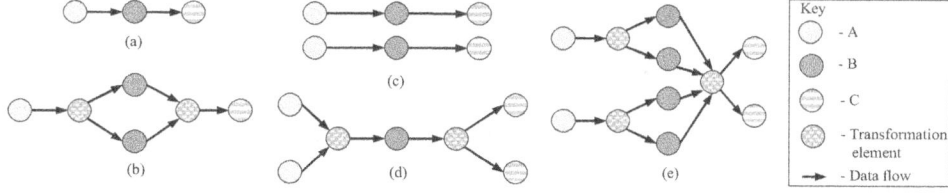

Figure 3: Some Sample Transformations using Tri-OP transformation. (a) Input operator blocks (b) Result of applying 1-2-1 transformation (c) Result of transforming by 2-1-2 (d) Result of transforming by 2-0-2 (e) Result of transforming by 2-2-2

Algorithm 3 transform(A_B_C, i, j, k)	Algorithm 4 weld(oblist, glen)	Algorithm 5 getmatchob(oblist, tList, fList, depth)
1: **if** i = 1 and j = 1 and k = 1 **then** 2: return A_B_C 3: **end if** 4: **if** all i, j, k are 0 or 1 **then** 5: return 6: **end if** 7: **if** i = 0 or k = 0 **then** 8: return 9: **end if** 10: **if** j = 0 **then** 11: return iA__B_kC 12: **end if** 13: **if** j = 1 and i = k **then** 14: return parallel(iA_iB_iC) 15: **end if** 16: return iA_(i×j)B_kC	1: fList ← emptyList 2: **for all** oblock in oblist **do** 3: **if** oblock is sourceoblock **then** 4: fList ← add(fList, oblock) 5: tList ← findoblist(oblist, oblock) 6: **if** tList not empty **then** 7: getmatchob(oblist, tList, fList, glen - 3) 8: **end if** 9: **end if** 10: **end for** 11: filter() 12: **for all** fusion in fusionList **do** 13: resprog ← fuse(oblist, fusion) 14: save(resprog) 15: **end for**	1: **for all** ob in tList **do** 2: **if** ob is sinkoblock **then** 3: fList.add(ob) 4: fusionList.add(fList) 5: **else** 6: **if** depth <= 0 **then** 7: return 8: **end if** 9: kList ← findoblist(oblist, ob) 10: **if** kList is not empty **then** 11: **for all** obk in kList **do** 12: fList.add(obk) 13: return getmatchob(obList, kList, fList, depth - 1) 14: **end for** 15: **end if** 16: **end if** 17: **end for**

The pseudocode of `getmatchob()` is shown in Algorithm 5. It finds matching operators for every operator in the transformed operator block list (oblist), and adds them to fusionList, which is a globally defined list that holds the final result. Next, it appends operator block ob to fList. A call to `getmatchob()` procedure returns a matched operator block list which keeps lists of matching operator blocks (fusions) in sequential order. After `getmatchob()` completes execution, the duplicate operator blocks in fusionList are removed by calling `filter()` procedure (Line 11 of Algorithm 4). Then `weld()` procedure fuses each and every fusion that is stored with in the fusionList to construct sample programs. A fusion in Lines 12-13 in Algorithm 4 refers to a sample program with operator blocks which are not fused yet. Merging of operator blocks located in each individual fusions is done by `fuse()` procedure (Line 13).

6. OPERATOR BLOCKS FUSION

A typical stream program may consist of minimum three operators. They are Source, a computational operator (e.g. Functor/Aggregate etc.), and Sink. Transformation of such program directly creates sample programs since the three operators represent three operator blocks. However, in most of the scenarios more than 3 operator blocks are present in stream programs. In such occasions more than one transformed operator blocks are created by `generate()`. These transformed operator blocks need to be stitched together meaningfully (i.e. with same semantics) to produce sample programs. Synthesis of sample programs in such occasions is called *Operator Blocks Fusion*.

A fusion mentioned in the previous section is a list of operator blocks which are arranged in a sequential order which makes a complete sample program (semantically equivalent to input program) if they are concatenated. Ordering of operator blocks is done based on the decision given by `is-match()` procedure call shown in Algorithm 7. The `is-match()` procedure determines whether two operator blocks

opb1 (iA_jB_kC) and opb2 (mX_nY_pZ) should be fused or not based on their operator types (A,B,C,X,Y,Z) and the transformation pattern values (i,j,k,m,n,p). For two transformed operator blocks opb1 and opb2 to match with each other, first and the second operators of opb2 should be the same as the second and third operators of opb1 (See Line 1 of Algorithm 7). (i.e. $X \equiv B$ and $Y \equiv C$). This is the primary requirement for opb1 to match with opb2. Next, if the opb2's last operator block (i.e. Z) is a Sink operator block then if m = 1 and n = p then opb1 and opb2 matches with each other (See Lines 4 to 7 of Algorithm 7). If opb2's last operator block is not a sink operator block then if the conditions k = (m×n) and m = 1 holds, opb1 and opb2 are considered matching with each other. (Note: the function names `fopb()`, `sopb()`, `topb()`, and `inopb()` correspond to first operator block, second operator block, third operator block, and index of operator block respectively).

7. TRANSFORMER BLOCKS

Hirundo uses a set of generic operator blocks called *Transformer Blocks* during transformation of a data flow graph. These are introduced in between the identified operator blocks to create coupling between resulting operator blocks (transformed operator blocks) of Tri-OP transformation.

`MUX-SINK` is a transformer block that multiplexes an input stream in to n number of sink operators (shown in (a) of Figure 4). The opposite of this operation, de-multiplexing of several streams in to a single sink operator is done by `DEMUX-SINK` (see (b) in Figure 4). `DEMUX-SOURCE` transformer block merges n number of source operators in to one single stream. Yet, multiple streams from n number of source operators can be obtained using `PARALLEL-SOURCE` transformer block. `MULTI-FUNCTOR` transformer block creates n number of functor blocks. Similar to `PARALLEL-SOURCE`, `PARALLEL-SINK` transformer block creates n number of sink operator blocks. A stream is converted to multiple streams using `MUX-STREAM` transformer block. `MUX-FUNCTOR-N-TO-M` trans-

Algorithm 6 findoblist(oblist, ob)	**Algorithm 7** ismatch(opb1, opb2)	**Algorithm 9** getprogramlabels(optrunList, n)
1: tList ← emptyList 2: **for all** oblock in oblist **do** 3: **if** ismatch(ob, oblock) **then** 4: tList.add(oblock) 5: **end if** 6: **end for** 7: return tList	1: **if** sopb(opb1) = fopb(opb2) **and** topb(opb1) = sopb(opb2) **then** 2: inopb1 ← getIndexes(opb1) 3: inopb2 ← getIndexes(opb2) 4: **if** inopb2[1] = 1 **then** 5: **if** topb(opb2) = 'SI' **and** inopb2[2] = inopb2[3] **then** 7: return true 8: **else if** inopb1[3] = (inopb2[1]*inopb2[2]) **then** 9: return true 10: **else** 11: return false 12: **end if** 13: **end if** 14: **end if**	1: inproglabels ← getinputproglabels() 2: alldict[label, avgdifflist] ← emptyDictionary 3: **for all** optrunid in optrunList **do** 4: labelslist ← getSampleProgLabels(optrunid) 5: filtlist ← removeInputProgLabels(labelslist, inproglabels) 6: labeldict[label, perfvalue] ← getperfvals(optrunid, filtlist) 7: perfdict[label, avgdiff] ← getAvgPerfvalDiffs(labeldict) 8: alldict.append(perfdict) 9: **end for** 10: rlabels ← sortUsingAveragePerfDiffAsc(alldict) 11: result_labels ← selectTopN(rlabels, n) 12: return result_labels

Algorithm 8 getmatchingoptruns(G, nodePerf, metrics, d, m, tschema)
1: optrunList ← getOptruns(metrics, tschema) 2: optrunList ← sortUsingTransformationDepth(optrunList, d) 3: optrunList ← sortUsingMatchingIndices(G, optrunList) 4: optrunList ← sortUsingMatchingNodes(nodePerf, optrunList) 5: optrunList ← selectTopN(optrunList, m) 6: return optrunList

former block creates n×m number of functor blocks accepting n input streams. TRANSFORMER-N-TO-M is a transformer block that accepts N number of input streams which can output M number of streams (see (i) of Figure 4). A slightly different transformer block to TRANSFORMER-N-TO-M called TRANSFORMER-MODULUS-N-TO-M accepts N input streams and outputs M streams. However, in the latter scenario, symmetry of the internal operators is not preserved. This can be observed from (j) of Figure 4.

Transformer blocks are created as supporting primitives for Tri-OP transformation process. They are reusable and useful when Hirundo is updated to support new operator types in future. While Tri-OP transformation algorithm concentrates on increasing/decreasing number of operator blocks in a data flow graph, transformer blocks concentrate on solving the problem of how to make links (i.e. streams) between the operators in transformed operator blocks. Transformer blocks should not be confused with similar constructs such as *Composite Operators* of IBM Stream Processing Language [15].

Furthermore, the decision of mapping output streams from split operators of transformer blocks such as TRANSFORMER-N-TO-M, TRANSFORMER-MODULUS-N-TO-M, etc. has been taken in order to preserve the isometry of data flow graph. Isometry of a data flow graph is an important factor for highly availability of a stream application [18].

8. SAMPLE PROGRAM RANKING

Hirundo's data flow graph transformation algorithm generates many sample programs for a given input program. E.g. 32 sample programs are generated for regex application during an optimization run with d = 4. Running all these sample programs for small time period may take time in the order of minutes. E.g. Running all the aforementioned 32 sample programs (+input program) in a System S environment with 8 nodes took 17 minutes and 22 seconds (an average calculated over 7 optimization runs). We observed that performance of a stream program in a certain environment can be repeated. Hence we can predict up to a certain level, what kind of performance could be obtained from a stream program using empirical data. We have implemented an algorithm (The Algorithms 8 and 9 corresponds to this prediction process.) in Hirundo that predicts similarity of optimization runs considering the parameters of structure of data flow graph (G), performance metrics used (e.g. throughput, elapsed time), optimization run depth (d), input data tuple schema (tschema). Hirundo

uses a relational database to store its information. Current optimization environment's profile information such as number of hosts, CPU, RAM capacity are stored in the database prior to any optimization attempt. All the important optimization run information (i.e. optimization session information) such as start time, end time, performance metrics used are recorded in the database. Furthermore, performance information (i.e. throughput, elapsed time, etc.) of each sample program which ran during the optimization session are also stored in this database.

In this mode of operation Hirundo predicts what kind of performance could be obtained from the input program. Algorithm 8 first selects a list of optimization runs based on the optimization metric used and the input data tuple schema. Next, it sorts the list based on the transformation depth and the structure of the input data flow graph (i.e. A,B,C values of the graph A_B_C). Finally the optimization runs are sorted based on node performance values, and top m optimization runs are selected as matching optimization runs. Next, these optimization run ids are fed to the getprogramlabels() procedure shown in Algorithm 9 to obtain sample program labels to run. For each optimization run, the performance differences of sample programs are gathered, and stored in a dictionary called alldict. The items in the dictionary are sorted based on their performance difference values in ascending order. The top n labels of this sorted list are selected as the candidate labels. These n labels correspond to the U_1 subset of the sample program labels mentioned in Section 4 (Methodology Section), and the remaining steps of the Methodology Section are followed to obtain a ranked list of sample programs (R_2) as the output. We use such method of two phase ranking in order to increase the accuracy of the end result. Section 12 demonstrates results we obtained by operating Hirundo in this mode.

9. PRESERVATION OF INPUT PROGRAM SEMANTICS

We took two key measures to ensure the semantically equivalence of the sample programs to their input program. We believe these measures preserve the semantics of all the input programs processed by Hirundo. First, Operator Block Fusion uses fusions that have the same operation type sequence similar to input program. Second measure is related to the problem of Stateful Operators in Parallel stream design pattern described in [6]. Hirundo provides the notion of annotations to ensure semantically correctness of sample programs with Stateful Operators. E.g. The sample

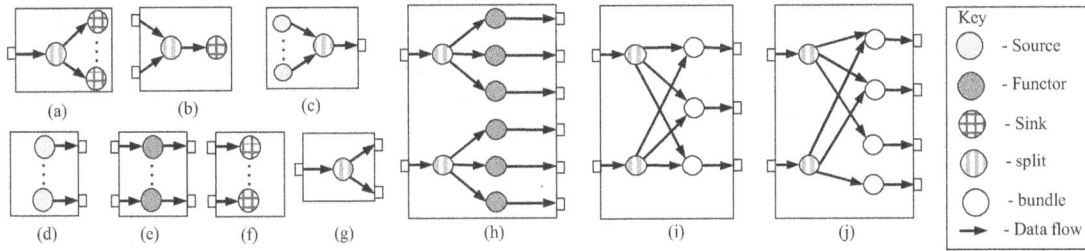

Figure 4: Some Sample Transformer blocks used by Hirundo. (a) `MUX-SINK` (b) `DEMUX-SINK` (c) `DEMUX-SOURCE` (d) `PARALLEL-SOURCE` (e) `MULTI-FUNCTOR` (f) `PARALLEL-SINK` (g) `MUX-STREAM` (h) `MUX-FUNCTOR-N-TO-M` (i) `TRANSFORMER-N-TO-M` (j) `TRANSFORMER-MODULUS-N-TO-M`

programs generated for the VWAP application shown in Figure 2 may produce semantically wrong code if AG,F2, and SI operator blocks are transformed to multiple operators by Hirundo. In order to avoid this, the SPADE code corresponding to AG,F2, and SI operators can be enclosed between two *Froze* annotation tags (these are marked as `#Hirundo-meta:Froze:Start` and `#Hirundo-meta:Froze:End` in program code). When code generator finds an operator block A_B_C having one or more operator blocks being marked as frozen, it makes sure that `transform()` procedure does not change the number of operator blocks in the corresponding transformed operator block that is output for A_B_C. Furthermore, we checked the output tuples of randomly chosen sample programs with each corresponding original input program's output and got confirmed that they produce the same outcome.

10. FAULT TOLERANCE OF HIRUNDO

Compared to many related work mentioned in Section 2, Hirundo emphasizes the importance of fault tolerance during automatic program optimization process. Hirundo strives to eliminate instance failures that might occur in the stream processing environment. An instance failure is just failure of a run-time instance (i.e. a process spawned by stream processing environment). Unexpected failures may occur in stream processing environment when such automatic optimization process has been conducted. While the stream processing run-time could continue with the remaining set of instances, it may not reflect the actual performance that could have been achieved by using a sample program. Ultimately this may lead to an inaccurate ranking of sample programs. Note that there are no such recording made during the experiments mentioned in this paper since all the faults were successfully resolved by Hirundo.

We have observed that certain large sample programs overload the run-time instances, and they might run out of memory creating instance failures. Finding the set of sample programs that provide highest performance without breaking the stream processing run-time environment's stability is a challenging issue. Hirundo uses `streamtool` of System S periodically to obtain the health information of the System S runtime, and compares those information with the runtime snapshot (original health record) obtained at the beginning of the optimization run to detect failures. (Note that at the very beginning of the optimization run, Hirundo displays the original health record to user, and gets it confirmed free of

faults). If found a failure, Hirundo tries to restart the runtime, and compares the health of the newly started runtime with the original health record. If the status of the runtime was restored, it starts running the interrupted job (sample program). It follows the same procedure during three consecutive failures. If it cannot succeed, it marks the sample program as a failure (by recording throughput as -1) and continues the optimization run.

11. IMPLEMENTATION

Hirundo has been implemented using Python programming language. It has been separated in to two modules called Main module and Worker module. Architecture of Hirundo is shown in Figure 5.

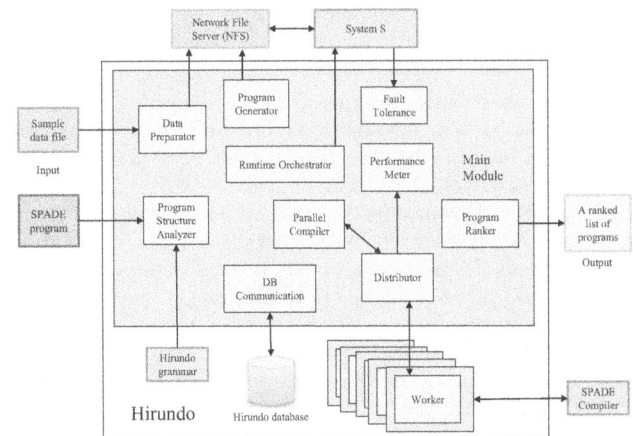

Figure 5: System Architecture of Hirundo.

Current version of Hirundo has been developed targeting stream programs written using SPADE language. Hence Hirundo depends on System S and SPADE compiler during its operations. It should be noted that, although System S is dependent on a shared file system such as NFS, Hirundo has been designed not to use such file systems for optimization runs. It uses local hard disks to store the data it handles during optimization runs. Hirundo uses a SQLite database to store its information. Main module has been separated in to ten sub modules based on different functionalities they handle. We briefly describe functions of important modules below.

341

11.1 Program Structure Analyzer

SPADE program analysis logic has been implemented in Program Structure Analyzer of Hirundo. As pointed out in Section 5.2, Hirundo uses a bespoke grammar written for parsing a SPADE program to identify its structure. Current implementation of Hirundo's grammar supports Source, Functor, Aggregate, Sink BIOPs, and UDOPs (with the use of annotations described in Section 9). This module uses an LALR parser [2]. Hirundo's parser has been developed using the GOLD parser generator developed by Cook *et al.* [9]. The grammar has been coded separately from Hirundo (independent of Python programming language), and can be modified easily using the GOLD parser generator [9]. Current version of the grammar consists of 34 rules. Only the rule that defines the structure of a program is shown in Figure 6. Program analyzer creates a representative graph G for the program it analyses if it can identify its structure. This graph keeps details of all the operators (vertices) identified from the program and the links between them.

```
<Program> ::= <PREAMBLE><SOURCE><FUNCTOR><SINK>
| <PREAMBLE><SOURCE><FUNCTOR><MUX-SINK>
| <PREAMBLE><AUTO-BUNDLE-SINGLE><PARALLEL-SOURCES-CSV><MUX-FUNCTOR-N-TO-M><DEMUX-STRM-M-N-To-1><SINK>
| <PREAMBLE><AUTO-BUNDLE-MULTI><PARALLEL-SOURCES-CSV><MULTI-FUNCTOR><TRANSFORMER-N-TO-M>
| <MUX-SINK-WITH-STRM-NAME>
| <PREAMBLE><PARALLEL-SOURCES-CSV><MULTI-FUNCTOR><PARALLEL-SINK>
| <PREAMBLE><AUTO-BUNDLE-SINGLE><PARALLEL-SOURCES-CSV><MULTI-FUNCTOR><DEMUX-SINK><SINK>
| <PREAMBLE><AUTO-BUNDLE-MULTI><SOURCE><MUX-SOURCE-CSV><MULTI-FUNCTOR><TRANSFORMER-N-TO-M><PARALLEL-SINK>
| <PREAMBLE><AUTO-BUNDLE-SINGLE><SOURCE><MUX-SOURCE-CSV><MULTI-FUNCTOR><DEMUX-SINK><SINK>
| <PREAMBLE><AUTO-BUNDLE-SINGLE><DEMUX-SOURCE-CSV><FUNCTOR><MUX-SINK>
| <PREAMBLE><AUTO-BUNDLE-MULTI><PARALLEL-SOURCES-CSV><MUX-FUNCTOR-N-TO-M><TRANSFORMERMODULUS>
| <MUX-SINK-WITH-STRM-NAME>
| <PREAMBLE><SOURCE><STRING-OF-FUNCTOR><SINK>
| <PREAMBLE><SOURCE><AGGREGATE><SINK>
| <PREAMBLE><SOURCE><STRING-OF-FUNCTOR><AGGREGATE><STRING-OF-FUNCTOR><SINK>
| <PREAMBLE><SOURCE><META><AGGREGATE><META><SINK>
| <PREAMBLE><SOURCE><STRING-OF-FUNCTOR><META><AGGREGATE><STRING-OF-FUNCTOR><META><SINK>
| <PREAMBLE><META><UDOP><META><STRING-OF-FUNCTOR><META><AGGREGATE><META><SINK>
```

Figure 6: A sample rule from Hirundo's Grammar.

11.2 Data Preparator

Unlike most static program optimizers, Hirundo runs selected sample programs for fixed time period in the stream processing environment to identify their performance. The sample programs require representative data during their execution. Data Preparator is the module that creates these required sample data. At the beginning of optimization process, user should provide a sample data file along with input program. This file is splitted in to total $[d(d+1)/2 - 1]$ number of files staring from the groups 2, 3, up to d. The number d is the depth value that is accepted by Tri-OP transformation algorithm. The files are splitted in this way since Tri-OP transformation with depth d may produce d number of maximum transformed source operator blocks for any optimization run. Furthermore, such splitting ensures that all the input data are received by all the source operators of the sample programs homogeneously. User should enter only required size input data file (smaller size file is preferred) to Hirundo since very large files impose unnecessary overhead on Hirundo during its optimization runs. Furthermore, we use a file rather than online data source in order to keep the input fixed during all the optimization attempts the input program faces since this could directly affect the end result of program ranking.

11.3 Parallel Compiler

Hirundo would have spent substantial portion of its processing time on compilation, if Hirundo were to compile all the sample programs on a single node. E.g. Compiling VWAP (25 programs), regex (33 programs), and Twitter (27 programs) applications described in this paper on a single node takes approximately 11, 43, 50 minutes respectively. To reduce total time taken for compilation we created a parallel compiler for Hirundo. Current version of Hirundo deploys one worker per each node of the node cluster of which it operates on during its instantiation. Parallel compiler assigns compilation task of a single program to one worker. We were able to reduce the percentage of time required for compilation of VWAP, regex, and Twitter applications to 5, 7, and 8 minutes resulting 51%, 84%, and 84% compilation time reduction respectively on 8 nodes.

12. EVALUATION

12.1 Experimental Environment and Methodology

The experiments were performed on a cluster of Linux Cent OS release 5.4 installed with IBM Infosphere Streams Version 1.2. Each machine (i.e. node) has a dual core AMD Opteron(tm) Processor 242, 1MB L2 cache per core, 8GB memory, 250GB hard drive, 1Gigabit Ethernet. In the first half of the experiments we disabled the sample program ranking of Hirundo, and made it to run all the sample programs it generated for a short period of time (less than 1 minute). In the second half we enabled the sample program ranking of Hirundo. In all of these experiments Hirundo ensured that the experiments are not affected by sudden instance failures by re-instantiating the run-time environment, and re-running the sample program that faced the instance failure. The graphs in Figures 8, 9, 10, and 11 show results of single runs (i.e. No average values were considered). We used three different real world stream applications during these evaluations. Note that program labels on X axis are shown increasing order of operator indexes from left to right. Each point corresponds to one sample program's performance during one optimization run.

The first application is the Volume Weighted Average Price Application (VWAP) shown in Figure 2. The data flow graph of VWAP application contains 5 operators including two Functors (F1 and F2) and an Aggregate operator (AG). F1 filters the tuples for valid records. AG finds the maximum/minimum of the trading prices using a sliding window of size 4 and outputs a tuple for each tuple it receives. F2 makes arithmetic operations on tuple data fields to create a volume weighted average price. The input data file size is 2.4 MB.

The second application is a data converter application (*regex*) (Shown in Figure 7 (a)). This application also consists of five operators including three functors (F1, F2, and F3). It converts an input data stream with date time data tuples represented as 2011-04-14 to 14-APR-2011. Furthermore, all the "00"s in the time portion of the tuple are replaced with "22"s. F1 filters the date time data tuples from the stream it receives from SI. Date time format conversion is done by F2. F3 does the replacement of "00"s with "22"s. Input data file size is 8.5 MB.

Third application is a Twitter hash tag counter application (*Twitter*). This is a 6 operator application (shown in Figure 7 (b)) including one UDOP (U), three Functors (F1, F2, and F3), and an Aggregate operator (AG). UDOP reads data

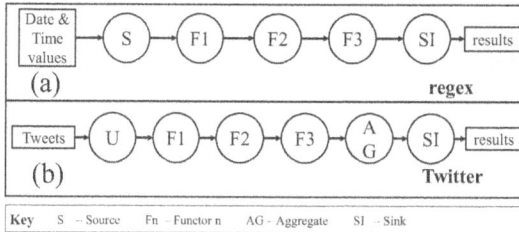

Figure 7: Data flow graphs of regex and Twitter applications.

from a dump of twitter data (size $\approx$ 181 MB). F1 tokenizes the tweets, and F2 extracts hash tags from the words. F3 eliminates empty tuples. AG aggregates hash tag tuples, emits the has tag count for every 10 tuples it receives, and emits summary of results for each tuple it receives.

12.2 Sample program performance

First, we disabled the performance prediction and sample program ranking feature of Hirundo. Therefore, the application ran the entire sample program space. We compared throughput of sample programs for three optimization runs using 8 nodes in each session. We use the term "Optimization run (Opt run)" to denote a single running of Hirundo in this mode. Our intention is to observe the performance characteristics of each sample program generated by Hirundo. Each optimization run had a transformation depth value of 4 for regex and Twitter. For VWAP we set the depth value to 8 since a depth of 4 produced few sample programs for VWAP application. Hirundo generated 32, 24, and 26 sample applications for regex, VWAP and Twitter respectively.

From the three graphs it can be observed that certain sample programs produce higher throughput compared to the input application (e.g. 4SCSV_2F_2AG_2F_2SI in the case of regex, 8SCSV_6F_F_AG_F_SI in the case of VWAP and U_4F_2F_F_AG_SI for Twitter). Note that the notation used for sample program labels represents the arrangement of operator blocks in the resulting sample programs. E.g. In Twitter sample application U_4F_2F_F_AG_SI, the label means there is one UDOP, four F1s, two F2s, one F3, one AG, and one SI.

12.3 Performance Prediction

We enabled the performance prediction and sample program ranking feature of Hirundo. In this mode each experiment completed in less than 15 minutes time, a 50% reduction of total experiment time compared to without use of performance prediction. The results are shown in the corresponding graphs on Figures 8,9, and 10. Two out of five sample programs had higher performance compared to regex application, whereas the sample programs pointed out for VWAP had higher performance for two out of the three optimization runs. In the case of Twitter application all the four sample programs predicted by Hirundo had higher performance compared to original Twitter application.

Next, we ran a completely different application (numapplong) which had never been optimized by Hirundo before (results shown in Figure 11). It has similar structure to regex application, but all the three functors chained together incremented an integer they received (each operator by 100).

Only one out of the four programs predicted by Hirundo had higher performance than numapplong application. However, after running two optimization runs in non-predictive mode we ran another optimization run with prediction enabled. Three out of five sample applications pointed by Hirundo had higher performance compared to the original version.

12.4 Performance Clusters

We conducted a cluster analysis on the data sets corresponding to Opt run 1, 2, and 3 of each performance curves of Figures 8,9, and 10. Our intention was to find the characteristics of data flow graphs which lead to higher performance. We used K-Means clustering [20] for this purpose since we needed to group the data points based on their performance values, and the data sets were of convex shape. We set the minimum gap between the clusters as 100B/s. The algorithm was implemented using Python and Scipy [25] and the results are shown in Figures 12, 13, and 14. We calculated average performance values of each clusters, and also recorded program labels if all the three data points corresponding to the three optimization runs fall in to a particular cluster.

VWAP data set resulted in 5 clusters. We saw that the cluster with the highest performance (6393B/s) had all the three data points corresponding to label 8SCSV_6F_AG_F_SI whereas the second highest cluster (3885B/s) had all the three data points corresponding to the label 8SCSV_4F_AG_-F_SI. However, two low performance clusters had all the data points corresponding to the labels SCSV_8F_AG_F_SI and 2SCSV_F_AG_F_SI. This indicates that having large number of source operators would produce high throughput in the case of VWAP application described in this paper.

The clustering results for Twitter application is somewhat different than the VWAP because Twitter application's UD-OP was frozen during program transformation. The highest performing cluster (961B/s) had all data points corresponding to the label U_4F_2F_F_AG_SI, whereas a medium performance cluster (2nd cluster from the lowest end, having 440B/s performance) had all the data points corresponding to labels U_2F_4F_F_AG_SI. The difference between these programs is that there are more mid level operators (F2, F3 in Figure 7) in low performing one, and there are more F1 operators in the high performance one. It is clear that having more tokenizer Functors (F1) has supported for high performance for Twitter sample applications.

Regex application's highest performing cluster did not include all the three points form any sample application. However, the second highest performing cluster (474.67KB/s) had all the three data points of SCSV_2F_2F_2F_2SI and 4SCSV_2F_2F_2F_2SI. The cluster with lowest performance (25KB/s) had all the points of labels 4SCSV_4F_2F_4F_4SI, 4SCSV_2F_2F_4F_4SI, SCSV_2F_4F_4F_4SI, SCSV_4F_2F_-4F_4SI. When comparing these two clusters it is clear that having a variety in the number of middle operators has produced less performance for regex application.

13. DISCUSSION AND LIMITATIONS

Our intention of this paper was to introduce a methodology for automatically producing optimized versions for a given data stream program. Our approach produced higher performance gains (1.7,2.3, and 2.9 times for regex, VWAP,

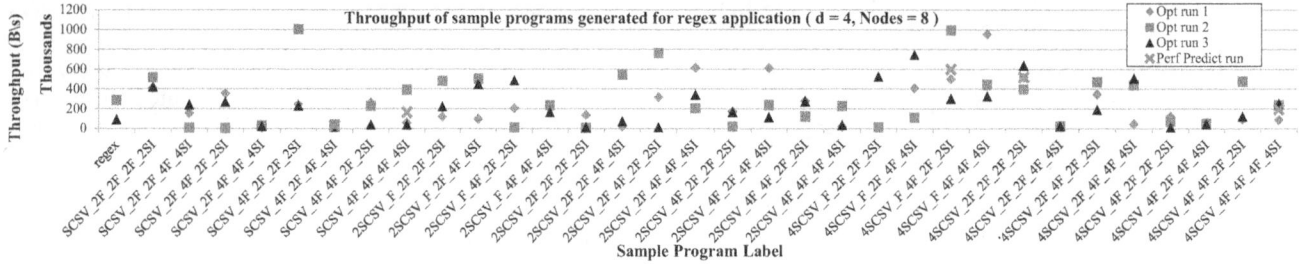

Figure 8: Comparison of three optimization runs (Opt run 1,2,3, and Perf Predict) with regex application using equal optimization parameters (d=4, nodecount=8)

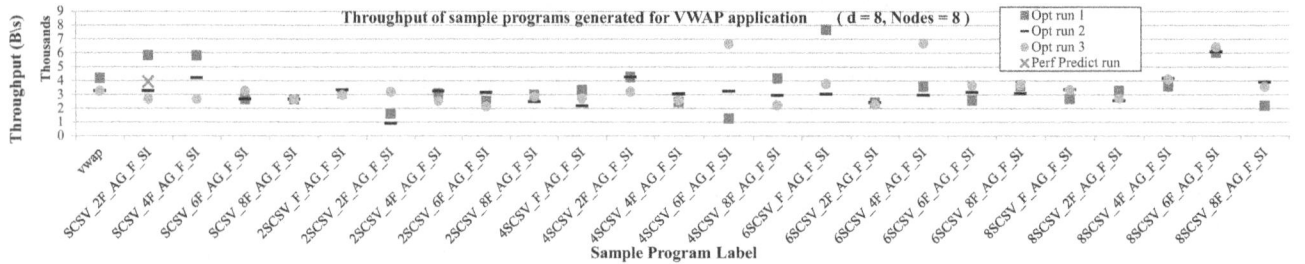

Figure 9: Comparison of four optimization runs (Opt run 1,2,3, and Perf Predict) with VWAP application using equal optimization parameters (d=8, nodecount=8)

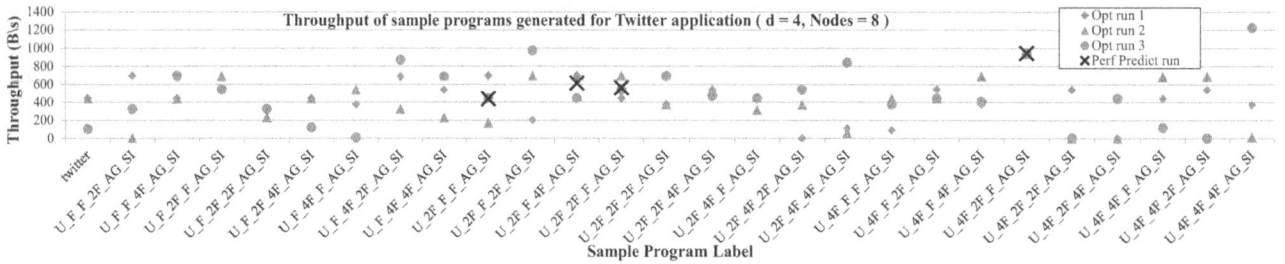

Figure 10: Comparison of four optimization runs (Opt run 1,2,3, and Perf Predict) with Twitter application using equal optimization parameters (d=4, nodecount=8)

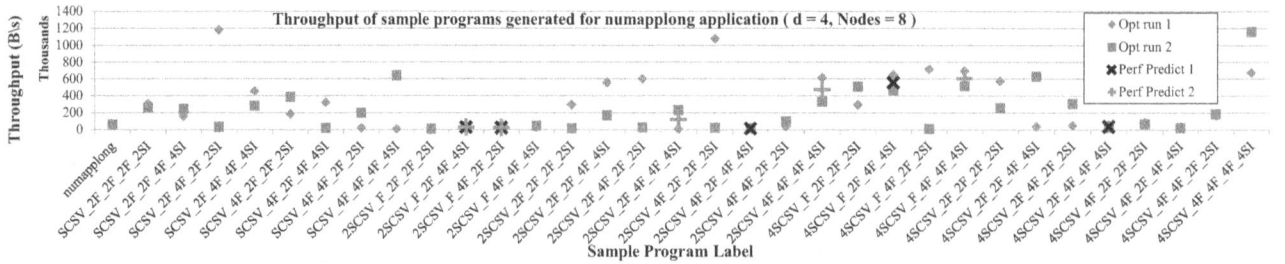

Figure 11: Comparison of four optimization runs of numapplong (Opt run 1,2,Perf Predict 1, and Perf Predict 2). Application uses equal optimization parameters in all runs (d=4, nodecount=8)

and Twitter applications respectively) exceeding the expected performance improvement (2 times) for two out of the three input programs.

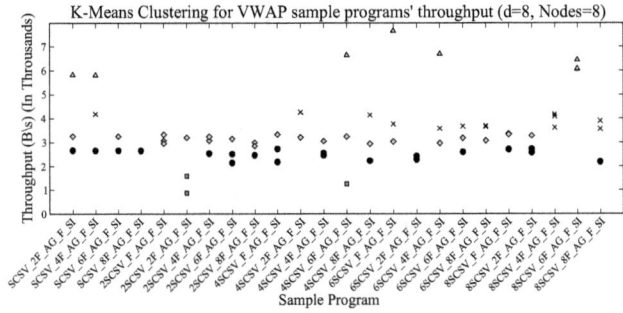

Figure 12: Results of applying K-Means clustering for VWAP sample program performance data.

While it is difficult to exactly characterize the structure of stream programs that deliver high throughput, it could be observed from the experiments that programs with higher number of source operators tend to produce more throughput. Furthermore, stream programs that had higher operator density in the middle part of their data flow graphs tend to produce less performance. One might argue that certain topologies of sample programs are favored by certain SPADE optimizations leading to higher performance in execution. However, the way how the operators are grouped during SPADE application compilation is at the discretion of the SPADE compiler [18], hence Hirundo can help programmers to identify common characteristics of high performance versions of their programs.

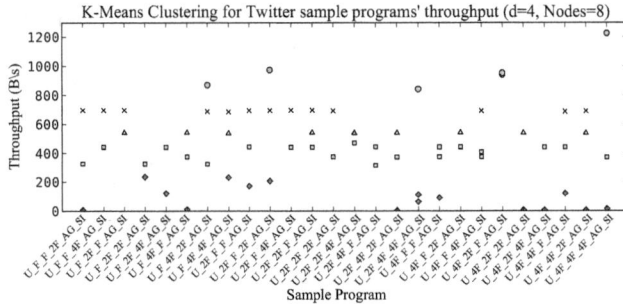

Figure 13: Results of applying K-Means clustering for Twitter sample program performance data.

Theoretically, Tri-Op transformation can generate sample programs with very large numbers of operators. However, we have observed that the upper limit of such transformation is imposed by the stream computing environment. We faced many instance failures with d = 8 optimization runs in our laboratory environment for applications such as regex. It should be noted that our method is capable of exploring the whole set of possible sample program combinations by varying the value of d.

Use of K-Means clustering on sample program database is a promising approach for finding performance characteristics of sample programs. However, in the current version of Hirundo we do not use K-Means clustering for identifying

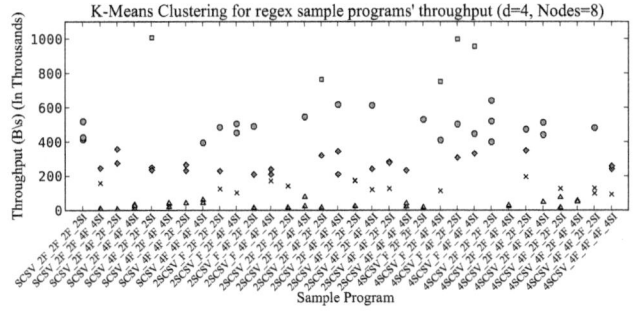

Figure 14: Results of applying K-Means clustering for regex sample program performance data.

sample labels with high performance. Instead, we use performance difference of sample programs in different optimization runs. We believe this approach is capable of pointing out specific sample programs with consistent high performance.

There are several limitations to Hirundo which we list here. Presently Hirundo's Program Analyzer can identify, and transform a class of stream programs which are made out of combinations of Source, Functor, Aggregate, Sink, and UDOP operators (with the use of annotations). These five types of operator blocks are sufficient to create many useful real world stream applications such as the ones discussed in this paper. However, there are other stream applications with different BIOP types such as Join, Sort, Punctor, etc. that we hope to integrate in to Hirundo's program analyzer's grammar, and transformation logic in future.

Moreover Hirundo assumes that programmer does not manually allocate node pools in his/her program (Node pool is a SPADE language construct that allows manual allocation of operators to specific hosts.).

14. CONCLUSION AND FURTHER WORK

In this paper we introduced a mechanism for automatically transforming data flow graph of stream programs to high performance, optimized versions. In achieving our aim, we introduced the notions of Tri-Operator transformation, transformation blocks, and operator block fusion for stream program transformation. Based on these concepts we developed Hirundo, a Python based performance optimization application for SPADE programs.

By setting d = 4, Hirundo created at least 25 sample programs with different performance levels for the input applications. Larger depth values produce even more sample programs. Therefore, we came to conclusion that Tri-Operator transformation is able to produce sufficiently large number of programs with variety of performance levels. The second conclusion we arrived at is that our approach is able to produce SPADE programs with consistent high throughput gains. We demonstrated this by optimizing three real world stream applications using Hirundo. Furthermore, the performance prediction mechanism we introduce showed its effectiveness by identifying a high performance sample program for a completely new application without exploring the whole sample program space. Another conclusion we arrived at is that having large number of source operators is likely to produce more throughput. Relatively high operator density in the middle regions of a data stream graph may produce less performance, hence stream programmers should avoid creating such programs. These two conclusions are supported by the observations made using K-Means clustering.

We plan to study different techniques for improving the performance prediction of Hirundo. We hope to improve the program structure analyzer and the program generator modules of Hirundo in future to support different other stream operator categories. We have begun to replace manual annotation mechanism by an automated procedure. We plan to do an in depth study on the performance characteristics of transformation blocks used in Hirundo's Program Generator module. We hope to improve Hirundo to identify important semantics of input programs, and incorporate those during its performance optimization process.

15. ACKNOWLEDGMENTS

This research was supported by the Japan Science and Technology Agency's CREST project titled "Development of System Software Technologies for post-Peta Scale High Performance Computing".

16. REFERENCES

[1] R. Ahmed and et al. Cost-based query transformation in oracle. VLDB '06, pages 1026–1036, 2006.

[2] A. W. Appel. *Modern compiler implementation in Java*. Cambridge University Press, 2002.

[3] A. Arasu, S. Babu, and J. Widom. The cql continuous query language: semantic foundations and query execution. *The VLDB Journal*, 15:121–142, June 2006.

[4] S. Babu. Towards automatic optimization of mapreduce programs. SoCC '10, pages 137–142, 2010.

[5] C. Ballard and et al. *IBM Infosphere Streams: Harnessing Data in Motion*. IBM, 2010.

[6] P. Banerjee and et al. The paradigm compiler for distributed-memory multicomputers. *Computer*, 28:37–47, Oct 1995.

[7] S. Bellamkonda and et al. Enhanced subquery optimizations in oracle. *Proc. VLDB Endow.*, 2:1366–1377, August 2009.

[8] B. Chapman, H. Herbeck, and H. Zima. Automatic support for data distribution. In *DMCC*, pages 51 –58, May 1991.

[9] D. Cook. Gold parsing system. URL: http://www.goldparser.org/, Dec. 2011.

[10] M. Dayarathna, S. Takeno, and T. Suzumura. A performance study on operator-based stream processing systems. In *IEEE IISWC*, 2011.

[11] B. Gedik, H. Andrade, and K.-L. Wu. A code generation approach to optimizing high-performance distributed data stream processing. In *CIKM '09*, pages 847–856, 2009.

[12] B. Gedik and et al. Spade: the system s declarative stream processing engine. In *SIGMOD '08*, pages 1123–1134, 2008.

[13] M. Hall and et al. Loop transformation recipes for code generation and auto-tuning. In *Languages and Compilers for Parallel Computing*, pages 50–64. 2010.

[14] H. Herodotou and et al. Query optimization techniques for partitioned tables. SIGMOD '11, pages 49–60, 2011.

[15] M. Hirzel and et al. Spl stream processing language specification. Nov 2009.

[16] IBM. Ibm infosphere streams version 1.2: Programming model and language reference. Feb 2010.

[17] N. Kabra and D. J. DeWitt. Efficient mid-query re-optimization of sub-optimal query execution plans. SIGMOD '98, pages 106–117, 1998.

[18] R. Khandekar and et al. Cola: Optimizing stream processing applications via graph partitioning. In *Middleware 2009*, pages 308–327. 2009.

[19] C. S. Liew and et al. Towards optimising distributed data streaming graphs using parallel streams. In *HPDC '10*, pages 725–736, 2010.

[20] S. Marsland. *Machine Learning : An Algorithmic Perspective*. Chapman & Hall/CRC, 2009.

[21] L. Neumeyer, B. Robbins, A. Nair, and A. Kesari. S4: Distributed stream computing platform. In *KDCloud 2010*, December 2010.

[22] D. Palermo, E. Hodges, and P. Banerjee. Compiler optimization of dynamic data distributions for distributed-memory multicomputers. In *Compiler Optimizations for Scalable Parallel Systems*, volume 1808, pages 445–484. 2001.

[23] J. Qin and et al. A novel graph based approach for automatic composition of high quality grid workflows. In *HPDC '09*, pages 167–176, 2009.

[24] R. Rea and K. Mamidipaka. Ibm infosphere streams: Enabling complex analytics with ultra-low latencies on data in motion. May 2009.

[25] Scipy. Scientific tools for python. URL: http://www.scipy.org/, 2011.

[26] S. Sodhi, J. Subhlok, and Q. Xu. Performance prediction with skeletons. *Cluster Computing*, 11:151–165, 2008.

[27] T. Suzumura, T. Yasue, and T. Onodera. Scalable performance of system s for extract-transform-load processing. In *SYSTOR '10*, pages 7:1–7:14, 2010.

[28] Z. Wang and M. F. O'Boyle. Partitioning streaming parallelism for multi-cores: a machine learning based approach. In *PACT '10*, pages 307–318, 2010.

[29] G. Yaikhom and et al. Federated enactment of workflow patterns. In *Euro-Par 2010 - Parallel Processing*, volume 6271, pages 317–328. 2010.

[30] L. T. Yang, X. Ma, and F. Mueller. Cross-platform performance prediction of parallel applications using partial execution. In *SC '05*, Washington, DC, USA, 2005.

[31] D. F. Yuan Yu, Michael Isard and M. Budiu. Dryadlinq: A system for general-purpose distributed data-parallel computing using a high-level language. OSDI '08, pages 1–14, 2008.

[32] X. J. Zhang and et al. Workload characterization for operator-based distributed stream processing applications. In *DEBS '10*, pages 235–247, 2010.

Author Index